CROSSWORD
LISTS

Fourth edition

Edited by
Anne Stibbs

A & C Black • London

1783-1874 Adam Black :· Enc.Brittanica — bought in 1827

First published 1989 by Bloomsbury Publishing Plc
Second edition published 1997
Third edition published 2000
Fourth edition published 2004
This combined edition published 2007 by
A&C Black Publishers Ltd, 38 Soho Square, London W1D 3HB
Reprinted 2008

A CIP record for this title is available from the British Library

ISBN 978 0 7136 8320 2

This book is produced using paper that is made from wood grown in managed, sustainable
forests. It is natural, renewable and recyclable. The logging and manufacturing processes
conform to the environmental regulations of the country of origin.

Text compiled and typeset by Market House Books Ltd., Aylesbury
Printed in Spain by GraphyCems

INTRODUCTION

This book is one of a series of reference books for crossword puzzles, including *Solving Cryptic Crosswords*, *Crossword Key*, the *Pocket Crossword Dictionary* and *Anagram Solver*. In this fourth edition we have substantially revised the existing text. We have also included many new lists (over 100). These cover such diverse topics as Swiss cantons, archaeology terms, stately homes, manned space programs, locomotives, members of the Commonwealth, etc. As in prevous editions we have listed words under categories – people, places, birds, animals, jewellery, canals, Greek gods, names of drinks, and so on, in the hope that the user can quickly find the required answer to a clue. We have chosen the contents for their usefulness and have tried to concentrate on words that actually appear in crosswords. We have also presented the information in the most helpful way. Usually, this means listing the words in length order – 3-letter, 4-letter, 5-letter words, etc., and then in alphabetical order within each section. In some cases we have used simple alphabetical or logical order and some information is presented in tabular form.

We have also included additional information in many of the lists; for example, the birth and death dates of people or the colours of gemstones. This is partly to help the reader find the correct word, but we also hope that owners of the book will find it a useful reference source in its own right.

While most of the lists are collections of things, there are also lists of types of words – for example, palindromes, back words, homophones (words that sound like others), abbreviations and acronyms, common two-word phrases, anagram indicators, and split-word indicators. The book also contains a short section of familiar quotations and some well-known foreign words and phrases. To help the reader find his or her way about, there is a Contents page that lists all the tables and lists in the order in which they appear in the book. In addition, there is an index in the back of the book. This gives the tables and lists in alphabetical order, but has also been expanded to include many more cross references. For instance, a reader interested in 'jewels' will be directed to the list of gemstones, 'girl' might indicate a girl's first name, listed under first names, and so on. The index also contains hints on solving cryptic clues. There are many conventions used by setters of crosswords – 'love' often indicates the letter O, 'cardinal' might be a compass point, N, S, E or W, 'twisted' could suggest an anagram, etc. A selection of these has been included in the index.

In using the book, the reader should also be aware of the inflection of words. The most common, for the purpose of crosswords, is the use of plurals, and it is usually apparent from the wording of the clue whether the answer is a singular or plural. When nouns have regular plurals, only the singular forms have been included. Another point is that verbs are invariably shown with -ize endings. The alternative -ise ending may have been used in the puzzle. The same principle applies to nouns with -ization.

Since the original publication of the book in 1989, a large number of useful comments and suggestions for additional lists have been received from readers. Many of these have been incorporated into both the 2000 edition and into this new and expanded fourth edition. The editor would like to thank these correspondents and also thank all the people who have been involved in the production of the book. Their names are listed under Acknowledgments.

Anne Stibbs
Aylesbury 2004

ACKNOWLEDGMENTS

Fran Alexander
Peter Blair
Beth Bonham
Eve Daintith
John Daintith
Jessica Foote
Joan Gallagher
Robert Kerr
Jonathan Law
Sandra McQueen
David Pickering
Kathy Rooney
Mark Salad
Jessica Scholes
Gwen Shaw
Kate Smith
Brenda Tomkins
Margaret Tuthill
Linda Wells
Edmund Wright

CONTENTS

GEOGRAPHY

COUNTRIES OF THE WORLD

AFGHANISTAN
  Capital: Kabul
  Currency: afghani [pul, *pl.* puli (*or* puls)]
ALBANIA
  Capital: Tirana (*or* Tiranë)
  Currency: lek, *pl.* lekë (*or* leks) [qindar (*or* qintar *or* qindarka)]
ALGERIA
  Capital: Algiers
  Currency: dinar [centime]
ANDORRA
  Capital: Andorra la Vella
  Currency: euro [cent]
ANGOLA
  Capital: Luanda
  Currency: kwanza [lwei]
ANTIGUA AND BARBUDA
  Capital: Saint John's
  Currency: East Caribbean dollar [cent]
ARGENTINA
  Capital: Buenos Aires
  Currency: peso [austral]
ARMENIA
  Capital: Yerevan
  Currency: dram [louma]
AUSTRALIA
  Capital: Canberra
  Currency: dollar [cent]
AUSTRIA
  Capital: Vienna
  Currency: euro [cent]
AZERBAIJAN
  Capital: Baku
  Currency: manat [gopik]
THE BAHAMAS
  Capital: Nassau
  Currency: dollar [cent]
BAHRAIN
  Capital: Manama
  Currency: dinar [fils]
BANGLADESH
  Capital: Dhaka
  Currency: taka [poisha]
BARBADOS
  Capital: Bridgetown
  Currency: dollar [cent]
BELARUS
  Capital: Minsk
  Currency: rouble [copeck (*or* kopek)]

BELAU
  Capital: Koror
  Currency: US dollar [cent]
BELGIUM
  Capital: Brussels
  Currency: euro [cent]
BELIZE
  Capital: Belmopan
  Currency: dollar [cent]
BENIN
  Capital: Porto-Novo
  Currency: CFA franc [centime]
BHUTAN
  Capital: Thimphu
  Currency: ngultrum, *pl.* ngultrum [chetrum]
BOLIVIA
  Capital: La Paz
  Currency: boliviano [centavo]
BOSNIA-HERCEGOVINA (*or* BOSNIA AND HERZEGOVINA)
  Capital: Sarajevo
  Currency: euro [cent]
BOTSWANA
  Capital: Gaborone
  Currency: pula [thebe]
BRAZIL
  Capital: Brasília
  Currency: real [centavo]
BRUNEI
  Capital: Bandar Seri Begawan
  Currency: dollar [sen]
BULGARIA
  Capital: Sofia
  Currency: lev, *pl.* leva (*or* levs) [stotinka, *pl.* stotinki]
BURKINA FASO
  Capital: Ouagadougou
  Currency: CFA franc [centime]
BURMA
  See MYANMAR
BURUNDI
  Capital: Bujumbura
  Currency: franc [centime]
CAMBODIA
  Capital: Phnom Penh
  Currency: riel [sen]
CAMEROON
  Capital: Yaoundé
  Currency: CFA franc [centime]

1

CANADA
Capital: Ottawa
Currency: dollar [cent]
CAPE VERDE
Capital: Praia
Currency: escudo [centavo]
CENTRAL AFRICAN REPUBLIC
Capital: Bangui
Currency: CFA franc [centime]
CHAD
Capital: N'Djaména
Currency: CFA franc [centime]
CHILE
Capital: Santiago
Currency: peso [centavo]
CHINA
Capital: Beijing (*or* Peking)
Currency: renminbi yuan [fen]
COLOMBIA
Capital: Bogotá
Currency: peso [centavo]
COMOROS
Capital: Moroni
Currency: franc [centime]
CONGO, DEMOCRATIC REPUBLIC OF
Capital: Kinshasa
Currency: franc [centime]
CONGO-BRAZZAVILLE, REPUBLIC OF
Capital: Brazzaville
Currency: CFA franc [centime]
COSTA RICA
Capital: San José
Currency: colón, *pl.* colónes (*or* colóns) [céntimo]
CÔTE D'IVOIRE
Capital: Yamoussoukro
Currency: CFA franc [centime]
CROATIA
Capital: Zagreb
Currency: kuna, *pl.* kune (*or* kuna) [lipa]
CUBA
Capital: Havana
Currency: peso [centavo]
CYPRUS
Capital: Nicosia (*or* Lefkosia)
Currency: pound [cent]
CZECH REPUBLIC
Capital: Prague
Currency: koruna [haler, *pl.* haleru (*or* haler *or* halura)]
DENMARK
Capital: Copenhagen
Currency: krone, *pl.* kroner (*or* kronen) [øre]
DJIBOUTI
Capital: Djibouti
Currency: franc [centime]
DOMINICA
Capital: Roseau
Currency: East Caribbean dollar [cent]
DOMINICAN REPUBLIC
Capital: Santo Domingo
Currency: peso [centavo]

EAST TIMOR
Capital: Dili
Currency: US dollar [cent]
ECUADOR
Capital: Quito
Currency: US dollar [cent]
EGYPT
Capital: Cairo
Currency: pound [piastre]
EL SALVADOR
Capital: San Salvador
Currency: colón, *pl.* colones (*or* colons) [centavo]
EQUATORIAL GUINEA
Capital: Malabo
Currency: CFA franc [centime]
ERITREA
Capital: Asmara
Currency: nakfa
ESTONIA
Capital: Tallinn
Currency: kroon, *pl.* krooni (*or* kroons) [sent (*or* cent), *pl.* senti]
ETHIOPIA
Capital: Addis Adaba
Currency: birr [cent]
FIJI
Capital: Suva
Currency: dollar [cent]
FINLAND
Capital: Helsinki
Currency: euro [cent]
FRANCE
Capital: Paris
Currency: euro [cent]
GABON
Capital: Libreville
Currency: CFA franc [centime]
THE GAMBIA
Capital: Banjul
Currency: dalasi [butut]
GEORGIA
Capital: Tbilisi
Currency: lari [tetri]
GERMANY
Capital: Berlin
Currency: euro [cent]
GHANA
Capital: Accra
Currency: cedi [pesewa]
GREECE
Capital: Athens
Currency: euro [cent]
GRENADA
Capital: St George's
Currency: East Caribbean dollar [cent]
GUATEMALA
Capital: Guatemala City
Currency: quetzal, *pl.* quetzales [centavo]
GUINEA
Capital: Conakry
Currency: franc [cauris (*or* centime)]

GUINEA-BISSAU
Capital: Bissau
Currency: CFA franc
GUYANA
Capital: Georgetown
Currency: dollar [cent]
HAITI
Capital: Port-au-Prince
Currency: gourde [centime]
HONDURAS
Capital: Tegucigalpa
Currency: lempira [centavo]
HUNGARY
Capital: Budapest
Currency: forint [fillér]
ICELAND
Capital: Reykjavik
Currency: króna, *pl.* krónur [eyrir, *pl.* aurar]
INDIA
Capital: New Delhi
Currency: rupee [paisa, *pl.* paise (*or* paisa)]
INDONESIA
Capital: Jakarta
Currency: rupiah [sen]
IRAN
Capital: Tehrān
Currency: rial
IRAQ
Capital: Baghdad
Currency: dinar [fils]
IRELAND, REPUBLIC OF
Capital: Dublin
Currency: euro [cent]
ISRAEL
Capital: Jerusalem
Currency: shekel (*or* sheqel) [agora, *pl.*
     agorot]
ITALY
Capital: Rome
Currency: euro [cent]
JAMAICA
Capital: Kingston
Currency: dollar [cent]
JAPAN
Capital: Tokyo
Currency: yen [sen]
JORDAN
Capital: Amman
Currency: dinar [fils]
KAZAKHSTAN
Capital: Astana (*or* Akmola)
Currency: tenge
KENYA
Capital: Nairobi
Currency: shilling [cent]
KIRIBATI
Capital: Tarawa
Currency: Australian dollar [cent]

KOREA, DEMOCRATIC PEOPLE'S
REPUBLIC OF (North Korea)
Capital: P'yŏngyang
Currency: won [chon (*or* jun)]
KOREA, REPUBLIC OF (South Korea)
Capital: Seoul
Currency: won [chon (*or* chun *or* jeon)]
KUWAIT
Capital: Kuwait City
Currency: dinar [fils]
KYRGYZSTAN
Capital: Bishkek
Currency: som [tyin]
LAOS
Capital: Vientiane
Currency: kip [at]
LATVIA
Capital: Riga
Currency: lat, *pl.* lati (*or* lats) [santimi]
LEBANON
Capital: Beirut
Currency: pound [piastre]
LESOTHO
Capital: Maseru
Currency: loti [sente, *pl.* lisente]
LIBERIA
Capital: Monrovia
Currency: dollar [cent]
LIBYA
Capital: Tripoli
Currency: dinar [dirham (*or* dirhem)]
LIECHTENSTEIN
Capital: Vaduz
Currency: Swiss franc [centime]
LITHUANIA
Capital: Vilnius
Currency: litas, *pl.* litai (*or* lits *or* litu) [centas,
     pl. centai (*or* centas)]
LUXEMBOURG
Capital: Luxembourg
Currency: euro [cent]
MACEDONIA
Capital: Skopje
Currency: dinar [para]
MADAGASCAR
Capital: Antananarivo
Currency: Malagasy franc [centime]
MALAWI
Capital: Lilongwe
Currency: kwacha [tambala]
MALAYSIA
Capital: Kuala Lumpur
Currency: ringgit (*or* dollar) [sen (*or* cent)]
MALDIVES
Capital: Malé
Currency: rufiyaa [laari (*or* lari *or* laree)]
MALI
Capital: Bamako
Currency: CFA franc [centime]
MALTA
Capital: Valletta
Currency: lira, *pl.* lire (*or* liras) [cent]

3

MARSHALL ISLANDS
Capital: Dalap-Uliga-Darrit
Currency: US dollar [cent]
MAURITANIA
Capital: Nouakchott
Currency: ouguiya (*or* ougiya) [khoum]
MAURITIUS
Capital: Port Louis
Currency: rupee [cent]
MEXICO
Capital: Mexico City
Currency: peso [centavo]
MICRONESIA, FEDERATED STATES OF
Capital: Palikir
Currency: US dollar [cent]
MOLDOVA
Capital: Kishinev (*or* Chişinău)
Currency: leu, *pl.* lei [ban, *pl.* bani]
MONACO
Capital: Monaco-Ville
Currency: euro [cent]
MONGOLIA
Capital: Ulaanbaatar (*or* Ulan Bator)
Currency: tugrik [möngö]
MOROCCO
Capital: Rabat
Currency: dirham (*or* dirhem) [centime]
MOZAMBIQUE
Capital: Maputo
Currency: metical [centavo]
MYANMAR (BURMA)
Capital: Yangôn (Rangoon)
Currency: kyat [pya]
NAMIBIA
Capital: Windhoek
Currency: dollar [cent]
NAURU
Capital: Yaren
Currency: Australian dollar [cent]
NEPAL
Capital: Kathmandu
Currency: rupee [paisa, *pl.* paise (*or* paisa)]
NETHERLANDS
Capital: Amsterdam
Currency: euro [cent]
NEW ZEALAND
Capital: Wellington
Currency: dollar [cent]
NICARAGUA
Capital: Managua
Currency: córdoba [centavo]
NIGER
Capital: Niamey
Currency: CFA franc [centime]
NIGERIA
Capital: Abuja
Currency: naira [kobo]
NORWAY
Capital: Oslo
Currency: krone, *pl.* kroner (*or* kronen) [øre]

OMAN
Capital: Muscat
Currency: rial [baiza]
PAKISTAN
Capital: Islamabad
Currency: rupee [paisa, *pl.* paise (*or* paisa)]
PANAMA
Capital: Panama City
Currency: balboa [centésimo (*or* cent)]
PAPUA NEW GUINEA
Capital: Port Moresby
Currency: kina [toea]
PARAGUAY
Capital: Asunción
Currency: guaraní [céntimo]
PAULA *See* BELAU
PERU
Capital: Lima
Currency: sol, *pl.* soles [cént]
PHILIPPINES
Capital: Manila
Currency: peso [centavo]
POLAND
Capital: Warsaw
Currency: złoty [grosz, *pl.* groszy]
PORTUGAL
Capital: Lisbon
Currency: euro [cent]
QATAR
Capital: Doha
Currency: riyal [dirham (*or* dirhem)]
ROMANIA
Capital: Bucharest
Currency: leu, *pl.* lei [ban, *pl.* bani]
RUSSIA
Capital: Moscow
Currency: rouble [kopeck (*or* copeck)]
RWANDA
Capital: Kigali
Currency: franc [centime]
SAINT KITTS (*or* CHRISTOPHER) AND NEVIS
Capital: Basseterre
Currency: East Caribbean dollar [cent]
SAINT LUCIA
Capital: Castries
Currency: East Caribbean dollar [cent]
SAINT VINCENT AND THE GRENADINES
Capital: Kingstown
Currency: East Caribbean dollar [cent]
SAMOA
Capital: Apia
Currency: tala [sene]
SAN MARINO
Capital: San Marino
Currency: euro [cent]
SÃO TOMÉ AND PRÍNCIPE
Capital: São Tomé
Currency: dobra [cêntimo]
SAUDI ARABIA
Capital: Riyadh
Currency: riyal [halala, *pl.* halala (*or* halalah *or* halalas)]

SENEGAL
Capital: Dakar
Currency: CFA franc [centime]
SERBIA AND MONTENEGRO
Capital: Belgrade
Currency: dinar [pura] and euro [cent]
SEYCHELLES
Capital: Victoria
Currency: rupee [cent]
SIERRA LEONE
Capital: Freetown
Currency: leone [cent]
SINGAPORE
Capital: Singapore
Currency: dollar [cent]
SLOVAKIA
Capital: Bratislava
Currency: koruna [haler (*or* halier), *pl.* haleru
  (*or* halierov *or* halura)]
SLOVENIA
Capital: Ljubljana
Currency: tolar, *pl.* tolarji (*or* tolars)
  [stotin]
SOLOMON ISLANDS
Capital: Honiara
Currency: dollar [cent]
SOMALIA
Capital: Mogadishu
Currency: shilling [cent]
SOUTH AFRICA
Capital: Pretoria
Currency: rand [cent]
SPAIN
Capital: Madrid
Currency: euro [cent]
SRI LANKA
Capital: Colombo
Currency: rupee [cent]
SUDAN
Capital: Khartoum
Currency: dinar
SURINAME
Capital: Paramaribo
Currency: guilder [cent]
SWAZILAND
Capital: Mbabane
Currency: Lilangeni [cent]
SWEDEN
Capital: Stockholm
Currency: krona, *pl.* kronor [öre]
SWITZERLAND
Capital: Bern
Currency: franc [centime]
SYRIA
Capital: Damascus
Currency: pound [piastre]
TAIWAN
Capital: Taipei
Currency: dollar [cent]
TAJIKSTAN
Capital: Dushanbe
Currency: rouble [tanga]

TANZANIA
Capital: Dodoma
Currency: shilling [cent]
THAILAND
Capital: Bangkok
Currency: baht [satang, *pl.* satang (*or* stangs
  or satangs)]
TOGO
Capital: Lomé
Currency: CFA franc [centime]
TONGA
Capital: Nuku'alofa
Currency: pa'anga [seniti]
TRINIDAD AND TOBAGO
Capital: Port of Spain
Currency: dollar [cent]
TUNISIA
Capital: Tunis
Currency: dinar [millime]
TURKEY
Capital: Ankara
Currency: lira, *pl.* lire [kurus]
TURKMENISTAN
Capital: Ashkhabad (*or* Ashgabat)
Currency: manat [tenge]
TUVALU
Capital: Fongafale
Currency: dollar [cent]
UGANDA
Capital: Kampala
Currency: shilling [cent]
UKRAINE
Capital: Kiev
Currency: hryvnya (*or* hryvna) [kopiyka]
UNITED ARAB EMIRATES
Capital: Abu Dhabi
Currency: dirham [fils]
UNITED KINGDOM
Capital: London
Currency: pound [penny, *pl.* pence]
UNITED STATES OF AMERICA
Capital: Washington, DC
Currency: dollar [cent]
URUGUAY
Capital: Montevideo
Currency: peso [centésimo]
UZBEKISTAN
Capital: Tashkent
Currency: sum, *pl.* sum (*or* sumy)
  [teen]
VANUATU
Capital: Vila
Currency: vatu [centime]
VATICAN CITY STATE
Capital: Vatican City
Currency: euro [cent]
VENEZUELA
Capital: Caracas
Currency: bolívar [céntimo]
VIETNAM
Capital: Hanoi
Currency: dong [xu]

YEMEN
Capital: Sana'a
Currency: riyal [fils]
ZAMBIA
Capital: Lusaka
Currency: kwacha [ngwee]

ZIMBABWE
Capital: Harare
Currency: dollar [cent]

DEPENDENCIES

AUSTRALIA
ASHMORE AND CARTIER ISLANDS
THE AUSTRALIAN ANTARCTIC TERRITORY
CHRISTMAS ISLAND
Principal Settlement: Flying Fish Cove
COCOS (KEELING) ISLANDS
Principal Settlement: West Island
CORAL SEA ISLANDS TERRITORY
HEARD ISLAND AND MCDONALD ISLAND
NORFOLK ISLAND
Capital: Kingstown

DENMARK
FAROE ISLANDS
Capital: Tórshavn
GREENLAND
Capital: Nuuk (Godthåb)

FRANCE
FRENCH GUIANA
Capital: Cayenne
FRENCH POLYNESIA
Capital: Papeete
GUADELOUPE
Capital: Basse-Terre
MARTINIQUE
Capital: Fort-de-France
MAYOTTE
Capital: Dzaoudzi
NEW CALEDONIA
Capital: Nouméa
RÉUNION
Capital: Saint-Denis
SAINT PIERRE AND MIQUELON
Capital: Saint-Pierre
WALLIS AND FUTUNA
Capital: Mata-Utu

THE NETHERLANDS
ARUBA
Capital: Oranjestad
NETHERLANDS ANTILLES
Capital: Willemstad

NEW ZEALAND
COOK ISLANDS
Capital: Avarua
NIUE
Capital: Alofi
THE ROSS DEPENDENCY
TOKELAU

NORWAY
BOUVET ISLAND
JAN MAYEN
PETER THE FIRST ISLAND
PRINCESS RAGNHILD LAND
QUEEN MAUD LAND
SVALBARD
Principal Settlement: Longyearbyen

UNITED KINGDOM
ANGUILLA
Capital: The Valley
BERMUDA
Capital: Hamilton
BRITISH ANTARCTIC TERRITORY
BRITISH INDIAN OCEAN TERRITORY
BRITISH VIRGIN ISLANDS
Capital: Road Town
CAYMAN ISLANDS
Capital: George Town
FALKLAND ISLANDS
Capital: Stanley
GIBRALTAR
Capital: Gibraltar
GUERNSEY
Capital: St Peter Port
ISLE OF MAN
Capital: Douglas
JERSEY
Capital: St Helier
MONTSERRAT
Capital: Plymouth
PITCAIRN ISLANDS
Sole town: Adamstown
SAINT HELENA
Capital: Jamestown

SOUTH GEORGIA AND THE SOUTH
  SANDWICH ISLANDS
TURKS AND CAICOS ISLANDS
  Capital: Cockburn Town

UNITED STATES
AMERICAN SAMOA
  Capital: Pago Pago

GUAM
  Capital: Agaña
NORTHERN MARIANA ISLANDS
  Principal Settlement: Saipan
PUERTO RICO
  Capital: San Juan
UNITED STATES VIRGIN ISLANDS
  Capital: Charlotte Amalie

CAPITALS

CAPITAL	COUNTRY	CAPITAL	COUNTRY
ABU DHABI	UNITED ARAB EMIRATES	BRAZZAVILLE	CONGO-BRAZZAVILLE
ABUJA	NIGERIA	BRIDGETOWN	BARBADOS
ACCRA	GHANA	BRUSSELS	BELGIUM
ADDIS ABABA	ETHIOPIA	BUCHAREST	ROMANIA
ADEN (*commercial*)	YEMEN	BUDAPEST	HUNGARY
ALGIERS	ALGERIA	BUENOS AIRES	ARGENTINA
AMMAN	JORDAN	BUJUMBURA	BURUNDI
AMSTERDAM	NETHERLANDS	CAIRO	EGYPT
ANDORRA LA VELLA	ANDORRA	CANBERRA	AUSTRALIA
ANKARA	TURKEY	CARACAS	VENEZUELA
ANTANANARIVO	MADAGASCAR	CASTRIES	SAINT LUCIA
APIA	SAMOA	CHIŞINĂU	MOLDOVA
ASHKHABAD (*OR* ASHGABAT)	TURKMENISTAN	COLOMBO	SRI LANKA
		CONAKRY	GUINEA
ASMARA	ERITREA	COPENHAGEN	DENMARK
ASTANA	KAZAKHSTAN	DAKAR	SENEGAL
ASUNCIÓN	PARAGUAY	DALAP-ULIGA-DARRIT	MARSHALL ISLANDS
ATHENS	GREECE		
BAGHDAD	IRAQ	DAMASCUS	SYRIA
BAKU	AZERBAIJAN	DHAKA (DACCA)	BANGLADESH
BAMAKO	MALI	DILI	EAST TIMOR
BANDAR SERI BEGAWAN	BRUNEI	DJIBOUTI	DJIBOUTI
		DODOMA	TANZANIA
BANGKOK	THAILAND	DOHA	QATAR
BANGUI	CENTRAL AFRICAN REPUBLIC	DUBLIN	IRELAND, REPUBLIC OF
BANJUL	THE GAMBIA	DUSHANBE	TAJIKISTAN
BASSETERRE	SAINT KITTS AND NEVIS	FONGAFALE	TUVALU
		FREETOWN	SIERRA LEONE
BEIJING	CHINA	GABORONE	BOTSWANA
BEIRUT	LEBANON	GEORGETOWN	GUYANA
BELGRADE	SERBIA AND MONTENEGRO	GUATEMALA CITY	GUATEMALA
		HANOI	VIETNAM
BELMOPAN	BELIZE	HARARE	ZIMBABWE
BERLIN	GERMANY	HAVANA	CUBA
BERN	SWITZERLAND	HELSINKI	FINLAND
BISHKEK	KYRGYZSTAN	HONIARA	SOLOMON ISLANDS
BISSAU	GUINEA-BISSAU	ISLAMABAD	PAKISTAN
BOGOTÁ	COLOMBIA	JAKARTA	INDONESIA
BRASÍLIA	BRAZIL	JERUSALEM	ISRAEL
BRATISLAVA	SLOVAKIA	KABUL	AFGHANISTAN

CAPITAL	COUNTRY	CAPITAL	COUNTRY
KAMPALA	UGANDA	PHNOM PENH	CAMBODIA
KATHMANDU	NEPAL	PORT-AU-PRINCE	HAITI
KHARTOUM	SUDAN	PORT LOUIS	MAURITIUS
KIEV	UKRAINE	PORT MORESBY	PAPUA NEW GUINEA
KIGALI	RWANDA	PORT OF SPAIN	TRINIDAD AND
KINGSTON	JAMAICA		TOBAGO
KINGSTOWN	SAINT VINCENT AND	PORTO-NOVO	BENIN
	THE GRENADINES	PRAGUE	CZECH REPUBLIC
KINSHASA	CONGO, DEMOCRATIC	PRAIA	CAPE VERDE
	REPUBLIC OF	PRETORIA	SOUTH AFRICA
KISHINEV	MOLDOVA	P'YONGYANG	NORTH KOREA
KOROR	BELAU	QUITO	ECUADOR
KUALA LUMPUR	MALAYSIA	RABAT	MOROCCO
KUWAIT CITY	KUWAIT	RANGOON	BURMA
LA PAZ	BOLIVIA	REYKJAVIK	ICELAND
LEFKOSIA	CYPRUS	RIGA	LATVIA
LIBREVILLE	GABON	RIYADH	SAUDI ARABIA
LILONGWE	MALAWI	ROME	ITALY
LIMA	PERU	ROSEAU	DOMINICA
LISBON	PORTUGAL	ST GEORGE'S	GRENADA
LJUBLJANA	SLOVENIA	SAINT JOHN'S	ANTIGUA AND
LOME	TOGO		BARBUDA
LONDON	UNITED KINGDOM	SANA'A (*administrative*)	YEMEN
LUANDA	ANGOLA	SAN JOSÉ	COSTA RICA
LUSAKA	ZAMBIA	SAN MARINO	SAN MARINO
LUXEMBOURG	LUXEMBOURG	SAN SALVADOR	EL SALVADOR
MADRID	SPAIN	SANTIAGO	CHILE
MALABO	EQUATORIAL GUINEA	SANTO DOMINGO	DOMINICAN
MALÉ	MALDIVES		REPUBLIC
MANAGUA	NICARAGUA	SÃO TOMÉ	SÃO TOMÉ AND
MANAMA	BAHRAIN		PRÍNCIPE
MANILA	PHILIPPINES	SARAJEVO	BOSNIA-
MAPUTO	MOZAMBIQUE		HERCEGOVINA
MASERU	LESOTHO	SEOUL	SOUTH KOREA
MBABANE	SWAZILAND	SINGAPORE	SINGAPORE
MEXICO CITY	MEXICO	SKOPJE	MACEDONIA
MINSK	BELARUS	SOFIA	BULGARIA
MOGADISHU	SOMALIA	STOCKHOLM	SWEDEN
MONACO-VILLE	MONACO	SUVA	FIJI
MONROVIA	LIBERIA	TAIPEI	TAIWAN
MONTEVIDEO	URUGUAY	TALLINN	ESTONIA
MORONI	COMOROS	TARAWA	KIRIBATI
MOSCOW	RUSSIA	TASHKENT	UZBEKISTAN
MUSCAT	OMAN	T'BILISI	GEORGIA
NAIROBI	KENYA	TEGUCIGALPA	HONDURAS
NASSAU	THE BAHAMAS	TEHRAN	IRAN
N'DJAMENA	CHAD	THIMPHU	BHUTAN
NEW DELHI	INDIA	TIRANA (*OR* TIRANË)	ALBANIA
NIAMEY	NIGER	TOKYO	JAPAN
NICOSIA	CYPRUS	TRIPOLI	LIBYA
NOUAKCHOTT	MAURITANIA	TUNIS	TUNISIA
NUKU'ALOFA	TONGA	ULAANBAATAR	MONGOLIA
OSLO	NORWAY	(*OR* ULAN BATOR)	
OTTAWA	CANADA	VADUZ	LIECHTENSTEIN
OUAGADOUGOU	BURKINA FASO	VALLETTA	MALTA
PALIKIR	MICRONESIA	VATICAN CITY	VATICAN CITY STATE
PANAMA CITY	PANAMA	VICTORIA	SEYCHELLES
PARAMARIBO	SURINAME	VIENNA	AUSTRIA
PARIS	FRANCE	VIENTIANE	LAOS
PEKING	CHINA	VILA	VANUATU

CAPITAL	COUNTRY	CAPITAL	COUNTRY
VILNIUS	LITHUANIA	YAMOUSSOUKRO	CÔTE D'IVOIRE
WARSAW	POLAND	YANGÔN	MYANMAR
WASHINGTON, DC	UNITED STATES OF AMERICA	YAOUNDÉ	CAMEROON
		YAREN	NAURU
WELLINGTON	NEW ZEALAND	YEREVAN	ARMENIA
WINDHOEK	NAMIBIA	ZAGREB	CROATIA

CURRENCIES

CURRENCY — COUNTRIES

AFGHANI — AFGHANISTAN

AGORA — ISRAEL

AGOROT — ISRAEL

AGOROTH — ISRAEL

AT — LAOS

AURAR — ICELAND

AUSTRAL — ARGENTINA

AUSTRALIAN DOLLAR — KIRIBATI, NAURU

BAHT — THAILAND

BAIZA — OMAN

BALBOA — PANAMA

BAN — MOLDOVA, ROMANIA

BANI — MOLDOVA, ROMANIA

BIRR — ETHIOPIA

BOLÍVAR — VENEZUELA

BOLIVIANO — BOLIVIA

BUTUT — THE GAMBIA

CAURIS — GUINEA

CEDI — GHANA

CENT — ANDORRA, ANTIGUA AND BARBUDA, ARUBA, AUSTRALIA, AUSTRIA, THE BAHAMAS, BARBADOS, BELGIUM, BELIZE, BERMUDA, BOSNIA-HERCEGOVINA, BRUNEI, CANADA, THE CAYMAN ISLANDS, CYPRUS, DOMINICA, EAST TIMOR, ECUADOR, EL SALVADOR, ETHIOPIA, FIJI, FINLAND, FRANCE, FRENCH GUIANA, GERMANY, GREECE, GRENADA, GUADELOUPE, GUAM, GUYANA, HONG KONG, IRELAND, JAMAICA, KENYA, KIRIBATI, KOSOVO, LIBERIA, LUXEMBOURG, MALAYSIA, MALTA, THE MARSHALL ISLANDS, MARTINIQUE, MAURITIUS, MAYOTTE, MICRONESIA, MONACO, MONTENEGRO, NAMIBIA, NAURU, THE NETHERLANDS, THE NETHERLANDS ANTILLES, NEW ZEALAND, THE NORTHERN MARIANA ISLANDS, PALAU, PORTUGAL, PUERTO RICO, RÉUNION, SAINT KITTS AND NEVIS, SAINT LUCIA, SAINT VINCENT AND THE GRENADINES, SAN MARINO, THE SEYCHELLES, SIERRA LEONE, SINGAPORE, THE SOLOMON ISLANDS, SOMALIA, SOUTH AFRICA, SPAIN, SRI LANKA, SURINAM, SWAZILAND, TAIWAN, TANZANIA, TRINIDAD AND TOBAGO, TUVALU, UGANDA, THE UNITED STATES, THE VATICAN CITY, THE VIRGIN ISLANDS, ZIMBABWE

CÉNT — PERU

CENTAI — LITHUANIA

CENTAS — LITHUANIA

CENTAVO — BOLIVIA, BRAZIL, CAPE VERDE, CHILE, COLOMBIA, CUBA, DOMINICAN REPUBLIC, ECUADOR, EL SALVADOR, GUATEMALA, HONDURAS, MEXICO, MOZAMBIQUE, NICARAGUA, PHILIPPINES

CENTÉSIMO — PANAMA, URUGUAY

CENTIME — ALGERIA, BENIN, BURKINA FASO, BURUNDI, CAMEROON, CENTRAL AFRICAN REPUBLIC, CHAD, COMOROS, CONGO, CÔTE D'IVOIRE, DJIBOUTI, EQUATORIAL GUINEA, GABON, GUINEA, HAITI, LIECHTENSTEIN, MADAGASCAR, MALI, MONACO, MOROCCO, NIGER, RWANDA, SENEGAL, SWITZERLAND, TOGO, VANUATU

CÉNTIMO — COSTA RICA, PARAGUAY, VENEZUELA

CÊNTIMO — SÃO TOMÉ AND PRÍNCIPE

CFA FRANC — BENIN, BURKINA FASO, CAMEROON, CENTRAL AFRICAN REPUBLIC, CHAD, COMOROS, CONGO, CÔTE D'IVOIRE, EQUATORIAL GUINEA, GABON, GUINEA-BISSAU, MALI, NIGER, SENEGAL, TOGO

CHETRUM — BHUTAN

CHON — SOUTH KOREA

CHUN — SOUTH KOREA

COLON — COSTA RICA

COLÓN — EL SALVADOR

COLONES — COSTA RICA, EL SALVADOR

COLONS — COSTA RICA, EL SALVADOR

COPECK — BELARUS, RUSSIA

COPEK — BELARUS, RUSSIA, TAJIKSTAN

CÓRDOBA — NICARAGUA

DALASI — THE GAMBIA

DINAR — BAHRAIN, IRAQ, JORDAN, KUWAIT,

9

LIBYA, MACEDONIA, SUDAN, TUNISIA, YUGOSLAVIA

DIRHAM (DIRHEM) — LIBYA, MOROCCO, QATAR, UNITED ARAB EMIRATES

DOBRA — SÃO TOMÉ AND PRÍNCIPE

DOLLAR — ANTIGUA AND BARBUDA, AUSTRALIA, THE BAHAMAS, BARBADOS, BELIZE, BERMUDA, THE BRITISH VIRGIN ISLANDS, BRUNEI, CANADA, THE CAYMAN ISLANDS, DOMINICA, EAST TIMOR, ECUADOR, EL SALVADOR, FIJI, GRENADA, GUATEMALA, GUYANA, HONG KONG, JAMAICA, KIRIBATI, LIBERIA, MALAYSIA, THE MARSHALL ISLANDS, MICRONESIA, NAMIBIA, NAURU, NEW ZEALAND, SAINT KITTS AND NEVIS, SAINT LUCIA, SAINT VINCENT AND THE GRENADINES, SINGAPORE, SOLOMON ISLANDS, TAIWAN, TRINIDAD AND TOBAGO, TUVALU, ZIMBABWE

DONG — VIETNAM

DRAM — ARMENIA

EAST CARIBBEAN DOLLAR — ANTIGUA AND BARBUDA, DOMINICA, GRENADA, SAINT KITTS AND NEVIS, SAINT LUCIA, SAINT VINCENT AND THE GRENADINES

ESCUDO — CAPE VERDE

EURO — ANDORRA, AUSTRIA, BELGIUM, BOSNIA-HERCEGOVINA, FINLAND, FRANCE, FRENCH GUIANA, GERMANY, GREECE, GUADELOUPE, IRELAND, ITALY, KOSOVO, LUXEMBOURG, MARTINIQUE, MAYOTTE, MONACO, MONTENEGRO, THE NETHERLANDS, PORTGUAL, RÉUNION, SAN MARINO, SPAIN, VATICAN CITY

EYRIR — ICELAND

FEN — CHINA

FILLÉR — HUNGARY

FILS — BAHRAIN, IRAQ, JORDAN, KUWAIT, UNITED ARAB EMIRATES, YEMEN

FORINT — HUNGARY

FRANC — BURUNDI, CONGO, DJIBOUTI, GUINEA, RWANDA, SWITZERLAND

GOPIK — AZERBAIJAN

GOURDE — HAITI

GROSZ — POLAND

GROSZY — POLAND

GUARANÍ — PARAGUAY

GUILDER — NETHERLANDS, SURINAME

HALALA — SAUDI ARABIA

HALER — CZECH REPUBLIC, SLOVAKIA

HALERU — CZECH REPUBLIC, SLOVAKIA

HALIER — SLOVAKIA

HALIEROV — SLOVAKIA

HALURA — CZECH REPUBLIC

HRYVNA — UKRAINE

HRYVNYA — UKRAINE

JEON — SOUTH KOREA

JUN — NORTH KOREA

KHOUM — MAURITANIA

KINA — PAPUA NEW GUINEA

KIP — LAOS

KOBO — NIGERIA

KOPECK — BELARUS, RUSSIA, TAJIKSTAN

KOPEK — BELARUS, RUSSIA, TAJIKSTAN

KOPIYKA — UKRAINE

KORUNA — CZECH REPUBLIC, SLOVAKIA

KRONA — SWEDEN

KRÓNA — ICELAND

KRONE — DENMARK, NORWAY

KRONEN — DENMARK, NORWAY

KRONER — DENMARK, NORWAY

KRONOR — SWEDEN

KRÓNUR — ICELAND

KROON — ESTONIA

KROONI — ESTONIA

KROONS — ESTONIA

KUNA — CROATIA

KUNE — CROATIA

KURUS — TURKEY

KURUSH — TURKEY

KWACHA — MALAWI, ZAMBIA

KWANZA — ANGOLA

KYAT — MYANMAR (BURMA)

LAARI — MALDIVES

LAREE — MALDIVES

LARI — GEORGIA, MALDIVES

LAT — LATVIA

LATI — LATVIA

LATS — LATVIA

LEI — MOLDOVA, ROMANIA

LEK — ALBANIA

LEKË — ALBANIA

LEKS — ALBANIA

LEMPIRA — HONDURAS

LEONE — SIERRA LEONE

LEU — MOLDOVA, ROMANIA

LEV — BULGARIA

LEVA — BULGARIA

LEVS — BULGARIA

LILANGENI — SWAZILAND

LIPA — CROATIA

LIRA — MALTA, TURKEY

LIRAS — MALTA, TURKEY

LIRE — MALTA, TURKEY,

LISENTE — LESOTHO

LITAI — LITHUANIA

LITAS — LITHUANIA

LITS — LITHUANIA

LITU — LITHUANIA

LOTI — LESOTHO

LOUMA — ARMENIA

LWEI — ANGOLA

MANAT — AZERBAIJAN, TURKMENISTAN

METICAL — MOZAMBIQUE

MILLIME — TUNISIA
MÖNGÖ — MONGOLIA
NAKFA — ERITREA
NAIRA — NIGERIA
NGULTRUM — BHUTAN
NGWEE — ZAMBIA
ØRE — DENMARK, NORWAY
ÖRE — SWEDEN
OUGIYA — MAURITANIA
OUGUIYA — MAURITANIA
PA'ANGA — TONGA
PAISA — INDIA, NEPAL, PAKISTAN
PAISE — INDIA, NEPAL, PAKISTAN
PARA — MACEDONIA, SERBIA AND
  MONTENEGRO
PENCE — UNITED KINGDOM
PENNIES — UNITED KINGDOM
PENNY — UNITED KINGDOM
PESEWA — GHANA
PESO — ARGENTINA, CHILE, COLOMBIA,
  CUBA, DOMINICAN REPUBLIC, MEXICO,
  PHILIPPINES, URUGUAY
PIASTRE — EGYPT, LEBANON, SYRIA
POISHA — BANGLADESH
POUND — CYPRUS, EGYPT, LEBANON,
  SYRIA, UNITED KINGDOM
PUL — AFGHANISTAN
PULA — BOTSWANA
PULI — AFGHANISTAN
PULS — AFGHANISTAN
PYA — MYANMAR (BURMA)
QINDAR — ALBANIA
QINDARKA — ALBANIA
QINTAR — ALBANIA
QUETZAL — GUATEMALA
QUETZALES — GUATEMALA
RAND — SOUTH AFRICA
REAL — BRAZIL
RENMINBI — CHINA
RIAL — IRAN, OMAN
RIYAL — YEMEN
RIEL — CAMBODIA
RINGGIT — MALAYSIA
RIYAL — QATAR, SAUDI ARABIA
ROUBLE — BELARUS, RUSSIA, TAJIKSTAN
RUFIYAA — MALDIVES
RUPEE — INDIA, MAURITIUS, NEPAL,
  PAKISTAN, SEYCHELLES, SRI LANKA
RUPIAH — INDONESIA

SANTIMI — LATVIA
SATANG — THAILAND
SATANGS — THAILAND
SEN — BRUNEI, CAMBODIA, INDONESIA,
  JAPAN, MALAYSIA
SENE — SAMOA
SENITI — TONGA
SENT — ESTONIA
SENTE — LESOTHO
SENTI — ESTONIA
SHEKEL — ISRAEL
SHEQEL — ISRAEL
SHILLING — KENYA, SOMALIA, TANZANIA,
  UGANDA
SOL — PERU
SOLES — PERU
SOM — KYRGYZSTAN
STANGS — THAILAND
STOTIN — SLOVENIA
STOTINKA — BULGARIA
STOTINKI — BULGARIA
SUM — UZBEKISTAN
SUMY — UZBEKISTAN
SWISS FRANC — LIECHTENSTEIN
TAKA — BANGLADESH
TALA — SAMOA
TAMBALA — MALAWI
TANGA — KAJIKSTAN
TEEN — UZBEKISTAN
TENGE — KAZAKHSTAN, TURKMENISTAN
TETRI — GEORGIA
THEBE — BOTSWANA
TOEA — PAPUA NEW GUINEA
TOLAR — SLOVENIA
TOLARJI — SLOVENIA
TOLARS — SLOVENIA
TUGRIK — MONGOLIA
TYIN — KYRGYZSTAN
US DOLLAR — BELAU, MARSHALL ISLANDS,
  MICRONESIA
VATU — VANUATU
WON — NORTH KOREA, SOUTH KOREA
XU — VIETNAM
YEN — JAPAN
YUAN — CHINA
ZLOTY — POLAND

FORMER EUROPEAN CURRENCIES

CENTESIMI — ITALY, SAN
  MARINO, VATICAN CITY
CENTESIMO — ITALY, SAN
  MARINO, VATICAN CITY
CENTIME — ANDORRA,
  BELGIUM, FRANCE,
  LUXEMBOURG
CÉNTIMO —
  ANDORRA,SPAIN
DEUTSCHE MARK —
  GERMANY
DEUTSCHMARK —
  GERMANY
DRACHMA — GREECE
DRACHMAE — GREECE
DRACHMAS — GREECE

ESCUDO — PORTUGAL
FRANC — BELGIUM,
  FRANCE, LUXEMBOURG
GROSCHEN — AUSTRIA
ITALIAN LIRA — SAN
  MARINO, VATICAN CITY
LEPTA — GREECE
LEPTON — GREECE
LIRA — ITALY
LIRAS — ITALY, SAN MARINO,
  VATICAN CITY
LIRE — ITALY, SAN MARINO,
  VATICAN CITY
MARKA — BOSNIA-
  HERCEGOVINA
MARKKA — FINLAND

PENCE — IRELAND,
  REPUBLIC OF
PENNI — FINLAND
PENNIÄ — FINLAND
PENNIES — IRELAND,
  REPUBLIC OF
PENNY — IRELAND,
  REPUBLIC OF
PESETA — ANDORRA, SPAIN
PFENNIG — GERMANY
PFENNIGE — GERMANY
PFENNIGS — GERMANY
PUNT — IRELAND, REPUBLIC
  OF
SCHILLING — AUSTRIA

ENGLISH COUNTIES AND SELECTED LOCAL AUTHORITIES

**AUTHORITY (Administrative
Centre)**

*AVON (Bristol)
BATH AND NORTH-EAST
  SOMERSET (Bath)
BEDFORD(SHIRE) (Bedford)
*BERKSHIRE (Reading)
BUCKINGHAM(SHIRE)
  (Aylesbury)
CALDERDALE (Halifax)
CAMBRIDGE(SHIRE)
  (Cambridge)
CHESHIRE (Chester)
*CLEVELAND
  (Middlesborough)
CORNWALL (Truro)
*CUMBERLAND (Carlisle)
CUMBRIA (Carlisle)
DERBY(SHIRE) (Matlock)
DEVON (Exeter)
DORSET (Dorchester)
DURHAM (Durham)
EAST RIDING (OF
  YORKSHIRE) (Beverley)
EAST SUSSEX (Lewes)
ESSEX (Chelmsford)
GLOUCESTER(SHIRE)
  (Gloucester)
†GREATER LONDON (London)
†GREATER MANCHESTER
  (Manchester)

HALTON (Runcorn)
HAMPSHIRE (Winchester)
*HEREFORD AND
  WORCESTER (Worcester)
HEREFORD(SHIRE)
  (Hereford)
HERTFORD(SHIRE) (Hertford)
*HUMBERSIDE (Beverley)
*HUNTINGDON(SHIRE)
  (Huntingdon)
ISLE OF WIGHT (Newport,
  IOW)
KENT (Maidstone)
KIRKLEES (Huddersfield)
LANCASHIRE (Preston)
LEICESTER(SHIRE)
  (Leicester)
LINCOLN(SHIRE) (Lincoln)
MEDWAY (Gillingham)
†MERSEYSIDE (Liverpool)
NORFOLK (Norwich)
NORTHAMPTON(SHIRE)
  (Northampton)
NORTH-EAST
  LINCOLNSHIRE (Grimsby)
NORTH LINCOLNSHIRE
  (Scunthorpe)
NORTH SOMERSET (Weston-
  super-Mare)
*NORTH RIDING (OF YORK-
  SHIRE) (Middlesbrough)
NORTH TYNESIDE (Wallsend)

NORTHUMBERLAND
  (Morpeth)
NORTH YORKSHIRE
  (Northallerton)
NOTTINGHAM(SHIRE)
  (Nottingham)
OXFORD(SHIRE) (Oxford)
REDCAR AND CLEVELAND
  (Redcar)
RUTLAND (Oakham)
SALOP (name for Shropshire
  between 1974 and 1980)
SHROPSHIRE (Shrewsbury)
SOMERSET (Taunton)
SOUTH GLOUCESTERSHIRE
  (Thornbury)
SOUTH TYNESIDE (South
  Shields)
†SOUTH YORKSHIRE
  (Barnsley)
STAFFORD(SHIRE) (Stafford)
SUFFOLK (Ipswich)
SURREY (Guildford)
*SUSSEX (Lewes)
TELFORD AND WREKIN
  (Telford)
†TYNE AND WEAR
  (Newcastle-Upon-Tyne)
WARWICK(SHIRE) (Warwick)
WEST BERKSHIRE
  (Newbury)

†WEST MIDLANDS
(Birmingham)
*WESTMORLAND (Kendal)
*WEST RIDING (OF
YORKSHIRE) (Wakefield)

WEST SUSSEX (Chichester)
†WEST YORKSHIRE
(Wakefield)
WILTSHIRE (Trowbridge)
WIRRAL (Birkenhead)

*WORCESTER(SHIRE)
(Worcester)

*indicates a former county
†metropolitan county

WELSH COUNTIES AND SELECTED LOCAL AUTHORITIES

**AUTHORITY (Administrative
Centre)**

*ANGLESEY (Llangefni)
BLAENAU GWENT (Ebbw
Vale)
*BRECON(SHIRE) (Brecon)
*CAERNARFON(SHIRE)
(Caernarfon)
*CARDIGAN(SHIRE)
(Aberystwyth)
CARMARTHEN(SHIRE)
(Carmarthen)
CEREDIGION (Aberaeron)
*CLWYD (Mold)
CONWY (Bodlondeb)

DENBIGH(SHIRE) (Ruthin)
*DYFED (Carmarthen)
FLINTSHIRE (Mold)
*GLAMORGAN (Cardiff)
*GWENT (Cwmbran)
GWYNEDD (Caernarfon)
*MERIONETH (Dolgellan)
*MID GLAMORGAN (Cardiff)
MONMOUTH(SHIRE)
(Cwmbran)
*MONTGOMERY(SHIRE)
(Welshpool)
NEATH PORT TALBOT
(Port Talbot)
PEMBROKE(SHIRE)
(Haverfordwest)

POWYS (Llandrindod Wells)
*RADNOR(SHIRE)
(Llandrindod Wells)
RHONDDA CYNON TAFF
(Clydach Vale)
*SOUTH GLAMORGAN
(Cardiff)
SWANSEA
(Swansea)
TORFAEN (Pontypool)
VALE OF GLAMORGAN
(Barry)
*WEST GLAMORGAN
(Swansea)
WREXHAM (Wrexham)

*indicates a former county

SCOTTISH REGIONS, COUNTIES, AND SELECTED LOCAL AUTHORITIES

**AUTHORITY (Administrative
Centre)**

ABERDEEN(SHIRE)
(Aberdeen)
ANGUS (Forfar)
ARGYLL AND BUTE
(Lochgilphead)
*ARGYLL (Lochgilphead)
*AYR(SHIRE) (Ayr)
*BANFF (Banff)
*BERWICK (Duns)
*BORDERS
*BUTE (Rothesay)
*CAITHNESS (Wick)
*CENTRAL (Stirling)
CLACKMANNAN(SHIRE)
(Alloa)
DUMFRIES AND GALLOWAY
(Dumfries)
*DUMFRIES (Dumfries)
*DUNBARTONSHIRE
(Dumbarton)
EAST AYRSHIRE (Kilmarnock)
EAST DUNBARTONSHIRE
(Kirkintilloch)
EAST LOTHIAN (Haddington)

EAST RENFREWSHIRE
(Giffnock)
EILEAN SIAR (Lewis)
FIFE (Glenrothes)
*GRAMPIAN (Aberdeen)
HIGHLAND (Inverness)
INVERCLYDE (Greenock)
*INVERNESS (Inverness)
*KINCARDINE(SHIRE)
(Stonehaven)
*KINROSS (Kinross)
*KIRKCUDBRIGHT
(Kirkcudbright)
*LANARK(SHIRE) (Hamilton)
*LOTHIAN (Edinburgh)
MIDLOTHIAN (Dalkeith)
MORAY (Elgin)
*NAIRN (Nairn)
NORTH AYRSHIRE (Irvine)
NORTH LANARKSHIRE
(Motherwell)
ORKNEY (Kirkwall)
*PEEBLES (Peebles)
PERTH AND KINROSS (Perth)
*PERTH(SHIRE) (Perth)
RENFREW(SHIRE) (Paisley)

*ROSS AND CROMARTY
(Dingwall)
*ROXBURGH (Newtown St.
Boswells)
SCOTTISH BORDERS
(Newton St. Boswells)
*SELKIRK (Selkirk)
SHETLAND (Lerwick)
SOUTH AYRSHIRE (Ayr)
SOUTH LANARKSHIRE
(Hamilton)
STIRLING (Stirling)
*STRATHCLYDE (Glasgow)
*SUTHERLAND (Golspie)
*TAYSIDE (Dundee)
WEST DUNBARTONSHIRE
(Dumbarton)
*WESTERN ISLES (Lewis)
(now Eilean Siar)
WEST LOTHIAN (Livingston)
*WIGTOWN(SHIRE)
(Stranraer)
ZETLAND (former name for
Shetland)

*indicates a former region or
county

13

PROVINCES AND COUNTIES OF IRELAND

PROVINCE
COUNTY (County Town)

CONNACHT
MAYO (Castlebar)
SLIGO (Sligo)
GALWAY (Galway)
LEITRIM (Carrick-on-Shannon)
ROSCOMMON (Roscommon)

LEINSTER
LOUTH (Dundalk)
MEATH (Trim)
CARLOW (Carlow)
DUBLIN (Dublin)
OFFALY (Tullamore)

KILDARE (Naas)
WEXFORD (Wexford)
WICKLOW (Wicklow)
KILKENNY (Kilkenny)
LAOIGHIS [or LAOIS or LEIX]
  (Portlaoighise or Portlaoise)
LONGFORD (Longford)
WESTMEATH (Mullingar)

MUNSTER
CORK (Cork)
CLARE (Ennis)
KERRY (Tralee)
LIMERICK (Limerick)
TIPPERARY (Clonmel)
WATERFORD (Waterford)

ULSTER
*DOWN (Downpatrick)
CAVAN (Cavan)
*ARMAGH (Armagh)
*ANTRIM (Belfast)
*TYRONE (Omagh)
DONEGAL (Lifford)
MONAGHAN (Monaghan)
*FERMANAGH (Enniskillen)
*LONDONDERRY
  (Londonderry)

  *indicates counties of N
  Ireland

AMERICAN STATES

STATE	ABBREVIATION	NICKNAME	CAPITAL
ALABAMA	ALA	COTTON	MONTGOMERY
ALASKA	ALAS	LAST FRONTIER	JUNEAU
ARIZONA	ARIZ	GRAND CANYON	PHOENIX
ARKANSAS	ARK	LAND OF OPPORTUNITY	LITTLE ROCK
CALIFORNIA	CAL	GOLDEN	SACRAMENTO
COLORADO	COLO	CENTENNIAL	DENVER
CONNECTICUT	CONN	CONSTITUTION	HARTFORD
DELAWARE	DEL	FIRST	DOVER
FLORIDA	FLA	SUNSHINE	TALLAHASSEE
GEORGIA	GA	EMPIRE STATE OF THE SOUTH	ATLANTA
HAWAII	HA	ALOHA	HONOLULU
IDAHO	IDA	GEM	BOISE
ILLINOIS	ILL	LAND OF LINCOLN	SPRINGFIELD
INDIANA	IND	HOOSIER	INDIANAPOLIS
IOWA	IA	HAWKEYE	DES MOINES
KANSAS	KAN	SUNFLOWER	TOPEKA
KENTUCKY	KY	BLUEGRASS	FRANKFORT
LOUISIANA	LA	PELICAN	BATON ROUGE
MAINE	ME	PINE TREE	AUGUSTA
MARYLAND	MD	OLD LINE	ANNAPOLIS
MASSACHUSETTS	MASS	BAY	BOSTON
MICHIGAN	MICH	WOLVERINE	LANSING
MINNESOTA	MINN	GOPHER	ST. PAUL
MISSISSIPPI	MISS	MAGNOLIA	JACKSON
MISSOURI	MO	SHOW ME	JEFFERSON CITY
MONTANA	MONT	TREASURE	HELENA
NEBRASKA	NEBR	CORNHUSKER	LINCOLN
NEVADA	NEV	SILVER	CARSON CITY
NEW HAMPSHIRE	NH	GRANITE	CONCORD
NEW JERSEY	NJ	GARDEN	TRENTON
NEW MEXICO	N MEX	LAND OF ENCHANTMENT	SANTA FÉ
NEW YORK	NY	EMPIRE	ALBANY

STATE	ABBREVIATION	NICKNAME	CAPITAL
NORTH CAROLINA	NC	TARHEEL	RALEIGH
NORTH DAKOTA	N DAK	FLICKERTAIL	BISMARCK
OHIO	OH	BUCKEYE	COLUMBUS
OKLAHOMA	OKLA	SOONER	OKLAHOMA CITY
OREGON	OREG	BEAVER	SALEM
PENNSYLVANIA	PA	KEYSTONE	HARRISBURG
RHODE ISLAND	RI	OCEAN	PROVIDENCE
SOUTH CAROLINA	SC	PALMETTO	COLUMBIA
SOUTH DAKOTA	S DAK	SUNSHINE	PIERRE
TENNESSEE	TENN	VOLUNTEER	NASHVILLE
TEXAS	TEX	LONE STAR	AUSTIN
UTAH	UT	BEEHIVE	SALT LAKE CITY
VERMONT	VT	GREEN MOUNTAIN	MONTPELIER
VIRGINIA	VA	OLD DOMINION	RICHMOND
WASHINGTON	WASH	EVERGREEN	OLYMPIA
WEST VIRGINIA	W VA	MOUNTAIN	CHARLESTON
WISCONSIN	WIS	BADGER	MADISON
WYOMING	WYO	EQUALITY	CHEYENNE

AUSTRALIAN STATES AND TERRITORIES

AUSTRALIAN CAPITAL TERRITORY	SOUTH AUSTRALIA
NEW SOUTH WALES	TASMANIA
NORTHERN TERRITORY	VICTORIA
QUEENSLAND	WESTERN AUSTRALIA

CANADIAN PROVINCES OR TERRITORIES

PROVINCE/TERRITORY	ABBREVIATION	PROVINCE/TERRITORY	ABBREVIATION
ALBERTA	AB	NOVA SCOTIA	NS
BRITISH COLUMBIA	BC	NUNAVUT	(not assigned)
MANITOBA	MB	ONTARIO	ON
NEW BRUNSWICK	NB	PRINCE EDWARD ISLAND	PE
NEWFOUNDLAND AND LABRADOR	NF	QUEBEC	QC
		SASKATCHEWAN	SK
NORTHWEST TERRITORIES	NT	YUKON TERRITORY	YT

NEW ZEALAND ISLANDS AND TERRITORIES

COOK ISLANDS	ROSS DEPENDENCY
NIUE	SOUTH ISLAND
NORTH ISLAND	TOKELAU

AUSTRIAN STATES

BURGENLAND
KARNTEN (CARINTHIA)
NIEDEROSTERREICH (LOWER AUSTRIA)
OBEROSTERREICH (UPPER AUSTRIA)
SALZBURG

STEIERMARK (STYRIA)
TIROL (TYROL)
VORARLBERG
WIEN (VIENNA)

FRENCH REGIONS

ALSACE
AQUITAINE
AUVERGNE
BASSE-NORMANDIE
BRITTANY (BRETAGNE)
BURGUNDY (BOURGOGNE)
CENTRE
CHAMPAGNE-ARDENNE
CORSE (CORSICA)
FRANCHE-COMTE
HAUTE-NORMANDIE

ILE-DE-FRANCE
LANGUEDOC-ROUSSILLON
LIMOUSIN
LORRAINE
MIDI-PYRENEES
NORD-PAS-DE-CALAIS
PAYS DE LA LORIE
PICARDIE
POITOU-CHARENTES
PROVENCE-ALPES-COTE D'AZUR
RHONE-ALPES

GERMAN STATES

BADEN-WURTTEMBERG
BAVARIA
BERLIN
BRANDENBURG
BREMEN
HAMBURG
HESSE
LOWER SAXONY

MECKLENBURG-WEST POMERANIA
NORTH RHINE-WESTPHALIA
RHINELAND-PALATINATE
SAAR
SAXONY
SAXONY-ANHALT
SCHLESWIG-HOLSTEIN
THURINGIA

SPANISH REGIONS

ANDALUSIA
ARAGON
ASTURIAS
CATALONIA
EXTREMADURA
GALICIA

MURCIA
NAVARRE
CASTILLA-LA MANCHA
CASTILLA Y LEON
VALENCIA

ITALIAN REGIONS

ABRUZZO (ABBRUZZI)
BASILICATA
BENEZIA GIULIA
CALABRIA
CAMPANIA
EMILIA ROMAGNA
FRIULI VENEZIA GIULIA
LAZIO
MARCHES (LE MARCHE)
LIGURIA
LOMBARDY (LOMBARDIA)

MOLISE
PIEMONT(E)
APULIA (PUGLIA)
SARDINIA (SARDEGNA)
SICILY (SICILIA)
TUSCANY (TOSCANA)
TRENTINO ALTO ADIGE
UMBRIA
VALLE D'AOSTA
VENETO

PORTUGUESE DISTRICTS AND AUTONOMOUS REGIONS

AVEIRO
BEJA
BRAGA
BRAGANCA
CASTELO BRANCO
COIMBRA
EVORA
FARO
GUARDA

LEIRIA
LISBON (LISBOA)
PORTALEGRE
OPORTO (PORTO)
SANTAREM
SETUBAL
VIANA DO CASTELO
VILA REAL
VISEU

SWISS CANTONS

APPENZELL INNER-RHODES
APPENZELL OUTER-RHODES
ARGOVIA
BASLE-COUNTRY
BASLE-TOWN
BERNE
FRIBOURG
GENEVA
GLARUS
GRISONS
JURA
LUCERNE
NEUCHATEL

NIDWALDEN
OBWALDEN
ST GALL
SCHAFFHAU
SCHWYZ
SOLOTHURN
THURGOVIA
TICINO
URI
VALAIS
VAUD
ZUG
ZURICH

INDIAN STATES AND UNION TERRITORIES

ANADAMAN AND NICOBAR ISLANDS
ANDHRA PRADESH
ARUNCHAL PRADESH
ASSAM
BIHAR
CHANDIGARH
DADRA AND NAGAR HAVELI
DAMAN AND DIU
DELHI
GOA
GUJARAT
HARYANA
HIMACHEL PRADESH
JAMMU AND KASHMIR
KARNATAKA
KERELA

LAKSHADWEEP
MADHYA PRADESH
MAHARASTRA
MANIPUR
MEGHALAYA
MIZORAM
NAGALAND
ORISSA
PONDICHERRY
PUNJAB
RAJASTHAN
SIKKIM
TAMIL NADU
TRIPURA
WEST BENGAL

PAKISTANI PROVINCES

BALOCHISTAN (BALUCHISTAN)
NORTHWEST FRONTIER PROVINCE

PUNJAB
SIND(H)

NIGERIAN STATES

ABIA
ABUJA, FEDERAL CAPITAL
  TERRITORY OF
ADAMAWA
AKWA IBOM
ANAMBRA
BAUCHI
BAYELSA
BERNUE
BORNO
CROSS RIVER
DELTA
EBONYI

EDO
EKITI
ENUGU
GOMBE
IMO
JIGAWA
KADUNA
KANO
KATSINA
KEBBI
KOGI
KWARA
LAGOS

NASSARAWA
NIGER
OGUN
ONDO
OSUN
OYO
PLATEAU
RIVERS
SOKOTO
TARABA
YOBE
ZAMFARA

RUSSIAN FEDERATION REPUBLICS

ADYGHEYA
ALTAI
BASHKORTOSTAN
BURYATIA
CHECHNYAT
CHUVASHIA
DAGHESTAN
INGUSHETIA
KABARDINO-BALKARIYA
KALMYKIYA
KARACHAYEVO-CHERKESSIYA

KARELIYA
KHAKASSIYA
KOMI
MARII-EL
MORDOVIYA
NORTHERN OSETIYA
SAKHA
TATARSTAN
TYVA
UDMURTIYA

CHINESE PROVINCES

ANHUI
BEIJING
FUJIAN
GANSU
GUANGDONG
GUIZHOU
GUNAGXI
HEBEI
HEILONGJIANG
HENAN

HUBEI
HUNAN
INNER MONGOLIA
JIANGSU
JIANGXI
JILIN
LIAONING
NINGXIA
QINGHAI
SHAANXI

SHANDONG
SHANGHAI
SHANXI
SICHUAN
TIANJIN
TIBET
XINJIANG
YUNNAN
ZHEJIANG

BRAZILIAN REGIONS

ACRE
ALAGOAS
AMAPA
AMAZONAS
BAHIA
CEARA
DISTRITO FEDERAL
ESPIRITO SANTO
GOIAS
MARANHAO
MATO GROSSO
MATO GROSSO DO SUL
MINAS GERAIS
PARANA

PARAIBA
PARA
PERNAMBUCO
PIAUI
RIO DE JANEIRO
RIO GRANDE DO NORTE
RIO GRANDE DO SUL
RONDONIA
RORAIMA
SANTA CATARINA
SERGIPE
SAO PAULO
TOCANTINS

TOWNS AND CITIES

AFGHANISTAN

5
HERAT
KABUL

8
KANDAHAR

ALBANIA

6
TIRANA
TIRANE

ALGERIA

4
ORAN

7
ALGIERS

ANGOLA

6
HUAMBO
LOBITO
LUANDA

ARGENTINA

7
CORDOBA
LA PLATA
ROSARIO

9
LA MATANZA

11
BAHIA BLANCA
BUENOS AIRES

AUSTRALIA

5
PERTH

6
DARWIN
HOBART
SYDNEY

8
ADELAIDE
BRISBANE
CANBERRA

9
MELBOURNE

9—continued
NEWCASTLE

12
ALICE SPRINGS

AUSTRIA

6
VIENNA

8
SALZBURG

9
INNSBRUCK

AZERBAIJAN

4
BAKU

BANGLADESH

5
DHAKA

10
CHITTAGONG

BELARUS

5
BREST
MINSK

BELGIUM

5
GHENT
LIÈGE
NAMUR
YPRES

6
BRUGES
DINANT
OSTEND

7
ANTWERP
MALINES

8
BRUSSELS

**BOSNIA-
  HERCEGOVINA**

5
TUZLA

6
MOSTAR

8
SARAJEVO

9
BANJA LUKA

BRAZIL

5
BELEM

6
MANAUS
RECIFE

8
BRASILIA
SALVADOR
SAO PAULO

11
PORTO ALEGRE

12
RIO DE JANEIRO

13
BELO HORIZONTE

BULGARIA

5
SOFIA
VARNA

BURMA
SEE MYANMAR

CANADA

6
OTTAWA
QUEBEC
REGINA

7
CALGARY
HALIFAX
ST JOHN'S
TORONTO

8
EDMONTON
HAMILTON
KINGSTON
MONTREAL
VICTORIA
WINNIPEG

9
VANCOUVER
SASKATOON

10
THUNDER BAY

11
FREDERICTON

12
NIAGARA FALLS

13
CHARLOTTETOWN

CHILE

8
SANTIAGO

10
VALPARAISO

CHINA

4
LUTA
SIAN

5
WUHAN

6
ANSHAN
CANTON
DAIREN
FUSHUN
HARBIN
MUKDEN
PEKING
TSINAN

7
BEIJING
KUNMING
LANCHOW
NANKING
TAIYUAN

8
SHANGHAI
SHENYANG
TIENTSIN

9
CHANGCHUN
CHUNGKING

10
PORT ARTHUR

COLOMBIA

4
CALI

6
BOGOTÁ

8
MEDELLÍN

9
CARTAGENA

12
BARRANQUILLA

15
SANTA FÉ DE
  BOGOTÁ

CONGO, DEMOCRA-
TIC REPUBLIC OF

6
BOKAVU

8
KINSHASA

10
LUBUMBASHI

CROATIA

5
SPLIT

6
ZAGREB

CUBA

6
HAVANA

14
SANTIAGO DE CUBA

CZECH REPUBLIC

4
BRNO

6
PRAGUE

DENMARK

5
ARHUS

6
ODENSE

10
COPENHAGEN

ECUADOR

5
QUITO

9
GUAYAQUIL

EGYPT

4
GIZA
SUEZ

5
ASWAN
CAIRO
LUXOR
TANTA

6
THEBES

7
MANSURA
MEMPHIS
ZAGAZIG

8
ISMAILIA
PORT SAID

10
ALEXANDRIA

ENGLAND

3
ELY
EYE
RYE
WEM

4
BATH
BRAY
BUDE
BURY
CLUN
DEAL
DISS
ETON
HOLT
HOVE
HULL
HYDE
INCE
LEEK
LOOE
LYDD
ROSS
RYDE
SHAP
WARE
WARK
YARM

4—continued
YORK

5
ACTON
ALTON
BACUP
BLYTH
BOURN
CALNE
CHARD
CHEAM
COLNE
COWES
CREWE
DERBY
DOVER
EGHAM
EPSOM
FILEY
FOWEY
FROME
GOOLE
HAWES
HEDON
HURST
HYTHE
LEEDS
LEIGH
LEWES
LOUTH
LUTON
MARCH
OLNEY
OTLEY
POOLE
REETH
RIPON
RISCA
RUGBY
SARUM
SELBY
STOKE
STONE
TEBAY
THAME
TRING
TRURO
WELLS
WIGAN

6
ALFORD
ALSTON
ASHTON
BARNET
BARROW
BARTON
BATLEY
BATTLE
BAWTRY
BEDALE
BELPER

6—continued
BODMIN
BOGNOR
BOLTON
BOOTLE
BOSTON
BRUTON
BUNGAY
BURTON
BUXTON
CASTOR
COBHAM
CROMER
DARWEN
DUDLEY
DURHAM
EALING
ECCLES
EPPING
EXETER
GORING
HANLEY
HARLOW
HARROW
HAVANT
HENLEY
HEXHAM
HOWDEN
ILFORD
ILKLEY
ILSLEY
JARROW
KENDAL
LEYTON
LONDON
LUDLOW
LYNTON
LYTHAM
MALDON
MALTON
MARLOW
MASHAM
MORLEY
NASEBY
NELSON
NESTON
NEWARK
NEWENT
NEWLYN
NEWTON
NORHAM
OAKHAM
OLDHAM
ORMSBY
OSSETT
OUNDLE
OXFORD
PENRYN
PEWSEY
PINNER
PUDSEY
PUTNEY

6–continued

RAMSEY
REDCAR
RIPLEY
ROMNEY
ROMSEY
RUGELY
SEAHAM
SEATON
SELSEY
SETTLE
SNAITH
ST IVES
STROOD
STROUD
SUTTON
THIRSK
THORNE
TOTNES
WALTON
WATTON
WESTON
WHITBY
WIDNES
WIGTON
WILTON
WITHAM
WITNEY
WOOLER
YEOVIL

7

ALNWICK
ANDOVER
APPLEBY
ARUNDEL
ASHFORD
AYLSHAM
BAMPTON
BANBURY
BARKING
BECCLES
BEDFORD
BELFORD
BERWICK
BEWDLEY
BEXHILL
BICKLEY
BILSTON
BOURTON
BOWFELL
BRANDON
BRISTOL
BRIXHAM
BROMLEY
BURNHAM
BURNLEY
BURSLEM
CAISTOR
CATFORD
CAWSTON
CHARING

7–continued

CHATHAM
CHEADLE
CHEDDAR
CHESHAM
CHESTER
CHORLEY
CLACTON
CLIFTON
CRAWLEY
CROYDON
DARSLEY
DATCHET
DAWLISH
DEVIZES
DORKING
DOUGLAS
DUNSTER
ELSTREE
ENFIELD
EVERTON
EVESHAM
EXMOUTH
FAREHAM
FARNHAM
FELTHAM
GLOSSOP
GOSPORT
GRIMSBY
HALIFAX
HAMPTON
HARWICH
HAWORTH
HELSTON
HEYWOOD
HITCHIN
HONITON
HORNSEA
HORNSEY
HORSHAM
IPSWICH
IXWORTH
KESWICK
KINGTON
LANCING
LANGTON
LEDBURY
LEYBURN
LINCOLN
MALVERN
MARGATE
MATLOCK
MOLESEY
MORETON
MORPETH
MOSSLEY
NEWBURY
NEWPORT
NORWICH
OLDBURY
OVERTON
PADSTOW

7–continued

PENRITH
POULTON
PRESCOT
PRESTON
RAINHAM
READING
REDHILL
REDRUTH
REIGATE
RETFORD
ROMFORD
ROSSALL
ROYSTON
RUNCORN
SALFORD
SALTASH
SANDOWN
SAXELBY
SEAFORD
SHIFNAL
SHIPLEY
SHIPTON
SILLOTH
SKIPTON
SPILSBY
STAINES
STILTON
ST NEOTS
SUDBURY
SUNBURY
SWANAGE
SWINDON
SWINTON
TAUNTON
TELFORD
TENBURY
TETBURY
THAXTED
TILBURY
TORQUAY
TWYFORD
VENTNOR
WALSALL
WALTHAM
WANTAGE
WAREHAM
WARWICK
WATCHET
WATFORD
WEOBLEY
WICKWAR
WINDSOR
WINSLOW
WINSTER
WISBECK
WORKSOP

8

ABINGDON
ALFRETON
ALNMOUTH

8–continued

AMESBURY
AMPTHILL
AXBRIDGE
AYCLIFFE
BAKEWELL
BARNSLEY
BERKELEY
BEVERLEY
BICESTER
BIDEFORD
BOLSOVER
BRACKLEY
BRADFORD
BRAMPTON
BRIDPORT
BRIGHTON
BROMYARD
BROSELEY
CAMBORNE
CARLISLE
CATERHAM
CHERTSEY
CLEVEDON
CLOVELLY
COVENTRY
CREDITON
DAVENTRY
DEBENHAM
DEDWORTH
DEPTFORD
DEWSBURY
EGREMONT
EVERSLEY
FAKENHAM
FALMOUTH
FOULNESS
GRANTHAM
GRANTOWN
HADLEIGH
HAILSHAM
HALSTEAD
HASTINGS
HATFIELD
HELMSLEY
HEREFORD
HERNE BAY
HERTFORD
HINCKLEY
HOLBEACH
HUNMANBY
ILKESTON
KEIGHLEY
KINGSTON
LAVENHAM
LECHLADE
LISKEARD
LONGTOWN
LYNMOUTH
MARYPORT
MIDHURST
MINEHEAD

8–continued

NANTWICH
NEWHAVEN
NUNEATON
ORMSKIRK
OSWESTRY
PENZANCE
PERSHORE
PETERLEE
PETWORTH
PEVENSEY
PLAISTOW
PLYMOUTH
RAMSGATE
REDDITCH
RICHMOND
RINGWOOD
ROCHDALE
ROTHBURY
SALTBURN
SANDGATE
SANDWICH
SEDBERGH
SHANKLIN
SHELFORD
SHIPSTON
SIDMOUTH
SKEGNESS
SLEAFORD
SOUTHEND
SPALDING
STAFFORD
ST ALBANS
STAMFORD
STANHOPE
STANWELL
ST HELENS
STOCKTON
STRATTON
SURBITON
SWAFFHAM
TAMWORTH
THETFORD
THORNABY
TIVERTON
TUNSTALL
UCKFIELD
UXBRIDGE
WALLASEY
WALLSEND
WANSTEAD
WESTBURY
WETHERAL
WETHERBY
WEYMOUTH
WOODFORD
WOOLWICH
WORTHING
YARMOUTH

9

ALDEBURGH

9–continued

ALDERSHOT
ALLENDALE
ALRESFORD
AMBLESIDE
ASHBOURNE
ASHBURTON
AVONMOUTH
AYLESBURY
BLACKBURN
BLACKPOOL
BLANDFORD
BLISWORTH
BRACKNELL
BRAINTREE
BRENTFORD
BRENTWOOD
BRIGHOUSE
BROUGHTON
CAMBRIDGE
CARNFORTH
CASTLETON
CHESILTON
CHINGFORD
CLITHEROE
CONGLETON
CRANBORNE
CRANBROOK
CREWKERNE
CRICKLADE
CUCKFIELD
DARTMOUTH
DEVONPORT
DONCASTER
DONINGTON
DROITWICH
DRONFIELD
DUNGENESS
DUNSTABLE
ELLESMERE
FAVERSHAM
FLEETWOOD
GATESHEAD
GODALMING
GRAVESEND
GREENWICH
GRINSTEAD
GUILDFORD
HARROGATE
HASLEMERE
HAVERHILL
HAWKHURST
HOLMFIRTH
ILCHESTER
IMMINGHAM
KETTERING
KING'S LYNN
KINGSWEAR
LAMBOURNE
LANCASTER
LEICESTER
LICHFIELD

9–continued

LIVERPOOL
LONGRIDGE
LOWESTOFT
LYME REGIS
LYMINGTON
MAIDSTONE
MANSFIELD
MIDDLETON
NEWCASTLE
NEWMARKET
NEW ROMNEY
NORTHWICH
OTTERBURN
PEMBRIDGE
PENISTONE
PENKRIDGE
PENYGHENT
PICKERING
ROCHESTER
ROTHERHAM
SALISBURY
SALTFLEET
SEVENOAKS
SHEERNESS
SHEFFIELD
SHERBORNE
SMETHWICK
SOUTHGATE
SOUTHPORT
SOUTHWELL
SOUTHWOLD
STARCROSS
ST AUSTELL
STEVENAGE
STOCKPORT
STOKESLEY
STOURPORT
STRATFORD
TARPORLEY
TAVISTOCK
TENTERDEN
TONBRIDGE
TOWCESTER
TYNEMOUTH
ULVERSTON
UPMINSTER
UPPINGHAM
UTTOXETER
WAINFLEET
WAKEFIELD
WARKWORTH
WEYBRIDGE
WHERNSIDE
WHITHAVEN
WIMBLEDON
WINCANTON
WOKINGHAM
WOODSTOCK
WORCESTER
WYMONDHAM

10

ACCRINGTON
ALDBOROUGH
ALTRINCHAM
BARNSTAPLE
BEDLINGTON
BELLINGHAM
BILLERICAY
BIRKENHEAD
BIRMINGHAM
BRIDGNORTH
BRIDGWATER
BROMSGROVE
BROXBOURNE
BUCKINGHAM
CANTERBURY
CARSHALTON
CHELMSFORD
CHELTENHAM
CHICHESTER
CHIPPENHAM
CHULMLEIGH
COGGESHALL
COLCHESTER
CULLOMPTON
DARLINGTON
DORCHESTER
DUKINFIELD
EASTBOURNE
ECCLESHALL
FARNINGHAM
FOLKESTONE
FRESHWATER
GILLINGHAM
GLOUCESTER
HALESWORTH
HARTLEPOOL
HASLINGDON
HEATHFIELD
HORNCASTLE
HORNCHURCH
HUNGERFORD
HUNSTANTON
HUNTINGDON
ILFRACOMBE
KENILWORTH
KINGSCLERE
KIRKOSWALD
LAUNCESTON
LEAMINGTON
LEOMINSTER
LITTLEPORT
MAIDENHEAD
MALMESBURY
MANCHESTER
MEXBOROUGH
MICHELDEAN
MIDDLEWICH
MILDENHALL
NAILSWORTH
NOTTINGHAM
OKEHAMPTON

10–continued
ORFORDNESS
PANGBOURNE
PATRINGTON
PEACEHAVEN
PONTEFRACT
PORTISHEAD
PORTSMOUTH
POTTER'S BAR
RAVENGLASS
ROCKINGHAM
SAXMUNDHAM
SHEPPERTON
SHERINGHAM
SHREWSBURY
STALBRIDGE
ST LEONARDS
STOWMARKET
SUNDERLAND
TEDDINGTON
TEIGNMOUTH
TEWKESBURY
THAMESMEAD
TORRINGTON
TROWBRIDGE
TWICKENHAM
WALSINGHAM
WARMINSTER
WARRINGTON
WASHINGTON
WEDNESBURY
WELLINGTON
WESTWARD HO
WHITCHURCH
WHITSTABLE
WHITTLESEY
WILLENHALL
WINCHELSEA
WINCHESTER
WINDERMERE
WINDLESHAM
WIRKSWORTH
WITHERNSEA
WOODBRIDGE
WORKINGTON

11
BASINGSTOKE
BEARMINSTER
BOGNOR REGIS
BOURNEMOUTH
BRIDLINGTON
BUNTINGFORD
CLEETHORPES
COCKERMOUTH
EAST RETFORD
GLASTONBURY
GREAT MARLOW
GUISBOROUGH
HALTWHISTLE
HAMPTON WICK
HATHERLEIGH

11–continued
HIGH WYCOMBE
INGATESTONE
LEYTONSTONE
LITTLESTONE
LUDGERSHALL
LUTTERWORTH
MABLETHORPE
MANNINGTREE
MARKET RASEN
MARLBOROUGH
MUCH WENLOCK
NEW BRIGHTON
NEWTON ABBOT
NORTHAMPTON
PETERSFIELD
POCKLINGTON
RAWTENSTALL
SCARBOROUGH
SHAFTESBURY
SOUTHAMPTON
SOUTH MOLTON
STALYBRIDGE
ST MARGARET'S
STOURBRIDGE
TATTERSHALL
WALLINGFORD
WALTHAMSTOW
WESTMINSTER
WHITECHURCH
WOODHALL SPA

12
ATTLEBOROUGH
BERKHAMPSTED
BEXHILL-ON-SEA
CASTLE RISING
CHESTERFIELD
CHRISTCHURCH
GAINSBOROUGH
GREAT GRIMSBY
GREAT MALVERN
HUDDERSFIELD
INGLEBOROUGH
LONG STRATTON
LOUGHBOROUGH
MACCLESFIELD
MILTON KEYNES
MORECAMBE BAY
NORTH BERWICK
NORTH SHIELDS
NORTH WALSHAM
PETERBOROUGH
SHOEBURYNESS
SHOTTESBROOK
SOUTH SHIELDS
STOKE-ON-TRENT

13
BARNARD CASTLE
BISHOP'S CASTLE
BOROUGHBRIDGE
BRIGHTLINGSEA

13–continued
BURTON-ON-TRENT
BURY ST EDMUNDS
CHIPPING ONGAR
FINCHAMPSTEAD
GODMANCHESTER
GREAT YARMOUTH
HIGHAM FERRERS
KIDDERMINSTER
KIRKBY STEPHEN
KNARESBOROUGH
LITTLEHAMPTON
LYTHAM ST ANNES
MARKET DEEPING
MARKET DRAYTON
MELCOMBE REGIS
MELTON MOWBRAY
MIDDLESBROUGH
NORTHALLERTON
SAFFRON WALDEN
SHEPTON MALLET
WOLVERHAMPTON
WOOTTON BASSET

14
BERWICK-ON-
  TWEED
BISHOP AUCKLAND
BISHOPS WALTHAM
CHIPPING BARNET
CHIPPING NORTON
HEMEL HEMPSTEAD
KIRKBY LONSDALE
MARKET
  BOSWORTH
MORTIMER'S CROSS
STOCKTON-ON-
  TEES
STONY STRATFORD
SUTTON COURTNEY
TUNBRIDGE WELLS
WELLINGBOROUGH
WEST HARTLEPOOL

15+
ASHTON-UNDER-
  LYNE
BARROW-IN-
  FURNESS
BISHOP'S
  STORTFORD
BURNHAM-ON-
  CROUCH
CASTLE
  DONINGTON
LEIGHTON
  BUZZARD
NEWCASTLE-ON-
  TYNE
ST LEONARDS-ON-
  SEA

15+–continued
STRATFORD-ON-
  AVON
SUTTON COLDFIELD
WELWYN GARDEN
  CITY
WESTON-SUPER-
  MARE

ERITREA

6
ASMARA
ASMERA

ESTONIA

7
TALLINN

FRANCE

3
AIX
PAU

4
ALBI
CAEN
LYON
METZ
NICE

5
ARLES
ARRAS
BREST
DIJON
EVIAN
LILLE
LYONS
MACON
NANCY
NIMES
PARIS
REIMS
ROUEN
TOURS
TULLE

6
AMIENS
BAYEUX
CALAIS
CANNES
DIEPPE
LE MANS
NANTES
RHEIMS
ST MALO
TOULON
VERDUN

7
AJACCIO
ALENÇON
AVIGNON
BAYONNE
DUNKIRK
LE HAVRE
LIMOGES
LOURDES
ORLÉANS

8
BESANÇON
BIARRITZ
BORDEAUX
BOULOGNE
CHARTRES
GRENOBLE
SOISSONS
ST TROPEZ
TOULOUSE

9
ABBEVILLE
CHERBOURG
DUNKERQUE
MARSEILLE
MONTAUBAN
PERPIGNAN
ST ETIENNE

10
MARSEILLES
MONTELIMAR
STRASBOURG
VERSAILLES

11
ARMENTIÈRES
MONTPELLIER

15
CLERMONT-
  FERRAND

GERMANY

4
BONN
GERA
KIEL
KÖLN
SUHL

5
ESSEN
HALLE
MAINZ
TRIER
WORMS

6
AACHEN
BERLIN
BOCHUM

6–continued
BREMEN
CASSEL
ERFURT
KASSEL
LÜBECK
MUNICH
TRÈVES

7
COBLENZ
COLOGNE
COTTBUS
DRESDEN
HAMBURG
HANOVER
HOMBURG
KOBLENZ
LEIPZIG
MÜNCHEN
POTSDAM
ROSTOCK
SPANDAU

8
AUGSBURG
DORTMUND
HANNOVER
MANNHEIM
NÜRNBERG
SCHWERIN

9
BRUNSWICK
DARMSTADT
FRANKFURT
MAGDEBURG
NUREMBERG
STUTTGART
WIESBADEN
WUPPERTAL

10
BADEN BADEN
BAD HOMBURG
DÜSSELDORF
HEIDELBERG

11
BRANDENBURG
SAARBRÜCKEN

13
AIX-LA-CHAPELLE
KARL-MARX-STADT

GREECE

6
ATHENS
SPARTA
THEBES

7
CORINTH

7–continued
MYCENAE
PIRAEUS

11
THESSALONIKI

HUNGARY

4
PÉCS
PUNE

8
BUDAPEST

INDIA

4
AGRA

5
AJMER
ALWAR
DELHI
KOTAH
PATNA
POONA
SIMLA
SURAT

6
BHOPAL
BOMBAY
HOWRAH
IMPHAL
INDORE
JAIPUR
JHANSI
KALYAN
KANPUR
KOHIMA
MADRAS
MEERUT
MUMBAI
MYSORE
NAGPUR
RAMPUR

7
BENARES
GWALIOR
JODHPUR
LUCKNOW

8
AGARTALA
AMRITSAR
CALCUTTA
CAWNPORE
JAMALPUR
LUDHIANA
SHILLONG
SRINAGAR
VADODARA

8–continued
VARANASI

9
AHMADABAD
ALLAHABAD
BANGALORE
HYDERABAD

10
CHANDIGARH
DARJEELING
JAMSHEDPUR
TRIVANDRUM

11
BHUBANESWAR

INDONESIA

5
MEDAN

7
BANDUNG
JAKARTA

8
SEMARANG
SURABAJA

9
PALEMBANG

IRAN

6
ABADAN
SHIRAZ
TABRIZ
TEHRAN

7
ISFAHAN
MASHHAD

IRAQ

5
BASRA
MOSUL

6
KIRKUK

7
BAGHDAD
KARBALA

**IRELAND, REPUBLIC
OF**

4
BRAY
COBH
CORK

4—continued
MUFF
NAAS
TRIM
TUAM

5
BALLA
BOYLE
CAVAN
CLARE
ENNIS
KELLS
SLIGO

6
ARKLOW
BANTRY
CALLAN
CARLOW
CARNEY
CASHEL
DUBLIN
GALWAY
SHRULE
TRALEE

7
ATHLONE
BLARNEY
CARRICK
CLONMEL
DONEGAL
DUNDALK
DUNMORE
KILDARE
LIFFORD
SHANNON
WEXFORD
WICKLOW
YOUGHAL

8
BALLYBAY
BUNCRANA
CLONTARF
DROGHEDA
KILKENNY
LIMERICK
LISTOWEL
LONGFORD
MAYNOOTH
MONAGHAN
RATHDRUM

9
CASTLEBAR
CONNEMARA
KILLARNEY
MULLINGAR
ROSCOMMON
TIPPERARY
TULLAMORE
WATERFORD

10
CASTLEFINN
KILCONNELL
SHILLELAGH
SKIBBEREEN
STRANORLAR

11
LETTERKENNY

12
DUN LAOGHAIRE

13
CASTLEBLAYNEY
INNISHTRAHULL
PORTLAOIGHISE

16
CARRICK-ON-
  SHANNON

ISRAEL

4
GAZA

5
HAIFA
JAFFA

7
TEL AVIV

9
BEERSHEBA
JERUSALEM

ITALY

4
BARI
PISA
ROME

5
GENOA
MILAN
OSTIA
PADUA
PARMA
SIENA
TURIN

6
MODENA
NAPLES
REGGIO
TRENTO
VENICE
VERONA

7
BOLOGNA
BERGAMO
BRESCIA
CATANIA

7—continued
FERRARA
MESSINA
PALERMO
PERUGIA
PESCARA
POMPEII
RAVENNA
SALERNO
SAN REMO
TRIESTE
VATICAN

8
CAGLIARI
FLORENCE
SYRACUSE

9
AGRIGENTO

JAPAN

4
FUGI
KOBE

5
KYOTO
OSAKA
TOKYO

6
NAGOYA
TOYOTA

7
FUKUOKA
HITACHI
SAPPORO

8
KAWASAKI
NAGASAKI
YOKOHAMA

9
HIROSHIMA

10
KITAKYUSHU

KAZAKHSTAN

6
ALMATY

9
KARAGANDA

KENYA

4
LAMU

7
MOMBASA

7—continued
NAIROBI

KOREA, SOUTH

5
SEOUL

9
PANMUNJON

KYRGYZSTAN

7
BISHPEK
PISHPEK

LATVIA

4
RIGA

LEBANON

4
TYRE

5
SIDON

6
BEIRUT

7
TRIPOLI

LIBYA

4
HOMS

6
TOBRUK

7
TRIPOLI

LITHUANIA

7
VILNIUS

MACEDONIA

6
SKOPJE

MALI

6
BAMAKO

8
TIMBUKTU

MEXICO

6
JUAREZ
PUEBLA

8
ACAPULCO
VERACRUZ

9
MONTERREY

11
GUADALAJARA

MOLDOVA

8
CHIŞINĂ
KISHINEV

MOROCCO

3
FEZ

5
RÀBAT

6
AGADIR
MEKNES

7
TANGIER

8
TANGIERS

9
MARRAKECH
MARRAKESH

10
CASABLANCA

MYANMAR

3
AVA

6
YANGON

7
RANGOON

8
MANDALAY

NETHERLANDS

5
BREDA
HAGUE

6
ARNHEM

6–continued
LEIDEN
LEYDEN

7
UTRECHT

8
THE HAGUE

9
AMSTERDAM
DORDRECHT
EINDHOVEN
ROTTERDAM

10
MAASTRICHT

NEW ZEALAND

6
NAPIER
NELSON

7
DUNEDIN

8
AUCKLAND

10
WELLINGTON

12
CHRISTCHURCH

NIGERIA

4
KANO

5
ABUJA
ENUGU
LAGOS

6
IBADAN

NORTHERN IRELAND

5
DOAGH
GLYNN
KEADY
LARNE
NEWRY
OMAGH
TOOME

6
ANTRIM
ARMAGH
AUGHER
BANGOR

6–continued
BELCOO
BERAGH
COMBER
LURGAN
RAPHOE

7
BELFAST
BELLEEK
CALEDON
CLOGHER
CRUMLIN
DERVOCK
DROMORE
FINAGHY
FINTONA
GILFORD
GLENARM
KILKEEL
LISBURN
POMEROY

8
AHOGHILL
ANNALONG
DUNGIVEN
HILLTOWN
HOLYWOOD
LIMAVADY
PORTRUSH
STRABANE
TRILLICK

9
BALLINTRA
BALLYMENA
BALLYMORE
BALLYNURE
BANBRIDGE
BUSHMILLS
CARNLOUGH
COLERAINE
COOKSTOWN
CRAIGAVON
CUSHENDUN
DUNGANNON
LISNASKEA
MONEYMORE
NEWCASTLE
PORTADOWN
RASHARKIN
ROSTREVOR
TANDRAGEE
TOVERMORE

10
ALDERGROVE
AUGHNACLOY
BALLYCLARE
BALLYGOWAN
BALLYMONEY
BALLYRONEY
CASTLEDERG

10–continued
COALISLAND
CUSHENDALL
DONAGHADEE
MARKETHILL
PORTAFERRY
SAINTFIELD
STRANGFORD
TANDERAGEE

11
BALLYCASTLE
BALLYGAWLEY
CARRICKMORE
CROSSMAGLEN
DOWNPATRICK
DRAPERSTOWN
ENNISKILLEN
LONDONDERRY
MAGHERAFELT
NEWTOWNARDS
PORTGLENONE
PORTSTEWART
RANDALSTOWN
RATHFRILAND
WARRENPOINT

12
BALLYHALBERT
BALLYNAHINCH
CASTLE DAWSON
CASTLEWELLAN
FIVEMILETOWN
HILLSBOROUGH
STEWARTSTOWN

13
BROOKE-BOROUGH
CARRICKFERGUS
CRAWFORDSBURN
DERRYGONNELLY

14
NEWTOWN
  STEWART

NORWAY

4
OSLO

6
BERGEN

9
TRONDHEIM

PAKISTAN

6
LAHORE
MULTAN
QUETTA

TOWNS AND CITIES

7
KARACHI

8
PESHAWAR

9
HYDERABAD
ISLAMABAD

10
FAISALABAD
GUJRANWALA
RAWALPINDI

PERU

4
LIMA

5
CUZCO

PHILIPPINES

6
MANILA

10
QUEZON CITY

POLAND

4
LODZ

5
POSEN

6
DANZIG
GDANSK
KRAKOW
LUBLIN
WARSAW

7
BRESLAU

8
PRZEMYSL

PORTUGAL

6
LISBON
OPORTO

RUSSIA

3&4
UFA
OMSK
PERM
TVER

5
KAZAN
PSKOV

6
MOSCOW
SAMARA

7
IRKUTSK
YAKUTSK

8
NOVGOROD
SMOLENSK

9
ASTRAKHAN
KALINGRAD
VOLGOGRAD

11
CHELYABINSK
NOVOSIBIRSK
VLADIVOSTOK

12
EKATERINBURG
ROSTOV-NA-DONU
ST PETERSBURG

14
NIZHNY NOVGOROD

SAUDI ARABIA

5
MECCA

6
JEDDAH
MEDINA
RIYADH

SCOTLAND

3
AYR
UIG

4
ALVA
BARR
DUNS
ELIE
KIRN
LUSS
NIGG
OBAN
REAY
RONA
STOW
WICK

5
ALLOA
ANNAN

5–continued
APPIN
AVOCH
AYTON
BANFF
BEITH
BRORA
BUNAW
BUSBY
CERES
CLOVA
CLUNE
CRAIL
CUPAR
DENNY
DOWNE
ELGIN
ELLON
ERROL
FYVIE
GOVAN
INSCH
ISLAY
KEISS
KEITH
KELSO
LAIRG
LARGO
LEITH
NAIRN
PERTH
SALEN
TROON

6
ABOYNE
ALFORD
BARVAS
BEAULY
BERVIE
BIGGAR
BO'NESS
BUCKIE
CARRON
CAWDOR
COMRIE
CRIEFF
CULLEN
CULTER
DOLLAR
DRYMEN
DUNBAR
DUNDEE
DUNLOP
DUNNET
DUNOON
DYSART
EDZELL
FINDON
FORFAR
FORRES
GIRVAN

6–continued
GLAMIS
HAWICK
HUNTLY
IRVINE
KILLIN
KILMUN
LANARK
LAUDER
LESLIE
LINTON
LOCHEE
MEIGLE
MOFFAT
PLADDA
RESTON
RHYNIE
ROSYTH
ROTHES
SHOTTS
THURSO
TONGUE
WISHAW
YARROW

7
AIRDRIE
BALFRON
BALLOCH
BANAVIE
BOWMORE
BRAEMAR
BRECHIN
BRODICK
CANOBIE
CANTYRE
CARBOST
CARGILL
CARLUKE
CRATHIE
CULROSS
CUMNOCK
DENHOLM
DOUGLAS
DUNKELD
DUNNING
EVANTON
FAIRLIE
FALKIRK
GALSTON
GIFFORD
GLASGOW
GLENCOE
GOLSPIE
GOUROCK
GRANTON
GUTHRIE
HALKIRK
KENMORE
KESSOCK
KILMORY
KILSYTH

7–continued
KINROSS
KINTORE
LAMLASH
LARBERT
LYBSTER
MACDUFF
MAYBOLE
MELDRUM
MELROSE
MELVICH
METHVEN
MILMUIR
MONIKIE
MUTHILL
NEWPORT
PAISLEY
PEEBLES
POLMONT
POOLEWE
PORTREE
PORTSOY
RENFREW
SADDELL
SARCLET
SCOURIE
SELKIRK
STANLEY
STRATHY
TARBERT
TARLAND
TAYPORT
TRANENT
TUNDRUM
TURRIFF
ULLSTER
YETHOLM

8
ABERDEEN
ABERLADY
ABINGTON
ARBROATH
ARMADALE
ARROCHAR
AULDEARN
BALLATER
BANCHORY
BARRHILL
BEATTOCK
BLANTYRE
BURGHEAD
CANISBAY
CARNWATH
CREETOWN
CROMARTY
DALKEITH
DALMALLY
DINGWALL
DIRLETON
DUFFTOWN
DUMFRIES

8–continued
DUNBEATH
DUNBLANE
DUNSCORE
EARLSTON
EYEMOUTH
FINDHORN
FORTROSE
GIFFNOCK
GLENLUCE
GREENLAW
GREENOCK
HAMILTON
INVERARY
INVERURY
JEANTOWN
JEDBURGH
KILBRIDE
KILNIVER
KILRENNY
KINGHORN
KIRKWALL
LANGHOLM
LATHERON
LEUCHARS
LOANHEAD
MARKINCH
MARYKIRK
MONIAIVE
MONTROSE
MONYMUSK
MUIRKIRK
NEILSTON
NEWBURGH
NEWMILNS
PENICUIK
PITSLIGO
POOLTIEL
QUIRAING
ROTHESAY
ST FERGUS
STIRLING
STRICHEN
TALISKER
TARANSAY
TRAQUAIR
ULLAPOOL
WHITHORN
WOODSIDE

9
ABERFELDY
ABERFOYLE
ARDROSSAN
BERRIDALE
BETTYHILL
BLACKLARG
BRACADALE
BRAERIACH
BROADFORD
BROUGHTON
BUCKHAVEN

9–continued
CAIRNTOUL
CALLANDER
CARSTAIRS
DUMBARTON
EDINBURGH
FERINTOSH
FOCHABERS
INCHKEITH
INVERARAY
INVERNESS
JOHNSTONE
KILDRUMMY
KINGUSSIE
KIRKCALDY
LEADHILLS
LOCHGELLY
LOCHINVAR
LOCHNAGAR
LOCKERBIE
LOGIERAIT
MAUCHLINE
MILNGAVIE
PETERHEAD
PITLOCHRY
PORT ELLEN
PRESTWICK
RICCARTON
RONALDSAY
ROTHIEMAY
SALTCOATS
SHIELDAIG
SLAMANNAN
ST ANDREWS
STEWARTON
ST FILLANS
STRANRAER
STRATHDON
STRONTIAN
THORNHILL
TOBERMORY
TOMINTOUL

10
ABBOTSFORD
ACHNASHEEN
ANSTRUTHER
APPLECROSS
ARDRISHAIG
AUCHINLECK
BALLANTRAE
BLACKADDER
CARNOUSTIE
CARSPHAIRN
CASTLETOWN
COATBRIDGE
COLDINGHAM
COLDSTREAM
DALBEATTIE
DRUMLITHIE
EAST LINTON
GALASHIELS

10–continued
GLENROTHES
JOHNSHAVEN
KILCREGGAN
KILLENAULE
KILMAINHAM
KILMALCOLM
KILMARNOCK
KILWINNING
KINCARDINE
KINGSBARNS
KIRKMAIDEN
KIRKOSWALD
KIRRIEMUIR
LENNOXTOWN
LESMAHAGOW
LINLITHGOW
LIVINGSTON
MILNATHORT
MOTHERWELL
PITTENWEEM
PORTOBELLO
RUTHERGLEN
STONEHAVEN
STONEHOUSE
STONEYKIRK
STRATHAVEN
STRATHEARN
STRATHMORE
TWEEDMOUTH
WEST CALDER
WILSONTOWN

11
ABERCHIRDER
BALQUHIDDER
BANNOCKBURN
BLAIR ATHOLL
BLAIRGOWRIE
CAMPBELTOWN
CHARLESTOWN
CUMBERNAULD
DRUMMELZIER
DUNFERMLINE
ECCLEFECHAN
FETTERCAIRN
FORT WILLIAM
FRASERBURGH
HELENSBURGH
INVERGORDON
KIRKMICHAEL
LOSSIEMOUTH
LOSTWITHIEL
MAXWELLTOWN
MUSSELBURGH
PORT GLASGOW
PORT PATRICK
PRESTONPANS
PULTNEYTOWN
STRATHBLANE

12
AUCHTERARDER

12–continued
BALLACHULISH
EAST KILBRIDE
FORT AUGUSTUS
GARELOCHHEAD
INNERLEITHEN
KINLOCHLEVEN
LAWRENCEKIRK
LOCHGILPHEAD
PORTMAHOMACK
STRATHPEFFER
TILLICOULTRY

13
AUCHTERMUCHTY
CASTLE DOUGLAS
COCKBURNSPATH
DALMELLINGTON
INVERKEITHING
INVERKEITHNIE
KIRKCUDBRIGHT
KIRKINTILLOCH
NEWTON STEWART
ROTHIEMURCHUS

SERBIA AND MONTENEGRO

3
NIŠ

7
NOVI SAD

8
BELGRADE

9
PODGORICA

SLOVAKIA

10
BRATISLAVA

SLOVENIA

9
LJUBLJANA

SOUTH AFRICA

6
DURBAN
SOWETO

8
CAPE TOWN
MAFEKING
PRETORIA

9
KIMBERLEY
LADYSMITH

10
ALEXANDRIA
EAST LONDON
SIMONSTOWN

11
GRAHAMSTOWN
SHARPEVILLE

12
BLOEMFONTEIN
JOHANNESBURG
Stellenbosch
13
PORT ELIZABETH

16
PIETERMARITZ-
  BURG

SPAIN

4
VIGO

5
CADIZ

6
BILBAO
MADRID
MALAGA

7
BADAJOZ
CORDOBA
GRANADA
SEVILLE

8
ALICANTE
PAMPLONA
VALENCIA
ZARAGOZA

9
BARCELONA
CARTAGENA
LAS PALMAS
SANTANDER
SARAGOSSA

12
SAN SEBASTIAN

SRI LANKA

5
GALLE
KANDY

7
COLOMBO

11
TRINCOMALEE

SUDAN

6
BERBER

7
DONGOLA

8
KHARTOUM
OMDURMAN

SWEDEN

5
MALMÖ

7
UPPSALA

8
GÖTEBORG

9
STOCKHOLM

10
GOTHENBURG

11
HELSINGBORG

SWITZERLAND

4
BÂLE
BERN

5
BASEL
BASLE

6
GENEVA
ZURICH

7
LUCERNE

8
LAUSANNE

SYRIA

4
HOMS

6
ALEPPO

7
PALMYRA

8
DAMASCUS

TAIWAN

6
TAIBEI
TAIPEI

9
KAO-HSIUNG

TAJIKSTAN

8
DUSHANBE

TANZANIA

6
DODOMA

8
ZANZIBAR

11
DAR ES SALAAM

TURKEY

5
ADANA
IZMIR

6
ANKARA
SMYRNA

7
ERZERUM

8
ISTANBUL

9
BYZANTIUM

14
CONSTANTINOPLE

TURKMENISTAN

9
ASHKHABAD

UKRAINE

4
KIEV
LVOV

5
YALTA

6
ODESSA

7
DONETSK

USA

4
GARY
LIMA
RENO
TROY
WACO
YORK

5
AKRON
BOISE
BRONX
BUTTE
FLINT
MIAMI
OMAHA
OZARK
SALEM
SELMA
TULSA
UTICA

6
ALBANY
AUSTIN
BANGOR
BILOXI
BOSTON
CAMDEN
CANTON
DALLAS
DAYTON
DENVER
DULUTH
EL PASO
EUGENE
FRESNO
LOWELL
MOBILE
NASSAU
NEWARK
OXNARD
PEORIA
ST PAUL
TACOMA
TOLEDO
TOPEKA
TUCSON
URBANA

7
ABILENE
ANAHEIM
ATLANTA
BOULDER
BUFFALO
CHICAGO
CONCORD
DETROIT
HAMPTON
HOBOKEN
HOUSTON

7–continued
JACKSON
KEY WEST
LINCOLN
MADISON
MEMPHIS
MODESTO
NEW YORK
NORFOLK
OAKLAND
ORLANDO
PHOENIX
RALEIGH
READING
ROANOKE
SAGINAW
SAN JOSÉ
SEATTLE
SPOKANE
ST LOUIS
WICHITA
YONKERS

8
BERKELEY
BROOKLYN
COLUMBUS
DEARBORN
GREEN BAY
HANNIBAL
HARTFORD
HONOLULU
LAKELAND
LAS VEGAS
NEW HAVEN
OAK RIDGE
PALO ALTO
PASADENA
PORTLAND
RICHMOND
SAN DIEGO
SANTA ANA
SAVANNAH
STAMFORD
STOCKTON
SYRACUSE
WHEELING

9
ANCHORAGE
ANNAPOLIS
ARLINGTON
BALTIMORE
BETHLEHEM
CAMBRIDGE
CHAMPAIGN
CHARLOTTE
CLEVELAND
DES MOINES
FAIRBANKS
FORT WAYNE
FORT WORTH
GALVESTON

9–continued
HOLLYWOOD
JOHNSTOWN
KALAMAZOO
LANCASTER
LEXINGTON
LONG BEACH
MANHATTAN
MILWAUKEE
NASHVILLE
NEW LONDON
NORTHEAST
PRINCETON
RIVERSIDE
ROCHESTER
WATERBURY
WORCESTER
YPSILANTI

10
ATOMIC CITY
BATON ROUGE
BIRMINGHAM
CHARLESTON
CINCINATTI
EVANSVILLE
GREENSBORO
GREENVILLE
HARRISBURG
HUNTSVILLE
JERSEY CITY
KANSAS CITY
LITTLE ROCK
LONG BRANCH
LOS ANGELES
LOUISVILLE
MIAMI BEACH
MONTGOMERY
NEW BEDFORD
NEW ORLEANS
PITTSBURGH
PROVIDENCE
SACRAMENTO
SAINT LOUIS
SAN ANTONIO
WASHINGTON
YOUNGSTOWN

11
ALBUQUERQUE
CEDAR RAPIDS
CHATTANOOGA
GRAND RAPIDS
MINNEAPOLIS
NEWPORT NEWS
PALM SPRINGS
SCHENECTADY
SPRINGFIELD

12
ATLANTIC CITY
BEVERLY HILLS
FAYETTEVILLE

12–continued
INDEPENDENCE
INDIANAPOLIS
JACKSONVILLE
NEW BRUNSWICK
NIAGARA FALLS
OKLAHOMA CITY
PHILADELPHIA
POUGHKEEPSIE
SALT LAKE CITY
SAN FRANCISCO
SANTA BARBARA

13
CORPUS CHRISTI
ST PETERSBURGH

14
FORT LAUDERDALE

15
COLORADO
  SPRINGS

UZBEKISTAN

8
TASHKENT

9
SAMARKAND

VENEZUELA

7
CARACAS

9
MARACAIBO

WALES

3
USK

4
BALA
HOLT
MOLD
PYLE
RHYL

5
BARRY
CHIRK
FLINT
NEATH
NEVIN
TENBY
TOWYN

6
AMLWCH
BANGOR
BRECON

6—continued
BUILTH
CONWAY
MARGAM
RUABON
RUTHIN

7
CARBURY
CARDIFF
CWMBRAN
DENBIGH
MAESTEG
NEWPORT
NEWTOWN
ST ASAPH
SWANSEA
WREXHAM

8
ABERAVON
ABERDARE
ABERGELE
BARMOUTH
BRIDGEND
CAERLEON
CARDIGAN
CHEPSTOW
DOLGELLY
EBBW VALE
HAWARDEN

8—continued
HOLYHEAD
HOLYWELL
KIDWELLY
KNIGHTON
LAMPETER
LLANELLI
LLANELLY
LLANRWST
MONMOUTH
PEMBROKE
RHAYADER
SKERRIES
SKIFNESS
TALGARTH
TREDEGAR
TREGARON

9
ABERAERON
ABERDOVEY
ABERFFRAW
BEAUMARIS
BODLONDEB
CARNARVON
CRICCIETH
FESTINIOG
FISHGUARD
LLANBERIS
LLANDUDNO

9—continued
NEW RADNOR
PONTYPOOL
PORTHCAWL
PORTMADOC
PWHLLHELI
WELSHPOOL

10
CADER IDRIS
CAERNARFON
CAERNARVON
CAPEL CURIG
CARMARTHEN
CRICKHOWEL
FFESTINIOG
LLANDOVERY
LLANFYLLIN
LLANGADOCK
LLANGOLLEN
LLANIDLOES
MONTGOMERY
PLINLIMMON
PONTYPRIDD
PORTH NIGEL
PORT TALBOT
PRESTEIGNE

11
ABERGAVENNY
ABERYSTWYTH

11—continued
CLYDACH VALE
MACHYNLLETH
OYSTERMOUTH

12
LLANDILOFAWR
LLANTRISSANT
YSTRAD MYNACH

13
HAVERFORDWEST
MERTHYR TYDFIL

YEMEN

4
ADEN
SAN'A

5
SANA'A

ZIMBABWE

6
HARARE

8
BULAWAYO

PORTS

ALGERIA

4
ORAN

6
SKIKDA

7
ALGIERS

9
PORT ARZEW

ANGOLA

6
LOBITO
LUANDA

ARGENTINA

7
LA PLATA

11
BUENOS AIRES

AUSTRALIA

6
SYDNEY

7
DAMPIER
GEELONG

8
ADELAIDE
BRISBANE

9
MELBOURNE

9—continued
NEWCASTLE

10
FREEMANTLE

11
PORT JACKSON

12
PORT ADELAIDE

BELGIUM

6
OSTEND

7
ANTWERP

9
ZEEBRUGGE

BENIN

7
COTONOU

9
PORTO NOVO

BRAZIL

4
PARA

5
BELEM

6
RECIFE
SANTOS

7
TOBARAO

10
PERNAMBUCO

12
RIO DE JANEIRO

BULGARIA

5
VARNA

BURMA

5
AKYAB

6
SITTWE

7
RANGOON

8
MOULMEIN

CAMEROON

6
DOUALA

CANADA

7
HALIFAX
KITIMAT

8
MONTREAL

9
CHURCHILL
ESQUIMALT
OWEN SOUND
VANCOUVER

11
THREE RIVERS

CHANNEL ISLANDS

8
ST HELIER

11
SAINT HELIER
ST PETER PORT

CHILE

5
ARICA

8
COQUIMBO

10
VALPARAISO

CHINA

4
AMOY

6
CHEFOO
HANKOW
SWATOW
WEIHAI

7
FOOCHOW
YINGKOW

8
SHANGHAI
TIENTSIN

10
PORT ARTHUR

COLUMBIA

9
CARTAGENA

12
BARRANQUILLA
BUENAVENTURA

**CONGO,
    DEMOCRATIC
    REPUBLIC OF**

6
MATADI

9
MBUJI-MAYI

CORSICA

6
BASTIA

7
AJACCIO

CUBA

6
HAVANA

14
SANTIAGO DE CUBA

CYPRUS

7
LARNACA

8
LIMASSOL

DENMARK

6
ODENSE

7
AALBORG
HORSENS

8
ELSINORE

9
HELSINGÖR

10
COPENHAGEN

13
FREDERIKSHAVN

ECUADOR

9
GUAYAQUIL

EGYPT

4
SUEZ

8
DAMIETTA
PORT SAID

10
ALEXANDRIA

ENGLAND

4
HULL

5
DOVER

6
LONDON

7
CHATHAM
GRIMSBY
HARWICH
TILBURY

8
FALMOUTH
NEWHAVEN
PENZANCE
PLYMOUTH
PORTLAND
SANDWICH
WEYMOUTH

9
AVONMOUTH
DEVONPORT
GRAVESEND

9—continued
KING'S LYNN
LIVERPOOL
NEWCASTLE
SHEERNESS

10
BARNSTAPLE
COLCHESTER
FELIXSTOWE
FOLKESTONE
HARTLEPOOL
PORTSMOUTH
SUNDERLAND
TEIGNMOUTH
WHITSTABLE

11
CINQUE PORTS
SOUTHAMPTON

12
NORTH SHIELDS
PORT SUNLIGHT

13
MIDDLESBROUGH

FINLAND

8
HELSINKI

FRANCE

5
BREST

6
CALAIS
CANNES
DIEPPE
TOULON

7
DUNKIRK
LE HAVRE

8
BORDEAUX
BOULOGNE
HONFLEUR

9
CHERBOURG
FOS-SUR-MER
MARSEILLE

10
LA ROCHELLE
MARSEILLES

FRENCH GUIANA

7
CAYENNE

PORTS

GERMANY

4
KIEL

5
EMDEN

6
BREMEN
WISMAR

7
HAMBURG
ROSTOCK

8
CUXHAVEN

9
FLENSBURG

10
TRAVEMÜNDE

11
BREMERHAVEN

13
WILHELMS-HAVEN

GHANA

4
TEMA

8
TAKORADI

GREECE

5
CANEA
CORFU

6
PATRAS
RHODES

7
PIRAEUS

8
NAVARINO

10
HERMOPOLIS

11
HERMOUPOLIS

HAWAII

8
HONOLULU

11
PEARL HARBOR

HUNGARY

8
BUDAPEST

INDIA

6
BOMBAY
COCHIN
HALDIA
KANDLA
MADRAS

8
CALCUTTA
COCANADA
KAKINADA

11
MASULIPATAM
PONDICHERRY

12
MASULIPATNAM

INDONESIA

6
PADANG

7
JAKARTA

8
MACASSAR
PARADEEP

IRAN

6
ABADAN

7
BUSHIRE

IRAQ

5
BASRA

IRELAND

4
COBH
CORK

7
DONEGAL
DUNDALK
YOUGHAL

12
DUN LAOGHAIRE

ISRAEL

4
ACRE
AKKO
ELAT

5
EILAT
HAIFA

6
ASHDOD

ITALY

4
BARI

5
GAETA
GENOA
OSTIA
TRANI

6
ANCONA
NAPLES
VENICE

7
LEGHORN
MARSALA
MESSINA
PALERMO
SALERNO
TRAPANI
TRIESTE

8
BRINDISI

IVORY COAST

7
ABIDJAN

JAMAICA

8
KINGSTON

9
PORT ROYAL

10
MONTEGO BAY

JAPAN

4
KOBE

5
KOCHI
OSAKA

8
HAKODATE
NAGASAKI
YOKOHAMA

9
HIROSHIMA
KAGOSHIMA

11
SHIMONOSEKI

KENYA

7
MOMBASA

KUWAIT

12
MINA AL-AHMADI

LEBANON

6
BEIRUT

LIBYA

7
TRIPOLI

8
BENGHAZI

MADAGASCAR

8
TAMATAVE

MALAYSIA

6
PENANG

9
PORT KLANG

10
GEORGE TOWN

12
KOTAKINABALU

MAURITANIA

10
NOUAKCHOTT

MAURITIUS

9
PORT LOUIS

MEXICO

7
GUAYMAS

8
VERACRUZ

MOROCCO

4
SAFI

5
CEUTA
RABAT

6
AGADIR
TETUÁN

7
MELILLA
MOGADOR
TANGIER

9
ESSAOUIRA

10
CASABLANCA

14
MINA HASSAN TANI

MOZAMBIQUE

5
BEIRA

6
MAPUTO

NETHERLANDS

5
DELFT

8
FLUSHING

9
AMSTERDAM
EUROPOORT
ROTTERDAM

10
VLISSINGEN

NEW ZEALAND

6
NELSON

8
AUCKLAND
GISBORNE

9
LYTTELTON

NIGERIA

5
LAGOS

12
PORT HARCOURT

NORTHERN IRELAND

5
LARNE

7
BELFAST

NORWAY

4
OSLO

6
BERGEN
LARVIK
NARVIK
TROMSØ

9
STAVANGER
TRONDHEIM

10
HAMMERFEST
KRISTIANIA

12
KRISTIANSAND

PAKISTAN

6
CHALNA

7
KARACHI

PANAMA

5
COLON

6
BALBOA

9
CRISTOBAL

PAPUA NEW GUINEA

11
PORT MORESBY

PERU

3
ILO

6
CALLAO

8
MATARINI

10
SAN JUAN BAY

PHILIPPINES

4
CEBU

6
MANILA

POLAND

6
DANZIG
GDANSK
GDYNIA

7
STETTIN

8
SZCZECIN

9
KOLOBRZEG

PORTUGAL

6
LISBON
OPORTO

PUERTO RICO

7
SAN JUAN

ROMANIA

10
CONSTANTSA

RUSSIA

8
PECHENGA
TAGANROG

9
ARCHANGEL

11
VLADIVOSTOK

12
ST PETERSBURG

SAUDI ARABIA

6
JEDDAH

SCOTLAND

4
TAIN
WICK

5
LEITH
SCAPA

6
DUNBAR
DUNDEE

8
GREENOCK

9
ARDROSSAN
SCAPA FLOW
STORNAWAY

11
GRANGEMOUTH
PORT GLASGOW

SENEGAL

5
DAKAR

SERBIA AND MONTENEGRO

3
BAR

5
KOTOR

7
CATTARO

SIERRA LEONE

8
FREETOWN

SOUTH AFRICA

6
DURBAN

8
CAPE TOWN

9
MOSSEL BAY

PORTS

9–continued
PORT NATAL

10
EAST LONDON
SIMONSTOWN

11
RICHARD'S BAY

13
PORT ELIZABETH

SOUTH KOREA

5
PUSAN

SPAIN

5
PALMA
PALOS

6
BILBAO
FERROL
MALAGA

7
CORUNNA
FUNCHAL

8
ALICANTE
ARRECIFE
LA CORUÑA

9
ALGECIRAS
BARCELONA
CARTAGENA
LAS PALMAS
PORT MAHON

SRI LANKA

5
GALLE

7
COLOMBO

SUDAN

6
SUAKIN

9
PORT SUDAN

SWEDEN

5
LULEA

5–continued
MALMÖ
WISBY
YSTAD

6
KÄLMAR

8
GÖTEBORG
HALMSTAD
NYKÖPING

9
STOCKHOLM

10
GOTHENBURG

11
HELSINGBORG

TAIWAN

6
TAINAN

7
KEELUNG

9
KAO-HSIUNG

TANZANIA

6
MTWARA

11
DAR ES SALAAM

**TRINIDAD AND
TOBAGO**

11
PORT-OF-SPAIN

TURKEY

5
IZMIR

6
SMYRNA

8
ISTANBUL

14
CONSTANTINOPLE

URUGUAY

10
MONTEVIDEO

USA

4
ERIE

7
DETROIT
HOUSTON
NEW YORK
NORFOLK
SEATTLE

8
NEW HAVEN

9
BALTIMORE
GALVESTON
NANTUCKET
PENSACOLA

10
BRIDGEPORT
CHARLESTON
JERSEY CITY
LOS ANGELES
NEW BEDFORD

10–continued
NEW ORLEANS
PERTH AMBOY
PORTSMOUTH

11
ROCK HARBOUR

12
SAN FRANCISCO

VENEZUELA

8
LA GUIARA

12
PUERTO HIERRO

13
PUERTO CABELLO

WALES

7
CARDIFF
SWANSEA

8
HOLYHEAD
LLANELLI
PEMBROKE

9
PORTMADOC

12
MILFORD HAVEN

YEMEN

4
ADEN

5
MOCHA

6
AHMEDI

7
HODEIDA

ISLANDS

3
RUM

4
ARAN
BALI
BUTE
CEBU
CUBA
EDGE
EIGG
GUAM
IONA
JAVA
JURA
MULL
OAHU
SARK
SKYE

5
ARRAN
BANKS
CERAM
CORFU
CAPRI
CRETE
DEVON
HAITI
IBIZA
ISLAY
LEWIS
LEYTE
LUNDY
LUZON
MALTA
PANAY
SAMAR
TIMOR

6
BAFFIN
BORNEO
CYPRUS
FLORES

6–continued
HAINAN
HARRIS
HAWAII
HONSHU
JERSEY
KODIAK
KYUSHU
LESBOS
MADURA
NEGROS
ORKNEY
PENANG
RHODES
SICILY
TAHITI
TAIWAN
TOBAGO

7
ANTIGUA
BAHRAIN
BARENTS
BERMUDA
CELEBES
CORSICA
CURAÇAO
GOTLAND
GRENADA
ICELAND
IRELAND
JAMAICA
MADEIRA
MAJORCA
MINDORO
OKINAWA
PALAWAN
RATHLIN
ROCKALL
ST KITTS
ST LUCIA
SHIKOKU
SUMATRA
WRANGEL

8
ALDERNEY
ANGLESEY
BARBADOS
DOMINICA
FAIR ISLE
GUERNSEY
HOKKAIDO
HONG KONG
MALAGASY
MALLORCA
MELVILLE
MINDANAO
ST HELENA
SAKHALIN
SARDINIA
SHETLAND
SOMERSET
SRI LANKA
SULAWESI
TASMANIA
TENERIFE
TRINIDAD
UNALASKA
VICTORIA
VITI LEVU
ZANZIBAR

9
ANTICOSTI
AUSTRALIA
ELLESMERE
GREENLAND
HALMAHERA
ISLE OF MAN
MANHATTAN
MAURITIUS
NANTUCKET
NEW GUINEA
ST VINCENT
SINGAPORE
VANCOUVER

10
CAPE BRETON

10–continued
GUADELOUPE
HISPANIOLA
LONG ISLAND
MADAGASCAR
MARTINIQUE
NEW BRITAIN
NEW IRELAND
NEW ZEALAND
PUERTO RICO

11
AXEL HEIBERG
GUADALCANAL
ISLE OF PINES
ISLE OF WIGHT

12
BOUGAINVILLE
GREAT BRITAIN
NEW CALEDONIA
NEWFOUNDLAND
NOVAYA ZEMLYA

13
NORTH EAST LAND
PRINCE OF WALES
PRINCE PATRICK
SANTA CATALINA

14
TIERRA DEL FUEGO

15
MARTHA'S
  VINEYARD
WEST SPITS-
  BERGEN

18
PRINCE EDWARD
  ISLAND

ISLAND GROUPS

ADMIRALTY ISLANDS
AEGEAN ISLANDS
    Cyclades
    Dodecanese
    Euboea
    N. Sporades
AEOLIAN ISLANDS (also called Lipari Islands)
AHVENANMAA (Finnish name for Aland Islands)
ALAND ISLANDS (Ahvenanmaa)
ALEUTIAN ISLANDS
    Unalaska
ANDREANOF ISLANDS
    Attu
    Near Islands
AMAGER ISLANDS
ANDAMAN AND NICOBAR ISLANDS
ANTARCTIC ARCHIPELAGO (former name of
    Palmer Archipelago)
ANTIGUA AND BARBUDA
    Antigua
    Barbuda
    Redonda
ANTIPODES ISLANDS
ARAN ISLANDS
    Aranmore (or Inishmore)
    Inisheer
    Inishmaan
ARRU (or ARU) ISLANDS
ASHMORE AND CARTIER ISLANDS
AUCKLAND ISLANDS
AUSTRAL ISLANDS (also called Tubuai Islands)
BAHAMAS (or Bahama) Islands
BALEARIC ISLANDS
    Cabrera
    Formentera
    Ibiza (Spanish name: Evissa)
    Majorca (Spanish name: Mallorca)
    Minorca (Spanish name: Menorca)
BATAN ISLANDS
BELAU ISLANDS
    Babelthuap
BISAYAS (Spanish name for Visayan Islands)
BISMARCK ARCHIPELAGO
    New Britain
    New Ireland
    Lavongai
    Admiralty Islands
BELAU ISLANDS (formerly called Palau or Pelew
    Islands)
BONIN ISLANDS (Japanese name: Ogasawara
    Gunto)
    Chichijima
BONVOULOIR ISLANDS

BRITISH VIRGIN ISLANDS
CAICOS ISLANDS
CANARY ISLANDS
    Fuerteventura
    Gomera
    Hierro
    La Palma
    Lanzarote
    Tenerife
CAROLINE ISLANDS
    Belau (formerly called Palau or Pelew Islands)
CAYMAN ISLANDS
CHANNEL ISLANDS
    Alderney
    Great Sark
    Guernsey
    Herm
    Jersey
    Jethou
    Little Sark
CHATHAM ISLANDS
CHISHIMA (Japanese name for Kuril Islands)
COCOS ISLANDS (also called Keeling Islands)
COOK ISLANDS
    Aitutaki
    Atiu
    Rarotonga
CYCLADES
    Náxos
DANISH WEST INDIES (former name of the US
    Virgin Islands)
D'ENTRECASTEAUX ISLANDS
DODECANESE ISLANDS
    Cos (or Kos)
    Rhodes
DIOMEDE ISLANDS
    Little Diomede
EAST CAROLINE ISLANDS
    Truk Islands
EAST NETHERLANDS ANTILLES
    Bonaire
EAST VIRGIN ISLANDS
    British Virgin Islands
EILEEN SIAR (another name for Outer Hebrides)
ELLICE ISLANDS (former name of Tuvalu Is-
    lands)
FAEROES (also called Faeroe Islands)
FALKLAND ISLANDS (Spanish name: Islas
    Malvinas)
    Palmer Islands
FARQUHAR ISLANDS
FIJI ISLANDS
    Vanua Levu
    Viti Levu

FRIENDLY ISLANDS (also called Tonga)
FRIESLAND ISLANDS
FURNEAUX ISLANDS
    Cape Barren
    Clarke
    Flinders Island
FUR SEAL ISLANDS (another name for the Pribilof Islands)
GALAPAGOS ISLANDS
    San Cristobal (also called Chatham Island)
GAMBIER ISLANDS (or Mangareva Islands)
    Rikitea
GILBERT ISLANDS (former name of Kiribati)
GREATER ANTILLES ISLANDS
    Cuba
    Hispaniola
    Jamaica
    Puerto Rico
GREATER SUNDA ISLANDS
    Borneo
    Java
    Nusa Tenggara
    Sulawesi
    Sumatra
GRENADINES
    Carriacou
GUADELOUPE ISLANDS
    Basse Terre
    Grande Terre
    Marie Galante
    North Saint Martin
HAWAII (formerly called Sandwich Islands)
    Kauai
    Maui
    Molokai
    Oahu
HEARD AND MCDONALD ISLANDS
INNER HEBRIDES ISLANDS
    Islay
    Jura
    Mull
    Skye
IONIAN ISLANDS
    Cephalonia
    Corfu
    Cythera
    Ithaca (Modern Greek Ithaki)
    Leukas (Spanish name: Santa Maura)
    Levkas
    Paxos
    Zante
JUAN FERNANDEZ ISLANDS
KIRIBATI (formerly Gilbert Islands)
    Banaba (Ocean Island)
    Gilbert Islands
    Phoenix Islands
KURIL ISLANDS (Japanese name: Chishima)
LACCADIVE, MINICOY, AND AMINDIVI

    ISLANDS (former name of the Lakshadweep Islands)
LADRONE ISLANDS (former name of the Mariana Islands)
LAGOON ISLANDS (former name of Tuvalu)
LAKSHADWEEP ISLANDS (formerly called Laccadive Minicoy and Amindivi Islands)
    Kavaratti
LEEWARD ISLANDS (French name: Isles sous le Vent)
    Anguilla
    Antigua
    Barbuda
    Dominica
    Guadeloupe Islands
    Montserrat
    Nevis
    Saba (Netherlands Antilles)
    St Barthelemy
    St Kitts
    St Martin North (Guadeloupe)
    St Martin South (Sint Maarten Netherlands Antilles)
    Sint Eustatius (Netherlands Antilles)
    Virgin Islands
LESSER ANTILLES (formerly called Caribbees)
    Barbados
    Leeward Islands
    Netherlands Antilles
    Tobago
    Trinidad
    Windward Islands
LESSER SUNDA ISLANDS (former name of Nusa Tenggara)
LINE ISLANDS (part of Kiribati)
    Fanning
    Jarvis
    Kiritimati (formerly called Christmas Island)
    Palmyra
    Tabuaeran
    Teraina
    Washington
LIPARI ISLANDS (also called Aeolian Islands)
    Stromboli
    Volcano
LOUISIADE ARCHIPELAGO
LOYALTY ISLANDS
MADEIRA
    Deserta
    Porto Santo
    Selvagen Islands
MALDIVE ISLANDS (or Maldives)
MALVINAS (Argentine name for the Falkland Islands)
MANGAREVA ISLANDS (see Gambier Islands)
MARIANA ISLANDS (former name of Ladrone Islands)
    Guam

ISLAND GROUPS

Saipan
Tinian Islands
MARQUESAS ISLANDS (French name: Iles Marquises)
Hiva Oa
Nuku Hiva
MARSHALL ISLANDS
Bikini
Eniwetok
Jaluit
Kwajalein
Majuro
Ralik (Sunset)and Ratak (Sunrise) chains
MASCARENE ISLANDS (French name: Iles Mascareignes)
Mauritius
Reunion
Rodrigues
MIDWAY ISLANDS
MOLUCCAS (or Maluku or the Molucca Islands) (formerly called Spice Islands)
Ambon
Ceram
Halmahera
NETHERLANDS ANTILLES
Bonaire
Curacao
Saba
Sint Maarten
Sint Eustatius
NEW GEORGIA ISLANDS
NEW SIBERIAN ISLANDS
Faddeyevskii
Kotelny
Lyakhov Islands
New Siberia
NORTHERN MARIANA ISLANDS
Saipan
NUSA TENGGARA (formerly called Lesser Sunda Islands)
Alor
Bali
Flores
Lombok
Sumba
Sumbawa
Timor
ORKNEYS
Hoy
Mainland (or Pomona)
Sanday
South Ronaldsay
Westray
OUTER HEBRIDES (Western Isles)
Harris
Lewis
Saint Kilda (also known as Hirta)
The Uists
PACIFIC ISLANDS
Belau

Caroline Islands
Marianas
Marshall Islands
PALAU ISLANDS (formerly called Belau Islands)
PALMER ARCHIPELAGO (formerly called Antarctic Archipelago)
PAPUA NEW GUINEA
Bismark Archipelago
D'Entrecasteaux Islands
E New Guinea
Louisiade Archipelago
Trobriand Islands
W Soloman Islands
Woodlark Island
PELAGIAN ISLANDS
Lampedusa
Lampione
Linosa
PELEW ISLANDS (formerly called Belau Islands)
PHILIPPINE ISLANDS
Visayan Islands
PHOENIX ISLANDS
PITCAIRN ISLANDS
Pitcairn
PRIBILOF ISLANDS (also called Fur Seal Islands)
QUEEN CHARLOTTE ISLANDS
QUEEN ELIZABETH ISLANDS
RYUKYU ISLANDS
Okinawa
SAFETY ISLANDS (French name: Iles du Salut)
SAMOA ISLANDS (formerly called Western Samoa)
Savai'i
Upolu
SANDWICH ISLANDS (former name of Hawaii)
SAN JUAN ISLANDS
SCHOUTEN ISLANDS
Biak
SCILLY ISLANDS (or Scillies)
SEA ISLANDS
SEYCHELLES
Alderbra
Desroches
Farquhar
La Digue
Mahe
Praslin
Silhouette
SHETLAND OR SHETLAND ISLANDS (formerly called Zetland)
Mainland
Unst
Yell
SOCIETY ISLANDS
Huahine
Leeward Islands
Moorea

Raiatea
Tahiti
Windward Islands
SOLOMON ISLANDS
Bougainville
Choiseul
Guadalcanal
Malaita
New Georgia Islands
San Cristobal
Santa Isabel
SOUTH GEORGIA AND THE SOUTH SAND-
WICH ISLANDS
SOUTH NETHERLANDS ANTILLES
Aruba
Bonaire
Curacao
SOUTH ORKNEY ISLANDS
SOUTH SEA ISLANDS
SOUTH SHETLAND ISLANDS
SOUTHWEST MOLUCCAS
Aru or Arru Islands
SPICE ISLANDS (former name of the Moluccas)
SPORADES
North Sporades
South Sporades
SULU ISLANDS
Basilan
Jolo
SUNDA ISLANDS OR SOENDA ISLANDS
Greater Sunda Islands
Nusa Tenggara (formerly called the Lesser
Sunda Islands)
THOUSAND ISLANDS
TOKELAU ISLANDS
Atafu
Fakaofo
Nukunono
TONGA (also called Friendly Islands)
Tongatapu
Tres Marias Islands
TRISTAN DA CUNHA ISLANDS
Tristan
TROBRIAND ISLANDS
Kiriwana
TRUK ISLANDS
TUAMOTU ARCHIPELAGO
Apataki
Fakarava
Rangiroa
TUBUAI ISLANDS (also called Austral Islands)
Tubuai
Rurutu

TURKS AND CAICOS ISLANDS
Grand Turk
Grand Caicos
Salt Cay
TUVALU ISLANDS (formerly called Lagoon
Islands or Ellice Islands)
Funafuti
VANUATU ISLANDS (formerly called New
Hebrides)
Espiritu Santo
VESTMANNAEYJAR ISLANDS (English name:
Westmann Islands)
Helgafell (volcano)
Surtsey (emerged 1963)
VIRGIN ISLANDS (British)
Anegada
Jost Van Dyke
Tortola
Virgin Gorda
VIRGIN ISLANDS (US) (formerly called Danish
West Indies)
Saint Croix (or Santa Cruz)
Saint John
Saint Thomas
VISAYAN ISLANDS (Spanish name: Bisayas)
Leyte
Negros
Panay
VOLCANO ISLANDS (Japanese name: Kazan
Retto)
Iwo Jima
WALLIS AND FUTUNA ISLANDS (or Isles de
Horne Islands)
Alofi
Futuna
Uvea
WEST CAROLINE ISLANDS
Babelthuap
Belau Islands
Yap Islands
WESTERN ISLES (another name for the Outer
Hebrides)
WEST SOCIETY ARCHIPELAGO
Maio (Tubuai Manu)
Mehetia
Moorea
Tetiaoro
WINDWARD ISLANDS (Spanish name: Islas de
Barlovento; French name: Iles du Vent)
Dominica
Martinique
Grenada
Northern Grenadines
St Lucia
St Vincent
YAP ISLANDS

OCEANS AND SEAS

3&4
ARAL (SEA)
AZOV (SEA OF)
DEAD (SEA)
JAVA (SEA)
KARA (SEA)
RED (SEA)
ROSS (SEA)
SAVA (SEA)

5
BANDA (SEA)
BLACK (SEA)
CHINA (SEA)
CORAL (SEA)
IRISH (SEA)
JAPAN (SEA OF)
NORTH (SEA)
TIMOR (SEA)

5–continued
WHITE (SEA)

6
AEGEAN (SEA)
ARCTIC (OCEAN)
BALTIC (SEA)
BERING (SEA)
CELTIC (SEA)
INDIAN (OCEAN)
INLAND (SEA)
IONIAN (SEA)
LAPTEV (SEA)
NANHAI (SEA)
TASMAN (SEA)
YELLOW (SEA)

7
ANDAMAN (SEA)
ARABIAN (SEA)

7–continued
ARAFURA (SEA)
BARENTS (SEA)
BEHRING (SEA)
CASPIAN (SEA)
DONG HAI (SEA)
GALILEE (SEA OF)
MARMARA (SEA OF)
OKHOTSK (SEA OF)
PACIFIC (OCEAN)
WEDDELL (SEA)

8
ADRIATIC (SEA)
AMUNDSEN (SEA)
ATLANTIC (OCEAN)
BEAUFORT (SEA)
HUANG HAI (SEA)
LIGURIAN (SEA)

8–continued
SARGASSO (SEA)
TIBERIAS (SEA OF)

9
ANTARCTIC (OCEAN)
CARIBBEAN (SEA)
EAST CHINA (SEA)
GREENLAND (SEA)

10+
BELLINGSHAUSEN
(SEA)
MEDITERRANEAN
(SEA)
PHILIPPINE (SEA)
SETO-NAIKAI (SEA)
SOUTH CHINA (SEA)

BAYS

3
ISE (Japan)
MAL (Republic of
Ireland)
TOR (England)

4
ACRE (Israel)
CLEW (Republic of
Ireland)
LUCE (Scotland)
LYME (England)
PIGS (Cuba)
VIGO (Spain)
WICK (Scotland)

5
ALGOA (South Africa)
CÁDIZ (Spain)
CASCO (USA)
DVINA (Russia)
FUNDY (Canada)
HAWKE (New
Zealand)
JAMES (Canada)
MILNE (New Guinea)
OMURA (Japan)
OSAKA (Japan)
SLIGO (Republic of
Ireland)
TABLE (South Africa)
TAMPA (USA)
TOKYO (Japan)
URADO (Japan)
VLORË (Albania)

6
ABUKIR (Egypt)
ALASKA (USA)
ARIAKE (Japan)
BAFFIN (Baffin Island,
Greenland)
BANTRY (Republic of
Ireland)
BENGAL (India,
Bangladesh,
Myanmar)
BISCAY (France,
Spain)
BOTANY (Australia)
CALLOA (Peru)
COLWYN (Wales)
DINGLE (Republic of
Ireland)
DUBLIN (Republic of
Ireland)
GALWAY (Republic of
Ireland)
GDANSK (Poland)
HUDSON (Canada)
JERVIS (Australia)
LOBITO (Angola)
MANILA (Philippines)
MOBILE (USA)
NAPLES (Italy)
NEWARK (USA)
PLENTY (New
Zealand)
RAMSEY (Isle of Man)

6–continued
TASMAN (New
Zealand)
TOYAMA (Japan)
TRALEE (Republic of
Ireland)
UNGAVA (Canada)
VYBORG (Finland)
WALVIS (Namibia)
WIGTON (Scotland)

7
ABOUKIR (Egypt)
BRITTAS (Republic of
Ireland)
CAPE COD (USA)
DELAGOA
(Mozambique)
DUNDALK (Republic
of Ireland)
FLORIDA (USA)
KAVÁLLA (Greece)
KILLALA (Republic of
Ireland)
MONTEGO (Jamaica)
MORETON (Australia)
NEW YORK (USA)
POVERTY (New
Zealand)
SETÚBAL (Portugal)
SWANSEA (Wales)
THUNDER (Canada)
TRINITY (Canada)
WALFISH (Namibia)

7–continued
WEXFORD (Republic
of Ireland)
YOUGHAL (Republic
of Ireland)

8
BIDEFORD (England)
BISCAYNE (USA)
BUZZARDS (USA)
CAMPECHE (Mexico)
CARDIGAN (Wales)
DELAWARE (USA)
DUNMANUS
(Republic of Ireland)
FALSE BAY (South
Africa)
GEORGIAN (Canada)
GWEEBARA
(Republic of Ireland)
HANGZHOU (China)
JIANZHOU (China)
PLYMOUTH (USA)
QUIBERON (France)
SAN PEDRO (USA)
SANTIAGO (Cuba)
ST BRIDES (Wales)
ST MICHEL (France)
TREMADOG (Wales)

9
BOMBETOKA
(Madagascar)
DISCOVERY
(Australia)

9–continued
ENCOUNTER
(Australia)
FAMAGUSTA (Cyprus)
FROBISHER
(Canada)
GIBRALTAR (Gibraltar,
Spain)
GUANABARA(Brazil)
INHAMBANE
(Mozambique)
LIVERPOOL
(England)
MAGDALENA
(Mexico)
MORECAMBE
(England)

9–continued
PLACENTIA(Canada)
ST AUSTELL
(England)
WHITE PARK
(Northern Ireland)

10
BALLYHEIGE
(Republic of Ireland)
BALLYTEIGE
(Republic of Ireland)
BARNSTAPLE
(England)
BRIDGWATER
(England)
CAERNARFON
(Wales)

10–continued
CAERNARVON
(Wales)
CARMARTHEN
(Wales)
CHESAPEAKE (USA)
CIENFUEGOS (Cuba)
GUANTÁNAMO
(Cuba)

11
BRIDLINGTON
(England)
LÜTZOW-HOLME
(Antarctica)
PORT PHILLIP
(Australia)

11–continued
TRINCOMALEE (Sri
Lanka)

12+
CORPUS CHRISTI
(USA)
ESPÍRITO SANTO
(Brazil)
MASSACHUSETTS
(USA)
NARRAGANSETT
(USA)
PASSAMAQUODDY
(Canada, USA)
SAN FRANCISCO
(USA)

STRAITS

4
BASS (Australia,
Tasmania)
COOK (New Zealand)
PALK (India, Sri
Lanka)

5
CANSO (Canada)
DAVIS (Canada,
Greenland)
DOVER (England,
France)
KERCH (Ukraine,
Russia)
KOREA (South Korea,
Japan)
MENAI (Wales)
SUMBA (Indonesia:
Sumba, Flores)
SUNDA (Indonesia:
Sumatra, Java)
TATAR (Russia)
TIRAN (Egypt, Saudi
Arabia)

6
BANGKA (Indonesia:
Bangka, Sumatra)
BERING (Alaska,
Russia)
HAINAN (China)
HORMUZ (Iran,
Oman)
HUDSON (Canada)
JOHORE (Malaysia,
Singapore)
LOMBOK (Indonesia:
Bali, Lombak)
SOEMBA (Indonesia:
Sumba, Flores)
TAIWAN (Taiwan,
China)
TORRES (Australia,
New Guinea)

7
BASILAN (Philippines:
Basilan, Mindanao)
DENMARK
(Greenland, Iceland)

7–continued
FLORIDA (USA,
Cuba)
FORMOSA (Taiwan,
China)
GEORGIA (Canada)
MAKASAR (Borneo,
Sulawesi)
MALACCA (Peninsular
Malaysia, Sumatra)
MESSINA (Sicily, Italy)
OTRANTO (Italy,
Albania)
SOENDRA (Indonesia:
Sumba, Java)
TSUGARU (Japan)

8
CLARENCE
(Australia)
MACASSAR (Borneo,
Sulawesi)
MACKINAC (Straits of;
USA)

8–continued
MAGELLAN (Chile,
Tierra del Fuego)
MAKASSAR (Borneo,
Sulawesi)
SURABAYA (Indo-
nesia: Java, Madura)

9
BELLE ISLE (Canada)
GIBRALTAR (Gibraltar,
Spain, Morocco)
LA PÉROUSE (Japan,
Russia)
SOERABAJA (Indo-
nesia: Java, Madura)

10+
GOLDEN GATE (USA)
JUAN DE FUCA
(Canada, USA)
SAN BERNARDINO
(Philippines: Luzon,
Samar)

LAKES, LOCHS, AND LOUGHS

3&4
ARAL (Kazahkstan,
Uzbekistan)
AWE (Scotland)
BALA (Wales)
CHAD (West Africa)

3&4–continued
COMO (Italy)
ERIE (Canada, USA)
EYRE (Australia)
KIVU (Congo,
Rwanda)

3&4–continued
NEMI (Italy)
NESS (Scotland)
TANA (Ethiopia)
VAN (Turkey)

5
FOYLE (Ireland)
GARDA (Italy)
GREAT (Australia)
GREAT (USA,
Canada)

RIVERS

5–continued
HURON (USA, Canada)
KIOGA (Uganda)
KYOGA (Uganda)
LÉMAN (Switzerland, France)
LEVEN (Scotland)
LOCHY (Scotland)
MAREE (Scotland)
NEAGH (Northern Ireland)
NYASA (Malawi, Tanzania,
  Mozambique)
ONEGA (Russia)
TAUPO (New Zealand)
URMIA (Iran)

6
ALBERT (Congo, Democratic
  Republic of, Uganda)
BAIKAL (Russia)
EDWARD (Congo, Democratic
  Republic of, Uganda)
GENEVA (Switzerland, France)
KARIBA (Zambia, Zimbabwe)
LADOGA (Russia)
LOMOND (Scotland)
LOP NOR (China)
MALAWI (Malawi, Tanzania,
  Mozambique)
MOBUTU (Congo, Democratic
  Republic of, Uganda)
NASSER (Egypt)
NATRON (Tanzania)
PEIPUS (Estonia, Russia)
POYANG (China)

6–continued
RUDOLF (Kenya, Ethiopia)
SAIMAA (Finland)
VÄNERN (Sweden)

7
BALATON (Hungary)
BELFAST (Northern Ireland)
DERWENT (England)
KATRINE (Scotland)
KOKO NOR (China)
LUCERNE (Switzerland)
NU JIANG (China, Burma)
ONTARIO (Canada, USA)
QINGHAI (China)
ST CLAIR (USA, Canada)
TORRENS (Australia)
TURKANA (Kenya, Ethiopia)

8
BALKHASH (Kazakhstan)
CHIEMSEE (Germany)
CONISTON (England)
DONGTING (China)
GRASMERE (England)
ISSYK KUL (Kyrgyzstan)
MAGGIORE (Italy, Switzerland)
MAZURIAN (Poland)
MENINDEE (Australia)
MICHIGAN (USA)
NEUSIEDL (Austria, Hungary)
SUPERIOR (USA, Canada)
TITICACA (Peru, Bolivia)
TONLE SAP (Cambodia)
TUNG-T'ING (China)

8–continued
VICTORIA (Uganda, Tanzania,
  Kenya)
WINNIPEG (Canada)

9
ATHABASCA (Canada)
BANGWEULU (Zambia)
CHAMPLAIN (USA)
CONSTANCE (Germany)
ENNERDALE (England)
GREAT BEAR (Canada)
GREAT SALT (USA)
MARACAIBO (Venezuela)
THIRLMERE (England)
TRASIMENO (Italy)
ULLSWATER (England)
WAST WATER (England)

10+
BUTTERMERE (England)
GREAT SLAVE (Canada)
IJSSELMEER (Netherlands)
KARA-BOGAZ-GOL
  (Turkmenistan)
OKEECHOBEE (USA)
STRANGFORD (Northern
  Ireland)
TANGANYIKA (Burundi,
  Congo, Democratic Republic
  of, Tanzania, Zambia)
VIERWALDSTÄTTERSEE
  (Switzerland)
WINDERMERE (England)

RIVERS

2&3
AIN (France)
ALN (England)
BUG (Ukraine, Poland,
  Germany)
CAM (England)
DEE (Scotland, Wales,
  England)
DON (Russia,
  Scotland, England,
  France, Australia)
EMS (Germany,
  Netherlands)
ESK (Australia)
EXE (England)
FAL (England)
FLY (Papua New
  Guinea)
HAN (China)
KWA (Congo, Demo-
  cratic Republic of)
LEA (England)

2&3–continued
LEE (Republic of
  Ireland)
LOT (France)
OB (Russia)
PO (Italy)
RED (USA)
RUR (Germany)
RYE (England)
TAY (Scotland)
URE (England)
USK (Wales, England)
WEY (England)
WYE (Wales, England)
YEO (England)

4
ADDA (Italy)
ADUR (England)
AIRE (England,
  France)

4–continued
AMUR (Mongolia,
  Russia, China)
ARNO (Italy)
ARUN (Nepal)
AUBE (France)
AVON (England)
BANN (Northern
  Ireland)
BEAS (India)
BURE (England)
CHER (France)
COLN (England)
DART (England)
DOON (Scotland)
DOVE (England)
EBRO (Spain)
EDEN (England,
  Scotland)
ELBE (Germany,
  Czech Republic)
EMBA (Kazakhstan)

4–continued
ISIS (England)
JUBA (E. Africa)
KAMA (Russia)
KURA (Turkey,
  Georgia, Azerbaijan)
LAHN (Germany)
LECH (Germany,
  Austria)
LENA (Russia)
LUNE (England)
LÜNE (Germany)
MAAS (Netherlands)
MAIN (Germany,
  Northern Ireland)
MIÑO (Spain)
MOLE (England)
NILE (Sudan, Egypt)
ODER (Germany,
  Czech Republic,
  Poland)
OHIO (USA)

4–continued

OISE (France)
OUSE (England)
OXUS (Turkmenistan, Uzbekistan)
PEEL (Australia, USA)
RAVI (India, Pakistan)
REDE (England)
RUHR (Germany)
SAAR (Germany, France)
SPEY (Scotland)
TAFF (Wales)
TAJO (Spain)
TARN (France)
TAWE (Wales)
TAWI (India)
TEES (England)
TEJO (Brazil)
TEST (England)
TYNE (Scotland, England)
URAL (Russia, Kazakhstan)
VAAL (South Africa)
WEAR (England)
YARE (England)

5

ADIGE (Italy)
AISNE (France)
ALLAN (Scotland, Syria)
ALLER (Spain, Germany)
ANNAN (Scotland)
BENUE (Nigeria)
BRENT (England)
CAMEL (England)
CHARI (Cameroon, Chad)
CLYDE (Scotland, Canada)
COLNE (England)
CONGO (Congo, Democratic Republic of)
DNEPR (Russia, Belarus, Ukraine)
DOUBS (France, Switzerland)
DOURO (Spain, Portugal)
DOVEY (Wales)
DRAVA (Italy, Austria, Yugoslavia, Hungary)
DUERO (Spain)
DVINA (Russia)
FORTH (Scotland)
FOYLE (Northern Ireland)

5–continued

FROME (Australia)
INDUS (India, Pakistan, China)
JAMES (USA, Australia)
JUMNA (India)
JURUÁ (Brazil)
KAFUE (Zambia)
KASAI (Angola, Congo, Democratic Republic of)
KUBAN (Russia)
LAGAN (Northern Ireland)
LIPPE (Germany)
LOIRE (France)
MARNE (France)
MAROS (Indonesia)
MEUSE (France, Belgium)
MINHO (Spain, Portugal)
MUREŞ (Romania, Hungary)
NEGRO (Spain, Brazil, Argentina, Bolivia, Paraguay, Uruguay, Venezuela)
NEMAN (Belarus, Lithuania)
NIGER (Nigeria, Mali, Guinea)
OTTER (England)
PEACE (Canada, USA)
PEARL (USA, China)
PECOS (USA)
PIAVE (Italy)
PURUS (Brazil)
RANCE (France)
RHINE (Switzerland, Germany, Netherlands)
SAALE (Germany)
SAÔNE (France)
SEINE (France)
SLAVE (Canada)
SNAKE (USA)
SOMME (France)
STOUR (England)
SWALE (England)
TAGUS (Portugal, Spain)
TAMAR (England)
TIBER (Italy)
TRENT (England)
TWEED (England, Scotland)
VOLGA (Russia, USA)
VOLTA (Ghana)

5–continued

WESER (Germany)
XINGU (Brazil)
ZAÏRE (Congo, Democratic Republic of)

6

ALLIER (France)
AMAZON (Peru, Brazil)
ANGARA (Russia)
BÍO-BÍO (Chile)
CHENAB (Pakistan)
CLUTHA (New Zealand)
COOPER (Australia)
COQUET (England)
CROUCH (England)
DANUBE (Germany, Austria, Romania, Hungary, Slovakia, Bulgaria)
DNESTR (Ukraine, Moldova)
ESCAUT (Belgium, France)
FRASER (Canada)
GAMBIA (The Gambia, Senegal)
GANGES (India)
GLOMMA (Norway)
HUDSON (USA)
HUNTER (Australia)
IRTYSH (China, Kazakhstan, Russia)
ITCHEN (England)
JAPURÁ (Brazil)
JORDAN (Israel, Jordan)
KOLYMA (Russia)
LIFFEY (Republic of Ireland)
LODDON (Australia, England)
MAMORÉ (Brazil, Bolivia)
MEDINA (USA)
MEDWAY (England)
MEKONG (Laos, China)
MERSEY (England)
MONNOW (England, Wales)
MURRAY (Australia, Canada)
NECKAR (Germany)
NEISSE (Poland, Germany)
OGOOUÉ (Gabon)
ORANGE (South Africa)
ORWELL (England)

6–continued

PARANÁ (Brazil)
PLATTE (USA)
RIBBLE (England)
ST JOHN (Liberia, USA)
SALADO (Argentina, Cuba, Mexico)
SEVERN (England)
SUTLEJ (Pakistan, India, China)
THAMES (England)
TICINO (Italy, Switzerland)
TIGRIS (Iraq, Turkey)
TUGELA (South Africa)
USSURI (China, USSR)
VIENNE (France)
VLTAVA (Czech Republic)
WABASH (USA)
WEAVER (England)
YELLOW (China, USA, Papua New Guinea)

7

BERMEJO (Argentina)
CAUVERY (India)
DAMODAR (India)
DARLING (Australia)
DERWENT (England)
DURANCE (France)
GARONNE (France)
GIRONDE (France)
HELMAND (Afghanistan)
HOOGHLY (India)
HUANG HO (China)
LACHLAN (Australia)
LIMPOPO (South Africa, Zimbabwe, Mozambique)
LUALABA (Congo, Democratic Republic of)
MADEIRA (Brazil)
MARAÑÓN (Brazil, Peru)
MARITSA (Bulgaria)
MOSELLE (Germany)
ORONTES (Syria)
PECHORA (Russia)
POTOMAC (USA)
SALWEEN (Myanmar, China)
SCHELDT (Belgium)
SENEGAL (Senegal)
SHANNON (Republic of Ireland)

7–continued

SONGHUA (Vietnam, China)
SUNGARI (China)
SUWANNEE (USA)
URUGUAY (Uruguay, Brazil)
VISTULA (Poland)
WAIKATO (New Zealand)
XI JIANG (China)
YANGTZE (China)
YENISEI (Russia)
ZAMBEZI (Zambia, Angola, Zimbabwe, Mozambique)

8

AMU DARYA (Turkmenistan, Uzbekistan)
ARAGUAIA (Brazil)
ARKANSAS (USA)
CANADIAN (USA)
CHARENTE (France)
COLORADO (USA)
COLUMBIA (USA)

8–continued

DEMERARA (Guyana)
DORDOGNE (France)
GODAVARI (India)
MANAWATU (New Zealand)
MENDERES (Turkey)
MISSOURI (USA)
PARAGUAY (Paraguay)
PUTUMAYO (Ecuador)
RÍO BRAVO (Mexico)
SAGUENAY (Canada)
SYR DARYA (Uzbekistan, Kazakhstan)
TORRIDGE (England)
TUNGUSKA (Russia)
VOLTURNO (Italy)
WANSBECK (England)
WINDRUSH (England)

9

ATHABASCA (Canada)
CHURCHILL (Canada)

9–continued

ESSEQUIBO (Guyana)
EUPHRATES (Iraq)
GREAT OUSE (England)
HSI CHIANG (China)
IRRAWADDY (Burma)
MACKENZIE (Australia)
MAGDALENA (Colombia)
RIO GRANDE (Jamaica)
TENNESSEE (USA)

10

CHANG JIANG (China)
CHAO PHRAYA (Thailand)
COPPERMINE (Canada)
HAWKESBURY (Australia)
SHENANDOAH (USA)
ST LAWRENCE (USA)

11

ASSINIBOINE (Canada)
BRAHMAPUTRA (China, India)
MISSISSIPPI (USA)
SUSQUEHANNA (USA)
YELLOWSTONE (USA)

12

GUADALQUIVIR (Spain)
MURRUMBIDGEE (Australia)
RÍO DE LA PLATA (Argentina, Uruguay)
SASKATCHEWAN (Canada)

MOUNTAINS AND HILLS

3

ASO (MT) (Japan)
IDA (MT) (Turkey)

4

ALPS (France, Switzerland, Italy, Austria)
BLUE (MTS) (Australia)
COOK (MT) (New Zealand)
ETNA (MT) (Sicily)
HARZ (MTS) (Germany)
JAYA (MT) (Indonesia)
JURA (MTS) (France, Switzerland)
OSSA (MT) (Australia)
RIGI (Switzerland)
URAL (MTS) (Russia)

5

ALTAI (MTS) (Russia, China, Mongolia)
ANDES (South America)

5–continued

ATHOS (MT) (Greece)
ATLAS (MTS) (Morocco, Algeria)
BLACK (MTS) (Wales)
COAST (MTS) (Canada)
EIGER (Switzerland)
ELGON (MT) (Uganda, Kenya)
GHATS (India)
KAMET (MT) (India)
KENYA (MT) (Kenya)
LENIN (PEAK) (Russia)
LOGAN (MT) (Canada)
PELÉE (MT) (Martinique)
ROCKY (MTS) (USA, Canada)
SAYAN (MTS) (Russia)
SNOWY (MTS) (Australia)
TATRA (MTS) (Poland, Slovakia)

5–continued

WEALD (THE) (England)

6

ANTRIM (HILLS) (Northern Ireland)
ARARAT (MT) (Turkey)
BALKAN (MTS) (Bulgaria)
CARMEL (MT) (Israel)
EGMONT (MT) (New Zealand)
ELBERT (MT) (USA)
ELBRUS (MT) (Russia, Georgia)
ELBURZ (MTS) (Iran)
EREBUS (MT) (Antartica)
HERMON (MT) (Syria, Lebanon)
HOGGAR (MTS) (Algeria)
KUNLUN (MTS) (China)
LADAKH (RANGE) (India)
MATOPO (HILLS) (Zimbabwe)

6–continued

MENDIP (HILLS) (England)
MOURNE (MTS) (Northern Ireland)
OLIVES (MT OF) (Israel)
PAMIRS (Tajikistan, China, Afghanistan)
PINDUS (MTS) (Greece, Albania)
TAURUS (MTS) (Turkey)
VOSGES (France)
ZAGROS (MTS) (Iran)

7

AHAGGAR (MTS) (Algeria)
BERNINA (Switzerland)
BROCKEN (Germany)
CHEVIOT (HILLS) (United Kingdom)
CHIANTI (Italy)
EVEREST (MT) (Nepal, China)
OLYMPUS (MT) (Greece)

7–continued
PALOMAR (MT) (USA)
RAINIER (MT) (USA)
RORAIMA (MT)
(Brazil, Guyana,
Venezuela)
RUAPEHU (MT) (New
Zealand)
SKIDDAW (England)
SLEMISH (Northern
Ireland)
SNOWDON (Wales)
SPERRIN (MTS)
(Northern Ireland)
ST ELIAS (MTS)
(Alaska, Yukon)
TIBESTI (MTS) (Chad,
Libya)
WICKLOW (MTS)
(Republic of Ireland)

8
ARDENNES
(Luxembourg,
Belgium, France)
BEN NEVIS (Scotland)
CAMBRIAN (MTS)
(Wales)
CAUCASUS (MTS)
(Georgia, Azerbaijan,
Armenia)
CÉVENNES (France)
CHILTERN (HILLS)
(England)
COTOPAXI (Ecuador)
COTSWOLD (HILLS)
(England)
FLINDERS (RANGE)
(Australia)
FUJIYAMA (Japan)
HYMETTUS (MT)
(Greece)
JUNGFRAU
(Switzerland)
KAIKOURA
(RANGES) (New
Zealand)
MUSGRAVE
(RANGES)
(Australia)
PENNINES (England)
PYRENEES (France,
Spain)
STANOVOI (RANGE)
(Russia)

8–continued
TIAN SHAN
(Tajikistan, China,
Mongolia)
VESUVIUS (Italy)

9
ACONCAGUA (MT)
(Argentina)
ALLEGHENY (MTS)
(USA)
ANNAPURNA (MT)
(Nepal)
APENNINES (Italy)
CAIRNGORM (MTS)
(Scotland)
DOLOMITES (Italy)
DUNSINANE
(Scotland)
GRAMPIANS
(Scotland)
HAMERSLEY
(RANGE) (Australia)
HELVELLYN(England)
HIMALAYAS (S. Asia)
HINDU KUSH (Central
Asia)
HUASCARÁN (Peru)
KARAKORAM
(RANGE) (China,
Pakistan, India)
KOSCIUSKO (MT)
(Australia)
MONT BLANC
(France, Italy)
NANDA DEVI (MT)
(India)
PACARAIMA (MTS)
(Brazil, Venezuela,
Guyana)
PARNASSUS (MT)
(Greece)
RUWENZORI (MTS)
(Congo, Democratic
Republic of, Uganda)
TIRICH MIR (MT)
(Pakistan)
ZUGSPITZE
(Germany)

10
ADIRONDACK (MTS)
(USA)
CADER IDRIS (Wales)
CANTABRIAN (MTS)
(Spain)

10–continued
CARPATHIAN (MTS)
(Slovakia, Poland,
Romania, Hungary,
Ukraine, Moldova)
CHIMBORAZO (MT)
(India)
DHAULAGIRI (MT)
(Nepal)
ERZGEBIRGE (Czech
Republic, Germany)
KEBNEKAISE
(Sweden)
LAMMERMUIR
(HILLS) (Scotland)
MACDONNELL
(RANGES)
(Australia)
MAJUBA HILL (South
Africa)
MATTERHORN
(Switzerland, Italy)
MIDDLEBACK
(RANGE) (Australia)
MONTSERRAT
(Spain)
MOUNT LOFTY
(RANGES)
(Australia)

11
ANTI-LEBANON
(MTS) (Lebanon,
Syria)
APPALACHIAN (MTS)
(USA)
DRAKENSBERG
(MTS) (South Africa)
JOTUNHEIMEN
(Norway)
KILIMANJARO (MT)
(Tanzania)
MONADHLIATH (MTS)
(Scotland)
NANGA PARBAT (MT)
(Pakistan)
SCAFELL PIKE
(England)
SIERRA MADRE
(Mexico)

12
CITLALTÉPETL
(Mexico)
GODWIN AUSTEN
(MT) (Pakistan)

12–continued
GOLAN HEIGHTS
(Syria)
GRAN PARADISO
(Italy)
INGLEBOROUGH
(England)
KANCHENJUNGA
(MT) (Nepal)
PEAK DISTRICT
(England)
POPOCATÉPETL
(MT) (Mexico)
SIDING SPRING (MT)
(Australia)
SIERRA MORENA
(Spain)
SIERRA NEVADA
(Spain, USA)
SLIEVE DONARD
(Northern Ireland)
WARRUMBUNGLE
(RANGE) (Australia)

13
CARRANTUOHILL
(Republic of Ireland)
COMMUNISM PEAK
(Tajikistan)
GROSSGLOCKNER
(Austria)
KANGCHENJUNGA
(MT) (Nepal)
KOMMUNIZMA PIK
(Tajikistan)
OJOS DEL SALADO
(Argentina, Chile)
SIERRA MAESTRA
(Cuba)

14+
BERNESE
OBERLAND
(Switzerland)
FICHTELGEBIRGE
(Germany)
FINSTERAARHORN
(Switzerland)
MACGILLICUDDY'S
REEKS (Republic of
Ireland)
SHIRÉ HIGHLANDS
(Malawi)

VOLCANOES

3
ASO (Japan)
AWU (Indonesia)

4
ETNA (Sicily)
FOGO (Cape Verde
 Islands)
GEDE (Indonesia)
KABA (Indonesia)
LAKI (Iceland)
NILA (Indonesia)
POAS (Costa Rica)
SIAU (Indonesia)
TAAL (Philippines)

5
AGUNG (Indonesia)
ASAMA (Japan)
ASKJA (Iceland)
DEMPO (Indonesia)
FUEGO (Guatemala)
HEKLA (Iceland)
KATLA (Iceland)
MANAM (Papua New
 Guinea)
MAYON (Philippines)
NOYOE (Iceland)
OKMOK (USA)
PALOE (Indonesia)
PELÉE (Martinique)
SPURR (USA)

6
ALCEDO (Galapagos
 Islands)
AMBRIM (Vanuatu)
BIG BEN (Heard
 Island)
BULENG (Indonesia)
COLIMA (Mexico)
DUKONO (Indonesia)
IZALCO (El Salvador)
KATMAI (USA)
LASCAR (Chile)
LASSEN (USA)
LLAIMA (Chile)
LOPEVI (Vanuatu)
MARAPI (Indonesia)

6–continued
MARTIN (USA)
MEAKAN (Japan)
MERAPI (Indonesia)
MIHARA (Japan)
O'SHIMA (Japan)
OSORNO (Chile)
PACAYA
 (Guatemala)
PAVLOF (USA)
PURACÉ (Colombia)
SANGAY (Ecuador)
SEMERU
 (Indonesia)
SLAMAT (Indonesia)
TACANA
 (Guatemala)
UNAUNA (Indonesia)

7
ATITLAN
 (Guatemala)
BÁRCENA (Mexico)
BULUSAN
 (Philippines)
DIDICAS (Philippines)
EL MISTI (Peru)
GALERAS (Colombia)
JORULLO (Mexico)
KILAUEA (USA)
OMETEPE
 (Nicaragua)
PUYEHUE (Chile)
RUAPEHU (New
 Zealand)
SABRINA (Azores)
SOPUTAN (Indonesia)
SURTSEY (Iceland)
TERNATE (Indonesia)
TJAREME (Indonesia)
TOKACHI (Japan)
TORBERT (USA)
TRIDENT (USA)
VULCANO (Italy)

8
BOGOSLOF (USA)

8–continued
CAMEROON
 (Cameroon)
COTOPAXI (Ecuador)
DEMAVEND (Iran)
FONUALEI (Tonga
 Islands)
FUJIYAMA (Japan)
HUALALAI (USA)
KERINTJI (Indonesia)
KRAKATAU
 (Indonesia)
KRAKATOA
 (Indonesia)
MAUNA LOA (USA)
NIUAFO'OU (Tonga)
RINDJANI (Indonesia)
SANGEANG
 (Indonesia)
TARAWERA (New
 Zealand)
VESUVIUS (Italy)
YAKEDAKE (Japan)

9
AMBUROMBU
 (Indonesia)
BANDAI-SAN (Japan)
CLEVELAND (USA)
COSEGUINA
 (Nicaragua)
COTACACHI
 (Ecuador)
GAMKONORA
 (Indonesia)
GRIMSVÖTN
 (Iceland)
MOMOTOMBO
 (Nicaragua)
MYOZIN-SYO (Japan)
NGAURUHOE (New
 Zealand)
PARICUTIN (Mexico)
RININAHUE (Chile)
SANTORINI (Greece)
STROMBOLI (Italy)
TONGARIRO (New
 Zealand)

10
ACATENANGO
 (Guatemala)
CAPELINHOS
 (Azores)
CERRO NEGRO
 (Nicaragua)
GUALLATIRI (Chile)
HIBOK HIBOK
 (Philippines)
LONG ISLAND (Papua
 New Guinea)
MIYAKEJIMA (Japan)
NYAMIAGIRA (Congo,
 Democratic Republic
 of)
NYIRAGONGO
 (Congo, Democratic
 Republic of)
SANTA MARIA
 (Guatemala)
SHISHALDIN (USA)
TUNGURAHUA
 (Ecuador)
VILLARRICA (Chile)

11
GREAT SITKIN (USA)
KILIMANJARO
 (Tanzania)
LA SOUFRIÈRE
 (Saint Vincent and
 the Grenadines)
TUPUNGATITO
 (Chile)
WHITE ISLAND (New
 Zealand)

12
HUAINAPUTINA
 (Peru)
POPOCATÉPETL
 (Mexico)

WATERFALLS

5
PILAO, SALTO (Brazil)

6
GIETRO, CASCADE DU (Switzerland)
YUTAJE, SALTO (Venezuela)

7
AA FALLS (USA)
RORAIMA, SALTO (Venezuela)
SELFOSS (Iceland)

8
ITUTINGA, CACHOEIRA (Brazil)
JOG FALLS (India)
KUKENAAM, SALTO (Venezuela)
LANGFOSS (Norway)

9
BRUFOSSEN (Norway)
DETTIFOSS (Iceland)
SIPI FALLS (Uganda)
TROU DE FER, CASCADES DE (Réunion)

10
AIMOO FALLS (USA)
ANGEL FALLS (Venezuela)
BLUFF FALLS (New Zealand)
GREAT FALLS (USA)
KJELFOSSEN (Norway)
LEVO SAVICE, SLAPOVI (Slovenia)
RHEINFALLE (Switzerland)
WAPTA FALLS (Canada)

11
BALAIFOSSEN (Norway)
BOYOMA FALLS (Congo)
BROWNE FALLS (New Zealand)
COHOES FALLS (USA)
DONTEFOSSEN (Norway)
HALOKU FALLS (USA)
IGUACU FALLS (Brazil, Argentina, Paraguay)
KAHIWA FALLS (USA)
KRUNEFOSSEN (Norway)
MADDEN FALLS (Canada)
MONGEFOSSEN (Norway)
OLMAAFOSSEN (Norway)
PAPALA FALLS (USA)
SPIREFOSSEN (Norway)
SUNDIFOSSEN (Norway)
TJOTAFOSSEN (Norway)
TUGELA FALLS (South Africa)
TYSSEFOSSEN (Norway)

12
IGUASSU FALLS (Brazil, Argentina, Paraguay)
LAEGDAFOSSEN (Norway)
LUNGAFOSSEN (Norway)
MARENGO FALLS (Australia)
MTARAZI FALLS (Zimbabwe)
NIAGARA FALLS (USA, Canada)

12-continued
ORMELIFOSSEN (Norway)
RUACANA FALLS (Namibia, Angola)
SPOKANE FALLS (USA)
STANLEY FALLS (former name for Boyoma Falls)
TRES HERMANAS, CATARATAS LAS (Peru)
WAIMANU FALLS (USA)
WAILELE FALLS (USA)

13
DIYALUMA FALLS (Sri Lanka)
HAFRAGILSFOSS (Iceland)
KAIETEUR FALLS (Guyana)
KAKAAUKI FALLS (USA)
KEANA'AWI FALLS (USA)
KOOTENAI FALLS (USA)
LAHOMENE FALLS (USA)
MARDALSFOSSEN (Norway)
MONUMENT FALLS (USA)
OLO'UPENA FALLS (USA)
PU'UKA'OKU FALLS (USA)
RAVINE BLANCHE, LA CASCADE DE (Réunion)
SENTINEL FALLS (USA)
SHOSHONE FALLS (USA)
STRUPENFOSSEN (Norway)
VICTORIA FALLS (Zimbabwe)
WAIHILAU FALLS (USA)
YOSEMITE FALLS (USA)

14
AUGRABIES FALLS (South Africa)
CHURCHILL FALLS (Canada)
DUDHSAGAR FALLS (India)
GOLD CREEK FALLS (Canada)
MURCHISON FALLS (Uganda)
PITCHFORK FALLS (USA)
SNOW CREEK FALLS (USA)
TYSSESTRENGENE (Norway)

15
BRIDAL VEIL FALLS (USA)
MANA'WAI'NUI FALLS (USA)
SILVER LAKE FALLS (USA)
SUTHERLAND FALLS (New Zealand)

16
ALFRED CREEK FALLS (Canada)
BASESEACHIC FALLS (Mexico)
PISSING MARE FALLS (Canada)
WILLIAMETTE FALLS (USA)
YELLOWSTONE FALLS (USA)

17
RAMNEFJELLSFOSSEN (Norway)
WHITE GLACIER FALLS (USA)

18+
AVALANCHE BASIN FALLS (USA)
COLONIAL CREEK FALLS (USA)
DESERTED RIVER FALLS (Canada)

DESERTS

18+—continued
KINGCOME VALLEY FALLS (Canada)
OSTRE TINJEFJELLFOSSEN (Norway)
SULPHIDE CREEK FALLS (USA)
YTSTE TINJEFJELLFOSSEN (Norway)

DESERTS

4
GILA
GOBI
THAR

5
NAMIB
NEFUD
NEGEV
OLMOS
ORDOS
SINAI
STURT

6
ARUNTA
GIBSON
MOJAVE

6—continued
NUBIAN
SAHARA
SYRIAN
UST'-URT

7
ALASHAN
ARABIAN
ATACAMA
KARA KUM
MORROPE
PAINTED
SECHURA
SIMPSON

8
COLORADO

8—continued
KALAHARI
KYZYL KUM
MUYUNKUM
VIZCAINO

9
BLACK ROCK
DASHT-I-LUT
DZUNGARIA

10
AUSTRALIAN
BET-PAK-DALA
GREAT SANDY
PATAGONIAN
RUB'AL KHALI

11
DASHT-I-KAVIR
DASHT-I-MARGO
DEATH VALLEY

13
GREAT SALT LAKE
GREAT VICTORIA

14
BOLSON DE MAPIMI

16
TURFAN
 DEPRESSION

NATIONAL PARKS

PARK	LOCATION	SPECIAL FEATURE
Abisko	Sweden	
Abruzzo	Italy	
Altos de Campana	Panama	
Amazônia	Brazil	
Angkor	Kampuchea	Khmer civilization remains
Arusha	Tanzania	
Atitlán	Guatemala	
Awāsh	Ethiopia	
Babiogórski	Poland	
Banff	Alberta, Canada	hot springs at Sulphur Mountain
Bayarischer Wald	Bavaria, West Germany	
Belovezhskaya	Belorussia	
Białowieski	Poland	
Brecon Beacons	Wales	
Cabo de Hornos	Chile	automatically operated lighthouse
Cairngorms	Scotland	
Canaima	Venezuela	Salto Angel
Cañon del Rio Blanco	Mexico	
Canyonlands	Utah, United States	landforms carved in the red sandstone
Carlsbad Caverns	New Mexico	largest area of caverns in the world
Carnarvon	Queensland	

PARK	LOCATION	SPECIAL FEATURE
Chobe	Botswana	
Corbett	Uttar Pradesh, India	
Cradle Mountain–Lake Saint Clair	Tasmania, Australia	
Daisetsuzan	Japan	
Dartmoor	England	
Denali	Alaska, United States	Mt. McKinley
Djung-kulon	Indonesia	
Etosha	Namibia	
Everglades	Florida, United States	
Exmoor	England	
Fiordland	New Zealand	
Franklin D. Roosevelt	Uruguay	
Fray Jorge	Chile	
Fuji-Hakone-Izu	Japan	
Fundy	New Brunswick, Canada	
Galápagos	Ecuador	giant iguanas and giant tortoises
Gemsbok	Botswana	
Gir Lion	Gujarāt, India	
Glacier	Montana, United States	
Gorongosa	Mozambique	
Grand Canyon	Arizona, United States	
Gran Paradiso	Italy	
Great Smoky Mountains	North Carolina & Tennessee, United States	
Hawaii Volcanoes	Hawaii, United States	
Henri Pittier	Venezuela	
Hohe Tauern	Austria	Krimmler Waterfall
Hortobágyi	Hungary	
Huascarán	Peru	Nevado Huascarán
Iguaçu	Brazil	Iguaçu Falls
Iguazú	Argentina	Iguazú River cliffs; Iguazú Falls
Isle Royale	Michigan, United States	
Ixtacihuatl-Popocatépetl	Mexico	
Jasper	Alberta, Canada	Columbia Icefield
Kabalega	Uganda	Kabalega Falls
Kafue	Zambia	
Kaieteur	Guyana	Kaieteur Falls
Kalahari Gemsbok	Cape of Good Hope, South Africa	
Karatepe-Asiantaş	Turkey	Hittite, Roman, and Phoenician civilizations ruins
Katmai	Alaska, United States	
Kaziranga	Assam, India	
Khao Yai	Thailand	
Kilimanjaro	Tanzania	
Komoé	Ivory Coast	
Kosciusko	New South Wales, Australia	Mt. Kosciusko
Kruger	Transvaal, South Africa	
Lake District	England	Lake Windermere
Loch Lomond and the Trossachs	Scotland	
Los Glaciares	Argentina	glacial landforms
Manovo-Gounda-Saint Floris	Central African Republic	
Manu	Peru	
Mayon Volcano	Phillippines	Mayon Volcano
Mesa Verde	Colorado, United States	remains of cliff dwellings of pre-Columbian Indians
Moçãmedes Reserva	Angola	

NATIONAL PARKS

PARK	LOCATION	SPECIAL FEATURE
Mount Apo	Phillippines	
Mount Aspiring	New Zealand	Mt. Aspiring
Mount Carmel	Israel	
Mount Cook	New Zealand	Mt. Cook; Tasman Glacier
Nahuel Huapi	Argentina	Mt. Tronador
Nairobi	Kenya	
Namib Desert	Namibia	
Norfolk Broads	England	
Northumberland	England	
North York Moors	England	
Odzala	Congo	
Olympic	Washington, USA	
Olympus	Greece	
Peak District	England	
Pellas-Ounastunturi	Finland	
Pembrokeshire Coast	Wales	
Petrified Forest	Arizona, United States	forests of petrified trees
Pfälzerwald	Rheinland-Pfalz, West Germany	
Pico de Orizaba	Mexico	Citlaltépetl volcano
Plitvička, Jezera	Croatia	
Puracé	Columbia	
Pyrénées Occidentales	France	
Rapa Nui	Chile	sites of an ancient civilization
Redwood	California, United States	
Retezat	Romania	
Rocky Mountain	Colorado, United States	
Rondane	Norway	
Ruwenzori	Uganda	
Sarek	Sweden	
Schweizerische	Switzerland	
Serengeti	Tanzania	
Setto-Naikai	Japan	
Sierra Nevada de Mérida	Venezuela	
Skaftafell Thingvellir	Iceland	
Snowdonia	Wales	Snowdon Peak
Stirling Range	Western Australia, Australia	
Stolby Zapovednik	Russia	
Tatransky Národni	Slovakia	
Tatrzański	Poland	
Teberdinsky Zapovednik	Russia	
Tikal	Guatemala	ruins of Mayan city
Tortuguero	Costa Rica	green sea turtles
Toubkal	Morocco	
Triglavski Narodni	Slovenia	Kanjavec Peak; Savica Waterfalls
Tsavo	Kenya	
Uluru	Northern Territory, Australia	Mt. Olga; Ayers Rock
Valle de Ordesa	Spain	
Vanoise	France	
Veluwezoom, Het	Netherlands	
Victoria Falls	Zimbabwe & Zambia	Victoria Falls
Virunga	Zaire	
Volcanoes	Rwanda	
Wankie	Zimbabwe	
Waterton Lakes	Alberta, Canada	
Waza	Cameroon	

PARK	LOCATION	SPECIAL FEATURE
Wood Buffalo	Alberta & Northwest Territories, Canada	reserve for bison herds
W. Parc	Benin, Niger, & Burkina Faso	
Yellowstone	Wyoming, Montana, & Idaho, United States	Old Faithful
Yoho	British Columbia, Canada	Takakkaw Falls
Yorkshire Dales	England	
Yosemite	California, United States	Yosemite Falls
Zion	Utah, United States	

ANIMALS AND PLANTS

ANIMALS

2&3
AI
APE
ASS
BAT
CAT
DOG
ELK
FOX
GNU
KOB
PIG
RAT
YAK

4
ANOA
BEAR
CAVY
CONY
DEER
GAUR
GOAT
HARE
IBEX
KUDU
LION
LYNX
MINK
MOLE
MULE
ORYX
PACA
PIKA
PUMA
SAKI
SEAL
SIKA
TAHR
TITI
URUS
VOLE
WOLF
ZEBU

5
ADDAX
BISON

5—continued
BONGO
CAMEL
CHIRU
CIVET
COATI
COYPU
DHOLE
DINGO
DRILL
ELAND
FOSSA
GAYAL
GENET
GORAL
HINNY
HORSE
HUTIA
HYENA
HYRAX
INDRI
KIANG
KOALA
LEMUR
LIGER
LLAMA
LORIS
MOOSE
MOUSE
NYALA
OKAPI
ORIBI
OTTER
OUNCE
PANDA
POTTO
RATEL
SABLE
SAIGA
SEROW
SHEEP
SHREW
SKUNK
SLOTH
STOAT
TAPIR
TIGER

5—continued
TIGON
WHALE
ZEBRA

6
AGOUTI
ALPACA
AOUDAD
ARGALI
AUROCH
AYE-AYE
BABOON
BADGER
BEAVER
BOBCAT
CATTLE
CHITAL
COLUGO
COUGAR
COYOTE
CUSCUS
DESMAN
DIK-DIK
DONKEY
DUGONG
DUIKER
ERMINE
FENNEC
FERRET
FISHER
GALAGO
GELADA
GERBIL
GIBBON
GOPHER
GRISON
GUENON
HYAENA
IMPALA
JACKAL
JAGUAR
JERBOA
LANGUR
MARGAY
MARMOT
MARTEN
MONKEY

6—continued
MUSK OX
NILGAI
NUMBAT
NUTRIA
OCELOT
OLINGO
ONAGER
POSSUM
RABBIT
RED FOX
RODENT
SEA COW
SERVAL
SIFAKA
TENREC
VERVET
VICUNA
WALRUS
WAPITI
WEASEL
WISENT
WOMBAT

7
ACOUCHI
ANT BEAR
BANTENG
BIGHORN
BLESBOK
BLUE FOX
BUFFALO
CANE RAT
CARACAL
CARIBOU
CHAMOIS
CHEETAH
COLOBUS
DASYURE
DOLPHIN
ECHIDNA
FELIDAE
GAZELLE
GEMSBOK
GERENUK
GIRAFFE
GLUTTON
GORILLA

7–continued

GRAMPUS
GUANACO
GYMNURE
HAMSTER
LEMMING
LEOPARD
LINSANG
MACAQUE
MAMMOTH
MANATEE
MARKHOR
MEERKAT
MOLE RAT
MOON RAT
MOUFLON
MUSKRAT
NARWHAL
NOCTULE
OPOSSUM
PACK RAT
PANTHER
PECCARY
POLECAT
PRIMATE
RACCOON
RED DEER
ROE DEER
RORQUAL
SEALION
SIAMANG
SOUSLIK
SUN BEAR
TAMARIN
TAMAROU
TARSIER
WALLABY
WARTHOG
WILDCAT
ZORILLA

8

AARDVARK
AARDWOLF
ANTEATER
ANTELOPE
AXIS DEER
BABIRUSA
BONTEBOK
BUSHBABY
BUSHBUCK
CACHALOT
CAPYBARA
CHIPMUNK
DORMOUSE
ELEPHANT
ENTELLUS
FRUIT BAT
HEDGEHOG
IRISH ELK
KANGAROO

8–continued

KINKAJOU
MANDRILL
MANGABEY
MARMOSET
MONGOOSE
MUSK DEER
MUSQUASH
PANGOLIN
PLATYPUS
PORPOISE
REEDBUCK
REINDEER
RUMINANT
SEA OTTER
SEI WHALE
SQUIRREL
STEINBOK
TALAPOIN
TAMANDUA
VISCACHA
WALLAROO
WATER RAT
WILD BOAR

9

ARCTIC FOX
ARMADILLO
BANDICOOT
BINTURONG
BLACK BEAR
BLACKBUCK
BLUE WHALE
BROWN BEAR
DEER MOUSE
DESERT RAT
DROMEDARY
FLYING FOX
GOLDEN CAT
GROUNDHOG
GUINEA PIG
HAMADRYAS
MONOTREME
MOUSE DEER
ORANG-UTAN
PACHYDERM
PALM CIVET
PAMPAS CAT
PHALANGER
POLAR BEAR
PORCUPINE
PRONGHORN
PROSIMIAN
SILVER FOX
SITATUNGA
SLOTH BEAR
SOLENODON
SPRINGBOK
THYLACINE
TREE SHREW
WATERBUCK

9–continued

WATER VOLE
WOLVERINE
WOODCHUCK

10

ANGWANTIBO
BARBARY APE
BOTTLENOSE
CACOMISTLE
CHEVROTAIN
CHIMPANZEE
CHINCHILLA
CHIROPTERA
FALLOW DEER
FIELDMOUSE
GOLDEN MOLE
HARTEBEEST
HONEY MOUSE
HOODED SEAL
JAGUARUNDI
KODIAK BEAR
MONA MONKEY
OTTER SHREW
PALLAS'S CAT
PILOT WHALE
PINE MARTEN
POUCHED RAT
PRAIRIE DOG
RACCOON DOG
RHINOCEROS
RIGHT WHALE
SPERM WHALE
SPRINGHAAS
TIMBER WOLF
VAMPIRE BAT
WATER SHREW
WHITE WHALE
WILDEBEEST

11

BARBASTELLE
BARKING DEER
DOUROUCOULI
FLYING LEMUR
GRASS MONKEY
GRIZZLY BEAR
HARBOUR SEAL
HONEY BADGER
KANGAROO RAT
KILLER WHALE
LEOPARD SEAL
PATAS MONKEY
PIPISTRELLE
PRAIRIE WOLF
RAT KANGAROO
RED SQUIRREL
SEROTINE BAT
SNOW LEOPARD

12

ELEPHANT SEAL

12–continued

HARVEST MOUSE
HIPPOPOTAMUS
HORSESHOE BAT
HOWLER MONKEY
JUMPING MOUSE
KLIPSPRINGER
MOUNTAIN LION
POCKET GOPHER
RHESUS MONKEY
ROAN ANTELOPE
SNOWSHOE HARE
SPIDER MONKEY
TREE KANGAROO
WATER BUFFALO
WOOLLY MONKEY

13

ANTHROPOID APE
CRABEATER SEAL
DORCAS GAZELLE
HUMPBACK WHALE
MARSUPIAL MOLE
ROYAL ANTELOPE
SABLE ANTELOPE
TASMANIAN WOLF

14

CAPUCHIN MONKEY
CLOUDED LEOPARD
FLYING SQUIRREL
GROUND SQUIRREL
MOUNTAIN BEAVER
NEW WORLD
  MONKEY
OLD WORLD
  MONKEY
PÈRE DAVID'S DEER
SPECTACLED BEAR
SQUIRREL MONKEY
TASMANIAN DEVIL

15+

CHINESE WATER
  DEER
DUCK-BILLED
  PLATYPUS
FLYING PHALANGER
PROBOSCIS
  MONKEY
PYGMY HIPPO-
  POTAMUS
SCALY-TAILED
  SQUIRREL
WHITE RHINO-
  CEROS
WOOLLY RHINO-
  CEROS
WOOLLY SPIDER
  MONKEY

ANIMALS AND THEIR GENDER

ANIMAL	MALE	FEMALE	ANIMAL	MALE	FEMALE
ANTELOPE	BUCK	DOE	HARE	BUCK	DOE
ASS	JACKASS	JENNYASS	HARTEBEAST	BULL	COW
BADGER	BOAR	SOW	HORSE	STALLION	MARE
BEAR	BOAR	SOW	IMPALA	RAM	EWE
BOBCAT	TOM	LIONESS	JACKRABBIT	BUCK	DOE
BUFFALO	BULL	COW	KANGAROO	BUCK	DOE
CAMEL	BULL	COW	LEOPARD	LEOPARD	LEOPARDESS
CARIBOU	STAG	DOE	LION	LION	LIONESS
CAT	TOM	QUEEN	MOOSE	BULL	COW
CATTLE	BULL	COW	OX	BULLOCK	COW
CHICKEN	COCK	HEN	PEACOCK	PEACOCK	PEAHEN
COUGAR	TOM	LIONESS	PHEASANT	COCK	HEN
COYOTE	DOG	BITCH	PIG	BOAR	SOW
DEER	STAG	DOE	RHINOCEROS	BULL	COW
DOG	DOG	BITCH	ROEDEER	ROEBUCK	DOEDEER
DONKEY	JACKASS	JENNYASS	SEAL	BULL	COW
DUCK	DRAKE	DUCK	SHEEP	RAM	EWE
ELAND	BULL	COW	SWAN	COB	PEN
ELEPHANT	BULL	COW	TIGER	TIGER	TIGRESS
FERRET	JACK	JILL	WALRUS	BULL	COW
FISH	COCK	HEN	WEASEL	BOAR	COW
FOX	FOX	VIXEN	WHALE	BULL	COW
GIRAFFE	BULL	COW	WOLF	DOG	BITCH
GOAT	BILLYGOAT	NANNYGOAT	ZEBRA	STALLION	MARE
GOOSE	GANDER	GOOSE			

ADJECTIVES

CREATURE	ADJECTIVE	CREATURE	ADJECTIVE
BEAR	URSINE	FROG	BATRACHIAN
BEE	APIAN	GOAT	CAPRINE; HIRCINE
BULL	TAURINE	GOOSE	ANSERINE
CAT	FELINE	HARE	LEPORINE
CHIPMUNK	SCIURINE	HORSE	EQUINE
CIVET	VIVERRINE	LION	LEONINE
COW	BOVINE	LIZARD	SAURIAN
CRAB	CRUSTACEAN or CRUSTACEOUS	LOBSTER	CRUSTACEAN or CRUSTACEOUS
DEER	CERVID or CERVINE	MONGOOSE	VIVERRINE
DOG	CANINE	MONKEY	SIMIAN
DOLPHIN	CETACEAN or CETACEOUS	MOUSE	MURINE
DONKEY	ASININE	PIG	PORCINE
EEL	ANGUILLIFORM	PORPOISE	CETACEAN or CETACEOUS
ELEPHANT	ELEPHANTINE	RAT	MURINE
FERRET	MUSTELINE	SEAL	OTARID; PHOCINE
FISH	PISCINE	SEA LION	OTARID
FOWL	GALLINACEOUS	SHEEP	OVINE
FOX	VULPINE		

CREATURE	ADJECTIVE	CREATURE	ADJECTIVE
SHRIMP	CRUSTACEAN *or* CRUSTACEOUS	TOAD	BATRACHIAN
		TORTOISE	CHELONIAN
SKUNK	MUSTELINE	TURTLE	CHELONIAN
SNAKE	ANGUINE; COLUBRINE; OPHIDIAN; SERPENTINE	VIPER	VIPERINE *or* VIPEROUS
		WEASEL	MUSTELINE
SPIDER	ARACHNOID	WHALE	CETACEAN *or* CETACEOUS
SQUIRREL	SCIURINE	WOLF	LUPINE
TERRAPIN	CHELONIAN	WORM	VERMIFORM

ANIMALS AND THEIR YOUNG

ANIMAL	YOUNG	ANIMAL	YOUNG
ANTELOPE	KID	HARE	LEVERET
BADGER	CUB	HARTEBEAST	CALF
BEAR	CUB	HAWK	CHICK
BEAVER	KITTEN	HORSE	FOAL
BOBCAT	KITTEN	JACKRABBIT	KITTEN
BUFFALO	CALF	KANGAROO	JOEY
CAMEL	CALF	LEOPARD	CUB
CARIBOU	FAWN	LION	CUB
CAT	KITTEN	MONKEY	INFANT
CATTLE	CALF	OX	STOT
CHICKEN	CHICK	PHEASANT	CHICK
COUGAR	KITTEN	PIG	PIGLET
COYOTE	PUPPY	RHINOCEROS	CALF
DEER	FAWN	ROEDEER	KID
DOG	PUPPY	SEAL	CALF
DUCK	DUCKLING	SHEEP	LAMB
ELAND	CALF	SKUNK	KITTEN
ELEPHANT	CALF	SWAN	CYGNET
ELK	CALF	TIGER	CUB
FISH	FRY	TOAD	TADPOLE
FROG	TADPOLE	WALRUS	CUB
FOX	CUB	WEASEL	KIT
GIRAFFE	CALF	WHALE	CALF
GOAT	KID	WOLF	CUB
GOOSE	GOSLING	ZEBRA	FOAL

ANIMAL SOUNDS

ANIMAL	SOUND	ANIMAL	SOUND
ASS	BRAY	BIRD	CALL
	HEE-HAW		SING
BEAR	GROWL		CHIRP
BEE	BUZZ		TWEET
	HUM		WARBLE
BEETLE	DRONE	BULL	BELLOW

ANIMAL HOMES

ANIMAL	SOUND	ANIMAL	SOUND
CAT	MEOW	GUINEA PIG	SQUEAK
	PURR	HIPPOPOTAMUS	BRAY
CHICKEN	CLUCK	HORSE	NEIGH
COCK	CROW		WHINNY
COW	MOO	HYENA	LAUGH
	LOW	KITTEN	MEW
CROW	CAW	LION	ROAR
CUCKOO	CUCKOO	MAGPIE	CHATTER
DEER	BELL	MONKEY	CHATTER
DOG	BARK		GIBBER
	YELP	MOUSE	SQUEAK
	BAY	MULE	BRAY
	YAP	NIGHTINGALE	WARBLE
	GROWL		PIPE
	SNARL		JUG-JUG
	HOWL	OWL	HOOT
	WHINE		SCREECH
DOLPHIN	CLICK	OX	LOW
DONKEY	BRAY		BELLOW
DOVE	COO	PARROT	SQUAWK
DUCK	QUACK	PEACOCK	SCREAM
EAGLE	SQUAWK		WAIL
	SCREAM	PIG	GRUNT
ELEPHANT	TRUMPET		OINK
FALCON	CHANT		SQUEAL
FLY	BUZZ	PIGEON	COO
FOX	BARK	RAVEN	CROAK
	YAP	RHINOCEROS	SNORT
	YELP	SEA GULLS	SQUAWK
FROG	CROAK		CRY
GIRAFFE	BLEAT	SEAL	BARK
	GRUNT	SHEEP	BLEAT
GOAT	BLEAT		BAA
GOOSE	HISS	SNAKE	HISS
	CACKLE	SWAN	HISS
	HONK	TIGER	GROWL
GRASSHOPPER	CHIRP	TURKEY	GOBBLE
	PITTER	WOLF	BAY
GROUSE	DRUM		HOWL

ANIMAL HOMES

ANIMAL	HOME	ANIMAL	HOME
ANT	HILL	BIRD	AVIARY
	FORMICARY		NEST
ARMADILLO	DUGOUT	CAT	CATTERY
BADGER	SETT		LAIR
	HOLE		DEN
BAT	ROOST	CHICKEN	COOP
	CAVE		BATTERY
BEAR	DEN		HENHOUSE
BEAVER	LODGE	COW	BYRE
BEE	HIVE		BARN

58

ANIMAL	HOME	ANIMAL	HOME
DOG	KENNEL	PHEASANT	NIDE
DOVE	DOVECOTE	PIG	PEN
EAGLE	EYRIE		STY
FOX	DEN	PIGEON	PIGEONCOTE
	LAIR		LOFT
	EARTH	RABBIT	WARREN
HARE	FORM		HUTCH
HERON	HERONRY		BURROW
HORNET	NEST	RAT	NEST
HORSE	STABLE		HOLE
	PADDOCK	RAVEN	RAVENRY
LION	DEN	SEAL	ROOKERY
MOLE	FORTRESS	SHEEP	FOLD
	HILL		PEN
	BURROW	SNAIL	SNAILERY
MOUSE	MOUSEHOLE	SNAKE	NEST
	MOUSERY	SPIDER	WEB
	NEST	SQUIRREL	DREY
OTTER	HOLT	SWAN	SWANNERY
	COUCH	TERMITE	MOUND
OWL	OWLERY	TIGER	LAIR
OX	CORRAL	WASP	NEST
	CRIB		VESPIARY
OYSTER	HIVE	WOLF	LAIR
PENGUIN	PENGUINERY		DEN

COLLECTIVE TERMS

ANIMAL	COLLECTIVE TERM	ANIMAL	COLLECTIVE TERM
ANTELOPE	HERD	ELAND	HERD
APE	SHREWDNESS	ELEPHANT	HERD
ASS	DROVE	ELK	GANG
BADGER	CETE	FERRET	BUSINESS
BEAR	SLEUTH	FISH	SCHOOL
BEAVER	COLONY	FOX	TROOP
BLOODHOUND	SUTE	GELDING	BRACE
BOAR	SOUNDER	GIRAFFE	HERD
BUFFALO	HERD	GOAT	FLOCK
CAMEL	TRAIN	GOOSE	GAGGLE
CARIBOU	HERD	HARE	HUSKE
CAT	CLUSTER	HARTEBEAST	HERD
CATTLE	HERD	HAWK	CAST
CHAMOIS	HERD	HORSE	HERD
CHICKEN	FLOCK	IMPALA	COUPLE
CHOUGH	CHATTERING	JACKRABBIT	HUSK
COLT	RAG	KANGAROO	TROOP
COOT	FLEET	KINE	DROVE
COYOTE	PACK	LEOPARD	LEAP
DEER	HERD	LION	PRIDE
DOG	PACK	MOLE	LABOUR
DOLPHIN	POD	MONKEY	TROOP
DONKEY	DROVE	MOOSE	HERD
DUCK	PADDLING	MOUSE	NEST

ANIMAL	COLLECTIVE TERM	ANIMAL	COLLECTIVE TERM
OX	TEAM	SHEEP	FLOCK
PEACOCK	PRIDE	SNAKE	KNOT
PHEASANT	BROOD	TOAD	NEST
PIG	TRIP	WALRUS	POD
RHINOCEROS	CRASH	WEASEL	PACK
ROEDEER	BEVY	WHALE	SCHOOL
ROOK	BUILDING	WOLF	PACK
SEAL	POD	ZEBRA	HERD

ANIMAL DISEASES AND INFECTIONS

3
EHV
EIA
GID
ORF
ROT

4
ROUP
SCUR

5
FARCY

6
APHTHA
CANKER
CAT FLU
CRUELS
EPULIS
GRAPES
GREASE
SPAVIN
STURDY
SWEENY
TEASER
WARBLE

7
BIGHEAD
FOOT ROT
FOUNDER

7–continued
GOLDEYE
MOONEYE
ONYCHIA
QUITTOR
REDFOOT
YELLOWS

8
FOG FEVER
JAUNDICE
LUMPY JAW
RINGWOMB
STAGGERS
SWAY-BACK
TOE CRACK
TREMBLES
WINDGALL

9
CLOACITIS
ECLAMPSIA
HOOFBOUND
MILK FEVER
RUBBER JAW
SAND COLIC
SAND CRACK
VENT GLEET
WHISTLING

10
BABESIOSIS
BLUETONGUE
BUMBLE-FOOT
HEART-WATER
KNEE SPAVIN
NYCTALOPIA
SADDLE GALL
SALLENDERS
SEBORRHOEA
SHOVEL BEAK
SOD DISEASE
TEXAS FEVER
WATERBRAIN

11
FOWL CHOLERA
WOODY TONGUE

12
BLACK DISEASE
BORNA DISEASE
HIP DYSPLASIA
MILK LAMENESS
MILK SICKNESS
QUARTER CRACK
WOODEN TONGUE

13
ACTINOMYCOSIS
BLIND STAGGERS

13–continued
BORDER DISEASE
MOON BLINDNESS

14
BABY PIG DISEASE
CALF DIPHTHERIA

15
BLACKWATER
  FEVER
EQUINE INFLUENZA
HYPOMAGNE-
  SAEMIA
LACTATION TETANY
MILLER'S DISEASE
PARTURIENT FEVER

16+
ACTINO BACILLOSIS
AFRICAN SWINE
  FEVER
ALTITUDE SICKNESS
CANINE PAR-
  VOVIRUS
MOUNTAIN SICK-
  NESS
NEW FOREST
  DISEASE

BREEDS OF CATS

3
REX

4
MANX

5
CREAM
SMOKE
TABBY

6
BIRMAN
HAVANA

7
BURMESE
PERSIAN
RED SELF
SIAMESE

7–continued
SPOTTED
TURKISH

8
DEVON REX
RED TABBY

9
BLUE CREAM

10
ABYSSINIAN
BROWN TABBY
CHINCHILLA
CORNISH REX

11
BLUE BURMESE
BRITISH BLUE

11–continued
COLOURPOINT
RUSSIAN BLUE
SILVER TABBY

12
BROWN BURMESE

13
CHESTNUT BROWN
RED ABYSSINIAN
TORTOISESHELL

14
LONG HAIRED BLUE
TORTIE AND WHITE

15
RED-POINT
SIAMESE

18
BLUE-POINTED
SIAMESE
SEAL-POINTED
SIAMESE
TORTIE-POINT
SIAMESE

19
LILAC-POINTED
SIAMESE
TABBY-POINTED
SIAMESE

20+
CHOCOLATE-
POINTED SIAMESE

BREEDS OF DOGS

3
PUG

4
PULI

5
BOXER
CORGI
HUSKY
SPITZ

6
BEAGLE
BORZOI
BRIARD
COLLIE
KELPIE
POODLE
SALUKI
SETTER

7
BASENJI
BULLDOG
GRIFFON
HARRIER
LOWCHEN
LURCHER
MALTESE
MASTIFF
POINTER
SAMOYED

7–continued
SHELTIE
SHIH TZU
SPANIEL
TERRIER
WHIPPET

8
ALSATIAN
CHOW CHOW
ELKHOUND
FOXHOUND
KEESHOND
MALEMUTE
PAPILLON
SHEEPDOG

9
CHIHUAHUA
DACHSHUND
DALMATIAN
DEERHOUND
GREAT DANE
GREYHOUND
LHASA APSO
PEKINGESE
RETRIEVER
SCHNAUZER
STAGHOUND
ST BERNARD

10
BLOODHOUND

10–continued
FOX TERRIER
OTTERHOUND
POMERANIAN
ROTTWEILER
SCHIPPERKE
WEIMARANER
WEIMERANER
WELSH CORGI

11
AFGHAN HOUND
BASSET HOUND
BULL MASTIFF
BULL TERRIER
IBIZAN HOUND
IRISH SETTER
SKYE TERRIER

12
CAIRN TERRIER
FINNISH SPITZ
IRISH TERRIER
JAPANESE CHIN
NEWFOUNDLAND
PHARAOH HOUND
SILKY TERRIER
WELSH TERRIER

13
AFFENPINSCHER
BORDER TERRIER

13–continued
BOSTON TERRIER
COCKER SPANIEL
ENGLISH SETTER
HUNGARIAN PULI

14
GERMAN SHEP-
HERD
IRISH WOLFHOUND

15
AIREDALE TERRIER
ALASKAN
MALAMUTE
GOLDEN
RETRIEVER
HUNGARIAN VIZSLA
LAKELAND TERRIER
SCOTTISH TERRIER
SEALYHAM TERRIER
SPRINGER SPANIEL

16
KERRY BLUE
TERRIER
PYRENEAN MOUN-
TAIN
SHETLAND SHEEP-
DOG
YORKSHIRE
TERRIER

17
BEDLINGTON TERRIER
DOBERMANN PINSCHER
LABRADOR RETRIEVER

18
JACK RUSSELL TERRIER
KING CHARLES SPANIEL

18—continued
LARGE MUNSTERLANDER
OLD ENGLISH SHEEPDOG
RHODESIAN RIDGEBACK

20+
DANDIE DINMONT TERRIER

20+—continued
STAFFORDSHIRE BULL
 TERRIER
WEST HIGHLAND WHITE
 TERRIER
WIREHAIRED POINTING
 GRIFFON

BREEDS OF HORSES AND PONIES

3
COB
DON

4
ARAB
BARB
FELL
POLO
RUSS

5
DALES
FJORD
HUCUL
KONIK
LOKAI
ORLOV
PINTO
SHIRE
TERSK
TIMOR
WELSH

6
ALBINO
BASUTO
EXMOOR
MERENS
MORGAN
TARPAN
VIATKA

7
CASPIAN
COMTOIS
CRIOLLO
FURIOSA
HACKNEY
JUTLAND
LLANERO
MUSTANG
NORIKER
QUARTER
SORRAIA

8
BUDEONNY

8—continued
CAMARGUE
DARTMOOR
GALICEÑO
HIGHLAND
HOLSTEIN
KABARDIN
KARABAIR
KARABAKH
LUSITANO
PALOMINO
SHETLAND

9
AKHAL-TEKE
ALTER-REAL
APPALOOSA
CONNEMARA
FALABELLA
HAFLINGER
KNABSTRUP
NEW FOREST
OLDENBURG
PERCHERON

9—continued
SCHLESWIG

10
ANDALUSIAN
AVELIGNESE
CLYDESDALE
GELDERLAND
HANOVERIAN
IRISH DRAFT
LIPIZZANER

11
NOVOKIRGHIZ

12
CLEVELAND BAY
SUFFOLK PUNCH
THOROUGHBRED

13
WELSH MOUNTAIN

16
TENNESSEE
 WALKING

BREEDS OF CATTLE

3
GIR

5
DEVON
KERRY
LUING

6
DEXTER
JERSEY
SUSSEX

7
BEEFALO
BRANGUS

8
AYRSHIRE
FRIESIAN
GALLOWAY
GUERNSEY
HEREFORD
HIGHLAND

8—continued
LIMOUSIN

9
CHAROLAIS
SHORTHORN
SIMMENTAL

10
BROWN SWISS
LINCOLN RED
MURRAY GREY

10—continued
WELSH BLACK

11
JAMAICA HOPE
MARCHIGIANA

13
ABERDEEN ANGUS
DROUGHTMASTER
TEXAS LONGHORN

BREEDS OF PIGS

5
DUROC
WELSH

8
PIETRAIN

8–continued
TAMWORTH

9
BERKSHIRE
HAMPSHIRE

10
LARGE WHITE

15
SWEDISH
LANDRACE

17
BRITISH SADDLE-
BACK
GLOUCESTER OLD
SPOT

BREEDS OF SHEEP

4
LONK
MULE
SOAY

5
CARDY
CHIOS
JACOB
LLEYN
MORFE
TEXEL

6
AWASSI
MASHAM

6–continued
MERINO
ROMNEY

7
CHEVIOT
GOTLAND
KARAKUL
LACAUNE
SUFFOLK

8
HERDWICK
LONGMYND
POLWARTH
PORTLAND

8–continued
SHETLAND

9
HEBRIDEAN
LONGWOOLS
OLDENBERG
ROUGH FELL
SWALEDALE
TEESWATER

10
CORRIEDALE
DORSET HORN
EXMOOR HORN
POLL DORSET

11
MANX LOGHTAN
WENSLEYDALE

13
WELSH MOUNTAIN
WILTSHIRE HORN

15
FRIES MELKSCHAAP

17
SCOTTISH BLACK-
FACE

18
WHITEFACED
WOODLAND

BREEDS OF POULTRY

4
BUFF (goose)

5
MARAN (chicken)
PEARL (guinea fowl)
PEKIN (duck)
ROMAN (goose)
ROUEN (duck)
WHITE (guinea fowl)

6
ANCONA (ohiokon)
CAYUGA (duck)
EMBDEN (goose)
SILKIE (chicken)

7
AFRICAN (goose)
CHINESE (goose)
CRESTED (duck)
DORKING (chicken)
LEGHORN (chicken)

7–continued
MUSCOVY (duck)
PILGRIM (goose)

8
LAVENDER (guinea
fowl)
TOULOUSE (goose)

9
AYLESBURY (duck)
WELSUMMER
(chicken)

10
BARNVELDER
(chicken)
BELTSVILLE (turkey)
BOURBON RED
(turkey)
INDIAN GAME
(chicken)

10–continued
ROSS RANGER
(chicken)
SEBASTOPOL
(goose)

11
CUCKOO MARAN
(chicken)
LIGHT SUSSEX
(chicken)

12
BLACK NORFOLK
(turkey)
INDIAN RUNNER
(duck)
NARRAGANSETT
(turkey)
PLYMOUTH ROCK
(chicken)
WHITE HOLLAND
(turkey)

13
BUFF ORPINGTON
(duck)
KHAKI CAMPBELL
(duck)
MAMMOTH BRONZE
(turkey)
WHITE AUSTRIAN
(turkey)

14
BLACK EAST INDIE
(duck)
RHODE ISLAND RED
(chicken)
WELSH HARLEQUIN
(duck)
WHITE WYANDOTTE
(chicken)

15
CAMBRIDGE
BRONZE (turkey)

POINTS OF A HORSE

CANNON BONE
CHEEK
CHEST
CHESTNUT
CHIN GROOVE
COFFIN BONE
CORONET
CREST
CROUP
DOCK
ELBOW
ERGOT
FEATHERS
FETLOCK
FETLOCK JOINT

FLANK
FOREARM
FORELOCK
FROG
GASKIN
GULLET
HEEL
HIND QUARTERS
HOCK
HOOF
KNEE
LOIN
MANE
NAVICULAR BONE
PASTERN

PEDAL BONE
POINT OF HIP
POINT OF SHOULDER
POLL
RIBS
SHANK
SHEATH
SHOULDER
SPLINT BONE
STIFLE
TAIL
TENDON
WINDPIPE
WITHERS

BIRDS

3
AUK
EMU
JAY
MOA
OWL
TIT
TUI

4
CHAT
COLY
COOT
CROW
DODO
DOVE
DUCK
GULL
HAWK
HUIA
IBIS
KAGU
KITE
KIWI
KNOT
LARK
LORY
RAIL
RHEA
ROOK
RUFF
SHAG
SKUA
SMEW
SWAN

4–continued
TEAL
TERN
WREN

5
BOOBY
CRAKE
CRANE
DIVER
EAGLE
EGRET
EIDER
FINCH
GOOSE
GREBE
HERON
HOBBY
MACAW
MYNAH
NODDY
OUZEL
PIPIT
PRION
QUAIL
RAVEN
ROBIN
SCAUP
SERIN
SNIPE
STILT
STORK

6
AVOCET

6–continued
BARBET
BULBUL
CANARY
CHOUGH
CONDOR
CUCKOO
CURLEW
DARTER
DIPPER
DRONGO
DUNLIN
FALCON
FULMAR
GANNET
GODWIT
HOOPOE
JABIRU
JACANA
KAKAPO
LINNET
MAGPIE
MARTIN
MERLIN
MOTMOT
ORIOLE
OSPREY
PARROT
PEEWIT
PETREL
PIGEON
PLOVER
PUFFIN
QUELEA

6–continued
RATITE
ROLLER
SHRIKE
SISKIN
TAKAHE
THRUSH
TOUCAN
TROGON
TURACO
TURKEY
WHIDAH
WHYDAH
WIGEON

7
ANTBIRD
BABBLER
BARN OWL
BITTERN
BLUETIT
BUNTING
BUSTARD
BUZZARD
COAL TIT
COURSER
DUNNOCK
EMU WREN
FANTAIL
FINFOOT
FISH OWL
GADWALL
GOSHAWK
GRACKLE
HARRIER

7–continued

HAWK OWL
HOATZIN
JACAMAR
JACKDAW
KESTREL
LAPWING
MALLARD
MANAKIN
MARABOU
MINIVET
MOORHEN
OILBIRD
ORTOLAN
OSTRICH
PEACOCK
PEAFOWL
PELICAN
PENGUIN
PINTAIL
POCHARD
QUETZAL
REDPOLL
REDWING
ROSELLA
SEAGULL
SERIEMA
SKIMMER
SKYLARK
SPARROW
SUNBIRD
SWALLOW
TANAGER
TINAMOU
TOURACO
VULTURE
WAGTAIL
WARBLER
WAXBILL
WAXWING
WRYBILL
WRYNECK

8

ACCENTOR
AVADAVAT
BATELEUR
BEE-EATER
BLACKCAP
BLUEBIRD
BOATBILL
BOBOLINK
CARACARA
CARDINAL
COCKATOO
CURASSOW
DABCHICK
DOTTEREL
EAGLE OWL
FISH HAWK
FLAMINGO
GAMEBIRD

8–continued

GARGANEY
GREAT TIT
GROSBEAK
HAWFINCH
HORNBILL
LOVEBIRD
LYREBIRD
MANNIKIN
MEGAPODE
MUTE SWAN
NIGHTJAR
NUTHATCH
OVENBIRD
OXPECKER
PARAKEET
PHEASANT
PYGMY OWL
REDSHANK
REDSTART
REEDLING
RIFLEMAN
ROCK DOVE
SCOPS OWL
SCREAMER
SEA EAGLE
SHELDUCK
SHOEBILL
SNOWY OWL
SONGBIRD
STARLING
SWIFTLET
TAWNY OWL
TITMOUSE
TRAGOPAN
WHEATEAR
WHIMBREL
WHINCHAT
WHIPBIRD
WHITE-EYE
WILDFOWL
WOODCHAT
WOODCOCK

9

ALBATROSS
BALD EAGLE
BLACKBIRD
BLACK SWAN
BOWERBIRD
BRAMBLING
BROADBILL
BULLFINCH
CASSOWARY
CHAFFINCH
COCKATIEL
CORMORANT
CORNCRAKE
CROSSBILL
CURRAWONG
FIELDFARE
FIRECREST

9–continued

FRANCOLIN
FRIARBIRD
FROGMOUTH
GALLINULE
GOLDCREST
GOLDENEYE
GOLDFINCH
GUILLEMOT
GYRFALCON
HILL MYNAH
KITTIWAKE
LITTLE OWL
MERGANSER
MOUSEBIRD
PARTRIDGE
PHALAROPE
PTARMIGAN
RAZORBILL
RED GROUSE
RIFLEBIRD
RING OUZEL
SANDPIPER
SCRUB BIRD
SNAKEBIRD
SNOW GOOSE
SPOONBILL
STONECHAT
THICKHEAD
THORNBILL
TRUMPETER
TURNSTONE

10

ARCTIC TERN
BEARDED TIT
BRENT GOOSE
BUDGERIGAR
CHIFFCHAFF
CRESTED TIT
DEMOISELLE
DIVING DUCK
FLYCATCHER
GRASSFINCH
GREENFINCH
GREENSHANK
GUINEA FOWL
HAMMERHEAD
HARPY EAGLE
HONEYEATER
HONEY GUIDE
HOODED CROW
JUNGLE FOWL
KINGFISHER
KOOKABURRA
MALLEE FOWL
MUTTONBIRD
NIGHT HERON
NUTCRACKER
PRATINCOLE
SACRED IBIS
SADDLEBACK

10–continued

SAGE GROUSE
SANDERLING
SANDGROUSE
SCREECH OWL
SHEARWATER
SHEATHBILL
SONG THRUSH
SUN BITTERN
TAILORBIRD
TROPIC BIRD
TURTLE DOVE
WEAVERBIRD
WOODPECKER
WOOD PIGEON
ZEBRA FINCH

11

BLACK GROUSE
BRUSH TURKEY
BUTCHERBIRD
BUTTON QUAIL
CANADA GOOSE
CARRION CROW
DIAMONDBIRD
FRIGATE BIRD
GNATCATCHER
GOLDEN EAGLE
HERRING GULL
HUMMINGBIRD
LAMMERGEIER
LAUGHING OWL
MOCKINGBIRD
MUSCOVY DUCK
NIGHTINGALE
REED WARBLER
SNOW BUNTING
SPARROWHAWK
STONE CURLEW
STORM PETREL
TREECREEPER
WALLCREEPER
WEAVERFINCH
WHITETHROAT
WOODCREEPER
WREN BABBLER

12

BURROWING OWL
CAPERCAILLIE
CUCKOO-SHRIKE
DABBLING DUCK
FAIRY PENGUIN
FLOWERPECKER
GREYLAG GOOSE
HEDGE SPARROW
HONEYCREEPER
HOUSE SPARROW
LANNER FALCON
MANDARIN DUCK
MARSH HARRIER
MISTLE THRUSH
MOURNING DOVE

ADJECTIVES

12—continued
PERCHING DUCK
SHOVELER DUCK
STANDARDWING
UMBRELLA BIRD
WHIPPOORWILL
YELLOWHAMMER

13
ADJUTANT STORK
AMERICAN EAGLE
BARNACLE GOOSE
CROCODILE BIRD

13—continued
ELEPHANT BIRDS
FAIRY BLUEBIRD
HARLEQUIN DUCK
HAWAIIAN GOOSE
LONG-TAILED TIT
OYSTERCATCHER
PASSERINE BIRD
SECRETARY BIRD
WHISTLING DUCK
WHOOPING CRANE

14
BEARDED VULTURE
BIRD OF PARADISE
DARWIN'S FINCHES
EMPEROR PENGUIN
GOLDEN PHEASANT
GRIFFON VULTURE
OWLET FROG-
  MOUTH
PLAINS-WANDERER

15+
BALTIMORE ORIOLE

15+—continued
GREAT CRESTED
  GREBE
IVORY-BILLED
  WOODPECKER
LAUGHING JACKASS
PASSENGER
  PIGEON
PEREGRINE FALCON
PHILIPPINE EAGLE
TYRANT FLY-
  CATCHER

ADJECTIVES

BIRD	ADJECTIVE	BIRD	ADJECTIVE
BIRD	AVIAN	PARROT	PSITTACINE
CROW	CORVINE	SONGBIRD	OSCINE
DOVE	COLUMBINE	SPARROW	PASSERINE
EAGLE	AQUILINE	SWALLOW	HIRUNDINE
FOWL	GALLINACEOUS	THRUSH	TURDINE

FISH

3
COD
DAB
EEL
GAR
IDE
RAY

4
BASS
CARP
CHAR
CHUB
DACE
DORY
FISH
GOBY
HAKE
LING
OPAH
ORFE
PIKE
RUDD
SHAD
SOLE

4—continued
TOPE
TUNA

5
BLEAK
BREAM
BRILL
DANIO
GRUNT
GUPPY
LOACH
MOLLY
PERCH
PORGY
ROACH
SAURY
SHARK
SKATE
SMELT
SPRAT
TENCH
TETRA
TROUT
TUNNY

6
BARBEL
BELUGA
BLENNY
BONITO
BOWFIN
BURBOT
GUNNEL
KIPPER
MARLIN
MINNOW
MULLET
PLAICE
PUFFER
REMORA
SAITHE
SALMON
TARPON
TURBOT
WEEVER
WRASSE

7
ALEWIFE
ANCHOVY

7—continued
BATFISH
CATFISH
CICHLID
CROAKER
DOGFISH
EELPOUT
GARFISH
GARPIKE
GOURAMI
GROUPER
GUDGEON
GURNARD
HADDOCK
HAGFISH
HALIBUT
HERRING
HOGFISH
ICEFISH
LAMPREY
MUDFISH
OARFISH
PIRANHA
POLLACK

7–continued
POMPANO
RATFISH
SARDINE
SAWFISH
SCULPIN
SEA BASS
SNAPPER
SUNFISH
TELEOST
TORPEDO
WHITING

8
ALBACORE
BLUEFISH
BRISLING
BROTULID
BULLHEAD
CAVE FISH
CHARACIN
CHIMAERA
DEVIL RAY
DRAGONET
DRUMFISH
FILEFISH
FLATFISH
FLATHEAD
FLOUNDER
FROGFISH
GOLDFISH
GRAYLING
JOHN DORY
LUNGFISH
MACKEREL
MANTA RAY
MONKFISH

8–continued
MOONFISH
MORAY EEL
PILCHARD
PIPEFISH
SAILFISH
SEA BREAM
SEA HORSE
SEA PERCH
SEA ROBIN
SKIPJACK
STINGRAY
STURGEON
SWAMP EEL
TOADFISH
WOLF FISH

9
ANGELFISH
BARRACUDA
BLUE SHARK
CLINGFISH
CONGER EEL
GLASSFISH
GLOBEFISH
GOOSEFISH
GRENADIER
KILLIFISH
LATIMERIA
LEMON SOLE
MURRAY COD
PEARLFISH
PIKEPERCH
PILOT FISH
PLACODERM
PORBEAGLE
RED MULLET

9–continued
RED SALMON
STARGAZER
STONE BASS
STONEFISH
SWORDFISH
SWORDTAIL
THREADFIN
TIGERFISH
TOP MINNOW
TRUNKFISH
WHITEBAIT
WHITEFISH
WRECKFISH
ZEBRA FISH

10
ANGLERFISH
ARCHER FISH
BOMBAY DUCK
COELACANTH
CORNETFISH
CYCLOSTOME
DAMSELFISH
DRAGONFISH
FLYING FISH
GHOST SHARK
GUITAR FISH
LUMPSUCKER
MIDSHIPMAN
MUDSKIPPER
NEEDLEFISH
NURSE SHARK
PADDLEFISH
PARROT FISH
PINK SALMON
PLACODERMI

10–continued
RIBBONFISH
SHIELD FERN
SILVERSIDE
TIGER SHARK
WHALE SHARK
WHITE SHARK

11
ELECTRIC EEL
ELECTRIC RAY
GOBLIN SHARK
HATCHETFISH
LANTERN FISH
MOORISH IDOL
STICKLEBACK
SURGEONFISH
TRIGGERFISH

12+
BASKING SHARK
CLIMBING PERCH
FIGHTING FISH
FOUR-EYED FISH
GREENLAND SHARK
HAMMERHEAD
  SHARK
LABYRINTH FISH
MACKEREL SHARK
MILLER'S THUMB
MOUTHBROODER
PORCUPINE FISH
REQUIEM SHARK
SCORPION FISH
SOCKEYE SALMON
THRESHER SHARK
YELLOWFIN TUNA

SEASHELLS

3
SUN

4
HARP

5
TULIP

6
NUTMEG

7
JUNONIA
SUNDIAL

8
DYE MUREX
LION'S PAW

8–continued
NOBLE PEN
PHEASANT
TURK'S CUP

9
ANGEL WING
BAT VOLUTE
BURSA FROG
GIANT CLAM
PINK CONCH
ROTA MUREX
SPINY VASE
TELESCOPE
TENT OLIVE
WEDGE CLAM

10
BLUE MUSSEL
CAMEO HELMT
COAT-OF-MAIL
CROWN CONCH
DELPHINULA
DRUPE SNAIL
EYED COWRIE
PAPERY RAPA
QUAHOG CLAM
SCALED WORM
WINGED FROG

11
BEAR PAW CLAM
CLIONE SNAIL
FRONS OYSTER

11–continued
GREEN TURBAN
HEART COCKLE
MUSIC VOLUTE
ONYX SLIPPER
OSTRICH FOOT
PAPER BUBBLE
PEARL OYSTER
SACRED CHANK
TEXTILE CONE
TIGER COWRIE

12
AMORIA VOLUTE
ATLANTIC CONE
FLORIDA MITER
GAUDY ASAPHIS

MARSUPIALS

12–continued
GOLDEN COWRIE
GOLDEN TELLIN
LIMA FILE CLAM
MONEY COWRIES
PACIFIC AUGER
PARTRIDGE TUN
PELICAN'S FOOT
SCOTCH BONNET
SPIKED LIMPET
SPINDLE TIBIA

13
ANGULAR VOLUTE
BABLYON TURRID
BLEEDING TOOTH
CARDINAL MITER
COMMERCIAL TOP
COSTATE COCKLE
FIGHTING CONCH
GEOGRAPHY CONE
JACKKNIFE CLAM
JAPANESE CONES
PAPER NAUTILUS
PRICKLY HELMET
RIDGED ABALONE
SPIRAL BABYLON
SUNRISE TELLIN
TURKEY WING ARK
VENUS COMB CLAM

14
CHANNELED WHELK
DISTAFF SPINDLE
ELEGANT FIMBRIA
EPISCOPAL MITER
IMPERIAL VOLUTE

14–continued
INDONESIAN CLAM
LEUCODON COWRIE
LEWIS' MOON SNAIL
LIGHTNING WHELK
PANAMANIAN CONE
PHILIPPINE CONE
POLYNESIAN CONE
TAPESTRY TURBAN
TRITON'S TRUMPET
VENUS COMB
MUREX

15
BITTERSWEET CLAM
BULL-MOUTH
HELMET
JAPANESE CARRIER
NEW ENGLAND
WHELK
PANAMANIAN
AUGER
PILGRIM'S SCALLOP
SUNBURST
CARRIER
TURRITELLA SNAIL
WATERING POT
CLAM
WEST INDIAN
CHANK
WEST AFRICAN
CONE

16
ASIAN MOON
SCALLOP

16–continued
ATLANTIC SURF
CLAM
DONKEY EAR
ABALONE
EDIBLE BAY
SCALLOP
FRILLED
DOGWINKLE
GLORY-OF-INDIA
CONE
ORANGE-MOUTH
OLIVE
PAGODA
PERIWINKLE
PERPLICATE
VOLUTE
PINK-MOUTHED
MUREX
ROOSTERTAIL
CONCH
WEDDING CAKE
VENUS

17
AUSTRALIAN
TRUMPET
CHAMBERED
NAUTILUS
FLORIDA HORSE
CONCH
PACIFIC WING
OYSTER
SANTA CRUZ
LATIAXIS
VIOLET SPIDER
CONCH

18
ATLANTIC DEER
COWRIE
GIANT KNOBBED
CERITH
GLORY-OF-THE-
SEAS CONE
GREAT KEYHOLE
LIMPET
PACIFIC GRINNING
TUN
PRECIOUS WENTLE-
TRAP
WHITE-SPOTTED
MARGIN

19
TANKERVILLE'S
ANCILLA

20+
ARTHRITIC SPIDER
CONCH
ATLANTIC THORNY
OYSTER
COLOURFUL
ATLANTIC MOON
ELEPHANT'S SNOUT
VOLUTE
IMBRICATE CUP-
AND-SAUCER
MIRACULOUS
THATCHERIA

MARSUPIALS

5
BILBY
KOALA

6
CUSCUS
NUMBAT
WOMBAT

7
DASYURE
DUNNART

7–continued
OPOSSUM
WALLABY

8
KANGAROO

9
BANDICOOT
KOALA BEAR
NATIVE CAT
PHALANGER

9–continued
SPRINGBOK
THYLACINE

10
HONEY MOUSE
SPRINGBUCK

11
DIPROTODONT
NOTOTHERIUM
PYGMY GLIDER

11–continued
RAT KANGAROO

13
MARSUPIAL MOLE
POLYPROTODONT

14
MARSUPIAL MOUSE
TASMANIAN DEVIL

15
FLYING PHALANGER

REPTILES AND AMPHIBIANS

3
ASP
BOA
OLM

4
FROG
NEWT
TOAD

5
ADDER
AGAMA
COBRA
GECKO
KRAIT
MAMBA
SIREN
SKINK
SNAKE
TOKAY
VIPER

6
CAYMAN
GAVIAL
IGUANA
LIZARD
MOLOCH
MUGGER
PYTHON
TAIPAN
TURTLE
ZALTYS

7
AXOLOTL
GHARIAL
REPTILE
TUATARA

8
ANACONDA
BASILISK
BULLFROG
CONGO EEL
MATAMATA
MOCCASIN
MUDPUPPY
PIT VIPER
RINGHALS
SEA SNAKE
SLOWWORM
TERRAPIN
TORTOISE
TREE FROG

9
ALLIGATOR
BLINDWORM
BOOMSLANG
BOX TURTLE
CAECILIAN
CHAMELEON
CROCODILE
HAIRY FROG
PUFF ADDER
TREE SNAKE

9–continued
VINE SNAKE
WART SNAKE
WHIP SNAKE

10
BLACK SNAKE
BUSHMASTER
CHUCKWALLA
CLAWED FROG
COPPERHEAD
CORAL SNAKE
FER-DE-LANCE
GLASS SNAKE
GRASS SNAKE
HELLBENDER
HORNED TOAD
NATTERJACK
POND TURTLE
SALAMANDER
SAND LIZARD
SIDEWINDER
WATER SNAKE
WORM LIZARD

11
AMPHISBAENA
CONSTRICTOR
COTTONMOUTH
DIAMONDBACK
FLYING SNAKE
GABOON VIPER
GILA MONSTER

11–continued
GOLIATH FROG
GREEN TURTLE
HORNED VIPER
MIDWIFE TOAD
RATTLESNAKE
SMOOTH SNAKE

12
FLYING LIZARD
HORNED LIZARD
KOMODO DRAGON

13
BEARDED LIZARD
FRILLED LIZARD
GIANT TORTOISE
MANGROVE SNAKE
MONITOR LIZARD
RUSSELL'S VIPER
SPADEFOOT TOAD
WATER MOCCASIN

14+
FIRE SALAMANDER
HAWKSBILL TURTLE
LEATHERBACK
  TURTLE
SNAKE-NECKED
  TURTLE
SOFT-SHELLED
  TURTLE

INSECTS

3
ANT
BEE
BUG
FLY

4
FLEA
GNAT
WASP

5
APHID
DRONE
LOUSE
MIDGE

6
BEDBUG
BEETLE
BOT FLY
CAPSID
CHAFER
CHIGOE
CICADA
EARWIG
GAD FLY
HORNET
LOCUST
LOOPER
MAGGOT
MANTIS
MAYFLY
SAWFL

6–continued
THRIPS
WEEVIL

7
ANTLION
ARMY ANT
BLOWFLY
CRICKET
CUTWORM
DIPTERA
FIRE ANT
FIREFLY
KATYDID
PROTURA
SANDFLY
STYLOPS

7–continued
TERMITE

8
ALDERFLY
ARMY WORM
BLACKFLY
BOOKWORM
CRANEFLY
FIREBRAT
FRUIT FLY
GALL WASP
GLOWWORM
GREENFLY
HONEY ANT
HONEYBEE
HORNTAIL

8–continued
HORSE FLY
HOUSEFLY
HOVERFLY
LACEWING
LADYBIRD
MASON BEE
MEALWORM
MEALYBUG
MOSQUITO
PHASMIDA
PLANT BUG
SHEEP KED
SILKWORM
SNAKEFLY
STINK BUG
STONEFLY
WATER BUG
WHITE FLY
WIREWORM
WOODWASP
WOODWORM

9
AMAZON ANT
ANOPHELES
BLOODWORM
BOOKLOUSE
BUMBLEBEE
CADDIS FLY
CHINCH BUG
COCKROACH
CORN BORER
DAMSELFLY
DOBSONFLY
DOR BEETLE

9–continued
DRAGONFLY
DRIVER ANT
GALL MIDGE
GROUND BUG
ICHNEUMON
LAC INSECT
OIL BEETLE
ROBBER FLY
SCREWWORM
SHIELD BUG
TSETSE FLY
WARBLE FLY
WHIRLIGIG

10
BARK BEETLE
BLUEBOTTLE
BOLL WEEVIL
COCKCHAFER
COLEOPTERA
DIGGER WASP
DROSOPHILA
DUNG BEETLE
FROGHOPPER
JUNE BEETLE
LEAF BEETLE
LEAF HOPPER
LEAF INSECT
PHYLLOXERA
POND SKATER
POTTER WASP
ROVE BEETLE
SILVERFISH
SPANISH FLY
SPIDER WASP

10–continued
SPITTLEBUG
SPRINGTAIL
STAG BEETLE
TREEHOPPER
WEBSPINNER
WOOLLY BEAR

11
ASSASSIN BUG
BACKSWIMMER
BLACK BEETLE
BRISTLETAIL
BUFFALO GNAT
BUSH CRICKET
CANTHARIDIN
CATERPILLAR
CLICK BEETLE
GRASSHOPPER
MOLE CRICKET
PLANT HOPPER
SCALE INSECT
SCORPION FLY
STICK INSECT
TIGER BEETLE
WATER BEETLE

12
CACTOBLASTIS
CARPENTER BEE
CARPET BEETLE
DIVING BEETLE
GROUND BEETLE
HERCULES MOTH
SCARAB BEETLE
SEXTON BEETLE

12–continued
WATER BOATMAN
WATER STRIDER

13
BLISTER BEETLE
BURYING BEETLE
COTTON STAINER
DADDY LONGLEGS
ELM BARK BEETLE
GIANT WATER BUG
GOLIATH BEETLE
LEAFCUTTER ANT
LEAFCUTTER BEE
SOLDIER BEETLE
WATER SCORPION

14+
AMBROSIA BEETLE
BOMBARDIER
 BEETLE
CABBAGE ROOT FLY
COLORADO BEETLE
CUCKOO-SPIT
 INSECT
DARKLING BEETLE
DEATHWATCH
 BEETLE
DEVIL'S COACH
 HORSE
HERCULES BEETLE
SLAVE-MAKING ANT
TORTOISE BEETLE

BUTTERFLIES

3&4
OWL
BLUE
LEAF
MONK

5
ARGUS
BROWN
DRYAD
FRIAR
HEATH
JOKER
NYMPH
SATYR
SNOUT
WHITE
ZEBRA

6
ACRAEA
APOLLO
COPPER
DIADEM
GLIDER
HERMIT
MORPHO

7
ADMIRAL
FESTOON
LEOPARD
MONARCH
RINGLET
SKIPPER
SULPHUR

8
BIRDWING
BLACK EYE
BLACK-TIP
CARDINAL
CHARAXES
CYMOTHOE
GRAYLING
MILKWEED

9
ATLAS BLUE
BATH WHITE
BRIMSTONE
CLEOPATRA
COMMODORE
GOLDEN TIP
HACKBERRY

9–continued
METALMARK
ORANGE TIP
SWORDTAIL
WALL BROWN
WOOD WHITE

10
ADONIS BLUE
ARCTIC BLUE
ARRAN BROWN
BLACK SATYR
BUSH BEAUTY
CRIMSON TIP
FRITILLARY
GATEKEEPER
GRASS JEWEL
HAIRSTREAK

10–continued
LARGE WHITE
PLAIN TIGER
RED ADMIRAL
SILVER-LINE
SMALL WHITE

11
AMANDA'S BLUE
FOREST QUEEN
GRASS YELLOW
MEADOW BROWN
PAINTED LADY

11–continued
PARNASSIANS
SWALLOWTAIL

12
DOTTED BORDER
MAP BUTTERFLY
MARBLED WHITE
SPECKLED WOOD
WHITE ADMIRAL

13
CLOUDED YELLOW
CHALK-HILL BLUE

13–continued
PEARL CRESCENT
PURPLE EMPEROR
TORTOISESHELL
WOODLAND BROWN

14
AFRICAN MIGRANT
COMMA BUTTERFLY
LEMON TRAVELLER
MOUNTAIN BEAUTY
PAINTED EMPRESS

15+
CAMBERWELL
 BEAUTY
GREAT SOOTY
 SATYR
MOTHER-OF-PEARL
 BLUE
NETTLE-TREE
 BUTTERFLY
PEACOCK
 BUTTERFLY
TWO-TAILED PASHA

MOTHS

2&3
IO
OWL

4
GOAT
HAWK
PUSS

5
ATLAS
EGGAR
FAIRY
GHOST
GYPSY
OWLET
REGAL

5–continued
SWIFT
TIGER
YUCCA

6
BURNET
CALICO
ERMINE
LAPPET

7
BAGWORM
CLOTHES
EMPEROR
FLANNEL
PYRALID

7–continued
TUSSOCK
URANIAS

8
CINNABAR
FORESTER
SILKWORM

9
AILANTHUS
BRAHMAEID
CARPENTER
CLEARWING
GEOMETRID
SALT MARSH
SATURNIID
UNDERWING

10
BLACK WITCH
LEAF ROLLER

11
HUMMINGBIRD
OLETHREUTID
PYROMORPHID

13
BLINDED SPHINX
GIANT SILKWORM

14
DEATH'S HEAD
 HAWK
PANDORA'S SPHINX

PLANTS AND FLOWERS

3
ABE
HOP
IVY
RYE

4
DOCK
FERN
FLAG (*Iris*)
FLAX
HEMP
IRIS (flag, sweet flag,
 gladdon)
JUTE

4–continued
LILY
PINK (carnation)
RAPE
REED
RICE
ROSE
RUSH
TARE
UPAS
WOAD

5
AGAVE

5–continued
ASTER (Michaelmas
 daisy)
AVENS
BRIAR
CANNA
CYCAD
DAISY
HENNA
JALAP
KUDZU
LOTUS
LUPIN
OXLIP (*Primula*)

5–continued
PANSY (*Viola*)
PEONY
PHLOX
POPPY
SEDGE
SENNA
SISAL
TULIP
VIOLA (pansy, violet)

6
ALLIUM
ALSIKE (clover)
BALSAM

6–continued
BLUETS
BRYONY
CACTUS
CLOVER (trefoil)
COLEUS
COTTON
COWPEA
CROCUS
DAHLIA
DARNEL
FESCUE
HYSSOP
MADDER
MEDICK
MILLET
NETTLE (*Urtica*)
ORCHID
PETREA
PEYOTE (cactus)
RATTAN
SALVIA
SPURGE
SQUILL (*Scilla*)
SUNDEW
TEASEL
THRIFT
TWITCH (couch grass)
VIOLET (*Viola*)
YARROW
ZINNIA

7
ACONITE
  (monkshood)
ALFALFA
ALKANET
ANEMONE
ASTILBE
BEGONIA
BISTORT (snakeroot)
BRACKEN (fern)
BUGLOSS
BULRUSH (reed
  mace)
BURDOCK
CAMPION
CATMINT
CLARKIA
COWSLIP (*Primula*)
DAY LILY
DOGBANE
DOG ROSE
FIGWORT
FREESIA
FROG-BIT
GENTIAN
GLADDON (*Iris*)
GUARANA
HEMLOCK
HENBANE

7–continued
HONESTY (*Lunaria*)
JONQUIL (*Narcissus*)
KINGCUP (marsh
  marigold)
LOBELIA
MILFOIL (yarrow)
MULLEIN (Aaron's
  rod)
OPUNTIA (prickly
  pear)
PAPYRUS
PETUNIA
PIGWEED
PRIMULA (cowslip,
  primrose)
RAGWORT
ROSELLE
SAGUARO
SANICLE
SPURREY
THISTLE
TIMOTHY
TOBACCO
TREFOIL (clover)
VERBENA (vervain)
VERVAIN (*Verbena*)

8
ACANTHUS
AGRIMONY
ARUM LILY (cuckoo-
  pint, lords-and-ladies)
ASPHODEL
AURICULA
BEDSTRAW
BERGENIA
BINDWEED
  (*Convolvulus*)
BLUEBELL
CATBRIER
CAT'S TAIL (reed-
  mace)
CHARLOCK
CLEAVERS (goose-
  grass)
CLEMATIS (old man's
  beard, traveller's joy)
CROWFOOT
CYLCAMEN
DAFFODIL
DIANTHUS
EELGRASS
EUCHARIS (amazon
  lily)
FLEABANE
FLEAWORT
FOXGLOVE (*Digitalis*)
FUMITORY
GERANIUM
  (*Pelargonium*)
GLOXINIA

8–continued
GOUTWEED (ground
  elder)
HAREBELL
HAWKWEED
HENEQUEN
HIBISCUS (rose of
  China, rose of
  Sharon)
HORNWORT
HYACINTH
ICE PLANT
KNAPWEED
LADY FERN
LARKSPUR
LUNGWORT
MARIGOLD
MILKWEED
MILKWORT
MOSS PINK (*Phlox*)
PLANTAIN
PLUMBAGO
POLYPODY
PRIMROSE (*Primula*)
REEDMACE (bulrush,
  cat's-tail)
ROCK ROSE
SAINFOIN
SALTWORT
SAMPHIRE
SCABIOUS
SEED FERN
SELF HEAL
SHAMROCK (clover,
  medick, wood sorrel)
SNOWDROP
SOAPWORT
SWEET PEA
TOAD LILY (fritillary)
TUBEROSE
VALERIAN
VERONICA
  (speedwell)
WAXPLANT
WOODBINE (virginia
  creeper)
WOODRUSH
WORMWOOD

9
AARON'S ROD
  (mullein)
AMARYLLIS
  (belladonna lily)
ANTHURIUM
AQUILEGIA
  (columbine)
ARROWROOT
BLUEGRASS
BROOMRAPE
BRYOPHYTE
BUCKWHEAT

9–continued
BUTTERCUP
CAMPANULA
  (Canterbury bell)
CANDYTUFT
CARNATION (pink)
CELANDINE
CHICKWEED
CINERARIA
COCKLEBUR
COCKSFOOT
  (orchard grass)
COLTSFOOT
COLUMBINE
  (*Aquilegia*)
CORDGRASS
CORN POPPY
CORYDALIS
CYMBIDIUM (orchid)
DANDELION
DEVIL'S FIG (prickly
  poppy)
DOG VIOLET
EDELWEISS
EGLANTINE (sweet
  briar)
EYEBRIGHT
GERMANDER
GLADIOLUS
GLASSWORT
GOLDENROD
  (*Solidago*)
GOOSEFOOT
  (pigweed)
GRASS TREE
GROUND IVY
GROUNDSEL
HELLEBORE
  (Christmas rose)
HERB PARIS
HOLLYHOCK
HORSETAIL
HOUSELEEK
IMPATIENS (touch-
  me-not, busy Lizzie)
JABORANDI
MARE'S TAIL
MONEYWORT
  (creeping jenny)
MONKSHOOD
  (aconite)
MOSCHATEL (town-
  hall clock)
NARCISSUS (jonquil)
PATCHOULI
PIMPERNEL
PYRETHRUM
QUILLWORT
ROYAL FERN
SAFFLOWER
SAXIFRAGE (London
  pride)

9—continued
SNAKEROOT (bistort)
SPEEDWELL
(*Veronica*)
SPIKENARD
STONECROP
SUNFLOWER
SWEET FLAG (*Iris*)
TORMENTIL
WATER LILY
WITCHWEED
WOUNDWORT

10
AGAPANTHUS
AMARANTHUS (love-
lies-bleeding)
AMAZON LILY
ASPIDISTRA
BELLADONNA
(deadly nightshade)
BUSY LIZZIE
BUTTERWORT
CHARMOMILE
CINQUEFOIL
CITRONELLA
CLIFFBREAK (fern)
CORNCOCKLE
CORNFLOWER
COUCH GRASS
(twitch, quack grass)
COW PARSLEY
CRANESBILL
CUCKOOPINT (arum
lily)
DAMASK ROSE
DRAGONROOT
DYER'S BROOM
FRITILLARY (snake's
head, leopard lily,
toad lily)
GAILLARDIA (blanket
flowers)
GOATSBEARD
GOOSEGRASS
(cleavers)
GRANADILLA
(passionflower)
GREENBRIER
(catbrier)
HELIOTROPE
HERB ROBERT
JIMSONWEED (thorn
apple)
LADY'S SMOCK
MARGUERITE (oxeye
daisy)
MIGNONETTE
MONTBRETIA
MOONFLOWER
(morning glory)
NASTURTIUM

10—continued
OPIUM POPPY
OXEYE DAISY
(marguerite)
PENNYROYAL
PERIWINKLE
POLYANTHUS
(*Primula*)
QUACK GRASS
(couch grass)
SHIELD FERN
SNAKE'S HEAD
SNAPDRAGON
(*Antirrhinum*)
SOW THISTLE
SPIDERWORT
SPLEENWORT
STITCHWORT
SWEET BRIAR
(eglantine)
THORN APPLE
(jimsonweed)
TOUCH-ME-NOT
WALLFLOWER
WATERCRESS
WELSH POPPY
WILLOWHERB
WOOD SORREL

11
ANTIRRHINUM (snap-
dragon)
BISHOP'S WEED
(ground elder)
BITTERSWEET
(woody nightshade)
BLADDERWORT
CALCEOLARIA
CANARY GRASS
CONVOLVULUS
(bindweed)
FIG MARIGOLD
FORGET-ME-NOT
GILLYFLOWER
(gilliflower, pink,
carnation)
GLOBE FLOWER
GROUND ELDER
(goutweed, bishop's
weed)
HELLEBORINE
(orchid)
HONEYSUCKLE
IPECACUANHA
KANGAROO PAW
LEOPARD LILY (fritil-
lary, blackberry lily)
LONDON PRIDE
(saxifrage)
LOVE-IN-A-MIST
MARRAM GRASS
MARSH MALLOW

11—continued
MEADOWSWEET
PAMPAS GRASS
PONTENTILLA
(cinquefoil)
PRICKLY PEAR
(cactus)
RAGGED ROBIN
RED-HOT POKER
ROSE OF CHINA
(*Hibiscus*)
RUBBER PLANT
SEA LAVENDER
SHRIMP PLANT
SPIDER PLANT
ST JOHN'S WORT
STRAWFLOWER
WELWITSCHIA
WINTERGREEN

12
AUTUMN CROCUS
(meadow saffron)
CENTURY PLANT
COMPASS PLANT
(turpentine plant)
GLOBE THISTLE
LADY'S SLIPPER
MONKEYFLOWER
MORNING GLORY
(moonflower)
OLD MAN CACTUS
OLD MAN'S BEARD
(*Clematis*)
ORCHARD GRASS
(cocksfoot)
PITCHER PLANT
PRICKLY POPPY
(devil's fig)
QUAKING GRASS
ROSE OF SHARON
(*Hibiscus*)
SOLOMON'S SEAL
SWEET WILLIAM
VENUS FLYTRAP

13
AFRICAN VIOLET
BIRD'S NEST FERN
BLEEDING HEART
CALYPSO ORCHID
CARRION FLOWER
CHRISTMAS ROSE
(hellebore)
CHRYSANTHEMUM
CREEPING JENNY
(moneywort)
ELEPHANT GRASS
GARLIC MUSTARD
(jack-by-the-hedge)
GRAPE HYACINTH
MARSH MARIGOLD
(kingcup)

13—continued
MEADOW SAFFRON
(autumn crocus)
PASSIONFLOWER
(granadilla)
RANUNCULACEAE
ROSE OF JERICHO
SLIPPER ORCHID
TOWNHALL CLOCK
(moschatel)
TRAVELLER'S JOY
(*Clematis*)
WINTER ACONITE

14
BELLADONNA LILY
(*Amaryllis*)
BLACKBERRY LILY
(leopard lily)
BLANKET FLOWERS
CANTERBURY BELL
(*Campanula*)
CASTOR-OIL PLANT
HEDGEHOG CACTUS
JACK-BY-THE-
HEDGE (garlic mus-
tard)
LORDS-AND-LADIES
(arum lily)
MAIDENHAIR FERN
TRUMPET CREEPER

15+
BIRD-OF-PARADISE
FLOWER
BIRD'S NEST
ORCHID
BLACK NIGHTSHADE
DEADLY NIGHT-
SHADE (belladonna)
DOG'S TOOTH
VIOLET
ENCHANTER'S
NIGHTSHADE
GRASS OF
PARNASSUS
LILY-OF-THE-VALLEY
LOVE-LIES-BLEED-
ING (*Amaranthus*)
MICHAELMAS DAISY
(*Aster*)
ORGAN-PIPE
CACTUS
SNOW-ON-THE-
MOUNTAIN
SQUIRTING
CUCUMBER
STAR OF
BETHLEHEM
TURPENTINE PLANT
(compass plant)
WOODY NIGHT-
SHADE (bittersweet)

PARTS OF A FLOWER

3	5-continued	7	9
LIP	STYLE	COROLLA	CAPITULUM
	TEPAL	NECTARY	GYNOECIUM
4	UMBEL	PANICLE	INVOLUCEL
CYME		PEDICEL	INVOLUCRE
SPUR	6	RHACHIS	POLLINIUM
	ANTHER		
5	CARPEL	8	10
BRACT	CATKIN	BRACTEDE	ANDROECIUM
CALYX	CORYMB	CYATHIUM	CARPOPHORE
GLUME	FLORET	FILAMENT	HYPANTHIUM
LEMMA	POLLEN	LADICULE	RECEPTACLE
OVARY	RACEME	NUCELLUS	
OVULE	SPADIX	PEDUNCLE	11
PALEA	SPATHE	PLACENTA	MONOCHASIUM
PETAL	STAMEN	SPIKELET	POLLEN GRAIN
SEPAL	STIGMA		
SPIKE			

PLANT PEOPLE

PLANT – named after

AUBRIETIA – Claude Aubriet 18th-century French painter of flowers and animals
BANKSIA – Sir Joseph Banks (1743–1820) British botanist and explorer
BARTSIA – Johann Bartsch (d. 1738) German botanist
BAUERA – Franz (1758–1840) and Ferdinand (1760–1826) Bauer, Australian botanical artists
BAUHINIA – Jean and Gaspard Bauhin 16th-century French herbalists
BEGONIA – Michel Bégon (1638–1710) French patron of science
BETONY – the Vettones an ancient Iberian tribe
BIGNONIA – the Abbé Jean-Paul Bignon (1662–1743)
BOLTONIA – James Bolton 18th-century English botanist
BOUGAINVILLEA – Louis Antoine de Bougainville (1729–1811) French navigator
BOYSENBERRY – Rudolph Boysen, US botanist who developed it
BRUCINE – James Bruce (1730–94) Scottish explorer of Africa
BUDDLEIA – A. Buddle (d. 1715) British botanist
CAMELLIA – Georg Josef Kamel (1661–1706) Moravian Jesuit missionary, who introduced it to
  Europe
CATTLEYA – William Cattley (d. 1832) English botanist
CLARKIA – William Clark (1770–1838) US explorer and frontiersman, who discovered it
CLAYTONIA – John Clayton (1693–1773) US botanist
CLINTONIA – De Witt Clinton (1769–1828) US politician and naturalist
COLLINSIA – Zaccheus Collins (1764–1831) US botanist
DAHLIA – Anders Dahl 18th-century Swedish botanist
DEUTZIA – Jean Deutz 18th-century Dutch patron of botany
DIEFFENBACHIA – Ernst Dieffenbach (d. 1855) German horticulturist
DOUGLAS FIR – David Douglas (1798–1834) Scottish botanist
ESCHSCHOLTZIA – J. F. von Eschscholtz (1743–1831) German naturalist
FORSYTHIA – William Forsyth (1737–1804) English botanist
FREESIA – F. H. T. Freese (d. 1876) German physician
FUCHSIA – Leonhard Fuchs (1501–66) German botanist
GAILLARDIA – Gaillard de Marentonneau 18th-century French amateur botanist
GALTONIA – Sir Francis Galton (1822–1911) English explorer and scientist

PLANT – named after

GARDENIA – Dr Alexander Garden (1730–91) US botanist
GAZANIA – Theodore of Gaza 1398–1478 translator of the botanical treatises of Theophrastus
GENTIAN – Gentius, a second-century BC Ilyrian king, reputedly the first to use it medicinally
GERBERA – Traugott Gerber (d. 1743) German naturalist
GLOXINIA – Benjamin P. Gloxin 18th-century German physician and botanist who first described it
GODETIA – C. H. Godet (d. 1879) Swiss botanist
GREVILLEA – C. F. Greville (1749–1809) a founder of the Royal Horticultural Society
GRINDELIA – David Hieronymus Grindel (1777–1836) Russian botanist
GUNNERA – J. E. Gunnerus (1718–73) Norwegian bishop and botanist
HAKEA – C. L. von Hake (d. 1818) German botanist
HEUCHERA – J. H. Heucher (1677–1747) German doctor and botanist
HOSTA – N. T. Host (1761–1834) Austrian physician
HOUSTONIA – Dr. William Houston (d. 1733) Scottish botanist
INCARVILLEA – Pierre d'Incarville (1706–57) French missionary
KALMIA – Peter Kalm (1715–79) Swedish botanist and pupil of Linnaeus
KNIPHOFIA – J. H. Kniphof (1704–63) German doctor and botanist
KOCHIA – W. D. J. Koch (1771–1849) German botanist
LAVATERA – the two brothers Lavater 18th-century Swiss doctors and naturalists
LEYLAND CYPRESS – C. J. Leyland (1849–1926) British horticulturalist
LOBELIA – Matthias de Lobel (1538–1616) Flemish botanist
LOGANBERRY – James H. Logan (1841–1928) US judge and horticulturist who first grew it (1881)
MACADAMIA – John Macadam (1827–65) Australian chemist
MAGNOLIA – Pierre Magnol (1638–1715) French botanist
MAHONIA – Bernard McMahon (d. 1816) US botanist
MONTBRETIA – A. F. E. Coquebert de Montbret (1780–1801) French botanist
PAULOWNIA – Anna Paulovna, daughter of Paul I of Russia
POINCIANA – M. de Poinci 17th-century governor of the French Antilles
RAUWOLFIA – Leonhard Rauwolf (d. 1596) German botanist
RUDBECKIA – Olaus Rudbeck (1630–1702) Swedish botanist
SAINTPAULIA – Baron W. von Saint Paul (d. 1910) German soldier who discovered it
SEQUOIA – Sequoya known also as George Guess (?1770–1843) US Indian scholar and leader
STRELITZIA – Charlotte of Mecklenburg-Strelitz (1744–1818) queen of Great Britain and Ireland
THUNBERGIA – K. P. Thunberg (1743–1822) Swedish traveller and botanist
TILLANDSIA – Elias Tillands (d. 1693) Finno-Swedish botanist
TIMOTHY GRASS – a Timothy Hanson, who brought it to colonial Carolina
TRADESCANTIA – John Tradescant (1570–1638) English botanist and gardener
WEIGELA – C. E. Weigel (1748–1831) German physician
WELLINGTONIA – the 1st Duke of Wellington
WELWITSCHIA – F. M. J. Welwitsch (1807–72) Portuguese botanist, born in Austria
WISTERIA – Caspar Wistar (1761–1818) US anatomist
YOUNGBERRY – B. M. Young, US fruit-grower who was first to cultivate it (circa 1900)
ZINNIA – J. G. Zinn (d. 1759) German botanist
ZOYSIA – Karl von Zois (d. 1800) German botanist

TREES AND SHRUBS

3	3–continued	4–continued	5–continued
ASH	TEA	KOLA (cola)	ASPEN
BOX	YEW	NIPA (palm)	BALSA
ELM	**4**	PALM	BEECH (*Fagus*)
FIG	ANIL	PINE	BIRCH
FIR	COCA	TEAK	BROOM
MAY (hawthorn)	DATE (palm)	**5**	CACAO
OAK	KAVA	ALDER	CAPER

5–continued
CEDAR
EBONY
ELDER
ERICA (heath, heather)
FURZE (gorse)
GORSE (furze)
HAZEL
HEATH (*Erica*)
HOLLY
KARRI
LARCH
LILAC
MAPLE
OSIER (willow)
PECAN (hickory)
ROWAN (mountain ash)
SAVIN (juniper)
YUCCA

6
ACACIA
AZALEA
BAMBOO
BANYAN
BAOBAB
BONSAI
BO TREE
CASSIA
DAPHNE
DATURA
DEODAR (cedar)
DERRIS
DURIAN
GINKGO (maidenhair tree)
GOMUTI (sugar palm)
JARRAH
JINBUL (coolabar)
JUJUBE
LAUREL
LOCUST (carob tree, St John's bread)
MIMOSA
MOOLAR (coolabar)
MYRTLE
NUTMEG
ORACHE
POPLAR
PRIVET
PROTEA
REDBUD (judas tree)
RED GUM (*Eucalyptus*)
SALLOW (willow)
SALVIA
SAPPAN
SPRUCE
WILLOW

7
AMBOYNA
ARBUTUS
BEBEERU (green-heart)
BLUE GUM (*Eucalyptus*)
CORK OAK
CYPRESS
DOGWOOD
DURMAST (oak)
FUCHSIA
GUM TREE (*Eucalyptus*)
HEATHER (*Erica*, ling)
HEMLOCK
HICKORY (pecan)
HOLM OAK (holly oak)
JASMINE
JUNIPER
MUGWORT (wormwood)
OIL PALM
PALMYRA
REDWOOD
ROSEBAY (oleander)
SEQUOIA (redwood, wellingtonia, big tree)
SOURSOP
SPIRAEA
SYRINGA (lilac, mock orange)

8
BARBERRY (*Berberis*)
BASSWOOD
BAYBERRY
BERBERIS (barberry)
BERGAMOT
BLACKBOX (coolabar)
BOX ELDER (maple)
CALABASH
CAMELLIA
CINCHONA
COOLABAR (jinbul, moolar, blackbox, dwarf box)
CORKWOOD (balsa)
DWARF BOX (coolabar)
EUONYMUS (spindle tree)
GARDENIA
GUAIACUM
HAWTHORN (may)
HORNBEAM
IRONWOOD
JAPONICA
LABURNUM (golden chain, golden rain)
LAVENDER

8–continued
MAGNOLIA (umbrella tree)
OLEANDER (rosebay)
QUANDONG
RAMBUTAN
ROSEWOOD
SAGO PALM
SALTBUSH
SILKY OAK
SWEET GUM
SWEETSOP
SYCAMORE (maple)
TAMARISK
TOLU TREE
VIBURNUM (snowball tree)
WISTERIA
WOODBINE (virginia creeper)
WORMWOOD (mugwort)

9
ARAUCARIA (monkey puzzle tree)
BEARBERRY
BUCKTHORN
CAROB TREE (locust)
CORAL TREE
EUPHORBIA (crown of thorns, poinsettia, snow-on-the-mountain)
FIRETHORN (pyracantha)
FLAME TREE (flamboyant)
FORSYTHIA (golden bell)
JACARANDA
JUDAS TREE (redbud)
KALANCHOE
KAURI PINE
MANGROVES
MISTLETOE
PLANE TREE
POINCIANA
POISON IVY
SASSAFRAS
SATINWOOD
SCREW PINE
STINKWOOD
STONE PINE
SWEETWOOD (greenheart)
TULIP TREE
WHITEBEAM

10
ARBOR VITAE
BIRD CHERRY

10–continued
BRAZILWOOD
COFFEE TREE
COTTONWOOD
DOUGLAS FIR
DRAGON TREE
EUCALYPTUS (blue gum, red gum)
FRANGIPANI (pagoda tree, temple flower)
GOLDEN BELL (forsythia)
GOLDEN RAIN - (laburnum)
GREENHEART (sweetwood, bebeeru)
JOSHUA TREE
MANGOSTEEN
MOCK ORANGE
PAGODA TREE (frangipani)
POINSETTIA
PYRACANTHA
RAFFIA PALM
RUBBER TREE
WITCH HAZEL
YELLOWWOOD

11
BOTTLEBRUSH
CABBAGE PALM
CAMPHOR TREE
CHAULMOOGRA
COTONEASTER
CYPRESS PINE
DAWN REDWOOD
GOLDEN CHAIN (laburnum)
GUELDER ROSE
HONEY LOCUST
JUMPING BEAN
MOUNTAIN ASH (rowan)
PENCIL CEDAR (juniper)
PHYLLANTHUS
SERVICE TREE
SLIPPERY ELM
SPINDLE TREE
STEPHANOTIS
TALIPOT PALM

12
CHERRY LAUREL
CREOSOTE BUSH
CUCUMBER TREE
CUSTARD APPLE (soursop, sweetsop)
INCENSE CEDAR
MONKEY PUZZLE
SNOWBALL TREE

12—continued
ST JOHN'S BREAD (locust)
SWAMP CYPRESS
TEMPLE FLOWER (frangipani)
TREE OF HEAVEN
UMBRELLA TREE (*Magnolia*)

13
BOUGAINVILLEA
BUTCHER'S BROOM
CROWN OF THORNS
HORSE CHESTNUT

13—continued
JAPANESE CEDAR
JAPANESE MAPLE
PAPER MULBERRY
PEACOCK FLOWER
  (flamboyant)
WAYFARING TREE

14+
FLAMBOYANT TREE (flame
  tree, peacock flower)
FLOWERING CURRANT

14+—continued
JERUSALEM CHERRY
MAIDENHAIR TREE
  (ginkgo)
STRAWBERRY TREE
TRAVELLER'S TREE
TURPENTINE TREE
VIRGINIA CREEPER
  (woodbine)

FRUIT, VEGETABLES, AND PULSES

3
FIG
PEA
YAM

4
BEET
EDDO (taro)
KALE
KIWI
LEEK
LIME (linden)
OKRA (lady's
  fingers, gumbo)
PEAR
PLUM
SLOE
TARO (eddo,
  dasheen,
  elephant's ear)

5
APPLE
CAROB
CHARD (swiss
  chard)
CRESS
GRAPE
GUAVA
GUMBO (okra)
LEMON
MANGO
MAIZE
MELON (musk,
  honeydew, can-
  teloupe, water)
OLIVE
ONION (spring
  onion, scallion)
PEACH
SWEDE

6
ALMOND
BANANA
CARROT
CASHEW
CELERY
CHERRY
CITRON
COB NUT
DAMSON
ENDIVE
GARLIC
LENTIL
LICHEE
LINDEN (lime)
LITCHI
LOQUAT
LYCHEE (litchi,
  lichee)
MANIOC
  (cassava)
MARROW
MEDLAR
ORANGE
PAWPAW
PEANUT
  (groundnut)
POTATO
PRUNUS (plum,
  almond, apri-
  cot, cherry)
QUINCE
RADISH
SORREL
SQUASH
TOMATO
TURNIP
WALNUT

7
ALFALFA
APRICOT

7—continued
AVOCADO
BRAMBLE
  (blackberry)
BULLACE (plum)
CABBAGE
CASSAVA
  (manioc)
CHICORY
CURRANT
DASHEEN (taro)
FILBERT
GENIPAP
GHERKIN
KUMQUAT
LETTUCE
PARSNIP
PUMPKIN
RHUBARB
SALSIFY
SATSUMA
  (tangerine)
SHALLOT
SPINACH

8
BEETROOT
BILBERRY
  (blaeberry,
  huckleberry,
  whortleberry)
BRASSICA
  (broccoli,
  cabbage)
BROCCOLI
CAPSICUM
  (sweet pepper,
  chilli, paprika)
CELERIAC (knob
  celery)
CHESTNUT
CHICK PEA

8—continued
CUCUMBER
DEWBERRY
EARTHNUT
  (groundnut)
EGGPLANT
  (aubergine)
KOHLRABI
  (cabbage)
MANDARIN
  (tangerine)
MULBERRY
MUNG BEAN
  (green gram)
MUSHROOM
OLEASTER
  (russian olive,
  trebizond date)
SCALLION
SUGAR PEA
SOYA BEAN
TAMARIND
ZUCCHINI
  (courgette)

9
ARTICHOKE
ASPARAGUS
AUBERGINE
  (eggplant)
BLAEBERRY
  (bilberry)
BROAD BEAN
CALABRESE
COCODEMER
COURGETTE
  (marrow,
  zucchini)
CRAB APPLE
CRANBERRY
CROWBERRY
DWARF BEAN

9—continued
GREENGAGE
GROUNDNUT
  (peanut, earth-
  nut)
MANGETOUT
NECTARINE
PERSIMMON
PETIT POIS
PINEAPPLE
PISTACHIO
RADICCHIO
RASPBERRY
SAPODILLA
STAR APPLE
SWEET CORN
TANGERINE

10
ADZUKI BEAN
BEAN SPROUT
BLACKBERRY
  (bramble)
BUTTER BEAN
CLEMENTINE
ELDERBERRY
FRENCH BEAN
  (kidney bean)
GOOSEBERRY
GRAPEFRUIT
  (*Citrus
  Paradisi*)
KIDNEY BEAN
LOGANBERRY
RED CABBAGE
REDCURRANT
RUNNER BEAN
SALAD ONION
SNAKE GOURD
STRAWBERRY
STRING BEAN
SWISS CHARD

11
CAULIFLOWER
COCONUT PALM
HORSERADISH
HUCKLEBERRY
 (bilberry)
POMEGRANATE

11–continued
SPRING ONION
SWEET POTATO

12+
BLACKCURRANT
BRUSSELS SPROUT

12+–continued
ELEPHANT'S EAR
 (taro)
JERUSALEM
 ARTICHOKE
LADY'S FINGERS
 (okra)

12+–continued
MANGEL-WURZEL
 (beet)
SAVOY CABBAGE
WATER CHESTNUT
WHORTLEBERRY
 (bilberry)

FUNGI

4
CÈPE

5
MOREL
YEAST

6
AGARIC
INK CAP

7
AMANITA
BLEWITS
BOLETUS
CANDIDA
TRUFFLE

8
DEATH CAP
MUSHROOM
PUFFBALL

9
CUP FUNGUS
EARTHSTAR
FLY AGARIC
PSILOCYBE
RUST FUNGI
STINKHORN
TOADSTOOL

10
BREAD MOULD

10–continued
CHAMPIGNON

11
ASCOMYCETES
ASPERGILLUS
CHANTERELLE
HONEY
 FUNGUS
PENICILLIUM
SLIME MOULDS

13
BRACKET
 FUNGUS

14
BASID-
 IOMYCETES

15
PARASOL
 MUSHROOM

FERNS

4
TREE

5
ROYAL

7
BRACKEN
OSMUNDA

8
LADY FERN

8–continued
POLYPODY
STAGHORN

9
BIRD'S NEST

10
CLIFFBRAKE
DRYOPTERIS
MAIDENHAIR
SPLEENWORT

11
HART'S
 TONGUE

GRASSES, SEDGES, AND RUSHES

3
FOG
OAT
RYE
TEF

4
BENT
CORN
REED
RICE
RUSH

5
BROME
DURRA
MAIZE
PADDY
PANIC
SEDGE
SPELT
WHEAT

6
BAMBOO

6–continued
BARLEY
DARNEL
FESCUE
FIORIN
MELICK
MILLET
QUITCH
REDTOP
ZOYSIA

7
BULRUSH
ESPARTO
FOXTAIL
PAPYRUS
SORGHUM
WILD OAT

8
CUTGRASS
DOG'S-TAIL
OAT-GRASS

8–continued
REED MACE
RYEGRASS
SPARTINA
SPINIFEX
TEOSINTE
WILD RICE
WOODRUSH

9
BLUEGRASS
BROOMCORN

9–continued
COCKSFOOT
CORDGRASS
CRABGRASS
GAMA GRASS
HAIR-GRASS
LYME GRASS
REED GRASS
STAR GRASS
SUGAR CANE
WIRE GRASS

10
BEACH GRASS

10–continued
BEARD GRASS
BUNCH GRASS
CHINA GRASS
COUCH GRASS
HERD'S-GRASS
INDIAN CORN
INDIAN RICE
LEMON GRASS
QUACK GRASS
SPEAR GRASS
SWORD GRASS

11
CANARY GRASS

11–continued
COTTON GRASS
FINGER GRASS
MARRAM GRASS
MEADOW GRASS
PAMPAS GRASS
SWITCH GRASS
TWITCH GRASS
VERNAL GRASS

12
BERMUDA GRASS
BRISTLE GRASS
BUFFALO GRASS
FEATHER GRASS

12–continued
ORCHARD GRASS
QUAKING GRASS
TIMOTHY GRASS
TUSSOCK GRASS
YORKSHIRE FOG

13+
ELEPHANT GRASS
KENTUCKY BLUE-
 GRASS
SQUIRREL-TAIL
 GRASS

PEOPLE

WORLD LEADERS

3

FOX, Charles James
(1749–1806; British Whig
politician)
FOX, Vincente (1942–   ;
Mexican politician)
LIE, Trygve (Halvdan)
(1896–1968; Norwegian
Labour politician)

4

BENN, Anthony Neil
Wedgwood (1925–   ; British
Labour politician)
BLUM, Léon (1872–1950;
French socialist)
BOSE, Subhas Chandra (c.
1897–c. 1945; Indian
nationalist leader)
COOK, Sir Joseph (1860–1947;
Australian statesman)
DÍAZ, Porfirio (1830–1915;
Mexican soldier)
FOOT, Michael (Mackintosh)
(1913–   ; British Labour
politician)
GORE, Al(bert) H., Jr
(1948–   ; US politician)
HOLT, Harold Edward
(1908–67; Australian
statesman)
HOWE, Sir Richard Edward
Geoffrey (1926–   ; British
Conservative politician)
HULL, Cordell (1871–1955; US
Democratic politician)
KING, Jr, Martin Luther
(1929–68; US Black civil-
rights leader)
KING, William Lyon Mackenzie
(1874–1950; Canadian
statesman)
KIRK, Norman Eric (1923–74;
New Zealand statesman)
KOHL, Helmut (1930–   ;
German statesman)
MEIR, Golda (1898–1978;
Israeli stateswoman)

4–continued

NAGY, Imre (1896–1958;
Hungarian statesman)
OWEN, Dr David (1938–   ;
British politician)
RHEE, Syngman (1875–1965;
Korean statesman)
RUSK, David Dean (1909–94;
US statesman)
TOJO (Hideki) (1884–1948;
Japanese general)
TONE, Theobald Wolfe
(1763–98; Irish nationalist)
TUTU, Desmond (1931–   ;
South African clergyman)
WARD, Sir Joseph George
(1856–1930; New Zealand
statesman)

5

AGNEW, Spiro Theodore
(1918–96; US Republican
politician)
AHERN, Bertie (1951–   ; Irish
statesman)
ASTOR, Nancy Witcher,
Viscountess (1879–1964;
British politician)
BANDA, Hastings Kamuzu
(1905–97; Malawi statesman)
BARAK, Ehud (1942–; Israeli
politician)
BEGIN, Menachem (1913–92;
Israeli statesman)
BERIA, Lavrenti Pavlovich
(1899–1953; Soviet politician)
BEVAN, Aneurin (1897–1960;
British Labour politician)
BEVIN, Ernest (1881–1951;
British politician)
BLAIR, Tony (1953–   ; British
politician)
BOTHA, Louis (1862–1919;
South African statesman)
BOTHA, Pieter Willem
(1916–   ; South African
statesman)

5–continued

CLARK, Charles Joseph
(1939–   ; Canadian
statesman)
CLARK, Helen (1950–   ; New
Zealand politician)
DAYAN, Moshe (1915–81;
Israeli general)
DEBRÉ, Michel (1912–96;
French statesman)
DESAI, Shri Morarji Ranchhodji
(1896–95; Indian statesman)
DE WET, Christian Rudolf
(1854–1922; Afrikaner
politician and soldier)
EBERT, Friedrich (1871–1925;
German statesman)
EMMET, Robert (1778–1803;
Irish nationalist)
FLOOD, Henry (1732–91; Irish
politician)
LAVAL, Pierre (1883–1945;
French statesman)
LENIN, Vladimir Ilich
(V I Ulyanov, 1870–1924;
Russian revolutionary)
LODGE, Henry Cabot
(1850–1924; US Republican
politician)
LYNCH, Jack (1917–99; Irish
statesman)
LYONS, Joseph Aloysius
(1879–1939; Australian
statesman)
MAJOR, John (1943–   ; British
politician)
MANIN, Daniele (1804–57;
Italian patriot)
MBEKI, Thabo (1942–   ;
South African politician)
MBOYA, Tom (1930–69;
Kenyan politician)
MENON, Krishna (Vengalil
Krishnan Krishna Menon,
1896–1974; Indian diplomat)
NEHRU, Jawaharlal
(1889–1964; Indian
statesman)

5–continued

NKOMO, Joshua (1917–99; Zimbabwean politician)
OBOTE, Apollo Milton (1925– ; Ugandan statesman)
PERÓN, Juan Domingo (1895–1974; Argentine statesman)
PUTIN, Vladimir (1952– ; Russian politician)
RABIN, Yitshak (1922–95; Israeli statesman)
SADAT, Anwar (1918–81; Egyptian statesman)
SMITH, Ian Douglas (1919– ; Rhodesian politician)
SMUTS, Jan Christiaan (1870–1950; South African statesman and general)
SPAAK, Paul Henri (1899–1972; Belgian statesman)
STEEL, David Martin Scott (1938– ; British politician)
VANCE, Cyrus (1917– ; US statesman)
VILLA, Pancho (Francesco V, (1878–1923; Mexican revolutionary)

6

ARAFAT, Yassir (1929– ; Palestinian leader)
ARROYO, Gloria Macapagal (1948– ; Filipino stateswoman)
BARTON, Sir Edmund (1849–1920; Australian statesman)
BHUTTO, Benazir (1953– ; Pakistani politician)
BHUTTO, Zulfikar Ali (1928–79; Pakistani statesman)
BORDEN, Sir Robert Laird (1854–1937; Canadian statesman)
BRANDT, Willy (1913–92; West German statesman)
BRIGHT, John (1811–89; British radical politician)
BRUTON, John Gerard (1947– ; Irish statesman)
BUTLER, Richard Austen, Baron (1902–82; British Conservative politician)
CHENEY, Richard Bruce (1941– ; US politician)
CHIRAC, Jacques (1932– ; French statesman)
COATES, Joseph Gordon (1878–1943; New Zealand statesman)

6–continued

COBDEN, Richard (1804–65; British politician and economist)
CRIPPS, Sir Richard Stafford (1889–1952; British Labour politician)
CURTIN, John Joseph (1885–1945; Australian statesman)
CURZON, George Nathaniel, 1st Marquess (1859–1925; British politician)
DAVITT, Michael (1846–1906; Irish nationalist)
DEAKIN, Alfred (1856–1919; Australian statesman)
DJILAS, Milovan (1911–95; Yugoslav politician)
DUBČEK, Alexander (1921–92; Czechoslovak statesman)
DULLES, John Foster (1888–1959; US Republican politician and diplomat)
ERHARD, Ludwig (1897–1977; German statesman)
FADDEN, Sir Arthur William (1895–1973; Australian statesman)
FISHER, Andrew (1862–1928; Australian statesman)
FLEURY, André Hercule de, Cardinal (1653–1743; French statesman)
FORBES, George William (1869–1947; New Zealand statesman)
FRANCO, Francisco (1892–1975; Spanish general and statesman)
FRASER, John Malcolm (1930– ; Australian statesman)
FRASER, Peter (1884–1950; New Zealand statesman)
GANDHI, Indira (1917–84; Indian stateswoman)
GANDHI, Mohandas Karamchand (1869–1948; Indian nationalist leader)
GÖRING, Hermann Wilhelm (1893–1946; German Nazi politician)
GORTON, John Grey (1911– ; Australian statesman)
GRIVAS, Georgios (1898–1974; Greek general)
HEALEY, Denis Winston (1917– ; British politician)
HOWARD, John (1939– ; Australian politician)

6–continued

HUGHES, William Morris (1864–1952; Australian statesman)
JUÁREZ, Benito Pablo (1806–72; Mexican statesman)
KAUNDA, Kenneth David (1924– ; Zambian statesman)
KRUGER, Stephanus Johannes Paulus (1825–1904; Afrikaner statesman)
MARCOS, Ferdinand Edralin (1917–89; Philippine statesman)
MASSEY, William Ferguson (1856–1925; New Zealand statesman)
MOBUTU, Sese Seko (Joseph Désiré M, (1930–97; Zaïrese statesman)
MOSLEY, Sir Oswald Ernald (1896–1980; British fascist)
NASSER, Gamal Abdel (1918–70; Egyptian statesman)
O'BRIEN, Conor Cruise (1917– ; Irish diplomat)
O'NEILL, Terence, Baron (1914–90; Northern Irish statesman)
PÉTAIN, Henri Philippe (1856–1951; French general and statesman)
POWELL, John Enoch (1912–98; British politician)
QUAYLE, Dan (1947– ; US politician)
REVERE, Paul (1735–1818; American revolutionary)
RHODES, Cecil John (1853–1902; South African financier and statesman)
SAVAGE, Michael Joseph (1872–1940; New Zealand statesman)
SEDDON, Richard John (1845–1906; New Zealand statesman)
SHARON, Ariel (1928– ; Israeli politician)
STALIN, Joseph (1879–1953; Soviet statesman)
SUÁREZ, Adolfo, Duke of (1932– ; Spanish statesman)
THORPE, John Jeremy (1929– ; British Liberal politician)
WATSON, John Christian (1867–1941; Australian statesman)

6–continued

WILKES, John (1725–97;
British journalist and
politician)

ZAPATA, Emiliano
(?1877–1919; Mexican
revolutionary)

7

ACHESON, Dean Gooderham
(1893–1971; US lawyer and
statesman)

ASHDOWN, Paddy (1941–   ;
Social and Liberal Democrat
politician)

ATATÜRK, Kemal (Mustafa
Kemal, 1881–1938; Turkish
statesman)

BATISTA (y Zaldívar),
Fulgencio (1901–73; Cuban
statesman)

BENNETT, Richard Bedford,
Viscount (1870–1947;
Canadian statesman)

BOLÍVAR, Simón (1783–1830;
South American statesman)

BORMANN, Martin (1900–45;
German Nazi leader)

CARDOSA, Fernando
Henrique (1931–   ; Brazilian
statesman)

CLINTON, Bill (1946–   ; US
statesman)

CLINTON, de Witt (1769–1828;
US statesman)

COLLINS, Michael
(1890–1922; Irish nationalist)

GADDAFI, Moammar Al- (or
Qaddafi, 1942–   ; Libyan
colonel and statesman)

GRATTAN, Henry (1746–1820;
Irish politician)

GRIMOND, Joseph (1913–93;
British politician)

GROMYKO, Andrei (1909–89;
Soviet statesman)

HIMMLER, Heinrich (1900–45;
German Nazi politician)

HOLLAND, Sir Sidney George
(1893–1961; New Zealand
statesman)

HUSSEIN (ibn Talal (1935–99;
King of Jordan)

HUSSEIN, Saddam (1937–   ;
Iraqi politician)

KEATING, Paul John (1944–   ;
Australian statesman)

JENKINS, Roy Harris
(1920–   ; British politician
and historian)

KINNOCK, Neil (1942–   ;
Labour politician)

7–continued

KOSYGIN, Aleksei Nikolaevich
(1904–80; Soviet statesman)

LUMUMBA, Patrice Hemery
(1925–61; Congolese
statesman)

MACLEOD, Iain Norman
(1913–70; British
Conservative politician)

MANDELA, Nelson (Rolihlahla)
(1918–   ; South African
lawyer and politician)

MAZZINI, Giuseppe (1805–72;
Italian patriot)

MCMAHON, William (1908–80;
Australian statesman)

MENZIES, Sir Robert Gordon
(1894–1978; Australian
statesman)

MINTOFF, Dominic (1916–   ;
Maltese statesman)

MOLOTOV, Vyacheslav
Mikhailovich (1890–1986;
Soviet statesman)

NYERERE, Julius Kambarage
(1922–99; Tanzanian
statesman)

PAISLEY, Ian (1926–   ;
Northern Irish politician)

PARNELL, Charles Stewart
(1846–91; Irish politician)

PEARSON, Lester Bowles
(1897–1972; Canadian
statesman)

RAFFLES, Sir Thomas
Stamford (1781–1826; British
colonial administrator)

SALAZAR, António de Oliveira
(1889–1970; Portuguese
dictator)

SCHMIDT, Helmut (1918–   ;
German statesman)

SCULLIN, James Henry (1876–
1953; Australian statesman)

SHASTRI, Shri Lal Bahadur
(1904–66; Indian statesman)

SUHARTO (1921–   ;
Indonesian statesman and
general)

TROTSKY, Leon (1879–1940;
Russian revolutionary)

TRUDEAU, Pierre Elliott
(1919–   ; Canadian
statesman)

VORSTER, Balthazar
Johannes (1915–83; South
African statesman)

WHITLAM, Edward Gough
(1916–   ; Australian
statesman)

YELTSIN, Boris (1931–   ;
Russian statesman)

8

ADENAUER, Konrad
(1876–1967; German
statesman)

AMIN DADA, Idi (c. 1925–   ;
Ugandan politician and
president)

ARISTIDE, Jean-Bertrand
(1953–   ; Haitian statesman)

AYUB KHAN, Mohammad
(1907–74; Pakistani
statesman)

BEN BELLA, Ahmed (1916–   ;
Algerian statesman)

BIN LADEN, Osama (1957–   ;
leader of al-Qaida terrorists)

BISMARCK, Otto Eduard
Leopold, Prince Von
(1815–98; Prussian
statesman)

BOUCHARD, Lucien (1938–   ;
Canadian politician)

BREZHNEV, Leonid Ilich
(1906–82; Soviet statesman)

BUKHARIN, Nikolai Ivanovich
(1888–1938; Soviet politician)

BULGANIN, Nikolai
Aleksandrovich (1895–1975;
Soviet statesman)

CHRÉTIEN, Jean (1934–   ;
Canadian statesman)

COSGRAVE, William Thomas
(1880–1965; Irish statesman)

CROSSMAN, Richard Howard
Stafford (1907–74; British
Labour politician)

DALADIER, Édouard (1884–
1970; French statesman)

DE GAULLE, Charles André
Joseph Marie (1890–1970;
French general and
statesman)

DE VALERA, Eamon
(1882–1975; Irish statesman)

DOLLFUSS, Engelbert (1892–
1934; Austrian statesman)

DUVALIER, François (1907–71;
Haitian politician)

EICHMANN, Adolf (1906–62;
German Nazi politician)

FRANKLIN, Benjamin
(1706–90; US diplomat)

GOEBBELS, Paul Joseph
(1897–1945; German Nazi
politician)

GRIFFITH, Arthur (1872–1922;
Irish journalist and nationalist)

HARRIMAN, William Averell
(1891–1986; US diplomat)

HASTINGS, Warren
(1732–1818; British colonial
administrator)

8–continued

HIROHITO (1901–89; Emperor of Japan)

HOLYOAKE, Sir Keith Jacka (1904–83; New Zealand statesman)

HONECKER, Erich (1912–94; East German statesman)

HUMPHREY, Hubert Horatio (1911–1978; US Democratic politician)

IBARRURI, Dolores (1895–1989; Spanish politician)

KENYATTA, Jomo (*c.* 1891–1978; Kenyan statesman)

KHOMEINI, Ayatollah Ruholla (1900–89; Iranian Shiite Muslim leader)

MALENKOV, Georgi Maksimilianovich (1902–88; Soviet statesman)

MCALEESE, Mary (1951– ; Irish politician)

MCCARTHY, Joseph Raymond (1908–57; US Republican senator)

MORRISON, Herbert Stanley, Baron (1888–1965; British Labour politician)

MUZOREWA, Bishop Abel Tendekayi (1925– ; Zimbabwean statesman)

O'CONNELL, Daniel (1775–1847; Irish politician)

O'HIGGINS, Bernardo (?1778–1842; Chilean national hero)

PINOCHET, Augusto (1915– ; Chilean general)

PODGORNY, Nikolai (1903–83; Soviet statesman)

POINCARÉ, Raymond (1860–1934; French statesman)

POMPIDOU, Georges Jean Raymond (1911–74; French statesman)

QUISLING, Vidkun Abraham Lauritz Jonsson (1887–1945; Norwegian army officer and Nazi collaborator)

RASPUTIN, Grigori Yefimovich (*c.* 1872–1916; Russian mystic)

SCHRÖDER, Gerhard (1944– ; German politician)

SIHANOUK, Norodim, Prince (1923– ; King of Cambodia)

SIKORSKI, Władysław (1881–1943; Polish general and statesman)

THATCHER, Margaret (1925– ; British stateswoman)

8–continued

ULBRICHT, Walter (1893–1973; East German statesman)

VERWOERD, Hendrik Frensch (1901–66; South African statesman)

WALDHEIM, Kurt (1918– ; Austrian diplomat and statesman)

WEIZMANN, Chaim Azriel (1874–1952; Israeli statesman)

WELENSKY, Sir Roy (1907–92; Rhodesian statesman)

WILLIAMS, Shirley Vivien Teresa Brittain (1930– ; British politician)

9

AGA KHAN IV (1936– ; Imam of the Ismaili sect of Muslims)

ANDREOTTI, Giulio (1919– ; Italian politician)

BEN-GURION, David (1886–1973; Israeli statesman)

CASTRO RUZ, Fidel (1926– ; Cuban statesman)

CHOU EN-LAI (*or* Zhou En Lai, 1898–1976; Chinese communist statesman)

CHURCHILL, Lord Randolph Henry Spencer (1849–95; British Conservative politician)

GAITSKELL, Hugh (1906–63; British politician)

GARIBALDI, Giuseppe (1807–82; Italian soldier)

GORBACHOV, Mikhail Sergeevich (1931– ; Soviet statesman)

HENDERSON, Arthur (1863–1935; British Labour politician)

HO CHI MINH (Nguyen That Thanh, 1890–1969; Vietnamese statesman)

KISSINGER, Henry Alfred (1923– ; US diplomat and political scientist)

LA GUARDIA, Fiorello Henry (1882–1947; US politician)

LUXEMBURG, Rosa (1871–1919; German revolutionary)

MACDONALD, James Ramsay (1866–1937; British statesman)

MACDONALD, Sir John Alexander (1815–91; Canadian statesman)

9–continued

MILOŠEVIĆ, Slobodan (1941– ; Serbian politician)

MUSSOLINI, Benito Amilcare Andrea (1883–1945; Italian fascist dictator)

PANKHURST, Emmeline (1858–1928; British suffragette)

STEVENSON, Adlai Ewing (1900–65; US Democratic politician)

10

ABDULLAH II (1962– ; King of Jordan)

BERNADOTTE, Jean Baptiste Jules (*c.* 1763–1844; French marshal)

BERLUSCONI, Silvio (1936– ; Italian politician)

CARRINGTON, Peter Alexander Rupert, 6th Baron (1919– ; British Conservative politician)

CLEMENCEAU, Georges (1841–1929; French statesman)

KHRUSHCHEV, Nikita Sergeevich (1894–1971; Soviet statesman)

LEE KUAN YEW (1923– ; Singaporean statesman)

MAO TSE-TUNG (*or* Mao Ze Dong, 1893–1976; Chinese communist statesman)

MITTERRAND, François Maurice (1916–96; French statesman)

RIBBENTROP, Joachim von (1893–1946; German Nazi politician)

VOROSHILOV, Kliment Yefremovich (1881–1969; Soviet marshal and statesman)

11

ABDUL RAHMAN, Tunku (1903–73; Malaysian statesman)

CASTLEREAGH, Robert Stewart, Viscount (1769–1822; British statesman)

DIEFENBAKER, John George (1895–1979; Canadian statesman)

HORE-BELISHA, Isaac Leslie, 1st Baron (1893–1957; British politician)

IZETBEGOVIĆ, Alija (1925– ; Bosnian politician)

11–continued

MAKARIOS III, Mikhail Khristodolou Mouskos (1913–77; Cypriot churchman and statesman)

MOUNTBATTEN (of Burma), Louis, 1st Earl (1900–79; British admiral and colonial administrator)

SELWYN LLOYD, John, Baron (1904–78; British Conservative politician)

WILBERFORCE, William (1759–1833; British philanthropist)

12

BANDARANAIKE, Solomon (1899–1959; Sri Lankan statesman)

12–continued

FREI MONTALVA, Eduardo (1911–82; Chilean statesman)

HAMMARSKJÖLD, Dag (1905–61; Swedish international civil servant)

MENDÈS-FRANCE, Pierre (1907–82; French statesman)

PAPADOPOULOS, George (1919– ; Greek colonel)

SHEVARDNADZE, Eduard Amvrosiyevich (1928– ; Georgian statesman)

13

CHIANG KAI-SHEK (or Jiang Jie Shi, 1887–1975; Nationalist Chinese soldier and statesman)

14

ALLENDE GOSSENS, Salvador (1908–73; Chilean statesman)

CLIVE OF PLASSEY, Robert, Baron (1725–74; British soldier and colonial administrator)

15

GISCARD D'ESTAING, Valéry (1926– ; French statesman)

20+

AYATOLLAH RUHOLLA KHOMEINI. See KHOMEINI, Ayatollah Ruholla.

HAILSHAM OF ST MARY-LEBONE, Baron (Quintin McGarel Hogg; 1907–)

MILITARY LEADERS

3

LEE, Robert E (1807–70; US Confederate commander)

NEY, Michel, Prince of Moscow (1769–1815; French marshal)

4

ALBA, Fernando Alvarez de Toledo, Duke of (1507–83; Spanish general)

BART, Jean (1650–1702; French admiral)

BYNG, George, Viscount Torrington (1663–1733; English admiral)

DIAZ, Porfirio (1830–1915; Mexican soldier)

FOCH, Ferdinand (1851–1929; French marshal)

HAIG, Douglas, 1st Earl (1861–1928; British field marshal)

HOOD, Samuel, 1st Viscount (1724–1816; British admiral)

HOWE, Richard, Earl (1726–99; British admiral)

JODL, Alfred (1890–1946; German general)

RAIS, Gilles de (or G de Retz 1404–40; French marshal)

RÖHM, Ernst (1887–1934; German soldier)

ROON, Albrecht, Graf von (1803–79; Prussian general)

4–continued

SAXE, Maurice, Comte de (1696–1750; Marshal of France)

SLIM, William Joseph, 1st Viscount (1891–1970; British field marshal)

TOGO (Heihachiro) (1847–1934; Japanese admiral)

5

ANDRÉ, John (1751–80; British soldier)

ANSON, George Anson, Baron (1697–1762; British admiral)

BLAKE, Robert (1599–1657; English admiral)

BLIGH, William (1754–1817; British admiral)

CIMON (d. c. 450 BC; Athenian general and politician)

DEWEY, George (1837–1917; US admiral)

DRAKE, Sir Francis (1540–96; English navigator and admiral)

EL CID (Rodrigo Diáz de Vivar, c. 1040–99; Spanish warrior)

GATES, Horatio (?1728–1806; American general)

HAWKE, Edward, 1st Baron (1705–81; British admiral)

JONES, John Paul (1747–92; American naval commander)

5–continued

LALLY, Thomas, Comte de (1702–66; French general)

LEVEN, Alexander Leslie, 1st Earl of (1580–1661; Scottish general)

MOORE, Sir John (1761–1809; British general)

MURAT, Joachim (1767–1815; French marshal)

PERRY, Matthew C (1794–1858; US naval officer)

PRIDE, Thomas (d. 1658; English parliamentary soldier)

SULLA, Lucius Cornelius (c. 138–78 BC; Roman dictator)

TILLY, Johan Tserclaes, Graf von (1559–1632; Bavarian general)

TROMP, Maarten (1598–1653; Dutch admiral)

WOLFE, James (1727–59; British soldier)

6

AETIUS, Flavius (d. 454 AD; Roman general)

ARNOLD, Benedict (1741–1801; American general)

BAYARD, Pierre Terrail, Seigneur de (c. 1473–1524; French soldier)

BEATTY, David, 1st Earl (1871–1936; British admiral)

6—continued

BENBOW, John (1653–1702; English naval officer)

CRONJE, Piet Arnoldus (c. 1840–1911; South African general)

CUSTER, George Armstrong (1839–76; US cavalry general)

DARLAN, Jean (Louis Xavier) François (1881–1942; French admiral)

DÖNITZ, Karl (1891–1981; German admiral)

DUNDEE, John Graham of Claverhouse, 1st Viscount (c. 1649–89; Scottish soldier)

DUNOIS, Jean d'Orléans, Comte de (1403–68; French general)

FISHER, John Arbuthnot, 1st Baron (1841–1920; British admiral)

FRENCH, John, 1st Earl of Ypres (1852–1925; British field marshal)

FULLER, J F C (1878–1966; British soldier)

GINKEL, Godert de, 1st Earl of Athlone (1644–1703; Dutch general)

GORDON, Charles George (1833–85; British general)

GRANBY, John Manners, Marquess of (1721–70; British soldier)

GREENE, Nathaneal (1742–86; American general)

HALSEY, William F (1882–1959; US admiral)

JOFFRE, Joseph Jacques Césaire (1852–1931; French marshal)

KEITEL, Wilhelm (1882–1946; German field marshal)

KLÉBER, Jean Baptiste (1753–1800; French general)

KONIEV, Ivan Stepanovich (1897–1973; Soviet marshal)

MARIUS, Gaius (c. 157–86 BC; Roman general)

MOLTKE, Helmuth, Graf von (1800–91; Prussian field marshal)

MOREAU, Jean Victor (1763–1813; French general)

NAPIER (of Magdala), Robert Cornelis, 1st Baron (1810–90; British field marshal)

NAPIER, Sir Charles James (1782–1853; British general)

6—continued

NARSES (c. 480–574 AD; Byzantine general)

NELSON, Horatio, Viscount (1758–1805; British admiral)

NIMITZ, Chester W (1885–1966; US admiral)

OUTRAM, Sir James (1803–63; British soldier)

PATTON, George S (1885–1945; US general)

PAULUS, Friedrich (1890–1957; German field marshal)

PÉTAIN, (Henri) Philippe (1856–1951; French general and statesman)

RAEDER, Erich (1876–1960; German admiral)

RAGLAN, Fitzroy James Henry Somerset, 1st Baron (1788–1855; British field marshal)

RODNEY, George Brydges, 1st Baron (1719–92; British admiral)

ROMMEL, Erwin (1891–1944; German general)

RUPERT, Prince (1619–82; Cavalry officer)

RUYTER, Michiel Adriaanszoon de (1607–76; Dutch admiral)

TEDDER, Arthur William, 1st Baron (1890–1967; British air marshal)

VERNON, Edward (1684–1757; British admiral)

WAVELL, Archibald Percival, 1st Earl (1883–1950; British field marshal)

WILSON, Henry Maitland, 1st Baron (1881–1964; British field marshal)

WILSON, Sir Henry Hughes (1864–1922; British field marshal)

ZHUKOV, Georgi Konstantinovich (1896–1974; Soviet marshal)

7

AGRIPPA, Marcus Vipsanius (?63–12 BC; Roman general)

ALLENBY, Edmund Henry Hynman, 1st Viscount (1861–1936; British field marshal)

ARTIGAS, José Gervasio (1764–1850; national hero of Uruguay)

7—continued

ATHLONE, Alexander Cambridge, 1st Earl of (1874–1957; British soldier)

BAZAINE, Achille François (1811–88; French marshal)

BERWICK, James Fitzjames, Duke of (1670–1734; Marshal of France)

BLÜCHER, Gebhard Leberecht von, Prince of Wahlstatt (1742–1819; Prussian general)

BRADLEY, Omar Nelson (1893–1981; US general)

DECATUR, Stephen (1779–1820; US naval officer)

DENIKIN, Anton Ivanovich (1872–1947; Russian general)

DOWDING, Hugh Caswall Tremenheere, 1st Baron (1882–1970; British air chief marshal)

FAIRFAX, Thomas, 3rd Baron (1612–71; English general)

JACKSON, Andrew (1767–1845; US statesman and general)

JACKSON, Stonewall (Thomas Jonathan J, 1824–63; US Confederate general)

KHAMENI, Ayatollah Seyed Ali (1940–   ; Iranian political and religious leader)

KOLCHAK, Alexander Vasilievich (1874–1920; Russian admiral)

LAMBERT, John (1619–83; English parliamentary general)

LYAUTEY, Louis Hubert Gonzalve (1854–1934; French marshal)

MASSÉNA, André (?1756–1817; French marshal)

METAXAS, Ioannis (1871–1941; Greek general)

MORTIER, Édouard Adolphe Casimir Joseph, Duc de Trévise (1768–1835; French marshal)

PHILLIP, Arthur (1738–1814; British admiral)

REGULUS, Marcus Attilus (d. c. 251 BC; Roman general)

ROBERTS, Frederick Sleigh, 1st Earl (1832–1914; British field marshal)

SHERMAN, William Tecumseh (1820–91; US Federal general)

7–continued

SHOVELL, Sir Cloudesley (1650–1707; English admiral)

SUVOROV, Aleksandr Vasilievich, Count (1729–1800; Russian field marshal)

TANCRED (c. 1078–1112; Norman Crusader)

TIRPITZ, Alfred von (1849–1930; German admiral)

TURENNE, Henri de la Tour d'Auvergne, Vicomte de (1611–75; French marshal)

VENDÔME, Louis Joseph, Duc de (1654–1712; French marshal)

VILLARS, Claude Louis Hector, Duc de (1653–1734; French marshal)

WALLACE, Lew (1827–1905; US soldier)

WINGATE, Orde Charles (1903–44; British soldier)

WRANGEL, Peter Nikolaievich, Baron (1878–1928; Russian general)

8

AGRICOLA, Gnaeus Julius (40–93 AD; Roman governor)

ANGLESEY, Henry William Paget, 1st Marquess of (1768–1854; British field marshal)

AUGEREAU, Pierre François Charles, Duc de Castiglione (1757–1816; French marshal)

BADOGLIO, Pietro (1871–1956; Italian general)

BERTRAND, Henri Gratien, Comte (1773–1844; French marshal)

BOURMONT, Louis Auguste Victor de Ghaisnes, Comte de (1773–1846; French marshal)

BURGOYNE, John (1722–92; British general)

CAMPBELL, Colin, Baron Clyde (1792–1863; British field marshal)

CARDIGAN, James Thomas Brudenell, 7th Earl of (1797–1868; British cavalry officer)

CARRANZA, Venustiano (1859–1920; Mexican statesman and soldier)

COCHRANE, Thomas, 10th Earl of Dundonald (1775–1860; British admiral)

CROMWELL, Oliver (1599–1658; English soldier and statesman)

8–continued

GUESCLIN, Bertrand du (c. 1320–80; French commander)

HANNIBAL (247–c. 183 BC; Carthaginian general)

IRONSIDE, William Edmund, 1st Baron (1880–1959; British field marshal)

JELLICOE, John Rushworth, 1st Earl (1859–1935; British admiral)

KORNILOV, Lavrentia Georgievich (1870–1918; Russian general)

LUCULLUS, Lucius Licinius (d. c. 57 BC; Roman general)

LYSANDER (d. 395 BC; Spartan general)

MARSHALL, George C (1880–1959; US general)

MONTCALM, Louis Joseph de Montcalm-Grozon, Marquis de (1712–59; French general)

O'HIGGINS, Bernardo (?1778–1842; Chilean national hero)

PERSHING, John J (1860–1948; US general)

SANDWICH, John Montagu, 4th Earl of (1718–92; first lord of the admiralty)

SHERIDAN, Philip H (1831–88; US Federal general)

STILICHO, Flavius (d. 408 AD; Roman general)

STILWELL, Joseph W (1883–1946; US general)

WOLSELEY, Garnet Joseph, 1st Viscount (1833–1913; British field marshal)

9

ANGOULÊME, Charles de Valois, Duc d' (1573–1650; French soldier)

ANTIPATER (397–319 BC; Macedonian general)

ANTONESCU, Ion (1882–1946; Romanian general)

ARISTIDES (the Just) (c. 520–c. 468 BC; Athenian statesman)

BONAPARTE, Napoleon (1769–1821; French emperor)

DUMOURIEZ, Charles François Du Périer (1739–1823; French general)

GNEISENAU, August, Graf Neithardt von (1760–1831; Prussian field marshal)

9–continued

GRENVILLE, Sir Richard (?1541–91; British sailor)

HASDRUBAL (d. 207 BC; Carthaginian general)

KITCHENER (of Khartoum), Horatio Herbert, 1st Earl (1850–1916; British field marshal)

LAFAYETTE, Marie Joseph Gilbert Motier, Marquis de (1757–1834; French general and politician)

MACARTHUR, Douglas (1880–1964; US general)

MARCELLUS, Marcus Claudius (d. 208 BC; Roman general)

MCCLELLAN, George B (1826–85; Federal general)

MILTIADES (c. 550–489 BC; Athenian general)

NEWCASTLE, William Cavendish, Duke of (1592–1676; English soldier)

OLDCASTLE, Sir John (c. 1378–1417; English soldier)

PRETORIUS, Andries (1799–1853; Afrikaner leader)

RUNDSTEDT, Gerd von (1875–1953; German field marshal)

SANTA ANNA, Antonio López de (1794–1876; Mexican soldier)

TRENCHARD, Hugh Montague, 1st Viscount (1873–1956; The first British air marshal)

10

ABERCROMBY, Sir Ralph (1734–1801; British general)

ALANBROOKE, Alan Francis Brooke, 1st Viscount (1883–1963; British field marshal)

ALCIBIADES (c. 450–404 BC; Athenian general and politician)

ANTIGONUS I (c. 382–301 BC; Macedonian general)

AUCHINLECK, Sir Claude (1884–1981; British field marshal)

BELISARIUS (c. 505–65 AD; Byzantine general)

BERNADOTTE, Jean Baptiste Jules (1763–1844)

CORNWALLIS, Charles, 1st Marquess (1738–1805; British general)

10–continued

CUMBERLAND, William Augustus, Duke of (1721–65; British general)

ENVER PASHA (1881–1922; Turkish soldier)

FLAMININUS, Titus Quinctius (c. 230–c. 174 BC; Roman general)

HINDENBURG, Paul von Beneckendorff und von (1847–1934; German general)

KESSELRING, Albert (1885–1960; German general)

KUBLAI KHAN (1215–94; Mongol conqueror of China)

MANNERHEIM, Carl Gustaf Emil, Baron von (1867–1951; Finnish general)

MONTGOMERY (of Alamein), Bernard Law, 1st Viscount (1887–1976; British field marshal)

OGLETHORPE, James Edward (1696–1785; English general)

RICHTHOFEN, Manfred, Freiherr von (1892–1918; German air ace)

SCHLIEFFEN, Alfred, Graf von (1833–1913; German general)

TIMOSHENKO, Semyon Konstantinovich (1895–1970; Soviet marshal)

VILLENEUVE, Pierre (1763–1806; French admiral)

10–continued

WELLINGTON, Arthur Wellesley, Duke of (1769–1852; British general)

11

ALBUQUERQUE, Alfonso de (1453–1515; Portuguese governor in India)

BADEN-POWELL, Robert Stephenson Smyth, 1st Baron (1857–1941; British general)

BEAUHARNAIS, Alexandre, Vicomte de (1760–94; French general)

BRAUCHITSCH, Walther von (1881–1948; German general)

COLLINGWOOD, Cuthbert, 1st Baron (1750–1810; British admiral)

EPAMINONDAS (c. 418–362 BC; Theban general)

LIDDELL HART, Sir Basil Henry (1895–1970; British soldier)

MARLBOROUGH, John Churchill, 1st Duke of (1650–1722; British general)

MÜNCHHAUSEN, Karl Friedrich, Freiherr von (1720–97; German soldier)

PONIATOWSKI, Józef (1763–1813; Marshal of France)

WALLENSTEIN, Albrecht Wenzel von (1583–1634; Bohemian-born general)

12

IBRAHIM PASHA (1789–1848; Ottoman general)

13

EUGÈNE OF SAVOY, Prince (1663–1736; Austrian general)

FABIUS MAXIMUS, Quintus (d. 203 BC; Roman general)

HAMILCAR BARCA (d. c. 229 BC; Carthaginian general)

14

BARCLAY DE TOLLY, Mikhail Bogdanovich, Prince (1761–1818; Russian field marshal)

CLIVE OF PLASSEY, Robert, Baron (1725–74; British soldier and colonial administrator)

15

CASSIUS LONGINUS, Gaius (d. 42 BC; Roman general)

SCIPIO AFRICANUS (236–183 BC; Roman general)

16

ALEXANDER OF TUNIS, Harold, 1st Earl (1891–1969; British field marshal)

17

HOWARD OF EFFINGHAM, Charles, 2nd Baron (1536–1624; English Lord High Admiral)

20+

BERNHARD OF SAXE-WEIMAR, Duke (1604–39; German general)

SCIPIO AEMILIANUS AFRICANUS (c. 185–129 BC; Roman general)

PRIME MINISTERS OF GREAT BRITAIN (FROM 1721)

NAME	(TERM)	NAME	(TERM)
ROBERT WALPOLE	(1721–42)	JOHN STUART, EARL OF BUTE	(1762–63)
SPENCER COMPTON, EARL OF WILMINGTON	(1742–43)	GEORGE GRENVILLE	(1763–65)
HENRY PELHAM	(1743–54)	CHARLES WATSON-WENTWORTH, MARQUIS OF ROCKINGHAM	(1765–66)
THOMAS PELHAM-HOLLES, DUKE OF NEWCASTLE	(1754–56)	WILLIAM PITT, EARL OF CHATHAM	(1766–68)
WILLIAM CAVENDISH, DUKE OF DEVONSHIRE	(1756–57)	AUGUSTUS HENRY FITZROY, DUKE OF GRAFTON	(1768–70)
THOMAS PELHAM-HOLLES, DUKE OF NEWCASTLE	(1757–62)	FREDERICK NORTH	(1770–82)

NAME	(TERM)	NAME	(TERM)
CHARLES WATSON-WENTWORTH, MARQUIS OF ROCKINGHAM	(1782)	JOHN RUSSELL, EARL RUSSELL	(1865–66)
		EDWARD STANLEY, EARL OF DERBY	(1866–68)
WILLIAM PETTY, EARL OF SHELBURNE	(1782–83)	BENJAMIN DISRAELI	(1868)
		WILLIAM EWART GLADSTONE	(1868–74)
WILLIAM HENRY CAVENDISH BENTINCK, DUKE OF PORTLAND	(1783)	BENJAMIN DISRAELI, EARL OF BEACONSFIELD	(1874–80)
		WILLIAM EWART GLADSTONE	(1880–85)
WILLIAM PITT (SON OF EARL OF CHATHAM)	(1783–1801)	ROBERT GASCOYNE-CECIL, MARQUIS OF SALISBURY	(1885–86)
HENRY ADDINGTON	(1801–04)	WILLIAM EWART GLADSTONE	(1886)
WILLIAM PITT	(1804–06)	ROBERT GASCOYNE-CECIL, MARQUIS OF SALISBURY	(1886–92)
WILLIAM WYNDHAM GRENVILLE, BARON GRENVILLE	(1806–07)	WILLIAM EWART GLADSTONE	(1892–94)
		ARCHIBALD PHILIP PRIMROSE, EARL OF ROSEBERY	(1894–95)
WILLIAM BENTINCK, DUKE OF PORTLAND	(1807–09)	ROBERT GASCOYNE-CECIL, MARQUIS OF SALISBURY	(1895–1902)
SPENCER PERCEVAL	(1809–12)	ARTHUR JAMES BALFOUR	(1902–05)
ROBERT BANKS JENKINSON, EARL OF LIVERPOOL	(1812–27)	HENRY CAMPBELL-BANNERMAN	(1905–08)
GEORGE CANNING	(1827)	HERBERT HENRY ASQUITH	(1908–16)
FREDERICK JOHN ROBINSON, VISCOUNT GODERICH	(1827–28)	DAVID LLOYD GEORGE	(1916–22)
ARTHUR WELLESLEY, DUKE OF WELLINGTON	(1828–30)	ANDREW BONAR LAW	(1922–23)
		STANLEY BALDWIN	(1923–24)
CHARLES GREY, EARL GREY	(1830–34)	JAMES RAMSAY MACDONALD	(1924)
WILLIAM LAMB, VISCOUNT MELBOURNE	(1834)	STANLEY BALDWIN	(1924–29)
		JAMES RAMSAY MACDONALD	(1929–35)
ROBERT PEEL	(1834–35)	STANLEY BALDWIN	(1935–37)
WILLIAM LAMB, VISCOUNT MELBOURNE	(1835–41)	NEVILLE CHAMBERLAIN	(1937–40)
ROBERT PEEL	(1841–46)	WINSTON CHURCHILL	(1940–45)
JOHN RUSSELL	(1846–52)	CLEMENT RICHARD ATTLEE	(1945–51)
EDWARD GEORGE GEOFFREY SMITH STANLEY, EARL OF DERBY	(1852)	WINSTON CHURCHILL	(1951–55)
		ANTHONY EDEN	(1955–57)
GEORGE HAMILTON GORDON, EARL OF ABERDEEN	(1852–55)	HAROLD MACMILLAN	(1957–63)
		ALEC DOUGLAS-HOME	(1963–64)
HENRY JOHN TEMPLE, VISCOUNT PALMERSTON	(1855–58)	HAROLD WILSON	(1964–70)
		EDWARD HEATH	(1970–74)
EDWARD STANLEY, EARL OF DERBY	(1858–59)	HAROLD WILSON	(1974–76)
		JAMES CALLAGHAN	(1976–79)
HENRY TEMPLE, VISCOUNT PALMERSTON	(1859–65)	MARGARET THATCHER	(1979–90)
		JOHN MAJOR	(1990–97)
		TONY BLAIR	(1997–)

THE PRESIDENTS OF THE UNITED STATES OF AMERICA

NAME	(TERM)	NAME	(TERM)
GEORGE WASHINGTON	(1789–97)	BENJAMIN HARRISON	(1889–93)
JOHN ADAMS	(1797–1801)	GROVER CLEVELAND	(1893–97)
THOMAS JEFFERSON	(1801–09)	WILLIAM MCKINLEY	(1897–1901)
JAMES MADISON	(1809–17)	THEODORE ROOSEVELT	(1901–09)
JAMES MONROE	(1817–25)	WILLIAM HOWARD TAFT	(1909–13)
JOHN QUINCY ADAMS	(1825–29)	WOODROW WILSON	(1913–21)
ANDREW JACKSON	(1829–37)	WARREN GAMALIEL HARDING	(1921–23)
MARTIN VAN BUREN	(1837–41)	CALVIN COOLIDGE	(1923–29)
WILLIAM HENRY HARRISON	(1841)	HERBERT CLARK HOOVER	(1929–33)
JOHN TYLER	(1841–45)	FRANKLIN DELANO ROOSEVELT	(1933–45)
JAMES KNOX POLK	(1845–49)	HARRY S. TRUMAN	(1945–53)
ZACHARY TAYLOR	(1849–50)	DWIGHT DAVID EISENHOWER	(1953–61)
MILLARD FILLMORE	(1850–53)	JOHN FITZGERALD KENNEDY	(1961–63)
FRANKLIN PIERCE	(1853–57)	LYNDON BAINES JOHNSON	(1963–69)
JAMES BUCHANAN	(1857–61)	RICHARD MILHOUS NIXON	(1969–74)
ABRAHAM LINCOLN	(1861–65)	GERALD RUDOLPH FORD	(1974–77)
ANDREW JOHNSON	(1865–69)	JAMES EARL CARTER	(1977–81)
ULYSSES SIMPSON GRANT	(1869–77)	RONALD WILSON REAGAN	(1981–89)
RUTHERFORD BIRCHARD HAYES	(1877–81)	GEORGE HERBERT WALKER BUSH	(1989–93)
JAMES ABRAM GARFIELD	(1881)	WILLIAM JEFFERSON CLINTON	(1993–2001)
CHESTER ALAN ARTHUR	(1881–85)	GEORGE WALKER BUSH	(2001–)
GROVER CLEVELAND	(1885–89)		

RULERS OF ENGLAND

KINGS OF KENT

HENGEST	(c. 455–488)
GERIC surnamed OISC	(488–?512)
OCTA	(?512–?)
EORMENRIC	(*N560)
ETHELBERT I	(560–616)
EADBALD	(616–640)
EARCONBERT	(640–664)
EGBERT I	(664–673)
HLOTHERE*	(673–685)
EADRIC*	(685–686)
SUAEBHARD*	(676–692)
OSWINI*	(?688–?690)
WIHTRED*	(690–725)
ETHELBERT II*	(725–762)
EADBERT*	(?725–?762)
ALRIC*	(c. 750s)
EARDWULF*	(747–762)
SIGERED*	(?762)
EANMUND*	(c. 759–765)
HEABERHT*	(764–765)
EGBERT II	(c. 765–780)
EALHMUND	(784–786)
EADBERT (PRAEN)	(796–798)
EADWALD	(?798 or 807)

CUTHRED	(798–807)
BALDRED	(?–825)

KINGS OF DEIRA

AELLI	(c. 560–590)
EDWIN	(?590–592)
ETHELFRITH	(592–616)
EDWIN	(616–632)
OSRIC	(632–633)
OSWALD (ST.)	(633–641)
OSWINE	(644–651)
ETHELWALD	(651–654)

KINGS OF NORTHUMBRIA

ETHELFRITH	(592–616)
EDWIN	(616–632)
OSWALD (ST.)	(633–641)
OSWIU	(654–670)
EGFRITH	(670–685)
ALDFRITH	(685–704)
OSRED I	(704–716)
COENRED	(716–718)
OSRIC	(718–729)
CEOLWULF	(729–737)

KINGS OF NORTHUMBRIA (cont.)

EADBERT	(737–758)
OSWULF	(c. 758)
ETHELWALD MOLL	(758–765)
ALCHRED	(765–774)
ETHELRED I	(774–778)
ELFWALD I	(778–788)
OSRED II	(788–790)
ETHELRED I	(790–796)
OSBALD	(796)
EARDWULF	(796–806)
ELFWALD II	(806–808)
EARDWULF	(?808)
EANRED	(808–840)
ETHELRED II	(840–844)
REDWULF	(844)
ETHELRED II	(844–849)
OSBERT	(849–862)
AELLE	(862–867)
EGBERT I	(867–873)
RICSIG	(873–876)
EGBERT II	(876–?878)

KINGS OF MERCIA

CEARL	(c. 600)
PENDA	(632–654)
WULFHERE	(657–674)
ETHELRED	(674–704)
COENRED	(704–709)
CEOLRED	(709–716)
ETHELBALD	(716–?757)
BEORNRED	(757)
OFFA	(757–796)
EGFRITH	(796)
COENWULF	(796–?821)
CEOLWULF I	(821–823)
BEORNWULF	(823–825)
LUDECAN	(825–827)
WIGLAF	(827–840)
BEORHTWULF	(840–852)
BURGRED	(852–874)
CEOLWULF II	(874–?883)

KINGS OF THE WEST SAXONS

CERDIC	(519–534)
CYNRIC	(534–560)
CEAWLIN	(560–591)
CEOL	(591–597)
CEOLWULF	(597–611)
CYNEGILS	(611–643)
CENWALH	(643–672)
SEAXBURH (Queen)	(?672–?674)
AESCWINE	(674–676)
CENTWINE	(676–685)
CAEDWALLA	(685–688)
INI	(688–726)
AETHELHEARD	(726–?740)
CUTHRED	(740–756)
SIGEBERHT	(756–757)

CYNEWULF	(757–786)
BEORHTRIC	(786–802)
EGBERT	(802–839)
ETHELWULF	(839–855)
ETHELBALD	(855–860)
ETHELBERT	(860–866)
ETHELRED	(866–871)
ALFRED	(871–899)
EDWARD THE ELDER	(899–925)
ATHELSTAN	(925–939)
EDMUND	(939–946)
EDRED	(946–955)

RULERS OF ENGLAND

EDWY	(955–959)
EDGAR	(959–975)
EDWARD THE MARTYR	(975–979)
ETHELRED	(979–1013)
SWEGN FORKBEARD	(1013–14)
ETHELRED	(1014–16)
EDMUND IRONSIDE	(1016)
CANUTE	(1016–35)
HAROLD HAREFOOT	(1035–40)
HARTACNUT	(1040–42)
EDWARD THE CONFESSOR	(1042–66)
HAROLD GODWINSON	(1066)
EDGAR ETHELING	(1066)
WILLIAM I (THE CONQUEROR)	(1066–87)
WILLIAM II (RUFUS)	(1087–1100)
HENRY I	(1100–35)
STEPHEN	(1135–54)
HENRY II	(1154–89)
RICHARD I	(1189–99)
JOHN	(1199–1216)
HENRY III	(1216–72)
EDWARD I	(1272–1307)
EDWARD II	(1307–27)
EDWARD III	(1327–77)
RICHARD II	(1377–99)
HENRY IV	(1399–1413)
HENRY V	(1413–22)
HENRY VI	(1422–61; 1470–71)
EDWARD IV	(1461–83)
EDWARD V	(1483)
RICHARD III	(1483–85)
HENRY VII	(1485–1509)
HENRY VIII	(1509–47)
EDWARD VI	(1547–53)
JANE (LADY JANE GREY)	(1553)
MARY	(1553–58)
PHILIP*	(1554–58)
ELIZABETH I	(1558–1603)
JAMES I	(1603–25)
CHARLES I	(1625–49)
THE COMMONWEALTH	(1649–60)
[OLIVER CROMWELL	(1653–58)
RICHARD CROMWELL	(1658–59)]
CHARLES II	(1660–85)
JAMES II	(1685–88)
WILLIAM AND MARY	(1689–1694)
WILLIAM III	(1694–1702)

ANNE	(1702–14)	EDWARD VII	(1901–10)
GEORGE I	(1714–27)	GEORGE V	(1910–36)
GEORGE II	(1727–60)	EDWARD VIII (DUKE OF	
GEORGE III	(1760–1820)	WINDSOR)	(1936)
GEORGE IV	(1820–30)	GEORGE VI	(1936–52)
WILLIAM IV	(1830–37)	ELIZABETH II	(1952–)
VICTORIA	(1837–1901)	* Joint rulers	

SCOTTISH RULERS

KENNETH I (MACALPIN)	(843–58)	EDGAR	(1097–1107)
DONALD I	(858–62)	ALEXANDER I	(1107–24)
CONSTANTINE I	(862–77)	DAVID I	(1124–53)
AEDH	(877–78)	MALCOLM IV	(1153–65)
GIRAC	(878–89)	WILLIAM THE LION	(1165–1214)
EOCHA	(878–89)	ALEXANDER II	(1214–49)
DONALD II	(889–900)	ALEXANDER III	(1249–86)
CONSTANTINE II	(900–43)	MARGARET, MAID OF NORWAY	(1286–90)
MALCOLM I	(943–54)	JOHN BALLIOL	(1292–96)
INDULPHUS	(954–62)	ROBERT I (BRUCE)	(1306–29)
DUFF	(962–66)	DAVID II	(1329–71)
COLIN	(966–71)	ROBERT II	(1371–90)
KENNETH II	(971–95)	ROBERT III	(1390–1406)
CONSTANTINE III	(995–97)	JAMES I	(1406–37)
KENNETH III	(997–1005)	JAMES II	(1437–60)
MALCOLM II	(1005–34)	JAMES III	(1460–88)
DUNCAN I	(1034–40)	JAMES IV	(1488–1513)
MACBETH	(1040–57)	JAMES V	(1513–42)
MALCOLM III	(1058–93)	MARY STUART,	
DONALD III (BANE)	(1093–94, 1094–97)	QUEEN OF SCOTS	(1542–67)
DUNCAN II	(1094)	JAMES VI OF SCOTLAND	(1567–1625)

ROMAN RULERS

NAME	(DATE OF OFFICE)	NERVA	(96–98)
(Usurpers in italics)		TRAJAN	(98–117)
		HADRIAN	(117–138)
AUGUSTUS	(27 BC–AD 14)	ANTONINUS PIUS	(138–161)
TIBERIUS	(14–37)	MARCUS AURELIUS	(161–180)
CALIGULA	(37–41)	LUCIUS VERUS	(161–169)
CLAUDIUS	(41–54)	COMMODUS	(180–192)
NERO	(54–68)	PERTINAX	(193)
GALBA	(68–69)	DIDUS JULIANUS	(193)
OTHO	(69)	NIGER	(193)
VITELLIUS	(69)	SEPTIMUS SEVERUS	(193–211)
VESPASIAN	(69–79)	CARACALLA	(211–217)
TITUS	(79–81)	GETA	(209–212)
DOMITIAN	(81–96)	MACRINUS	(217–218)

ROMAN RULERS (continued)

ELAGABALUS	(218–222)
ALEXANDER SEVERUS	(222–235)
MAXIMIN I	(235–238)
GORDIAN I	(238)
GORDIAN II	(238)
BALBINUS	(238)
MAXIMUS	(238)
GORDIAN III	(238–244)
PHILIP	(244–249)
DECIUS	(249–251)
HOSTILIAN	(251)
GALLUS	(251–253)
AEMILIAN	(253)
VALERIAN	(253–260)
GALLIENUS	(253–268)
CLAUDIUS II	(268–269)
QUINTILLUS	(269–270)
AURELIAN	(270–275)
TACITUS	(275–276)
FLORIAN	(276)
PROBUS	(276–282)
CARUS	(282–283)
CARINUS	(283–285)
NUMERIAN	(283–284)
†DIOCLETIAN	(284–305; abdicated)
*MAXIMIAN	(286–305; 306–308)
*CONSTANTIUS I	(305–306)
†GALERIUS	(305–311)
*SEVERUS	(306–307)
†LICINIUS	(308–324)
MAXIMIN	(310–313)
*MAXENTIUS	(306–312)
CONSTANTINE I (THE GREAT)	(312–337)
CONSTANTINE II	(337–340)
CONSTANS	(337–350)

CONSTANTIUS II	(337–361)
MAGNENTIUS	(350–351)
JULIAN	(360–363)
JOVIAN	(363–364)
*VALENTINIAN I	(364–375)
†VALENS	(364–378)
†PROCOPIUS	(365–366)
*GRATIAN	(375–383)
*VALENTINIAN II	(375–392)
THEODOSIUS I	(379–395)
†ARCADIUS	(395–408)
*HONORIUS	(395–423)
CONSTANTINE III	(407–411)
†THEODOSIUS II	(408–450)
*CONSTANTIUS III	(421–423)
VALENTINIAN III	(423–455)
†MARCIAN	(450–457)
**PETRONIUS MAXIMUS*	(455)
*AVITUS	(455–456)
†LEO I	(457–474)
*MAJORIAN	(457–461)
*LIBIUS SEVERUS	(461–467)
*ANTHEMIUS	(467–472)
**OLYBRIUS*	(472–473)
GLYCERIUS	(473)
*JULIUS NEPOS	(474–475)
†LEO II	(474)
†ZENO	(474–491)
**ROMULUS AUGUSTULUS*	(475–476)

*Emperors of the Western Roman Empire only

†Emperors of the Eastern Roman Empire (at Constantinople) before the fall of Rome (476). (For Eastern emperors after 476, *see* BYZANTINE RULERS.)

BYZANTINE RULERS

Name	(Date of office)
(Usurpers in italics)	
ZENO	(474–491)
BASILICUS	(475–76)
ANASTASIUS I	(491–518)
JUSTIN I	(518–527)
JUSTINIAN I	(527–565)
JUSTIN II	(565–578)
TIBERIUS II CONSTANTINE	(578–582)
MAURICE TIBERIUS	(582–602)
PHOCAS	(602–610)
HERACLIUS	(610–641)
HERACLIUS CONSTANTINE	(641)
HERACLONAS	(641)
CONSTANS II	(641–668)
CONSTANTINE IV	(668–685)

JUSTINIAN II RHINOTMETUS	(685–695, 705–711)
LEONTIUS	(695–698)
TIBERIUS III	(698–705)
PHILIPPICUS	(711–713)
ANASTASIUS II	(713–716)
THEODOSIUS III	(716–717)
LEO III	(717–741)
CONSTANTINE V COPRONYMUS	(741–775)
LEO IV	(775–780)
CONSTANTINE VI	(780–797)
IRENE	(797–802)
NICEPHORUS I	(802–811)
STAURACIUS	(811)
MICHAEL I RHANGABE	(811–813)
LEO V	(813–820)

MICHAEL II BALBUS	(820–829)
THEOPHILUS	(829–842)
MICHAEL III	(842–867)
BASIL I	(867–886)
LEO VI	(886–912)
ALEXANDER	(912–913)
CONSTANTINE VII PORPHYROGENITUS	(913–959)
ROMANUS I LECAPENUS	(920–944)
ROMANUS II	(959–963)
NICEPHOROUS II PHOCAS	(963–969)
JOHN I TZIMISCES	(969–976)
BASIL II BULGAROCTONUS	(976–1025)
CONSTANTINE VIII	(1025–28)
ROMANUS III ARGYRUS	(1028–34)
MICHAEL IV	(1034–41)
MICHAEL V CALAPHATES	(1041–42)
ZOE	(1042–56)
CONSTANTINE IX MONOMACHUS	(1042–55)
THEODORA	(1055–56)
MICHAEL VI STRATIOTICUS	(1056–57)
ISAAC I COMNENUS	(1057–59)
CONSTANTINE X DUCAS	(1059–67)
ROMANUS IV DIOGENES	(1067–71)
MICHAEL VII DUCAS	(1071–78)
NICEPHORUS III BOTANIATES	(1078–81)
ALEXIUS I COMNENUS	(1081–1118)
JOHN II COMNENUS	(1118–43)
MANUEL I COMNENUS	(1143–80)
ALEXIUS II COMNENUS	(1180–83)
ANDRONICUS I COMNENUS	(1183–85)

ISAAC II ANGELUS	(1185–95, 1203–04)
ALEXIUS III ANGELUS	(1195–1203)
ALEXIUS V DUCAS MURTZUPHLUS	(1204)
*BALDWIN I	(1204–06)
*HENRY	(1206–16)
*PETER	(1217)
*YOLANDE	(1217–19)
*ROBERT	(1219–28)
*BALDWIN II	(1228–61)
*JOHN	(1231–37)
†CONSTANTINE (XI) LASCARIS	(1204–05?)
†THEODORE I LASCARIS	(1205*N22)
†JOHN III DUCAS VATATZES	(1222–54)
†THEODORE II LASCARIS	(1254–58)
†JOHN IV LASCARIS	(1258–61)
MICHAEL VIII PALAEOLOGUS	(1261–82)
ANDRONICUS II PALAEOLOGUS	(1282–1328)
ANDRONICUS III PALAEOLOGUS	(1328–41)
JOHN V PALAEOLOGUS	(1341–76, 1379–90, 1390–91)
JOHN VI CANTACUZENUS	(1347–54)
ANDRONICUS IV PALAEOLOGUS	(1376–77)
JOHN VII PALAEOLOGUS	(1390)
MANUEL II PALAEOLOGUS	(1391–1425)
JOHN VIII PALAEOLOGUS	(1421–48)
CONSTANTINE XI PALAEOLOGUS	(1448–53)

*Latin emperors

†Nicaean emperors

ANCIENT EGYPTIAN RULERS

DYNASTIES
(all dates are BC):

Earliest dynasties

I	3200–3000
II	3000–2780

Old Kingdom

III	2780–2720
IV	2720–2560
V	2560–2420
VI	2420–2270

First Intermediate Period

VII–VIII	2270–2240
IX–X	2240–2100

Middle Kingdom

XI	2100–2000
XII	2000–1788

Second Intermediate Period

XIII–XVI	1788–1600
XVII	1600–1555

The Empire

XVIII	1555–1350
XIX	1350–1200
XX	1200–1090
XXI	1090–945
XXII	945–c. 745
XXIII	c. 745–718
XXIV	718–712

Late Period

XXV	712–663
XXVI	663–525
XXVII	525–332
XXVIII	405–399
XXIX	399–379
XXX	379–341
Ptolemaic	323–30

ANCIENT EGYPTIAN RULERS (continued)

NARMER	
MENES	
AHA	
DEN	
HETEPSEKHEMWY	
RENEB	
NYNETJER	
PERIBSEN	
KHASEKHEM	
KHASEKHEMWY	
SANAKHTE	
DJOSER	
NETJERYKHET	
SEKHEMKHET	
KHABA	
HUNI	
SNEFRU	
KHUFU	
CHEOPS	
REDJEDEF	
SHEPSESKAF	
KHAFRE	
USERKAF	
SAHURE	
NEFERIAKARE	
RENEFEREF	
NUSERRE	
MENKAUHOR	
DJEDKARE IZEZI	
UNAS	
TETI	
PEPI I	
MERENRE	
PEPI II	
IBI	
NEFERKARE	
KHETY	
MERIKARE	
INYOTEF I	(2081–2065 BC)
INYOTEF II	(2065–2016 BC)
INYOTEF III	(2016–2008 BC)
MENTUHOTEP I	(2008–1957 BC)
MENTUHOTEP II	(1957–1945 BC)
MENTUHOTEP III	(1945–1938 BC)
AMENEMHET I	(1938–1908 BC)
SESOSTRIS I	(1918–1875 BC)
AMENEMHET II	(1876–1842 BC)
SESOSTRIS II	(1844–1837 BC)
SESOSTRIS III	(1836–1818 BC)
AMENEMHET III	(1818–1770 BC)
AMENEMHET IV	(1770–1760 BC)
SEBEKNEFRU	(1760–1756 BC)
APOPIS	
KAMOSE	
AHMOSE	(c. 1539–1514 BC)
AMENHOTEP I	(c. 1514–1493 BC)
THUTMOSE I	(1493–c. 1482 BC)
THUTMOSE II	(c. 1482–1479 BC)
THUTMOSE III	(1479–1426 BC)
HATSHEPSUT	(c. 1481–c. 1458 BC)

AMENHOTEP II	(c. 1426–1400 BC)
THUTMOSE IV	(1400–1390 BC)
AMENHOTEP III	(1390–1353 BC)
AMENHOTEP IV	(1353–1336 BC)
AKHENATON	(1353–1336 BC)
SMENKHKARE	(1335–1332 BC)
TUTANKHATEN	(1352–c. 1323 BC)
TUTANKHAMEN	(1352–c. 1323 BC)
AY	(1323–1319 BC)
HOREMHEB	(1319–c. 1292 BC)
RAMSES I	(1292–1290 BC)
SETI I	(1290–1279 BC)
RAMSES II	(1279–1213 BC)
MARNEPTAH	(1213–1204 BC)
SETI II	(1204–1198 BC)
SIPTAH	(1198–1193 BC)
TAUSERT	(1193–1190 BC)
SETNAKHT	(1190–1187 BC)
RAMSES III	(1187–1156 BC)
RAMSES IV	(1156–1150 BC)
RAMSES V	(1150–1145 BC)
RAMSES VI	(1145–1137 BC)
RAMSES VII	(1137–c. 1132 BC)
RAMSES VIII	(c. 1132–1126 BC)
RAMSES IX	(1126–1108 BC)
RAMSES X	(1108–1104 BC)
RAMSES XI	(1104–c. 1075 BC)
SMENDES	(c. 1075 BC)
PINUDJEM I	
PSUSENNES I	(c. 1045–c. 997 BC)
AMENEMOPE	(c. 998–c. 989 BC)
OSORKON I	(c. 979–c. 973 BC)
PSUSENNES II	(c. 964–c. 950 BC)
SHESHONK	(c. 950–929 BC)
OSORKON II	(c. 929–c. 914 BC)
OSORKON III	(c. 888–c. 860 BC)
OSORKON IV	(c. 777–c. 750 BC)
KASHTA	
SHEPENWEPE I	
AMONIRDIS I	
BOCCHORIS	(c. 722–c. 715 BC)
SHABAKA	(c. 719–703 BC)
SHEBITKU	(703–690 BC)
TAHARQA	(690–664 BC)
TANUTAMON	(664 BC)
PSAMTIK I	(664–610 BC)
PSAMMETICHUS I	(664–610 BC)
NECHO II	(610–595 BC)
PSAMTIK II	(595–589 BC)
APRIES	(589–570 BC)
AMASIS II	(570–526 BC)
AHMOSE II	(570–526 BC)
CAMBYSES II	(526–522 BC)
DARIUS I	(522–486 BC)
ARTAXERXES I	(465–424 BC)
DARIUS II	(424–404 BC)
AMYRTAEUS	(404–399 BC)
ACHORIS	(393–380 BC)
NEPHERITES II	(380 BC)
NECTANEBO I	(380–362 BC)
TACHOS	(c. 365–360)
NECTANEBO II	(360–343 BC)

PTOLEMY I SOTER	(305–282 BC)	PTOLEMY VIII	(145–116 BC)
PTOLEMY II PHILADELPHUS	(285–246 BC)	EURGETES II	
PTOLEMY III EVERGETES	(246–222 BC)	PHYSCON	
PTOLEMY IV PHILOPATOR	(222–205 BC)	PTOLEMY XII AULETES	(80–51 BC)
PTOLEMY V EPIPHANES	(205–180 BC)	PTOLEMY XIII	(51–47 BC)
PTOLEMY VI PHILOMETOR	(180–145 BC)	CLEOPATRA VII	(51–30 BC)

ARTISTS, SCULPTORS, AND ARCHITECTS

3

ARP, Jean (1887–1966; French sculptor and poet)

DOU, Gerrit (1613–75; Dutch painter)

FRY, Roger (1866–1934; British painter and art critic)

LIN, Maya (1959– ; US sculptor and architect)

LOW, Sir David (1871–1963; New Zealand-born cartoonist)

4

ADAM, Robert (1728–92; British architect and interior designer)

CAPP, Al (Alfred Caplin, 1909–79; US cartoonist)

CUYP, Aelbert Jacobsz (1620–91; Dutch landscape painter)

DADD, Richard (1817–86; British painter)

DALI, Salvador (1904–89; Spanish surrealist painter)

DORÉ, Gustave (1832–83; French illustrator, painter, and sculptor)

DUFY, Raoul (1877–1953; French painter)

EMIN, Tracey (1963– ; British artist)

ERTÉ (Romain de Tirtoff, 1892–1990; French fashion illustrator and designer, born in Russia)

ETTY, William (1787–1849; British painter)

GABO, Naum (Naum Neemia Pevsner, 1890–1977; Russian sculptor)

GOES, Hugo van der (c. 1440–82; Flemish painter)

GOYA, Francesco de (1746–1828; Spanish painter)

4–continued

GRIS, Juan (José Victoriano González, 1887–1927; Spanish-born cubist painter)

GROS, Antoine Jean, Baron (1771–1835; French painter)

HALS, Frans (c. 1581–1666; Dutch painter)

HILL, David Octavius (1802–70; Scottish painter and photographer)

HUNT, William Holman (1827–1910; British painter)

JOHN, Augustus (1878–1961; British painter)

KAHN, Louis Isadore (1901–74; US architect)

KENT, William (1685–1748; English architect, landscape gardener, and interior designer)

KLEE, Paul (1879–1940; Swiss painter and etcher)

LAMB, Henry (1885–1960; Australian-born British painter)

LELY, Sir Peter (Pieter van der Faes, 1618–80; English portrait painter of Dutch descent)

LOOS, Adolph (1870–1933; Austrian architect)

MAES, Nicolas (or N Maas, 1634–93; Dutch painter)

MARC, Franz (1880–1916; German expressionist painter)

MIRÓ, Joan (1893–1983; Spanish painter)

NASH, John (1752–1835; British architect)

NASH, Paul (1889–1946; British painter)

NEER, Aert van der (c. 1603–77; Dutch landscape painter)

OPIE, John (1761–1807; British portrait and history painter)

4–continued

RENI, Guido (1575–1642; Italian painter)

ROSA, Salvator (1615–73; Italian painter and etcher)

SHAW, Norman (1831–1912; British architect)

WARD, Sir Leslie (1851–1922; British caricaturist)

WEST, Benjamin (1738–1820; British painter of American birth)

WOOD, Christopher (1901–30; English painter)

WOOD, Grant (1892–1942; US painter)

WOOD, John, of Bath (1704–54; English architect)

WREN, Sir Christopher (1632–1723; English architect and scientist)

ZORN, Anders (1860–1920; Swedish artist)

5

AALTO, Alvar (1898–1976; Finnish architect)

ATGET, Eugène (1856–1927; French photographer)

BACON, Francis (1909–92; British painter, born in Dublin)

BACON, John (1740–99; British neoclassical sculptor)

BAKST, Léon (Lev Samoilovich Rosenberg, 1866–1924; Russian artist)

BALLA, Giacomo (1871–1958; Italian futurist painter)

BARRY, Sir Charles (1795–1860; British architect)

BLAKE, Peter (1932– ; British artist)

BLAKE, Quentin (1932– ; British artist)

BOSCH, Hieronymus (Jerome van Aeken, c. 1450–c. 1516; Dutch painter)

5–continued

BOUTS, Dierick (c. 1400–75; Netherlandish painter)

BROWN, Capability (Lancelot B, 1716–83; British landscape gardener)

BROWN, Ford Madox (1821–93; British painter, born in Calais)

BURRA, Edward (1905–76; British painter)

CAMPI, Giulio (1502–72; Italian Renaissance architect)

COROT, Jean Baptiste Camille (1796–1875; French landscape painter)

CRANE, Walter (1845–1915; British illustrator, painter, and designer of textiles and wallpaper)

CROME, John (1768–1821; British landscape painter and etcher)

DAGLY, Gerhard (c. 1653–?1714; Belgian artist)

DANBY, Francis (1793–1861; Irish painter)

DANCE, George (c. 1700–68; British architect)

DAVID, Gerard (c. 1460–1523; Netherlandish painter)

DAVID, Jacques Louis (1748–1825; French painter)

DEGAS, Edgar (1834–1917; French painter and sculptor)

DENIS, Maurice (1870–1943; French painter, designer, and art theorist)

DÜRER, Albrecht (1471–1528; German painter)

ENSOR, James Sydney, Baron (1860–1949; Belgian painter)

ERNST, Max (1891–1976; German artist)

FOLEY, John Henry (1818–74; British sculptor)

FREUD, Lucian (1922–   ; German-born British painter)

GADDI, Taddeo (c. 1300–?1366; Florentine painter)

GEHRY, Frank Owen (1929–   ; US architect)

GIBBS, James (1682–1754; British architect)

GILES, Carl Ronald (1916–95; British cartoonist)

GORKY, Arshile (Vosdanig Adoian, 1905–48; US painter, born in Armenia)

GOYEN, Jan Josephszoon van (1596–1656; Dutch landscape painter and etcher)

5–continued

GRANT, Duncan James Corrowr (1885–1978; British painter and designer)

GROSZ, George (1893–1959; German painter and draughtsman)

HIRST, Damien (1965–   ; British artist and sculptor)

HOMER, Winslow (1836–1910; US painter)

HOOCH, Pieter de (1629–c. 1684; Dutch painter)

HORTA, Victor (1861–1947; Belgian architect)

JOHNS, Jasper (1930–   ; US artist)

JONES, Inigo (1573–1652; English classical architect)

KEENE, Charles Samuel (1823–91; British artist and illustrator)

KLIMT, Gustav (1862–1918; Viennese Art Nouveau artist)

KLINT, Kaare (1888–1954; Danish furniture designer)

LEACH, Bernard (1887–1979; British potter, born in Hong Kong)

LEECH, John (1817–64; British caricaturist)

LÉGER, Fernand (1881–1955; French painter)

LE VAU, Louis (1612–70; French baroque architect)

LIPPI, Fra Filippo (c. 1406–69; Florentine painter)

LOTTO, Lorenzo (c. 1480–1556; Venetian painter)

LOWRY, L S (1887–1976; British painter)

MACKE, August (1887–1914; German painter)

MANET, Edouard (1832–83; French painter)

MENGS, Anton Raphael (1728–79; German painter)

METSU, Gabriel (1629–67; Dutch painter)

MONET, Claude (1840–1926; French impressionist painter)

MOORE, Henry (1898–1986; British sculptor)

MOSES, Grandma (Anna Mary Robertson M, 1860–1961; US primitive painter)

MUNCH, Edvard (1863–1944; Norwegian painter and printmaker)

MYRON (5th century BC; Athenian sculptor)

5–continued

NADAR (Gaspard Felix Tournachon, 1820–1910; French photographer and caricaturist)

NERVI, Pier Luigi (1891–1979; Italian architect)

NOLAN, Sir Sidney (1917–92; Australian painter)

NOLDE, Emil (E Hansen, 1867–1956; German expressionist painter and printmaker)

OUDRY, Jean-Baptiste (1686–1755; French rococo painter and tapestry designer)

PHYFE, Duncan (or Fife, 1768–1854; US cabinetmaker and furniture designer, born in Scotland)

PIPER, John (1903–92; British painter and writer)

PUGIN, Augustus Welby Northmore (1812–52; British architect and theorist)

REDON, Odilon (1840–1916; French symbolist painter and lithographer)

RICCI, Sebastiano (1659–1734; Venetian painter)

RILEY, Bridget Louise (1931–   ; British painter)

RODIN, Auguste (1840–1917; French sculptor)

SCOTT, Sir George Gilbert (1811–78; British architect)

SHAHN, Ben (1898–1969; Lithuanian-born US artist)

SOANE, Sir John (1753–1837; British architect)

STEEN, Jan (c. 1626–79; Dutch painter)

STOSS, Veit (c. 1445–1533; German gothic sculptor and woodcarver)

TOBEY, Mark (1890–1976; US painter)

VICKY (Victor Weisz, 1913–66; British cartoonist, born in Berlin)

WATTS, George Frederick (1817–1904; British artist)

WYATT, James (1747–1813; British architect)

6

ALBERS, Josef (1888–1976; German abstract painter)

6–continued

ARCHER, Thomas (1668–1743; English baroque architect)

BEATON, Sir Cecil (1904–80; British photographer)

BEHZAD (*c.* 1455–*c.* 1536; Persian painter)

BENTON, Thomas Hart (1889–1975; US painter)

BEWICK, Thomas (1753–1828; British wood engraver)

BOUDIN, Eugène (1824–98; French painter)

BOULLE, André Charles (*or* Buhl, 1642–1732; French cabinetmaker)

BRANDT, Bill (1905–83; British photographer)

BRAQUE, Georges (1882–1963; French painter)

BRATBY, John (1928–92; British painter and writer)

BREUER, Marcel Lajos (1902–81; US architect, born in Hungary)

BUFFET, Bernard (1928–99; French painter)

BUTLER, Reg Cotterell (1913–81; British sculptor)

CALDER, Alexander (1898–1976; US sculptor)

CALLOT, Jacques (*c.* 1592–1635; French graphic artist)

CANOVA, Antonio (1757–1822; Italian sculptor)

CASSON, Sir Hugh (1910–99; British architect)

CLOUET, Jean (*c.* 1485–1540; French portrait painter)

COOPER, Samuel (1609–72; British miniaturist)

COSWAY, Richard (1742–1821; British portrait miniaturist)

COTMAN, John Sell (1782–1842; British landscape watercolourist and etcher)

DERAIN, André (1880–1954; French postimpressionist painter)

DE WINT, Peter (1784–1849; British landscape painter)

EAKINS, Thomas (1844–1916; US painter)

FLORIS, Cornelis (1514–75; Flemish artist)

FLORIS, Frans (*c.* 1516–70; Flemish artist)

FOSTER, Norman (1935– ; British architect)

6–continued

FULLER, Richard Buckminster (1895–1983; US inventor and architect)

FUSELI, Henry (Johann Heinrich Füssli, 1741–1825; British painter of Swiss birth)

GÉRARD, François, Baron (1770–1837; French painter)

GIOTTO (Giotto di Bondone, *c.* 1266–1337; Italian painter and architect)

GIRTIN, Thomas (1775–1802; British landscape painter)

GOUJON, Jean (*c.* 1510–68; French Renaissance sculptor)

GREUZE, Jean-Baptiste (1725–1805; French painter)

GUARDI, Francesco (1712–93; Venetian painter)

HOLLAR, Wenceslaus (1607–77; Bohemian etcher)

HOUDON, Jean Antoine (1741–1828; French sculptor)

INGRES, Jean-Auguste-Dominique (1780–1867; French painter)

ISABEY, Jean Baptiste (1767–1855; French portrait painter and miniaturist)

JOCHHO (d. 1057; Japanese sculptor)

KNIGHT, Dame Laura (1877–1970; British painter)

LASDUN, Sir Denys (1914– ; British architect)

LA TOUR, Georges de (1593–1652; French painter)

LA TOUR, Maurice-Quentin de (1704–88; French portrait pastellist)

LE BRUN, Charles (1619–90; French history and portrait painter and designer)

LE NAIN, Antoine (*c.* 1588–1648; French painter)

LE NAIN, Louis (*c.* 1593–1648; French painter)

LE NAIN, Mathieu (*c.* 1607–77; French painter)

LESCOT, Pierre (*c.* 1510–78; French architect)

LONGHI, Pietro (Pietro Falca, 1702–85; Venetian painter)

LURÇAT, Jean (1892–1966; French painter)

MARINI, Marino (1901–80; Italian sculptor and painter)

MARTIN, John (1789–1854; British painter)

6–continued

MASSYS, Quentin (*or* Matsys, Messys, Metsys, *c.* 1466–1530; Flemish painter)

MILLET, Jean François (1814–75; French painter)

MOREAU, Gustave (1826–98; French symbolist painter)

MORONI, Giovanni Battista (*c.* 1525–78; Italian painter)

MORRIS, William (1834–96; British designer and artist)

OLIVER, Isaac (?1556–1617; English portrait miniaturist, born in France)

OROZCO, José (1883–1949; Mexican mural painter)

OSTADE, Adrian van (1610–85; Dutch painter and etcher)

PALMER, Samuel (1805–81; British landscape painter and etcher)

PAXTON, Sir Joseph (1801–65; British architect)

PISANO, Andrea (Andrea de Pontedera, *c.* 1290–1348; Italian sculptor)

PISANO, Nicola (*c.* 1220–*c.* 1278; Italian sculptor)

RENOIR, Pierre Auguste (1841–1919; French impressionist painter)

RIBERA, José de (*or* Jusepe R, 1591– 1652; Spanish-born painter and etcher)

RIVERA, Diego (1886–1957; Mexican mural painter)

ROMNEY, George (1734–1802; British portrait painter)

ROTHKO, Mark (Marcus Rothkovitch, 1903–70; Russian-born US painter)

RUBENS, Peter Paul (1577–1640; Flemish painter)

SCARFE, Gerald (1936– ; British cartoonist)

SEARLE, Ronald William Fordham (1920– ; British cartoonist)

SESSHU (Sesshu Toyo, 1420–1506; Japanese landscape painter)

SEURAT, Georges (1859–91; French painter)

SIGNAC, Paul (1863–1935; French painter and art theorist)

SISLEY, Alfred (1839–99; Impressionist painter)

SLUTER, Claus (*c.* 1345–1406; Dutch sculptor)

6–continued

SPENCE, Sir Basil (1907–76; British architect)

STUBBS, George (1724–1806; British animal painter)

TANGUY, Yves (1900–55; French surrealist painter)

TISSOT, James Joseph Jacques (1836–1902; French painter and etcher)

TITIAN (Tiziano Vecellio, c. 1488–1576; Venetian painter)

TURNER, Joseph Mallord William (1775–1851; British landscape and marine painter)

VASARI, Giorgio (1511–74; Italian painter, architect, and writer)

VOYSEY, Charles Francis Annesley (1857–1941; British architect and designer)

WARHOL, Andy (Andrew Warhola, 1926–87; US pop artist)

WEYDEN, Rogier van der (c. 1400–64; Flemish painter)

WILKIE, Sir David (1785–1841; Scottish painter)

WILSON, Richard (1714–82; British landscape painter)

WRIGHT, Frank Lloyd (1869–1959; US architect)

XIA GUI (or Hsia Knei, c. 1180–c. 1230, Chinese landscape painter)

ZEUXIS (late 5th century BC; Greek painter)

7

ALBERTI, Leon Battista (1404–72; Italian Renaissance architect)

ALLSTON, Washington (1779–1843; US Romantic painter)

ANTENOR (late 6th century BC; Athenian sculptor)

APELLES (4th century BC; Greek painter)

ASTBURY, John (1688–1743; English potter)

BARLACH, Ernst (1870–1938; German expressionist sculptor and playwright)

BASSANO, Jacopo (Jacopo or Giacomo da Ponte, c. 1517–92; Italian painter)

BEHRENS, Peter (1868–1940; German architect)

BELLINI, Jacopo (c. 1400–c. 1470; Venetian painter)

7–continued

BERNINI, Gian Lorenzo (1598–1680; Italian sculptor and architect)

BONNARD, Pierre (1867–1947; French painter)

BORGLUM, Gutzon (1867–1941; US sculptor)

BOUCHER, François (1703–70; French rococo painter)

BROUWER, Adriaen (c. 1605–38; Flemish painter)

CAMERON, Julia Margaret (1815–79; British photographer, born in Calcutta)

CASSATT, Mary (1844–1926; US painter)

CELLINI, Benvenuto (1500–71; Florentine goldsmith and sculptor)

CENNINI, Cennino (c. 1370–c. 1440; Florentine painter)

CÉZANNE, Paul (1839–1906; French postimpressionist painter)

CHAGALL, Marc (1887–1985; Russian-born painter and printmaker)

CHARDIN, Jean-Baptiste-Siméon (1699–1779; French painter)

CHIRICO, Giorgio de (1888–1978; Italian painter)

CHRISTO (1935– ; Bulgarian-born artist)

CIMABUE, Giovanni (Cenni de Peppi, c. 1240–c. 1302; Florentine painter)

CLODION (Claude Michel, 1738–1814; French rococo sculptor)

COURBET, Gustave (1819–77; French painter)

DAUMIER, Honoré (1808–79; French caricaturist, painter, and sculptor)

DELORME, Philibert (?1510–70; French Renaissance architect)

DELVAUX, Paul (1897–94; Belgian painter)

DUCHAMP, Marcel (1887–1968; French artist)

EL GRECO (Domenikos Theotokopoulos, 1541–1614; Painter of Greek parentage, born in Crete)

EPSTEIN, Sir Jacob (1880–1959; British sculptor)

EXEKIAS (6th century BC; Athenian potter and vase painter)

7–continued

FABERGÉ, Peter Carl (1846–1920; Russian goldsmith and jeweller)

FLAXMAN, John Henry (1755–1826; British sculptor and book illustrator)

FONTANA, Domenico (1543–1607; Italian architect)

FOUQUET, Jean (c. 1420–81; French painter and manuscript illuminator)

GAUGUIN, Paul (1848–1903; French postimpressionist painter)

GIBBONS, Grinling (1648–1721; English wood carver and sculptor)

GILLRAY, James (1756–1815; British caricaturist)

GOZZOLI, Benozzo (Benozzo di Lese, 1420–97; Florentine painter)

GROPIUS, Walter (1883–1969; German architect)

GUARINI, Guarino (1624–83; Italian baroque architect)

HASSALL, John (1868–1948; British artist)

HERRERA, Juan de (1530–97; Spanish architect)

HOBBEMA, Meindert (1638–1709; Dutch landscape painter)

HOCKNEY, David (1937– ; British painter, draughtsman, and printmaker)

HOGARTH, William (1697–1764; British painter and engraver)

HOKUSAI (Katsushika H, 1760–1849; Japanese painter and book illustrator)

HOLLAND, Henry (1745–1806; British architect)

HOPPNER, John (1758–1810; British portrait painter)

ICTINUS (5th century BC; Greek architect)

JOHNSON, Cornelius (Janssen van Ceulen, 1593–1661; English portrait painter)

KNELLER, Sir Godfrey (1646–1723; English portrait painter)

LALIQUE, René (1860–1945; French Art Nouveau jeweller and glassmaker)

LAMERIE, Paul de (1688–1751; English silversmith)

L'ENFANT, Pierre-Charles (1754–1825; US architect and town planner of French birth)

7–continued

LE NÔTRE, André (1613–1700; French landscape gardener)

LIMBURG, Pol de (active c. 1400–c. 1416; French manuscript illuminator)

LIMOSIN, Léonard (or Limousin, c. 1505–c. 1577; French artist)

LOCHNER, Stefan (c. 1400–51; German painter)

LUTYENS, Sir Edwin Landseer (1869–1944; British architect)

MACLISE, Daniel (1806–70; Irish portrait and history painter)

MADERNA, Carlo (1556–1629; Roman architect)

MAILLOL, Aristide (1861–1944; French sculptor)

MANSART, François (or Mansard, 1596–1666; French classical architect)

MARTINI, Simone (c. 1284–1344; Italian painter)

MATISSE, Henri (1869–1954; French painter and sculptor)

MEMLING, Hans (or Memlinc, c. 1430–1494; German painter)

MILLAIS, Sir John Everett (1829–96; British painter)

MORANDI, Giorgio (1890–1964; Italian still-life painter and etcher)

MORISOT, Berthe (1841–95; French painter)

MORLAND, George (1763–1804; British painter)

MURILLO, Bartolomé Esteban (1617–82; Spanish painter)

NEUMANN, Balthasar (1687–1753; German architect)

O'KEEFFE, Georgia (1887–1986; US painter)

ORCAGNA, Andrea (Andrea di Cione, c. 1308–c. 1368; Florentine artist)

PALISSY, Bernard (1510–89; French potter)

PASMORE, Victor (1908–98; British artist)

PATINIR, Joachim (or Patenier, c. 1485–1524; Flemish painter)

PEVSNER, Antoine (1886–1962; Russian sculptor and painter)

PHIDIAS (c. 490–c. 417 BC; Athenian sculptor)

7–continued

PICABIA, Francis (1879–1953; French painter and writer)

PICASSO, Pablo (1881–1973; Spanish artist)

POLLOCK, Jackson (1912–56; US painter)

POUSSIN, Nicolas (1594–1665; French painter)

PRUD'HON, Pierre Paul (1758–1823; French painter and draughtsman)

RACKHAM, Arthur (1867–1939; British watercolourist and book illustrator)

RAEBURN, Sir Henry (1756–1823; Scottish portrait painter)

RAPHAEL (Raffaello Sanzio, 1483–1520; Italian Renaissance painter and architect)

REDOUTÉ, Pierre Joseph (1759–1841; French flower painter)

ROBERTS, Tom (1856–1931; Australian painter, born in Britain)

ROUAULT, Georges (1871–1958; French artist)

RUBLYOV, Andrey (or A Rublev, c. 1370–1430; Russian icon painter)

SARGENT, John Singer (1856–1925; US portrait painter, born in Florence)

SCHIELE, Egon (1890–1918; Austrian expressionist painter)

SEGHERS, Hercules Pieterzoon (c. 1589–c. 1638; Dutch landscape painter and etcher)

SHEPARD, Ernest Howard (1879–1976; British artist)

SICKERT, Walter Richard (1860–1942; British impressionist, born in Munich)

SNOWDON, Antony Armstrong-Jones, Earl of (1930– ; British photographer)

SNYDERS, Frans (1579–1657; Flemish animal painter)

SOUTINE, Chaim (1893–1943; Lithuanian-born painter, who emigrated to Paris)

SPENCER, Sir Stanley (1891–1959; British painter)

TENNIEL, Sir John (1820–1914; British cartoonist and book illustrator)

7–continued

TIBALDI, Pellegrino (1527–96; Italian architect and painter)

TIEPOLO, Giovanni Battista (1696–1770; Venetian rococo painter)

UCCELLO, Paolo (P di Dono, 1397–1475; Florentine painter and craftsman)

UTRILLO, Maurice (1883–1955; French painter)

VAN DYCK, Sir Anthony (or Vandyke, 1599–1641; Flemish baroque painter)

VAN EYCK, Jan (c. 1390–1441; Flemish painter)

VAN GOGH, Vincent (1853–90; Dutch postimpressionist painter)

VERMEER, Jan (1632–75; Dutch painter)

VIGNOLA, Giacomo da (1507–73; Roman mannerist architect)

WATTEAU, Antoine (1684–1721; French rococo painter)

ZADKINE, Ossip (1890–1967; French sculptor of Russian birth)

ZOFFANY, Johann (c. 1733–1810; German-born English painter)

ZUCCARO, Federico (1543–1609; Italian painter)

ZUCCARO, Taddeo (1529–66; Italian painter)

8

AALTONEN, Wäinö (1894–1966; Finnish sculptor)

AMMANATI, Bartolommeo (1511–92; Florentine architect and sculptor)

ANGELICO, Fra (Guido di Pietro, c. 1400–55; Italian painter)

ANNIGONI, Pietro (1910–88; Italian painter)

ANTELAMI, Benedetto (active 1177–1233; Italian sculptor)

BECKMANN, Max (1884–1950; German expressionist painter)

BOCCIONI, Umberto (1882–1916; Italian futurist painter and sculptor)

BRAMANTE, Donato (1444–1514; Italian Renaissance architect)

BRANCUSI, Constantin (1876–1957; Romanian sculptor)

8–continued

BRONZINO, Il (Agnolo di Cosimo, 1503–72; Florentine mannerist painter)

CARRACCI, Annibale (1560–1609; Italian painter)

CASTAGNO, Andrea del (Andrea di Bartolo de Simone, c. 1421–57; Italian painter)

CHAMBERS, Sir William (1723–96; British architect and interior designer)

CRESSENT, Charles (1685–1768; French cabinetmaker)

CRIVELLI, Carlo (c. 1430–95; Venetian painter)

DAUBIGNY, Charles-François (1817–78; French landscape painter)

DELAUNAY, Robert (1885–1941; French painter)

DRYSDALE, Sir Russell (1912–81; Australian painter, born in England)

DUBUFFET, Jean (1901–85; French painter and sculptor)

FILARETE (Antonio Averlino, c. 1400–c. 1469; Italian Renaissance architect)

FRAMPTON, Sir George James (1860–1928; British sculptor)

GHIBERTI, Lorenzo (c. 1378–1455; Florentine Renaissance sculptor)

GIORDANO, Luca (1632–1705; Neapolitan painter, nicknamed LUCA FA PRESTO)

GOSSAERT, Jan (c. 1478–c. 1532; Flemish painter)

GUERCINO (Giovanni Francesco Barbieri, 1591–1666; Italian painter)

HEPWORTH, Dame Barbara (1903–75; British sculptor)

HILLIARD, Nicholas (1547–1619; English portrait miniaturist)

JACOBSEN, Arne (1902–71; Danish architect and designer of furniture and wallpaper)

JONGKIND, Johan Barthold (1819–91; Dutch landscape painter and etcher)

JORDAENS, Jakob (1593–1678; Flemish painter)

KIRCHNER, Ernst Ludwig (1880–1938; German expressionist painter and printmaker)

8–continued

LANDSEER, Sir Edwin Henry (1802–73; British artist)

LAWRENCE, Sir Thomas (1769–1830; British painter)

LIPCHITZ, Jacques (1891–1973; Lithuanian cubist sculptor)

LOMBARDO, Pietro (c. 1438–1515; Italian sculptor and architect)

LYSIPPUS (4th century BC; Court sculptor of Alexander the Great)

MAGRITTE, René (1898–1967; Belgian surrealist painter)

MALEVICH, Kazimir (1878–1935; Russian painter and art theorist)

MANTEGNA, Andrea (c. 1431–1506; Italian Renaissance painter and engraver)

MASACCIO (Tommaso di Giovanni di Simone Guidi, 1401–28; Florentine painter)

MASOLINO (Tommaso di Cristoforo Fini, 1383–?1447; Italian painter)

MEEGEREN, Hans van (1889–1947; Dutch painter)

MONDRIAN, Piet (Pieter Cornelis Mondriaan, 1872–1944; Dutch painter)

MULREADY, William (1786–1863; British painter)

MUNNINGS, Sir Alfred (1878–1959; British painter)

NIEMEYER, Oscar (1907– ; Brazilian architect)

PALLADIO, Andrea (1508–80; Italian architect)

PIRANESI, Giambattista (1720–78; Italian etcher)

PISSARRO, Camille (1830–1903; French impressionist painter)

PONTORMO, Jacopo da (J Carrucci, 1494–1557; Italian mannerist painter)

REYNOLDS, Sir Joshua (1723–92; British portrait painter)

ROBINSON, William Heath (1872–1944; British cartoonist and book illustrator)

ROUSSEAU, Henri (1844–1910; French painter)

ROUSSEAU, Théodore (1812–67; French Romantic painter)

RUISDAEL, Jacob van (?1628–82; Dutch landscape painter)

8–continued

SAARINEN, Eero (1910–61; US architect, born in Finland)

SASSETTA (Stefano di Giovanni, c. 1392–c. 1450; Italian painter)

SEVERINI, Gino (1883–1966; Italian painter)

SHERATON, Thomas (1751–1806; British furniture designer)

SOUFFLOT, Jacques Germain (1713–80; French architect)

SULLIVAN, Louis Henry (1856–1924; US architect)

TERBORCH, Gerard (1617–81; Dutch painter)

VANBRUGH, Sir John (1664–1726; English architect)

VASARELY, Victor (1908–97; Hungarian-born painter)

VERONESE, Paolo (P Caliari, 1528–88; Italian painter)

VLAMINCK, Maurice de (1876–1958; French painter)

VUILLARD, Édouard (1868–1940; French artist)

WEDGWOOD, Josiah (1730–95; British potter, industrialist, and writer)

WHISTLER, James McNeill (1834–1903; US painter)

WHISTLER, Rex (1905–44; British artist)

WOOLLETT, William (1735–85; British engraver)

ZURBARÁN, Francisco de (1598–1664; Spanish painter)

9

ALTDORFER, Albrecht (c. 1480–1538; German artist)

BARTHOLDI, Frédéric August (1834–1904; French sculptor)

BEARDSLEY, Aubrey Vincent (1872–98; British illustrator)

BONINGTON, Richard Parkes (1801–28; British painter)

BORROMINI, Francesco (1599–1667; Italian baroque architect)

BOURDELLE, Émile (1861–1929; French sculptor)

CANALETTO (Antonio Canal, 1697–1768; Venetian painter)

CARPACCIO, Vittore (c. 1460–c. 1525; Venetian painter)

CAVALLINI, Pietro (c. 1250–c. 1330; Italian painter)

Rembrandt (1606–1669) ARTISTS, SCULPTORS, AND ARCHITECTS

9–continued

COCKERELL, Charles Robert
(1788–1863; British architect)

CONSTABLE, John
(1776–1837; British
landscape painter)

CORNELIUS, Peter von
(1783–1867; German painter)

CORREGGIO (Antonio Allegri,
c. 1494–1534; Italian
Renaissance painter)

DE KOONING, Willem
(1904–89; US painter of
Dutch birth)

DELACROIX, Eugène
(1798–1863; French
Romantic painter)

DELAROCHE, Paul
(1797–1859; French history
and portrait painter)

DONATELLO (Donato de
Nicolo di Betti Bardi, c.
1386–1466; Florentine
sculptor)

FABRITIUS, Carel (1622–54;
Dutch painter)

FEININGER, Lyonel
(1871–1956; US painter and
illustrator)

FRAGONARD, Jean Honoré
(1732–1806; French rococo
painter)

FRIEDRICH, Caspar David
(1774–1840; German
Romantic landscape painter)

GÉRICAULT, Théodore
(1791–1824; French painter)

GIORGIONE (c. 1477–1510;
Italian painter)

GREENAWAY, Kate
(1846–1901; British artist and
book illustrator)

GREENOUGH, Horatio (1805–
52; US neoclassical sculptor)

GRÜNEWALD, Matthias
(Mathis Gothardt, d. 1528;
German painter)

HAWKSMOOR, Nicholas
(1661–1736; English baroque
architect)

HIROSHIGE (Ando Tokitaro,
1797–1858; Japanese colour
print artist)

HONTHORST, Gerrit von
(1590–1656; Dutch painter)

JAWLENSKY, Alexey von
(1864–1941; Russian
expressionist painter)

KANDINSKY, Wassily
(1866–1944; Russian
expressionist painter and art
theorist)

9–continued

KAUFFMANN, Angelica
(1741–1807; Swiss painter)

KOKOSCHKA, Oskar
(1886–1980; Austrian expressionist painter and writer)

LISSITZKY, El (Eliezer L,
1890–1941; Russian painter
and architect)

MEŠTROVIĆ, Ivan
(1883–1962; US sculptor,
born in Yugoslavia)

MUYBRIDGE, Eadweard
(Edward James Muggeridge,
1830–1904; US
photographer, born in Britain)

NICHOLSON, Ben
(1894–1982; British artist)

NOLLEKENS, Joseph
(1737–1823; British
neoclassical sculptor)

OLDENBURG, Claes;
(1929–   ; US sculptor, born
in Sweden)

PISANELLO (Antonio Pisano,
c. 1395–c. 1455; Italian
international gothic painter,
draughtsman, and medallist)

ROUBILLAC, Louis François (or
L F Roubiliac, 1695–1762;
French sculptor)

SIQUEIROS, David Alfaro
(1896–1974; Mexican painter)

STIEGLITZ, Alfred (1864–1946;
US photographer)

THORNHILL, Sir James
(1675–1734; English baroque
decorative painter)

VELÁZQUEZ, Diego Rodriguez
de Silva (1599–1660; Spanish
painter)

VITRUVIUS (Marcus Vitruvius
Pollio, 1st century BC; Roman
architect)

WOUWERMAN, Philips
(1619–68; Dutch painter)

10

ALMA-TADEMA, Sir Lawrence
(1836–1912; Dutch painter)

ALTICHIERO (c. 1330–c. 1390;
Italian painter)

ARCHIPENKO, Alexander
(1887–1964; Russian-born
sculptor and painter)

ARCIMBOLDO, Giuseppe
(1527–93; Mannerist painter)

BERRUGUETE, Alonso (c.
1488–1561; Castillian painter)

BERRUGUETE, Pedro (c.
1450–c. 1504; Castillian
painter)

10–continued

BOTTICELLI, Sandro
(Alessandro di Mariano
Filipepi, c. 1445–1510;
Florentine Renaissance
painter)

BURLINGTON, Richard Boyle,
3rd Earl of (1694–1753;
English architect)

BURNE-JONES, Sir Edward
Coley (1833–98; Pre-
Raphaelite painter)

CARAVAGGIO (Michelangelo
Merisi, 1573–1610; Italian
painter)

CHAMPAIGNE, Philippe de
(1602–74; French portrait
painter)

CRUIKSHANK, George
(1792–1872; British
caricaturist, painter, and
illustrator)

EUPHRONIOS (late 6th–early
5th centuries BC; Athenian
potter and vase painter)

GIACOMETTI, Alberto
(1901–66; Swiss sculptor and
painter)

LORENZETTI, Ambrogio (c.
1290–?1348; Italian painter)

MACKINTOSH, Charles Rennie
(1868–1928; Scottish
architect and designer)

MEISSONIER, Jean-Louis-
Ernest (1815–91; French
painter)

MODIGLIANI, Amedeo
(1884–1920; Italian painter
and sculptor)

MOHOLY-NAGY, László
(1895–1946; Hungarian artist)

MOTHERWELL, Robert
(1915–91; US abstract
painter)

POLLAIUOLO, Antonio (c.
1432–98; Florentine
Renaissance artist)

POLYCLITUS (5th century BC;
Greek sculptor)

PRAXITELES (mid-4th century
BC; Athenian sculptor)

RICHARDSON, Henry Hobson
(1838–86; US architect)

ROWLANDSON, Thomas
(1756–1827; British
caricaturist)

SCHWITTERS, Kurt
(1887–1958; German artist
and poet)

SENEFELDER, Aloys
(1771–1834; German
playwright and engraver)

101

10–continued

SIGNORELLI, Luca (c. 1441–1523; Italian Renaissance painter)

SUTHERLAND, Graham Vivian (1903–80; British artist)

TANGE KENZO (1913– ; Japanese architect)

TINTORETTO (Jacopo Robusti, 1518–94; Venetian painter)

VAN DE VELDE, Henry (1863–1957; Belgian Art Nouveau architect, interior designer, and painter)

VERROCCHIO, Andrea del (Andrea del Cione, c. 1435–88; Italian sculptor, painter, and goldsmith)

WATERHOUSE, Alfred (1830–1905; British architect)

ZUCCARELLI, Francesco (1702–88; Italian painter)

11

ABERCROMBIE, Sir Patrick (1879–1957; British architect)

BARTOLOMMEO, Fra (Baccio della Porta, c. 1472–1517; Florentine Renaissance painter)

BUTTERFIELD, William (1814–1900; British architect)

CALLICRATES (5th century BC; Athenian architect)

CALLIMACHUS (late 5th century BC; Greek sculptor)

CHIPPENDALE, Thomas (1718–79; British cabinetmaker)

CHODOWIECKI, Daniel Nikolaus (1726–1801; German painter and engraver)

DELLA ROBBIA, Luca (1400–82; Florentine Renaissance sculptor)

DOMENICHINO (Domenico Zampieri, 1581–1641; Italian painter)

GHIRLANDAIO, Domenico (Domenico di Tommaso Bigordi, 1449–94; Florentine painter)

GIAMBOLOGNA (Giovanni da Bologna or Jean de Boulogne, 1529–1608; Italian mannerist sculptor)

GISLEBERTUS (early 12th century; French romanesque sculptor)

11–continued

HEPPLEWHITE, George (d. 1786; British furniture designer and cabinetmaker)

LE CORBUSIER (Charles-Édouard Jeanneret, 1887–1965; French architect, born in Switzerland)

TERBRUGGHEN, Hendrik (1588–1629; Dutch painter)

THORVALDSEN, Bertel (or B Thorwaldsen, 1768–1844; Danish sculptor)

12

BRUNELLESCHI, Filippo (1377–1446; Italian architect)

FANTIN-LATOUR, Henri (1836–1904; French painter)

GAINSBOROUGH, Thomas (1727–88; British portrait and landscape painter)

GAUDÍ Y CORNET, Antonio (1852–1926; Spanish architect)

GIULIO ROMANO (Giulio Pippi, c. 1499–1546; Italian mannerist painter and architect)

LICHTENSTEIN, Roy (1923–97; US painter)

LUCA FA PRESTO (Nickname of Luca Giordano)

PALMA VECCHIO, Jacopo (J Negretti, c. 1480–1528; Italian painter)

PARMIGIANINO (Girolamo Francesco Maria Mazzola, 1503–40; Italian painter)

PINTURICCHIO (Bernardino di Betto, c. 1454–1513; Italian Renaissance painter)

RAUSCHENBERG, Robert (1925– ; US artist)

VIOLLET-LE-DUC, Eugène Emmanuel (1814–79; French architect and author)

WINTERHALTER, Franz Xavier (1806–73; German painter and lithographer)

13

LORENZO MONACO (Piero di Giovanni, c. 1370–1425; Italian painter)

PIERO DI COSIMO (P di Lorenzo, 1462–1521; Florentine Renaissance painter)

WILLIAMS-ELLIS, Sir Clough (1883–1978; Welsh architect)

14

ANDREA DEL SARTO (Andrea d'Agnolo, 1486–1530; Italian painter)

BÉRAIN THE ELDER, Jean (1637–1711; French designer, engraver, and painter)

CARTIER-BRESSON, Henri (1908–2004; French photographer)

CLAUDE LORRAINE (Claude Gellée, 1600–82; French landscape painter)

COUSIN THE ELDER, Jean (1490–1560; French artist and craftsman)

GAUDIER-BRZESKA, Henri (1891–1915; French sculptor)

LUCAS VAN LEYDEN (Lucas Hugensz or Jacobsz, c. 1494–1533; Dutch artist)

MIES VAN DER ROHE, Ludwig (1886–1969; German architect)

15

CRANACH THE ELDER, Lucas (Lucas Müller, 1472–1553; German artist)

HARDOUIN-MANSART, Jules (1646–1708; French baroque architect)

KITAGAWA UTAMARO (1753–1806; Japanese artist)

LEONARDO DA VINCI (1452–1519; Italian artistic and scientific genius of the Renaissance)

TOULOUSE-LAUTREC, Henri de (1864–1901; French artist)

16

BRUEGHEL THE ELDER, Pieter (or Bruegel, 1525–69; Flemish painter)

FISCHER VON ERLACH, Johann Bernhard (1656–1723; Austrian architect)

PUVIS DE CHAVANNES, Pierre (1824–98; French painter)

REMBRANDT VAN RIJN (1606–69; Dutch painter and etcher)

UTAGAWA KUNIYOSHI (Igusa Magosaburo, 1797–1861; Japanese painter and printmaker)

17

DOMENICO VENEZIANO (active *c.* 1438–1461; Italian painter)

GENTILE DA FABRIANO (Niccolo di Giovanni di Massio, *c.* 1370–1427; Florentine painter)

HERRERA THE YOUNGER, Francisco de (1622–85; Spanish baroque painter and architect)

HOLBEIN THE YOUNGER, Hans (*c.* 1497–1543; German painter)

TENIERS THE YOUNGER, David (1610–90; Flemish painter)

18

ANTONELLO DA MESSINA (*c.* 1430–*c.* 1479; Italian painter)

JACOPO DELLA QUERCIA (*c.* 1374–1438; Italian Renaissance sculptor)

LEIGHTON OF STRETTON, Frederic, Baron (1830–96; British painter and sculptor)

19

DUCCIO DI BUONINSEGNA (*c.* 1255–*c.* 1318; Italian painter)

PIERO DELLA FRANCESCA (*c.* 1420–92; Italian Renaissance painter)

20

DESIDERIO DA SETTIGNANO (*c.* 1430–64; Italian Renaissance sculptor)

MICHELANGELO BUONARROTI (1475–1564; Italian sculptor, painter, and architect)

MICHELOZZO DI BARTOLOMMEO (1396–1472; Florentine Renaissance sculptor and architect)

WRITERS, PLAYWRIGHTS, AND POETS

Alasdair Gray : - "Lanark"

2

FO, Dario (1926– ; Italian playwright)

3

ECO, Umberto (1932– ; Italian writer)

FRY, Christopher (C Harris, 1907– ; British dramatist)

GAY, John (1685–1732; British poet and dramatist)

KYD, Thomas (1558–94; English dramatist)

PAZ, Octavio (1914–98; Mexican poet)

SUE, Eugène (Joseph Marie S, 1804–57; French novelist)

4

AGEE, James (1909–55; US poet and novelist)

AMIS, Kingsley (1922–95; British novelist and poet)

AMIS, Martin (1949– ; British novelist)

ASCH, Sholem (1880–1957; Jewish novelist)

BANA (7th century AD; Sanskrit writer)

BAUM, L Frank (1856–1919; US novelist)

BENN, Gottfried (1886–1956; German poet)

BLOK, Aleksandr Aleksandrovich (1880–1921; Russian symbolist poet)

4–continued

BÖLL, Heinrich (1917–85; German novelist)

BOLT, Robert Oxton (1924–95; British dramatist)

BOND, Edward (1934– ; British dramatist)

BUCK, Pearl S (1892–1973; US novelist)

CARY, Joyce (1888–1957; British novelist)

CRUZ, Sor Juana Inéz de la (1651–95; Mexican poet)

DAHL, Roald (1916–90; British author)

DEUS, João de (1830–96; Portuguese poet)

DU FU (*or* Tu Fu; 712–70 AD; Chinese poet)

FORD, Ford Madox (Ford Hermann Hueffer, 1873–1939; British novelist)

FORD, John (1586–*c.* 1640; English dramatist)

FOXE, John (1516–87; English religious writer)

GALT, John (1779–1839; Scottish novelist)

GIDE, André (1869–1951; French novelist and critic)

GRAY, Thomas (1716–71; British poet)

GUNN, Thomson W (1929– ; British poet)

HARE, Sir David (1947– ; British playwright)

4–continued

HART, Moss (1904–61; US dramatist)

HILL, Geoffrey (1932– ; British poet)

HOGG, James (1770–1835; Scottish poet and writer)

HOOD, Thomas (1799–1845; British poet)

HOPE, Anthony (Sir Anthony Hope Hawkins; 1863–1933; British novelist)

HUGO, Victor (1802–85; French poet, dramatist, and novelist)

HUNT, Leigh (1784–1859; British poet and journalist)

KING, Stephen Edwin (1947– ; US novelist)

KIVI, Alexis (A Stenvall, 1834–72; Finnish poet, dramatist, and novelist)

LAMB, Charles (1775–1834; British essayist and critic)

LEAR, Edward (1812–88; British artist and poet)

LIVY (Titus Livius, 59 BC–17 AD; Roman writer)

LOTI, Pierre (Julien Viaud; 1850–1923; French novelist)

LYLY, John (*c.* 1554–1606; English dramatist and writer)

MANN, Thomas (1875–1955; German novelist)

Alastair Reid :- Poet/Translator b. Whithorn 1926-2014

WRITERS, PLAYWRIGHTS, AND POETS

4–continued

MUIR, Edwin (1887–1959;
Scottish poet)
NASH, Ogden (1902–71; US
humorous writer)
NEXØ, Martin Andersen
(1869–1954; Danish novelist)
OVID (Publius Ovidius Naso 43
BC–17 AD; Roman poet)
OWEN, Wilfred (1893–1918;
British poet)
POPE, Alexander (1688–1744;
British poet)
READ, Sir Herbert (1893–1968;
British poet)
RHYS, Jean (1894–1979;
British novelist)
RICH, Adrienne (1929– ; US
poet)
ROTH, Philip (1933– ; US
novelist)
ROWE, Nicholas (1674–1718;
British dramatist)
RUIZ, Juan (c. 1283–c. 1350;
Spanish poet)
SADE, Donatien Alphonse
François, Marquis de
(1740–1814; French novelist)
SA'DI (Mosleh al-Din S,
c. 1215–92; Persian poet)
SAKI (H H Munro, 1870–1916;
British humorous short-story
writer)
SAND, George (Aurore Dupin,
Baronne Dudevant, 1804–76;
French novelist)
SETH, Vikram (1952– ;
Indian-born novelist)
SHAW, George Bernard
(1856–1950; Irish dramatist)
SNOW, C P, Baron (1905–80;
British novelist)
TATE, Allen (1899–1979; US
poet and critic)
TATE, Nahum (1652–1715;
British poet)
URFÉ, Honoré d' (1568–1625;
French novelist)
VEGA, Lope Félix de
(1562–1635; Spanish poet
and dramatist)
WAIN, John (1925–94; British
novelist and poet)
WARD, Artemus (Charles
Farrar Browne, 1834–67; US
humorous writer)
WARD, Mrs Humphry
(1851–1920; British novelist)
WEBB, Mary (1881–1927;
British novelist)

4–continued

WEST, Dame Rebecca (Cicely
Isabel Fairfield, 1892–1983;
British novelist and journalist)
WEST, Nathanael (Nathan
Weinstein, 1903–40; US
novelist)
WOOD, Mrs Henry (1814–87;
British novelist)
WREN, P C (1885–1941;
British novelist)
WYSS, Johann Rudolph
(1782–1830; Swiss writer)
ZOLA, Émile (1840–1902;
French novelist)

5

ADAMS, Henry (1838–1918;
US historian)
ADAMS, Richard (1920– ;
British novelist)
AGNON, Shmuel Yosef
(Samuel Josef Czaczkes,
1888–1970; Jewish novelist)
ALBEE, Edward (1928– ; US
dramatist)
ARANY, János (1817–82;
Hungarian poet)
AUDEN, W H (1907–73; British
poet)
BABEL, Isaac Emmanuilovich
(1894–1941; Russian short-
story writer)
BANKS, Iain Menzies
(1954– ; Scottish novelist)
BARTH, John (1930– ; US
novelist)
BATES, H E (1905–74; British
writer)
BEHAN, Brendan (1923–64;
Irish playwright)
BELLO, Andrés (1781–1865;
Venezuelan scholar and poet)
BELYI, Andrei (Boris
Nikolaevich Bugaev,
1880–1934; Russian poet)
BEMBO, Pietro (1470–1547;
Italian scholar)
BENDA, Julien (1867–1956;
French novelist and
philosopher)
BENÉT, Stephen Vincent
(1898–1943; US poet and
novelist)
BETTI, Ugo (1892–1953; Italian
dramatist)
BOWEN, Elizabeth
(1899–1973; British novelist,
born in Dublin)
BRANT, Sebastian
(?1458–1521; German poet)

5–continued

BROCH, Hermann
(1886–1951; Austrian
novelist)
BUNIN, Ivan Alekseevich
(1879–1953; Russian poet
and novelist)
BURNS, Robert (1759–96;
Scottish poet)
BUTOR, Michel (1926– ;
French experimental novelist
and critic)
BYATT, A S (1936– ; British
writer)
BYRON, George Gordon, Lord
(1788–1824; British poet)
CAMUS, Albert (1913–60;
French novelist)
CAREW, Thomas (c.
1595–1640; British poet)
CLARE, John (1793–1864;
British poet)
COLUM, Padraic (Patrick Colm;
1881–1972; Irish poet)
CRAIK, Dinah Maria Mulock
(1826–87; British novelist)
CRANE, Hart (1899–1932; US
poet)
CRANE, Stephen (1871–1900;
US novelist)
DARÍO, Rubén (Félix García
Sarmiento; 1867–1916;
Nicaraguan poet)
DEFOE, Daniel (1660–1731;
British novelist)
DONNE, John (1572–1631;
English poet)
DOYLE, Sir Arthur Conan
(1859–1930; British author)
DOYLE, Roddy (1958– ; Irish
novelist)
DUMAS, Alexandre (1802–70;
French novelist and dramatist)
DURAS, Marguerite (1914– ;
French novelist)
ELIOT, George (Mary Ann
Evans, 1819–80; British
novelist)
ELIOT, T S (1888–1965; Anglo-
American poet, critic, and
dramatist)
ELYOT, Sir Thomas (c.
1490–1546; English scholar)
EWALD, Johannes (1743–81;
Danish poet and playwright)
FRIEL, Brian (1929– ; Irish
playwright)
FROST, Robert Lee
(1874–1963; US poet)
GENET, Jean (1910–86;
French novelist and dramatist)

104

Sharp :-Alan : born 1934
Lorca : Federico Garcia (Spanish) b 1898 - 36

5—continued

GOGOL, Nikolai Vasilievich (1809–52; Russian novelist and dramatist)

GORKI, Maksim (Aleksei Maksimovich Peshkov; 1868–1936; Russian novelist)

GOSSE, Sir Edmund (1849–1928; British critic)

GOWER, John (c. 1330–1408; English poet)

GRASS, Günter (1927– ; German novelist and poet)

GREEN, Henry (Henry Vincent Yorke; 1905–73; British novelist)

HAFIZ, Shams al-Din Muhammad (?1326–90; Persian lyric poet)

HALLE, Adam de la (c. 1240–90; French poet and musician)

HARDY, Thomas (1840–1928; British novelist and poet)

HARTE, Brett (1836–1902; US short-story writer)

HAŠEK, Jaroslav (1883–1923; Czech novelist)

HEINE, Heinrich (1797–1856; German Jewish poet and writer)

HENRY, O (William Sidney Porter, 1862–1910; US short-story writer)

HESSE, Hermann (1877–1962; German novelist and poet)

HOMER (8th century BC; Greek epic poet)

HOOFT, Pieter Corneliszoon (1581–1647; Dutch poet)

IBSEN, Henrik (1828–1906; Norwegian playwright and poet)

JAMES, Henry (1843–1916; US novelist and critic)

JAMES, P D (1920– ; British novelist)

JARRY, Alfred (1873–1907; French dramatist)

JONES, David (1895–1974; Anglo-Welsh writer)

JONES, Le Roi (1934– ; US dramatist and poet)

JOYCE, James (1882–1941; Irish novelist and poet)

KAFKA, Franz (1883–1924; Czech writer)

KEATS, John (1795–1821; British poet)

KEMAL, Namik (1840–88; Turkish poet, novelist, and dramatist)

5—continued

KESEY, Ken (1935– ; US novelist)

LEWIS, C S (1898–1963; British writer)

LEWIS, Matthew Gregory (1775–1818; British novelist)

LEWIS, Sinclair (1885–1951; US novelist)

LEWIS, Wyndham (1882–1957; British novelist)

LODGE, David (1935– ; British novelist)

LODGE, Thomas (1558–1625; English poet, dramatist, and writer)

LOWRY, Malcolm (1909–57; British novelist)

LUCAN (Marcus Annaeus Lucanus, 39–65 AD; Roman poet)

MAMET, David (1947– ; US playwright)

MAROT, Clément (1496–1544; French poet)

MARSH, Dame Ngaio (1899–1981; New Zealand detective-story writer)

MARTÍ, José Julián (1853–95; Cuban poet)

MASON, A E W (1865–1948; British novelist)

MILNE, A A (1882–1956; British novelist and dramatist)

MOORE, Marianne (1887–1972; US poet)

MOORE, Thomas (1779–1852; Irish poet)

MURRY, John Middleton (1889–1957; British literary critic)

MUSIL, Robert (1880–1942; Austrian novelist)

MYERS, F W H (1843–1901; British essayist and poet)

NASHE, Thomas (1567–c. 1601; British dramatist)

NOYES, Alfred (1880–1958; British poet)

ODETS, Clifford (1906–63; US dramatist)

O'HARA, John (1905–70; US novelist)

OPITZ, Martin (1597–1639; German poet)

ORCZY, Baroness Emmusca (1865–1947; British novelist)

OTWAY, Thomas (1652–85; British dramatist)

OUIDA (Marie Louise de la Ramée, 1839–1908; British novelist)

5—continued

PAN GU (or P'an Ku; 32–92 AD; Chinese historian)

PATON, Alan (1903–88; South African novelist)

PEAKE, Mervyn (1911–68; British novelist)

PEELE, George (1556–96; English dramatist)

PÉGUY, Charles (1873–1914; French poet and essayist)

PERSE, Saint-John (Alexis Saint-Léger, 1887–1975; French poet)

PLATH, Sylvia (1932–63; US poet and writer)

POUND, Ezra (1885–1972; US poet and critic)

POWYS, John Cowper (1872–1963; British novelist)

PRIOR, Matthew (1664–1721; British poet)

PULCI, Luigi (1432–84; Italian poet)

RAINE, Kathleen (1908– ; British poet)

READE, Charles (1814–84; British novelist)

RILKE, Rainer Maria (1875–1926; Austrian poet)

ROLFE, Frederick William (1860–1913; British novelist)

SACHS, Hans (1494–1576; German poet and folk dramatist)

SACHS, Nelly (1891–1970; German Jewish poet and dramatist)

SAGAN, Françoise (Françoise Quoirez, 1935– ; French writer)

SCOTT, Sir Walter (1771–1832; Scottish novelist)

SETON, Ernest Thompson (1860–1946; US writer)

SHUTE, Nevil (Nevil Shute Norway, 1899–1960; British novelist)

SIMMS, William Gilmore (1806–70; US novelist)

SMART, Christopher (1722–71; British poet)

SMITH, Stevie (Florence Margaret S, 1902–71; British poet)

SPARK, Muriel (1918– ; British novelist)

STAËL, Anne Louise Germaine Necker, Madame de (1766–1817; French writer)

STEIN, Gertrude (1874–1946; US writer)

5–continued

STORM, Theodor Woldsen
(1817–1888; German writer)

STOWE, Harriet Beecher
(1811–96; US novelist)

SVEVO, Italo (Ettore Schmitz,
1861–1928; Italian novelist)

SWIFT, Graham (1946– ;
British novelist)

SWIFT, Jonathan (1667–1745;
Anglo-Irish poet and satirist)

SYNGE, John Millington
(1871–1909; Anglo-Irish
dramatist)

TASSO, Torquato (1544–95;
Italian poet)

TIECK, Ludwig (1773–1853;
German writer)

TWAIN, Mark (Samuel
Langhorne Clemens,
1835–1910; US novelist)

UDALL, Nicholas (1505–56;
English dramatist)

VARRO, Marcus Terentius
(116–27 BC; Roman poet)

VERNE, Jules (1828–1905;
French writer)

VIDAL, Gore (1925– ; US
novelist and essayist)

VIGNY, Alfred de (1797–1863;
French poet, novelist, and
dramatist)

WALEY, Arthur (1889–1966;
British translator and poet)

WAUGH, Evelyn (1903–66;
British novelist)

WEISS, Peter (1916–82; German dramatist and novelist)

WELLS, H G (1866–1946;
British novelist)

WHITE, Patrick (1912–90;
Australian novelist)

WHITE, T H (1906–64; British
novelist)

WILDE, Oscar (O Fingal
O'Flahertie Wills W,
1854–1900; British dramatist
and poet)

WOLFE, Charles (1791–1823;
Irish poet)

WOLFE, Thomas (1900–38;
US novelist)

WOOLF, Virginia (1882–1941;
British novelist)

WYATT, Sir Thomas (1503–42;
English poet)

YEATS, William Butler
(1865–1939; Irish poet and
dramatist)

YONGE, Charlotte (1823–1901;
British novelist)

5–continued

ZWEIG, Arnold (1887–1968;
East German-Jewish novelist)

ZWEIG, Stefan (1881–1942;
Austrian Jewish writer)

6

ACCIUS, Lucius (170–c. 85 BC;
Roman tragic dramatist)

ADAMOV, Arthur (1908–70;
French dramatist)

ALCOTT, Louisa May
(1832–88; US novelist)

ALDISS, Brian W (1925– ;
British novelist)

ALEMÁN, Mateo (1547–?1614;
Spanish writer)

ALGREN, Nelson (1909–81;
US novelist)

AMBLER, Eric (1909– ;
British novelist)

ANDRIĆ, Ivo (1892–1975;
Serbian writer)

ARAGON, Louis (1897–1982;
French poet, novelist, and
journalist)

ASCHAM, Roger (1515–68;
English scholar and writer)

ASIMOV, Isaac (1920–92; US
science fiction writer, born in
Russia)

AUBREY, John (1626–97;
English antiquary)

AUSTEN, Jane (1775–1817;
British novelist)

AZORÍN (José Martinéz Ruíz,
1874–1967; Spanish novelist,
essayist, and critic)

AZUELA, Mariano (1873–1952;
Mexican novelist)

BALZAC, Honoré de
(1799–1850; French novelist)

BARHAM, Richard Harris
(1788–1845; British
humorous writer)

BARKER, George (1913–91;
British poet)

BARNES, William (1801–86;
British poet)

BAROJA, Pío (1872–1956;
Spanish novelist)

BARRÈS, Maurice (1862–1923;
French writer)

BARRIE, Sir James
(1860–1937; British dramatist
and novelist)

BELLAY, Joachim de (1522–60;
French poet)

BELLOC, Hilaire (1870–1953;
British poet and essayist)

BELLOW, Saul (1915– ;
Canadian-born US novelist)

6–continued

BESANT, Sir Walter
(1836–1901; British novelist)

BIALIK, Chaim Nachman
(1873–1934; Jewish poet and
translator)

BIERCE, Ambrose Gwinnett
(1842–?1914; US writer)

BINCHY, Maeve (1940– ; Irish
novelist)

BINYON, Laurence
(1869–1943; British poet)

BLYTON, Enid (1897–1968;
British writer of children's
books)

BORGES, Jorge Luis
(1899–1986; Argentinian
writer)

BORROW, George Henry
(1803–81; British writer)

BRECHT, Bertolt (1898–1956;
German dramatist and poet)

BRETON, André (1896–1966;
French poet)

BRIDIE, James (Osborne
Henry Mavor; 1888–1951;
British dramatist)

BRONTË, Anne (1820–49;
British novelist)

BRONTË, Charlotte (1816–55;
British novelist)

BRONTË, Emily (1818–48;
British novelist)

BROOKE, Rupert (1887–1915;
British poet)

BROWNE, Sir Thomas
(1605–82; English writer)

BRYANT, William Cullen
(1794–1878; US poet,
journalist, and critic)

BUCHAN, John, 1st Baron
Tweedsmuir (1875–1940;
British novelist)

BUNYAN, John (1628–88;
English writer)

BÜRGER, Gottfried (1747–94;
German poet)

BURNEY, Fanny (Mrs Frances
Burney D'Arblay; 1752–1840;
British novelist)

BUTLER, Samuel (1612–80;
British satirical poet)

BUTLER, Samuel (1835–1902;
British novelist)

CAMÕES, Luís de (c. 1524–80;
Portuguese poet)

CAPOTE, Truman (1924–84;
US novelist)

CARSON, Rachel Louise
(1907–64; US science writer)

6—continued

CAVAFY, Constantine (C Kavafis, 1863–1933; Greek poet)

CÉLINE, Louis Ferdinand (L F Destouches, 1884–1961; French novelist)

CIBBER, Colley (1671–1757; British dramatist)

CLANCY, Tom (1947– ; US novelist)

CLARKE, Marcus (1846–81; Australian novelist, born in London)

COLMAN, George (1732–94; British dramatist)

CONRAD, Joseph (Teodor Josef Konrad Watęcz Korzeniowski, 1857–1924; Polish-born British novelist)

COOPER, James Fenimore (1789–1851; US novelist)

COWLEY, Abraham (1618–67; English poet)

COWPER, William (1731–1800; British poet)

CRABBE, George (1754–1832; British poet)

CRONIN, A J (1896–1981; British novelist)

DANIEL, Samuel (?1562–1619; English poet, dramatist, and critic)

DAUDET, Alphonse (1840–97; French novelist)

DAVIES, W H (1871–1940; British poet)

DEKKER, Thomas (c. 1572–1632; British dramatist and pamphleteer)

DOWSON, Ernest (1867–1900; British poet)

DRYDEN, John (1631–1700; British poet)

DUNBAR, William (c. 1460–c. 1530; Scots poet)

ÉLUARD, Paul (Eugène Grindel, 1895–1952; French poet)

EMPSON, Sir William (1906–84; British poet and critic)

ENNIUS, Quintus (238–169 BC; Roman poet)

EVELYN, John (1620–1706; English diarist)

FOUQUÉ, Friedrich Heinrich Karl, Baron de la Motte (1777–1843; German novelist and dramatist)

FOWLES, John (1926– ; British novelist)

6—continued

FRANCE, Anatole (Jacques Anatole François Thibault 1844–1924; French novelist)

FRISCH, Max (1911–91; Swiss dramatist and novelist)

FUGARD, Athol (1932– ; South African dramatist)

FULLER, Roy (1912–91; British poet and novelist)

FULLER, Thomas (1608–61; British historian)

GEORGE, Stefan (1868–1933; German poet)

GIBBON, Edward (1737–94; British historian)

GIBRAN, Khalil (1883–1931; Lebanese mystic and poet)

GOETHE, Johann Wolfgang von (1749–1832; German poet)

GRAVES, Robert (1895–1985; British poet, critic, and novelist)

GREENE, Graham (1904–91; British novelist)

GREENE, Robert (c. 1558–92; English dramatist)

HAMSUN, Knut (1859–1952; Norwegian novelist)

HARRIS, Joel Chandler (1848–1908; US novelist and short-story writer)

HEANEY, Seamus (1939– ; Irish poet)

HEBBEL, Friedrich (1813–63; German dramatist)

HELLER, Joseph (1923– ; US novelist)

HESIOD (8th century BC; Greek poet)

HILTON, James (1900–54; British novelist)

HOLMES, Oliver Wendell (1809–94; US essayist and poet)

HORACE (Quintus Horatius Flaccus; 65–8 BC; Roman poet)

HUDSON, W H (1841–1922; British naturalist and writer)

HUGHES, Richard (1900–76; British novelist)

HUGHES, Ted (1930–98; British poet)

HUGHES, Thomas (1822–96; British writer)

IRVING, Washington (1783–1859; US short-story writer)

ISAACS, Jorge (1837–95; Colombian novelist)

6—continued

JENSEN, Johannes (1873–1950; Danish novelist and poet)

JONSON, Ben (1572–1637; English dramatist and poet)

KAISER, Georg (1878–1945; German dramatist)

KELLER, Gottfried (1819–90; German-Swiss poet and novelist)

KLEIST, Heinrich von (1777–1811; German dramatist)

LACLOS, Pierre Choderlos de (1741–1803; French novelist)

LANDOR, Walter Savage (1775–1864; British poet and prose writer)

LANIER, Sidney (1842–81; US poet)

LARKIN, Philip (1922–85; British poet)

LAWLER, Ray (1921– ; Australian dramatist)

LE FANU, Sheridan (1814–73; Irish novelist)

LEONOV, Leonid (1899–1994; Soviet novelist and playwright)

LESAGE, Alain-René (1668–1747; French novelist)

LIVELY, Penelope (1933– ; British novelist)

LONDON, Jack (1876–1916; US novelist)

LOWELL, Amy (1874–1925; US poet)

LOWELL, James Russell (1819–91; US poet)

LOWELL, Robert (1917–77; US poet)

LU HSÜN (or Chou Shu-jen 1881–1936; Chinese writer)

MACHEN, Arthur (1863–1947; Welsh novelist)

MAILER, Norman (1923– ; US novelist and journalist)

MALORY, Sir Thomas (?1400–71; English writer)

MCEWAN, Ian (1948– ; British novelist)

MERCER, David (1928–80; British dramatist)

MILLAY, Edna St Vincent (1892–1950; US poet)

MILLER, Arthur (1915– ; US dramatist)

MILLER, Henry (1891–1980; US novelist)

MILTON, John (1608–74; English poet)

6–continued

MOLNÁR, Ferenc (1878–1952; Hungarian dramatist)

MORGAN, Charles (1894–1958; British novelist and dramatist)

MÖRIKE, Eduard Friedrich (1804–75; German poet and novelist)

MOTION, Andrew (1952– ; British poet and writer)

MUNTHE, Axel (1857–1949; Swedish author)

MUSSET, Alfred de (1810–57; French poet and dramatist)

NERUDA, Pablo (Neftalí Ricardo Reyes 1904–73; Chilean poet)

NERVAL, Gérard de (Gérard Labrunie 1808–55; French poet)

NESBIT, Edith (1858–1924; British children's writer)

O'BRIEN, Flann (Brian O'Nolan 1911–66; Irish novelist and journalist)

O'CASEY, Sean (1880–1964; Irish dramatist)

O'NEILL, Eugene (1888–1953; US dramatist)

ORWELL, George (Eric Blair; 1903–50; British novelist, born in India)

PARKER, Dorothy Rothschild (1893–1967; US humorous writer)

PAVESE, Cesare (1908–50; Italian novelist and poet)

PETÖFI, Sándor (1823–49; Hungarian poet)

PINDAR (518–438 BC; Greek poet)

PINERO, Sir Arthur Wing (1855–1934; British dramatist)

PINTER, Harold (1930– ; British dramatist)

PIOZZI, Hester Lynch (1741–1821; British writer)

PLOMER, William (1903–73; South African poet and novelist)

PORTER, Katherine Anne (1890–1980; US short-story writer and novelist)

PORTER, Peter (1929– ; British poet)

POTTER, Beatrix (1866–1943; British children's writer)

POTTER, Stephen (1900–70; British writer)

6–continued

POWELL, Anthony (1905– ; British novelist)

PROUST, Marcel (1871–1922; French novelist)

RACINE, Jean (1639–99; French dramatist)

RAMSAY, Allan (?1685–1758; Scottish poet)

RANSOM, John Crowe (1888–1974; US poet)

RUNYON, Damon (1884–1946; US humorous writer)

SAPPER (H C McNeile, 1888–1937; British novelist)

SAPPHO (c. 612–c. 580 BC; Greek poet)

SARDOU, Victorien (1831–1908; French dramatist)

SARTRE, Jean-Paul (1905–80; French philosopher, novelist, dramatist, and critic)

SAVAGE, Richard (c. 1696–1743; British poet)

SAYERS, Dorothy L (1893–1957; British writer)

SIDNEY, Sir Philip (1554–86; English poet)

SILONE, Ignazio (Secondo Tranquilli, 1900–78; Italian novelist)

SINGER, Isaac Bashevis (1904–91; US novelist and short-story writer)

SMILES, Samuel (1812–1904; British writer)

STEELE, Sir Richard (1672–1729; British essayist and dramatist)

STERNE, Laurence (1713–68; British novelist)

STOKER, Bram (Abraham S, 1847–1912; Irish novelist)

STOREY, David (1933– ; British novelist and dramatist)

SURREY, Henry Howard, Earl of (1517–47; English poet)

SYMONS, Arthur (1865–1945; British poet and critic)

TAGORE, Rabindranath (1861–1941; Indian poet)

THOMAS, Dylan (1914–53; Welsh poet)

THOMAS, Edward (1878–1917; British poet)

TOLLER, Ernst (1893–1939; German playwright and poet)

TRAVEN, B (Berick Traven Torsvan, 1890–1969; US novelist)

6–continued

UHLAND, Ludwig (1787–1862; German poet)

UNDSET, Sigrid (1882–1949; Norwegian novelist)

UPDIKE, John (1932– ; US novelist and short-story writer)

VALÉRY, Paul (1871–1945; French poet, essayist, and critic)

VILLON, François (1431–?1463; French poet)

VIRGIL (Publius Vergilius Maro, 70–19 BC; Roman poet)

VONDEL, Joost van den (1587–1679; Dutch dramatist and poet)

WALLER, Edmund (1606–87; British poet)

WALTON, Izaak (1593–1683; English writer)

WARTON, Joseph (1722–1800; British poet and critic)

WELDON, Fay (1931– ; British writer)

WERFEL, Franz (1890–1945; Austrian Jewish poet, dramatist, and novelist)

WESKER, Arnold (1932– ; British dramatist)

WILDER, Thornton (1897–1975; US novelist and dramatist)

WILSON, Colin (1931– ; British critic and novelist)

WILSON, Edmund (1895–1972; US critic and essayist)

WILSON, Sir Angus (1913–91; British novelist)

WOTTON, Sir Henry (1568–1639; English poet)

WRIGHT, Judith (1915– ; Australian poet)

WRIGHT, Richard (1908–60; US novelist and critic)

7

ADDISON, Joseph (1672–1719; British essayist and poet)

AELFRIC (c. 955–c. 1020; Anglo-Saxon prose writer)

ALARCÓN, Pedro Antonio de (1833–91; Spanish novelist)

ALBERTI, Raphael (1902–99; Spanish poet)

ALCAEUS (6th century BC; Greek lyric poet)

ALDANOV, Mark (M Aleksandrovich Landau, 1886–1957; Russian novelist)

7–continued

ALDRICH, Thomas Bailey (1836–1907; US short- story writer and poet)

ALEGRÍA, Ciro (1909–61; Peruvian novelist)

ALFIERI, Vittorio, Count (1749–1803; Italian poet and dramatist)

ALLENDE, Isabel (1942– ; Peruvian novelist)

ANEIRIN (6th century AD; Welsh poet)

ARETINO, Pietro (1492–1556; Italian satirist)

ARIOSTO, Ludovico (1474–1533; Italian poet)

ARRABAL, Fernando (1932– ; Spanish playwright and novelist)

BALCHIN, Nigel (1908–70; British novelist)

BALDWIN, James Arthur (1924–87; US novelist, essayist, and dramatist)

BARBOUR, John (1316–95; Scottish poet)

BECKETT, Samuel (1906–89; Irish novelist, dramatist, and poet)

BEDDOES, Thomas Lovell (1803–49; British poet)

BENNETT, Arnold (1837–1931; British novelist)

BENTLEY, Edmund Clerihew (1875–1956; British writer)

BERGMAN, Hjalmar (1883–1931; Swedish novelist and dramatist)

BLUNDEN, Edmund Charles (1896–1974; British poet and critic)

BOIARDO, Matteo Maria, Conte di Scandiano (1441–94; Italian poet)

BOILEAU(-Despréaux), Nicolas (1636–1711; French poet and critic)

BOSWELL, James (1740–95; Scottish writer)

BO ZHU YI (or Po Chü-i; 772–846; Chinese poet)

BRADLEY, Andrew Cecil (1851–1935; British literary critic)

BRIDGES, Robert Seymour (1844–1930; British poet)

BÜCHNER, Georg (1813–37; German dramatist)

BURGESS, Anthony (John Burgess Wilson; 1917–93; British novelist and critic)

7–continued

BURNETT, Frances Eliza Hodgson (1849–1924; British novelist)

CAEDMON (d. c. 680 AD; English poet)

CAO CHAN (or Zao Zhan; ?1715–63; Chinese novelist)

CAROSSA, Hans (1878–1956; German novelist)

CARROLL, Lewis (Charles Lutwidge Dodgson; 1832–98; British writer)

CHAPMAN, George (c. 1560–1634; British poet and dramatist)

CHAUCER, Geoffrey (c. 1342–1400; English poet)

CHEKHOV, Anton Pavlovich (1860–1904; Russian dramatist and short-story writer)

CHÉNIER, André de (1762–94; French poet, born in Istanbul)

CHU YUAN (c. 343 BC–c. 289 BC; Chinese poet)

CLAUDEL, Paul (1868–1955; French dramatist and poet)

CLELAND, John (1709–89; English novelist)

COCTEAU, Jean (1889–1963; French poet and artist)

COETZEE, J M (1940– ; South African novelist)

COLETTE (Sidonie-Gabrielle C, 1873–1954; French novelist)

COLLINS, William (1721–59; British poet)

COLLINS, William Wilkie (1824–89; British novelist)

CORELLI, Marie (1854–1924; British novelist)

CRASHAW, Richard (c. 1613–49; British poet)

CREELEY, Robert (1926– ; US poet)

DA PONTE, Lorenzo (1749–1838; Italian author)

DELEDDA, Grazia (1871–1936; Italian novelist)

DICKENS, Charles (1812–70; British novelist)

DINESEN, Isak (Karen Blixen, Baroness Blixen-Finecke, 1885–1962; Danish author)

DOUGLAS, Gavin (?1474–1522; Scottish poet)

DOUGLAS, Norman (1868–1952; British novelist)

DRABBLE, Margaret (1939– ; British novelist)

7–continued

DRAYTON, Michael (1563–1631; English poet)

DREISER, Theodore (1871–1945; US novelist)

DUHAMEL, Georges (1884–1966; French novelist)

DUNSANY, Edward John Moreton Drax Plunkett, 18th Baron (1878–1957; Irish author)

DURRELL, Lawrence George (1912–90; British novelist and poet, born in India)

EMERSON, Ralph Waldo (1803–82; US essayist and poet)

ERCILLA, Alonso de (1533–94; Spanish poet)

EUPOLIS (late 5th century BC; Greek dramatist)

FERRIER, Susan Edmonstone (1782–1854; Scottish novelist)

FEYDEAU, Georges (1862–1921; French playwright)

FIRBANK, Ronald (1886–1926; British novelist)

FLECKER, James Elroy (1884–1915; British poet)

FLEMING, Ian (1908–64; British author)

FLEMING, Paul (1609–40; German poet)

FONTANE, Theodor (1819–98; German novelist)

FORSTER, E M (1879–1970; British novelist)

FOSCOLO, Ugo (1778–1827; Italian poet)

FRENEAU, Philip (1752–1832; US poet)

FRÖDING, Gustaf (1860–1911; Swedish lyric poet)

GAARDER, Jostein (1952– ; Norwegian novelist)

GASKELL, Elizabeth Cleghorn (1810–65; British novelist)

GAUTIER, Théophile (1811–72; French poet)

GILBERT, Sir William Schwenk (1836–1911; British comic dramatist)

GISSING, George Robert (1857–1903; British novelist)

GOLDING, William (1911–93; British novelist)

GOLDONI, Carlo (1707–93; Italian comic playwright)

GRAHAME, Kenneth (1859–1932; British children's writer)

7–continued

GRISHAM, John (1955– ; US novelist)

GUARINI, Giovanni Battista (1538–1612; Italian poet)

HAGGARD, Sir H Rider (1856–1925; British novelist)

HAMMETT, Dashiell (1894–1961; US novelist)

HARTLEY, L P (1895–1972; British novelist)

HELLMAN, Lillian (1905–84; US dramatist)

HERBERT, George (1593–1633; English poet)

HERRICK, Robert (1591–1674; English poet)

HEYWOOD, Thomas (*c.* 1574–1641; English dramatist)

HOLBERG, Ludvig, Baron (1684–1754; Danish playwright and poet)

HOPKINS, Gerard Manley (1844–89; British poet)

HOUSMAN, A E (1859–1936; British poet and scholar)

IBN EZRA, Abraham Ben Meir (1093–1167; Hebrew poet and scholar)

IONESCO, Eugène (1912–94; French dramatist)

JEFFERS, Robinson (1887–1962; US poet)

JIMÉNEZ, Juan Ramón (1881–1958; Spanish poet)

JUVENAL (Decimus Junius Juvenalis, *c.* 60–*c.* 130 AD; Roman satirist)

KÄSTNER, Erich (1899–1974; German novelist and poet)

KAUFMAN, George S (1889–1961; US dramatist)

KENDALL, Henry (1841–82; Australian poet)

KEROUAC, Jack (1922–69; US novelist)

KIPLING, Rudyard (1865–1936; British writer and poet)

KLINGER, Friedrich Maximilian von (1752–1831; German dramatist)

LABICHE, Eugène (1815–88; French dramatist)

LARDNER, Ring (1885–1933; US short-story writer)

LAXNESS, Halldór (1902–98; Icelandic novelist and essayist)

LAYAMON (early 13th century; English poet)

7–continued

LEACOCK, Stephen (1869–1944; English-born Canadian humorist)

LE CARRÉ, John (David Cornwell, 1931– ; British novelist)

LESSING, Doris (1919– ; British novelist)

LESSING, Gotthold Ephraim (1729–81; German dramatist and writer)

LINDSAY, Vachel (1879–1931; US poet)

LYDGATE, John (*c.* 1370–*c.* 1450; English poet)

MACHAUT, Guillaume de (*c.* 1300–77; French poet)

MALAMUD, Bernard (1914–86; US novelist)

MALRAUX, André (1901–76; French novelist and essayist)

MANZONI, Alessandro (1785–1873; Italian poet and novelist)

MARLOWE, Christopher (1564–93; English dramatist and poet)

MARRYAT, Captain Frederick (1792–1848; British novelist)

MARSTON, John (1576–1634; English dramatist)

MARTIAL (Marcus Valerius Martialis, *c.* 40–*c.* 104 AD; Roman poet)

MARVELL, Andrew (1621–78; English poet)

MASTERS, Edgar Lee (1868–1950; US poet)

MAUGHAM, W Somerset (1874–1965; British novelist and dramatist)

MAURIAC, François (1885–1970; French novelist)

MAUROIS, André (Émile Herzog; 1885–1967; French biographer, novelist, and critic)

MÉRIMÉE, Prosper (1803–70; French novelist)

MISHIMA, Yukio (Kimitake Hiraoka; 1925–70; Japanese novelist and playwright)

MISTRAL, Frédéric (1830–1914; French poet)

MISTRAL, Gabriela (Lucila Godoy Alcayaga, 1889–1957; Chilean poet)

MOLIÈRE (Jean-Baptiste Poquelin, 1622–73; French dramatist)

7–continued

MONTAGU, Lady Mary Wortley (1689–1762; English writer)

MONTALE, Eugenio (1896–1981; Italian poet)

MORAVIA, Alberto (Alberto Pincherle, 1907–90; Italian novelist)

MURDOCH, Dame Iris (1919–99; British novelist)

NABOKOV, Vladimir (1899–1977; US novelist)

NAEVIUS, Gnaeus (*c.* 270–*c.* 200 BC; Roman poet)

NAIPAUL, V S (1932– ; West Indian novelist)

NOVALIS (Friedrich Leopold, Freiherr von Hardenberg; 1772–1801; German poet and writer)

O'CONNOR, Frank (Michael O'Donovan; 1903–66; Irish short-story writer)

OSBORNE, John (1929–94; British dramatist)

PATMORE, Coventry (1823–96; British poet)

PEACOCK, Thomas Love (1785–1866; British satirical novelist)

PLAUTUS, Titus Maccius (*c.* 254–184 BC; Roman dramatist)

PRÉVERT, Jacques (1900–77; French poet)

PUSHKIN, Aleksandr (1799–1837; Russian poet, novelist, and dramatist)

PYNCHON, Thomas (1937– ; US novelist)

QUENEAU, Raymond (1903–79; French novelist and poet)

RANSOME, Arthur Mitchell (1884–1967; British journalist and children's writer)

REGNIER, Henri François Joseph de (1864–1936; French poet)

RICHLER, Mordecai (1931– ; Canadian novelist)

RIMBAUD, Arthur (1854–91; French poet)

ROLLAND, Romain (1866–1944; French novelist, dramatist, and essayist)

ROMAINS, Jules (Louis Farigoule; 1885–1972; French poet, novelist, and dramatist)

Arthur Rimbaud 1854-91 (French)

7–continued

RONSARD, Pierre de (1524–85; French poet)

ROSTAND, Edmond (1868–1918; French dramatist)

ROUSSEL, Raymond (1877–1933; French writer and dramatist)

ROWLING, Joanne Kathleen (1965– ; British children's writer)

RUSHDIE, Salman (1947– ; British novelist)

SAROYAN, William (1908–81; US dramatist and fiction writer)

SASSOON, Siegfried (1886–1967; British poet and writer)

SCARRON, Paul (1610–60; French poet, dramatist, and satirist)

SEFERIS, George (Georgios Seferiadis, 1900–71; Greek poet)

SHAFFER, Peter (1926– ; British dramatist)

SHELLEY, Percy Bysshe (1792–1822; British poet)

SIMENON, Georges (1903–89; Belgian novelist)

SIMONOV, Konstantin (1915–79; Soviet novelist, playwright, poet, and journalist)

SITWELL, Edith (1887–1964; British poet and writer)

SKELTON, John (c. 1460–1529; English poet)

SOUTHEY, Robert (1774–1843; British poet and writer)

SOYINKA, Wole (1934– ; Nigerian dramatist and poet)

SPENDER, Sir Stephen (1909–95; British poet and critic)

SPENSER, Edmund (c. 1552–99; English poet)

STEVENS, Wallace (1879–1955; US poet)

SURTEES, Robert Smith (1803–64; British novelist)

TERENCE (Publius Ierentius Afer, c. 185–c. 159 BC; Roman dramatist)

THESPIS (6th century BC; Greek poet)

THOMSON, James (1700–48; British poet)

THURBER, James (1894–1961; US humorous writer and cartoonist)

7–continued

TOLKIEN, J R R (1892–1973; British scholar and writer)

TOLSTOY, Leo, Count (1828–1910; Russian writer)

TRAVERS, Ben (1886–1980; British dramatist)

TUTUOLA, Amos (1920–97; Nigerian writer)

VAN DUYN, Mona (1921– ; US poet)

VAUGHAN, Henry (c. 1622–95; English poet)

VICENTE, Gil (c. 1465–1536; Portuguese dramatist)

WALLACE, Edgar (1875–1932; British novelist)

WALPOLE, Sir Hugh (1884–1941; British novelist)

WEBSTER, John (c. 1580–c. 1625; English dramatist)

WHARTON, Edith (1862–1937; US novelist)

WHITMAN, Walt (1819–92; US poet)

WIELAND, Christoph Martin (1733–1813; German novelist and poet)

YESENIN, Sergei Aleksandrovich (1895–1925; Russian poet)

8

ABU NUWAS (c. 762–c. 813 AD; Arab poet)

ANACREON (6th century BC; Greek lyric poet)

ANCHIETA, José de (1534–97; Portuguese poet)

ANDERSEN, Hans Christian (1805–75; Danish author)

ANDERSON, Sherwood (1876–1941; US author)

APULEIUS, Lucius (2nd century AD; Roman writer and rhetorician)

ARMITAGE, Simon Robert (1963– ; British poet and writer)

ASTURIAS, Miguel Ángel (1899–1974; Guatemalan novelist and poet)

BANDEIRA, Manuel Carneiró de Sousa (1886–1968; Brazilian poet)

BANVILLE, Théodore Faullain de (1823–89; French poet)

BARBUSSE, Henri (1873–1935; French novelist)

BEAUMONT, Francis (1584–1616; British dramatist)

8–continued

BEAUVOIR, Simone de (1908–86; French novelist and essayist)

BECKFORD, William (?1760–1844; British writer)

BEERBOHM, Sir Max (1872–1956; British caricaturist and writer)

BELINSKY, Vissarion (1811–48; Russian literary critic)

BENCHLEY, Robert Charles (1889–1945; US humorist)

BERANGER, Pierre Jean de (1780–1857; French poet and songwriter)

BERNANOS, Georges (1888–1948; French novelist)

BETJEMAN, Sir John (1906–84; British poet)

BJØRNSON, Bjørnstjerne (1832–1910; Norwegian novelist, poet, and playwright)

BRADBURY, Ray (1920– ; US science-fiction writer)

BRENTANO, Clemens (1778–1842; German writer)

BROOKNER, Anita (1928– ; British writer and art historian)

BROWNING, Robert (1812–89; British poet)

CAMPBELL, Roy (1901–57; South African poet)

CAMPBELL, Thomas (1777–1844; British poet)

CARDUCCI, Giosuè (1835–1907; Italian poet and critic)

CASTILHO, Antonio Feliciano de (1800–75; Portuguese poet)

CATULLUS, Valerius (c. 84–c. 54 BC; Roman poet)

CHANDLER, Raymond (1888–1959; US novelist)

CHARTIER, Alain (c. 1385–c. 1440; French poet and prose writer)

CHRISTIE, Dame Agatha (1891–1976; British author of detective fiction and playwright)

CLAUDIAN (c. 370–404 AD; Roman poet)

CONGREVE, William (1670–1729; British dramatist)

CONSTANT, Benjamin (1767–1830; French novelist)

CORNWELL, Patricia (1956– ; US novelist)

WRITERS, PLAYWRIGHTS, AND POETS

8–continued

CROMPTON, Richmal (Richmal Crompton Lamburn, 1890–1969; British children's author)

CUMMINGS, e e (1894–1962; US poet)

CYNEWULF (early 9th century AD; Anglo-Saxon religious poet)

DAVENANT, Sir William (1606–68; English dramatist and poet)

DAY LEWIS, C (1904–72; British poet and critic)

DE LA MARE, Walter (1873–1956; British poet, novelist, and anthologist)

DONLEAVY, J P (1926– ; Irish-American novelist)

ETHEREGE, Sir George (c. 1635–c. 1692; English dramatist)

FARQUHAR, George (1678–1707; Irish dramatist)

FAULKNER, William (1897–1962; US novelist)

FIELDING, Henry (1707–54; British novelist and dramatist)

FIRDAUSI (Abul Qasim Mansur; c. 935–c. 1020; Persian poet)

FLAUBERT, Gustave (1821–80; French novelist)

FLETCHER, John (1579–1625; English dramatist)

FORESTER, C S (1899–1966; British novelist)

GINSBERG, Allen (1926–97; US poet)

GONCOURT, Edmond de (1822–96; French writer)

HENRYSON, Robert (15th century; Scottish poet)

HOCHHUTH, Rolf (1933– ; Swiss dramatist)

HUYSMANS, Joris Karl (1848–1907; French novelist)

JEAN PAUL (Johann Paul Friedrich Richter, 1763–1825; German novelist)

KALIDASA (5th century AD; Indian poet)

KENEALLY, Thomas (1935– ; Australian writer)

KINGSLEY, Charles (1819–79; British writer)

KOESTLER, Arthur (1905–83; British writer)

KOTZEBUE, August von (1761–1819; German dramatist and novelist)

8–continued

LAFORGUE, Jules (1860–87; French poet)

LAGERLÖF, Selma Ottiliana Lovisa (1858–1940; Swedish novelist)

LANGLAND, William (c. 1330–c. 1400; English poet)

LAS CASES, Emmanuel, Comte de (1776–1842; French writer)

LAWRENCE, D H (1885–1930; British novelist, poet, and painter)

LEOPARDI, Giacomo (1798–1837; Italian poet)

LOCKHART, John Gibson (1794–1854; Scottish biographer and journalist)

LONGINUS (1st century AD; Greek rhetorician)

LOVELACE, Richard (1618–57; English Cavalier poet)

MACAULAY, Dame Rose (1881–1958; British novelist)

MACLEISH, Archibald (1892–1982; US poet)

MACNEICE, Louis (1907–63; Irish-born British poet)

MALHERBE, François de (1555–1628; French poet and critic)

MALLARMÉ, Stéphane (1842–98; French poet)

MARGOLIS, Donald (1955– ; US playwright)

MARIVAUX, Pierre Carlet de Chamblain de (1688–1763; French dramatist)

MARQUAND, J P (1893–1960; US novelist)

MCCARTHY, Mary (1912–89; US novelist)

MELVILLE, Herman (1819–91; US novelist)

MENANDER (c. 341–c. 290 BC; Greek dramatist)

MEREDITH, George (1828–1909; British poet and novelist)

MICHELET, Jules (1798–1874; French historian)

MITCHELL, Margaret (1909–49; US novelist)

MORRISON, Toni (1931– ; US writer)

NEKRASOV, Nikolai Alekseevich (1821–78; Russian poet)

NICOLSON, Sir Harold (1886–1968; British literary critic)

8–continued

ONDAATJE, Michael (1943– ; Canadian writer)

PALGRAVE, Francis Turner (1824–97; British poet and anthologist)

PERELMAN, S J (1904–79; US humorous writer)

PERRAULT, Charles (1628–1703; French poet and fairytale writer)

PETRARCH (Francesco Petrarca, 1304–74; Italian poet)

PHAEDRUS (1st century AD; Roman writer)

PHILEMON (c. 368–c. 264 BC; Greek dramatist)

PLUTARCH (c. 46–c. 120 AD; Greek biographer and essayist)

RABELAIS, François (1483–1553; French satirist)

RADIGUET, Raymond (1903–23; French novelist)

RATTIGAN, Sir Terence (1911–77; British dramatist)

REMARQUE, Erich Maria (1898–1970; German novelist)

RICHARDS, Frank (Charles Hamilton, 1876–1961; British children's writer)

RUNEBERG, Johan Ludvig (1804–77; Finnish poet)

SALINGER, J D (1919– ; US novelist)

SANDBURG, Carl (1878–1967; US poet)

SARAMAGO, José (1922– ; Portuguese writer)

SARRAUTE, Nathalie (1900–99; French novelist, born in Russia)

SCALIGER, Julius Caesar (1484–1558; Italian humanist scholar)

SCHILLER, Friedrich (1759–1805; German dramatist, poet, and writer)

SHADWELL, Thomas (c. 1642–92; British dramatist)

SHERIDAN, Richard Brinsley (1751–1816; Anglo-Irish dramatist)

SILLITOE, Alan (1928– ; British novelist)

SINCLAIR, Upton (1878–1968; US novelist)

8–continued

SMOLLETT, Tobias (1721–71; British novelist)

SPILLANE, Mickey (Frank Morrison S, 1918– ; US detective-story writer)

STENDHAL (Henri Beyle, 1783–1842; French novelist)

STOPPARD, Sir Tom (1937– ; British dramatist)

SUCKLING, Sir John (1609–42; English poet and dramatist)

SU DONG PO (or Su Tung-p'o, 1036–1101; Chinese poet)

TALIESIN (6th century AD; Welsh poet)

TENNYSON, Alfred, Lord (1809–92; British poet)

THOMPSON, Francis (1859–1907; British poet and critic)

TIBULLUS, Albius (c. 55–c. 19 BC; Roman poet)

TOURNEUR, Cyril (c. 1575–1626; English dramatist)

TRAHERNE, Thomas (c. 1637–74; English poet)

TRILLING, Lionel (1905–75; US literary critic)

TROLLOPE, Anthony (1815–82; British novelist)

TULSIDAS (c. 1532–1623; Indian poet)

TURGENEV, Ivan (1818–83; Russian novelist)

VERLAINE, Paul (1844–96; French poet)

VOLTAIRE (François-Marie Arouet, 1694–1778; French writer)

VONNEGUT, Kurt (1922– ; US novelist)

WEDEKIND, Frank (1864–1918; German dramatist)

WHITTIER, John Greenleaf (1807–92; US poet)

WILLIAMS, Tennessee (1911–83; US dramatist)

WILLIAMS, William Carlos (1883–1963; US poet)

ZAMYATIN, Yevgenii Ivanovich (1884–1937; Russian novelist)

9

AESCHYLUS (c. 525–456 BC; Greek tragic dramatist)

AINSWORTH, W Harrison (1805–82; British historical novelist)

9–continued

AKHMATOVA, Anna (Anna Andreevna Gorenko, 1889–1966; Russian poet)

ALDINGTON, Richard (1892–1962; British poet, novelist, and biographer)

ALLINGHAM, Margery (1904–66; British detective-story writer)

ARBUTHNOT, John (1667–1735; Scottish writer)

AYCKBOURN, Alan (1939– ; British dramatist)

BLACKMORE, R D (1825–1900; British historical novelist)

BLACKWOOD, Algernon Henry (1869–1951; British novelist and short-story writer)

BLEASDALE, Alan (1946– ; British playwright)

BOCCACCIO, Giovanni (1313–75; Italian writer and poet)

BURROUGHS, Edgar Rice (1875–1950; US novelist)

BURROUGHS, William (1914–97; US novelist)

CERVANTES, Miguel de (1547–1616; Spanish novelist)

CHARTERIS, Leslie (L Charles Bowyer Yin, 1907–93; British novelist)

CHURCHILL, Charles (1731–64; British poet)

COLERIDGE, Samuel Taylor (1772–1834; British poet)

CORNEILLE, Pierre (1606–84; French dramatist)

D'ANNUNZIO, Gabriele (1863–1938; Italian poet, novelist, and dramatist)

DE LA ROCHE, Mazo (1885–1961; Canadian novelist)

DE QUINCEY, Thomas (1785–1859; British essayist and critic)

DICKINSON, Emily (1830–86; US poet)

DOOLITTLE, Hilda (1886–1961; US poet)

DOS PASSOS, John (1896–1970; US novelist)

DU MAURIER, George (1834–96; British caricaturist and novelist)

ECKERMANN, Johann Peter (1792–1854; German writer)

EDGEWORTH, Maria (1767–1849; Anglo-Irish writer)

9–continued

EHRENBERG, Iliya Grigorievich (1891–1967; Soviet author)

EURIPIDES (c. 480–406 BC; Greek dramatist)

FROISSART, Jean (1337–c. 1400; French chronicler and poet)

GIRAUDOUX, Jean (1882–1944; French dramatist and novelist)

GOLDSMITH, Oliver (1730–74; Anglo-Irish writer)

GONCHAROV, Ivan Aleksandrovich (1812–91; Russian novelist)

GOTTSCHED, Johann Christoph (1700–66; German critic)

GREENWOOD, Walter (1903–74; British novelist)

HAUPTMANN, Gerhart (1862–1946; German dramatist)

HAWTHORNE, Nathaniel (1804–64; US novelist and short-story writer)

HEMINGWAY, Ernest (1899–1961; US novelist)

HIGHSMITH, Patricia (1921–95; US author of crime fiction)

HÖLDERLIN, Friedrich (1770–1843; German poet)

ISHERWOOD, Christopher (1904–86; British novelist)

JEFFERIES, Richard (1848–87; British novelist and naturalist)

KLOPSTOCK, Friedrich Gottlieb (1724–1803; German poet)

LA BRUYÈRE, Jean de (1645–96; French satirist)

LA FAYETTE, Mme de (Marie Madeleine, Comtesse de L F, 1634–93; French novelist)

LAMARTINE, Alphonse de (1790–1869; French poet)

LAMPEDUSA, Giuseppe Tomasi di (1896–1957; Italian novelist)

LERMONTOV, Mikhail (1814–41; Russian poet and novelist)

LINKLATER, Eric (1889–1974; Scottish novelist)

LLEWELLYN, Richard (R D V L Lloyd, 1907–83; Welsh novelist)

WRITERS, PLAYWRIGHTS, AND POETS

9–continued

LOMONOSOV, Mikhail Vasilievich (1711–65; Russian poet)

LOVECRAFT, H P (1890–1937; US novelist and short-story writer)

LUCRETIUS (Titus Lucretius Carus, c. 95–c. 55 BC; Roman philosopher and poet)

MACKENZIE, Sir Compton (1883–1972; British novelist)

MALAPARTE, Curzio (Kurt Erich Suckert; 1898–1957; Italian novelist and dramatist)

MANSFIELD, Katherine (Kathleen Mansfield Beauchamp, 1888–1923; New Zealand short-story writer)

MARINETTI, Filippo Tommaso (1876–1944; Italian poet and novelist)

MARTINEAU, Harriet (1802–76; British writer)

MASEFIELD, John (1878–1967; British poet)

MASSINGER, Philip (1583–1640; English dramatist)

MCCULLERS, Carson (1917–67; US novelist and playwright)

MIDDLETON, Thomas (1580–1627; English dramatist)

MONSARRAT, Nicholas (John Turney, 1910–79; British novelist)

MONTAIGNE, Michel de (1533–92; French essayist)

MUTANABBI, Abu At-Tayyib Ahmad Ibn Husayn al- (915–65 AD; Arab poet)

O'FLAHERTY, Liam (1897–1984; Irish novelist)

PARKINSON, Northcote (1909–93; British author)

PASTERNAK, Boris (1890–1960; Russian poet and novelist)

POLIZIANO (or Politian; 1454–94; Italian poet and scholar)

PRATCHETT, Terence (1948– ; British writer)

PRITCHETT, V S (1900–97; British short-story writer and critic)

RADCLIFFE, Ann (1764–1823; British novelist)

ROCHESTER, John Wilmot, 2nd Earl of (1647–80; British poet)

9–continued

SACKVILLE, Thomas, 1st Earl of Dorset (1536–1608; British poet and dramatist)

SCHREINER, Olive (1855–1920; South African novelist)

SHENSTONE, William (1714–63; British poet)

SHOLOKHOV, Mikhail (1905–84; Soviet novelist)

SOPHOCLES (c. 496–406 BC; Greek dramatist)

STEINBECK, John (1902–68; US novelist)

STEVENSON, Robert Louis (1850–94; British novelist)

STURLUSON, Snorri (1178–1241; Icelandic poet)

SWINBURNE, Algernon Charles (1837–1909; British poet)

THACKERAY, William Makepeace (1811–63; British novelist)

TSVETAEVA, Marina (1892–1941; Russian poet)

UNGARETTI, Giuseppe (1888–1970; Italian poet)

VERHAEREN, Émile (1844–96; Belgian poet)

VITTORINI, Elio (1908–66; Italian novelist)

WERGELAND, Henrik Arnold (1808–45; Norwegian poet)

WODEHOUSE, Sir P G (1881–1975; US humorous writer)

WYCHERLEY, William (1640–1716; English dramatist)

10

BAINBRIDGE, Beryl (1934– ; British novelist and playwright)

BAUDELAIRE, Charles (1821–67; French poet)

BILDERDIJK, Willem (1756–1831; Dutch poet and dramatist)

CAVALCANTI, Guido (c. 1255–1300; Italian poet)

CHATTERJEE, Bankim Chandra (1838–94; Indian novelist)

CHATTERTON, Thomas (1752–70; British poet)

CHESTERTON, G K (1874–1936; British essayist, novelist, and poet)

CONSCIENCE, Hendrik (1812–83; Flemish novelist)

10–continued

DAZAI OSAMU (Tsushima Shuji; 1909–48; Japanese novelist)

DIO CASSIUS (c. 150–235 AD; Roman historian)

DRINKWATER, John (1882–1937; British poet and dramatist)

DÜRRENMATT, Friedrich (1921–90; Swiss dramatist and novelist)

FITZGERALD, Edward (1809–83; British poet)

FITZGERALD, F Scott (1896–1940; US novelist)

GALSWORTHY, John (1867–1933; British novelist and dramatist)

JEAN DE MEUN (c. 1240–c. 1305; French poet)

KHLEBNIKOV, Velimir (Victor K, 1885–1922; Russian poet)

LA FONTAINE, Jean de (1621–95; French poet)

LAGERKVIST, Pär (1891–1974; Swedish novelist, poet, and dramatist)

LONGFELLOW, Henry Wadsworth (1807–82; US poet)

MACDIARMID, Hugh (Christopher Murray Grieve, 1892–1978; Scottish poet)

MANDELSTAM, Osip (1891–?1938; Russian poet)

MAUPASSANT, Guy de (1850–93; French short-story writer and novelist)

MCGONAGALL, William (1830–1902; Scottish poet)

MICKIEWICZ, Adam (1798–1855; Polish poet)

OSTROVSKII, Aleksandr Nikolaevich (1823–86; Russian dramatist)

PIRANDELLO, Luigi (1867–1936; Italian dramatist and novelist)

PROPERTIUS, Sextus (c. 50–c. 16 BC; Roman poet)

RICHARDSON, Henry Handel (Ethel Florence R, 1870–1946; Australian novelist)

RICHARDSON, Samuel (1689–1761; British novelist)

RUTHERFORD, Mark (William Hale White, 1831–1913; British novelist)

10–continued

SCHNITZLER, Arthur
(1862–1931; Austrian Jewish
dramatist and novelist)
STRINDBERG, August
(1849–1912; Swedish
dramatist and writer)
TANNHÄUSER (c. 1200–c.
1270; German poet)
THEOCRITUS (c. 310–250 BC;
Greek poet)
VAN DER POST, Sir Laurens
(1906–96; South African
novelist)
WILLIAMSON, Henry
(1895–1977; British novelist)
WORDSWORTH, William
(1770–1850; British poet)
XENOPHANES (6th century
BC; Greek poet)

11

ANZENGRUBER, Ludwig
(1839–89; Austrian dramatist
and novelist)
APOLLINAIRE, Guillaume
(Wilhelm de Kostrowitzky,
1880–1918; French poet)
ARCHILOCHUS (c. 680–c. 640
BC; Greek poet)
BACCHYLIDES (c. 516–c. 450
BC; Greek lyric poet)
BLESSINGTON, Marguerite,
Countess of (1789–1849;
Irish author)
CALLIMACHUS (c. 305–c. 240
BC; Greek poet)
CASTIGLIONE, Baldassare
(1478–1529; Italian writer)
DOSTOIEVSKI, Fedor
Mikhailovich (1821–81;
Russian novelist)
EICHENDORFF, Josef, Freiherr
von (1788–1857; German
writer)
GARCÍA LORCA, Federico
(1898–1936; Spanish poet
and dramatist)
GRILLPARZER, Franz
(1791–1872; Austrian
dramatist)
KAZANTZAKIS, Nikos
(1885–1957; Greek novelist
and poet)
LAUTRÉAMONT, Comte de
(Isidore Ducasse, 1846–70;
French writer)
MAETERLINCK, Maurice
(1862–1949; Belgian poet
and dramatist)

11–continued

MATSUO BASHO (Matsuo
Munefusa, 1644–94;
Japanese poet)
MAYAKOVSKII, Vladimir
(1893–1930; Russian poet)
MONTHERLANT, Henry de
(1896–1972; French novelist
and dramatist)
'OMAR KHAYYAM
(?1048–?1122; Persian poet)
PÉREZ GALDÓS, Benito
(1843–1920; Spanish
novelist)
SHAKESPEARE, William
(1564–1616; English
dramatist)
SIENKIEWICZ, Henryk
(1846–1916; Polish novelist)
STIERNHIELM, Georg Olofson
(1598–1672; Swedish poet)
YEVTUSHENKO, Yevgenii
(1933– ; Soviet poet)

12

ARISTOPHANES (c. 450–c.
385 BC; Greek comic
dramatist)
BEAUMARCHAIS, Pierre-
Augustin Caron de (1732–99;
French dramatist)
BLASCO IBÁÑEZ, Vicente
(1867–1928; Spanish
novelist)
FERLINGHETTI, Lawrence
(1919– ; US poet)
FEUCHTWANGER, Lion
(1884–1958; German novelist
and dramatist)
HOFMANNSTHAL, Hugo von
(1874–1929; Austrian poet
and dramatist)
LÓPEZ DE AYALA, Pero (c.
1332–c. 1407; Spanish poet
and chronicler)
MARTIN DU GARD, Roger
(1881–1958; French novelist)
MATTHEW PARIS (c. 1200–59;
English chronicler)
ROBBE-GRILLET, Alain
(1922– ; French novelist)
SAINT EXUPÉRY, Antoine de
(1900–44; French novelist)
SOLZHENITSYN, Aleksandr
(1918– ; Russian novelist)
VOZNESENSKII, Andrei
(1933– ; Soviet poet)

13

BERTRAN DE BORN
(?1140–?1215; French
troubadour poet)

13–continued

CASTELO BRANCO, Camilo
(1825–95; Portuguese
novelist)
CHATEAUBRIAND, Vicomte de
(1768–1848; French writer)
CSOKONAI VITÉZ, Mihaly
(1773–1805; Hungarian poet)
GARCÍA MÁRQUEZ, Gabriel
(1928– ; Colombian
novelist)
HARISHCHANDRA (1850–85;
Hindi poet, dramatist, and
essayist, also known as
Bharatendu)
MARIE DE FRANCE (12th
century AD; French poet)
TIRSO DE MOLINA (Gabriel
Téllez, c. 1584–1648;
Spanish dramatist)
ZEAMI MOTOKIYO (1363–c.
1443; Japanese playwright)

14

BRILLAT-SAVARIN, Anthelme
(1755–1826; French writer)
COMPTON-BURNETT, Dame
Ivy (1892–1969; British
novelist)
DAFYDD AP GWILYM (c.
1320–c. 1380; Welsh poet)
DANTE ALIGHIERI
(1265–1321; Italian poet)
DROSTE-HÜLSHOFF, Annette
von (1797–1848; German
poet and novelist)
GÓNGORA Y ARGOTE, Luis
de (1561–1627; Spanish
poet)
GRIMMELSHAUSEN, Hans
Jacob Christoph von (c.
1625–76; German novelist)
JACOPONE DA TODI (c.
1236–1306; Italian religious
poet)
LECONTE DE LISLE, Charles
Marie René (1818–94; French
poet)
OEHLENSCHLÄGER, Adam
(1779–1850; Danish poet and
playwright)
PRÉVOST D'EXILES, Antoine
François, Abbé (1697–1763;
French novelist)
SULLY-PRUDHOMME, René
François Armand
(1839–1907; French poet)
WOLLSTONECRAFT, Mary
(1759–97; British writer)
ZORRILLA Y MORAL, José
(1817–93; Spanish poet and
dramatist)

15

ALARCÓN Y MENDOZA, Juan Ruiz de (1581–1639; Spanish dramatist)

DIODORUS SICULUS (1st century BC; Greek historian)

PLINY THE YOUNGER (Gaius Plinius Caecilius Secundus, c. 61–c. 113 AD; Roman writer)

16

CHRÉTIEN DE TROYES (12th century AD; French poet)

CYRANO DE BERGERAC, Savinien (1619–55; French writer and dramatist)

KAWABATA YASUNARI (1899–1972; Japanese novelist)

PETRONIUS ARBITER (1st century AD; Roman satirist)

17

CALDERÓN DE LA BARCA, Pedro (1600–81; Spanish dramatist)

17–continued

GUILLAUME DE LORRIS (13th century; French poet and author)

TANIZAKI JUN-ICHIRO (1886–1965; Japanese novelist)

18

APOLLONIUS OF RHODES (3rd century BC; Greek epic poet)

KAKINOMOTO HITOMARO (c. 680–710; Japanese poet)

THOMAS OF ERCELDOUNE (13th century; English poet and prophet)

19

BENOIT DE SAINTE-MAURE (12th century AD; French poet)

CHIKAMATSU MONZAEMON (Sugimori Nobumori; 1653–1724; Japanese dramatist)

VILLIERS DE L'ISLE-ADAM, Philippe Auguste, Comte de (1838–89; French poet, novelist, and dramatist)

20+

BERNARDIN DE SAINT-PIERRE, Jacques Henri (1737–1814; French naturalist and writer)

DIONYSIUS OF HALICARNASSUS (1st century BC; Greek historian)

DRUMMOND OF HAWTHORNDEN, William (1585–1649; Scots poet)

ECHEGARAY Y EIZAGUIRRE, José (1832–1916; Spanish dramatist)

GOTTFRIED VON STRASSBURG (13th century; German poet)

WALTHER VON DER VOGELWEIDE (c. 1170–c. 1230; German poet)

WOLFRAM VON ESCHENBACH (c. 1170–c. 1220; German poet)

PHILOSOPHERS

Ayn Rand U.S. Writer/Phil.

4

AYER, Sir Alfred (Jules) (1910–89; British philosopher)

HUME, David (1711–76; Scottish philosopher and historian)

KANT, Immanuel (1724–1804; German philosopher)

MACH, Ernst (1838–1916; Austrian physicist and philosopher)

MARX, Karl (Heinrich) (1818–83; German philosopher)

MILL, James (1773–1836; Scottish writer and philosopher)

MORE, Henry (1614–87; English philosopher)

MOZI (or Motzu; ?470–?391 BC; Chinese philosopher)

RAZI, ar (or Rhazes; c. 865–c. 928 AD; Persian physician and philosopher)

REID, Thomas (1710–96; Scottish philosopher)

RYLE, Gilbert (1900–76; British philosopher)

4–continued

VICO, Giambattista (or Giovanni Battista Vico; 1668–1744; Italian historical philosopher)

WEIL, Simone (1909–43; French mystic and philosopher)

5

AMIEL, Henri Frédéric (1821–81; Swiss philosopher and writer)

BACON, Francis, 1st Baron Verulam, Viscount St Albans (1561–1626; English lawyer and philosopher)

BENDA, Julien (1867–1956; French novelist and philosopher)

BODIN, Jean (1530–96; French philosopher and jurist)

BRUNO, Giordano (1548–1600; Italian philosopher)

BUBER, Martin (1878–1965; Austrian-born Jewish religious philosopher)

5–continued

BURKE, Edmund (1729–97; British political philosopher and politician)

CHU XI (or Chu Hsi; 1130–1200; Chinese philosopher)

COMTE, Auguste (1798–1857; French philosopher)

CROCE, Benedetto (1866–1952; Italian philosopher)

DEWEY, John (1859–1952; US philosopher and educationalist)

FLUDD, Robert (1574–1637; English physician and philosopher)

FROMM, Erich (1900–80; US psychologist and philosopher)

HEGEL, Georg Wilhelm Friedrich (1770–1831; German philosopher)

IQBAL, Sir Mohammed (?1875–1938; Indian Muslim poet and philosopher)

5–continued

LACAN, Jacques (Marie Emile) (1901–81; French psycho-analyst and philosopher)

LOCKE, John (1632–1704; English philosopher)

MOORE, G(eorge); E(dward) (1873–1958; British philosopher)

PLATO (429–347 BC; Greek philosopher)

QUINE, Willard van Orman (1908–; US philosopher)

RAMUS, Petrus (Pierre de la Ramée; 1515–72; French humanist philosopher and logician)

RENAN, (Joseph; Ernest (1823–92; French philosopher and theologian)

SMITH, Adam (1723–90; Scottish moral philosopher and political economist)

SOREL, Georges (1847–1922; French social philosopher)

6

ADORNO, Theodor (Wiesengrund) (1903–64; German philosopher)

AGNESI, Maria Gaetana (1718–99; Italian mathematician and philosopher)

ARENDT, Hannah (1906–75; German-born US political philosopher)

AUSTIN, John Langshaw (1911–60; British philosopher)

BERLIN, Sir Isaiah (1909–97; Latvian-born British philosopher and historian)

CARNAP, Rudolf (1891–1970; German-born logical positivist philosopher)

COUSIN, Victor (1792–1867; French philosopher)

FICHTE, Johann Gottlieb (1762–1814; German philosopher)

GODWIN, William (1756–1836; British political philosopher and novelist)

HERDER, Johann Gottfried (1744–1803; German philosopher and poet)

HERZEN, Aleksandr (Ivanovich) (1812–70; Russian political philosopher)

HOBBES, Thomas (1588–1679; English political philosopher)

6–continued

KRIPKE, Saul (1940– ; US philosopher)

LUKACS, Giorgi (1885–1971; Hungarian Marxist philosopher)

ORESME, Nicole d' (c. 1320–82; French philosopher and churchman)

PEIRCE, Charles Sanders (1839–1914; US philosopher and logician)

POPPER, Sir Karl Raimund (1902–94; Austrian-born philosopher)

SARTRE, Jean-Paul (1905–80; French philosopher, novelist, dramatist, and critic)

TAGORE, Rabindranath (1861–1941; Indian poet, philosopher, and teacher)

7

ABELARD, Peter (1079–1142; French philosopher)

ALKINDI, Abu Yusuf Ya'qub ibn Ishaq (died c. 870; Muslim Arab philosopher)

AQUINAS, St Thomas (c. 1225–74; Italian Dominican theologian, scholastic philosopher, and Doctor of the Church)

ARNAULD, Antoine (1612–94; French theologian, philosopher, and logician)

BENTHAM, Jeremy (1748–1832; British philosopher)

BERGSON, Henri (1859–1941; French philosopher and psychologist)

BLONDEL, Maurice (1861–1949; French philosopher)

BRADLEY, Francis Herbert (1846–1924; British philosopher)

BURIDAN, Jean (c. 1297–c. 1358; French scholastic philosopher)

CHARRON, Pierre (1541–1603; French theologian and philosopher)

DERRIDA, Jacques (1930– ; French philosopher)

DESTUTT, Antoine Louis Claude, Comte de Tracy (1754–1836; French philosopher and politician)

7–continued

DIDEROT, Denis (1713–84; French philosopher and writer)

EDWARDS, Jonathan (1703–58; American theologian and philosopher)

ERIGENA, John Scotus (c. 800–c. 877; Irish-born medieval philosopher)

GENTILE, Giovanni (1875–1944; Italian philosopher)

GUARINI, Guarino (1624–83; Italian baroque architect, philosopher, and mathematician)

HUSSERL, Edmund (1859–1938; German philosopher)

HYPATIA (d. 415 AD; Neoplatonist philosopher and mathematician)

JASPERS, Karl (Theodor) (1883–1969; German philosopher)

LEIBNIZ, Gottfried Wilhelm (1646–1716; German philosopher and mathematician)

MENCIUS (Mengzi or Mengtzu; 371–289 BC; Chinese moral philosopher)

MUMFORD, Lewis (1895–1990; US social philosopher)

MURDOCH, Dame Iris (1919–99; British novelist and philosopher)

PROCLUS (410–85 AD; Neoplatonist philosopher)

PYRRHON (or Pyrrho; c. 360–c. 270 BC; Greek philosopher)

RUSSELL, Bertrand Arthur William, 3rd Earl (1872–1970; British philosopher)

SANKARA (or Shankara; 8th century AD; Hindu philosopher)

SCHLICK, Moritz (1882–1936; German philosopher)

SCRUTON, Roger (Vernon) (1944–; British philosopher and cultural historian)

SPENCER, Herbert (1820–1903; British philosopher)

SPINOZA, Benedict (or Baruch de S.; 1632–77; Dutch philosopher, theologian, and scientist)

8

ALFARABI, Mohammed ibn Tarkhan (d. 950; Muslim philosopher, physician, mathematician, and musician)

AVERROES (Ibn Rushd; 1126–98; Muslim philosopher)

AVICENNA (980–1037; Persian philosopher and physician)

BERDYAEV, Nikolai (1874–1948; Russian mystical philosopher)

BERKELEY, George (1685–1753; Irish bishop and idealist philosopher)

BOETHIUS, Anicius Manlius Severinus (c. 480–524 AD; Roman statesman and philosopher)

BRENTANO, Franz (1838–1916; German psychologist and philosopher)

CASSIRER, Ernst (1874–1945; German philosopher and historian)

EPICURUS (341–270 BC; Greek philosopher)

FOUCAULT, Michel (1926–84; French philosopher)

GASSENDI, Pierre (1592–1655; French physicist and philosopher)

GEULINCX, Arnold (1624–69; Belgian-born philosopher)

HAN FEI ZI (d. 233 BC; Chinese diplomat and philosopher of law)

HARTMANN, Eduard von (1842–1906; German philosopher)

HARTMANN, Nicolai (1882–1950; Russian-born German philosopher)

KROCHMAL, Nachman (1785–1840; Jewish philosopher)

PLOTINUS (205–70 AD; Greek philosopher)

PORPHYRY (232–305 AD; Syrian-born philosopher)

RAMANUJA (11th century AD; Indian-born Hindu philosopher and theologian)

ROSCELIN (died c. 1125; French scholastic philosopher)

ROUSSEAU, Jean Jacques (1712–78; French philosopher and writer)

8–continued

SIDGWICK, Henry (1838–1900; British moral philosopher)

SOCRATES (c. 469–399 BC; Athenian philosopher)

SOLOVIOV, Vladimir Sergevich (1853–1900; Russian philosopher and poet)

SPENGLER, Oswald (1880–1936; German philosopher)

STRAWSON, Sir Peter Frederick (1919–; British philosopher)

VOLTAIRE (François-Marie Arouet; 1694–1778; French philosopher)

ZHUANGZI (or Chuangtzu; c. 369–286 BC; Chinese philosopher)

9 Anderson, John (1893-1962;

ALTHUSSER, Louis (1918–90; Algerian-born French philosopher)

ARISTOTLE (384–322 BC; Greek philosopher and scientist)

BOSANQUET, Bernard (1848–1923; British philosopher)

CLEANTHES (c. 310–230 BC; Greek philosopher)

CONDILLAC, Étienne Bonnot de (1715–80; French philosopher and psychologist)

CONDORCET, Marie Jean Antoine de Caritat, Marquis de (1743–94; French philosopher and politician)

CONFUCIUS (Kong Zi or K'ungfutzu; c. 551–479 BC; Chinese philosopher)

DESCARTES, René (1596–1650; French philosopher)

EPICTETUS (c. 60–110 AD; Stoic philosopher)

FEUERBACH, Ludwig Andreas (1804–72; German philosopher)

HEIDEGGER, Martin (1889–1976; German philosopher)

HELVÉTIUS, Claude Adrien (1715–71; French philosopher)

HUTCHESON, Francis (1694–1746; Scottish philosopher)

9–continued

LEUCIPPUS (5th century BC; Greek philosopher)

LUCRETIUS (Titus Lucretius Carus; c. 95–c. 55 BC; Roman philosopher and poet)

NAGARJUNA (c. 150–c. 250 AD; Indian Buddhist monk and philosopher)

NIETZSCHE, Friedrich (1844–1900; German philosopher)

PLEKHANOV, Georgi Valentinovich (1857–1918; Russian revolutionary and Marxist philosopher)

PUFENDORF, Samuel von (1632–94; German philosopher)

SANTAYANA, George (1863–1952; Spanish-born US philosopher and poet)

SCHELLING, Friedrich (1775–1854; German philosopher)

WHITEHEAD, A(lfred); N(orth) (1861–1947; British philosopher and mathematician)

10

ANAXAGORAS (c. 500–428 BC; Greek philosopher)

ANAXIMENES (died c. 528 BC; Greek philosopher)

ARISTIPPUS (c. 435–c. 356 BC; Greek philosopher)

BAUMGARTEN, Alexander Gottlieb (1714–62; German philosopher)

CAMPANELLA, Tommaso (1568–1639; Italian philosopher and Dominican friar)

CUMBERLAND, Richard (1631–1718; English moral philosopher)

DEMOCRITUS (c. 460–370 BC; Greek philosopher and scientist)

DUNS SCOTUS, John (c. 1260–1308; Scottish-born Franciscan philosopher)

EMPEDOCLES (c. 490–430 BC; Sicilian Greek philosopher)

FONTENELLE, Bernard le Bovier de (1657–1757; French philosopher)

HERACLITUS (c. 535–c. 475 BC; Greek philosopher)

IBN GABIROL, Solomon (c. 1021–c. 1058; Spanish-born Jewish philosopher and poet)

10–continued

IBN KHALDUN (1332–1406; Arab historian and philosopher)

MAIMONIDES, Moses (1135–1204; Jewish philosopher and physician)

PARMENIDES (c. 510–c. 450 BC; Greek philosopher)

PYTHAGORAS (6th century BC; Greek philosopher and religious leader)

SWEDENBORG, Emanuel (1688–1772; Swedish scientist, mystic, and philosopher)

ZENO OF ELEA (born c. 490 BC; Greek philosopher)

11

BOLINGBROKE, Henry St John, 1st Viscount (1678–1751; English statesman and philosopher)

COLLINGWOOD, R(obin); G(eorge) (1889–1943; British philosopher)

JUDAH HALEVI (or Halevy; c. 1075–1141; Jewish poet and philosopher)

KIERKEGAARD, Søren (1813–55; Danish philosopher)

MALEBRANCHE, Nicolas (1638–1715; French philosopher and theologian)

MENDELSSOHN, Moses (1729–86; German Jewish philosopher)

11–continued

MONTESQUIEU, Charles Louis de Secondat, Baron de (1689–1755; French historical philosopher and writer)

VIVEKANANDA, Swami (1862–1902; Hindu philosopher)

ANAXIMANDER (c. 610–c. 546 BC; Greek philosopher)

ANTISTHENES (c. 445–c. 360 BC; Greek philosopher)

12

MERLEAUPONTY, Maurice (1908–61; French philosopher)

PHILO JUDAEUS (c. 30 BC–45 AD; Jewish philosopher)

SCHOPENHAUER, Arthur (1788–1860; German philosopher)

THEOPHRASTUS (c. 370–286 BC; Greek philosopher and scientist)

UNAMUNO Y JUGO, Miguel de (1864–1936; Spanish writer and philosopher)

WITTGENSTEIN, Ludwig (1889–1951; Austrian philosopher)

ZENO OF CITIUM (c. 335–262 BC; Greek philosopher)

13

DIO CHRYSOSTOM (2nd century AD; Greek philosopher and orator)

13–continued

ORTEGA Y GASSET, José (1883–1955; Spanish philosopher and writer)

14

ALBERTUS MAGNUS, St (c. 1200–80; German bishop, philosopher, and Doctor of the Church)

WOLLSTONECRAFT, Mary (1759–97; British writer)

15

JOHN OF SALISBURY (c. 1115–80; English philosopher)

WILLIAM OF OCKHAM (c. 1285–1349; English scholastic philosopher)

16

ALEXANDER OF HALES (c. 1170–1245; English scholastic philosopher)

17

APOLLONIUS OF TYANA (1st century AD; Pythagorean philosopher)

BERNARD OF CHARTRES (died c. 1130; French scholastic philosopher)

18

PICO DELLA MIRANDOLA, Giovanni, Conte (1463–94; Italian Renaissance philosopher)

MUSICIANS AND COMPOSERS

3

BAX, Sir Arnold Edward Trevor (1883–1953; British composer)

4

ADAM, Adolphe-Charles (1803–56; French composer)

ARNE, Thomas Augustine (1710–78; British composer)

BACH, Johann Sebastian (1685–1750; German composer and keyboard player)

BERG, Alban (1885–1935; Austrian composer)

4–continued

BING, Sir Rudolf (1902– ; British opera administrator)

BLOW, John (1649–1708; English composer)

BÖHM, Karl (1894–1981; Austrian conductor)

BULL, John (c. 1562–1628; English composer and organist)

BUSH, Alan Dudley (1900– ; British composer)

BUTT, Dame Clara (1873–1936; British contralto singer)

4–continued

BYRD, William (?1543–1623; English composer)

CAGE, John (1912–92; US composer)

HESS, Dame Myra (1890–1965; British pianist)

IVES, Charles (1874–1954; US composer)

LALO, Édouard (1823–92; French composer)

LILL, John (1944– ; British pianist)

LIND, Jenny (1820–87; Swedish soprano)

4–continued

NONO, Luigi (1924–90; Italian composer)

ORFF, Carl (1895–1982; German composer and conductor)

PÄRT, Arvo (1935– ; Estonian composer)

WOLF, Hugo (1860–1903; Austrian composer)

WOOD, Sir Henry (1869–1944; British conductor)

5

ADAMS, John Coolidge (1947– ; US composer)

ALKAN, Charles Henri Valentin (C H V Morhange, 1813–88; French pianist and composer)

ALLEN, Thomas (1944– ; British operatic baritone)

ARRAU, Claudio (1903–91; Chilean pianist)

AUBER, Daniel François Esprit (1782–1871; French composer)

AURIC, Georges (1899–1983; French composer)

BAKER, Dame Janet (1933– ; British mezzo-soprano)

BERIO, Luciano (1925– ; Italian composer)

BIZET, Georges (Alexandre César Léopold B, 1838–75; French composer)

BLISS, Sir Arthur Edward Drummond (1891–1975; British composer)

BLOCH, Ernest (1880–1959; Swiss-born composer)

BOEHM, Theobald (1794–1881; German flautist)

BOULT, Sir Adrian (1889–1983; British conductor)

BOYCE, William (c. 1710–79; British composer)

BREAM, Julian Alexander (1933– ; British guitarist and lutenist)

BRIAN, Havergal (1876–1972; British composer)

BRUCH, Max (1838–1920; German composer)

BÜLOW, Hans Guido, Freiherr von (1830–94; German pianist and conductor)

DAVIS, Sir Andrew (1944– ; British conductor)

DAVIS, Sir Colin (1927– ; British conductor)

D'INDY, Vincent (1851–1931; French composer)

5–continued

DUFAY, Guillaume (c. 1400–74; Burgundian composer)

DUKAS, Paul (1865–1935; French composer)

DUPRÉ, Marcel (1886–1971; French composer)

ELGAR, Sir Edward (1857–1934; British composer)

EVANS, Sir Geraint (1922–92; Welsh baritone)

FALLA, Manuel de (1876–1946; Spanish composer)

FAURÉ, Gabriel (1845–1924; French composer and organist)

FIELD, John (1782–1837; Irish pianist and composer)

FRIML, Rudolph (1879–1972; Czech-born composer and pianist)

GIGLI, Beniamino (1890–1957; Italian tenor)

GLASS, Philip (1937– ; US composer)

GLUCK, Christoph Willibald (1714–87; German composer)

GOBBI, Tito (1915–84; Italian baritone)

GOEHR, Alexander (1932– ; British composer)

GRIEG, Edvard Hagerup (1843–1907; Norwegian composer)

GROVE, Sir George (1820–1900; British musicologist)

HALLÉ, Sir Charles (Karl Hallé, 1819–1895; German conductor and pianist)

HAYDN, Franz Joseph (1732–1809; Austrian composer)

HENZE, Hans Werner (1926– ; German composer)

HOLST, Gustav (1874–1934; British composer and teacher)

IBERT, Jacques (1890–1962; French composer)

LEHÁR, Franz (Ferencz L, 1870–1948; Hungarian composer)

LISZT, Franz (Ferencz L, 1811–86; Hungarian pianist and composer)

LOCKE, Matthew (c. 1622–77; English composer)

LULLY, Jean Baptiste (Giovanni Battista Lulli, 1632–87; French composer)

MELBA, Dame Nellie (Helen Porter Armstrong, 1861–1931; Australian soprano)

5–continued

MOORE, Gerald (1899–1987; British pianist)

MUNCH, Charles (1892–1968; French conductor)

OGDON, John (1937–89; British pianist)

PARRY, Sir Hubert (1848–1918; British composer)

PATTI, Adelina (Adela Juana Maria, 1843–1919; Italian-born operatic soprano)

PEARS, Sir Peter (1910–86; British tenor)

RAVEL, Maurice (1875–1937; French composer)

REGER, Max (1873–1916; German composer, organist, and teacher)

SATIE, Erik (1866–1925; French composer)

SHARP, Cecil (1859–1924; British musician)

SOLTI, Sir Georg (1912–97; Hungarian-born British conductor)

SOUSA, John Philip (1854–1933; US composer and bandmaster)

SPOHR, Louis (Ludwig S, 1784–1859; German violinist and composer)

STERN, Isaac (1920– ; Russian-born US violinist)

SZELL, George (1897–1970; Hungarian conductor)

TEYTE, Dame Maggie (1888–1976; British soprano)

VERDI, Giuseppe (1813–1901; Italian composer)

WEBER, Carl Maria von (1786–1826; German composer)

WEILL, Kurt (1900–50; German composer)

WIDOR, Charles Marie (1844–1937; French organist and composer)

6

ARNOLD, Malcolm (1921– ; British composer)

BARBER, Samuel (1910–81; US composer)

BARTÓK, Béla (1881–1945; Hungarian composer)

BATTLE, Kathleen (1948– ; US soprano)

BISHOP, Sir Henry Rowley (1786–1855; British composer and conductor)

Stephen Foster (1826-64) (Camptown Races)

6–continued

BOULEZ, Pierre (1925– ; French composer and conductor)

BRAHMS, Johannes (1833–97; German composer)

BRIDGE, Frank (1879–1941; British composer)

BURNEY, Charles (1726–1814; British musicologist, organist, and composer)

BUSONI, Ferruccio (1866–1924; Italian virtuoso pianist and composer)

CALLAS, Maria (Maria Anna Kalageropoulos, 1923–77; US-born soprano)

CARTER, Elliott (1908– ; US composer)

CARUSO, Enrico (1873–1921; Italian tenor)

CASALS, Pablo (Pau C, 1876–1973; Spanish cellist, conductor, and composer)

CHOPIN, Frédéric (François, 1810–49; Polish composer)

CLARKE, Jeremiah (?1673–1707; English composer and organist)

CORTOT, Alfred (1877–1962; French pianist and conductor)

COWELL, Henry (1897–1965; US composer)

CURWEN, John (1816–80; British teacher who perfected the Tonic Sol-fa system)

CURZON, Sir Clifford (1907–82; British pianist)

DAVIES, Sir Peter Maxwell (1934– ; British composer)

DELIUS, Frederick (1862–1934; British composer)

DIBDIN, Charles (1745–1814; British composer, actor, and singer)

DUPARC, Henri (Marie Eugène Henri Foucques D, 1848–1933; French composer)

DVOŘÁK, Antonín (1841–1904; Czech composer)

ENESCO, Georges (G Enescu, 1881–1955; Romanian violinist and composer)

FLOTOW, Friedrich von (1812–83; German composer)

FRANCK, César Auguste (1822–90; Belgian composer, organist, and teacher)

6–continued

GALWAY, James (1939– ; Irish flautist)

GLINKA, Mikhail Ivanovich (1804–57; Russian composer)

GOUNOD, Charles François (1818–93; French composer)

GRÉTRY, André Ernest Modeste (1741–1813; Belgian composer)

GROVES, Sir Charles (1915–92; British conductor)

HALÉVY, Jacques François (Fromental Elias Levy, 1799–1862; French composer)

HANDEL, George Frederick (1685–1759; German composer)

HARRIS, Roy (1898–1979; US composer)

HOTTER, Hans (1909– ; German baritone)

HUMMEL, Johann Nepomuk (1778–1837; Hungarian pianist and composer)

JOCHUM, Eugen (1902–87; German conductor)

KODÁLY, Zoltan (1882–1967; Hungarian composer)

KRENEK, Ernst (1900–91; Austrian composer)

LASSUS, Roland de (c. 1532–94; Flemish composer)

LIGETI, György (1923– ; Hungarian composer)

MAAZEL, Lorin (1930– ; US conductor)

MAHLER, Gustav (1860–1911; Austrian composer and conductor)

MORLEY, Thomas (1557–1603; English composer, music printer and organist)

MOZART, Wolfgang Amadeus (1756–91; Austrian composer)

PREVIN, André (Andreas Ludwig Priwin, 1929– ; German-born conductor, pianist, and composer)

RAMEAU, Jean Philippe (1683–1764; French composer)

RATTLE, Sir Simon (1955– ; British conductor)

RUBBRA, Edmund (1901–86; British composer)

SCHÜTZ, Heinrich (1585–1672; German composer)

6–continued

TALLIS, Thomas (c. 1505–85; English composer)

VARÈSE, Edgard (1883–1965; French composer)

WAGNER, Richard (1813–83; German composer)

WALTER, Bruno (B W Schlesinger, 1876–1962; German conductor)

WALTON, Sir William (1902–83; British composer)

WEBERN, Anton von (1883–1945; Austrian composer)

7

ALBÉNIZ, Isaac Manuel Francisco (1860–1909; Spanish composer and pianist)

ALLEGRI, Gregorio (1582–1652; Italian composer)

ANTHEIL, George (1900–59; US composer)

BABBITT, Milton (1916– ; US composer)

BEECHAM, Sir Thomas (1879–1961; British conductor)

BELLINI, Vincenzo (1801–35; Italian opera composer)

BENNETT, Richard Rodney (1936– ; British composer)

BENNETT, Sir William Sterndale (1816–75; British pianist)

BERLIOZ, Hector (1803–69; French composer and conductor)

BORODIN, Aleksandr Porfirevich (1833–87; Russian composer)

BRENDEL, Alfred (1931– ; Austrian pianist)

BRAXTON, Anthony (1945– ; US composer)

BRITTEN, Benjamin, Baron (1913–76; British composer and pianist)

CABALLÉ, Montserrat (1933– ; Spanish soprano)

CACCINI, Giulio (c. 1545–c. 1618; Italian singer and composer)

CAMPION, Thomas (or Campian, 1567–1620; English composer)

CAVALLI, Francesco (1602–76; Italian composer)

COPLAND, Aaron (1900–90; US composer)

7–continued

CORELLI, Arcangelo (1653–1713; Italian violinist and composer)

DEBUSSY, Claude (1862–1918; French composer)

DELIBES, Leo (1836–91; French composer)

DOMINGO, Placido (1941– ; Spanish tenor)

DOWLAND, John (1563–1626; English composer and lutenist)

FARNABY, Giles (c. 1565–1640; English composer)

FERRIER, Kathleen (1912–53; British contralto)

GALUPPI, Baldassare (1706–85; Venetian composer)

GARRETT, Lesley (1955– ; British soprano)

GIBBONS, Orlando (1583–1625; English composer, organist, and virginalist)

GIULINI, Carlo Maria (1914– ; Italian conductor)

GORECKI, Henryk (1933– ; Polish composer)

HAMMOND, Dame Joan (1912–96; British soprano)

HOFMANN, Joseph Casimir (1876–1957; Polish-born pianist)

IRELAND, John Nicholson (1879–1962; British composer)

JANÁČEK, Leoš (1854–1928; Czech composer)

JOACHIM, Joseph (1831–1907; Hungarian violinist and composer)

KARAJAN, Herbert von (1908–89; Austrian conductor)

KUBELIK, Rafael (1914–96; Czech conductor)

LAMBERT, Constant (1905–51; British composer and conductor)

LEHMANN, Lilli (1848–1929; German soprano)

LEHMANN, Lotte (1885–1976; German soprano)

MALCOLM, George John (1917– ; British harpsichordist)

MARTINŮ, Bohuslav (1890–1959; Czech composer)

MENOTTI, Gian Carlo (1911– ; Italian-born US composer)

7–continued

MENUHIN, Sir Yehudi (1916–99; British violinist)

MILHAUD, Darius (1892–1974; French composer)

MONTEUX, Pierre (1875–1964; French conductor)

NICOLAI, Otto Ehrenfried (1810–49; German conductor and composer)

NIELSEN, Carl (1865–1931; Danish composer and conductor)

NIKISCH, Arthur (1855–1922; Hungarian conductor)

NILSSON, Birgit Marta (1918– ; Swedish soprano)

OKEGHEM, Jean d' (c. 1425–c. 1495; Flemish composer)

ORMANDY, Eugene (E Blau, 1899–1985; Hungarian-born US conductor)

PÉROTIN (Latin name: Perotinus Magnus, c. 1155–c. 1202; French composer)

POULENC, Francis (1899–1963; French composer)

PUCCINI, Giacomo (1858–1924; Italian opera composer)

PURCELL, Henry (1659–95; English composer and organist)

RICHTER, Hans (1843–1916; Hungarian conductor)

RICHTER, Sviatoslav (1915–97; Ukrainian pianist)

RODRIGO, Joaquín (1902– ; Spanish composer)

ROSSINI, Gioacchino Antonio (1792–1868; Italian composer)

ROUSSEL, Albert (1869–1937; French composer)

RUGGLES, Carl (1876–1971; US composer)

SALIERI, Antonio (1750–1825; Italian composer and conductor)

SARGENT, Sir Malcolm (1895–1967; British conductor)

SCHUMAN, William (1910–91; US composer)

SLATKIN, Leonard (1944– ; US conductor)

SMETANA, Bedřich (1824–84; Bohemian composer)

SOLOMON (S Cutner, 1902– ; British pianist)

STAINER, Sir John (1840–1901; British composer and organist)

7–continued

STAMITZ, Johann (Jan Stamic, 1717–57; Bohemian composer)

STRAUSS, Richard (1864–1949; German composer and conductor)

THIBAUD, Jacques (1880–1953; French violinist)

THOMSON, Virgil (1896–1989; US composer and conductor)

TIPPETT, Sir Michael (1905–98; British composer)

VIVALDI, Antonio (1678–1741; Italian composer and violinist)

WARLOCK, Peter (Philip Heseltine, 1894–1930; British composer and music scholar)

WEELKES, Thomas (c. 1575–1623; English composer and organist)

WELLESZ, Egon (1885–1974; Austrian composer)

XENAKIS, Yannis (1922– ; Greek composer)

8

ALBINONI, Tomaso (1671–1750; Italian composer)

ANSERMET, Ernest (1883–1969; Swiss conductor)

BERKELEY, Sir Lennox Randal Francis (1903–89; British composer)

BRUCKNER, Anton (1824–96; Austrian composer and organist)

CHABRIER, Emmanuel (1841–94; French composer)

CHAUSSON, Ernest (1855–99; French composer)

CIMAROSA, Domenico (1749–1801; Italian composer)

CLEMENTI, Muzio (1752–1832; Italian pianist and composer)

COUPERIN, François (1668–1733; French composer)

DOHNÁNYI, Ernö (Ernst von D, 1877–1960; Hungarian composer and pianist)

FLAGSTAD, Kirsten Malfrid (1895–1962; Norwegian soprano)

GARDINER, Sir John Eliot (1943– ; British conductor)

GERSHWIN, George (Jacob Gershvin, 1898– 1937; US composer)

8–continued

GESUALDO, Carlo, Prince of Venosa (c. 1560–1631; Italian composer)

GLAZUNOV, Aleksandr Konstantinovich (1865–1936; Russian composer)

GOOSSENS, Sir Eugene (1893–1962; British conductor and composer)

GRAINGER, Percy Aldridge (1882–1961; Australian composer and pianist)

GRANADOS, Enrique (1867–1916; Spanish composer and pianist)

HONEGGER, Arthur (1892–1955; French composer)

HOROWITZ, Vladimir (1904–89; Russian pianist)

KREISLER, Fritz (1875–1962; Austrian violinist)

MACONCHY, Dame Elizabeth (1907–94; British composer)

MARENZIO, Luca (1553–99; Italian composer)

MASCAGNI, Pietro (1863–1945; Italian composer)

MASSENET, Jules (1842–1912; French composer)

MELCHIOR, Lauritz (1890–1973; Danish tenor)

MESSAGER, André (1853–1929; French composer and conductor)

MESSIAEN, Olivier (1908–92; French composer, organist, and teacher)

MILSTEIN, Nathan (1904–92; US violinist)

MUSGRAVE, Thea (1928– ; Scottish composer)

OISTRAKH, David (1908–75; Russian violinist)

PAGANINI, Niccolò (1782–1840; Italian violinist)

PHILIDOR, André Danican (d. 1730; French musician)

RESPIGHI, Ottorino (1879–1936; Italian composer)

SCHNABEL, Artur (1882–1951; Austrian pianist)

SCHUBERT, Franz (1797–1828; Austrian composer)

SCHULLER, Gunther (1925– ; US composer)

SCHUMANN, Elisabeth (1885–1952; German-born soprano)

8–continued

SCHUMANN, Robert (1810–56; German composer)

SCRIABIN, Alexander (1872–1915; Russian composer and pianist)

SESSIONS, Roger (1896–1985; US composer)

SIBELIUS, Jean (Johan Julius Christian S, 1865–1957; Finnish composer)

STANFORD, Sir Charles (1852–1924; Irish composer)

SULLIVAN, Sir Arthur (1842–1900; British composer)

TAVERNER, John (c. 1495–1545; English composer)

TE KANAWA, Dame Kiri (1944– ; New Zealand soprano)

TELEMANN, Georg Philipp (1681–1767; German composer)

VICTORIA, Tomás Luis de (c. 1548–1611; Spanish composer)

WILLIAMS, John (1941– ; Australian guitarist)

WILLIAMS, John Towner (1932– ; US composer)

ZABALETA, Nicanor (1907–93; Spanish harpist)

9

ADDINSELL, Richard (1904–77; British composer)

ASHKENAZY, Vladimir (1937– ; Russian pianist and conductor)

BALAKIREV, Mili Alekseevich (1837–1910; Russian composer)

BARENBOIM, Daniel (1942– ; Israeli pianist and composer)

BEETHOVEN, Ludwig van (1770–1827; German composer)

BERNSTEIN, Leonard (1918–90; US conductor, composer, and pianist)

BOULANGER, Nadia (1887–1979; French composer, teacher, and conductor)

BUXTEHUDE, Dietrich (1637–1707; Danish organist and composer)

CHALIAPIN, Feodor Ivanovich (1873–1938; Russian bass)

CHERUBINI, Maria Luigi (1760–1842; Italian composer)

9–continued

CHRISTOFF, Boris (1919–93; Bulgarian singer)

DOLMETSCH, Arnold (1858–1940; British musician and instrument maker)

DONIZETTI, Gaetano (1797–1848; Italian composer)

DUNSTABLE, John (d. 1453; English composer)

HINDEMITH, Paul (1895–1963; German composer and viola player)

HODDINOTT, Alun (1929– ; Welsh composer)

KLEMPERER, Otto (1885–1973; German conductor)

LANDOWSKA, Wanda (1877–1959; Polish-born harpsichordist)

MACKERRAS, Sir Charles (1925– ; US-born Australian conductor)

MALIPIERO, Gian Francesco (1882–1973; Italian composer and teacher)

MEYERBEER, Giacomo (Jacob Liebmann Beer, 1791–1864; German composer and pianist)

OFFENBACH, Jacques (J Eberst, 1819–80; French composer)

PAVAROTTI, Luciano (1935– ; Italian tenor)

PERGOLESI, Giovanni (1710–36; Italian composer)

SCARLATTI, Domenico (1685–1757; Italian composer, harpsichordist, and organist)

STOKOWSKI, Leopold (1882–1977; British-born conductor)

TORTELIER, Paul (1914–90; French cellist)

TOSCANINI, Arturo (1867–1957; Italian conductor)

10

BARBIROLLI, Sir John (1899–1970; British conductor)

BIRTWISTLE, Harrison (1934– ; British composer)

BOCCHERINI, Luigi (1743–1805; Italian violoncellist and composer)

GALLI-CURCI, Amelita (1882–1963; Italian soprano)

MUSICIANS AND COMPOSERS

10—continued

LOS ANGELES, Victoria de (1923– ; Spanish soprano)

MENGELBERG, William (1871–1951; Dutch conductor)

MONTEVERDI, Claudio (1567–1643; Italian composer)

MUSSORGSKI, Modest Petrovich (1839–81; Russian composer)

PADEREWSKI, Ignacy (1860–1941; Polish pianist and composer)

PALESTRINA, Giovanni Pierluigi da (?1525–94; Italian composer)

PENDERECKI, Krzysztof (1933– ; Polish composer)

PRAETORIUS, Michael (M Schultheiss, 1571–1621; German composer)

RAWSTHORNE, Alan (1905–71; British composer)

RUBINSTEIN, Anton (1829–94; Russian pianist and composer)

RUBINSTEIN, Artur (1888–1982; Polish-born pianist)

SAINT-SAËNS, Camille (1835–1921; French composer, conductor, pianist, and organist)

SCHOENBERG, Arnold (1874–1951; Austrian-born composer)

SKALKOTTAS, Nikos (1904–49; Greek composer)

STRADIVARI, Antonio (?1644–1737; Italian violin maker)

STRAVINSKY, Igor (1882–1971; Russian-born composer)

SUTHERLAND, Dame Joan (1926– ; Australian soprano)

10—continued

TETRAZZINI, Luisa (1871–1940; Italian soprano)

VILLA-LOBOS, Heitor (1887–1959; Brazilian composer)

11

CHARPENTIER, Gustave (1860–1956; French composer)

FURTWÄNGLER, Wilhelm (1886–1954; German conductor)

HUMPERDINCK, Engelbert (1854–1921; German composer)

LEONCAVALLO, Ruggiero (1858–1919; Italian composer)

LESCHETIZKY, Theodor (1830–1915; Polish pianist and piano teacher)

LLOYD WEBBER, Andrew (1948– ; British composer)

LLOYD WEBBER, Julian (1951– ; British cellist)

LUTOSLAWSKI, Witold (1913–94; Polish composer)

MENDELSSOHN, Felix (Jacob Ludwig Felix Mendelssohn-Bartholdy, 1809–47; German composer)

RACHMANINOV, Sergei (1873–1943; Russian composer, pianist, and conductor)

SCHWARZKOPF, Elisabeth (1915– ; German soprano)

STOCKHAUSEN, Karlheinz (1928– ; German composer)

SZYMANOWSKI, Karol (1882–1937; Polish composer)

TCHAIKOVSKY, Peter Ilich (1840–93; Russian composer)

WOLF-FERRARI, Ermanno (1876–1948; Italian composer)

12

DALLAPICCOLA, Luigi (1904–1975; Italian composer and pianist)

GUIDO D'AREZZO (c. 990–c. 1050; Italian monk and musical theorist)

KHACHATURIAN, Aram Ilich (1903–78; Soviet composer, born in Armenia)

KOUSSEVITSKY, Sergei (1874–1951; Russian composer)

13

ROUGET DE L'ISLE, Claude Joseph (1760–1836; French composer)

14

FISCHER-DIESKAU, Dietrich (1925– ; German baritone)

JAQUES-DALCROZE, Émile (1865–1950; Swiss composer)

JOSQUIN DES PREZ (c. 1450–1521; Flemish composer)

RIMSKY-KORSAKOV, Nikolai (1844–1908; Russian composer)

15

COLERIDGE-TAYLOR, Samuel (1875–1912; British composer)

VAUGHAN WILLIAMS, Ralph (1872–1958; British composer)

17

STRAUSS THE YOUNGER, Johann (1825–99; Austrian violinist, conductor, and composer)

STAGE AND SCREEN PERSONALITIES

3

BOW, Clara (US film actress)
COX, Robert (English comic actor)
FOY, Eddie (US actor)
HAY, Will (British comedian)
LEE, Gypsy Rose (US entertainer)
RAY, Satyajit (Indian film director)
RIX, Sir Brian (British actor)
SIM, Alastair (Scottish actor)

4

ARNE, Susanna Maria (British actress)
BIRD, Theophilus (English actor)
BOND, Edward (British dramatist)
CANE, Andrew (English actor)
CHAN, Jackie (Hong Kong actor-director)
COBB, Lee J (US actor)
COOK, Peter (British comedy actor)
DALY, Augustin (US theatre manager)
DEAN, James (US film actor)
DIAZ, Cameron (US film actress)
DUFF, Mrs (US actress)
DUSE, Eleonora (Italian actress)
FORD, John (US film director)
FORD, Harrison (US film actor)
GISH, Lillian (US actress)
GOLD, Jimmy (British comedian)
GRAY, Dulcie (British actress)
GRAY, 'Monsewer' Eddie (British comedian)
HALL, Sir Peter (British theatre director)
HOPE, Bob (US comedian, born in Britain)
KEAN, Edmund (British actor)
KNOX, Teddy (British comedian)
LAHR, Bert (US actor)
LANG, Fritz (German film director)
LEAN, Sir David (British film director)
LUNT, Alfred (US actor)
NUNN, Trevor (British theatre director)

4–continued

OWEN, Alun Davies (British dramatist)
PAGE, Geraldine (US actress)
PIAF, Edith (French cabaret and music-hall performer)
RANK, J Arthur (British industrialist and film executive)
REED, Sir Carol (British film director)
REID, Beryl (British actress)
RIGG, Diana (British actress)
SHER, Anthony (British actor)
TATE, Harry (British music-hall comedian)
TREE, Sir Herbert Beerbohm (British actor and theatre manager)
WEST, Mae (US actress)

5

ALLEN, Chesney (British comedian)
ALLEN, Woody (US film actor and director)
ARMIN, Robert (British actor)
ASTON, Anthony (Irish actor)
BADEL, Alan (British actor)
BARON, André (French actor)
BARON, Michel (French actor)
BARRY, Elizabeth (English actress)
BARRY, Spranger (Irish actor)
BATES, Alan (British actor)
BETTY, William Henry West (British boy actor)
BLOOM, Claire (British actress)
BOOTH, Barton (British actor)
BOOTH, Edwin Thomas (US actor)
BOOTH, Junius Brutus (US actor)
BOYER, Charles (French film actor)
BRICE, Fanny (US actress)
BROOK, Peter (British theatre director)
BROWN, Pamela (British actor)
BRYAN, Dora (British actress)
CAINE, Sir Michael (British film actor)
CAPRA, Frank (US film director, born in Italy)
CAREY, Joyce (British actress)
CARNÉ, Marcel (French film director)
CLAIR, René (French film director)

5–continued

CLIVE, Kitty (British actress)
CLOSE, Glenn (US actress)
CONTI, Italia (British actress)
DAVIS, Bette (US film actress)
DENCH, Dame Judi (British actress)
EDWIN, John (British actor)
EKHOF, Konrad (German actor and director)
EVANS, Dame Edith (British actress)
FLYNN, Errol (Australian actor, born in Tasmania)
FONDA, Henry (US film actor and director)
GABIN, Jean (French film actor)
GABLE, Clark (US film actor)
GARBO, Greta (Swedish actress)
GOZZI, Carlo (Italian dramatist)
GRANT, Cary (US film actor, born in England)
GWYNN, Nell (English actress)
HAIGH, Kenneth (British actor)
HANDL, Dame Irene (British actress)
HANKS, Tom (US actor)
HAWKS, Howard (US film director)
HICKS, Sir Seymour (British actor-manager)
IRONS, Jeremy (British actor)
KAZAN, Elia (US stage and film director and novelist)
KELLY, Grace (US film actress)
KORDA, Sir Alexander (British film producer and director)
LA RUE, Danny (British female impersonator)
LEIGH, Vivien (British actress)
LENYA, Lotte (German actress and singer)
LIFAR, Serge (Russian ballet dancer and choreographer)
LLOYD, Harold (US film comedian)
LLOYD, Marie (British music-hall entertainer)
LOPEZ, Jennifer (J-Lo; Puerto Rican film actress and singer)
LOREN, Sophia (Italian film actress)
LOSEY, Joseph (US film director)
LUCAS, George (US film director)

5—continued

MAYER, Louis B (US film producer, born in Russia)

MILES, Bernard (British theatre director and actor)

MILLS, Sir John (British actor)

MOORE, Dudley (British actor and songwriter)

NERVO, Jimmy (British comedian)

NIVEN, David (British film actor)

PAIGE, Elaine (British actress and singer)

PASCO, Richard (British actor)

PETIT, Roland (French ballet dancer and choreographer)

POLUS (Greek tragic actor)

POPOV, Oleg Konstantinovich (Russian clown)

POWER, Tyrone (US actor)

PRYCE, Jonathan (British actor)

ROBEY, Sir George Edward (British music-hall comedian)

SMITH, Maggie Natalie (British actress)

TERRY, Dame Ellen Alice (British actress)

TOPOL, Chaim (Israeli actor)

TRACY, Spencer (US film actor)

TUTIN, Dorothy (British actress)

WAJDA, Andrzej (Polish film director)

WAYNE, John (US film actor)

6

ADRIAN, Max (British actor)

AINLEY, Henry (British actor)

AITKEN, Maria (British actress)

ALIZON (French actor)

ALLEYN, Edward (English actor)

ALTMAN, Robert (US film director)

ARNAUD, Yvonne Germaine (French actress)

ARTAUD, Antonin (French actor, poet, producer, and theoretician of the theatre)

ASHTON, Sir Frederick (British ballet dancer and choreographer, born in Ecuador)

ATKINS, Eileen (British actress)

BACALL, Lauren (US film actress)

BALCON, Sir Michael (British film producer)

BARDOT, Brigitte (French film actress)

6—continued

BARNUM, Phineas Taylor (US showman)

BAYLIS, Lilian (British theatre manager)

BEATTY, Warren (US film actor)

BÉJART, Joseph (French actor)

BÉJART, Maurice (French ballet dancer and choreographer)

BENSON, Sir Frank (British actor-manager)

BLASIS, Carlo (Italian dance teacher)

BOCAGE (French actor)

BOGART, Humphrey (US film actor)

BRANDO, Marlon (US actor)

BRIERS, Richard (British actor)

BROOKE, Gustavus Vaughan (British actor)

BROUGH, Lionel (British actor)

BROWNE, Robert (English actor)

BRYANT, Michael (British actor)

BUÑUEL, Luis (Spanish film director)

BURTON, Richard Walter (British actor, born in Wales)

CAGNEY, James (US actor)

CALLOW, Simon (British actor)

CANTOR, Eddie (US singer and actor)

CASSON, Sir Lewis (British actor and director)

CIBBER, Colley (British actor-manager)

COLMAN, Ronald (British actor)

CONWAY, William Augustus (British actor)

COOPER, Dame Gladys (British actress)

COOPER, Gary (US film actor)

COWARD, Sir Noël (British dramatist, composer, and actor)

COWELL, Joe Leathley (British actor)

CRANKO, John (British choreographer, born in South Africa)

CROSBY, Bing (US popular singer and film actor)

CURTIS, Tony (US film actor)

DE NIRO, Robert (US film actor)

DE SICA, Vittorio (Italian film director)

DEVINE, George Alexander Cassady (British theatre manager, director, and actor)

DIGGES, Dudley (British actor)

6—continued

DISNEY, Walt (US film producer and animator)

DRAPER, Ruth (US actress)

DREYER, Carl Theodor (Danish film director)

DUNCAN, Isadora (US dancer)

FIELDS, Gracie (British popular entertainer)

FIELDS, W C (US actor)

FINLAY, Frank (British actor)

FINNEY, Albert (British actor)

FLEURY (French actor)

FOKINE, Michel (Russian ballet dancer and choreographer)

FORMAN, Miloš (Czech film director)

FORMBY, George (British music hall singer)

FOSTER, Jodie (US actress)

GIBSON, Mel (Australian film actor and director)

GODARD, Jean-Luc (French film director)

GONG LI (Chinese actress)

GORING, Marius (British actor)

GRAHAM, Martha (US ballet dancer and choreographer)

GUITRY, Sacha (French actor and dramatist)

HARLOW, Jean (US film actress)

HERZOG, Werner (German film director)

HILLER, Dame Wendy (British actress)

HOWARD, Leslie (British actor of Hungarian descent)

HUSTON, John (US film director)

IRVING, Sir Henry (British actor and manager)

JACOBI, Derek (British actor)

JOLSON, Al (US actor and singer)

JORDAN, Dorothy (British actress)

JOUVET, Louis (French actor and theatre director)

KEATON, Buster (US comedian of silent films)

KEMBLE, John Philip (British actor and manager)

KENDAL, Felicity (British actress)

KIDMAN, Nicole (Australian film actress)

LANDEN, Dinsdale (British actor)

LAUDER, Sir Harry (Scottish singer and music-hall comedian)

6–continued

LEMMON, Jack (US actor)
LESSER, Anton (British actor)
LILLIE, Beatrice Gladys (British actress, born in Canada)
LIPMAN, Maureen (British actress)
MARTIN, Mary (US actress)
MARTIN, Steve (US film actor)
MASSEY, Daniel (British actor)
MASSEY, Raymond Hart (Canadian actor)
MCEWAN, Geraldine (British actress)
MCKERN, Leo (Australian actor)
MERMAN, Ethel (US actress)
MONROE, Marilyn (US film actress)
MORLEY, Robert (British actor)
MURPHY, Eddie (US film actor)
NEWMAN, Paul (US film actor)
O'TOOLE, Peter (British actor)
PACINO, Al (US actor)
PETIPA, Marius (French dancer and choreographer)
PORTER, Eric (British actor)
QUAYLE, Sir Anthony (British actor)
RACHEL (French actress)
RÉJANE (French actress)
ROBSON, Dame Flora (British actress)
ROGERS, Ginger (US actress and singer)
ROWLEY, Thomas (English dramatist and actor)
SHUTER, Ned (British actor)
SINDEN, Donald (British actor)
SNIPES, Wesley (US actor)
SPACEY, Kevin (US actor)
STEELE, Tommy (British singer and actor)
STREEP, Meryl (US actress)
SUZMAN, Janet (British actress)
TAYLOR, Elizabeth (US film actress, born in England)
TEARLE, Godfrey Seymour (British actor)
TEMPLE, Shirley (US film actress)
TILLEY, Vesta (British music-hall entertainer)
WARREN, William (US actor, born in Britain)
WELLES, Orson (US film actor and director)
WILDER, Billy (US film director, born in Austria)
WOLFIT, Sir Donald (British actor and manager)

7

ACHURCH, Janet (British actress)
ACKLAND, Joss (British actor)
AESOPUS, Claudius (Roman tragic actor)
ALLGOOD, Sara (Irish actress)
ANTOINE, André (French actor, director, and theatre manager)
BEAUVAL (French actor)
BELLAMY, George Anne (British actress)
BENNETT, Hywel (British actor, born in Wales)
BENNETT, Jill (British actress)
BERGMAN, Ingmar (Swedish film and stage director)
BERGMAN, Ingrid (Swedish actress)
BERGNER, Elisabeth (Austrian actress)
BLAKELY, Colin (British actor)
BOGARDE, Dirk (British film actor of Dutch descent)
BRANAGH, Kenneth (British actor)
BRESSON, Robert (French film director)
BURBAGE, Richard (English actor)
BUSSELL, Darcey (British ballet dancer)
CALVERT, Louis (British actor)
CAMERON, James (Canadian film director)
CAMPION, Jane (New Zealand film director)
CASARÉS, Maria (French actress)
CELESTE, Céline (French actress)
CHABROL, Claude (French film director)
CHAPLIN, Charlie (US film actor, born in Britain)
CLOONEY, George (US film actor)
COLBERT, Claudette (US film actress, born in France)
COLLIER, Constance (British actress)
COMPTON, Fay (British actress)
CONDELL, Henry (English actor)
CONNERY, Sir Sean (Scottish film actor)
COPPOLA, Francis Ford (US film director)
CORALLI, Jean (Italian ballet dancer and choreographer)

7–continued

CORNELL, Katharine (US actress)
COSTNER, Kevin (US film actor and director)
DEBURAU, Jean-Gaspard (French pantomimist, born in Bohemia)
DÉJAZET, Pauline-Virginie (French actress)
DELYSIA, Alice (French actress and singer)
DE MILLE, Cecil B (US film producer and director)
DENEUVE, Catherine (French film actress)
DENISON, Michael (British actor)
DOGGETT, Thomas (British actor)
DOTRICE, Roy (British actor)
DOUGLAS, Kirk (US film actor)
DOUGLAS, Michael (US film actor)
DURANTE, Jimmy (US actor and singer, known as 'Schnozzle')
ELLIOTT, Denholm (British actor)
FELLINI, Federico (Italian film director)
FIENNES, Ralph (British actor)
FONTEYN, Dame Margot (British ballet dancer)
GARLAND, Judy (US singer and film actress)
GARRICK, David (English actor)
GIELGUD, Sir John (British actor)
GINGOLD, Hermione (British actress)
GOLDWYN, Samuel (US film producer)
GREGORY, Lady Augusta (Irish theatre patron and dramatist)
GUTHRIE, Tyrone (British theatre director)
HANCOCK, Sheila (British actress)
HANCOCK, Tony (British comedian)
HAWTREY, Sir Charles (British actor-manager)
HEPBURN, Audrey (British actress)
HEPBURN, Katharine (US actress)
HOFFMAN, Dustin (US film actor)
HOPKINS, Sir Anthony (British actor)

7–continued

HORDERN, Sir Michael (British actor)
HOUDINI, Harry (US magician)
IFFLAND, August Wilhelm (German actor)
JACKSON, Glenda (British actress)
JOHNSON, Dame Celia (British actress)
KARLOFF, Boris (British character actor)
KUBRICK, Stanley (US film writer, director, and producer)
LACKAYE, Wilton (US actor)
LANGTRY, Lillie (British actress, known as the 'Jersey Lily')
LAROQUE (French actor)
LÉOTARD, Jules (French acrobat and music-hall performer)
MADONNA (US pop singer and film actress)
MARCEAU, Marcel (French mime)
MARKOVA, Dame Alicia (British ballet dancer)
MASSINE, Léonide (Russian ballet dancer and choreographer)
MCKENNA, Siobhán (Irish actress)
MCQUEEN, Steve (US film actor)
MICHELL, Keith (Australian actor)
NUREYEV, Rudolf (Russian ballet dancer)
OLIVIER, Laurence Kerr, Lord (British actor)
OXBERRY, William (British actor)
PAVLOVA, Anna (Russian ballet dancer)
PAXINOU, Katina (Greek actress)
PLUMMER, Christopher (Canadian actor)
PORTMAN, Eric (British actor)
QUILLEY, Denis (British actor)
RAMBERT, Dame Marie (British ballet dancer and choreographer)
REDFORD, Robert (US film actor)
RISTORI, Adelaide (Italian actress)
ROBARDS, Jason (US actor)
ROBBINS, Jerome (US ballet dancer and choreographer)

7–continued

ROBERTS, Julia (US film actress)
ROBESON, Paul Bustil (US Black actor)
RUSSELL, Ken (British film director)
SALVINI, Tommaso (Italian actor)
SELLERS, Peter (British comic actor)
SIDDONS, Sarah (English actress)
STEWART, James (US film actor)
STRITCH, Elaine (US actress)
TEMPEST, Dame Marie (British actress)
ULANOVA, Galina (Russian ballet dancer)
USTINOV, Peter Alexander (British actor, director, and dramatist)
VESTRIS, Madame (British actress)
WINSLET, Kate (British film actress)
WITHERS, Googie (British actress)

8

ABINGTON, Frances (British actress)
ALDRIDGE, Ira Frederick (US actor)
ANDERSON, Dame Judith (Australian actress)
ANDREINI, Francesco (Italian actor-manager and playwright)
ANDREINI, Giovann Battista (Italian actor)
ANDREINI, Isabella (Italian actress)
ASHCROFT, Dame Peggy (British actress)
BADDELEY, Hermione (British actress)
BANCROFT, Anne (US actress)
BANKHEAD, Tallulah (US actress)
BARRAULT, Jean-Louis (French actor and director)
BERKELEY, Busby (US dance director)
BRASSEUR, Pierre (French actor)
BUCHANAN, Jack (Scottish actor-manager)
CALDWELL, Zoë (Australian actress)

8–continued

CAMPBELL, Mrs Patrick (British actress)
CHANNING, Carol (US actress and singer)
CLEMENTS, Sir John (British actor-manager)
CRAWFORD, Joan (US film actress)
CRAWFORD, Michael (British actor)
DANCOURT, Florent (French actor and playwright)
DE LA TOUR, Frances (British actress)
DE VALOIS, Dame Ninette (British ballet dancer and choreographer, born in Ireland)
DEVRIENT, Ludwig (German actor)
DICAPRIO, Leonardo (US film actor)
DIETRICH, Marlene (German film actress and singer)
DUFRESNE (French actor)
EASTWOOD, Clint (US film actor and director)
ESTCOURT, Richard (English actor)
FLAHERTY, Robert (US film director)
FLANAGAN, Bud (British comedian)
FLORENCE, William Jermyn (US actor)
FLORIDOR (French actor)
GRENFELL, Joyce (British actress)
GRIERSON, John (British film director)
GRIMALDI, Joseph (British clown)
GUINNESS, Sir Alec (British actor)
HARRISON, Rex (British actor)
HELPMANN, Sir Robert Murray (Australian ballet dancer, choreographer, and actor)
KUROSAWA, Akira (Japanese film director)
KYNASTON, Ned (English actor)
LANSBURY, Angela (US actress)
LAUGHTON, Charles (British actor)
LAWRENCE, Gertrude (British actress)
LEIGHTON, Margaret (British actress)

8–continued

MACLAINE, Shirley (US actress)
MACREADY, William Charles (British actor and theatre manager)
MATTHEWS, Jessie (British actress)
MCKELLEN, Ian (British actor)
MERCOURI, Melina (Greek actress and politician)
NAUGHTON, Charlie (British comedian)
NAZIMOVA, Alla (Russian actress)
NIJINSKY, Vaslav (Russian ballet dancer)
PALTROW, Gwyneth (US film actress)
PFEIFFER, Michelle (US actress)
PICKFORD, Mary (Canadian-born US film actress)
POLANSKI, Roman (Polish film director, born in Paris)
REDGRAVE, Corin (British actor)
REDGRAVE, Lynn (British actress)
REDGRAVE, Sir Michael (British actor)
REDGRAVE, Vanessa (British actress)
ROBINSON, Edward G (US film actor, born in Romania)
SCOFIELD, Paul (British actor)
SCORSESE, Martin (US film director)
SELZNICK, David O (US film producer)
STROHEIM, Erich von (US film director and actor)
THOMPSON, Emma (British actress)
VISCONTI, Luchino (Italian film director)
WHITELAW, Billie (British actress)
WILLIAMS, Kenneth (British comic actor)
WILLIAMS, Michael (British actor)
WILLIAMS, Robin (US film actor)
ZIEGFELD, Florenz (US theatrical producer)

9

ALMODÓVAR, Pedro (Spanish film director)
ANTONIONI, Michelangelo (Italian film maker)

9–continued

BARKWORTH, Peter (British actor)
BARRYMORE, Ethel (US actress)
BARRYMORE, John (US actor)
BARRYMORE, Lionel (US actor)
BARRYMORE, Maurice (British actor)
BELLECOUR (French actor)
BELLEROSE (French actor-manager)
BERIOSOVA, Svetlana (Russian ballet dancer)
BERNHARDT, Sarah (French actress)
BETTERTON, Thomas (English actor)
BLANCHETT, Cate (Australian actress)
CHEN KAIGE (Chinese film director)
CHEVALIER, Maurice (French singer and actor)
COURTENAY, Tom (British actor)
DEPARDIEU, Gérard (French film actor)
DIAGHILEV, Sergei (Russian ballet impresario)
DU MAURIER, Sir Gerald (British actor-manager)
FAIRBANKS, Douglas (US film actor)
FAVERSHAM, William (US actor)
FERNANDEL (French comedian)
FEUILLÈRE, Edwige (French actress)
FISHBURNE, Larry (US actor)
GRAMATICA, Irma (Italian actress)
GROSSMITH, George (British actor)
GRÜNDGENS, Gustav (German actor)
LAPOTAIRE, Jane (British actress)
MACMILLAN, Sir Kenneth (British ballet dancer and choreographer)
MONCRIEFF, Gladys (Australian actress)
NICHOLSON, Jack (US film actor)
PECKINPAH, Sam (US film director)
PLEASENCE, Donald (British actor)

9–continued

PLOWRIGHT, Joan Anne (British actress)
PREMINGER, Otto (US film director, born in Austria)
REINHARDT, Max (Austrian theatre director)
SPIELBERG, Steven (US film director)
STERNBERG, Josef von (US film director, born in Austria)
STREISAND, Barbra (US singer and actress)
THORNDIKE, Dame Sybil (British actress)
VALENTINO, Rudolf (US film actor, born in Italy)

10

BALANCHINE, George (US ballet dancer and choreographer, born in Russia)
BASSERMANN, Albert (German actor)
BELLEROCHE (French actor)
BERTOLUCCI, Bernardo (Italian film director)
BOUCICAULT, 'Dot' (British actor-manager)
BOUCICAULT, Nina (British actress)
CARTWRIGHT, William (English actor)
CUNNINGHAM, Merce (US dancer and choreographer)
D'OYLY CARTE, Richard (British theatre impresario and manager)
EISENSTEIN, Sergei (Russian film director)
FASSBINDER, Rainer Werner (German film director)
LITTLE TICH (British music-hall comedian)
LITTLEWOOD, Joan (British theatre director)
MONTFLEURY (French actor)
RICHARDSON, Ian (British actor)
RICHARDSON, Sir Ralph (British actor)
ROSSELLINI, Roberto (Italian film director)
RUTHERFORD, Dame Margaret (British actress)
WASHINGTON, Denzil (US film actor)
WOFFINGTON, Peg (Irish actress)
ZEFFIRELLI, G Franco (Italian director and stage designer)

Tarkovsky, Andrei
Russian film maker

129

11
BEAUCHÂTEAU (French actor)
BIANCOLELLI, Giuseppe
Domenico (French actor)
BRACEGIRDLE, Anne (English
actress)
BRAITHWAITE, Dame Lilian
(British actress)
COURTNEIDGE, Dame Cicely
(British actress)
DAUVILLIERS (French actor)
MACLIAMMÓIR, Micheál (Irish
actor and dramatist)
MASTROIANNI, Marcello
(Italian actor)

11–continued
MISTINGUETT (French singer
and comedienne)
SCHLESINGER, John (British
film and theatre director)

12
BRUSCAMBILLE (French
actor)
MARX BROTHERS (US family
of comic film actors)
STANISLAVSKY, Konstantin
(Russian actor and theatre
director)

13
ROSCIUS GALLUS, Quintus
(Roman comic actor)

14
MIZOGUCHI KENJI (Japanese
film director)

15
FFRANGCON-DAVIES, Gwen
(British actress)
FORBES-ROBERTSON, Sir
Johnston (British actor-
manager)
GRANVILLE-BARKER, Harley
(British theatre director)
KOBAYASHI MASAKI
(Japanese film director)

SCIENTISTS

3
DAM, Carl Peter Henrik
(1895–1976; Danish
biochemist)
KAY, John (1704–c. 1764;
British inventor)
LEE, Tsung-Dao (1926–   ; US
physicist)
OHM, Georg Simon (1787–
1854; German physicist)
RAY, John (1627–1705; English
naturalist)

4
ABEL, Niels Henrik (1802–29;
Norwegian mathematician)
ABEL, Sir Frederick Augustus
(1827–1902; British chemist)
ADER, Clément (1841–1926;
French engineer and inventor)
AIRY, Sir George Biddell
(1801–92; British astronomer)
BAER, Karl Ernest von
(1792–1876; Russian
embryologist)
BENZ, Karl (1844–1929;
German engineer)
BIRÓ, Laszlo (1900–85;
Hungarian inventor)
BOHR, Niels Henrik David
(1885–1962; Danish
physicist)
BORN, Max (1882–1970;
British physicist)
BOSE, Sir Jagadis Chandra
(1858–1937; Indian plant
physiologist and physicist)

4–continued
COHN, Ferdinand Julius
(1839–1884; German
botanist)
COKE, Thomas William, of
Holkham, Earl of Leicester
(1752–1842; British
agriculturalist)
EADS, John Buchanan
(1820–87; US civil engineer)
FUST, Johann (1400–66;
German printer)
GOLD, Thomas (1920–2004;
Austrian-born astronomer)
GRAY, Asa (1810–88; US
botanist)
HAHN, Otto (1879–1968;
German chemist and
physicist)
HESS, Victor Francis
(1883–1964; US physicist)
KOCH, Robert (1843–1910;
German bacteriologist)
LAUE, Max Theodor Felix Von
(1879–1960; German
physicist)
LOEB, Jacques (1859–1924;
US zoologist)
MACH, Ernst (1838–1916;
Austrian physicist)
MAYO (family of US medical
researchers)
OTIS, Elisha Graves (1811–61;
US inventor)
OTTO, Nikolaus August
(1832–91; German engineer)

4–continued
RABI, Isidor Isaac (1898–88;
US physicist)
RYLE, Sir Martin (1918–84;
British astronomer)
SWAN, Sir Joseph Wilson
(1828–1914; British physicist)
TODD, Alexander Robertus,
Baron (1907–97; British
biochemist)
UREY, Harold Clayton
(1893–1981; US physicist)
YANG, Chen Ning (1922–   ;
US physicist)

5
ADAMS, John Couch
(1819–92; English
astronomer)
AIKEN, Howard Hathaway
(1900–73; US mathematician)
AMICI, Giovanni Battista
(1786–1863; Italian
astronomer, microscopist, and
optical instrument maker)
ASTON, Francis William
(1877–1945; British chemist)
AVERY, Oswald Theodore
(1877–1955; Canadian
bacteriologist)
BACON, Roger (c. 1214–c.
1292; English scientist)
BAILY, Francis (1774–1844;
British amateur astronomer)
BAKER, Sir Benjamin
(1840–1907; British civil
engineer)

5–continued

BANKS, Sir Joseph (1743–1820; British botanist and explorer)

BATES, Henry Walter (1825–92; British naturalist and explorer)

BEEBE, Charles William (1877–1962; US explorer and naturalist)

BETHE, Hans Albrecht (1906– ; US physicist)

BLACK, Joseph (1728–99; Scottish physician and chemist)

BLOCH, Felix (1905–83; US physicist)

BONDI, Sir Hermann (1919– ; British cosmologist and mathematician)

BOOLE, George (1815–64; British mathematician)

BOSCH, Carl (1874–1940; German chemist)

BOTHE, Walther Wilhelm Georg Franz (1891–1957; German experimental physicist)

BOVET, Daniel (1907–92; Swiss pharmacologist)

BOWEN, Norman Levi (1887–1956; Canadian experimental petrologist)

BOWER, Frederick Orpen (1855–1948; British botanist)

BOYLE, Robert (1627–91; British physicist and chemist)

BRAGG, Sir William Henry (1862–1942; British physicist)

BRAHE, Tycho (1546–1601; Danish astronomer)

BROWN, Robert (1773–1858; Scottish botanist)

BÜRGE, Joost (1552–1632; Swiss mathematician)

CHAIN, Sir Ernst Boris (1906–79; British biochemist)

CRICK, Francis Harry Compton (1916–2004; British biophysicist)

CURIE, Marie (1867–1934; Polish chemist)

CURIE, Pierre (1859–1906; French physicist)

DEBYE, Peter Joseph Wilhelm (1884–1966; Dutch physicist and chemist)

DIELS, Otto Paul Hermann (1876–1954; German chemist)

DIRAC, Paul Adrien Maurice (1902–84; British physicist)

5–continued

ELTON, Charles (1900–91; British zoologist)

EULER, Leonhard (1707–83; Swiss mathematician)

EVANS, Oliver (1755–1819; American engineer)

FABRE, Jean Henri (1823–1915; French entomologist)

FABRY, Charles (1867–1945; French physicist)

FERMI, Enrico (1901–54; US physicist)

FREGE, Gottlob (1848–1925; German mathematician and logician)

GABOR, Dennis (1900–79; British electrical engineer)

GALLE, Johann Gottfried (1812–1910; German astronomer)

GAUSS, Karl Friedrich (1777–1855; German mathematician)

GEBER (14th century; Spanish alchemist)

GIBBS, Josiah Willard (1839–1903; US physicist)

GÖDEL, Kurt (1906–78; US mathematician)

HABER, Fritz (1868–1934; German chemist and inventor)

HARDY, Godfrey Harold (1877–1947; British mathematician)

HENRY, Joseph (1797–1878; US physicist)

HERTZ, Heinrich Rudolf (1857–94; German physicist)

HOOKE, Robert (1635–1703; British physicist)

HOYLE, Sir Fred (1915– ; British astronomer)

JEANS, Sir James Hopwood (1877–1946; British mathematician and astronomer)

JOULE, James Prescott (1818–89; British physicist)

KOLBE, Hermann (1818–84; German chemist)

KREBS, Sir Hans Adolf (1900–81; British biochemist)

KROTO, Sir Harold (1939– ; British chemist)

LAWES, Sir John Bennet (1814–1900; British agriculturalist)

LIBBY, Willard Frank (1908–80; US chemist)

LODGE, Sir Oliver Joseph (1851–1940; British physicist)

5–continued

LYELL, Sir Charles (1797–1875; British geologist)

MAYER, Julius Robert Von (1814–78; German physicist)

MONGE, Gaspard (1746–1818; French mathematician)

MONOD, Jacques-Lucien (1910–76; French biochemist)

NOBEL, Alfred Bernhard (1833–96; Swedish chemist)

NOBLE, Sir Andrew (1831–1915; British physicist)

PAULI, Wolfgang (1900–58; US physicist)

POPOV, Aleksandr Stepanovich (1859–1905; Russian physicist)

PROUT, William (1785–1850; British chemist and physiologist)

RAMAN, Sir Chandrasekhara Venkata (1888–1970; Indian physicist)

REBER, Grote (1911– ; US astronomer)

RHINE, Joseph Banks (1895–1980; US psychologist)

ROSSE, William Parsons, 3rd Earl Of (1800–67; Irish astronomer)

SEGRÈ, Emilio (1905–89; US physicist)

SMITH, Sir Keith Macpherson (1890–1955; Australian aviator)

SODDY, Frederick (1877–1956; British chemist)

STAHL, Georg Ernst (1660–1734; German physician and chemist)

TATUM, Edward Lawrie (1909–75; US geneticist)

VOLTA, Alessandro Giuseppe Antonio Anastasio, Count (1745–1827; Italian physicist)

WEBER, Ernst Heinrich (1795–1878; German physiologist)

WHITE, Gilbert (1720–93; English naturalist)

YOUNG, Thomas (1773–1829; British physician and physicist)

6

ACHARD, Franz Karl (1753–1821; German chemist)

ADRIAN, Edgar Douglas, 1st Baron (1889–1977; British physiologist)

131

6–continued

AGNESI, Maria Gaetana (1718–99; Italian mathematician)

ALFVÉN, Hannes Olof Gösta (1908–95; Swedish astrophysicist)

AMPÈRE, André Marie (1775–1836; French physicist)

APPERT, Nicolas (1750–1841; French inventor)

ARCHER, Frederick Scott (1813–57; British inventor and sculptor)

BAEYER, Adolf Von (1835–1917; German chemist)

BEADLE, George Wells (1903–89; US geneticist)

BODONI, Giambattista (1740–1813; Italian printer)

BOLYAI, János (1802–60; Hungarian mathematician)

BONNET, Charles (1720–93; Swiss naturalist)

BORDET, Jules Jean Baptiste Vincent (1870–1961; Belgian bacteriologist)

BOVERI, Theodor Heinrich (1862–1915; German cell biologist)

BRAMAH, Joseph (1748–1814; British engineer and inventor)

BRIGGS, Henry (1561–1630; English mathematician)

BRUNEL, Isambard Kingdom (1806–59; British engineer)

BUFFON, Georges Louis Leclerc, Comte de (1707–88; French naturalist)

BUNSEN, Robert Wilhelm (1811–99; German chemist)

CALVIN, Melvin (1911–97; US biochemist)

CANTOR, Georg (1845–1918; Russian mathematician)

CARNOT, Sadi (1796–1832; French scientist and soldier)

CARREL, Alexis (1873–1944; French surgeon)

CARVER, George Washington (1864–1943; US agriculturalist)

CAUCHY, Augustin Louis, Baron (1789–1857; French mathematician)

CAXTON, William (c. 1422–91; The first English printer)

CAYLEY, Arthur (1821–95; British mathematician)

6–continued

CAYLEY, Sir George (1773–1857; British engineer and pioneer designer of flying machines)

CUVIER, Georges, Baron (1769–1832; French zoologist)

DALTON, John (1766–1844; British chemist)

DARWIN, Charles Robert (1809–1882; British naturalist)

DE BARY, Heinrich Anton (1831–88; German botanist)

DE DUVE, Christian (1917– ; Belgian biochemist)

DREYER, Johan Ludvig Emil (1852–1926; Danish astronomer)

ECKERT, John Presper (1919–95; US electronics engineer)

ENDERS, John Franklin (1897–1985; US microbiologist)

ENGLER, Gustav Heinrich Adolf (1844–1930; German botanist)

EUCLID (c. 300 BC; Greek mathematician)

FERMAT, Pierre de (1601–65; French mathematician)

FINSEN, Niels Ryberg (1860–1904; Danish physician)

FOKKER, Anthony Hermann Gerard (1890–1939; Dutch aircraft manufacturer)

FRANCK, James (1882–1964; US physicist)

FRISCH, Karl Von (1886–1982; Austrian zoologist)

FRISCH, Otto Robert (1904–79; Austrian-born physicist)

FULTON, Robert (1765–1815; American inventor)

GALOIS, Évariste (1811–32; French mathematician)

GALTON, Sir Francis (1822–1911; British scientist)

GEIGER, Hans (1882–1945; German physicist)

GESNER, Conrad (1516–65; Swiss physician)

GRAHAM, Thomas (1805–69; British physicist)

HALLEY, Edmund (1656–1742; British astronomer)

HEVESY, George Charles Von (1885–1966; Hungarian-born chemist)

6–continued

HOOKER, Sir William Jackson (1785–1865; British botanist)

HUBBLE, Edwin Powell (1889–1953; US astronomer)

HUTTON, James (1726–97; Scottish physician)

HUXLEY, Thomas Henry (1825–95; British biologist)

JANSKY, Karl Guthe (1905–50; US radio engineer)

JENSON, Nicolas (c. 1420–80; French printer)

JOLIOT, Frédéric (1900–59; French physicist)

KELVIN, William Thomson, 1st Baron (1824–1907; Scottish physicist)

KEPLER, Johannes (1571–1630; German astronomer)

KINSEY, Alfred (1894–1956; US zoologist and sociologist)

LANDAU, Lev Davidovich (1908–68; Soviet physicist)

LARTET, Édouard Armand Isidore Hippolyte (1801–71; French archaeologist)

LIEBIG, Justus, Baron Von (1803–73; German chemist)

LORENZ, Konrad (1903–89; Austrian zoologist)

LOVELL, Sir Bernard (1913– ; British astronomer)

LOWELL, Percival (1855–1916; US astronomer)

MARKOV, Andrei Andreevich (1856–1922; Russian mathematician)

MARTIN, Archer John Porter (1910– ; British biochemist)

MARTIN, Pierre-Émile (1824–1915; French engineer)

MCADAM, John Loudon (1756–1836; British inventor)

MENDEL, Gregor Johann (1822–84; Austrian botanist)

MORGAN, Thomas Hunt (1866–1945; US geneticist)

MORLEY, Edward Williams (1838–1923; US chemist)

MORRIS, Desmond John (1928– ; British zoologist)

MULLER, Hermann Joseph (1890–1967; US geneticist)

MÜLLER, Paul Hermann (1899–1965; Swiss chemist)

NAPIER, John (1550–1617; Scottish mathematician)

NERNST, Walther Hermann (1864–1941; German physical chemist)

6–continued

NEWTON, Sir Isaac
(1642–1727; British physicist
and mathematician)

OLBERS, Heinrich Wilhelm
Matthäus (1758–1840;
German astronomer)

PASCAL, Blaise (1623–62;
French mathematician and
physicist)

PENNEY, William George,
Baron (1909–91; British
mathematician)

PERKIN, Sir William Henry
(1838–1907; British chemist)

PERRIN, Jean-Baptiste
(1870–1942; French
physicist)

PLANCK, Max Karl Ernst
Ludwig (1858–1947; German
physicist)

POWELL, Cecil Frank
(1903–69; British physicist)

PROUST, Joseph-Louis
(1754–1826; French chemist)

RAMSAY, Sir William
(1852–1916; Scottish
chemist)

RENNIE, John (1761–1821;
British civil engineer)

SANGER, Frederick (1918– ;
British biochemist)

SAVERY, Thomas (c.
1650–1715; English engineer)

SLOANE, Sir Hans
(1660–1753; British physician
and naturalist)

STOKES, Sir George Gabriel
(1819–1903; British physicist
and mathematician)

STRUVE, Otto (1897–1963; US
astronomer)

SUTTON, Walter Stanborough
(1877–1916; US geneticist)

TALBOT, William Henry Fox
(1800–77; British botanist and
physicist)

TAYLOR, Brook (1685–1737;
English mathematician)

TAYLOR, Frederick Winslow
(1856–1915; US engineer)

TELLER, Edward (1908– ;
US physicist)

TOWNES, Charles Hard
(1915– ; US physicist)

VAUBAN, Sébastian Le Prestre
de (1633–1707; French
military engineer)

WALLIS, Sir Barnes
(1887–1979; British
aeronautical engineer)

6–continued

WALTON, Ernest Thomas Sin-
ton (1903–95; Irish physicist)

WATSON, James Dewey
(1928– ; US geneticist)

WIENER, Norbert (1894–1964;
US mathematician)

WIGNER, Eugene Paul
(1902–95; US physicist)

WILSON, Charles Thomson
Rees (1869–1959; British
physicist)

WILSON, Edmund Beecher
(1856–1939; US biologist)

WÖHLER, Friedrich (1800–82;
German chemist)

WRIGHT, Orville (1871–1948;
US aviator)

YUKAWA, Hideki (1907–81;
Japanese physicist)

ZEEMAN, Pieter (1865–1943;
Dutch physicist)

7

AGASSIZ, Jean Louis
Rodolphe (1807–73; Swiss
natural historian)

ALVAREZ, Luis Walter
(1911–88; US physicist)

AUDUBON, John James
(1785–1851; US naturalist)

BABBAGE, Charles
(1792–1871; British
mathematician)

BARDEEN, John (1908–91; US
physicist)

BARNARD, Edward Emerson
(1857–1923; US astronomer)

BATESON, William
(1861–1926; British biologist)

BATTANI, Al- (c. 858–929;
Islamic astronomer)

BERGIUS, Friedrich
(1884–1949; German
chemist)

BORLAUG, Norman (1914– ;
US plant breeder)

BROUWER, Luitzen Egbertus
Jan (1881–1966; Dutch
mathematician)

BURBANK, Luther (1849–1926;
US plant breeder)

CANDELA, Felix (1910– ;
Mexican engineer)

CARDANO, Girolamo (1501–
76; Italian mathematician)

COMPTON, Arthur Holly
(1892–1962; US physicist)

CORRENS, Carl Erich
(1864–1933; German botanist
and geneticist)

7–continued

COULOMB, Charles Augustin
de (1736–1806; French
physicist)

CROOKES, Sir William
(1832–1919; British physicist)

CURTISS, Glenn (1878–1930;
US aviator and aeronautical
engineer)

DAIMLER, Gottlieb (1834–
1900; German inventor)

DANIELL, John Frederic
(1790–1845; British chemist)

DE LA RUE, Warren (1815–89;
British astronomer)

DE VRIES, Hugo Marie
(1848–1935; Dutch botanist)

DOPPLER, Christian Johann
(1803–53; Austrian physicist)

DRIESCH, Hans Adolf Eduard
(1867–1941; German
zoologist)

EICHLER, August Wilhelm
(1839–87; German botanist)

FARADAY, Michael (1791–
1867; British chemist and
physicist)

FEYNMAN, Richard Phillips
(1918–88; US physicist)

FISCHER, Emil Hermann
(1852–1919; German
chemist)

FLEMING, Sir John Ambrose
(1849–1945; British electrical
engineer)

FOURIER, Jean Baptiste
Joseph, Baron (1768–1830;
French mathematician and
physicist)

FRESNEL, Augustin Jean
(1788–1827; French
physicist)

GAGARIN, Yuri Alekseevich
(1934–68; Soviet cosmonaut)

GALVANI, Luigi (1737–98;
Italian physician)

GILBERT, William (1544–1603;
English physicist)

GODDARD, Robert Hutchings
(1882–1945; US physicist)

GREGORY, James (1638–75;
Scottish mathematician and
astronomer)

HAECKEL, Ernst Heinrich
(1834–1919; German
zoologist)

HAWORTH, Sir Walter Norman
(1883–1950; British
biochemist)

HELMONT, Jan Baptist van
(1580–1644; Belgian
alchemist and physician)

133

7–continued

HERMITE, Charles (1822–1901; French mathematician)

HILBERT, David (1862–1943; German mathematician)

HODGKIN, Alan Lloyd (1914– ; British physiologist)

HODGKIN, Dorothy Mary Crowfoot (1910–95; British biochemist)

HOPKINS, Sir Frederick Gowland (1861–1947; British biochemist)

HUGGINS, Sir William (1824–1910; British astronomer)

HUYGENS, Christiaan (1629–95; Dutch astronomer and physicist)

JUSSIEU (French family of botanists)

KAPITZA, Peter Leonidovich (1894–1984; Soviet physicist)

KENDALL, Edward Calvin (1886–1972; US biochemist)

KENDREW, Sir John Cowdery (1917–97; British biochemist)

KHORANA, Har Gobind (1922– ; US biochemist)

KIDINNU (4th century BC; Babylonian mathematician and astronomer)

KOZIREV, Nikolai Aleksandrovich (1908– ; Russian astronomer)

LALANDE, Joseph-Jérôme le Français de (1732–1807; French astronomer)

LAMARCK, Jean-Baptiste de Monet, Chevalier de (1744–1829; French naturalist)

LAMBERT, Johann Heinrich (1728–77; German mathematician and astronomer)

LANGLEY, Samuel Pierpont (1834–1906; US astronomer)

LAPLACE, Pierre Simon, Marquis de (1749–1827; French mathematician and astronomer)

LESSEPS, Ferdinand de (1805–94; French diplomat)

LOCKYER, Sir Joseph Norman (1836–1920; British astronomer)

LORENTZ, Hendrick Antoon (1853–1928; Dutch physicist)

7–continued

LUMIÈRE, Auguste (1862–1954; French photographer and inventor)

LYSENKO, Trofim Denisovich (1898–1976; Soviet biologist)

MARCONI, Guglielmo (1874–1937; Italian electrical engineer)

MAXWELL, James Clerk (1831–79; Scottish physicist)

MEITNER, Lise (1878–1968; Austrian physicist)

MESSIER, Charles (1730–1817; French astronomer)

MOSELEY, Henry Gwyn Jeffries (1887–1915; British physicist)

NEUMANN, John Von (1903–57; US mathematician)

OERSTED, Hans Christian (1777–1851; Danish physicist)

ONSAGER, Lars (1903–76; US chemist)

OSTWALD, Wilhelm (1853–1932; German chemist)

PARSONS, Sir Charles Algernon (1854–1931; British engineer)

PASTEUR, Louis (1822–95; French chemist and microbiologist)

PAULING, Linus Carl (1901–94; US chemist)

PICCARD (family of Swiss scientists)

POISSON, Siméon Dénis (1781–1840; French mathematician)

PRANDTL, Ludwig (1875–1953; German physicist)

PTOLEMY (or Claudius Ptolemaeus, 2nd century AD; Egyptian mathematician, astronomer, and geographer)

PURCELL, Edward Mills (1912–97; US physicist)

RÉAUMUR, René-Antoine Ferchault de (1683–1757; French physicist)

RIEMANN, Georg Friedrich Bernhard (1826–66; German mathematician)

RUMFORD, Benjamin Thompson, Count (1753–1814; American-born scientist)

SANDAGE, Allan Rex (1926– ; US astronomer)

SCHEELE, Carl Wilhelm (1742–86; Swedish chemist)

7–continued

SCHWANN, Theodor (1810–82; German physiologist)

SEABORG, Glenn Theodore (1912– ; US physicist)

SHEPARD, Jr, Allan Bartlett (1923– ; US astronaut)

SIEMENS, Ernst Werner von (1816–92; German electrical engineer)

SIMPSON, George Gaylord (1902– ; US palaeontologist)

SZILARD, Leo (1898–1964; US physicist)

TELFORD, Thomas (1757–1834; British civil engineer)

THENARD, Louis-Jacques (1777–1857; French chemist)

THOMSON, Sir Joseph John (1856–1940; British physicist)

TUPOLEV, Andrei Niklaievich (1888–1972; Soviet designer)

TYNDALL, John (1820–93; Irish physicist)

VAVILOV, Nikolai Ivanovich (1887–1943; Soviet plant geneticist)

WAKSMAN, Selman Abraham (1888–1973; US microbiologist)

WALLACE, Alfred Russel (1823–1913; British naturalist)

WEGENER, Alfred Lothar (1880–1930; German geologist)

WILKINS, Maurice Hugh Frederick (1916– ; New Zealand physicist)

WINSTON, Robert (1940– ; British obstetrician and gynaecologist)

ZIEGLER, Karl (1898–1973; German chemist)

8

AGRICOLA, Georgius (1494–1555; German physician and mineralogist)

ANDERSON, Carl David (1905–91; US physicist)

ÅNGSTRÖM, Anders Jonas (1814–74; Swedish physicist and astronomer)

AVOGADRO, Amedeo, Conte di Quaregna e Ceretto (1776–1856; Italian physicist)

BAKEWELL, Robert (1725–95; British agriculturalist)

BESSEMER, Sir Henry (1813–98; British engineer and inventor)

8—continued

BIRKHOFF, George David (1864–1944; US mathematician)

BJERKNES, Vilhelm Friman Koren (1862–1951; Norwegian meteorologist and physicist)

BLACKETT, Patrick Maynard Stuart, Baron (1897–1974; British physicist)

BRATTAIN, Walter Houser (1902–87; US physicist)

BREWSTER, Sir David (1781–1868; Scottish physicist)

BRIDGMAN, Percy Williams (1882–1961; US physicist)

BRINDLEY, James (1716–72; British canal builder)

BUSHNELL, David (1742–1824; US inventor; built the first submarine)

CALMETTE, Albert Léon Charles (1863–1933; French bacteriologist)

CHADWICK, Sir James (1891–1974; British physicist)

CLAUSIUS, Rudolf Julius Emanuel (1822–88; German physicist)

CULPEPER, Nicholas (1616–54; English physician)

DEDEKIND, Richard (1831–1916; German mathematician)

DE MORGAN, Augustus (1806–71; British mathematician and logician)

EINSTEIN, Albert (1879–1955; German physicist)

ERICSSON, John (1803–89; US naval engineer and inventor)

FOUCAULT, Jean Bernard Léon (1819–68; French physicist)

GASSENDI, Pierre (1592–1655; French physicist)

GELL-MANN, Murray (1929– ; US physicist)

GUERICKE, Otto Von (1602–86; German physicist)

HAMILTON, Sir William Rowan (1805–65; Irish mathematician)

HERSCHEL, Sir William (1738–1822; British astronomer)

8—continued

ILYUSHIN, Sergei Vladimirovich (1894–1977; Soviet aircraft designer)

IPATIEFF, Vladimir Nikolaievich (1867–1952; US physicist)

JACQUARD, Joseph-Marie (1752–1834; French inventor)

KENNELLY, Arthur Edwin (1861–1939; US electrical engineer)

KLAPROTH, Martin Heinrich (1743–1817; German chemist)

KOROLIOV, Sergei Pavlovich (1906–66; Soviet aeronautical engineer)

LAGRANGE, Joseph Louis, Comte de (1736–1813; French mathematician and astronomer)

LANGMUIR, Irving (1881–1957; US chemist)

LAWRENCE, Ernest Orlando (1901–58; US physicist)

LEGENDRE, Adrien Marie (1752–1833; French mathematician)

LEMAÎTRE, Georges Édouard, Abbé (1894–1966; Belgian priest and astronomer)

LEUCKART, Karl Georg Friedrich Rudolph (1822–98; German zoologist)

LINNAEUS, Carolus (Carl Linné; 1707–78; Swedish botanist)

LIPSCOMB, William Nunn (1919– ; US chemist)

LONSDALE, Dame Kathleen (1903–71; Irish physicist)

MAUDSLAY, Henry (1771–1831; British engineer)

MCMILLAN, Edwin Mattison (1907–91; US physicist)

MERCATOR, Gerardus (1512–94; Flemish geographer)

MEYERHOF, Otto Fritz (1884–1951; US biochemist)

MILLIKAN, Robert Andrews (1868–1953; US physicist)

MILSTEIN, César (1927– ; British molecular biologist)

MITCHELL, Reginald Joseph (1895–1937; British aeronautical engineer)

MULLIKEN, Robert Sanderson (1896–1986; US chemist and physicist)

8—continued

NEWCOMEN, Thomas (1663–1729; English blacksmith and inventor of steam engine)

OLIPHANT, Sir Mark Laurence Elwin (1901– ; Australian physicist)

POINCARÉ, Jules Henri (1854–1912; French mathematician)

RAYLEIGH, John William Strutt, 3rd Baron (1842–1919; British physicist)

RHETICUS (1514–76; German mathematician)

ROBINSON, Sir Robert (1886–1975; British chemist)

ROEBLING, John Augustus (1806–69; US engineer)

ROENTGEN, Wilhelm Konrad (1845–1923; German physicist)

SABATIER, Paul (1854–1941; French chemist)

SAKHAROV, Andrei Dimitrievich (1921–89; Soviet physicist)

SHOCKLEY, William Bradfield (1910–89; US physicist)

SHRAPNEL, Henry (1761–1842; British army officer, who invented the shrapnel shell)

SIKORSKY, Igor Ivan (1889–1972; US aeronautical engineer)

STIRLING, James (1692–1770; Scottish mathematician)

VAN ALLEN, James Alfred (1914– ; US physicist)

VAN'T HOFF, Jacobus Henricus (1852–1911; Dutch chemist)

WEISMANN, August Friedrich Leopold (1834–1914; German biologist)

WOODWARD, Robert Burns (1917–79; US chemist)

ZERNICKE, Frits (1888–1966; Dutch physicist)

ZWORYKIN, Vladimir Kosma (1889–1982; US physicist)

9

ABU AL-WAFA (940–98 AD; Persian mathematician and astronomer)

ARMSTRONG, Edwin Howard (1890–1954; US electrical engineer)

9–continued

ARMSTRONG, William George, Baron (1810–1900; British engineer)

ARRHENIUS, Svante August (1859–1927; Swedish physicist and chemist)

BECQUEREL, Henri (1852–1908; French physicist)

BERNOULLI (family of Swiss mathematicians and physicists)

BERTHELOT, Marcelin (1827–1907; French chemist)

BERZELIUS, Jöns Jakob, Baron (1779–1848; Swedish chemist)

BOLTZMANN, Ludwig Eduard (1844–1906; Austrian physicist)

BRONOWSKI, Jacob (1908–74; British mathematician)

CAVENDISH, Henry (1731–1810; British physicist)

CHEBISHEV, Pafnuti Lvovich (1821–94; Russian mathematician)

CHERENKOV, Pavel Alekseievich (1904–90; Russian physicist)

COCKCROFT, Sir John Douglas (1897–1967; British physicist)

CORNFORTH, Sir John Warcup (1917– ; Australian chemist)

D'ALEMBERT, Jean Le Rond (1717–83; French mathematician)

DAUBENTON, Louis Jean Marie (1716–1800; French naturalist)

DAVENPORT, Charles Benedict (1866–1944; US zoologist)

EDDINGTON, Sir Arthur Stanley (1882–1944; British theoretical astronomer)

ENDLICHER, Stephan Ladislaus (1804–49; Hungarian botanist)

FIBONACCI, Leonardo (c. 1170–c. 1230; Italian mathematician)

FLAMSTEED, John (1646–1719; English astronomer)

GAY-LUSSAC, Joseph Louis (1778–1850; French chemist and physicist)

HEAVISIDE, Oliver (1850–1925; British physicist)

9–continued

HELMHOLTZ, Hermann Ludwig Ferdinand Von (1821–94; German physicist and physiologist)

HOPKINSON, John (1849–98; British physicist and electrical engineer)

JOHANNSEN, Wilhelm Ludvig (1857–1927; Danish geneticist)

JOSEPHSON, Brian David (1940– ; British physicist)

KIRCHHOFF, Gustav Robert (1824–87; German physicist)

KURCHATOV, Igor Vasilievich (1903–60; Soviet physicist)

LANKESTER, Sir Edwin Ray (1847–1929; British zoologist)

LAVOISIER, Antoine Laurent (1743–94; French chemist)

LEDERBERG, Joshua (1925– ; US geneticist)

LEVERRIER, Urbain Jean Joseph (1811–77; French astronomer)

LIOUVILLE, Joseph (1809–82; French mathematician)

MACINTOSH, Charles (1766–1843; Scottish chemist)

MACMILLAN, Kirkpatrick (d. 1878; Scottish inventor)

MICHELSON, Albert Abraham (1852–1931; US physicist)

NICHOLSON, William (1753–1815; British chemist)

NIRENBERG, Marshall Warren (1927– ; US biochemist)

PELLETIER, Pierre Joseph (1788–1842; French chemist)

PRIESTLEY, Joseph (1733–1804; British chemist)

REMINGTON, Eliphalet (1793–1863; US inventor)

SCHLEIDEN, Matthias Jakob (1804–81; German botanist)

STEINMETZ, Charles Proteus (1865–1923; US electrical engineer)

TINBERGEN, Nikolaas (1907–94; Dutch zoologist and pioneer ethologist)

ZSIGMONDY, Richard Adolph (1865–1929; Austrian chemist)

ZUCKERMAN, Solly, Baron (1904–93; British anatomist)

10

ARCHIMEDES (c. 287–c. 212 BC; Greek mathematician and inventor)

10–continued

ARROWSMITH, Aaron (1750–1823; British cartographer)

BARKHAUSEN, Heinrich (1881–1956; German physicist)

BERTHOLLET, Claude Louis, Comte (1748–1822; French chemist and physician)

BLENKINSOP, John (1783–1831; British engineer)

CANNIZZARO, Stanislao (1826–1910; Italian chemist)

COPERNICUS, Nicolaus (1473–1543; Polish astronomer)

DOBZHANSKY, Theodosius (1900–75; US geneticist)

FITZGERALD, George Francis (1851–1901; Irish physicist)

FOURNEYRON, Benoît (1802–67; French engineer)

FRAUNHOFER, Joseph Von (1787–1826; German physicist)

HEISENBERG, Werner Karl (1901–76; German physicist)

HIPPARCHUS (c. 190–c. 120 BC; Greek astronomer)

HOFMEISTER, Wilhelm Friedrich Benedict (1824–77; German botanist)

INGENHOUSZ, Jan (1730–99; Dutch physician and plant physiologist)

KOLMOGOROV, Andrei Nikolaevich (1903–87; Soviet mathematician)

LILIENTHAL, Otto (1848–96; German aeronautical engineer)

LIPPERSHEY, Hans (d. c. 1619; Dutch lens grinder)

MAUPERTUIS, Pierre Louis Moreau de (1698–1759; French mathematician)

MENDELEYEV, Dimitrii Ivanovich (1834–1907; Russian chemist)

METCHNIKOV, Ilya Ilich (1845–1916; Russian zoologist)

RUTHERFORD, Ernest, 1st Baron (1871–1937; English physicist)

SOMMERFELD, Arnold Johannes Wilhelm (1868–1951; German physicist)

STAUDINGER, Hermann (1881–1965; German chemist)

10–continued

STEPHENSON, George (1781–1848; British engineer)

SWAMMERDAM, Jan (1637–80; Dutch naturalist and microscopist)

TORRICELLI, Evangelista (1608–47; Italian physicist)

TOURNEFORT, Joseph Pitton de (1656–1708; French botanist)

TREVITHICK, Richard (1771–1833; British engineer)

WATSON-WATT, Sir Robert Alexander (1892–1973; Scottish physicist)

WHEATSTONE, Sir Charles (1802–75; British physicist)

11

AL-KHWARIZMI, Muhammed Ibn Musa (c. 780–c. 850 AD; Arabic mathematician)

BASKERVILLE, John (1706–75; British printer)

BHOSKHARA II (1114–c. 1185; Indian mathematician)

CHAMBERLAIN, Owen (1920–   ; US physicist)

GOLDSCHMIDT, Richard Benedict (1878–1958; US geneticist)

HINSHELWOOD, Sir Cyril Norman (1897–1967; British chemist)

JOLIOT-CURIE, Irène (1896–1956; French physicist)

LE CHÂTELIER, Henri-Louis (1850–1936; French chemist)

LEEUWENHOEK, Antonie van (1632–1723; Dutch scientist)

LOBACHEVSKI, Nikolai Ivanovich (1793–1856; Russian mathematician)

11–continued

NOSTRADAMUS (1503–66; French physician and astrologer)

OPPENHEIMER, J Robert (1904–67; US physicist)

SCHRÖDINGER, Erwin (1887–1961; Austrian physicist)

SHERRINGTON, Sir Charles Scott (1857–1952; British physiologist)

SPALLANZANI, Lazzaro (1729–99; Italian physiologist)

TSIOLKOVSKI, Konstantin Eduardovich (1857–1935; Russian aeronautical engineer)

VAN DER WAALS, Johannes Diderik (1837–1923; Dutch physicist)

12

AMBARTSUMIAN, Viktor Amazaspovich (1908–96 Armenian astrophysicist)

SZENT-GYÖRGYI, Albert (1893–1986; US biochemist)

13

ARAGO FRANÇOIS (1786–1853; French astronomer and physicist)

CHANDRASEKHAR, Subrahmanyan (1910–95; US astronomer)

REGIOMONTANUS (1436-76; German astronomer and mathematician)

14

GALILEO GALILEI (1564–1642; Italian mathematician, physicist, and astronomer)

15

EUDOXUS OF CNIDUS (c. 408–c. 355 BC; Greek astronomer and mathematician)

16

HERO OF ALEXANDRIA (mid-1st century AD; Greek engineer and mathematician)

17

APOLLONIUS OF PERGA (c. 261–c. 190 BC; Greek mathematician)

18

ARISTARCHUS OF SAMOS (c. 310–230 BC; Greek astronomer)

LECOQ DE BOISBAUDRAN, Paul-Émile (1838–1912; French chemist)

PAPPUS OF ALEXANDRIA (3rd century BC; Greek mathematician)

19

DIOSCORIDES PEDANIUS (c. 40–c. 90 AD; Greek physician)

KEKULÉ VON STRADONITZ, Friedrich August (1829–96; German chemist)

20+

IOPHANTUS OF ALEXANDRIA (mid-3rd century AD; Greek mathematician)

ERATOSTHENES OF CYRENE (c. 276–c. 194 BC; Greek astronomer)

GEOFFROY SAINT-HILAIRE, Étienne (1772–1844; French naturalist)

SOSIGENES OF ALEXANDRIA (1st century BC; Greek astronomer)

COMPUTER SCIENTISTS

4

BINA, Eric US computer scientist

CERF, Vinton G US computer scientist

HOFF, Marcian Edward (1937–) US computer engineer

JOBS, Steven Paul (1955–) US computer engineer and entrepreneur

KAHN, Robert (1938–) US computer scientist

ZUSE, Konrad (1910–95) German computer engineer

5

AIKEN, Howard Hathaway (1900–73) US computer pioneer

BYRON, Augusta Ada, Countess of Lovelace (1815–52) British computer pioneer

KNUTH, Donald Ervin (1938–) US computer programmer

LENAT, Douglas (1950–) US computer scientist

OLSEN, Kenneth Harry (1926–) US computer engineer and entrepreneur

6

AMDAHL, Gene Myron (1922–) US computer engineer

6–continued

BACKUS, John (1924–) US computer scientist

ECKERT, John Presper, Jr (1919–1995) US computer scientist

HOPPER, Grace (1906–92) US mathematician and computer scientist

KAPOOR, Mitchell David (1950–) US computer scientist

MINSKY, Marvin Lee (1927–) US computer scientist

NELSON, Ted (1937–) US computer scientist

NEWELL, Allan (1927–) US computer scientist

POSTEL, Jonathan (1943–98) US computer scientist

SCHANK, Roger Carl (1946–) US computer scientist

WILKES, Maurice Vincent (1913–) British computer scientist

7

KILDALL, Gary (1942–95) US computer scientist

MAUCHLY, John William (1907–80) US computer engineer

STIBITZ, George Robert (1904–95) US computer pioneer

8

BRICKLIN, Daniel (1951–) US computer engineer

STRACHEY, Christopher (1916–75) British computer scientist

WINOGRAD, Terry Allen (1946–) US computer scientist

9

ATANASOFF, John Vincent (1904–95) US physicist and computer pioneer

ENGLEBART, Douglas (1925–) US computer scientist

FORRESTER, Jay (1918–) US computer engineer

MCCARTHY, John (1927–) US computer scientist

10

ANDREESSEN, Marc (1971–) US computer scientist

BERNERS-LEE, Tim (1955–) British computer scientist

FEIGENBAUM, Edward Albert (1936–) US computer scientist

HOFSTADTER, Douglas Richard (1945–) US computer scientis

ENGINEERS AND INVENTORS

4

BELL, Alexander Graham (1847–1922) Scottish-born US inventor of the telephone

DAVY, Humphry (1778–1829) English inventor of the Davy lamp

HOWE, Elias (1819–67) US inventor of the sewing machine

IVES, Frederick Eugene (1856–1937) US inventor of halftone photography

LAND, Edwin Herbert (1909–91) US inventor of the Polaroid Land camera

4–continued

MOON, William (1818–94) British inventor of the Moon writing system

TULL, Jethro (1674–1741) English inventor of the seed drill

WATT, James (1736–1819) Scottish engineer and inventor who developed the steam engine

5

BAIRD, John Logie (1888–1946) Scottish inventor of television

CREED, Frederick (1871–1957) Canadian inventor of the teleprinter

5–continued

CYRIL, Saint (?827–869) Greek Christian theologian, inventor of the Cyrillic alphabet

DALEN, Nils Gustaf (1869–1937) Swedish inventor of an automatic light-controlled valve

HOOKE, Robert (1635–1703) English physicist, chemist, and inventor of the Gregorian telescope and a balance spring for watches

MAXIM, Hiram Stevens (1840–1916) British inventor of the first automatic machine gun

5–continued

MORSE, Samuel (1791–1872) US inventor of electric telegraph and Morse code

NOBEL, Alfred (1833–96) Swedish inventor of dynamite

TESLA, Nikola (1857–1943) US inventor of transformers, generators, and dynamos

6

ARCHER, Frederick Scott (1813–57) British inventor of wet collodion photographic process

BAYLIS, Trevor (1937–) British inventor of clockwork radio

DU MONT, Allen Balcom (1901–65) US inventor and developer of cathode-ray tube

DUNLOP, John (1840–1921) Scottish inventor of pneumatic tyre

EDISON, Thomas Alva (1847–1931) US inventor of phonograph, electric lamp, microphone, etc.

NAPIER, John (1550–1617) Scottish inventor of logarithms

NIEPCE, Joseph-Nicéphore (1765–1833) French inventor who produced first photographic image and first permanent camera photograph

PITMAN, Sir Isaac (1813–97) British inventor of a system of shorthand

SHOLES, Christopher Latham (1819–90) US inventor of the typewriter

SINGER, Isaac Merrit (1811–75) US inventor of chain-stitch sewing machine

6–continued

WILSON, Charles (1869–1959) Scottish inventor of the cloud chamber

7

BABBAGE, Charles (1792–1871) English inventor of a calculating machine (forerunner of modern electronic computers)

BRAILLE, Louis (1809–52) French inventor of the Braille system of raised writing

LAENNEC, René (1781–1826) French inventor of the stethoscope

NASMYTH, James (1808–90) British inventor of the steam hammer

SIEMENS, Ernst Werner von (1816–92) German inventor and pioneer in telegraphy

WHITNEY, Eli (1765–1825) US inventor of a mechanical cotton gin

WHITTLE, Frank (1907–96) British inventor of the jet engine

8

CROMPTON, Samuel (1753–1827) British inventor of the spinning mule

DAGUERRE, Louise (1789–1851) French inventor of photographic processes

DE FOREST, Lee (1873–1961) US inventor of radio equipment

GOODYEAR, Charles (1800–60) US inventor of vulcanized rubber

LAWRENCE, Ernest (1901–58) US inventor of the cyclotron

8–continued

LIPPMANN, Gabriel (1845–1921) French inventor of a process of colour photography

ZAMENHOF, Lazarus (1859–1917) Polish inventor of Esperanto

9

ARKWRIGHT, Richard (1732–92) English inventor of the spinning wheel

COCKERELL, Christopher (1910–99) British inventor of the hovercraft

FOX TALBOT, William (1800–77) British pioneer of photography

GUTENBERG, Johann (?1398–1468) German inventor of printing by movable type

MCCORMICK, Cyrus Hall (1809–84) US inventor of the reaping machine

10

CARTWRIGHT, Edmund (1743–1823) British inventor of the power loom

FAHRENHEIT, Gabriel (1686–1736) German inventor of the mercury thermometer

HARGREAVES, James (d. 1778) English inventor of the spinning jenny

MONTGOLFIER, Jacques (1745–99) and Joseph (1740–1810) French inventors who built the first practical hot-air balloon

STEPHENSON, George (1781-1848) British inventor of the first successful steam locomotive

ENTREPRENEURS AND INDUSTRIALISTS

3

LAW, John (1671–1729) Scottish financier

4

FORD, Henry (1863–1947) US manufacturer

OWEN, Robert (1771–1858) Welsh industrialist

RANK, J Arthur, 1st Baron (1888–1972) British industrialist

TATE, Henry (1819–99) British manufacturer

5

DAWES, Charles Gates (1865–1951) US financier

FARGO, William (1818–81) US businessman

GATES, Bill (1955–   ) US businessman

GETTY, J(ean) Paul (1892–1976) US oil executive

WELLS, Henry (1805–78) US businessman

6

GEORGE, Edward (1938–   ) British banker

HAMLYN, Paul, Baron (1926–   ) British businessman

HUGHES, Howard (1905–76) US industrialist

MORGAN, John Pierpont (1837–1913) US financier

NECKER, Jacques (1732–1804) French financier

RHODES, Cecil John (1853–1902) British financier

TURNER, Robert Edward, III (1938–   ) US businessman

7

BOULTON, Matthew (1728–1809) British manufacturer

BRANSON, Richard (1950–   ) British entrepreneur

BUGATTI, Ettore (1881–1947) Italian manufacturer

CADBURY, George (1839–1922) British industrialist

DAIMLER, Gottlieb (1834–1900) German manufacturer

EASTMAN, George (1854–1932) US manufacturer

GRESHAM, Thomas (?1519–79) English financier

ONASSIS, Aristotle (1906–1975) Turkish-born Argentinian shipowner

PEABODY, George (1795–1869) US merchant

RODDICK, Anita (1942–   ) British entrepreneur

WHITNEY, Eli (1765–1825) US manufacturer

8

CARNEGIE, Andrew (1835–1919) US manufacturer

MICHELIN, André (1853–1931) French industrialist

NUFFIELD, William Richard Morris (1877–1963) English manufacturer

PATERSON, William (1658–1719) Scottish merchant

8–continued

RATHENAU, Walther (1867–1922) German industrialist

SINCLAIR, Clive (1940–   ) British entrepreneur

9

ARKWRIGHT, Sir Richard (1732–92) English manufacturer

MACARTHUR, John (1767–1834) Australian entrepreneur

WEDGEWOOD, Josiah (1730–95) British industrialist

WOOLWORTH, Frank Winfield (1852–1919) US merchant

10

CHARDONNET, (Louis Marie) Hilaire Bernigaud (1839–1924) French industrialist

GULBENKIAN, Calouste Sarkis (1869–1955) British industrialist

LEVERHULME, 1st Viscount (1851–1925) English industrialist

ROTHSCHILD, Lionel Nathan, Baron de Rothschild (1809–1879) British banker

VANDERBILT, Cornelius (1794–1877) US shipowner

11

ROCKEFELLER, John D (1839–1937) US industrialist

FASHION DESIGNERS

3

SUI, Anna (1955–) US fashion designer

4

DIOR, Christian (1905–57) French fashion designer

HEAD, Edith (1907–81) US fashion designer

KORS, Michael (1959–) US fashion designer

LANG, Helmut (1956–) Austrian fashion designer

WANG, Vera (1949–) US fashion designer

5

DOLCE, Domenico (1958–) Italian fashion designer

FARHI, Nicole (1946–) French fashion designer

FERRE, Gianfranco (1944–) Italian fashion designer

FREUD, Bella (1961–) British fashion designer

GUCCI, Guccio (1881–1953) Italian fashion designer

KARAN, Donna (1948–) US fashion designer

KLEIN, Calvin (1942– –) US fashion designer

PRADA, Miuccia (1949–) Italian fashion designer

QUANT, Mary (1934–) British fashion designer

RICCI, Nina (1883–1970) Italian fashion designer

WORTH, Charles Frederick (1825–95) British fashion designer

6

ARMANI, Giorgio (1936– –) Italian fashion designer

ASHLEY, Laura (1925–85) British fashion designer

CARDIN, Pierre (1922–) French fashion designer

CHANEL, Gabrielle (Coco) (1883–1971) French fashion designer

CONRAN, Jasper (1959–) British fashion designer

6–continued

JACOBS, Marc (1963–) US fashion designer

LAUREN, Ralph (1939–) US fashion designer

MIYAKE, Issey (1935–) Japanese fashion designer

MUGLER, Thierry (1948–) French fashion designer

SANDER, Jil (1943–) German fashion designer

UNGARO, Emanuel (1934–) French fashion designer

7

BALMAIN, Pierre Alexandre (1914–82) French fashion designer

BLAHNIK, Manolo (1943–) Spanish Czech fashion designer

GABBANA, Stefano (1962–) Italian fashion designer

HAMNETT, Katharine (1948–) British fashion designer

HERRERA, Carolina (1939–) US fashion designer

LACROIX, Christian (1951–) French fashion designer

MCQUEEN, Alexander (1969–) British fashion designer

VERSACE, Donatella (1955–) Italian fashion designer

VERSACE, Gianni (1946–97) Italian fashion designer

VUITTON, Louis (1821–92) Swiss fashion designer

8

BURBERRY, Thomas (1835–1926) British fashion designer

CERRUTTI, Nino (1930–) Italian fashion designer

FERRETTI, Alberta (1950–) Italian fashion designer

GALLIANO, John (1960–) British fashion designer

8–continued

GAULTIER, Jean–Paul (1952–) French fashion designer

GIVENCHY, Hubert de (1927–) French fashion designer

HARTNELL, Norman Sir (1901–79) British fashion designer

HILFIGER, Tommy (1951–) US fashion designer

OLDFIELD, Bruce (1950–) British fashion designer

WESTWOOD, Vivienne (1941–) British fashion designer

9

COURREGES, André (1923–) French fashion designer

DE LA RENTA, Oscar (1936–) Dominican fashion designer

FERRAGAMO, Salvatore (1898–1960) Italian fashion designer

LAGERFELD, Karl (1938–) German fashion designer

MACDONALD, Julien (1972–) British fashion designer

MCCARTNEY, Stella (1971–) British fashion designer

VALENTINO (Garavani) (1932–) Italian fashion designer

10+

BALENCIAGA, Cristobal (1895–1972) Spanish fashion designer

SAINT-LAURENT, Yves (1936–) French fashion designer

SCHIAPARELLI, Elsa (1890–1970) Italian fashion designer

VON FURSTENBERG, Diane (1946–) Belgian fashion designer

ECONOMISTS

4

LIST, Friedrich (1789–1846;
German economist)

MARX, Karl (Heinrich; (1818–
83; German philosopher,
economist, and revolutionary)

WARD, Barbara, Baroness
Jackson (1914–81; British
economist and
conservationist)

WEBB, Sidney (James;, Baron
Passfield (1859–1947; British
economist and socialist)

5

DEFOE, Daniel (1660–1731;
British novelist, economist,
and journalist)

FOGEL, Robert William
(1926–   ; US historian and
economist)

HAYEK, Friedrich August von
(1899–1992; British
economist)

MEADE, James Edward
(1907–95; British economist)

PASSY, Frédéric (1822–1912;
French economist and
politician)

PIGOU, Arthur Cecil (1877–
1954; British economist)

SMITH, Adam (1723–90;
Scottish moral philosopher
and political economist)

TOBIN, James (1918–   ; US
economist)

6

ANGELL, Sir Norman (1874–
1967; British author, economist, and Labour politician)

6–continued

BARUCH, Bernard
(1870–1965; US economist)

COBDEN, Richard (1804–65;
British politician and
economist)

DELORS, Jacques (Lucien
Jean; (1925–   ; French
politician and economist)

ERHARD, Ludwig (1897–1977;
German statesman and
economist)

FRISCH, Ragnar (1895–1973;
Norwegian economist)

JEVONS, William Stanley
(1835–1882; British
economist, logician, and
statistician)

KEYNES, John Maynard, 1st
Baron (1883–1946; British
economist)

MONNET, Jean (1888–1979;
French economist)

MYRDAL, Gunnar (1898–1987;
Swedish sociologist and
economist)

PARETO, Vilfredo (1848–1932;
Italian economist and
sociologist)

TURGOT, Anne Robert
Jacques, Baron de l'Aulne
(1727–81; French economist)

7

BAGEHOT, Walter (1826–77;
British economist, political
theorist, literary critic, and
journalist)

KUZNETS, Simon (1901–85;
US economist)

7–continued

MALTHUS, Thomas Robert
(1766–1834; British
clergyman and economist)

QUESNAY, François
(1694–1774; French
economist)

RICARDO, David (1772–1823;
British political economist)

TOYNBEE, Arnold (1852–83;
British economist and
philanthropist)

WOOTTON, Barbara, Baroness
(1897–1988; British
educationalist and economist

8

BECCARIA, Cesare Bonesana,
Marchese de (1738–94;
Italian legal theorist and
political economist)

FRIEDMAN, Milton (1912–   ;
US economist)

MANSHOLT, Sicco (1908–95;
Dutch politician and
economist)

PHILLIPS, A W (1914–75;
British economist)

9

BEVERIDGE, William Henry
Beveridge, 1st Baron
(1879–1963; British
economist, writer, and
academic)

GALBRAITH, John Kenneth
(1908–   ; US economist)

TINBERGEN, Jan (1903–94;
Dutch economist)

NOBEL PRIZE WINNERS

PHYSICS

1901	W RÖNTGEN (GER)
1902	H ANTOON LORENTZ (NETH)
	P ZEEMAN (NETH)
1903	A BECQUEREL (FR)
	P CURIE (FR)
	M CURIE (FR)
1904	LORD RAYLEIGH (GB)
1905	P LENARD (GER)
1906	SIR J J THOMSON (GB)
1907	A A MICHELSON (US)
1908	G LIPPMANN (FR)
1909	G MARCONI (ITALY)
	K BRAUN (GER)
1910	J VAN DER WAALS (NETH)
1911	W WIEN (GER)
1912	N G DALÉN (SWED)

1913	H KAMERLINGH ONNES (NETH)		R MÖSSBAUER (GER)
1914	M VON LAUE (GER)	1962	L D LANDAU (USSR)
1915	SIR W BRAGG (GB)	1963	J H D JENSEN (GER)
	SIR L BRAGG (GB)		M G MAYER (US)
1916	(NO AWARD)		E P WIGNER (US)
1917	C BARKLA (GB)	1964	C H TOWNES (US)
1918	M PLANCK (GER)		N G BASOV (USSR)
1919	J STARK (GER)		A M PROKHOROV (USSR)
1920	C GUILLAUME (SWITZ)	1965	J S SCHWINGER (US)
1921	A EINSTEIN (SWITZ)		R P FEYNMAN (US)
1922	N BOHR (DEN)		S TOMONAGA (JAPAN)
1923	R MILLIKAN (US)	1966	A KASTLER (FR)
1924	K SIEGBAHN (SWED)	1967	H A BETHE (US)
1925	J FRANCK (GER)	1968	L W ALVAREZ (US)
	G HERTZ (GER)	1969	M GELL-MANN (US)
1926	J PERRIN (FR)	1970	H ALVÉN (SWED)
1927	A H COMPTON (US)		L NÉEL (FR)
	C WILSON (GB)	1971	D GABOR (GB)
1928	SIR O RICHARDSON (GB)	1972	J BARDEEN (US)
1929	PRINCE L DE BROGLIE (FR)		L N COOPER (US)
1930	SIR C RAMAN (INDIA)		J R SCHRIEFFER (US)
1931	(NO AWARD)	1973	L ESAKI (JAPAN)
1932	W HEISENBERG (GER)		I GIAEVER (US)
1933	P A M DIRAC (GB)		B JOSEPHSON (GB)
	E SCHRÖDINGER (AUSTRIA)	1974	SIR M RYLE (GB)
1934	(NO AWARD)		A HEWISH (GB)
1935	SIR J CHADWICK (GB)	1975	J RAINWATER (US)
1936	V HESS (AUSTRIA)		A BOHR (DEN)
	C ANDERSON (US)		B MOTTELSON (DEN)
1937	C DAVISSON (US)	1976	B RICHTER (US)
	SIR G P THOMSON (GB)		S TING (US)
1938	E FERMI (ITALY)	1977	P W ANDERSON (US)
1939	E LAWRENCE (US)		SIR N F MOTT (GB)
1943	O STERN (US)		J H VAN VLECK (US)
1944	I RABI (US)	1978	P L KAPITSA (USSR)
1945	W PAULI (AUSTRIA)		A A PENZIAS (US)
1946	P BRIDGMAN (US)		R W WILSON (US)
1947	SIR E APPLETON (GB)	1979	S L GLASHOW (US)
1948	P BLACKETT (GB)		A SALAM (PAK)
1949	H YUKAWA (JAPAN)		S WEINBERG (US)
1950	C POWELL (GB)	1980	J CRONIN (US)
1951	SIR J COCKCROFT (GB)		V FITCH (US)
	E WALTON (IRE)	1981	K SIEGBAHN (SWED)
1952	F BLOCH (US)		N BLOEMBERGEN (US)
	E PURCELL (US)		A SCHAWLOW (US)
1953	F ZERNIKE (NETH)	1982	K G WILSON (US)
1954	M BORN (GB)	1983	S CHANDRASEKHAR (US)
	W BOTHE (GER)		W FOWLER (US)
1955	W LAMB, JR (US)	1984	C RUBBIA (ITALY)
	P KUSCH (US)		S VAN DER MEER (NETH)
1956	W SHOCKLEY (US)	1985	K VON KLITZING (GER)
	J BARDEEN (US)	1986	E RUSKA (GER)
	W BRATTAIN (US)		G BINNIG (GER)
1957	TSUNG-DAO LEE (CHINA)		H ROHRER (SWITZ)
	C N YANG (CHINA)	1987	A MÜLLER (SWITZ)
1958	P A CHERENKOV (USSR)		G BEDNORZ (GER)
	I M FRANK (USSR)	1988	L M LEDERMAN (US)
	I Y TAMM (USSR)		M SCHWARTZ (US)
1959	E SEGRÈ (US)		J STEINBERGER (GER)
	O CHAMBERLAIN (US)	1989	H DEHMELT (US)
1960	D GLASER (US)		W PAULM (GER)
1961	R HOFSTADTER (US)		N RAMSEY (US)

1990	J FRIEDMAN (US)
	H KENDALL (US)
	R TAYLOR (CAN)
1991	P De GENNES (FR)
1992	G CHARPAK (FR)
1993	R HULSE (US)
	J TAYLOR (US)
1994	B BROCKHOUE (CAN)
	C SHULL (US)
1995	M PERL (US)
	F REINES (US)
1996	D M LEE (US)
	D D OSCHEROF (US)
	R C RICHARDSON (US)
1997	S CHU (US)
1998	R B LAUGHLIN (US)
	H L STÖRMER (GER)
	D C TSUI (US)
1999	G 't HOOFT (NETH)
	M J G VELTMAN (NETH)
2000	Z I ALFEROV (RUS)
	H KOEMER (GER)
	J S KILBY (US)
2001	E A CORNELL (US)
	W KETTERLE (GER)
	C E WIEMAN (US)
2002	R DAVIS JR (US)
	M KOSHIBA (JAPAN)
	R GIACCONI (US)
2004	A A ABRIKOSOV (US)
	V L GINZBURG (RUS)
	A J LEGGETT (US)

CHEMISTRY

1901	J V HOFF (NETH)
1902	E FISCHER (GER)
1903	S ARRHENIUS (SWED)
1904	SIR W RAMSAY (GB)
1905	A VON BAEYER (GER)
1906	H MOISSAN (FR)
1907	E BUCHNER (GER)
1908	LORD RUTHERFORD (GB)
1909	W OSTWALD (GER)
1910	O WALLACH (GER)
1911	M CURIE (FR)
1912	V GRIGNARD (FR)
	P SABATIER (FR)
1913	A WERNER (SWITZ)
1914	T RICHARDS (US)
1915	R WILLSTÄTTER (GER)
1916	(NO AWARD)
1917	(NO AWARD)
1918	F HABER (GER)
1919	(NO AWARD)
1920	W NERNST (GER)
1921	F SODDY (GB)
1922	F ASTON (GB)
1923	F PREGL (AUSTRIA)
1924	(NO AWARD)
1925	R ZSIGMONDY (AUSTRIA)
1926	T SVEDBERG (SWED)

1927	H WIELAND (GER)
1928	A WINDAUS (GER)
1929	SIR A HARDEN (GB)
	H VON EULER-CHELPIN (SWED)
1930	H FISCHER (GER)
1931	K BOSCH (GER)
	F BERGIUS (GER)
1932	I LANGMUIR (US)
1933	(NO AWARD)
1934	H UREY (US)
1935	F JOLIOT-CURIE (FR)
	I JOLIOT-CURIE (FR)
1936	P DEBYE (NETH)
1937	SIR W HAWORTH (GB)
	P KARRER (SWITZ)
1938	R KUHN (GER)
1939	A BUTENANDT (GER)
	L RUZICKA (SWITZ)
1943	G DE HEVESY (HUNG)
1944	O HAHN (GER)
1945	A VIRTANEN (FIN)
1946	J SUMNER (US)
	J NORTHROP (US)
	W STANLEY (US)
1947	SIR R ROBINSON (GB)
1948	A TISELIUS (SWED)
1949	W GIAUQUE (US)
1950	O DIELS (GER)
	K ALDER (GER)
1951	E MCMILLAN (US)
	G SEABORG (US)
1952	A MARTIN (GB)
	R SYNGE (GB)
1953	H STAUDINGER (GER)
1954	L C PAULING (US)
1955	V DU VIGNEAUD (US)
1956	N SEMYONOV (USSR)
	SIR C HINSHELWOOD (GB)
1957	SIR A TODD (GB)
1958	F SANGER (GB)
1959	J HEYROVSKY (CZECH)
1960	W LIBBY (US)
1961	M CALVIN (US)
1962	J C KENDREW (GB)
	M F PERUTZ (GB)
1963	G NATTA (ITALY)
	K ZIEGLER (GER)
1964	D M C HODGKIN (GB)
1965	R B WOODWARD (US)
1966	R S MULLIKEN (US)
1967	M EIGEN (GER)
	R G W NORRISH (GB)
	G PORTER (GB)
1968	L ONSAGER (US)
1969	D H R BARTON (GB)
	O HASSEL (NOR)
1970	L F LELOIR (ARG)
1971	G HERZBERG (CAN)
1972	C B ANFINSEN (US)
	S MOORE (US)
	W H STEIN (US)
1973	E FISCHER (GER)

	G WILKINSON (GB)
1974	P J FLORY (US)
1975	J W CORNFORT (AUSTR)
	V PRELOG (SWITZ)
1976	W M LIPSCOMB (US)
1977	I PRIGOGINE (BELGIUM)
1978	P MITCHELL (GB)
1979	H C BROWN (US)
	G WITTIG (GER)
1980	P BERG (US)
	W GILBERT (US)
	F SANGER (GB)
1981	K FUKUI (JAPAN)
	R HOFFMANN (POL)
1982	A KLUG (GB)
1983	H TAUBE (US)
1984	R B MERRIFIELD (US)
1985	H HAUPTMAN (US)
	J KARLE (US)
1986	D HERSCHBACH (US)
	Y TSEH LEE (US)
	J POLANYI (CAN)
1987	D CRAM (US)
	J LEHN (FR)
	C PEDERSEN (US)
1988	J DIESENHOFER (GER)
	R HUBER (GER)
	H MICHEL (GER)
1989	S ALTMAN (US)
	T CECH (US)
1990	E CORY (US)
1991	R ERNST (SWITZ)
1992	R MARCUS (CAN)
1993	K MULLIS (US)
	M SMITH (US)
1994	G OLAH (US)
1995	P CRUTZEN (NETH)
	M MOLINA (MEX)
	F ROWLAND (US)
1996	SIR H KROTO (GB)
	R CURL (US)
	R SMALLEY (US)
1997	P D BOYER (US)
	J C SKOU (DEN)
	J E WALKER (GB)
1998	W KOHN (US)
	J A POPE (GB)
1999	A H ZEWAIL (EGYPT & US)
2000	A J HEEGER (US)
	A G MACDIARMID (US)
	H SHIRAKAWA (JAPAN)
2001	W S KNOWLES (US)
	R NOYORI (JAPAN)
	K B SHARPLESS (US)
2002	J B FENN (US)
	K TANAKA (JAPAN)
	K WUTHRICH (SWITZ)
2003	P AGRE (US)
	R MACKINNON (US)

PHYSIOLOGY OR MEDICINE

1901	E VON BEHRING (GER)
1902	SIR R ROSS (GB)
1903	N R FINSEN (DEN)
1904	I PAVLOV (RUSS)
1905	R KOCH (GER)
1906	C GOLGI (ITALY)
	S RAMÓN Y CAJAL (SPAIN)
1907	A LAVERAN (FR)
1908	P EHRLICH (GER)
	I MECHNIKOV (RUSS)
1909	E KOCHER (SWITZ)
1910	A KOSSEL (GER)
1911	A GULLSTRAND (SWED)
1912	A CARREL (FR)
1913	C RICHET (FR)
1914	R BÁRÁNY (AUSTRIA)
1915	(NO AWARD)
1916	(NO AWARD)
1917	(NO AWARD)
1919	J BORDET (BELG)
1920	A KROGH (DEN)
1921	(NO AWARD)
1922	A V HILL (GB)
	O MEYERHOF (GER)
1923	SIR F G BANTING (CAN)
	J J R MACLEOD (GB)
1924	W EINTHOVEN (NETH)
1925	(NO AWARD)
1926	J FIBIGER (DEN)
1927	J W VON JAUREGG (AUSTRIA)
1928	C NICOLLE (FR)
1929	C EIJKMAN (NETH)
	SIR F HOPKINS (GB)
1930	K LANDSTEINER (US)
1931	O WARBURG (GER)
1932	E D ADRIAN (GB)
	SIR C SHERRINGTON (GB)
1933	T H MORGAN (US)
1934	G R MINOT (US)
	W P MURPHY (US)
	G H WHIPPLE (US)
1935	H SPEMANN (GER)
1936	SIR H H DALE (GB)
	O LOEWI (GER)
1937	A SZENT-GYÖRGYI (HUNG)
1938	C HEYMANS (BELG)
1939	G DOMAGK (GER)
1943	H DAM (DEN)
	E A DOISY (US)
1944	J ERLANGER (US)
	H S GASSER (US)
1945	SIR A FLEMING (GB)
	E B CHAIN (GB)
	LORD FLOREY (AUSTR)
1946	H J MULLER (US)
1947	C F CORI (US)
	G T CORI (US)
	B HOUSSAY (ARG)
1948	P MÜLLER (SWITZ)
1949	W R HESS (SWITZ)

	A E MONIZ (PORT)
1950	P S HENCH (US)
	E C KENDALL (US)
	T REICHSTEIN (SWITZ)
1951	M THEILER (S AF)
1952	S A WAKSMAN (US)
1953	F A LIPMANN (US)
	SIR H A KREBS (GB)
1954	J F ENDERS (US)
	T H WELLER (US)
	F ROBBINS (US)
1955	A H THEORELL (SWED)
1956	W FORSSMANN (GER)
	D RICHARDS (US)
	A F COURNAND (US)
1957	D BOVET (ITALY)
1958	G W BEADLE (US)
	E L TATUM (US)
	J LEDERBERG (US)
1959	S OCHOA (US)
	A KORNBERG (US)
1960	F MACFARLANE BURNET (AUSTR)
	P B MEDAWAR (GB)
1961	G VON BÉKÉSY (US)
1962	F H C CRICK (GB)
	J D WATSON (US)
	M WILKINS (GB)
1963	SIR J C ECCLES (AUSTR)
	A L HODGKIN (GB)
	A F HUXLEY (GB)
1964	K BLOCH (US)
	F LYNEN (GER)
1965	F JACOB (FR)
	A LWOFF (FR)
	J MONOD (FR)
1966	C B HUGGINS (US)
	F P ROUS (US)
1967	H K HARTLINE (US)
	G WALD (US)
	R A GRANIT (SWED)
1968	R W HOLLEY (US)
	H G KHORANA (US)
	M W NIRENBERG (US)
1969	M DELBRÜCK (US)
	A D HERSHEY (US)
	S E LURIA (US)
1970	J AXELROD (US)
	SIR B KATZ (GB)
	U VON EULER (SWED)
1971	E W SUTHERLAND, JR (US)
1972	G M EDELMAN (US)
	R R PORTER (GB)
1973	K VON FRISCH (GER)
	K LORENZ (GER)
	N TINBERGEN (NETH)
1974	A CLAUDE (US)
	C DE DUVE (BELG)
	G E PALADE (BELG)
1975	D BALTIMORE (US)
	R DULBECCO (US)
	H M TEMIN (US)
1976	B S BLUMBERG (US)
	D G GAJDUSEK (US)

1977	R S YALOW (US)
	R GUILLEMIN (US)
	A V SCHALLY (US)
1978	W ARBER (SWITZ)
	D NATHANS (US)
	H SMITH (US)
1979	A M CORMACK (US)
	G N HOUNSFIELD (GB)
1980	G SNELL (US)
	J DAUSSET (FR)
	B BENACERRAF (US)
1981	R SPERRY (US)
	D HUBEL (US)
	T WIESEL (SWED)
1982	S K BERGSTROM (SWED)
	B I SAMUELSON (SWED)
	J R VANE (GB)
1983	B MCCLINTOCK (US)
1984	N K JERNE (DEN)
	G J F KÖHLER (GER)
	C MILSTEIN (GB)
1985	J GOLDSTEIN (US)
	M BROWN (US)
1986	S COHEN (US)
	R LEVI-MONTALCINI (ITALY)
1987	S TONEGAWA (JAPAN)
1988	J W BLACK (GB)
	G B ELION (US)
	G H HITCHINGS (US)
1989	M BISHOP (US)
	H VARMUS (US)
1990	J MURRAY (US)
	E THOMAS (US)
1991	E NEHER (GER)
	B SAKMANN (GER)
1992	E FISCHER (US)
	E KREBS (US)
1993	R ROBERTS (US)
	P SHARP (US)
1994	A GILMAN (US)
	M RODBELL (US)
1995	E LEWIS (US)
	C NÜESSLEIN-VOLHARD (GER)
	E WIESCHAUS (US)
1996	P DOHERTY (AUSTR)
	R ZINKERNAGEL (SWITZ)
1997	S B PRUSINER (US)
1998	R F FURCHGOTT (US)
	L J IGNARRO (US)
	F MURAD (US)
1999	G BLOBEL (US)
2000	A CARLSSON (SWED)
	P GREENGARD (US)
	E R KANDEL (US)
2001	L H HARTWELL (US)
	R T HUNT (GB)
	P M NURSE (GB)
2002	S BRENNER (GB)
	H R HORVITZ (US)
	J E SULSTON (GB)
2003	P C LAUTERUR (US)
	P MANSFIELD (GB)

LITERATURE

1901	S PRUDHOMME (FR)
1902	T MOMMSEN (GER)
1903	B BJØRNSON (NOR)
1904	F MISTRAL (FR)
	J ECHEGARAY Y EIZAGUIRRE
	(SPAIN)
1905	H SIENKIEWICZ (POL)
1906	G CARDUCCI (ITALY)
1907	R KIPLING (GB)
1908	R EUCKEN (GER)
1909	S LAGERLÖF (SWED)
1910	P VON HEYSE (GER)
1911	M MAETERLINCK (BELG)
1912	G HAUPTMANN (GER)
1913	SIR R TAGORE (INDIA)
1914	(NO AWARD)
1915	R ROLLAND (FR)
1916	V VON HEIDENSTAM (SWED)
1917	K GJELLERUP (DEN)
	H PONTOPPIDAN (DEN)
1919	C SPITTELER (SWITZ)
1920	K HAMSUN (NOR)
1921	A FRANCE (FR)
1922	J BENAVENTE Y MARTINEZ
	(SPAIN)
1923	W B YEATS (IRE)
1924	W S REYMONT (POL)
1925	G B SHAW (IRE)
1926	G DELEDDA (ITALY)
1927	H BERGSON (FR)
1928	S UNDSET (NOR)
1929	T MANN (GER)
1930	S LEWIS (US)
1931	E A KARLFELDT (SWED)
1932	J GALSWORTHY (GB)
1933	I BUNIN (USSR)
1934	L PIRANDELLO (ITALY)
1935	(NO AWARD)
1936	E O'NEILL (US)
1937	R M DU GARD (FR)
1938	P BUCK (US)
1939	F E SILLANPÄÄ (FIN)
1940	(NO AWARD)
1941	(NO AWARD)
1942	(NO AWARD)
1943	(NO AWARD)
1944	J V JENSEN (DEN)
1945	G MISTRAL (CHILE)
1946	H HESSE (SWITZ)
1947	A GIDE (FR)
1948	T S ELIOT (GB)
1949	W FAULKNER (US)
1950	B RUSSELL (GB)
1951	P F LAGERKVIST (SWED)
1952	F MAURIAC (FR)
1953	SIR WINSTON CHURCHILL (GB)
1954	E HEMINGWAY (US)
1955	H K LAXNESS (ICE)
1956	J R JIMÉNEZ (SPAIN)
1957	A CAMUS (FR)

1958	B L PASTERNAK (DECLINED
	AWARD) (USSR)
1959	S QUASIMODO (ITALY)
1960	S J PERSE (FR)
1961	I ANDRIĆ (YUGOS)
1962	J STEINBECK (US)
1963	G SEFERIS (GR)
1964	J-P SARTRE (DECLINED AWARD)
	(FR)
1965	M SHOLOKHOV (USSR)
1966	S Y AGNON (ISR)
	N SACHS (SWED)
1967	M A ASTURIAS (GUAT)
1968	K YASUNARI (JAPAN)
1969	S BECKETT (IRE)
1970	A I SOLZHENITSYN (USSR)
1971	P NERUDA (CHILE)
1972	H BÖLL (GER)
1973	P WHITE (AUSTR)
1974	E JOHNSON (SWED)
	H MARTINSON (SWED)
1975	E MONTALE (ITALY)
1976	S BELLOW (US)
1977	S ALEIXANDRE (SPAIN)
1978	I B SINGER (US)
1979	O ELYTIS (GREECE)
1980	C MILOSZ (US)
1981	E CANETTI (BULG)
1982	G GARCIA MARQUEZ (COLOMBIA)
1983	W GOLDING (GB)
1984	J SEIFERT (CZECH)
1985	C SIMON (FR)
1986	W SOYINKA (NIGERIA)
1987	J BRODSKY (US)
1988	N MAHFOUZ (EGYPT)
1989	C J CELA (SPAIN)
1990	O PAZ (MEX)
1991	N GORDIMER (S AF)
1992	D WALCOTT (ST LUCIA)
1993	T MORRISON (US)
1994	KENSABURO OË (JAPAN)
1995	S HEANEY (US)
1996	W SZYMBORSKA (POL)
1997	D FO (ITALY)
1998	J SARAMAGO (PORT)
1999	G GRASS (GER)
2000	G XINGJIAN (FRANCE)
2001	V S NAIPAUL (GB)
2002	I KERTESZ (HUNGARY)
2003	J M COETZEE (SA)

PEACE

1901	J H DUNANT (SWITZ)
	F PASSY (FR)
1902	E DUCOMMUN (SWITZ)
	C A GOBAT (SWITZ)
1903	SIR W CREMER (GB)
1904	INSTITUTE OF INTERNATIONAL
	LAW (FOUNDED, 1873)
1905	BARONESS VON SUTTNER
	(AUSTRIA)

1906	T ROOSEVELT (US)	1949	LORD BOYD-ORR (GB)
1907	E TEODORO MONETA (ITALY)	1950	R BUNCHE (US)
	L RENAULT (FR)	1951	L JOUHAUX (FR)
1908	K P ARNOLDSON (SWED)	1952	A SCHWEITZER (FR)
1909	BARON D'ESTOURNELLES DE	1953	G C MARSHALL (US)
	CONSTANT (FR)	1954	OFFICE OF THE UNITED NATIONS
	A BEERNAERT (BELG)		HIGH COMMISSIONER FOR
1910	INTERNATIONAL PEACE BUREAU		REFUGEES (FOUNDED, 1951)
	(FOUNDED, 1891)	1955	(NO AWARD)
1911	T ASSER (NETH)	1956	(NO AWARD)
	A FRIED (AUSTRIA)	1957	L B PEARSON (CAN)
1912	E ROOT (US)	1958	D G PIRE (BELG)
1913	H LAFONTAINE (BELG)	1959	P J NOEL-BAKER (GB)
1914	(NO AWARD)	1960	A J LUTHULI (S AF)
1915	(NO AWARD)	1961	D HAMMARSKJÖLD (SWED)
1916	(NO AWARD)	1962	L C PAULING (US)
1917	INTERNATIONAL RED CROSS	1963	INTERNATIONAL RED CROSS
	COMMITTEE (FOUNDED, 1863)		COMMITTEE (FOUNDED, 1863)
1918	(NO AWARD)		LEAGUE OF RED CROSS
1919	W WILSON (US)		SOCIETIES (GENEVA)
1920	L BOURGEOIS (FR)	1964	M LUTHER KING, JR (US)
1921	K BRANTING (SWED)	1965	UNITED NATIONS CHILDREN'S
	C L LANGE (NOR)		FUND (FOUNDED, 1946)
1922	F NANSEN (NOR)	1966	(NO AWARD)
1923	(NO AWARD)	1967	(NO AWARD)
1924	(NO AWARD)	1968	R CASSIN (FR)
1925	SIR A CHAMBERLAIN (GB)	1969	INTERNATIONAL LABOUR
	C G DAWES (US)		ORGANISATION (FOUNDED,
1926	A BRIAND (FR)		1919)
	G STRESEMANN (GER)	1970	N E BORLAUG (US)
1927	F BUISSON (FR)	1971	W BRANDT (GER)
	L QUIDDE (GER)	1972	(NO AWARD)
1928	(NO AWARD)	1973	H KISSINGER (US)
1929	F B KELLOGG (US)		LE DUC THO (DECLINED AWARD)
1930	N SÖDERBLOM (SWED)		(N VIET)
1931	J ADDAMS (US)	1974	S MACBRIDE (IRE)
	N M BUTLER (US)		E SATO (JAPAN)
1932	(NO AWARD)	1975	A S SAKHAROV (USSR)
1933	SIR N ANGELL (GB)	1976	MRS B WILLIAMS (N IRE)
1934	A HENDERSON (GB)		MISS M CORRIGAN (N IRE)
1935	C VON OSSIETZKY (GER)	1977	AMNESTY INTERNATIONAL
1936	C S LAMAS (ARG)		(FOUNDED IN UK, 1961)
1937	VISCOUNT CECIL OF CHELWOOD	1978	A SADAT (EGYPT)
	(GB)		M BEGIN (ISR)
1938	NANSEN INTERNATIONAL OFFICE	1979	MOTHER TERESA (YUGOS)
	FOR REFUGEES (FOUNDED,	1980	A P ESQUIVEL (ARG)
	1931)	1981	OFFICE OF THE U N HIGH
1939	(NO AWARD)		COMMISSION FOR REFUGEES
1940	(NO AWARD)		(FOUNDED, 1951)
1941	(NO AWARD)	1982	A GARCIA ROBLES (MEX)
1942	(NO AWARD)		MRS A MYRDAL (SWED)
1943	(NO AWARD)	1983	L WALESA (POL)
1944	INTERNATIONAL RED CROSS	1984	BISHOP D TUTU (S AF)
	COMMITTEE (FOUNDED, 1863)	1985	INTERNATIONAL PHYSICIANS FOR
1945	C HULL (US)		THE PREVENTION OF NUCLEAR
1946	E G BALCH (US)		WAR (FOUNDED, 1980)
	J R MOTT (US)	1986	E WIESEL (US)
1947	AMERICAN FRIENDS' SERVICE	1987	OSCAR ARIAS SÁNCHEZ (COSTA
	COMMITTEE (US)		RICA)
	FRIENDS' SERVICE COUNCIL	1988	THE UNITED NATIONS PEACE-
	(LONDON)		KEEPING FORCES
1948	(NO AWARD)	1989	DALAI LAMA (TIBET)

1990	M GORBACHOV (RUSS)	1979	T W SCHULTZ (US)
1991	A SAN SUU KYI (BURMESE)		A LEWIS (GB)
1992	R MENCHU	1980	L R KLEIN (US)
1993	F W DE KLERK (S AF)	1981	J TOBIN (US)
	N MANDELA (S AF)	1982	G J STIGLER (US)
1994	Y ARAFAT (PALESTINE)	1983	G DEBREU (US)
	S PERES (ISR)	1984	R STONE (GB)
	Y RABIN (ISR)	1985	F MODIGLIANI (US)
1995	J ROTBLAT (GB)	1986	J M BUCHANAN, JR (US)
1996	J RAMOS-HORTA (E TIMOR)	1987	R M SOLOW (US)
	C BELO (E TIMOR)	1988	M ALLAIS (FR)
1997	THE INTERNATIONAL CAMPAIGN	1989	T HAAVELMO (NOR)
	TO BAN LANDMINES	1990	H MARKOWITZ (US)
1998	J HUME (N IRE)		W F SHARPE (US)
	D TRIMBLE (N IRE)		M MILLER (US)
1999	MÉDICINS SANS FRONTIÈRES	1991	R H COASE (GB)
2000	K DAE-JUNG (SOUTH KOREA)	1992	G S BECKER (US)
2001	UNITED NATIONS	1993	R FOGEL (US)
	K ANNAN (GHANA)		D NORTH (US)
2002	J CARTER (US)	1994	J HARSANYI (US)
2003	S EBADI (IRAN)		J NASH (US)
			R SELTON (GER)
		1995	R LUCAS (US)
ECONOMICS		1996	J MIRRLEES (GB)
			W VICKREY (CAN)
1969	R FRISCH (NOR)	1997	R C MERTON (US)
	J TINBERGEN (NETH)		M S SCHOLES (US)
1970	P A SAMUELSON (US)	1998	A SEN (INDIA)
1971	S KUZNETS (US)	1999	R A MUNDELL (CAN)
1972	R HICKS (GB)	2000	J J HECKMAN (US)
	K J ARROW (US)		D L MCFADDEN (US)
1973	W LEONTIEF (US)	2001	G A AKERLOF (US)
1974	G MYRDAL (SWED)		A M SPENCE (US)
	F A VON HAYEK (GB)		J E STIGLITZ (US)
1975	L KANTOROVICH (USSR)	2002	D KAHNEMAN (US)
	T C KOOPMANS (US)		V L SMITH
1976	M FRIEDMAN (US)	2003	R F ENGLE (US)
1977	B OHLIN (SWED)		C W J GRANGER (GB)
	J E MEADE (GB)		
1978	H A SIMON (US)		

EXPLORERS, PIONEERS, AND ADVENTURERS

John Ross (1777-1856)

4

BYRD, Richard E (1888–1957; US explorer)

CANO, Juan Sebastián del (c. 1400–1520, Spanish navigator)

COOK, Captain James (1728–79; British navigator)

DIAS, Bartolomeu (c. 1450–c. 1500; Portuguese navigator)

EYRE, Edward John (1815–1901; British explorer)

GAMA, Vasco da (c. 1469–1524; Portuguese navigator)

4–continued

HUME, Hamilton (1797–1873; Australian explorer)

HUNT, John, Baron (1910– ; British mountaineer)

KIDD, William (c. 1645–1701; Scottish sailor)

PARK, Mungo (1771–c. 1806; Scottish explorer)

POLO, Marco (c. 1254–1324; Venetian traveller)

ROSS, Sir James Clark (1800–62; British explorer)

4–continued

SOTO, Hernando de (?1496–1542; Spanish explorer)

5

BAKER, Sir Samuel White (1821–93; British explorer)

BARTH, Heinrich (1821–65; German explorer and geographer)

BOONE, Daniel (1734–1820; American pioneer)

BRUCE, James (1730–94; British explorer)

5–continued

BURKE, Robert O'Hara (1820–61; Irish explorer)

CABOT, John (Giovanni Caboto, *c.* 1450–*c.* 1499; Italian explorer)

DAVIS, John (*or* J Davys *c.* 1550–1605; English navigator)

FUCHS, Sir Vivian (1908–99; British explorer)

LAIRD, Macgregor (1808–61; Scottish explorer)

OATES, Lawrence Edward Grace (1880–1912; British explorer)

OÑATE, Juan de (d. 1630; Spanish conquistador)

PARRY, Sir William Edward (1790–1855; British navigator)

PEARY, Robert Edwin (1856–1920; US explorer)

SCOTT, Robert Falcon (1868–1912; British explorer)

SMITH, Dick (1944– ; Australian adventurer)

SPEKE, John Hanning (1827–64; British explorer)

STURT, Charles (1795–1869; British explorer)

TEACH, Edward (d. 1718; British pirate)

6

ALCOCK, Sir John (1892–1919; British aviator)

BAFFIN, William (*c.* 1584–1622; English navigator)

BALBOA, Vasco Núñez de (*c.* 1475–1517; Spanish explorer)

BERING, Vitus Jonassen (1681–1741; Danish navigator)

BRAZZA, Pierre Paul François Camille Savorgnan de (1852–1905; French explorer)

BROOKE, Sir James (1803–68; British explorer)

BURTON, Sir Richard (1821–90; British explorer)

CABRAL, Pedro Álvares (?1467–1520; Portuguese navigator)

CARSON, Kit (Christopher C, 1809–68; US frontiersman)

CORTÉS, Hernán (1485–1547; Spanish conquistador)

HUDSON, Henry (d. 1611; English navigator)

MORGAN, Sir Henry (*c.* 1635–88; Welsh buccaneer)

6–continued

NANSEN, Fridtjof (1861–1930; Norwegian explorer)

NOBILE, Umberto (1885–1978; Italian aviator)

STUART, John McDouall (1815–66; Scottish explorer)

TASMAN, Abel Janszoon (*c.* 1603–*c.* 1659; Dutch navigator)

7

BARENTS, Willem (*c.* 1550–97; Dutch navigator)

BLÉRIOT, Louis (1872–1936; French aviator)

BRANSON, Richard (1950– ; British entrepreneur and adventurer)

CARPINI, Giovanni da Pian del (*c.* 1180–*c.* 1252; Italian traveller)

CARTIER, Jacques (1491–1557; French navigator)

CÓRDOBA, Francisco Fernández de (d. 1518; Spanish explorer)

COVILHÃ, Pêro da (*c.* 1460–*c.* 1526; Portuguese explorer)

DAMPIER, William (*c.* 1652–1715; English explorer)

EARHART, Amelia (1898–1937; US aviator)

FIENNES, Sir Ranulph (1944– ; British explorer)

FRÉMONT, John C (1813–90; US explorer)

GILBERT, Sir Humphrey (*c.* 1539–83; English navigator)

HAWKINS, Sir John (1532–95; English navigator)

HILLARY, Sir Edmund (1919– ; New Zealand mountaineer and explorer)

HINKLER, Herbert John Lewis (1892–1933; Australian aviator)

LA SALLE, Robert Cavelier, Sieur de (1643–87; French explorer)

MCCLURE, Sir Robert John Le Mesurier (1807–73; Irish explorer)

PIZARRO, Francisco (*c.* 1475–1541; Spanish conquistador)

PYTHEAS (4th century BC; Greek navigator)

RALEIGH, Sir Walter (1554–1618; British explorer)

SELKIRK, Alexander (1676–1721; Scottish sailor)

7–continued

STANLEY, Sir Henry Morton (1841–1904; British explorer)

WILKINS, Sir George Hubert (1888–1958; British explorer)

WRANGEL, Ferdinand Petrovich, Baron von (1794–1870; Russian explorer)

8

AMUNDSEN, Roald (1872–1928; Norwegian explorer)

COLUMBUS, Christopher (1451–1506; Italian navigator)

COUSTEAU, Jacques Yves (1910–97; French underwater explorer)

FLINDERS, Matthew (1774–1814; British navigator and hydrographer)

FRANKLIN, Sir John (1786–1847; British explorer)

MAGELLAN, Ferdinand (*c.* 1480–1521; Portuguese explorer)

MARCHAND, Jean Baptiste (1863–1934; French explorer)

VESPUCCI, Amerigo (1454–1512; Italian navigator)

9

BLANCHARD, Jean Pierre François (1753–1809; French balloonist)

CHAMPLAIN, Samuel de (1567–1635; French explorer)

FROBISHER, Sir Martin (*c.* 1535–94; English navigator)

HEYERDAHL, Thor (1914– ; Norwegian ethnologist)

IBERVILLE, Pierre Le Moyne, Sieur d' (1661–1706; French-Canadian explorer)

LEICHARDT, Ludwig (1813–48; German explorer)

LINDBERGH, Charles A (1902–74; US aviator)

MARQUETTE, Jacques (1637–75; French explorer)

PAUSANIAS (2nd century AD; Greek traveller)

RASMUSSEN, Knud Johan Victor (1879–1933; Danish explorer)

VANCOUVER, George (*c.* 1758–98; British navigator)

VELÁSQUEZ, Diego (?1465–1522; Spanish explorer)

10

BARBAROSSA (Khayr ad-Din,
d. 1546; Turkish pirate)
ERIC THE RED (late 10th
century; Norwegian explorer)
SHACKLETON, Sir Ernest
Henry (1874–1922; British
explorer)

11

IBN BATTUTAH (1304–?1368;
Arab traveller)
LA CONDAMINE, Charles
Marie de (1701–74; French
geographer)
LIVINGSTONE, David
(1813–73; Scottish
missionary and explorer)

11–continued

PONCE DE LEON, Juan
(1460–1521; Spanish
explorer)

12

BOUGAINVILLE, Louis Antoine
de (1729–1811; French
navigator)
LEIF ERIKSSON (11th century;
Icelandic explorer)
NORDENSKJÖLD, Nils Adolf
Erik, Baron (1832–1901;
Swedish navigator)

14

BELLINGSHAUSEN, Fabian
Gottlieb, Baron von (1778–
1852; Russian explorer)
DUMONT D'URVILLE, Jules
Sébastien César (1790–1842;
French navigator)

17

HENRY THE NAVIGATOR
(1394–1460; Portuguese
navigator and patron of
explorers)

SPORTSMEN AND WOMEN

Jim Alder :- Marathon gold medal 1966

3

ALI, Muhammad (Cassius
Marcellus Clay, 1942–   ; US
boxer)
COE, Sebastian (1956–   ;
British middle-distance
runner)
LEE, Bruce (1940–73; US
kungfu expert)

4

ASHE, Arthur (1943–93; US
tennis player)
BORG, Bjorn (1956–   ;
Swedish tennis player)
CLAY, Cassius. See Ali,
Muhammad
CRAM, Steve (1960–   ; British
middle-distance runner)
DUKE, Geoffrey E (1923–   ;
British racing motorcyclist)
GRAF, Steffi (1969–   ;
German tennis player)
HILL, Damon (1960–   ; British
motor-racing driver)
HILL, Graham (1929–75;
British motor-racing driver)
HOAD, Lewis Alan (1934–94;
Australian tennis player)
HUNT, James (1947–93; British
motor-racing driver)
JOHN, Barry (1945–   ; Welsh
Rugby Union footballer)
KHAN, Imran (1952–   ;
Pakistani cricketer)
KING, Billie Jean (born Moffitt,
1943–   ; US tennis player)

4–continued

LARA, Brian (1969–   ; West
Indian cricketer)
LOMU, Jonah (1975–   ; New
Zealand Rugby Union
footballer)
MILO (late 6th century BC;
Greek wrestler)
MOSS, Stirling (1929–   ;
British motor-racing driver)
OWEN, Michael (1979–   ;
British Association footballer)
PELÉ (1940–   ; Brazilian
Association footballer)
WADE, Virginia (1945–   ;
British tennis player)

5

BLAKE, Peter (1948–   ; New
Zealand yachtsman)
BLYTH, Chay (1940–   ; British
yachtsman)
BRUNO, Frank (1961–   ;
British heavyweight boxer)
BUDGE, Don (1916–2000; US
tennis player)
BUENO, Maria (1939–   ;
Brazilian tennis player)
BUSBY, Matt (1909–94; British
Association footballer)
CLARK, Jim (1937–68; British
motor-racing driver)
COURT, Margaret (born Smith,
1942–   ; Australian tennis
player)
CURRY, John Anthony
(1949–94; British ice skater)

5–continued

EVERT, Christine (1954–   ;
US tennis player)
FALDO, Nick (1957–   ; British
golfer)
GRACE, William Gilbert
(1848–1915; British cricketer)
GREIG, Tony (1946–   ;
Rhodesian-born cricketer)
HAGEN, Walter Charles
(1892–1969; US professional
golfer)
HOBBS, Jack (1882–1963;
British cricketer)
HOGAN, Ben (1912–   ; US
professional golfer)
HOYLE, Edmond (1672–1769;
British authority on card
games)
JEEPS, Dickie (1931–   ;
British Rugby Union
footballer)
JONES, Bobby (1902–71; US
amateur golfer)
LAUDA, Niki (1949–   ;
Austrian motor-racing driver)
LAVER, Rod (1938–   ;
Australian tennis player)
LEWIS, Carl (1961–   ; US
athlete)
LEWIS, Lennox (1965–   ;
British boxer)
LLOYD, Clive (1944–   ; West
Indian cricketer)
LOUIS, Joe (1914–81; US
boxer)

5–continued

MEADE, Richard (1938– ;
British three-day-event horse
rider)

MEADS, Colin Earl (1935– ;
New Zealand Rugby Union
footballer)

MOORE, Bobby (1941–93;
British Association footballer)

NURMI, Paavo Johannes
(1897–1973; Finnish middle-
distance and long-distance
runner)

OVETT, Steve (1955– ; British
middle-distance runner)

OWENS, Jesse (1913–80; US
sprinter, long jumper, and
hurdler)

PERRY, Fred (1909–95; British
tennis and table-tennis player)

SELES, Monica (1973– ; US
tennis player)

SENNA, Ayrton (1960–94;
Brazilian motor-racing driver)

SMITH, Harvey (1938–
British showjumper and
equestrian)

SPITZ, Mark Andrew (1950– ;
US swimmer)

TYSON, Mike (1966– ; US
boxer)

VIREN, Lasse Arttturi (1949– ;
Finnish middle-distance and
long-distance runner)

WALSH, Courtney (1962– ;
Jamaican cricketer)

WARNE, Shane (1969– ;
Australian cricketer)

WAUGH, Mark (1965– ;
Australian cricketer)

WAUGH, Stephen (1965– ;
Australian cricketer)

WOODS, Tiger (1975– ; US
golfer)

6

AGASSI, Andre (1970– ; US
tennis player)

BLANCO, Serge (1965– ;
French Rugby Union
footballer)

BORDER, Allan (1955– ;
Australian cricketer)

BOTHAM, Ian (1955– ; British
cricketer)

BROOME, David (1940– ;
British showjumper)

BROUGH, Louise (1923– ;
US tennis player)

BUTTON, Jenson (1980– ;
British motor-racing driver)

6–continued

CAWLEY, Evonne (*born*
Goolagong, 1951– ;
Australian tennis player)

CRUYFF, Johann (1947– ;
Dutch Association footballer)

D'INZEO, Colonel Piero
(1923– ; Italian show
jumper and equestrian)

EDBERG, Stefan (1966– ;
Swedish tennis player)

FANGIO, Juan Manuel
(1911–95; Argentinian motor-
racing driver)

HADLEE, Sir Richard
(1951– ; New Zealand
cricketer)

HENDRY, Stephen (1969– ;
British snooker player)

HENMAN, Tim (1974– ;
British tennis player)

HINGIS, Martina (1980– ;
Swiss tennis player)

HUTTON, Len (1916–90;
British cricketer)

KARPOV, Anatoly (1951– ;
Russian chess player)

KEEGAN, Kevin (1951– ;
British footballer)

LASKER, Emanuel
(1868–1941; German chess
player)

MORPHY, Paul Charles
(1837–84; US chess player)

PALMER, Arnold (1929– ; US
golfer)

RAMSEY, Alf (1922–99; British
Association footballer)

RHODES, Wilfred (1877–1973;
British cricketer)

SHEENE, Barry (1950– ;
British racing motorcyclist)

SMYTHE, Pat (1928– ; British
showjumper and equestrian)

SOBERS, Gary (1936– ;
West Indian cricketer)

TUNNEY, Gene (1897–1978;
US boxer)

7

AMBROSE, Curtly (1963– ;
West Indian cricketer)

BECKHAM, David (1975– ;
British footballer)

BRABHAM, Jack (1926–
Australian motor-racing
driver)

BRADMAN, Donald George
(1908– ; Australian
cricketer)

CANTONA, Eric (1966– ;
French footballer)

7–continued

CARLING, William (1965– ;
British Rugby Union
footballer)

CARNERA, Primo (1906–67;
Italian boxer)

COMPTON, Denis (1918–97;
British cricketer)

CONNORS, Jimmy (1952– ;
US tennis player)

COWDREY, Colin (1932– ;
British cricketer)

DEMPSEY, Jack (1895–1983;
US boxer)

EDWARDS, Johnathan
(1966– ; British athlete)

FISCHER, Bobby (1943– ;
US chess player)

FRAZIER, Joe (1944– ; US
boxer)

GUNNELL, Sally (1966– ;
British athlete)

HAMMOND, Wally (1903–65;
British cricketer)

HUSSAIN, Nasser (1968– ;
British cricketer)

JOHNSON, Michael (1967– ;
US sprinter)

LENGLEN, Suzanne
(1899–1938; French tennis
player)

LINEKER, Gary (1960– ;
British footballer)

MCBRIDE, Willie John
(1939– ; Irish Rugby Union
footballer)

MCENROE, John (1959– ;
US tennis player)

MANSELL, Nigel (1953– ;
British motor-racing driver)

PINSENT, Matthew (1970– ;
British oarsman)

SAMPRAS, Pete (1971– ; US
tennis player)

SPASSKY, Boris (1937– ;
Russian chess player)

STEWART, Jackie (1939– ;
British motor-racing driver)

SURTEES, John (1934– ;
British racing motorcyclist and
motor-racing driver)

TREVINO, Lee (1939– ; US
golfer)

TRUEMAN, Fred (1931– ;
British cricketer)

WHYMPER, Edward (1840–
1911; British mountaineer)

WINKLER, Hans Günter
(1926– ; German
showjumper)

ZÁTOPEK, Emil (1922– ;
Czech long-distance runner)

8

AGOSTINI, Giacomo (1944– ;
Italian racing motorcyclist)

ALEKHINE, Alexander
(1892–1946; French chess
player)

ATHERTON, Michael (1968– ;
British cricketer)

CAMPBELL, Sir Malcolm
(1885–1949; British land- and
water-speed racing driver)

CHARLTON, Bobby (1937– ;
British Association footballer)

CHRISTIE, Linford (1960– ;
British sprinter)

COMANECI, Nadia (1961– ;
Romanian gymnast)

HAILWOOD, Mike (1940–81;
British racing motorcyclist)

HAKKINEN, Mika (1968– ;
Finnish motor-racing driver)

HAWTHORN, Mike (1929–58;
British motor-racing driver)

JOSELITO (1895–1920;
Spanish matador)

KAPIL DEV, (1959– ; Indian
cricketer)

KORCHNOI, Victor (1931– ;
Soviet-born chess player)

LINDWALL, Raymond Russell
(1921–96; Australian
cricketer)

MATTHEWS, Stanley
(1915–2000; British
Association footballer)

NEWCOMBE, John (1944– ;
Australian tennis player)

NICKLAUS, Jack William
(1940– ; US golfer)

REDGRAVE, Steven (1962– ;
British oarsman)

RICHARDS, Sir Gordon
(1904–86; British jockey)

RICHARDS, Viv (1952– ;
West Indian cricketer)

ROBINSON, Sugar Ray
(1920–89; US boxer)

ROSEWALL, Ken (1934– ;
Australian tennis player)

8–continued

RUSEDSKI, Greg (1973– ;
Canadian-born British tennis
player)

SULLIVAN, John Lawrence
(1858–1918; US boxer)

THOMPSON, Daley (1958– ;
British decathlete)

WILLIAMS, J P R (1949– ;
Welsh Rugby Union
footballer)

WILLIAMS, SERENA
(1981– ; US tennis player)

WILLIAMS, VENUS (1980– ;
US tennis player)

9

BANNISTER, Roger (1929– ;
British middle-distance
runner)

BONINGTON, Chris (1934– ;
British mountaineer)

BOTVINNIK, Mikhail Moiseivich
(1911–95; Russian chess
player)

COULTHARD, David (1971– ;
British motor-racing driver)

DAVENPORT, Lindsay
(1976– ; US tennis player)

D'OLIVIERA, Basil Lewis
(1931– ; South African-born
cricketer)

GASCOIGNE, Paul (1967– ;
British footballer)

GOOLAGONG, Evonne. *See*
Cawley, Evonne

LLEWELLYN, Harry (1911– ;
British showjumper and
equestrian)

PETROSIAN, Tigran
Vartanovich (1929–84; Soviet
chess player)

SCHMELING, Max (1905– ;
German boxer)

SUTCLIFFE, Herbert
(1894–1978; British cricketer)

SZEWINSKA, Irena (1946– ;
Polish athlete)

TENDULKAR, Sachin
(1973– ; Indian cricketer)

9–continued

UNDERWOOD, Rory
(1963– ; British Rugby
Union football player)

10

CARPENTIER, Georges
(1894–1975; French boxer)

CULBERTSON, Ely
(1891–1955; US bridge
authority)

IMRAN KHAN (1952– ;
Pakistani cricketer)

JUANTORENA, Alberto
(1951– ; Cuban middle-
distance runner)

SCHUMACHER, Michael
(1969– ; German motor-
racing driver)

WILLS MOODY, Helen
(1905–98; US tennis player)

11

BALLESTEROS, Severiano
(1957– ; Spanish golfer)

CONSTANTINE, Learie
Nicholas, Baron (1902–71;
West Indian cricketer)

FITZSIMMONS, Bob
(1862–1917; New Zealand
boxer)

NAVRATILOVA, Martina
(1956– ; Czech-born US
tennis player)

WEISSMULLER, Johnny
(1904–84; US swimmer)

12

GREY-THOMPSON, Tanni
(1969– ; British wheelchair
athlete)

KNOX-JOHNSTON, Sir Robin
(1939– ; British yachtsman)

19

CAPABLANCA Y GRAUPERA,
José Raúl (1888–1942;
Cuban chess player)

RANJITSINHJI VIBHAJI,
Kumar Shri, Maharajah Jam
Sahib of Nawanagar
(1872–1933; Indian cricketer)

MURDERERS

MURDERER	YEAR	DETAILS
ALLEN, Peter and WELBY, John	1964	Murdered John West. Last two men to be hanged in Britain.
BENTLEY, Derek and CRAIG, Christoper	1952	Both men were convicted of the murder of PC Miles. Bentley was hanged, although he did not fire a shot, on the grounds that he had incited his younger partner to murder. Craig, who was too young for the death sentence, was imprisoned until 1963. This case caused considerable public disquiet and was used in the abolition-of-hanging debate.
BORDEN, Lizzie	1892	Accused of the murder of her father and stepmother in Fall River, Massachusetts, but was acquitted. Public opinion was that she was guilty. Lizzie Borden took an axe And gave her mother forty whacks. When she saw what she had done, She gave her father forty-one.
BRADY, Ian and HINDLEY, Myra	1966	Sentenced to life imprisonment for the brutal murder of five children. They were known as the Moors murders as at least three children were killed and buried on the Lancashire moors; some of the bodies were never recovered.
BURKE, William and HARE, William	1827–28	Burke was sentenced to death for the murder of Mary Patterson, James Wilson, and Margaret Docherty; Hare was granted immunity from prosecution by offering to turn King's Evidence. Burke and Hare, with the help of their partners, lured victims to their lodging house, murdered them and sold their bodies to an Edinburgh anatomist, Dr Knox. They are known to have murdered 16 people over a period of nine months, although the exact total is unknown.
BUSH, Edwin	1961	Hanged for the murder of Mrs Elsie Batten. He was identified from an indentikit portrait – the first use of the system in Britain.
CHAPMAN, George	1897–1902	Hanged for the murders of Mary Spink, Bessie Taylor, and Maud Marsh. The three women (all of whom were apparently married to Chapman) were poisoned with antimony. The police who arrested him believed that Chapman may have been 'Jack the Ripper'.
CHRISTIE, John	1943–53	Hanged for the murder of his wife, Ethel Christie, whose body was found under the floorboards of 10 Rillington Place, London. The bodies of five other women were found behind the kitchen wall and buried in the garden.
CORDER, William	1827	Sentenced to death for the murder of Maria Marten. Although her family had been led to believe that she was happily married and living on the Isle of Wight, her mother had a dream that she had been murdered and buried in the Red Barn on Corder's father's farm. Her body was found there.
COTTON, Mary Ann	1872	Hanged for the murder of her stepson Charles Cotton. She was estimated to have killed 14 victims who were diagnosed as having died of gastric fever. She was arrested following the discovery of arsenic in the body of

her stepson and the bodies of her husband, baby, and two stepchildren were exhumed. They were also found to have died of arsenical poisoning.

CRIPPEN, Dr Hawley Harvey	1910	US doctor who poisoned his actress wife Cora (called Belle Elmore) in London. He attempted to escape to America with his mistress Ethel LeNeve on the *SS Montrose*, but was arrested on board following one of the first uses of ship-to-shore radio.
ELLIS, Ruth	1955	Convicted of the murder of her boyfried David Blakely. Last woman to be hanged in Britain.
HAIGH, John	1949	Hanged for the murder of Olivia Durand-Deacon. Haigh thought he could not be tried for murder as he had destroyed the body in an acid bath. However, the discovery of gallstones, bone fragments, and false teeth meant that the remains could be identified.
HALLIWELL, Kenneth	1967	Murdered his lover, the British dramatist Joe Orton (1933–67).
HANRATTY, James	1961	Hanged for the murder of Michael Gregsten, after a trial lasting 21 days. Controversy surrounded the verdict. Much of the evidence was based on the identification of Hanratty by Valerie Storie (Gregsten's lover, who was present at the murder). Hanratty's alibi that he had been in Rhyl when the murder was committed was disbelieved. The uncertainty relating to the verdict added fuel to the campaign against hanging. In 2001 Hanratty's remains were exhumed to enable DNA comparison of the body with samples found at the crime scene. These matched and in 2002 the Court of Criminal Appeal ruled that Hanratty's conviction was not unsound and that there were no grounds for a posthumous pardon.
JACK THE RIPPER	1888	Brutally murdered at least five prostitutes in the Whitechapel area. There has been great controversy about the identity of the murderer.
KENT, Constance	1860	Sentenced to death, commuted to life imprisonment, for the murder of her half-brother, Francis. In 1885 she was released and went to Australia, where she trained as a nurse under the name of Ruth Kaye. She successfully rebuilt her life and died in 1944, at the age of 100.
NEILSON, Donald	1974–75	Sentenced to life imprisonment for the murder of four men. He was know as 'The Black Panther'.
NILSEN, Denis	1979–83	Convicted of the murder of six men after the discovery of human remains in a manhole at the side of the flats where he lived. He boasted of killing over 15 men in total.
PEACE, Charles	1876	Hanged for the murder of Arthur Dyson. Peace was a burglar who carried the 'tools of his trade' in a violin case. His activities were spread over a 25 year period, during which he became notorious.
ROBINSON, John	1927	Suffocated Minnie Alice Bonati. He dismembered her body and hid it in a trunk which he handed to the left-luggage office at Charing Cross station.
SHIPMAN, Harold	?1974–98	A GP, Shipman was jailed in 2000 for the murder of 15 of his patients, although the total number of his victims is believed to be at least 215. He was found dead, hanging from the window bars of his prison cell, in 2004.

SMITH, George (*alias* Oliver Love, George Rose, Henry Williams, Oliver James, John Lloyd)	1912	Hanged for the murder of Bessie Mundy. The story became known as 'The Brides in the Bath' when it was revealed that Smith bigamously married his victims and, in three instances, killed them in their baths. In each inquest a verdict of accidental drowning was brought in, and Smith claimed the possessions or life insurance of his 'wife'.
STRATTON, Alfred and Albert	1905	Convicted of the murders of Mr and Mrs Farrow. The case made legal history because the jury was convinced of the guilt of the two brothers after a fingerprint found at the scene of the crime was found to match that of Alfred Stratton.
SUTCLIFFE, Peter	1975–80	Sentenced to life imprisonment following the murder of 13 women. Known as the 'Yorkshire Ripper', Sutcliffe claimed he had a mission from God to kill prostitutes (although several of his victims were not prostitutes).
TURPIN, Dick	1735	Hanged at York for the murder of Thomas Morris. Notorious for highway robberies, a reward of £200 was placed on his head.
WEST, Frederick and Rosemary	?1970–94	Frederick West committed suicide before his trial for the murder of 12 young women. Rosemary West was sentenced to life imprisonment for the murder of 10 young women.

THE ARTS

ART TERMS

2
OP

3
FEC
INC
OIL
POP

4
BODY
BUST
CAST
DADA
HERM
KORE
SIZE
SWAG
TERM
WASH

5
BRUSH
BURIN
CHALK
EASEL
FECIT
GESSO
GLAZE
MODEL
NAIVE
PIETÀ
PUTTO
SALON
SCULP
SECCO
SEPIA
STYLE
TONDO

6
ASHCAN
BISTRE
CANVAS
CUBISM
FRESCO
GOTHIC
GROUND
KIT-CAT

6–continued
KITSCH
KOUROS
LIMNER
MAESTÀ
MEDIUM
MOBILE
MOSAIC
PASTEL
PATINA
PENCIL
PURISM
RELIEF
ROCOCO
SCHOOL
SKETCH
STUCCO
STYLUS
TUSCAN
VEDUTA
VERISM

7
ACADEMY
ARCHAIC
ATELIER
BAROQUE
BAUHAUS
BITUMEN
BODEGÓN
CABINET
CAMAÏEU
CARTOON
COLLAGE
COSMATI
DIPTYCH
DRAWING
ECORCHÉ
ETCHING
GOUACHE
IMPASTO
INCIDIT
LINOCUT
LOST WAX
MODELLO
MONTAGE
PALETTE

7–continued
PIGMENT
POCHADE
REALISM
SCUMBLE
SFUMATO
SINOPIA
TEMPERA
VANITAS
VARNISH
WOODCUT

8
ABSTRACT
AIR-BRUSH
ALLEGORY
ANCIENTS
AQUATINT
ARMATURE
ARRICCIO
BARBIZON
BOZZETTO
CARYATID
CHARCOAL
DRÔLERIE
DRYPOINT
EMULSION
FIXATIVE
FROTTAGE
FUTURISM
GRAFFITI
HATCHING
INTAGLIO
INTONACO
MANDORLA
MAQUETTE
PASTICHE
PLEURANT
POUNCING
PREDELLA
REPOUSSÉ
SCULPSIT
STAFFAGE
TACHISME
TESSERAE
TRECENTO
TRIPTYCH

8–continued
VENETIAN

9
ALLA PRIMA
ANTI-CERNE
AQUARELLE
AUTOGRAPH
BRUSHWORK
BYZANTINE
CAPRICCIO
COLOURIST
DISTEMPER
ENGRAVING
GRISAILLE
GROTESQUE
INTIMISME
LANDSCAPE
MAHLSTICK
MAULSTICK
MEZZOTINT
MINIATURE
POLYPTYCH
PRIMITIVE
SCULPTURE
STILL LIFE
STIPPLING
SYMBOLISM
TENEBRISM
VORTICISM

10
ARRICCIATO
ART NOUVEAU
ASSEMBLAGE
AUTOMATISM
AVANTGARDE
BIOMORPHIC
CARICATURE
CIRE-PERDUE
CRAQUELURE
FLORENTINE
METALPOINT
MONOCHROME
MORBIDEZZA
NATURALISM
PENTIMENTO
PROVENANCE

157

10–continued
QUADRATURA
REPOUSSOIR
ROMANESQUE
SURREALISM
SYNTHETISM
TURPENTINE
XYLOGRAPHY

11
BAMBOCCANTI
BIEDERMEIER
CAROLINGIAN
CHIAROSCURO

11–continued
CONTÉ CRAYON
DIVISIONISM
ECLECTICISM
ILLUSIONISM
IMPRIMATURA
LITHOGRAPHY
MASTERPIECE
PERSPECTIVE
PICTURESQUE
POINTILLISM
PORTRAITURE
RENAISSANCE

11–continued
RETROUSSAGE
STYLIZATION
SUPREMATISM
TROMPE L'OEIL
WATERCOLOUR

12
ACRYLIC PAINT
ANAMORPHOSIS
CLOISONNISME
CONTRAPPOSTO
COUNTERPROOF
ILLUMINATION

12–continued
PRECISIONISM
QUATTROCENTO
SUPERREALISM

13
ARCHITECTONIC
EXPRESSIONISM
FÊTE CHAMPÊTRE
IMPRESSIONISM
PAPIERS COLLÉS

14
CONSTRUCTIVISM

ART SCHOOLS AND STYLES

4
DADA

5
OP ART

6
CUBISM
KITSCH
POP ART
PURISM
ROCOCO
VERISM

7
ART BRUT
ART DECO
BAROQUE
DE STIJL
FAUVISM
FOLK ART
JUNK ART
LAND ART
ORPHISM
REALISM
TACHISM

8
FUTURISM
MOGUL ART
NAIVE ART
RAYONISM

9
INTIMISME
MANNERISM
MINOAN ART
SYMBOLISM
VORTICISM

10
ARTE POVERA
ART NOUVEAU
CLASSICISM
ISLAMIC ART
JUGENDSTIL
KINETIC ART
MINIMALISM
NATURALISM
OTTOMAN ART
SURREALISM
SYNTHETISM

11
ABSTRACT ART
ART INFORMEL
AVANT-GARDE
BLAUE REITER
CLOISONNISM
CONCRETE ART
DIVISIONISM
GRAND MANNER
POINTILLISM
REGIONALISM
ROMANTICISM
SUPREMATISM

11–continued
SYNCHRONISM

12
BYZANTINE ART
CAMDEN SCHOOL
MAGIC REALISM
MOZARABIC ART
PHOTOREALISM
PRECISIONISM
PRIMITIVE ART

13
CONCEPTUAL ART
EXPRESSIONISM
FIGURATIVE ART
IMPRESSIONISM
NEOCLASSICISM
POSTMODERNISM
SIENESE SCHOOL
SOCIAL REALISM

14
ACTION PAINTING
CONSTRUCTIVISM
NEOROMANTICISM
PERFORMANCE ART
RENAISSANCE ART
VENETIAN SCHOOL

16
ENVIRONMENTAL
    ART

16–continued
FLORENTINE
    SCHOOL
NEOEXPRESSION-
    ISM
NEOIMPRESSION-
    ISM
NEUE SACH-
    LICHKEIT
PRE-RAPHAELITISM
SOCIALIST REALISM
TRANSAVANT-
    GARDE

18+
ABSTRACT EXPRES-
    SIONISM
AESTHETIC MOVE-
    MENT
ARTS AND CRAFTS
    MOVEMENT
HIGH RENAISSANCE
    ART
INTERNATIONAL
    GOTHIC
METAPHYSICAL
    PAINTING
PLEIN-AIR PAINTING
POSTIMPRESSION-
    ISM
REPRESENTATIONAL
    ART

ARCHITECTURAL TERMS

3
BAY
CAP
DIE
EYE
KEY

4
AMBO
ANTA
APSE
ARCH
BAND
BEAD
BELL
BOSS
DADO
DAIS
DOME
FRET
FROG
FUST
NAVE
PELE
STOA

5
AISLE
AMBRY
ARRIS
ATTIC
CONGÉ
CROWN
CRYPT
DORIC
FOILS
GABLE
GLYPH
HELIX
INLAY
IONIC
LOBBY
NEWEL
ROMAN
SCAPE
SHAFT
SHANK
TALON
TENIA
TUDOR
VERGE

6
ABACUS
ACCESS
ALCOVE
ARCADE
ATRIUM

6–continued
ATTICK
AUMBRY
BELFRY
BONNET
BROACH
CANOPY
CHEVET
COLUMN
CORONA
CRENEL
CUPOLA
DAGGER
DENTIL
DIAPER
FAÇADE
FILLET
FINIAL
FLÈCHE
FRESCO
FRIEZE
GABLET
GAZEBO
GOTHIC
GUTTAE
HEROIC
LESENE
LINTEL
LINTOL
LOGGIA
LOUVRE
MANTEL
MERLON
METOPE
MUTULE
NORMAN
OCULUS
PAGODA
PATERA
PLINTH
PULPIT
QUADRA
REGULA
ROCOCO
SCAPUS
SCROLL
SEDILE
SOFFIT
TROPHY
URELLA
VESTRY
VOLUTE
WREATH
XYSTUS
ZIG-ZAG

7
ANNULET

7–continued
ARCH RIB
ASTYLAR
BALCONY
BAROQUE
BASTION
BOULTIN
BUTMENT
CAPITAL
CAVETTO
CHANCEL
CHEVRON
CORNICE
CROCHET
CROCKET
DISTYLE
ECHINUS
ENCARPA
ENTASIS
EUSTYLE
FESTOON
FLEURON
FLUTING
GADROON
GALILEE
GALLERY
LACUNAR
LANTERN
LATTICE
LEQUEAR
LUNETTE
NARTHEX
NULLING
OBELISK
ORATORY
PARVISE
PORTAIL
PORTICO
POSTERN
PTEROMA
REEDING
REGENCY
REREDOS
ROSETTE
ROTUNDA
ROUNDEL
SCALLOP
SPANISH
SYSTYLE
TESSARA
TONDINO
TRACERY
TRUMEAU

8
ABUTMENT
ACANTHUS

8–continued
AEDICULA
APOPHYGE
ASTRAGAL
ATLANTES
BALUSTER
BARTIZAN
BASILICA
BEAK HEAD
CARYATID
CIMBORIO
CINCTURE
CRENELLE
CRESTING
CYMATIUM
DIASTYLE
DIPTERAL
DOG-TOOTH
EDGE ROLL
EXTRADOS
FORMERET
GARGOYLE
INTRADOS
KEEL ARCH
KEYSTONE
LICH GATE
LYCH GATE
MISERERE
PAVILION
PEDESTAL
PEDIMENT
PILASTER
PREDELLA
PULPITUM
ROCAILLE
SPANDREL
SPANDRIL
TORCHING
TRANSEPT
TRIGLYPH
TYMPANUM
VERANDAH
VIGNETTE
WAINSCOT

9
ACROPOLIS
ANTEFIXAE
ANTHEMION
APEX STONE
ARABESQUE
ARCH BRICK
ARCHIVOLT
ATTIC BASE
BIRD'S BEAK
BYZANTINE
CAMPANILE
CANEPHORA

9—continued
CARTOUCHÈ
CAULICOLI
CLOISTERS
COLONNADE
COMPOSITE
DRIPSTONE
FOLIATION
GROTESQUE
HEXASTYLE
HYPOCAUST
HYPOSTYLE
INGLE NOOK
LABEL STOP
LACUNARIA
LINENFOLD
MEZZANINE
MOULDINGS
OCTASTYLE
PALLADIAN
REFECTORY
SGRAFFITO

9—continued
STRAPWORK
STYLOBATE
TRABEATED
TRIFORIUM
TRILITHON
VESTIBULE
ZOOPHORUS

10
ACROTERION
AMBULATORY
ARAEOSTYLE
ARCHITRAVE
BALDACHINO
BALL FLOWER
BALUSTRADE
BATTLEMENT
CINQUEFOIL
COLONNETTE
CORINTHIAN
EGG AND DART
ENRICHMENT

10—continued
HAGIOSCOPE
LADY CHAPEL
LANCET ARCH
MISERICORD
MODILLIONS
PIETRA DURA
PRESBYTERY
PYCNOSTYLE
QUATREFOIL
ROMANESQUE
ROOD SCREEN
ROSE WINDOW
SEXPARTITE
TETRASTYLE
TRACHELION

11
CASTELLATED
ENTABLATURE
FAN VAULTING
HARELIP ARCH
LEADED LIGHT

11—continued
MANTELPIECE
MANTELSHELF
ORIEL WINDOW
RENAISSANCE
RETICULATED

12
AMPHITHEATRE
BLIND TRACERY
COCKLE STAIRS
EGG AND TONGUE
LANCET WINDOW
PORTE-COCHÈRE

13
AMPHI-PROSTYLE

14
ANGULAR CAPITAL
FLYING BUTTRESS
HYPOTRACHELION

ANTIQUE-TRADE TERMS

3
WAF

4
COST
KITE
LUMP
RING

5
AGGRO
FOLKY
FRESH
LYLE'S
MOODY
REPRO
RIGHT
ROUGH
RUN UP

5—continued
TOUCH
TRADE
VICKY

6
LOOKER
MADE-UP
PERIOD
PUNTER
RUNNER
SMALLS
TOTTER

7
BREAKER
CALL-OUT
CUT DOWN
KNOCKER

7—continued
MILLER'S

8
AS BOUGHT
BENT GEAR
BOUGHT IN
CHAIRMAN
DOWN TO ME
ESTIMATE
FOLLOWER
MARRIAGE
SCLENTER

9
CLEARANCE
INNER RING
SIX AND TWO

10
COMMERCIAL
FOUR AND TWO
OFF THE WALL
OLD FRIENDS

11
EIGHT AND TWO
HAMMER PRICE
OUT OF THE AIR
SIGHT UNSEEN

12+
COLLECTOR'S ITEM
KNOCKING DOWN

TYPES OF GLASS

4
AMEN
COIN
DAUM
KNOP
LAVA
RUBY
SLAG

5
AGATE
CAMEO
FLUTE
GALLE
GRAAL
WEALD

6
CLICHY
CLUTHA
GOBLET
HUMPEN

6—continued
MURANO
NEVERS
RUMMER

7
AMPULLA
BACCHUS
BRISTOL
BURMESE
FAVRILE
HYALITH
LALIQUE
LOBMEYR
NAILSEA
OPALINE
POTSDAM
RATAFIA
STAINED
TIFFANY

8
AIRTWIST
BACCARAT
BOHEMIAN
CUT GLASS
FACET CUT
FRIGGERS
INTAGLIO
JACOBITE
VAUXHALL
VENETIAN
WALDGLAS

9
CHALCEDON
HARRACHOV
LITHYALIN
MOSS AGATE
NEWCASTLE
PEACH BLOW
PEACH SKIN

9—continued
PILLAR CUT

10
AVENTURINE
FLUGELGLAS
MILLEFIORI
PILKINGTON

11
HOCHSCHNITT
OPAQUE TWIST
PATE-DE-VERRE
RAVENSCROFT
STANGENGLAS
STOURBRIDGE
WHITEFRIARS

16
ZWISCHENGOLD-
  GLAS

TYPES OF WOOD

3
ASH
BOX
ELM
OAK
YEW

4
DEAL
LIME
PINE
TEAK

5
CEDAR

5—continued
EBONY
HOLLY
IROKO
LARCH
MAPLE
THUJA
THUYA

6
CHERRY
PADAUK
PADOUK
WALNUT
WILLOW

7
AMBOYNA
CYPRESS
LOGWOOD

8
CHESTNUT
FUMED OAK
HARDWOOD
HAREWOOD
KINGWOOD
MAHOGANY
MULBERRY
PEARWOOD
ROSEWOOD

9
MARQUETRY
STAINWOOD

11
LIGNUM VITAE

13
ITALIAN WALNUT
MACASSAR EBONY
PARTRIDGE-WOOD

14
COROMANDEL
  WOOD
INDIAN ROSEWOOD

FURNITURE

3
COT

4
CRIB
DESK
SOFA

5
BENCH
BERTH
CHEST
COUCH
DIVAN
FUTON
STALL
STOOL
Z-BED

6
BUREAU
CRADLE
DAY BED
LOWBOY
SETTEE
SETTLE

7
BUNK BED
CABINET
CAMP BED
CASSONE
COMMODE
DRESSER
HAMMOCK
HIGHBOY
LECTERN
SHELVES
SOFA BED
TALLBOY
TWIN BED
WHATNOT

8
ARMCHAIR
BAR STOOL
BOOKCASE
BOX CHAIR
END TABLE
LOVE SEAT
RECLINER
TEA TABLE
WARDROBE
WATER BED

9
BOOKSHELF
CAMP CHAIR
CANE CHAIR
CARD TABLE
CLUB CHAIR
DAVENPORT
DECK CHAIR
DOUBLE BED
EASY CHAIR
EMPIRE BED
HIGH CHAIR
HOPE CHEST
PIER TABLE
SIDEBOARD
SIDE CHAIR
SIDE TABLE
SINGLE BED
WING CHAIR
WORK TABLE

10
BUCKET SEAT
CANTERBURY
CHOIR STALL
ESCRITOIRE
FEATHER BED
SECRETAIRE
TRUCKLE BED

11
BARREL CHAIR
CANOPIED BED
CARVER CHAIR
COFFEE TABLE
COLONIAL BED
DINING CHAIR
DINING TABLE
FOLDAWAY BED
GAMING TABLE
KING-SIZE BED
LOUNGE CHAIR
MORRIS CHAIR
PANELLED BED
READING DESK
ROLL-TOP DESK
SHAKER CHAIR
STUDIO COUCH
SWIVEL CHAIR
WOODEN CHAIR
WRITING DESK

12
BEDSIDE TABLE
BOSTON ROCKER
BOTTOM DRAWER
CHAISE LONGUE
CHESTERFIELD
CHINA CABINET
CONSOLE TABLE
FOLDING CHAIR
GATE-LEG TABLE
GRECIAN COUCH
KITCHEN TABLE
KNEE-HOLE DESK
LEATHER CHAIR
LIBRARY TABLE
MILKING STOOL
NURSING CHAIR
QUEEN-SIZE BED
ROCKING CHAIR

12–continued
SLANT-TOP DESK
SLOPE-TOP DESK
WELSH DRESSER
WINDSOR CHAIR
WRITING TABLE

13
BENTWOOD CHAIR
CAPTAIN'S CHAIR
DOUBLE DRESSER
DRESSING TABLE
DRINKS CABINET
DROP-LEAF TABLE
FOUR-POSTER BED
LIQUOR CABINET
MIRROR CABINET
PEDESTAL TABLE
PEMBROKE TABLE
SHERATON CHAIR
STRAIGHT CHAIR

14
CHEST OF
  DRAWERS
CORNER
  CUPBOARD
PANEL-BACK CHAIR
QUEEN-ANNE CHAIR
RECLINING CHAIR
WHEEL-BACK CHAIR

15+
COCKTAIL CABINET
CONVERTIBLE SOFA
LADDER-BACK
  CHAIR
UPHOLSTERED
  CHAIR

FURNITURE TERMS

3
EAR

4
BAIL
BULB
HUSK
OGEE
SWAG

5
APRON
BEVEL
BOMBÉ
CLEAT
DOWEL
FRETS
GESSO
INLAY

5–continued
LOPER
OVOLO
SHELL
SKIRT
SPLAT
SQUAB
STILE

6
DIAPER
FIGURE
FILLET
FINIAL
FLY-LEG
FRIEZE
LINING
MUNTIN

6—continued
ORMOLU
PATERA
PATINA
PLINTH
REBATE
RUNNER
SCROLL
VENEER
VOLUTE

7
AMORINI
BANDING
BEADING
BLISTER
BUN FOOT
CARCASE
CASTORS
CHAMFER
CORNICE
EN SUITE
FLUTING
GALLERY
HIPPING
LOZENGE
LUNETTE
PAD FOOT
PAW FOOT
REEDING
ROUNDEL

7—continued
SALTIRE
TAMBOUR
TURNING

8
ACANTHUS
ARCADING
ASTRAGAL
BALUSTER
BOW FRONT
CABOCHON
DOVETAIL
HOOP BACK
LION MASK
MOULDING
PEDIMENT
PIE CRUST
PILASTER
RAM'S HEAD
SABRE LEG
SUNBURST
SWAN-NECK
TERMINAL
WAINSCOT

9
ANTHEMION
ARABESQUE
BLIND FRET
CAMEO BACK

9—continued
CARTOUCHE
DROP FRONT
FALL FRONT
GUILLOCHE
LINENFOLD
MARQUETRY
MEDALLION
PARQUETRY
RULE JOINT
SHOE-PIECE
SPADE FOOT
SPOON BACK
STRAPWORK
STRETCHER
STRIATION
STRINGING

10
BOULLE WORK
BREAK-FRONT
EGG-AND-DART
ESCUTCHEON
GADROONING
KEY PATTERN
LADDER BACK
MITRE JOINT
MONOPODIUM
QUARTERING
SERPENTINE
SHIELD-BACK

10—continued
UNDER-BRACE

11
BALL-AND-CLAW
BALLOON BACK
BRACKET FOOT
CABRIOLE LEG
CHIP-CARVING
COCKBEADING
COUNTERSINK
CUP-AND-COVER
LATTICEWORK
SPIRAL TWIST

12
CRESTING RAIL
DISHED CORNER
FIELDED PANEL
OYSTER VENEER

13+
BARLEY-SUGAR
    TWIST
BOBBIN TURNING
BROKEN PEDIMENT
CHANNEL MOULDING
COLUMN TURNING
MORTISE-AND-
    TENON

POTTERY AND PORCELAIN

3&4
AULT
BOW
MING
TANG

5
DELFT
DERBY
IMARI
SPODE

6
BISQUE
RRETBY
CANTON
MINTON
PARIAN
RUSKIN
SEVRES

7
BELLEEK
BISCUIT
BRISTOL

7—continued
CHELSEA
DOULTON
FAIENCE
ITALIAN
MEISSEN
MOULDED
NEW HALL
REDWARE
SATSUMA
TOBY JUG

8
CANEWARE
CAUGHLEY
CHAFFERS
COALPORT
FAIRINGS
MAIOLICA
MAJOLICA
NANTGARW
PLYMOUTH
SALOPIAN
SLIPWARE
WEDGWOOD

9
AGATE WARE
CHINA CLAY
CRACKLING
CREAMWARE
DAVENPORT
HARD PASTE
LINTHORPE
LIVERPOOL
LOWESTOFT
MOORCROFT
PEARLWARE
PRATTWARE
SOFT PASTE
STONEWARE
WORCESTER

10
CANTON WARE
CHINA STONE
LUSTREWARE
MARTINWARE
PILKINGTON
POLYCHROME
ROCKINGHAM

10—continued
SALT-GLAZED
STONE CHINA
TERRACOTTA

11
BLACK BASALT
CAPODIMONTE
EARTHENWARE
FAMILLE ROSE
FAMILLE VERT
LONGTON HALL
PATE-SUR-PATE

12+
ASIATIC PHEASANT
BLUE AND WHITE
CAMBRIAN POTTERY
MASON'S
    IRONSTONE CHINA
NAGASAKI WARE
STAFFORDSHIRE
WILLOW PATTERN

LITERARY TERMS

3
ODE
WIT

4
EPIC
FOOT
IAMB
MYTH

5
ELEGY
FABLE
GENRE
ICTUS
IRONY
LYRIC
METRE
NOVEL
OCTET
PROSE
RHYME
STYLE
THEME
VERSE

6
BALLAD
BATHOS
CESURA
CLICHÉ
DACTYL
HUBRIS
LAMENT
MONODY
OCTAVE
PARODY
PATHOS
SATIRE
SCHOOL
SEPTET
SESTET

6–continued
SIMILE
SONNET
STANZA
STRESS
SYMBOL

7
CAESURA
CONCEIT
COUPLET
DICTION
ELISION
EPIGRAM
EPISTLE
EPITAPH
EUPHONY
FABLIAU
HUMOURS
IMAGERY
NEMESIS
PARADOX
PROSODY
PYRRHIC
REALISM
SPONDEE
SUBPLOT
TRAGEDY
TROCHEE

8
ALLEGORY
ANAPAEST
AUGUSTAN
DIDACTIC
ELEMENTS
EXEMPLUM
EYE RHYME
METAPHOR
OXYMORON
PASTORAL
QUATRAIN

8–continued
RHETORIC
SCANSION
SYLLABLE
TRIMETER

9
AMBIGUITY
ASSONANCE
BURLESQUE
CATHARSIS
CLASSICAL
EUPHEMISM
FREE VERSE
HALF RHYME
HEXAMETER
HYPERBOLE
MONOMETER
OCTAMETER
PARARHYME

10
BLANK VERSE
CARICATURE
DENOUEMENT
EPIC SIMILE
HEPTAMETER
MOCK HEROIC
NATURALISM
PENTAMETER
PICARESQUE
SPOONERISM
SUBJECTIVE
TETRAMETER

11
ANACHRONISM
COURTLY LOVE
END STOPPING
ENJAMBEMENT
GOTHIC NOVEL
HORATIAN ODE

11–continued
MALAPROPISM
NOBLE SAVAGE
OBJECTIVITY
TRAGICOMEDY

12
ALLITERATION
ONOMATOPOEIA

13
ANTHROPOMORPH
HEROIC COUPLET
INTERNAL RHYME

14
EXISTENTIALISM
FEMININE ENDING
MILTONIC SONNET
ROMANTIC POETRY
SENTIMENTALITY

15
MASCULINE ENDING
PATHETIC FALLACY
PERSONIFICATION

16
PETRARCHAN
   SONNET

18
METAPHYSICAL
   POETRY
NEGATIVE
   CAPABILITY
OMNISCIENT
   NARRATOR

20+
STREAM OF
   CONSCIOUSNESS

FIGURES OF SPEECH

ALLITERATION
ANACOLUTHON
ANADIPLOSIS
ANAPHORA
ANTISTROPHE
ANTITHESIS
APOSIOPESIS
APOSTROPHE

ASSONANCE
ASYNDETON
CHIASMUS
CONSONANCE
HYPERBATON
HYPERBOLE
IRONY
LITOTES

METAPHOR
METONYMY
PERIPHRASIS
PERSONIFICATION
SIMILE
SYNECDOCHE

PRINTING AND PUBLISHING TERMS

2&3	5–continued	6–continued	8–continued	9–continued
CCR	INSET	OFFSET	BODY TEXT	DRY OFFSET
CPU	LITHO	ORPHAN	BUNDLING	ENDMATTER
CRT	POINT	OZALID	CONTENTS	ENDPAPERS
DTP	PROOF	QUARTO	CONTRACT	EVEN PAGES
FIT	RECTO	RASTER	CONTRAST	FREELANCE
KEY	REPRO	READER	DATABASE	HALF-SHEET
LAY	RESET	REVIEW	DELETION	HALF TITLE
OCR	ROMAN	SIZING	DIGITISE	HARDBOUND
PE	ROUGH	SPREAD	DROP CAPS	HARDCOVER
SC	RUN-ON	UNSEWN	EMBOSSED	HIGHLIGHT
	SERIF	WEIGHT	EMULSION	KEYSTROKE
4	SHEET		EPIGRAPH	LANDSCAPE
BOLD	SPACE	**7**	EPILOGUE	LIMPBOUND
BOOK	SPINE	ACETATE	FOOTNOTE	LOOSE LEAF
CAPS	VERSO	ACRYLIC	FORE-EDGE	LOWER CASE
CASE	WIDOW	ADVANCE	FOREWORD	MARKETING
COPY		ARTWORK	GATEFOLD	MICROFILM
CROP	**6**	BINDING	GILT EDGE	MILLBOARD
DATA	AUTHOR	BROMIDE	GLOSSARY	OVERPRINT
EDIT	BLOW UP	BUCKRAM	GRAMMAGE	OXIDATION
FILM	CENTRE	CALIPER	GRAPHICS	PAGE PROOF
FLAP	CHEMAC	CAPTION	HALFTONE	PAPER TAPE
FOIL	CICERO	CHAPTER	HARDBACK	PERFECTOR
FOLD	COLUMN	COLLATE	HARD COPY	REMAINDER
FONT	CREASE	DENSITY	HEADLINE	SANS SERIF
FOOT	CREDIT	DIAGRAM	KEYBOARD	SIGNATURE
HEAD	CUT-OFF	DUOTONE	LAMINATE	SMALL CAPS
LEAF	DAGGER	EDITION	LANGUAGE	SUB-EDITOR
LINE	DAMPER	FEATURE	LIGATURE	SUBSCRIPT
MATT	DECKLE	FIGURES	OFFPRINT	TITLE PAGE
PAGE	DELETE	FLYLEAF	PACKAGER	TRANSPOSE
PICA	DESIGN	FOLD-OUT	PHOTOSET	TWO-COLOUR
PULP	DRYING	HEADING	PORTRAIT	UNDERLINE
REAM	EDITOR	IMPRINT	PRE-PRESS	UPPER CASE
SEWN	EM-DASH	JUSTIFY	PRINT RUN	WATERMARK
SKID	EN-DASH	KEYLINE	SIDE HEAD	WORDSPACE
TEXT	ERRATA	KNOCK UP	SLIP CASE	
TRIM	FIGURE	LEADING	STILLAGE	**10**
TYPE	FILTER	MASKING	SUBTITLE	BACKLINING
WOVE	FIXING	OUTWORK	SUPERIOR	BACK MARGIN
	FOOTER	PASTE-UP	TAILBAND	BACKMATTER
5	FORMAT	PICKING	TEXT AREA	BIBLE PAPER
AGENT	GLOSSY	PREFACE	TYPEFACE	BOOK BINDER
ALIGN	GUTTER	PRELIMS	TYPESIZE	BOOK JACKET
BLOCK	HEADER	PRINTER		CORRECTION
BLURB	INDENT	REISSUE	**9**	DEDICATION
COVER	JACKET	REPRINT	BLANK PAGE	DIAZO PRINT
DRAFT	LAYOUT	ROYALTY	BLUEPRINT	DIDOT POINT
DUMMY	LEADED	TYPESET	BOOK PROOF	HOUSE STYLE
ERROR	LEGEND	UPRIGHT	CASE BOARD	IMPOSITION
FIBRE	MAKE-UP		CHARACTER	IMPRESSION
FLUSH	MANILA	**8**	CO-EDITION	IN REGISTER
FOLIO	MARK-UP	ABRIDGED	COLLOTYPE	LAMINATION
FOUNT	MARGIN	ADDENDUM	COPYRIGHT	MANUSCRIPT
GLOSS	MASKING	APPENDIX	CROP MARKS	METAL PLATE
GRAIN	MOCK-UP	ASCENDER	DANDY ROLL	MICROFICHE
IMAGE	OCTAVO	BAD BREAK	DESCENDER	MONOCHROME
INDEX		BASE LINE		

10–continued
OVERMATTER
PAGINATION
PAPER PLATE
PERFORATED
PRODUCTION
RANGED LEFT
REVERSE OUT
SEPARATION
SUBHEADING
SUPPLEMENT
TAIL MARGIN
THUMB INDEX
TITLE VERSO
TYPE HEIGHT
TYPESCRIPT

11
ADVANCE COPY
ADVERTISING
ANTIQUE WOVE
CASE BINDING
CHAPTER HEAD
CONTRIBUTOR
COPY EDITING
COPYFITTING
DIRECT LITHO
DROPPED HEAD
ENLARGEMENT
FACING PAGES
FILMSETTING
FLAT ARTWORK
FRONT MATTER
GALLEY PROOF
HYPHENATION
KEYBOARDING
KNIFE FOLDER
LETTERSPACE
LINE ARTWORK
LINE DRAWING
LINE SPACING
MIDDLE TONES
MULTICOLOUR
OFFSET LITHO
ORIGINATION
OVEREXPOSED
POSTER PAPER
PROCESS INKS
PROOFREADER
RAGGED RIGHT
RANGED RIGHT
RUBBER PLATE
RUNNING HEAD
SPECIAL SORT

11–continued
STRIPPING IN
SUPERSCRIPT
UNJUSTIFIED

12
BIBLIOGRAPHY
BIMETAL PLATE
BLADE-COATING
CENTRESPREAD
CHARACTER SET
CHEMICAL PULP
CLOTH BINDING
CODING SYSTEM
DOUBLE-COLUMN
FILM NEGATIVE
FILM POSITIVE
FRONTISPIECE
ILLUSTRATION
INTRODUCTION
LEATHERBOUND
MARBLED PAPER
MILL FINISHED
PARALLEL FOLD
PASS FOR PRESS
PERFECT BOUND
POSITIVE FILM
QUARTER-BOUND
RANGED CENTER
REPRODUCTION
SADDLE STITCH
SIDE-STITCHED
SINGLE-COLOUR
SINGLE-COLUMN
SOFTWOOD PULP
THERMOGRAPHY
TRANSPARENCY
UNDEREXPOSED

13
BASE ALIGNMENT
BLACK AND WHITE
BLACK HALFTONE
BLIND BLOCKING
CONDENSED TYPE
CYLINDER PRESS
FILM PROCESSOR
FOREIGN RIGHTS
GRAPHIC DESIGN
JUSTIFICATION
LINING FIGURES
LITHO PRINTING
PROCESS COLOUR
REGISTER MARKS
RIGHT-HAND PAGE

13–continued
SPECIFICATION
SPIRAL BINDING
STRIKE-THROUGH
TRIMETAL PLATE
UNTRIMMED SIZE

14
CATHODE RAY TUBE
CODE CONVERSION
CONCERTINA FOLD
CROSS REFERENCE
CUT-OUT HALFTONE
DIGITAL READ-OUT
FRONT-END SYSTEM
LEATHER BINDING
PERFECT BINDING
PRINTER'S ERROR
SCREEN PRINTING

15
ANTI SET-OFF
SPRAY
CALENDERED
PAPER
CAST COATED
PAPER
COFFEE-TABLE
BOOK
DIRECT SCREENING
FLATBED PRINTING
GRAVURE PRINTING
OLD-STYLE FIG-
URES
PICTURE RE-
SEARCH

16
ACKNOWLEDGE-
MENTS
AUTOPOSITIVE FILM
AUTOREVERSAL
FILM
COLD MELT ADHE-
SIVE
CYRILLIC ALPHABET
DOUBLE-PAGE
SPREAD
INTERLINE SPACING
LINE ILLUSTRATION
PROCESS ENGRAV-
ING
PROOFREADER'S
MARK

16–continued
ROUNDED AND
BACKED
VANITY PUBLISHING

17
ALL RIGHTS RE-
SERVED
DIFFUSION TRANS-
FER
FOLDED AND GATH-
ERED
INCLUSIVE TYPE
AREA

18+
ACADEMIC
PUBLISHING
ACHROMATIC
SEPARATION
CENTRAL
PROCESSING
UNIT
COLD-SET WEB
PRINTING
COMPLEMENTARY
COLOUR REMOVAL
DESK-TOP
PUBLISHING
DISCRETIONARY
HYPHEN
DRY-TRANSFER
LETTERING
ELECTRONIC
PUBLISHING
FOUR-COLOUR
PRINTING
FOUR-COLOUR
SEPARATION
HOT METAL
COMPOSITION
HYPHENATION AND
JUSTIFICATION
LINE AND TONE
COMBINATION
OPTICAL
CHARACTER
RECOGNITION
PROOF
CORRECTION
MARKS
SILK-SCREEN
PRINTING
VERTICAL
JUSTIFICATION

BOOK AND PAPER SIZES

4
DEMY
POST
POTT

5
CROWN
FOLIO
ROYAL

6
MEDIUM
OCTAVO
QUARTO

8
FOOLSCAP
IMPERIAL

9
DUODECIMO
LARGE POST
SMALL DEMY

10
ATLAS FOLIO
CROWN FOLIO
DOUBLE DEMY
DOUBLE POST
LARGE CROWN
OCTODECIMO
ROYAL FOLIO
SMALL ROYAL
SUPER ROYAL

11
CROWN OCTAVO
CROWN QUARTO
DOUBLE CROWN
DOUBLE ROYAL
MEDIUM FOLIO
ROYAL OCTAVO
ROYAL QUARTO
SEXTODECIMO

12
MEDIUM OCTAVO
MEDIUM QUARTO

13
ELEPHANT FOLIO

14
CROWN SIXTEENMO
DOUBLE FOOLSCAP
IMPERIAL OCTAVO
ROYAL SIXTEENMO

15+
CROWN SIXTY-FOURMO
CROWN THIRTY-TWOMO
DOUBLE ELEPHANT FOLIO
MEDIUM SIXTEENMO
MEDIUM SIXTY-FOURMO
MEDIUM THIRTY-TWOMO
QUADRASEGISIMO-OCTAVO
ROYAL SIXTY-FOURMO
ROYAL THIRTY-TWOMO
SEXAGESIMO-QUARTO
TRIGESIMO-SEGUNDO

ARCHAEOLOGY TERMS

2&3
AMS
AXE
CRM
DIG
DNA
EDM
GIS
GPR
TL

4
ALUM
CIST
CLAY
COIN
MAYA
SILT
SITE
SLIP
SOIL
TANG
TELL
TROY
WOOD

5
BLADE
BONES
CAIRN
CHERT
DECAY
FLINT
GENUS
HENGE
HOARD
MOUND
PALEO-
QUERN
ROMAN
STONE
TOMBS
TOOLS

6
AEGEAN
BARROW
BEAKER
BURIAL
DEBRIS
GENDER
GOTHIC
GRAVES

6–continued
ICE AGE
INSULA
METALS
MIDDEN
PALAEO-
TUMULI
VARVES
VILLAS

7
AEOLIAN
AZILIAN
CAPSIAN
CONTEXT
ECOLOGY
FEATURE
HOMINID
ICE CORE
IRON AGE
ISOTOPE
LAKE BED
OLDOWAN
POMPEII
POTTERY
SCRAPER

8
AMPHORAE
ARTEFACT
CHELLEAN
CROP MARK
CULTURES
EVIDENCE
GLACIALS
HALF-LIFE
HERITAGE
HILLFORT
KNAPPING
MEGALITH
METAL ORE
MUD-BRICK
OBSIDIAN
PEAT BOGS
SAVAGERY
SECTIONS
STONE AGE
TYPOLOGY

9
ACHEULIAN
BARBARISM
BIOSPHERE
BRONZE AGE

9–continued
COMPONENT
ETHNICITY
EVOLUTION
FIELDWORK
FIRED CLAY
HUT CIRCLE
JEWELLERY
MICROLITH
NEOLITHIC
PRIMITIVE
SEDIMENTS
SERIATION
SOLUTREAN
SYMBOLISM
TAPHONOMY
THREE AGES
TREE RINGS

10
ANGLO-SAXON
ASSEMBLAGE
CHRONOLOGY
CLACTONIAN
COPROLITES
DERIVATIVE
EARTHWORKS

10–continued
EGYPTOLOGY
EXCAVATION
GRAVE GOODS
GRAVETTIAN
HAMBURGIAN
LOWER PHASE
MESOLITHIC
METALLURGY
MOUSTERIAN
PALAEODIET
PALAEOSOLS
PALYNOLOGY
POSITIVISM
PREHISTORY
RIFT VALLEY
SETTLEMENT
STONEHENGE
STONE TOOLS
UPPER PHASE
WEATHERING

11
ABBEVILLIAN
ANTIQUARIES
ASSOCIATION
AURIGNACIAN
BURIAL MOUND
CALIBRATION
CRESWELLIAN
CROSS-DATING
ETHNOGRAPHY
FIELD SURVEY
FIELD SYSTEM
FOUNDATIONS
INSCRIPTION
MAGDALENIAN
MESOPOTAMIA
MIDDLE PHASE
NEANDERTHAL
NEW STONE AGE
OLD STONE AGE
PERIGORDIAN
PHOTOGRAPHY
PREHISTORIC
RADIOCARBON
RENAISSANCE
RITUAL SITES
ROMANTICISM
SEABED CORES

12
ANTHROPOLOGY
ARCHITECTURE
CALENDAR YEAR
CARBON DATING
CAVE DWELLERS
CHALCOLITHIC
CIVILIZATION
CONSERVATION
CRO-MAGNON MAN
DIFFUSIONISM
ETHNOGRAPHIC

12–continued
FIELDWALKING
INTERGLACIAL
LAKE DWELLERS
LEVALLOISIAN
LUMINESCENCE
MAGNETOMETER
OLDUVAI GORGE
PALAEOBOTANY
PALAEOLITHIC
POLLEN GRAINS
RELATIVE AGES
ROSETTA STONE
SHELL MIDDENS
STONE CIRCLES
STRATIGRAPHY

13
ARCHAEOLOGIST
CLIFF DWELLERS
DOMESTICATION
ENLIGHTENMENT
FOLSOM CULTURE
GEOCHRONOLOGY
HUNTER-GATHERER
MAGNETIC FIELD
PARADIGM SHIFT
PROCESSUALISM
REMOTE SENSING
SAMIAN POTTERY
SITE FORMATION
VOLCANIC GLASS
WATTLE AND DAUB

14
ABSOLUTE DATING
ANTHROPOLOGIST
ANTIQUARIANISM
CHATELPERRONIAN
GEOLOGICAL TIME
MAGNETIC DATING
NEW ARCHAEOL-
  OGY
RELATIVE DATING
STRATIFICATION
THREE AGE SYSTEM
TREE-RING DATING
ZOOARCHAEOLOGY

15
BOX TRENCH SYS-
  TEM
CLIMATIC FACTORS
CUP AND RING
  MARKS
GEOLOGICAL
  ROCKS
ISOTOPE ANALYSIS
MATERIAL CULTURE
NOBLE SAVAGE
  MYTH
PALAEOMAGNETISM

15–continued
PRESSURE-FLAKING
RELATIVE SYSTEMS
SOCIAL EVOLUTION

16
ARCHAEOASTRON-
  OMY
ARCHAEOMAGNET-
  ISM
BULB OF PERCUS-
  SION
CALIBRATION
  CURVE
CHARACTERIZATION
DENDROCHRONOL-
  OGY
ETHNOARCHAEOL-
  OGY
FIELD ARCHAEOL-
  OGY
GEOLOGICAL
  STRATA
ORGANIC
  MATERIALS
PALAEODEMOGRA-
  PHY
RADIOACTIVE
  DECAY
TERMINUS ANTE
  QUEM
TERMINUS POST
  QUEM
VOLCANIC
  DEPOSITS

17
ABSOLUTE
  TECHNIQUE
AERIAL ARCHAEOL-
  OGY
AERIAL PHOTOGRA-
  PHY
EXCAVATION
  METHODS
GEOMAGNETIC
  SURVEY
GEOPHYSICAL
  SURVEY
LANDSCAPE
  FEATURES
MAGNETIC SURVEY-
  ING
MIDDLE RANGE
  THEORY
OBSIDIAN HYDRA-
  TION
PALAEOENVIRON-
  MENT
POSTGLACIAL
  PERIOD
RADIOCARBON
  DATING

17–continued
RESCUE ARCHAE-
  OLOGY
RESISTIVITY
  METERS
SELECTIVE BREED-
  ING

18
CHRONOMETRIC
  DATING
DOMESTICATED
  PLANTS
FORMATION
  PROCESSES
MAGNETOMETER
  SURVEY
NORTH-SOUTH
  REVERSAL
OPEN-AREA
  EXCAVATION
SALVAGE ARCHAE-
  OLOGY

19
BIBLICAL ARCHAE-
  OLOGY
CLIMATOSTRATIG-
  RAPHY
DOMESTICATED
  ANIMALS
ETHNOARCHAEO-
  LOGICAL
MEDIEVAL ARCHAE-
  OLOGY
NEOLITHIC REVOLU-
  TION
RADIOACTIVE
  ISOTOPES

20
CLASSICAL AR-
  CHAEOLOGY
GEOPHYSICAL
  TECHNIQUE
LANDSCAPE
  ARCHAEOLOGY
POTASSIUM-ARGON
  DATING
RADIOMETRIC
  TECHNIQUE
RESISTIVITY
  SURVEYING

21
ABSOLUTE DATING
  SYSTEMS
ARCHAEOMAGNETIC
  DATING
HISTORICAL
  ARCHAEOLOGY
INDUSTRIAL
  ARCHAEOLOGY

MUSEUMS AND GALLERIES

AMERICAN MUSEUM (Bath)
ART GALLERY (Aberdeen)
ART GALLERY AND MUSEUM (Glasgow)
ASHMOLEAN (Oxford)
BALTIC CENTRE FOR CONTEMPORARY ART,
THE (Gateshead)
BARBARA HEPWORTH MUSEUM (St Ives)
BEAMISH OPEN AIR MUSEUM (County
Durham)
BEATLES STORY (Liverpool)
BIG PIT MINING MUSEUM (Blaenafon)
BLISTS HILL MUSEUM (Ironbridge Gorge)
BRIGHTON MUSEUM AND ART GALLERY
(Brighton)
BRISTOL INDUSTRIAL MUSEUM (Bristol)
BRITISH MUSEUM (London)
BUCKLER'S HARD (Beaulieu)
BUILDING OF BATH MUSEUM (Bath)
BURRELL COLLECTION (Glasgow)
CADBURY WORLD (Bournville)
CASTLE MUSEUM (Norwich)
CENTRE FOR ALTERNATIVE TECHNOLOGY
(Machynlleth)
CHELTENHAM ART GALLERY AND MUSEUM
(Cheltenham)
CITY ART GALLERY (Leeds)
CITY MUSEUM AND ART GALLERY
(Birmingham)
CITY MUSEUM AND ART GALLERY (Bristol)
COALPORT CHINA MUSEUM (Ironbridge
Gorge)
CRICH NATIONAL TRAMWAY MUSEUM (Crich)
D-DAY MUSEUM (Portsmouth)
DESIGN MUSEUM (London)
DULWICH PICTURE GALLERY (London)
FITZWILLIAM MUSEUM (Cambridge)
GOONHILLY EARTH STATION (Lizard
Peninsular)
HUNTERIAN ART GALLERY (Glasgow)
IMPERIAL WAR MUSEUM (London)
IMPERIAL WAR MUSEUM (Duxford)

KELVINGROVE ART GALLERY AND MUSEUM
(Glasgow)
LIVERPOOL MUSEUM (Liverpool)
LLECHWEDD SLATE CAVERNS (Blaenau)
LONDON DUNGEON (London)
LONDON TRANSPORT MUSEUM (London)
LOWRY GALLERY (Manchester)
MADAME TUSSAUD'S (London)
MANCHESTER ART GALLERY (Manchester)
MARITIME AND INDUSTRIAL MUSEUM
(Swansea)
MARITIME MUSEUM (Southampton)
MILLENNIUM GALLERIES (Sheffield)
MUSEUM OF IRON (Ironbridge Gorge)
MUSEUM OF ISLAY LIFE (Islay)
MUSEUM OF LONDON (London)
MUSEUM OF NORTH DEVON (Barnstaple)
MUSEUM OF OXFORD (Oxford)
MUSEUM OF SCIENCE AND INDUSTRY
(Manchester)
MUSEUM OF SCOTLAND (Edinburgh)
MUSEUM OF TRANSPORT (Glasgow)
MUSEUM OF VICTORIAN SCIENCE (Whitby)
NATIONAL COAL MINING MUSEUM (Wakefield)
NATIONAL FISHING HERITAGE CENTRE
(Grimsby)
NATIONAL GALLERY (London)
NATIONAL GALLERY OF MODERN ART &
DEAN GALLERY (Edinburgh)
NATIONAL GALLERY OF SCOTLAND
(Edinburgh)
NATIONAL HORESRACING MUSEUM
(Newmarket)
NATIONAL MARITIME MUSEUM (Greenwich)
NATIONAL MOTOR MUSEUM (Beaulieu)
NATIONAL MUSEUM OF PHOTOGRAPHY,
FILM AND TELEVISION (Bradford)
NATIONAL MUSEUM OF WALES (Cardiff)
NATIONAL PORTRAIT GALLERY (London)
NATIONAL RAILWAY MUSEUM (York)
NATURAL HISTORY MUSEUM (London)

169

NORTH CORNWALL MUSEUM AND GALLERY (Camelford)
NORTH DEVON MARITIME MUSEUM (Appledore)
OXFORD STORY, THE (Oxford)
PITT RIVERS MUSEUM (Oxford)
PLANETARIUM (London)
POLDARK MINE (Lizard Peninsular)
QUEEN'S GALLERY, Buckingham Palace (London)
RAF ROYAL AIR FORCE MUSEUM (Hendon)
ROMAN BATHS MUSEUM (Bath)
ROYAL ALBERT MEMORAIL MUSEUM AND ART GALLERY (Exeter)
ROYAL ARMOURIES MUSEUM (Leeds)
ROYAL CORNWALL (Truro)
ROYAL NAVAL MUSEUM (Portsmouth)
ROYAL OBSERVATORY GREENWICH (Greenwich)
ROYAL PUMP ROOM MUSEUM (Harrogate)
SAINSBURY CENTRE FOR VISUAL ARTS (Norwich)

SCIENCE MUSEUM (London)
SCOTTISH FISHERIES MUSEUM (Anstruther)
SCOTTISH NATIONAL PORTRAIT GALLERY (Edinburgh)
SHERLOCK HOLMES MUSEUM (London)
ST MUNGO'S MUSEUM OF RELIGIOUS LIFE AND ART (Glasgow)
TATE LIVERPOOL (Liverpool)
TATE MODERN (London)
TATE ST IVES (St Ives)
THACKERY MEDICAL MUSEUM (Leeds)
UNIVERSITY MUSEUM (Oxford)
VERULAMIUM MUSEUM (St Albans)
VICTORIA AND ALBERT MUSEUM (London)
WALKER ART GALLERY (Liverpool)
WALLACE COLLECTION (London)
WHEAL MAWRTYN CHINA CLAY MUSEUM (Carthew)
YORK CASTLE MUSEUM (York)
YORK CITY ART GALLERY (York)
YORKSHIRE SCULPTURE PARK (Wakefield)
YORVIK VIKING CENTRE (York)

STATELY HOMES

A LA RONDE (Devonshire)
ABBOTSFORD HOUSE (Scottish borders)
ALTHORP HOUSE (Northamptonshire)
ARLINGTON COURT (Devon)
AUDLEY END (Essex)
BLENHEIM PALACE (Oxfordshire)
BLICKLING HALL (Norfolk)
BOWOOD HOUSE (Wiltshire)
BROADLANDS (Hampshire)
BURGHLEY HOUSE (Lincolnshire)
BURTON AGNES (East Yorkshire)
BURTON CONSTABLE (East Yorkshire)
CASTLE HOWARD (Yorkshire)
CHARLECOTE PARK (Warwickshire)
CHATSWORTH HOUSE (Derbyshire)
CHISWICK HOUSE (London)
CLANDON PARK (Surrey)
CLAYDON HOUSE (Buckinghamshire)
CLIVEDEN (Buckinghamshire)
CORSHAM COURT (Wiltshire)
DALEMAIN (Cumbria)
FAIRFAX HOUSE (York)
FOUNTAINS HALL (North Yorkshire)
GLYNDE PLACE (East Sussex)
GOODWOOD HOUSE (West Sussex)
GREAT DIXTER (East Sussex)
HADDON HALL (Derbyshire)
HAMPTON COURT (Surrey)
HARDWICK HALL (Derbyshire)
HAREWOOD HOUSE (West Yorkshire)
HATFIELD HOUSE (Hertfordshire)
HOLKER HALL (Cumbria)

HOLKHAM HALL (Norfolk)
HOPETOUN HOUSE (West Lothian)
HUGHENDEN MANOR (Buckinghamshire)
HUTTON-IN-THE-FOREST (Cumbria)
ICKWORTH HOUSE (Suffolk)
KEDLESTON HALL (Derbyshire)
KELMSCOTT MANOR (Oxfordshire)
KINGSTON LACY (Dorset)
KNEBWORTH HOUSE (Hertfordshire)
KNOLE (Kent)
LANHYDROCK (Cornwall)
LEIGHTON HALL (Lancashire)
LEVENS HALL (Cumbria)
LITTLE MORETON HALL (Cheshire)
LONGLEAT (Wiltshire)
MELLERSTAIN HOUSE (Scottish Borders)
MONTACUTE HOUSE (Dorset)
MOSELEY OLD HALL (Staffordshire)
NEWBY HALL (North Yorkshire)
NUNNINGTON HALL (York)
OSBOURNE HOUSE (Isle of Wight)
OXBURGH HALL (Norfolk)
PACKWOOD HOUSE (Warwickshire)
PENSHURST PLACE (Kent)
PETWORTH HOUSE (West Sussex)
PLAS NEWYDD (Denbighshire)
PLAS-YN-RHIW (Gwynedd)
QUENBY HALL (Leicestershire)
ROYAL PAVILION (Brighton)
SALTRAM HOUSE (Devon)
SANDRINGHAM (Norfolk)
SCONE PALACE (Perthshire)

SNOWSHILL MANOR (Gloucestershire)
SOMERLEYTON HALL (Suffolk)
SPEKE HALL (Merseyside)
STOURHEAD (Wiltshire)
STRATFIELD SAYE (Hampshire/Berkshire border)

SYON HOUSE (London)
TRAQUAIR HOUSE (Scottish Borders)
WADDESDON MANOR (Buckinghamshire)
WIGHTWICK MANOR (West Midlands)
WILTON HOUSE (Wiltshire)

ABBEYS AND PRIORIES

ABBEY DORE (Herefordshire)
ANGLESEY ABBEY (Cambridgeshire)
BATH ABBEY (Bath)
BATTLE ABBEY (East Sussex)
BEAULIEU ABBEY (Hampshire)
BOLTON PRIORY (North Yorkshire)
BUCKFAST ABBEY (Devon)
BUCKLAND ABBEY (Devon)
BYLAND ABBEY (North Yorkshire)
CARTMEL PRIORY (Cumbria)
CASTLE ACRE PRIORY (Norfolk)
CHRISTCHURCH PRIORY (Dorset)
DRYBURGH ABBEY (Scottish Borders)
EASBY ABBEY (North Yorkshire)
FOUNTAINS ABBEY (North Yorkshire)
FURNESS ABBEY (Cumbria)
GLASTONBURY (Somerset)
HEXHAM ABBEY (Northumberland)
INCHMAHOME PRIORY (Stirling)
JEDBURGH ABBEY (Scottish Borders)

KELSO ABBEY (Scottish Borders)
KIRKHAM PRIORY (North Yorkshire)
KIRKSTALL ABBEY (West Yorkshire)
LACOCK ABBEY (Wiltshire)
LANERCOST PRIORY (Cumbria)
LINDISFARNE PRIORY (Northumberland)
LLANTHONY PRIORY (Gwent)
MELROSE ABBEY (Scottish Borders)
MOUNT GRACE PRIORY (North Yorkshire)
RIEVAULX ABBEY (North Yorkshire)
SELBY ABBEY (West Yorkshire)
SHERBORNE ABBEY (Dorset)
ST MARY'S ABBEY (York)
ST NICHOLAS PRIORY (Devon)
TINTERN ABBEY (Gwent)
TORRE ABBEY (Devon)
WHALLEY ABBEY (Lancashire)
WHITBY ABBEY (North Yorkshire)
WOBURN ABBEY (Bedfordshire)

BRITISH CASTLES

3&4
DEAL (England)
DRUM (Scotland)
ETAL (England)
RABY (England)
ROSS (Ireland)
RYE (England)

5
AYDON (England)
BLACK (Ireland)
BOWES (England)
CABRA (Ireland)
CAREW (Wales)
CONWY (Wales)
CORFE (England)
DOUNE (Scotland)
DOVER (England)
EWLOE (Wales)
FLINT (Wales)

5–continued
FYVIE (Scotland)
HEVER (England)
LEEDS (England)
LEWES (England)
UPNOR (England)
WHITE (Wales)

6
BODIAM (England)
BOLTON (England)
BROUGH (England)
CAMBER (England)
DUBLIN (Ireland)
DUFFUS (Scotland)
EDZELL (Scotland)
FRASER (Scotland)
GLAMIS (Scotland)
HAILES (Scotland)
HUNTLY (Scotland)

6–continued
KELLIE (Scotland)
MORTON (Scotland)
NEWARK (England)
NORHAM (England)
NUNNEY (England)
ODIHAM (England)
ORFORD (England)
PENHOW (Wales)
RAGLAN (Wales)
ROTHES (Scotland)
TIORAM (Scotland)
TOTNES (England)
WALDEN (England)
WALMER (England)

7
ALNWICK (England)
APPLEBY (England)
ARUNDEL (England)

BRITISH CASTLES

7–continued
BARNARD (England)
BEESTON (England)
BERWICK (England)
BLARNEY (Ireland)
CARDIFF (Wales)
CARRICK (Ireland)
CRATHES (Scotland)
DENBIGH (Wales)
DINEFWR (Wales)
DONEGAL (Ireland)
DUNSTER (England)
FARNHAM (England)
HARLECH (Wales)
LINCOLN (England)
LYDFORD (England)
OLD WICK, Castle of
  (Scotland)
PENRITH (England)
PRUDHOE (England)
ST MAWES (England)
SKIPSEA (England)
SKIPTON (England)
STALKER (Scotland)
THREAVE (Scotland)
TUTBURY (England)
WARWICK (England)
WEOBLEY (Wales)
WICKLOW (Ireland)
WINDSOR (England)

8
ABERDOUR (Scotland)
ARDVRECK (Scotland)
BALVENIE (Scotland)
BAMBURGH (England)
BROUGHAM (England)
BUNRATTY (Ireland)
CARLISLE (England)
CHEPSTOW (Wales)
CORGARFF (Scotland)
CRICHTON (Scotland)
DELGATIE (Scotland)
DIRLETON (Scotland)
DRISHANE (Ireland)
DRYSLWYN (Wales)
DUNGIVEN (Ireland)
EYNSFORD (England)
GOODRICH (England)
GROSMONT (Wales)
HADLEIGH (England)
HELMSLEY (England)
KIDWELLY (Wales)
KILCHURN (Scotland)
LONGTOWN (England)
PEMBROKE (Wales)
PEVENSEY (England)
PORTLAND (England)
RICHMOND (England)
STIRLING (Scotland)
TAMWORTH (England)

8–continued
TINTAGEL (England)
TOLQUHON (Scotland)
URQUHART (Scotland)
YARMOUTH (England)

9
BEAUMARIS (Wales)
CARDONESS (Scotland)
CASTLE ROS (Ireland)
CLAYPOTTS (Scotland)
CRICCIETH (Wales)
DARTMOUTH (England)
DROMOLAND (Ireland)
DUNNOTTAR (Scotland)
EDINBURGH (Scotland)
EDLINGHAM (England)
FINDLATER (Scotland)
GUILDFORD (England)
HEDINGHAM (England)
KILDRUMMY (Scotland)
KINGSWEAR (England)
LAUGHARNE (Wales)
LLANTILIO (Wales)
LLAWHADEN (Wales)
MANORBIER (Wales)
MIDDLEHAM (England)
PENDENNIS (England)
PENDRAGON (England)
PICKERING (England)
RESTORMEL (England)
ROCHESTER (England)
SHANKHILL (Ireland)
SKENFRITH (Wales)
SPOFFORTH (England)
TANTALLON (Scotland)
WARKWORTH (England)

10
AUCHINDOUN (Scotland)
BALLYMALOO (Ireland)
CAERNARFON (Wales)
CAERPHILLY (Wales)
CASTLE ACRE (England)
CASTLE SHAN (Ireland)
COLCHESTER (England)
CRAIGIEVAR (Scotland)
DONNINGTON (England)
GLENBUCHAT (Scotland)
KENILWORTH (England)
KILLYLEAGH (Ireland)
LAUNCESTON (England)
LINLITHGOW (Scotland)
OKEHAMPTON (England)
OLD WARDOUR (England)

11
BALLYCASTLE (Ireland)
BARDEN TOWER (England)
BAYARD'S COVE (England)
BERKHAMSTED (England)
CARISBROOKE (England)

11–continued
CARRIGONNON (Ireland)
CASTELL COCH (Wales)
CASTLE KELLY (Ireland)
CASTLE SHANE (Ireland)
CHILLINGHAM (England)
CONISBROUGH (England)
CRAIGMILLAR (Scotland)
DOLWYDDELAN (Wales)
EILEAN DONAN (Scotland)
FRAMLINGHAM (England)
LINDISFARNE (England)
LLANSTEFFAN (Wales)
MACLELLAN'S (Scotland)
PORTCHESTER (England)
RAVENSCRAIG (Scotland)
SCARBOROUGH (England)
TATTERSHALL (England)
TILBURY FORT (England)

12
BERRY POMEROY (England)
CAERLAVEROCK (Scotland)
CARREG CENNEN (Wales)
CASTELL Y BERE (Wales)
CASTLE FRASER (Scotland)
CASTLE RISING (England)
DUNSTANBURGH (England)
HERSTMONCEUX (England)
HUNTINGTOWER (Scotland)
SHERBORNE OLD (England)
SPYNIE PALACE (Scotland)

13
BALLINDALLOCH (Scotland)
CASTLE DONOVAN (Ireland)
CASTLE STALKER (Scotland)
KNARESBOROUGH (England)
ST CATHERINE'S (England)
TOWER OF LONDON
  (England)

14
CASTLE CAMPBELL
  (Scotland)
FALKLAND PALACE (Scotland)

15+
CLIFFORD'S TOWER
  (England)
CLOUGH BALLYMORE
  (Ireland)
FARLEIGH HUNGERFORD
  (England)
ORCHARDTON TOWER
  (Scotland)
SINCLAIR GIRNIGOE
  (Scotland)
ST MICHAEL'S MOUNT
  (England)
WINCHESTER GREAT HALL
  (England)

MUSICAL TERMS

TERM – definition

1 & 2
F – loud
FF - very loud
MF – half loud
P – soft
PP – very soft
SF – strongly accented

3
BIS – repeat
DIM – becoming softer
PED – abbr. for pedal
PIÙ – more
PIZ – plucked
RFZ – accentuated
RIT – slowing down, holding back
SFZ – strongly accented
TEN – held
VIF – lively (Fr.)

4
CODA – final part of a movement
MOTO – motion
RALL – slowing down
SINO – up to; until
TIEF – deep; low (Ger.)

5
AD LIB – at will
ASSAI – very
BUFFO – comic
DOLCE – sweet
FORTE – loud
LARGO – very slow
LENTO – slowly
MESTO – sad, mournful
MEZZO – half
MOLTO – very much
MOSSO – moving, fast
PIANO – soft
QUASI – almost, as if
SEGNO – sign
SENZA – without
SOAVE – sweet; gentle
STARK – strong, loud (Ger.)
TACET – instrument is silent
TANTO – so much
TEMPO – the speed of a composition
TUTTI – all
ZOPPA – in syncopated rhythm

6
ADAGIO – slow
AL FINE – to the end

6–continued
CHIUSO – stopped (of a note); closed
DA CAPO – from the beginning
DEHORS – outside; prominent
DIVISI – divided
DOPPIO – double
FACILE – easy, fluent
LEGATO – bound, tied (of notes), smoothly
MARCIA – march
NIENTE – nothing
NOBILE – noble
RETENU – held back
SEMPRE – always, still
SUBITO – immediately
TENUTO – held

7
AGITATO – agitated; rapid tempo
ALLEGRO – lively, brisk
AL SEGNO – as far as the sign
AMOROSO – loving, emotional
ANIMATO – spirited
ATTACCA – attack; continue without a pause
CALANDO – ebbing; lessening of tempo
CODETTA – small coda; to conclude a passage
CON BRIO – with vigour
DOLENTE – sorrowful
ESTINTO – extremely softly, almost without tone
GIOCOSO – merry; playful
MARCATO – accented
MORBIDO – soft, delicate
PESANTE – heavily, firmly
SCHNELL – fast (Ger.)
SFOGATO – effortless; in a free manner
SORDINO – mute
STRETTO – accelerating or intensifying; overlapping of entries of fugue

8
A BATTUTA – return to strict time
A PIACERE – as you please
BRILLANT – brilliant
COL CANTO – accompaniment to follow solo line
COL LEGNO – to strike strings with stick of the bow
CON FUOCO – fiery; vigorous
DAL SEGNO – from the sign
IN MODO DI – in the manner of

8–continued
MAESTOSO – majestic
MODERATO – moderately
PORTANDO – carrying one note into the next
RITENUTO – slowing down, holding back
SOURDINE – mute (Fr.)
STACCATO – detached
VIVEMENT – lively (Fr.)

9
ADAGIETTO – quite slow
CANTABILE – in a singing fashion
CANTILENA – lyrical, flowing
CRESCENDO – becoming louder
FIORITURA – decoration of a melody
GLISSANDO – sliding scale played on instrument
MENO MOSSO – slower pace
MEZZA VOCE – at half power
OBBLIGATO – not to be omitted
PIUTTOSTO – somewhat
PIZZICATO – plucked
SCHNELLER – faster (Ger.)
SFORZANDO – strongly accented
SIN'AL FINE – up to the end
SLENTANDO – slowing down
SOSTENUTO – sustained
SOTTO VOCE – quiet subdued tone

10
AFFETTUOSO – tender
ALLA CACCIA – in hunting style
ALLARGANDO – broadening; more dignified
ALLEGRETTO – quite lively, brisk
DIMINUENDO – becoming softer
FORTISSIMO – very loud
MEZZOFORTE – half loud
NOBILMENTE – nobly
PERDENDOSI – dying away gradually
PIANISSIMO – very soft
PORTAMENTO – carrying one note into the next
RAVVIVANDO – quickening
RITARDANDO – slowing down, holding back

173

10–continued
SCHERZANDO – joking; playing
SCHLEPPEND – dragging; deviating from correct speed (Ger.)
SCORREVOLE – gliding; fluent
STRINGENDO – tightening; intensification

11
ACCELERANDO – accelerating
AFFRETTANDO – hurrying
MINACCIANDO – menacing
RALLENTANDO – slowing down
RINFORZANDO – accentuated

12
ALLA CAPPELLA – in church style
LEGGERAMENTE – lightly

13
LEGGIERAMENTE – lightly

TONIC SOL-FA

DOH   RAY   ME   FAH   SOH   LAH   TE

MUSICAL INSTRUMENTS

2
UD (lute)
YÜ (scraper)

3
BIN (vina)
KIT (fiddle)
LUR (horn)
OUD (ud)
SAZ (lute)
SHÔ (mouth organ)
TAR (drum; lute)
UTI (lute)

4
BATA (drum)
BIWA (lute)
CH'IN (zither)
DRUM
FIFE
FUYE (flute)
GONG
HARP
HORN
KENA (quena)
KHEN (mouth organ)
KOTO (zither)
LIRA (fiddle)
LUTE
LYRA (lyre)
LYRE
MU YÜ (drum)
MVET (zither)

4–continued
OBOE
OUTI (lute)
P'I P'A (lute)
PIPE
ROTE (lyre)
RUAN (lute)
SONA (shawm)
TRO-U (fiddle)
URUA (clarinet)
VINA (stringed instrument related to sitar)
VIOL
WHIP (percussion)
ZOBO (mirliton)

5
AULOI (shawm)
BANJO
BELLS
BHAYA (kettledrum)
BUGLE
BUMPA (clarinet)
CELLO
CHANG (dulcimer)
CHIME
CLAVE
COBZA (lute)
CORNU (trumpet)
CRWTH (lyre)

5–continued
DAULI (drum)
DHOLA (drum)
DOBRO (guitar)
ERH-HU (fiddle)
FIDEL (fiddle)
FIDLA (zither)
FLUTE
GAITA (bagpipe)
GAJDY (bagpipe)
GUSLE (fiddle)
HURUK (drum)
KAKKO (drum)
KANUN (qanun)
KAZOO (mirliton)
KERAR (lyre)
KO-KIU (fiddle)
MBILA (xylophone)
NGOMA (drum)
NGURU (flute)
OKEDO (drum)
ORGAN
PIANO
PI NAI (shawm)
PU-ILU (clappers)
QANUN (zither)
QUENA (flute)
RASPA (scraper)
REBAB (fiddle)
REBEC (fiddle)
SARON (metallophone)

5–continued
SHAWM
SHENG (mouth organ)
SITAR (lute)
TABLA (drum)
TABOR (drum)
TAIKO (drum)
TIBIA (shawm)
TIPLE (shawm)
TI-TZU (flute)
TUDUM (drum)
TUMYR (drum)
TUPAN (drum)
VIOLA
YUN LO (gong)
ZURLA (shawm)
ZURNA (shawm)

6
ALBOKA (hornpipe)
ARGHUL (clarinet)
BAGANA (lyre)
BINIOU (bagpipe)
CARNYX (trumpet)
CHAKAY (zither)
CHA PEI (lute)
CORNET
CURTAL (double reed)
DARBUK (drum)

6–continued
FANDUR (fiddle)
FIDDLE
FUJARA (flute)
GEKKIN (lute)
GENDER (metallophone)
GONGUE (percussion)
GUITAR
HU CH'IN (fiddle)
HUMMEL (zither)
KENONG (gong)
KISSAR (lyre)
KOBORO (drum)
LIRICA (fiddle)
LIRONE (fiddle)
LITUUS (trumpet)
LONTAR (clappers)
MAYURI (lute)
MOROPI (drum)
NAKERS (drums)
NAQARA (drums)
NTENGA (drum)
O-DAIKO (drum)
OMBGWE (flute)
P'AI PAN (clappers)
POMMER (shawm)

6–continued
RACKET (double
  reed)
RAMKIE (lute)
RATTLE
REBECK (fiddle)
SANTIR (dulcimer)
SHAING (horn)
SHAKER
SHANAI (shawm)
SHIELD (percussion)
SHOFAR (horn)
SOPILE (shawm)
SPINET
SPOONS (clappers)
SRALAY (shawm)
SURNAJ (shawm)
SWITCH (percussion)
SYRINX (panpipe)
TAM-TAM (gong)
TOM-TOM (drum)
TXISTU (flute)
VALIHA (zither)
VIELLE (fiddle)
VIOLIN
YANGUM (dulcimer)
ZITHER

7
ADENKUM (stamping
  tube)
ALPHORN (trumpet)
ANKLUNG (rattle)
ATUMPAN (kettledrum)
BAGPIPE
BARYTON (viol)
BASSOON
BODHRAN (drum)
BONNANG (gong)
BOW HARP
BOX LYRE
BUCCINA (trumpet)
BUISINE (trumpet)
BUMBASS
CELESTE
CHANGKO (drum)
CITTERN
CORNETT
COWBELL
CROTALS
  (percussion)
CYMBALS
DA-DAIKO (drum)
DIPLICE (clarinet)
DUGDUGI (drum)
ENZENZE (zither)
FITHELE (fiddle)
GADULKA (fiddle)
GITTERN
GLING-BU (flute)
HULA IPU
  (percussion)

7–continued
INGUNGU (drum)
ISIGUBU (drum)
KACHAPI (zither)
KALUNGU (talking
  drum)
KAMANJE (fiddle)
KANTELE (zither)
KEMANAK (clappers)
KITHARA (lyre)
KOMUNGO (zither)
MACHETE (lute)
MANDOLA (lute)
MARACAS
  (percussion)
MASENQO (fiddle)
MIGYAUN (zither)
MOKUGYO (drum)
MURUMBU (drum)
MUSETTE (bagpipe)
MUSETTE (shawm)
OBUKANO (lyre)
OCARINA (flute)
OCTAVIN (wind)
ORPHICA (piano)
PANDORA (cittern)
PANPIPE
PIANINO
PIBCORN (hornpipe)
PICCOLO
PIFFARO (shawm)
QUINTON (viol)
RESHOTO (drum)
RINCHIK (cymbals)
SACKBUT (trombone)
SALPINX (trumpet)
SAMISEN (lute)
SANTOOR (dulcimer)
SARANGI (fiddle)
SARINDA (fiddle)
SAW-THAI (fiddle)
SAXHORN
SAXTUBA
SERPENT
SHIWAYA (flute)
SISTRUM (rattle)
SORDINE (kit)
SORDONE (double
  reed)
SPAGANE (clappers)
TAM ÂM LA (gong)
TAMBURA (lute)
TERBANG (drum)
THEORBO (lute)
TIKTIRI (clarinet)
TIMPANI
TRUMPET
TSUZUMI (drum)
UJUSINI (flute)
UKULELE
VIHUELA (guitar)
VIOLONE (viol)

7–continued
WHISTLE
YUN NGAO (gong)
ZUMMARA (clarinet)

8
ALGHAITA (shawm)
ALTOHORN
AUTOHARP
BANDOURA (lute)
BASS DRUM
BASS HORN
BOMBARDE (shawm)
BOUZOUKI (lute)
BOWL LYRE
BUZZ DISK
CALLIOPE
  (mechanical organ)
CARILLON
CHIME BAR
CIMBALOM (dulcimer)
CIPACTLI (flute)
CLAPPERS
CLARINET
CLAVICOR (brass
  family)
CLAW BELL
COURTAUT (double
  reed)
CRECELLE (cog
  rattle)
CRUMHORN (double
  reed)
DULCIMER
DVOYNICE (flute)
GONG DRUM
HANDBELL
HAND HORN
HAWKBELL
JEW'S HARP
KAYAKEUM (zither)
KHUMBGWE (flute)
LANGLEIK (zither)
LANGSPIL (zither)
LAP ORGAN
  (melodeon)
MANDOLIN (lute)
MELODEON
MELODICA
MIRLITON (kazoo)
MRIDANGA (drum)
OLIPHANT (horn)
O-TSUZUMI (drum)
OTTAVINO (virginal)
P'AI HSIAO (panpipe)
PENORCON (cittern)
POCHETTE (kit)
PSALTERY (zither)
PUTORINO (trumpet)
RECORDER
RKAN-DUNG
  (trumpet)

8–continued
RKAN-LING (horn)
RONÉAT-EK
  (xylophone)
SAN HSIEN (lute)
SIDE DRUM
SLIT DRUM
SONAJERO (rattle)
SRINGARA (fiddle)
SURBAHAR (lute)
TALAMBAS (drum)
TARABUKA (drum)
TAROGATO (clarinet;
  shawm)
TIMBALES (drum)
TRIANGLE
TRO-KHMER (fiddle)
TROMBONE
VIOLETTA (viol)
VIRGINAL
YANGCHIN (dulcimer)
YUEH CH'IN (lute)
ZAMPOGNA
  (bagpipe)

9
ACCORDION
ANGLE HARP
ARPANETTA (zither)
BALALAIKA (lute)
BANDURRIA (lute)
BANJOLELE
BASSONORE
  (bassoon)
BOMBARDON (tuba)
CASTANETS
CHALUMEAU
  (clarinet)
COG RATTLE
COMPONIUM
  (mechanical organ)
CORNEMUSE
  (bagpipe)
CORNOPEAN (brass
  family)
CROOK HORN
DAIBYOSHI (drum)
DARABUKKE (drum)
DJUNADJAN (zither)
DUDELSACK
  (bagpipes)
DVOJACHKA (flute)
EUPHONIUM (brass
  family)
FLAGEOLET (flute)
FLEXATONE
  (percussion)
GONG AGENG
HACKBRETT
  (dulcimer)
HARMONICA
HARMONIUM

9–continued
HYDRAULIS (organ)
KELONTONG (drum)
KÖNIGHORN (brass
  family)
LAUNEDDAS (clarinet)
MANDOBASS (lute)
MANDOLONE (lute)
MORIN-CHUR (fiddle)
ORPHARION (cittern)
PICCO PIPE (flute)
PIEN CH'ING
  (lithophone)
ROMMELPOT (drum)
SAXOPHONE
TALLHARPA (lyre)
TOTOMBITO (zither)
TUBA-DUPRÉ
WOOD BLOCK
WURLITZER
XYLOPHONE
XYLORIMBA
  (xylophone)

10
BANANA DRUM
BARREL DRUM
BASSANELLO (double
  reed)
BASSET HORN
BIBLE REGAL (organ)
BICITRABIN (vina)
BIRD SCARER
BONGO DRUMS
BULL-ROARER
CHENGCHENG
  (cymbals)
CHITARRONE (lute)
CLAVICHORD
CLAVIORGAN
COLASCIONE (lute)
CONTRABASS
  (double bass)
COR ANGLAIS
DIDGERIDOO
  (trumpet)
DOUBLE BASS
FLUGELHORN

10–continued
FRENCH HORN
GEIGENWERK
  (mechanical
  harpsichord)
GONG CHIMES
GRAND PIANO
HANDLE DRUM
HURDY GURDY
KETTLEDRUM
LITHOPHONE
  (percussion)
MANDOCELLO (lute)
MELLOPHONE (horn)
MOSHUPIANE (drum)
MOUTH ORGAN
OPHICLEIDE (brass
  family)
RANASRINGA (horn)
SAXOTROMBA
SHAKUHACHI (flute)
SOUSAPHONE
SPITZHARFE (zither)
SYMPHONIUM
  (mouth organ)
TAMBOURINE (drum)
TEPONAZTLI (drum)
THUMB PIANO (jew's
  harp)
TIN WHISTLE
TLAPIZTALI (flute)
TSURI DAIKO (drum)

11
AEOLIAN HARP
ANGEL CHIMES
BARREL ORGAN
BELL CITTERN
BIVALVE BELL
BLADDER PIPE
BOARD ZITHER
CLAPPER BELL
FIPPLE FLUTE
GAMBANG KAYA
  (xylophone)
GUITAR-BANJO
HAND TRUMPET
HARPSICHORD

11–continued
HECKELPHONE
  (oboe)
NYCKELHARPA
PAIMENSARVI (horn)
PANHUÉHUETL
  (drum)
SARON DEMONG
  (metallophone)
SLEIGH BELLS
SPIKE FIDDLE
THEORBO-LUTE
UCHIWA DAIKO
  (drum)
VIOLA D'AMORE
  (viol)
VIOLONCELLO

12
DIPLO-KITHARA
  (zither)
GANSA GAMBANG
  (metallophone)
GANSA JONGKOK
  (metallophone)
GLOCKENSPIEL
  (metallophone)
GUITAR-VIOLIN
HI-HAT CYMBALS
KANTELEHARPE
  (lyre)
MANDOLINETTO
  (ukulele)
PEACOCK SITAR
  (lute)
RAUSCHPFEIFE
  (double reed)
SARRUSOPHONE
  (brass)
SHOULDER HARP
STOCK-AND-HORN
  (hornpipe)
TIPPOO'S TIGER
  (organ)
TUBULAR BELLS
VIOLA DA GAMBA
  (viol)
WHISTLE FLUTE

13
COCKTAIL DRUMS
CONTRABASSOON
DOUBLE BASSOON
  (contrabassoon)
HARDANGERFELE
  (fiddle)
HECKELCLARINA
  (clarinet)
SAVERNAKE HORN
SCHRILLPFEIFE
  (flute)
SLIDE TROMBONE
VIOLA BASTARDA
  (viol)

14
CLARINET D'AMORE
CLAVICYTHERIUM
  (harpsichord)
CYTHARA ANGLICA
  (harp)
JINGLING JOHNNY
TLAPANHUÉHUETL
  (drum)
TRICCABALLACCA
  (clappers)

15
CLASSICAL GUITAR
MOOG
  SYNTHESIZER
TURKISH CRESCENT
  (jingling johnny)

16
CHINESE WOOD
  BLOCK
CHITARRA
  BATTENTE (guitar)
CYLINDRICAL
  DRUMS
DEUTSCHE
  SCHALMEI (double
  reed)
STRUMENTO DI
  PORCO (zither)

BALLET TERMS

4
BRAS
DEMI
JETÉ
PLIÉ
POSÉ

SAUT
TUTU
VOLÉ

5
ARQUÉ

5–continued
BARRE
BATTU
BEATS
BRISÉ
COLLÉ

5–continued
COUPÉ
DÉCOR
ÉLÈVE
FONDU
LIGNE

5–continued
PASSÉ
PIQUÉ
PIVOT
PORTÉ
ROSIN
SAUTÉ
SERRÉ
TOMBÉ

6
APLOMB
À TERRE
ATTACK
BAISSÉ
BALLON
CAMBRÉ
CHAINÉ
CHANGÉ
CHASSÉ
CROISÉ
DÉGAGÉ
DÉTIRÉ
DEVANT
ÉCARTÉ
ÉFFACÉ
ÉLANCÉ
ENTRÉE
ÉPAULÉ
ÉTENDU
ÉTOILE
FAILLI
JARRET
MONTER

6–continued
PENCHÉ
POINTE
RELEVÉ
RETIRÉ
VOYAGÉ

7
ALLONGÉ
ARRONDI
ATTAQUE
BALANCÉ
DANSEUR
DÉBOITÉ
ÉCHAPPÉ
EMBOITÉ
ÉTENDRE
FOUETTÉ
JARRETÉ
LEOTARD
MAILLOT
MARQUER
POISSON
RAMASSÉ
RETOMBÉ
SISSONE
SOUTENU
TAQUETÉ

8
ASSEMBLÉ
ATTITUDE
BACK BEND

8–continued
BALLONNÉ
BALLOTTÉ
BATTERIE
CABRIOLE
CAGNEAUX
CORYPHÉE
DANSEUSE
DÉBOULÉS
DERRIÈRE
DÉTOURNÉ
GLISSADE
PISTOLET
RENVERSÉ
SERPETTE
SPOTTING
STULCHIK
TONNELET

9
ARABESQUE
BALLABILE
COU DE PIED
DÉVELOPPÉ
ÉLÉVATION
ENTRECHAT
ENVELOPPÉ
ÉQUILIBRE
HORTENSIA
JUPONNAGE
LIMBERING
MARCHEUSE
PAS DE DEUX
PIROUETTE

9–continued
RACCOURCI
RÉVÉRENCE
REVOLTADE

10
BATTEMENTS
ENLÈVEMENT
ÉPAULEMENT
SOUBRESAUT
TAQUETERIE

11
CONTRETEMPS
PAS DE BASQUE

12
CHOREOGRAPHY
ENCHAÎNEMENT
GARGOUILLADE

13
CHOREOGRAPHER
CORPS DE BALLET

14
CLOSED POSITION
DIVERTISSEMENT
PRIMA BALLERINA

15
AUTOUR DE LA
  SALLE

17
RÉGISSEUR-
  GÉNÉRALE

NOVEL TITLES

NOVEL (Author)

3
SHE (H Rider Haggard)

4
DR NO (Ian Fleming)
EMMA (Jane Austen)
GIGI (Colette)
NANA (Émile Zola)

5
CHÉRI (Colette)
KIPPS (H G Wells)
SCOOP (Evelyn Waugh)
SYBIL (Benjamin Disraeli)
ZADIG (Voltaire)

6
AMELIA (Henry Fielding)
BEN HUR (Lew Wallace)
CHOCKY (John Wyndham)

6–continued
LOLITA (Vladimir Nabokov)
PAMELA (Henry Fielding)
ROB ROY (Walter Scott)

7
CAMILLA (Fanny Burney)
CANDIDE (Voltaire)
CECILIA (Fanny Burney)
DRACULA (Bram Stoker)
EREWHON (Samuel Butler)
EVELINA (Fanny Burney)
IVANHOE (Walter Scott)
REBECCA (Daphne Du
  Maurier)
SHIRLEY (Charlotte Brontë)
THE FALL (Albert Camus)
ULYSSES (James Joyce)

8
ADAM BEDE (George Eliot)
CRANFORD (Mrs Gaskell)

8–continued
JANE EYRE (Charlotte Brontë)
LUCKY JIM (Kingsley Amis)
SWAN SONG (John
  Galsworthy)
THE IDIOT (Fyodor
  Mikhailovich Dostoevsky)
THE MAGUS (John Fowles)
THE REBEL (Albert Camus)
TOM JONES (Henry Fielding)
VILLETTE (Charlotte Brontë)
WAVERLEY (Walter Scott)

9
AGNES GREY (Anne Brontë)
BILLY LIAR (Keith Waterhouse)
CONINGSBY (Benjamin
  Disraeli)
DUBLINERS (James Joyce)
GLENARVON (Lady Caroline
  Lamb)

9–continued

HARD TIMES (Charles Dickens)
I CLAUDIUS (Robert Graves)
KIDNAPPED (R L Stevenson)
LOVE STORY (Erich Segal)
ROGUE MALE (Geoffrey Household)
THE CHIMES (Charles Dickens)
THE DEVILS (Fyodor Mikhailovich Dostoevsky)
THE HEROES (Charles Kingsley)
THE HOBBIT (J R R Tolkien)
THE PLAGUE (Albert Camus)
VICE VERSA (F Anstey)

10

ANIMAL FARM (George Orwell)
BLEAK HOUSE (Charles Dickens)
CANCER WARD (Alexander Solzhenitsyn)
CLAYHANGER (Arnold Bennett)
DON QUIXOTE (Cervantes)
GOLDFINGER (Ian Fleming)
IN CHANCERY (John Galsworthy)
KENILWORTH (Walter Scott)
LORNA DOONE (R D Blackmore)
PERSUASION (Jane Austen)
THE RAINBOW (D H Lawrence)
TITUS ALONE (Mervyn Peake)
TITUS GROAN (Mervyn Peake)
VANITY FAIR (William Makepeace Thackeray)

11

BLACK BEAUTY (Anna Sewell)
BURMESE DAYS (George Orwell)
CAKES AND ALE (W Somerset Maugham)
COUSIN BETTE (Honoré de Balzac)
DAISY MILLER (Henry James)
GORMENGHAST (Mervyn Peake)
LITTLE WOMEN (Louisa M Alcott)
LOST HORIZON (James Hilton)
MIDDLEMARCH (George Eliot)
MRS DALLOWAY (Virginia Woolf)
OLIVER TWIST (Charles Dickens)
SILAS MARNER (George Eliot)
THE BIG SLEEP (Raymond Chandler)
THE OUTSIDER (Albert Camus)
WAR AND PEACE (Leo Tolstoy)
WOMEN IN LOVE (D H Lawrence)

12

ANNA KARENINA (Leo Tolstoy)
A SEVERED HEAD (Iris Murdoch)
BARNABY RUDGE (Charles Dickens)
BRIGHTON ROCK (Graham Greene)
CASINO ROYALE (Ian Fleming)
DOMBEY AND SON (Charles Dickens)
FRANKENSTEIN (Mary Shelley)
GUY MANNERING (Walter Scott)
HEADLONG HALL (Thomas Love Peacock)
LITTLE DORRIT (Charles Dickens)
MADAME BOVARY (Gustave Flaubert)
MOLL FLANDERS (Daniel Defoe)
OF MICE AND MEN (John Steinbeck)
ROGUE JUSTICE (Geoffrey Household)
ROOM AT THE TOP (John Braine)

12–continued

THE DECAMERON (Boccaccio)
THE GO-BETWEEN (L P Hartley)
THE LOST WORLD (Arthur Conan Doyle)
THE MOONSTONE (Wilkie Collins)
THE PROFESSOR (Charlotte Brontë)

13

A KIND OF LOVING (Stan Barstow)
A MODERN COMEDY (John Galsworthy)
BRAVE NEW WORLD (Aldous Huxley)
DANIEL DERONDA (George Eliot)
DOCTOR ZHIVAGO (Boris Pasternak)
JACOB FAITHFUL (Captain Marryat)
JUST-SO STORIES (Rudyard Kipling)
LES MISÉRABLES (Victor Hugo)
LIVE AND LET DIE (Ian Fleming)
LIZA OF LAMBETH (W Somerset Maugham)
MANSFIELD PARK (Jane Austen)
NORTH AND SOUTH (Mrs Gaskell)
PINCHER MARTIN (William Golding)
SKETCHES BY BOZ (Charles Dickens)
SMILEY'S PEOPLE (John Le Carré)
SONS AND LOVERS (D H Lawrence)
TARKA THE OTTER (Henry Williamson)
THE BLUE LAGOON (H de Vere Stacpoole)
THE CHRYSALIDS (John Wyndham)
THE GOLDEN BOWL (Henry James)
THE HISTORY MAN (Malcolm Bradbury)
THE LAST TYCOON (F Scott Fitzgerald)
THÉRÈSE RAQUIN (Émile Zola)
ZULEIKA DOBSON (Max Beerbohm)

14

A MAN OF PROPERTY (John Galsworthy)
A ROOM OF ONE'S OWN (Virginia Woolf)
A ROOM WITH A VIEW (E M Forster)
A TOWN LIKE ALICE (Neville Shute)
CHANGING PLACES (David Lodge)
CIDER WITH ROSIE (Laurie Lee)
CROTCHET CASTLE (Thomas Love Peacock)
DEATH ON THE NILE (Agatha Christie)
DECLINE AND FALL (Evelyn Waugh)
FrANNY AND ZOOEY (J D Salinger)
GOODBYE, MR CHIPS (James Hilton)
JUDE THE OBSCURE (Thomas Hardy)
LORD OF THE FLIES (William Golding)
NIGHTMARE ABBEY (Thomas Love Peacock)
OUR MAN IN HAVANA (Graham Greene)
PICKWICK PAPERS (Charles Dickens)
RITES OF PASSAGE (William Golding)
ROBINSON CRUSOE (Daniel Defoe)
THE AMBASSADORS (Henry James)
THE CORAL ISLAND (R M Ballantyne)
THE FIRST CIRCLE (Alexander Solzhenitsyn)
THE FORSYTE SAGA (John Galsworthy)
THE GREAT GATSBY (F Scott Fitzgerald)
THE KRAKEN WAKES (John Wyndham)
THE LONG GOODBYE (Raymond Chandler)
THE SECRET AGENT (Joseph Conrad)
THE SILVER SPOON (John Galsworthy)
THE TIME MACHINE (H G Wells)
THE WATER-BABIES (Charles Kingsley)

14–continued
THE WHITE MONKEY (John Galsworthy)
THE WOODLANDERS (Thomas Hardy)
TREASURE ISLAND (R L Stevenson)
TRISTRAM SHANDY (Laurence Sterne)
WHAT MAISIE KNEW (Henry James)

15
A CHRISTMAS CAROL (Charles Dickens)
A FAREWELL TO ARMS (Ernest Hemingway)
A PASSAGE TO INDIA (E M Forster)
COLD COMFORT FARM (Stella Gibbons)
EUSTACE AND HILDA (L P Hartley)
GONE WITH THE WIND (Margaret Mitchell)
GOODBYE TO BERLIN (Christopher Isherwood)
NORTHANGER ABBEY (Jane Austen)
OUR MUTUAL FRIEND (Charles Dickens)
PORTRAIT OF A LADY (Henry James)
PORTRAIT OF CLARE (Francis Brett Young)
STRAIT IS THE GATE (André Gide)
THE COUNTRY GIRLS (Edna O'Brien)
THE INVISIBLE MAN (H G Wells)
THE SECRET GARDEN (Frances Hodgson Burnett)
THE SILMARILLION (J R R Tolkien)
THE TRUMPET MAJOR (Thomas Hardy)
THE WHITE COMPANY (Arthur Conan Doyle)
THE WOMAN IN WHITE (Wilkie Collins)
THREE MEN IN A BOAT (Jerome K Jerome)

16
A CLOCKWORK ORANGE (Anthony Burgess)
A TALE OF TWO CITIES (Charles Dickens)
DAVID COPPERFIELD (Charles Dickens)
GULLIVER'S TRAVELS (Jonathan Swift)
MARTIN CHUZZLEWIT (Charles Dickens)
MR MIDSHIPMAN EASY (Captain Marryat)
NICHOLAS NICKLEBY (Charles Dickens)
TENDER IS THE NIGHT (F Scott Fitzgerald)
TEN LITTLE NIGGERS (Agatha Christie)
THE GRAPES OF WRATH (John Steinbeck)
THE PLUMED SERPENT (D H Lawrence)
THE SCARLET LETTER (Nathaniel Hawthorne)
WUTHERING HEIGHTS (Emily Brontë)

17
ALICE IN WONDERLAND (Lewis Carroll)
DR JEKYLL AND MR HYDE (R L Stevenson)
GREAT EXPECTATIONS (Charles Dickens)
KING SOLOMON'S MINES (H Rider Haggard)
MY BROTHER JONATHAN (Francis Brett Young)
POINT COUNTER POINT (Aldous Huxley)
PRIDE AND PREJUDICE (Jane Austen)
THE DEVILS OF LOUDUN (Aldous Huxley)
THE DIARY OF A NOBODY (G and W Grossmith)
THE LORD OF THE RINGS (J R R Tolkien)
THE MIDWICH CUCKOOS (John Wyndham)
THE MILL ON THE FLOSS (George Eliot)
THE WAR OF THE WORLDS (H G Wells)
THE WINGS OF THE DOVE (Henry James)
WIVES AND DAUGHTERS (Mrs Gaskell)

18
A HIGH WIND IN JAMAICA (Richard Hughes)
ANNA OF THE FIVE TOWNS (Arnold Bennett)
CRIME AND PUNISHMENT (Fyodor Dostoevsky)
NINETEEN EIGHTY-FOUR (George Orwell)
SWALLOWS AND AMAZONS (Arthur Ransome)
THE CATCHER IN THE RYE (J D Salinger)
THE MOON AND SIXPENCE (W Somerset Maugham)
THE OLD MAN AND THE SEA (Ernest Hemingway)
THE PRISONER OF ZENDA (Anthony Hope)
THE THIRTY-NINE STEPS (John Buchan)
THE THREE MUSKETEERS (Alexandre Dumas)

19
BRIDESHEAD REVISITED (Evelyn Waugh)
FOR WHOM THE BELL TOLLS (Ernest Hemingway)
SENSE AND SENSIBILITY (Jane Austen)
THE DAY OF THE TRIFFIDS (John Wyndham)
THE GULAG ARCHIPELAGO (Alexander Solzhenitsyn)
THE HISTORY OF MR POLLY (H G Wells)
THE MAN IN THE IRON MASK (Alexandre Dumas)
THE OLD CURIOSITY SHOP (Charles Dickens)
THE PILGRIM'S PROGRESS (John Bunyan)
THE RIDDLE OF THE SANDS (Erskine Childers)
THE SCARLET PIMPERNEL (Baroness Orczy)
THE SCREWTAPE LETTERS (C S Lewis)
THE VICAR OF WAKEFIELD (Oliver Goldsmith)
THE WIND IN THE WILLOWS (Kenneth Grahame)
TOM BROWN'S SCHOOLDAYS (Thomas Hughes)

20+
A CONNECTICUT YANKEE IN KING ARTHUR'S COURT (Mark Twain)
A DANCE TO THE MUSIC OF TIME (Anthony Powell)
AS I WALKED OUT ONE MIDSUMMER MORNING (Laurie Lee)
CHILDREN OF THE NEW FOREST (Captain Marryat)
FAR FROM THE MADDING CROWD (Thomas Hardy)
JOHN HALIFAX, GENTLEMAN (Mrs Craik)
KEEP THE ASPIDISTRA FLYING (George Orwell)
LADY CHATTERLEY'S LOVER (D H Lawrence)
LARK RISE TO CANDLEFORD (Flora Thompson)
LITTLE LORD FAUNTLEROY (Frances Hodgson Burnett)
MURDER ON THE ORIENT EXPRESS (Agatha Christie)
OUT OF THE SILENT PLANET (C S Lewis)
AROUND THE WORLD IN EIGHTY DAYS (Jules Verne)

20+—continued

TESS OF THE D'URBERVILLES (Thomas Hardy)

THE ADVENTURES OF HUCKLEBERRY FINN (Mark Twain)

THE ADVENTURES OF TOM SAWYER (Mark Twain)

THE BEAUTIFUL AND DAMNED (F Scott Fitzgerald)

THE BRIDE OF LAMMERMOOR (Walter Scott)

THE BROTHERS KARAMAZOV (Fyodor Mikhailovich Dostoevsky)

THE CRICKET ON THE HEARTH (Charles Dickens)

THE FRENCH LIEUTENANT'S WOMAN (John Fowles)

THE HEART OF MIDLOTHIAN (Walter Scott)

THE HISTORY OF HENRY ESMOND (William Makepeace Thackeray)

THE HONOURABLE SCHOOLBOY (John Le Carré)

THE INNOCENCE OF FATHER BROWN (G K Chesterton)

THE ISLAND OF DOCTOR MOREAU (H G Wells)

20+—continued

THE LAST OF THE MOHICANS (James Fenimore Cooper)

THE MEMOIRS OF SHERLOCK HOLMES (Arthur Conan Doyle)

THE MYSTERIES OF UDOLPHO (Mrs Radcliffe)

THE MYSTERIOUS AFFAIR AT STYLES (Agatha Christie)

THE MYSTERY OF EDWIN DROOD (Charles Dickens)

THE PICTURE OF DORIAN GRAY (Oscar Wilde)

THE PRIME OF MISS JEAN BRODIE (Muriel Spark)

THE RED BADGE OF COURAGE (Stephen Crane)

THE RETURN OF THE NATIVE (Thomas Hardy)

THE TENANT OF WILDFELL HALL (Anne Brontë)

TINKER, TAILOR, SOLDIER, SPY (John Le Carré)

TWENTY THOUSAND LEAGUES UNDER THE SEA (Jules Verne)

TWO YEARS BEFORE THE MAST (Richard Henry Dana)

UNDER THE GREENWOOD TREE (Thomas Hardy)

PLAY TITLES

TITLE (Playwright)

4

LOOT (Joe Orton)

ROSS (Terence Rattigan)

5

CASTE (T W Robertson)

FAUST (Goethe)

MEDEA (Euripides)

ROOTS (Arnold Wesker)

6

GHOSTS (Henrik Ibsen)

HAMLET (William Shakespeare)

HENRY V (William Shakespeare)

PHÈDRE (Jean Racine)

PLENTY (David Hare)

STRIFE (John Galsworthy)

7

AMADEUS (Peter Shaffer)

ATHALIE (Jean Racine)

CANDIDA (G B Shaw)

ELECTRA (Sophocles)

GALILEO (Bertolt Brecht)

HENRY IV (William Shakespeare)

7—continued

HENRY VI (William Shakespeare)

JUMPERS (Tom Stoppard)

MACBETH (William Shakespeare)

OTHELLO (William Shakespeare)

THE LARK (Jean Anouilh)

THE ROOM (Harold Pinter)

VOLPONE (Ben Jonson)

8

ANTIGONE (Sophocles)

HAY FEVER (Noël Coward)

KING JOHN (William Shakespeare)

KING LEAR (William Shakespeare)

PERICLES (William Shakespeare)

PETER PAN (J M Barrie)

TARTUFFE (Molière)

THE BIRDS (Aristophanes)

THE FROGS (Aristophanes)

THE MISER (Molière)

9

ALL MY SONS (Arthur Miller)

9—continued

BILLY LIAR (Willis Hall and Keith Waterhouse)

CAVALCADE (Noël Coward)

CYMBELINE (William Shakespeare)

DR FAUSTUS (Christopher Marlowe)

FLARE PATH (Terence Rattigan)

GOLDEN BOY (Clifford Odets)

HAPPY DAYS (Samuel Beckett)

HENRY VIII (William Shakespeare)

PYGMALION (G B Shaw)

RICHARD II (William Shakespeare)

SAINT JOAN (G B Shaw)

THE CIRCLE (W Somerset Maugham)

THE CRITIC (Sheridan)

THE DEVILS (John Whiting)

THE RIVALS (Sheridan)

10

ALL FOR LOVE (John Dryden)

ANDROMAQUE (Jean Racine)

AURENG-ZEBE (John Dryden)

10–continued
CORIOLANUS (William Shakespeare)
I AM A CAMERA (John Van Druten)
OEDIPUS REX (Sophocles)
RICHARD III (William Shakespeare)
THE BACCHAE (Euripides)
THE BALCONY (Jean Genet)
THE HOSTAGE (Brendan Behan)
THE SEAGULL (Anton Chekhov)
THE TEMPEST (William Shakespeare)
UNCLE VANYA (Anton Chekhov)

11
A DOLL'S HOUSE (Henrik Ibsen)
AS YOU LIKE IT (William Shakespeare)
JOURNEY'S END (R C Sherriff)
LOVE FOR LOVE (William Congreve)
PANDORA'S BOX (Frank Wedekind)
ROOKERY NOOK (Ben Travers)
THE BANKRUPT (Alexander Ostrovsky)
THE CONTRAST (Royall Tyler)
THE CRUCIBLE (Arthur Miller)
THE WILD DUCK (Henrik Ibsen)

12
AFTER THE FALL (Arthur Miller)
ANNA CHRISTIE (Eugene O'Neill)
BEDROOM FARCE (Alan Ayckbourn)
BLITHE SPIRIT (Noël Coward)
BLOOD WEDDING (García Lorca)
CHARLEY'S AUNT (Brandon Thomas)
DUEL OF ANGELS (Jean Giraudoux)
JULIUS CAESAR (William Shakespeare)
MAJOR BARBARA (G B Shaw)
PRIVATE LIVES (Noël Coward)
THE ALCHEMIST (Ben Jonson)
THE ANATOMIST (James Bridie)
THE APPLE CART (G B Shaw)
THE BROKEN JUG (Heinrich von Kleist)
THE CARETAKER (Harold Pinter)
THE MOUSETRAP (Agatha Christie)
THREE SISTERS (Anton Chekhov)
TWELFTH NIGHT (William Shakespeare)

13
ARMS AND THE MAN (G B Shaw)
A TASTE OF HONEY (Shelagh Delaney)
HOBSON'S CHOICE (Harold Brighouse)
LE MISANTHROPE (Molière)
QUALITY STREET (J M Barrie)
THE ACHARNIANS (Aristophanes)
THE DUMB WAITER (Harold Pinter)
THE JEW OF MALTA (Christopher Marlowe)
THE LINDEN TREE (J B Priestley)
THE MAGISTRATE (Pinero)
THE MATCHMAKER (Thornton Wilder)
THE WHITE DEVIL (John Webster)
THE WINSLOW BOY (Terence Rattigan)
TIMON OF ATHENS (William Shakespeare)
UNDER MILK WOOD (Dylan Thomas)

14
AN IDEAL HUSBAND (Oscar Wilde)
MAN AND SUPERMAN (G B Shaw)

14–continued
ROMEO AND JULIET (William Shakespeare)
SEPARATE TABLES (Terence Rattigan)
THE CORN IS GREEN (Emlyn Williams)
THE COUNTRY GIRL (Clifford Odets)
THE DEEP BLUE SEA (Terence Rattigan)
THE FIRE-RAISERS (Max Frisch)
THE GHOST SONATA (August Strindberg)
THE OLD BACHELOR (William Congreve)
THE PHILANDERER (G B Shaw)
THE TROJAN WOMEN (Euripides)
THE WINTER'S TALE (William Shakespeare)
THIS HAPPY BREED (Noël Coward)

15
BARTHOLOMEW FAIR (Ben Jonson)
DANGEROUS CORNER (J B Priestley)
DESIGN FOR LIVING (Noël Coward)
HEARTBREAK HOUSE (G B Shaw)
LOOK BACK IN ANGER (John Osborne)
MARRIAGE À LA MODE (John Dryden)
PRESENT LAUGHTER (Noël Coward)
THE CONSTANT WIFE (W Somerset Maugham)
THE ICEMAN COMETH (Eugene O'Neill)
TITUS ANDRONICUS (William Shakespeare)
TWO NOBLE KINSMEN (William Shakespeare)
VENICE PRESERVED (Thomas Otway)
WAITING FOR GODOT (Samuel Beckett)

16
A CUCKOO IN THE NEST (Ben Travers)
AN INSPECTOR CALLS (J B Priestley)
CAT ON A HOT TIN ROOF (Tennessee Williams)
DEATH OF A SALESMAN (Arthur Miller)
LOVE'S LABOUR'S LOST (William
    Shakespeare)
PILLARS OF SOCIETY (Henrik Ibsen)
RING ROUND THE MOON (Jean Anouilh)
THE ADDING MACHINE (Elmer Rice)
THE AMERICAN DREAM (Edward Albee)
THE BIRTHDAY PARTY (Harold Pinter)
THE CHERRY ORCHARD (Anton Chekhov)
THE COCKTAIL PARTY (T S Eliot)
THE FAMILY REUNION (T S Eliot)
THE MASTER BUILDER (Henrik Ibsen)
WHAT THE BUTLER SAW (Joe Orton)

17
A MAN FOR ALL SEASONS (Robert Bolt)
AN ITALIAN STRAW HAT (Eugène Labiche)
ARSENIC AND OLD LACE (Joseph Kesselring)
BAREFOOT IN THE PARK (Neil Simon)
JUNO AND THE PAYCOCK (Sean O'Casey)
MEASURE FOR MEASURE (William
    Shakespeare)
ROMANOFF AND JULIET (Peter Ustinov)
THE BEAUX' STRATAGEM (George Farquhar)
THE COMEDY OF ERRORS (William
    Shakespeare)
THE DEVIL'S DISCIPLE (G B Shaw)
THE DOCTOR'S DILEMMA (G B Shaw)
THE DUCHESS OF MALFI (John Webster)
THE GLASS MENAGERIE (Tennessee Williams)

17–continued
THE GOOD-NATURED MAN (Oliver Goldsmith)
THE SCHOOL FOR WIVES (Molière)
THE SUPPLIANT WOMEN (Aeschylus)
'TIS PITY SHE'S A WHORE (John Ford)

18
AN ENEMY OF THE PEOPLE (Henrik Ibsen)
ANTONY AND CLEOPATRA (William Shakespeare)
CAESAR AND CLEOPATRA (G B Shaw)
FIVE FINGER EXERCISE (Peter Shaffer)
FRENCH WITHOUT TEARS (Terence Rattigan)
LADY WINDERMERE'S FAN (Oscar Wilde)
SHE STOOPS TO CONQUER (Oliver Goldsmith)
SUDDENLY LAST SUMMER (Tennessee Williams)
THE BROWNING VERSION (Terence Rattigan)
THE ROMANS IN BRITAIN (Howard Brenton)
TROILUS AND CRESSIDA (William Shakespeare)

19
ANDROCLES AND THE LION (G B Shaw)
CHIPS WITH EVERYTHING (Arnold Wesker)
MUCH ADO ABOUT NOTHING (William Shakespeare)
TAMBURLAINE THE GREAT (Christopher Marlowe)
THE MERCHANT OF VENICE (William Shakespeare)
THE SCHOOL FOR SCANDAL (Sheridan)
THE TAMING OF THE SHREW (William Shakespeare)
WHAT EVERY WOMAN KNOWS (J M Barrie)

20+
ACCIDENTAL DEATH OF AN ANARCHIST (Dario Fo)

20+–continued
ALL GOD'S CHILLUN GOT WINGS (Eugene O'Neill)
ALL'S WELL THAT ENDS WELL (William Shakespeare)
A MIDSUMMER NIGHT'S DREAM (William Shakespeare)
A STREETCAR NAMED DESIRE (Tennessee Williams)
A WOMAN OF NO IMPORTANCE (Oscar Wilde)
CAPTAIN BRASSBOUND'S CONVERSION (G B Shaw)
ENTERTAINING MR SLOANE (Joe Orton)
INADMISSIBLE EVIDENCE (John Osborne)
MOURNING BECOMES ELECTRA (Eugene O'Neill)
MURDER IN THE CATHEDRAL (T S Eliot)
ROSENCRANTZ AND GUILDENSTERN ARE DEAD (Tom Stoppard)
THE ADMIRABLE CRICHTON (J M Barrie)
THE BARRETTS OF WIMPOLE STREET (Rudolf Besier)
THE CAUCASIAN CHALK CIRCLE (Bertolt Brecht)
THE GOVERNMENT INSPECTOR (Nikolai Gogol)
THE IMPORTANCE OF BEING EARNEST (Oscar Wilde)
THE LADY'S NOT FOR BURNING (Christopher Fry)
THE MERRY WIVES OF WINDSOR (William Shakespeare)
THE SECOND MRS TANQUERAY (Pinero)
THE TWO GENTLEMEN OF VERONA (William Shakespeare)
WHO'S AFRAID OF VIRGINIA WOOLF? (Edward Albee)

FICTIONAL CHARACTERS

CHARACTER (*Title*, Author)

3
FOX, Brer (*Uncle Remus*, J C Harris)
GOG (*The Tower of London*, W H Ainsworth)
HUR, Judah (*Ben Hur*, L Wallace)
JIM, 'Lord' (*Lord Jim*, J Conrad)
KIM (*Kim*, Rudyard Kipling)
LEE, General Robert E (*Abraham Lincoln*, J Drinkwater)
LEE, Lorelei (*Gentlemen Prefer Blondes*, Anita Loos)
OWL (*Winnie the Pooh*, A A Milne)
ROO (*Winnie the Pooh*, A A Milne)
TOM (*The Water Babies*, C Kingsley)

3–continued
TOM, 'Uncle' (*Uncle Tom's Cabin*, Harriet B Stowe)

4
ABEL (*Middlemarch*, George Eliot)
CASS, Eppie (*Silas Marner*, George Eliot)
CASY, Rev Jim (*The Grapes of Wrath*, J Steinbeck)
CUFF, Sergeant (*The Moonstone*, W Collins)
DEAN, Ellen (*Wuthering Heights*, Emily Brontë)
EAST (*Tom Brown's Schooldays*, T Hughes)
EASY, John (*Mr Midshipman Easy*, Captain Marryat)
EYRE, Jane (*Jane Eyre*, Charlotte Brontë)
FAWN, Lord Frederic (*Phineas Finn*, A Trollope)

4–continued

FELL, Dr Gideon (*The Black Spectacles*, J Dickson Carr)

FINN, Huckleberry (*Huckleberry Finn*, *Tom Sawyer*, M Twain)

FINN, Phineas (*Phineas Finn*, A Trollope)

GRAY, Dorian (*The Picture of Dorian Gray*, Oscar Wilde)

GRAY, Nelly (*Faithless Nelly Gray*, T Hood)

GUNN, Ben (*Treasure Island*, R L Stevenson)

HOOK, Captain James (*Peter Pan*, J M Barrie)

HYDE, Edward (*Dr Jekyll and Mr Hyde*, R L Stevenson)

JUDY (*Wee Willie Winkie*, R Kipling)

LAMB, Leonard (*Middlemarch*, George Eliot)

MOLE, Mr (*The Wind in the Willows*, K Grahame)

NANA (*Peter Pan*, J M Barrie)

NASH, Richard (Beau) (*Monsieur Beaucaire*, Booth Tarkington)

PUCK (Robin Goodfellow) (*Puck of Pook's Hill*, R Kipling)

RAMA (Tiger Tiger) (*The Jungle Book*, R Kipling)

REED, Mrs (*Jane Eyre*, Charlotte Brontë)

RIDD, John (*Lorna Doone*, R D Blackmore)

SEAL, Basil (*Put Out More Flags*, E Waugh)

SMEE (*Peter Pan*, J M Barrie)

TOAD, Mr (*The Wind in the Willows*, K Grahame)

TROY, Sergeant Francis (*Far from the Madding Crowd*, T Hardy)

VANE, Harriet (*Strong Poison*, Dorothy L Sayers)

VANE, Lady Isabel (*East Lynne*, Mrs Henry Wood)

WOLF, 'Brer' (*Uncle Remus*, J C Harris)

5

ADLER, Irene (*The Adventures of Sherlock Holmes*, A Conan Doyle)

AKELA (*The Jungle Book*, R Kipling)

ALIBI, Tom (*Waverley*, W Scott)

ATHOS (*The Three Musketeers*, Alexandre Dumas)

BALOO (*The Jungle Book*, R Kipling)

BLAKE, Franklin (*The Moonstone*, W Collins)

BONES, Captain Billy (*Treasure Island*, R L Stevenson)

BOOBY, Sir Thomas (*Joseph Andrews*, H Fielding)

BRUFF (*The Moonstone*, W Collins)

BULBO, Prince (*The Rose and the Ring*, W M Thackeray)

CHANT, Mercy (*Tess of the D'Urbervilles*, T Hardy)

CLACK, Drusilla (*The Moonstone*, W Collins)

CLARE, Angel (*Tess of the D'Urbervilles*, T Hardy)

DARCY, Fitzwilliam (*Pride and Prejudice*, Jane Austen)

DEANS, Effie/Jeanie (*The Heart of Midlothian*, W Scott)

DIXON, James (*Lucky Jim*, K Amis)

DOONE, Lorna (*Lorna Doone*, R D Blackmore)

5–continued

EAGER, Rev Cuthbert (*Room with a View*, E M Forster)

FANNY (*Fanny's First Play*, G B Shaw)

FLYNN, Father James (*The Dubliners*, J Joyce)

GESTE, Beau (*Beau Geste*, P C Wren)

GWYNN, Nell (*Simon Dale*, A Hope)

HANDS, Israel (*Treasure Island*, R L Stevenson)

HATCH, Bennet (*The Black Arrow*, R L Stevenson)

JONES, Tom (*Tom Jones*, H Fielding)

KANGA (*Winnie the Pooh*, A A Milne)

KIPPS, Arthur (*Kipps*, H G Wells)

LEIGH, Captain Sir Amyas (*Westward Ho!*, C Kingsley)

MAGOG (*The Tower of London*, W H Ainsworth)

MARCH, Amy/Beth/Josephine (Jo)/Meg (*Little Women*, etc, Louisa M Alcott)

MERCY (*Pilgrim's Progress*, J Bunyan)

MITTY, Walter (*The Secret Life of Walter Mitty*, J Thurber)

MOORE, Mrs (*A Passage to India*, E M Forster)

O'HARA, Kimball (*Kim*, Rudyard Kipling)

O'HARA, Scarlett (*Gone with the Wind*, Margaret Mitchell)

OTTER, Mr (*The Wind in the Willows*, K Grahame)

PAGET, Jean (*A Town like Alice*, N Shute)

POLLY, Alfred (*The History of Mr Polly*, H G Wells)

POOLE, Grace (*Jane Eyre*, Charlotte Brontë)

PORGY (*Porgy*, Du Bose Heyward)

PRISM, Miss Laetitia (*The Importance of Being Earnest*, Oscar Wilde)

PUNCH (*Wee Willie Winkie*, R Kipling)

READY, Masterman (*Masterman Ready*, F Marryat)

REMUS, Uncle (*Uncle Remus* series, J C Harris)

RYDER, Charles (*Brideshead Revisited*, E Waugh)

SALLY (*Sally in Our Alley*, H Carey)

SAMBO (*Just So Stories*, R Kipling)

SHARP, Rebecca (Becky) (*Vanity Fair*, W M Thackeray)

SLOPE, Rev Obadiah (*Barchester Towers*, A Trollope)

SLOTH (*Pilgrim's Progress*, J Bunyan)

SMITH, Winston (*1984*, G Orwell)

SNOWE, Lucy (*Villette*, Charlotte Brontë)

TARKA (*Tarka the Otter*, H Williamson)

THUMB, Tom (*The Tale of Two Bad Mice*, Beatrix Potter)

TOPSY (*Uncle Tom's Cabin*, Harriet B Stowe)

UNCAS (*The Last of the Mohicans*, J Fennimore Cooper)

6

AITKEN (*Prester John*, J Buchan)

ARAMIS (*The Three Musketeers*, Alexandre Dumas)

AYESHA (*She*, H Rider Haggard)

6–continued

BENNET, Catherine/Elizabeth/Jane/Lydia/Mary (*Pride and Prejudice*, Jane Austen)

BESSIE (*Jane Eyre*, Charlotte Brontë)

BINKIE, Lady Grizzel (*Vanity Fair*, W M Thackeray)

BOVARY, Emma (*Madame Bovary*, G Flaubert)

BUTLER, Rhett (*Gone with the Wind*, Margaret Mitchell)

CACKLE (*Vanity Fair*, W M Thackeray)

CARDEW, Cecily (*The Importance of Being Earnest*, Oscar Wilde)

CRUSOE, Robinson (*Robinson Crusoe*, D Defoe)

DANGLE (*The Critic*, R B Sheridan)

EEYORE (*Winnie the Pooh*, A A Milne)

ELAINE (*Idylls of the King*, Lord Tennyson)

'FRIDAY' (*Robinson Crusoe*, D Defoe)

FRITHA (*The Snow Goose*, P Gallico)

GARTER, Polly (*Under Milk Wood*, D Thomas)

GATSBY, Major Jay (*The Great Gatsby*, F Scott Fitzgerald)

GEORGE (*Three Men in a Boat*, J K Jerome)

GERARD, Etienne (*The Exploits of Brigadier Gerard*, A Conan Doyle)

GILPIN, John (*John Gilpin*, W Cowper)

GLOVER, Catherine (*The Fair Maid of Perth*, W Scott)

GORDON, Squire (*Black Beauty*, A Sewell)

GRIMES (*The Water Babies*, C Kingsley)

HANNAY, Richard (*The Thirty-Nine Steps*, J Buchan)

HARKER, Jonathan/Minna (*Dracula*, Bram Stoker)

HARMAN, Joe (*A Town like Alice*, N Shute)

HAROLD, Childe (*Childe Harold's Pilgrimage*, Lord Byron)

HEARTS, King of/Knave of/Queen of (*Alice in Wonderland*, L Carroll)

HOLMES, Mycroft (*The Return of Sherlock Holmes*, A Conan Doyle)

HOLMES, Sherlock (*A Study in Scarlet, The Sign of Four, The Hound of the Baskervilles*, etc, A Conan Doyle)

HOOPER, Fanny (*Fanny by Gaslight*, M Sadleir)

JEEVES (*Thank you, Jeeves*, P G Wodehouse)

JEKYLL, Henry (*Dr Jekyll and Mr Hyde*, R L Stevenson)

LAURIE (*Little Women*, Louisa M Alcott)

LAURIE, Annie (*Annie Laurie*, Douglass)

LEGREE, Simon (*Uncle Tom's Cabin*, Harriet B Stowe)

LINTON, Edgar (*Wuthering Heights*, Emily Brontë)

MANGAN, Boss (*Heartbreak House*, G B Shaw)

MANSON, Dr Andrew (*The Citadel*, A J Cronin)

MARPLE, Jane (*A Pocket Full of Rye*, Agatha Christie)

MERLIN (*Idylls of the King*, Lord Tennyson)

MODRED, Sir (*Idylls of the King*, Lord Tennyson)

MOREAU, André-Louis (*Scaramouche*, R Sabatini)

6–continued

MOREAU, Dr (*The Island of Dr Moreau*, H G Wells)

MORGAN, Angharad/Huw (*How Green Was My Valley*, R Llewellyn)

MORGAN, Organ (*Under Milk Wood*, D Thomas)

MOWGLI (*The Jungle Book*, R Kipling)

NUTKIN, Squirrel, (*The Tale of Squirrel Nutkin*, Beatrix Potter)

OMNIUM, Duke of (Family name Palliser) (*The Barsetshire series*, Angela Thirkell)

PICKLE, Peregrine (*Peregrine Pickle*, T Smollett)

PIGLET, Henry Pootel (*Winnie the Pooh*, A A Milne)

POIROT, Hercule (*The Mysterious Affair at Styles*, Agatha Christie)

RABBIT (*Winnie the Pooh*, A A Milne)

RABBIT, 'Brer' (*Uncle Remus*, J C Harris)

RABBIT, The White (*Alice in Wonderland*, L Carroll)

RIVERS, St John (*Jane Eyre*, Charlotte Brontë)

RUSTUM (*Sohrab and Rustum*, M Arnold)

SAWYER, Tom (*The Adventures of Tom Sawyer*, M Twain)

SHANDY, Tristram (*Tristram Shandy*, L Sterne)

SILVER, Long John (*Treasure Island*, R L Stevenson)

SIMNEL, Lambert (*Perkin Warbeck*, John Ford)

SOHRAB (*Sohrab and Rustum*, M Arnold)

TEMPLE, Miss (*Jane Eyre*, Charlotte Brontë)

THORNE, Dr Thomas (*Doctor Thorne*, A Trollope)

THORPE, Isabella (*Northanger Abbey*, Jane Austen)

TILNEY, Henry (*Northanger Abbey*, Jane Austen)

TURNER, Jim (Captain Flint) (*Swallows and Amazons*, A Ransome)

UMPOPA (*King Solomon's Mines*, H Rider Haggard)

WALKER, John/Roger/Susan/Titty/Vicky (*Swallows and Amazons*, A Ransome)

WESTON, Mrs (*Emma*, Jane Austen)

WILKES, Ashley/India (*Gone with the Wind*, Margaret Mitchell)

WIMSEY, Lord Peter Death Bredon (*Whose Body?*, Dorothy L Sayers)

7

AISGILL, Alice (*Room at the Top*, J Braine)

BAGSTER (*Middlemarch*, George Eliot)

BEESLEY (*Lucky Jim*, Kingsley Amis)

BINGLEY, Charles (*Pride and Prejudice*, Jane Austen)

BRANDON, Colonel (*Sense and Sensibility*, Jane Austen)

CANDOUR, Mrs (*The School for Scandal*, R B Sheridan)

CHESNEY, Jack (*Charley's Aunt,* Brandon Thomas)

COLLINS, Rev William (*Pride and Prejudice*, Jane Austen)

CYPRESS, Mr (*Nightmare Abbey*, T L Peacock)

7—continued

DANVERS, Mrs (*Rebecca*, Daphne du Maurier)
DESPAIR, Giant (*Pilgrim's Progress*, J Bunyan)
DRACULA, Count (*Dracula*, Bram Stoker)
EPICENE (*Epicene*, B Jonson)
FAIRFAX, Gwendolen (*The Importance of Being Earnest*, Oscar Wilde)
FAIRFAX, Jane (*Emma*, J Austen)
FAIRFAX, Mrs (*Jane Eyre*, Charlotte Brontë)
FAIRLIE, Frederick (*Woman in White*, W Collins)
FAUSTUS (*The History of Dr Faustus*, C Marlowe)
FORSYTE, Fleur/Irene/Jolyon/Jon/Soames (*The Forsyte Saga*, J Galsworthy)
GALAHAD (*Idylls of the King*, Lord Tennyson)
GERAINT (*Idylls of the King*, Lord Tennyson)
GRANTLY, Bishop of Barchester (*The Warden, Barchester Towers*, A Trollope)
HAWKINS, Jim (*Treasure Island*, R L Stevenson)
HENTZAU, Rupert of (*The Prisoner of Zenda*, A Hope)
HERRIES, Francis (*Rogue Herries*, H Walpole)
HIGGINS, Henry (*Pygmalion*, G B Shaw)
IVANHOE, Wilfred, Knight of (*Ivanhoe*, W Scott)
JENKINS, Rev Eli (*Under Milk Wood*, D Thomas)
KEELDAR, Shirley (*Shirley*, Charlotte Brontë)
LAMPTON, Joe (*Room at the Top*, J Braine)
LATIMER, Darsie (*Redgauntlet*, W Scott)
LAWLESS (*The Black Arrow*, R L Stevenson)
LINCOLN, Abraham (*Abraham Lincoln*, J Drinkwater)
LUCIFER (*Faustus*, C Marlowe)
MARKHAM, Gilbert (*The Tenant of Wildfell Hall*, Anne Brontë)
MESSALA (*Ben Hur*, L Wallace)
MICHAEL, Duke of Strelsau (*The Prisoner of Zenda*, A Hope)
MINIVER, Mrs Caroline (*Mrs Miniver*, Jan Struther)
MORLAND, Catherine (*Northanger Abbey*, Jane Austen)
NOKOMIS (*Song of Hiawatha*, H W Longfellow)
PORTHOS (*The Three Musketeers*, Alexandre Dumas)
PROUDIE, Dr/Mrs (*Framley Parsonage*, A Trollope)
RAFFLES, A J (*Raffles* series, E W Hornung)
RANDALL, Rebecca (*Rebecca of Sunnybrook Farm*, Kate D Wiggin)
RATTLER, Martin (*Martin Hattler*, R M Ballantyne)
REBECCA (*Rebecca*, Daphne du Maurier)
REBECCA (*Rebecca of Sunnybrook Farm*, Kate D Wiggin)
RED KING (*Alice Through the Looking Glass*, L Carroll)
ROBSART, Amy (*Kenilworth*, W Scott)
SANDERS (Sandi) (*Sanders of the River*, E Wallace)

7—continued

SHELTON, Richard (*The Black Arrow*, R L Stevenson)
SHIPTON, Mother (*The Luck of Roaring Camp*, Bret Harte)
SMOLLET, Captain (*Treasure Island*, R L Stevenson)
SORRELL, Christopher (Kit) (*Sorrell and Son*, W Deeping)
ST CLARE, Evangeline (Little Eva) (*Uncle Tom's Cabin*, Harriet B Stowe)
TIDDLER, Tom (*Adam's Opera*, Clemence Dane)
WARBECK, Perkin (*Perkin Warbeck*, John Ford)
WESTERN, Mrs/Sophia/Squire, (*Tom Jones*, H Fielding)
WILLIAM (*Just William*, Richmal Crompton)
WINSLOW, Ronnie (*The Winslow Boy*, T Rattigan)
WOOSTER, Bertie (*Thank You, Jeeves*, P G Wodehouse)

8

ABSOLUTE, Sir Anthony (*The Rivals*, R B Sheridan)
ANGELICA (*The Rose and the Ring*, W M Thackeray)
APOLLYON (*Pilgrim's Progress*, J Bunyan)
ARMITAGE, Jacob (*The Children of the New Forest*, Captain Marryat)
BACKBITE, Sir Benjamin (*The School for Scandal*, R B Sheridan)
BAGHEERA (*The Jungle Book*, R Kipling)
BLACK DOG (*Treasure Island*, R L Stevenson)
CARRAWAY, Nick (*The Great Gatsby*, F Scott Fitzgerald)
CASAUBON, Rev Edward, (*Middlemarch*, George Eliot)
CRAWFURD, David (*Prester John*, J Buchan)
CRICHTON, Bill (*The Admirable Crichton*, J M Barrie)
DASHWOOD, Henry (*Sense and Sensibility*, Jane Austen)
DE BOURGH, Lady Catherine (*Pride and Prejudice*, Jane Austen)
DE WINTER, Maximilian (*Rebecca*, Daphne du Maurier)
EARNSHAW, Catherine (*Wuthering Heights*, Emily Brontë)
EVERDENE, Bathsheba (*Far from the Madding Crowd*, T Hardy)
FFOULKES, Sir Andrew (*The Scarlet Pimpernel*, Baroness Orczy)
FLANDERS, Moll (*Moll Flanders*, D Defoe)
FLASHMAN (*Tom Brown's Schooldays*, T Hughes)
GLORIANA (*The Faërie Queen*, E Spenser)
GOLLANTZ, Emmanuel (*Young Emmanuel*, N Jacob)
GULLIVER, Lemuel (*Gulliver's Travels*, J Swift)
GUNGA DIN (*Barrack-room Ballads*, R Kipling)
HIAWATHA (*The Song of Hiawatha*, H W Longfellow)

8–continued

KNIGHTLY, George (*Emma*, J Austen)

LANCELOT, Sir (*Idylls of the King*, Lord Tennyson)

LANGUISH, Lydia (*The Rivals*, R B Sheridan)

LAURENCE, Theodore (*Little Women*, Louisa M Alcott)

LESSWAYS, Hilda (*The Clayhanger Trilogy*, Arnold Bennett)

LESTRADE, of Scotland Yard (*A Study in Scarlet*, A Conan Doyle)

LOCKWOOD (*Wuthering Heights*, Emily Brontë)

MACAVITY (*Old Possum's Book of Practical Cats*, T S Eliot)

MALAPROP, Mrs (*The Rivals*, R B Sheridan)

MARY JANE (*When We Were Very Young*, A A Milne)

MORIARTY, Professor James (*Memoirs of Sherlock Holmes*, A Conan Doyle)

O'FERRALL, Trilby (*Trilby*, George du Maurier)

OLIFAUNT, Nigel (*The Fortunes of Nigel*, W Scott)

O'TRIGGER, Sir Lucius (*The Rivals*, R B Sheridan)

PALLISER, Lady Glencora/Plantagenet (*Phineas Finn*, A Trollope)

PRIMROSE, Dr Charles (*The Vicar of Wakefield*, O Goldsmith)

QUANTOCK, Mrs Daisy (*Queen Lucia*, E F Benson)

RED QUEEN (*Alice Through the Looking Glass*, L Carroll)

SHOTOVER, Captain (*Heartbreak House*, G B Shaw)

ST BUNGAY, Duke of (*Phineas Finn*, A Trollope)

SVENGALI (*Trilby*, George du Maurier)

THATCHER, Becky (*The Adventures of Tom Sawyer*, M Twain)

TRISTRAM (*Idylls of the King*, Lord Tennyson)

TULLIVER, Maggie/Tom (*The Mill on the Floss*, George Eliot)

VERINDER, Lady Julia (*The Moonstone*, W Collins)

WATER RAT (Ratty) (*The Wind in the Willows*, K Grahame)

WAVERLEY, Edward (*Waverley*, W Scott)

WHITEOAK (family) (*The Whiteoak Chronicles*, Mazo de la Roche)

WHITE-TIP (*Tarka the Otter*, Henry Williamson)

WHITTIER, Pollyanna (*Pollyanna*, Eleanor H Porter)

WILLIAMS, Percival William (*Wee Willie Winkie*, R Kipling)

WORTHING, John (*The Importance of Being Earnest*, Oscar Wilde)

9

ABBEVILLE, Horace (*Cannery Row*, J Steinbeck)

ABLEWHITE, Godfrey (*The Moonstone*, W Collins)

ALLWORTHY, Squire (*Tom Jones*, H Fielding)

9–continued

BABBERLEY, Lord Fancourt (*Charley's Aunt*, Brandon Thomas)

BARRYMORE (*The Hound of the Baskervilles*, A Conan Doyle)

BRACKNELL, Lady (*The Importance of Being Earnest*, Oscar Wilde)

BULSTRODE, Nicholas (*Middlemarch*, George Eliot)

CHAINMAIL (*Crotchet Castle*, T L Peacock)

CHRISTIAN (*Pilgrim's Progress*, J Bunyan)

CHURCHILL, Frank (*Emma*, Jane Austen)

D'ARTAGNAN (*The Three Musketeers*, Alexandre Dumas)

DOOLITTLE, Eliza (*Pygmalion*, G B Shaw)

GREYSTOKE, Lord (*Tarzan* series, E R Burroughs)

GUINEVERE (*Idylls of the King*, Lord Tennyson)

INDIAN JOE (*The Adventures of Tom Sawyer*, M Twain)

LEICESTER, Earl of (*Kenilworth*, W Scott)

MACGREGOR, Robin (*Rob Roy*, W Scott)

MARCH HARE, The (*Alice in Wonderland*, L Carroll)

MARCHMAIN, Lady Cordelia/Lady Julia/Lord Sebastian/ Marquis of/Teresa/The Earl of Brideshead (*Brideshead Revisited*, E Waugh)

MEHITABEL, the cat (*Archy and Mehitabel*, D Marquis)

MERRILIES, Meg (*Guy Mannering*, W Scott)

MINNEHAHA (*The Song of Hiawatha*, H W Longfellow)

MONCRIEFF, Algernon (*The Importance of Being Earnest*, Oscar Wilde)

PENDENNIS, Arthur (Pen) (*Pendennis*, W M Thackeray)

PERCIVALE (*Idylls of the King*, Lord Tennyson)

RED KNIGHT (*Alice Through the Looking Glass*, L Carroll)

ROCHESTER, Bertha/Edward Fairfax (*Jane Eyre*, Charlotte Brontë)

SHERE KHAN (Lungri) (*The Jungle Book*, R Kipling)

SOUTHDOWN, Earl of (*Vanity Fair*, W M Thackeray)

TAMERLANE (*Tamerlane*, N Rowe)

TANQUERAY, Aubrey (*The Second Mrs Tanqueray*, A W Pinero)

TIGER LILY (*Peter Pan*, J M Barrie)

TRELAWNEY, Rose (*Trelawney of the Wells*, A W Pinero)

TRELAWNEY, Squire (*Treasure Island*, R L Stevenson)

TWITCHETT, Mrs Tabitha (*The Tale of Tom Kitten*, Beatrix Potter)

VIRGINIAN, The (*The Virginian*, O Wister)

WAYNFLETE, Lady Cicely (*Captain Brassbound's Conversion*, G B Shaw)

WOODHOUSE, Emma/Isabella (*Emma*, Jane Austen)

10

ABRAMS MOSS (*Pendennis*, W M Thackeray)
ALLAN-A-DALE (*Ivanhoe*, W Scott)
ARROWPOINT (*Daniel Deronda*, George Eliot)
BELLADONNA (*Vanity Fair*, W M Thackeray)
CHALLENGER, Professor (*The Lost World*, A Conan Doyle)
CRIMSWORTH, William (*The Professor*, Charlotte Brontë)
EVANGELINE (*Evangeline*, H W Longfellow)
FAUNTLEROY, Lord Cedric Errol (*Little Lord Fauntleroy*, F H Burnett)
GOODFELLOW, Robin (*St Ronan's Well*, W Scott)
HEATHCLIFF (*Wuthering Heights*, Emily Brontë)
HORNBLOWER, Horatio (The *Hornblower* series, C S Forester)
HUNCA MUNCA (*The Tale of Two Bad Mice*, Beatrix Potter)
HUNTER-DUNN, Joan (*A Subaltern's Love Song*, J Betjeman)
JACKANAPES (*Jackanapes*, Juliana H Ewing)
LETHBRIDGE, Daphne (*The Dark Tide*, Vera Brittain)
MAN IN BLACK (*A Citizen of the World*, O Goldsmith)
MAULEVERER, Lord (*Cranford*, Mrs Gaskell)
MOCK TURTLE, THE (*Alice in Wonderland*, L Carroll)
PUDDLEDUCK, Jemima (*The Tale of Jemima Puddleduck*, Beatrix Potter)
QUATERMAIN, Allan (*King Solomon's Mines*, H Rider Haggard)
STARKADDER, Judith/Old Mrs (*Cold Comfort Farm*, Stella Gibbons)
TINKER BELL (*Peter Pan*, J M Barrie)
TWEEDLEDEE (*Alice Through the Looking-Glass*, L Carroll)
TWEEDLEDUM (*Alice Through the Looking-Glass*, L Carroll)
UNDERSHAFT, Barbara (*Major Barbara*, G B Shaw)
WILLOUGHBY, John (*Sense and Sensibility*, Jane Austen)
WINDERMERE, Lord Arthur/Margaret (*Lady Windermere's Fan*, Oscar Wilde)

11

ADDENBROOKE, Bennett (*Raffles*, E W Hornung)
DURBEYFIELD, Tess (*Tess of the D'Urbervilles*, T Hardy)
JABBERWOCKY (*Alice Through the Looking-Glass*, L Carroll)
MONTMORENCY, the dog (*Three Men in a Boat*, J K Jerome)
REDGAUNTLET, Sir Arthur Darsie (*Redgauntlet*, W Scott)
TAMBURLAINE (*Tamburlaine*, C Marlowe)
TAM O'SHANTER (*Tam O'Shanter*, R Burns)
TIGGY-WINKLE, Mrs (*The Tale of Mrs Tiggy-Winkle*, Beatrix Potter)
TITTLEMOUSE, Mrs Thomasina (*The Tale of Mrs Tittlemouse*, Beatrix Potter)

12

BROCKLEHURST (*Jane Eyre*, Charlotte Brontë)
CAPTAIN FLINT (*Swallows and Amazons*, A Ransome)
FRANKENSTEIN, Victor (*Frankenstein*, M W Shelley)
HUMPTY-DUMPTY (*Alice Through the Looking-Glass*, L Carroll)
PENNYFEATHER, Paul (*Decline and Fall*, E Waugh)

13

WINNIE-THE-POOH (Edward Bear) (*Winnie-the-Pooh*, A A Milne)

14

MEPHISTOPHELES (*Doctor Faustus*, C Marlowe)
RIKKI-TIKKI-TAVI (*The Jungle Book*, R Kipling)
SAMUEL WHISKERS (*The Tale of Samuel Whiskers*, Beatrix Potter)
WORLDLY-WISEMAN (*Pilgrim's Progress*, J Bunyan)

15

OGMORE-PRITCHARD, Mrs (*Under Milk Wood*, D Thomas)
VALIANT-FOR-TRUTH (*Pilgrim's Progress*, J Bunyan)
VIOLET ELIZABETH (*Just William*, Richmal Crompton)

DICKENSIAN CHARACTERS

CHARACTER (Novel)

2
JO (*Bleak House*)

3
AMY (*Oliver Twist*)

3—continued
BET, Betsy (*Oliver Twist*)
BUD, Rosa (*Edwin Drood*)
CLY (*A Tale of Two Cities*)
GAY, Walter (*Dombey and Son*)
JOE (*Pickwick Papers*)
TOX, Miss (*Dombey and Son*)

4
ANNE (*Dombey and Son*)
BAPS (*Dombey and Son*)
BEGS, Mrs Ridger (*David Copperfield*)
BRAY, Madeline (*Nicholas Nickleby*)

4–continued

BRAY, Walter (*Nicholas Nickleby*)
DICK, Mr (*Oliver Twist*)
DUFF (*Oliver Twist*)
FIPS, Mr (*Martin Chuzzlewit*)
FOGG (*Pickwick Papers*)
GAMP, Mrs Sarah (*Martin Chuzzlewit*)
GRIP (*Barnaby Rudge*)
HAWK, Sir Mulberry (*Nicholas Nickleby*)
HEEP, Uriah (*David Copperfield*)
HUGH (*Barnaby Rudge*)
JOWL, Mat (*The Old Curiosity Shop*)
JUPE, Cecilia (*Hard Times*)
KAGS (*Oliver Twist*)
KNAG, Miss (*Nicholas Nickleby*)
LIST, Isaac (*The Old Curiosity Shop*)
MANN, Mrs (*Oliver Twist*)
MARY (*Pickwick Papers*)
MELL, Charles (*David Copperfield*)
MIFF, Mrs (*Dombey and Son*)
OMER (*David Copperfield*)
PEAK (*Barnaby Rudge*)
PELL, Solomon (*Pickwick Papers*)
PEPS, Dr Parker (*Dombey and Son*)
POTT, Minverva (*Pickwick Papers*)
'RIAH (*Our Mutual Friend*)
RUGG, Anastasia (*Little Dorrit*)
TIGG, Montague (*Martin Chuzzlewit*)
WADE, Miss (*Little Dorrit*)
WEGG, Silas (*Our Mutual Friend*)

5

ADAMS, Jack (*Dombey and Son*)
ALLEN, Arabella/Benjamin (*Pickwick Papers*)
BATES, Charley (*Oliver Twist*)
BETSY (*Pickwick Papers*)
BRASS, Sally/Sampson (*The Old Curiosity Shop*)
BRICK, Jefferson (*Martin Chuzzlewit*)
BROWN, Alice/Mrs (*Dombey and Son*)
CASBY, Christopher (*Little Dorrit*)
CHICK, John/Louisa (*Dombey and Son*)
CLARE, Ada (*Bleak House*)

5–continued

CLARK (*Dombey and Son*)
CLIVE (*Little Dorrit*)
CROWL (*Nicholas Nickleby*)
CRUPP, Mrs (*David Copperfield*)
DAISY, Solomon (*Barnaby Rudge*)
DAVID (*Nicholas Nickleby*)
DAWES, Mary (*Dombey and Son*)
DINGO, Professor (*Bleak House*)
DIVER, Colonel (*Martin Chuzzlewit*)
DONNY, Mrs (*Bleak House*)
DOYCE, Daniel (*Little Dorrit*)
DROOD, Edwin (*Edwin Drood*)
DUMPS, Nicodemus (*Pickwick Papers*)
FAGIN (*Oliver Twist*)
FLITE, Miss (*Bleak House*)
GILES (*Oliver Twist*)
GILLS, Solomon (*Dombey and Son*)
GOWAN, Harry (*Little Dorrit*)
GREEN, Tom (*Barnaby Rudge*)
GRIDE, Arthur (*Nicholas Nickleby*)
GUPPY, William (*Bleak House*)
HEXAM, Charlie/Jesse/Lizzie (*Our Mutual Friend*)
JANET (*David Copperfield*)
JONES, Mary (*Barnaby Rudge*)
KROOK (*Bleak House*)
LOBBS, Maria/'Old' (*Pickwick Papers*)
LORRY, Jarvis (*A Tale of Two Cities*)
LUCAS, Solomon (*Pickwick Papers*)
LUPIN, Mrs (*Martin Chuzzlewit*)
MEALY (*David Copperfield*)
'MELIA (*Dombey and Son*)
MIGGS, Miss (*Barnaby Rudge*)
MILLS, Julia (*David Copperfield*)
MOLLY (*Great Expectations*)
MOULD (*Martin Chuzzlewit*)
NANCY (*Oliver Twist*)
NANDY, John Edward (*Little Dorrit*)
NOGGS, Newman (*Nicholas Nickleby*)
PERCH (*Dombey and Son*)
PINCH, Ruth/Tom (*Martin Chuzzlewit*)
PRICE, 'Tilda (*Nicholas Nickleby*)
PROSS, Miss/Solomon (*A Tale of Two Cities*)
QUALE (*Bleak House*)

5–continued

QUILP, Daniel (*The Old Curiosity Shop*)
RUDGE, Barnaby/Mary (*Barnaby Rudge*)
SALLY, Old (*Oliver Twist*)
SCOTT, Tom (*The Old Curiosity Shop*)
SHARP (*David Copperfield*)
SIKES, Bill (*Oliver Twist*)
SLURK (*Pickwick Papers*)
SLYME, Chevy (*Martin Chuzzlewit*)
SMIKE (*Nicholas Nickleby*)
SNOBB, The Hon (*Nicholas Nickleby*)
SQUOD, Phil (*Bleak House*)
STAGG (*Barnaby Rudge*)
TOOTS, Mr P (*Dombey and Son*)
TRABB (*Great Expectations*)
TRENT, Frederick/Nellie (*The Old Curiosity Shop*)
TWIST, Oliver (*Oliver Twist*)
VENUS, Mr (*Our Mutual Friend*)
WATTY (*Pickwick Papers*)

6

BADGER, Dr Bayham/Laura/Malta/Matthew/Quebec/Woolwich (*Bleak House*)
BAILEY, Benjamin (*Martin Chuzzlewit*)
BAILEY, Captain (*David Copperfield*)
BAMBER, Jack (*Pickwick Papers*)
BANTAM, Angelo Cyrus (*Pickwick Papers*)
BARKER, Phil (*Oliver Twist*)
BARKIS (*David Copperfield*)
BARLEY, Clara (*Great Expectations*)
BARNEY (*Oliver Twist*)
BEDWIN, Mrs (*Oliver Twist*)
BETSEY, Jane (*Dombey and Son*)
BITZER (*Hard Times*)
BOFFIN, Henrietta/Nicodemus (*Our Mutual Friend*)
BONNEY (*Nicholas Nickleby*)
BRIGGS (*Dombey and Son*)
BUMBLE (*Oliver Twist*)
BUNSBY, Captain (*Dombey and Son*)
BUZFUZ, Sergeant (*Pickwick Papers*)
CARKER, Harriet/James/John (*Dombey and Son*)
CARTON, Sydney (*A Tale of Two Cities*)

6–continued

CHEGGS, Alick (*The Old Curiosity Shop*)
CLARKE (*Pickwick Papers*)
CODGER, Mrs (*Martin Chuzzlewit*)
CODLIN, Thomas (*The Old Curiosity Shop*)
CONWAY, General (*Barnaby Rudge*)
CORNEY, Mrs (*Oliver Twist*)
CURDLE (*Nicholas Nickleby*)
CUTLER, Mr/Mrs (*Nicholas Nickleby*)
CUTTLE, Captain Ned (*Dombey and Son*)
DARNAY, Charles (*A Tale of Two Cities*)
DARTLE, Rosa (*David Copperfield*)
DENNIS, Ned (*Barnaby Rudge*)
DIBABS, Mrs (*Nicholas Nickleby*)
DODSON (*Pickwick Papers*)
DOMBEY, Fanny/Florence/Louisa/Paul (*Dombey and Son*)
DORKER (*Nicholas Nickleby*)
DORRIT, Amy/Edward/Fanny/Frederick/William (*Little Dorrit*)
DOWLER, Captain (*Pickwick Papers*)
FEEDER (*Dombey and Son*)
FEENIX (*Dombey and Son*)
FIZKIN, Horatio (*Pickwick Papers*)
FOLIAR (*Nicholas Nickleby*)
GEORGE (*The Old Curiosity Shop*)
GEORGE (*Pickwick Papers*)
GEORGE, Mr (*Bleak House*)
GORDON, Lord George (*Barnaby Rudge*)
GRAHAM, Mary (*Martin Chuzzlewit*)
GROVES, 'Honest' James (*The Old Curiosity Shop*)
GUNTER (*Pickwick Papers*)
HARMON, John (*Our Mutual Friend*)
HARRIS, Mrs (*Martin Chuzzlewit*)
HAWDON, Captain (*Bleak House*)
HIGDEN, Betty (*Our Mutual Friend*)
HOMINY, Major (*Martin Chuzzlewit*)
HOWLER, Rev M (*Dombey and Son*)
JARLEY, Mrs (*The Old Curiosity Shop*)
JASPER, Jack (*Edwin Drood*)
JINGLE, Alfred (*Pickwick Papers*)
KETTLE, La Fayette (*Martin Chuzzlewit*)
LAMMLE, Alfred (*Our Mutual Friend*)
LOBLEY (*Edwin Drood*)
LUMLEY, Dr (*Nicholas Nickleby*)
MAGNUS, Peter (*Pickwick Papers*)
MALDEN, Jack (*David Copperfield*)
MARLEY, Jacob (*A Christmas Carol*)
MARTON (*The Old Curiosity Shop*)
MAYLIE, Harrie/Mrs/Rose (*Oliver Twist*)
MERDLE, Mr (*Little Dorrit*)
MILVEY, Rev Frank (*Our Mutual Friend*)
MIVINS (*Pickwick Papers*)
MODDLE, Augustus (*Martin Chuzzlewit*)
MORFIN (*Dombey and Son*)
MULLET, Professor (*Martin Chuzzlewit*)
NIPPER, Susan (*Dombey and Son*)
PANCKS (*Little Dorrit*)
PERKER (*Pickwick Papers*)
PHUNKY (*Pickwick Papers*)
PIPKIN, Nathaniel (*Pickwick Papers*)

6–continued

PIRRIP, Philip (*Great Expectations*)
POCKET, Herbert/Matthew/Sarah (*Great Expectations*)
POGRAM, Elijah (*Martin Chuzzlewit*)
RADDLE, Mr and Mrs (*Pickwick Papers*)
RIGAUD, Monsieur (*Little Dorrit*)
SAPSEA, Thomas (*Edwin Drood*)
SAWYER, Bob (*Pickwick Papers*)
SCALEY (*Nicholas Nickleby*)
SLEARY, Josephine (*Hard Times*)
'SLOPPY' (*Our Mutual Friend*)
SOWNDS (*Dombey and Son*)
STRONG, Dr (*David Copperfield*)
TACKER (*Martin Chuzzlewit*)
TAPLEY, Mark (*Martin Chuzzlewit*)
TARTAR (*Edwin Drood*)
TIPPIN, Lady (*Our Mutual Friend*)
TISHER, Mrs (*Edwin Drood*)
TOODLE (*Dombey and Son*)
TUPMAN, Tracy (*Pickwick Papers*)
VARDEN, Dolly/Gabriel (*Barnaby Rudge*)
VHOLES (*Bleak House*)
VUFFIN (*The Old Curiosity Shop*)
WALKER, Mick (*David Copperfield*)
WARDLE, Emily/Isabella/Mr/Rachel (*Pickwick Papers*)
WELLER, Sam/Tony (*Pickwick Papers*)
WILFER, Bella/Lavinia/Reginald (*Our Mutual Friend*)
WILLET, Joe/John (*Barnaby Rudge*)
WINKLE, Nathaniel (*Pickwick Papers*)
WOPSLE (*Great Expectations*)

7

BAILLIE, Gabriel (*Pickwick Papers*)
BANGHAM, Mrs (*Little Dorrit*)
BARBARA (*The Old Curiosity Shop*)
BARBARY, Miss (*Bleak House*)
BARDELL, Mrs Martha/Tommy (*Pickwick Papers*)
BAZZARD (*Edwin Drood*)
BELLING, Master (*Nicholas Nickleby*)
BLIMBER, Dr (*Dombey and Son*)
BLOTTON (*Pickwick Papers*)
BOBSTER, Cecilia/Mr (*Nicholas Nickleby*)
BOLDWIG, Captain (*Pickwick Papers*)
BROGLEY (*Dombey and Son*)
BROOKER (*Nicholas Nickleby*)
BROWDIE, John (*Nicholas Nickleby*)
BULLAMY (*Martin Chuzzlewit*)
CHARLEY (*David Copperfield*)
CHESTER, Edward/Sir John (*Barnaby Rudge*)
CHILLIP, Dr (*David Copperfield*)
CHIVERY, John (*Little Dorrit*)
CHOLLOP, Hannibal (*Martin Chuzzlewit*)
CHUFFEY (*Martin Chuzzlewit*)
CLEAVER, Fanny (*Our Mutual Friend*)
CLENNAM, Arthur (*Little Dorrit*)
CLUBBER, Sir Thomas (*Pickwick Papers*)
CRACKIT, Toby (*Oliver Twist*)
CRAWLEY, Young Mr (*Pickwick Papers*)
CREAKLE (*David Copperfield*)

7–continued

CREWLER, Mrs/Rev Horace/Sophy (*David Copperfield*)
CRIMPLE, David (*Martin Chuzzlewit*)
CROOKEY (*Pickwick Papers*)
DAWKINS, Jack (*Oliver Twist*)
DEDLOCK, Sir Leicester/Volumnia (*Bleak House*)
DEFARGE, Madame (*A Tale of Two Cities*)
DOLLOBY (*David Copperfield*)
DRUMMLE, Bentley (*Great Expectations*)
DUBBLEY (*Pickwick Papers*)
DURDLES (*Edwin Drood*)
EDMUNDS, John (*Pickwick Papers*)
ESTELLA (*Great Expectations*)
FLEMING, Agnes (*Oliver Twist*)
GABELLE, Theophile (*A Tale of Two Cities*)
GARGERY, Biddy/Joe/Pip (*Great Expectations*)
GARLAND, Abel/Mrs/Mr (*The Old Curiosity Shop*)
GASPARD (*A Tale of Two Cities*)
GAZINGI, Miss (*Nicholas Nickleby*)
GENERAL, Mrs (*Little Dorrit*)
GILBERT, Mark (*Barnaby Rudge*)
GRANGER, Edith (*Dombey and Son*)
GRIDLEY (*Bleak House*)
GRIMWIG (*Oliver Twist*)
GRUDDEN, Mrs (*Nicholas Nickleby*)
HAGGAGE, Dr (*Little Dorrit*)
HEYLING, George (*Pickwick Papers*)
JAGGERS (*Great Expectations*)
JELLYBY, Caddy/Mrs/Peepy (*Bleak House*)
JINKINS (*Martin Chuzzlewit*)
JOBLING, Dr John (*Martin Chuzzlewit*)
JOBLING, Tony (*Bleak House*)
JOHNSON, Mr (*Nicholas Nickleby*)
JORKINS (*David Copperfield*)
KEDGICK, Captain (*Martin Chuzzlewit*)
KENWIGS, Morleena (*Nicholas Nickleby*)
LARKINS, Mr (*David Copperfield*)
LEEFORD, Edward (*Oliver Twist*)
LEWSOME (*Martin Chuzzlewit*)
MALLARD (*Pickwick Papers*)
MANETTE, Dr/Lucie (*A Tale of Two Cities*)
MEAGLES (*Little Dorrit*)
MINERVA (*Pickwick Papers*)
MOWCHER, Miss (*David Copperfield*)
NADGETT (*Martin Chuzzlewit*)
NECKETT, Charlotte/Emma/Tom (*Bleak House*)
NUBBLES, Christopher (*The Old Curiosity Shop*)
NUPKINS, George (*Pickwick Papers*)
PAWKINS, Major (*Martin Chuzzlewit*)
PILKINS, Dr (*Dombey and Son*)
PIPCHIN, Mrs (*Dombey and Son*)
PODSNAP, Georgiana/Mr (*Our Mutual Friend*)
QUINION (*David Copperfield*)
SAMPSON, George (*Our Mutual Friend*)
SCADDER, Zephaniah (*Martin Chuzzlewit*)
SCROOGE, Ebenezer (*A Christmas Carol*)
SIMMONS, William (*Martin Chuzzlewit*)
SKEWTON, Hon Mrs (*Dombey and Son*)
SKYLARK, Mr (*David Copperfield*)
SLAMMER, Dr (*Pickwick Papers*)

7–continued

SLUMKEY, Hon Samuel (*Pickwick Papers*)
SNAGSBY (*Bleak House*)
SNAWLEY (*Nicholas Nickleby*)
SNUBBIN, Sergeant (*Pickwick Papers*)
SPARSIT, Mrs (*Hard Times*)
SPENLOW, Dora (*David Copperfield*)
SQUEERS, Fanny/Wackford (*Nicholas Nickleby*)
STARTOP (*Great Expectations*)
STRYVER, C J (*A Tale of Two Cities*)
TAMAROO, Miss (*Martin Chuzzlewit*)
TODGERS, Mrs (*Martin Chuzzlewit*)
TROTTER, Job (*Pickwick Papers*)
TRUNDLE (*Pickwick Papers*)
WACKLES, Jane/Melissa/Sophie (*The Old Curiosity Shop*)
WATKINS (*Nicholas Nickleby*)
WEMMICK (*Great Expectations*)
WICKHAM, Mrs (*Dombey and Son*)
WITHERS (*Dombey and Son*)

8

AKERSHEM, Sophronia (*Our Mutual Friend*)
BAGSTOCK, Major (*Dombey and Son*)
BARNWELL, B B (*Martin Chuzzlewit*)
BILLIKIN, Mrs (*Edwin Drood*)
BLATHERS (*Oliver Twist*)
BOYTHORN, Lawrence (*Bleak House*)
BRAVASSA, Miss (*Nicholas Nickleby*)
BROWNLOW, Mr (*Oliver Twist*)
CLAYPOLE, Noah (*Oliver Twist*)
CLUPPINS (*Pickwick Papers*)
CRADDOCK, Mrs (*Pickwick Papers*)
CRATCHIT, Belinda/Bob/Tiny Tim (*A Christmas Carol*)
CRIPPLES, Mr (*Little Dorrit*)
CRUMMLES, Ninetta/Vincent (*Nicholas Nickleby*)
CRUNCHER, Jeremiah/Jerry (*A Tale of Two Cities*)
CRUSHTON, Hon Mr (*Pickwick Papers*)
DATCHERY, Dick (*Edwin Drood*)
D'AULNAIS (*A Tale of Two Cities*)
FINCHING, Mrs Flora (*Little Dorrit*)
FLEDGEBY, Old/Young (*Our Mutual Friend*)
GASHFORD (*Barnaby Rudge*)
HAREDALE, Emma/Geoffrey/Reuben (*Barnaby Rudge*)
HAVISHAM, Miss (*Great Expectations*)
HORTENSE (*Bleak House*)
JARNDYCE, John (*Bleak House*)
LA CREEVY, Miss (*Nicholas Nickleby*)
LANDLESS, Helena/Neville (*Edwin Drood*)
LANGDALE (*Barnaby Rudge*)
LENVILLE (*Nicholas Nickleby*)
LITTIMER (*David Copperfield*)
LOSBERNE (*Oliver Twist*)
MAGWITCH, Abel (*Great Expectations*)
MARY ANNE (*David Copperfield*)
MATTHEWS (*Nicholas Nickleby*)
MICAWBER, Wilkins (*David Copperfield*)
MUTANHED, Lord (*Pickwick Papers*)

8–continued

NICKLEBY, Godfrey/Kate/Nicholas/Ralph (*Nicholas Nickleby*)
PEGGOTTY, Clara/Daniel/Ham/Little Em'ly (*David Copperfield*)
PICKWICK, Samuel (*Pickwick Papers*)
PLORNISH, Thomas (*Little Dorrit*)
POTATOES (*David Copperfield*)
SCADGERS, Lady (*Hard Times*)
SKIFFINS, Miss (*Great Expectations*)
SKIMPOLE, Arethusa/Harold/Kitty/Laura (*Bleak House*)
SKITTLES, Sir Barnet (*Dombey and Son*)
SMIGGERS, Joseph (*Pickwick Papers*)
SPARKLER, Edmund (*Little Dorrit*)
STIGGINS (*Pickwick Papers*)
TRADDLES, Tom (*David Copperfield*)
TROTWOOD, Betsey (*David Copperfield*)
WESTLOCK, John (*Martin Chuzzlewit*)
WRAYBURN, Eugene (*Our Mutual Friend*)

9

BELVAWNEY, Miss (*Nicholas Nickleby*)
BERINTHIA (*Dombey and Son*)
BLACKPOOL, Stephen (*Hard Times*)
BOUNDERBY, Josiah (*Hard Times*)
CHARLOTTE (*Oliver Twist*)
CHEERYBLE, Charles/Frank/Ned (*Nicholas Nickleby*)
CHICKWEED, Conkey (*Oliver Twist*)
CHUCKSTER (*The Old Curiosity Shop*)
COMPEYSON (*Great Expectations*)
FIBBITSON, Mrs (*David Copperfield*)
GRADGRIND, Louisa/Thomas (*Hard Times*)
GREGSBURY (*Nicholas Nickleby*)
GREWGIOUS (*Edwin Drood*)
HARTHOUSE, James (*Hard Times*)
HEADSTONE, Bradley (*Our Mutual Friend*)
LIGHTWOOD, Mortimer (*Our Mutual Friend*)
LILLYVICK (*Nicholas Nickleby*)
MANTALINI, Mr (*Nicholas Nickleby*)
MURDSTONE, Edward/Jane (*David Copperfield*)
OLD BARLEY (*Great Expectations*)
PARDIGGLE, Francis/O A (*Bleak House*)
PECKSNIFF, Charity/Mercy/Seth (*Martin Chuzzlewit*)
PRISCILLA (*Bleak House*)
RIDERHOOD, Pleasant/Roger (*Our Mutual Friend*)
SMALLWEED, Bartholomew/Joshua/Judy (*Bleak House*)
SMORLTORK, Count (*Pickwick Papers*)

9–continued

SNODGRASS, Augustus (*Pickwick Papers*)
SUMMERSON, Esther (*Bleak House*)
SWIVELLER, Richard (*The Old Curiosity Shop*)
TAPPERTIT, Simon (*Barnaby Rudge*)
VENEERING, Anastasia/Hamilton (*Our Mutual Friend*)
VERISOPHT, Lord Frederick (*Nicholas Nickleby*)
WICKFIELD, Agnes/Mr (*David Copperfield*)
WITHERDEN, Mr (*The Old Curiosity Shop*)
WOODCOURT, Allan (*Bleak House*)

10

AYRESLEIGH, Mr (*Pickwick Papers*)
CHUZZLEWIT, Anthony/Diggory/George/Jonas/Martin/Mrs Ned/Toby (*Martin Chuzzlewit*)
CRISPARKLE, Rev Septimus (*Edwin Drood*)
FLINTWINCH, Affery/Ephraim/Jeremiah (*Little Dorrit*)
MACSTINGER, Mrs (*Dombey and Son*)
ROUNCEWELL, Mrs (*Bleak House*)
SNEVELLICI, Miss (*Nicholas Nickleby*)
SOWERBERRY (*Oliver Twist*)
STARELEIGH, Justice (*Pickwick Papers*)
STEERFORTH, James (*David Copperfield*)
TATTYCORAM (*Little Dorrit*)
TURVEYDROP, Prince (*Bleak House*)
TWINKLETON, Miss (*Edwin Drood*)
WATERBROOK (*David Copperfield*)
WITITTERLY, Julia (*Nicholas Nickleby*)

11

COPPERFIELD, Clara/David (*David Copperfield*)
'DISMAL JIMMY' (*Pickwick Papers*)
'GAME CHICKEN', The (*Dombey and Son*)
MARCHIONESS, The (*The Old Curiosity Shop*)
PUMBLECHOOK (*Great Expectations*)
SPOTTLETOES, Mrs (*Martin Chuzzlewit*)
ST EVREMONDE, Marquis de/Marquise de (*A Tale of Two Cities*)
SWEEDLEPIPE, Paul (*Martin Chuzzlewit*)
TULKINGHORN (*Bleak House*)

12

HONEYTHUNDER, Luke (*Edwin Drood*)
'SHINY WILLIAM' (*Pickwick Papers*)
SWEET WILLIAM (*The Old Curiosity Shop*)
TITE-BARNACLE, Clarence/Ferdinand/Junior/Lord Decimus/Mr (*Little Dorrit*)

15

VON KOELDWETHOUT (*Nicholas Nickleby*)

SHAKESPEAREAN CHARACTERS

CHARACTER (*Play*)

3
HAL (*1 Henry IV*)
NYM (*Henry V, The Merry Wives of Windsor*)

4
ADAM (*As You Like It*)
AJAX (*Troilus and Cressida*)
EROS (*Antony and Cleopatra*)
FORD, Mistress (*The Merry Wives of Windsor*)
GREY (*Henry V*)
HERO (*Much Ado About Nothing*)
IAGO (*Othello*)
IRAS (*Antony and Cleopatra*)
LEAR (*King Lear*)
PAGE, Mistress (*The Merry Wives of Windsor*)
PETO (*2 Henry IV*)
PUCK (*A Midsummer Night's Dream*)
SNUG (*A Midsummer Night's Dream*)

5
AARON (*Titus Andronicus*)
ARIEL (*The Tempest*)
BELCH, Sir Toby (*Twelfth Night*)
BLUNT (*2 Henry IV*)
CAIUS, Doctor (*The Merry Wives of Windsor*)
CELIA (*As You Like It*)
CLEON (*Pericles*)
CORIN (*As You Like It*)
DIANA (*All's Well that Ends Well*)
EDGAR (*King Lear*)
ELBOW (*Measure for Measure*)
FESTE (*Twelfth Night*)
FLUTE (*A Midsummer Night's Dream*)
FROTH (*Measure for Measure*)
GOBBO, Launcelot (*The Merchant of Venice*)
JULIA (*The Two Gentlemen of Verona*)
LAFEW (*All's Well That Ends Well*)
MARIA (*Love's Labour's Lost, Twelfth Night*)
PARIS (*Troilus and Cressida*)
PERCY (*1 Henry IV*)
PHEBE (*As You Like It*)
PINCH (*The Comedy of Errors*)

5–continued
POINS (*1 Henry IV, 2 Henry IV*)
PRIAM (*Troilus and Cressida*)
REGAN (*King Lear*)
ROMEO (*Romeo and Juliet*)
SNOUT (*A Midsummer Night's Dream*)
TIMON (*Timon of Athens*)
TITUS (*Titus Andronicus*)
VIOLA (*Twelfth Night*)

6
AEGEON (*The Comedy of Errors*)
ALONSO (*The Tempest*)
ANGELO (*Measure for Measure*)
ANTONY (*Antony and Cleopatra*)
ARCITE (*The Two Noble Kinsmen*)
ARMADO (*Love's Labour's Lost*)
AUDREY (*As You Like It*)
BANQUO (*Macbeth*)
BIANCA (*The Taming of the Shrew, Othello*)
BOTTOM (*A Midsummer Night's Dream*)
BRUTUS (*Coriolanus, Julius Caesar*)
CASSIO (*Othello*)
CHIRON (*Titus Andronicus*)
CLOTEN (*Cymbeline*)
DENNIS (*As You Like It*)
DROMIO (*The Comedy of Errors*)
DUMAIN (*Love's Labour's Lost*)
DUNCAN (*Macbeth*)
EDMUND (*King Lear*)
EMILIA (*Othello, The Two Noble Kinsmen*)
FABIAN (*Twelfth Night*)
FENTON (*The Merry Wives of Windsor*)
FULVIA (*Antony and Cleopatra*)
HAMLET (*Hamlet*)
HECATE (*Macbeth*)
HECTOR (*Troilus and Cressida*)
HELENA (*A Midsummer Night's Dream, All's Well That Ends Well*)
HERMIA (*A Midsummer Night's Dream*)
IMOGEN (*Cymbeline*)
JULIET (*Romeo and Juliet, Measure for Measure*)

6–continued
LUCIUS (*Titus Andronicus*)
MARINA (*Pericles*)
MUTIUS (*Titus Andronicus*)
OBERON (*A Midsummer Night's Dream*)
OLIVER (*As You Like It*)
OLIVIA (*Twelfth Night*)
ORSINO (*Twelfth Night*)
OSWALD (*King Lear*)
PISTOL (*2 Henry IV, Henry V, The Merry Wives of Windsor*)
POMPEY (*Measure for Measure, Antony and Cleopatra*)
PORTIA (*The Merchant of Venice*)
QUINCE (*A Midsummer Night's Dream*)
RUMOUR (*2 Henry IV*)
SCROOP (*Henry IV*)
SILVIA (*The Two Gentlemen of Verona*)
TAMORA (*Titus Andronicus*)
THASIA (*Pericles*)
THURIO (*The Two Gentlemen of Verona*)
TYBALT (*Romeo and Juliet*)
VERGES (*Much Ado About Nothing*)

7
ADRIANA (*The Comedy of Errors*)
AEMILIA (*The Comedy of Errors*)
AGRIPPA (*Antony and Cleopatra*)
ALARBUS (*Titus Andronicus*)
ANTONIO (*The Merchant of Venice, The Tempest*)
BEROWNE (*Love's Labour's Lost*)
BERTRAM (*All's Well That Ends Well*)
CALCHAS (*Troilus and Cressida*)
CALIBAN (*The Tempest*)
CAPULET (*Romeo and Juliet*)
CESARIO (*Twelfth Night*)
CLAUDIO (*Much Ado About Nothing, Measure for Measure*)
COSTARD (*Love's Labour's Lost*)
DIONYZA (*Pericles*)
DOUGLAS (*1 Henry IV*)
ESCALUS (*Measure for Measure*)

SHAKESPEAREAN CHARACTERS

7–continued

FLAVIUS (*Timon of Athens*)
FLEANCE (*Macbeth*)
GONERIL (*King Lear*)
GONZALO (*The Tempest*)
HORATIO (*Hamlet*)
HOTSPUR (*1 Henry IV*)
IACHIMO (*Cymbeline*)
JACQUES (*As You Like It*)
JESSICA (*The Merchant of Venice*)
LAERTES (*Hamlet*)
LAVINIA (*Titus Andronicus*)
LEONTES (*The Winter's Tale*)
LORENZO (*The Merchant of Venice*)
LUCIANA (*The Comedy of Errors*)
MACBETH (*Macbeth*)
MACDUFF (*Macbeth*)
MALCOLM (*Macbeth*)
MARIANA (*Measure for Measure, All's Well That Ends Well*)
MARTIUS (*Titus Andronicus*)
MIRANDA (*The Tempest*)
NERISSA (*The Merchant of Venice*)
OCTAVIA (*Antony and Cleopatra*)
OPHELIA (*Hamlet*)
ORLANDO (*As You Like It*)
OTHELLO (*Othello*)
PALAMON (*The Two Noble Kinsmen*)
PAULINA (*The Winter's Tale*)
PERDITA (*The Winter's Tale*)
PISANIO (*Cymbeline*)
PROTEUS (*The Two Gentlemen of Verona*)
QUICKLY, Mistress (*1 Henry IV, 2 Henry IV, The Merry Wives of Windsor*)
QUINTUS (*Titus Andronicus*)
SHALLOW, Justice (*2 Henry IV, The Merry Wives of Windsor*)
SHYLOCK (*The Merchant of Venice*)
SILENCE (*2 Henry IV*)
SILVIUS (*As You Like It*)
SLENDER (*The Merry Wives of Windsor*)
SOLINUS (*The Comedy of Errors*)
THESEUS (*A Midsummer Night's Dream, The Two Noble Kinsmen*)
TITANIA (*A Midsummer Night's Dream*)
TROILUS (*Troilus and Cressida*)

7–continued

ULYSSES (*Troilus and Cressida*)
WILLIAM (*As You Like It*)

8

ACHILLES (*Troilus and Cressida*)
AUFIDIUS (*Coriolanus*)
BAPTISTA (*The Taming of the Shrew*)
BARDOLPH (*Henry IV, Henry V, The Merry Wives of Windsor*)
BASSANIO (*The Merchant of Venice*)
BEATRICE (*Much Ado About Nothing*)
BELARIUS (*Cymbeline*)
BENEDICK (*Much Ado About Nothing*)
BENVOLIO (*Romeo and Juliet*)
CHARMIAN (*Antony and Cleopatra*)
CLAUDIUS (*Hamlet*)
COMINIUS (*Coriolanus*)
CORDELIA (*King Lear*)
CRESSIDA (*Troilus and Cressida*)
DIOMEDES (*Antony and Cleopatra, Troilus and Cressida*)
DOGBERRY (*Much Ado About Nothing*)
DON PEDRO (*Much Ado About Nothing*)
FALSTAFF (*The Merry Wives of Windsor, Henry IV*)
FLORIZEL (*The Winter's Tale*)
GERTRUDE (*Hamlet*)
GRATIANO (*The Merchant of Venice*)
HERMIONE (*The Winter's Tale*)
ISABELLA (*Measure for Measure*)
LUCENTIO (*The Taming of the Shrew*)
LYSANDER (*A Midsummer Night's Dream*)
MALVOLIO (*Twelfth Night*)
MENENIUS (*Coriolanus*)
MERCUTIO (*Romeo and Juliet*)
MONTAGUE (*Romeo and Juliet*)
MORTIMER (*1 Henry IV*)
OCTAVIUS (*Antony and Cleopatra*)
PANDARUS (*Troilus and Cressida*)
PAROLLES (*All's Well That Ends Well*)
PERICLES (*Pericles*)

8–continued

PHILOTEN (*Pericles*)
POLONIUS (*Hamlet*)
PROSPERO (*The Tempest*)
RODERIGO (*Othello*)
ROSALIND (*As You Like It*)
ROSALINE (*Love's Labour's Lost*)
SICINIUS (*Coriolanus*)
STEPHANO (*The Tempest*)
TRINCULO (*The Tempest*)
VIOLENTA (*All's Well That Ends Well*)
VOLUMNIA (*Coriolanus*)

9

AGUECHEEK, Sir Andrew (*Twelfth Night*)
ANTIOCHUS (*Pericles*)
ARVIRAGUS (*Cymbeline*)
BASSIANUS (*Titus Andronicus*)
BRABANTIO (*Othello*)
CAMBRIDGE (*Henry V*)
CLEOPATRA (*Antony and Cleopatra*)
CYMBELINE (*Cymbeline*)
DEMETRIUS (*A Midsummer Night's Dream, Antony and Cleopatra, Titus Andronicus*)
DESDEMONA (*Othello*)
ENOBARBUS (*Antony and Cleopatra*)
FERDINAND (*Loves Labours Lost, The Tempest*)
FREDERICK (*As You Like It*)
GLENDOWER, Owen (*1 Henry IV*)
GUIDERIUS (*Cymbeline*)
HELICANUS (*Pericles*)
HIPPOLYTA (*A Midsummer Night's Dream, The Two Noble Kinsmen*)
HORTENSIO (*The Taming of the Shrew*)
KATHERINA (*The Taming of the Shrew*)
KATHERINE (*Henry V, Love's Labour's Lost*)
MAMILLIUS (*The Winter's Tale*)
PATROCLUS (*Troilus and Cressida*)
PETRUCHIO (*The Taming of the Shrew*)
POLIXENES (*The Winter's Tale*)
SEBASTIAN (*The Tempest, Twelfth Night*)
TEARSHEET, Doll (*2 Henry IV*)
VALENTINE (*The Two Gentlemen of Verona*)

9—continued
VINCENTIO (*Measure for Measure, The Taming of the Shrew*)

10
ALCIBIADES (*Timon of Athens*)
ANTIPHOLUS (*The Comedy of Errors*)
CORIOLANUS (*Coriolanus*)
FORTINBRAS (*Hamlet*)
JAQUENETTA (*Love's Labour's Lost*)
LONGAVILLE (*Love's Labour's Lost*)
LYSIMACHUS (*Pericles*)

10—continued
POSTHUMOUS (*Cymbeline*)
SATURNINUS (*Titus Andronicus*)
TOUCHSTONE (*As You Like It*)

11
ROSENCRANTZ (*Hamlet*)

12
GUILDENSTERN (*Hamlet*)

14
CHRISTOPHER SLY (*The Taming of the Shrew*)

CHARACTERS FROM JANE AUSTEN

CHARACTER (Novel)

ALLEN, Mr/Mrs (*Northanger Abbey*)
BATES, Mrs (*Emma*)
BENNET, Jane/Elizabeth/Catherine/Mary/Lydia (*Pride and Prejudice*)
BENWICK, Captain (*Persuasion*)
BERTRAM, Lady Maria/Sir Thomas/ Rev Edmund/Maria/Julia (*Mansfield Park*)
BINGLEY, Charles/Caroline/Louisa (*Pride and Prejudice*)
BRANDON, Colonel (*Sense and Sensibility*)
CAMPBELL, Colonel/Jane (*Emma*)
CHURCHILL, Frank (*Emma*)
CLAY, Mrs (*Persuasion*)
COLLINS, Rev William (*Pride and Prejudice*)
CRAWFORD, Henry/Mary/Admiral (*Mansfield Park*)
CROFT, Admiral (*Persuasion*)
DARCY, Fitzwilliam/Lady Anne/Georgiana (*Pride and Prejudice*)
DASHWOOD, Henry/John/Fanny/Elinor/ Marianne/Margaret (*Sense and Sensibility*)
DE BOURGH, Lady Catherine (*Pride and Prejudice*)
DIXON, Mr (*Emma*)
ELTON (*Emma*)
FAIRFAX, Jane (*Emma*)
FERRARS, Edward/Robert (*Sense and Sensibility*)
FITZWILLIAM, Colonel (*Pride and Prejudice*)
FORSTER, Colonel/Harriet (*Pride and Prejudice*)
GARDINER, Edward (*Pride and Prejudice*)
GODDARD, Mrs (*Emma*)
GRANT, Rev Dr (*Mansfield Park*)
HARVILLE, Captain (*Persuasion*)
HAYTER, Mrs (*Persuasion*)

HURST, Louisa (*Pride and Prejudice*)
JENNINGS, Mrs (*Sense and Sensibility*)
KNIGHTLEY, George/John/Isabella (*Emma*)
LUCAS, Sir William/Charlotte/Marie (*Pride and Prejudice*)
MARTIN, Robert (*Emma*)
MIDDLETON, Sir John (*Sense and Sensibility*)
MORLAND, Catherine/James/Sarah/George/ Harriet (*Northanger Abbey*)
MUSGROVE, Mary/Richard/Charles/Henrietta/Laura (*Persuasion*)
NORRIS, Mrs/Rev Mr (*Mansfield Park*)
PALMER, Mrs Charlotte (*Sense and Sensibility*)
PERRY (*Emma*)
PHILLIPS, Mrs (*Pride and Prejudice*)
PRICE, Mrs Frances/Lieutenant/Fanny/ William/Susan (*Mansfield Park*)
RUSHWORTH, Maria/James (*Mansfield Park*)
RUSSELL, Lady (*Persuasion*)
SHEPHERD, John (*Persuasion*)
SMITH, Harriet (*Emma*)
SMITH, Mrs (*Persuasion*)
SMITH, Mrs (*Sense and Sensibility*)
STEELE, Anne/Lucy (*Sense and Sensibility*)
THORPE, Mrs/Isabella/John/Edward/William (*Northanger Abbey*)
TILNEY, Henry/Eleanor/General/Captain Fred (*Northanger Abbey*)
WENTWORTH, Captain Frederick (*Persuasion*)
WESTON, Mrs (*Emma*)
WICKHAM, George (*Pride and Prejudice*)
WILLIAMS, Eliza (*Sense and Sensibility*)
WILLOUGHBY, John (*Sense and Sensibility*)
WOODHOUSE, Emma/Isabella (*Emma*)
YATES, Hon John (*Mansfield Park*)

CHARACTERS FROM LEWIS CARROLL'S 'ALICE' BOOKS

4
DODO
LION
LORY

5
ALICE
DINAH
HATTA
KITTY
MOUSE

6
EAGLET
HAIGHA

6–continued
PIGEON
WALRUS

7
DUCHESS
GRYPHON
OYSTERS
PIG-BABY
UNICORN

8
DORMOUSE
FLAMINGO
RED QUEEN

9
CARPENTER
MAD HATTER
MARCH HARE
RED KNIGHT
WHITE KING

10
MOCK TURTLE
TWEEDLEDEE
TWEEDLEDUM
WHITE QUEEN

11
CATERPILLAR

11–continued
CHESHIRE CAT
FISH FOOTMAN
FROG FOOTMAN
WHITE KNIGHT
WHITE RABBIT

12
HUMPTY DUMPTY
KING OF HEARTS

13
BILL THE LIZARD
FATHER WILLIAM
KNAVE OF HEARTS
QUEEN OF HEARTS

CHARACTERS FROM TROLLOPE

'BARSETSHIRE' NOVELS:
The Warden
Barchester Towers
Doctor Thorne
Framley Parsonage
The Small House at Allington
The Last Chronicle of Barset

3
FAY, Marion (*Marion Fay*)
RAY, Rachel (*Rachel Ray*)

4
BOLD, John (*The Warden*)
DALE, Lily (*The Small House at Allington; The Last Chronicle of Barset*)
DALE, Squire (*The Small House at Allington; The Last Chronicle of Barset*)
DUNN, Onesiphorus (*The Last Chronicle of Barset*)
FAWN, Lord (*The Eustace Diamonds*)
FINN, Phineas (*Phineas Finn; Phineas Redux*)
GREX, Lady Mabel (*The Duke's Children*)
GREY, Dolly (*Mr Scarborough's Family*)
GREY, John (*Can You Forgive Her?*)
MONK, Joshua (*Phineas Finn*)
ORME, Sir Peregrine (*Orley Farm*)
ROBY, Thomas (*The Prime Minister*)
VOSS, Michel (*The Golden Lion of Granpere*)

5
CRUMP, Mrs (*The Small House at Allington*)
EAMES, Johnny (*The Small House at Allington; The Last Chronicle of Barset*)
GREEN, Archibald (*The Conors of Castle Conor*)
JONES, Henry (*Cousin Henry*)

'PALLISER' NOVELS:
Can You Forgive Her?
Phineas Finn
The Eustace Diamonds
Phineas Redux
The Prime Minister
The Duke's Children

5–continued
JONES, Indefer (*Cousin Henry*)
JONES, Mrs Montacute (*Is He Popenjoy?*)
KELLY, Martin (*The Kellys and the O'Kellys*)
LOPEZ, Ferdinand (*The Prime Minister*)
LOVEL, Earl (*Frederick*) (*Lady Anna*)
LOVEL, Lady Anna (*Lady Anna*)
LYNCH, Simeon (*The Kellys and the O'Kellys*)
MASON, Lady (*Orley Farm*)
MASON, Mrs (*Orley Farm*)
MAULE, Gerard (*Phineas Redux*)
MOGGS, Ontario (*Ralph the Heir*)
ONGAR, Lady Julia (*The Claverings*)
ONGAR, Lord (*The Claverings*)
ORIEL, Rev. Caleb (*Doctor Thorne*)
PENGE, Caroline (*The US Senator*)
PRIME, Dorothea (*Rachel Ray*)
PRONG, Rev. Samuel (*Rachel Ray*)
RODEN, George (*Marion Fay*)
ROWAN, Luke (*Rachel Ray*)
SCOTT, Clementina (*The Three Clerks*)
SCOTT, Mrs Val (*The Three Clerks*)
SLOPE, Rev. Obadiah (*Barchester Towers*)
TIFTO, Major (*The Duke's Children*)
TUDOR, Alaric (*The Three Clerks*)
TUDOR, Charley (*The Three Clerks*)

CHARACTERS FROM TROLLOPE

6

ARABIN, Rev. Francis (*Barchester Towers*)
AYLMER, Lady (*The Belton Estate*)
BELTON, Will (*The Belton Estate*)
BODKIN, Sir Borcas (*Marion Fay*)
BOODLE, Captain ('Doodles') (*The Claverings*)
BURTON, Florence (*The Claverings*)
BURTON, Theodore (*The Claverings*)
CASHEL, Lord and Lady (*The Kellys and the O'Kellys*)
DORMER, Ayala (*Ayala's Angel*)
DORMER, Lucy (*Ayala's Angel*)
FRENCH, Arabella (*He Knew He Was Right*)
FRENCH, Camilla (*He Knew He Was Right*)
GIBSON, Rev. Mr (*He Knew He Was Right*)
GLOMAX, Captain (*The US Senator*)
GRAHAM, Felix (*Orley Farm*)
HURTLE, Winifred (*The Way We Live Now*)
LUFTON, Lord (*Framley Parsonage*)
MCKEON, Tony (*The Macdermots of Ballycloran*)
MORRIS, Lucy (*The Eustace Diamonds*)
MORTON, Reginald (*The US Senator*)
M'RUEN, Jabez (*The Three Clerks*)
NEEFIT, Mr (*Ralph the Heir*)
NEEFIT, Polly (*Ralph the Heir*)
NERONI, Signora Vesey (Barchester Towers)
NEWTON, Ralph (*Ralph the Heir*)
NORMAN, Harry (*The Three Clerks*)
O'GRADY, Sam (*Castle Richmond*)
O'KELLY, Frank (*The Kellys and the O'Kellys*)
O'KELLY, Guss (*The Kellys and the O'Kellys*)
O'KELLY, Sophy (*The Kellys and the O'Kellys*)
OMNIUM, Duke of ('Palliser' novels)
PETRIE, Wallachia (*He Knew He Was Right*)
PUFFLE, Mrs ('Barsetshire' novels)
ROWLEY, Nora (*He Knew He Was Right*)
STUBBS, Colonel Jonathan (*Ayala's Angel*)
THOMAS, John (*The Small House at Allington*)
THORNE, Doctor (*Doctor Thorne*)
THORNE, Mary (*Doctor Thorne*)
TOWERS, Tom (*The Warden*)
USHANT, Lady (*The US Senator*)
USSHER, Myles (*The Macdermots*)
WORTLE, Dr and Mrs (*Dr Wortle's School*)

7

AMEDROZ, Clara (*The Belton Estate*)
BANMANN, Baroness (*Is He Popenjoy?*)
BERTRAM, George (*The Bertrams*)
BONTEEN, Mr (*Phineas Redux*)
BRATTLE, Carry (*The Vicar of Bullhampton*)
CARBURY, Felix (*The Way We Live Now*)
CARBURY, Henrietta (*The Way We Live Now*)
CARBURY, Lady (*The Way We Live Now*)
COMFORT, Rev. Charles (*Rachel Ray*)
CRAWLEY, Grace ('Barsetshire' novels)
CRAWLEY, Rev. Josiah (*Framley Parsonage*; The Last Chronicle of Barset)
CROSBIE, Adolphus (*The Small House at Allington*)
DE BARON, Jack (*Is He Popenjoy?*)
DE GUEST, Earl (*The Small House at Allington*)

7–continued

DESMOND, Lady (*Castle Richmond*)
DOSSETT, Aunt and Uncle (*Ayala's Angel*)
EMILIUS, Rev. Joseph ('Palliser' novels)
EUSTACE, John (*The Eustace Diamonds*)
EUSTACE, Lizzie (*The Eustace Diamonds*)
EUSTACE, Sir Florian (*The Eustace Diamonds*)
FENWICK, Rev. Frank (*The Vicar of Bullhampton*)
GERMAIN, Lord and Lady George (*Is He Popenjoy?*)
GILMORE, Harry (*The Vicar of Bullhampton*)
GOESLER, Madame Max (*Phineas Finn*)
GOTOBED, Elias (*The US Senator*)
GRANTLY, Archdeacon ('Barsetshire' novels)
GRESHAM, Fanny (*Framley Parsonage*)
GRESHAM, Frank (*Doctor Thorne*)
GRESLEY, Lord Alfred (*Sir Harry Hotspur of Humblethwaite*)
HARDING, Rev. Septimus (*The Warden*)
HOTSPUR, Emily (*Sir Harry Hotspur of Humblethwaite*)
HOTSPUR, George (*Sir Harry Hotspur of Humblethwaite*)
KENNEDY, Lady Laura (*Phineas Finn*; Phineas Redux)
LOWTHER, Mary (*The Vicar of Bullhampton*)
MASTERS, Gregory (*The US Senator*)
MASTERS, Mary (*The US Senator*)
MILDMAY, Aunt Ju (*Is He Popenjoy?*)
NEVILLE, Fred (*An Eye for an Eye*)
O'MAHONY, Gerald (*The Hard Leaguers*)
O'MAHONY, Rachel (*The Hard Leaguers*)
PEACOCK, Mr and Mrs (*Dr Wortle's School*)
PROSPER, Peter (*Mr Scarborough's Family*)
PROTEST, Lady Selina (*Is He Popenjoy?*)
PROUDIE, Augusta ('Barsetshire' novels)
PROUDIE, Bishop ('Barsetshire' novels)
PROUDIE, Mrs ('Barsetshire' novels)
PROUDIE, Netta ('Barsetshire' novels)
ROBARTS, Fanny (*Framley Parsonage*)
ROBARTS, Lucy (*Framley Parsonage*)
ROBARTS, Mrs Mark (*Framley Parsonage*)
ROBARTS, Rev. Mark (*Framley Parsonage*)
RUFFORD, Lord (*The US Senator*)
SOWERBY, Nathaniel (*Framley Parsonage*)
THWAITE, Daniel (*Lady Anna*)
TOOGOOD, Mr (*The Last Chronicle of Barset*)
TREFOIL, Arabella (*The US Senator*)
TREGEAR, Frank (*The Duke's Children*)
TRINGLE, Sir Thomas (*Ayala's Angel*)
TRINGLE, Tom (*Ayala's Angel*)
VAVASOR, Alice (*Can You Forgive Her?*)
VAVASOR, George (*Can You Forgive Her?*)
VAVASOR, John (*Can You Forgive Her?*)
VAVASOR, Kate (*Can You Forgive Her?*)
WESTEND, Sir Warwick (*The Three Clerks*)
WESTERN, Cecilia (*Kept in the Dark*)
WESTERN, George (*Kept in the Dark*)
WHARTON, Abel (*The Prime Minister*)
WHARTON, Emily (*The Prime Minister*)
WYNDHAM, Fanny (*The Kellys and the O'Kellys*)

CHARACTERS FROM WALTER SCOTT

3
LEE, Alice (*Woodstock*)
LEE, Colonel Albert (*Woodstock*)
LEE, Sir Henry (*Woodstock*)

4
DODS, Meg (*St Ronan's Well*)
GRAY, Gideon (*The Surgeon's Daughter*)
GRAY, Menie (*The Surgeon's Daughter*)
LYLE, Annot (*A Legend of Montrose*)
VERE, Isabella (*The Black Dwarf*)

5
BINKS, Sir Bingo (*St Ronan's Well*)
BUNCE, Jack (*The Pirate*)
EWART, Nanty (*Redgauntlet*)
DEANS, Davie (*The Heart of Midlothian*)
DEANS, Effie (*The Heart of Midlothian*)
DEANS, Jeanie (*The Heart of Midlothian*)
GURTH (*Ivanhoe*)
ISAAC (the Jew) (*Ivanhoe*)
SMITH, Henry (*The Fair Maid of Perth*)
SMITH, Wayland (*Kenilworth*)
TROIL, Brenda (*The Pirate*)
TROIL, Magnus (*The Pirate*)
TROIL, Minna (*The Pirate*)
TROIL, Ulla (*The Pirate*)
WAMBA (*Ivanhoe*)

6
ALBANY, Duke of (*The Fair Maid of Perth*)
ASHTON, Lucy (*The Bride of Lammermoor*)
ASHTON, Sir William (*The Bride of Lammermoor*)
AVENEL, Mary (*The Monastery*)
AVENEL, Roland (*The Abbot*)
BERTHA (*Count Robert of Paris*)
BUTLER, Reuben (*The Heart of Midlothian*)
CEDRIC (*Ivanhoe*)
DE LACY, Damian (*The Betrothed*)
DE LACY, Hugo (*The Betrothed*)
DE LACY, Randel (*The Betrothed*)
DE VERE, Arthur (*Anne of Geierstein*)
ELLIOT, Hobbie (*The Black Dwarf*)
GEDDES, Joshua (*Redgauntlet*)
GLOVER, Catharine (*The Fair Maid of Perth*)
GLOVER, Simon (*The Fair Maid of Perth*)
GRAEME, Magdalen (*The Abbot*)
GRAEME, Roland (*The Abbot*)
HALCRO, Claud (*The Pirate*)
JAMES I (*The Fortunes of Nigel*)
JARVIE, Bailie Nicol (*Rob Roy*)
LE DAIN, Oliver (*Quentin Durward*)
MANLEY, Sir Edward (*The Black Dwarf*)
MORTON, Henry (*Old Mortality*)
OXFORD, Earl of (*Anne of Geierstein*)
PHILIP (of France) (*The Talisman*)
RAMSAY, Margaret (*The Fortunes of Nigel*)
ROWENA (*Ivanhoe*)

6–continued
SEYTON, Catherine (*The Abbot*)
SLUDGE, Dickie (*Kenilworth*)
TALBOT, Colonel (*Waverley*)
TYRREL, Francis (*St Ronan's Well*)
VARNEY, Richard (*Kenilworth*)
VERNON, Diana (*Rob Roy*)
WARDEN, Henry (*The Monastery*)

7
BALFOUR, John (*Old Mortality*)
BERTRAM (*Castle Dangerous*)
BERTRAM, Harry (*Guy Mannering*)
BUCKLAW, Laird of (*The Bride of Lammermoor*)
DINMONT, Dandie (*Guy Mannering*)
DOUGLAS, Sir James (*Castle Dangerous*)
DURWARD, Quentin (*Quentin Durward*)
EVERARD, Colonel Markham (*Woodstock*)
FENELLA (*Peveril of the Peak*)
GLOSSIN (*Guy Mannering*)
GWENWYN (*The Betrothed*)
HARTLEY, Adam (*The Surgeon's Daughter*)
KENNETH, Sir (*The Talisman*)
LANGLEY, Sir Frederick (*The Black Dwarf*)
LATIMER, Darsie (*Redgauntlet*)
MACTURK, Captain (*St Ronan's Well*)
M'AULAY, Allan (*A Legend of Montrose*)
MERTOUM, Basil (*The Pirate*)
MERTOUM, Mordaunt (*The Pirate*)
MOWBRAY, Clara (*St Ronan's Well*)
NEVILLE, Major (*The Antiquary*)
OLDBUCK, Jonathan (*The Antiquary*)
PEEBLES, Peter (*Redgauntlet*)
PEVERIL, Julian (*Peveril of the Peak*)
PEVERIL, Sir Geoffrey (*Peveril of the Peak*)
REBECCA (*Ivanhoe*)
ROBSART, Amy (*Kenilworth*)
ROBSART, Sir Hugh (*Kenilworth*)
ROTHSAY, Duke of (*The Fair Maid of Perth*)
SALADIN (*The Talisman*)
SAMPSON, Dominie (*Guy Mannering*)
SHAFTON, Sir Piercie (*The Monastery*)
TOMKINS, Joseph (*Woodstock*)
WARDOUR, Isabella (*The Antiquary*)
WARDOUR, Sir Arthur (*The Antiquary*)

8
BEAN LEAN, Donald (*Waverley*)
BERENGER, Eveline (*The Betrothed*)
BONIFACE, Abbot (*The Monastery*)
BURGUNDY, Duke of (*Anne of Geierstein*)
CAMPBELL, Sir Duncan (*A Legend of Montrose*)
CONACHAR (*The Fair Maid of Perth*)
CROMWELL, Oliver (*Woodstock*)
DALGARNO, Lord (*The Fortunes of Nigel*)
DALGETTY, Captain Dugald (*A Legend of Montrose*)
DE WALTON, Sir John (*Castle Dangerous*)
EVANDALE, Lord (*Old Mortality*)

8–continued

FAIRFORD, Alan (*Redgauntlet*)
GALEOTTI, Martius (*Quentin Durward*)
GARDINER, Colonel James (*Waverley*)
HEREWARD (*Count Robert of Paris*)
HYDER ALI (*The Surgeon's Daughter*)
L'HERMITE, Tristan (*Quentin Durward*)
MENTEITH, Earl of (*A Legend of Montrose*)
M'INTYRE, Hector (*The Antiquary*)
OLIFAUNT, Nigel (*The Fortunes of Nigel*)
RAMORNEY, Sir John (*The Fair Maid of Perth*)
STAUNTON, George (*The Heart of Midlothian*)
TRAPBOIS (*The Fortunes of Nigel*)
TRUMBULL, Thomas (*Redgauntlet*)
WAVERLEY, Edward (*Waverley*)
WAVERLEY, Sir Everard (*Waverley*)
WILDRAKE, Roger (*Woodstock*)

9

ARMSTRONG, Grace (*The Black Dwarf*)
BELLENDEN, Edith (*Old Mortality*)
BELLENDEN, Lady Margaret (*Old Mortality*)
BIEDERMAN, Arnold (*Anne of Geierstein*)
BRENHILDA (*Count Robert of Paris*)
BRIENNIUS, Nicephorus (*Count Robert of Paris*)
CHIFFINCH (*Peveril of the Peak*)
CHRISTIAN, Edward (*Peveril of the Peak*)
CLEVELAND, Clement (*The Pirate*)
DE BERKELY, Lady Augusta (*Castle Dangerous*)
DE LA MARCK, William (*Quentin Durward*)
DE VALENCE, Aymer (*Castle Dangerous*)
ELIZABETH, Queen (*Kenilworth*)
FRIAR TUCK (*Ivanhoe*)
GELLATLEY, Davie (*Waverley*)
HAGENBACH, Archibald of (*Anne of Geierstein*)
MACGREGOR, Rob Roy (*Rob Roy*)
MANNERING, Colonel Guy (*Guy Mannering*)
MANNERING, Julia (*Guy Mannering*)
MERRILIES, Meg (*Guy Mannering*)
MIDDLEMAS, Richard (*The Surgeon's Daughter*)
MONIPLIES, Richard (*The Fortunes of Nigel*)
OCHILTREE, Edie (*The Antiquary*)
PHILIPSON (*Anne of Geierstein*)
ROBIN HOOD (*Ivanhoe*)
TOUCHWOOD, Mr (*St Ronan's Well*)
YELLOWLEY, Barbara (*The Pirate*)
YELLOWLEY, Triptolemus (*The Pirate*)

10

ATHELSTANE (of Coningsburgh) (*Ivanhoe*)
BERENGARIA, Queen (*The Talisman*)
BUCKINGHAM (*Peveril of the Peak*)
HATTERAICK, Dirk (*Guy Mannering*)
HOLDENOUGH, Rev. Nehemiah (*Woodstock*)
LOWESTOFFE, Templar (*The Fortunes of Nigel*)
MACWHEEBLE, Duncan (*Waverley*)
MONTFERRAT, (Conrade of) (*The Talisman*)
MURDOCKSON, Meg (*The Heart of Midlothian*)
PENFEATHER, Lady Penelope (*St Ronan's Well*)
RAVENSWOOD, Lord (*The Bride of Lammermoor*)
RAVENSWOOD, Master of (*The Bride of Lammermoor*)

10–continued

SADDLETREE, Bartoline (*The Heart of Midlothian*)
SNAILSFOOT, Bryce (*The Pirate*)
SUDDLECHOP, Dame Ursula (*The Fortunes of Nigel*)
TRESSILIAN, Edmund (*Kenilworth*)

11

ANNA COMNENA (*Count Robert of Paris*)
BALDERSTONE, Caleb (*The Bride of Lammermoor*)
BRADWARDINE, Baron of (*Waverley*)
BRADWARDINE, Rose (*Waverley*)
BRIDGENORTH, Alic (*Peveril of the Peak*)
BRIDGENORTH, Major (*Peveril of the Peak*)
DUMBIEDIKES, Laird of (*The Heart of Midlothian*)
ETHERINGTON, Earl of (*St Ronan's Well*)
FAIRSERVICE, Andrew (*Rob Roy*)
GLENDINNING, Edward (*The Monastery*)
GLENDINNING, Halbert (*The Monastery*)
GLENDINNING, Simon (*The Monastery*)
MONTREVILLE, Madame (*The Surgeon's Daughter*)
PLANTAGENET, Edith (*The Talisman*)
REDGAUNTLET, Sir Arthur Darsie (*Redgauntlet*)
TIPPOO SAHIB (*The Surgeon's Daughter*)

12

BOIS-GUILBERT, Sir Brian de (*Ivanhoe*)
FRONT-DE-BOEUF, Sir Reginald (*Ivanhoe*)
MALAGROWTHER, Sir Mungo (*The Fortunes of Nigel*)
OSBALDISTONE, Francis (*Rob Roy*)
OSBALDISTONE, Rashleigh (*Rob Roy*)
OSBALDISTONE, Sir Hildebrand (*Rob Roy*)

13

DOUSTERSWIVEL (*The Antiquary*)
FATHER EUSTACE (*The Monastery*)
MADGE WILDFIRE (*The Heart of Midlothian*)

14

CHARLES THE BOLD (*Anne of Geierstein; Quentin Durward*)
ROBERT THE BRUCE (*Castle Dangerous*)

15+

ELSHENDER THE RECLUSE (*The Black Dwarf*)
ELSHIE OF THE MUCKLESTANES (*The Black Dwarf*)
FLIBBERTIGIBBET (*Kenilworth*)
HERRIES OF BIRRENSWORK (*Redgauntlet*)
ISABELLE DE CROYE (*Quentin Durward*)
KNIGHT OF THE LEOPARD (*The Talisman*)
MAC-IVOR VICH IAN VOHR OF GLEN-NAQUOICH, Fergus (*Waverley*)
MAC-IVOR VICH IAN VOHR OF GLEN-NAQUOICH, Flora (*Waverley*)
NORNA OF THE FITFUL-HEAD (*The Pirate*)
TORQUIL OF THE OAK (*The Fair Maid of Perth*)
WANDERING WILLIE (*Redgauntlet*)
WILFRED OF IVANHOE (*Ivanhoe*)

CHARACTERS FROM TOLKIEN'S 'LORD OF THE RINGS'

3&4

ENT – one of the tree-people

ORC – nasty goblin-like creature – many served Saruman and Sauron

SAM – see Gamgee, Sam

TOOK, Peregrin – (hobbit) member of the Fellowship, known as Pippin

5

ARWEN – (elf) daughter of Elrond – she married Aragorn and became Queen when he was crowned King – also known as the Evenstar

DROGO – see Baggins, Drogo

EOMER – (man) Marshal of the Riders of Rohan – became King of Rohan after his uncle Théoden's death

EOWYN – (woman) Lady of Rohan, she was Théoden's niece and Éomer's sister

FRODO – see Baggins, Frodo

GIMLI – dwarf and member of the Fellowship

GLOIN – (dwarf) Gimli's father

MERRY – see Brandybuck, Meriadoc

NARYA – one of the Rings of Power – belonged to Gandalf

NENYA – one of the Rings of Power – belonged to Galadriel

STING – sword belonging to Bilbo Baggins, which he gave to Frodo Baggins – glows blue when Orcs are near

UGLUK – an Uruk-hai

VILYA – one of the Rings of Power, belonged to Elrond

6

BALROG – a creature of fire in the mines of Moria

COTTON, Rosie – (hobbit) who marries Sam Gamgee

DEAGOL – (hobbit) cousin of Sméagol – found the Ring in a river and was killed by Sméagol

ELROND – (elf) Lord of Rivendell and father of Arwen

GAMGEE, Samwise – (hobbit) best friend of Frodo Baggins and member of the Fellowship – known as Sam

GOLLUM – pitiful creature obsessed by the Ring, named for his gurgling cough. He was once a hobbit called Sméagol

HALDIR – (elf) escorted the Fellowship into Lothlórien

HOBBIT – little people, also known as 'halflings'

NARSIL – the broken sword with which Isildur cut the Ring from Sauron's hand – repaired in Rivendell for Aragorn's use – rechristened Anduril

NAZGUL – another name for a Ringwraith

PIPPIN – see Took, Peregrin

SAURON – The Dark Lord and Master of the Ring

6–continued

SHELOB – huge carnivorous spider who lives in the mountains on the edge of Mordor – killed by Sam Gamgee

THEODEN – (man) King of Rohan – died in battle and was succeeded by his nephew, Éomer

7

ANDURIL – name given to the sword Narsil, after being reforged

ARAGORN – (man and ranger) sometimes known as Strider – heir of Isildur and Member of the Fellowship – named Elessar (meaning Elfstone) when he is crowned King

BAGGINS, Bilbo – (hobbit) Frodo's uncle

BAGGINS, Drogo – (hobbit) Frodo's father

BAGGINS, Frodo – (hobbit) ring-bearer and member of the Fellowship – Bilbo's nephew

BOROMIR – (man) member of the Fellowship, brother of Faramir and son of Denethor

ELENDIL – (man) Isildur's father and ancestor of Aragorn. He was once King of Gondor

ELESSAR – see Aragorn

FARAMIR – (man) Captain of Gondor – brother of Boromir and son of Denethor

GANDALF – wizard and member of the Fellowship – his Elvish name is Mithrandir

GWAIHIR – great eagle who rescued Gandalf from Isengard and Frodo and Sam from Mount Doom

ISILDUR – (man) son of Elendil and ancestor of Aragorn – he cut the Ring from Sauron's finger

LEGOLAS – see Greenleaf, Legolas

MITHRIL – dwarf-made chainmail originally belonging to Bilbo Baggins – he gave it to Frodo for the journey to Mordor

SARUMAN – a wizard

SMEAGOL – Gollum's name when he was a hobbit

STRIDER – a name by which Aragorn is sometimes known

URUK-HAI – a particularly large and violent breed of Orc

8

ARATHORN – (man) Aragorn's father

BOMBADIL, Tom – master of wood, water, and hill – gives shelter to the four hobbits on their journey to Rivendell

CELEBORN – (elf) Lord of Lórien

DENETHOR – (man) ruling Steward of Gondor in the absence of a King – also the father of Boromir and Faramir

EVENSTAR – see Arwen

9

BUTTERBUR, Barliman – (man) Landlord of the Prancing Pony

9–continued

CELEBRIAN – (elf) Wife of Elrond and mother of Arwen (daughter of Galadriel and Celeborn)

GALADRIEL – (elf) Lady of Lórien and Arwen's grandmother

GLAMDRING – sword belonging to Gandalf

GREENLEAF, Legolas – (elf) member of the Fellowship – son of Thranduil, the Elven-king of Mirkwood

SHADOWFAX – horse originally belonging to King Théoden, ridden by Gandalf

THRANDUIL – (elf) Legolas's father and Elven-king of Mirkwood

TREEBEARD – an Ent in the forest of Fangorn – oldest living thing in Middle-earth

UNDERHILL, Mr – alias used by Frodo on the journey to Mordor

10+

BLACK RIDER – another name for a Ringwraith

BRANDYBUCK, Meriadoc – (hobbit) member of the Fellowship, known as Merry

GLORFINDEL – (elf) escorted Aragorn and the hobbits to Rivendell

MITHRANDIR – see Gandalf

RINGWRAITHS – nine shadows of men who are the servants of Sauron – also known as the Nazgul or the Black Riders

SACKVILLE-BAGGINS – (hobbits) cousins of Bilbo Baggins

WITCH-KING – the Lord of the Nazgul, sometimes fully known as the Witch-king of Angmar

WORMTONGUE, Gríma – (man) servant of Théoden but secretly in league with Saruman

CHARACTERS FROM ROWLING'S 'HARRY POTTER'

3

OGG – gamekeeper at Hogwarts when Arthur and Molly Weasley were students

PYE, Augustus – trainee Healer at St Mungo's Hospital for Magical Maladies

TOM – landlord of the Leaky Cauldron, the London pub that provides the entrance to Diagon Alley

4

BANE – centaur who lives in the Forbidden Forest

BELL, Katie – student at Hogwarts and Chaser for the Gryffindor Quidditch team

BOTT, Bertie – maker of the Every Flavour Beans

DOGE, Elphias – member of the Order of the Phoenix

GRIM, the – spectral black dog that is an omen of death

FANG – large boarhound belonging to Hagrid

FIGG, Arabella – a fellow resident of Privet Drive, where the Dursley family and Harry live

NOTT, Theodore – student at Hogwarts and friend of Draco Malfoy

WOOD, Oliver – student at Hogwarts – one-time captain and Keeper for the Gryffindor Quidditch team

5

AUROR – catcher of dark wizards – works for the Ministry of Magic

AVERY – a Death Eater

BASIL – keeper of the Portkeys for the Quidditch World Cup

BINNS, Professor – History of Magic teacher at Hogwarts

BLACK, Alphard – Sirius Black's uncle

5–continued

BLACK, Elladora – Sirius Black's aunt

BLACK, Mrs – Sirius Black's mother – a firm believer in pure-blood wizardry

BLACK, Regulus – Sirius Black's brother and a Death Eater

BLACK, Sirius – Harry's godfather and a member of the Order of the Phoenix – school friend of Peter Pettigrew, James Potter, and Remus Lupin – escaped from the wizard prison Azkaban, where he was falsely held for multiple murders

BONES, Amelia – head of the Department of Magical Law Enforcement at the Ministry of Magic

BONES, Edgar – brother of Amelia Bones and an original member of the Order of the Phoenix

BONES, Susan – niece of Amelia Bones, student at Hogwarts

BROWN, Lavender – student at Hogwarts, usually to be found with Parvati Patil

CHANG, Cho – student at Hogwarts and Seeker for the Ravenclaw Quidditch team

CRAGG, Elfrida – former headmistress of Hogwarts, whose portrait hangs in St Mungo's Hospital for Magical Maladies

DOBBY – A male house-elf

ERROL – ancient owl belonging to the Weasley family

FILCH, Argus – caretaker at Hogwarts

FLINT, Marcus – student at Hogwarts and captain of the Slytherin Quidditch team

FUDGE, Cornelius – Minister for Magic

GOYLE, Gregory – student at Hogwarts and one of Draco Malfoy's cronies

GRAWP – Hagrid's giant half-brother

CHARACTERS FROM ROWLING'S 'HARRY POTTER'

5–continued

HOOCH, Madam – teacher of Flying lessons and Quidditch at Hogwarts

JONES, Hestia – member of the Order of the Phoenix

LUPIN, Remus – Harry's third Defence Against the Dark Arts teacher – a werewolf and school friend of Peter Pettigrew, James Potter, and Sirius Black – member of the Order of the Phoenix

MOODY, Alastor 'Mad-Eye' – ex-Auror and a member of the Order of the Phoenix

MOONY – school nickname for Remus Lupin when he was in his animagus form (a werewolf)

MUNCH, Eric – Security watchwizard at the Ministry of Magic

OGDEN, Tiberius – an Elder at the Wizengamot (wizard court)

PATIL, Padma and Parvati – twin sisters and students at Hogwart's

PINCE, Madam – librarian at Hogwarts

PRANG, Ernie – driver of the Knight Bus, a bus that magically transports wizard folk up and down the UK

PUCEY, Adrian – student at Hogwarts and player for the Slytherin Quidditch team

RONAN – centaur who lives in the Forbidden Forest

SMITH, Zacharias – student at Hogwarts

SNAPE, Professor Severus – Potions teacher at Hogwarts, head of Slytherin house, and a member of the Order of the Phoenix

SQUIB – name for somebody born into a wizarding family who has no magical powers

TONKS, Andromeda – Nymphadora Tonks's mother and a cousin of Sirius Black

TONKS, Nymphadora – an Auror and member of the Order of the Phoenix – a metamorphmagus (can change her appearance at will)

TONKS, Ted – Nymphadora Tonks's father

VANCE, Emmeline – member of the Order of the Phoenix

VEELA – beautiful women who enchant men, especially by dancing, but become physically ugly when unhappy – Bulgaria's mascots at the Quidditch World Cup

WINKY – female house-elf

6

ABBOTT, Hannah – student at Hogwarts

ARAGOG – huge spider brought up by Hagrid – lives in the Forbidden Forest

BAGMAN, Ludo – Head of the Department of Magical Games and Sports at the Ministry of Magic

CRABBE, Mr – Vincent Crabbe's father and a Death Eater

CRABBE, Vincent – student at Hogwarts and one of Draco Malfoy's cronies

CROUCH, Barty, Jr – a Death Eater who impersonated 'Mad-Eye' Moody for the whole of Harry's fourth year of school

6–continued

CROUCH, Barty, Sr – one-time head of the Department of International Magical Cooperation at the Ministry of Magic

DAVIES, Roger – student at Hogwarts and captain of the Ravenclaw Quidditch team

DIGGLE, Dedalus – member of the Order of the Phoenix

DIPPET, Professor Armando Albus Dumbledore's predecessor as Headmaster of Hogwarts

FAWKES – Phoenix belonging to Albus Dumbledore – provided the feather that lies inside the wands of Harry and Voldemort

FLAMEL, Nicholas – responsible for making the Philosopher's Stone – worked on alchemy with Albus Dumbledore

FLUFFY – huge, three-headed dog that guarded the trapdoor through which the Philosopher's Stone was hidden

HAGRID, Rubeus – gamekeeper and teacher of the Care of Magical Creatures at Hogwarts

HEDWIG – snowy white owl belonging to Harry Potter

HERMES – screech owl belonging to Percy Weasley

JORDAN, Lee – student at Hogwarts and best friend of Fred and George Weasley

JUGSON – a Death Eater

KARKUS – a giant

MALFOY, Draco – student at Hogwarts and enemy of Harry Potter – became Seeker for the Slytherin Quidditch team in Harry's second year of school

MALFOY, Lucius – Draco Malfoy's father – a Death Eater and supporter of Voldemort

MALFOY, Narcissa – Draco Malfoy's mother and a cousin of Sirius Black

MALKIN, Madam – owns and runs the robe shop in Diagon Alley

MAXIME, Madame Olympe – headmistress of Beauxbatons Academy – a giantess

MUGGLE – name for a non-magic person

MURCUS – head of the merpeople who live in the lake at Hogwarts

NAGINI – snake-like creature whose venom helped restore Voldemort to human form

NORRIS, Mrs – cat with lamp-like eyes belonging to Argus Filch

PEEVES – resident poltergeist at Hogwarts

POTTER, Harry – boy wizard and central character – famously survived a murder attempt by Lord Voldemort, which left a lightning-shaped scar on his forehead – one of the champions of the Triwizard Tournament and Seeker for the Gryffindor Quidditch team – can speak Parseltongue (snake language)

POTTER, James – Harry's father who was Head Boy while at Hogwarts and school friend of Sirius Black, Remus Lupin, and Peter Pettigrew

6–continued

POTTER, Lily – Harry's mother and Petunia Dursley's sister – was Head Girl at Hogwarts and an original member of the Order of the Phoenix

PRONGS – school nickname for James Potter when he was in his animagus form (a stag)

RAGNOK – a goblin

RIDDLE, Tom – Voldemort's original name

RIPPER – Marge Dursley's pet dog

ROSIER – a Death Eater

SPROUT, Professor – Herbology teacher at Hogwarts and head of Hufflepuff house

STROUT, Miriam – a healer at St Mungo's Hospital for Magical Maladies, in charge of the ward where Broderick Bode died

THOMAS, Dean – student at Hogwarts and friend of Harry and Ron Weasley

TREVOR – pet toad belonging to Neville Longbottom

VECTOR, Professor – Arithmancy teacher at Hogwarts

VIOLET – portrait painting of a witch who is good friends with the Fat Lady

WILKES – a Death Eater

7

BAGNOLD, Millicent – Cornelius Fudge's predecessor as Minister for Magic

CADOGAN, Sir – portrait painting at Hogwarts

CREEVEY, Colin – student at Hogwarts

CREEVEY, Dennis – Colin Creevey's younger brother, student at Hogwarts

DERWENT, Dilys – former headmistress of Hogwarts, now present in a portrait painting in Albus Dumbledore's office – was a Healer at St Mungo's Hospital for Magical Maladies

DIGGORY, Cedric – student and Prefect at Hogwarts – one of the champions in the Triwizard Tournament – killed by Peter Pettigrew on Voldemort's orders

DURSLEY, Dudley – Harry's bullying, overweight cousin

DURSLEY, Petunia – Harry's aunt – sister of Lily Potter

DURSLEY, Vernon – Harry's uncle

EVERARD – former headmaster of Hogwarts, now present in a portrait painting in Albus Dumbledore's office

FAT LADY – portrait painting at Hogwarts through which the Gryffindor students enter their Tower

FENWICK, Benjy – an original member of the Order of the Phoenix, killed by Death Eaters

FIRENZE – centaur who lives in the Forbidden Forest next to Hogwarts

GOSHAWK, Miranda – author of the Standard Book of Spells (in various grades)

GRANGER, Hermione – best friend of Harry and Ron Weasley

HOPKIRK, Mafalda – employee of the Improper Use of Magic Office at the Ministry of Magic

7–continued

JOHNSON, Angelina – student at Hogwarts and Chaser for the Gryffindor Quidditch team

JORKINS, Bertha – employee of the Ministry of Magic who was killed by Voldemort

MACNAIR, Walden – executioner at Buckbeak's trial – a Death Eater

NORBERT – dragon of the Norwegian Ridgeback variety – later taken to Romania by Charlie Weasley

PADFOOT – school nickname for Sirius Black when he was in his animagus form (a large black dog)

PERKINS – elderly colleague of Arthur Weasley's at the Ministry of Magic

PODMORE, Sturgis – member of the Order of the Phoenix

POMFREY, Madam Poppy – school nurse at Hogwarts

PREWETT, Fabian and Gideon – original members of the Order of the Phoenix

PRINGLE, Apollyon – caretaker at Hogwarts when Arthur and Molly Weasley were students

SKEETER, Rita – reporter for the Daily Prophet – can transform into a beetle

SPINNET, Alicia – student at Hogwarts and Chaser for the Gryffindor Quidditch team

TRAVERS – a Death Eater

WEASLEY, Arthur – Ron Weasley's father and a member of the Order of the Phoenix – works at the Ministry of Magic and is fascinated by anything to do with Muggles

WEASLEY, Bill – older brother of Ron – worked in Egypt breaking curses for Gringotts Wizarding Bank before moving back to England to join the Order of the Phoenix

WEASLEY, Charlie – older brother of Ron Weasley – former Hogwarts Quidditch captain, now studying dragons in Romania – member of the Order of the Phoenix

WEASLEY, Fred and George – Identical twins and older brothers of Ron Weasley – fond of practical jokes – were beaters for the Gryffindor Quidditch team

WEASLEY, Ginny – younger sister of Ron Weasley – replaced Harry as Seeker for the Gryffindor Quidditch team for part of Harry's fifth year

WEASLEY, Molly – Ron Weasley's mother and a member of the Order of the Phoenix

WEASLEY, Percy – older brother of Ron Weasley – prefect and Head Boy at Hogwarts – left to work at the Ministry of Magic

WEASLEY, Ron – best friend of Harry and Hermione Granger – became both a Prefect and Keeper for the Gryffindor Quidditch team in Harry's fifth year of school

8

BASILISK – large serpent-like creature that petrified those who looked it in the eye

8–continued

BUCKBEAK – a hippogriff (a cross between a horse and an eagle) belonging to Hagrid and later Sirius Black

DEARBORN, Caradoc – an original member of the Order of the Phoenix

DELACOUR, Fleur – one of the champions of the Triwizard Tournament (representing Beauxbatons Academy of Magic) – became an employee at Gringott's Wizarding Bank – partly a Veela

DELACOUR, Gabrielle – Fleur Delacour's younger sister, used as a hostage for a challenge in the Triwizard Tournament

DIMITROV – player for the Bulgarian Quidditch World Cup team

FAT FRIAR – One of the resident ghosts at Hogwarts

FINNIGAN, Seamus – student at Hogwarts and friend of Harry

FLETCHER, Mundungus – member of the Order of the Phoenix

FLITWICK, Professor – teacher of Charms at Hogwarts

GRIPHOOK – a goblin at Gringotts Wizarding Bank

KREACHER – house-elf belonging to both the Black and the Malfoy families

LOCKHART, Gilderoy – Harry's second teacher of Defence Against the Dark Arts

LOVEGOOD, Luna – student at Hogwarts

MAGORIAN – a centaur who lives in the Forbidden Forest

MCKINNON, Marlene – an original member of the Order of the Phoenix, killed by Death Eaters

MEADOWES, Dorcas – an original member of the Order of the Phoenix, killed by Voldemort

MELIFLUA, Araminta – distant relative of Sirius Black

MUDBLOOD – vulgar name for somebody with non-magic parents

MULCIBER – a Death Eater

NIGELLUS, Phineas – Sirius Black's great-great-grandfather

QUIRRELL, Professor – Harry's first Defence Against the Dark Arts teacher

ROOKWOOD, Algernon – a Death Eater

ROSMERTA, Madam – landlady of the Three Broomsticks Inn at Hogsmeade

SCABBERS – seemingly useless rat belonging to Ron Weasley – turned out to be Peter Pettigrew in his animagus form

SHUNPIKE, Stan – conductor on the Knight Bus, a bus that magically transports wizard folk up and down the UK

SINISTRA, Professor – Astronomy teacher at Hogwarts

TENEBRUS – a Thestral (winged horse creatures that pull carriages) – first of its kind born in the Hogwarts forest

8–continued

UMBRIDGE, Professor Dolores – Harry's fifth Defence Against the Dark Arts teacher who replaced Albus Dumbledore as headteacher for a time in Harry's fifth year of school

WORMTAIL – school nickname for Peter Pettigrew when he was in his animagus form (a rat)

9

BLETCHLEY, Miles – student at Hogwarts and Keeper for the Slytherin Quidditch team

BULSTRODE, Millicent – student at Hogwarts and one of Draco Malfoy's cronies

DEMENTORS – menacing guards of the Azkaban prison

EDGECOMBE, Marietta – student at Hogwarts and friend of Cho Chang

FORTESCUE – previous headmaster of Hogwarts, now resident in a portrait painting in Albus Dumbledore's office

FORTESCUE, Florean – owns and runs the ice cream parlour in Diagon Alley

FRIDWULFA – Hagrid's giantess mother

GOLDSTEIN, Anthony – student at Hogwarts

KARKAROFF, Professor Igor – headmaster of Durmstrang school, former Death Eater

LESTRANGE, Bellatrix – wife of Rodolphus Lestrange – a Death Eater and cousin of Sirius Black

LESTRANGE, Rabastan – brother of Rodolphus Lestrange – a Death Eater

LESTRANGE, Rodolphus – husband of Bellatrix Lestrange – Death Eater

MACMILLAN, Ernie – student at Hogwarts

PARKINSON, Pansy – student at Hogwarts and friend of Draco Malfoy

PETTIGREW, Peter – school friend of Sirius Black, James Potter, and Remus Lupin – betrayed James and Lily Potter and then hid out in the form of Scabbers the rat

PUDDIFOOT, Madam – owner of the tea shop in Hogsmeade

RAVENCLAW, Rowena – one of the four founders of Hogwarts – creator of Ravenclaw house

SLINKHARD, Wilbert – author of 'Defensive Magical Theory'

SLYTHERIN, Salazar – one of the four founders of Hogwarts and creator of Slytherin house – known for being a parselmouth

SMETHWYCK, Hippocrates – healer-in-Charge at St Mungo's Hospital for Magical Maladies

TRELAWNEY, Cassandra – great-great-grandmother of Sybill Trelawney – a celebrated seer

TRELAWNEY, Professor Sybill – Divination teacher at Hogwarts

VOLDEMORT, Lord – dark wizard

10

DUMBLEDORE, Aberforth – Albus Dumbledore's brother and an original member of the Order of the Phoenix

DUMBLEDORE, Albus – headmaster of Hogwarts

GRYFFINDOR, Godric – one of the four founders of Hogwarts – creator of Gryffindor house

HUFFLEPUFF, Helga – one of the founders of Hogwarts – creator of Hufflepuff house

LONGBOTTOM, Algie – Neville Longbottom's great uncle

LONGBOTTOM, Alice – Neville Longbottom's mother and an original member of the Order of the Phoenix

LONGBOTTOM, Frank – Neville Longbottom's father and an original member of the Order of the Phoenix

LONGBOTTOM, Neville – friend of Harry, Ron Weasley, and Hermione Granger

MARCHBANKS, Griselda – an Elder at the Wizengamot and head of the Wizarding Examinations Authority

MCGONAGALL, Professor Minerva – transfiguration teacher, deputy headmistress, and head of Gryffindor house – a member of the Order of the Phoenix

OLLIVANDER, Mr – owns and runs the wand shop in Diagon Alley

RACKHARROW, Urquhart – portrait painting at St Mungo's Hospital for Magical Maladies

SCRIMGEOUR – employee at the Ministry of Magic

SORTING HAT – talking wizard's hat (originally belonging to Godric Gryffindor) that famously sorts students into houses on their arrival at the Hogwarts

10–continued

WARRINGTON – student at Hogwarts and player for the Slytherin Quidditch team

11

BLOODY BARON – one of the resident ghosts at Hogwarts

CROOKSHANKS – large ginger cat belonging to Hermione Granger

DEATH EATERS – supporters of Voldemort

SHACKLEBOLT, Kingsley – an Auror and member of the Order of the Phoenix

UNSPEAKABLE – name for employees who work in the Department of Mysteries at the Ministry of Magic (so-called because their work is top secret)

12+

DE MIMSY-PORPINGTON, Sir Nicholas – One of the resident ghosts at Hogwarts, more commonly known as 'Nearly Headless Nick'

FINCH-FLETCHLEY, Justin – student at Hogwarts who was petrified by the Basilisk

GOLGOMATH – a giant

GRUBBLY-PLANK, Professor Wilhelmina – teacher who temporarily took over Hagrid's Care of Magical Creatures classes

MOANING MYRTLE – ghost of a student that haunts one of the girl's bathrooms – killed by the Basilisk when Tom Riddle was at Hogwarts

NEARLY HEADLESS NICK – one of the resident ghosts at Hogwarts (full name Sir Nicholas de Mimsy-Porpington)

PIGWIDGEON 'Pig' – tiny, hyperactive owl given to Ron Weasley by Sirius Black to replace Scabbers the rat

WEIRD SISTERS, the – famous wizarding music group who play at the Yule Ball

LOVERS OF FACT AND FICTION

ANNA KARENINA AND LEON VRONSKI
ANTONY AND CLEOPATRA
AUCASSIN AND NICOLETTE
BEATRICE AND BENEDICK
BONNIE AND CLYDE
BYRON AND LADY CAROLINE LAMB
CHARLES II AND NELL GWYN
CHARLES PARNELL AND KITTY O'SHEA
CHOPIN AND GEORGE SAND
DANTE AND BEATRICE
DAPHNIS AND CHLOE
DARBY AND JOAN
DAVID AND BATHSHEBA
DIDO AND AENEAS
EDWARD VII AND LILLIE LANGTRY
EDWARD VIII AND WALLIS SIMPSON
ELIZABETH BARRETT AND ROBERT
  BROWNING
ELIZABETH BENNETT AND FITZWILLIAM
  DARCY
EROS AND PSYCHE
GEORGE IV AND MARIA FITZHERBERT
GERTRUDE STEIN AND ALICE B TOKLAS
HARLEQUIN AND COLUMBINE
HEATHCLIFF AND CATHY
HELOISE AND ABELARD
HERO AND LEANDER
HORATIO NELSON AND LADY EMMA
  HAMILTON

HUMPHREY BOGART AND LAUREN BACALL
JANE EYRE AND EDWARD ROCHESTER
JOHN OF GAUNT AND KATHERINE
  SWYNFORD
LADY CHATTERLEY AND MELLORS
LANCELOT AND GUINEVERE
NAPOLEON AND JOSEPHINE
ODYSSEUS AND PENELOPE
OSCAR WILDE AND LORD ALFRED DOUGLAS
PAOLO AND FRANCESCA
PARIS AND HELEN
PETRARCH AND LAURA
PORGY AND BESS
PYGMALION AND GALATEA
PYRAMUS AND THISBE
RICHARD BURTON AND ELIZABETH TAYLOR
RIMBAUD AND VERLAINE
ROBIN HOOD AND MAID MARIAN
ROMEO AND JULIET
ROSALIND AND ORLANDO
SAMSON AND DELILAH
SCARLETT O'HARA AND RHETT BUTLER
SPENCER TRACEY AND KATHARINE
  HEPBURN
TRISTAN AND ISOLDE
TROILUS AND CRESSIDA
VIRGINIA WOOLF AND VITA SACKVILLE-
  WEST
W B YEATS AND MAUD GONNE

FICTIONAL DETECTIVES

CHARACTER	(Creator)
MARTIN AINSWORTH	(Michael Underwood)
SUPERINTENDENT RODERICK ALLEYN	(Ngaio Marsh)
INSPECTOR ENRIQUE ALVAREZ	(Roderic Jeffries)
SIR JOHN APPLEBY	(Michael Innes)
SERGEANT NICK ATTWELL	(Michael Underwood)
INSPECTOR BILL AVEYARD	(James Fraser)
PROFESSOR ANDREW BASNETT	(E X Ferrars)
SUPERINTENDENT BATTLE	(Agatha Christie)
SERGEANT WILLIAM BEEF	(Leo Bruce)
TOMMY AND TUPPENCE BERESFORD	(Agatha Christie)
COLONEL PETER BLAIR	(J R L Anderson)
INSPECTOR BLAND	(Julian Symons)
DR WILLIAM BLOW	(Kenneth Hopkins)
INSPECTOR SALVADOR BORGES	(John and Emery Bonett)
DAME BEATRICE BRADLEY	(Gladys Mitchell)
CONSTABLE JOHN BRAGG	(Henry Wade)
MILES BREDON	(Ronald A Knox)
ERNST BRENDEL	(J C Masterman)

INSPECTOR JOHN BRENTFORD	(S B Hough)
RONALD BRIERCLIFFE	(Francis Beeding)
INSPECTOR DAVID BROCK	(R J White)
SUPERINTENDENT JOHN BROCK	(John Bingham)
FATHER BROWN	(G K Chesterton)
JANE AND DAGOBERT BROWN	(Delano Ames)
INSPECTOR THOMAS BRUNT	(John Buxton Hilton)
INSPECTOR BURNIVEL	(Edward Candy)
BROTHER CADFAEL	(Ellis Peters)
INSPECTOR THOMAS CADOVER	(Michael Innes)
RONALD CAMBERWELL	(J S Fletcher)
ALBERT CAMPION	(Margery Allingham)
	(Youngman Carter)
JOHN CARLYLE	(Henry Calvin)
SUPERINTENDENT CHARLESWORTH	(Christianna Brand)
AMBROSE CHITTERWICK	(Anthony Berkeley)
JOSHUA CLUNK	(H C Bailey)
INSPECTOR COCKRILL	(Christianna Brand)
MRS CRAGGS	(H R F Keating)
INSPECTOR CRAMBO	(Julian Symons)
PROFESSOR THEA CRAWFORD	(Jessica Mann)
SERGEANT CRIBB	(Peter Lovesey)
TESSA CRICHTON	(Anne Morice)
SERGEANT CUFF	Wilkie Collins
SUPERINTENDENT ADAM DALGLIESH	(P D James)
PROFESSOR DALY	(Eilís Dillon)
SUPERINTENDENT ANDREW DALZIEL	(Reginald Hill)
CHARMIAN DANIELS	(Jennie Melville)
DR R V DAVIE	(V C Clinton-Baddeley)
CAROLUS DEENE	(Leo Bruce)
INSPECTOR PIET DEVENTER	(J R L Anderson)
SUPERINTENDENT DITTERIDGE	(E X Ferrars)
KENNETH DUCANE (VANDOREN)	(John Bingham)
SUPERINTENDENT DUFFY	(Nigel FitzGerald)
TOBY DYKE	(E X Ferrars)
ROSA EPTON	(Michael Underwood)
MAJOR FAIDE	(Henry Wade)
KATE FANSLER	(Amanda Cross)
GIDEON FELL	(John Dickson Carr)
SUPERINTENDENT GEORGE, DOMINIC, AND BUNTY FELSE	(Ellis Peters)
GERVASE FEN	(Edmund Crispin)
INSPECTOR FINCH (RUDD)	(June Thomson)
INSPECTOR SEPTIMUS FINCH	(Margaret Erskine)
REGGIE FORTUNE	(H C Bailey)
SUPERINTENDENT FRANCIS FOY	(Lionel Black)
VIRGINIA FREER	(E X Ferrars)
INSPECTOR JOSEPH FRENCH	(Freeman Wills Crofts)
DR HENRY FROST	(Josephine Bell)
INSPECTOR MATTHEW FURNIVAL	(Stella Phillips)
INSPECTOR ROBERT FUSIL	(Michael Alding)
SUPERINTENDENT GEORGE GENTLY	(Alan Hunter)
COLONEL ANTHONY GETHRYN	(Philip MacDonald)
INSPECTOR GANESH GHOTE	(H R F Keating)
LINDSAY GORDON	(Val McDermid)
COLONEL ALISTER GRANBY	(Francis Beeding)
INSPECTOR ALAN GRANT	(Gordon Daviot)
	(Josephine Tey)
CELIA GRANT	(John Sherwood)
DR PATRICK GRANT	(Margaret Yorke)
CORDELIA GRAY	(P D James)
EMMA GREAVES	(Lionel Black)

SID HALLEY	(Dick Francis)
SUPERINTENDENT HANNASYDE	(Georgette Heyer)
PAUL HARRIS	(Gavin Black)
JIMMIE HASWELL	(Herbert Adams)
INSPECTOR HAZLERIGG	(Michael Gilbert)
INSPECTOR HEMINGWAY	(Georgette Heyer)
SHERLOCK HOLMES	(Arthur Conan Doyle)
CHARLES HONEYBATH	(Michael Innes)
TAMARA HOYLAND	(Jessica Mann)
INSPECTOR HARRY JAMES	(Kenneth Giles)
INSPECTOR BENJAMIN JURNET	(S T Haymon)
SUPERINTENDENT RICHARD JURY	(Martha Grimes)
INSPECTOR KELSEY	(Emma Page)
INSPECTOR MIKE KENNY	(Eilís Dillon)
SUPERINTENDENT SIMON KENWORTHY	(John Buxton Hilton)
INSPECTOR DON KERRY	(Jeffrey Ashford)
INSPECTOR KYLE	(Roy Vickers)
GERALD LEE	(Kenneth Hopkins)
CORPORAL JUAN LLORCA	(Delano Ames)
INSPECTOR HENRY LOTT	(Henry Wade)
LOVEJOY	(Jonathan Gash)
ADAM LUDLOW	(Simon Nash)
SUPERINTENDENT MACDONALD	(E C R Lorac)
MAIGRET	(Georges Simenon)
ANTONY MAITLAND	(Sara Woods)
DAN MALLETT	(Frank Parrish)
INSPECTOR MALLETT	(Cyril Hare)
PROFESSOR GIDEON MANCIPLE	(Kenneth Hopkins)
PROFESSOR MANDRAKE	(John and Emery Bonett)
SUPERINTENDENT SIMON MANTON	(Michael Underwood)
PHILIP MARLOWE	(Raymond Chandler)
MISS JANE MARPLE	(Agatha Christie)
INSPECTOR GEORGE MARTIN	(Francis Beeding)
PERRY MASON	(Erle Stanley Gardner)
SUPERINTENDENT GEORGE MASTERS	(Douglas Clark)
KINSEY MILLHONE	(Sue Grafton)
SUPERINTENDENT STEVEN MITCHELL	(Josephine Bell)
INSPECTOR MONTERO	(Simon Nash)
INSPECTOR MORSE	(Colin Dexter)
ARIADNE OLIVER	(Agatha Christie)
DAI OWEN	(Henry Calvin)
CHARLES PARIS	(Simon Brett)
INSPECTOR PETER PASCOE	(Reginald Hill)
AMELIA PEABODY	(Elizabeth Peters)
DOUGLAS PERKINS	(Marian Babson)
SERGEANT PATRICK PETRELLA	(Michael Gilbert)
MIKAEL PETROS	(James Anderson)
FRANCIS PETTIGREW	(Cyril Hare)
SUPERINTENDENT JAMES PIBBLE	(Peter Dickinson)
SUPERINTENDENT ARNOLD PIKE	(Philip MacDonald)
MISS MELINDA PINK	(Gwen Moffat)
INSPECTOR THOMAS AND CHARLOTTE E PITT	(Anne Perry)
INSPECTOR POINTER	(A Fielding)
HERCULE POIROT	(Agatha Christie)
SUPERINTENDENT TOM POLLARD	(Elizabeth Lemarchand)
INSPECTOR JOHN POOL	(Henry Wade)
THOMAS PRESTON	(Francis Beeding)
DR LANCELOT PRIESTLEY	(John Rhode)
INSPECTOR WALTER PURBRIGHT	(Colin Watson)
DR HENRY PYM	(W J Burley)
INSPECTOR DOUGLAS QUANTRILL	(Sheila Radley)

ELLERY QUEEN	(Ellery Queen)
COLONEL RACE	(Agatha Christie)
SUPERINTENDENT GEORGE ROGERS	(Jonathan Ross)
INSPECTOR RUDD (FINCH)	(June Thomson)
ALAN RUSSELL	(Nigel FitzGerald)
DR KAY SCARPETTA	(Patricia Cornwell)
ROGER SHERINGHAM	(Anthony Berkeley)
JEMIMA SHORE	(Antonia Fraser)
MAUD SILVER	(Patricia Wentworth)
INSPECTOR C D SLOAN	(Catherine Aird)
SUPERINTENDENT BEN SPENCE	(Michael Allen)
MATTHEW STOCK	(Leonard Tourney)
NIGEL STRANGEWAYS	(Nicholas Blake)
JEREMY STURROCK	(Jeremy Sturrock)
PROFESSOR HILARY TAMAR	(Sarah Caudwell)
INSPECTOR LUKE THANET	(Dorothy Simpson)
KATE THEOBALD	(Lionel Black)
LIZZIE THOMAS	(Anthony Oliver)
DR JOHN THORNDYKE	(R Austin Freeman)
SUPERINTENDENT GEORGE THORNE	(John Penn)
SUPERINTENDENT HENRY AND EMILY TIBBETT	(Patricia Moyes)
MARK TREASURE	(David Williams)
PHILIP TRENT	(E C Bentley)
SUPERINTENDENT PERRY TRETHOWAN	(Robert Barnard)
MISS AMY TUPPER	(Josephine Bell)
V I WARSHAWSKI	(Sara Paretsky)
MALCOLM WARREN	(C H B Kitchin)
CLAUD WARRINGTON-REEVE	(Josephine Bell)
JOHN WEBBER	(Anthony Oliver)
INSPECTOR REGINALD WEXFORD	(Ruth Rendell)
INSPECTOR WILKINS	(James Anderson)
INSPECTOR WILKINS	(Francis Beeding)
LORD PETER WIMSEY	(Dorothy L Sayers)
DR DAVID WINTRINGHAM	(Josephine Bell)
NERO WOLFE	(Rex Stout)
SUPERINTENDENT CHARLES WYCLIFFE	(W J Burley)

GILBERT AND SULLIVAN

OPERAS	**Alternative title**
THESPIS	(The Gods Grown Old)
TRIAL BY JURY	
THE SORCERER	
HMS PINAFORE	(The Lass that Loved a Sailor)
THE PIRATES OF PENZANCE	(The Slave of Duty)
PATIENCE	(Bunthorne's Bride)
IOLANTHE	(The Peer and the Peri)
PRINCESS IDA	(Castle Adamant)
THE MIKADO	(The Town of Titipu)
RUDDIGORE	(The Witch's Curse)
THE YEOMEN OF THE GUARD	(The Merryman and his Maid)
THE GONDOLIERS	(The King of Barataria)
UTOPIA, LIMITED	(The Flowers of Progress)
THE GRAND DUKE	(The Statutory Duel)

CHARACTERS (*Operas*)

4

ADAM (*Ruddigore*)
ELLA (*Patience*)
GAMA (*Princess Ida*)
INEZ (*The Gondoliers*)
JANE (*Patience*)
KATE (*The Pirates of Penzance*)
KO-KO (*The Mikado*)
LUIZ (*The Gondoliers*)
RUTH (*The Pirates of Penzance*)

5

ALINE (*The Sorcerer*)
CELIA (*Iolanthe*)
CYRIL (*Princess Ida*)
EDITH (*The Pirates of Penzance*)
EDWIN (*Trial by Jury*)
FLETA (*Iolanthe*)
LEILA (*Iolanthe*)
MABEL (*The Pirates of Penzance*)
TESSA (*The Gondoliers*)

6

ALEXIS (*The Sorcerer*)
ANGELA (*Patience*)
ISABEL (*The Pirates of Penzance*)
PEEP-BO (*The Mikado*)
SAPHIR (*Patience*)
YUM-YUM (*The Mikado*)

7

CASILDA (*The Gondoliers*)
FLORIAN (*Princess Ida*)
KATISHA (*The Mikado*)
LEONARD (*The Yeomen of the Guard*)
MELISSA (*Princess Ida*)
PHYLLIS (*Iolanthe*)
POOH-BAH (*The Mikado*)

8

ANGELINA (*Trial by Jury*)
FREDERIC (*The Pirates of Penzance*)
GIANETTA (*The Gondoliers*)
HILARION (*Princess Ida*)
IOLANTHE (*Iolanthe*)
NANKI-POO (*The Mikado*)
PATIENCE (*Patience*)
PISH-TUSH (*The Mikado*)
SERGEANT (*The Pirates of Penzance*)
STREPHON (*Iolanthe*)

9

BUNTHORNE (*Patience*)
JACK POINT (*The Yeomen of the Guard*)
JOSEPHINE (*HMS Pinafore*)
PITTI-SING (*The Mikado*)

10

DAME HANNAH (*Ruddigore*)
HILDEBRAND (*Princess Ida*)
LADY PSYCHE (*Princess Ida*)
PIRATE KING (*The Pirates of Penzance*)
ROSE MAYBUD (*Ruddigore*)
SIR RODERIC (*Ruddigore*)

11

DICK DEADEYE (*HMS Pinafore*)
LADY BLANCHE (*Princess Ida*)
MAD MARGARET (*Ruddigore*)
MOUNTARARAT (*Iolanthe*)
PRINCESS IDA (*Princess Ida*)

12

ELSIE MAYNARD (*The Yeomen of the Guard*)
PHOEBE MERYLL (*The Yeomen of the Guard*)
SIR MARMADUKE (*The Sorcerer*)

13

LADY SANGAZURE (*The Sorcerer*)
MARCO PALMIERI (*The Gondoliers*)
ROBIN OAKAPPLE (*Ruddigore*)

14

COLONEL FAIRFAX (*The Yeomen of the Guard*)
DAME CARRUTHERS (*The Yeomen of the Guard*)
RALPH RACKSTRAW (*HMS Pinafore*)

15

CAPTAIN CORCORAN (*HMS Pinafore*)
DUKE OF DUNSTABLE (*Patience*)
DUKE OF PLAZA TORO (*The Gondoliers*)
EARL OF TOLLOLLER (*Iolanthe*)
LITTLE BUTTERCUP (*HMS Pinafore*)
SIR JOSEPH PORTER (*HMS Pinafore*)
WILFRED SHADBOLT (*The Yeomen of the Guard*)

16

COLONEL CALVERLEY (*Patience*)
GIUSEPPE PALMIERI (*The Gondoliers*)
RICHARD DAUNTLESS (*Ruddigore*)

18

ARCHIBALD GROSVENOR (*Patience*)

19

JOHN WELLINGTON WELLS (*The Sorcerer*)
MAJOR-GENERAL STANLEY (*The Pirates of Penzance*)

20

SIR DESPARD MURGATROYD (*Ruddigore*)
SIR RICHARD CHOLMONDELEY (*The Yeomen of the Guard*)

CHARACTERS FROM OPERA

CHARACTER (*Opera*, Composer)

3
LIU (*Turandot*, Puccini)

4
AIDA (*Aida*, Verdi)
ELSA (*Lohengrin*, Wagner)
ERDA (*Das Rheingold, Götterdämmerung, Siegfried*, Wagner)
ERIK (*The Flying Dutchman*, Wagner)
FROH (*Das Rheingold*, Wagner)
GORO (*Madame Butterfly*, Puccini)
KATE (*Madame Butterfly*, Puccini)
LOGE (*Das Rheingold*, Wagner)
LUNA, THE COUNT OF (*Il Trovatore*, Verdi)
MARY (*The Flying Dutchman*, Wagner)
MIME (*Das Rheingold, Götterdämmerung, Siegfried*, Wagner)
MIMI (*La Bohème*, Puccini)
OCHS, BARON (*Der Rosenkavalier*, Strauss)
PANG (*Turandot*, Puccini)
PING (*Turandot*, Puccini)
PONG (*Turandot*, Puccini)

5
BERTA (*The Barber of Seville*, Rossini)
BONZE, THE (*Madame Butterfly*, Puccini)
CALAF (*Turandot*, Puccini)
EDGAR; EDGARDO (*Lucy of Lammermoor*, Donizetti)
FREIA (*Das Rheingold*, Wagner)
GILDA (*Rigoletto*, Verdi)
HAGEN (*Götterdämmerung*, Wagner)
LUCIA See LUCY ASHTON
PETER (*Hansel and Gretel*, Humperdinck)
SENTA (*The Flying Dutchman*, Wagner)
TIMUR (*Turandot*, Puccini)
WITCH (*Hansel and Gretel*, Humperdinck)
WOTAN, THE WANDERER (*Das Rheingold, Die Walküre, Götterdämmerung, Siegfried*, Wagner)

6
AILSIE; ALISA (*Lucy of Lammermoor*, Donizetti)
ALTOUM, THE EMPEROR (*Turandot*, Puccini)
ANNINA (*Der Rosenkavalier*, Strauss; (*La Traviata*, Verdi)
ARTURO See ARTHUR BUCKLAW
BENOIT (*La Bohème*, Puccini)
CARMEN (*Carmen*, Bizet)
DALAND (*The Flying Dutchman*, Wagner)
DONNER (*Das Rheingold*, Wagner)
FAFNER (*Das Rheingold, Götterdämmerung, Siegfried*, Wagner)
FASOLT (*Das Rheingold*, Wagner)
FIGARO (*The Barber of Seville*, Rossini; *The Marriage of Figaro*, Mozart)
FRICKA (*Das Rheingold, Die Walküre, Götterdämmerung*, Wagner)

6–continued
GRETEL (*Hansel and Gretel*, Humperdinck)
HANSEL (*Hansel and Gretel*, Humperdinck)
MANTUA,THE DUKE OF (*Rigoletto*, Verdi)
NORINA (*Don Pasquale*, Donizetti)
NORMAN; NORMANNO (*Lucy of Lammermoor*, Donizetti)
ORTRUD (*Lohengrin*, Wagner)
PAMINA (*The Magic Flute*, Mozart)
RAMFIS; RAMPHIS (*Aida*, Verdi)
ROSINA (*The Barber of Seville*, Rossini)
SOPHIE (*Der Rosenkavalier*, Strauss)
SUZUKI (*Madame Butterfly*, Puccini)
TAMINO (*The Magic Flute*, Mozart)
ZUNIGA (*Carmen*, Bizet)

7
AMNERIS (*Aida*, Verdi)
ANTONIO (*The Marriage of Figaro*, Mozart)
AZUCENA (*Il Trovatore*, Verdi)
BARTOLA, DR (*The Marriage of Figaro*, Mozart)
BARTOLO, DR (*The Barber of Seville*, Rossini)
COLLINE (*La Bohème*, Puccini)
DESPINA (*Cosi Fan Tutte*, Mozart)
DON JOSÉ (*Carmen*, Bizet)
EDGARDO See EDGAR
ERNESTO (*Don Pasquale*, Donizetti)
FANINAL (*Der Rosenkavalier*, Strauss)
GERTRUD (*Hansel and Gretel*, Humperdinck)
GETRUNE (*Götterdämmerung*, Wagner)
GRENVIL, DR (*La Traviata*, Verdi)
GUNTHER (*Götterdämmerung*, Wagner)
HUNDING (*Die Walküre*, Wagner)
LEONORA (*Il Trovatore*, Verdi)
MANRICO (*Il Trovatore*, Verdi)
MASETTO (*Don Giovanni*, Mozart)
MICAELA (*Carmen*, Bizet)
MUSETTA (*La Bohème*, Puccini)
RADAMES (*Aida*, Verdi)
RAMPHIS See RAMFIS
RODOLFO (*La Bohème*, Puccini)
SANDMAN (*Hansel and Gretel*, Humperdinck)
SCARPIA, BARON (*Tosca*, Puccini)
SUSANNA (*The Marriage of Figaro*, Mozart)
ZERLINA (*Don Giovanni*, Mozart)

8
ALBERICH (*Das Rheingold, Götterdämmerung, Siegfried*, Wagner)
ALMAVIVA, COUNTESS (*The Marriage of Figaro*, Mozart)
ALMAVIVA, COUNT (*The Barber of Seville*, Rossini; *The Marriage of Figaro*, Mozart)
AMONASRO (*Aida*, Verdi)
DEW FAIRY (*Hansel and Gretel*, Humperdinck)
FERRANDO (*Cosi Fan Tutte*, Mozart; *Il Trovatore*, Verdi)
FIORELLO (*The Barber of Seville*, Rossini)
GERHILDE (*Die Walküre*, Wagner)

211

CHARACTERS FROM OPERA

8–continued

HELMWIGE (*Die Walküre*, Wagner)
MARCELLO (*La Bohême*, Puccini)
MARIANNE (*Der Rosenkavalier*, Strauss)
NORMANNO *See* NORMAN
OCTAVIAN (*Der Rosenkavalier*, Strauss)
ORTLINDE (*Die Walküre*, Wagner)
PAPAGENA (*The Magic Flute*, Mozart)
PAPAGENO (*The Magic Flute*, Mozart)
RAIMONDO *See* BIDE-THE-BENT
SARASTRO (*The Magic Flute*, Mozart)
SIEGMUND (*Die Walküre*, Wagner)
SIEGRUNE (*Die Walküre*, Wagner)
SPOLETTA (*Tosca*, Puccini)
TURANDOT, PRINCESS (*Turandot*, Puccini)
WOGLINDE (*Das Rheingold*, *Götterdämmerung*, Wagner)
YAMADORI, PRINCE (*Madame Butterfly*, Puccini)

9

ANGELOTTI (*Tosca*, Puccini)
BARBARINA (*The Marriage of Figaro*, Mozart)
CHERUBINO (*The Marriage of Figaro*, Mozart)
DON CURZIO (*The Marriage of Figaro*, Mozart)
DONNA ANNA (*Don Giovanni*, Mozart)
DORABELLA (*Cosi Fan Tutte*, Mozart)
ESCAMILLO (*Carmen*, Bizet)
GRIMGERDE (*Die Walküre*, Wagner)
GUGLIELMO (*Cosi Fan Tutte*, Mozart)
LEPORELLO (*Don Giovanni*, Mozart)
LOHENGRIN (*Lohengrin*, Wagner)
MADDALENA (*Rigoletto*, Verdi)
MALATESTA, DR (*Don Pasquale*, Donizetti)
PINKERTON, LIEUTENANT B F (*Madame Butterfly*, Puccini)
ROSSWEISS (*Die Walküre*, Wagner)
SCHAUNARD (*La Bohême*, Puccini)
SHARPLESS (*Madame Butterfly*, Puccini)
SIEGFRIED (*Götterdämmerung*, *Siegfried*, Wagner)
SIEGLINDE (*Die Walküre*, Wagner)
VALZACCHI (*Der Rosenkavalier*, Strauss)
WALTRAUTE (*Die Walküre*, *Götterdämmerung*, Wagner)
WELLGUNDE (*Das Rheingold*, *Götterdämmerung*, Wagner)

10

BRÜNNHILDE (*Die Walküre*, *Götterdämmerung*, *Siegfried*, Wagner)
DON ALFONSO (*Cosi Fan Tutte*, Mozart)
DON BASILIO (*The Barber of Seville*, Rossini; *The Marriage of Figaro*, Mozart)
DON OTTAVIO (*Don Giovanni*, Mozart)
FIORDILIGI (*Cosi Fan Tutte*, Mozart)
FLOSSHILDE (*Das Rheingold*, *Götterdämmerung*, Wagner)
LUCY ASHTON; LUCIA (*Lucy of Lammermoor*, Donizetti)
MARCELLINA (*The Marriage of Figaro*, Mozart)
MONOSTATOS (*The Magic Flute*, Mozart)

11

BIDE-THE-BENT; RAIMONDO (*Lucy of Lammermoor*, Donizetti)
DON GIOVANNI (*Don Giovanni*, Mozart)
DONNA ELVIRA (*Don Giovanni*, Mozart)
DON PASQUALE (*Don Pasquale*, Donizetti)
FLORIO TOSCA (*Tosca*, Puccini)
HENRY ASHTON; ENRICO (*Lucy of Lammermoor*, Donizetti)
MARSCHALLIN (*Der Rosenkavalier*, Strauss)
SPARAFUCILE (*Rigoletto*, Verdi)

12

COMMENDATORE, THE (*Don Giovanni*, Mozart)
FLORA BERVOIX (*La Traviata*, Verdi)
SCHWERTLEITE (*Die Walküre*, Wagner)

13

ARTHUR BUCKLAW; ARTURO (*Lucy of Lammermoor*, Donizetti)

14+

ALFREDO GERMONT (*La Traviata*, Verdi)
FRIEDRICH VON TELRAMUND (*Lohengrin*, Wagner)
GIORGIO GERMONT (*La Traviata*, Verdi)
HENRY I OF GERMANY (*Lohengrin*, Wagner)
MADAME BUTTERFLY (*Madame Butterfly*, Puccini)
MARIO CAVARADOSSI (*Tosca*, Puccini)
VIOLETTA VALERY (*La Traviata*, Verdi)

CHARACTERS FROM NURSERY RHYMES

3
CAT
COW
NAN
TOM

4
DISH
JACK
JILL
JOHN
JUDY
MARY
PAUL

5
BAKER, THE
PETER
POLLY
PUNCH
ROBIN
SANDY
SPOON
SUKEY
TAFFY

6
FIDDLE
JOHNNY

7
BUTCHER, THE
RICHARD

8
BILLY BOY
DAME TROT
LADYBIRD
PUSSY CAT
THUMBKIN

9
AIKEN DRUM
COCK ROBIN
GREEDY NAN
JACK SPRAT
JENNY WREN
JOHN SMITH
LITTLE DOG
WILLY WOOD

10
BLACK SHEEP
DAPPLE GREY
KING ARTHUR
LUCY LOCKET
MARGERY DAW
PETER PIPER
SLEEPY-HEAD
TOMMY STOUT
TWEEDLEDEE
TWEEDLEDUM

11
BESSY BROOKS
ELSIE MARLEY
FARMER GILES
JACK AND JILL
JEMMY DAWSON
JOHNNY GREEN
JUMPING JOAN
KITTY FISHER
OLD KING COLE
SIMPLE SIMON
TOMMY O'LINN
TOMMY SNOOKS
BETTY PRINGLE
BOBBY SHAFTOE
DARBY AND JOAN
DISH AND SPOON
DOCTOR FOSTER
FARMER'S WIFE
HUMPTY DUMPTY
KING OF HEARTS
LITTLE BO-PEEP
NOTHING-AT-ALL
PETER AND PAUL
PUNCH AND JUDY
ROBERT BARNES
ROBERT ROWLEY
YANKEE DOODLE

13
ANTHONY ROWLEY
CHARLEY BARLEY
DOCTOR FAUSTUS
FATHER FRANCIS
GEORGIE PORGIE
GREGORY GRIGGS

13–continued
JOHNNY PRINGLE
KNAVE OF HEARTS
LITTLE BOY BLUE
MRS SHECKLETON
QUEEN OF HEARTS
SOLOMON GRUNDY

14
DAFFY DOWN DILLY
OLD MOTHER GOOSE
ROBIN REDBREAST
THREE BLIND MICE

15
HECTOR PROTECTOR
LITTLE BETTY BLUE
LITTLE TOM TINKER
ROBIN AND RICHARD
WEE WILLIE WINKIE

16
CANDLESTICK MAKER, THE
LITTLE JACK HORNER
LITTLE MISS MUFFET
OLD MOTHER HUBBARD
OLD MOTHER SHUTTLE

17
INCEY WINCEY SPIDER
LITTLE TOMMY TUCKER

18+
ELSPETH, BETSY, AND BESS
GOOSEY GOOSEY GANDER
LITTLE NANCY ETTICOAT
LITTLE POLLY FLINDERS
LITTLE TOMMY TITTLE-
  MOUSE
MATTHEW MARK LUKE AND
  JOHN
OLD MOTHER TWITCHETT
OLD WOMAN WHO LIVED IN
  A SHOE
THE CAT AND THE FIDDLE
THE GRAND OLD DUKE OF
  YORK
THEOPHILUS THISTLEDOWN
THREE LITTLE KITTENS
WILLIAM MCTRIMBLETOE

HISTORY, POLITICS, GOVERNMENT, AND LAW

OLD NAMES OF COUNTRIES

CURRENT NAME	OLD NAME(S) (MOST RECENT FIRST)
BANGLADESH	EAST PAKISTAN
BELAU	PALAU (*OR* PELEW)
BELIZE	BRITISH HONDURAS
BENIN	DAHOMEY
BOLIVIA	UPPER PERU
BOTSWANA	BECHUANALAND
BURKINA FASO	UPPER VOLTA
CAYMAN ISLANDS	LAS TORTUGAS

CONGO,
  DEMOCRATIC
  REPUBLIC OF
	ZAÏRE; CONGO;
	  BELGIAN CONGO;
	  CONGO FREE STATE

ETHIOPIA	ABYSSINIA
GHANA	GOLD COAST
GUINEA	FRENCH GUINEA; RIVIÈRES DU SUD
GUINEA-BISSAU	PORTUGUESE GUINEA
GUYANA	BRITISH GUIANA
HAITI	SAINT-DOMINIQUE
INDONESIA	DUTCH EAST INDIES
IRAN	PERSIA
IRAQ	MESOPOTAMIA

IRELAND,
  REPUBLIC OF
	EIRE; IRISH FREE
	  STATE

JORDAN	TRANSJORDAN
KENYA	EAST AFRICA PROTECTORATE
KIRIBATI	GILBERT ISLANDS
LESOTHO	BASUTOLAND
MADAGASCAR	MALAGASY REPUBLIC
MALAWI	NYASALAND

CURRENT NAME	OLD NAME(S) (MOST RECENT FIRST)
MALDIVES	MALDIVE ISLANDS
MALI	FRENCH SUDAN

MONGOLIA	MONGOLIAN PEOPLE'S
	  REPUBLIC; OUTER
	  MONGOLIA

MYANMAR	BURMA
NAMIBIA	SOUTH WEST AFRICA
NAURU	PLEASANT ISLAND
NEW ZEALAND	STATEN LAND
NIUE	SAVAGE ISLAND
OMAN	MUSCAT AND OMAN
PUERTO RICO	PORTO RICO
SERBIA AND MONTENEGRO	YUGOSLAVIA
SINGAPORE	TUMASIK (*OR* TEMASEK)
SRI LANKA	CEYLON
SURINAME	DUTCH GUIANA
TAIWAN	FORMOSA
TANZANIA	TANGANYIKA
THAILAND	SIAM
TOGO	FRENCH TOGOLAND
TUNISIA	CARTHAGE
TURKEY	OTTOMAN EMPIRE
TUVALU	ELLICE ISLANDS
UNITED ARAB EMIRATES	TRUCIAL STATES
VANUATU	NEW HEBRIDES
ZAMBIA	NORTHERN RHODESIA
ZIMBABWE	RHODESIA; SOUTHERN

OLD NAMES OF CAPITAL AND MAJOR CITIES

CURRENT NAME	OLD NAME(S) (MOST RECENT FIRST)	CURRENT NAME	OLD NAME(S) (MOST RECENT FIRST)
ALMATY	ALMA-ATA; VERNY	KIROV	VYATKA
ANTANANARIVO	TANANARIVE	KOROR	CORRORA
ASTANA	AKMOLA	LUANDA	SÃO PAULO DE
BANDAR SERI	BRUNEI TOWN		LOANDA
BEGAWAN		MALABO	SANTA ISABEL
BANJUL	BATHURST	MAPUTO	LOURENÇO MARQUES
BEIJING	PEI-P'ING (OR	MEXICO CITY	TENOCHTITLÁN
(OR PEKING)	BEIBING); TA-TU	MONTREAL	VILLE-MARIE
BISHKEK	FRUNZE	MUMBAI	BOMBAY
(OR PISHPEK)		NABEREZHNYE	BREZHNEV; CHELNY
BOGOTÁ	BACATÁ	CHELNY	
BUJUMBURA	USUMBURA	NAPLES	NEAPOLIS
CAIRO	EL QAHIRA;	N'DJAMENA	FORT LAMY
	EL FUSTAT	NIZHNY	GORKY (OR GORKI)
CARACAS	SANTIAGO DE LEÓN	NOVGOROD	
DE CARACAS		NOUMÉA	PORT-DE-FRANCE
CHARLOTTE	SAINT THOMAS	NUUK	GODTHAÅB
AMALIE		OTTAWA	BYTOWN
CONSTANTINE	CIRTA	OSLO	KRISTIANIA
DHAKA	DACCA	PAGO PAGO	PANGO PANGO
DNEPROPETROVSK	EKATERINOSLAV	PALIKIR	KOLONIA
DONETSK	STALINO; YUZOVKA	PERM	MOLOTOV
DÚN LAOGHAIRE	KINGSTOWN;	SAMARA	KUYBYSHEV
	DUNLEARY	SANTO DOMINGO	CIUDAD TRUJILLO
DUSHANBE	STALINABAD;	SOFIA	SERDICA
	DYUSHAMBE	ST PETERSBURG	LENINGRAD;
EKATERINBURG	SVERDLOVSK		PETROGRAD
EAST LONDON	PORT REX	T'BILISI	TIFLIS
FAISALABAD	LYALLPUR	THESSALONÍKI	SALONIKA;
FORT-DE-FRANCE	FORT ROYAL		THESSALONICA
GABERONE	GABERONES	TOKYO	EDO
HARARE	SALISBURY	TRIPOLI	OEA
HO CHI MINH CITY	SAIGON	UJANG PANDANG	MACASSAR (OR
ISTANBUL	CONSTANTINOPLE;		MAKASAR)
	BYZANTIUM	ULAANBAATAR	URGA
IZMIR	SMYRNA	VADODARA	BARODA
JAKARTA	BATAVIA	VOLGOGRAD	STALINGRAD;
KANPUR	CAWNPORE		TSARITSYN
KINSHASA	LÉOPOLDVILLE		

ROMAN NAMES OF CITIES

ROMAN NAME – BRITISH NAME

ANDERITUM – PEVENSEY
AQUAE SULIS – BATH
CALLEVA – SILCHESTER
CAMULODUNUM – COLCHESTER
CORINIUM – CIRENCESTER
DANUM – DONCASTER
DEVA – CHESTER
DURNOVARIA – DORCHESTER
DUROLIPONTE – GRANTCHESTER
DUROVERNUM – CANTERBURY
EBORACUM – YORK
GLEVUM – GLOUCESTER
ISARIUM – ALDEBOROUGH
ISCA – CAERLEON
ISCA – EXETER
LETOCETUM – WALL
LINDINIS – ILCHESTER
LINDUM – LINCOLN
LONDINIUM – LONDON
LUGUVALIUM – CARLISLE
MAMUCIUM – MANCHESTER
MORIDUNUM – CARMARTHEN
NOVIOMAGUS – CHICHESTER
PETURIA – BROUGH
POTUS ADURNI – PORTCHESTER
RATAE – LEICESTER
SARUM – SALISBURY
SEGONTIUM – CAERNARFON
TAMIUM – CARDIFF
VENTA – CAERWENT
VENTA – WINCHESTER
VERTIS – WORCESTER
VERULAMIUM – ST ALBANS
VIROCONIUM – WROXETER

CELTIC TRIBES OF BRITAIN

ATREBATES
BRIGANTES
CALEDONII
CANTIUM
CATUVELLAUNI
CORIELTAUVI
CORNOVII
DECEANGELI
DEMETAE
DOBUNNI
DRUIDS
DUROTRIGES
ICENI
NOVANTAE
ORDOVICES
PARISI
SELGOVAE
SILURES
TAXALI
TRINOVANTES
VACOMAGI
VENICONES
VOTADINI

THE EUROPEAN UNION

STATE	ACCESSION YEAR	STATE	ACCESSION YEAR
AUSTRIA	1995	LATVIA	2004
BELGIUM	1958	LITHUNIA	2004
CYPRUS	2004	LUXEMBOURG	1958
CZECH REPUBLIC	2004	MALTA	2004
DENMARK	1973	NETHERLANDS	1958
ESTONIA	2004	POLAND	2004
FINLAND	1995	PORTUGAL	1986
FRANCE	1958	SLOVAKIA	2004
GERMANY	1958	SLOVENIA	2004
GREECE	1981	SPAIN	1986
HUNGARY	2004	SWEDEN	1995
IRELAND	1973	UK	1973
ITALY	1958		

MEMBERS OF THE COMMONWEALTH

ANTIGUA AND BARBUDA
AUSTRALIA
THE BAHAMAS
BANGLADESH
BARBADOS
BELIZE
BOTSWANA
BRUNEI DARUSSALAM
CAMEROON
CANADA
CYPRUS
DOMINICA
FIJI ISLANDS
THE GAMBIA
GHANA
GRENADA
GUYANA
INDIA
JAMAICA

KENYA
KIRIBATI
LESOTHO
MALAWI
MALAYSIA
MALDIVES
MALTA
MAURITIUS
MOZAMBIQUE
NAMIBIA
NAURU
NEW ZEALAND
NIGERIA
PAKISTAN
PAPUA NEW GUINEA
ST KITTS AND NEVIS
ST LUCIA
ST VINCENT AND THE
    GRENADINES

SAMOA
SEYCHELLES
SIERRA LEONE
SINGAPORE
SOLOMON ISLANDS
SOUTH AFRICA
SRI LANKA
SWAZILAND
TONGA
TRINIDAD AND TOBAGO
TUVALU
UGANDA
UNITED KINGDOM
UNITED REPUBLIC OF TAN-
    ZANIA
VANUATU
ZAMBIA

MEMBERS OF NATO

BELGIUM
BULGARIA
CANADA
CZECH REPUBLIC
DENMARK
ESTONIA
FRANCE
GERMANY
GREECE

HUNGARY
ICELAND
ITALY
LATVIA
LITHUANIA
LUXEMBOURG
NETHERLANDS
NORWAY
POLAND

PORTUGAL
ROMANIA
SLOVAKIA
SLOVENIA
SPAIN
TURKEY
UNITED KINGDOM
UNITED STATES

POLITICAL PARTIES AND MOVEMENTS IN THE UK

A NEW PARTY FOR BRITAIN
ALLIANCE FOR GREEN SOCIALISM
ALLIANCE PARTY OF NORTHERN IRELAND
ASSOCIATION OF CONSERVATIVE CLUBS
BOW GROUP
BRITANNIA PARTY
BRITISH FIELD SPORTS SOCIETY
BRITISH NATIONAL PARTY
BRUGES GROUP
CAMPAIGN FOR AN INDEPENDENT BRITAIN.
CAMPAIGN FOR CONSERVATIVE
  DEMOCRACY
CAMPAIGN FOR NUCLEAR DISARMAMENT
CAMPAIGN FOR POLITICAL ECOLOGY
CHARITY COMMISSION
CHARTER FOR BASIC DEMOCRATIC RIGHTS
CHARTER MOVEMENT
CHRISTIAN PEOPLES ALLIANCE
COMMON GOOD
COMMUNIST ACTION
COMMUNIST PARTY IN WALES
COMMUNIST PARTY OF BRITAIN
COMMUNIST PARTY OF GREAT BRITAIN
COMMUNITY ACTION PARTY
COMMUNITY ALLIANCE
COMMUNITY REPRESENTATIVE PARTY
CONNOLLY ASSOCIATION
CONSENSUS
CONSERVATIVE CHRISTIAN FELLOWSHIP
CONSERVATIVE PARTY
CONSERVATIVE WAY FORWARD
CONSTITUTIONAL MONARCHY ASSOCIATION
COOPERATIVE PARTY
COUNTRYSIDE PARTY
DEMOCRATIC PARTY
DEMOCRATIC UNIONIST PARTY
ENGLAND DEVOLVE!
ENGLAND FIRST PARTY
ENGLISH DEMOCRATS
ENGLISH INDEPENDENCE PARTY
ENVIRONMENTAL PROTEST IN BRITAIN
FEDERATION OF STUDENT NATIONALISTS
FREEDOM PARTY
FRIENDS OF THE EARTH
GRAND ORANGE LODGE OF IRELAND
GREEN PARTY
GREEN SOCIALIST NETWORK
GREENPEACE
IMPERIAL PARTY
IMPERIAL TORIES
INDEPENDENT GREEN VOICE
INDEPENDENT LABOUR NETWORK
INDEPENDENT WORKING CLASS
  ASSOCIATION
INSTITUTE OF RADICAL REFORM
IRISH REPUBLICAN SOCIALIST MOVEMENT
IRISH REPUBLICAN SOCIALIST PARTY
LABOUR FRIENDS OF ISRAEL

LABOUR PARTY
LAND IS OURS
LEAGUE AGAINST CRUEL SPORTS
LIBERAL DEMOCRATS
LIBERAL PARTY
LIGALI PARTY
MEBYON KERNOW
MONARCHIST LEAGUE
MOVEMENT AGAINST THE MONARCHY
NATIONAL DEMOCRATS
NATIONAL FRONT
NATURAL LAW PARTY
NORTHERN IRELAND WOMEN'S COALITION
OFFICIAL MONSTER RAVING LOONY PARTY
OPERATION CHRISTIAN VOTE
ORGANISATION OF FREE DEMOCRATS
PENSIONERS PARTY
PEOPLE AGAINST BUREAUCRACY ACTION
  GROUP
PLAID CYMRU
PROGRESSIVE UNIONIST PARTY
PROLIFE ALLIANCE
RAINBOW DREAM TICKET PARTY
RED ACTION
REFERENDUM PARTY
REVOLUTIONARY COMMUNIST GROUP
SCIENTISTS FOR LABOUR
SCOTTISH CONSERVATIVE AND UNIONIST
  PARTY
SCOTTISH INDEPENDENCE PARTY
SCOTTISH NATIONAL PARTY
SCOTTISH REPUBLICAN SOCIALIST
  MOVEMENT
SCOTTISH UNIONIST PARTY
SDLP
SINN FEIN
SOCIAL DEMOCRATIC AND LABOUR PARTY
SOCIAL JUSTICE PARTY
SOCIALIST ALLIANCE
SOCIALIST EQUALITY PARTY
SOCIALIST LABOUR PARTY
SOCIALIST PARTY
SOCIALIST WORKERS PARTY
THIRD WAY
THRONE OUT
TROOPS OUT MOVEMENT
UK LIBERTARIAN ALLIANCE
ULSTER NATION
ULSTER THIRD WAY
ULSTER UNIONIST PARTY
UNITED KINGDOM INDEPENDENCE PARTY
UNITED KINGDOM UNIONIST PARTY
WHITE NATIONALIST PARTY
WORKERS PARTY
WORKERS PARTY OF IRELAND
WORKERS' REVOLUTIONARY PARTY
YOUTH FOR A FREE EUROPE

LEGAL TERMS

2&3	5–continued	6–continued	6–continued
BAN	BRIEF	ANSWER	RESCUE
BAR	BRING	APPEAL	RETAIN
CAV	CHEAT	ARREST	RETURN
DOE	CHOSE	ASSETS	REVIEW
FEE	CLAIM	ASSIGN	SAVING
JUS	CLOSE	ATTACH	SCRIPT
NP	COUNT	ATTORN	SPECIE
ROE	COURT	CAMERA	SUITOR
RUN	COVIN	CAPIAS	TENDER
USE	DEMUR	CAVEAT	TROVER
	DEVIL	CESSER	VACANT
4	DONEE	CHARGE	VACATE
ABLE	DONOR	COMMON	VENTER
AVER	ENTER	CONVEY	VERIFY
AVOW	ESTOP	COVERT	VIEWER
BAIL	FOLIO	CY PRES	
BANC	IN REM	DEFEAT	**7**
BILL	ISSUE	DELICT	ACCUSED
BOND	JOINT	DEMAND	AFFIANT
COST	JURAT	DEPONE	ALIENEE
DEED	LAPSE	DEPOSE	ALIENOR
FACT	LIBEL	DEVISE	ALIMONY
FEME	LIMIT	DICTUM	AMNESTY
FIND	MESNE	DISBAR	ANCIENT
FLAW	MORAL	DOCKET	APPROVE
FREE	NAKED	DOMAIN	ASSAULT
GIST	OVERT	DURESS	BEQUEST
HEAR	PANEL	ENJOIN	CAPITAL
LAND	PAROL	EQUITY	CAUTION
LIEN	PETTY	ESCROW	CODICIL
MISE	PLEAD	ESTRAY	COMMUTE
MUTE	POSSE	EXTENT	CONDONE
NISI	PRIVY	FOREST	CONNIVE
NUDE	PROOF	GUILTY	CONVERT
OATH	PROVE	HOLDER	CRUELTY
OPEN	REMIT	INFANT	CULPRIT
PLEA	REPLY	INFIRM	CURATOR
REST	SHORE	INJURY	DAMAGES
ROUT	SOUND	INTENT	DAMNIFY
RULE	SQUAT	JUNIOR	DEFAULT
SOLE	STALE	LACHES	DEFENCE
TERM	TALES	MALICE	DERAIGN
TORT	TENOR	MATTER	DETINUE
UDAL	THING	MAYHEM	DEVOLVE
USER	TITLE	MERGER	DIES NON
VIEW	TRIAL	MOTION	DOWABLE
WAIF	VENUE	NONAGE	EMPANEL
WAND	WASTE	OWELTY	ENGROSS
	WRONG	PLAINT	ESCHEAT
5		PRAYER	ESTREAT
ABATE	**6**	PREFER	EXAMINE
ADOPT	ABATOR	RECOUP	EXECUTE
ADULT	ACCRUE	REJOIN	EXHIBIT
AGIST	ACTION	RELIEF	EX PARTE
ALIBI	AFFIRM	REMAND	FICTION
ARRAY	AFFRAY	REMISE	FILIATE
AVOID	AMERCE	REPORT	FINDING
AWARD			

7–continued

FOREIGN
FOREMAN
FORFEIT
GARNISH
GRANTEE
GRANTOR
IMPLEAD
JOINDER
JUS SOLI
JUSTIFY
LARCENY
MANAGER
MENS REA
MISUSER
MOVABLE
NONSUIT
OBSCENE
ONEROUS
OPENING
PORTION
PRECEPT
PRESUME
PURVIEW
RECITAL
RECOVER
REFEREE
RELATOR
RELEASE
REPLEVY
RESIDUE
REVERSE
SCANDAL
SETTLOR
SEVERAL
SLANDER
TESTIFY
VESTURE
WARRANT

8

ABEYANCE
ABSOLUTE
ACT OF GOD
ALIENATE
APPELLEE
ASSIGNEE
ASSIGNOR
AVULSION
BAILABLE
BEQUEATH
BONDSMAN
CAVEATOR
CHANCERY
CITATION
COMPOUND
CONTINUE
COPYHOLD
COVENANT
DEAD HAND
DECEDENT
DEED POLL

8–continued

DEMURRER
DEPONENT
DETAINER
DISCLAIM
DISTRAIN
DISTRESS
DIVIDEND
DOMINION
DOTATION
ESTOPPEL
ESTOVERS
EVIDENCE
EXECUTOR
FELO DE SE
FEME SOLE
FIDUCIAL
FORJUDGE
FUNGIBLE
GRAVAMEN
GUARDIAN
HAND DOWN
HANDLING
HEIRSHIP
HERITAGE
IN CAMERA
INNUENDO
INSANITY
INSTRUCT
JEOPARDY
JOINTURE
JURATORY
MANDAMUS
MATERIAL
MITTIMUS
MONOPOLY
MORTMAIN
NON PROS
NOVATION
NUISANCE
OBLIVION
OCCUPANT
PERSONAL
PETITION
PLEADING
PREMISES
PRESENTS
PROPERTY
QUESTION
REBUTTER
RECOVERY
RELATION
REPLEVIN
SCHEDULE
SCIENTER
SOLATIUM
SOLUTION
SPINSTER
STRANGER
SUI JURIS
TORTIOUS
TRANSFER

8–continued

TRAVERSE
TRESPASS
VOIR DIRE

9

ABANDONEE
ACCESSARY
ACCRETION
ADMINICLE
AFFIDAVIT
ALIENABLE
APPELLANT
APPELLATE
APPENDANT
ARBITRARY
ASSUMPSIT
AUTHORITY
AVOIDANCE
BAILIWICK
BLASPHEMY
BONA FIDES
CARTULARY
CHALLENGE
CHAMPERTY
COMPETENT
CONDITION
COVERTURE
CUSTOMARY
DEBATABLE
DEFALCATE
DEMANDANT
DESERTION
DEVISABLE
DILIGENCE
DISAFFIRM
DISCHARGE
DISCOMMON
DISCOVERT
DISCOVERY
DISTRAINT
EQUITABLE
EXCEPTION
EXECUTRIX
EXEMPLIFY
FIDUCIARY
FILIATION
FORECLOSE
FOREJUDGE
GARNISHEE
GRAND JURY
GUARANTEE
IMMOVABLE
IMPERFECT
INSTANTER
INTENTION
INTERVENE
JOINTRESS
LITIGABLE
MORTGAGEE
MUNIMENTS
OCCUPANCY

9–continued

ONOMASTIC
PECUNIARY
PLEADINGS
PRECEDENT
PREJUDICE
PRESCRIBE
PRINCIPAL
PROPONENT
QUITCLAIM
RECAPTION
RE-EXAMINE
REJOINDER
RES GESTAE
RESIDUARY
SEQUESTER
SERVITUDE
SEVERABLE
SEVERANCE
SOLEMNITY
SPECIALTY
STATEMENT
SUBROGATE
SURCHARGE
SURRENDER
TESTAMENT
TESTIMONY
TRADITION
VEXATIOUS
VOLUNTARY
VOLUNTEER

10

ABSENTE REO
ACTIONABLE
ADMISSIBLE
AGGRAVATED
ALIENATION
AMBULATORY
APOTHECARY
APPEARANCE
ASSIGNMENT
ATTACHMENT
AUTOMATISM
BENEFICIAL
BILL OF SALE
CASE STATED
CERTIORARI
CESSIONARY
CIVIL DEATH
COEXECUTOR
COGNIZABLE
COGNIZANCE
COMMITMENT
COMMUTABLE
COMPETENCY
CONCLUSION
CONNIVANCE
CONSENSUAL
CONSORTIUM
CONSTITUTE
CONTRACTOR

10–continued
CONVERSION
CONVEYANCE
COPARCENER
COPYHOLDER
DEFAMATION
DEFEASIBLE
DEPOSITION
DISINHERIT
DISORDERLY
DISTRAINEE
DISTRINGAS
EMBLEMENTS
FEME COVERT
GRATUITOUS
GROUND RENT
HEREDITARY
HOMOLOGATE
IMPARTIBLE
IMPEDIMENT
INCAPACITY
INDUCEMENT
INJUNCTION
IN PERSONAM
INTERPLEAD
LIMITATION
MEMORANDUM
MISJOINDER
NEGLIGENCE
NEXT FRIEND
NONJOINDER
OBLIGATION
PERCEPTION
PEREMPTORY
PERSONALTY
POSSESSORY
PRE-EMPTION
PREFERENCE
PRIVILEGED
PRIZE COURT
PROPOSITUS
RECOGNIZEE
RECOGNIZOR
RESCISSION
RESOLUTIVE
RESPONDENT
SECULARIZE
SETTLEMENT
SIGN MANUAL
SMART MONEY
SPOLIATION
STILLICIDE
SUBMISSION
SURPLUSAGE
SUSPENSION
TORT-FEASOR
TRIAL COURT
ULTRA VIRES
UNILATERAL

11
AFFIRMATION

11–continued
ARBITRATION
ASSIGNATION
BED AND BOARD
BENEFICIARY
CLASS ACTION
COMPLAINANT
CONTENTIOUS
COPARCENARY
DECLARATION
DECLARATORY
DESCENDIBLE
DISCONTINUE
DISTRIBUTEE
DISTURBANCE
ENCUMBRANCE
EXAMINATION
FIERI FACIAS
FORBEARANCE
FORNICATION
GARNISHMENT
HYPOTHECATE
INCOMPETENT
INCORPOREAL
INHERITANCE
LOCUS STANDI
MAINTENANCE
MALFEASANCE
MARE CLAUSUM
MARE LIBERUM
MATTER OF LAW
MINISTERIAL
MISFEASANCE
MISPLEADING
NECESSARIES
NONFEASANCE
NUDUM PACTUM
PORT OF ENTRY
PRESENTMENT
PRESUMPTION
PROCURATION
PROCURATORY
PROHIBITION
QUO WARRANTO
REPLICATION
RESERVATION
RES JUDICATA
RESTITUTION
SCIRE FACIAS
SEARCH ORDER
SELF-DEFENCE
SEQUESTRATE
SPECIAL CASE
SUBROGATION
SURREBUTTAL
SURREBUTTER
UNAVOIDABLE

12
ACCUSATORIAL
AMICUS CURIAE
BONA VACANTIA

12–continued
CODIFICATION
COMPURGATION
CONSTRUCTIVE
CONVENTIONAL
CO-RESPONDENT
CROSS-EXAMINE
DENUNCIATION
DETERMINABLE
DISTRIBUTION
ENCUMBRANCER
FORCE MAJEURE
HABEAS CORPUS
INDEFEASIBLE
INSTRUCTIONS
INTERPLEADER
JUS SANGUINIS
MANSLAUGHTER
MATTER OF FACT
MISADVENTURE
OBITER DICTUM
ONUS PROBANDI
PENDENTE LITE
PRESCRIPTION
RECEIVERSHIP
RECOGNIZANCE
SURREJOINDER
TRAFFIC COURT
UNAPPEALABLE
UNCOVENANTED
VENIRE FACIAS
VERIFICATION

13
A MENSA ET THORO
ATTORNEY-AT-LAW
BODY CORPORATE
BREACH OF TRUST
BURDEN OF PROOF
CERTIFICATION
CIVIL MARRIAGE
CONSIDERATION
CONSOLIDATION
CORPUS DELICTI
CRIMEN INJURIA
DETERMINATION
EMINENT DOMAIN
INQUISITORIAL
INTERLOCUTORY
IRREPLEVIABLE
JURIDICAL DAYS
NOLLE PROSEQUI
PARAPHERNALIA
PATERNITY SUIT
PREMEDITATION
PRIMOGENITURE
PROBABLE CAUSE
RECRIMINATION
SEQUESTRATION
TREASURE-TROVE

14
DIRECT EVIDENCE

14–continued
FAMILY DIVISION
GRANT OF PROBATE
MENTAL DISORDER
NOLO CONTENDERE
NON PROSEQUITUR
PUBLIC NUISANCE
TIME IMMEMORIAL
ULTIMOGENITURE
UNINCORPORATED
UTTER BARRISTER

15
BREACH OF PROMISE
DISORDERLY HOUSE
HEARSAY EVIDENCE
IMPRESCRIPTIBLE
INTERROGATORIES
OFFICIAL REFEREE
RES IPSA LOQUITUR
SPECIAL PLEADING
WRIT OF EXECUTION

16
AFFILIATION ORDER
ANTON PILLER ORDER

16–continued
ARREST OF JUDGMENT
BREACH OF THE PEACE
DEFERRED SENTENCE
EXEMPLARY DAMAGES
LITIGATION FRIEND
MAREVA INJUNCTION
MENTAL IMPAIRMENT
PERSONAL PROPERTY
PUBLIC PROSECUTOR
STATEMENT OF CLAIM
STATEMENTS OF CASE
TRANSITORY ACTION
UNLAWFUL ASSEMBLY

17
DISORDERLY CONDUCT
FALSE IMPRISONMENT
INSURABLE INTEREST
PERSISTENT CRUELTY

18
AGGRAVATED TRESPASS
CORPUS JURIS CIVILIS
COURT OF COMMON PLEAS
CUMULATIVE EVIDENCE

18–continued
FACULTY OF ADVOCATES
PARTICULARS OF CLAIM
PECUNIARY ADVANTAGE
PLACE OF SAFETY ORDER
PRIMA-FACIE EVIDENCE

19
ADMINISTRATION ORDER
PROSECUTING ATTORNEY
RESTRICTIVE COVENANT
SPECIFIC PERFORMANCE

20+
CONTRIBUTORY
 NEGLIGENCE
DIMINISHED
 RESPONSIBILITY
INDETERMINATE SENTENCE
LETTERS OF
 ADMINISTRATION
OBTAINING BY DECEPTION
PSYCHOPATHIC DISORDER
STATUTORY DECLARATION
UNREASONABLE
 BEHAVIOUR

SCIENCE AND TECHNOLOGY

BRANCHES OF SCIENCE

6
BOTANY
OPTICS

7
ALGEBRA
ANATOMY
BIOLOGY
ECOLOGY
GEOLOGY
OTOLOGY
PHYSICS
ZOOLOGY

8
ANALYSIS
APIOLOGY
BRYOLOGY
CALCULUS
CYTOLOGY
ETHOLOGY
GEOMETRY
MEDICINE
MYCOLOGY
ONCOLOGY
TOPOLOGY
VIROLOGY

9
ACAROLOGY
ACOUSTICS
ASTRONOMY
CHEMISTRY
COSMOGONY
COSMOLOGY
DENTISTRY
HISTOLOGY
LITHOLOGY
MECHANICS
NEUROLOGY
OSTEOLOGY
PATHOLOGY
PETROLOGY

9–continued
PHYTOLOGY
RADIOLOGY
RHINOLOGY
SELENLOGY

10
ARITHMETIC
CARDIOLOGY
EMBRYOLOGY
ENTOMOLOGY
IMMUNOLOGY
METALLURGY
MINERALOGY
OCEANOLOGY
ODONTOLOGY
PALYNOLOGY
PHYSIOLOGY
POTAMOLOGY
SEISMOLOGY
SPELEOLOGY
TOXICOLOGY
TRICHOLOGY

11
AERONAUTICS
CLIMATOLOGY
DERMATOLOGY
ELECTRONICS
GERONTOLOGY
GROUP THEORY
HAEMATOLOGY
HERPETOLOGY
ICHTHYOLOGY
INFORMATICS
LIFE SCIENCE
MATHEMATICS
METEOROLOGY
ORNITHOLOGY
PAEDIATRICS
STOMATOLOGY
VOLCANOLOGY
VULCANOLOGY

12
ANTHROPOLOGY
ASTROBIOLOGY
ASTRONAUTICS
ASTROPHYSICS
BACTERIOLOGY
BIOCHEMISTRY
EARTH SCIENCE
EPIDEMIOLOGY
ETHNOBIOLOGY
GEOCHEMISTRY
MICROBIOLOGY
NUMBER THEORY
OCEANOGRAPHY
ORTHODONTICS
PARASITOLOGY
PHARMACOLOGY
SPECTROSCOPY

13
ENDOCRINOLOGY
GEOMORPHOLOGY
HEALTH PHYSICS
HELMINTHOLOGY
OPHTHALMOLOGY
PALAEONTOLOGY

14
ASTROCHEMISTRY
BIOINFORMATICS
COLEOPTEROLOGY
PHYTOCHEMISTRY
THERMODYNAMICS

15
CHEMICAL PHYSICS
COMPUTER SCI-
  ENCE
CRYSTALLOGRAPHY
PHYSICAL SCIENCE
PHYSIOCHEMISTRY
PURE MATHEMATICS

16
CIVIL ENGINEERING
GASTROENTER-
  OLOGY
INTEGRAL
  CALCULUS
ORGANIC
  CHEMISTRY

17
EUCLIDEAN
  GEOMETRY
PHYSICAL
  CHEMISTRY

18
APPLIED
  MATHEMATICS
CELESTIAL
  MECHANICS
INORGANIC
  CHEMISTRY
PALAEOANTHRO-
  POLOGY

19
CHEMICAL
  ENGINEERING

20+
AERONAUTICAL
  ENGINEERING
DIFFERENTIAL
  CALCULUS
ELECTRICAL
  ENGINEERING
INFORMATION
  TECHNOLOGY
MECHANICAL
  ENGINEERING
NONEUCLIDEAN
  GEOMETRY

WEIGHTS AND MEASURES

2
CM
DR
FT
GR
HL
IN
KG
KM
LB
MG
ML
MM
OZ
YD

3
AMP
ARE
BAR
BEL
BIT
CWT
DWT
ELL
ERG
LUX
MHO
MIL
MIM
NIT
OHM
RAD
REM
ROD
TON
TUN

4
ACRE
BALE
BARN
BOLT
BYTE
CASK
CORD
CRAN
DRAM
DYNE
FOOT
GILL
GRAM
HAND
HIDE
HOUR
INCH
KILO
KNOT

4–continued
LINE
LINK
MILE
MOLE
NAIL
PECK
PHON
PHOT
PICA
PINT
PIPE
POLE
REAM
ROOD
SLUG
SPAN
TORR
TROY
VOLT
WATT
YARD

5
CABLE
CARAT
CHAIN
CRITH
CUBIT
CURIE
CUSEC
CYCLE
DEBYE
FARAD
FERMI
GAUGE
GAUSS
GRAIN
HENRY
HERTZ
JOULE
LITRE
LUMEN
METRE
MINIM
NEPER
OUNCE
PERCH
POINT
POISE
POUND
QUART
QUIRE
STADE
STERE
STILB
STOKE

5–continued
STONE
TESLA
THERM
TOISE
TONNE
WEBER

6
AMPERE
BARREL
BUSHEL
CANDLE
CENTAL
DEGREE
DENIER
DRACHM
FATHOM
FIRKIN
GALLON
GRAMME
KELVIN
LEAGUE
MEGOHM
MICRON
MINUTE
NEWTON
PARSEC
PASCAL
RADIAN
RÉAMUR
SECOND
STOKES

7
CALORIE
CANDELA
CENTNER
COULOMB
DECIBEL
DIOPTER
FARADAY
FURLONG
GILBERT
HECTARE
KILOBAR
KILOTON
LAMBERT
MAXWELL
MEGATON
OERSTED
POUNDAL
QUARTER
QUINTAL
RÖNTGEN
SCRUPLE
SIEMENS

8
ÅNGSTROM
CHALDRON
HOGSHEAD
KILOGRAM
KILOWATT
QUADRANT
MEGAWATT
MICROOHM
WATT-HOUR

9
BOARD-FOOT
CENTIGRAM
CUBIC FOOT
CUBIC INCH
CUBIC YARD
DECALITRE
DECAMETRE
DECILITRE
DECIMETRE
FOOT-POUND
HECTOGRAM
KILOCYCLE
KILOHERTZ
KILOLITRE
KILOMETRE
LIGHT-YEAR
MEGACYCLE
MEGAFARAD
MEGAHERTZ
METRIC TON
MICROGRAM
MICROWATT
MILLIGRAM
NANOMETRE
SCANTLING
STERADIAN

10+
BARLEYCORN
CENTILITRE
CENTIMETRE
CUBIC METRE
DECAGRAMME
DECIGRAMME
FLUID OUNCE
HECTOLITRE
HORSEPOWER
HUNDREDWEIGHT
KILOGRAMME
MICROFARAD
MILLILITRE
MILLIMETRE
NANOSECOND
PENNYWEIGHT

10+—continued
RUTHERFORD
SQUARE
  CENTIMETRE
SQUARE INCH

10+—continued
SQUARE
  KILOMETRE
SQUARE MILE
SQUARE YARD

PAPER MEASURES

4
BALE
COPY
DEMY
POST
POTT
REAM

5
ATLAS
BRIEF
CROWN
DRAFT
QUIRE

5—continued
ROYAL

6
BAG CAP
BUNDLE
CASING
MEDIUM

7
EMPEROR
KENT CAP

8
ELEPHANT

8—continued
FOOLSCAP
HAVEN CAP
IMPERIAL

9
CARTRIDGE
COLOMBIER
LARGE POST
MUSIC DEMY

10
DOUBLE DEMY
DOUBLE POST
GRAND EAGLE

10—continued
SUPER ROYAL

11
ANTIQUARIAN
IMPERIAL CAP
PINCHED POST

14
DOUBLE ELEPHANT

15
DOUBLE LARGE
  POST

ELEMENTARY PARTICLES

2
XI

3
ETA
PHI
PSI

4
KAON
MUON
PION

5
BOSON
GLUON
MESON
OMEGA
QUARK
SIGMA

6
BARYON
HADRON
LAMBDA
LEPTON

6—continued
PHOTON
PROTON

7
FERMION
HYPERON
NEUTRON
TACHYON

8
DEUTERON
ELECTRON

8—continued
GRAVITON
NEUTRINO
POSITRON

9
NEUTRETTO

12
ANTIPARTICLE
BETA PARTICLE

13
ALPHA PARTICLE

THE CHEMICAL ELEMENTS

NAME	(SYMBOL)						
		DUBNIUM	(DB)	MEITNERIUM	(MT)	RUTHENIUM	(RU)
		DYSPROSIUM	(DY)	MENDELEVIUM	(MD)	SAMARIUM	(SM)
ACTINIUM	(AC)	EINSTEINIUM	(ES)	MERCURY	(HG)	SCANDIUM	(SC)
ALUMINIUM	(AL)	ERBIUM	(ER)	MOLYBDENUM	(MO)	SELENIUM	(SE)
AMERICIUM	(AM)	EUROPIUM	(EU)	NEODYMIUM	(ND)	SILICON	(SI)
ANTIMONY	(SB)	FERMIUM	(FM)	NEON	(NE)	SILVER	(AG)
ARGON	(AR)	FLUORINE	(F)	NEPTUNIUM	(NP)	SODIUM	(NA)
ARSENIC	(AS)	FRANCIUM	(FR)	NICKEL	(NI)	STRONTIUM	(SR)
ASTATINE	(AT)	GADOLINIUM	(GD)	NIOBIUM	(NB)	SULPHUR	(S)
BARIUM	(BA)	GALLIUM	(GA)	NITROGEN	(N)	TANTALUM	(TA)
BERKELIUM	(BK)	GERMANIUM	(GE)	NOBELIUM	(NO)	TECHNETIUM	(TC)
BERYLLIUM	(BE)	GOLD	(AU)	OSMIUM	(OS)	TELLURIUM	(TE)
BISMUTH	(BI)	HAFNIUM	(HF)	OXYGEN	(O)	TERBIUM	(TB)
BOHRIUM	(BH)	HASSIUM	(HS)	PALLADIUM	(PD)	THALLIUM	(TL)
BORON	(B)	HELIUM	(HE)	PHOSPHORUS	(P)	THORIUM	(TH)
BROMINE	(BR)	HOLMIUM	(HO)	PLATINUM	(PT)	THULIUM	(TM)
CADMIUM	(CD)	HYDROGEN	(H)	PLUTONIUM	(PU)	TIN	(SN)
CAESIUM	(CS)	INDIUM	(IN)	POLONIUM	(PO)	TITANIUM	(TI)
CALCIUM	(CA)	IODINE	(I)	POTASSIUM	(K)	TUNGSTEN	(W)
CALIFORNIUM	(CF)	IRIDIUM	(IR)	PRASEODYMIUM		URANIUM	(U)
CARBON	(C)	IRON	(FE)		(PR)	VANADIUM	(V)
CERIUM	(CE)	KRYPTON	(KR)	PROMETHIUM	(PM)	WOLFRAM	(W)
CHLORINE	(CL)	LANTHANUM	(LA)	PROTACTINIUM	(PA)	XENON	(XE)
CHROMIUM	(CR)	LAWRENCIUM	(LR)	RADIUM	(RA)	YTTERBIUM	(YB)
COBALT	(CO)	LEAD	(PB)	RADON	(RN)	YTTRIUM	(Y)
COLUMBIUM	(CB)	LITHIUM	(LI)	RHENIUM	(RE)	ZINC	(ZN)
COPPER	(CU)	LUTETIUM	(LU)	RHODIUM	(RH)	ZIRCONIUM	(ZR)
CURIUM	(CM)	MAGNESIUM	(MG)	ROENTGENIUM	(RG)		
DARMSTADTIUM	(DS)	MANGANESE	(MN)	RUBIDIUM	(RB)		

COMMON CHEMICALS

4	6–continued	7–continued	8–continued	10
ALUM	PHENOL	QUINONE	PEROXIDE	CAPRIC ACID
LIME	POTASH	REALGAR	PHOSGENE	CYANIC ACID
UREA	QUINOL	RED LEAD	PLUMBAGO	FORMIC ACID
	SILICA	SODA ASH	PROPANOL	LACTIC ACID
5	XYLENE	STYRENE	SODA LIME	LAURIC ACID
BORAX		TOLUENE	SODAMIDE	MUSTARD GAS
ETHER	7		STRONTIA	NITRIC ACID
FREON	ACETATE	8		OXALIC ACID
FURAN	ALUMINA	BERYLLIA	9	PICRIC ACID
HALON	AMMONIA	CATECHOL	ACETYLENE	SLAKED LIME
	ANILINE	CHLORIDE	AQUA REGIA	TANNIC ACID
6	BENZENE	CINNABAR	BLANC FIXE	WATER GLASS
BARYTA	BORAZON	CORUNDUM	BORIC ACID	ZINC BLENDE
CETANE	BROMIDE	CYANOGEN	BROMOFORM	
CRESOL	CALOMEL	FLUORIDE	FERROCENE	11
DIOXAN	CAMPHOR	FLUORITE	IODIC ACID	ACRYLIC ACID
ETHANE	CHLORAL	FORMALIN	LIMEWATER	BENZOIC ACID
HEXANE	CYANIDE	MAGNESIA	PHOSPHINE	BUTYRIC ACID
IODIDE	ETHANOL	MELAMINE	PROPYLENE	CAPROIC ACID
LITHIA	HEPTANE	METHANOL	QUICKLIME	CAUSTIC SODA
LITMUS	PENTANE	NEOPRENE	SALTPETRE	DIPHOSPHINE

11–continued
FUMARIC ACID
IODOMETHANE
LAUGHING GAS
MALONIC ACID
NITRIC OXIDE
NITROUS ACID
PRUSSIC ACID
SAL AMMONIAC
STEARIC ACID
SUGAR OF LEAD
WASHING SODA

12
ACETALDEHYDE
BENZALDEHYDE
BENZOQUINONE
CAPRYLIC ACID
CARBOLIC ACID
CARBONIC ACID
DECANOIC ACID
ETHYL ALCOHOL
FLUOROCARBON
FORMALDEHYDE
FULMINIC ACID
GREEN VITRIOL
HYDROQUINONE
NITROBENZENE
NITROUS OXIDE
OIL OF VITRIOL
PERMANGANATE

12–continued
PHTHALIC ACID
TARTARIC ACID

13
ISOCYANIC ACID
METHANOIC ACID
METHYL ALCOHOL
PROPANOIC ACID
SILVER NITRATE
SODIUM CYANIDE
SULPHURIC ACID
VINYL CHLORIDE

14
CALCIUM CARBIDE
CARBON MONOXIDE
CHLORAL HYDRATE
COPPER SULPHATE
HYDROIODIC ACID
METHYL CHLORIDE
NITROCELLULOSE
PHOSPHORIC ACID
SODIUM CHLORIDE
SODIUM SULPHATE
SULPHUR DIOXIDE
TETRAETHYL LEAD

15
ABSOLUTE
ALCOHOL

15–continued
BLEACHING
POWDER
HYDROBROMIC ACID
HYDROCYANIC ACID
HYDROGEN
CYANIDE
NITROGEN DIOXIDE
PHOSPHOROUS
ACID
SODIUM HYDROXIDE
SULPHUR TRIOXIDE
TETRAHYDRO-
FURAN

16
CALCIUM
CARBONATE
CALCIUM
HYDROXIDE
HYDROCHLORIC
ACID
HYDROFLUORIC
ACID
HYDROGEN
FLUORIDE
HYDROGEN
PEROXIDE
HYPOCHLOROUS
ACID

16–continued
NITROGEN
MONOXIDE

17
BICARBONATE OF
SODA
MAGNESIUM
CHLORIDE
POTASSIUM
CHLORIDE
SODIUM
BICARBONATE
VANADIUM
PENTOXIDE

18
CHLOROFLUORO-
CARBON
DIMETHYL
SULPHOXIDE
MAGNESIUM
CARBONATE

19+
BUCKMINSTER-
FULLERENE
CARBON TETRA-
CHLORIDE
POTASSIUM
BICARBONATE
POTASSIUM
PERMANGANATE

ALLOYS

ALLOY – main components

4
ALNI – iron, nickel, aluminium,
copper
BETA – titanium, aluminium,
vanadium, chromium

5
ALPHA – titanium, aluminium,
tin, copper, zirconium, nio-
bium, molybdenum
BRASS – copper, zinc
INVAR – iron, nickel
MAZAC – zinc, aluminium,
magnesium, copper
MONEL – nickel, cobalt, iron
STEEL – iron, carbon

6
ALNICO – aluminium, nickel,
cobalt

6–continued
BABBIT – tin, lead, antimony,
copper
BRONZE – copper, tin
CUNICO – iron, cobalt, copper,
nickel
CUNIFE – iron, cobalt, nickel
FEROBA – iron, barium oxide,
iron oxide
PEWTER – tin, lead
SOLDER – lead, tin (soft), cop-
per, zinc (brazing)

7
ALCOMAX – aluminium, cobalt,
nickel, copper, lead, niobium
ALUMNEL – aluminium,
chromium
AMALGAM – mercury, various
CHROMEL – nickel, chromium

7–continued
COLUMAN – iron, chromium,
nickel, aluminium, nobium,
copper
ELINVAR – iron, nickel,
chromium, tungsten
INCONEL – nickel, chromium,
iron
KANTHAL – chromium, alu-
minium, iron
MUMETAL – iron, nickel, copper, chromium
NIMONIC – nickel, chromium,
iron, titanium, aluminium,
manganese, silicon

8
CAST IRON – carbon, iron
DOWMETAL – magnesium,
aluminium, zinc, manganese
GUNMETAL – copper, tin, zinc
HIPERNIK – nickel, iron

227

8–continued
KIRKSITE – zinc, aluminium, copper
MANGANIN – copper, manganese, nickel
NICHROME – nickel, iron, chromium
VICALLOY – iron, cobalt, vanadium
ZIRCALOY – zirconium, tin, iron, nickel,
   chromium

9
DURALUMIN – aluminium, copper, silicon, mag-
   nesium, manganese, zinc
HASTELLOY – nickel, molybdenum, iron,
   chromium, cobalt, tungsten
PERMALLOY – nickel, iron
PERMINVAR – nickel, iron, cobalt
TYPE METAL – lead, tin, antimony

10
CONSTANTAN – copper, nickel
MISCH METAL – cerium, various
MUNTZ METAL – copper, zinc
ROSE'S METAL – bismuth, lead, tin
SUPERALLOY – type of stainless steel
WOOD'S METAL – lead, tin, bismuth, cadmium

11
CUPRONICKEL – copper, nickel
ELECTROTYPE – lead, tin, antimony
SUPERMALLOY – iron, nickel
SUPERMENDUR – iron, cobalt

12
FERROSILICON – iron, silicon
GERMAN SILVER – copper, nickel, zinc, lead, tin
SILVER SOLDER – copper, silver, zinc

13
FERROCHROMIUM – iron, chromium
FERROTUNGSTEN – iron, tungsten
FERROVANADIUM – iron, vanadium

14
ADMIRALTY METAL – copper, zinc
BRITANNIA METAL – tin, antimony, copper
FERROMANGANESE – iron, manganese
PHOSPHOR BRONZE – copper, tin, phosphorus
STAINLESS STEEL – iron, chromium, vanadium

TYPES OF CHEMICAL COMPOUND

4
ACID
BASE

5
ALDOL
AMIDE
AMINE
ARENE
ARYNE
AZINE
ESTER
ETHER
KETAL
OXIDE
OXIME
SUGAR
YLIDE

6
ACETAL
ALKALI
ALKANE
ALKENE
ALKYNE
BORANE
CRESOL
HALIDE
IODIDE
KETENE
KETONE

6–continued
LACTAM
LACTIM
LACTOL
OLEFIN
PHENOL
PURINE
PURINE

7
ALCOHOL
BENZYNE
CARBIDE
CHELATE
COMPLEX
EPOXIDE
LACTONE
OZONIDE
QUINONE

8
ALDEHYDE
ALKOXIDE
ANNULENE
AROMATIC
CARBINOL
CARBONYL
CHLORIDE
CORONAND
CRYPTAND
CRYPTATE

8–continued
CUMULENE
FLUORIDE
HELICENE
PEROXIDE

9
ACETYLENE
AMINO ACID
ANHYDRIDE
FATTY ACID
FULLERENE
HEMIKETAL
IMINO ACID
NAPHTHENE

10
ACYL HALIDE
CALIXARENE
CROWN ETHER
CYCLOPHANE
HEMIACETAL
PIANO STOOL
PYRIMIDINE
PYRIMIDINE
SACCHARIDE

11
ALKYL HALIDE
CYCLOALKANE
CYCLOALKENE
CYCLOALKYNE

11–continued
HETEROARENE
HETEROARYNE
HYDROCARBON
METALLOCENE

12
CARBOHYDRATE
HALF SANDWICH
HETEROCYCLIC
INTERHALOGEN

13
ACID ANHYDRIDE
SPIRO COMPOUND

14
CARBOXILIC ACID
PSEUDOAROMATIC

15+
CHARGE TRANSFER
   COMPOUND
COORDINATION
   COMPOUND
DOUBLE DECKER
   SANDWICH
NITROGENOUS
   BASE
SANDWICH
   COMPOUND

BIOCHEMICAL COMPOUNDS

3
ADP
AMP
ATP
COA
DNA
FAD
FMN
NAD
RNA

4
HAEM
HEME
NADP
UREA

5
ACTIN
AUXIN
DNASE
EOSIN
HEMIN
KININ
LYASE
MUCIN
OPSIN
PRION
RENIN

6
BIOTIN
CASEIN
CHITIN
FIBRIN
FLAVIN
GLUCAN
GLUTEN
GLYCAN
INULIN
KINASE
LIGASE
LIGNIN
LIPASE
LUTEIN
MYOSIN
NIACIN
PECTIN
PEPSIN
PURINE
RENNIN
S PHASE
STARCH
STEROL
TANNIN
URACIL

7
ADENINE
ALBUMEN

7–continued
ALBUMIN
AMYLASE
AMYLOSE
CHOLINE
COCAINE
CODEINE
CYSTINE
DEXTRIN
ELASTIN
ESTRIOL
ESTRONE
FLAVONE
FRUCTAN
GASTRIN
GUANINE
HEPARIN
HORMONE
INHIBIN
INSULIN
KERATIN
MELANIN
OPSONIN
PEPTIDE
PROTEIN
PTYALIN
QUININE
RELAXIN
RETINAL
STEROID
TERPENE
THYMINE
TRYPSIN
URIDINE

8
ANAPHASE
ATROPINE
CAFFEINE
CAROTENE
CATALASE
COLLAGEN
CORTISOL
CREATINE
CYTIDINE
CYTOKINE
CYTOSINE
ESTROGEN
EXOTOXIN
FLAVONOL
GLOBULIN
GLUCAGON
GLYCEROL
GLYCOGEN
INOSITOL
KILOBASE
LECITHIN
LYSOSOME

8–continued
LYSOZYME
MANNITOL
MEGABASE
MORPHINE
NEOTONIN
NUCLEASE
OXYTOCIN
PROPHASE
PROTEASE
PYRUVATE
RETINENE
RIBOZYME
SECRETIN
THIAMINE
THROMBIN
TROPONIN
URIC ACID

9
ACETYL COA
ADENOSINE
AFLATOXIN
BILIRUBIN
CELLULASE
CORTISONE
CYTOKININ
DEAMINASE
ENDORPHIN
ENDOTOXIN
ESTRADIOL
FLAVONOID
FOLIC ACID
GLYCERIDE
GLYCOSIDE
GUANOSINE
HISTAMINE
HYDROLASE
KAIROMONE
LUCIFERIN
MELATONIN
METAPHASE
MYOGLOBIN
NINHYDRIN
PEPTIDASE
PORPHYRIN
PROLACTIN
PROTAMINE
RHODOPSIN
SEROTONIN
TELOPHASE
THYMIDINE
THYROXINE
UBIQUITIN

10
ACTOMYOSIN
ADRENALINE
BILIVERDIN

10–continued
BRADYKININ
CADAVERINE
CALCIFEROL
CALCITONIN
CAROTENOID
CITRULLINE
COLCHICINE
CREATININE
CYTOCHROME
ENCEPHALIN
ENKEPHALIN
ERGOSTEROL
FERREDOXIN
GLYCOLIPID
HOMOGLYCAN
INTERFERON
INTERPHASE
LIPOIC ACID
LIPOTROPIN
LYMPHOKINE
NUCLEOSIDE
NUCLEOTIDE
PENICILLIN
PHYCOBILIN
POLYMERASE
PROHORMONE
PROTEINASE
PUTRESCINE
PYRIDOXINE
PYRIMIDINE
RIBOFLAVIN
STRYCHNINE
TOCOPHEROL
UBIQUINONE

11
ACTINOMYCIN
ALDOSTERONE
AMYLOPECTIN
ANGIOTENSIN
ANTHOCYANIN
CARBOXYLASE
CHLOROPHYLL
CHOLESTEROL
CYTOKERATIN
ECDYSTERONE
EPINEPHRINE
EUCHROMATIN
EXONUCLEASE
FUCOXANTHIN
FUMARIC ACID
GIBBERELLIN
GLUTATHIONE
HAEMOCYANIN
HAEMOGLOBIN
INTERLEUKIN
MENAQUINONE

229

ORGANIC ACIDS

11—continued
MUCOPROTEIN
MYCOPROTEIN
NUCLEIC ACID
PHAEOPHYTIN
POLYPEPTIDE
PROGESTOGEN
PROTHROMBIN
THEOBROMINE
THYROTROPIN
TRANSFERASE
TRYPSINOGEN
VASOPRESSIN
XANTHOPHYLL

12
ABSCISIC ACID
ANDROSTERONE
ASCORBIC ACID
ENDONUCLEASE
ENTEROKINASE
FLAVOPROTEIN
GLYCOPROTEIN
GONADOTROPIN
HAEMATOXYLIN
HAEMERYTHRIN
NEUROHORMONE
PHOSPHOLIPID
PHYTOHORMONE
PROGESTERONE
PROTEOGLYCAN
RIBONUCLEASE
SOMATOSTATIN

12—continued
SOMATOTROPIN
TESTOSTERONE
TETRAPYRROLE
THEOPHYLLINE
TRANSAMINASE
VIOLAXANTHIN
VISUAL PURPLE

13
ACETYLCHOLINE
CATECHOLAMINE
CORTICOTROPIN
DECARBOXYLASE
DEHYDROGENASE
HEMICELLULOSE
NICOTINIC ACID
NORADRENALINE
NUCLEOPROTEIN
OXYHEMOGLOBIN
PHYCOERYTHRIN
PHYLLOQUINONE
PROSTAGLANDIN
PROTEIN KINASE
SCLEROPROTEIN

14
CORTICOSTEROID
CORTICOSTERONE
CYANOCOBALAMIN
GLUCOCORTICOID
HYALURONIC ACID
HYDROCORTISONE
IMMUNOGLOBULIN

14—continued
NOREPINEPHRINE
PHOSPHOPROTEIN

15
CHOLECALCIFEROL
CHOLECYSTOKININ
ENTEROPEPTIDASE
EXORIBONUCLEASE
GIBBERELLIC ACID
HETEROCHROMATIN
OXALOACETIC ACID
PANTOTHENIC ACID
PHOSPHOCREATINE
RIBONUCLEIC ACID

16
ENDORIBONUCLE-
ASE
METALLOPOR-
PHYRIN
TRIIODOTHYRONINE

17
AUTOIMMUNE DIS-
EASE
DEOXYRIBONUCLE-
ASE
GLYCOSAMINOGLY-
CAN
MINERALOCORTI-
COID

18
LIPOPOLYSACCHA-
RIDE

18—continued
MUCOPOLYSACCHA-
RIDE

19
DEOXYCORTICOS-
TERONE
PTEROYLGLUTAMIC
ACID

20+
ACETYL-
CHOLINESTERASE
ADENOSINE
DIPHOSPHATE
ADENOSINE
MONOPHOSPHATE
ADENOSINE
TRIPHOSPHATE
DEOXYRIBO-
NUCLEIC ACID
FLAVIN ADENINE
DINUCLEOTIDE
FLAVIN MONO-
NUCLEOTIDE
NICOTINAMIDE
ADENINE DINU-
CLEOTIDE
RESTRICTION
ENDONUCLEASE
REVERSE TRAN-
SCRIPTASE
RIBULOSE BISPHOS-
PHATE

ORGANIC ACIDS

5
MALIC (hydroxybutanedioic)
OLEIC (octadec-9-enoic)

6
ACETIC (ethanoic)
ADIPIC (hexanedioic)
CAPRIC (decanoic)
CITRIC (2-hydroxy-propane-
1,2,3-tricarboxylic)
FORMIC (methanoic)
LACTIC (2-hydroxypropanoic)
LAURIC (dodecanoic)
MALEIC (cis-butenedioic)
OXALIC (ethanedioic)

7
BEHENIC (docosanoic)
BUTYRIC (butanoic)
CAPROIC (hexanoic)
CEROTIC (hexacosanoic)
ENATHIC (heptanoic)
FUMARIC (trans-butenedioic)
MALONIC (propanedioic)
STEARIC (octadecanoic)
VALERIC (pentanoic)

8
CAPRYLIC (octanoic)
GLUTARIC (pentanedioic)
GLYCOLIC (hydroxyethanoic)

8—continued
LINOLEIC (octadeca-9,12-
dienoic)
MYRISTIC (tetradecanoic)
PALMITIC (hexadecanoic)
SUCCINIC (butanedioic)

9
ARACHIDIC (eicosanoic)
LINOLENIC (octadeca-9,12,15-
trienoic)

10
LIGNOCERIC (tetracosanoic)
PELARGONIC (nonanoic)
PROPRIONIC (propanoic)

AMINO ACIDS

6
LYSINE
SERINE
VALINE

7
ALANINE
GLYCINE
LEUCINE

7–continued
PROLINE

8
ARGININE
CYSTEINE
TYROSINE

9
ASPARTINE

9–continued
GLUTAMINE
HISTIDINE
ORNITHINE
THREONINE

10
ASPARAGINE
CITRULLINE

10–continued
ISOLEUCINE
METHIONINE
TRYPTOPHAN

12
ASPARTIC ACID
GLUTAMIC ACID

13
PHENYLALANINE

SUGARS

6
ALDOSE
HEXOSE
KETOSE
RIBOSE

7
AMYLOSE
GLUCOSE
LACTOSE
MALTOSE

7–continued
MANNOSE
PENTOSE
SUCROSE

8
DEXTROSE
FRUCTOSE
FURANOSE
MANNITOL
PYRANOSE

9
CANE SUGAR
GALACTOSE
MILK SUGAR

10
ALDOHEXOSE
GRAPE SUGAR
KETOHEXOSE
SACCHARIDE

11
ALDOPENTOSE
KETOPENTOSE

12
DISACCHARIDE

14
MONOSACCHARIDE

MATHEMATICAL TERMS

3
SET
SUM

4
BASE
CUBE
MEAN
NODE
RING
ROOT
SINE
SURD

5
ARRAY
DIGIT
FIELD
GROUP
LIMIT
LOCUS
POWER
PROOF

5–continued
RATIO
UNITY

6
COSINE
FACTOR
GOOGOL
MATRIX
MEDIAN
ORIGIN
SCALAR
SECANT
SERIES
SQUARE
SUBSET
TENSOR
VECTOR

7
ALGEBRA
DIVISOR
FORMULA

7–continued
FRACTAL
INTEGER
INVERSE
MODULUS
PRODUCT
TANGENT
UNKNOWN

8
ABSCISSA
ADDITION
ANALYSIS
BINOMIAL
CALCULUS
COSECANT
CUBE ROOT
DIVISION
EQUATION
EXPONENT
FRACTION
FUNCTION
FUZZY SET

8–continued
GRADIENT
IDENTITY
JULIA SET
LIE GROUP
MULTIPLE
OPERATOR
QUOTIENT
SOLUTION
VARIABLE

9
ALGORITHM
ASYMPTOTE
CANTOR SET
CONJUGATE
COTANGENT
EXPANSION
FACTORIAL
INTEGRAND
INTERCEPT
ITERATION
LOGARITHM

9–continued
NUMERATOR
PARAMETER
RECURSION
REMAINDER
SET THEORY
SUB-GROUP
TRANSFORM

10
DERIVATIVE
DIFFERENCE
EIGENVALUE
FRACTAL SET
GAME THEORY
GOOGOLPLEX
INEQUALITY
MULTIPLIER
PERCENTILE
POLYNOMIAL
QUATERNION
REAL NUMBER
RECIPROCAL
SQUARE ROOT

11
ALIQUOT PART
BANACH SPACE
CHAOS THEORY
COEFFICIENT
DENOMINATOR
DETERMINANT
EIGENVECTOR
GALOIS GROUP
GROUP THEORY
INTEGRATION
KLEIN BOTTLE
MAGIC SQUARE
MARKOV CHAIN
MÖBIUS STRIP
PERMUTATION
POWER SERIES
PRIME NUMBER
SUBTRACTION
VENN DIAGRAM
WHOLE NUMBER

12
BAYES' THEOREM
DECIMAL POINT
GÖDEL NUMBERS
HILBERT SPACE
LONG DIVISION
MULTIPLICAND
NEWTON METHOD
NUMBER THEORY
SIMPSON'S RULE
SQUARE NUMBER
SUBSTITUTION
TAYLOR SERIES

13
ANTILOGARITHM
ARGAND DIAGRAM

13–continued
COMPLEX NUMBER
EIGENFUNCTION
EUCLID'S AXIOMS
EULER'S FORMULA
EXTRAPOLATION
FOURIER SERIES
GAUSS'S THEOREM
GEOMETRIC MEAN
GREEN'S THEOREM
INTERPOLATION
L'HÔPITAL'S RULE
MANDELBROT SET
ORDINAL NUMBER
PERFECT NUMBER
PERFECT SQUARE
QUEUING THEORY
STOKES' THEOREM

14
ARITHMETIC MEAN
ASSOCIATIVE LAW
BOOLEAN ALGEBRA
CARDINAL NUMBER
CAUCHY SEQUENCE
COMMUTATIVE LAW
EULER'S CONSTANT
HYPERBOLIC SINE
LINEAR EQUATION
MULTIPLICATION
NATURAL NUMBERS
NULL HYPOTHESIS
PROPER FRACTION
RATIONAL NUMBER
ROOT-MEAN-SQUARE
VULGAR FRACTION

15
BESSEL FUNCTIONS
BINOMIAL THEOREM
DIFFERENTIATION
DIRICHLET SERIES
DISTRIBUTIVE LAW
FOURIER ANALYSIS
HERMITIAN MATRIX
IMAGINARY NUMBER
LAPLACE OPERATOR
LEIBNIZ'S THEOREM
MACLAURIN SERIES
MERSENNE NUMBERS
MIDPOINT THEOREM
PASCAL'S TRIANGLE
RUSSELL'S PARADOX
STATIONARY POINT

16
BERNOULLI NUMBERS
DEFINITE INTEGRAL
DE MOIVRE'S FORMULA
FIBONACCI NUMBERS
HILBERT'S PROBLEMS
HYPERBOLIC COSINE
IMPROPER FRACTION

16–continued
INTEGRAL CALCULUS
IRRATIONAL NUMBER
LAGRANGE'S THEOREM
MONTE CARLO METHOD
NATURAL LOGARITHM
POLAR COORDINATES
RECURRING DECIMAL
REMAINDER THEOREM
REPEATING DECIMAL

17
APOLLONIUS' THEOREM
CATASTROPHE THEORY
COMMON DENOMINATOR
EUCLIDEAN GEOMETRY
HYPERBOLIC TANGENT
PARTIAL DERIVATIVE
POINT OF INFLECTION
SIGNIFICANT FIGURE
TRANSFINITE NUMBER

18
COORDINATE GEOMETRY
FERMAT'S LAST THEOREM
FOUR-COLOUR THEOREM
INDEFINITE INTEGRAL
LEAST SQUARES METHOD
NAPIERIAN LOGARITHM
PYTHAGORAS' THEOREM
RIEMANNIAN GEOMETRY

19
BRIGGSIAN LOGARITHMS
DIOPHANTINE EQUATION
EXPONENTIAL FUNCTION
HARMONIC PROGRESSION
HIGHEST COMMON FACTOR
LEGENDRE POLYNOMIALS
POISSON DISTRIBUTION

20+
ARITHMETIC PROGRESSION
CARTESIAN COORDINATES
CHINESE REMAINDER
  THEOREM
DIFFERENTIAL CALCULUS
DIFFERENTIAL EQUATION
GAUSSIAN DISTRIBUTION
GEOMETRIC PROGRESSION
INFINITESIMAL CALCULUS
LOBACHEVSKIAN
  GEOMETRY
LOWEST COMMON
  DENOMINATOR
LOWEST COMMON
  MULTIPLE
SIMULTANEOUS EQUATIONS
STIRLING'S APPROXIMATION
TRIGONOMETRIC FUNCTION
TRANSCENDENTAL
  FUNCTION

GEOMETRIC FIGURES AND CURVES

3
ARC

4
CONE
CUBE
KITE
LINE
LOOP
LUNE
OVAL
ROSE
ZONE

5
CHORD
CONIC
HELIX
LOCUS
NAPPE
OGIVE
PLANE
PRISM
RHOMB
SHEET
SOLID
TORUS
WEDGE
WITCH

6
CIRCLE
CONOID
FOLIUM
LAMINA
NORMAL
OCTANT
PENCIL
RADIUS
SECTOR
SPHERE
SPIRAL
SPLINE
SQUARE

7
ANNULUS
CISSOID
CYCLOID
DECAGON
ELLIPSE
EVOLUTE
FRACTAL
HEXAGON
LIMAÇON
OCTAGON
PERIGON
POLYGON
PYRAMID
RHOMBUS
SEGMENT
SURFACE
TANGENT
TREFOIL
TRIDENT

8
CARDIOID
CATENARY
CATENOID
CONCHOID
CONICOID
CYLINDER
ENVELOPE
EPICYCLE
EXCIRCLE
FRUSTRUM
GEODESIC
HEPTAGON
INCIRCLE
INVOLUTE
PARABOLA
PENTAGON
PRISMOID
QUADRANT
RHOMBOID
ROULETTE
SPHEROID
TRACTRIX

8–continued
TRIANGLE
TROCHOID

9
ANTIPRISM
CRUCIFORM
DIRECTRIX
DODECAGON
ELLIPSOID
HYPERBOLA
ISOCHRONE
KOCH CURVE
LOXODROME
MULTIFOIL
PENTAGRAM
PENTANGLE
RHUMB LINE
SINE CURVE
STROPHOID
TRAPEZIUM
TRAPEZOID

10
ACUTE ANGLE
ANCHOR RING
CYLINDROID
EPICYCLOID
HEMISPHERE
HEXAHEDRON
KAPPA CURVE
LEMNISCATE
OCTAHEDRON
PARABOLOID
PEANO CURVE
POLYHEDRON
PRISMATOID
QUADRANGLE
QUADREFOIL
RIGHT ANGLE
SEMICIRCLE
SERPENTINE
TRISECTRIX

11
CORNU SPIRAL
EPITROCHOID
HEPTAHEDRON
HYPERBOLOID
HYPOCYCLOID
ICOSAHEDRON
KLEIN BOTTLE
LATUS RECTUM
MÖBIUS STRIP
OBTUSE ANGLE
PENTAHEDRON
REFLEX ANGLE
TAUTOCHRONE
TETRAHEDRON

12
HYPOTROCHOID
PSEUDOSPHERE
RHOMBOHEDRON
SIGMOID CURVE

13
CIRCUMFERENCE
CUBOCTAHEDRON
PARALLELOGRAM
PARALLELOTOPE
PEDAL TRIANGLE
PERPENDICULAR
QUADRILATERAL

14
SNOWFLAKE CURVE

15
BRACHISTOCHRONE
SCALENE TRIANGLE

17
ICOSIDODECA-
HEDRON
ISOSCELES
TRIANGLE

19
EQUILATERAL
TRIANGLE

ELECTRONIC COMPONENTS

3
FET
LED
RCD

4
CHIP
FUSE

4–continued
GATE

5
CHOKE
DIODE
IGFET
RELAY

5–continued
SHUNT
VALVE

6
BRIDGE
DYNAMO
FILTER

6–continued
JUGFET
MOSFET
SWITCH
TRIODE

7
AMMETER

7–continued
BATTERY
COUNTER
MAGNETO
PENTODE
SPEAKER
TETRODE

8
ARMATURE
BISTABLE
FLIP-FLOP
INDUCTOR
RESISTOR
RHEOSTAT
SOLENOID
VARACTOR
WINDINGS

9
AMPLIFIER
CAPACITOR
GUNN DIODE
MICROCHIP
RECTIFIER
THYRISTOR

9–continued
VOLTMETER
WAVEGUIDE

10
ALTERNATOR
ATTENUATOR
MICROPHONE
OSCILLATOR
TRANSDUCER
TRANSISTOR
ZENER DIODE

11
ELECTRON GUN
LOUDSPEAKER
SILICON CHIP
TRANSFORMER

12
ELECTRON LENS
ELECTRON TUBE
GALVANOMETER
LOGIC CIRCUIT
OSCILLOSCOPE
PHOTOCATHODE

13
SEMICONDUCTOR

14
CIRCUIT BREAKER
PRINTED CIRCUIT

15+
ELECTRON
 MULTIPLIER

15+–continued
FIELD-EFFECT
 TRANSISTOR
INTEGRATED
 CIRCUIT
LIGHT-EMITTING
 DIODE
N-TYPE SEMI-
 CONDUCTOR
PHOTOMULTIPLIER
P-TYPE SEMI-
 CONDUCTOR
THERMIONIC
 CATHODE
WHEATSTONE
 BRIDGE

COMPUTER TERMS

1 & 2
K
AI
BS
CD
CR
DP
GB
IC
IE
IP
IT
KB
LF
MB
NL
OS
PC
UI
WP

3
AGP
BBS
BIT
BUG
BUS
CAD
CAL
CAM
CBL
CGI
COM
CPU
CRT
CUT

3–continued
DAT
DNS
DSL
DTP
DVD
EGA
EPS
FAQ
FYI
GIF
GIG
GUI
IAP
ICR
IDE
IRQ
ISP
JOB
KEY
LAN
LCD
MEG
NET
NIC
NLQ
OCR
OEM
PDA
PIN
POS
RAM
RGB
RIP
ROM

3–continued
RTF
RUN
UPS
URL
USB
VDA
VDU
VPN
WAN
WEB
WWW
XML
ZIP

4
ADSL
ANSI
BAUD
BEEP
BIOS
BOOT
BURN
BYTE
CELL
CHAT
CHIP
CMYK
COPY
CORE
CROP
DATA
DISK
DRAG
DRAM
DUMP

4–continued
ECHO
EDIT
EPOS
EXIT
FILE
FIND
FLAG
FLOP
FONT
GEEK
GOTO
HOST
HTML
HTTP
HUNG
ICON
ISDN
JAVA
JPEG
KILL
LOOP
MENU
MIDI
MPEG
MTBF
NERD
NODE
PACK
PATH
PORT
POST
PROM
RAID
SAVE

4–continued
SCAN
SCSI
SGML
SLOT
SOHO
SPAM
SRAM
UNDO
VOIP
WAND
WIFI
WORD
WORM
ZOOM

5
ABORT
ALIAS
ARRAY
ASCII
BASIC
BATCH
BLINK
BLOCK
BOARD
CACHE
CD-ROM
CLICK
CLONE
CODEC
CRASH
CYCLE
DEBUG
EMAIL
EPROM

5–continued	6–continued	7–continued	8–continued	9–continued
ERASE	DRIVER	CRACKER	DOT PITCH	CLOCK RATE
ERROR	ESCAPE	CRAWLER	DOWNLOAD	CONFIGURE
FIELD	FILTER	DECIMAL	DOWNTIME	CYBERCAFE
FLAME	FORMAT	DEFAULT	EMOTICON	DATA ENTRY
FLOOD	GOPHER	DENSITY	ETHERNET	DECOMPILE
FORUM	HACKER	DESKTOP	EXTRANET	DIGITIZER
GUSET	HANDLE	DINGBAT	FEED BACK	DIRECTORY
IMAGE	HEADER	DISPLAY	FILENAME	DOWNGRADE
INDEX	HOT FIX	DYNAMIC	FIREWALL	EASTER EGG
INPUT	IMPORT	END USER	FIRMWARE	E-COMMERCE
KIOSK	JUMPER	EURONET	FREEWARE	EXTENSION
LOCAL	KERMIT	FIDONET	GIGABYTE	FIXED DISK
LOGIN	KEYPAD	FRACTAL	GRAPHICS	FLOWCHART
LOGON	LAPTOP	GAME PAD	HALFWORD	GREY SCALE
MACRO	LAYOUT	GARBAGE	HARD DISK	HANDSHAKE
MEDIA	LOGOFF	GATEWAY	HARDWIRE	HASH TABLE
MERGE	LOGOUT	HASHING	HELP DESK	HEARTBEAT
MODEM	MEMORY	HISTORY	HOME PAGE	HEURISTIC
MOUSE	NEWBIE	HOT SPOT	INTERNET	HIGHLIGHT
OCTAL	NYBBLE	INSTALL	INTRANET	HYPERLINK
PAINT	ON-LINE	JOURNAL	JOYSTICK	HYPERTEXT
PASTE	OUTPUT	MAILBOX	KEYBOARD	INFECTION
PATCH	PACKET	MESSAGE	KILOBYTE	ININSTALL
PIXEL	PARITY	MONITOR	LANGUAGE	INTERFACE
POP-UP	PARSER	NESTING	LIGHT PEN	INTERRUPT
PURGE	PIRACY	NETWORK	LINEFEED	IP ADDRESS
QUEUE	PORTAL	NEWLINE	MEGABYTE	MAGIC WAND
SLAVE	QWERTY	OFF-LINE	NAVIGATE	MAINFRAME
SLEEP	RASTER	PALMTOP	NOTEBOOK	MICROCHIP
SPOOL	RECORD	PARSING	OPERATOR	NEWSGROUP
TABLE	REMOTE	PLOTTER	PASSWORD	OVERWRITE
TWAIN	ROUTER	PRINTER	PLATFORM	PHREAKING
VIRUS	SCREEN	PRIVACY	PRINTOUT	POP-UP-MENU
WHOIS	SCRIPT	PROGRAM	PROTOCOL	PRIME TIME
WRITE	SCROLL	RESTORE	QUADWORD	PROCESSOR
	SECTOR	SCANNER	REAL TIME	RENDERING
6	SERVER	SORTING	RECOVERY	SHAREWARE
ACCESS	SMILEY	SPYWARE	REGISTER	SMART CARD
ALT KEY	SPIDER	STORAGE	REPEATER	SOUND CARD
APPLET	SPRITE	TASK BAR	RETRIEVE	STREAMING
ATTACK	STRING	TIMEOUT	ROBOTICS	THESAURUS
BACKUP	THREAD	TOOL BAR	SECURITY	TRACKBALL
BANNER	TROJAN	TOOLBOX	SOFTWARE	USER GROUP
BINARY	UNPACK	UPGRADE	TEMPLATE	VOICE MAIL
BITMAP	UPLOAD	WYSIWYG	TERMINAL	WALLPAPER
BITNET	USENET		TYPEFACE	WEBMASTER
BOOT UP	VECTOR	**8**	UNDELETE	WRAP-AROUND
BRANCH	WIZARD	ALIASING	WILD CARD	
BRIDGE		ANALYZER		**10**
BROWSE	**7**	BETA TEST	**9**	ANNOTATION
BUFFER	ADDRESS	BOOKMARK	ALGORITHM	BIOMETRICS
BULLET	ARCHIVE	CALL BACK	ASSEMBLER	CLOCK CYCLE
BUTTON	ARPANET	CHAT ROOM	BACKSPACE	CLOCK SPEED
CLIENT	BARCODE	CHECK BOX	BANDWIDTH	CYBERSPACE
COOKIE	BROWSER	COMPILER	BENCHMARK	DATA TABLET
CURSOR	CHANNEL	COMPRESS	BOOTSTRAP	DIAGNOSTIC
DAEMON	CHIPSET	COMPUTER	BROADBAND	DOWNSIZING
DECODE	CLIP ART	DESELECT	BROADCAST	ENCRYPTION
DELETE	COMMAND	DIGITIZE	CARTRIDGE	FILE SERVER
DIAL-UP	COMPILE	DINGBATS	CHARACTER	FLOPPY DISK
DOMAIN	COUNTER	DISKETTE	CLIPBOARD	MULTIMEDIA

10–continued
NAVIGATION
NETIQUETTE
NEWSLETTER
OPEN SOURCE
PEER-TO-PEER
PERIPHERAL
PREPROCESS
PROGRAMMER
REWRITABLE
SERIAL PORT
SOURCE CODE
TEXT EDITOR
TRANSISTOR
VACUUM TUBE
WEB ADDRESS
WHITEBOARD

11
ACCUMULATOR
ADDRESS BOOK
APPLICATION
BAND PRINTER
BELT PRINTER
BETA TESTING
BOILER PLATE
CLICKSTREAM
COMPACT DISK
COMPILATION
COMPRESSION
COPROCESSOR
CUT AND PASTE
CYBERNETICS
DOTS PER INCH
DRUM PRINTER
INTELLIGENT
INTERACTIVE
INTERPRETER
LINE PRINTER
MOTHERBOARD
MULTIPLEXER
OPTICAL DISK
PLUG AND PLAY
POINT OF SALE
PRINT SERVER
PROGRAMMING
SCREEN SAVER
SEMANTIC NET
SPREADSHEET
STAR NETWORK
SYNCHRONOUS
TIME SHARING
TRANSCEIVER
TROJAN HORSE
VIRTUAL DISK
WORKSTATION

12
ALPHANUMERIC
ASSEMBLY CODE
ASYNCHRONOUS
BROADCASTING
BUBBLE MEMORY

12–continued
CHAIN PRINTER
CHARACTER SET
CLICK AND DRAG
COLOR PRINTER
CONTROL PANEL
DEVICE DRIVER
DIRECT ACCESS
ENCRYPTION
EXPERT SYSTEM
GRAPHICS CARD
HOUSEKEEPING
LASER PRINTER
MINICOMPUTER
MULTITASKING
OPTICAL MOUSE
PARALLEL PORT
PROGRAM SUITE
PULL-DOWN MENU
SEARCH ENGINE
SPELL CHECKER
USER-FRIENDLY
WORLDWIDE WEB

13
ADMINISTRATOR
AUTHORING TOOL
BAR-CODE READER
BARREL PRINTER
BULLETIN BOARD
COMPATIBILITY
CYBERCOMMERCE
DATA STRUCTURE
DOT COM COMPANY
DYNAMIC MEMORY
FLOPTICAL DISK
GRID COMPUTING
HYPERTEXT LINK
IMPACT PRINTER
INK-JET PRINTER
LETTER QUALITY
MICROCOMPUTER
NEURAL NETWORK
PRIMARY MEMORY
SUPERCOMPUTER
TELECOMMUTING
USER INTERFACE
WINDOW MANAGER
WORD PROCESSOR

14
CARRIAGE RETURN
CATHODE-RAY TUBE
DATA PROCESSING
ELECTRONIC MAIL
FLAT-BED PLOTTER
FRAGMENTATTION
MULTITHREADING
PAPER-TAPE PUNCH
READ-ONLY MEM-
ORY
RICH TEXT FORMAT
SYSTEMS ANALYST

14–continued
SYSTEM SOFTWARE
THEOREM PROVING
UTILITY PROGRAM
VIRTUAL REALITY
VOICE ACTIVATED
VOLATILE MEMORY
WORD PROCESSING

15
ACOUSTIC COU-
PLER
BATCH PROCESSING
BUNDLED SOFT-
WARE
CHARACTER
STRING
CONTROL SE-
QUENCE
CRYOGENIC MEM-
ORY
DATABASE PRO-
GRAM
ELECTRONIC BRAIN
MULTIPROCESSING
OPERATING SYSTEM
PAPER-TAPE
READER
RULE-BASED SYS-
TEM
SPELLING CHECKER
TERMINAL DISPLAY
WIDE AREA NET-
WORK
WIRELESS NET-
WORK

16
BUBBLE-JET
PRINTER
COMPILED LAN-
GUAGE
DIAL-IP NETWORK-
ING
DIGITAL AUDIO TAPE
DOMAIN NAME SYS-
TEM
DOT-MATRIX
PRINTER
INSTANT MESSAG-
ING
INTERNET PROTO-
COL
LOCAL AREA NET-
WORK
PERSONAL COM-
PUTER
SOLID-STATE MEM-
ORY
TELECONFERENC-
ING
TOKEN RING NET-
WORK

16–continued
TURNKEY OPERA-
TION
VIDEO DISPLAY UNIT

17
DAISYWHEEL
PRINTER
DESKTOP PUBLISH-
ING
HIGH-LEVEL LAN-
GUAGE
INTEGRATED CIR-
CUIT
NEAR LETTER QUAL-
ITY
OPTICAL RESOLU-
TION
PARALLEL PROCES-
SOR
PERSONAL ORGA-
NIZER

18
FOR YOUR INFOR-
MATION
IONOGRAPHIC
PRINTER
PRINTABLE CHAR-
ACTER
RANDOM-ACCESS
MEMORY
RELATIONAL DATA-
BASE
SPREADSHEET PRO-
GRAM
UNIVERSAL SERIAL
BUS

19
BULLETIN BOARD
SYSTEM
COMPUTER-AIDED
DESIGN
PERCEPTUAL COM-
PUTING
PROGRAMMING
LANGUAGE
SEMICONDUCTOR
MEMORY
TOUCHSCREEN
SOFTWARE
UNIVERSL POWER
SUPPLY

20
APPLICATIONS
SOFTWARE
HEXADECIMAL
CHARACTER
HIERARCHICAL
DATABASE
LIQUID CRYSTAL
DISPLAY

20–continued
MODULATOR-DEMODULA-
TOR

21
CENTRAL PROCESSING
UNIT
COMPUTER-BASED LEARN-
ING
DIGITAL SUBSCRIBER LINE
INFORMATION TECHNOL-
OGY
VIRTUAL PRIVATE NETWORK

22
ARTIFICIAL INTELLIGENCE
COMMON GATEWAY INTER-
FACE
GRAPHICAL USER INTER-
FACE
INTERNET ACCESS
PROVIDER
MEAN TIME BETWEEN FAIL-
URE

22–continued
WHAT YOU SEE IS WHAT
YOU GET

23+
ACCELERATED GRAPHICS
PORT
COMPUTER-AIDED MANU-
FACTURE
COMPUTER-ASSISTED
LEARNING
ENHANCED GRAPHICS
ADAPTER
FLOATING-POINT OPERA-
TION
FREQUENTLY ASKED QUES-
TIONS
INTEGRATED DRIVE ELEC-
TRONICS
INTERNET SERVICE
PROVIDER
NATURAL-LANGUAGE PRO-
CESSING

23+–continued
PERSONAL DIGITAL ASSIS-
TANT
TOUCHSCREEN HARDCOPY
DEVICE
UNINTERRUPTIBLE POWER
SUPPLY
OPTICAL CHARACTER
RECOGNITION
PROGRAMMABLE READ-
ONLY MEMORY
INDUSTRY STANDARD AR-
CHITECTURE
SMALL COMPUTER SYS-
TEMS INTERFACE
INTELLIGENT CHARACTER
RECOGNITION
INTEGRATED SERVICES DIG-
ITAL NETWORK
ERASABLE PROGRAMMABLE
READ-ONLY MEMORY

COMPUTER LANGUAGES

4GL
ADA
ALGOL
APL
ASSEMBLER
ASSEMBLY
  LANGUAGE
AUTOCODE
C
C++
COBOL

COMAL
COMMON LISP
CORAL
CPL
CSL
EULISP
FORTH
FORTRAN
IPL
JAVA
JOVIAL

LISP
LOGO
MACLISP
PASCAL
PILOT
PL/1
PL/360
POP-11
POP-2
POSTSCRIPT
PROLOG

QUICKBASIC
RPG
SGML
SNOBOL
UCSD PASCAL
VBA
VISUAL BASIC
VISUAL BASIC FOR
  APPLICATIONS
VISUAL C++
WORD BASIC

PLANETS AND SATELLITES

MAIN PLANETS (NAMED SATELLITES)

MERCURY
VENUS
EARTH (MOON)
MARS (PHOBOS, DEIMOS)
JUPITER (METIS, ADRASTEA, AMALTHEA,
  THEBE, IO, EUROPA, GANYMEDE,
  CALLISTO, LEDA, HIMALIA, LYSITHEA,
  ELARA, IOCASTE, PRAXIDIKE, HARPALYKE,
  ANANKE, ISONOE, ERINOME, TAYGETE,
  CHALDENE, CARME, PASIPHAE, KALYKE,
  MAGACLITE, SINOPE, CALLIRRHOE)
SATURN (PAN, ATLAS, PROMETHEUS,
  PANDORA, EPIMETHEUS, JANUS, MIMAS,
  ENCELADUS, TETHYS, TELESTO, CALYPSO,
  DIONE, HELENE, RHEA, TITAN, HYPERION,
  IAPETUS, PHOEBE)
URANUS (MIRANDA, ARIEL, UMBRIEL,
  TITANIA, OBERON, CALIBAN, STEPHANO,
  SYCORAX, PROSPERO, SETEBOS,
  CORDELIA, OPHELIA, BIANCA, CRESSIDA,
  DESDEMONA, JOLIET, PORTIA, ROSALIND,
  BELINDA, PUCK, CALIBAN, SYCORAX)

NEPTUNE (TRITON, NEREID, NAIAD,
  THALASSA, DESPINA, LARISSA, GALATEA,
  PROTEUS, LARISSA)
PLUTO (CHARON)

MINOR PLANETS AND PLANETOIDS

ACHILLES	GEOGRAPHOS
ADONIS	HEBE
AGAMEMNON	HEPHAISTOS
AMOR	HERMES
APOLLO	HIDALGO
ASTRAEA	HYGIEA
ATEN	ICARUS
CASTALIA	IDA
CERES	IRIS
CHIRON	JUNO
DACTYL	MATHILDE
DAVIDA	PALLAS
EROS	QUAOAR
EUNOMIA	SEDNA
EUPHROSYNE	TOUTATIS
EUROPA	VESTA
GASPRA	

COMETS

4	7	9	12	15
FAYE	BENNETT	COMAS SOLÀ	PONS-	GIACOBINI-
	D'ARREST	CROMMELIN	WINNECKE	ZINNER
5	VÄISÄLÄ	HYAKUTAKE		GRIGG-
BIELA	WHIPPLE		**13**	SKIELLERUP
ENCKE		**10**	SHOEMAKER-	
KOPFF	**8**	PONS-BROOKS	LEVY	
	BORRELLY	SCHAUMASSE	STEPHAN-	
6	DAYLIGHT		OTERMA	
HALLEY	HALE-BOPP	**11**		
OLBERS	KOHOUTEK	AREND-	**14**	
TUTTLE	WESTPHAL	ROLAND	BRONSEN-	
		SWIFT-TUTTLE	METCALF	

NAMED NEAREST AND BRIGHTEST STARS

4
ROSS
VEGA
WOLF

5
CYGNI
DENEB
RIGEL
SIRUS
SPICA

6
ADHARA

6–continued
ALTAIR
CASTOR
CRUCIS
KRUGER
LUYTEN
POLLUX
SHAULA
SIRIUS

7
ANTARES
CANOPUS

7–continued
CAPELLA
LALANDE
PROCYON
REGULUS
TAU CETI

8
ACHERNAR
ARCTURUS
BARNARD'S
CENTAURI
KAPTEYN'S

9
ALDEBARAN
BELLATRIX
FOMALHAUT

10+
BETELGEUSE
EPSILON INDI
ALPHA CENTAURI
EPSILON ERIDANI
PROXIMA CENTAURI

THE CONSTELLATIONS

3
ARA
LEO

4
APUS
CRUX
GRUS
LYNX
LYRA
PAVO
VELA

5
ARIES
CETUS
DRACO
HYDRA
INDUS
LEPUS
LIBRA
LUPUS
MENSA
MUSCA

5–continued
NORMA
ORION
PYXIS
VIRGO

6
ANTLIA
AQUILA
AURIGA
BOÖTES
CAELUM
CANCER
CARINA
CORVUS
CRATER
CYGNUS
DORADO
FORNAX
GEMINI
HYDRUS
OCTANS
PICTOR

6–continued
PISCES
PUPPIS
SCUTUM
TAURUS
TUCANA
VOLANS

7
CEPHEUS
COLUMBA
LACERTA
PEGASUS
PERSEUS
PHOENIX
SAGITTA
SERPENS
SEXTANS

8
AQUARIUS
CIRCINUS
EQUULEUS
ERIDANUS

8–continued
HERCULES
LEO MINOR
SCORPIUS
SCULPTOR

9
ANDROMEDA
CENTAURUS
CHAMELEON
DELPHINUS
MONOCEROS
OPHIUCHUS
RETICULUM
URSA MAJOR
URSA MINOR
VULPECULA

10
CANIS MAJOR
CANIS MINOR
CASSIOPEIA
HOROLOGIUM
TRIANGULUM

11
CAPRICORNUS
SAGITTARIUS
TELESCOPIUM

12+
CAMELOPAR-
   DALIS
CANES
   VENATICI
COMA
   BERENICES
CORONA AUS-
   TRALIS
CORONA
   BOREALIS
MICRO-
   SCOPIUM
PISCIS
   AUSTRINUS
TRIANGULUM
   AUSTRALE

METEOR SHOWERS

6
LYRIDS
URSIDS

7
CYGNIDS
LEONIDS

7–continued
TAURIDS

8
CEPHEIDS
GEMINIDS
ORIONIDS

8–continued
PERSEIDS

10
AUSTRALIDS
OPHIUCHIDS
PHOENICIDS

11
QUADRANTIDS

12
CAPRICORNIDS

ASTRONOMERS ROYAL

JOHN FLAMSTEED (1675–1719)
EDMUND HALLEY (1720–42)
JAMES BRADLEY (1742–62)
NATHANIEL BLISS (1762–64)
NEVIL MASKELYNE (1765–1811)
JOHN POND (1811–35)
SIR GEORGE BIDDELL AIRY (1835–81)
SIR WILLIAM H. M. CHRISTIE (1881–1910)

SIR FRANK WATSON DYSON (1910–33)
SIR HAROLD SPENCER JONES (1933–55)
SIR RICHARD WOOLLEY (1955–71)
SIR MARTIN RYLE (1972–82)
SIR FRANCIS GRAHAM-SMITH (1982–91)
SIR ARNOLD WOLFENDALE (1991–95)
SIR MARTIN REES (1995–   )

MANNED SPACE PROGRAMS

VOSTOK (Russian; 1961-63)
MERCURY (US; 1961-63)
VOSKHOD (Russian; 1964-65)
GEMINI (US; 1965-66)
APOLLO (US; 1967-72)
SOYUZ (Russian; 1967-   )

SALYUT (Russian; 1971-86)
SKYLAB (US; 1973-79)
SPACE SHUTTLE (US; 1981-   )
SPACELAB (US; 1983-92)
MIR (Russian; 1986-99
INTERNATIONAL SPACE STATION (1998-   )

GEOLOGICAL TIME SCALE

ERA	PERIOD	EPOCH
CENOZOIC	QUATERNARY	HOLOCENE
		PLEISTOCENE
	TERTIARY	PLIOCENE
		IOCENE
		OLIGOCENE
		EOCENE
		PALAEOCENE
MESOZOIC	CRETACEOUS	
	JURASSIC	
	TRIASSIC	
PALAEOZOIC	PERMIAN	
	CARBONIFEROUS	
	DEVONIAN	
	SILURIAN	
	ORDOVICIAN	
	CAMBRIAN	
PRECAMBRIAN	PRECAMBRIAN	

PREHISTORIC ANIMALS

8
EOHIPPUS
RUTIODON
SMILODON

9
IGUANODON
TRACHODON

10
ALLOSAURUS
ALTISPINAX
BAROSAURUS
DIPLODOCUS
DRYOSAURUS
EUPARKERIA
MESOHIPPUS
ORTHOMERUS
PLIOHIPPUS
PTERANODON
STEGOCERAS

11
ANATOSAURUS
ANCHISAURUS
APATOSAURUS
APHANERAMMA
CETIOSAURUS

11–continued
COELOPHYSIS
DEINONYCHUS
KRITOSAURUS
MANDASUCHUS
MERYCHIPPUS
MONOCLONIUS
POLACANTHUS
PTERODACTYL
RIOJASAURUS
SAUROLOPHUS
SCOLOSAURUS
SPINOSAURUS
STEGOSAURUS
TARBOSAURUS
TRICERATOPS

12
ANKYLOSAURUS
BRONTOSAURUS
CAMPTOSAURUS
CERATOSAURUS
CHASMOSAURUS
DEINOCHEIRUS
HYLAEOSAURUS
KENTROSAURUS
LAMBEOSAURUS

12–continued
MEGALOSAURUS
ORNITHOMIMUS
OURANOSAURUS
PLATEOSAURUS
TICINOSUCHUS

13
BRACHIOSAURUS
COMPSOGNATHUS
CORYTHOSAURUS
DESMATOSUCHUS
DILOPHOSAURUS
EDMONTOSAURUS
ERYTHROSUCHUS
HYPSELOSAURUS
HYPSILOPHODON
LESOTHOSAURUS
PANOPLOSAURUS
PENTACERATOPS
PROTOCERATOPS
PTERODACTYLUS
SCELIDOSAURUS
SCLEROMOCHLUS
STYRACOSAURUS
TENONTOSAURUS
TYRANNOSAURUS

14
BALUCHITHERIUM
CETIOSAURISCUS
CHASMATOSAURUS
EUOPLOCEPHALUS
MASSOSPONDYLUS
PSITTACOSAURUS
THESCELOSAURUS

15
PARASAUROLOPHUS
PROCHENEOSAURUS

16
PACHYRHINO-
  SAURUS
PROCOMPSO-
  GNATHUS

17
HETERODONTO-
  SAURUS

18
PACHYCEPHALO-
  SAURUS

EARLY HOMINIDS

AFRICAN EVE (*Australopithecus afarensis*)
BODO SKULL (*Homo heidelbergensis*)
BOXGROVE MAN (*Homo heidelbergensis*)
CRO-MAGNON MAN (*Homo sapiens*)
FLAT-FACED KENYA MAN (*Kenyanthropus platyops*)
HANDY MAN (*Homo habllis*)
HEIDELBERG MAN (*Homo heidelbergensis*)
HERTO MAN (*Homo sapiens idaltu*)
JAVA MAN (*Homo erectus*)
KABWE SKULL (*Homo heidelbergensis*)
KENYA MAN (*Kenyanthropus platyops*)
LUCY (*Australopithecus afarensis*)
MAUER MANDIBLE (*Homo heidelbergensis*)

MILLENNIUM MAN (*Orrorin turgensis*)
MITOCHONDRIAL EVE
MUNGO MAN (*Homo sapiens*)
NANJING MAN (*Homo erectus*)
NEBRASKA MAN (*fake*)
PEKING MAN (*Homo erectus*)
PILTDOWN MAN (*fake*)
QATZEH SKULL (*Homo heidelbergensis*)
RHODESIAN MAN (*Homo heidelbergensis*)
SOUTHERN APE (*Australopithecus*)
TAUNG CHILD (*Australopithecus afarensis*)
TURKANA BOY (*Homo erectus*)
UPRIGHT MAN (*Homo erectus*)

ROCKS AND MINERALS

4
GOLD
MICA
OPAL
RUBY
TALC

5
AGATE
BERYL
BORAX
EMERY
FLINT
SHALE
SHARD
SKARN
TOPAZ
TRONA

6
ACMITE
ALBITE
ARKOSE
AUGITE
BARITE
BASALT
COPPER
DACITE
DUNITE
GABBRO
GALENA
GARNET
GNEISS
GYPSUM
HALITE
HAÜYNE
HUMITE
ILLITE
LEVYNE
MINIUM
NORITE
NOSEAN
PELITE
PYRITE
PYROPE
QUARTZ
RUTILE
SALITE
SCHIST
SCHORL
SILICA
SILVER
SPHENE
SPINEL
URTITE
ZIRCON

7
ALNOITE

7–continued
ALTAITE
ALUNITE
ANATASE
APATITE
ARSENIC
AXINITE
AZURITE
BARYTES
BAUXITE
BIOTITE
BISMUTH
BORNITE
BRECCIA
BRUCITE
CALCITE
CALOMEL
CELSIAN
CITRINE
COESITE
CUPRITE
DIAMOND
DIORITE
EMERALD
EPIDOTE
FELSITE
FOYAITE
GAHNITE
GEDRITE
GRANITE
GUMMITE
HELVITE
HESSITE
HOPEITE
HUNTITE
IJOLITE
JADEITE
KAINITE
KERNITE
KYANITE
LEUCITE
LIGNITE
MELLITE
MULLITE
OLIVINE
ORTHITE
RASPITE
REALGAR
SPARITE
SYENITE
SYLVITE
THORITE
THULITE
ZEOLITE
ZINCITE
ZOISITE

8
AEGIRINE
ALLANITE
ALUNOGEN
ANALCIME
ANALCITE
ANDESINE
ANDORITE
ANKERITE
ANTIMONY
ARCANITE
AUGELITE
AUTUNITE
BASANITE
BIXBYITE
BLOEDITE
BLUE JOHN
BOEHMITE
BORACITE
BRAGGITE
BRAUNITE
BRAVOITE
BRONZITE
BROOKITE
CALAMINE
CHIOLITE
CHLORITE
CHROMITE
CINNABAR
CORUNDUM
CROCOITE
CRYOLITE
CUBANITE
DATOLITE
DIALLAGE
DIASPORE
DIGENITE
DIOPSIDE
DIOPTASE
DOLERITE
DOLOMITE
ECLOGITE
ENARGITE
EPSOMITE
ESSEXITE
EULYTITE
EUXENITE
FAYALITE
FELDSPAR
FLUORITE
GIBBSITE
GOETHITE
GRAPHITE
HANKSITE
HAWAIITE
HEMATITE
HYACINTH
IDOCRASE

8–continued
ILMENITE
IODYRITE
JAROSITE
LAZURITE
LIMONITE
LITHARGE
MARSHITE
MEIONITE
MELANITE
MELILITE
MESOLITE
MIERSITE
MIMETITE
MONAZITE
MONETITE
MYLONITE
NEPHRITE
ORPIMENT
PARISITE
PERIDOTE
PERTHITE
PETALITE
PLATINUM
PORPHYRY
PREHNITE
PSAMMITE
PYRIBOLE
PYROXENE
RHYOLITE
ROCKSALT
SANIDINE
SAPPHIRE
SELLAITE
SIDERITE
SMECTITE
SODALITE
STANNITE
STEATITE
STIBNITE
STILBITE
STOLSITE
STRUVITE
TITANITE
TONALITE
TRACHYTE
VARISITE
VATERITE
WEHRLITE
WURTZITE
XENOTIME

9
ACANTHITE
ALMANDINE
ALUMINITE
AMPHIBOLE
ANDRADITE

9–continued
ANGLESITE
ANHYDRITE
ANORTHITE
ARAGONITE
ARGENTITE
ATACAMITE
BENITOITE
BRIMSTONE
BROMYRITE
BUNSENITE
BYTOWNITE
CARNALITE
CARNOTITE
CELESTITE
CERUSSITE
CHABAZITE
CHINACLAY
COBALTITE
COLUMBITE
COPIAPITE
COTUNNITE
COVELLITE
DANBURITE
DERBYLITE
DIATOMITE
ENSTATITE
ERYTHRITE
EUCAIRITE
EUCLASITE
EUDIALITE
FERBERITE
FIBROLITE
FLUORSPAR
GEHLENITE
GMELINITE
GOSLARITE
GRANULITE
GREYWACKE
GROSSULAR
GRUNERITE
HARMOTOME
HERCYNITE
HERDERITE
HORNSTONE
KAOLINITE
KIESERITE
LANARKITE
LAWSONITE
LEUCITITE
LIMESTONE
LODESTONE
MAGNESITE
MAGNETITE
MALACHITE
MALIGNITE
MANGANITE
MARCASITE

9–continued

MARGARITE
MARIALITE
MENDIPITE
MICROLITE
MIGMATITE
MILLERITE
MISPICKEL
MONZONITE
MORDENITE
MUGEARITE
MUSCOVITE
NANTOKITE
NATROLITE
NEPHELINE
NICCOLITE
OLDHAMITE
OLIVENITE
PECTOLITE
PENNINITE
PERCYLITE
PERICLASE
PHENAKITE
PHONOLITE
PIGEONITE
PISTACITE
POLLUCITE
POWELLITE
PROUSTITE
PULASKITE
QUARTZITE
RHODONITE
SANDSTONE
SCAPOLITE
SCHEELITE
SCOLECITE
SCORODITE
SMALLTITE
SOAPSTONE
SPODUMENE
STRENGITE
SYLVANITE
TACHYLITE
TANTALITE
TAPIOLITE
THERALITE
THOLEIITE
TREMOLITE
TRIDYMITE
TURQUOISE
URANINITE
VIVIANITE
WAGNERITE
WAVELLITE
WILLEMITE
WITHERITE
WULFENITE
ZEUNERITE

10

ACTINOLITE
ÅKERMANITE

10–continued

ALABANDITE
ANDALUSITE
ANKARAMITE
ARSENOLITE
BOROLONITE
BOURNONITE
BRONZITITE
CACOXENITE
CALEDONITE
CANCRINITE
CERVANTITE
CHALCEDONY
CHALCOCITE
CHLORITOID
CHRYSOLITE
CLAUDETITE
CLINTONITE
COLEMANITE
CONNELLITE
COQUIMBITE
CORDIERITE
DOUGLASITE
DYSCRASITE
EMPLECTITE
EMPRESSITE
EPIDIORITE
FORSTERITE
GANOMALITE
GARNIERITE
GAYLUSSITE
GEIKIELITE
GLAUBERITE
GLAUCONITE
GREENSTONE
HAMBERGITE
HEULANDITE
HORNBLENDE
HUEBNERITE
IGNIMBRITE
JAMESONITE
KIMBERLITE
LANTHANITE
LAUMONTITE
LAURIONITE
LEPIDOLITE
LHERZOLITE
LIMBURGITE
MASCAGNITE
MATLOCKITE
MEERSCHAUM
MELILITITE
MELTEIGITE
MICROCLINE
MIRABILITE
MOISSANITE
NEWBERYITE
OLIGOCLASE
ORTHOCLASE
PARAGONITE
PEKOVSKITE
PERIDOTITE

10–continued

PERTHOSITE
PHLOGOPITE
PHOSGENITE
PIEMONTITE
POLYBASITE
PYRALSPITE
PYROCHLORE
PYROLUSITE
PYRRHOTITE
RHYODACITE
RICHTERITE
RIEBECKITE
SAFFLORITE
SAMARSKITE
SAPPHIRINE
SERPENTINE
SHONKINITE
SPERRYLITE
SPHALERITE
STAUROLITE
STERCORITE
STISHOVITE
TESCHENITE
THENARDITE
THOMSONITE
THORIANITE
TORBERNITE
TOURMALINE
TRAVERTINE
TROEGERITE
ULLMANNITE
ULVÓSPINEL
VANADINITE
VITROPHYRE
WEBSTERITE
WHEWELLITE
WOLFRAMITE
ZINCBLENDE

11

ALLEMONTITE
AMBLYGONITE
ANORTHOSITE
APOPHYLLITE
BADDELEYITE
BERTRANDITE
BERYLLONITE
BROCHANTITE
CALCARENITE
CALCILUTITE
CALCIRUDITE
CARBONATITE
CARBORUNDUM
CASSITERITE
CERARGYRITE
CHARNOCKITE
CHIASTOLITE
CHLOANTHITE
CHONDRODITE
CHRYSOBERYL
CHRYSOCOLLA

11–continued

CLINOCHLORE
COBALTBLOOM
DAUBREELITE
EGLESTONITE
FERROAUGITE
FRANKLINITE
GLAUBER SALT
GLAUCOPHANE
GREENOCKITE
HARZBURGITE
HASTINGSITE
HAUSMANNITE
HYPERSTHENE
ICELAND SPAR
KATOPHORITE
LAPIS LAZULI
LEADHILLITE
LOELLINGITE
MANGANOSITE
MELANTERITE
MOLYBDENITE
MONTROYDITE
NEPHELINITE
NORDMARKITE
PENFIELDITE
PENTLANDITE
PHILLIPSITE
PITCHBLENDE
PLAGIOCLASE
PSILOMELANE
PUMPELLYITE
PYRARGYRITE
PYROCHROITE
RADIOLARITE
ROCK CRYSTAL
SILLIMANITE
SMITHSONITE
SPESSARTITE
TITANAUGITE
TRIPHYLLITE
VALENTINITE
VERMICULITE
VESUVIANITE
VILLIAUMITE
ZINNWALDITE

12

ANORTHOCLASE
ARSENOPYRITE
BISMUTHINITE
BOULANGERITE
CALCISILTITE
CHALCANTHITE
CHALCOPYRITE
CLAY MINERALS
CLINOPTOLITE
CLINOZOISITE
CRISTOBALITE
EDDINGTONITE
FELDSPATHOID
FERGUSSONITE

12–continued
FLUORAPATITE
GROSSULARITE
HEDENBERGITE
HEMIMORPHITE
LUXULLIANITE
METACINNABAR
MONTICELLITE
PYROMORPHITE
PYROPHYLLITE
RHODOCROSITE
SENARMONTITE
SKUTTERUDITE
STRONTIANITE
SYENODIORITE
TERLINGUAITE

12–continued
TETRAHEDRITE
THOMSENOLITE
TRACHYBASALT
WOLLASTONITE

13
ANTHOPHYLLITE
BREITHAUPTITE
CLINOPYROXENE
CUMMINGTONITE
JACUPIRANGITE
KALIOPHYLLITE
LEPIDOCROCITE
LITCHFIELDITE
ORTHOPYROXENE
QUARTZARENITE

13–continued
RHODOCHROSITE
STILPNOMELANE
THERMONATRITE
UNCOMPAHGRITE

14
CRYOLITHIONITE
HYDROMAGNESITE
LECHATELIERITE
LITHIOPHYLLITE
ORTHOQUARTZITE
PSEUDOBROOKITE
RAMMELSBERGITE
TRACHYANDESITE
XANTHOPHYLLITE

15
MONTMORILLONITE
PSEUDOTACHYLITE
STIBIOTANTALITE

16
GALENABISMUTHITE
ORTHOFERROSILITE
PHARMA-
  COSIDERITE

17
HYDRO-
  GROSSULARITE
TELLURO-
  BISMUTHITE

ORES

ELEMENT – ore(s)

3
TIN – cassiterite

4
IRON – haematite, magnetite
LEAD – galena
ZINC – sphalerite, smithsonite, calamine

5
BORON – kernite

6
BARIUM – barite, witherite
CERIUM – monazite, bastnaesite
COBALT – cobaltite, smaltite, erythrite
COPPER – malachite, azurite, chalcopyrite, bornite, cuprite
ERBIUM – monazite, bastnaesite
INDIUM – sphalerite, smithsonite, calamine
NICKEL – pentlandite, pyrrhotite
OSMIUM – iridosime
RADIUM – pitchblende, carnotite
SILVER – argentite, horn silver
SODIUM – salt

7
ARSENIC – realgar, orpiment, arsenopyrite
CADMIUM – greenockite

7–continued
CAESIUM – lepidolite, pollucite
CALCIUM – limestone, gypsum, fluorite
HAFNIUM – zircon
HOLMIUM – monazite
LITHIUM – lepidolite, spodumene
MERCURY – cinnabar
NIOBIUM – columbite-tantalite, pyrochlore, euxenite
RHENIUM – molybdenite
SILICON – silica
THORIUM – monazite
THULIUM – monazite
URANIUM – pitchblende, uraninite, carnotite
YTTRIUM – monazite

8
ANTIMONY – stibnite
CHROMIUM – chromite
LUTETIUM – monazite
PLATINUM – sperrylite
RUBIDIUM – lepidolite
SAMARIUM – monazite, bastnaesite
SCANDIUM – thortveitite, davidite
SELENIUM – pyrites
TANTALUM – columbite-tantalite
THALLIUM – pyrites
TITANIUM – rutile, ilmenite, sphere
TUNGSTEN – wolframite, scheelite

8–continued
VANADIUM – carnotite, roscoelite, vanadinite

9
ALUMINIUM – bauxite
BERYLLIUM – beryl
GERMANIUM – germanite, argyrodite
LANTHANUM – monazite, bastnaesite
MAGNESIUM – magnesite, dolomite
MANGANESE – pyrolusite, rhodochrosite
NEODYMIUM – monazite, bastnaesite
POTASSIUM – sylvite, carnallite, polyhalite
RUTHENIUM – pentlandite, pyroxinite
STRONTIUM – celestite, strontianite
YTTERBIUM – monazite

10
DYSPROSIUM – monazite, bastnaesite
GADOLINIUM – monazite, bastnaesite
MOLYBDENUM – molybdenite, wulfenite
PHOSPHORUS – apatite

12
PRASEODYMIUM – monazite, bastnaesite
PROTACTINIUM – pitchblende

GEMSTONES

STONE (colour)

4
JADE (green, mauve, brown)
ONYX (various colours, banded)
OPAL (white, milky blue, or black with rainbow-coloured reflections)
RUBY (red)

5
AGATE (brown, red, blue, green, yellow)
BERYL (green, blue, pink)

5–continued
TOPAZ (usually yellow or colourless)

6
GARNET (red)
ZIRCON (all colours)

7
CITRINE (yellow)
DIAMOND (colourless)
EMERALD (green)

8
AMETHYST (purple)
SAPPHIRE (blue and other colours except red)

8–continued
SUNSTONE (whitish-red-brown flecked with gold)

9
MALACHITE (dark green-brown banded)
MOONSTONE (white with bluish tinge)
SOAPSTONE (white or greenish)
TURQUOISE (greenish-blue)

10
AQUAMARINE (turquoise, greenish-blue)

10–continued
BLOODSTONE (green with red spots)
CHALCEDONY (red, brown, grey, or black)
SERPENTINE (usually green or white)
TOURMALINE (all colours)

11
LAPIS LAZULI (deep blue)

CLOUD CLASSIFICATION

ALTOCUMULUS
ALTOSTRATUS
CIRROCUMULUS

CIRROSTRATUS
CIRRUS
CUMULONIMBUS

CUMULUS
NIMBOSTRATUS

STRATOCUMULUS
STRATUS

NOTABLE WINDS

4
BERG
BISE
BORA
FÖHN

5
BURAN
FOEHN
GIBLI
ZONDA

6
AUSTRU
GHIBLI
HABOOB
KAMSIN
SANIEL
SIMOOM
SOLANO

7
CHINOOK
ETESIAN

7–continued
GREGALE
KHAMSIN
MELTEMI
MISTRAL
MONSOON
PAMPERO
SIROCCO

8
LEVANTER
LIBECCIO

8–continued
PAPAGAYO
SANTA ANA
WILLIWAW

9
HARMATTAN
LIBECCHIO
SNOW EATER

10
CAPE DOCTOR
EUROCLYDON

10–continued
TRAMONTANA
TRAMONTANE
WET CHINOOK
WILLY-WILLY

11
TEHUANTEPEC

12+
BRICKFIELDER
SOUTHERLY BUSTER

ECONOMIC TERMS AND THEORIES

3
GDP
GNP

4
FIFO

5
SLUMP

7
DUOPOLY
MARXISM
NEW DEAL
SLAVERY
STATICS
SURPLUS

8
FUNGIBLE
LENINISM
MONOPOLY
PROPERTY

9
BOOM CYCLE
BUST CYCLE
FREE TRADE
INELASTIC
LIQUIDITY
OLIGOPOLY
PUT OPTION
RECESSION

10
ADDED VALUE
BEAR MARKET
BROAD MONEY
BULL MARKET
CAPITALISM
DEPRESSION

10–continued
FISCAL DRAG
FREE MARKET
INVESTMENT
MONETARISM
PROTECTION
TRADE CYCLE
TROTSKYISM
VALUE ADDED

11
COLONIALISM
COMPETITION
CONSUMERISM
DEMAND CURVE
IMPERIALISM
MARGINALISM
MATERIALISM
NARROW MONEY
PHYSIOCRACY
REVISIONISM
STAGFLATION
SYNDICALISM

12
ECONOMETRICS
ECONOMIC RENT
FISCAL POLICY
FIVE-YEAR PLAN
GOLD STANDARD
KEYNESIANISM
MARKET FORCES
MERCANTILISM
MIXED ECONOMY
NEW ECONOMICS
PRODUCTIVITY
PUBLIC SECTOR
SURPLUS VALUE
TRADE BARRIER

13
DEMAND ECONOMY
EXCHANGE VALUE
FUTURES MARKET
NEO-CLASSICISM
OPTIONS MARKET
PRIVATE SECTOR

14
BALANCED BUDGET
COMMAND
  ECONOMY
CORPORATE STATE
ECONOMIC
  GROWTH
ECONOMIC POLICY
MACROECONOMICS
MICROECONOMICS
MONETARY POLICY
NATIONAL INCOME
WINDFALL PROFIT

15
AGGREGATE
  DEMAND
INFLATIONARY GAP
POSITIONAL GOODS
SUPPLY AND
  DEMAND
TOTALITARIANISM
VELOCITY OF
  MONEY
WAGE-PRICE SPIRAL

16
COST OF
  PRODUCTION
DEFICIT FINANCING
DIVISION OF
  LABOUR

16–continued
ECONOMIES OF
  SCALE
INSTITUTIONALISM
RETAIL PRICE INDEX
WELFARE ECONOM-
  ICS

17
MEANS OF PRODUC-
  TION

18
DIMINISHING
  RETURNS
ECONOMIC CLASSI-
  CISM
ELASTICITY OF
  DEMAND
PERFECT COMPETI-
  TION

19+
DIALECTICAL MA-
  TERIALISM
ECONOMIC EQUILIB-
  RIUM
GROSS DOMESTIC
  PRODUCT
GROSS NATIONAL
  PRODUCT
LAISSEZ-FAIRE
  ECONOMICS
PRICES AND
  INCOMES
  POLICY
SUPPLY-SIDE
  ECONOMICS

MEDICINE AND HEALTH

MEDICAL FIELDS AND SPECIALITIES

7
ANATOMY
MYOLOGY
OTOLOGY
UROLOGY

8
CYTOLOGY
EUGENICS
NOSOLOGY
ONCOLOGY
SEROLOGY

9
AETIOLOGY
ANDROLOGY
AUDIOLOGY
HISTOLOGY
NECROLOGY
NEUROLOGY
ORTHOTICS
OSTEOLOGY
PATHOLOGY
PLEOPTICS
RADIOLOGY
RHINOLOGY

10
CARDIOLOGY
EMBRYOLOGY
GERIATRICS
IMMUNOLOGY
MORPHOLOGY
NEPHROLOGY
OBSTETRICS
ORTHOPTICS
PROCTOLOGY
PSYCHOLOGY
SEMEIOLOGY
TERATOLOGY

11
DERMATOLOGY
GERONTOLOGY
GYNAECOLOGY
HAEMATOLOGY
LARYNGOLOGY
LOGOPAEDICS
PAEDIATRICS
RADIOGRAPHY
STOMATOLOGY

12
CYTOGENETICS
EPHEBIATRICS
EPIDEMIOLOGY
ORTHOPAEDICS
PHARMACOLOGY
RADIOBIOLOGY
RHEUMATOLOGY
SYNDESMOLOGY
THERAPEUTICS
TRAUMATOLOGY

13
ENDOCRINOLOGY
OPHTHALMOLOGY
PSYCHOMETRICS

14
OTOLARYNGOLOGY
SYMPTOMATOLOGY

15
DERMATOGLYPHICS
NEUROPHYSIOLOGY
PSYCHOPATHOLOGY

16
GASTRO-
  ENTEROLOGY
PSYCHO-
  GERIATRICS
PSYCHO-
  PHYSIOLOGY

17+
COGNITIVE
  PSYCHOLOGY
INTERVENTIONAL
  RADIOLOGY
NUCLEAR
  CARDIOLOGY
OTORHINO-
  LARYNGOLOGY
PSYCHO-
  LINGUISTICS
PSYCHO-
  PHARMACOLOGY

MAJOR ARTERIES

AORTA
BRACHIAL
CAROTID
FEMORAL

HEPATIC
ILIAC
INNOMINATE
MESENTERIC

PULMONARY
RADIAL
RENAL
SUBCLAVIAN

THORACIC
TIBIAL
ULNAR

MAJOR VEINS

BASILIC
BRACHIAL
CEPHALIC
FEMORAL
HEPATIC

HEPATIC PORTAL
ILIAC
INFERIOR VENA
  CAVA
JUGULAR

PULMONARY
RENAL
SAPHENOUS
SUBCLAVIAN

SUPERIOR VENA
  CAVA
SUPRARENAL
TIBIAL

ALTERNATIVE THERAPIES

4
YOGA

5
REIKI

6
T'AI CHI

7
CHI KUNG
CUPPING
FASTING
HEALING
MASSAGE
ROLFING
SHIATSU

8
AYURVEDA
FENG SHUI

9
BREATHING
DREAMWORK
RADIONICS
SHAMANISM

10
ART THERAPY
BIORHYTHMS
HELLERWORK
HOMEOPATHY
MEDITATION
MYOTHERAPY
OSTEOPATHY
RELAXATION

11
ACUPRESSURE
ACUPUNCTURE

11–continued
BATES METHOD
BIOFEEDBACK
COUNSELLING
FELDENKRAIS
MOXIBUSTION
NATUROPATHY
PSYCHODRAMA
REFLEXOLOGY

12
AROMATHERAPY
CHIROPRACTIC
HYDROTHERAPY
HYPNOTHERAPY
LIGHT THERAPY
SOUND THERAPY
TREE REMEDIES

13
BIOENERGETICS
COLOUR THERAPY
FOOD COMBINING
PSYCHOTHERAPY
VISUALIZATION

14
BOWEN TECHNIQUE
CRYSTAL HEALING
DIETARY THERAPY
FLOWER REMEDIES
GESTALT THERAPY
HERBAL MEDICINE
ROSEN TECHNIQUE
TRAGER APPROACH

15
CELLOID MINERALS
ENCOUNTER
  GROUPS

15–continued
ENERGY THERAPIES
GEOPATHIC ENERGY
MACROBIOTIC DIET
MAGNETIC THERAPY
POLARITY THERAPY
PSIONIC MEDICINE
PSYCHOSYNTHESIS
SCHUESSLER SALTS
THALASSOTHERAPY

16
COGNITIVE
  THERAPY
FLOTATION
  THERAPY
SPIRITUAL HEALING
THERAPEUTIC
  TOUCH

17
AUTOGENIC
  TRAINING
COLONIC
  IRRIGATION
CRANIAL
  OSTEOPATHY

18
ALEXANDER
  TECHNIQUE
APPLIED
  KINESIOLOGY
BACH FLOWER
  REMEDIES
MEGAVITAMIN
  THERAPY
NUTRITIONAL
  THERAPY

19
CRANIOSACRAL
  THERAPY
EXPRESSION
  THERAPIES

20+
BIOCHEMIC TISSUE
  SALTS
CHINESE HERBAL
  MEDICINE
ELECTROCRYSTAL
  THERAPY
ELECTROMAGNETIC
  THERAPY
ENVIRONMENTAL
  THERAPIES
EXTERNAL
  VISUALIZATION
GEM AND MINERAL
  ESSENCES
INTERNAL
  VISUALIZATION
METAMORPHIC
  TECHNIQUE
ORIENTAL HERBAL
  MEDICINE
TRADITIONAL
  CHINESE
  MEDICINE
TRANSACTIONAL
  ANALYSIS
TRANSCENDENTAL
  MEDITATION

THE EAR

ANVIL
AUDITORY NERVE
BASILAR
  MEMBRANE
COCHLEA
EARDRUM
EUSTACHIAN TUBE
FENESTRA OVALIS
FENESTRA
  ROTUNDA

HAMMER
INCUS
INNER EAR
LABYRINTH
MALLEUS
MEMBRANE OF
  REISSNER
MIDDLE EAR
ORGAN OF CORTI
OSSICLES

OVAL WINDOW
PINNA
RECEPTOR CELLS
ROUND WINDOW
SACCULE
SCALA MEDIA
SCALA TYMPANI
SCALA VESTIBULI
SEMICIRCULAR
  CANAL

STAPES
STIRRUP
TECTORIAL
  MEMBRANE
TUNNEL OF CORTI
TYMPANIC
  MEMBRANE
UTRICLE
VESTIBULAR NERVE

THE EYE

AQUEOUS HUMOUR
BLIND SPOT
CHOROID
CILIARY BODY
CONE
CONJUNCTIVA

CORNEA
EYELASH
FOVEA
HYALOID CANAL
IRIS
LACRIMAL GLAND

LENS
MEIBOMIAN GLAND
OPTIC NERVE
PUPIL
RETINA
ROD

SCLERA
VITREOUS HUMOUR
YELLOW SPOT

MUSCLES

4	7–continued	8–continued	9–continued	11
PSOAS	ILIACUS	SERRATUS	SUPINATOR	ORBICULARIS
	TRICEPS	SKELETAL	TRAPEZIUS	STERNOHYOID
5		TIBIALIS	VOLUNTARY	
TERES	8			12
	ANCONEUS	9	10	STYLOGLOS-
SUS
6	MASSETER	DEPRESSOR	BRACHIALIS	
BICEPS	OPPONENS	ILIOPSOAS	BUCCINATOR	13+
RECTUS	PECTORAL	MYLOHYOID	EPICRANIUS	GASTROCNE-
MIUS
SOLEUS	PERONEUS	OBTURATOR	HYOGLOSSUS	STERNOMAS-
TOID
VASTUS	PLATYSMA	POPLITEUS	QUADRICEPS	STERNOCLEI-
DOMASTOID
	POSTURAL	QUADRATUS	STYLOHYOID	
7	RHOMBOID	SARTORIUS	TEMPORALIS	
DELTOID	SCALENUS	SPHINCTER		
GLUTEUS				

BONES

3	6–continued	7–continued	9–continued	12–continued
RIB	FIBULA	PATELLA	NASAL BONE	SPINAL COL-
UMN
	HALLUX	PHALANX	PHALANGES	TEMPORAL
BONE
4	HAMMER	SCAPULA	THIGHBONE	
ULNA	PELVIS	STERNUM	WRISTBONE	13
	RACHIS	STIRRUP		OCCIPITAL
BONE
5	RADIUS		10	SESAMOID
BONES
ANVIL	SACRUM	8	ASTRAGALUS	SHOULDER
BLADE
COSTA	STAPES	BACKBONE	BREASTBONE	ZYGOMATIC
BONE
FEMUR	TARSAL	CLAVICLE	CANNON BONE	
ILIUM	TARSUS	HEEL BONE	COLLARBONE	14+
INCUS		MANDIBLE	HAUNCH BONE	INNOMINATE
BONE
PUBIS	7	SCAPHOID	METACARPAL	VERTEBRAL
COLUMN
SKULL	CRANIUM	SHINBONE	METACARPUS	
SPINE	HIPBONE	SPHENOID	METATARSAL	
TALUS	HUMERUS	VERTEBRA	METATARSUS	
TIBIA	ISCHIUM			
VOMER	JAWBONE	9	11	
	KNEECAP	ANKLEBONE	ETHMOID BONE	
6	KNEEPAN	CALCANCUS	FLOATING RIB	
CARPAL	MALLEUS	CHEEKBONE	FRONTAL BONE	
CARPUS	MASTOID	FUNNY BONE		
COCCYX	MAXILLA	HYOID BONE	12	
CUBOID		MAXILLARY	PARIETAL BONE	

GLANDS

5
LIVER
SWEAT

6
BUCCAL
PINEAL
TARSAL
THYMUS

7
ADRENAL
COWPER'S

7–continued
GASTRIC
MAMMARY
PAROTID
THYROID

8
BRUNNER'S
DUCTLESS
EXOCRINE
PANCREAS
PROSTATE

8–continued
SALIVARY

9
ENDOCRINE
MEIBOMIAN
PITUITARY
PREPUTIAL
SEBACEOUS

10
BARTHOLIN'S
SUBLINGUAL

10–continued
SUPRARENAL
VESTIBULAR

11
LIEBERKÜHN'S
PARATHYROID

12
SUBMAXILLARY

13
BULBOURETHRAL
SUBMANDIBULAR

SURGICAL OPERATIONS

7
MYOTOMY – MUSCLE
LOBOTOMY – NERVE FIBRES
  FROM FRONTAL LOBE OF
  BRAIN

8
MYECTOMY – MUSCLE
TENOTOMY – TENDON
VAGOTOMY – VAGUS NERVE
VASOTOMY – SPERM DUCT

9
AMNIOTOMY – AMNIOTIC
  MEMBRANES
COLECTOMY – COLON
COLOSTOMY – COLON
COLPOTOMY – VAGINA
CORDOTOMY – PART OF
  SPINAL CORD
CYSTOTOMY – BLADDER
GONIOTOMY – DUCT IN EYE
ILEECTOMY – ILEUM
ILEOSTOMY – ILEUM
IRIDOTOMY – IRIS
LEUCOTOMY – NERVE
  FIBRES IN BRAIN
LITHOTOMY – KIDNEY
  STONE
LOBECTOMY – LOBE OF AN
  ORGAN
MYOPLASTY – MUSCLE
NEUROTOMY – NERVE
OSTECTOMY – BONE
OSTEOTOMY – BONE
OTOPLASTY – EAR
PUBIOTOMY – PUBIC BONE

9–continued
PYELOTOMY – PELVIS OF
  KIDNEY
RHIZOTOMY – NERVE
  ROOTS
THYROTOMY – THYROID
  GLAND
TOPECTOMY – PART OF
  BRAIN
VALVOTOMY –HEART VALVE
VASECTOMY – SPERM DUCT

10
ANTRECTOMY – PART OF
  STOMACH
ANTROSTOMY – BONE
  CAVITY
APICECTOMY – ROOT OF
  TOOTH
ARTHROTOMY – JOINT
  CAPSULE
CAECOSTOMY – CAECUM
CORDECTOMY – VOCAL
  CORD
CRANIOTOMY – SKULL
CYSTECTOMY – BLADDER
CYSTOSTOMY – BLADDER
EMBRYOTOMY – FETUS
ENTEROTOMY – INTESTINE
EPISIOTOMY – VAGINAL
  OPENING
GASTROTOMY – STOMACH
HYMENOTOMY – HYMEN
IRIDECTOMY – IRIS
JEJUNOTOMY – JEJUNUM
KERATOTOMY – CORNEA
LAPAROTOMY – ABDOMEN

10–continued
LUMPECTOMY – BREAST
  TUMOUR
MASTECTOMY – BREAST
MYOMECTOMY – FIBROIDS
NEPHROTOMY – KIDNEY
NEURECTOMY – NERVE
ORBITOTOMY – BONE
  AROUND EYE
OVARIOTOMY – OVARY
PHLEBOTOMY – VEIN
PLEUROTOMY – PLEURAL
  MEMBRANE
PROCTOTOMY – RECTUM
  OR ANUS
RACHIOTOMY – BACKBONE
SCLEROTOMY – WHITE OF
  EYE
SCROTOTOMY – SCROTUM
STERNOTOMY – BREAST-
  BONE
TARSECTOMY – ANKLE
  BONES *OR* EYELID TISSUE
TENOPLASTY – TENDON
THYMECTOMY – THYMUS
  GLAND
UVULECTOMY – UVULA
VARICOTOMY – VARICOSE
  VEIN
VITRECTOMY – VITREUS
  HUMOUR
VULVECTOMY – VULVA

11
ANGIOPLASTY – BLOOD
  VESSEL
ARTERIOTOMY – ARTERY

11—continued
ARTHRECTOMY – JOINT
CAPSULOTOMY – LENS
CAPSULE OF EYE
COLPOPLASTY – VAGINA
CYSTOPLASTY – BLADDER
EMBOLECTOMY – EMBOLUS,
BLOOD CLOT
ENTERECTOMY – INTESTINE
ENTEROSTOMY – SMALL
INTESTINE
FRAENECTOMY – TISSUE
BENEATH TONGUE
GASTRECTOMY – STOMACH
GASTROSTOMY – STOMACH
GENIOPLASTY – CHIN
GLOSSECTOMY – TONGUE
HELCOPLASTY – SKIN
ULCERS
HEPATECTOMY – LIVER
HYSTEROTOMY – WOMB
INCUDECTOMY – MIDDLE
EAR OSSIDE
JEJUNECTOMY – JEJUNUM
JEJUNOSTOMY – JEJUNUM
KERATECTOMY – CORNEA
LABIOPLASTY –LIPS
LARYNGOTOMY – LARYNX
MAMMOPLASTY – BREAST
MYRINGOTOMY – EARDRUM
NEPHRECTOMY – KIDNEY
NEPHROSTOMY – KIDNEY
OMENTECTOMY – PERI-
TONEUM OF STOMACH
ORCHIDOTOMY – TESTIS
OVARIECTOMY – OVARY
PAPILLOTOMY – PART OF
BILE DUCT
PHLEBECTOMY – VEIN
PLEURECTOMY – PLEURAL
MEMBRANE
POLYPECTOMY – POLYP
PROCTECTOMY – RECTUM
PYELOPLASTY – PELVIS OF
KIDNEY
PYLORECTOMY – PART OF
STOMACH
RHINOPLASTY – NOSE
SCLERECTOMY – WHITE OF
EYE
SPLENECTOMY – SPLEEN
SYNOVECTOMY – MEM-
BRANE AROUND JOINT
TARSOPLASTY – EYELID
THALAMOTOMY – PART OF
BRAIN
THORACOTOMY – CHEST
CAVITY
TRACHEOTOMY – WINDPIPE
TYMPANOTOMY – EARDRUM
URETEROTOMY – URETER
URETHROTOMY – URETHRA

11—continued
VALVULOTOMY – HEART
VALVE
VARICECTOMY – VARICOSE
VEINS
VESICOSTOMY – BLADDER

12
ARTERIECTOMY – ARTERY
ARTHROPLASTY – JOINT
CHEILOPLASTY – LIPS
CINGULECTOMY – PART OF
BRAIN
DUODENOSTOMY –
DUODENUM
GASTROPLASTY – STOMACH
GINGIVECTOMY – GUM
TISSUE
HERNIOPLASTY – HERNIA
HYSTERECTOMY – WOMB
KERATOPLASTY – CORNEA
LARYNGECTOMY – LARYNX
MASTOIDOTOMY – MASTOID
BONE
MENISCECTOMY – KNEE
CARTILAGE
OOPHORECTOMY –OVARY
ORCHIDECTOMY – TESTIS
PALATOPLASTY – CLEFT
PALATE
PALLIDECTOMY – PART OF
BRAIN
PHALLOPLASTY – PENIS
PYLOROPLASTY – STOMACH
OUTLET
STAPEDECTOMY – THIRD
EAR OSSICLE
THORACECTOMY – RIB
THROMBECTOMY – BLOOD
CLOT
TONSILLOTOMY – TONSIL
TRACHEOSTOMY – WIND
PIPE
TURBINECTOMY – BONE IN
NOSE
URETERECTOMY – URETER
URETEROSTOMY – URETER
URETHROSTOMY –
URETHRA
VAGINOPLASTY – VAGINA

13
ADENOIDECTOMY
ADENOIDS
ARTERIOPLASTY – ARTERY
CARDIOMYOTOMY –
STOMACH OPENING
DERMATOPLASTY – SKIN
HEMICOLECTOMY – PART OF
COLON
HEPATICOSTOMY – LIVER
ILEOCOLOSTOMY – ILEUM
AND COLON

13—continued
MASTOIDECTOMY –
MASTOID
MYRINGOPLASTY –
EARDRUM
NEURONOPLASTY – NERVES
OESOPHAGOTOMY –
GULLET
OPHTHALMOTOMY – EYE
PANCREATOTOMY –
PANCREAS
PERINEOPLASTY – VAGINAL
OPENING
PHALANGECTOMY – FINGER
OR TOE BONES
PHARYNGECTOMY –
PHARYNX
PHRENICECTOMY –
PHRENIC NERVE
PNEUMONECTOMY – LUNG
PROSTATECTOMY –
PROSTATE GLAND
PYLOROMYOTOMY –
STOMACH OUTLET
SALPINGECTOMY –
FALLOPIAN TUBE
SALPINGOSTOMY –
FALLOPIAN TUBE
SIGMOIDECTOMY – PART OF
COLON
STAPHYLECTOMY – UVULA
SYMPATHECTOMY –
SYMPATHETIC NERVE
SYMPHYSIOTOMY – FRONT
OF PELVIS
THORACOPLASTY – CHEST
CAVITY
THYROIDECTOMY –
THYROID GLAND
TONSILLECTOMY – TONSILS
TRABECULOTOMY – DUCT IN
EYE
MYRINGOTOMY, TYMPAN-
OTOMY – EARDRUM
TYMPANOPLASTY –
EARDRUM
URETEROPLASTY – URETER
URETHROPLASTY –
URETHRA
VASOVASOSTOMY – REJOIN-
ING OF SEVERED SPERM
DUCT
VESICULECTOMY – SEMINAL
VESICLE

14
APPENDICOSTOMY –
APPENDIX
BLEPHAROPLASTY –EYELID
CHOLECYSTOTOMY – GALL
BLADDER

251

14–continued
CHOLEDOCHOTOMY – BILE DUCT
CLITORIDECTOMY – CLITORIS
ENDARTERECTOMY – INNER WALL OF ARTERY
EPIDIDYMECTOMY – SPERM DUCT
HYPOPHYSECTOMY – PITUITARY GLAND
OESOPHAGOSTOMY – GULLET
OPHTHALMECTOMY – EYE
PANCREATECTOMY – PANCREAS
SEQUESTRECTOMY – DEAD BONE
SPHINCTEROTOMY – SPHINCTER MUSCLE
TRABECULECTOMY – PART OF EYE

15
CHOLECYSTECTOMY – GALL BLADDER
ILEOPROCTOSTOMY – ILEUM AND RECTUM
JEJUNOILEOSTOMY – JEJUNUM AND ILEUM
LITHONEPHROTOMY – KIDNEY STONE
LYMPHADENECTOMY – LYMPH NODE
NEPHROLITHOTOMY – KIDNEY STONE
PYELOLITHOTOMY – KIDNEY STONE

16
PERICARDIOSTOMY – MEMBRANE AROUND HEART
PROCTOCOLECTOMY – RECTUM AND COLON
SPHINCTERECTOMY – SPHINCTER MUSCLE
STRICTUROPLASTY – STRICTURE
VENTRICULOSTOMY – CAVITY OF BRAIN

17
GASTROENTEROSTOMY – STOMACH AND SMALL INTESTINE

17–continued
GASTROJEJUNOSTOMY – STOMACH AND JEJUNUM
HAEMORRHOIDECTOMY – HAEMORRHOIDS
PARATHYROIDECTOMY – PARATHYROID GLAND

18
COLPOPERINEOPLASTY – VAGINAL OPENING
EPIDIDYMOVASOSTOMY – SPERM DUCTS
GASTRODUODENOSTOMY – STOMACH AND DUODENUM
URETEROENTEROSTOMY – URETER AND BOWEL
VASO-EPIDIDYMOSTOMY – SPERM DUCTS

19
CHOLECYSTENTEROSTOMY – GALL BLADDER AND SMALL INTESTINE
URETERONEOCYSTOSTOMY – URETER AND BLADDER
URETEROSIGMOIDOSTOMY – URETER AND PART OF BOWEL

20+
CHOLECYSTODUODENOSTOMY – GALL BLADDER AND DUODENUM
CHOLECYSTOGASTROSTOMY – GALL BLADDER AND STOMACH
DACRYOCYSTORHINOSTOMY – TEAR SAC AND NOSE
GASTRO-OESOPHAGOSTOMY – STOMACH AND GULLET
TRANSURETERO-URETEROSTOMY – ONE URETER TO THE OTHER

MEDICATION

4
DOPA

5
ALOES
JALAP
L-DOPA
OPIUM
SENNA

6
HEROIN
OUBAIN

7
ACONITE
ASPIRIN
BROMIDE
CALOMEL
CASCARA

7–continued
CHLORAL
CODEINE
DAPSONE
DIGOXIN
DOXEPIN
EMETINE
HEPARIN
HIRUDIN
INSULIN
MENTHOL
METHOIN
MOGADON
MUSTINE
PULVULE
QUININE
SOTALOL
SURAMIN
TYLOCIN

8
ANTABUSE
BARBITAL
COLCYNTH
COLISTIN
DIAZEPAM
ETHOTOIN
FRADICIN
GLUCAGON
HYOSCINE
LAETRILE
LEVODOPA
MANNITOL
MAZINDOL
MORPHINE
NAPROXEN
NEOMYCIN
OXAZEPAM
PIMOZIDE

8–continued
SUBTILIN
URETHANE
VIOMYCIN
WARFARIN

9
ALOXIPRIN
AMILORIDE
AZAPETINE
BARBITONE
BECLAMIDE
BENZHEXOL
BIPERIDEN
BISACODYL
BISULPHAN
BLEOMYCIN
BUCLIZINE
BUPHENINE

9–continued
CARBACHOL
CARBROMAL
CASTOR OIL
CLEMIZOLE
CLONIDINE
CLOPAMIDE
CORTISONE
CYCLIZINE
DIGITALIS
DIGITOXIN
DITHRANOL
EPSOM SALT
ETOGLUCID
FRUSEMIDE
GALLAMINE
GLYMIDINE
IPRINDOLE
ISONIAZID

9–continued
KANAMYCIN
LORAZEPAM
MECLOZINE
MEGESTROL
MELPHALAN
MEPACRINE
MESTRANOL
METFORMIN
METHADONE
MIANSERIN
MYCOMYCIN
NADROLONE
NIALAMIDE
NICOTINYL
NIFURATEL
NUX VOMICA
OESTROGEN
OXACILLIN
PETHIDINE
PHENAZONE
PHENETOIN
POLYMIXIN
PRIMIDONE
PROMAZINE
PROQUANIL
PYOCYANIN
QUINIDINE
RIFAMYCIN
RIMITEROL
STANOLONE
SULTHIAME
TRICLOFOS
TROXIDONE
VANOMYCIN

10
ALPRENOLOL
AMANTADINE
AMPICILLIN
ANTAZOLINE
BASITRACIN
BENORYLATE
CANDICIDIN
CARBOMYCIN
CEPHALEXIN
CLOFIBRATE
CLONAZEPAM
CLORINDOLE
COLCHICINE
CROTAMITON
CYTARABINE
DICOUMAROL
DIPENZEPIN
DIPIPANONE
DISULFIRAM
ERYTHRITOL
ETHAMBUTOL
ETHINAMATE
ETHYNODIOL
FENOPROFEN
FLURAZEPAM

10–continued
FRAMYCETIN
GENTAMYCIN
ICHTHAMMOL
IMIPRAMINE
IPRONIAZID
ISOXUPRINE
KETOPROFEN
LINCOMYCIN
MEPERIDINE
MEPHENESIN
MEPYRAMINE
METHYLDOPA
METOLAZONE
METOPROLOL
NITRAZAPAM
NOVOBIOCIN
OXPRENADOL
OXYPERTINE
PAPAVERINE
PENICILLIN
PHENACETIN
PHENELZINE
PHOLCODINE
PICROTOXIN
PIPERAZINE
PREDNISONE
PRIMAQUINE
PROBENECID
PROPANOLOL
PYOCYANASE
RESORCINOL
RIFAMPICIN
SALBUTAMOL
STRYCHNINE
TOLAZAMIDE
TOLAZOLINE
TROMETAMOL
URAMUSTINE

11
ACETANILIDE
ACTINOMYCIN
ALKA SELTZER
ALLOPURINOL
AMOBARBITAL
AMODIAQUINE
AMPHETAMINE
AMYL NITRITE
ANILERIDINE
APOMORPHINE
BETHANIDINE
CAPREOMYCIN
CARBIMAZOLE
CARISPRODOL
CLINDAMYCIN
CLOREXOLONE
CYCLOSERINE
CYPROTERONE
DESERPIDINE
DESIPRAMINE
DIAMORPHINE

11–continued
DIENOESTROL
DOXORUBICIN
DOXYCYCLINE
ETHEBENECID
ETHIONAMIDE
ETHISTERONE
HALOPERIDOL
HYDROXYUREA
HYDROXYZINE
HYOSCYAMINE
IDOXURIDINE
IPECACUANHA
LEVORPHANOL
MAPROTILINE
MATHIMAZOLE
MEPROBAMATE
METHENOLONE
METHICILLIN
METHOXAMINE
MITHRAMYCIN
NAPHAZOLINE
NIKETHAMIDE
PAPAVERETUM
PARACETAMOL
PARALDEHYDE
PAROMOMYCIN
PENTAZOCINE
PHENAZOCINE
PHENETURIDE
PHENINDIONE
PHENIRAMINE
PHENTERMINE
PRENYLAMINE
PROGESTOGEN
TERBUTALINE
THEOBROMINE
THIOGUANINE
THIOPENTONE
THYMOXAMINE
TRIAMTERENE
TRIAZIQUONE
TYROTHRYCIN
VASOPRESSIN
VINBLASTINE
VINCRISTINE

12
AMPHOTERICIN
AZATHIOPRINE
BROMO SELTZER
CHLORAMBUCIL
CHLORBUTANOL
CHLORDANTOIN
CHLORHEXADOL
CLOMIPRAMINE
CYCLANDELATE
DEBRISOQUINE
DICHLOROPHEN
DISOPYRAMIDE
DROSTANOLONE
ERYTHROMYCIN

12–continued
ETHOSUXIMIDE
FENFLURIDINE
FLUOXURIDINE
FLUPHENAZINE
FLUSPIRILENE
GLAUBER'S SALT
GRISEOFULVIN
GUAIPHENESIN
GUANETHIDINE
HYDRALLAZINE
HYDRARGAPHEN
INDOMETHACIN
ISOPRENALINE
LIOTHYRONINE
LYNOESTRENOL
MANNOMUSTINE
MECAMYLAMINE
METHANDRIONE
METHAQUALONE
METHOTREXATE
METHYPRYLONE
METHYSERGIDE
OLEANDOMYCIN
ORPHENADRINE
OXOLINIC ACID
OXYMESTERONE
PERPHENAZINE
PHENSUXIMIDE
PHENTOLAMINE
PHILOCARPINE
PIPERIDOLATE
PODOPHYLLINE
PREDNISOLONE
PROCARBAZINE
PROCYCLIDINE
PROMETHAZINE
PROTHIPENDYL
PYRAZINAMIDE
ROCHELLE SALT
SALICYLAMIDE
SELTZER WATER
STILBOESTROL
STREPTOMYCIN
SULPHADOXINE
TETRACYCLINE
THEOPHYLLINE
THIACETAZONE
THIORIDAZINE
TRIMEPRAZINE
TRIMIPRAMINE
TRYPARSAMIDE
VALPROIC ACID

13
ACETAZOLAMIDE
ACETOHEXAMIDE
ALLYLESTRENOL
AMINOPHYLLINE
AMITRIPTYLINE
BETAMETHASONE
BUTOBARBITONE

13–continued
CARBAMAZEPINE
CARBENICILLIN
CARBINOXAMINE
CEPHALOGLYCIN
CEPHALORIDINE
CEPHALOSPORIN
CHLORMEZANONE
CO-TRIMOXAZOLE
DEXAMETHASONE
DIATHIAZININE
DIHYDRALAZINE
DIPHENOXYLATE
DIPROPHYLLINE
GLIBENCLAMIDE
HEXOBARBITONE
MEFANAMIC ACID
METHANDERIONE
METHAPYRILENE
METHYLENE BLUE
MITROBRONITOL
NALIDIXIC ACID
NORTRYPTYLINE
ORCIPRENALINE
PENICILLAMINE
PHENMETRAZINE
PHENOTHIAZINE
PHENYLEPHRINE
PHYSOSTIGMINE
PROPANTHELINE
PROTHIONAMIDE
PROTRIPTYLINE
SALICYLIC ACID
SPECTINOMYCIN
SULPHADIAZINE
THIOPROPAZATE
TRIAMCINOLONE

14
ACETYLCYSTEINE
AMYLOBARBITONE
BECLOMETHASONE
BENDROFLUAZIDE
BENZODIAZEPINE
CHLORAL HYDRATE
CHLORCYCLIZINE
CHLOROPYRILENE
CHLOROTHIAZIDE
CHLORPROMAZINE
CHLORPROPAMIDE
CHLORTHALIDONE
CROMOLYN SODIUM
CYCLOBARBITONE
CYCLOPENTAMINE
CYCLOPENTOLATE
CYPROHEPTADINE
DEXAMPHETAMINE
DEXTROMORAMIDE

14–continued
DIETHYLPROPION
DIHYDROCODEINE
DIMENHYDRINATE
DIMETHISTERONE
DYDROGESTERONE
ETHACRYNIC ACID
ETHYLOESTRENOL
FLUFENAMIC ACID
GLUTETHIMIDINE
HEPTABARBITONE
HYDROCORTISONE
LIQUID PARAFFIN
MERCAPTOPURINE
METHOSERPIDINE
MILK OF MAGNESIA
NITROFURANTOIN
NORETHISTERONE
PARAMETHADIONE
PENTOBARBITONE
PHENETHICILLIN
PHENYLBUTAZONE
SEIDLITZ POWDER
SODIUM SULPHATE
SULPHACETAMIDE
SULPHADIDIMINE
SULPHAFURAZOLE
SULPHISOXAZOLE
XYLOMETAZOLINE

15
CHLORAMPHENICOL
CHLORMETHIAZOLE
CHLORPROTHIXENE
DEXTROTHYROXINE
DIMETHOTHIAZINE
DIPHENHYDRAMINE
FLUDROCORTISONE
METHYLCELLULOSE
NITROGEN MUSTARD
NORETHANDROLONE
OXYPHENBUTAZONE
OXYTETRACYCLINE
PENTAERYTHRITOL
PHENAZOPYRIDINE
PHENOLPHTHALEIN
SULPHAMETHIZOLE
SULPHAQUANIDINE
SULPHINPYRAZOLE
THYROCALCITONIN
TRANYLCYPROMINE
TRIFLUOPERAZINE

16
BENZYL PENICILLIN
BROMOPHENIRAMINE
CHLORDIAZEPOXIDE
CHLOROTRIANISENE
CHLORPHENIRAMINE

16–continued
CHLORPHENOXAMINE
CHLORPHENTERMINE
CYCLOPENTHIAZIDE
CYCLOPHOSPHAMIDE
DEXTROMETHORPHAN
LITHIUM CARBONATE
METHOXYPHENAMINE
PARAFORMALDEHYDE
PHENOXYBENZAMINE
PROCHLORPERAZINE
TETRAHYDROZOLINE

17
BICARBONATE OF SODA
CEPHALOTHIN SODIUM
CHLORTETRACYCLINE
CHOLINE SALICYLATE
CLOXACILLIN SODIUM
DICHLOROPHENAMIDE
DIHYDROERGOTAMINE
ETHINYLOESTRADIOL
MAGNESIUM SULPHATE
METHOTRIMEPRAZINE
METHYLAMPHETAMINE
SODIUM BICARBONATE
SULPHAMETHOXAZOLE

18
DEXTROPROPOXYPHENE
DICHLORALPHENAZONE
DIMETHYLSULPHOXIDE
HYDROXYAMPHETAMINE
MAGNESIUM CARBONATE
MAGNESIUM HYDROXIDE
METHYLTESTOSTERONE
PROCAINE PENICILLIN

19
DIETHYLSTILBESTEROL
DIHYDROSTREPTOMYCIN
ETHYL BISCOUMACETATE
GLYCERINE TRINITRATE
HYDROCHLOROTHIAZIDE
HYDROXYPROGESTERONE
HYDROXYSTILBAMIDINE
MEDROXYPROGESTERONE
PHENYLPROPANOLAMINE

20+
BENTHAZINE PENICILLIN
BROMODIPHENYLHYDRAINE
CHLORAZEPATE POTASSIUM
CHOLINE THEOPHYLLINATE
DIMETHYLCHLORTETRACY-
  CLINE
PARA-AMINOSALICYLIC ACID
PHENOXYMETHYLPENI-
  CILLIN
PHTHALYLSULPHATHIAZOLE

PSYCHOLOGY TERMS

2&3
ID
IQ
ADD
DSM
ECT
EGO
PVS
REM

4
AMOK
FEAR
KORO
MIND
PICA
PTSD
SADS
SANE
SKEW

5
ANIMA
BINGE
FUGUE
FUROR
HABIT
IMAGO
LATAH
MANIA

6
ABULIA
AFFECT
ANIMUS
ANOMIA
AUTISM
CENSOR
DÉJÀ VU
ENGRAM
EONISM
FADING
LIBIDO
MENCAP
MUTISM
PHOBIA
PSYCHE
SADISM
SCHISM
SODOMY
STRESS
TRANCE

7
AMENTIA
AMNESIA
ANXIETY
AROUSAL
BONDING
BULIMIA

7–continued
COMPLEX
COUVADE
DEREISM
ECSTASY
EIDETIC
ELATION
EMOTION
EMPATHY
FANTASY
IMAGERY
INSIGHT
LERESIS
OPERANT
PARADOX
PSYCHIC
SHAPING
T-GROUP
WINDIGO
ZOOPSIA

8
ANALYSIS
ANOREXIA
APHRENIA
ASTHENIC
ATARAXIA
AVOIDANT
BISEXUAL
BLOCKING
CHAINING
CONATION
CONFLICT
DELUSION
DEMENTIA
DOPAMINE
DYSBULIA
DYSLOGIA
EUPHORIA
EXPOSURE
FREUDIAN
FROTTAGE
GENOGRAM
HEBETUDE
HYSTERIA
IDEATION
ILLUSION
INSANITY
INSTINCT
LOBOTOMY
NEUROSIS
ONEIRISM
PARANOIA
PARANOID
PSELLISM
REACTIVE
SUPEREGO

9
ADDICTION
AEROPHAGY
AGROMANIA
AKATHISIA
ANALYSAND
ANHEDONIA
ARCHETYPE
ASYNDESIS
AUTOSCOPY
BABY BLUES
CATALEPSY
CATATONIA
COCAINISM
COGNITION
DYSPHEMIA
DYSSOCIAL
ECHOLALIA
EROTICISM
EXTROVERT
FETISHISM
FLASHBACK
FRIGIDITY
GEOPHAGIA
HYPOBULIA
HYPOMANIA
IDEOMOTOR
IMITATION
IMPLOSION
INTROVERT
LALLATION
LEUCOTOMY
MASOCHISM
MENTAL AGE
MODELLING
MONOMANIA
NEOLOGISM
OBSESSION
OBSESSIVE
PALILALIA
PRECOCITY
PROMPTING
PSYCHOSIS
PYROMANIA
SCULPTING
SPLITTING
SURROGATE
SYMBOLISM
VOYEURISM
ZOOPHOBIA

10
ABREACTION
ALIENATION
ANANKASTIC
APOTREPTIC
ATTACHMENT
BELL AND PAD

10–continued
BORDERLINE
CHILD ABUSE
CITALOPRAM
CLUTTERING
COMPULSION
CONVERSION
COPROLALIA
DEPENDENCE
DEPRESSION
DIPSOMANIA
DIVAGATION
DROMOMANIA
ECHOPRAXIA
EROTOMANIA
EXALTATION
EXTINCTION
FOLIE À DEUX
GESTALTISM
HANDEDNESS
HYPNAGOGIC
HYPOTHYMIA
HYSTERICAL
IMPRINTING
LESBIANISM
LOGORRHOEA
MONOPHOBIA
NARCISSISM
NECROMANIA
NEGATIVISM
OLANZAPINE
PAEDERASTY
PARAMNESIA
PAREIDOLIA
PAROXETINE
PERCEPTION
PITHIATISM
POLYPHAGIA
PROJECTION
PSYCHIATRY
PSYCHOLOGY
PSYCHOPATH
REGRESSION
REPRESSION
RUMINATION
SAMARITANS
SATYRIASIS
SERTINDOLE
SERTRALINE
STAMMERING
STEREOTYPY
STUTTERING
SUGGESTION
WITHDRAWAL
XENOPHOBIA
ZOOPHILISM

11
AGORAPHOBIA
ALEXITHYMIA
AMBIVALENCE
BIOFEEDBACK
COUNSELLING
CYCLOTHYMIA
DOUBLE-BIND
DYSPAREUNIA
ECHOKINESIS
GANSER STATE
GLOSSOLALIA
HEBEPHRENIA
HYPERPRAXIA
HYPNOPOMPIC
IDIOT SAVANT
KLEPTOMANIA
LYCANTHROPY
MEGALOMANIA
MELANCHOLIA
NEUROTICISM
NYCTOPHILIA
NYCTOPHOBIA
NYCTOPHONIA
NYMPHOMANIA
ORIENTATION
PAEDOPHILIA
PALIPHRASIA
PARAGRAPHIA
PARAPHRENIA
PARASUICIDE
PERSONALITY
PSYCHODRAMA
PSYCHOGENIC
RETARDATION
RETROGRAPHY
RISPERIDONE
ROLE PLAYING
SAD SYNDROME
SCHIZOTYPAL
SEXUAL ABUSE
SUBLIMATION
THALAMOTOMY
UNCONSCIOUS

12
BEHAVIOURISM
CANCER PHOBIA
CINGULECTOMY
CONDITIONING
DISPLACEMENT
DISSOCIATION
EXTRAVERSION
EXTROVERSION
FEINGOLD DIET
FLAGELLATION
GROUP THERAPY
HALFWAY HOUSE
HYPERGRAPHIA
HYPERKINESIA
HYPOCHONDRIA
INTRAVERSION

12–continued
INTROJECTION
INTROVERSION
NECROPHILISM
NEURASTHENIA
ONOMATOMANIA
PALINGRAPHIA
PHANEROMANIA
PREPAREDNESS
PSEUDOPLEGIA
PSYCHIATRIST
PSYCHOLOGIST
PSYCHOTICISM
SOMNAMBULISM
SUBCONSCIOUS
SUBSTITUTION
TIME SAMPLING
TRANSFERENCE
TRANSVESTISM

13
ANTIPSYCHOTIC
CONFABULATION
CROSS-DRESSING
DEREALIZATION
EVENT SAMPLING
EXHIBITIONISM
FAMILY THERAPY
HALLUCINATION
HOMOSEXUALITY
MENTAL ILLNESS
NORMALIZATION
PANIC DISORDER
PERSEVERATION
PHARMACOMANIA
PSYCHOKINESIS
PSYCHOMETRICS
PSYCHOSOMATIC
PSYCHOSURGERY
PSYCHOTHERAPY
REINFORCEMENT
RORSCHACH TEST
SCHIZOPHRENIA
SLEEP-WALKING
SOMNILOQUENCE
TWILIGHT STATE
VERBIGERATION

14
AUTOSUGGESTION
CLAUSTROPHOBIA
DISORIENTATION
DRUG DEPENDENCE
EFFORT SYNDROME
ENCOUNTER
  GROUP
IDENTIFICATION
MENTAL HANDICAP
NOCTAMBULATION
OEDIPUS COMPLEX
ONOMATOPOIESIS
PARAPSYCHOLOGY
PROJECTIVE TEST

14–continued
PSYCHOANALYSIS
PSYCHONEUROSIS
RETT'S SYNDROME
SECURITY OBJECT
SENILE DEMENTIA
TRANSSEXUALISM
WECHSLER SCALES

15
ANOREXIA
  NERVOSA
AVERSION THERAPY
BIPOLAR DISORDER
CAPGRAS'
  SYNDROME
CONDUCT
  DISORDER
DYSMORPHOPHO-
  BIA
ELECTRONARCOSIS
FREE ASSOCIATION
HELLER'S
  SYNDROME
HETEROSEXUALITY
NEUROPSYCHIATRY
PSEUDOMUTUALITY
PSYCHOPATHOLOGY
RATIONALIZATION
RETENTION DEFECT
SEXUAL DEVIATION
THOUGHT
  STOPPING

16
BEHAVIOUR
  THERAPY
BRIQUET'S
  SYNDROME
COGNITIVE
  THERAPY
CORE-AND-
  CLUSTER
DEFENCE
  MECHANISM
EXPRESSED
  EMOTION
FRAGILE-X
  SYNDROME
GLOBUS
  HYSTERICUS
INTELLIGENCE TEST
LOCKED-IN
  SYNDROME
MENTAL
  DEFICIENCY
MENTAL HEALTH
  ACTS
MENTAL
  IMPAIRMENT
NERVOUS
  BREAKDOWN

16–continued
OVERCOMPENSA-
  TION
PSYCHOGERI-
  ATRICS
PSYCHOPHYSIOL-
  OGY
SPECIAL HOSPITALS
TRICHOTILLOMANIA

17
AFFECTIVE
  DISORDER
ASPERGER'S
  SYNDROME
BELLE
  INDIFFERENCE
CIRCUMSTANTIAL-
  ITY
DEPERSONALIZA-
  TION
DYSMNESIC
  SYNDROME
DYSTHYMIC
  DISORDER
FLEXIBILITAS CEREA
MENTAL
  RETARDATION
PSYCHOLINGUIS-
  TICS
REACTION
  FORMATION
RELAXATION
  THERAPY
SEPARATION
  ANXIETY
TOURETTE'S
  SYNDROME

18
ASSOCIATION OF
  IDEAS
ATTACHMENT
  DISORDER
CONVERSION
  DISORDER
DOPAMINE
  HYPOTHESIS
GRADED SELF-
  EXPOSURE
INFERIORITY
  COMPLEX
KNIGHT'S-MOVE
  THOUGHT
KORSAKOFF'S
  SYNDROME
LEARNING
  DISABILITY
RESPONSE
  PREVENTION
SENSORY
  DEPRIVATION

PHOBIAS BY NAME

ACAROPHOBIA – ITCHING, MITES
ACERBOPHOBIA – SOURNESS
ACEROPHOBIA – SOURNESS
ACHLUOPHOBIA – DARKNESS
ACOUSTICOPHOBIA – SOUND
ACROPHOBIA – HIGH PLACES, SHARPNESS
AEROPHOBIA – DRAUGHTS
AGORAPHOBIA – CROWDS, OPEN PLACES
AGYROPHOBIA – STREETS (CROSSING)
AILUROPHOBIA – CATS
ALGOPHOBIA – PAIN
ALTOPHOBIA – HIGH PLACES
AMATHOPHOBIA – DUST
ANAEMOPHOBIA – ANAEMIA
ANCRAOPHOBIA – WIND
ANDROPHOBIA – MEN
ANGINOPHOBIA – NARROWNESS
ANGLOPHOBIA – ENGLISH
ANTHOPHOBIA – FLOWERS
ANTHROPOPHOBIA – PEOPLE
ANTLOPHOBIA – FLOODS
APEIROPHOBIA – INFINITY
APIPHOBIA – BEES
ARACHNEPHOBIA – SPIDERS
ASTHENOPHOBIA – WEAKNESS
ASTRAPHOBIA – LIGHTNING
ASTRAPOPHOBIA – LIGHTNING
ATELOPHOBIA – IMPERFECTION
ATEPHOBIA – RUIN
AULOPHOBIA – FLUTES
AUROPHOBIA – GOLD
AUTOPHOBIA – LONELINESS
BACILLOPHOBIA – MICROBES
BACTERIOPHOBIA – BACTERIA
BALLISTOPHOBIA – BULLETS
BAROPHOBIA – GRAVITY
BATHOPHOBIA – DEPTH
BATOPHOBIA – HIGH BUILDINGS, HIGH
  PLACES
BATRACHOPHOBIA – REPTILES
BELONEPHOBIA – NEEDLES
BLENNOPHOBIA – SLIME
BROMIDROSIPHOBIA – BODY ODOUR
BRONTOPHOBIA – THUNDER
CARDIOPHOBIA – HEART DISEASE
CHAETOPHOBIA – HAIR
CHEIMAPHOBIA – COLD
CHEIMATOPHOBIA – COLD
CHIONOPHOBIA – SNOW
CHLOEROPHOBIA – CHOLERA
CHROMETOPHOBIA – MONEY
CHROMOPHOBIA – COLOUR
CHRONOPHOBIA – TIME (DURATION)
CIBOPHOBIA – FOOD
CLAUSTROPHOBIA – ENCLOSED PLACES
CLINOPHOBIA – BED (GOING TO BED)
CNIDOPHOBIA – INSECT STINGS
COITOPHOBIA – COITUS
COMETOPHOBIA – COMETS

COPROPHOBIA – FAECES
COPROSTASOPHOBIA – CONSTIPATION
CREMNOPHOBIA – PRECIPICES
CRYOPHOBIA – ICE, FROST
CRYSTALLOPHOBIA – CRYSTALS
CYMOPHOBIA – WAVES
CYNOPHOBIA – DOGS
DEMONOPHOBIA – DEMONS
DEMOPHOBIA – CROWDS
DERMATOPATHOPHOBIA – SKIN DISEASE
DERMATOSIOPHOBIA – SKIN
DIABETOPHOBIA – DIABETES
DIKEPHOBIA – JUSTICE
DORAPHOBIA – FUR
DROMOPHOBIA – MOTION
ECCLESIOPHOBIA – CHURCH
ECOPHOBIA – HOME
EISOPTROPHOBIA – MIRRORS
ELECTROPHOBIA – ELECTRICITY
ELEUTHEROPHOBIA – FREEDOM
EMETOPHOBIA – VOMITING
ENETOPHOBIA – PINS
ENTOMOPHOBIA – INSECTS
EOSOPHOBIA – DAWN
ERGOPHOBIA – WORK
ERMITOPHOBIA – LONELINESS
EROTOPHOBIA – SEX
ERYTHROPHOBIA – BLUSHING
FEBRIPHOBIA – FEVER
FRANCOPHOBIA – FRENCH
GALLOPHOBIA – FRENCH
GAMETOPHOBIA – MARRIAGE
GENOPHOBIA – SEX
GEPHYROPHOBIA – BRIDGES (CROSSING)
GERMANOPHOBIA – GERMANS
GEUMATOPHOBIA – TASTE
GLOSSOPHOBIA – SPEECH
GRAPHOPHOBIA – WRITING
GYNEPHOBIA – WOMEN
HADEPHOBIA – HELL
HAGIOPHOBIA – SAINTS
HAMARTOPHOBIA – SIN
HAPHOPHOBIA – TOUCH
HAPTOPHOBIA – TOUCH
HARPAXOPHOBIA – ROBBERS
HEDONOPHOBIA – PLEASURE
HELIOPHOBIA – SUN
HELMINTHOPHOBIA – WORMS
HAEMAPHOBIA – BLOOD
HAEMATOPHOBIA – BLOOD
HAEMOPHOBIA – BLOOD
HERPETOPHOBIA – REPTILES
HIEROPHOBIA – PRIESTS
HIPPOPHOBIA – HORSES
HODOPHOBIA – TRAVEL
HOMICHLOPHOBIA – FOG
HORMEPHOBIA – SHOCK
HYDROPHOBIA – WATER
HYDROPHOBOPHOBIA – RABIES

HYGROPHOBIA – DAMPNESS
HYPEGIAPHOBIA – RESPONSIBILITY
HYPNOPHOBIA – SLEEP
HYPSOPHOBIA – HIGH PLACES
ICHTHYOPHOBIA – FISH
IDEOPHOBIA – IDEAS
JAPANOPHOBIA – JAPANESE
JUDEOPHOBIA – JEWS
KAKORRAPHIAPHOBIA – FAILURE
KATAGELOPHOBIA – RIDICULE
KENOPHOBIA – VOID
KERAUNOPHOBIA – THUNDER
KINETOPHOBIA – MOTION
KLEPTOPHOBIA – STEALING
KONIOPHOBIA -DUST
KOPOPHOBIA – FATIGUE
LALIOPHOBIA – SPEECH
LALOPHOBIA – SPEECH
LIMNOPHOBIA – LAKES
LINONOPHOBIA – STRING
LOGOPHOBIA – WORDS
LYSSOPHOBIA – INSANITY
MANIPHOBIA – INSANITY
MASTIGOPHOBIA – BEATING
MECHANOPHOBIA – MACHINERY
MENINGITOPHOBIA – MENINGITIS
METALLOPHOBIA – METAL
MICROBIOPHOBIA – MICROBES
MICROPHOBIA – SMALL THINGS
MONOPHOBIA – LONELINESS
MUSICOPHOBIA – MUSIC
MUSOPHOBIA – MICE
MYSOPHOBIA – DIRT
MYXOPHOBIA – SLIME
NECROPHOBIA -CORPSES
NEGROPHOBIA – NEGROES
NEOPHOBIA – NEW THINGS
NEPHOPHOBIA – CLOUDS, DISEASE
NYCTOPHOBIA – NIGHT
OCHLOPHOBIA – MOBS
OCHOPHOBIA – VEHICLES
ODONTOPHOBIA – TEETH
OECOPHOBIA – HOME
OIKOPHOBIA – HOME
OLFACTOPHOBIA – SMELL
OMMETAPHOBIA – EYES
ONOMATOPHOBIA – NAMES
OPHICIOPHOBIA – SNAKES
OPHIOPHOBIA – SNAKES
OPHRESIOPHOBIA – SMELL
ORNITHOPHOBIA – BIRDS
OSMOPHOBIA – SMELL
OURANOPHOBIA – HEAVEN
PAEDOPHOBIA – CHILDREN
PANPHOBIA – EVERYTHING
PANTOPHOBIA – EVERYTHING
PAPAPHOBIA – POPE
PARASITOPHOBIA – PARASITES
PARTHENOPHOBIA – YOUNG GIRLS
PATHOPHOBIA – DISEASE
PATROIOPHOBIA – HEREDITY
PECCATIPHOBIA – SIN

PEDICULOPHOBIA – LICE
PENIAPHOBIA – POVERTY
PHAGOPHOBIA – SWALLOWING
PHARMACOPHOBIA – DRUGS
PHASMOPHOBIA – GHOSTS
PHILOSOPHOBIA – PHILOSOPHY
PHOBOPHOBIA – FEAR, SPEECH
PHOTOPHOBIA – LIGHT
PHRONEMOPHOBIA – THINKING
PHTHISIOPHOBIA – TUBERCULOSIS
PNEUMATOPHOBIA – SPIRITS
PNIGEROPHOBIA – SMOTHERING
PNIGOPHOBIA – SMOTHERING
POGONOPHOBIA – BEARDS
POINEPHOBIA – PUNISHMENT
POLITICOPHOBIA – POLITICS
POTAMOPHOBIA – RIVERS
POTOPHOBIA – DRINK
PTERONOPHOBIA – FEATHERS
PYROPHOBIA – FIRE
RECTOPHOBIA – RECTUM
RHABDOPHOBIA – MAGIC
RUSSOPHOBIA – RUSSIANS
RYPOPHOBIA – SOILING
SATANOPHOBIA – SATAN
SCABIOPHOBIA – SCABIES
SCIOPHOBIA – SHADOWS
SCOTOPHOBIA – DARKNESS
SIDEROPHOBIA – STARS
SINOPHOBIA – CHINESE
SITOPHOBIA – FOOD
SNAKEPHOBIA – SNAKES
SPERMATOPHOBIA – GERMS
SPERMOPHOBIA – GERMS
STASOPHOBIA – STANDING
STYGIOPHOBIA – HELL
SYMMETROPHOBIA – SYMMETRY
SYPHILOPHOBIA – SYPHILIS
TACHOPHOBIA – SPEED
TELEPHONOPHOBIA – TELEPHONE
TERATROPHOBIA – MONSTERS
TEUTONOPHOBIA – GERMANS
THAASOPHOBIA – IDLENESS
THALASSOPHOBIA – SEA
THANATOPHOBIA – DEATH
THEOPHOBIA – GOD
THERMOPHOBIA – HEAT
THIXOPHOBIA – TOUCH
TOCOPHOBIA – CHILDBIRTH
TONITROPHOBIA – THUNDER
TOPOPHOBIA – PLACES
TOXICOPHOBIA – POISON
TOXIPHOBIA – POISON
TOXOPHOBIA – POISON
TRAUMATOPHOBIA – INJURY
TREMOPHOBIA – TREMBLING
TRICHOPATHOPHOBIA – HAIR DISEASE
TRICHOPHOBIA – HAIR
TRICINOPHOBIA – TRICHINOSIS
TRISKAIDEKAPHOBIA – THIRTEEN
TRYPANOPHOBIA – INOCULATION
TUBERCULOPHOBIA – TUBERCULOSIS

TYRANNOPHOBIA – TYRANTS
URANOPHOBIA – HEAVEN
UROPHOBIA – URINE
VACCINOPHOBIA – INOCULATION

VENEROPHOBIA – VENEREAL DISEASE
VERMIPHOBIA – WORMS
XENOPHOBIA – FOREIGNERS
ZELOPHOBIA – JEALOUSY

PHOBIAS BY FEAR

ANAEMIA – ANAEMOPHOBIA
BACTERIA – BACTERIOPHOBIA
BEARDS – POGONOPHOBIA
BEATING – MASTIGOPHOBIA
BED (GOING TO BED) – CLINOPHOBIA
BEES – APIPHOBIA
BIRDS – ORNITHOPHOBIA
BLOOD – HAEMAPHOBIA, HAEMATOPHOBIA,
 HAEMOPHOBIA
BLUSHING – ERYTHROPHOBIA
BODY ODOUR – BROMIDROSIPHOBIA
BRIDGES (CROSSING) – GEPHYROPHOBIA
BULLETS – BALLISTOPHOBIA
CATS – AILUROPHOBIA
CHILDBIRTH – TOCOPHOBIA
CHILDREN – PAEDOPHOBIA
CHINESE – SINOPHOBIA
CHOLERA – CHLOEROPHOBIA
CHURCH – ECCLESIOPHOBIA
CLOUDS – NEPHOPHOBIA
COITUS – COITOPHOBIA
COLD – CHEIMAPHOBIA, CHEIMATOPHOBIA
COLOUR – CHROMOPHOBIA
COMETS – COMETOPHOBIA
CONSTIPATION – COPROSTASOPHOBIA
CORPSES – NECROPHOBIA
CROWDS – AGORAPHOBIA, DEMOPHOBIA
CRYSTALS – CRYSTALLOPHOBIA
DAMPNESS – HYGROPHOBIA
DARKNESS – ACHLUOPHOBIA,
 SCOTOPHOBIA
DAWN – EOSOPHOBIA
DEATH – THANATOPHOBIA
DEMONS – DEMONOPHOBIA
DEPTH – BATHOPHOBIA
DIABETES – DIABETOPHOBIA
DIRT – MYSOPHOBIA
DISEASE – NEPHOPHOBIA, PATHOPHOBIA
DOGS – CYNOPHOBIA
DRAUGHTS – AEROPHOBIA
DRINK – POTOPHOBIA
DRUGS – PHARMACOPHOBIA
DUST – AMATHOPHOBIA
ELECTRICITY – ELECTROPHOBIA
ENCLOSED PLACES – CLAUSTROPHOBIA
ENGLISH – ANGLOPHOBIA
EVERYTHING – PANPHOBIA, PANTOPHOBIA
EYES – OMMETAPHOBIA
FAECES – COPROPHOBIA
FAILURE – KAKORRAPHIAPHOBIA
FATIGUE – KOPOPHOBIA

FEAR – PHOBOPHOBIA
FEATHERS – PTERONOPHOBIA
FEVER – FEBRIPHOBIA
FIRE – PYROPHOBIA
FISH – ICHTHYOPHOBIA
FLOODS – ANTLOPHOBIA
FLOWERS – ANTHOPHOBIA
FLUTES – AULOPHOBIA
FOG – HOMICHLOPHOBIA
FOOD – CIBOPHOBIA, SITOPHOBIA
FOREIGNERS – XENOPHOBIA
FREEDOM – ELEUTHEROPHOBIA
FRENCH – FRANCOPHOBIA, GALLOPHOBIA
FROST – CRYOPHOBIA
FUR – DORAPHOBIA
GERMANS – GERMANOPHOBIA
GERMANS – TEUTONOPHOBIA
GERMS – SPERMATOPHOBIA,
 SPERMOPHOBIA
GHOSTS – PHASMOPHOBIA
GOD – THEOPHOBIA
GOLD – AUROPHOBIA
GRAVITY – BAROPHOBIA
HAIR – CHAETOPHOBIA, TRICHOPHOBIA
HAIR DISEASE – TRICHOPATHOPHOBIA
HEART DISEASE – CARDIOPHOBIA
HEAT – THERMOPHOBIA
HEAVEN – OURANOPHOBIA, URANOPHOBIA
HELL – HADEPHOBIA, STYGIOPHOBIA
HEREDITY – PATROIOPHOBIA
HIGH BUILDINGS – BATOPHOBIA
HIGH PLACES – ACROPHOBIA, ALTOPHOBIA,
 BATOPHOBIA, HYPSOPHOBIA
HOME – ECOPHOBIA, OECOPHOBIA,
 OIKOPHOBIA
HORSES – HIPPOPHOBIA
ICE – CRYOPHOBIA
IDEAS – IDEOPHOBIA
IDLENESS – THAASOPHOBIA
IMPERFECTION – ATELOPHOBIA
INFINITY – APEIROPHOBIA
INJURY – TRAUMATOPHOBIA
INOCULATION – TRYPANOPHOBIA,
 VACCINOPHOBIA
INSANITY – LYSSOPHOBIA, MANIPHOBIA
INSECTS – ENTOMOPHOBIA
INSECT STINGS – CNIDOPHOBIA
ITCHING – ACAROPHOBIA
JAPANESE – JAPANOPHOBIA
JEALOUSY – ZELOPHOBIA
JEWS – JUDEOPHOBIA

JUSTICE – DIKEPHOBIA
LAKES – LIMNOPHOBIA
LICE – PEDICULOPHOBIA
LIGHTNING – ASTRAPHOBIA,
  ASTRAPOPHOBIA
LIGHT – PHOTOPHOBIA
LONELINESS – AUTOPHOBIA,
  ERMITOPHOBIA, MONOPHOBIA
MACHINERY – MECHANOPHOBIA
MAGIC – RHABDOPHOBIA
MARRIAGE – GAMETOPHOBIA
MEN – ANDROPHOBIA
MENINGITIS – MENINGITOPHOBIA
METAL – METALLOPHOBIA
MICE – MUSOPHOBIA
MICROBES – BACILLOPHOBIA,
  MICROBIOPHOBIA
MIRRORS – EISOPTROPHOBIA
MITES – ACAROPHOBIA
MOBS – OCHLOPHOBIA
MONEY – CHROMETOPHOBIA
MONSTERS – TERATROPHOBIA
MOTION – DROMOPHOBIA
MOTION – KINETOPHOBIA
MUSIC – MUSICOPHOBIA
NAMES – ONOMATOPHOBIA
NARROWNESS – ANGINOPHOBIA
NEEDLES – BELONEPHOBIA
NEGROES – NEGROPHOBIA
NEW THINGS – NEOPHOBIA
NIGHT – NYCTOPHOBIA
OPEN PLACES – AGORAPHOBIA
PAIN – ALGOPHOBIA
PARASITES – PARASITOPHOBIA
PEOPLE – ANTHROPOPHOBIA
PHILOSOPHY – PHILOSOPHOBIA
PINS – ENETOPHOBIA
PLACES – TOPOPHOBIA
PLEASURE – HEDONOPHOBIA
POISON – TOXICOPHOBIA, TOXOPHOBIA
POLITICS – POLITICOPHOBIA
POPE – PAPAPHOBIA
POVERTY – PENIAPHOBIA
PRECIPICES – CREMNOPHOBIA
PRIESTS – HIEROPHOBIA
PUNISHMENT – POINEPHOBIA
RABIES – HYDROPHOBOPHOBIA
RECTUM – RECTOPHOBIA
REPTILES – BATRACHOPHOBIA,
  HERPETOPHOBIA
RESPONSIBILITY – HYPEGIAPHOBIA
RIDICULE – KATAGELOPHOBIA
RIVERS – POTAMOPHOBIA
ROBBERS – HARPAXOPHOBIA
RUIN – ATEPHOBIA
RUSSIANS – RUSSOPHOBIA
SAINTS – HAGIOPHOBIA
SATAN – SATANOPHOBIA
SCABIES – SCABIOPHOBIA
SEA – THALASSOPHOBIA
SEX – EROTOPHOBIA, GENOPHOBIA
SHADOWS – SCIOPHOBIA

SHARPNESS – ACROPHOBIA
SHOCK – HORMEPHOBIA
SIN – HAMARTOPHOBIA, PECCATIPHOBIA
SKIN – DERMATOSIOPHOBIA
SKIN DISEASE – DERMATOPATHOPHOBIA
SLEEP – HYPNOPHOBIA
SLIME – BLENNOPHOBIA, MYXOPHOBIA
SMALL THINGS – MICROPHOBIA
SMELL – OLFACTOPHOBIA,
  OPHRESIOPHOBIA, OSMOPHOBIA
SMOTHERING – PNIGEROPHOBIA
SNAKES – OPHICIOPHOBIA, SNAKEPHOBIA
SNOW – CHIONOPHOBIA
SOILING – RYPOPHOBIA
SOUND – ACOUSTICOPHOBIA
SOURNESS – ACERBOPHOBIA
SPEECH – GLOSSOPHOBIA, LALIOPHOBIA,
  PHONOPHOBIA
SPEED – TACHOPHOBIA
SPIDERS – ARACHNEPHOBIA
SPIRITS – PNEUMATOPHOBIA
STANDING – STASOPHOBIA
STARS – SIDEROPHOBIA
STEALING – KLEPTOPHOBIA
STREETS (CROSSING) – AGYROPHOBIA
STRING – LINONOPHOBIA
SUN – HELIOPHOBIA
SWALLOWING – PHAGOPHOBIA
SYMMETRY – SYMMETROPHOBIA
SYPHILIS – SYPHILOPHOBIA
TASTE – GEUMATOPHOBIA
TEETH – ODONTOPHOBIA
TELEPHONE – TELEPHONOPHOBIA
THINKING – PHRONEMOPHOBIA
THIRTEEN – TRISKAIDEKAPHOBIA
THUNDER – BRONTOPHOBIA, THUNDER,
  KERAUNOPHOBIA, TONITROPHOBIA
TIME (DURATION) – CHRONOPHOBIA
TOUCH – HAPTOPHOBIA, THIXOPHOBIA
TRAVEL – HODOPHOBIA
TREMBLING – TREMOPHOBIA
TRICHINOSIS – TRICINOPHOBIA
TUBERCULOSIS – PHTHISIOPHOBIA,
  TUBERCULOPHOBIA
TYRANTS – TYRANNOPHOBIA
URINE – UROPHOBIA
VEHICLES – OCHOPHOBIA
VENEREAL DISEASE – VENEROPHOBIA
VOID – KENOPHOBIA
VOMITING – EMETOPHOBIA
WATER – HYDROPHOBIA
WAVES – CYMOPHOBIA
WEAKNESS – ASTHENOPHOBIA
WIND – ANCRAOPHOBIA
WOMEN – GYNEPHOBIA
WORDS – LOGOPHOBIA
WORK – ERGOPHOBIA
WORMS – HELMINTHOPHOBIA,
  VERMIPHOBIA
WRITING – GRAPHOPHOBIA
YOUNG GIRLS – PARTHENOPHOBIA

RELIGION AND MYTHOLOGY

BOOKS OF THE BIBLE

BIBLICAL CHARACTERS

OLD TESTAMENT

AARON – elder brother of Moses; 1st high priest of Hebrews

ABEL – second son of Adam and Eve; murdered by brother Cain

ABRAHAM – father of Hebrew nation

ABSALOM – David's spoilt third son; killed after plotting against his father

ADAM – the first man created; husband of Eve

BAAL – fertility god of Canaanites and Phoenicians

BATHSHEBA – mother of Solomon

BELSHAZZAR – last king of Babylon, son of Nebuchadnezzar; Daniel interpreted his vision of writing on the wall as foretelling the downfall of his kingdom

BENJAMIN – youngest son of Jacob and Rachel. His descendants formed one of the 12 tribes of Israel

CAIN – first son of Adam and Eve; murdered his brother Abel

DANIEL – prophet at the court of Nebuchadnezzar with a gift for interpreting dreams

DAVID – slayed the giant Goliath

DELILAH – a Philistine seducer and betrayer of Samson

ELIJAH – Hebrew prophet, taken into heaven in a fiery chariot

ELISHA – prophet and disciple of Elijah

ENOCH – father of Methuselah

EPHRAIM – son of Joseph; founded one of the 12 tribes of Israel

ESAU – elder of Isaac's twin sons; tricked out of his birthright by his younger brother Jacob

ESTHER – beautiful Israelite woman; heroically protected her people

EVE – first woman; created as companion for Adam in Garden of Eden

EZEKIEL – prophet of Israel captured by Babylonians

GIDEON – Israelite hero and judge

GOLIATH – Philistine giant killed by David

HEZEKIAH – king of Judah (c 715–686 BC)

ISAAC – son of Abraham and Sarah, conceived in their old age; father of Jacob and Esau

ISAIAH – the greatest old testament prophet

ISHMAEL – Abraham's son by Hagar, handmaiden to his wife, Sarah; rival of Isaac

ISRAEL – new name given to Jacob after his reconciliation with Esau

JACOB – second son of Isaac and Rebekah, younger twin of Esau whom he tricked out of his inheritance. The 12 tribes of Israel were named after his sons and grandsons

JEREMIAH – one of the great prophets; foretold destruction of Jerusalem

JEZEBEL – cruel and lustful wife of Ahab, king of Israel

JOB – long-suffering and pious inhabitant of Uz

JONAH – after ignoring God's commands he was swallowed by a whale

JONATHAN – eldest son of Saul and close friend of David

JOSEPH – favourite son of Jacob and Rachel with his "coat of many colours"; sold into slavery by his jealous brothers

JOSHUA – succeeded Moses and led Israelites against Canaan. He defeated Jericho where the walls fell down

JUDAH – son of Jacob and Leah; founded tribe of Judah

LOT – nephew of Abraham; he escaped the destruction of Sodom, but his wife was turned into a pillar of salt for looking back

METHUSELAH – son of Enoch, the oldest person ever (969 years)

MIRIAM – sister of Aaron and Moses whom she looked after as a baby; prophetess and leader of Israelites

MOSES – Israel's great leader and lawgiver, he led the Israelites out of captivity in Egypt to the promised land of Canaan. Received ten commandments from Jehovah on Mt Sinai

NATHAN – Hebrew prophet at courts of David and Solomon

NEBUCHADNEZZAR – king of Babylon

NOAH – grandson of Methuselah, father of Shem, Ham, and Japheth; built ark to save his family and all animal species from the great flood

REBEKAH – wife of Isaac, mother of Jacob and Esau

RUTH – Moabite who accompanied her mother-in-law Naomi to Bethlehem. Remembered for her loyalty

SAMSON – Israelite judge of great physical strength; seduced and betrayed by Delilah

SAMUEL – prophet and judge of Israel

SARAH – wife of Abraham, mother of Isaac

SAUL – first king of Israel

SOLOMON – son of David and Bathsheba; remembered for his great wisdom and wealth

NEW TESTAMENT

ANDREW – fisherman and brother of Peter; one of 12 Apostles

BARABAS – Cypriot missionary; introduced Paul to the Church

BARABBAS – robber and murderer; in prison with Jesus and released instead of him

BARTHOLOMEW – possibly same person as Nathaniel, one of the 12 Apostles

CAIAPHAS – high priest of the Jews; Jesus brought to him after arrest

GABRIEL – angel who announced birth of Jesus to Mary; and of John the Baptist to Zechariah

HEROD – 1. the Great, ruled when Jesus was born 2. Antipas, son of Herod the Great, ruled when John the Baptist was murdered 3. Agrippa, killed James (brother of John) 4. Agrippa II, before whom Paul was tried

JAMES – 1. the Greater, one of 12 Apostles, brother of John 2. the Less, one of 12 Apostles 3. leader of the Church in Jerusalem and author of the New Testament epistle

JESUS – founder of Christianity

JOHN – youngest of 12 Apostles

JOHN THE BAPTIST – announced coming of Jesus, and baptized him

JOSEPH – 1. husband of Mary the mother of Jesus 2. of Arimathea, a secret disciple of Jesus

JUDAS ISCARIOT – the disciple who betrayed Jesus

LAZARUS – brother of Mary and Martha, raised from the dead by Jesus

LUKE – companion of Paul, author of Luke and Acts

MARK – author of the gospel; companion of Paul, Barnabas, and Peter

MARTHA – sister of Mary and Lazarus, friend of Jesus

MARY – 1. mother of Jesus 2. sister of Martha and Lazarus 3. Magdalene, cured by Jesus and the first to see him after the resurrection

MATTHEW – one of 12 Apostles, author of the gospel

MATTHIAS – chosen to replace the apostle Judas

MICHAEL – a chief archangel

NATHANIEL – see Bartholomew

NICODEMUS – a Pharisee who had a secret meeting with Jesus

PAUL – formerly Saul of Tarsus, persecutor of Christians; renamed after his conversion. Apostle to the Gentiles and author of epistles

PETER – Simon, one of 12 Apostles; denied Jesus before the crucifixion but later became leader of the Church

PHILIP – one of 12 Apostles

PILATE – Roman procurator of Judea; allowed Jesus to be crucified

SALOME – **1.** wife of Zebedee, mother of James and John **2.** daughter of Herodias; danced before Herod for the head of John the Baptist

SAUL – *see* Paul

SIMON – **1.** Simon Peter *see* Peter **2.** the Canaanite, one of 12 Apostles **3.** one of Jesus' four brothers **4.** the leper, in whose house Jesus was anointed **5.** of Cyrene, carried the cross of Jesus **6.** the tanner, in whose house Peter had his vision

STEPHEN – Christian martyr, stoned to death

THOMAS – one of 12 Apostles, named 'Doubting' because he doubted the resurrection

TIMOTHY – Paul's fellow missionary; two of Paul's epistles are to him

TITUS – convert and companion of Paul, who wrote him one epistle

PATRON SAINTS

NAME (Patron of)

AGATHA (bell-founders)
ALBERT THE GREAT (students of natural sciences)
ANDREW (Scotland)
BARBARA (gunners and miners)
BERNARD OF MONTJOUX (mountaineers)
CAMILLUS (nurses)
CASIMIR (Poland)
CECILIA (musicians)
CHRISTOPHER (wayfarers)
CRISPIN (shoemakers)
DAVID (Wales)
DIONYSIUS (DENIS) OF PARIS (France)
DUNSTAN (goldsmiths, jewellers, and locksmiths)
DYMPNA (insane)

ELIGIUS *or* ELOI (metalworkers)
ERASMUS (sailors)
FIACRE (gardeners)
FRANCES CABRINI (emigrants)
FRANCES OF ROME (motorists)
FRANCIS DE SALES (writers)
FRANCIS XAVIER (foreign missions)
FRIDESWIDE (Oxford)
GEORGE (England)
GILES (cripples)
HUBERT (huntsmen)
JEROME EMILIANI (orphans and abandoned children)
JOHN OF GOD (hospitals and booksellers)
JUDE (hopeless causes)

JULIAN (innkeepers, boatmen, travellers)
KATHERINE OF ALEXANDRIA (students, philosophers, and craftsmen)
LUKE (physicians and surgeons)
MARTHA (housewives)
NICHOLAS (children, sailors, unmarried girls, merchants, pawnbrokers, apothecaries, and perfumeries)
PATRICK (Ireland)
PETER NOLASCO (midwives)
SAVA (Serbian people)
VALENTINE (lovers)
VITUS (epilepsy and nervous diseases)
WENCESLAS (Czechoslovakia)
ZITA (domestic servants)

RELIGIOUS ORDERS

AUGUSTINIAN
BARNABITE
BENEDICTINE
BRIGITTINE
CAMALDOLESE
CAPUCHINS
CARMELITE

CARTHUSIAN
CISTERCIAN
DOMINICAN
FRANCISCAN
HOSPITALLERS
JERONYMITE
MINIMS

POOR CLARES
PREMONSTRATEN-SIAN
SALESIAN
SERVITE
SYLVESTRINE
TEMPLARS

THEATINE
TRAPPIST
TRINITARIAN
URSULINE
VISITANDINE, VISITATION

RELIGIOUS MOVEMENTS

3
BON
I AM
ZEN

4
AINU

5
BOSCI
ISLAM
KEGON
THAGS
THUGS

6
BABISM
PARSIS
SHINTO
TAOISM
VOODOO

7
AJIVIKA
BAHAISM
GIDEONS
JAINISM
JUDAISM
JUMPERS
LAMAISM
MORMONS

7–continued
PARSEES
QUAKERS
SHAKERS
SIKHISM
WAHABIS
ZIONISM

8
ABELIANS
ABELITES
ACOEMETI
ADAMITES
ADMADIYA
AHMADIYA
AMARITES
BAPTISTS
BUDDHISM
HINDUISM
HUMANISM
MAR THOMA
NICHIREN
NOSAIRIS
STUDITES

9
CALVINISM
CHUNTOKYO
FRANKISTS
HICKSITES

9–continued
HUGUENOTS
JANSENISM
METHODIST
PANTHEISM

10
ABSTINENTS
ADVENTISTS
AGONIZANTS
AMBROSIANS
BUCHANITES
CALIXTINES
PURATINISM

11
ABODE OF LOVE
ABRAHAMITES
ANABAPTISTS
ANGLICANISM
ARMINIANISM
BASILIDEANS
BERNARDINES
CATHOLICISM
COVENANTERS

12
ABECEDARIANS
BENEDICTINES
CHRISTIANITY

12–continued
SPIRITUALISM
UNITARIANISM

13
MOHAMMEDANISM
PROTESTANTISM
REDEMPTORISTS
SALVATION ARMY

14
CONGREGATIONAL
FUNDAMENTALISM

15
PRESBYTERIANISM

16
CHRISTIAN SCIENCE
PLYMOUTH
  BRETHREN
ROMAN
  CATHOLICISM

17
ANTIPAEDO-
  BAPTISTS
CONGREGATIONAL-
  ISM
JEHOVAH'S
  WITNESSES

CLERGY

ARCHBISHOP
ARCHDEACON
BISHOP
CANON

CARDINAL
CHAPLAIN
CURATE
DEACON

DEAN
ELDER
MINISTER
PADRE

PARSON
POPE
PRIEST

RECTOR
VICAR
VICAR-FORANE

POPES

POPE (DATE OF ACCESSION)

ST PETER (42)
ST LINUS (67)
ST ANACLETUS (Cletus) (76)
ST CLEMENT I (88)
ST EVARISTUS (97)

ST ALEXANDER I (105)
ST SIXTUS I (115)
ST TELESPHORUS (125)
ST HYGINUS (136)
ST PIUS I (140)
ST ANICETUS (155)
ST SOTERUS (166)

ST ELEUTHERIUS (175)
ST VICTOR I (189)
ST ZEPHYRINUS (199)
ST CALLISTUS I (217)
ST URBAN I (222)
ST PONTIAN (230)
ST ANTERUS (235)

ST FABIAN (236)
ST CORNELIUS (251)
ST LUCIUS I (253)
ST STEPHEN I (254)
ST SIXTUS II (257)
ST DIONYSIUS (259)
ST FELIX I (269)
ST EUTYCHIAN (275)
ST CAIUS (283)
ST MARCELLINUS (296)
ST MARCELLUS I (308)
ST EUSEBIUS (309)
ST MELCHIADES (311)
ST SYLVESTER I (314)
ST MARCUS (336)
ST JULIUS I (337)
LIBERIUS (352)
ST DAMASUS I (366)
ST SIRICIUS (384)
ST ANASTASIUS I (399)
ST INNOCENT I (401)
ST ZOSIMUS (417)
ST BONIFACE I (418)
ST CELESTINE I (422)
ST SIXTUS III (432)
ST LEO I (the Great) (440)
ST HILARY (461)
ST SIMPLICIUS (468)
ST FELIX III (483)
ST GELASIUS I (492)
ANASTASIUS II (496)
ST SYMMACHUS (498)
ST HORMISDAS (514)
ST JOHN I (523)
ST FELIX IV (526)
BONIFACE II (530)
JOHN II (533)
ST AGAPETUS I (535)
ST SILVERIUS (536)
VIGILIUS (537)
PELAGIUS I (556)
JOHN III (561)
BENEDICT I (575)
PELAGIUS II (579)
ST GREGORY I (the Great) (590)
SABINIANUS (604)
BONIFACE III (607)
ST BONIFACE IV (608)
ST DEUSDEDIT (Adeodatus I) (615)
BONIFACE V (619)
HONORIUS I (625)
SEVERINUS (640)
JOHN IV (640)
THEODORE I (642)
ST MARTIN I (649)
ST EUGENE I (654)
ST VITALIAN (657)
ADEODATUS II (672)
DONUS (676)
ST AGATHO (678)

ST LEO II (682)
ST BENEDICT II (684)
JOHN V (685)
CONON (686)
ST SERGIUS I (687)
JOHN VI (701)
JOHN VII (705)
SISINNIUS (708)
CONSTANTINE (708)
ST GREGORY II (715)
ST GREGORY III (731)
ST ZACHARY (741)
STEPHEN II (III)* (752)
ST PAUL I (757)
STEPHEN III (IV) (768)
ADRIAN I (772)
ST LEO III (795)
STEPHEN IV (V) (816)
ST PASCHAL I (817)
EUGENE II (824)
VALENTINE (827)
GREGORY IV (827)
SERGIUS II (844)
ST LEO IV (847)
BENEDICT III (855)
ST NICHOLAS I (858)
ADRIAN II (867)
JOHN VIII (872)
MARINUS I (882)
ST ADRIAN III (884)
STEPHEN V (VI) (885)
FORMOSUS (891)
BONIFACE VI (896)
STEPHEN VI (VII) (896)
ROMANUS (897)
THEODORE II (897)
JOHN IX (898)
BENEDICT IV (900)
LEO V (903)
SERGIUS III (904)
ANASTASIUS III (911)
LANDUS (913)
JOHN X (914)
LEO VI (928)
STEPHEN VII (VIII) (928)
JOHN XI (931)
LEO VII (936)
STEPHEN VIII (IX) (939)
MARINUS II (942)
AGAPETUS II (946)
JOHN XII (955)
LEO VIII (963)
BENEDICT V (964)
JOHN XIII (965)
BENEDICT VI (973)
BENEDICT VII (974)
JOHN XIV (983)
JOHN XV (985)
GREGORY V (996)
SYLVESTER II (999)
JOHN XVII (1003)
JOHN XVIII (1004)

SERGIUS IV (1009)
BENEDICT VIII (1012)
JOHN XIX (1024)
BENEDICT IX (1032)
GREGORY VI (1045)
CLEMENT II (1046)
BENEDICT X (1047)
DAMASUS II (1048)
ST LEO IX (1049)
VICTOR II (1055)
STEPHEN IX (X) (1057)
NICHOLAS II (1059)
ALEXANDER II (1061)
ST GREGORY VII (1073)
VICTOR III (1086)
URBAN II (1088)
PASCHAL II (1099)
GELASIUS II (1118)
CALLISTUS II (1119)
HONORIUS II (1124)
INNOCENT II (1130)
CELESTINE II (1143)
LUCIUS II (1144)
EUGENE III (1145)
ANASTASIUS IV (1153)
ADRIAN IV (1154)
ALEXANDER III (1159)
LUCIUS III (1181)
URBAN III (1185)
GREGORY VIII (1187)
CLEMENT III (1187)
CELESTINE III (1191)
INNOCENT III (1198)
HONORIUS III (1216)
GREGORY IX (1227)
CELESTINE IV (1241)
INNOCENT IV (1243)
ALEXANDER IV (1254)
URBAN IV (1261)
CLEMENT IV (1265)
GREGORY X (1271)
INNOCENT V (1276)
ADRIAN V (1276)
JOHN XXI (1276)
NICHOLAS III (1277)
MARTIN IV (1281)
HONORIUS IV (1285)
NICHOLAS IV (1288)
ST CELESTINE V (1294)
BONIFACE VIII (1294)
BENEDICT XI (1303)
CLEMENT V (1305)
JOHN XXII (1316)
BENEDICT XII (1334)
CLEMENT VI (1342)
INNOCENT VI (1352)
URBAN V (1362)
GREGORY XI (1370)
URBAN VI (1378)
BONIFACE IX (1389)
INNOCENT VII (1404)
GREGORY XII (1406)

265

MARTIN V (1417)
EUGENE IV (1431)
NICHOLAS V (1447)
CALLISTUS III (1455)
PIUS II (1458)
PAUL II (1464)
SIXTUS IV (1471)
INNOCENT VIII (1484)
ALEXANDER VI (1492)
PIUS III (1503)
JULIUS II (1503)
LEO X (1513)
ADRIAN VI (1522)
CLEMENT VII (1523)
PAUL III (1534)
JULIUS III (1550)
MARCELLUS II (1555)
PAUL IV (1555)
PIUS IV (1559)
ST PIUS V (1566)
GREGORY XIII (1572)
SIXTUS V (1585)

URBAN VII (1590)
GREGORY XIV (1590)
INNOCENT IX (1591)
CLEMENT VIII (1592)
LEO XI (1605)
PAUL V (1605)
GREGORY XV (1621)
URBAN VIII (1623)
INNOCENT X (1644)
ALEXANDER VII (1655)
CLEMENT IX (1667)
CLEMENT X (1670)
INNOCENT XI (1676)
ALEXANDER VIII (1689)
INNOCENT XII (1691)
CLEMENT XI (1700)
INNOCENT XIII (1721)
BENEDICT XIII (1724)
CLEMENT XII (1730)
BENEDICT XIV (1740)
CLEMENT XIII (1758)
CLEMENT XIV (1769)

PIUS VI (1775)
PIUS VII (1800)
LEO XII (1823)
PIUS VIII (1829)
GREGORY XVI (1831)
PIUS IX (1846)
LEO XIII (1878)
ST PIUS X (1903)
BENEDICT XV (1914)
PIUS XI (1922)
PIUS XII (1939)
JOHN XXIII (1958)
PAUL VI (1963)
JOHN PAUL I (1978)
JOHN PAUL II (1978)
*Stephen II died before conse-
    cration and was dropped from
    the list of popes in 1961;
    Stephen III became
    Stephen II

ARCHBISHOPS OF CANTERBURY

**ARCHBISHOP
(DATE OF ACCESSION)**

AUGUSTINE (597)
LAURENTIUS (604)
MELLITUS (619)
JUSTUS (624)
HONORIUS (627)
DEUSDEDIT (655)
THEODORUS (668)
BEORHTWEALD (693)
TATWINE (731)
NOTHELM (735)
CUTHBEORHT (740)
BREGUWINE (761)
JAENBEORHT (765)
ÆTHELHEARD (793)
WULFRED (805)
FEOLOGILD (832)
CEOLNOTH (833)
ÆTHELRED (870)
PLEGMUND (890)
ÆTHELHELM (914)
WULFHELM (923)
ODA (942)
ÆLFSIGE (959)
BEORHTHELM (959)
DUNSTAN (960)
ÆTHELGAR (988)
SIGERIC SERIO (990)
ÆLFRIC (995)

ÆLFHEAH (1005)
LYFING (1013)
ÆTHELNOTH (1020)
EADSIGE (1038)
ROBERT OF JUMIÈGES
    (1051)
STIGAND (1052)
LANFRANC (1070)
ANSELM (1093)
RALPH D'ESCURES (1114)
WILLIAM OF CORBEIL (1123)
THEOBALD OF BEC (1139)
THOMAS BECKET (1162)
RICHARD OF DOVER (1174)
BALDWIN (1184)
REGINALD FITZJOCELIN
    (1191)
HUBERT WALTER (1193)
REGINALD (1205)
JOHN DE GRAY (1205)
STEPHEN LANGTON (1213)
WALTER OF EVESHAM (1128)
RICHARD GRANT
    (Wethershed) (1229)
RALPH NEVILL (1231)
JOHN OF SITTINGBOURNE
    (1232)
JOHN BLUND (1232)
EDMUND RICH (1234)
BONIFACE OF SAVOY (1245)

ADAM OF CHILLENDEN
    (1270)
ROBERT KILWARDBY (1273)
ROBERT BURNELL (1278)
JOHN PECHAM (1279)
ROBERT WINCHELSEY
    (1295)
THOMAS COBHAM (1313)
WALTER REYNOLDS (1314)
SIMON MEPHAM (1328)
JOHN STRATFORD (1334)
JOHN OFFORD (1348)
THOMAS BRADWARDINE
    (1349)
SIMON ISLIP (1349)
SIMON LANGHAM (1366)
WILLIAM WHITTLESEY (1369)
SIMON SUDBURY (1375)
WILLIAM COURTENAY (1381)
THOMAS ARUNDEL (1397)
ROGER WALDEN (1398)
THOMAS ARUNDEL (1399)
HENRY CHICHELE (1414)
JOHN STAFFORD (1443)
JOHN KEMPE (1452)
THOMAS BOURGCHIER
    (1454)
JOHN MORTON (1486)
HENRY DEANE (1501)
WILLIAM WARHAM (1504)
THOMAS CRANMER (1533)

REGINALD POLE (1556)
MATTHEW PARKER (1559)
EDMUND GRINDAL (1576)
JOHN WHITGIFT (1583)
RICHARD BANCROFT (1604)
GEORGE ABBOT (1611)
WILLIAM LAUD (1633)
WILLIAM JUXON (1660)
GILBERT SHELDON (1663)
WILLIAM SANCROFT (1678)
JOHN TILLOTSON (1691)
THOMAS TENISON (1695)
WILLIAM WAKE (1716)
JOHN POTTER (1737)
THOMAS HERRING (1747)
MATTHEW HUTTON (1757)

THOMAS SECKER (1758)
FREDERICK CORNWALLIS
 (1768)
JOHN MOORE (1783)
CHARLES MANNERS
 SUTTON (1805)
WILLIAM HOWLEY (1828)
JOHN BIRD SUMNER (1848)
CHARLES THOMAS
 LONGLEY (1862)
ARCHIBALD CAMPBELL TAIT
 (1868)
EDWARD WHITE BENSON
 (1883)
FREDERICK TEMPLE (1896)

RANDALL THOMAS
 DAVIDSON (1903)
COSMO GORDON LANG
 (1928)
GEOFFREY FRANCIS FISHER
 (1945)
ARTHUR MICHAEL RAMSEY
 (1961)
FREDERICK DONALD
 COGGAN (1974)
ROBERT ALEXANDER
 KENNEDY RUNCIE (1980)
GEORGE LEONARD CAREY
 (1991)
ROWAN DOUGLAS WILLIAMS
 (2002)

RELIGIOUS TERMS

2
BA
HO
OM

3
ALB
ARA
AUM
HAJ
PEW
PIX
PYX
YAD

4
AMBO
APSE
AZAN
BEMA
BUJI
BULL
COPE
COWL
FONT
HADJ
HAJJ
HALO
HELL
HOOD
HOST
HYMN
JUBE
KAMA
KNOP
LENT
MACE
MASS
NAOS
NAVE

4–continued
OLAH
RAMA
SOMA
TIEN
VOID
WAKE
YOGA

5
ABBOT
ABYSS
AGATI
AISLE
ALLEY
ALTAR
AMBRY
AMICE
ANGEL
APRON
ARMOR
BANNS
BASON
BEADS
BIBLE
BIMAH
BODHI
BRIEF
BUGIA
BURSE
COTTA
CREED
CROSS
CRUET
DIKKA
EMETH
EPHOD
FALDA
GOHEI
HYLIC

5–continued
IHRAM
KALPA
KARMA
LAVER
LIMBO
MOTZI
NICHE
PASCH
PESAH
PESHA
PSALM
ROSHI
SHIVA
STOUP
SYNOD
TOTEM
USHER
VEDAS
WAFER

6
ABBACY
ABODAH
ADVENT
AGUNAH
AHIMSA
AKASHA
AKEDAH
AL CHET
ANOINT
ANTHEM
AUMBRY
AVODAH
BARSOM
BAT KOL
BEADLE
BELFRY
CANTOR
CHOHAN

6–continued
CHOVAH
CHRISM
CLERGY
DHARMA
DHYANA
DITTHI
DOSSAL
DUCHAN
EASTER
FLECHE
FRATER
GLORIA
HEAVEN
HEKHAL
HESPED
KAIROS
KIBLAH
KISMET
KITTEL
LITANY
MANTRA
MATINS
MISSAL
NIGGUN
NIMBUS
ORATIO
ORISON
PARVIS
PESACH
PRAYER
PULPIT
ROCHET
ROSARY
SANGHA
SERMON
SERVER
SHARI'A
SHRIVE

6–continued
SPIRIT
SUTRAS
TAUHID
TIPPET
VERGER
VESTRY

7
ACCIDIA
ACCIDIE
ACOLYTE
AGRAPHA
AMPULLA
ANGELUS
APOSTIL
APOSTLE
APPAREL
ASHAMNU
ATHEISM
AUREOLE
BADCHAN
BANKERS
BAPTISM
BATHING
BELL COT
BERAKAH
BIRETTA
CASSOCK
CHALICE
CHAMETZ
CHANCEL
CHANTRY
CHAPTER
CHAZZAN
CHRISOM
COLLECT
COMPLIN
CORNICE
CROSIER

7–continued
CROZIER
DHARANI
DIOCESE
DIPTYCH
EILETON
FISTULA
GAYATRI
GELILAH
GEULLAH
GRADINE
GREMIAL
HASSOCK
HEATHEN
HEKDESH
INTROIT
KHEREBU
LECTERN
LOCULUS
MANIPLE
MINARET
MOZETTA
NARTHEX
NIRVANA
NOCTURN
PALLIUM
PENANCE
PILGRIM
PURUSHA
REQUIEM
REREDOS
SAMSARA
STHIBEL
TALLITH
TONSURE
TRINITY
TZADDIK
VESPERS
WORSHIP

8
ABLUTION
ABSTEMII
A CAPELLA
AFFLATUS

8–continued
AFFUSION
AFIKOMEN
AGNUS DEI
ANTIPHON
ARMORIUM
AUTO DA FE
AVE MARIA
BEADROLL
BELL COTE
BEMIDBAR
BENEFICE
BREVIARY
BUTSUDEN
CANCELLI
CANTICLE
CIBORIUM
CINCTURE
COMPLINE
CONCLAVE
CORPORAL
CRUCIFIX
DALMATIC
DIKERION
DISCIPLE
DOXOLOGY
EPIPHANY
EVENSONG
FRONTLET
HABDALAH
MANIPULE
NATIVITY
NER TAMID
NIVARANA
OBLATION
PAROKHET
PASSOVER
PREDELLA
RESPONSE
SACRISTY
SURPLICE
TASHLICH
TRIPTYCH
VESTMENT

9
ADIAPHORA
ANAMNESIS
APOCRYPHA
ARBA KOSOT
ARCHANGEL
ASPERSION
CANDLEMAS
CARTOUCHE
CATACOMBS
CATECHISM
CERECLOTH
CHALITZAH
CHRISTMAS
COLLATION
COMMUNION
EPHPHETHA
EUCHARIST
FALDSTOOL
FLABELLUM
FORMULARY
MUNDATORY
OFFERTORY
PACE-AISLE
PURGATORY
SANCTUARY
YOM KIPPUR

10
ABSOLUTION
AGATHOLOGY
ALLOCUTION
AMBULATORY
ANTECHAPEL
APOCALYPSE
BALDACHINO
BAR MITZVAH
BAS MITZVAH
BAT MITZVAH
BENEDICTUS
CATAFALQUE
CLERESTORY
CUTTY STOOL
HAGIOSCOPE
INDULGENCE

10–continued
INTINCTION
INVOCATION
LADY CHAPEL
PRESBYTERY
SEXAGESIMA

11
ABBREVIATOR
ABOMINATION
AGNOSTICISM
ALITURGICAL
ANTEPENDIUM
ANTIMINSION
ASPERGILLUM
BENEDICTION
CHRISTENING
HUMERAL VEIL
INQUISITION
INVESTITURE
SCRIPTORIUM

12
ANTILEGOMENA
ARON HA-KODESH
ASH WEDNESDAY
CONFIRMATION
CONGREGATION
SEPTUAGESIMA

13
BEATIFICATION
BIRKAT HA-MAZON
EPITRACHELION

14
FOLDED CHASUBLE
MAUNDY THURSDAY

17
CONSUBSTANTIA-
TION

RELIGIOUS BUILDINGS

3
WAT

4
CELL
KIRK

5
ABBEY
BET AM
CELLA

5–continued
DUOMO
HONDO
JINGU
JINJA

6
CHAPEL
CHURCH
MOSQUE
PAGODA

6–continued
PRIORY

7
CHANTRY
CONVENT
DEANERY
MINSTER

8
BASILICA

8–continued
CLOISTER
HOUNFORT
LAMASERY

9
BADRINATH
CATHEDRAL
MONASTERY
SYNAGOGUE

12
BET HA-
  KNESSET
BET HA-
  MIDRASH
CHAPTER HOUSE
MEETINGHOUSE

13
ANGELUS
  TEMPLE

RELIGIOUS FESTIVALS

Date	Festival	Religion
Jan	Epiphany	Christian
Jan	Imbolc	Pagan
Jan, Feb	New Year	Chinese
Feb, Mar	Shrove Tuesday	Christian
Feb, Mar	Ash Wednesday	Christian
Feb, Mar	Purim	Jewish
Feb, Mar	Mahashivaratri	Hindu
Feb, Mar	Holi	Hindu
Mar, Apr	Easter	Christian
Mar, Apr	Passover	Jewish
Mar, Apr	Holi Mohalla	Sikh
Mar, Apr	Rama Naumi	Hindu
Mar, Apr	Ching Ming	Chinese
Apr	Baisakhi	Sikh
Apr	Beltane	Pagan
Apr, May	Lailat ul-Isra wal Mi'raj	islamic
Apr, May	Lailat ul-Bara'h	Islamic
Apr, May	Vesak	Buddhist
May, June	Shavuoth	Jewish
May, June	Lailat ul-Qadr	Islamic
May, June	Eid ul-Fitr	Islamic
May, June	Martyrdom of Guru Arjan	Sikh
June	Dragon Boat Festival	Chinese
June	Summer Solstice	Pagan
July	Dhammacakka	Buddhist
July	Eid ul-Adha	Islamic
Aug	Raksha Bandhan	Hindu
Aug	Lammas	Pagan
Aug, Sept	Janmashtami	Hindu
Sept	Moon Festival	Chinese
Sept, Oct	Rosh Hashana	Jewish
Sept, Oct	Yom Kippur	Jewish
Sept, Oct	Succoth	Jewish
Oct	Dusshera	Hindu
Oct	Samhain	Pagan
Oct, Nov	Diwali	Hindu, Sikh
Nov	Birthday of Guru Nanak	Sikh
Nov	Bodhi Day	Buddhist
Dec	Christmas	Christian
Dec	Hanukkah	Jewish
Dec	Winter Festival	Chinese
Dec	Winter Solstice	Pagan
Dec, Jan	Birthday of Guru Gobind Singh	Sikh
Dec, Jan	Martyrdom of Guru Tegh Bahadur	Sikh

HINDU DEITIES

ADITI - goddess of heaven; mother of the gods
AGNI - god of fire
AHI or IHI - the Sistrum Player
AMARAVATI - city of the gods
AMRITA - water of life
BALI - demon who became king of heaven and earth
BRAHMA - the Creator
DEVI - a mother goddess
DITI - mother of the demons
GANDHARVAS - celestial musicians
GANESHA - god of literature, wisdom, and prosperity
GARUDA - the devourer, identified with fire and the sun
HANUMAN - a monkey chief
INDRA - king of the gods; god of war and storm
JYESTHA - goddess of misfortune

KAMA - god of desire
KARTTIKEYA - war-god; god of bravery
KUBERA - god of wealth; guardian of the north
LAKSHMI - goddess of fortune
MANASA - sacred mountain and lake
PRITHIVI - earth-goddess; goddess of fertility
SARANYU - goddess of the clouds
SARASVATI - goddess of speech
SHITALA - goddess of smallpox
SHIVA - the Destroyer
SOMA - ambrosial offering to the gods
SUGRIVA - monkey king
SURYA - the sun-god
VAYU - god of the wind
VISVAKARMA - architect for the gods
VISHNU - the Preserver
YAMA - king of the dead
VARUNA - god of water

GREEK AND ROMAN MYTHOLOGY

MYTHOLOGICAL CHARACTERS

ACHILLES – Greek hero; invulnerable except for his heel

ADONIS – renowned for his beauty

AGAMEMNON – king of Mycenae

AJAX – Greek warrior

ATLAS – bore heaven on his shoulders

BELLEROPHON – Corinthian hero who rode winged horse Pegasus

BOREAS – the north wind

CERBERUS – three-headed dog, guarded Hades

CHARON – boatman who rowed dead across river Styx

CHARYBDIS – violent whirlpool

CIRCE – sorceress who had the power to turn men into beasts

CYCLOPS – one of a race of one-eyed giants (cyclopes)

DAEDALUS – craftsman; designed and built the labyrinth in Crete

GORGONS – three sisters (Stheno, Euryale, and Medusa) who had snakes for hair and whose appearance turned people to stone

HADES – the Underworld

HELEN OF TROY – famed for her beauty; cause of Trojan war

HERACLES – famed for his courage and strength; performed the twelve labours

HERCULES – Roman name for HERACLES

HYDRA – many-headed snake

JASON – led the Argonauts in search of the Golden Fleece

LETHE – river in Hades whose water caused forgetfulness

MIDAS – King of Phrygia whose touch turned everything to gold

MINOTAUR – monster with the head of a bull and the body of a man. It was kept in the Cretan labyrinth and fed with human flesh

NARCISSUS – beautiful youth who fell in love with his own reflection

ODYSSEUS – Greek hero of the Trojan war

OEDIPUS – king of Thebes; married his mother

OLYMPUS – a mountain; the home of the gods

ORPHEUS – skilled musician

PANDORA – the first woman; opened the box that released all varieties of evil

PERSEUS – Greek hero who killed the Gorgon Medusa

POLYPHEMUS – leader of the Cyclopes

ROMULUS – founder of Rome

SATYRS – hoofed spirits of forests, fields, and streams

SCYLLA – six-headed sea monster

SIBYL – a prophetess

SIRENS – creatures depicted as half women, half birds, who lured sailors to their deaths

STYX – main river of Hades, across which Charon ferried the souls of the dead

THESEUS – Greek hero who killed the Cretan Minotaur

ULYSSES – Roman name for ODYSSEUS

GREEK GODS (ROMAN EQUIVALENT)

APHRODITE – goddess of beauty and love (VENUS)

APOLLO – god of poetry, music, and prophecy (APOLLO)

ARES – god of war (MARS)

ARTEMIS – goddess of the moon (DIANA)

ASCLEPIUS – god of medical art (AESCULAPIUS)

ATHENE – goddess of wisdom (MINERVA)

CHARITES – 3 daughters of Zeus: Euphrosyne, Aglaia, and Thalia; personified grace, beauty, and charm (GRACES)

CRONOS – god of agriculture (SATURN)

DEMETER – goddess of agriculture (CERES)

DIONYSUS – god of wine and fertility (BACCHUS)

EOS – goddess of dawn (AURORA)

EROS – god of love (CUPID)

FATES – 3 goddesses who determine man's destiny: Clotho, Lachesis, and Atropos

HEBE – goddess of youth (JUVENTAS)

HECATE – goddess of witchcraft (HECATE)

HELIOS – god of the sun (SOL)

HEPHAESTUS – god of destructive fire (VULCAN)

HERA – queen of heaven, goddess of women and marriage (JUNO)

HERMES – messenger of gods (MERCURY)

HESTIA – goddess of the hearth (VESTA)

HYPNOS – god of sleep (SOMNUS)

NEMESIS – goddess of retribution

PAN – god of woods and fields (FAUNUS)

PERSEPHONE – goddess of the Underworld (PROSERPINE)

PLUTO – god of the Underworld (PLUTO)

PLUTUS – god of wealth

POSEIDON – god of the sea (NEPTUNE)

RHEA – goddess of nature (CYBELE)

SELENE – goddess of the moon (LUNA)

THANATOS – god of death (MORS)

ZEUS – supreme god; god of sky and weather (JUPITER)

ROMAN GODS (GREEK EQUIVALENT)

AESCULAPIUS (ASCLEPIUS)
APOLLO (APOLLO)
AURORA (EOS)
BACCHUS (DIONYSUS)
CERES (DEMETER)
CUPID (EROS)
CYBELE (RHEA)
DIANA (ARTEMIS)
FAUNUS (PAN)
GRACES (CHARITES)
HECATE (HECATE)
JUNO (HERA)
JUPITER (ZEUS)
JUVENTAS (HEBE)

LUNA (SELENE)
MARS (ARES)
MERCURY (HERMES)
MINERVA (ATHENE)
MORS (THANATOS)
NEPTUNE (POSEIDON)
PLUTO (PLUTO)
PROSERPINE (PERSEPHONE)
SATURN (CRONOS)
SOL (HELIOS)
SOMNUS (HYPNOS)
VENUS (APHRODITE)
VESTA (HESTIA)
VULCAN (HEPHAESTUS)

THE TWELVE LABOURS OF HERCULES

THE NEMEAN LION
THE LERNAEAN HYDRA
THE WILD BOAR OF ERYMANTHUS
THE STYMPHALIAN BIRDS
THE CERYNEIAN HIND
THE AUGEAN STABLES
THE CRETAN BULL
THE MARES OF DIOMEDES
THE GIRDLE OF HIPPOLYTE
THE CATTLE OF GERYON
THE GOLDEN APPLES OF THE HESPERIDES
THE CAPTURE OF CERBERUS

THE NINE MUSES

CALLIOPE (EPIC POETRY)
CLIO (HISTORY)
ERATO (LOVE POETRY)
EUTERPE (LYRIC POETRY)
MELPOMENE (TRAGEDY)
POLYHYMNIA (SACRED SONG)
TERPSICHORE (DANCING)
THALIA (COMEDY)
URANIA (ASTRONOMY)

NORSE MYTHOLOGY

AEGIR – god of the sea

ALFHEIM – part of Asgard inhabited by the light elves

ASGARD – the home of the gods

ASK – name of the first man, created from a fallen tree

BALDER – god of the summer sun

BRAGI – god of poetry

EIR – goddess of healing

EMBLA – name of first woman, created from a fallen tree

FORSETI – god of justice

FREY – god of fertility and crops

FREYJA – goddess of love and night

FRIGG – Odin's wife; supreme goddess

GUNGNIR – Odin's magic spear

HEIMDAL – guardian of Asgard

HEL – goddess of the dead

HÖDUR – god of night

IDUN – wife of Bragi; guardian of the golden apples of youth

LOKI – god of evil

MIDGARD – the world of men

NORNS – three goddesses of destiny: Urd (Fate), Skuld (Being), and Verdandi (Necessity)

ODIN – supreme god; god of battle, inspiration, and death

RAGNAROK – final battle between gods and giants, in which virtually all life is destroyed

SIF – wife of Thor; her golden hair was cut off by Loki

SLEIPNIR – Odin's eight-legged horse

THOR – god of thunder

TYR – god of war

VALHALLA – hall in Asgard where Odin welcomed the souls of heroes killed in battle

VALKYRIES – nine handmaidens of Odin who chose men doomed to die in battle

YGGDRASILL – the World Tree, an ash linking all the worlds

YMIR – giant from whose body the world was formed

EGYPTIAN MYTHOLOGY

AMON-RA – supreme god
ANUBIS – jackel-headed son of Osiris; god of the dead
BES – god of marriage
GEB – earth-god
HATHOR – cow-headed goddess of love
HORUS – hawk-headed god of light
ISIS – goddess of fertility
MAAT – goddess of law, truth, and justice
MIN – god of virility
MONT – god of war
MUT – wife of Amon-Ra
NEHEH – god of eternity

NUN or NU – the primordial Ocean
NUT – goddess of the sky
OSIRIS – ruler of the afterlife
PTAH – god of the arts
RA – the sun god
RENPET – goddess of youth
SEKHMET – goddess of war
SET or SETH – god of evil
SHU – god of air
TEFNUT – goddess of dew and rain
THOTH – god of wisdom
UPUAUT – warrior-god; god of the dead

NORTH AMERICAN MYTHOLOGY

ADLIVUN – Eskimo land of the unhappy dead
AGLOOKIK – Eskimo spirit of hunters
AHSONNUTLI – chief god of the Navaho Indians
AKYCHA – the Sun
ANGAKOO – Eskimo shaman
ANGUTA – Eskimo ruler of the underworld
ANINGAN – the Moon
BIG OWL – cannibalistic monster of the Apache Indians
COYOTE – trickster god
DZOAVITS – Shoshone ogre
GLOOSKAP – agent of good; made the sky, earth, creatures, and mankind
HIAWATHA – legendary sage of the Iroquois Indians who founded the League of Five Nations
HINO – Iroquois god of thunder
HINUN – thunder spirit of the Iroquois Indians
ICTINIKE – trickster god of the Sioux Indians
MALSUM – agent of evil; made the mountains, valleys, snakes

NANA BOZHO (MANA BOZHO) – trickster god of the Algonquins
NANOOK – the Bear (the Pleiades)
NAPI – chief god of the Blackfoot
NATOS – sun god of the Blackfoot Indians
NAYENEZGANI – hero of Navaho legend; name means 'slayer of evil gods'
NEGAFOK – cold weather spirit
SEDNA – the great Sea Mother; Eskimo goddess of the underworld and sea
SPIDER WOMAN – benevolent creature who helped Nayenezgani defeat the powers of evil
TIRAWA – chief god of the Pawnee, who created the world and set the course of the sun, moon, and stars
TORNAQ – familiar of a shaman
TSOHANOAI – Navaho sun god, who carries the sun on his back across the sky
WAKONDA – great god of the Sioux Indians whose name means 'great power above'
WONOMI – sky god of the Maidu Indians who was abandoned in favour of Coyote

CENTRAL AND SOUTH AMERICAN MYTHOLOGY

AH PUCH – Maya god of death
BACHUE – mother goddess and protector of crops
BOCHICA – Colombian founder hero; appears as an old bearded man
CHAC – Maya rain god
CINTEOTL – Aztec god of maize
COATLICUE – Aztec earth goddess; a devouring

goddess who was only satisfied by human flesh and blood
CUPAY (SUPAY) – Inca god of death
EHECATL – Aztec god of the winds who introduced sexual love to mankind
GUINECHEN – chief deity of Araucanian Indians, associated with fertility
HUITZILOPOCHTLI – chief god of the Aztecs

INTI – sun god from whom Inca dynasty traced its descent

ITZAMNA – chief god of the Maya

IXCHEL – Maya moon goddess

IXTAB – Maya goddess of suicide

IXTLILTON – Aztec god of medicine

KUAT – sun god of the Mamaiurans

MIXCOATL – Aztec god of the chase

MONTEZUMA – Aztec god whose name was taken from the last emperor

PACHAMAMA – Earth goddess of the Incas

PILLAN – thunder god of Araucanian Indians

QUETZALCOATL – a priest-king of Central America; the snake-bird god or plumed serpent

TEZCATLIPOCA – Aztec god of summer sun; bringer of harvests as well as drought

TLALOC – rain god of Central America, worshipped by the Toltecs and Aztecs

TUPAN – thunder god of the Guarani Indians

VAICA – magician and medicine-man of the Jurunas

VIRACOCHA – creator god of the Incas

XIPETOTEC – Aztec god of agriculture and self-torture; his name means 'flayed lord'

XOCHIQUETZAL – Aztec goddess of flowers and fruits

AUSTRALIAN MYTHOLOGY

AKURRA – serpent god

ALCHERA – 'Dreamtime', primeval time when the ancestors sang the world into existence

ARUNKULTA – Aranda spirit of evil

BAGADJIMBIRI – ancestral creator of gods

BIAME – god of creation

BIRRAHGNOOLOO – chief wife of Biame

BOLUNG – serpent god; giver of life

BOOMERANG – symbolizes the rainbow and the connection of opposites (e.g. heaven and earth)

BRALGU – island of the dead

BUNJIL – god of creation

BUNYIP – monster and giver of mystic healing rites

DILGA – earth goddess

DJANBUN – many who turned into a platypus after blowing too hard on a fire-stick

KAPOO – ancestral kangaroo who gave cats their spots

MANGAR-KUNGER-KUNJA – great lizard ancestor of the Aranda

MARINDI – ancestral dog whose blood turned the rocks red

PUNDJEL – creator god who made the first human being

WATI-KUTJARA – two lizard men of Central Australia

YURLUNYUR – ancestor of the Murngin of the northern Australia, known as the great copper python or the rainbow serpent

AFRICAN MYTHOLOGY

ABASSI – sky god of the Efik

ADROA – creator god of the Lugbara

ADU OGYINAE – first man of the Ashanti

ALA – mother goddess of the Ibo, eastern Nigeria

AMMA – an egg; seed of the cosmos; god of creation

ANANSI – W African trickster god

ASA – supreme god of the Akamba

BUMBA – creator god of the Bushongo of the Democratic Republic of Congo

CHINAWEJI – serpent; founder of the universe

CHUKU – supreme god of the Ibo, eastern Nigeria

DXUI – first god of creation

ESHU – messenger between High God and humans

ESHU – trickster god of the Yoruba who carried messages from the gods to mankind

EVENING STAR – wife of MWETSI, bearer of animals and people

FARO – maker of the sky

GU – heavenly blacksmith

IFA – god of medicine and prophecy

IMANA – supreme god of the Banyarwanda, Rwanda

JOK – creator god of the Alur

KAANG – creator god of the southwest African Bushmen

LEZA – supreme god of the Bantu

MAWU-LISA – twin creator gods

MBOOM – god of creation

MINIA – serpent; founder of the universe

MORNING STAR – wife of MWETSI, bearer of grass, shrubs, etc.

MOYNA – hero who invented the bull-roarer

MULUNGU – all-knowing sky god of the Nyamwezi

MWARI – High God
MWETSI – the first man
NANA – earth goddess of the Yoruba
NGAAN – god of creation
NGEWO – sky god of the Miende
NOMMO – a creator god
NTORO – the soul, in the beliefs of the Ashanti
NYAME – mother goddess

OGUN – war god of the Yoruba
PEMBA – maker of the earth
RUHANGA – high god of the Bangoro
UNKULUNKULU – supreme god of the Zulus
WELE – chief god of the Abaluyia of Kenya
WOOD – name of all the nine children of MBOOM

ARTHURIAN LEGEND

AGRAVAIN – younger brother of Gawain, helped expose Lancelot's and Guinevere's adultery to Arthur

AMFORTAS – Fisher King who looked after the Grail

ARTHUR – legendary British leader of the Knights of the Round Table

AVALON – wonderful island where Arthur was taken to be healed of this wounds

BORS – only knight to achieve the quest of the Holy Grail, and to survive and return to Arthur's court

CAMELOT – capital of Arthur's kingdom

ECTOR – foster father of Arthur, father of Kay

EXCALIBUR – Arthur's magic sword

GALAHAD – son of Lancelot; purest of the Knights of the Round Table; succeeded in the quest of the Grail

GAWAIN – nephew of Arthur, son of Morgan Le Fay; searched for the Grail

GRAIL (SANGREAL, THE HOLY GRAIL) – said to be the vessel of the Last Supper; in the custody of the Fisher King

GUINEVERE – wife of Arthur, lover of Lancelot

IGRAINE – wife of Uther Pendragon; mother of Arthur and Morgan le Fay

KAY – foster brother of Arthur

LADY OF THE LAKE – enchantress who raised Lancelot and gave Arthur Excalibur

LANCELOT or LAUNCELOT – knight and lover of Queen Guinevere

LUCAN – most trusted of Arthur's friends

MERLIN – magician and bard who prepared Arthur for kingship

MORDRED or MODRED – son of Arthur and his half-sister Morgause

MORGAN LE FAY – sorceress and healer; half-sister of Arthur

MORGAUSE – half-sister of Arthur; mother of Mordred, Gawain, Gareth, and Agravain

NIMUE – enchantress with whom Merlin fell in love

PERCIVAL or PERCEVAL – knight who vowed to seek the Grail

UTHER PENDRAGON – father of Arthur

VIVIANE – the Lady of the Lake

CELTIC MYTHOLOGY

ANGUS – Irish god of love

ANNWN – the Underworld in Welsh mythology

ANU – earth goddess, mother of the gods of Ireland

ARAWN – Welsh king of the Underworld (Annwn)

BALOR – Irish one-eyed god of death

BANSHEE – English name for Bean Sidhe, the Irish fairy, whose wailing foretells the approach of death

BECUMA – Irish goddess, who was banished to earth

BELINUS – god of the sun

BELTAIN – first day of summer – 1st May

BRANWEN – daughter of Llyr

BRIGIT, BRIGHID – bringer of the spring – became St Bride

CERNUNNOS – god of wild beasts

CIAN – Irish father of the sun god Lugh

COCIDIUS – god of hunting

CONN – high king of Ireland

COVENTINA – goddess of water

CU CHULAINN – Irish hero, foster-son of King Conchobhar

DAGHDHA, THE – The Good God (of Ireland)

DANA – Irish mother goddess

DIAN-CECHT – Irish god of medicine

DIERDRE – daughter of the Ulster lord Felim Mac Dall who was forced to marry Conchobhar, and never smiled again

DONN – Irish god of the dead

EPONA – goddess of horsemen and animals

FINN MAC COOL (FINGAL) – legendary Irish hero who obtained wisdom from the salmon of knowledge (Fintan)

FLIDHAIS – goddess of the moon and hunting
GREEN MAN – fertility god
GWYDION – Welsh priest-king and magician
GWYNN – Welsh god of the Underworld
HERNE – the hunter
LUGH – Irish sun god
MABON – god of youth
MANANNAN – Irish sea god
MEDB – legendary Queen of Connacht –
  possibly prototype of Mab, British Queen of the
  fairies
MORRIGAN – Irish goddess of war
NUADA – high king of Ireland

OENGHUS – god of love
OSSIAN – Irish hero
PRYDERI – son of Pwyll and Rhiannon, who
  eventually succeeded his father as lord of Dyfed
PWYLL – Chief of Annwn (Prince of Dyfed)
RHIANNON – wife of Pwyll who was falsely
  accused of killing her son
SAMHAIN – first day of winter – 1st November
SHEELA-NA-GIG – goddess of fertility
SIDHE – Irish fairies of the Otherworld
TALIESIN – Welsh wizard who knew the secrets
  of the past, present, and future
TARANIS – the thunderer

MYTHOLOGICAL AND IMAGINARY BEINGS

3
ELF
NIX
ORC
ROC

4
FAUN
JINN
OGRE
PUCK
YETI

5
DEMON
DWARF
FAIRY
FIEND
GENIE
GHOST
GHOUL
GIANT
GNOME
GOLEM

5–continued
HARPY
JOTUN
LAMIA
NYMPH
PIXIE
PRETA
SATYR
SYLPH
TROLL

6
AFREET
AZAZEL
BUNYIP
DAEMON
DRAGON
DYBBUK
FAFNIR
FURIES
GOBLIN
HOBBIT
KELPIE

6–continued
KOBOLD
KRAKEN
RAVANA
SINBAD
SPHINX
SPRITE
UNDINE
ZOMBIE

7
AMAZONS
BANSHEE
BROWNIE
CENTAUR
CHIMERA
GREMLIN
GRENDEL
GRIFFIN
INCUBUS
LORELEI
MERMAID
PHOENIX

7–continued
SILENUS
UNICORN
VAMPIRE

8
BABA YAGA
BARGHEST
BASILISK
BEHEMOTH
QUEEN MAB
SUCCUBUS
WEREWOLF

9
GILGAMESH
HOBGOBLIN
MANTICORE
NIBELUNGS
PIED PIPER
ROBIN HOOD

10
HIPPOGRIFF

10–continued
LEPRECHAUN
SALAMANDER
SANTA CLAUS

11
AMPHISBAENA
HIPPOCAMPUS
POLTERGEIST
RIP VAN
  WINKLE
SCHEHERE-
  ZADE

12+
ABOMINABLE
  SNOWMAN
FATHER
  CHRISTMAS
LOCH NESS
  MONSTER
ROBIN
  GOODFELLOW

CHARACTERS FROM THE TALES OF ROBIN HOOD

ALAN A DALE
FRIAR TUCK
GUY OF GISBORNE
KING RICHARD THE
  LIONHEART
LITTLE JOHN

MAID MARIAN
MERRY MEN
MUCH THE MILLER
PRINCE JOHN
SHERIFF OF NOTTINGHAM
WILL SCARLET

WORK

PROFESSIONS, TRADES, AND OCCUPATIONS

2
GP
MD
MO
PM

3
DOC
DON
GYP
PRO
REP
SPY
VET

4
AMAH
AYAH
BABU
BARD
BOSS
CHAR
CHEF
COOK
CREW
DIVA
DYER
GANG
GRIP
HACK
HAND
HEAD
HERD
HIND
MAGI
MAID
MATE
MIME
PAGE
PEON
POET
SEER
SERF
SYCE
TOUT
WARD
WHIP

5
ACTOR
AD-MAN
AGENT
BAKER
BONZE
BOOTS
BOSUN
CADDY
CLERK
CLOWN
COACH
COMIC
CRIER
CRIMP
CURER
DAILY
ENVOY
EXTRA
FAKIR
FENCE
FIFER
FILER
FINER
FLIER
GIPSY
GLUER
GROOM
GUARD
GUIDE
GUILD
HAKIM
HARPY
HELOT
HIRER
HIVER
HOPPO
LEECH
LUTER
MASON
MEDIC
MINER
NAVVY
NURSE
OILER
OWLER
PILOT

5–continued
PIPER
PLYER
PUPIL
QUACK
QUILL
RABBI
RATER
REEVE
RUNER
SCOUT
SEWER
SHOER
SLAVE
SMITH
SOWER
STAFF
SWEEP
TAMER
TAWER
TAXER
TILER
TUNER
TUTOR
TYLER
USHER
VALET
VINER

6
AIRMAN
ARCHER
ARTIST
AURIST
AUTHOR
BAGMAN
BAILER
BAILOR
BALKER
BANKER
BARBER
BARGEE
BARKER
BARMAN
BATMAN
BEARER
BINDER
BOFFIN

6–continued
BOOKIE
BOWMAN
BREWER
BROKER
BUGLER
BURLER
BURSAR
BUSKER
BUTLER
CABBIE
CABMAN
CALKER
CANNER
CARTER
CARVER
CASUAL
CENSOR
CLERGY
CLERIC
CODIST
COINER
COMBER
CONDER
COOLIE
COOPER
COPPER
CO-STAR
COSTER
COWBOY
COWMAN
CRITIC
CUTLER
CUTTER
DANCER
DEALER
DIGGER
DOCKER
DOCTOR
DOWSER
DRAPER
DRAWER
DRIVER
DROVER
EDITOR
FABLER
FACTOR

6–continued
FARMER
FELLER
FICTOR
FISHER
FITTER
FLAYER
FORGER
FOWLER
FRAMER
FULLER
GAFFER
GANGER
GAOLER
GAUCHO
GAUGER
GIGOLO
GILDER
GILLIE
GLAZER
GLOVER
GRAVER
GROCER
GUIDER
GUIDON
GUNMAN
GUNNER
HARPER
HATTER
HAWKER
HEALER
HEAVER
HODMAN
HOOPER
HORNER
HOSIER
HUNTER
INTERN
ISSUER
JAILER
JAILOR
JOBBER
JOCKEY
JOINER
JOWTER
JURIST
KEELER

6–continued	6–continued	6–continued	7–continued	7–continued
KEEPER	RECTOR	TUBMAN	BOATMAN	FLESHER
KILLER	REGENT	TURNER	BONDMAN	FLORIST
LACKEY	RELIEF	TYCOON	BOOKMAN	FLUNKEY
LANDER	RENTER	TYPIST	BOTTLER	FLUTIST
LASCAR	RIGGER	USURER	BRIGAND	FOOTBOY
LAWYER	RINGER	VACHER	BUILDER	FOOTMAN
LECTOR	ROBBER	VALUER	BURGLAR	FOOTPAD
LENDER	ROOFER	VAMPER	BUTCHER	FOREMAN
LOADER	ROOTER	VANMAN	BUTTONS	FOUNDER
LOGMAN	SACKER	VASSAL	CALLBOY	FRISEUR
LUMPER	SAILOR	VENDER	CAMBIST	FROGMAN
MARKER	SALTER	VENDOR	CARRIER	FUELLER
MATRON	SALVOR	VERGER	CASEMAN	FURRIER
MEDICO	SAPPER	VERSER	CASHIER	GATEMAN
MENDER	SARTOR	VIEWER	CATERER	GIRDLER
MENIAL	SAWYER	WAITER	CAULKER	GLAZIER
MENTOR	SCRIBE	WALLER	CELLIST	GLEANER
MERCER	SEA-DOG	WARDEN	CHANTER	GLEEMAN
MILKER	SEALER	WARDER	CHAPMAN	GLOSSER
MILLER	SEAMAN	WARPER	CHEMIST	GRAFFER
MINTER	SEINER	WASHER	CHORIST	GRAFTER
MONGER	SEIZOR	WEAVER	CLEANER	GRAINER
MORISK	SELLER	WEEDER	CLICKER	GRANGER
MUMMER	SERVER	WELDER	CLIPPIE	GRANTEE
MUMPER	SETTER	WHALER	COALMAN	GRANTOR
MYSTIC	SEXTON	WORKER	COBBLER	GRAZIER
NAILER	SHROFF	WRIGHT	COCKLER	GRINDER
NOTARY	SINGER	WRITER	COLLIER	GYMNAST
NURSER	SIRCAR		CO-PILOT	HACKLER
OBOIST	SKIVVY	**7**	COPYIST	HARPIST
OILMAN	SLATER	ABACIST	CORONER	HAULIER
ORATOR	SLAVER	ABIGAIL	CORSAIR	HELOTRY
OSTLER	SLAVEY	ACOLYTE	COUNSEL	HERBIST
PACKER	SLEUTH	ACOLYTH	COURIER	HERDMAN
PARSON	SNARER	ACROBAT	COWHERD	HERITOR
PASTOR	SOCMAN	ACTRESS	COWPOKE	HIGGLER
PAVIER	SORTER	ACTUARY	CROFTER	HOGHERD
PAVIOR	SOUTER	ALEWIFE	CROPPER	HOSTLER
PEDANT	SPICER	ALMONER	CURATOR	INDEXER
PEDLAR	SQUIRE	ANALYST	CURRIER	INLAYER
PENMAN	STAGER	APPOSER	CUSTODE	IRONIST
PICKER	STOKER	ARABIST	DANSEUR	JANITOR
PIEMAN	STORER	ARBITER	DENTIST	JUGGLER
PIRATE	SUTLER	ARTISAN	DIALIST	JUNKMAN
PITMAN	TABLER	ARTISTE	DIETIST	JURYMAN
PLATER	TAILOR	ASSAYER	DITCHER	KEELMAN
PLAYER	TAMPER	ASSIZER	DOMINIE	KNACKER
PORTER	TANNER	ASSURED	DOORMAN	KNITTER
POTBOY	TASKER	ASSURER	DRAGMAN	LACEMAN
POTTER	TASTER	AUDITOR	DRAPIER	LINKBOY
PRIEST	TELLER	AVIATOR	DRAWBOY	LINKMAN
PRUNER	TERMER	AWARDER	DRAYMAN	LOCKMAN
PURSER	TESTER	BAILIFF	DREDGER	LOMBARD
QUERRY	TILLER	BANDMAN	DRESSER	MALTMAN
RABBIN	TINKER	BARMAID	DROGMAN	MANAGER
RAGMAN	TINMAN	BELLBOY	DRUMMER	MANGLER
RANGER	TINNER	BELLHOP	DUSTMAN	MARBLER
RATTER	TOLLER	BEST BOY	FARRIER	MARCHER
READER	TOUTER	BIRDMAN	FASCIST	MARINER
REAPER	TRACER	BLASTER	FIDDLER	MARSHAL
REAVER	TRADER	BLENDER	FIREMAN	MATADOR

7–continued	7–continued	8–continued	8–continued	8–continued
MATELOT	SNIPPER	BANDSMAN	FABULIST	LINESMAN
MEALMAN	SOCAGER	BARGEMAN	FACTOTUM	LUMBERER
MEATMAN	SOLDIER	BEARHERD	FALCONER	MAGICIAN
MIDWIFE	SOLOIST	BEDESMAN	FAMULIST	MAGISTER
MILKMAN	SPENCER	BEDMAKER	FARMHAND	MALTSTER
MODISTE	SPINNER	BIT-MAKER	FERRYMAN	MASSEUSE
MONEYER	SPOTTER	BLEACHER	FIGURANT	MEASURER
MONITOR	STAINER	BOATSMAN	FILMSTAR	MECHANIC
MOOTMAN	STAMPER	BONDMAID	FINISHER	MEDALIST
MOULDER	STAPLER	BONDSMAN	FISHWIFE	MELODIST
NEWSBOY	STATIST	BOTANIST	FLATFOOT	MERCATOR
OCULIST	STEERER	BOWMAKER	FLAUTIST	MERCHANT
OFFICER	STEWARD	BOXMAKER	FLETCHER	METAL-MAN
ORDERER	SURGEON	BREWSTER	FODDERER	MILKMAID
ORDERLY	SWABBER	BROACHER	FORESTER	MILLHAND
PACKMAN	SWEEPER	CABIN BOY	FORGEMAN	MILLINER
PAGEBOY	TABORER	CELLARER	FUGLEMAN	MINISTER
PAINTER	TALLIER	CERAMIST	GANGSTER	MINSTREL
PALMIST	TAPSTER	CHANDLER	GARDENER	MODELLER
PANTLER	TAXI-MAN	CHOIRBOY	GAVELMAN	MULETEER
PEDDLER	TEACHER	CIDERIST	GENDARME	MURALIST
PIANIST	TIPSTER	CLAQUEUR	GLASSMAN	MUSICIAN
PICADOR	TRACKER	CLOTHIER	GOATHERD	NEWSHAWK
PLANNER	TRAINER	COACHMAN	GOVERNOR	NOVELIST
PLANTER	TRAPPER	CO-AUTHOR	GUARDIAN	ONION-MAN
PLEADER	TRAWLER	CODIFIER	GUNSMITH	OPERATOR
PLUMBER	TRIMMER	COISTRIL	HAMMERER	OPTICIAN
POACHER	TRUCKER	COLLATOR	HANDMAID	ORDAINER
POSTBOY	TRUSTEE	COMEDIAN	HANDYMAN	ORDINAND
POSTMAN	TUMBLER	COMPILER	HATMAKER	ORGANIST
PRESSER	TURNKEY	COMPOSER	HAYMAKER	OUTRIDER
PRESTOR	VINTNER	CONJURER	HEAD COOK	OVERSEER
PRINTER	VIOLIST	CONVEYOR	HEADSMAN	PARGETER
PUDDLER	WAGONER	COURTIER	HELMSMAN	PARODIST
RANCHER	WARRIOR	COW-LEECH	HENCHMAN	PENMAKER
REALTOR	WEBSTER	COXSWAIN	HERDSMAN	PERFUMER
REFINER	WEIGHER	CROUPIER	HIRELING	PETERMAN
RIVETER	WHEELER	CUTPURSE	HISTRION	PEWTERER
ROADMAN	WHETTER	DAIRYMAN	HOME HELP	PICAROON
ROASTER	WIREMAN	DANSEUSE	HOTELIER	PLOUGHER
RUSTLER	WOODMAN	DECKHAND	HOUSEBOY	POLISHER
SACRIST	WOOLMAN	DEFENDER	HUCKSTER	PORTRESS
SADDLER	WORKMAN	DESIGNER	HUNTSMAN	POSTILER
SAMPLER	WRAPPER	DIRECTOR	IMPORTER	POTMAKER
SAMURAI		DOG-LEECH	IMPROVER	PREACHER
SCOURER	**8**	DOMESTIC	INKMAKER	PREFACER
SCRAPER	ADSCRIPT	DOUGHBOY	INVENTOR	PRELUDER
SERVANT	AERONAUT	DRAGOMAN	JAPANNER	PRESSMAN
SETTLER	ALGERINE	DRUGGIST	JET PILOT	PROBATOR
SHARPER	ANALYSER	EDUCATOR	JEWELLER	PROCURER
SHEARER	APHORIST	EMBALMER	JONGLEUR	PROMOTER
SHIPPER	APIARIST	EMISSARY	KIPPERER	PROMPTER
SHOPBOY	APRON-MAN	ENGINEER	LABOURER	PROSAIST
SHOWMAN	ARBORIST	ENGRAVER	LANDGIRL	PROVIDER
SHUNTER	ARMORIST	ENROLLER	LANDLADY	PSALMIST
SILKMAN	ARMOURER	EPIC POET	LANDLORD	PUBLICAN
SIMPLER	ARRESTOR	ESSAYIST	LAPIDARY	PUGILIST
SKINNER	ASSESSOR	ESSOINER	LARCENER	PURVEYOR
SKIPPER	ATTORNEY	EXORCIST	LARDERER	QUARRIER
SLIPPER	BAGMAKER	EXPLORER	LEADSMAN	RAFTSMAN
SMELTER	BAGPIPER	EXPORTER	LECTURER	RANCHERO

8–continued	8–continued	9–continued	9–continued
RAPPEREE	TORTURER	BURNISHER	EMBEZZLER
RECEIVER	TOYMAKER	BUS DRIVER	ENAMELLER
REGRATER	TRIPEMAN	CAB DRIVER	ENGINEMAN
RELESSEE	TRUCKMAN	CAFÉ OWNER	ENGROSSER
RELESSOR	TURNCOCK	CAMERAMAN	EPITOMIST
REPAIRER	TURNSPIT	CAR DRIVER	ERRAND BOY
REPORTER	TUTORESS	CARETAKER	ESTIMATOR
RESETTER	UNIONIST	CARPENTER	EXAMINANT
RESTORER	VALUATOR	CARVANEER	EXCAVATOR
RETAILER	VINTAGER	CASEMAKER	EXCERPTOR
RETAINER	VIRTUOSO	CATECHIST	EXCHANGER
REVIEWER	VOCALIST	CELLARMAN	EXCISEMAN
REWRITER	VOLUMIST	CHARWOMAN	EXECUTIVE
RIVETTER	WAITRESS	CHAUFFEUR	EXERCITOR
ROMANCER	WALKER-ON	CHEAPJACK	EXORCISER
RUGMAKER	WARDRESS	CHORISTER	FABRICANT
RUMOURER	WARRENER	CLARIFIER	FASHIONER
SALESMAN	WATCHMAN	CLERGYMAN	FELT-MAKER
SATIRIST	WATERMAN	CLINICIAN	FIGURANTE
SAWBONES	WET NURSE	CLOGMAKER	FILM ACTOR
SCULLION	WHALEMAN	COALMINER	FILM EXTRA
SCULPTOR	WHITENER	COALOWNER	FILM-MAKER
SEAMSTER	WHITSTER	COLLECTOR	FINANCIER
SEA-ROVER	WIGMAKER	COLOURIST	FIRE-EATER
SEASONER	WINNOWER	COLUMNIST	FISH-CURER
SEEDSMAN	WOOL-DYER	COMPRADOR	FISHERMAN
SEMPSTER	WRESTLER	CONCIERGE	FISH-WOMAN
SERVITOR		CONDUCTOR	FLAG-MAKER
SHEARMAN	**9**	CONSERVER	FLAX-WENCH
SHEPHERD	ALCHEMIST	COSMONAUT	FLYFISHER
SHIPMATE	ALLUMINOR	COST CLERK	FREELANCE
SHIP'S BOY	ANATOMIST	COSTUMIER	FREIGHTER
SHOPGIRL	ANNOTATOR	COURTESAN	FRIPPERER
SHOWGIRL	ANNOUNCER	COUTURIER	FRUITERER
SIDESMAN	ARBORATOR	COWFEEDER	FURBISHER
SIMPLIST	ARCHERESS	COWKEEPER	FURNISHER
SKETCHER	ARCHITECT	CRACKSMAN	GALVANIST
SMUGGLER	ARCHIVIST	CRAFTSMAN	GASFITTER
SPACEMAN	ART CRITIC	CRAYONIST	GAZETTEER
SPEARMAN	ART DEALER	CYMBALIST	GEM-CUTTER
SPEEDCOP	ARTIFICER	DAILY HELP	GEOLOGIST
SPURRIER	ASTRONAUT	DAIRYMAID	GLADIATOR
STARCHER	ATTENDANT	DECORATOR	GLUEMAKER
STITCHER	AUTHORESS	DECRETIST	GOLDSMITH
STOCKMAN	BALLADIST	DESK CLERK	GONDOLIER
STOREMAN	BALLERINA	DETECTIVE	GOSPELLER
STRIPPER	BANK AGENT	DICE-MAKER	GOVERNESS
STRUMMER	BARRISTER	DIE-SINKER	GROUNDMAN
STUNTMAN	BARROW BOY	DIETETIST	GUARDSMAN
SUPPLIER	BEEFEATER	DIETITIAN	GUERRILLA
SURVEYOR	BEEKEEPER	DIRECTRIX	GUITARIST
SWINDLER	BIOLOGIST	DISPENSER	GUN-RUNNER
TABOURER	BOATSWAIN	DISSECTOR	HARLEQUIN
TALLYMAN	BODYGUARD	DISTILLER	HARMONIST
TAVERNER	BOILERMAN	DOCTORESS	HARPOONER
TEAMSTER	BONDSLAVE	DRAFTSMAN	HARVESTER
THATCHER	BONDWOMAN	DRAMATIST	HELLENIST
THESPIAN	BOOKMAKER	DRAWLATCH	HERBALIST
THRESHER	BOOTBLACK	DRUM-MAKER	HERBARIAN
TIN MINER	BOOTMAKER	DRYSALTER	HERBORIST
TINSMITH	BUCCANEER	ECOLOGIST	HERB-WOMAN

279

9—continued

HIRED HAND
HIRED HELP
HISTORIAN
HOG-RINGER
HOMEOPATH
HOP-PICKER
HOSTELLER
HOUSEMAID
HOUSEWIFE
HYGIENIST
HYPNOTIST
INCUMBENT
INGRAFTER
INNHOLDER
INNKEEPER
INSCRIBER
INSPECTOR
INTENDANT
IRONSMITH
ITINERANT
JACK-SMITH
JOB-MASTER
KENNEL-MAN
LACEMAKER
LACQUERER
LADY'S MAID
LAND AGENT
LANDREEVE
LARCENIST
LAUNDERER
LAUNDRESS
LEGIONARY
LIBRARIAN
LINOTYPER
LIONTAMER
LIVERYMAN
LOAN AGENT
LOCKMAKER
LOCKSMITH
LOG-ROLLER
LUMBERMAN
MACHINIST
MAGNETIST
MAJORDOMO
MALE MODEL
MALE NURSE
MAN-AT-ARMS
MANNEQUIN
MECHANIST
MEDALLIST
MEMOIRIST
MERCENARY
MESMERIST
MESSENGER
METALLIST
METRICIAN
MILL-OWNER
MODELGIRL
MORTICIAN
MUFFIN-MAN
MUSKETEER

9—continued

MUSKETOON
MYOLOGIST
NAVIGATOR
NEGOTIANT
NEOLOGIAN
NEOLOGIST
NEWSAGENT
NURSEMAID
ODD JOB MAN
OFFICE BOY
OPERATIVE
ORDINATOR
OSTEOPATH
OTOLOGIST
OUTFITTER
PASQUILER
PAYMASTER
PEDAGOGUE
PERFORMER
PHYSICIAN
PHYSICIST
PINKMAKER
PITSAWYER
PLANISHER
PLASTERER
PLOUGHBOY
PLOUGHMAN
PLURALIST
POETASTER
POINTSMAN
POLICEMAN
POP ARTIST
PORTERESS
PORTRAYER
PORTREEVE
POSTILION
POSTWOMAN
POULTERER
PRACTISER
PRECENTOR
PRECEPTOR
PREDICANT
PRELECTOR
PRIESTESS
PRIVATEER
PROFESSOR
PROFILIST
PROVEDORE
PUBLICIST
PUBLISHER
PULPITEER
PUPPETEER
PYTHONESS
QUALIFIER
QUARRYMAN
RACKETEER
RAILMAKER
RECRUITER
REFORMIST
REHEARSER
RIBBONMAN

9—continued

ROADMAKER
ROPEMAKER
ROUNDSMAN
RUM-RUNNER
SACRISTAN
SAFEMAKER
SAILMAKER
SCARIFIER
SCAVENGER
SCENARIST
SCHOLIAST
SCHOOLMAN
SCIENTIST
SCRIVENER
SCYTHEMAN
SEA-ROBBER
SECRETARY
SHIPOWNER
SHIP'S MATE
SHOEBLACK
SHOEMAKER
SIGHTSMAN
SIGNALMAN
SINOLOGUE
SOAPMAKER
SOLICITOR
SONNETEER
SORCERESS
STABLEBOY
STABLEMAN
STAGEHAND
STATIONER
STAY-MAKER
STEERSMAN
STEVEDORE
SUBEDITOR
SUCCENTOR
SUR-MASTER
SWAN-UPPER
SWINEHERD
SWITCHMAN
SWORDSMAN
SYNDICATE
SYNOPTIST
TABLEMAID
TACTICIAN
TAILORESS
TEATASTER
TENTMAKER
TEST PILOT
THERAPIST
THEURGIST
THROWSTER
TIMBERMAN
TIREWOMAN
TOOLSMITH
TOWN CLERK
TOWNCRIER
TRADESMAN
TRAGEDIAN
TRAVELLER

9—continued

TREASURER
TREPANNER
TRIBUTARY
TRUMPETER
TYMPANIST
USHERETTE
VARNISHER
VERSIFIER
VETTURINO
VEXILLARY
VIOLINIST
VOLCANIST
VOLTIGEUR
WADSETTER
WARRANTEE
WARRANTER
WASHERMAN
WAXWORKER
WHITESTER
WINEMAKER
WOOD-REEVE
WORKWOMAN
ZOOKEEPER
ZOOLOGIST
ZOOTOMIST

10

ABLE SEAMAN
ACCOMPTANT
ACCOUCHEUR
ACCOUNTANT
ACOLOTHIST
ADVERTISER
AEROLOGIST
AGROLOGIST
AGRONOMIST
AIR HOSTESS
AIR STEWARD
ALGEBRAIST
AMANUENSIS
APOTHECARY
APPRENTICE
ARBALISTER
ARBITRATOR
ASTROLOGER
ASTRONOMER
ATMOLOGIST
AUCTIONEER
AUDIT CLERK
BALLOONIST
BALLPLAYER
BANDMASTER
BASEBALLER
BASSOONIST
BEADSWOMAN
BEAUTICIAN
BELL-HANGER
BELL-RINGER
BIOCHEMIST
BIOGRAPHER
BLACKSMITH

10–continued

BLADESMITH
BLOCKMAKER
BLUEJACKET
BOMBARDIER
BONDSWOMAN
BONESETTER
BOOKBINDER
BOOKHOLDER
BOOKKEEPER
BOOKSELLER
BOOTLEGGER
BRICKLAYER
BRICKMAKER
BRUSHMAKER
BUREAUCRAT
BUTTERWIFE
CARTOONIST
CARTWRIGHT
CASH-KEEPER
CAT BREEDER
CAT BURGLAR
CERAMICIST
CHAIR-MAKER
CHARGEHAND
CHARIOTEER
CHIRURGEON
CHORUS GIRL
CHRONICLER
CIRCUITEER
CLAIM AGENT
CLAPPER BOY
CLOCKMAKER
CLOG DANCER
CLOTH MAKER
COACHMAKER
COAL-BACKER
COAL-FITTER
COALHEAVER
COAL-MASTER
CO-ASSESSOR
COASTGUARD
COLLOCUTOR
COLLOQUIST
COLPORTEUR
COMEDIENNE
COMPOSITOR
COMPOUNDER
CONCORDIST
CONTRACTOR
CONTROLLER
COPYHOLDER
COPYWRITER
CORDWAINER
COUNSELLOR
CULTIVATOR
CUSTOMS MAN
CYTOLOGIST
DELINEATOR
DIRECTRESS
DISC JOCKEY
DISCOUNTER

10–continued

DISCOVERER
DISHWASHER
DISPATCHER
DISTRAINER
DISTRAINOR
DOCKMASTER
DOG BREEDER
DOG-FANCIER
DOORKEEPER
DRAMATURGE
DRESSMAKER
DRUMMER-BOY
DRY CLEANER
EMBLAZONER
EMBOWELLER
ENAMELLIST
EPHEMERIST
EPITAPHIST
EPITOMIZER
EVANGELIST
EXAMINATOR
EXPLORATOR
EYE-SERVANT
FELL-MONGER
FILE-CUTTER
FILIBUSTER
FILM EDITOR
FIREMASTER
FIRE-WORKER
FISHMONGER
FLIGHT CREW
FLOWERGIRL
FLUVIALIST
FOLK-DANCER
FOLK-SINGER
FORECASTER
FRAME-MAKER
FREEBOOTER
FUND RAISER
GAMEKEEPER
GAME WARDEN
GEAR-CUTTER
GEISHA GIRL
GENETICIST
GEOGRAPHER
GLEE-SINGER
GLOSSARIST
GLUE-BOILER
GOLD-BEATER
GOLD-DIGGER
GOLD-WASHER
GOVERNANTE
GRAMMARIAN
GUNSLINGER
HACKNEY-MAN
HALL PORTER
HANDMAIDEN
HARVESTMAN
HATCHELLER
HEAD PORTER
HEAD WAITER

10–continued

HIEROPHANT
HIGHWAYMAN
HORN PLAYER
HOROLOGIST
HORSECOPER
HORSE-LEECH
HOUSE AGENT
HUCKSTRESS
HUSBANDMAN
INOCULATOR
INSTITUTOR
INSTRUCTOR
INTERAGENT
IRONMONGER
IRONWORKER
JOURNALIST
JOURNEYMAN
KENNELMAID
KEYBOARDER
LAUNDRYMAN
LAW OFFICER
LEGISLATOR
LIBRETTIST
LIGHTERMAN
LIME-BURNER
LINOTYPIST
LIQUIDATOR
LOBSTERMAN
LOCK-KEEPER
LUMBERJACK
MAGISTRATE
MANAGERESS
MANICURIST
MANSERVANT
MATCHMAKER
MEAT-HAWKER
MEDICAL MAN
MILITIAMAN
MILLWRIGHT
MINERALIST
MINISTRESS
MINTMASTER
MISSIONARY
MOONSHINER
NATURALIST
NAUTCH GIRL
NEGOTIATOR
NEWSCASTER
NEWS EDITOR
NEWSVENDOR
NEWSWRITER
NIGHT NURSE
NOSOLOGIST
NURSERYMAN
OBITUARIST
OIL PAINTER
ORCHARDIST
OSTEOLOGER
OVERLOOKER
PANEGYRIST
PANTRYMAID

10–continued

PARK-KEEPER
PARK-RANGER
PASQUILANT
PASTRY-COOK
PATHFINDER
PAWNBROKER
PEARL-DIVER
PEDIATRIST
PEDICURIST
PELTMONGER
PENOLOGIST
PERRUQUIER
PHARMACIST
PHILOLOGER
PIANO TUNER
PICKPOCKET
PLATELAYER
PLAYWRIGHT
POLITICIAN
PORTIONIST
POSTILLION
POSTMASTER
PRESCRIBER
PRIMA DONNA
PRIVATE EYE
PROCURATOR
PROGRAMMER
PRONOUNCER
PROPRIETOR
PROSPECTOR
PROTRACTOR
PROVEDITOR
PUNCTURIST
PYROLOGIST
QUIZ-MASTER
RAILWAYMAN
RAT-CATCHER
RECITALIST
RESEARCHER
RINGMASTER
ROADMENDER
ROPEDANCER
ROUGHRIDER
SAFEBLOWER
SALES FORCE
SALESWOMAN
SCHOOLMARM
SCRUTINEER
SCULPTRESS
SEA-CAPTAIN
SEAMSTRESS
SECOND MATE
SEMINARIST
SERVING-MAN
SEXOLOGIST
SHIP-BROKER
SHIP-HOLDER
SHIPMASTER
SHIPWRIGHT
SHOPFITTER
SHOPKEEPER

10–continued

SHOPWALKER
SIGNWRITER
SILENTIARY
SILK-MERCER
SILK-WEAVER
SINOLOGIST
SKIRMISHER
SLOP SELLER
SNEAK THIEF
SOAP-BOILER
SPECIALIST
STAFF NURSE
STEERSMATE
STEWARDESS
STIPULATOR
STOCKTAKER
STONE-BORER
STONEMASON
STRATEGIST
STREET-WARD
SUPERCARGO
SUPERVISER
SURCHARGER
SURFACE-MAN
SWAN-KEEPER
SYMPHONIST
TALLY CLERK
TASKMASTER
TAXI-DRIVER
TEA-BLENDER
TEA PLANTER
TECHNICIAN
TECHNOCRAT
THEOGONIST
THEOLOGIAN
THEOLOGIST
THRENODIST
TIMEKEEPER
TRACTARIAN
TRADE UNION
TRAFFIC COP
TRAFFICKER
TRAM-DRIVER
TRANSACTOR
TRANSLATOR
TRAWLERMAN
TREASURESS
TROUBADOUR
TYPESETTER
UNDERTAKER
VETERINARY
VICTUALLER
VIVANDIÈRE
VOCABULIST
WAINWRIGHT
WARRIORESS
WATCHMAKER
WATERGUARD
WHARFINGER
WHITESMITH
WHOLESALER

10–continued

WINEGROWER
WINE-WAITER
WIREWORKER
WOODCARVER
WOODCUTTER
WOOD-MONGER
WOODWORKER
WOOL-CARDER
WOOL-COMBER
WOOL-DRIVER
WOOL-GROWER
WOOL-SORTER
WOOL-TRADER
WOOL-WINDER
YARDMASTER
ZINC-WORKER
ZOOGRAPHER
ZYMOLOGIST

11

ACCOMPANIST
ACCOUCHEUSE
ACOUSTICIAN
ADJUDICATOR
ALLOPATHIST
ANNUNCIATOR
ANTIQUARIAN
APPLE-GROWER
ARBITRATRIX
ARMY OFFICER
ARQUEBUSIER
ARTILLERIST
AUDIO TYPIST
AUSCULTATOR
BANK CASHIER
BANK MANAGER
BARGEMASTER
BASKETMAKER
BATTI-WALLAH
BATTOLOGIST
BEACHCOMBER
BELL-FOUNDER
BILL-STICKER
BIRD-CATCHER
BIRD-FANCIER
BIRD-WATCHER
BOATBUILDER
BODY SERVANT
BOILERSMITH
BONDSERVANT
BROADCASTER
BULLFIGHTER
CANDLEMAKER
CAR SALESMAN
CAT'S-MEAT-MAN
CHAIR-MENDER
CHALK-CUTTER
CHAMBERMAID
CHIFFONNIER
CHIROLOGIST
CHIROMANCER

11–continued

CHIROPODIST
CHOIRMASTER
CHRONOLOGER
CINDER-WENCH
CLOCK-SETTER
CLOTH-WORKER
COAL-WHIPPER
COFFIN-MAKER
COLLAR-MAKER
CONDISCIPLE
CONDOTTIERE
CONDUCTRESS
CONFEDERATE
CONGRESSMAN
CONSECRATOR
CONSERVATOR
CONVEYANCER
COPPERSMITH
COSMOGONIST
COSMOLOGIST
CRANE DRIVER
CRIMEWRITER
CUB REPORTER
CYPHER CLERK
DELIVERY MAN
DEMOGRAPHER
DISPENSATOR
DRAUGHTSMAN
DUTY OFFICER
ELECTRICIAN
EMBLEMATIST
EMBROIDERER
ENTERTAINER
ESTATE AGENT
ETHNOLOGIST
ETYMOLOGIST
EXECUTIONER
EXTORTIONER
FACE-PAINTER
FACTORY HAND
FAITH HEALER
FANCY-MONGER
FIELD WORKER
FIGURE-MAKER
FILING CLERK
FINESTILLER
FIRE INSURER
FLAX-DRESSER
FLESH-MONGER
FOURBISSEUR
FRINGE-MAKER
FRUIT PICKER
FUNAMBULIST
GALLEY-SLAVE
GENEALOGIST
GHOSTWRITER
GLASS-BENDER
GLASS-BLOWER
GLASS-CUTTER
GLASS-WORKER
GRAVE-DIGGER

11–continued

GREENGROCER
HABERDASHER
HAGIOLOGIST
HAIRDRESSER
HAIR STYLIST
HARDWAREMAN
HEDGE-PRIEST
HEDGE-WRITER
HIEROLOGIST
HISTOLOGIST
HORSE DOCTOR
HORSE TRADER
HOSPITALLER
HOTEL-KEEPER
HOUSEMASTER
HOUSEMOTHER
HYMNOLOGIST
ILLUMINATOR
ILLUSIONIST
ILLUSTRATOR
INFANTRYMAN
INSTITUTIST
INTERPRETER
INTERVIEWER
IRON-FOUNDER
IVORY-CARVER
IVORY-TURNER
IVORY-WORKER
KITCHENMAID
LAMPLIGHTER
LAND STEWARD
LAUNDRYMAID
LEADING LADY
LEDGER CLERK
LIFEBOATMAN
LIGHTKEEPER
LINEN DRAPER
LITHOLOGIST
LITHOTOMIST
LORRY DRIVER
MADRIGALIST
MAIDSERVANT
MAMMALOGIST
MASTER BAKER
MECHANICIAN
MEDICINE MAN
MEMORIALIST
MERCHANTMAN
METAL WORKER
MINIATURIST
MONEY-BROKER
MONEY-LENDER
MONOGRAPHER
MULE-SPINNER
MUSIC CRITIC
MUSIC MASTER
MYOGRAPHIST
MYSTERIARCH
MYTHOLOGIST
NECROLOGIST
NECROMANCER

11—continued

NEEDLEWOMAN
NEUROLOGIST
NEUROTOMIST
NIGHT PORTER
NIGHTWORKER
NOMENCLATOR
NUMISMATIST
OFFICE STAFF
ONION-SELLER
OPERA SINGER
OPHIOLOGIST
ORIENTALIST
ORTHOPEDIST
OSTEOLOGIST
PAMPHLETEER
PANEL-BEATER
PANTOMIMIST
PAPERHANGER
PARLOURMAID
PATHOLOGIST
PATTENMAKER
PEARLFISHER
PETROLOGIST
PETTIFOGGER
PHILATELIST
PHILOLOGIST
PHONOLOGIST
PHYTOLOGIST
POLYPHONIST
PORK BUTCHER
PORTRAITIST
PRECEPTRESS
PRINT-SELLER
PROBATIONER
PROMULGATOR
PROOFREADER
PROPERTY MAN
PROPRIETRIX
QUESTIONARY
RADIOLOGIST
RAG MERCHANT
REPRESENTER
REPUBLISHER
RHETORICIAN
ROADSWEEPER
SAFEBREAKER
SANDWICH MAN
SANSCRITIST
SAXOPHONIST
SCOUTMASTER
SCRAPDEALER
SCRIP-HOLDER
SECRET AGENT
SEDITIONARY
SERVANT GIRL
SERVING-MAID
SHARE-BROKER
SHEEPFARMER
SHEPHERDESS
SHIPBREAKER
SHIPBUILDER

11—continued

SHIP'S MASTER
SHOPSTEWARD
SILK-THROWER
SILVERSMITH
SLAUGHTERER
SLAVE-DRIVER
SLAVE-HOLDER
SMALLHOLDER
SOCIOLOGIST
STAGE-DRIVER
STEEPLEJACK
STOCKBROKER
STOCKJOBBER
STONECUTTER
STOREKEEPER
SUNDRIESMAN
SYSTEM-MAKER
TAXIDERMIST
TELEGRAPHER
TELEPHONIST
TICKET AGENT
TOASTMASTER
TOBACCONIST
TOOTH-DRAWER
TOPOGRAPHER
TORCH-BEARER
TOWN PLANNER
TOXOPHILITE
TRAIN-BEARER
TRANSCRIBER
TRANSPORTER
TRAVEL AGENT
TYPE-FOUNDER
TYPOGRAPHER
UNDERBEARER
UNDERLETTER
UNDERWRITER
UPHOLSTERER
VERSEMONGER
VINE-DRESSER
WASHERWOMAN
WATCHKEEPER
WAX-CHANDLER
WHEEL-CUTTER
WHEELWRIGHT
WHITEWASHER
WITCH-DOCTOR
WOOL-STAPLER
XYLOPHONIST
ZOOGRAPHIST

12

ACCORDIONIST
ACTOR MANAGER
AMBULANCE MAN
ANAESTHETIST
ANIMALCULIST
ARCHEOLOGIST
ARTILLERYMAN
BALLET DANCER
BALLET MASTER

12—continued

BANTAMWEIGHT
BELLOWS-MAKER
BIBLIOLOGIST
BIBLIOPEGIST
BIBLIOPOLIST
BOOKING CLERK
BUS CONDUCTOR
CABINET-MAKER
CALLIGRAPHER
CARICATURIST
CARPET-FITTER
CARTOGRAPHER
CATACLYSMIST
CEROGRAPHIST
CHEESEMONGER
CHIEF CASHIER
CHIMNEY-SWEEP
CHIROPRACTOR
CHRONOLOGIST
CHURCHWARDEN
CIRCUIT RIDER
CIVIL SERVANT
CLARINETTIST
CLERK OF WORKS
CLOTH-SHEARER
COACH-BUILDER
COLEOPTERIST
COMMISSIONER
CONCHOLOGIST
CONFECTIONER
CORN CHANDLER
COSMOGRAPHER
COSTERMONGER
CRAFTS-MASTER
CRANIOLOGIST
CRYPTOGAMIST
DANCE HOSTESS
DEEP-SEA DIVER
DEMONOLOGIST
DEMONSTRATOR
DENDROLOGIST
DRAMATURGIST
ECCLESIASTIC
EGYPTOLOGIST
ELECUTIONIST
ENGINE-DRIVER
ENTOMOLOGIST
ENTOMOTOMIST
ENTREPRENEUR
ESCAPOLOGIST
ETHNOGRAPHER
EXPERIMENTER
FAMILY DOCTOR
FARM LABOURER
FILM DIRECTOR
FILM PRODUCER
FIRST OFFICER
FLYING DOCTOR
FOOTPLATEMAN
GEOMETRICIAN
GERIATRICIAN

12—continued

GLASS-GRINDER
GLOSSOLOGIST
GREASEMONKEY
GUILD BROTHER
GYMNOSOPHIST
GYNECOLOGIST
HAGIOGRAPHER
HALIOGRAPHER
HARNESS-MAKER
HEAD GARDENER
HOMEOPATHIST
HORSE-BREAKER
HORSE-COURSER
HORSE-KNACKER
HOTEL MANAGER
HOUSEBREAKER
HOUSEPAINTER
HOUSE STEWARD
HOUSE SURGEON
HYDROGRAPHER
HYDROPATHIST
HYPOTHECATOR
IMMUNOLOGIST
IMPROPRIATOR
INSTRUCTRESS
INVOICE CLERK
JERRY-BUILDER
JOINT-TRUSTEE
JURISCONSULT
JUVENILE LEAD
KING'S COUNSEL
KNIFE-GRINDER
KNIFE-THROWER
LABOURING MAN
LAND SURVEYOR
LATH-SPLITTER
LEADER-WRITER
LEXICOLOGIST
LITHOGRAPHER
LONGSHOREMAN
LOSS ADJUSTER
LUMBER-DEALER
MAITRE D'HOTEL
MAKE-UP ARTIST
MALACOLOGIST
MANUAL WORKER
MANUFACTURER
MASS PRODUCER
MEAT-SALESMAN
METALLURGIST
MEZZO SOPRANO
MICROSCOPIST
MINERALOGIST
MISCELLANIST
MONEY-CHANGER
MONOGRAPHIST
MORRIS-DANCER
MOSAIC-ARTIST
MOSAIC-WORKER
MYTHOGRAPHER
NEWSPAPERMAN

12–continued

NUTRITIONIST
OBSTETRICIAN
OFFICE JUNIOR
ONEIROCRITIC
ORCHESTRATOR
ORGAN-BUILDER
ORGAN-GRINDER
ORTHODONTIST
ORTHOGRAPHER
OVARIOTOMIST
PAPER-STAINER
PATTERN-MAKER
PEDIATRICIAN
PHONOGRAPHER
PHOTOGRAPHER
PHRENOLOGIST
PHYSIOLOGIST
PLANT MANAGER
PLOUGHWRIGHT
PLUMBER'S MATE
PLYER-FOR-HIRE
POSTMISTRESS
PRACTITIONER
PRESS OFFICER
PRESTIGIATOR
PRISON WARDER
PRIZE-FIGHTER
PROFESSIONAL
PROPAGANDIST
PROPRIETRESS
PSYCHIATRIST
PSYCHOLOGIST
PUBLICITY MAN
PUPIL-TEACHER
PUPPET-PLAYER
QUARRY MASTER
RACING DRIVER
RADIOGRAPHER
RECEPTIONIST
REMEMBRANCER
RESTAURATEUR
RIDING-MASTER
RIGHT-HAND MAN
RUBBER-GRADER
SALES MANAGER
SCENE-PAINTER
SCENE-SHIFTER
SCHOOLMASTER
SCREENWRITER
SCRIPTWRITER
SCULLERY-MAID
SEED-MERCHANT
SEISMOLOGIST
SHARECROPPER
SHARPSHOOTER
SHIP CHANDLER
SHIP'S HUSBAND
SHOE-REPAIRER
SILVER-BEATER
SLAUGHTERMAN
SNAKE-CHARMER

12–continued

SOCIAL WORKER
SOIL MECHANIC
SPECIAL AGENT
SPEECHWRITER
SPICE-BLENDER
SPORTSCASTER
SPORTSWRITER
STAGE MANAGER
STATISTICIAN
STENOGRAPHER
STONEBREAKER
STONEDRESSER
STONESQUARER
STREET-TRADER
STREET-WALKER
SUGAR-REFINER
TAX-COLLECTOR
TECHNOLOGIST
TELEGRAPH BOY
TELEGRAPHIST
TEST ENGINEER
THERAPEUTIST
THIEF-CATCHER
TICKET-PORTER
TIMBER TRADER
TOLL-GATHERER
TOURIST AGENT
TOXICOLOGIST
TRADESPEOPLE
TRANSPLANTER
TRICHOLOGIST
UNDERMANAGER
UNDERSERVANT
VETERINARIAN
WAITING-WOMAN
WAREHOUSEMAN
WATER DIVINER
WINE MERCHANT
WOOD-ENGRAVER
WORKS MANAGER
ZINCOGRAPHER

13

ADMINISTRATOR
AGRICULTURIST
ANTIQUE DEALER
ARACHNOLOGIST
ARCHAEOLOGIST
ARITHMETICIAN
ARTICLED CLERK
ASSYRIOLOGIST
BARBER-SURGEON
BIBLIOGRAPHER
CALICO-PRINTER
CAMPANOLOGIST
CARTOGRAPHIST
CHARTOGRAPHER
CHICKEN-FARMER
CHIROGRAPHIST
CHOREOGRAPHER
CHRONOGRAPHER

13–continued

CIVIL ENGINEER
CLEARSTARCHER
COFFEE-PLANTER
COMETOGRAPHER
CONTORTIONIST
CONTRABANDIST
COTTON-SPINNER
COUNTER-CASTER
COUNTERFEITER
CRANIOSCOPIST
CRYPTOGRAPHER
DANCING MASTER
DEIPNOSOPHIST
DERMATOLOGIST
DIAGNOSTICIAN
DIAMOND-CUTTER
DRAUGHTSWOMAN
DRAWING-MASTER
DRESS DESIGNER
DRILL SERGEANT
ELECTROPLATER
ELECTROTYPIST
EMIGRATIONIST
ENCYCLOPEDIST
ENTOZOOLOGIST
EPIGRAMMATIST
ESTATE MANAGER
FENCING-MASTER
FORTUNE-TELLER
FREIGHT-BROKER
GALVANOLOGIST
GASTRILOQUIST
GLOSSOGRAPHER
GLYPHOGRAPHER
GROUND-BAILIFF
GYNAECOLOGIST
HARBOUR MASTER
HIEROGLYPHIST
HORSE-MILLINER
HOSPITAL NURSE
ICHTHYOLOGIST
INDUSTRIALIST
INTELLIGENCER
JOINT-EXECUTOR
LETTER-CARRIER
LETTER-FOUNDER
LEXICOGRAPHER
LIGHTHOUSE-MAN
MAID-OF-ALL-WORK
MASTER-BUILDER
MASTER MARINER
MATHEMATICIAN
MELODRAMATIST
METAPHYSICIAN
METEOROLOGIST
METOPOSCOPIST
MUSIC MISTRESS
NIGHT-WATCHMAN
OLD-CLOTHES-MAN
ORNITHOLOGIST
ORTHOGRAPHIST

13–continued

PARK ATTENDANT
PERIODICALIST
PHARMACEUTIST
PHYSIOGNOMIST
PHYSIOGRAPHER
POSTURE-MASTER
POULTRY FARMER
PRIVATEERSMAN
PROCESS-SERVER
PSALMOGRAPHER
PSYCHOANALYST
PTERIDOLOGIST
PUBLIC SPEAKER
QUEEN'S COUNSEL
RACING-TIPSTER
REVOLUTIONARY
REVOLUTIONIST
RUBBER-PLANTER
SAILING MASTER
SCHOOLTEACHER
SCIENCE MASTER
SHOP ASSISTANT
SILK-THROWSTER
SINGING-MASTER
STATION-MASTER
STENOGRAPHIST
STEREOSCOPIST
STETHOSCOPIST
STREET-SWEEPER
SUB-CONTRACTOR
SUPERINTENDER
SUPERNUMERARY
THAUMATURGIST
THIMBLE-RIGGER
TOLL COLLECTOR
TRADE UNIONIST
TRAMCAR-DRIVER
TRAM CONDUCTOR
VENTRILOQUIST
VIOLONCELLIST
WINDOW-CLEANER
WINDOW-DRESSER
WOOLLEN-DRAPER
WRITING-MASTER

14

ADMINISTRATRIX
ANTHROPOLOGIST
AUTOBIOGRAPHER
BACTERIOLOGIST
BALLET MISTRESS
BILLIARD-MARKER
BILLIARD-PLAYER
CHAMBER-COUNSEL
CHIMNEY-SWEEPER
CITIZEN-SOLDIER
CLASSICS MASTER
COLOUR SERGEANT
COMMISSIONAIRE
DANCING PARTNER
DISCOUNT-BROKER

14–continued
ECCLESIOLOGIST
EDUCATIONALIST
ENCYCLOPAEDIST
EXCHANGE-BROKER
GRAMMATICASTER
HANDICRAFTSMAN
HERESIOGRAPHER
HORTICULTURIST
HOUSE DECORATOR
HOUSE FURNISHER
LANGUAGE MASTER
LEATHER-DRESSER
MANUAL LABOURER
MARKET-GARDENER
MEDICAL OFFICER
MERCHANT-TAILOR
MISCELLANARIAN
MONEY-SCRIVENER
MOTHER-SUPERIOR
MUSIC PUBLISHER

14–continued
NAVAL PENSIONER
OPTHALMOLOGIST
PAINTER-STAINER
PHARMACOLOGIST
PNEUMATOLOGIST
PSALMOGRAPHIST
RECEPTION CLERK
REPRESENTATIVE
SCHOOLMISTRESS
SHIP'S-CARPENTER
SIDEROGRAPHIST
SPECTACLE-MAKER
SPECTROSCOPIST
SUPERINTENDENT
SYSTEMS ANALYST
TALLOW CHANDLER
WATER-COLOURIST
WEATHER PROPHET

15
ARBORICULTURIST

15–continued
ASSISTANT MASTER
BOW STREET
 RUNNER
CROSSING-
 SWEEPER
CRUSTACEOLOGIST
DANCING MISTRESS
DIAMOND
 MERCHANT
DOMESTIC SERVANT
FORWARDING
 AGENT
GENTLEMAN-
 FARMER
HACKNEY
 COACHMAN
HEART SPECIALIST
HELMINTHOLOGIST
HIEROGRAMMATIST
HISTORIOGRAPHER

15–continued
INSTRUMENTALIST
INSURANCE BROKER
MUSICAL DIRECTOR
NUMISMATOLOGIST
PALAEONTOLOGIST
PLATFORM-
 SPEAKER
PORTRAIT-PAINTER
PROGRAMME
 SELLER
PROVISION DEALER
RAILWAY ENGINEER
RESURRECTIONIST
SCRIPTURE-
 READER
SLEEPING PARTNER
STRETCHER-
 BEARER
TICKET COLLECTOR
TIGHTROPE
 WALKER

TOOLS

3
AWL
AXE
BIT
DIE
FAN
GAD
GIN
HOD
HOE
JIG
LOY
SAW
ZAX

4
ADZE
BILL
BORE
BROG
BURR
CART
CELT
CRAB
FILE
FORK
FROW
GAGE
HINK
HOOK
JACK

4–continued
LAST
LOOM
MALL
MAUL
MULE
NAIL
PICK
PIKE
PLOW
RAKE
RASP
RULE
SOCK
SPUD
TRUG
VICE
WHIM

5
ANVIL
AUGER
BEELE
BENCH
BESOM
BETTY
BEVEL
BLADE
BORER
BRACE
BURIN

5–continued
CHUCK
CHURN
CLAMP
CLAMS
CLASP
CLEAT
CRAMP
CRANE
CROOM
CROZE
CUPEL
DOLLY
DRILL
FLAIL
FLANG
FORGE
GAUGE
GAVEL
GOUGE
HOIST
INCUS
JACKS
JEMMY
JIMMY
KNIFE
LATHE
LEVEL
LEVER
MOWER
PARER

5–continued
PLANE
PLUMB
PREEN
PRISE
PRONG
PUNCH
QUERN
QUOIN
RATCH
RAZOR
SARSE
SCREW
SPADE
SPIKE
SPILE
SPILL
SWAGE
TEMSE
TOMMY
TONGS
TROMP
TRONE
WEDGE
WINCH

6
BARROW
BENDER
BLOWER
BODKIN

6–continued

BORCER
BOW-SAW
BRAYER
BROACH
BURTON
CHASER
CHISEL
COLTER
CREVET
CRUSET
DIBBER
DIBBLE
DOFFER
DREDGE
DRIVER
FANNER
FAUCET
FERRET
FOLDER
GIMLET
GRAVER
HACKLE
HAMMER
HARROW
JAGGER
JIGGER
JIG SAW
LADDER
MALLET
MORTAR
MULLER
OLIVER
PALLET
PENCIL
PESTLE
PITSAW
PLANER
PLIERS
PLOUGH
PONTEE
POOLER
RAMMER
RASPER
REAPER
RIDDLE
RIPSAW
RUBBER
SANDER
SAW-SET
SCREEN
SCYTHE
SEGGER
SHEARS
SHOVEL
SICKLE
SIFTER
SKEWER
SLEDGE
SLICER
SQUARE
STIDDY

6–continued

STITHY
STRIKE
TACKLE
TENTER
TREPAN
TROWEL
TUBBER
TURREL
WIMBLE
WRENCH

7

BOASTER
BRADAWL
CAPSTAN
CATLING
CAUTERY
CHAMFER
CHIP-AXE
CHOPPER
CLEAVER
COULOIR
COULTER
CRAMPON
CRISPER
CROWBAR
CUVETTE
DERRICK
DIAMOND
DOG-BELT
DRUDGER
FISTUCA
FORCEPS
FRETSAW
FRUGGIN
GRADINE
GRAINER
GRAPNEL
GRUB AXE
HACKSAW
HANDSAW
HATCHET
HAY FORK
JOINTER
MANDREL
MATTOCK
NIPPERS
NUT HOOK
PICKAXE
PIERCER
PINCERS
PLUMMET
POLE AXE
POUNDER
PRICKER
SALT-PAN
SCALPEL
SCAUPER
SCRAPER
SCREWER
SCRIBER

7–continued

SEED LOP
SPADDLE
SPANNER
SPITTLE
SPRAYER
STROCAL
TENONER
THIMBLE
TRESTLE
TRIBLET
T-SQUARE
TWIBILL
TWISTER
WHIP-SAW
WHITTLE
WOOLDER

8

BARK MILL
BAR SHEAR
BEAKIRON
BENCH PEG
BILL HOOK
BISTOURY
BLOOMARY
BLOWLAMP
BLOWPIPE
BOATHOOK
BOWDRILL
BULL NOSE
BUTTERIS
CALIPERS
CANTHOOK
CROW MILL
CRUCIBLE
DIE STOCK
DOWEL BIT
DRILL BOW
EDGE TOOL
FILATORY
FIRE KILN
FLAME GUN
FLAX COMB
GAVELOCK
GEE CRAMP
HANDLOOM
HANDMILL
HAND VICE
HAY KNIFE
HORSE HOE
LAPSTONE
LEAD MILL
MITRE BOX
MOLEGRIP
MUCK RAKE
NUT SCREW
OILSTONE
PAINT PAD
PANEL SAW
PICKLOCK
PINCHERS

8–continued

PLUMB BOB
POLISHER
POWER SAW
PRONG-HOE
PUNCHEON
REAP HOOK
SAW WREST
SCISSORS
SCUFFLER
SLATE AXE
STILETTO
STRICKLE
TENON SAW
THROSTLE
TOOTH KEY
TWEEZERS
TWIST BIT
WATERCAN
WATER RAM
WEED HOOK
WINDLASS
WINDMILL

9

BELT PUNCH
BENCH HOOK
BOLT AUGER
BOOT CRIMP
CANKER BIT
CANNIPERS
CAN OPENER
CENTRE BIT
COMPASSES
CORKSCREW
COTTON GIN
CRAMP IRON
CURRY COMB
CUTTER BAR
DOG CLUTCH
DRAW KNIFE
DRAW-PLATE
EXCAVATOR
EYELETEER
FILLISTER
FINING POT
FORK CHUCK
GAS PLIERS
HAMMER AXE
HANDBRACE
HANDSCREW
HANDSPIKE
HOLING AXE
HUMMELLER
IMPLEMENT
JACKKNIFE
JACKPLANE
JACKSCREW
LACE FRAME
LAWNMOWER
NAIL PUNCH
NUT WRENCH

9–continued
PITCH FORK
PLANE IRON
PLANISHER
PLUMBLINE
PLUMBRULE
SCREWJACK
SCRIBE AWL
SHEARLEGS
SHEEP HOOK
STEELYARD
SUGAR MILL
TIN OPENER
TRY SQUARE
TURF SPADE
TURN BENCH
TURNSCREW
WATERMILL

10
BUSH HARROW
CLASPKNIFE
CLAWHAMMER
COLD CHISEL
CRANE'S BILL
CULTIVATOR
DRAY PLOUGH
DRIFT BOLTS
DRILLPRESS
DRILLSTOCK
EMERY WHEEL
FIRING IRON
GRINDSTONE
INSTRUMENT
MASONRY BIT
MASTICATOR
MITRE BLOCK
MOTOR MOWER
MOULD BOARD
PAINTBRUSH
PERFORATOR
PIPE WRENCH
POINTED AWL
SCREW PRESS
SLEEK STONE
SNOWPLOUGH
SPOKESHAVE
STEAM PRESS
STEPLADDER

10–continued
TENTERHOOK
THUMBSCREW
THUMBSTALL
TILT HAMMER
TRIP HAMMER
TURF CUTTER
TURNBUCKLE
WATERCRANE
WATERGAUGE
WATERLEVEL
WHEEL BRACE

11
BRACE-AND-BIT
BREAST DRILL
CHAFF CUTTER
CHAIN BLOCKS
CHAIN WRENCH
CHEESE PRESS
COUNTERSINK
CRAZING MILL
CRISPING PIN
CROSSCUT SAW
DRILL BARROW
DRILL HARROW
DRILL PLOUGH
FANNING MILL
GRUBBING HOE
HELVEHAMMER
JAGGING IRON
MACHINE TOOL
MONKEY BLOCK
PAINT ROLLER
PLOUGHSHARE
PRUNING HOOK
RABBET PLANE
REAPING-HOOK
SAWING STOOL
SCREWDRIVER
SINGLE-EDGED
SKIM COULTER
SNATCH BLOCK
SPIRIT LEVEL
SQUARING ROD
STEAM HAMMER
STONE HAMMER
STRAW CUTTER
STRIKE BLOCK

11–continued
STUBBLE RAKE
SWARD CUTTER
SWINGPLOUGH
TAPEMEASURE
TURFING IRON
TWO-FOOT RULE
WARPING HOOK
WARPING POST
WEEDING FORK
WEEDING HOOK
WEEDING RHIM
WHEELBARROW

12
BARKING IRONS
BELT ADJUSTER
BRANDING IRON
BREASTPLOUGH
CAULKING TOOL
COUNTER GAUGE
CRADEL SCYTHE
CRAMPING IRON
CRIMPING IRON
CRISPING IRON
CURLING TONGS
DRILL GRUBBER
DRIVING SHAFT
DRIVING WHEEL
EMERY GRINDER
FLOUR DRESSER
GLASS FURNACE
HYDRAULIC RAM
MANDREL LATHE
MARLINE SPIKE
MONKEY WRENCH
PRUNING KNIFE
PULLEY BLOCKS
RUNNING BLOCK
SCRIBING IRON
SLEDGE HAMMER
SLIDING BEVEL
SOCKET CHISEL
STONE BREAKER
STRAIGHTEDGE
SWINGLE KNIFE
TOUCH NEEDLES
TRENCH PLOUGH
TURFING SPADE

12–continued
TURNING LATHE
WATER BELLOWS
WEEDING TONGS

13
CHOPPING BLOCK
CHOPPING KNIFE
CYLINDER PRESS
ELECTRIC DRILL
GRAPPLING-IRON
HYDRAULIC JACK
PACKING NEEDLE
SCRIBING BLOCK
SEWING MACHINE
SOLDERING BOLT
SOLDERING IRON
SOWING MACHINE
SPINNING JENNY
SPINNING WHEEL
STOCKING FRAME
SUBSOIL PLOUGH
TWO-HOLE PLIERS
WEEDING CHISEL

14
BLOWING MACHINE
CARDING MACHINE
DRAINING ENGINE
DRAINING PLOUGH
PENUMATIC DRILL
REAPING MACHINE
SMOOTHING PLANE
SWINGLING KNIFE
THRUSTING SCREW
WEEDING FORCEPS

15
CARPENTER'S
  BENCH
CRIMPING MACHINE
DREDGING MACHINE
DRILLING MACHINE
ENTRENCHING
  TOOL
PESTLE AND
  MORTAR
PUMP SCREW-
  DRIVER
WEIGHING MACHINE

MILITARY TERMS

TITLES

ROYAL AIR FORCE RANKS

MARSHAL OF THE RAF
AIR CHIEF MARSHAL
AIR MARSHAL
AIR VICE-MARSHAL
AIR COMMODORE
GROUP CAPTAIN
WING COMMANDER
SQUADRON LEADER
FLIGHT LIEUTENANT
FLYING OFFICER
PILOT OFFICER
MASTER PILOT
WARRANT OFFICER
FLIGHT SERGEANT
CHIEF TECHNICIAN
SERGEANT
CORPORAL
JUNIOR TECHNICIAN
SENIOR AIRCRAFTMAN
LEADING AIRCRAFTMAN

ARMY RANKS

FIELD MARSHAL
GENERAL
LIEUTENANT-GENERAL
MAJOR-GENERAL
BRIGADIER
COLONEL
LIEUTENANT-COLONEL
MAJOR
CAPTAIN
LIEUTENANT
SECOND-LIEUTENANT
REGIMENTAL SERGEANT-
  MAJOR
SERGEANT-MAJOR
STAFF/COLOUR-SERGEANT
SERGEANT
CORPORAL
LANCE-CORPORAL
PRIVATE

ROYAL NAVY RANKS

ADMIRAL OF THE FLEET
ADMIRAL
VICE-ADMIRAL
REAR-ADMIRAL
COMMODORE
CAPTAIN
COMMANDER
LIEUTENANT-COMMANDER
LIEUTENANT
SUB-LIEUTENANT
MIDSHIPMAN
WARRANT OFFICER
CHIEF PETTY OFFICER
PETTY OFFICER
LEADING RATE
ABLE RATE
ORDINARY RATE

BRITISH DECORATIONS AND MEDALS

AIR FORCE CROSS (AFC)
AIR FORCE MEDAL (AFM)
ALBERT MEDAL (AM)
CONSPICUOUS GALLANTRY MEDAL (CGM)
DISTINGUISHED FLYING CROSS (DFC)
DISTINGUISHED FLYING MEDAL (DFM)
DISTINGUISHED SERVICE CROSS (DSC)
DISTINGUISHED SERVICE MEDAL (DSM)

GEORGE CROSS (GC)
GEORGE MEDAL (GM)
MEDAL FOR DISTINGUISHED CONDUCT IN
  THE FIELD (DCM)
MILITARY CROSS (MC)
MILITARY MEDAL (MM)
THE DISTINGUISHED SERVICE ORDER (DSO)
VICTORIA CROSS (VC)

US DECORATIONS AND MEDALS

AIR FORCE CROSS
AIRMAN'S MEDAL
BRONZE STAR MEDAL
COAST GUARD MEDAL
DISTINGUISHED SERVICE CROSS
DISTINGUISHED FLYING CROSS
DISTINGUISHED SERVICE MEDAL
LEGION OF MERIT

MEDAL OF HONOR
NAVY CROSS
NAVY/MARINE CORPS MEDAL
PURPLE HEART MEDAL
SILVER STAR MEDAL
SOLDIER'S MEDAL
SUPERIOR SERVICE MEDAL

BATTLES

2
RÉ, ÎLE DE (1627, Anglo-French Wars)

3
ACS (1849, Hungarian Rising)
AIX, ÎLE D' (1758, Seven Years' War)
DEE, BRIG OF (1639, Bishops' War)
GOA (1511, 1570, Portuguese Conquest)
HUÉ (1968, Vietnam War)
ULM (1805, Napoleonic Wars)

4
ACRE (1189–1191, Third Crusade; 1291,
    Crusader-Turkish Wars; 1799, French
    Revolutionary Wars; 1840, Egyptian Revolt)
AGRA (1803, Second British-Maratha War; 1857,
    Indian Mutiny)
ALMA (1854, Crimean War)
AONG (1857, Indian Mutiny)
ARAS (1775, First British-Maratha War)
AVUS (198 BC, Second Macedonian War)
BAZA (1489, Spanish-Muslim Wars)
BEDR (623, Islamic Wars)
BEGA (1696, Ottoman Wars)
CUBA (1953, Castro Revolt)
DEEG (1780, First British-Maratha War; 1804,
    Second British-Maratha War)
GAZA (332 BC, Alexander's Asiatic Campaigns;
    312 BC, Wars of Alexander's Successors; 1917,
    World War I)
GELT, THE (1570, Anglo-Scottish Wars)
GUAM (1944, World War II)
JENA (1806, Napoleonic Wars)
KARS (1855, Crimean War)
KIEV (1941, World War II)
KULM (1813, Napoleonic Wars)
LAON (1814, Napoleonic Wars)
LECK, THE (1632, Thirty Years' War)
LENS (1648, Thirty Years' War)
LÓDŹ (1914, World War I)
MAIN, THE (9 BC, Germanic War)
MAYA, COLDE (1813, Peninsular War)
METZ (1870, Franco-Prussian War)
NEON (354 BC, Sacred War)
NILE (1798, French Revolutionary Wars)
NIVE (1813, Peninsular War)
NOVI (1799, French Revolutionary Wars)
ONAO (1857, Indian Mutiny)
ORAN (1509, Spanish Invasion of Morocco;
    1940, World War II)
OREL (1943, World War II)
RAAB (1809, Napoleonic Wars)
ROME (387 BC, First Invasion of the Gauls; 408,
    Wars of the Western Roman Empire; 472,
    Ricimer's Rebellion; 537, 546, Wars of the
    Byzantine Empire; 1082, Norman Seizure;
    1527, Wars of Charles V; 1849, Italian Wars of
    Independence)

4–continued
SCIO (1769, Ottoman Wars)
SOHR (1745, War of the Austrian Succession)
ST LÔ (1944, World War II)
TOBA (1868, Japanese Revolution)
TROY (1100 BC)
TRUK (1944, World War II)
VEII (405 BC, Rise of Rome)
ZELA (67 BC, Third Mithridatic War; 47 BC, Wars
    of the First Triumvirate)

5
ACCRA (1824, 1825, First British-Ashanti War)
ADUWA (1896, Italian Invasion of Ethiopia)
ALAMO, STORMING OF THE (1836, Texan
    Rising)
ALLIA, THE (390 BC, The First Invasion of the
    Gauls)
ALSEN (1864, Schleswig-Holstein War)
ANZIO (1944, World War II)
ARGOS (195 BC, Roman Invasion of Greece)
ARIUS (214 BC, The Wars of the Hellenistic
    Monarchies)
ARRAH (1857, Indian Mutiny)
ARRAS (1654, Wars of Louis XIV; 1917, World
    War I)
A SHAU (1966, Vietnam War)
AURAY (1364, Hundred Years' War)
BAHUR (1752, Seven Years' War)
BANDA (1858, Indian Mutiny)
BANDS, THE (961, Danish Invasion of Scotland)
BEREA (1852, Kaffir Wars)
BETWA, THE (1858, Indian Mutiny)
BOYNE, THE (1690, War of the Grand Alliance)
BREST (1512, War of the Holy League)
BRILL (1572, Netherlands War of Independence)
BURMA (1942, 1943, World War II)
BUXAR (1764, British Conquest of Bengal)
CADIZ (1587, Anglo-Spanish War)
CAIRO (1517, Ottoman Wars)
CARPI (1701, War of the Spanish Succession)
CEŞME (1770, Ottoman Wars)
CRÉCY (1346, Hundred Years' War)
CRETE (1941, World War II)
DAK TO (1967, Vietnam War)
DELHI (1297, First Tatar Invasion of India; 1398,
    Second Tatar Invasion; 1803, Second British-
    Maratha War; 1804, Second British-Maratha
    War; 1857, Indian Mutiny)
DOUAI (1710, War of the Spanish Succession)
DOURO (1809, Peninsular War)
DOVER (1652, Anglo-Dutch Wars)
DOWNS, THE (1666, Anglo-Dutch Wars)
ELENA (1877, Russo-Turkish War)
EL TEB (1884, British-Sudan Campaigns)
EMESA (272, Wars of the Roman Empire)
ENGEN (1800, French Revolutionary Wars)

5–continued

EYLAU (1807, Napoleonic Wars)
GENOA (1746, Patriotic Rising; 1795, 1800, French Revolutionary Wars)
GOITS (1848, Italian Wars of Independence)
GUBAT (1885, British Sudan Campaigns)
HANAU (1813, Napoleonic Wars)
HIPPO (430, Wars of the Western Roman Empire)
IMOLA (1797, French Revoutionary Wars)
ISSUS (333 BC, Alexander's Asiatic Campaigns; 1488, Ottoman Wars)
JASSY (1620, Ottoman Wars)
KAGUL (1770, Ottoman Wars)
KALPI (1858, Indian Mutiny)
KAREE (1900, Second Boer War)
KAZAN (1774, Cossack Rising)
KOLIN (1757, Seven Years' War)
KOTAH (1858, Indian Mutiny)
LAGOS (1693, War of the Grand Alliance)
LA PAZ (1865, Bolivian Civil War)
LARGS (1263, Norse Invasion of Scotland)
LEWES (1264, Barons' Wars)
LEYTE (1944, World War II)
LIÈGE (1914, World War I)
LIGNY (1815, Napoleonic Wars)
LILLE (1708, War of the Spanish Succession)
LISSA (1866, Seven Weeks' War)
LUZON (1945, World War II)
LYONS (197, Civil Wars of the Roman Empire)
MAIDA (1806, Napoleonic Wars)
MALTA (1565, Ottoman Wars; 1798, French Revolutionary Wars; 1942, World War II)
MARNE (1914, 1918, World War I)
MAXEN (1759, Seven Years' War)
MUDKI (1845, First British-Sikh War)
MUNDA (45 BC, Civil War of Caesar and Pompey)
MURSA (351, Civil Wars of the Roman Empire)
MYLEX (36 BC, Wars of the Second Triumvirate)
NAMUR (1914, World War I)
PARIS (1814, Napoleonic Wars; 1870, Franco-Prussian War)
PATAY (1429, Hundred Years' War)
PODOL (1866, Seven Weeks' War)
PRUTH, THE (1770, Ottoman Wars)
RAMLA (1177, Crusader-Turkish Wars)
REDAN, THE GREAT (1855, Crimean War)
REIMS (1814, Napoleonic Wars)
ROUEN (1418, Hundred Years' War)
SEDAN (1870, Franco-Prussian War)
SELBY (1644, English Civil War)
SEOUL (1950, Korean War)
SLUYS (1340, Hundred Years' War)
SOMME (1916, 1918, World War I)
SPIRA (1703, War of the Spanish Succession)
SPURS (1302, Flemish War; 1513, Anglo-French Wars)
STOKE (1487, Lambert Simnel's Rebellion)
TAMAI (1884, British Sudan Campaigns)
TEXEL (1653, Anglo-Dutch Wars)
TOURS (732, Muslim Invasion of France)

5–continued

TUNIS (255 BC, First Punic War; 1270, Eighth Crusade)
TURIN (312, Civil Wars of the Roman Empire; 1706, War of the Spanish Succession)
UTICA (49 BC, Civil War of Caesar and Pompey; 694, Muslim Conquest of Africa)
VALMY (1792, French Revolutionary Wars)
VARNA (1444, Anti-Turkish Crusade; 1828, Ottoman Wars)
VARUS, DEFEAT OF (AD 9, Wars of the Roman Empire)
VASAQ (1442, Ottoman Wars)
WAVRE (1815, Napoleonic Wars)
WÖRTH (1870, Franco-Prussian War)
YPRES (1914, 1915, 1917, World War I)
ZENTA (1679, Ottoman Wars)
ZNAIM (1809, Napoleonic Wars)

6

AACHEN (1944, World War II)
ABUKIR (1799, 1801, French Revolutionary Wars)
ABU KRU (1885, British Sudan Campaigns)
ACTIUM (31 BC, Wars of the Second Triumvirate)
ALEPPO (638, Muslim Invasion of Syria; 1400, Tatar Invasion of Syria; 1516, Ottoman Wars)
ALFORD (1645, English Civil War)
ALIWAL (1846, First British-Sikh War)
AMIENS (1870, Franco-Prussian War)
ANGORA (1402, Tatar Invasion of Asia Minor)
ARBELA (331 BC, Alexander's Asiatic Campaigns)
ARCOLA (1796, French Revolutionary Wars)
ARGAON (1803, Second British-Maratha War)
ARKLOW (1798, Irish Rebellion)
ARNHEM (1944, World War II)
ARSOUF (1191, Third Crusade)
ARTOIS (1915, World War I)
ASHTEE (1818, Third British-Maratha War)
ASIAGO (1916, World War I)
ASPERN (1809, Napoleonic Wars)
ASSAYE (1803, Second British-Maratha War)
ATBARA (1898, British Sudan Campaigns)
AZORES (1591, Anglo-Spanish War)
BARDIA (1941, World War II)
BARNET (1471, Wars of the Roses)
BASING (871, Danish Invasion of Britain)
BAYLEN (1808, Peninsular War)
BEAUGÉ (1421, Hundred Years' War)
BENDER (1768, Ottoman Wars)
BERGEN (1759, Seven Years' War)
BEYLAN (1831, Egyptian Revolt)
BILBAO (1937, Spanish Civil War)
BUSACO (1810, Peninsular War)
CALAIS (1346, Hundred Years' War; 1558, Anglo-French Wars)
CAMDEN (1780, American Revolutionary War)
CAMPEN (1759, Seven Years' War)
CHANDA (1818, Third British-Maratha War)
CHIARI (1701, War of the Spanish Succession)
CHIZAI (1372, Hundred Years' War)

6–continued

DANZIG (1627, Thirty Years' War; 1807, 1813, Napoleonic Wars)
DARGAI (1897, British Northwest Frontier Campaign)
DELPHI (355 BC, Sacred War)
DENAIN (1712, War of the Spanish Succession)
DESSAU (1626, Thirty Years' War)
DIEPPE (1942, World War II)
DJERBA (1560, Ottoman Wars)
DOLLAR (875, Danish Invasions of Scotland)
DUNBAR (1296, 1339, Wars of Scottish Independence; 1650, Cromwell's Scottish Campaign)
DUNDEE (1899, Second Boer War)
DÜPPEL (1864, Schleswig-Holstein War)
ERBACH (1800, French Revolutionary Wars)
FERKEH (1896, British Sudan Campaigns)
GAZALA (1942, World War II)
GEBORA (1811, Peninsular War)
GERONA (1809, Peninsular War)
GHAZNI (1839, First British-Afghan War)
GISORS (1197, Anglo-French Wars)
GROZKA (1739, Ottoman Wars)
HALLUE (1870, Franco-Prussian War)
HARLAW (1411, Scottish Civil Wars)
HASHIN (1885, British Sudan Campaigns)
HAVANA (1748, War of the Austrian Succession; 1762, Seven Years' War)
HEXHAM (1464, Wars of the Roses)
HÖCHST (1622, Thirty Years' War)
INCHON (1950, Korean War)
INGOGO (1881, First Boer War)
ISMAIL (1790, Ottoman Wars)
ISONZO (1915, World War I)
JERSEY (1550, Anglo-French Wars)
JHANSI (1857, Indian Mutiny)
KHELAT (1839, First British-Afghan War)
KIRKEE (1817, Third British-Maratha War)
KOKEIN (1824, First Burma War)
KOTZIN (1622, 1673, Ottoman Wars)
KRONIA (1738, Ottoman Wars)
LANDAU (1702, War of the Spanish Succession)
LANDEN (1693, War of the Grand Alliance)
LAWARI (1803, Second British-Maratha War)
LE MANS (1871, Franco-Prussian War)
LERIDA (1642, 1647, Thirty Years' War)
LONATO (1796, French Revolutionary Wars)
LUTTER (1626, Thirty Years' War)
LÜTZEN (1632, Thirty Years' War; 1813, Napoleonic Wars)
MADRAS (1746, War of the Austrian Succession; 1758, Seven Years' War)
MADRID (1936, Spanish Civil War)
MAIDAN (1842, First British-Afghan War)
MAJUBA (1881, First Boer War)
MALAGA (1487, Spanish-Muslim Wars; 1704, War of the Spanish Succession)
MALAYA (1941, World War II)
MALDON (991, Danish Invasions of Britain)
MANILA (1898, Spanish-American War)
MANTUA (1797, French Revolutionary Wars)
MARGUS (285, Civil Wars of the Roman Empire)

6–continued

MEDOLA (1796, French Revolutionary Wars)
MERTON (871, Danish Invasions of Britain)
MEXICO (1520, Conquest of Mexico)
MINDEN (1759, Seven Years' War)
MOHACZ (1526, 1687, Ottoman Wars)
MORAWA (1443, Ottoman Wars)
MOSCOW (1941, World War II)
MUKDEN (1905, Russo-Japanese War; 1948, Chinese Civil War)
MULTAN (1848, Second British-Sikh War)
MUTINA (43 BC, Roman Civil Wars)
MYTTON (1319, Wars of Scottish Independence)
NACHOD (1866, Seven Weeks' War)
NÁJARA (1367, Hundred Years' War)
NASEBY (1645, English Civil War)
NICAEA (1097, First Crusade)
NORWAY (1940, World War II)
OCKLEY (851, Danish Invasions of Britain)
OLMÜTZ (1758, Seven Years' War)
OPORTO (1809, Peninsular War)
ORTHEZ (1814, Peninsular War)
OSTEND (1601, Netherlands War of Independence)
OSWEGO (1756, Seven Years' War)
OTUMBA (1520, Spanish Conquest of Mexico)
PEKING (1214, Tatar Invasion of China)
PLEI ME (1965, Vietnam War)
PLEVNA (1877, Russo-Turkish War)
POLAND (1939, World War II)
PONANI (1780, First British-Mysore War)
PRAGUE (1620, Thirty Years' War; 1757, Seven Years' War)
QUEBEC (1759, 1760, Seven Years' War)
RABAUL (1943, World War II)
RAPHIA (217 BC, Wars of the Hellenistic Monarchies)
RASZYN (1809, Napoleonic Wars)
RHODES (1480, Ottoman Wars)
RIVOLI (1797, French Revolutionary Wars)
ROCROI (1643, Thirty Years' War)
ROLICA (1808, Peninsular War)
RUMANI (1915, World War I)
SACILE (1809, Napoleonic Wars)
SADOWA (1866, Seven Weeks' War)
SAIGON (1968, Vietnam War)
SAINTS, THE (1782, American Revolutionary War)
SANGRO (1943, World War II)
SHILOH (1862, American Civil War)
SICILY (1943, World War II)
SINOPE (1853, Crimean War)
SORATA (1780, Inca Rising)
STE FOY (1760, Seven Years' War)
ST KITS (1667, Anglo-Dutch Wars)
TAURIS (47 BC, Civil War of Caesar and Pompey)
THURII (282 BC, Roman Civil Wars)
TOBRUK (1941, 1942, World War II)
TOFREK (1885, British-Sudan Campaigns)
TORGAU (1760, Seven Years' War)
TOULON (1707, War of the Spanish Succession; 1744, War of the Austrian Succession; 1793, French Revolutionary Wars)

6–continued

TOWTON (1461, Wars of the Roses)
TSINAN (1948, Chinese Civil War)
TUDELA (1808, Peninsular War)
ULUNDI (1879, Zulu-British War)
USHANT (1794, French Revolutionary Wars)
VENICE (1848, Italian Wars of Independence)
VERDUN (1916, World War I)
VERONA (312, Civil Wars of the Roman Empire)
VIENNA (1529, 1683, Ottoman Wars)
WAGRAM (1809, Napoleonic Wars)
WARSAW (1831, Second Polish Rising; 1914, World War I; 1918, Russo-Polish War; 1939, 1944, World War II)
WERBEN (1631, Thirty Years' War)
WIAZMA (1812, Napoleonic Wars)
ZÜRICH (1799, French Revolutionary Wars)

7

ABRAHAM, PLAINS OF (1759, Seven Years' War)
ABU KLEA (1885, British Sudan Campaigns)
ALBUERA (1811, Peninsular War)
ALGIERS (1775, Spanish-Algerian War; 1816, Bombardment of)
ALIGARH (1803, First British-Maratha War)
ALKMAAR (1573, Netherlands War of Independence; 1799, French Revolutionary Wars)
ALMORAH (1815, British-Gurkha War)
ALNWICK (1093, Anglo-Scottish Wars)
AMOAFUL (1874, Second British-Ashanti War)
ANTIOCH (1097, First Crusade)
ANTWERP (1576, Netherlands War of Independence; 1832, Liberation of Belgium; 1914, World War I)
ARIKERA (1791, Second British-Mysore War)
ASCALON (1099, First Crusade)
ASHDOWN (871, Danish Invasion of Britain)
ATHENRY (1316, Conquest of Ireland)
AUGHRIM (1691, War of the English Succession)
BAGHDAD (1401, Mongul Invasion of Mesopotamia)
BALKANS (1940, 1944, World War II)
BAROSSA (1811, Peninsular War)
BASSANO (1796, French Revolutionary Wars)
BASSEIN (1780, First British-Maratha War)
BATAVIA (1811, Napoleonic Wars)
BAUTZEN (1813, Napoleonic Wars)
BELMONT (1899, Second Boer War)
BENBURB (1646, Great Irish Rebellion)
BÉTHUNE (1707, War of the Spanish Succession)
BIBERAC (1796, French Revolutionary Wars)
BOURBON (1810, Napleonic Wars)
BRESLAU (1757, Seven Years' War)
BRIENNE (1814, Napoleonic Wars)
BULL RUN (1861, 1862, American Civil War)
CADSAND (1357, Hundred Years' War)
CALAFAT (1854, Crimean War)
CALICUT (1790, Second British-Mysore War)
CARIGAT (1791, Second British-Mysore War)
CASSINO (1944, World War II)

7–continued

CHETATÉ (1854, Crimean War)
COLENSO (1899, Second Boer War)
COLOMBO (1796, French Revolutionary Wars)
CORINTH (394 BC, Corinthian War; 1862, American Civil War)
CORONEL (1914, World War I)
CORUMBA (1877, Paraguayan War)
CORUNNA (1809, Peninsular War)
CRAONNE (1814, Napoleonic Wars)
CRAVANT (1423, Hundred Years' War)
CREFELD (1758, Seven Years' War)
CROTOYE (1347, Hundred Years' War)
CURICTA (49 BC, Civil War of Caesar and Pompey)
DEORHAM (577, Wessex against the Welsh)
DODOWAH (1826, First British-Ashanti War)
DRESDEN (1813, Napleonic Wars)
DUNDALK (1318, Scottish Invasion of Ireland)
DUNKELD (1689, Jacobite Rising)
DUNKIRK (1940, World War II)
DUPPLIN (1332, Baliol's Rising)
ECKMÜHL (1809, Napoleonic Wars)
ELK HORN (1862, American Civil War)
ESSLING (1809, Napoleonic Wars)
EVESHAM (1265, Barons' War)
FALKIRK (1298, Wars of Scottish Independence; 1746, The Forty-five Rebellion)
FERRARA (1815, Napoleon's Hundred Days)
FLEURUS (1622, Thirty Years' War; 1690, War of the Grand Alliance; 1794, French Revolutionary Wars)
FLODDEN (1513, Anglo-Scottish Wars)
FRANLIN (1864, American Civil War)
FULFORD (1066, Norse Invasion of England)
GALICIA (1914, World War I)
GATE PAH (1864, Maori-British War)
GHERAIN (1763, British Conquest of Bengal)
GHOAINE (1842, First British-Afghan War)
GORARIA (1857, Indian Mutiny)
GORLICE (1915, World War I)
GRASPAN (1899, Second Boer War)
GRENADA (1779, American Revolutionary War; 1983, American Invasion)
GUJERAT (1849, Second British-Sikh War)
GWALIOR (1780, First British-Maratha War; 1858, Indian Mutiny)
HAARLEM (1572, Netherlands War of Independence)
HASLACH (1805, Napoleonic Wars)
HOOGHLY, THE (1759, Anglo-Dutch Wars in India)
IWO-JIMA (1945, World War II)
JAMAICA (1655, Anglo-Spanish Wars)
JAVA SEA (1942, World War II)
JITGURH (1815, British Gurkha War)
JUTLAND (1916, World War I)
KALUNGA (1814, British-Gurkha War)
KAMBULA (1879, Zulu War)
KASHGAL (1883, British Sudan Campaigns)
KHARKOV (1942, 1943, World War II)
KHE SANH (1968, Vietnam War)

7—continued

KILSYTH (1645, English Civil War)
KINEYRI (1848, Second British-Sikh War)
KINLOSS (1009, Danish Invasion of Scotland)
KINSALE (1601, O'Neill's Rebellion)
KRASNOI (1812, Napoleonic Wars)
LA HOGUE (1692, War of the Grand Alliance)
L'ECLUSE (1340, Hundred Years' War)
LEGHORN (1653, Anglo-Dutch Wars)
LEIPZIG (1631, Thirty Years' War; 1813, Napoleonic Wars)
LEUTHEN (1757, Seven Years' War)
LINCOLN, FAIR OF (1217, First Barons' War)
LINDLEY (1900, Second Boer War)
LOCNINH (1967, Vietnam War)
LUCKNOW (1857, Indian Mutiny)
MAIWAND (1880, Second British-Afghan War)
MALAKOV (1855, Crimean War)
MANSÛRA (1250, Seventh Crusade)
MARENGO (1800, French Revolutionary Wars)
MARGATE (1387, Hundred Years' War)
MAROSCH, THE (101, Roman Empire Wars)
MATAPAN, CAPE (1941, World War II)
MEMPHIS (1862, American Civil War)
METHVEN (1306, Wars of Scottish Independence)
MINORCA (1756, Seven Years' War; 1762, American Revolutionary War)
MOGILEV (1812, Napoleonic Wars)
MOSKOWA (1812, Napoleonic Wars)
NAM DONG (1964, Vietnam War)
NANKING (1949, Chinese Civil War)
NEUWIED (1797, French Revolutionary Wars)
NEWBURN (1640, Anglo-Scottish Wars)
NEWBURY (1643, 1644, English Civil War)
NEW ROSS (1798, Irish Rebellion)
NIAGARA (1759, Seven Years' War)
NIVELLE (1813, Peninsular War)
OKINAWA (1945, World War II)
OOSCATA (1768, First British-Mysore War)
OPEQUAN (1864, American Civil War)
ORLÉANS (1428, Hundred Years' War)
PARKANY (1663, Ottoman Wars)
PLASSEY (1757, Seven Years' War)
POLOTSK (1812, Napoleonic Wars)
PRESTON (1648, English Civil War; 1715, The Fifteen Rebellion)
PULTUSK (1806, Napoleonic Wars)
RASTADT (1796, French Revolutionary Wars)
READING (871, Danish Invasions of Britain)
RIO SECO (1808, Peninsular War)
RUMANIA (1916, World War I)
RUSPINA (46 BC, Civil War of Caesar and Pompey)
SABUGAL (1811, Peninsular War)
SAGUNTO (1811, Peninsular War)
SALERNO (1943, World War II)
SAN JUAN (1898, Spanish-American War)
SCUTARI (1474, Ottoman Wars)
SEALION, OPERATION (1940, World War II)
SENEKAL (1900, Second Boer War)
SHARQAT (1918, World War I)

7—continued

SINUIJU (1951, Korean War)
SKALITZ (1866, Seven Weeks' War)
SOBRAON (1846, First British-Sikh War)
ST DENIS (1567, French Religious Wars; 1837, French-Canadian Rising)
ST LUCIA (1794, French Revolutionary Wars)
SURINAM (1804, Napoleonic Wars)
TALNEER (1818, Third British-Maratha War)
TANJORE (1758, Seven Years' War; 1773, First British-Mysore War)
TARANTO (1940, World War II)
THAPSUS (46 BC, Civil War of Caesar and Pompey)
TREBBIA (1799, French Revolutionary Wars)
TRIPOLI (643, Muslim Conquest of Africa)
TUNISIA (1942, World War II)
UKRAINE (1943, World War II)
VIMEIRO (1808, Peninsular War)
VINAROZ (1938, Spanish Civil War)
VITORIA (1813, Peninsular War)
WARBURG (1760, Seven Years' War)
WARGAOM (1779, First British-Maratha War)
WEPENER (1900, Second Boer War)
WIMPFEN (1622, Thirty Years' War)
WINKOVO (1812, Napoleonic Wars)

8

ABERDEEN (1644, English Civil War)
ABU HAMED (1897, British Sudan Campaigns)
ACAPULCO (1855, Mexican Liberal Rising)
ALICANTE (1706, War of the Spanish Succession)
AMALINDE (1818, Kaffir Wars)
ANTIETAM (1862, American Civil War)
ASIRGHAR (1819, Third British-Maratha War)
ASSUNDUN (1016, Danish Invasions of Britain)
ATLANTIC (1917, World War I)
AULDEARN (1645, English Civil War)
AZIMGHUR (1858, Indian Mutiny)
BAGRADAS (49 BC, Wars of the First Triumvirate)
BASTOGNE (1944, World War II)
BEDA FOMM (1941, World War II)
BELGRADE (1456, 1717, 1789, Ottoman Wars)
BEREZINA (1812, Napoleonic Wars)
BEYMAROO (1841, First British-Afghan War)
BISMARCK (1941, World War II)
BLENHEIM (1704, War of the Spanish Succession)
BLUEBERG (1806, Napoleonic Wars)
BORODINO (1812, Napoleonic Wars)
BOULOGNE (1544, Anglo-French Wars)
BOUVINES (1214, Anglo-French Wars)
BROOKLYN (1776, American Revolutionary War)
CALCUTTA (1756, Seven Years' War)
CALDIERO (1796, French Revolutionary Wars; 1805, Napoleonic Wars)
CARLISLE (1745, The Forty-five Rebellion)
CARRICAL (1758, Seven Years' War)
CARTHAGE (533, Byzantine Empire Wars)
CASTELLA (1813, Peninsular War)

8–continued

CAWNPORE (1857, Indian Mutiny)
CHERITON (1644, English Civil War)
CLONTARF (1014, Norse Invasion of Ireland)
COCHEREL (1364, Hundred Years' War)
CORAL SEA (1942, World War II)
CULLODEN (1746, The Forty-five Rebellion)
CZARNOVO (1806, Napoleonic Wars)
DAMASCUS (1918, World War I)
DOMINICA (1782, American Revolutionary War)
DROGHEDA (1641, Great Irish Rebellion; 1649, Cromwell's Campaign in Ireland)
DRUMCLOG (1679, Covenanters' Rising)
EDGEHILL (1642, English Civil War)
ESPINOSA (1808, Peninsular War)
ETHANDUN (878, Danish Invasions of Britain)
FAIR OAKS (1862, American Civil War)
FLANDERS (1940, World War II)
FLORENCE (406, Wars of the Western Roman Empire)
FLUSHING (1809, Napoleonic Wars)
FORMIGNY (1450, Hundred Years' War)
FREIBURG (1644, Thirty Years' War)
FRETEVAL (1194, Anglo-French Wars)
GAULAULI (1858, Indian Mutiny)
GITSCHIN (1866, Seven Weeks' War)
GOODWINS, THE (1666, Anglo-Dutch Wars)
GRAF SPEE (1939, World War II)
GÜNZBURG (1805, Napoleonic Wars)
HASTINGS (1066, Norman Conquest)
HERACLEA (280 BC, Pyrrhus' Invasion of Italy; 313, Roman Civil Wars)
HERRINGS, THE (1429, Hundred Years' War)
HONG KONG (1941, World War II)
INKERMAN (1854, Crimean War)
JEMAPPES (1792, French Revolutionary Wars)
KANDAHAR (1648, Perso-Afghan Wars; 1834, Afghan Tribal Wars; 1880, Second British-Afghan War)
KATZBACH (1813, Napoleonic Wars)
KHARTOUM (1884, British-Sudan Campaigns)
KIRBEKAN (1885, British Sudan Campaigns)
KORYGAOM (1818, Third British-Maratha War)
KUMANOVO (1912, 1st Balkan War)
LANGPORT (1645, English Civil War)
LANGSIDE (1568, Scottish Civil Wars)
LE CATEAU (1914, World War I)
LEITSKAU (1813, Napoleonic Wars)
LIEGNITZ (1760, Seven Years' War)
LOBOSITZ (1756, Seven Years' War)
LUNCARTY (980, Danish Invasions of Scotland)
LYS RIVER (1918, World War I)
MAFEKING (1899, Second Boer War)
MAHIDPUR (1817, Third British-Maratha War)
MARATHON (490 BC, Persian-Greek Wars)
MEDELLIN (1809, Peninsular War)
MEDENINE (1943, World War II)
MESSINES (1917, World War I)
MONTREAL (1760, Seven Years' War)
MORTLACK (1010, Danish Invasions of Scotland)
MORTMANT (1814, Napoleonic Wars)

8–continued

MÖSKIRCH (1800, French Revolutionary Wars)
MOUSCRON (1794, French Revolutionary Wars)
MÜHLBERG (1547, German Reformation Wars)
MUSA BAGH (1858, Indian Mutiny)
NAVARINO (1827, Greek War of Independence)
OMDURMAN (1898, British-Sudan Campaigns)
ONESSANT (1778, American Revolutionary War)
OSTROWNO (1812, Napoleonic Wars)
OVERLORD, OPERATION (1944, World War II)
PALO ALTO (1846, American-Mexican War)
PEA RIDGE (1862, American Civil War)
PESHAWAR (1001, Afghan Invasion of India)
PHILIPPI (42 BC, Roman Civil Wars)
POITIERS (507, Gothic Invasion of France; 1356, Hundred Years' War)
PORTLAND (1653, Anglo-Dutch Wars)
PYRAMIDS (1798, French Revolutionary Wars)
PYRENEES (1813, Peninsular War)
RICHMOND (1862, American Civil War)
ROSSBACH (1757, Seven Years' War)
ROVEREDO (1796, French Revolutionary Wars)
SAALFELD (1806, Napoleonic Wars)
SAPIENZA (1490, Ottoman Wars)
SARATOGA (1777, American Revolutionary War)
SHOLAPUR (1818, Third British-Maratha War)
SIDASSIR (1799, Third British-Mysore War)
SILISTRA (1854, Crimean War)
SMOLENSK (1708, Great Northern War; 1812, Napoleonic Wars; 1941, World War II)
SORAUREN (1813, Peninsular War)
SPION KOP (1900, Second Boer War)
ST ALBANS (1455, 1461, Wars of the Roses)
STANDARD, THE (1138, Anglo-Scottish Wars)
STE CROIX (1807, Napoleonic Wars)
ST GEORGE (1500, Ottoman Wars)
ST MIHIEL (1918, World War I)
STOCKACH (1799, French Revolutionary Wars)
ST PRIVAT (1870, Franco-Prussian War)
STRATTON (1643, English Civil War)
ST THOMAS (1807, Napoleonic Wars)
TALAVERA (1809, Peninsular War)
THETFORD (870, Danish Invasions of England)
TIBERIAS (1187, Crusader-Saracen Wars)
TOULOUSE (1814, Peninsular War)
TRINIDAD (1797, French Revolutionary Wars)
TSINGTAO (1914, World War I)
VALLETTA (1798, French Revolutionary Wars)
VALUTINO (1812, Napoleonic Wars)
VERNEUIL (1424, Hundred Years' War)
VILLIERS (1870, Franco-Prussian War)
WATERLOO (1815, Napoleonic Wars)
WIESLOCH (1622, Thirty Years' War)
YORKTOWN (1781, American Revolutionary War; 1862, American Civil War)
ZORNDORF (1758, Seven Years' War)

9

ABENSBERG (1809, Napoleonic Wars)
AGINCOURT (1415, Hundred Years' War)
AHMADABAD (1780, First British-Maratha War)

9—continued

AHMED KHEL (1880, Second British-Afghan War)

AIGUILLON (1347, Hundred Years' War)

ALCÁNTARA (1580, Spanish Conquest of Portugal; 1706, War of the Spanish Succession)

ALRESFORD (1644, English Civil War)

ALTENDORF (1632, Thirty Years' War)

AMSTETTEN (1805, Napoleonic Wars)

ANGOSTURA (1847, American-Mexican War; 1868, Paraguayan War)

ASKULTSIK (1828, Ottoman Wars)

AUERSTADT (1806, Napoleonic Wars)

AYLESFORD (456, Jutish Invasion of Britain)

BALACLAVA (1854, Crimean War)

BALLYMORE (1798, Irish Rebellion)

BANGALORE (1791, Second British-Mysore War)

BARCELONA (1705, War of the Spanish Succession; 1938, Spanish Civil War)

BERGFRIED (1807, Napleonic Wars)

BHURTPORE (1805, Second British-Maratha War; 1827, Second Siege of)

BLUFF COVE (1982, Falkland Isles)

BOIS-LE-DUC (1794, French Revolutionary Wars)

BORGHETTO (1796, French Revolutionary Wars)

BRENTFORD (1642, English Civil War)

BRIG OF DEE (1639, Bishops' Wars)

BUCHAREST (1771, Ottoman Wars)

BURNS HILL (1847, Kaffir Wars)

BYZANTIUM (318 BC, Wars of Alexander's Successors; 323, Civil Wars of the Roman Empire)

CAPE HENRY (1781, American Revolutionary War)

CAPORETTO (1917, World War I)

CASILINUM (554, Byzantine Empire Wars)

CASTILLON (1453, Hundred Years' War)

CHAMPAGNE (1915, World War I)

CHARASIAB (1879, Second British-Afghan War)

CROSSKEYS (1862, American Civil War)

CUDDALORE (1783, American Revolutionary War)

DENNEWITZ (1813, Napoleonic Wars)

DORYLAEUM (1097, First Crusade)

DUNSINANE (1054, Anglo-Scottish Wars)

EBRO RIVER (1938, Spanish Civil War)

EDERSBERG (1809, Napoleonic Wars)

EDGEWORTH (1469, Wars of the Roses)

EL ALAMEIN (1942, World War II)

ELCHINGEN (1805, Napoleonic Wars)

ELLANDUNE (825, Wessex versus Mercia)

EMPINGHAM (1470, Wars of the Roses)

FIVE FORKS (1865, American Civil War)

FRIEDLAND (1807, Napoleonic Wars)

FRONTIERS, BATTLE OF THE (1914, World War I)

GALLIPOLI (1915, World War I)

GIBRALTAR (1704, War of the Spanish Succession; 1779, American Revolutionary War)

GLADSMUIR (1745, The Forty-five Rebellion)

9—continued

GLEN FRUIN (1604, Scottish Civil Wars)

GLENLIVET (1594, Huntly's Rebellion)

GRAMPIANS, THE (Roman Invasion of Scotland)

GUINEGATE (1513, Anglo-French Wars)

GUMBINNEN (1914, World War I)

HEILSBERG (1807, Napoleonic Wars)

HOCHKIRCH (1758, Seven Years' War)

HÖCHSTÄDT (1800, French Revolutionary Wars)

JERUSALEM (70 AD, Jewish Wars of Roman Empire; 637, Muslim Invasion of Syria; 1099, First Crusade; 1187, Crusader-Turkish Wars; 1917, World War I; 1948, Israeli-Arab Wars)

JUGDULLUK (1842, First British-Afghan War)

KASSASSIN (1882, Egyptian Revolt)

KIMBERLEY (1899, Second Boer War)

KISSINGEN (1866, Seven Weeks' War)

LADYSMITH (1899, Second Boer War)

LANG'S NECK (1881, First Boer War)

LANSDOWNE (1643, English Civil Wars)

LENINGRAD (1944, World War II)

LEXINGTON (1775, American Revolutionary War; 1861, American Civil War)

LEYTE GULF (1944, World War II)

LÖWENBERG (1813, Napoleonic Wars)

MAGDEBURG (1631, Thirty Years' War)

MALAVILLY (1799, Third British-Mysore War)

MANGALORE (1783, First British-Mysore War)

MANSFIELD (1864, American Civil War)

MARIA ZELL (1805, Napoleonic Wars)

MARSAGLIA (1693, War of the Grand Alliance)

MILLESIMO (1796, French Revolutionary Wars)

MOHRUNGEN (1807, Napoleonic Wars)

MONTEREAU (1814, Napoleonic Wars)

MONTERREY (1846, Amercian-Mexican War)

MUKWANPUR (1816, British-Gurkha War)

NASHVILLE (1863, American Civil War)

NAULOCHUS (36 BC, Wars of the Second Triumvirate)

NAVARRETE (1367, Hundred Years' War)

NEGAPATAM (1746, War of the Austrian Succession; 1781, Second British Mysore War; 1782, American Revolutionary War)

NEW GUINEA (1942, World War II)

NEW MARKET (1864, American Civil War)

NICOPOLIS (1396, Ottoman Wars; 1877, Russo-Turkish War)

NUJUFGHUR (1857, Indian Mutiny)

OCEAN POND (1864, American Civil War)

OLTENITZA (1853, Crimean War)

OTTENBURN (1300, Wars of Scottish Independence)

OUDENARDE (1708, War of the Spanish Succession)

PHARSALUS (48 BC, Civil War of Caesar and Pompey; 1897, Greco-Turkish Wars)

POLLICORE (1781, First British-Mysore War)

PORTO NOVO (1781, First British-Mysore War)

PRIMOLANÓ (1796, French Revolutionary Wars)

PRINCETON (1777, American Revolutionary War)

9–continued

RAMILLIES (1706, War of the Spanish Succession)
RAMNUGGUR (1849, Second British-Sikh War)
RATHMINES (1649, Cromwell's Campaign in Ireland)
RHINELAND, THE (1945, World War II)
ROSEBURGH (1460, Anglo-Scottish Wars)
SADULAPUR (1848, Second British-Sikh War)
SALAMANCA (1812, Peninsular War; 1858, Mexican Liberal Rising)
SANTANDER (1937, Spanish Civil War)
SARAGOSSA (1700, War of the Spanish Succession; 1808, Peninsular War)
SEDGEMOOR (1685, Monmouth's Rebellion)
SEVENOAKS (1450, Cade's Rebellion)
SHEERNESS (1667, Anglo-Dutch Wars)
SHERSTONE (1016, Danish Invasion of England)
SHOLINGUR (1781, First British-Mysore War)
SINGAPORE (1942, World War II)
SITABALDI (1817, Third British-Maratha War)
SOUTHWARK (1450, Cade's Rebellion)
STADTLOHN (1623, Thirty Years' War)
STAFFARDA (1690, War of the Grand Alliance)
STORMBERG (1899, Second Boer War)
ST QUENTIN (1557, Franco-Spanish Wars; 1871, Franco-Prussian War)
STRALSUND (1628, Thirty Years' War; 1715, Great Northern War)
SUDDASAIN (1848, Second British-Sikh War)
TARRAGONA (1811, Peninsular War)
TCHERNAYA (1855, Crimean War)
TOLENTINO (1815, Napoleonic Wars)
TOU MORONG (1966, Vietnam War)
TOURCOING (1794, French Revolutionary Wars)
TRAFALGAR (1805, Napoleonic Wars)
TRAUTENAU (1866, Seven Weeks' War)
TREBIZOND (1461, Ottoman Wars)
TRINKITAT (1884, British-Sudan Campaigns)
VAALKRANZ (1900, Second Boer War)
VAUCHAMPS (1814, Napoleonic Wars)
VICKSBURG (1862, American Civil War)
VIMY RIDGE (1917, World War I)
WAKEFIELD (1460, Wars of the Roses)
WANDIWASH (1760, Seven Years' War; 1780, First British-Mysore War)
WORCESTER (1651, English Civil War)
WÜRTZBURG (1796, French Revolutionary Wars)

10

ADRIANOPLE (1205, Fourth Crusade; 1913, First Balkan War)
ALEXANDRIA (642, Muslim Invasion of Egypt; 1801, British Invasion of Egypt; 1881, Egyptian Revolt)
ANCRUM MOOR (1545, Anglo-Scottish Wars)
ARTOIS-LOOS (1915, World War I)
AUSTERLITZ (1805, Napoleonic Wars)
BALL'S BLUFF (1861, American Civil War)

10–continued

BEACHY HEAD (1690, War of the Grand Alliance)
BEAUSÉJOUR (1755, Seven Year's War)
BENNINGTON (1777, American Revolutionary War)
BLACKWATER (1598, O'Neill's Rebellion)
BLORE HEATH (1459, Wars of the Roses)
BRANDYWINE (1777, American Revolutionary War)
BRUNANBURH (937, Danish Invasion)
BUENA VISTA (1846, American-Mexican War)
CAMPERDOWN (1797, French Revolutionary Wars)
CEDAR CREEK (1864, American Civil War)
CHARLESTON (1863, American Civil War)
CHEVY CHASE (1388, Wars of Scottish Independence)
CHIPPENHAM (878, Danish Invasions of Britain)
COPENHAGEN (1801, French Revolutionary Wars; 1807, Napoleonic Wars)
DALMANUTHA (1900, Second Boer War)
DOGGER BANK (1781, American Revolutionary War; 1915, World War I)
DUNGANHILL (1647, Great Irish Rebellion)
DYRRACHIUM (48 BC, Civil War of Caesar and Pompey)
ENGLEFIELD (871, Danish Invasion of Britain)
FEROZESHAH (1845, First British-Sikh War)
FETHANLEAG (584, Saxon Conquests)
FUTTEYPORE (1857, Indian Mutiny)
GAINES' MILL (1862, American Civil War)
GERMANTOWN (1777, American Revolutionary War)
GETTYSBURG (1863, American Civil War)
GLEN MALONE (1580, Colonization of Ireland)
GORODECZNO (1812, Napoleonic Wars)
GOTHIC LINE (1944, World War II)
GRANT'S HILL (1758, Seven Years' War)
GRAVELINES (1558, Franco-Spanish Wars)
GRAVELOTTE (1870, Franco-Prussian War)
GUADELOUPE (1794, French Revolutionary Wars)
HABBANIYAH (1941, World War II)
HASTENBECK (1757, Seven Years' War)
HEATHFIELD (633, Mercia against Northumbria)
HELIGOLAND (1807, Napoleonic Wars)
HELIOPOLIS (1800, French Revolutionary Wars)
HELLESPONT (323, War of the Two Empires)
HOLLABRUNN (1805, Napleonic Wars)
INVERLOCHY (1645, English Civil War)
JELLALABAD (1842, First British-Afghan War)
KHOJAH PASS (1842, First British-Afghan War)
KÖNIGGRÄTZ (1866, Seven Weeks' War)
KORNSPRUIT (1900, Second Boer War)
KUNERSDORF (1759, Seven Years' War)
KUT-EL-AMARA (1915, World War I)
LA FAVORITA (1797, French Revolutionary Wars)
LAKE GEORGE (1755, Seven Years' War)
LA ROCHELLE (1372, Hundred Years' War; 1627, French Religious Wars)
LA ROTHIÈRE (1814, Napoleonic Wars)

10–continued

LOUDON HILL (1307, Wars of Scottish Independence)

LOUISBOURG (1745, War of the Austrian Succession; 1758, Seven Years' War)

LÜLEBÜRGAZ (1912, Balkan Wars)

LUNDY'S LANE (1814, War of 1812)

MAASTRICHT (1579, Netherlands War of Independence)

MAHARAJPUR (1843, Gwalior Campaign; 1857, Indian Mutiny)

MARETH LINE (1943, World War II)

MARIENDAHL (1645, Thirty Years' War)

MARTINIQUE (1794, French Revolutionary Wars; 1809, Napoleonic Wars)

MASERFIELD (642, Northumbria against Mercia)

MICHELBERG (1805, Napoleonic Wars)

MONTEBELLO (1800, French Revolutionary Wars; 1859, Italian Wars of Independence)

MONTENOTTE (1796, French Revolutionary Wars)

MONTEVIDEO (1807, Napoleonic Wars; 1843, 1851, 1863, Uruguayan Civil War)

MONTFAUCON (886, Norman Invasion of France)

MONTMIRAIL (1814, Napoleonic Wars)

MOUNT TABOR (1799, French Revolutionary Wars)

NAROCH LAKE (1916, World War I)

NEERWINDEN (1693, War of the Grand Alliance; 1793, French Revolutionary Wars)

NEW ORLEANS (1814, War of 1812; 1862, American Civil War)

NÖRDLINGEN (1634, 1645, Thirty Year's War)

OSTROLENKA (1853, Crimean War)

PAARDEBERG (1900, Second Boer War)

PANDU NADDI (1857, Indian Mutiny)

PEN SELWOOD (1016, Danish Invasions of Britain)

PEREMBACUM (1780, First British-Mysore War)

PERRYVILLE (1862, American Civil War)

PERSEPOLIS (316 BC, Wars of Alexander's Successors)

PETERSBURG (1864, American Civil War)

PIAVE RIVER (1918, World War I)

PONT VALAIN (1370, Hundred Years' War)

PORT ARTHUR (1894, Sino-Japanese War; 1904, Russo-Japanese War)

PORT HUDSON (1863, American Civil War)

QUATRE BRAS (1815, Napoleonic Wars)

RAKERSBERG (1416, Ottoman Wars)

RUHR POCKET (1945, World War II)

SANNA'S POST (1900, Second Boer War)

SANTA LUCIA (1842, Rio Grande Rising)

SAVANDROOG (1791, Second British-Mysore War)

SEINE MOUTH (1416, Hundred Years' War)

SEVASTOPOL (1854, Crimean War)

SEVEN PINES (1862, American Civil War)

SHREWSBURY (1403, Percy's Rebellion)

SHROPSHIRE (AD 50, Roman Conquest of Britain)

10–continued

SIDI REZEGH (1941, World War II)

SOLWAY MOSS (1542, Anglo-Scottish Wars)

STALINGRAD (1942, World War II)

STEENKERKE (1692, War of the Grand Alliance)

STILLWATER (1777, American Revolutionary War)

STONE RIVER (1862, American Civil War)

TALANA HILL (1899, Second Boer War)

TANNENBERG (1914, World War I)

TEL-EL-KEBIR (1882, Egyptian Revolt)

TETTENHALL (910, Danish Invasions of England)

TEWKESBURY (1471, Wars of the Roses)

TIPPERMUIR (1644, English Civil War)

TRAVANCORE (1789, Second British-Mysore War)

WARTEMBERG (1813, Napoleonic Wars)

WATTIGNIES (1793, French Revolutionary Wars)

WILDERNESS, THE (1864, American Civil War)

WINCHESTER (1863, American Civil War)

11

ALAM EL HALFA (1942, World War II)

ALESSANDRIA (1799, French Revolutionary Wars)

AN LAO VALLEY (1966, Vietnam War)

BANNOCKBURN (1314, Wars of Scottish Independence)

BELLEAU WOOD (1918, World War I)

BISMARCK SEA (1943, World War II)

BLANQUEFORT (1450, Hundred Years' War)

BRAMHAM MOOR (1408, Northumberland's Rebellion)

BREITENFELD (1642, Thirty Years' War)

BRENNEVILLE (1119, Anglo-French Wars)

BUENOS AIRES (1806, 1807, Napoleonic Wars; 1874, Mitre's Rebellion)

BUNKER'S HILL (1775, American Revolutionary War)

CAMELODUNUM (43, Roman Invasion of Britain)

CARBIESDALE (1650, English Civil War)

CARENAGE BAY (1778, American Revolutionary War)

CASTIGLIONE (1706, War of the Spanish Succession; 1796, French Revolutionary Wars)

CHAMPAUBERT (1814, Napoleonic Wars)

CHATTANOOGA (1863, American Civil War)

CHICKAMAUGA (1863, American Civil War)

CHILIANWALA (1849, Second British-Sikh War)

CHRYSOPOLIS (324, War of the Two Empires)

COLDHARBOUR (1864, American Civil War)

DIAMOND HILL (1900, Second Boer War)

DINGAAN'S DAY (1838, Afrikaner-Zulu War)

DRIEFONTEIN (1900, Second Boer War)

DÜRRENSTEIN (1805, Napoleonic Wars)

ELANDS RIVER (1900, Second Boer War)

FARRUKHABAD (1804, Second British-Maratha War)

FERRYBRIDGE (1461, Wars of the Roses)

FISHER'S HILL (1864, American Civil War)

11–continued

FORT ST DAVID (1758, Seven Years' War)
GIBBEL RUTTS (1798, Irish Rebellion)
GROSS-BEEREN (1813, Napoleonic Wars)
GUADALAJARA (1937, Spanish Civil War)
GUADALCANAL (1942, World War II)
HADRIANOPLE (323, War of the Two Empires; 378, Second Gothic Invasion of the East)
HALIDON HILL (1333, Wars of Scottish Independence)
HEAVENFIELD (634, Northumbria against the British)
HOHENLINDEN (1800, French Revolutionary Wars)
HONDSCHOOTE (1793, French Revolutionary Wars)
ÎLE DE FRANCE (1810, Napoleonic Wars)
ISANDHLWANA (1879, Zulu-British War)
LANGENSALZA (1866, Seven Weeks' War)
LONDONDERRY (1689, War of the Grand Alliance)
LOSTWITHIEL (1644, English Civil War)
MALVERN HILL (1862, American Civil War)
MARSTON MOOR (1644, English Civil War)
MASULIPATAM (1759, Seven Years' War)
MERSA MATRÛH (1942, World War II)
MILL SPRINGS (1862, American Civil War)
MODDER RIVER (1899, Second Boer War)
MONTE LEZINO (1796, French Revolutionary Wars)
MONTMORENCI (1759, Seven Years' War)
MORSHEDABAD (1763, British Conquest of Bengal)
NOISSEVILLE (1870, Franco-Prussian War)
NORTHAMPTON (1460, Wars of the Roses)
PEARL HARBOR (1941, World War II)
PEIWAR KOTAL (1878, Second British-Afghan War)
PHILIPHAUGH (1645, English Civil War)
PIETER'S HILL (1900, Second Boer War)
PONDICHERRY (1748, War of the Austrian Succession; 1760, Seven Years' War; 1778, 1783, American Revolutionary War)
PRESTONPANS (1745, The Forty-five Rebellion)
QUIBERON BAY (1759, Seven Years' War)
RAJAHMUNDRY (1758, Seven Years' War)
REDDERSBERG (1900, Second Boer War)
RHEINFELDEN (1638, Thirty Years' War)
RIETFONTEIN (1899, Second Boer War)
RORKE'S DRIFT (1879, Zulu-British War)
ROWTON HEATH (1645, English Civil War)
SALDANHA BAY (1796, French Revolutionary Wars)
SAN GIOVANNI (1799, French Revolutionary Wars)
SAUCHIE BURN (1488, Rebellion of the Scottish Barons)
SHERIFFMUIR (1715, The Fifteen Rebellion)
SIDI BARRÂNI (1940, World War II)
TAILLEBOURG (1242, Anglo-French Wars)
TARAWA-MAKIN (1943, World War II)
TEL-EL-MAHUTA (1882, Egyptian Revolt)

11–continued

TELLICHERRY (1780, First British-Mysore War)
TEUTTLINGEN (1643, Thirty Years' War)
TICONDEROGA (1758, Seven Years' War; 1777, American Revolutionary War)
TRINCOMALEE (1759, Seven Years' War; 1767, First British-Mysore War; 1782, American Revolutionary War)
VINEGAR HILL (1798, Irish Rebellion)
WALTERSDORF (1807, Napoleonic Wars)
WEDNESFIELD (911, Danish Invasions of England)
WEISSENBURG (1870, Franco-Prussian War)
WHITE RUSSIA (1943, World War II)

12

ADWALTON MOOR (1643, English Civil War)
ALGEÇIRAS BAY (1801, French Revolutionary Wars)
ARCIS-SUR-AUBE (1814, Napoleonic Wars)
ATHERTON MOOR (1643, English Civil War)
BANDA ISLANDS (1796, French Revolutionary Wars)
BERGEN-OP-ZOOM (1747, War of the Austrian Succession; 1799, French Revolutionary Wars)
BLOEMFONTEIN (1900, Second Boer War)
BRADDOCK DOWN (1643, English Civil War)
CHICKAHOMINY (1864, American Civil War)
ELANDSLAAGTE (1899, Second Boer War)
EUTAW SPRINGS (1781, American Revolutionary War)
FORT DONELSON (1862, American Civil War)
HAMPTON ROADS (1862, American Civil War)
HARPER'S FERRY (1862, American Civil War)
HEDGELEY MOOR (1464, Wars of the Roses)
HENGESTESDUN (837, Danish Invasions of Britain)
HOMILDON HILL (1402, Anglo-Scottish Wars)
KIRCH-DENKERN (1761, Seven Years' War)
KÖNIGSWARTHA (1813, Napoleonic Wars)
KURSK SALIENT (1943, World War II)
LYNN HAVEN BAY (1781, American Revolutionary War)
MIDWAY ISLAND (1942, World War II)
MÜNCHENGRÄTZ (1866, Seven Weeks' War)
MURFREESBORO (1862, American Civil War)
NECHTAN'S MERE (685, Northumbrian Invasion of Scotland)
OONDWA NULLAH (1763, British Conquest of Bengal)
PENOBSCOT BAY (1779, American Revolutionary War)
PETERWARDEIN (1716, Ottoman Wars)
PINKIE CLEUGH (1547, Anglo-Scottish Wars)
PORT REPUBLIC (1862, American Civil War)
PRAIRIE GROVE (1862, American Civil War)
RICH MOUNTAIN (1861, American Civil War)
RONCESVALLES (1813, Peninsular War)
ROUNDWAY DOWN (1643, English Civil War)
RULLION GREEN (1666, Covenanters' Rising)
SAN SEBASTIAN (1813, Peninsular War; 1836, First Carlist War)

12–continued

SECUNDERBAGH (1857, Indian Mutiny)
SERINGAPATAM (1792, Second British-Mysore War; 1799, Third British-Mysore War)
SOUTHWOLD BAY (1672, Anglo-Dutch Wars)
SPOTSYLVANIA (1864, American Civil War)
TET OFFENSIVE, THE (1968, Vietnam War)
WILLIAMSBURG (1862, American Civil War)
WILSON'S CREEK (1861, American Civil War)
WROTHAM HEATH (1554, Wyatt's Insurrection)

13

AIX-LA-CHAPELLE (1795, French Revolutionary Wars)
BADULI-KI-SERAI (1857, Indian Mutiny)
BELLE-ÎLE-EN-MER (1759, 1761, Seven Years' War; 1795, French Revolutionary Wars)
BOROUGHBRIDGE (1322, Rebellion of the Marches)
BOSWORTH FIELD (1485, Wars of the Roses)
CAPE ST VINCENT (1797, French Revolutionary Wars)
CEDAR MOUNTAIN (1862, American Civil War)
CHANDERNAGORE (1757, Seven Years' War)
CIUDAD RODRIGO (1812, Peninsular War)
FALKLAND ISLES (1914, World War I; 1982, Falklands War)
FARQUHAR'S FARM (1899, Second Boer War)
FORT FRONTENAC (1758, Seven Years' War)
FRANKENHAUSEN (1525, Peasants' War)
GLENMARRESTON (683, Angles' Invasion of Britain)
HORNS OF HATTIN (1187, Crusader-Saracen Wars)
INVERKEITHING (1317, Anglo-Scottish Wars)
KASSERINE PASS (1943, World War II)
KILLIECRANKIE (1689, Jacobite Rising)
LITTLE BIG HORN (1876, Sioux Rising)
MAGERSFONTEIN (1899, Second Boer War)
MASURIAN LAKES (1914, 1915, World War I)
MOLINOS DEL REY (1808, Peninsular War)
MOUNT SELEUCUS (353, Civil Wars of the Roman Empire)
NEVILLE'S CROSS (1346, Anglo-Scottish Wars)
NEWTOWN BUTLER (1689, War of the Grand Alliance)
NORTHALLERTON (1138, Anglo-Scottish Wars)
NORTH FORELAND (1666, Anglo-Dutch Wars)
PASSCHENDAELE (1917, World War I)
PELELIU-ANGAUR (1944, World War II)
PHILIPPINE SEA (1944, World War II)
PORTO PRAIA BAY (1781, American Revolutionary War)
ROANOKE ISLAND (1862, American Civil War)
SOUTH MOUNTAIN (1862, American Civil War)
SPANISH ARMADA (1588, Anglo-Spanish War)
SUDLEY SPRINGS (1862, American Civil War)
WHITE OAK SWAMP (1862, American Civil War)
YOUGHIOGHENNY (1754, Seven Years' War)
ZUSMARSHAUSEN (1647, Thirty Years' War)

14

BERWICK-ON-TWEED (1296, Wars of Scottish Independence)
BOTHWELL BRIDGE (1679, Covenanters' Rising)
BRISTOE STATION (1863, American Civil War)
CAPE FINISTERRE (1747, War of the Austrian Succession; 1805, Napoleonic Wars)
CHALGROVE FIELD (1643, English Civil War)
CHÂTEAU-THIERRY (1814, Napoleonic Wars)
CONSTANTINOPLE (668, Muslim Invasion of Europe; 1203–04, Fourth Crusade; 1261, Reconquest by Byzantines; 1422, Ottoman Invasion of Europe; 1453, Turkish Conquest)
CROPREDY BRIDGE (1644, English Civil War)
DRUMMOSSIE MOOR (1746, The Forty-five Rebellion)
FREDERICKSBURG (1862, American Civil War)
FUENTES DE OÑORO (1811, Peninsular War)
KOVEL-STANISLAV (1916, World War I)
LA BELLE FAMILLE (1759, Seven Years' War)
LOOSECOAT FIELD (1470, Wars of the Roses)
MARIANA ISLANDS (1944, World War II)
MORTIMER'S CROSS (1461, Wars of the Roses)
NICHOLSON'S NECK (1899, Second Boer War)
PEACH TREE CREEK (1864, American Civil War)
PUSAN PERIMETER (1950, Korean War)
ROUVRAY-ST-DENIS (1429, Hundred Years' War)
SANTIAGO DE CUBA (1898, Spanish-American War)
SAVAGE'S STATION (1862, American Civil War)
SECESSIONVILLE (1862, American Civil War)
SINAI PENINSULA (1956, Israeli-Arab War)
SOLOMON ISLANDS (1942, World War II)
STAMFORD BRIDGE (1066, Norse Invasion of Britain; 1453, Wars of the Roses)
STIRLING BRIDGE (1297, Wars of Scottish Independence)
VITTORIO VENETO (1918, World War I)

15

ALEUTIAN ISLANDS (1943, World War II)
AMATOLA MOUNTAIN (1846, Kaffir Wars)
APPOMATTOX RIVER (1865, American Civil War)
BATTLE OF BRITAIN (1940, World War II)
BEAVER'S DAM CREEK (1862, American Civil War)
FRANKFURT-ON-ODER (1631, Thirty Years' War)
GROSS-JÄGERSDORF (1757, Seven Years' War)
HELIGOLAND BIGHT (1914, World War I)
KHOORD KABUL PASS (1842, First British-Afghan War)
MALOYAROSLAVETS (1812, Napoleonic Wars)
MISSIONARY RIDGE (1863, American Civil War)
PLAINS OF ABRAHAM (1759, Seven Years' War)
SEVEN DAYS' BATTLE (1862, American Civil War)
SPANISH GALLEONS (1702, War of the Spanish Succession)

16
BATAAN-CORREGIDOR (1941, World War II)
BRONKHORST SPRUIT (1880, First Boer War)
CAMBRAI-ST QUENTIN (1918, World War I)
CHANCELLORSVILLE (1863, American Civil War)
FORT WILLIAM HENRY (1757, Seven Years' War)
KINNESAW MOUNTAIN (1864, American Civil War)
MONONGAHELA RIVER (1755, Seven Years' War)
SALUM-HALFAYA PASS (1941, World War II)

17
BURLINGTON HEIGHTS (1813, War of 1812)
DODECANESE ISLANDS (1943, World War II)
GUSTAV-CASSINO LINE (1943, World War II)
INHLOBANE MOUNTAIN (1879, Zulu War)
KWAJALEIN-ENIWETOK (1944, World War II)
LA FÈRE CHAMPENOISE (1814, Napoleonic Wars)

17—continued
PITTSBURGH LANDING (1862, American Civil War)
POLAND-EAST PRUSSIA (1944, World War II)
VAN TUONG PENINSULA (1965, Vietnam War)

18
GUILFORD COURTHOUSE (1781, American Revolutionary War)
MEUSE-ARGONNE FOREST (1918, World War I)

19
CHU PONG-IA DRANG RIVER (1965, Vietnam War)
'GLORIOUS FIRST OF JUNE' (1794, French Revolutionary Wars)

20+
RHINE AND THE RUHR POCKET, THE (1945, World War II)
SHANNON AND CHESAPEAKE (1813, War of 1812)
THIRTY-EIGHTH PARALLEL (1951, Korean War)

WARS

AMERICAN CIVIL WAR	1861–65	PENINSULAR WAR	1808–14
BALKAN WARS	1912–13	PERSIAN WARS	5th century BC
BOER WAR	1880–81,	PUNIC WARS	264–241 BC,
	1899–1902		218–201 BC,
BOSNIAN CIVIL WAR	1992–95		149–146 BC
CRIMEAN WAR	1853–56	RUSSIAN CIVIL WAR	1918–21
ENGLISH CIVIL WAR	1642–49	RUSSO–JAPANESE WAR	1904–05
FALKLANDS WAR	1982	SAMNITE WARS	343–341 BC,
FIRST WORLD WAR	1914–18		316–314 BC,
FRANCO–PRUSSIAN WAR	1870–71		298–290 BC
FRENCH AND INDIAN WAR	1754–63	SECOND WORLD WAR	1939–45
FRENCH INDOCHINA WAR	1946–54	SEVEN YEARS WAR	1756–63
FRENCH WARS OF RELIGION	1562–98	SINO–JAPANESE WARS	1894–95,
GALLIC WARS	58–51 BC		1937–45
GREAT NORTHERN WAR	1700–21	SIX DAY WAR	1967
GULF WAR	1991	SPANISH–AMERICAN WAR	1898
HUNDRED YEARS WAR	1337–1453	SPANISH CIVIL WAR	1936–39
IRAN–IRAQ WAR	1980–88	THIRTY YEARS WAR	1618–48
KOREAN WAR	1950–53	VIETNAM WAR	1954–75
MACEDONIAN WARS	214–205 BC,	WAR OF 1812	1812–14
	200–196 BC,	WAR OF AMERICAN	1775–83
	171–168 BC,	INDEPENDENCE	
	149–148 BC	WAR OF THE AUSTRIAN	1740–48
MEXICAN WAR	1846–48	SUCCESSION	
NAPOLEONIC WARS	1805–15	WAR OF THE SPANISH	1701–14
OPIUM WARS	1839–42,	SUCCESSION	
	1856–60	WARS OF THE ROSES	1455–85
PELOPONNESIAN WARS	431–404 BC	YOM KIPPUR WAR	1973

ARMOUR

4	6–continued	7–continued	8–continued	10
JACK	CRENEL	FRONTAL	COLLERET	AVENTAILLE
MAIL	CRINET	GAUCHET	COLLETIN	BANDED MAIL
	CUELLO	GOUCHET	CORSELET	BARREL HELM
5	GORGET	GREAVES	CRINIERE	BRICHETTES
ARMET	GUSSET	HAUBERK	GAUNTLET	BRIGANDINE
BACYN	HEAUME	HOGUINE	HALECRET	CROISSANTS
BUFFE	HELMET	LANIERS	JAMBEAUX	ECREVISSES
CREST	MASCLE	MURSAIL	JAZERANT	EMBOITMENT
CULET	MESAIL	PANACHE	PAULDRON	FLANCHARDS
GIPON	MORIAN	PLACARD	PECTORAL	LAMBREQUIN
IMBER	MORION	POITRAL	PLASTRON	
JUPEL	SALADE	SURCOAT	SABATONS	**11**
JUPON	SHIELD	VISIERE	SOLARETS	BREASTPLATE
LAMES	TABARD		SOLERETS	BREASTSTRAP
SALET	UMBRIL	**8**	TESTIERE	BRIGANDYRON
VISOR		ALLECRET		BRIGANTAYLE
	7	BARDINGS	**9**	CHAPEL DE
6	AILETES	BASCINET	BAINBERGS	FER
ALETES	BACINET	BAUDRICK	BEINBERGS	ESPALLIERES
BASNET	BALDRIC	BRASSARD	CHAIN MAIL	PLATE ARMOUR
BHANJU	BARBUTE	BRAYETTE	CHAMPFRON	
BRACER	BASINET	BUFF COAT	CHAUSSONS	**13**
BRIDLE	BUCKLER	BURGINOT	EPAULETTE	ARMING
BRUGNE	CHAUCES	BURGONET	HAUSSE-COL	DOUBLET
CALOTE	CORSLET	CABASSET	JACK BOOTS	
CAMAIL	CRUPPER	CHAMPONS	POURPOINT	**15**
CASQUE	CUIRASS	CHANFRON	REREBRACE	IMBRICATE
CASSIS	CUISSES	CHAUCHES	SABATYNES	ARMOUR
CELATE	CULESET	CHAUSSES		
CHEEKS	FENDACE	COD PIECE		

WEAPONS

2	4–continued	5–continued	5–continued	6
NU	BOMB	ANLAS	KILIJ	AMUKTA
V1	CLUB	ARROW	KNIFE	ARMLET
V2	DIRK	ASWAR	KUKRI	BARKAL
	FANG	BATON	KYLIE	BARONG
3	FOIL	BIDAG	LANCE	BASTON
AXE	KORA	BILBO	LATCH	BODKIN
BOW	KRIS	BOLAS	PILUM	BULLET
DAG	MACE	BOSON	PRODD	CANNON
DAS	MINE	BHAND	RIFLE	CARCAS
GUN	PIKE	ESTOC	SABRE	CEMTEX
GYN	SHOT	FLAIL	SHELL	CUDGEL
TNT	TANK	FUSEE	SLING	DAGGER
	TOCK	FUSIL	SPEAR	DAISHO
4	TUCK	GUPTI	STAKE	DRAGON
ADZE		H-BOMB	STAVE	DUM-DUM
BARB	**5**	KERIS	SWORD	DUSACK
BILL	A-BOMB	KHORA	TACHI	EXOCET
BOLO	ANCUS	KILIG	WADDY	KATANA
BOLT	ANKUS			

6–continued

KERRIE
KHANDA
KIKUKI
KODOGU
MASSUE
MAZULE
MORTAR
MUSKET
NAPALM
PARANG
PETARD
PISTOL
POP GUN
QILLIJ
QUIVER
RAMROD
RAPIER
ROCKET
SCYTHE
SEMTEX
SUMPIT
TALWAR
VGO GUN

7

ASSEGAI
AWL-PIKE
BALASAN
BALISTA
BAYONET
BELFREY
BILIONG
BOMBARD
BOURDON
BREN GUN
CALIVER
CALTRAP
CARABEN
CARBINE
CARREAU
CHAKRAM
CHALCOS
CHOPPER
CURRIER
CUTLASS
DUDGEON
DUSSACK
FAUCHON
FIRE-POT
GRENADE
HALBARD
HALBART
HALBERD
HAND GUN

7–continued

HARPOON
KASTANE
KINDJAL
LONG BOW
MISSILE
MUSQUET
PONIARD
PUNT GUN
QUARREL
SHASHQA
SHINKEN
STEN GUN
TORPEDO
TRIDENT

8

AMUSETTE
ARBALEST
ARBALETE
ARQUEBUS
ATOM BOMB
AXE-KNIFE
BASELARD
BASILARD
BLOWPIPE
BUZZBOMB
CALTHORP
CANISTER
CARABINE
CATAPULT
CHACHEKA
CLADIBAS
CLAYMORE
CROSSBOW
DERINGER
DESTRIER
FALCHION
FALCONET
FAUCHARD
FIRELOCK
HACKBUTT
HAIL SHOT
HAQUEBUT
HASSEGAI
HOWITZER
LAND MINE
PETRONEL
POIGNARD
QUERQUER
REPEATER
REVOLVER
SCIMITAR
SHAMSHIR
SHRAPNEL

8–continued

SPONTOON
SUMPITAN
TOMAHAWK
TOMMY GUN

9

ACK-ACK GUN
ARTILLERY
BADELAIRE
BANDELEER
BANDOLIER
BANNEROLE
BATTLE-AXE
BIG BERTHA
BOOMERANG
CARRONADE
CARTOUCHE
CARTRIDGE
CHAIN SHOT
DETONATOR
DOODLE-BUG
FALCASTRA
FLAGELLUM
FLAMBERGE
FLINTLOCK
GELIGNITE
GRAPESHOT
GUNPOWDER
HARQUEBUS
KNOBSTICK
MATCHLOCK
MAZZUELLE
MILLS BOMB
MUSKETOON
POM-POM GUN
SLUNG SHOT
TRUNCHEON

10

ARTILLATOR
BANDEROLLE
BRANDESTOC
BROAD ARROW
BROADSWORD
CANNON BALL
FIRE-STICKS
FLICK KNIFE
FLYING BOMB
GATLING GUN
KNOBKERRIE
LETTER BOMB
LIMPET MINE
MACHINE GUN
PEA-SHOOTER

10–continued

POWDERHORN
SIDEWINDER
SMALL SWORD
SWORD STICK

11

ANTI-TANK GUN
ARMOURED CAR
BLUNDERBUSS
HAND GRENADE
KHYBER KNIFE
MISERICORDE
NEUTRON BOMB

12

BATTERING RAM
BREECH LOADER
BRIDLE CUTTER
FIRE CARRIAGE
FLAME-THROWER
HYDROGEN BOMB

13

BRASS KNUCKLES
DUELLING SWORD
GUIDED MISSILE
KNUCKLE DUSTER
THROWING KNIFE

14

DUELLING PISTOL
INCENDIARY BOMB
NUCLEAR WEAPONS
ROCKET LAUNCHER
SAWN-OFF
  SHOTGUN

15

ANTI-AIRCRAFT GUN

16

BALLISTIC MISSILE

17

ANTI-PERSONNEL
  MINE

18

HEAT-SEEKING
  MISSILE

20+

DOUBLE-
  BARRELLED
  SHOTGUN

TRANSPORT

VEHICLES

3
BMX
BUS
CAB
CAR
FLY
GIG
VAN

4
AUTO
BIKE
CART
DRAG
DRAY
EKKA
HACK
JEEP
LUGE
SHAY
SLED
TAXI
TRAM
TRAP
TUBE
WAIN

5
ARABA
BRAKE
BUGGY
COACH
COUPÉ
CRATE
CYCLE
DANDY
DOOLY
LORRY
METRO
MOPED
MOTOR
PALKI
SEDAN
SULKY
TONGA
TRAIN
TRUCK
WAGON

6
BERLIN
CALASH
CHAISE
DIESEL
FIACRE
GO-CART
HANSOM
HEARSE
HOTROD
HURDLE
JALOPY
JITNEY
LANDAU
LIMBER
LITTER
MAGLEV
MODEL-T
ROCKET
SALOON
SLEDGE
SLEIGH
SNOCAT
SURREY
TANDEM
TANKER
TOURER
TRICAR
WEASEL

7
AUTOBUS
AUTOCAR
BICYCLE
BOB-SLED
BRITZKA
BROWSER
CALÈCHE
CARAVAN
CAROCHE
CHARIOT
COASTER
DOG-CART
DROSHKY
FLIVVER
GROWLER
HACKERY
HARD-TOP

7–continued
OFF-ROAD
OMNIBUS
OPEN-CAR
PHÆTON
PULLMAN
SCOOTER
SHUNTER
SIDE-CAR
TALLY-HO
TAXI-CAB
TILBURY
TRACTOR
TRAILER
TROLLEY
TUMBRIL
TWO-DOOR
UNICORN
VIS-À-VIS
WHISKEY

8
BAROUCHE
BRANCARD
BROUGHAM
CABLE-CAR
CAPE-CART
CARRIAGE
CARRIOLE
CLARENCE
CURRICLE
DEAD-CART
DORMEUSE
FOUR-DOOR
HORSE-BUS
HORSE-CAB
HORSE-VAN
ICE-YACHT
KIBITZKA
MONORAIL
MOTOR-CAR
MOTOR-VAN
OLD CROCK
PONY-CART
PUSH-BIKE
QUADRIGA
RICKSHAW
ROADSTER

8–continued
RUNABOUT
SOCIABLE
STAFF CAR
STEAM-CAR
TOBOGGAN
TRICYCLE
UNICYCLE
VICTORIA

9
AMBULANCE
BOAT-TRAIN
BOB-SLEIGH
BUBBLECAR
BUCKBOARD
CABRIOLET
CHAR-À-BANC
DILIGENCE
ESTATE-CAR
FUNICULAR
HORSE-CART
LIMOUSINE
MAIL-COACH
MILKFLOAT
MILK TRAIN
MONOCYCLE
MOTOR-BIKE
PALANKEEN
PALANQUIN
RACING CAR
SPORTS CAR
STREET-CAR
STRETCHER
TARANTASS
TIN LIZZIE
TWO-SEATER
WAGONETTE

10
AUTOMOBILE
BAIL GHARRY
BEACHWAGON
BLACK MARIA
FIRE-ENGINE
FOUR-IN-HAND
GOODS TRAIN
JINRICKSHA

303

10–continued
LOCAL TRAIN
LOCOMOTIVE
MOTOR-COACH
MOTOR-CYCLE
NIGHT TRAIN
OUTSIDE CAR
PADDYWAGON
PEDAL-CYCLE
PONY-ENGINE
POST-CHAISE
RATTLETRAP
SEDAN-CHAIR
SHANDRYDAN
SINCLAIR C5
SNOWPLOUGH
STAGE-COACH
STAGE-WAGON
STATE COACH
TROLLEY-BUS
TROLLEY-CAR
TWO-WHEELER
VELOCIPEDE

11
BONE-BREAKER
BULLOCK-CART
CONVERTIBLE
DIESEL TRAIN
FOUR-WHEELER
GUN-CARRIAGE
JAUNTING-CAR
JINRICKSHAW
LANDAULETTE
MAIL-PHÆTON
QUADRICYCLE
SIT-UP-AND-BEG
SOUPED-UP CAR
STEAM-ENGINE
STEAM-ROLLER
THIKA-GHARRY
WHITECHAPEL

12
COACH AND FOUR
DÉSOBLIGEANT
DOUBLE-DECKER

12–continued
EXPRESS TRAIN
FREIGHT TRAIN
HORSE-AND-CART
LUGGAGE TRAIN
PANTECHNICON
PUFFING BILLY
RAILWAY TRAIN
SINGLE-DECKER
STATION-WAGON
STEAM-OMNIBUS
THROUGH TRAIN

13
CYCLE-RICKSHAW
ELECTRIC TRAIN
GOVERNESS-CART
HORSE-CARRIAGE
PENNYFARTHING
PEOPLE CARRIER
RACING CHARIOT
SHOOTING-BRAKE

14
FOUR-WHEEL DRIVE
PASSENGER TRAIN
RIDING-CARRIAGE
TRACTION ENGINE

15
HACKNEY-CARRIAGE
PRAIRIE-SCHOONER

16
MOTORIZED
  BICYCLE
UNDERGROUND
  TRAIN

17
HORSELESS
  CARRIAGE

18
TRAVELLING
  CARRIAGE

SHIPS AND BOATS

3
ARK
COG
HOY
TUG

4
ARGO
BARK
BOAT
BRIG
BUSS
DHOW
DORY
GRAB
JUNK
PROA
PUNT
RAFT
SAIC
SNOW
TROW
YAWL

5
BARGE
CANOE
COBLE
DANDY
FERRY
FUNNY

5–continued
KAYAK
KETCH
LINER
NOBBY
PRAHU
SHELL
SKIFF
SLOOP
SMACK
TRAMP
U-BOAT
UMIAK
XEBEC
YACHT

6
BARQUE
BAWLEY
BIREME
CAIQUE
CARVEL
CUTTER
DINGHY
DOGGER
DUG-OUT
GALLEY
HOOKER
HOPPER
LAUNCH
LORCHA

6–continued
LUGGER
PACKET
RANDAN
SAMPAN
SEALER
SLAVER
TANKER
TENDER
WHALER

7
BUMBOAT
CARAVEL
CARRACK
CLIPPER
COASTER
COLLIER
CORACLE
CORSAIR
CURRACH
DREDGER
DRIFTER
DROMOND
FELUCCA
FLY-BOAT
FRIGATE
GABBARD
GALLEON
GONDOLA
JANGADA

7–continued
PINNACE
PIRAGUA
POLACCA
POLACRE
ROWBOAT
SCULLER
STEAMER
TARTANE
TOWBOAT
TRAWLER
TRIREME
WAR SHIP

8
BILANDER
BUDGEROW
COCKBOAT
CORVETTE
CRUMSTER
DAHABIYA
FIRESHIP
FOLDBOAT
GALLIVAT
LIFEBOAT
LONG-BOAT
MAIL-SHIP
NOAH'S ARK
OUTBOARD
SAILBOAT
SCHOONER

8–continued
SHOWBOAT

9
BUCENTAUR
CARGO-BOAT
CATAMARAN
CRIS-CRAFT
FREIGHTER
HOUSE BOAT
JOLLY-BOAT
LIGHTSHIP
MOTORBOAT
MOTORSHIP
MUD-HOPPER
OUTRIGGER
RIVER-BOAT
ROTOR SHIP
SHIP'S BOAT

9–continued
SLAVE-SHIP
SPEEDBOAT
STEAMBOAT
STEAMSHIP
STORESHIP
SUBMARINE

10
BANANA-BOAT
BRIGANTINE
PADDLE-BOAT
PICKET BOAT
PIRATE-SHIP
PRISON-SHIP
QUADRIREME
ROWING BOAT
TEA-CLIPPER
TRAIN-FERRY

10–continued
VIKING-SHIP
WIND-JAMMER

11
BARQUENTINE
CHASSE-MARÉE
COCKLE-SHELL
DOUBLE-CANOE
FISHING-BOAT
HOPPER-BARGE
MAIL-STEAMER
PENTECONTER
PILOT VESSEL
QUINQUEREME
SAILING-SHIP
THREE-MASTER

12
CABIN-CRUISER

12–continued
ESCORT VESSEL
FISHING SMACK
HOSPITAL SHIP
MERCHANT SHIP
PLEASURE BOAT
SAILING BARGE
STERN-WHEELER

13
HERRING-FISHER
PASSENGER SHIP
TRANSPORT SHIP

14
CHANNEL STEAMER
COASTING VESSEL
FLOATING PALACE
OCEAN
  GREYHOUND

AIRCRAFT

3
JET

4
KITE

5
PLANE

6
AIR CAR
BOMBER
GLIDER

7
AIRSHIP
BALLOON
BIPLANE

7–continued
CLIPPER
FIGHTER
JUMP-JET
SHUTTLE

8
AEROSTAT
AIRPLANE
AUTOGIRO
CONCORDE
JUMBO-JET
ROTODYNE
SEA-PLANE
TRIPLANE
TURBO-JET
WARPLANE

8–continued
ZEPPELIN

9
AEROPLANE
DIRIGIBLE
MAIL-PLANE
MONOPLANE
SAILPLANE
TURBO-PROP

10
FLYING-BOAT
GAS-BALLOON
HELICOPTER
HOVERCRAFT
HYDROPLANE

11
FIRE-BALLOON

12
FREIGHT-PLANE

13
STRATOCRUISER

14
FLYING BEDSTEAD
PASSENGER PLANE

18
MONTGOLFIER
  BALLOON

INTERNATIONAL AIRPORTS

ARLANDA (Stockholm)
ATATURK (Istanbul)
BARAJAS (Madrid)
CHARLES DE GAULLE (Paris)
CHANGI (Singapore)
CHIANG KAI-SHEK (Taipei)
COINTRIN (Geneva)
DALLAS-FORT WORTH
  (Dallas)

DORVAL (Montreal)
DOUGLAS (Charlotte)
DULLES (Washington)
ECHTERDINGEN (Stuttgart)
FINDEL (Luxembourg)
FORNEBU (Oslo)
GATWICK (London)
HARTSFIELD (Atlanta)
HEATHROW (London)

HELSINKI-VANTAA (Helsinki)
HONGQIAO (Shanghai)
HOPKINS (Cleveland)
JOHN F KENNEDY (New York)
(BENITO) JUAREZ (Mexico
  City)
KIMPO (Seoul)
KING KHALED (Riyadh)
KINGSFORD SMITH (Sydney)

LA GUARDIA (New York)
LEONARDO DA VINCI (FIUMICINO) Rome
LINATE (Milan)
LINDBERGH FIELD (San Diego)
LOGAN (Boston)
LUIS MUÑOZ MARIN (San Juan)

MCCARRAN (Las Vegas)
MIRABEL (Montreal)
NARITA (Tokyo)
NINOY AQUINO (Manila)
O'HARE (Chicago)
OKECIE (Warsaw)
ORLY (Paris)
PEARSON (Toronto)
ST PAUL (Minneapolis)

SCHIPHOL (Amsterdam)
SHEREMETYEVO (Moscow)
SKY HARBOR (Phoenix)
SOEKARNO HATTA (Jakarta)
STANSTED (London)
SUBANG (Kuala Lumpur)
TEGEL (Berlin)
TULLAMARINE (Melbourne)
WAYNE COUNTY (Detroit)

AIRLINE FLIGHT CODES

CODE	AIRLINE
AAF	Aigle Azur
AAG	Air Atlantique
AAL	American A/L
AAN	Oasis
ABB	Air Belgium
ABR	Hunting
ACA	Air Canada
ACF	Air Charter Intl
ADR	Adria A/W
AEA	Air Europa
AEF	Aero Lloyd
AFL	Aeroflot
AFM	Affretair
AFR	Air France
AGX	Aviogenex
AHK	Air Hong Kong
AIA	Air Atlantis
AIC	Air-India
AIH	Airtours
ALK	Air Lanka
AMC	Air Malta
AMM	Air 2000
AMT	American Trans Air
ANA	All Nippon A/W
ANZ	Air New Zealand
AOM	Air Outre Mer
APW	Arrow Air
ARG	Argentine A/W
ATI	ATI
ATT	Aer Turas
AUA	Austrian A/L
AUR	Aurigny A/S
AVA	Avianca
AWC	Titan A/W
AYC	Aviaco
AZA	Alitalia
AZI	Air Zimbabwe
AZR	Air Zaire
BAC	BAC Leasing
BAF	British Air Ferries
BAL	Britannia A/L
BAW	British Airways

BBB	Balair
BBC	Bangladesh Biman
BCS	European A/T
BEA	Brymon European
BEE	Busy Bee
BER	Air Berlin
BIH	British Intl Heli
BMA	British Midland
BRA	Braathens
BWA	BWIA
BZH	Brit Air
CCA	CAAC
CDN	Canadian A/L Intl
CFE	City Flyer
CFG	Condor
CIC	Celtic Air
CKT	Caledonian
CLH	Lufthansa CityLine
CLX	Cargolux
CMM	Canada 3000 A/L
CNB	Air Columbus
COA	Continental A/L
CPA	Cathay Pacific
CRL	Corse Air
CRX	Crossair
CSA	Czech A/L
CTA	CTA
CTN	Croatia A/L
CYP	Cyprus A/W
DAH	Air Algerie
DAL	Delta A/L
DAT	Delta Air Transport
DLH	Lufthansa
DMA	Maersk Air
DQI	Cimber Air
DYA	Alyemda
EGY	Egypt Air
EIA	Evergreen Intl
EIN	Aer Lingus
ELY	El Al
ETH	Ethiopian A/L
EUI	Euralair
EWW	Emery
EXS	Channel Express

EXX	Air Exel UK
FDE	Federal Express
FIN	Finnair
FOB	Ford
FOF	Fred Olsen
FUA	Futura
FXY	Flexair
GBL	GB Airways
GEC	German Cargo
GFA	Gulf Air
GFG	Germania
GHA	Ghana A/W
GIA	Garuda
GIL	Gill Air
GNT	Business Air
GRN	Greenair
HAL	Hawaiian Air
HAS	Hamburg A/L
HLA	HeavyLift
HLF	Hapag-Lloyd
IAW	Iraqi A/W
IBE	Iberia
ICE	Icelandair
IEA	Inter European
INS	Instone A/L
IRA	Iran Air
IST	Istanbul A/L
ITF	Air Inter
JAL	Japan A/L
JAT	JAT
JAV	Janes Aviation
JEA	Jersey European A/W
KAC	Kuwait A/W
KAL	Korean Air
KAR	Kar-Air
KIS	Contactair
KLM	KLM
KQA	Kenya A/W
LAA	Libyan Arab A/L
LAZ	Bulgarian A/L
LDA	Lauda Air
LEI	Air UK Leisure
LGL	Luxair
LIB	Air Liberte

LIN	Linjeflyg	RBA	Royal Brunei	TMA	Trans Mediterranean
LIT	Air Littoral	RIA	Rich Intl	TOW	Tower Air
LKA	Alkair	RJA	Royal Jordanian	TRA	Transavia
LOG	Loganair	RNA	Royal Nepal A/L	TSC	Air Transat
LOT	Polish A/L (LOT)	ROT	Tarom	TSW	TEA Basle
LTE	LTE	RWD	Air Rwanda	TWA	TWA
LTS	LTU Sud	RYR	Ryanair	TWE	Transwede
LTU	LTU	SAA	South African A/W	TYR	Tyrolean
MAH	Malev	SAB	Sabena	UAE	Emirates A/L
MAS	Malaysian A/L	SAS	SAS	UAL	United A/L
MAU	Air Mauritius	SAW	Sterling A/W	UGA	Uganda A/L
MDN	Meridiana	SAY	Suckling A/W	UKA	Air UK
MEA	Middle East A/L	SDI	Saudi	UKR	Air Ukraine
MNX	Manx A/L	SEY	Air Seychelles	ULE	Air UK Leisure
MON	Monarch A/L	SIA	Singapore A/L	UPA	Air Foyle
MOR	Morefly	SJM	Southern AT	UPS	United Parcels
MPH	Martinair	SLA	Sobelair	USA	USAir
NAD	Nobleair	SPP	Spanair	UTA	UTA
NAW	Newair	STR	Stellair	UYC	Cameroon A/L
NEX	Northern Executive	SUD	Sudan A/W	VIA	Viasa
NGA	Nigeria A/W	SUT	Sultan Air	VIR	Virgin Atlantic
NSA	Nile Safaris	SWE	Swedair	VIV	Viva Air
NWA	Northwest A/L	SWR	Swissair	VKG	Scanair
NXA	Nationair	SXS	Sun Express	VRG	Varig
OAL	Olympic A/L	SYR	Syrian Arab	WDL	WDL
OYC	Conair	TAP	Air Portugal	WOA	World A/W
PAL	Philippine A/L	TAR	Tunis Air	ZAC	Zambia A/W
PGA	Portugalia	TAT	TAT	ZAS	ZAS A/L of Egypt
PGT	Pegasus	TCT	TUR European		
PIA	Pakistan Intl	THA	Thai A/W Intl	A/W = Airways	
QFA	Qantas	THG	Thurston	A/L = Airlines	
QSC	African Safaris	THY	Turkish A/L	A/T = Air Transport	
RAM	Royal Air Maroc	TLE	Air Toulouse	A/S = Aero Service	

MOTORING TERMS

2	4–continued	6–continued	7–continued	8–continued
CC	TYRE	GASKET	GEARBOX	MOUNTING
		HEATER	OIL SEAL	RADIATOR
3	**5**	HUB CAP		ROTOR ARM
BHP	BRAKE	IDLING	**8**	SELECTOR
CAM	CHOKE	PISTON	ADHESION	SILENCER
FAN	SERVO	REBORE	BRAKE PAD	SMALL END
HUB	SHAFT	STROKE	BULKHEAD	STEERING
JET	VALVE	TAPPET	CALLIPER	THROTTLE
REV	WHEEL	TORQUE	CAMSHAFT	TRACK ROD
ROD		TUNING	CROSS-PLY	
	6		CYLINDER	**9**
4	BIG END	**7**	DIPSTICK	BRAKESHOE
AXLE	BONNET	BATTERY	FLYWHEEL	CONDENSER
BOOT	CAMBER	BEARING	FUEL PUMP	DISC BRAKE
BUSH	CLUTCH	BRACKET	IGNITION	DRUM BRAKE
COIL	DAMPER	CHASSIS	KICK-DOWN	GEAR STICK
GEAR	DECOKE	DYNAMIC	KNOCKING	GENERATOR
HORN	DYNAMO	EXHAUST	LIVE AXLE	HALF-SHAFT
LOCK	ENGINE	FAN BELT	MANIFOLD	HANDBRAKE
SUMP	FILTER			

9–continued
INDUCTION
MISFIRING
OVERDRIVE
OVERSTEER
PROP SHAFT
RADIAL-PLY
SIDE VALVE
SPARK PLUG
TWO-STROKE
UNDERSEAL
WHEELBASE

10
AIR CLEANER
ALTERNATOR
BRAKE FLUID
CRANKSHAFT
DETONATION
DRIVE SHAFT
FOUR-STROKE
GUDGEON PIN
HORSEPOWER

10–continued
PISTON RING
REV COUNTER
SUSPENSION
TACHOMETER
THERMOSTAT
UNDERSTEER
WINDSCREEN

11
ANTI-ROLL BAR
CARBURETTER
CARBURETTOR
COMPRESSION
CROSSMEMBER
DISTRIBUTOR
SERVO SYSTEM
SYNCHROMESH

12
ACCELERATION
CYLINDER HEAD
DIESEL ENGINE

12–continued
DIFFERENTIAL
SPARKING PLUG
SUPERCHARGER
TRANSMISSION
TURBOCHARGER
VISCOUS DRIVE

13
COOLING SYSTEM
DECARBONIZING
FUEL INJECTION
OVERHEAD VALVE
POWER STEERING
RACK-AND-PINION
SHOCK ABSORBER
SLAVE CYLINDER
SPARK IGNITION

14
FOUR-WHEEL DRIVE
PROPELLER SHAFT
UNIVERSAL JOINT

15
FRONT-WHEEL
  DRIVE
HYDRAULIC SYSTEM
PETROL INJECTION

17
INDUCTION
  MANIFOLD
REVOLUTION
  COUNTER

19
CROWN WHEEL AND
  PINION

20+
AUTOMATIC
  TRANSMISSION
INDEPENDENT
  SUSPENSION
POWER ASSISTED
  STEERING

INTERNATIONAL CAR REGISTRATIONS

REGISTRATION LETTER
  Country

A	Austria	GH	Ghana	NIG	Niger	RU	Burundi
AL	Albania	GR	Greece	NL	Netherlands	RWA	Rwanda
AUS	Australia	H	Hungary	NZ	New Zealand	S	Sweden
B	Belgium	HK	Hong Kong	P	Portugal	SD	Swaziland
BDS	Barbados	HKJ	Jordan	PA	Panama	SF	Finland
BG	Bulgaria	I	Italy	PAK	Pakistan	SGP	Singapore
BR	Brazil	IL	Israel	PE	Peru	SME	Surinam
BRG	Guyana	IND	India	PI	Philippines	SN	Senegal
BRN	Bahrain	IR	Iran	PL	Poland	SYR	Syria
BS	Bahamas	IRL	Ireland	PY	Paraguay	T	Thailand
C	Cuba	IRQ	Iraq	R	Romania	TG	Togo
CDN	Canada	IS	Iceland	RA	Argentina	TN	Tunisia
CH	Switzerland	J	Japan	RB	Botswana	TR	Turkey
CI	Côte d'Ivoire	JA	Jamaica	RC	China	TT	Trinidad and
CO	Colombia	KWT	Kuwait	RCA	Central African		Tobago
CR	Costa Rica	L	Luxembourg		Republic	U	Uruguay
CY	Cyprus	LAO	Laos	RCB	Congo	USA	United States
D	Germany	LB	Liberia	RCH	Chile		of America
DK	Denmark	LS	Lesotho	RH	Haiti	VN	Vietnam
DZ	Algeria	M	Malta	RI	Indonesia	WAL	Sierra Leone
E	Spain	MA	Morocco	RIM	Mauritania	WAN	Nigeria
EC	Ecuador	MAL	Malaysia	RL	Lebanon	WS	Western
F	France	MEX	Mexico	RM	Malagasy		Samoa
FL	Liechtenstein	MS	Mauritius		Republic	YV	Venezuela
GB	Great Britain	MW	Malawi	RMM	Mali	Z	Zambia
GCA	Guatemala	N	Norway	ROK	South Korea	ZA	South Africa

NAUTICAL TERMS

3
AFT
BOW
FID
LEE

4
ALEE
BEAM
BITT
BOOM
FORE
HOLD
HULL
KEEL
KNOT
LIST
MATE
POOP
PORT
PROW
STAY
STEM
WAKE
WARP

5
ABAFT
ABEAM
ABOUT
ALOFT
AVAST
BELAY
BELLS
BILGE
BOSUN
CABLE

5–continued
CAULK
CLEAT
DAVIT
HATCH
HAWSE
STERN
TRICK
TRUCK
WAIST
WEIGH
WINCH

6
BRIDGE
BUNKER
FATHOM
FENDER
FLUKES
FO'C'SLE
GALLEY
HAWSER
JETSAM
LEAGUE
LEEWAY
OFFING
PURSER
SHROUD
YAWING

7
ADMIRAL
BALLAST
BOLLARD
BULWARK
CAPSTAN
CATWALK

7–continued
COAMING
DRAUGHT
FLOTSAM
GANGWAY
GRAPNEL
GUNWALE
INBOARD
LANYARD
MOORING
QUARTER
RIGGING
SEA MILE
TONNAGE
TOPSIDE
WATCHES

8
BINNACLE
BOWSPRIT
BULKHEAD
COXSWAIN
DOG WATCH
HALYARDS
HATCHWAY
LARBOARD
PITCHING
RATLINES
SCUPPERS
SPLICING
TAFFRAIL
WINDLASS
WINDWARD

9
AMIDSHIPS
COMPANION

9–continued
CROW'S NEST
FREEBOARD
SHIP'S BELL
STARBOARD
WATER-LINE

10
BATTEN DOWN
DEADLIGHTS
DEADWEIGHT
FIRST WATCH
FORE-AND-AFT
FORECASTLE
NIGHT WATCH

11
MIDDLE WATCH
QUARTER-DECK
WEATHER SIDE

12
DISPLACEMENT
JACOB'S LADDER
MARLINE SPIKE
NAUTICAL MILE
PLIMSOLL LINE

13
QUARTERMASTER

14
SUPERSTRUCTURE

15
COMPANION-
  LADDER
DAVY JONES'
  LOCKER

SHIPPING AREAS NAMED IN WEATHER FORECASTS

BAILEY
BISCAY
CROMARTY
DOGGER
DOVER
FAEROES
FAIR ISLE
FASTNET
FINISTERRE
FISHER

FORTH
FORTIES
GERMAN BIGHT
HEBRIDES
HUMBER
IRISH SEA
LUNDY
MALIN
PLYMOUTH
PORTLAND

ROCKALL
SHANNON
SOLE
SOUTH-EAST ICELAND
THAMES
TYNE
VIKING
WIGHT

BRITISH CANALS

4
BUDE
5
CHARD
DERBY
NEATH
CRINAN

6
DUDLEY
EXETER
KETLEY
LYDNEY
OAKHAM
OXFORD
SANKEY
TYRONE

7
CHESTER
EREWASH
REGENTS
SWANSEA
TENNANT

8
BARNSLEY
CARLISLE
COVENTRY
CROMFORD
GRANTHAM
MONKLAND
ROCHDALE
ST HELENS

9
BAYBRIDGE
DROITWICH
ELLESMERE
LANCASTER
LOUTH SHIP

9–continued
NEWRY SHIP
TAVISTOCK
ULVERSTON

10
BIRMINGHAM
CALEDONIAN
COALISLAND
COOMBE HILL
DONNINGTON
GRAND TRUNK (Trent and Mersey)
GRAND UNION
LLANGOLLEN
NOTTINGHAM
PEAK FOREST
SHREWSBURY
TORRINGTON

11
BASINGSTOKE
BRIDGEWATER
STOURBRIDGE

12
CALDON BRANCH (Trent and Mersey)
CHESTERFIELD
GRAND WESTERN
MACCLESFIELD
THANET BRANCH

13
ABERDEENSHIRE
FORTH AND CLYDE
GRAND JUNCTION
KENNET AND AVON
ROYAL MILITARY
WILTS AND BERKS

14
ASHBY-DE-LA-ZOUCH
GLAMORGANSHIRE
MANCHESTER SHIP
STAFFS AND WORCS
TRENT AND MERSEY

15
ASHTON-UNDER-LYNE
MONTGOMERYSHIRE
RAMSDENS-SIR JOHN
SHROPSHIRE UNION
THAMES AND SEVERN

16
WARWICK AND NAPTON

17
LEEDS AND LIVERPOOL
SOMERSETSHIRE COAL
STRATFORD-UPON-AVON

18
HUDDERSFIELD NARROW
NEWCASTLE-UNDER-LYME
WYRLEY AND ESSINGTON

19
ELLESMERE AND CHESTER

20
LISKEARD AND LOO UNION
PORTSMOUTH AND ARUNDEL
STOURBRIDGE EXTENSION

21
BRIDGEWATER AND TAUNTON
MONMOUTHSHIRE AND BRECON
WORCESTER AND BIRMINGHAM

23+
BRECKNOCK AND ABERGAVENNY
CHELMSFORD AND BLACKWATER
CLIFTON AND KEARSLEY-FLETCHER
EDINBURGH AND GLASGOW UNION
GLASGOW, PAISLEY, AND ADROSSAN
GLOUCESTER AND BERKELEY SHIP
HEREFORDSHIRE AND GLOUCESTER
LEICESTER AND NORTHANTS UNION
SHEFFIELD AND SOUTH YORKSHIRE

WORLD CANALS

3&4
EST, DE L' (FRANCE)
ERIE (New York State Barge) (USA)
GOTA (SWEDEN)
KIEL (DENMARK)
MIDI, DU (FRANCE)
SUEZ (EGYPT)

5
EIDER (DENMARK)
GRAND (CHINA)
GRAND (IRELAND)
KINDA (SWEDEN)
LINDO (SWEDEN)
RHINE (GERMANY)
TRENT (CANADA)
UNION (USA)

6
ALBERT (BELGIUM)
ALSACE (FRANCE)
BIRARE (FRANCE)
CENTRE, DU (BELGIUM)
EUROPA (GERMANY)
LEHIGH (USA)
MORRIS (USA)

6–continued
PANAMA
RIDEAU (CANADA)
SAIMAA (FINLAND)
SANTEE (USA)
VIRIDI (FRANCE)

7
AUGUSTA (USA)

7–continued
CAPE COD (USA)
CHAMBLY (CANADA)
CHEMUNG (USA)
CORINTH (GREECE)
JULIANA (HOLLAND)
LOUVAIN, DE (BELGIUM)
LUDWIGS (GERMANY)
ORLEANS (FRANCE)
WELLAND (CANADA)

8
MARCHAND (FRANCE)
NOORDZEE (HOLLAND)
TELEMARK (NORWAY)

9
BOURGOGNE (FRANCE)
CHAMPLAIN (USA)
DALSLANDS (SWEDEN)
LANGUEDOC (FRANCE)
MIDDLESEX (USA)
ST QUENTIN (FRANCE)
STECKNITZ (GERMANY)

10
BEREGUARDO (ITALY)
MITTELLAND (GERMANY)
RHONE A SETE (FRANCE)
SCHUYLKILL (USA)
TROLLHATTE (SWEDEN)

11
DISMAL SWAMP (USA)
DORTMUND-EMS
(GERMANY)
HOUSTON SHIP (USA)

11–continued
MARNE AU RHIN, DE LA
(FRANCE)
NORTH BRANCH (USA)
OHIO AND ERIE (USA)
RHINE-DANUBE (GERMANY)
RHONE AU RHIN (FRANCE)
WILLEBROECK (BELGIUM)

12
CROSS-FLORIDA (USA)
FRANCHE-COMTE (FRANCE)
MARNE LATERAL (FRANCE)
MIAMI AND ERIE (USA)
NANTES A BREST (FRANCE)
PENNSYLVANIA (USA)

13
AISNE A LA MARNE
(FRANCE)
BEAVER AND ERIE (USA)
MARNE A LA SAONE
(FRANCE)
SAMBRE AND OISE
(FRANCE)
WABASH AND ERIE (USA)

14
AMSTERDAM-RHINE
(HOLLAND)
GHENT-TERNEUZEN
(BELGIUM/HOLLAND)

15
MARSEILLES-RHONE
(FRANCE)

16
BLUE RIDGE PARKWAY (USA)
NORTH HOLLAND SHIP
ST LAWRENCE SEAWAY
(USA)
SAULT SAINTE MARIE (USA)
SOUTH HADLEY FALLS (USA)

17
BRUSSELS-CHARLEROI
(BELGIUM)
CHESAPEAKE AND OHIO
(USA)
DELAWARE AND HUDSON
(USA)
LATERAL A LA GARONNE
(FRANCE)
NEW YORK STATE BARGE
(formerly Erie) (USA)

19+
CHESAPEAKE AND
DELAWARE (USA)
CHICAGO SHIP AND
SANITARY (USA)
ILLINOIS AND MICHIGAN
WATERWAY (USA)
JAMES RIVER AND
KANAWHA (USA)
PENNSYLVANIA AND ERIE
(USA)
PENNSYLVANIA AND OHIO
(USA)

MOTORWAY SERVICE STATIONS

5
BIRCH (M62)
FLEET (M3)
KEELE (M6)
MAGOR (M4)
TEBAY (M6)

6
CORLEY (M6)
DURHAM (A1M)
EXETER (M5)
GRETNA (A74M)
HESTON (M4)
MEDWAY (M2)
OXFORD (M40)

7
CHESTER (M56)
GORDANO (M5)

7–continued
KINROSS (M90)
MEMBURY (M4)
RADWELL (A1M)
READING (M4)
TELFORD (M54)
TROWELL (M1)
WARWICK (M40)
WOODALL (M1)

8
ABINGTON (M74)
BOTHWELL (M74)
FRANKLEY (M5)
HAMILTON (M74)
HARTHILL (M8)
ROWNHAMS (M27)
SANDBACH (M6)
SARN PARK (M4)

8–continued
STAFFORD (M6)
STANFORD (M20)
STIRLING (M9/M80)
THURROCK (M25)
TIBSHELF (M1)

9
KIRBY HILL (A1M)
KNUTSFORD (M6)
LANCASTER (M6)
MAIDSTONE (M20)
SEDGEMOOR (M5)
STRENSHAM (M5)

10
BOLTON WEST (M61)
BRIDGWATER (M5)
BURTONWOOD (M57)

LOCOMOTIVES

10–continued
CULLOMPTON (M5)
HILTON PARK (M6)
ROSSINGTON (M18)
SEVERN VIEW (M4)
SOUTH MIMMS (A1M/M25)
SOUTHWAITE (M6)
TODDINGTON (M1)
WASHINGTON (A1M)
WATFORD GAP (M1)
WINCHESTER (M3)

11
CARDIFF GATE (M4)
CARDIFF WEST (M4)
CLACKET LANE (M25)

11–continued
FERRYBRIDGE (A1M/M62)
HOPWOOD PARK (M42)
MICHAEL WOOD (M5)
PORT ABRAHAM (M4)
SWANSEA WEST (M4)
WOOLLEY EDGE (M1)

12
TAUNTON DEANE (M5)

13
HARTSHEAD MOOR (M62)
LEIGH DELAMERE (M4)
LONDON GATEWAY (M1)
ROTHERSTHORPE (M1)

14
ANNANDALE WATER (A74M)
CHERWELL VALLEY (M40)
DONCASTER NORTH
  (M18/M180)
DONNINGTON PARK (M1)
KILLINGTON LAKE (M6)
NEWPORT PAGNELL (M1)

15
CHARNOCK RICHARD (M6)

19
LEICESTER FOREST EAST
  (M1)

LOCOMOTIVES

4
DART
ISAR

5
ARROW
BEUTH
CAMEL
COMET
GOTHA
QUEEN
SEEVE

6
DRAGON
METEOR
MINORU
MOABIT
PLANET
ROCKET

7
AMERICA
BATAVIA
CARDEAN
CORSAIR
FIRE FLY
GENERAL
JUPITER

7–continued
MALLARD
NOVELTY
PHOENIX
TORNADO
WANNSEE

8
ATLANTIC
CYCLOPED
DER ADLER
HERCULES
IRON DUKE
MAJESTIC
PYRACMON
REINGOLD
TOM THUMB
VAUXHALL

9
BLUE GOOSE
IRISH MAIL
NEWCASTLE
NORTH STAR

10
CALEDONIAN
DORCHESTER
EXPERIMENT

10–continued
LOCOMOTION
SANS PAREIL
WYLAM DILLY

11
HENRY OAKLEY
JEANIE DEANS
ROYAL GEORGE
WILLIAM DEAN

12
GREAT WESTERN
NORTHUMBRIAN
NUNNEY CASTLE
OLD IRONSIDES
PERSEVERENCE
PHILADELPHIA
PINES EXPRESS
PRINCE ALFRED
PUFFING BILLY

13
COALBROOKDALE
GENERAL LOWELL
SAINT NICHOLAS

14
CENTRAL VERMONT

14–continued
CYRUS K HOLLIDAY
DANTE ALIGHIERI
FLYING SCOTSMAN
ROBERT THE DEVIL

15
BROTHER
  JONATHAN
PENDENNIS CASTLE

17
DUCHESS OF
  HAMILTON
PLANET CENTENAR-
  IAN
SIR WILLIAM
  STANIER

18+
BEST FRIEND OF
  CHARLSTON
EMPIRE STATE EX-
  PRESS
TWENTIETH CEN-
  TURY LIMITED
WASHINGTON
  COUNTY FARMER

CLOTHES, MATERIALS, AND FASHION

CLOTHES

3	4–continued	5–continued	5–continued	6–continued
ABA	MASK	BOINA	PANTS	BEAVER
ALB	MAXI	BOOTS	PARKA	BÈQUIN
BAL	MIDI	BURKA	PILCH	BERTHA
BAS	MINI	BUSBY	PIRNY	BICORN
BAT	MITT	CABAS	PUMPS	BIETLE
BIB	MUFF	CADET	SABOT	BIGGIN
BRA	MULE	CAPPA	SAREE	BIKINI
COP	PUMP	CHALE	SCARF	BIRRUS
FEZ	ROBE	CHAPS	SHAKO	BISHOP
HAT	RUFF	CHOGA	SHAWL	BLAZER
LEI	SARI	CHOLI	SHIFT	BLIAUD
OBI	SASH	CLOAK	SHIRT	BLOUSE
TAM	SAYA	CORDY	SKIRT	BOATER
	SHOE	COTTA	SMOCK	BODICE
4	SLIP	COTTE	SNOOD	BOLERO
ABBA	SLOP	CREST	STOCK	BONNET
AGAL	SOCK	CROWN	STOLA	BOOTEE
ALBA	SPAT	CURCH	STOLE	BOWLER
APEX	SUIT	CYLAS	TAILS	BOXERS
BAJU	TABI	CYMAR	TEDDY	BRACAE
BARB	TOGA	DERBY	TIARA	BRACES
BECK	TOGS	DHOTI	TONGS	BRAGAS
BELT	TOPI	EPHOD	TOPEE	BRAIES
BENN	TUTU	FICHU	TOQUE	BRETON
BOTA	VAMP	FROCK	TREWS	BRIEFS
BUSK	VEIL	GANSY	TUNIC	BROGAN
CACK	VEST	GILET	VISOR	BROGUE
CAPE	WRAP	GIPPO	VIZOR	BUSKIN
CLOG		GLOVE	WEEDS	BYRNIE
COAT	**5**	HABIT		BYRRUS
COPE	ABNET	HULLS	**6**	CABAAN
COTE	ACTON	IHRAM	ABOLLA	CADDIE
COWL	AEGIS	JABOT	ALMUCE	CAFTAN
DAPS	AMICE	JAMAH	ANADEM	CALASH
DIDO	AMPYX	JEANS	ANALAV	CALCEI
DISK	APRON	JELAB	ANKLET	CALIGA
GARB	ARCAN	JUPON	ANORAK	CALPAC
GETA	ARMET	LAMMY	ARCTIC	CAMAIL
GOWN	ARMOR	LODEN	ARTOIS	CAMISA
HAIK	ASCOT	LUNGI	BALKAN	CAMISE
HOOD	BARBE	MIDDY	BANYAN	CAPOTE
HOSE	BARRY	MUFTI	BARRET	CAPUCE
IZAR	BENJY	NUBIA	BARVEL	CAPUTI
JAMA	BERET	PAGNE	BASQUE	CARACO
KEPI	BLAKE	PAGRI	BAUTTA	CASQUE
KILT	BLUEY	PALLA	BEANIE	CASTOR

6–continued

CAUSIA
CESTUS
CHADAR
CHITON
CHOKER
CILICE
CIMIER
CLAQUE
CLOCHE
COBCAB
COCKET
CORNET
CORONA
CORSET
COTHUM
COVERT
CRAVAT
DIADEM
DICKEY
DIRNDL
DOLMAN
DOMINO
DUSTER
EARCAP
FEDORA
FILLET
GAITER
GANSEY
GARTER
GAUCHO
GILLIE
GUIMPE
HALTER
HENNIN
HUIPIL
JACKET
JERKIN
JERSEY
JUBBAH
JUMPER
KABAYA
KIMONO
KIRTLE
KITTEL
LAMMIE
LOAFER
LUNGEE
MAGYAR
MANTEE
MANTLE
MANTUA
MITTEN
MOBCAP
MOGGAN
OUTFIT
PEG-TOP
PEPLOS
PEPLUM
PILEUS
PINNER
PIRNIE

6–continued

PONCHO
PUGREE
PUTTEE
RAGLAN
REEFER
RUFFLE
SANDAL
SARONG
SERAPE
SHIMMY
SHORTS
SHROUD
SLACKS
SONTAG
STEP-IN
SUN HAT
TABARD
TAMISE
TIGHTS
TIPPET
TOP HAT
TOPPER
TRILBY
TRUNKS
T-SHIRT
TUCKER
TURBAN
TUXEDO
TWEEDS
ULSTER
UNDIES
UPLIFT
VAMPAY
VESTEE
WIMPLE
WOOLLY
ZOUAVE

7

AMICTUS
APPAREL
ARISARD
ARM BAND
BABOOSH
BALDRIC
BALTEUS
BANDEAU
BANDORE
BARBUTE
BAROQUE
BASHLYK
BASINET
BAVETTE
BAVOLET
BEDIZEN
BELCHER
BERDASH
BERETTA
BETSIES
BIRETTA
BOTTINE

7–continued

BOX CAPE
BOX COAT
BRIMMER
BROIGNE
BURNOUS
BUSSKIN
CALEÇON
CALOTTE
CAMOURO
CANEZOU
CAPE HAT
CAPUCHE
CAPULET
CASAQUE
CASSOCK
CATSKIN
CAUBEEN
CEREVIS
CHAINSE
CHALWAR
CHAPLET
CHEMISE
CHEVRON
CHIMERE
CHIP HAT
CHLAMYS
CHOPINE
CHOU HAT
CHRISOM
CHUDDAR
CHUDDER
COMMODE
CORONEL
CORONET
COSSACK
COXCOMB
CREPIDA
CRISPIN
CUCULLA
CUIRASS
CULOTTE
CURCHEF
CUTAWAY
DOPATTA
DOUBLET
DRAWERS
DULBAND
DUL HOSE
EARMUFF
ETON CAP
EVERETT
FANCHON
FASHION
FILIBEG
FLATCAP
GARMENT
GHILLIE
G STRING
GUM BOOT
GUM SHOE
GYM SHOE

7–continued

HANDBAG
HIGH-LOW
HOMBURG
HOSIERY
JODHPUR
KLOMPEN
LAYETTE
LEOTARD
MAILLOT
MANTEAU
MONTERA
MONTERO
MUFFLER
OLIVERS
OVERALL
OXFORDS
PANTIES
PARASOL
PATTERN
PELISSE
PETASOS
PIERROT
PILLBOX
PLUVIAL
PUGGREE
PYJAMAS
RAIMENT
REGALIA
ROMPERS
RUBBERS
SARAFAN
SCOGGER
SHALWAR
SILK HAT
SINGLET
SKI BOOT
SLIPPER
SLYDERS
SMICKET
SNEAKER
SOUTANE
SPENCER
SPORRAN
SULTANE
SUN SUIT
SURCOAT
SURTOUT
SWEATER
TANK TOP
TEA GOWN
TOP BOOT
TOP COAT
TRAHEEN
TRICORN
TUNICLE
TWIN SET
UNIFORM
VEILING
WATTEAU
WEDGIES
WING TIE

7–continued

WOOLLEN
WRAPPER
YASHMAK
Y-FRONTS
ZIMARRA

8

ABBÉ CAPE
ALL-IN-ONE
ANALABOS
ANTELOPE
BABUSHKA
BALADRAN
BALMORAL
BANDANNA
BARBETTE
BASQUINE
BATH ROBE
BEARSKIN
BED SOCKS
BENJAMIN
BIGGONET
BINNOGUE
BLOOMERS
BODY COAT
BOMBARDS
BOOT-HOSE
BOTTEKIN
BREECHES
BURGONET
BURNOOSE
BYCOCKET
CABASSET
CAMISOLE
CANOTIER
CAPE COAT
CAPELINE
CAPRIOLE
CAPUCINE
CAPUTIUM
CARCANET
CARDIGAN
CARDINAL
CAROLINE
CASAQUIN
CATERCAP
CHANDAIL
CHAPERON
CHAQUETA
CHASUBLE
CHAUSSES
CHONGSAM
COLOBIUM
COPATAIN
CORSELET
COUCH HAT
COVERALL
CRUSH HAT
CUCULLUS
DANCE SET
DANDY HAT

8–continued
DJELLABA
DOM PEDRO
DORMEUSE
DUCK-BILL
DUNCE CAP
DUST COAT
DUTCH CAP
FALDETTA
FLANNELS
FLIMSIES
FOOTWEAR
GAMASHES
GAUNTLET
GUERNSEY
HALF-HOSE
HALF SLIP
HEADGEAR
JACK BOOT
JUDO COAT
JUMP SUIT
KERCHIEF
KNICKERS
KNITWEAR
LARRIGAN
LAVA-LAVA
LEGGINGS
LINGERIE
LIRIPIPE
MANTELET
MANTILLA
MOCCASIN
NECKLACE
NIGHTCAP
OPERA HAT
OVERALLS
OVERCOAT
OVERSHOE
PARAMENT
PEASECOD
PEIGNOIR
PHILIBEG
PILEOLUS
PINAFORE
PLASTRON
PLATINUM
PLIMSOLL
PULLOVER
SABOTINE
SKULL-CAP
SLIP-OVER
SNOWSHOE
SOMBRERO
STOCKING
SURPLICE
SWIM SUIT
TAIL COAT
TAILLEUR
TARBOOSH
TOQUETTE
TRAINERS
TRENCHER

8–continued
TRICORNE
TROUSERS
TWO-PIECE
WOOLLENS
WOOLLIES
ZOOT SUIT

9
AFTERWELT
ALPARGATA
ALPINE HAT
ANKLE BOOT
APON DRESS
ARMILAUSA
BABY SKIRT
BALAYEUSE
BALL DRESS
BALMACAAN
BAMBIN HAT
BANDOLEER
BARCELONA
BEAVERTOP
BED JACKET
BEEGUM HAT
BELL SKIRT
BILLICOCK
BILLYCOCK
BLOUSETTE
BODY LINEN
BOURRELET
BRASSIÈRE
BROADBRIM
BRODEQUIN
BRUNSWICK
BYZANTINE
CABRIOLET
CAPE DRESS
CAPE STOLE
CARTWHEEL
CASENTINO
CASQUETTE
CASSIMERE
CHEMILOON
CHIN-CLOTH
CHIVARRAS
CHOLO COAT
COAT DRESS
COAT SHIRT
COCKED HAT
COOLIE HAT
COPINTANK
CORNERCAP
COVERSLUT
COWBOY HAT
CREEDMORE
CRINOLINE
DOG COLLAR
DOMINICAL
DRESS COAT
DRESS SHOE
DRESS SUIT

9–continued
DUNGAREES
DUNSTABLE
ESCOFFIAN
FORAGE CAP
FROCK COAT
FULL DRESS
GABARDINE
GABERDINE
GARIBALDI
GLENGARRY
GREATCOAT
HEADDRESS
HEADPIECE
HELMET CAP
HOURI-COAT
HOUSE-COAT
HULA SKIRT
INVERNESS
JOCKEY CAP
JULIET CAP
LOINCLOTH
MILLINERY
NECKCLOTH
NIGHTGOWN
OUTERWEAR
OVERDRESS
OVERSHIRT
OVERSKIRT
PANAMA HAT
PANTALETS
PANTOFFLE
PANTY HOSE
PEA JACKET
PETTICOAT
PILOT COAT
PLUS FOURS
POLONAISE
QUAKER HAT
REDINGOTE
SANBENITO
SHAKSHEER
SHINTIYAN
SHOVEL HAT
SLOPPY JOE
SLOUCH HAT
SNEAKERS
SOU'WESTER
STOMACHER
STRING TIE
SUNBONNET
SURCINGLE
TENT DRESS
THIGH BOOT
TROUSSEAU
TRUNK-HOSE
UNDERCOAT
UNDERGOWN
UNDERVEST
UNDERWEAR
VESTMENTS
VICTORINE

9–continued
WAISTCOAT
WATCH COAT
WIDE-AWAKE
WITCH'S HAT
WYLIECOAT

10
ANGELUS CAP
APRON TUNIC
BABY BONNET
BASIC DRESS
BATHING CAP
BEER JACKET
BELLBOY CAP
BERRETTINO
BIBI BONNET
BICYCLE BAL
BLOUSE COAT
BOBBY SOCKS
BOSOM SHIRT
BOUDOIR CAP
BRIGANDINE
BRUNCH COAT
BUCKET TOPS
BUMPER BRIM
BUSH JACKET
BUSK JACKET
CALZONERAS
CANVAS SHOE
CAPE COLLAR
CAPPA MAGNA
CARMAGNOLE
CERVELIÈRE
CHARTREUSE
CHATELAINE
CHEMISETTE
CHIGNON CAP
CHOUQUETTE
CLOCK-MUTCH
COOLIE COAT
COQUELUCHE
CORPS PIQUÉ
COSSACK CAP
COTE-HARDIE
COUVRE-CHEF
COVERCHIEF
COVERT COAT
CROSSCLOTH
CUMMERBUND
DANCE DRESS
DESHABILLE
DINNER SUIT
DIPLOIDIAN
DOUILLETTE
DRESS PLAID
DRESS SHIRT
DUFFEL COAT
ECLIPSE TIE
ESPADRILLE
ETON JACKET
EUGÉNIE HAT

10–continued

FANCY DRESS
FASCINATOR
FLYING SUIT
FORE-AND-AFT
FUSTANELLA
GARMENTURE
GRASS SKIRT
HAREM SKIRT
HUG-ME-TIGHT
JIGGER COAT
LIRIPIPIUM
LOUNGE SUIT
LUMBERJACK
MESS JACKET
NIGHTDRESS
NIGHTSHIRT
OPERA CLOAK
OVERBLOUSE
OVERGAITER
OXFORD BAGS
OXFORD GOWN
PANTALOONS
PICTURE HAT
PITH HELMET
POKE BONNET
PORK PIE HAT
RIDING-HOOD
SERVICE CAP
SHIRTWAIST
SPORTS COAT
SPORT SHIRT
SPORTSWEAR
STICHARION
STRING VEST
SUNDAY BEST
SUSPENDERS
SWEAT SHIRT
THREE-PIECE
TRENCH COAT
UNDERDRESS
UNDERLINEN
UNDERPANTS
UNDERSHIRT
UNDERSKIRT
VELDSCHOEN
WINDSOR TIE
WING COLLAR

11

ALSATIAN BOW
BATHING SUIT
BIB-AND-BRACE
BOILED SHIRT
BOXER SHORTS
BRACONNIÈRE
BREECHCLOTH
BRITISH WARM
CANCAN DRESS
CAVALIER HAT
CHAPEAU BRAS
CHAPEL DE FER

11–continued

CIRCASSIENE
COMBINATION
CORSET COVER
COWBOY BOOTS
DANCING CLOG
DEERSTALKER
DINNER DRESS
EMPIRE SKIRT
ESPADRILLES
EVENING GOWN
EVENING SLIP
FORMAL DRESS
FORTUNY GOWN
GALLIGASKIN
HOBBLE SKIRT
HOSTESS GOWN
HOUPPELANDE
HUNTING BOOT
MIDDY BLOUSE
NECKERCHIEF
OVERGARMENT
PANTY GIRDLE
RIDING HABIT
RUBBER APRON
RUNNING SHOE
RUSSIAN BOOT
SEWING APRON
SNAP-BRIM HAT
SOUP-AND-FISH
SOUTHWESTER
SPATTERDASH
STOCKING CAP
STRING GLOVE
SWAGGER COAT
TAM-O'SHANTER
TYROLEAN HAT
UNDERGIRDLE
UNDERTHINGS
WALKING SHOE
WEDDING GOWN
WEDDING VEIL
WELLINGTONS
WINDBREAKER
WINDCHEATER

12

AMISH COSTUME
BALKAN BLOUSE
BALLOON SKIRT
BASEBALL BOOT
BATTLE JACKET
BELLY DOUBLET
BLOOMER DRESS
BUSINESS SUIT
CAMICIA ROSSA
CAVALIER BOOT
CHEMISE DRESS
CHEMISE FROCK
CHESTERFIELD
CHUKKER SHIRT
CIGARETTE MIT

12–continued

CORSET BODICE
COTTAGE CLOAK
CRUSADER HOOD
DINNER JACKET
DIVIDED SKIRT
DORIC CHILTON
DRESS CLOTHES
DRESSING GOWN
EASTER BONNET
ENGLISH DRAPE
EVENING DRESS
EVENING SHOES
EVENING SKIRT
HANDKERCHIEF
HEADKERCHIEF
HELMET BONNET
KNEE BREECHES
LOUNGING ROBE
MANDARIN COAT
MONKEY JACKET
MORNING DRESS
MOTORING VEIL
PEDAL PUSHERS
PENITENTIALS
QUAKER BONNET
ROLL-ON GIRDLE
SCOTCH BONNET
SHIRTWAISTER
SLEEPING COAT
SLEEPING SUIT
SMALLCLOTHES
STOVEPIPE HAT
SUGAR-LOAF HAT
TAILORED SUIT
TEN-GALLON HAT
TROUSERETTES
UNDERCLOTHES
UNDERGARMENT
WIDE-AWAKE HAT
ZOUAVE JACKET

13

ACROBATIC SHOE
AFTER-SKI SOCKS
BACK-STRAP SHOE
BEEFEATER'S HAT
BELLBOY JACKET
BUNGALOW APRON
COACHMAN'S COAT
COMBING JACKET
COTTAGE BONNET
DRESSING SAQUE
ELEVATOR SHOES
HAWAIIAN SKIRT
MOTHER HUBBARD
MOURNING DRESS
NORFOLK JACKET
PEEK-A-BOO WAIST
PRINCESS DRESS
SAM BROWNE BELT
SMOKING JACKET

13–continued

SPORTS CLOTHES
SUSPENDER-BELT
TEDDYBEAR COAT
TRUNK-BREECHES
UNDERCLOTHING

14

AFTERNOON DRESS
BATHING COSTUME
BICYCLE CLIP HAT
CACHE-POUSSIÈRE
CAMOUFLAGE SUIT
CARDIGAN BODICE
CONGRESS GAITOR
CONTINENTAL HAT
DRESSING JACKET
DRESSMAKER SUIT
EGYPTIAN SANDAL
EVENING SWEATER
KNICKERBOCKERS
SHOOTING JACKET

15

CARDIGAN SWEATER
CHAPEAU FRANÇAIS
CHEMISE À LA REINE
CHEVALIER BONNET
ENVELOPE CHEMISE
FAIR ISLE SWEATER
MONTGOMERY
  BERET

16

BUTCHER BOY
  BLOUSE
CALMEL'S HAIR
  SHAWL
CHICKEN SKIN
  GLOVE
EISENHOWER
  JACKET
GOING-AWAY
  COSTUME
SWADDLING
  CLOTHES

17

CHEMISE À
  L'ANGLAISE
COAL SCUTTLE
  BONNET
CONFIRMATION
  DRESS
FOUNDATION
  GARMENT
SWALLOW-TAILED
  COAT

18

BETHLEHEM
  HEADDRESS
CHARLOTTE
  CORDAY CAP

MATERIALS

3	5–continued	6–continued	6–continued	7–continued
ABB	LAPIN	CANGAN	SHODDY	ETAMINE
BAN	LINEN	CANVAS	SISSOL	FAKE FUR
FUR	LINON	CASTOR	SKIVER	FISHNET
NET	LISLE	CATGUT	SOUPLE	FITCHEW
REP	LUREX	CHILLO	TARTAN	FLANNEL
	MOIRE	CHINTZ	TINSEL	FOULARD
4	NINON	CHROME	TISSUE	FUR FELT
ACCA	NYLON	CHUNAN	TRICOT	FUSTIAN
ALMA	ORLON	COBURG	TUSSAH	GALATEA
BAKU	PEKIN	CONTRO	TUSSEH	GINGHAM
BRIN	PIQUÉ	COSSAS	VELURE	GOBELIN
BURE	PLUSH	CÔTELÉ	VELVET	GROGRAM
CALF	PRINT	CREPON	VICUNA	GUANACO
CORD	RAYON	CROISE	WINCEY	GUIPURE
CREA	SATIN	CUBICA	WITNEY	HESSIAN
FELT	SCRIM	DAMASK		HOLLAND
FUJI	SERGE	DIAPER	**7**	JACONET
GROS	SISAL	DIMITY	ACRILON	JAP SILK
HEMP	SISOL	DJERSA	ACRYLIC	KASHMIR
HIDE	STRAW	DOMETT	ALAMODE	KIDSKIN
JEAN	STUFF	DOWLAS	ART SILK	LEATHER
LACE	SUEDE	DUCAPE	BAGGING	LEGHORN
LAMÉ	SURAH	ÉPONGE	BATISTE	LIBERTY
LAWN	TAMMY	ERMINE	BATTING	MINIVER
MULL	TISSU	FABRIC	BEMBERG	MOROCCO
PELT	TOILE	FAILLE	BRABANT	NANKEEN
ROAN	TULLE	FISHER	BUNTING	NETTING
SILK	TWEED	FORFAR	BUSTIAN	OILSKIN
SKIN	TWILL	FRIEZE	CAMBAYE	ORGANDY
VAIR	UNION	GALYAC	CAMBRIC	ORGANZA
WOOL	VOILE	GALYAK	CANTON	OTTOMAN
		GRENAI	CAPENET	PAISLEY
5	**6**	GURRAH	CARACAL	PARAGON
ABACA	ALACHA	KERSEY	CARACUL	PERCALE
ACELE	ALASKA	LAMPAS	CATALIN	PIGSKIN
ACETA	ALPACA	LASTEX	CHALLIS	RACCOON
ARDIL	ANGORA	LINENE	CHAMOIS	RAWHIDE
BAIZE	ARALAC	MADRAS	CHARVET	RAW SILK
BASCO	ARIDEX	MELTON	CHEKMAK	ROMAINE
CADIS	ARMURE	MERINO	CHEVIOT	SACKING
CAFFA	BALINE	MILIUM	CHEYNEY	SAFFIAN
CASHA	BARÉGE	MOHAIR	CHIFFON	SATINET
CLOTH	BENGAL	MOUTON	COOTHAY	SUITING
CRAPE	BERBER	MULMUL	COWHIDE	TAFFETA
CRASH	BIRETZ	MUSLIN	DAMMASÉ	TEXTILE
CRISP	BLATTA	NAPERY	DELAINE	TICKING
CROWN	DOTANY	OXFORD	DOESKIN	TIE SILK
DENIM	BUREAU	PAILLE	DORNICK	TIFFANY
DORIA	BURLAP	PONGEE	DRABBET	TUSSORE
FITCH	BURNET	POPLIN	DRUGGET	VALENCE
GAUZE	BURRAH	RIBBON	DUCHESS	VELOURS
GENET	BYSSUS	RUBBER	DURANCE	VISCOSE
GUNNY	CAFFOY	SAMITE	DUVETYN	VIYELLA
HONAN	CALICO	SATEEN	EARL GLO	WEBBING
JUPON	CAMACA	SAXONY	ÉPINGLÉ	WOOLLEN
KAPOK	CAMLET	SENNIT	ESPARTO	WORSTED
LAINE				

8

AGA BANEE
ALOE LACE
ARMOZEEN
ARMOZINE
ART LINEN
BAGHEERA
BARATHEA
BARRACAN
BAUDEKIN
BEUTANOL
BLANCARD
BOBBINET
BOMBAZET
BOX CLOTH
BUCKSKIN
BUFFSKIN
CALFSKIN
CAPESKIN
CASHMERE
CELANESE
CELENESE
CHAMBRAY
CHARMEEN
CHENILLE
CHIRIMEN
CHIVERET
CORDUROY
COTELINE
CRETONNE
DIAPHANE
DRAP D'ÉTÉ
DUCHESSE
ÉCRU SILK
EOLIENNE
ESTAMENE
EVERFAST
FARADINE
FLORENCE
GOATSKIN
GOSSAMER
HOMESPUN
INDIENNE
KOLINSKY
LAMBSKIN
LUSTRINE
LUSTRING
MARABOUT
MARCELLA
MAROCAIN
MATERIAL
MILANESE
MOGADORE
MOLESKIN
MOQUETTE
MUSLINET
MUSQUASH
NAINSOOK
OILCLOTH
ORGANDIE
PURE SILK
SARCENET

8–continued

SARSENET
SEALSKIN
SHAGREEN
SHANTUNG
SHIRTING
SHOT SILK
TAPESTRY
TARLATAN
TARLETAN
TOILINET
VALENCIA
WAX CLOTH
WHIPCORD
WILD SILK
ZIBELINE

9

ADA CANVAS
AGRA GAUZE
ASBESTALL
ASTRAKHAN
BARK CLOTH
BARK CREPE
BENGALINE
BOMBAZINE
BOMBYCINE
BOOK CLOTH
BOOK LINEN
BROCATELL
BYRD CLOTH
CALAMANCO
CANNEQUIN
CATALOWNE
CHARMEUSE
CHINA SILK
COTTONADE
COTTON REP
CREPELINE
CRINOLINE
CUT VELVET
DACCA SILK
ÉCRU CLOTH
ÉLASTIQUE
FLANNELET
FUR FABRIC
GABARDINE
GEORGETTE
GRENADINE
GROSGRAIN
HAIRCLOTH
HORSEHAIR
HUCKABACK
LONGCLOTH
MARCELINE
MESSALINE
MOSS CREPE
ORGANZINE
PATCHWORK
PETERSHAM
SACKCLOTH
SAIL CLOTH

9–continued

SATINETTE
SHARKSKIN
SHEEPSKIN
SNAKESKIN
STOCKINET
SWANSDOWN
TARPAULIN
TOWELLING
TRICOTINE
VELVETEEN
WORCESTER

10

ABBOT CLOTH
AIDA CANVAS
ANGOLA YARN
AUSTINIZED
BALBRIGGAN
BARLEYCORN
BAUM MARTEN
BEAVERETTE
BEAVERTEEN
BOOK MUSLIN
BOUCLÉ YARN
BROADCLOTH
BROAD GOODS
CADET CLOTH
CAMBRESINE
CHINO CLOTH
CIRCASSIAN
CONGO CLOTH
CREPE LISSE
DRESS LINEN
GRASS CLOTH
HOP SACKING
HORSECLOTH
IRISH LINEN
MARSEILLES
MOUSSELINE
PEAU DE SOIE
PIECE GOODS
PILOT CLOTH
SEERSUCKER
SUEDE CLOTH
TERRY CLOTH
TOILINETTE
WINCEYETTE

11

ABRADED YARN
AERATED YARN
ALBERT CREPE
ARABIAN LACE
ARMURE-LAINE
BABY FLANNEL
BAG SHEETING
BANDLE LINEN
BASKET CLOTH
BATH COATING
BEDFORD CORD
BOMBER CLOTH
BRUSHED WOOL

11–continued

CANTON CREPE
CANTON LINEN
CHAMOISETTE
CHEESECLOTH
CHESS CANVAS
CHINA COTTON
CLAY WORSTED
COTTON CREPE
DACCA MUSLIN
DIAPER CLOTH
DOTTED SWISS
DRAP DE BERRY
DREADNOUGHT
DRUID'S CLOTH
DU PONT RAYON
ESKIMO CLOTH
EVERLASTING
FLANNELETTE
HARRIS TWEED
IRISH POPLIN
LEATHERETTE
MARQUISETTE
NAPA LEATHER
NUN'S VEILING
OVERCOATING
PANNE VELVET
POODLE CLOTH
POULT-DE-SOIE
SCOTCH PLAID
SPONGE CLOTH
TOILE DE JOUY
WAFFLE CLOTH

12

ACETATE RAYON
BALLOON CLOTH
BERLIN CANVAS
BOLIVIA CLOTH
BOLTING CLOTH
BRILLIANTINE
BROWN HOLLAND
BRUSHED RAYON
BUTCHER LINEN
CARACUL CLOTH
CAVALRY TWILL
CONVENT CLOTH
COTTON VELVET
CRINKLE CLOTH
CROISÉ VELVET
DENMARK SATIN
DOUBLE DAMASK
DRESS FLANNEL
ELEMENT CLOTH
EMPRESS CLOTH
GLAZED CHINTZ
MUTATION MINK
SHETLAND WOOL
SLIPPER SATIN
SUMMER ERMINE
VISCOSE RAYON
WELSH FLANNEL

13
AIRPLANE CLOTH
AMERICAN CLOTH
ARMURE-SATINÉE
BRITTANY CLOTH
CANTON FLANNEL
CARDINAL CLOTH
CASEMENT CLOTH
CLOISTER CLOTH
COSTUME VELVET
COTTON FLANNEL
COTTON SUITING
COTTON WORSTED
CRUSHED VELVET
DIAGONAL CLOTH
DIAPER FLANNEL
EGYPTIAN CLOTH

13–continued
END-TO-END CLOTH
LINSEY-WOOLSEY
PATENT LEATHER
RUSSIA LEATHER

14
ALGERIAN STRIPE
AMERICAN COTTON
ARGENTINE CLOTH
BANDOLIER CLOTH
BARONETTE SATIN
BROADTAIL CLOTH
CORKSCREW TWILL
EGYPTIAN COTTON
ELECTORAL CLOTH
FRUIT OF THE LOOM

14–continued
HONEYCOMB CLOTH
JACQUARD FABRIC
SHEPHERD'S PLAID

15
ABSORBENT
 COTTON
ADMIRALITY CLOTH
CACHEMIRE DE SOIE
CAMEL'S HAIR
 CLOTH
EMBROIDERY LINEN
OSTRICH FEATHERS
PARACHUTE FABRIC
SEA-ISLAND COTTON
SHIRTING FLANNEL

15–continued
TATTERSALL CHECK
TATTERSALL PLAID
TROPICAL SUITING

16
CANDLEWICK
 FABRIC
CONSTITUTION
 CORD
MERCERIZED
 COTTON
TURKISH
 TOWELLING

17
CROSS-STITCH
 CANVAS

COSMETICS

4
KOHL

5
ROUGE
TONER

7
BLUSHER
BRONZER
LIP BALM
MASCARA

8
CLEANSER

8–continued
EYE CREAM
EYELINER
FACE MASK
LIP GLOSS
LIPLINER
LIPSTICK
TWEEZERS

9
COLD CREAM
CONCEALER
EYESHADOW
FACE SCRUB

9–continued
SPOT CREAM

10
FOUNDATION
NIGHT CREAM

11
LOOSE POWDER
MOISTURIZER

13
EYEBROW PENCIL
EYELASH CURLER
PRESSED POWDER

14
FALSE EYELASHES
LIQUID EYELINER

15+
ANTI-AGEING
 CREAM
EYE MAKEUP RE-
 MOVER
ILLUMINATING
 CREAM
TINTED MOISTUR-
 IZER

HAIRDRESSING

3
BOB
BUN
GEL
WAX
WIG

4
AFRO
COMB
CROP
PERM
SHAG
TINT
TRIM

5
BRAID
BRUSH
PLAIT
QUIFF
RAZOR
SERUM

6
FRINGE
MOHAWK
MOUSSE
MULLET
POMADE
'RACHEL'
TOUPEE

7
BEEHIVE
BLOWDRY
BOWL CUT
BUNCHES
CHIGNON
CREW-CUT
CURLERS
FLAT-TOP
MOHICAN
PAGEBOY
PINCURL
ROLLERS
SHAMPOO
TOPKNOT

7–continued
UPSWEEP

8
AFRO COMB
CHONMAGE
CLIPPERS
CORN-ROWS
CRIMPERS
CURTAINS
DUCKTAIL
PIGTAILS
PONYTAIL
RINGLETS
SCISSORS
SKINHEAD

8–continued
SUMO KNOT
UNDERCUT

9
BEATLE CUT
FEATHERED
HAIRBRUSH
HAIRDRYER
HAIRSPRAY
LOWLIGHTS
POMPADOUR

10
DREADLOCKS
FRENCH KNOT
HIGHLIGHTS

11
CONDITIONER
FRENCH PLAIT

12
CURLING TONGS

13
PERMANENT WAVE
SETTING LOTION

14
HAIR EXTENSIONS

15+
HEAT PROTECTION
SPRAY

15+–continued
PERMANENT COL-
OUR
SHORT BACK AND
SIDES
STRAIGHTENING
IRONS
TEMPORARY COL-
OUR

JEWELLERY

3
JET

4
COIL
HORN
JADE
ONYX
OPAL
RUBY

5
AMBER
BADGE
BEADS
BERYL
BEZEL
CAMEO
CHAIN
CLASP
CORAL
DROPS
EBONY
IVORY
PANEL
PASTE
TIARA
TOPAZ

6
AGATES
AMULET
BANGLE
BROOCH
CHOKER
CHROME
COPPER
DIADEM
GARNET
IOLITE
JASPER
LOCKET
MOSAIC

6–continued
NIELLO
PEARLS
PLIQUE
ROSARY
SCROLL
SPINEL
ZIRCON

7
ABALONE
BANDEAU
CIRCLET
CITRINE
CLUSTER
COLLETS
CORONET
CRYSTAL
EMERALD
GARLAND
KUNZITE
LALIQUE
PENDANT
PERIDOT
PIERCED
PLAQUES
RHODIUM

8
AMETHYST
AMETRINE
AMMONITE
BRACELET
CRUCIFIX
DIAMANTE
EN BRANCH
ENGRAVED
FILIGREE
FIRE OPAL
HAIR COMB
HEMATITE
HORN COMB

8–continued
INTAGLIO
MAQUETTE
NAIL-HEAD
NECKLACE
OPENWORK
PAILLONS
PASTICHE
REPOUSSE
SAPPHIRE
SARDONYX
SHAGREEN
STAR RUBY

9
ALUMINIUM
BRIOLETTE
CAIRNGORM
CARBUNCLE
CARBUNCLE
CELLULOID
FRENCH JET
LOVE JEWEL
MALACHITE
MARCASITE
MOONSTONE
PEARL DROP
PINNACLED
PORCELAIN
RELIQUARY
SEED PEARL
SIMULATED
STOMACHER
TANZANITE
TERMINALS
TURQUOISE
WING PEARL

10
AQUAMARINE
CANNA BEADS
CHAKRA BEAD

10–continued
DEMI-PARURE
ENAMELLING
FLEUR-DE-LIS
GOLD THREAD
MEDALLIONS
PENDOLOQUE
QUATREFOIL
ROSE QUARTZ
SHELL CAMEO
SIGNET RING
SILVER GILT
TOURMALINE

11
ALEXANDRITE
CHRYSOBERYL
CHRYSOLITES
CHRYSOPRASE
GOLDEN BERYL
GRANULATION
LAPIS-LAZULI
MICRO MOSAIC
OMBRE ENAMEL
ROCK CRYSTAL
TRANSLUCENT

12
BAROQUE PEARL
BLUE SAPPHIRE
CHALCEDONIES
FACETED STONE
FROSTED GLASS
NEPHRITE DROP
PINK SAPPHIRE
SILVER THREAD
STAR SAPPHIRE

13
CARLO GUILIANO
DOG-TOOTH PEARL
HAIR ORNAMENTS
MOTHER OF PEARL

13–continued
PECTORAL CROSS
STAR SAPPHIRES
TORTOISESHELL
YELLOW SAPHIRE

14
CABOCHON ZIRCON
MORGANITE BERYL
STERLING SILVER
TREFOIL SETTING

15
CABOCHON
  EMERALD
CANDY TWIST CHAIN
CHAMPLEVE
  ENAMEL

15–continued
CLOISONNE
  ENAMEL
CORSAGE
  ORNAMENT
DEMANTOID-
  GARNET
GREEN
  TOURMALINE
MANDARINE
  GARNET
PLASTER MAQUETTE
RHODOLITE
  GARNET
RUTILATED QUARTZ
TSAVORITE GARNET
WROUGHT
  WIREWORK

16
CRUCIFORM
  PENDANT
IRIDESCENT
  ENAMEL
SOLITAIRE DIAMOND
TABLE CUT
  DIAMOND

17
ARTICULATED
  SILVER
CABOCHON
  TURQUOISE
MARRIAGE
  JEWELLERY
PLIQUE-A-JOUR
  ENAMEL

17–continued
PARAIBA
  TOURMALINE
TORTOISESHELL
  COMB

18+
ORANGE BLOSSOM
  JEWELLERY
PADPARASCHA
  SAPPHIRE
POLYCHROME
  CHAMPLEVE
  ENAMELS
RUBELLITE
  TOURMALINE

FOOD AND DRINK

COOKERY TERMS

4
BARD
BEAT
BLEU (AU)
BOIL
BONE
CHOP
COAT
HANG
HASH
LARD
PIPE
RARE
TOSS

5
BASTE
BERNY
BLANC (À)
BLANC (AU)
BROIL
BROWN
BRULÉ
CARVE
CHILL
CROWN
DAUBE
DRAIN
DRESS
GLAZE
GRILL
KNEAD
MELBA
PLUCK
POACH
POINT (À)
PROVE
PURÉE

5—continued
REINE (À LA)
ROAST
RUB IN
SAUTÉ
SCALD
STEAM
SWEAT
TRUSS

6
AURORE
BRAISE
CONFIT
CRÉOLE (À LA)
DECANT
DESALT
DIABLE (À LA)
FILLET
FONDUE
GRATIN
GREASE
MAISON
MIGNON
NATURE
REDUCE
SIMMER
ZEPHYR

7
AL DENTE
ARRÊTER
BLANCHE
BLONDIR
CHEMISE (EN)
COLBERT
CROUTON
DEGLAZE

7—continued
EMINCER
FLAMBER
GRECQUE (À LA)
MARENGO
MÉDICIS
NIÇOISE (À LA)
REFRESH
SUPRÊME
TARTARE (À LA)

8
ALLONGER
ANGLAISE (À L')
APPAREIL
ASSATION
BARBECUE
BELLEVUE (EN)
BRETONNE (À LA)
CATALANE (À LA)
CHAMBORD
CHASSEUR
CHEMISER
CRUDITÉS
DAUPHINE (À LA)
DEVILLED
DUCHESSE (À LA)
EMULSION
ESCALOPE
FLAMANDE (À LA)
INFUSION
JULIENNE
MACERATE
MARINATE
MEUNIÈRE (À LA)
PISTACHE
POT-ROAST
SURPRISE (EN)

9
ACIDULATE
BAKE BLIND
CANELLING
DETAILLER
DIEPPOISE (À LA)
ESPAGNOLE (À L')
FRICASSÉE
KNOCK BACK
LIÉGEOISE (À LA)
LYONNAISE (À LA)
MARINIÈRE (À LA)
MEDALLION
MILANAISE (À LA)

10
ANTILLAISE (À L')
BALLOTTINE
BLANQUETTE
BONNE FEMME
BORDELAISE (À LA)
BOULANGÈRE (À LA)
CHAUD-FROID
DIJONNAISE (À LA)
FLORENTINE (À LA)
PROVENÇALE (À LA)

11
BELLE-HÉLÈNE
BOURGUIGNON
CHARCUTERIE
DAUPHINOISE (À LA)
HOLLANDAISE (À LA)

13
BOURGUIGNONNE
(À LA)
CLARIFICATION
DEEP-FAT FRYING

KITCHEN UTENSILS AND TABLEWARE

3
CUP
HOB
JAR
JUG
LID

3—continued
MUG
PAN
POT
TIN
WOK

4
BOWL
DISH
EWER
FORK

4—continued
MILL
RACK
SPIT
TRAY

5
BAHUT
BASIN
BOARD
CHOPE
CHURN
FLUTE
GRILL
KNIFE
LADLE
MIXER
MOULD
PELLE
PLATE
PRESS
RUSSE
SIEVE
SPOON
STEEL
STRAW
TONGS
WHISK

6
BASKET
BUCKET
CARAFE
CLOCHE
COOLER
CRIBLE
DIABLE
EGG CUP
FUNNEL
GOBLET
GRADIN
GRATER
KETTLE
MINCER
MORTAR
MUSLIN
PESTLE
PICHET
PITTER
POÊLON
SAUCER
SHAKER
SHEARS
SIPHON
SKEWER

6–continued
STRING
TAJINE
TOUPIN
TUREEN

7
ALEMBIC
ATTELET
BLENDER
BROILER
CAISSES
CHINOIS
CHIP PAN
CHOPPER
COCOTTE
DRAINER
DREDGER
ÉCUELLE
GRINDER
MARMITE
PITCHER
RAMEKIN
RONDEAU
SALT BOX
SAMOVAR
SKILLET
SKIMMER
SPATULA
SYRINGE
TÂTE-VIN
TOASTER

8
CAQUELON
CAULDRON
COLANDER
CRÊPE PAN
CROCKERY
DAUBIÈRE
EGG TIMER
FLAN RING
HOTPLATE
MAZAGRAN
MOUVETTE
SAUCEPAN
SAUTÉ PAN
SCISSORS
STOCKPOT

8–continued
STRAINER
TART RING
TASTE-VIN
TRENCHER

9
ALCARRAZA
AUTOCLAVE
BAIN-MARIE
BAKING TIN
CAFETIÈRE
CASSEROLE
COMPOTIER
CORKSCREW
CRUMB TRAY
DÉCOUPOIR
FISH SLICE
FRYING-PAN
KILNER JAR
MANDOLINE
MIJOTEUSE
PASTRY BAG
PIPING BAG
RING MOULD
SALAD BOWL
SAUCEBOAT
SHARPENER
STEAK BATT
TISANIÈRE
TOURTIÈRE

10
APPLE-CORER
CAISSETTES
CASSOLETTE
CHOPSTICKS
CRUET STAND
DIPPING PIN
FISH KETTLE
LIQUIDISER
MUSTARD POT
PERCOLATOR
ROLLING PIN
ROTISSERIE
SALAMANDER
SALT CELLAR
SALTING TUB
SLOW COOKER

10–continued
STERILIZER
WAFFLE IRON

11
BAKING SHEET
BRAISING PAN
CANDISSOIRE
CHAFING DISH
CHEESECLOTH
COFFEE MAKER
DOUGH TROUGH
DRIPPING PAN
FRUIT STONER
GARGOULETTE
JAMBONNIÈRE
NUTCRACKERS
PASTRY BRUSH
PASTRY WHEEL
SERVING DISH
THERMOMETER
YOGURT-MAKER

12
CARVING KNIFE
DEEP-FAT FRYER
MEASURING JUG
PALETTE KNIFE
PASTRY CUTTER
TURBOT KETTLE

13
BUTCHER'S BLOCK
FOOD PROCESSOR
ICE-CREAM MAKER
KITCHEN SCALES
LARDING NEEDLE
PRESERVING JAR
SACCHAROMETER
VEGETABLE DISH

14
JUICE EXTRACTOR
KNEADING TROUGH
KNIFE SHARPENER
PRESSURE COOKER
TRUSSING NEEDLE

16
MEAT-CARVING
  TONGS

BAKING

3
BAP
BUN
COB
FAR
PIE

4
BABA
CAKE
CHOU
FLAN
PAVÉ

4–continued
RUSK
TART

5
BAGEL
BÂTON

5–continued
BREAD
CRÊPE
FLÛTE
ICING
PLAIT

CEREALS

5—continued
SABLÉ
SCONE
STICK
TOAST

6
COOKIE
CORNET
ÉCLAIR
LEAVEN
MUFFIN
OUBLIE
ROCHER
TOURTE
WAFFLE

7
BAKLAVA
BANNOCK
BISCUIT
BLOOMER
BRIOCHE
CHAPATI

7—continued
COTTAGE
CRACKER
CRUMPET
FICELLE
FRITTER
GALETTE
PALMIER
PANCAKE
PRALINE
PRETZEL
STOLLEN
STRUDEL
TARTINE
TARTLET

8
AMANDINE
BAGUETTE
BARM CAKE
BÂTONNET
BISCOTTE
DOUGHNUT
DUCHESSE

8—continued
DUMPLING
EMPANADA
FROSTING
GRISSINI
SANDWICH
SPLIT TIN
TORTILLA
TURNOVER

9
ALLUMETTE
BARQUETTE
CROISSANT
FEUILLETÉ
FRIANDISE
KUGELHOPF
PETIT FOUR
VOL-AU-VENT

10
CRISPBREAD
FRANGIPANE
PÂTISSERIE

10—continued
PUFF PASTRY
RELIGIEUSE
SHORTBREAD
SPONGE CAKE

11
CHOUX PASTRY
LINZERTORTE
PETIT-BEURRE
PROFITEROLE

12
LANGUE-DE-CHAT
PUMPERNICKEL
SPONGE FINGER

13
GENOESE SPONGE

14
PAIN AU CHOCOLAT

15
SAVOY SPONGE
  CAKE

CEREALS

3
RYE

4
BRAN
CORN
OATS
RICE

5
MAIZE
SPELT
WHEAT

6
BARLEY
BULGUR

6—continued
MÉTEIL
MILLET

7
BURGHUL
FROMENT
SORGHUM

9
BUCKWHEAT

12
CRACKED WHEAT

CHEESES

4
BRIE (France)
CURD (CHEESE)
EDAM (Netherlands)
FETA (Greece)
TOME (France)

5
BANON (France)
BRICK (US)
CABOC (Scotland)
COMTÉ (France)
DANBO (Denmark)

5—continued
DERBY (England)
FETTA (Greece)
GOUDA (Netherlands)
HERVE (Belgium)
LEIGH (England)
MOLBO (Denmark)
MUROL (France)
NIOLO (Corsica)
TAMIÉ (France)

6
ASIAGO (Italy)

6—continued
BAGNES (Switzerland)
BRESSE (France)
CACHAT (France)
CANTAL (France)
CENDRÉ (France)
DUNLOP (Scotland)
FOURME (France)
GAPRON (France)
GÉROMÉ (France)
HALUMI (Greece)
HRAMSA (Scotland)

6—continued
LEIDEN (Netherlands)
MORVEN (Scotland)
OLIVET (France)
POURLY (France)
ROLLOT (France)
SALERS (France)
SAMSOË (Denmark)
SBRINZ (Switzerland)
SURATI (India)
TILSIT (Switzerland)
VENACO (Corsica)

7
BONDARD (France)
BRINZEN (Hungary)
BROCCIO (Corsica)
BROCCIU (Corsica)
BROUSSE (France)
BRUCCIU (Corsica)
BRYNDZA (Hungary)
CABÉCOU (France)
CHEDDAR (England)
CROWDIE (Scotland)
DAUPHIN (France)
DEMI-SEL (France)
FONTINA (Italy)
GAPERON (France)
GJETÖST (Norway)
GRUYÈRE (France; Switzerland)
JONCHÉE (France)
LANGRES (France)
LEVROUX (France)
LIMBURG (Belgium)
LIVAROT (France)
MACQUÉE (France)
MONT-D'OR (France)
MORBIER (France)
MÜNSTER (France)
NANTAIS (France)
PICODON (France)
QUARGEL (Austria)
RICOTTA (Italy)
SAPSAGO (Switzerland)
STILTON (England)
VENDÔME (France)

8
AUVERGNE (France)
AYRSHIRE (Scotland)
BEAUFORT (France)
BEL PAESE (Italy)
BERGKÄSE (Austria)
BOULETTE (France)
CHAOURCE (France)
CHESHIRE (England)
EDELPILZ (Germany)
EMMENTAL (Switzerland)
EPOISSES (France)
MANCHEGO (Spain)

8–continued
PARMESAN (Italy)
PECORINO (Italy)
PÉLARDON (France)
REMOUDOU (Belgium)
SCAMORZE (Italy)
TALEGGIO (Italy)
VACHERIN (Switzerland)
VALENÇAY (France)

9
APPENZELL (Switzerland)
BROODKAAS (Netherlands)
CAITHNESS (Scotland)
CAMBOZOLA (Italy; Germany)
CAMEMBERT (France)
CHABICHOU (France)
CHEVRETON (France)
EMMENTHAL (Switzerland)
EXCELSIOR (France)
GAMMELÖST (Norway)
LA BOUILLE (France)
LEICESTER (England)
LIMBURGER (Belgium)
MAROILLES (France)
MIMOLETTE (France)
PAVÉ D'AUGE (France)
PORT-SALUT (France)
PROVOLONE (Italy)
REBLOCHON (France)
ROQUEFORT (France)

10
CAERPHILLY (Wales)
DANISH BLUE (Denmark)
DOLCELATTE (Italy)
GLOUCESTER (England)
GORGONZOLA (Italy)
LANCASHIRE (England)
MOZZARELLA (Italy)
NEUFCHÂTEL (Switzerland)
PITHIVIERS (France)
RED WINDSOR (England)
SAINGORLON (France)
STRACCHINO (Italy)

11
CARRÉ DE L'EST (France)

11–continued
COEUR DE BRAY (France)
COULOMMIERS (France)
KATSHKAWALJ (Bulgaria)
PETIT-SUISSE (France)
PONT-L'ÉVÊQUE (France)
SAINTE-MAURE (France)
SAINT-PAULIN (France)
SCHABZIEGER (Switzerland)
TÊTE-DE-MOINE (Switzerland)
WEISSLACKER (Germany)
WENSLEYDALE (England)

12
CACIOCAVALLO (Italy)
RED LEICESTER (England)
SOUMAINTRAIN (France)

13
SAINT-NECTAIRE (France)
SELLES-SUR-CHER (France)

14
BRILLAT-SAVARIN (France)
FEUILLE DE DREUX (France)
LAGUIOLE-AUBRAC (France)
SAINT-FLORENTIN (France)
SAINT-MARCELLIN (France)
TRAPPISTENKÄSE (Germany)

15
BOUTON-DE-CULOTTE
  (France)

16
DOUBLE GLOUCESTER
  (England)

17
RIGOTTE DE PELUSSIN
  (France)

18
CHEVROTIN DES ARAVIS
  (France)
CROTTIN DE CHAVIGNOL
  (France)

19
POULIGNY-SAINT-PIERRE
  (France)

HERBS AND SPICES

3	5	6	6–continued
BAY	ANISE	BETONY	PEPPER
RUE	BASIL	BORAGE	SAVORY
	CHIVE	BURNET	SESAME
4	CLOVE	CICELY	SORREL
BALM	CUMIN	FENNEL	
DILL	TANSY	GARLIC	**7**
MINT	THYME	GINGER	BONESET
SAGE		LOVAGE	CARAWAY

7–continued
CHERVIL
COMFREY
DITTANY
MUSTARD
OREGANO
PAPRIKA
PARSLEY
PERILLA
PIMENTO
SAFFRON
SALSIFY

7–continued
TABASCO
VANILLA

8
ALLSPICE
ANGELICA
CAMOMILE
CARDAMOM
CARDAMON
CINNAMON
DROPWORT
FEVERFEW

8–continued
MARJORAM
ROSEMARY
TARRAGON
TURMERIC

9
CHAMOMILE
CORIANDER
FENUGREEK
SPEARMINT

10+
ASAFOETIDA
BLACK-EYED SUSAN
HERB OF GRACE
HORSERADISH
HOTTENTOT FIG
OYSTER PLANT
PEPPERMINT
POT MARIGOLD
VEGETABLE OYSTER

JOINTS OF MEAT

BEEF
BRISKET
CHUCK
FILLET STEAK
FLANK
FORE RIB
LEG
NECK
RIB
ROLLED RIBS

RUMP
SHIN
SILVERSIDE
SIRLOIN
T-BONE
TOPSIDE
UNDERCUT STEAK

PORK
BELLY

BLADE
HAND
HOCK
LEG
LEG FILLET
LOIN
SHOULDER
SPARE RIB
TENDERLOIN
TROTTER

LAMB
BEST END OF NECK
BREAST
CHUMP
CHUMP CHOPS
LEG
LOIN
SCRAG-END
SHOULDER

TYPES OF PASTA

4
PIPE

5
PENNE

6
BIGOLI
DITALI
RISONI
ROTINI

7
CAPELLI

7–continued
FUSILLI
LASAGNE
LUMACHE
NOODLES
RAVIOLI
ROTELLE

8
BUCATINI
DITALINI
DITALONI
FARFALLE

8–continued
FETTUCCE
FIDELINI
GRAMIGNA
LINGUINE
MACARONI
RIGATONI
STELLINE
TAGLIONI
TRENETTE

9
AGNOLOTTI

9–continued
ANNELLINI
MANICOTTI
SPAGHETTI
TUFFOLONI

10
CANNELLONI
CONCHIGLIE
CRAVATTINE
FARFALLINE
FETTUCCINE
TAGLIOLINI
TORTELLINI

TORTELLONI
VERMICELLI

11
CAPPELLETTI
ORECCHIETTE
PAPPARDELLE
SPAGHETTINI
SPAGHETTONE
TAGLIATELLE
TORTIGLIONI

12
PAGLIA E FIENO

BEANS AND PEAS

6
LENTIL

7
PEA-BEAN
RED BEAN

8
CHICKPEA
LIMA BEAN
MUNG BEAN
SOYA BEAN

8–continued
SPLIT PEA
SUGAR PEA

9
BROAD BEAN

9–continued
FLAGEOLET
GARDEN PEA
HORSE BEAN
MANGETOUT

9–continued
PETIT POIS
PINTO BEAN

10
ADZUKI BEAN

10–continued
BEAN SPROUT
BUTTER-BEAN
FRENCH BEAN
KIDNEY BEAN
RUNNER BEAN

10–continued
STRING BEAN
WAX-POD BEAN

11
HARICOT BEAN

12
SUGAR SNAP PEA

13
BLACK-EYED BEAN
SCARLET RUNNER

VEGETABLES

3
YAM

4
AARD
BEAN
BEET
KALE
LEEK
OKRA
TARO

5
CHARD
CRESS
GOURD
GUMBO
ONION
SAVOY
SWEDE

6
CARROT
CELERY
ENDIVE
FENNEL
LENTIL
MANIOC

6–continued
MARROW
ORACHE
PEPPER
POTATO
RADISH
SQUASH
TOMATO
TURNIP

7
CABBAGE
CARDOON
CASSAVA
CHAYOTE
CHERVIL
CHICORY
GHERKIN
LETTUCE
MUSTARD
PAK-CHOI
PARSNIP
PUMPKIN
SALSIFY
SEA KALE
SHALLOT
SPINACH

7–continued
SUCCORY

8
BEETROOT
BROCCOLI
CAPSICUM
CELERIAC
CUCUMBER
EGGPLANT
KOHLRABI
PIMIENTO
RUTABAGA
SCALLION
ZUCCHINI

9
ARTICHOKE
ASPARAGUS
AUBERGINE
CALABRESE
COURGETTE
CURLY KALE
MANGETOUT
SWEET CORN

10
BREADFRUIT

10–continued
SCORZONERA
WATERCRESS

11
AVOCADO PEAR
CAULIFLOWER
OYSTER PLANT
SPINACH BEET
SWEET POTATO

12
BAMBOO SHOOTS
CORN ON THE COB
MARROW SQUASH

13
CHINESE LEAVES
WATER CHESTNUT

14
BRUSSELS SPROUT
CHINESE CABBAGE
DISHCLOTH GOURD

18
JERUSALEM ARTI-
    CHOKE

FRUITS AND NUTS

3
FIG

4
BAEL
DATE
KAKI
LIME
NIPA
PEAR
PLUM
SLOE

5
ACORN
APPLE

5–continued
CAROB
GOURD
GRAPE
GUAVA
LEMON
MANGO
MELON
OLIVE
PEACH
PECAN

6
ALMOND
ANANAS
BABACO

6–continued
BANANA
CASHEW
CHERRY
CITRON
COB-NUT
CONKER
DAMSON
DURIAN
FEIJOA
GUM NUT
HOGNUT
JUJUBE
LONGAN
LOQUAT

6–continued
LYCHEE
MEDLAR
MOMBIN
MUSCAT
ORANGE
PAWPAW
PEANUT
PIGNUT
PIPPIN
POMELO
QUINCE
SAL NUT
TOMATO
WALNUT

7
APRICOT
AVOCADO
BULLACE
COCONUT
COLA NUT
COSTARD
CURRANT
FILBERT
GEEBUNG
GENIPAP
KUMQUAT
PALM NUT
PINE NUT
SATSUMA

DESSERTS

7–continued
SOURSOP
TANGELO

8
ARECA NUT
BARBERRY
BAYBERRY
BEECHNUT
BERGAMOT
BETEL-NUT
BILBERRY
BREADNUT
CHESTNUT
COC-DE-MER
COCOANUT
DEWBERRY
EARTH-NUT
HAZELNUT
MANDARIN
MINNEOLA
MULBERRY
PLANTAIN
QUANDONG
RAMBUTAN
SOUR PLUM
SWEETSOP
TAMARIND
TAYBERRY

9
BAKEAPPLE

9–continued
BEARBERRY
BITTERNUT
BLUEBERRY
BRAZIL NUT
BUTTERNUT
CANDLENUT
CARAMBOLA
CHERIMOYA
CHINCAPIN
COFFEE NUT
CRAB APPLE
CRANBERRY
CROWBERRY
GREENGAGE
GROUNDNUT
GRUGRU NUT
HACKBERRY
IVORY-NUT
JACKFRUIT
KIWI FRUIT
LITCHI NUT
MOCKERNUT
MUSK MELON
MYROBALAN
NECTARINE
PERSIMMON
PINEAPPLE
PISTACHIO
RASPBERRY
SAPODILLA

9–continued
SOUR GOURD
STAR FRUIT
TAMARILLO
TANGERINE
UGLI FRUIT

10
BLACKBERRY
BREADFRUIT
CHINABERRY
CHOKEBERRY
CLEMENTINE
ELDERBERRY
GOOSEBERRY
GRANADILLA
GRAPEFRUIT
HICKORY NUT
JABOTICABA
LOGANBERRY
MANGOSTEEN
MANZANILLA
MONKEY-NUT
REDCURRANT
SAOUARI NUT
SOUR CHERRY
SOUR ORANGE
STAR-APPLE
STRAWBERRY
TREE TOMATO
WATERMELON

10–continued
YOUNGBERRY

11
BOYSENBERRY
COQUILLA NUT
HUCKLEBERRY
LINGONBERRY
POMEGRANATE
PRICKLY PEAR
SALMONBERRY
SHARON FRUIT
SPICE-BERRY
WHITE WALNUT

12
BLACKCURRANT
BURRAWANG NUT
MACADAMIA NUT
PASSION FRUIT
SERVICE-BERRY
WHITE CURRANT
WHORTLEBERRY
WINTER CHERRY

13
ALLIGATOR PEAR
DWARF CHESTNUT
HORSE CHESTNUT
QUEENSLAND NUT
SWEET CHESTNUT
WATER CHESTNUT

DESSERTS

4
FOOL
WHIP

5
JELLY

6
CAJETA
JUNKET
KISSEL
MOUSSE
SORBET
SUNDAE
TRIFLE
YOGURT

7
BAKLAVA
COBBLER
COMPOTE
CRUMBLE
CUSTARD
GRANITA
JAM TART

7–continued
PARFAIT
PAVLOVA
SOUFFLE
SPUMONI
TAPIOCA

8
APPLE PIE
FRUIT CUP
ICE CREAM
PANDOWDY
ROLY POLY
SEMOLINA
TIRAMISU
WATER ICE

9
BAVAROISE
ENTREMETS
FRUIT FLAN
TIPSY CAKE

10
BANOFFI PIE

10–continued
BLANCMANGE
BROWN BETTY
EGG CUSTARD
FRESH FRUIT
FRUIT SALAD
PEACH MELBA
SHOOFLY PIE
ZABAGLIONE

11
BAKED ALASKA
BANANA SPLIT
EVE'S PUDDING
PLUM PUDDING
RICE PUDDING
SPOTTED DICK
STEWED FRUIT
SUET PUDDING
TREACLE TART

12
APFELSTRUDEL
CREME
  CARAMEL

13
CREPES
  SUZETTE
DAIRY ICE
  CREAM
SPONGE PUD-
  DING
SUMMER PUD-
  DING

14
APPLE CHAR-
  LOTTE
CABINET PUD-
  DING
CHARLOTTE
  RUSSE
FLOATING IS-
  LAND
STEAMED PUD-
  DING

16
CHRISTMAS
  PUDDING

16–continued
DEATH BY
  CHOCOLATE
VIENNOISE
  PUDDING

17
BLACK FOREST
  GATEAU
MISSISSIPPI
  MUD PIE
UPSIDE DOWN
  PUDDING

18
KNICKER-
  BOCKER
  GLORY

21
BREAD AND
  BUTTER PUD-
  DING

CAKES

4
BABA

5
SCONE
TORTE
ECLAIR

6
GATEAU
KUCHEN
MUFFIN
PARKIN

7
BAKLAVA
BANNOCK
BROWNIE
CRULLER
CUPCAKE
HOECAKE

7–continued
PANCAKE
PAVLOVA
STRUDEL
TEACAKE
YULE LOG

8
DOUGHNUT
FLAPJACK
MERINGUE
PANDOWDY
PLUM CAKE
ROCK CAKE
SEEDCAKE

9
ANGEL CAKE
DROP SCONE
FAIRY CAKE

9–continued
FRUIT CAKE
GENOA CAKE
LARDY-CAKE
MADELEINE
POUND CAKE
QUEEN CAKE
SHORTCAKE
SWISS ROLL
TIPSY-CAKE

10
ALMOND CAKE
BATTENBURG
CHEESECAKE
DUNDEE CAKE
ECCLES CAKE
FRANGIPANE
KOEKSISTER
LADYFINGER

10–continued
MARBLE CAKE
SIMNEL CAKE
SPONGE CAKE

11
GINGERBREAD
MADEIRA CAKE
WEDDING CAKE

12
BAKEWELL TART
DANISH PASTRY
MILLEFEUILLE

14
DEVIL'S FOOD CAKE
UPSIDE-DOWN CAKE
VICTORIA SPONGE

SAUCES

3
SOY

4
MINT
NOIR

5
AIOLI
VERTE

6
BATARD
BUTTER
HOISIN

6–continued
MADERE
MORNAY
ROBERT
TOMATO

7
BLANCHE
COLBERT
MADEIRA
ROUILLE
SOUBISE
SUPREME
TARTARE
VELOUTE

8
ALBUFERA
BARBEQUE
BECHAMEL
CHASSEUR
DUXELLES
NORMANDE
POIVRADE

9
BEARNAISE
LYONNAISE
PICQUANTE
RICHELIEU

10
BORDELAISE
MAYONNAISE
SARLADAISE

11
HOLLANDAISE
VINAIGRETTE

12
SWEET-AND-SOUR

13
BOURGUIGNONNE

EASTERN EUROPEAN DISHES

4
KIEV
UKHA

5
BABKA
BIGOS
BITKI
BLINI
KASHA
LATKE

5–continued
LOSOS
MIASO
RAKOV
SCHEE
ZRAZY

6
BORSCH
CAVIAR
KULICH

6–continued
PASKHA

7
BANITSA
BLINTZE
BORSHCH
GOULASH
GRIBNOY
PELMENI
SELEDKA

7–continued
ZAKUSKY

8
BOTVINYA
DRANNIKY
GROBNAUA
HOLUBTSI
KRABOVIY
KREPLACH
KURINAYA

8–continued
MYASNOYE
RAZNOSOI
SHASHLYK
SOLYANKA
TURSCHIA

9
BLINCHIKI
CHEBUREKI
POD SHUBOY

329

9–continued
STROGANOV
TYUKLEVES

10
BOUZHENINA
OGURTCHIKY

10–continued
PAPRIKACHE
STOLICHNIY
STROGANOFF

15+
FARSH PO TATARSKY

15+–continued
GOLUBTZY OVOSH-
NIE
GRIBNY MARINO-
VANNIE
KOTLETY
POZHARSKI

15+–continued
MIASNIE GOLUBTZY
SOLYANKA
MIASNAYA

INDIAN DISHES

3
DAL

4
DHAL
NAAN
PETIS
PURI

5
BHAJI
DORMA
DURMA
KARHI
KOFTA
KORMA
POORI
RAITA
RISTA
TIKKA

6
KARAHI
KORMAH
MADRAS
MASALA
RAITHA
SAMBAL
SAMOSA

7
BIRIANI
BIRYANI
CHAHKEE
CHAPATI
DHANSAK
DO PIAZA
PAPADUM
PARATHA
SHIRMAL

8
POPPADOM

8–continued
TANDOORI
VINDALOO

9
ALOO BHAJI
GOBHI MHAS
JHAL FARZI
ROGAN JOSH

10
ALOO GOSCHT
BOMBAY ALOO
MALAI SEEKH
METHI GOSHT
MURGH TIKKA
SAMBAL ALOO

11
BARRAH KABAB

12
GOSHT KHUBANI

12–continued
KADHAI JHINGA
MAKHANI MURGH
MOORGHI KHARI

13
GOSHT GULMARGI
KHEEMA DO-PIAZA
MACHCHI BADAMI
PESHAWARI RAAN
TANDOORI MURGH

14
PESHAWARI GOSHT

15+
MURGH HARA
MASALA
MURGH KORMA
SHAHI
MURGH-ALOO
BHOONA

CHINESE DISHES

4
MA-LA

5
SATAY

6
DIM SUM
TIAO-MA
TUNG-PO
WONTON
WUN TUN

7
CHA SHAO

7–continued
FOO YUNG
GAN-CHAO
GAN-SHAO
GUAI-WEI
HANG-YOU
TIANG-ZU
YU-XIANG

8
CHOP SUEY
CHOW MEIN

9
SPARERIBS
STIR FRIED

10
PEKING DUCK
SPRING ROLL

11
MOO SHOO PORK
PANCAKE ROLL

12
EGG FRIED RICE
PRAWN CRACKER
SWEET AND SOUR

13
BIRD'S NEST SOUP
SHARK'S FIN SOUP

15
PEKING ROAST
DUCK
YANGCHOW NOO-
DLES

18
CANTONESE ROAST
DUCK
CRISPY AROMATIC
DUCK
CRISPY FRIED SEA-
WEED

DRINKS

WINES AND APERITIFS

4
FINO
HOCK
PORT
SACK

5
BYRRH
CRÉPY
FITOU
MÉDOC
MOSEL
RIOJA
TAVEL
TOKAY

6
ALSACE
BANDOL
BAROLO
BARSAC
BEAUNE
CAHORS
CASSIS
CHINON
CLARET
FRANGY
GRAVES
MÁLAGA
SAUMUR
SHERRY
VOLNAY

7
ALIGOTÉ
CAMPARI
CHABLIS
CHIANTI
CLAIRET
CRÉMANT
FALERNO
GAILLAC
MADEIRA
MARGAUX
MARSALA
MARTINI
MOSELLE
ORVIETO
POMMARD
RETSINA
VOUVRAY

8
BORDEAUX
BROUILLY
DUBONNET
GIGONDAS
MERCUREY
MONTAGNY
MONTILLA
MUSCADET
PAUILLAC
RIESLING
ROSÉ WINE
SANCERRE

8–continued
SANTENAY
VALENÇAY
VERMOUTH
VIN JAUNE

9
BOURGUEIL
CHAMPAGNE
CLAIRETTE
CÔTE-RÔTIE
HERMITAGE
LAMBRUSCO
MEURSAULT
MONTLOUIS
SAUTERNES

10
BARBARESCO
BEAUJOLAIS
BULL'S BLOOD
MANZANILLA
MONTRACHET
RICHEBOURG
RIVESALTES
VINHO VERDE

11
ALOXE-CORTON
AMONTILLADO
MONBAZILLAC
POUILLY-FUMÉ
SAINT JULIEN

12
CÔTES-DU-
  RHÔNE
ROMANÉE-
  CONTI
SAINT-EMILION
SAINT ES-
  TEPHE
VALPOLICELLA
VOSNE-RO-
  MANÉE

13
CHÂTEAU
  D'YQUEM
CHÂTEAU
  LAFITE
CHÂTEAU LA-
  TOUR
ENTRE-DEUX-
  MERS
POUILLY-
  FUISSÉ

14
CHÂTEAU MAR-
  GAUX
CÔTES-DU-
  VENTOUX
GEWÜRZ-
  TRAMINER

15
CÔTES-DE-
  PROVENCE
CÔTES-DU-VI-
  VARAIS
CROZES-
  HERMITAGE
MOREY-SAINT-
  DENIS

16
CHAMBOLLE-
  MUSIGNY
GEVREY-
  CHAMBERTIN
SAVIGNY-
  LÈS-BEAUNE

17
CÔTES-DU-
  ROUSSILLON
NUITS-SAINT-
  GEORGES

18
BLANQUETTE
  DE LIMOUX

19
CHASSAGNE-
  MONTRACHET

COCKTAILS AND MIXED DRINKS

3
FIX
KIR
NOG

4
FIZZ
FLIP
GROG
RAKI
SOUR

5
JULEP
NEGUS
PUNCH
TODDY

6
BEADLE
BISHOP
GIMLET

POSSET

7
MARTINI
SANGRIA
SIDECAR
WALDORF

8
APPLE CAR
DAIQUIRI
GIN AND IT
GIN SLING
HIGHBALL
NIGHTCAP
PINK LADY
WHIZ BANG

9
ALEXANDER
APPLEJACK
BEE'S KNEES

9–continued
BUCK JONES
BUCKS FIZZ
COMMODORE
MANHATTAN
MINT JULEP
MOONLIGHT
MOONSHINE
MULLED ALE
WHITE LADY

10
ANGEL'S KISS
ARCHBISHOP
BLACK MARIA
BLOODY MARY
HORSE'S NECK
MERRY WIDOW
MULLED WINE
PINA COLADA
RUM COLLINS

10–continued
TOM COLLINS

11
BEACHCOMBER
BLACK VELVET
FALLEN ANGEL
JOHN COLLINS
WASSAIL BOWL

12
CHURCHWAR-
  DEN
ELEPHANT'S
  EAR
FINE AND
  DANDY
OLD-FASH-
  IONED
WHITE GIN
  SOUR

13
CHAMPAGNE
  BUCK
CORPSE RE-
  VIVER
KNICKER-
  BOCKER
MAIDEN'S
  PRAYER
PLANTER'S
  PUNCH
PRAIRIE OYS-
  TER

16
BETWEEN THE
  SHEETS
HARVEY
  WALLBANGER

BEERS AND BEVERAGES

3	**5**	**6**	**8**	**10**
ALE	CIDER	BITTER	GUINNESS	BARLEY BEER
	KVASS	LAMBIC	HYDROMEL	BARLEY WINE
4	LAGER	SHANDY		
MEAD	PERRY			
MILD	STOUT			

SPIRITS

3	**6**	**7**	**8–continued**
GIN	BOUKHA	AKVAVIT	FALERNUM
RUM	BRANDY	AQUAVIT	SCHNAPPS
	CHICHA	BACARDI	**9**
4	COGNAC	BOUKHRA	SLIVOVITZ
ARAK	GRAPPA	BOURBON	
MARC	KIRSCH	SCHNAPS	**10**
OUZO	MESCAL	TEQUILA	RYE WHISKEY
	METAXA	WHISKEY	**11**
5	PASTIS		AGUARDIENTE
CHOUM	PERNOD	**8**	
VODKA	PULQUE	ARMAGNAC	
	WHISKY	CALVADOS	

LIQUEURS

4	**7**	**9**	**12**
SAKÉ	ALCAMAS	ARQUEBUSE	CHERRY BRANDY
SAKI	ALLASCH	COINTREAU	CRÈME DE CACAO
	BAILEYS	FRAMBOISE	GRAND MARNIER
5	CURAÇAO	GUIGNOLET	**13**
ANISE	ESCUBAC	MIRABELLE	CRÈME DE MENTHE
ANRAM	RATAFIA	TRIPLE SEC	
	SAMBUCA		**15**
6		**10**	SOUTHERN
CASSIS	**8**	BROU DE NOIX	COMFORT
KÜMMEL	ABSINTHE	CHARTREUSE	**17**
MÉLISS	ADVOCAAT	MARASCHINO	AMARETTO DI
QETSCH	ANISETTE		SARANNO
SCUBAC	DRAMBUIE	**11**	
STREGA	PERSICOT	BENEDICTINE	
	PRUNELLE	TRAPPISTINE	

NON-ALCOHOLIC DRINKS

3	**5**	**7–continued**	**9–continued**
CHA (TEA)	LASSI	CORDIAL	MILKSHAKE
TEA	WATER	DIABOLO	ORANGEADE
		LIMEADE	
4	**6**	SELTZER	**10**
CHAR (TEA)	COFFEE		GINGER BEER
COLA	ORGEAT	**8**	TONIC WATER
MATÉ	TISANE	LEMONADE	**12**
SODA		**9**	MINERAL WATER
	7	GRENADINE	
	BEEF TEA		

SPORT AND RECREATION

SPORTS

4
GOLF
JUDO
PATO
POLO

5
BOWLS
FIVES
KENDO
RALLY
RODEO

6
AIKIDO
BOULES
BOXING
HOCKEY
KARATE
KUNG FU
PELOTA
ROWING
SHINTY
SKIING
TENNIS

7
ANGLING
ARCHERY
BOWLING
CRICKET
CROQUET
CURLING
FENCING
HURLING
JUJITSU
KABADDI
KARTING

7–continued
NETBALL
RACKETS
SHOT PUT

8
BASEBALL
BIATHLON
CANOEING
COURSING
DRESSAGE
FALCONRY
GYMKHANA
HANDBALL
HURDLING
LACROSSE
LONG JUMP
MARATHON
PETANQUE
PING-PONG
ROUNDERS
SHOOTING
SPEEDWAY
SWIMMING
TUG OF WAR

9
ATHLETICS
BADMINTON
DECATHLON
ICE HOCKEY
MOTO-CROSS
POLE VAULT
SKYDIVING
TAE KWON-DO
WATER POLO
WRESTLING

10
BASKETBALL
DRAG RACING
FLAT RACING
FOXHUNTING
GYMNASTICS
ICE SKATING
REAL TENNIS
RUGBY UNION
TRIPLE JUMP
VOLLEYBALL

11
BEARBAITING
BLOOD SPORTS
BOBSLEDDING
BULLBAITING
DISCUS THROW
HAMMER THROW
HANG-GLIDING
HORSE RACING
HORSE TRAILS
MARTIAL ARTS
MOTOR RACING
PARACHUTING
PENTHATHLON
RUGBY LEAGUE
SEPAK TAKRAW
TABLE TENNIS
TOBOGGANING
WATER SKIING

12
BULLFIGHTING
CABER TOSSING
COCKFIGHTING
ETON WALL GAME

12–continued
JAVELIN THROW
ORIENTEERING
PIGEON RACING
POINT-TO-POINT
STEEPLECHASE

13
EQUESTRIANISM
HARNESS RACING
SKATEBOARDING
SQUASH RACKETS
WEIGHT LIFTING

14
FOOTBALL LEAGUE
MOUNTAINEERING
STOCK-CAR RACING

15
GREYHOUND
   RACING

16
AMERICAN
   FOOTBALL
MOTORCYCLE
   RACING

18
CLAY-PIGEON
   SHOOTING
FREESTYLE
   WRESTLING

19
ASSOCIATION
   FOOTBALL

GAMES

2
GO

4
POOL

5
BINGO

5–continued
CAVES
CHESS
CRAPS
DARTS
FIVES
SHOGI

5–continued
SPOOF

6
CLUEDO
PAC-MAN
QUOITS

6–continued
TIPCAT

7
DOBBERS
MAHJONG
MARBLES

7–continued
MATADOR
PACHISI
SNOOKER
YAHTZEE

8
BACCARAT
BIRD CAGE
DADDLUMS
DOMINOES
DRAUGHTS
LIAR DICE

8–continued
MONOPOLY
ROULETTE
SCRABBLE
SKITTLES

9
AUNT SALLY
BILLIARDS
POKER DICE
SNAKE-EYES
STOOL BALL

10
BACKGAMMON
BAT AND TRAP
CASABLANCA
RUNNING OUT

11
TIDDLYWINKS

12
BAR BILLIARDS
KNUR AND SPELL
SHOVE HA'PENNY

13
SPACE INVADERS

14
TRIVIAL PURSUIT

16
SNAKES AND
   LADDERS

20
DEVIL AMONG THE
   TAILORS

CARD GAMES

3
LOO
PAN
RUM

4
BRAG
JASS
KLOB
SNAP
SPIT
VINT

5
BINGO
BOURE
CINCH
COMET
DARDA
OMBRE
PEDRO
PITCH
POKER
POQUE
RUMMY
SAMBA
WHIST
YUKON

6
BOO-RAY
BOSTON
BRIDGE
CASINO
CHEMMY
ÉCARTÉ
EIGHTS
EUCHRE
FAN-TAN
GAIGEL
GO FISH
JULEPE

6–continued
MAU-MAU
PIQUET
POCHEN
POKINO
QUINZE
RED DOG
SEVENS
SMUDGE
TRUMPS
YABLON

7
AUTHORS
BELOTTE
BEZIQUE
BOLIVIA
CANASTA
COLONEL
COONCAN
OLD MAID
PONTOON
PRIMERA
PRIMERO
SET-BACK
SEVEN-UP
SNOOKER
SOLOMON
SPINADO
TRIUMPH

8
ACE-DEUCE
CANFIELD
CONQUIAN
CRIBBAGE
GIN RUMMY
IMPERIAL
IRISH LOO
KLONDIKE
LAST CARD

8–continued
LOW PITCH
NAPOLEON
OKLAHOMA
PATIENCE
PINOCHLE
ROCKAWAY
ROLLOVER
SIXTY SIX
SLAPJACK

9
BLACKJACK
DRAW POKER
FORTY FIVE
IN-BETWEEN
OPEN POKER
SOLITAIRE
SOLO WHIST
SPOIL FIVE
STUD POKER
THIRTY ONE
VINGT-ET-UN
WILD JACKS

10
DRAW CASINO
JOKER PITCH
PANGUINGUE
PISHE PASHA
PUT AND TAKE
TABLANETTE
THIRTY FIVE
WELLINGTON

11
BOSTON WHIST
BRIDGE WHIST
CATCH THE TEN
CHEMIN DE FER
CLOSED POKER
CRAZY EIGHTS

11–continued
DOUBLE RUMMY
FIVE CARD LOO
FIVE HUNDRED
GERMAN WHIST
HUMBUG WHIST
KLABBERJASS
RACING DEMON
ROYAL CASINO
RUSSIAN BANK
SCOTCH WHIST
SLIPPERY SAM
SPADE CASINO

12
AUCTION PITCH
DOMINO FAN-TAN
JACK CHANGE IT
SWEDISH RUMMY

13
AUCTION BRIDGE
CONCENTRATION
HAPPY FAMILIES
OLD MAN'S BUNDLE
SIX SPOT RED DOG
STRAIGHT POKER

14
BACCARET BANQUE
CHINESE BEZIQUE
CONTRACT BRIDGE
FRENCH PINOCHLE
FROGS IN THE
   POND
RACEHORSE PITCH
RUBICON BEZIQUE
SIX DECK BEZIQUE
SPITE AND MALICE

15
AROUND THE
   CORNER

15–continued
AUCTION PINOCHLE
BANKER AND
  BROKER
HOLLYWOOD EIGHTS

16
CONTINENTAL RUMMY
DOUBLE DUMMY WHIST

16–continued
EIGHT DECK
  BEZIQUE
TRENTE ET QUARANTE
TRUMP HUMBUG WHIST

17+
BEAT YOUR
  NEIGHBOUR

17+–continued
BEGGAR-MY-
  NEIGHBOUR
BEGGAR-YOUR-NEIGHBOUR
FIVE HUNDRED
  BEZIQUE
ROUND THE
  CORNER RUMMY

BRIDGE TERMS

3
BID
FIT

4
ACOL
CALL
DEAL
GAME
LEAD
RUFF
VOID

5
ALERT
DUMMY
ENTRY
GUARD
REBID
TABLE

6
DOUBLE
GERBER
HONOUR
LENGTH
MISFIT
REVOKE
RUBBER
SYSTEM
TENACE
TIMING

7
AUCTION

7–continued
CONTROL
CUE BIDS
DISCARD
FINESSE
JUMP BID
PARTNER
SIGNALS
STAYMAN
STOPPER

8
CONTRACT
DECLARER
DIRECTOR
LIMIT BID
MCKENNEY
OVERCALL
OVER RUFF
REDOUBLE
RESPONSE
SIDE SUIT

9
BLACKWOOD
DOUBLETON
GRAND SLAM
LAVINTHAL
MAJOR SUIT
MINOR SUIT
OVER TRICK
PART SCORE
SACRIFICE
SINGLETON

9–continued
SMALL SLAM
SOLID SUIT

10
CONVENTION
FORCING BID
LINE OF PLAY
REVERSE BID
SYSTEM CARD
UNBALANCED
UNDER TRICK
VULNERABLE

11
DOUBLE DUMMY
MATCH POINTS
OPENING LEAD
PARTNERSHIP
THIRD IN HAND

12
BALANCED HAND
BIDDABLE SUIT
BIDDING SPACE
DISTRIBUTION
FOURTH IN HAND
INTERVENTION
JUMP OVERCALL
PLAYING TRICK
SEMI-BALANCED

13
COMMUNICATION
NOT VULNERABLE

13–continued
PRE-EMPTIVE BID
TAKE OUT DOUBLE
TOUCHING SUITS
TWO-SUITED HAND

14
COMPETITIVE BID
DESTRUCTIVE BID
GRAND SLAM
  FORCE
REBIDDABLE SUIT

15
CONSTRUCTIVE BID
DUPLICATE BRIDGE
INVITATIONAL BID
PLAYING STRENGTH
THREE-SUITED
  HAND

16+
CONTESTED
  AUCTION
MIRROR
  DISTRIBUTION
NEGATIVE
  RESPONSE
PHANTOM
  SACRIFICE
POSITIVE
  RESPONSE
SINGLE SUITED
  HAND

POKER HANDS

ROYAL FLUSH	FULL HOUSE	THREE OF A KIND
STRAIGHT FLUSH	FLUSH	TWO PAIRS
FOUR OF A KIND	STRAIGHT	ONE PAIR

DANCES

3	5–continued	7–continued	8	9–continued
DOG	SIBYL	ARNAOUT	ALEGRIAS	PASO DOBLE
GIG	STOMP	BABORÁK	Ã MOLESON	PASSEPIED
JIG	TANGO	BALL PLA	AURRESKU	POLONAISE
OLE	TRATA	BAMBUCO	BALZTANZ	QUADRILLE
	TWIST	BANJARA	BULL-FOOT	QUICKSTEP
4	VELAL	BATUQUE	CACHUCHA	RENNINGEN
AHIR	WALTZ	BHARANG	CAKEWALK	ROCK 'N' ROLL
BUMP		BOURRÉE	CANACUAS	SARABANDE
CANA	**6**	CANARIE	CANDIOTE	SATECKOVA
HAKA	ABUANG	CANARIO	CHARRADA	TAMBORITO
HORA	AMENER	CINQ PAS	COURANTE	TROYANATS
JIVE	ATINGA	CSARDAS	FANDANGO	
JOTA	BATUTA	FORLANA	GALLIARD	**10**
POGO	BOLERO	FOX-TROT	GYMNASKA	ATNUMOKITA
SHAG	BOOGIE	FURIANT	HABANERA	BANDLTANTZ
VIRA	CALATA	FURLANA	HAND JIVE	BATON DANCE
	CANARY	GAVOTTE	HORNPIPE	BERGERETTA
5	CAN-CAN	GERANOS	HUAPANGO	CHANIOTIKO
BARIS	CAROLE	GLOCSEN	MAILEHEN	CHARLESTON
BULBA	CEBELL	GOMBEYS	MOHOBELO	ESPRINGALE
CAROL	CHA CHA	GONDHAL	MOONWALK	FACKELTANZ
CONGA	DJOGED	GOSHIKI	MUTCHICO	FARANDOULO
CUECA	EIXIDA	HIMINAU	OXDANSEN	FURRY DANCE
DANSA	GANGAR	JABADAO	PERICOTE	GAY GORDONS
DEBKA	GIENYS	LAMENTO	RIGAUDON	HOKEY-COKEY
GAVOT	HUSTLE	LANCERS	RUTUBURI	KYNDELDANS
GIGUE	JACARA	LANDLER	TSAMIKOS	LAUTERBACH
GOPAK	JARABE	LLORONA		LOCOMOTION
HALOA	JARANA	MADISON	**9**	RUNNING SET
HOPAK	KAGURA	MAYPOLE	BAGUETTES	STRATHSPEY
KUMMI	KALELA	MAZURKA	BAILECITO	STRIP TEASE
L'AG-YA	MINUET	MEASURE	BARN DANCE	SURUVAKARY
LIMBO	PAVANE	MILONGA	BOULANGER	TARANTELLA
LOURE	PESSAH	MUNEIRA	CARDADORA	TRENCHMORE
MAMBO	POLSKA	PASILLO	CLOG DANCE	TURKEY TROT
NAZUN	SHIMMY	PERICON	COTILLION	
NUMBA	TIRANA	PLANXTY	ECOSSAISE	**11**
OKINA	VALETA	PURPURI	FARANDOLE	BABORASCHKA
POLKA	VELETA	SARDANA	GALLEGADA	BLACKBOTTOM
RUEDA	YUMARI	SATACEK	HAJDUTÂNC	DANSURINGUR
RUMBA		SIKINIK	HORN DANCE	DITHYRAMBOS
SALSA	**7**	TANDAVA	JITTERBUG	FLORAL DANCE
SAMBA	ABRASAX	TANTARA	KOLOMEJKA	GHARBA
SARBA	ABRAXAS	TRAIPSE	MISTLETOE	DANCE
SHAKE	AHIDOUS	WAKAMBA	MOKOROTLO	LAMBETH WALK
SIBEL	APARIMA			LINE DANCING

11–continued
MORRIS DANCE
PALAIS GLIDE
PAMPERRUQUE
ROCK AND ROLL
SCHOTTISCHE
SQUARE DANCE
TEWRDANNCKH

12
BREAKDANCING

12–continued
CREUX DE VERVI
DAMHSA NAM BOC
DANSE MACABRE
FUNKY CHICKEN
GREEN GARTERS
REEL O'TULLOCH

13
EIGHTSOME REEL
GHILLIE CALLUM

13–continued
HIGHLAND FLING

14
BABBITY BOWSTER
COUNTRY BUMPKIN
MILKMAIDS' DANCE
STRIP THE WILLOW

15
MILITARY TWO-STEP

15–continued
SELLINGER'S
  ROUND

17
HASTE TO THE
  WEDDING

18
SIR ROGER DE
  COVERLEY

HOBBIES AND CRAFTS

3
DIY

5
BATIK
BINGO

6
BONSAI
SEWING

7
COLLAGE
COOKERY
CROCHET
KEEP FIT
MACRAMÉ
MOSAICS
ORIGAMI
POTTERY
READING
TATTING
TOPIARY
WEAVING

8
AEROBICS
APPLIQUÉ
BASKETRY
CANEWORK

8–continued
FRETWORK
KNITTING
LAPIDARY
PAINTING
QUILTING
SPINNING
TAPESTRY
WOODWORK

9
ASTROLOGY
ASTRONOMY
DÉCOUPAGE
GARDENING
GENEALOGY
MARQUETRY
PALMISTRY
PATCHWORK
PHILATELY
RUG MAKING

10
BEE-KEEPING
BEER MAKING
CROSSWORDS
EMBROIDERY
ENAMELLING
KITE FLYING

10–continued
LACE MAKING
UPHOLSTERY
WINE MAKING

11
ARCHAEOLOGY
BARK RUBBING
BOOK BINDING
CALLIGRAPHY
DRESS MAKING
HANG GLIDING
LEPIDOPTERY
MODEL MAKING
PHOTOGRAPHY
STENCILLING
VINTAGE CARS

12
BEACH COMBING
BIRD WATCHING
BRASS RUBBING
CANDLE-MAKING
FLOWER DRYING
TROPICAL FISH

13
FOSSIL HUNTING
JIG-SAW PUZZLES
MODEL RAILWAYS

13–continued
TRAIN SPOTTING

14
BADGER WATCHING
CAKE DECORATING
COIN COLLECTING
FLOWER PRESSING
GLASS ENGRAVING
PIGEON FANCYING

15
FLOWER
  ARRANGING
LAMPSHADE
  MAKING
SHELL COLLECTING
STAMP COLLECTING

16
AMATEUR
  DRAMATICS
AUTOGRAPH
  HUNTING

19
BUTTERFLY
  COLLECTING

GAMES POSITIONS

3
END

4
POST
PROP
SLIP
WING

5
GUARD
GULLY
MID-ON
PIVOT

6
ATTACK

6–continued
BATTER
BOWLER
CENTER
CENTRE
HOOKER
LONG ON

6–continued
MID-OFF
SAFETY
TACKLE

7
BATSMAN
CATCHER

7–continued
DEFENCE
FIELDER
FORWARD
LEG SLIP
LONG LEG
LONG OFF

337

7–continued
OFFENSE
PITCHER
STRIKER
SWEEPER

8
FULLBACK
HALFBACK
LEFT BACK
LEFT HALF
LEFT WING
MIDFIELD
SPLIT END
TAILBACK
THIRD MAN
TIGHT END
WINGBACK

9
INFIELDER
MID WICKET
NOSE GUARD
NUMBER ONE
NUMBER TWO

9–continued
RIGHT BACK
RIGHT HALF
RIGHT WING
SCRUM HALF
SHORTSTOP
SQUARE LEG

10
CENTRE BACK
CENTRE HALF
CORNERBACK
COVER POINT
EXTRA COVER
GOAL ATTACK
GOALKEEPER
INSIDE LEFT
LINEBACKER
NUMBER FOUR
OUTFIELDER
SILLY MID-ON
WING ATTACK

11
DEEP FINE LEG

11–continued
FLANKER BACK
GOAL DEFENCE
GOAL SHOOTER
INSIDE RIGHT
LEFT FIELDER
LEFT FORWARD
NUMBER THREE
OUTSIDE LEFT
QUARTERBACK
RUNNING BACK
SILLY MID-OFF
WING DEFENCE
WING FORWARD

12
FIRST BASEMAN
OUTSIDE RIGHT
LEFT-WING BACK
RIGHT FIELDER
RIGHT FORWARD
SHORT FINE LEG
STAND OFF HALF
THIRD BASEMAN
THREE-QUARTER

12–continued
WICKETKEEPER
WIDE RECEIVER

13
CENTRE FIELDER
CENTRE FORWARD
POPPING CREASE
RIGHT-WING BACK
SECOND BASEMAN

14
LEFT-CENTRE BACK
LEFT DEFENSEMAN
SHORT SQUARE LEG

15+
FORWARD SHORT
  LEG
LEFT-WING
  FORWARD
RIGHT-CENTRE
  BACK
RIGHT
  DEFENSEMAN
RIGHT-WING
  FORWARD

STADIUMS AND VENUES

AINTREE (horse racing)
ANAHEIM STADIUM, CALIFORNIA (baseball)
ASCOT (horse racing)
AZTECA STADIUM, MEXICO CITY (football)
BELFRY, THE (golf)
BELMONT PARK, LONG ISLAND (horse racing)
BERNABAU STADIUM, MADRID (football)
BIG FOUR CURLING RINK (curling)
BRANDS HATCH (motor racing)
BROOKLANDS (motor racing)
CAESAR'S PALACE, LAS VEGAS (boxing)
CARDIFF ARMS PARK (rugby union)
CENTRAL STADIUM, KIEV (football)
CLEVELAND MUNICIPAL STADIUM (baseball)
CORPORATION STADIUM, CALICUR (cricket)
CROKE PARK, DUBLIN (Gaelic football, hurling)
CRUCIBAL, SHEFFIELD (snooker)
CRYSTAL PALACE (athletics)
DAYTONA INTERNATIONAL SPEEDWAY (motor
  racing, motor cycling)
EDEN GARDENS, CALCUTTA (cricket)
EDGBASTON (cricket)
EPSOM DOWNS (horse racing)
FORUM, THE (gymnastics)
FRANCORCHAMPS, BELGIUM (motor racing)
HAMPDEN PARK, GLASGOW (football)
HEADINGLEY (cricket)
HEYSEL STADIUM, BRUSSELS (football)
LAHORE (cricket)

LANDSDOWNE ROAD, BELFAST (rugby union)
LENIN STADIUM, MOSCOW (football)
LORDS CRICKET GROUND (cricket)
LOUISIANA SUPERDOME (most sports)
MARACANA STADIUM, BRAZIL (football)
MEADOWBANK (athletics)
MEMORIAL COLISEUM, LOS ANGELES (most
  sports)
MOOR PARK, RICKMANSWORTH (golf)
MUNICH OLYMPIC STADIUM (athletics, football)
MURRAYFIELD (rugby union)
NEWMARKET (horse racing)
NOU CAMP, BARCELONA (football)
ODSAL STADIUM, BRADFORD (rugby league)
OLD TRAFFORD (cricket)
OVAL, THE (cricket)
ST ANDREWS (golf)
SENAYAN MAIN STADIUM, JAKARTA (cricket)
SHANGHAI STADIUM (gymnastics)
SILVERSTONE (motor racing)
STAHOV STADIUM, PRAGUE (gymnastics)
TRENT BRIDGE (cricket)
TEXAS STADIUM (most sports)
TWICKENHAM (rugby union)
WEMBLEY CONFERENCE CENTRE (darts)
WEMBLEY STADIUM (football, rugby)
WHITE CITY (greyhound racing)
WIMBLEDON (tennis)
WINDSOR PARK, BELFAST (football)

TROPHIES, EVENTS, AND AWARDS

ADMIRAL'S CUP (sailing)
AFRICAN NATIONS CUP (football)
AIR CANADA SILVER BROOM (curling)
ALL-IRELAND CHAMPIONSHIP (Gaelic football)
ALL-IRELAND CHAMPIONSHIPS (hurling)
ALPINE CHAMPIONSHIPS (skiing)
AMERICA'S CUP (sailing)
ASHES (cricket)
BADMINTON THREE DAY EVENT (equestrian)
BBC SPORTS PERSONALITY OF THE YEAR (all-round)
BENSON & HEDGES CUP (cricket)
BOAT RACE (rowing)
BRITISH OPEN CHAMPIONSHIP (golf)
BRONZE MEDAL (most sports)
CAMANACHD ASSOCIATION CHALLENGE CUP (shinty)
CHELTENHAM AND GLOUCESTER TROPHY (cricket)
CHELTENHAM GOLD CUP (horse racing)
CLASSICS (horse racing)
COMMONWEALTH GAMES (athletics)
CORNHILL TEST (cricket)
DAVIS CUP (tennis)
DAYTONA 500 (motor racing)
DECATHLON (athletics)
DERBY (horse racing)
EMBASSY WORLD INDOOR BOWLS CROWN (bowls)
EMBASSY WORLD PROFESSIONAL SNOOKER CHAMPIONSHIP (snooker)
ENGLISH GREYHOUND DERBY (greyhound racing)
EUROPEAN CHAMPION CLUBS CUP (football)
EUROPEAN CHAMPIONS CUP (basketball)
EUROPEAN CHAMPIONSHIPS (football)
EUROPEAN CUP WINNERS' CUP (football)
EUROPEAN FOOTBALLER OF THE YEAR (football)
EUROPEAN SUPER CUP (football)
FEDERATION CUP (tennis)

FOOTBALL ASSOCIATION CHALLENGE CUP (football)
FOOTBALL ASSOCIATION CHARITY SHIELD (football)
FOOTBALL LEAGUE CHAMPIONSHIP (football)
FOOTBALL LEAGUE CUP (football)
FULL CAP (football, rugby)
FWA FOOTBALLER OF THE YEAR (football)
GILLETTE CUP (cricket)
GOLDEN BOOT AWARD (football)
GOLD MEDAL (most sports)
GORDEN INTERNATIONAL MEDAL (curling)
GRAND NATIONAL (greyhound racing)
GRAND NATIONAL STEEPLECHASE (horse racing)
GRAND PRIX (motor racing)
GUINNESS TROPHY (tiddlywinks)
HARMSWORTH TROPHY (power boat racing)
HENLEY REGATTA (rowing)
HENRI DELANEY TROPHY (football)
HIGHLAND GAMES (athletics)
ICY SMITH CUP (ice hockey)
INDIANAPOLIS 500 (motor racing)
INTERNATIONAL CHAMPIONSHIP (bowls)
INTERNATIONAL CROSS-COUNTRY CHAMPIONSHIP (athletics)
INTERNATIONAL INTER-CITY INDUSTRIAL FAIRS CUP (football)
IROQUOIS CUP (lacrosse)
ISLE OF MAN TT (motorcycle racing)
JOHN PLAYER CUP (rugby league)
JOHN PLAYER LEAGUE (cricket)
JULES RIMET TROPHY (football)
KING GEORGE V GOLD CUP (equestrian)
KINNAIRD CUP (fives)
LE MANS 24 HOUR (motor racing)
LITTLEWOODS CHALLENGE CUP (football)

LOMBARD RALLY (motor rallying)
LONSDALE BELT (boxing)
MACROBERTSON INTERNATIONAL SHIELD (croquet)
MAN OF THE MATCH (football)
MARATHON (athletics)
MIDDLESEX SEVENS (rugby union)
MILK CUP (football)
MILK RACE (cycling)
MONTE CARLO RALLY (motor rallying)
MOST VALUABLE PLAYER (American football)
NATIONAL ANGLING CHAMPIONSHIP (angling)
NATIONAL HUNT JOCKEY CHAMPIONSHIP (horse racing)
NATIONAL WESTMINSTER BANK TROPHY (cricket)
NORDIC CHAMPIONSHIPS (skiing)
OAKS (horse racing)
OLYMPIC GAMES (most sports)
ONE THOUSAND GUINEAS (horse racing)
OPEN CROQUET CHAMPIONSHIP (croquet)
OXFORD BLUE (most sports)
PALIO (horse racing)
PENTATHLON (athletics)
PFA FOOTBALLER OF THE YEAR (football)
PRUDENTIAL WORLD CUP (cricket)
QUEEN ELIZABETH II CUP (equestrian)
RAC TOURIST TROPHY (motor racing)
ROSE BOWL (American football)
ROYAL HUNT CUP (horse racing)
RUGBY LEAGUE CHALLENGE CUP (rugby league)
RUNNERS-UP MEDAL (most sports)
RYDER CUP (golf)
SCOTTISH FOOTBALL ASSOCIATION CUP (football)
SILVER MEDAL (most sports)
SIMOD CUP (football)
SKOL CUP (football)
SOUTH AMERICAN CHAMPIONSHIP (football)

STANLEY CUP (ice hockey)
ST LEGER (horse racing)
STRATHCONA CUP (curling)
SUPER BOWL (American
football)
SUPER CUP (handball)
SWAYTHLING CUP (table
tennis)
THOMAS CUP (badminton)
TOUR DE FRANCE (cycling)
TRIPLE CROWN (rugby union)

TWO THOUSAND GUINEAS
(horse racing)
UBER CUP (badminton)
UEFA CUP (Union of European
Football Associations) (foot-
ball)
UNIROYAL WORLD JUNIOR
CHAMPIONSHIPS (curling)
WALKER CUP (golf)
WIGHTMAN CUP (sailing)
WIMBLEDON (tennis)

WINGFIELD SKULLS (rowing)
WINNERS MEDAL (most
sports)
WOODEN SPOON (! most
sports)
WORLD CLUB CHAMPION-
SHIP (football)
WORLD MASTERS
CHAMPIONSHIPS (darts)
WORLD SERIES (baseball)
YELLOW JERSEY (cycling)

FIRST-CLASS CRICKETING COUNTIES

DERBYSHIRE
DURHAM
ESSEX
GLAMORGAN
GLOUCESTERSHIRE

HAMPSHIRE
KENT
LANCASHIRE
LEICESTERSHIRE
MIDDLESEX

NORTHAMPTON-
SHIRE
NOTTINGHAMSHIRE
SOMERSET
SURREY

SUSSEX
WARWICKSHIRE
WORCESTERSHIRE
YORKSHIRE

CRICKETING TERMS AND EXPRESSIONS

3
BAT
BYE
CUT
LBW
RUN
TON

4
BAIL
DUCK
HOOK
OVER
WIDE

5
BOSIE
COVER
GULLY
MID-ON
POINT
SWEEP

6
BEAMER
BOWLED
BOWLER
CAUGHT
CREASE
GOOGLY
HOWZAT!

6–continued
LEG BYE
LONG ON
MAIDEN
MID-OFF
NO-BALL
RUN OUT
SCORER
SEAMER
UMPIRE
WICKET
YORKER

7
BATSMAN
BOUNCER
CENTURY
COW-SHOT
FIELDER
FINE LEG
FLIPPER
INNINGS
LATE CUT
LEG SLIP
LEG SPIN
LONG HOP
LONG LEG
LONG OFF
OFF SPIN
SHOOTER

7–continued
STRIKER
STUMPED

8
BOUNDARY
CHINAMAN
HAT-TRICK
HOW'S THAT!
LONGSTOP
SHORT LEG
THE SLIPS
THIRD MAN

9
BATSWOMAN
HIT WICKET
IN-SWINGER
LEG GLANCE
MID-WICKET
OVERTHROW
SQUARE CUT
SQUARE LEG
STICKY DOG
TEST MATCH
THE COVERS

10
ALL-ROUNDER
GOLDEN DUCK
NON-STRIKER

10–continued
OUT-SWINGER
SIGHT-SCREEN
SILLY MID-ON
SILLY POINT
TOP-SPINNER
TWELFTH MAN

11
DAISY-CUTTER
SILLY MID-OFF

12
RETURN CREASE
REVERSE SWEEP
STICKY WICKET
STONEWALLING
WICKETKEEPER

13
BATTING CREASE
DEEP SQUARE LEG
POPPING CREASE

14+
BODY-LINE BOWLING
LEG BEFORE
WICKET
LEG-SIDE FIELDER
LEG-THEORY
BOWLING
OFFSIDE FIELDER

GRAND PRIX CIRCUITS

GRAND PRIX	Circuit		
		EUROPEAN	Nürburgring, Germany
		FRENCH	Magny-Cours
AUSTRALIAN	Melbourne	GERMAN	Hockenheim
AUSTRIAN	Spielberg	HUNGARIAN	Hungaroring
BAHRAINI	Bahrain International	ITALIAN	Monza
	Circuit	JAPANESE	Suzuka
BELGIAN	Spa-Francorchamps	MALAYSIAN	Kuala Lumpur
BRAZILIAN	São Paulo	MONACO	Monte Carlo
BRITISH	Silverstone	SAN MARINO	Imola, Italy
CANADIAN	Montreal	SPANISH	Barcelona
CHINESE	Shangai	UNITED STATES	Indianapolis

MAJOR RUGBY UNION CLUBS

3
GHK

4
BATH
GALA
SALE

5
FLYDE
LEEDS
NEATH
ORREL
OTLEY
RUGBY
WASPS

6
CURRIE
EXETER
HAVANT
HAWICK
MORLEY

7
BEDFORD

7—continued
BRISTOL
CARDIFF
CLIFTON
MELROSE
MOSELEY
NEWPORT
READING
REDRUTH
SHANNON
SWANSEA
WALSALL

8
ABERAVON
ASPATRIA
BRIDGEND
COVENTRY
EBBW VALE
LLANELLI
RICHMOND
SARACENS
TREORCHY
WATERLOO

9
BALLYMENA
GARRYOWEN
HARROGATE
HERIOT'S FP
JEDFOREST
LANDSDOWE
LEICESTER
NEWBRIDGE
NEWCASTLE
OLD WESLEY
ROTHERHAM
WAKEFIELD

10
BARBARIANS
BLACKHEATH
GLOUCESTER
HARLEQUINS
INSTONIANS
NOTTINGHAM
PONTYPRIDD
WATSONIANS

11
ABERTILLERY
BOROUGHMUIR
LONDON IRISH
LONDON WELSH
NORTHAMPTON
ROSSLYN PARK

12
OLD BELVEDERE
YOUNG MUNSTER

14
LONDON SCOTTISH
STIRLING COUNTY
WEST HARTLEPOOL

16+
BLACKROCK
  COLLEGE
CORK
  CONSTABULARY
EDINBURGH
  ACADEMICALS
LIVERPOOL ST
  HELENS

RUGBY LEAGUE CLUBS

4
HULL
YORK

5
LEEDS
WIGAN

6
BATLEY
WIDNES

7
BRAMLEY
HALIFAX

7—continued
SWINTON

8
CARLISLE
DEWSBURY
ST HELENS

9
HIGHFIELD

10
CASTLEFORD
WARRINGTON
WHITEHAVEN

11
OLDHAM BEARS
SALFORD REDS

12
BARROW
  BRAVES

12–continued
HUDDERSFIELD
HUNSLET HAWKS

13
BRADFORD BULLS
LONDON
  BRONCOS

14
WORKINGTON TOWN

15+
CHORLEY
  CHIEFTAINS
DONCASTER
  DRAGONS

15+—continued
FEATHERSTONE
  ROVERS
HULL KINGSTON
  ROVERS
KEIGHLEY
  COUGARS
LEIGH CENTURIONS

15+—continued
PARIS SAINT
  GERMAIN
ROCHDALE
  HORNETS
SHEFFIELD EAGLES
WAKEFIELD TRINITY

BRITISH FOOTBALL TEAMS

TEAM	GROUND	NICKNAME
ABERDEEN	PITTODRIE STADIUM	DONS
AIRDRIEONIANS	BROOMFIELD PARK	DIAMONDS; WAYSIDERS
ALBION ROVERS	CLIFTON HALL	WEE ROVERS
ALDERSHOT	RECREATION GROUND	SHOTS
ALLOA	RECREATION PARK	WASPS
ARBROATH	GAYFIELD PARK	RED LICHTIES
ARSENAL	HIGHBURY	GUNNERS
ASTON VILLA	VILLA PARK	VILLANS
AYR UNITED	SOMERSET PARK	HONEST MEN
BARNSLEY	OAKWELL GROUND	TYKES; REDS; COLLIERS
BERWICK RANGERS	SHIELFIELD PARK	BORDERERS
BIRMINGHAM CITY	ST ANDREWS	BLUES
BLACKBURN ROVERS	EWOOD PARK	BLUE & WHITES; ROVERS
BLACKPOOL	BLOMMFIELD ROAD	SEASIDERS
BOLTON WANDERERS	BURNDEN PARK	TROTTERS
BOURNEMOUTH	DEAN COURT	CHERRIES
BRADFORD CITY	VALLEY PARADE	BANTAMS
BRECHIN CITY	GLEBE PARK	CITY
BRENTFORD	GRIFFIN PARK	BEES
BRIGHTON & HOVE ALBION	GOLDSTONE GROUND	SEAGULLS
BRISTOL CITY	ASHTON GATE	ROBINS
BRISTOL ROVERS	TWERTON PARK	PIRATES
BURNLEY	TURF MOOR	CLARETS
BURY	GIGG LANE	SHAKERS
CAMBRIDGE UNITED	ABBEY STADIUM	UNITED
CARDIFF CITY	NINIAN PARK	BLUEBIRDS
CARLISLE UNITED	BRUNTON PARK	CUMBRIANS; BLUES
CELTIC	CELTIC PARK	BHOYS
CHARLTON ATHLETIC	THE VALLEY	ADDICKS; ROBINS; VALIANTS
CHELSEA	STAMFORD BRIDGE	BLUES
CHESTER CITY	SEALAND ROAD	BLUES
CHESTERFIELD	RECREATION GROUND	BLUES; SPIREITES
CLYDEBANK	KILBOWIE PARK	BANKIES
CLYDE	FIRHILL PARK	BULLY WEE
COLCHESTER UNITED	LAYER ROAD	U'S
COVENTRY CITY	HIGHFIELD ROAD	SKY BLUES
COWDENBEATH	CENTRAL PARK	COWDEN
CREWE ALEXANDRA	GRESTY ROAD	RAILWAYMEN
CRYSTAL PALACE	SELHURST PARK	EAGLES
DARLINGTON	FEETHAMS GROUND	QUAKERS
DERBY COUNTY	BASEBALL GROUND	RAMS
DONCASTER ROVERS	BELLE VUE GROUND	ROVERS
DUMBARTON	BOGHEAD PARK	SONS
DUNDEE	DENS PARK	DARK BLUES; DEE
DUNDEE UNITED	TANNADICE PARK	TERRORS

TEAM	GROUND	NICKNAME
DUNFERMLINE ATHLETIC	EAST END PARK	PARS
EAST FIFE	BAYVIEW PARK	FIFERS
EAST STIRLINGSHIRE	FIRS PARK	SHIRE
EVERTON	GOODISON PARK	TOFFEES
EXETER CITY	ST JAMES PARK	GRECIANS
FALKIRK	BROCKVILLE PARK	BAIRNS
FORFAR ATHELTIC	STATION PARK	SKY BLUES
FULHAM	CRAVEN COTTAGE	COTTAGERS
GILLINGHAM	PRIESTFIELD STADIUM	GILLS
GRIMSBY TOWN	BLUNDELL PARK	MARINERS
HALIFAX TOWN	SHAY GROUND	SHAYMEN
HAMILTON ACADEMICAL	DOUGLAS PARK	ACCES
HARTLEPOOL UNITED	VICTORIA GROUND	POOL
HEART OF MIDLOTHIAN	TYNECASTLE PARK	HEARTS
HEREFORD UNITED	EDGAR STREET	UNITED
HIBERNIAN	EASTER ROAD	HIBEES
HUDDERSFIELD TOWN	LEEDS ROAD	TERRIERS
HULL CITY	BOOTHFERRY PARK	TIGERS
IPSWICH TOWN	PORTMAN ROAD	BLUES; TOWN
KILMARNOCK	RUGBY PARK	KILLIE
LEEDS UNITED	ELLAND ROAD	UNITED
LEICESTER CITY	FILBERT STREET	FILBERTS; FOXES
LEYTON ORIENT	BRISBANE ROAD	O'S
LINCOLN CITY	SINCIL BANK	RED IMPS
LIVERPOOL	ANFIELD	REDS; POOL
LUTON TOWN	KENILWORTH ROAD	HATTERS
MANCHESTER CITY	MAINE ROAD	BLUES
MANCHESTER UNITED	OLD TRAFFORD	RED DEVILS
MANSFIELD TOWN	FIELD MILL GROUND	STAGS
MEADOWBANK THISTLE	MEADOWBANK STADIUM	THISTLE; WEE JAGS
MIDDLESBROUGH	AYRESOME PARK	BORO
MILLWALL	THE DEN	LIONS
MONTROSE	LINKS PARK	GABLE ENDERS
MORTON	CAPPIELOW PARK	TON
MOTHERWELL	FIR PARK	WELL
NEWCASTLE UNITED	ST JAMES PARK	MAGPIES
NORTHAMPTON TOWN	COUNTY GROUND	COBBLERS
NORWICH CITY	CARROW ROAD	CANARIES
NOTTINGHAM FOREST	CITY GROUND	REDS; FOREST
NOTTS COUNTY	MEADOW LANE	MAGPIES
OLDHAM ATHLETIC	BOUNDARY PARK	LATICS
OXFORD UNITED	MANOR GROUND	U'S
PARTICK THISTLE	FIRHILL PARK	JAGS
PETERBOROUGH UNITED	LONDON ROAD	POSH
PLYMOUTH ARGYLE	HOME PARK	PILGRIMS
PORTSMOUTH	FRATTON PARK	POMPEY
PORT VALE	VALE PARK	VALIANTS
PRESTON NORTH END	DEEPDALE	LILYWHITES; NORTH END
QUEEN OF THE SOUTH	PALMERSTON PARK	DOONHAMERS
QUEEN'S PARK	HAMPDEN PARK	SPIDERS
QUEEN'S PARK RANGERS	LOFTUS ROAD	RANGERS; R'S
RAITH ROVERS	STARK'S PARK	ROVERS
RANGERS	IBROX STADIUM	GERS
READING	ELM PARK	ROYALS
ROCHDALE	SPOTLAND	DALE
ROTHERHAM UNITED	MILLMOOR GROUND	MERRY MILLERS
SCARBOROUGH	SEAMER ROAD	BORO
SCUNTHORPE UNITED	GLANFORD PARK	IRON
SHEFFIELD UNITED	BRAMALL LANE	BLADES
SHEFFIELD WEDNESDAY	HILLSBOROUGH	OWLS

TEAM	GROUND	NICKNAME
SHREWSBURY TOWN	GAY MEADOW	SHREWS; TOWN
SOUTHAMPTON	DELL	SAINTS
SOUTHEND UNITED	ROOTS HALL	SHRIMPERS
STENHOUSEMUIR	OCHILVIEW PARK	WARRIORS
STIRLING ALBION	ANNFIELD PARK	ALBION
ST JOHNSTONE	MUIRTON PARK	SAINTS
ST MIRREN	LOVE STREET	BUDDIES; PAISLEY SAINTS
STOCKPORT COUNTY	EDGELEY PARK	COUNTY; HATTERS
STOKE CITY	VICTORIA GROUND	POTTERS
STRANRAER	STAIR PARK	BLUES
SUNDERLAND	ROKER PARK	ROKERITES
SWANSEA CITY	VETCH FIELD	SWANS
SWINDON TOWN	COUNTY GROUND	ROBINS
TORQUAY UNITED	PLAINMOOR GROUND	GULLS
TOTTENHAM HOTSPUR	WHITE HART LANE	SPURS
TRANMERE ROVERS	PRENTON PARK	ROVERS
WALSALL	FELLOWS PARK	SADDLERS
WATFORD	VICARAGE ROAD	HORNETS
WEST BROMWICH ALBION	HAWTHORNS	THROSTLES; BAGGIES; ALBION
WEST HAM UNITED	UPTON PARK	HAMMERS
WIGAN ATHLETIC	SPRINGFIED PARK	LATICS
WIMBLEDON	PLOUGH LANE	DONS
WOLVERHAMPTON WANDERERS	MOLINEUX	WOLVES
WREXHAM	RACECOURSE GROUND	ROBINS
YORK CITY	BOOTHAM CRESCENT	MINSTERMEN

EUROPEAN FOOTBALL CLUBS

AUSTRIA

RAPID VIENNA
SALZBURG

BELGIUM

ANDERLECHT
EKEREN
FC BRUGES
ROYAL ANTWERP
STANDARD LIEGE

CROATIA

HAJOUK SPLIT

CZECH REPUBLIC

SLAVIA PRAGUE
SPARTA PRAGUE

DENMARK

BRONDBY

FRANCE

AUXERRE

BASTIA
BORDEAUX
LE HAVRE
LILLE
LYONS
MARSEILLES
METZ
MONACO
MONTPELLIER
NANTES
NICE
PARIS SAINT
  GERMAIN
STRASBOURG

GERMANY

BAYER
  LEVERKUSEN
BAYERN MUNICH
BORUSSIA
  MÖNCHENGLAD-
  BACH
BRANN BERGEN
COLOGNE
DUISBURG
HANSA ROSTOCK

KARLSRUHE
MUNICH
WERDER BREMEN
VFB STUTTGART

GREECE

AEK ATHENS
GALATASARAY
OLYMPIAKOS
PANATHINAIKOS

ITALY

AC MILAN
AS ROMA
ATALANTA
BOLOGNA
CAGLIARI
FIORENTINA
INTER MILAN
INTERNAZIONALE
JUVENTUS
LAZIO
NAPOLI
PARMA
PERUGIA

PIACENZA
SAMPDORIA
VERONA
VICENZA

NETHERLANDS

AJAX
FC VOLENDAM
FEYENOORD
FORTUNA SITTARD
JC KERKRADE
PSV EINDHOVEN
RKC WAALWIJK
TILBURG
UTRECHT
VITESSE ARNHEM

PORTUGAL

AMADORA
BENFICA
BOAVISTA
BRAGA
FARENSE
FC PORTO
SETUBAL

SPORTING LISBON

SPAIN
ATLÉTICO DE
  BILBAO
ATLÉTICO DE
  MADRID
BARCELONA
ESPAÑOL
RACING SANTANDER

REAL MADRID
REAL SOCIEDAO
REAL ZARAGOZA
SEVILLA
SPORTING GIJÓN
VALLENCIA

POLAND
LEGIA WARSAW

ROMANIA
STEAVA
  BUCHAREST

RUSSIA
CSKA MOSCOW
SPARTAK MOSCO

SWEDEN
AIK STOCKHOLM
IFK GOTHENBURG

UKRAINE
DYNAMO KIEV

AMERICAN FOOTBALL TEAMS

ATLANTA FALCONS
BUFFALO BILLS
CHICAGO BEARS
CLEVELAND BROWNS
DALLAS COWBOYS
DENVER BRONCOS
DETROIT LIONS
GREEN BAY PACKERS
HOUSTON OILERS

INDIANAPOLIS COLTS
KANSAS CITY CHIEFS
LOS ANGELES RAIDERS
LOS ANGELES RAMS
MIAMI DOLPHINS
MINNESOTA VIKINGS
NEW ENGLAND PATRIOTS
NEW ORLEANS SAINTS
NEW YORK GIANTS

NEW YORK JETS
PHILADELPHIA EAGLES
PHOENIX CARDINALS
PITTSBURGH STEELERS
SAN DIEGO CHARGERS
SAN FRANCISCO 49ERS
SEATTLE SEAHAWKS
TAMPA BAY BUCCANEERS
WASHINGTON REDSKINS

AMERICAN BASEBALL TEAMS

ATLANTA BRAVES
BALTIMORE ORIOLES
BOSTON RED SOX
BROOKLYN DODGERS
CALIFORNIA ANGELS
CHICAGO WHITE SOX
CINCINNATI REDS
CLEVELAND INDIANS
DETROIT TIGERS

KANSAS CITY ROYALS
LOS ANGELES DODGERS
MILWAUKEE BRAVES
MINNESOTA TWINS
NEW YORK GIANTS
NEW YORK METS
NEW YORK YANKEES
OAKLAND ATHLETICS
PHILADELPHIA PHILLIES

PITTSBURGH PIRATES
ST LOUIS BROWNS
ST LOUIS CARDINALS
SAN FRANCISCO GIANTS
TEXAS RANGERS
TORONTO BLUE JAYS
WASHINGTON SENATORS

GARDENING

GARDENING TERMS

2	4	4–continued	5–continued	5–continued
PH	BOLE	SNAG	CROSS	MULCH
	BULB	SPIT	CROWN	PRUNE
3	LIME		FORCE	SHRUB
BUD	LOAM	**5**	GENUS	SPORT
POT	NODE	BLIND	GRAFT	STAKE
	PEAT	BLOOM	HARDY	TILTH

345

5–continued
TRUSS
TUBER

6
ALPINE
ANNUAL
CLOCHE
CORDON
DIBBER
FLORET
HYBRID
MANURE
RUNNER
STRAIN
SUCKER

7
COMPOST
CUTTING
FRIABLE
LATERAL
NEUTRAL
PERGOLA
RHIZOME

8
ACID SOIL
AERATION
BIENNIAL
DEAD-HEAD
PINCH OUT
PRICK OUT
SEEDLING

8–continued
STANDARD

9
BLANCHING
CHLOROSIS
DECIDUOUS
EVERGREEN
FUNGICIDE
HALF HARDY
HEELING-IN
PERENNIAL
ROOTSTOCK
SIDE SHOOT

10
BASAL SHOOT

10–continued
CALCAREOUS
FERTILIZER
HERBACEOUS
VARIEGATED

11
GERMINATION
INSECTICIDE
POLLINATION
PROPAGATION

12+
ALKALINE SOIL
BASTARD
TRENCHING
BEDDING PLANT
HARDENING OFF

GARDEN FLOWERS

4
FLAX
GEUM
IRIS
SAGE

5
AJUGA
ASTER
ASTER
AVENS
BUGLE
DAISY
HOSTA
INULA
LINUM
LUPIN
PANSY
PEONY
PHLOX
PINKS
POPPY
SEDUM
VIOLA

6
BELLIS
BORAGE
CALTHA
CLEOME
COBAEA
COSMEA
COSMOS
DAHLIA
ECHIUM
IBERIS
MALOPE
NEPETA
PAEONY
RESEDA
SALVIA
SPURGE

6–continued
STOCKS
VIOLET
YARROW
ZINNIA

7
ALKANET
ALTHAEA
ALYSSUM
ANCHUSA
ANEMONE
ARUNCUS
ASTILBE
BEGONIA
BUGBANE
CAMPION
CATMINT
CELOSIA
CLARKIA
DAY LILY
GAZANIA
GODETIA
HONESTY
IPOMOEA
KINGCUP
LIATRIS
LINARIA
LIRIOPE
LOBELIA
LUNARIA
LYCHNIS
LYTHRUM
MILFOIL
MIMULUS
MONARDA
MULLEIN
NEMESIA
NIGELLA
PAPAVER
PETUNIA
PRIMULA

7–continued
STACHYS
STATICE
TAGETES
URSINIA
VERBENA

8
ACANTHUS
ACHILLEA
ACONITUM
AGERATUM
ARCTOTIS
BARTONIA
BERGAMOT
BERGENIA
BRUNNERA
CLEMATIS
DIANTHUS
DICENTRA
DROPWORT
ECHINOPS
EREMURUS
ERIGERON
ERYNGIUM
FEVERFEW
FLEABANE
FOXGLOVE
GERANIUM
HELENIUM
HEUCHERA
HIBISCUS
KNAPWEED
KNOTWEED
LARKSPUR
LATHYRUS
LAUATERA
LILY TURF
LIMONIUM
LUNGWORT
MACLEAYA
MYOSOTIS

8–continued
PHACELIA
PHYSALIS
PRIMROSE
PRUNELLA
SCABIOSA
SCABIOUS
SEA HOLLY
SELF-HEAL
SIDALCEA
SOAPWORT
SOLIDAGO
STOKESIA
SUN PLANT
SWEET PEA
TIARELLA
TICKSEED
TOADFLAX
TROLLIUS
VENIDIUM
VERONICA
VISCARIA

9
ANAPHALIS
AQUILEGIA
ASTRANTIA
BIG BETONY
BUTTERCUP
CALENDULA
CAMPANULA
CANDYTUFT
CARNATION
CENTAUREA
COLUMBINE
COREOPSIS
DICTAMNUS
DIGITALIS
DORONICUM
ECHINACEA
EPIMEDIUM
EUPHORBIA

9–continued
GOLDEN ROD
HELIOPSIS
HOLLYHOCK
IMPATIENS
KNIPHOFIA
LAMB'S EARS
LIGULARIA
MALCOLMIA
MATTHIOLA
MEADOW RUE
MOLUCELLA
MONKSHOOD
NAVELWORT
NEMOPHILA
NICOTIANA
OENOTHERA
PENSTEMON
POLYGONUM
PORTULACA
PYRETHRUM
RODGERSIA
RUDBECKIA
SAPONARIA
SAXIFRAGE
SNAKEROOT
SPEEDWELL
STONECROP
SUNFLOWER
VERBASCUM

10
ACROLINIUM
AGAPANTHUS
AGROSTEMMA
ALCHEMILLA
AMARANTHUS
BARRENWORT
BELLFLOWER
BISHOP'S HAT
BUSY LIZZIE
CATANANCHE

10–continued
CHINA ASTER
CIMICIFUGA
CINQUEFOIL
CONEFLOWER
CORN COCKLE
CORNFLOWER
CORTADERIA
CUPID'S DART
DELPHINIUM
FOAM FLOWER
GAILLARDIA
GAYFEATHER
GOAT'S BEARD
GYPSOPHILA
HELIANTHUS
HELIOTROPE
HELLEBORUS
INDIAN PINK
KAFFIR LILY
LENTEN ROSE
LIMNANTHES
LYSIMACHIA
MASTERWORT
MATRICARIA
MECONOPSIS
MIGNONETTE
NASTURTIUM
OMPHALODES
PLATYCODON
PLUME POPPY
POLEMONIUM
POTENTILLA
PULMONARIA
RANUNCULUS
SNAPDRAGON
SNEEZEWORT
SPIDERWORT
THALICTRUM
THUNBERGIA
TROPAEOLUM
WALLFLOWER

11
AFRICAN LILY
ANTIRRHINUM
BABY'S BREATH
BEARD TONGUE
BLAZING STAR
BOUNCING BET
BURNING BUSH
CALCEOLARIA
CENTRANTHUS
CHEIRANTHUS
CONVOLVULUS
CORAL FLOWER
CRANE'S-BILL
FILIPENDULA
FLOSS FLOWER
FORGET-ME-NOT
FOXTAIL LILY
GLOBE FLOWER
HELICHRYSUM
INCARVILLEA
LADY'S MANTLE
LOOSESTRIFE
LOVE-IN-A-MIST
PAMPAS GRASS
PHYSOSTEGIA
POLYGONATUM
POT MARIGOLD
RED HOT POKER
RED VALERIAN
SCHIZANTHUS
SEA LAVENDER
SHASTA DAISY
STOKES' ASTER
STRAW FLOWER
XERANTHEMUM

12
AFRICAN DAISY
ALSTROEMERIA
ANNUAL MALLOW
BABY BLUE EYES
BLUE-EYED MARY
CALLISTEPHUS

12–continued
ESCHSCHOLZIA
GLOBE THISTLE
HELIOTROPIUM
HEMEROCALLIS
JACOB'S LADDER
LEOPARD'S BANE
MONKEY FLOWER
MORNING GLORY
PERUVIAN LILY
PLANTAIN LILY
SALPIGLOSSIS
SCHIZOSTYLIS
SOLOMON'S SEAL
SPIDER FLOWER
SWEET ALYSSUM
SWEET WILLIAM
TOBACCO PLANT
TRADESCANTIA

13
BALLOON FLOWER
BEAR'S BREECHES
BLANKET FLOWER
BLEEDING HEART
CATHEDRAL BELL
CHRISTMAS ROSE
CHRYSANTHEMUM
DIMORPHOTHECA
MARSH MARIGOLD
OBEDIENT PLANT
PAINTED TONGUE
PRAIRIE MALLOW
SLIPPER FLOWER
VIRGINIA STOCK

14
BELLS OF IRELAND
BLACK-EYED SUSAN
CANTERBURY BELL
CHINESE LANTERN
FLOWER OF AN
  HOUR
FRENCH MARIGOLD

14–continued
POOR MAN'S
  ORCHID
STAR OF THE VELDT
YOUTH AND OLD
  AGE

15
AFRICAN MARIGOLD
EVENING PRIMROSE
JAPANESE
  ANEMONE
MICHAELMAS DAISY

16
BACHELOR'S
  BUTTONS
CALIFORNIAN
  POPPY
COMMON
  IMMORTELLE
LIVINGSTONE DAISY
MESEMBRYAN-
  THEMUM
PEARL
  EVERLASTING
POACHED EGG
  FLOWER
PURPLE CONE-
  FLOWER

17+
CHINESE BELL-
  FLOWER
CHINESE TRUMPET
  FLOWER
EVERLASTING
  FLOWER
LOVE-LIES-
  BLEEDING
MONARCH OF THE
  VELDT
PURPLE
  LOOSESTRIFE

ROCKERY PLANTS

4
GEUM

5
ASTER
DRABA
DRYAS
MAZUS
PHLOX
SEDUM

6
ACAENA
ARABIS
ERINUS
IBERIS

6–continued
ONOSMA
OXALIS
SILENE
THRIFT

7
ALYSSUM
ARMERIA
ASTILBE
CAT'S EAR
GENTIAN
LEWISIA
LINNAEA
LYCHNIS

7–continued
MIMULUS
MORISIA
PIGROOT
PLEIONE
RAMONDA
RAOULIA
SEA PINK
SHORTIA

8
ACHILLEA
ARENARIA
AUBRIETA
DIANTHUS

8–continued
ERIGERON
ERYSIMUM
FLEABANE
GENTIANA
GERANIUM
GROMWELL
HABERLEA
HEPATICA
ORIGANUM
ROCK ROSE
SANDWORT
SNOWBELL
UVULARIA

9
ANACYCLUS
ANDROSACE
AUBRIETIA
BLOODROOT
CAMPANULA
CANDYTUFT
CERASTIUM
EDELWEISS
HOUSELEEK
HYPERICUM
PENSTEMON
POLYGONUM
ROCK CRESS
SAPONARIA

9—continued
SAXIFRAGA
SAXIFRAGE
STONECROP
VERBASCUM

10
AETHIONEMA
ALPINE GEUM
ANTENNARIA
BELLFLOWER
CYANANTHUS
LYSIMACHIA
PULSATILLA
SOLDANELLA
THROATWORT

10—continued
TWIN FLOWER

11
DODECATHEON
DONKEY PLANT
HELICHRYSUM
MOSS CAMPION
ROCKERY PINK
ROCK JASMINE
ROCK MULLEIN
SANGUINARIA
SEMPERVIVUM
VANCOUVERIA
WALDSTEINIA

12
ALPINE YARROW
HELIANTHEMUM
LEONTOPODIUM
LITHOSPERMUM
MONKEY FLOWER
PASQUE FLOWER
ROCK SOAPWORT
SHOOTING STAR
SISYRINCHIUM
ST JOHN'S WORT
WHITLOW GRASS

13+
ALPINE
  WALLFLOWER

13+—continued
CREEPING JENNY
EVERLASTING
  FLOWER
INSIDE-OUT
  FLOWER
MOUNTAIN AVENS
MOUNT ATLAS
  DAISY
NEW ZEALAND
  BURR
ROCK CINQUEFOIL
SNOW-IN-SUMMER
SUMMER
  STARWORT
WHITE ROCK CRESS

BULBS

4
IRIS
IXIA
LILY

5
CANNA
TULIP

6
ALLIUM
CRINUM
CROCUS
LILIUM
NERINE
OXALIS
SCILLA
SORREL
TULIPA

7
ANEMONE
BEGONIA
FREESIA
IPHEION
MUSCARI
QUAMASH

8
BLUEBELL
BRODIAEA
CAMASSIA
CORN LILY
CYCLAMEN
DAFFODIL
ERANTHIS
GALTONIA
HYACINTH
LEUCOJUM
SNOWDROP
SPARAXIS
TIGRIDIA
TRILLIUM
TRITONIA

9
AMARYLLIS
COLCHICUM
CROCOSMIA
GALANTHUS
GLADIOLUS
NARCISSUS
SNOWFLAKE
SWORD LILY
WAKE ROBIN

10
ACIDATHERA
CHIONODOXA
FRITILLARY
HYACINTHUS
INDIAN SHOT
MONTBRETIA
PUSCHKINIA
RANUNCULUS
WINDFLOWER

11
BLAZING STAR
CONVALLARIA
ERYTHRONIUM
FRITILLARIA
STERNBERGIA
TIGER FLOWER

12
AUTUMN CROCUS
CARDIOCRINUM
ORNITHOGALUM

13
GRAPE HYACINTH
STRIPED SQUILL
WINTER ACONITE

14
BELLADONNA LILY
GLORY OF THE
  SNOW
SUMMER HYACINTH

15
DOG'S-TOOTH
  VIOLET
FLOWERING GARLIC
HARLEQUIN
  FLOWER
LILY OF THE VALLEY
STAR OF
  BETHLEHEM
TURBAN
  BUTTERCUP

16+
GIANT HIMALAYAN
  LILY
SPRING
  STARFLOWER
YELLOW STAR
  FLOWER

WATER-GARDEN PLANTS

4
GEUM
IRIS
RUSH

5
CALLA
CAREX
CHARA
HOSTA
LEMNA
RHEUM

5—continued
SEDGE
TRAPA
TYPHA

6
ACORUS
ALISMA
AZOLLA
CALTHA
COTULA
ELODEA

6—continued
JUNCUS
MENTHA
NUPHAR
PISTIA

7
ARUNCUS
ASTILBE
BOG ARUM
BOG BEAN
BONESET

7—continued
BULRUSH
BUR-REED
BUTOMUS
CYPERUS
DAY LILY
GUNNERA
LOBELIA
LYCHNIS
LYTHRUM
MIMULUS
ONOCLEA

7—continued
OSMUNDA
PRIMULA
SCIRPUS
TILLAEA

8
DROPWORT
DUCKWEED
FROG-BIT
GLYCERIA
HORNWORT

8–continued
HOTTONIA
KNOTWEED
MYOSOTIS
NYMPHAEA
ORONTIUM
POND LILY
PONDWEED
REEDMACE
SAURURUS
TROLLIUS
VERONICA

9
ARROW ARUM
ARROWHEAD
BROOKLIME
CARDAMINE
EICHORNIA
FAIRY MOSS
HAIRGRASS
HYPERICUM
LIGULARIA
PELTANDRA
POLYGONUM
RODGERSIA
ROYAL FERN
STONEWORT
SWEET FLAG
WATER LILY
WATER MINT

10
APONOGETON
ELEOCHARIS
ERIOPHORUM
EUPATORIUM
FONTINALIS
GOAT'S BEARD
GOLDEN CLUB
GOLDEN RAYS
HOUTTUYNIA
KAFFIR LILY
LYSICHITON
LYSIMACHIA
MATTEUCCIA
MENYANTHES
NYMPHOIDES
PONTEDERIA
RANUNCULUS
SAGITTARIA
SPARGANIUM
STRATIOTES
WATER AVENS
WATER GRASS
WILLOW MOSS

11
BLADDERWORT
CALLITRICHE
COTTON GRASS
FILIPENDULA
GLOBE FLOWER

11–continued
HYDROCHARIS
LOOSESTRIFE
POTAMOGETON
RAGGED ROBIN
UTRICULARIA
WATER FRINGE
WATER VIOLET

12
CUCKOO FLOWER
GOLDFISH WEED
HEMEROCALLIS
LAGAROSIPHON
LIZARD'S TAIL
MONKEY FLOWER
MYRIOPHYLLUM
PELTIPHYLLUM
PICKEREL WEED
PLANTAIN LILY
SCHIZOSTYLIS
SKUNK CABBAGE
WATER LETTUCE
WATER MILFOIL
WATER SOLDIER
ZANTEDESCHIA

13
CERATOPHYLLUM
FLOWERING RUSH
GOLDEN BUTTONS
MARSH MARIGOLD

13–continued
SENSITIVE FERN
UMBRELLA GRASS
UMBRELLA PLANT
WATER CHESTNUT
WATER HAWTHORN
WATER HYACINTH
WATER PLANTAIN
WATER STARWORT
WHITE ARUM LILY

14
PARROT'S FEATHER
PRICKLY RHUBARB
SWAMP
  STONECROP
WATER BUTTERCUP

15+
CANADIAN
  PONDWEED
MARSH ST JOHN'S
  WORT
ORNAMENTAL
  RHUBARB
OSTRICH FEATHER
  FERN
PURPLE LOOSE-
  STRIFE
WATER FORGET-ME-
  NOT

ANGLING TERMS

3
DUN
FLY
NET
PEG
RIB
ROD
TAG
TIP

4
BAIT
DAND
CAST
GAFF
HEMP
HOOK
LEAD
LINE
LURE
PLUG
POLE

4–continued
REEL
SHOT
TAIL
WORM

5
BLANK
CREEL
FLOAT
FLOSS
JOKER
LEGER
PASTE
QUILL
SPOON
WHISK

6
CASTER
DRY FLY
HACKLE
MAGGOT

6–continued
MARKER
PALMER
PINKIE
PRIEST
SLIDER
SPIGOT
SQUATT
STRIKE
SWIVEL
WET FLY
ZOOMER

7
ANTENNA
BALE ARM
BRISTLE
DAPPING
DUBBING
KEEP NET
MISSILE
PLUMMET

7–continued
ROD REST
ROD RING
SPINNER
WAGGLER

8
BACK SHOT
DEAD BAIT
FREELINE
LEGERING
LINE BITE
SPECIMEN
STOP KNOT
SWINGTIP

9
BITE ALARM
BLOODWORM
BLUED HOOK
CLOUD BAIT
DISGORGER
GORGE BAIT

9–continued
MICRO SHOT
MIDGE HOOK
QUIVERTIP
ROACH POLE
TYING SILK
WAGGY LURE
WIRE TRACE

10
BREAD FLAKE
BREAD PUNCH
CADDIS HOOK
COFFIN LEAD
DOUBLE HOOK
FLYBODY FUR
GROUND BAIT

10–continued
HAIR-AND-FUR
LANDING NET
SNAP TACKLE
STICK FLOAT
SWIM FEEDER

11
ARLESEY BOMB
BAIT DROPPER
BUBBLE FLOAT
DEVON MINNOW
DOUGH-BOBBIN
FOUL-HOOKED
GALLOWS TOOL
LOADED FLOAT
PATERNOSTER
SPARKLE BODY

11–continued
WHIP-FINISH
WING-CUTTER

12
BARBLESS HOOK
DETACHED BODY
DRY-FLY HACKLE
PARACHUTE FLY
SLIDING FLOAT

13
BUTT INDICATOR
CENTRE-PIN REEL
FLEXI-TAIL LURE

14
BLOCKEND FEEDER
BREAKING STRAIN

14–continued
GRUB-SHRIMP
  HOOK
MULTIPLIER REEL

15+
DANISH DRY FLY
  HOOK
DETACHED-BODY
  HOOK
FLAT-BODIED
  NYMPH HOOK
PARACHUTE-FLY
  HOOK
SWEDISH DRY FLY
  HOOK
YORKSHIRE SEDGE
  HOOK

SEWING TECHNIQUES

6
FACING

7
BASTING
BINDING
CUTWORK
DARNING
MITRING
RUCHING
TUCKING

8
APPLIQUE
COUCHING
LAID WORK
PLEATING
QUILTING
RUFFLING
SHIRRING
SMOCKING

9
DRAWN-WORK
FAGGOTING
GATHERING
PATCHWORK
WHITEWORK

10
CROCHETING
EMBROIDERY
OVERSEWING

10–continued
SCALLOPING

11
FINE-DRAWING
NEEDLEPOINT
OVERCASTING
OVERLOCKING

12
TOPSTITCHING

SEWING STITCHES

4
TACK

9
CROW'S FOOT
GROS POINT
HEMSTITCH
TOPSTITCH

10
BACKSTITCH
FRENCH KNOT
LOCK STITCH
OVERSTITCH
PETIT POINT

10–continued
STAY STITCH
STEM STITCH
TENT STITCH
WHIP-STITCH

11
BLIND STITCH
CHAIN STITCH
CROSS STITCH
NEEDLEPOINT
SATIN STITCH
TAILOR'S TACK

12
KETTLE STITCH

13
BLANKET STITCH
FEATHER STITCH
RUNNING STITCH

15
LAZY DAISY STITCH

16
BUTTONHOLE STITCH
FLORENTINE STITCH

17
HERRINGBONE STITCH

KNITTING TERMS

4
WARP
YARN

5
CHAIN
GRAFT

6
ARGYLE

7
CROCHET
RASCHEL
RIBBING
WORSTED

8
FAIR ISLE
INCREASE
INTARSIA

9
FISHERMAN
FOUNDATION

10
MOSS STITCH
PURL STITCH
SLIP-STITCH

11
CABLE STITCH
PLAIN STITCH

11–continued
SHELL-STITCH

12
GARTER STITCH

13
TRELLIS STITCH

14
DOUBLE KNITTING
STOCKING STITCH

GOLF TERMS

3
ACE
LIE
PAR
PGA
PIN
TEE

4
BITE
BUTT
FORE!
HEEL
HOOK
IRON
LOFT
PUTT
SOLE
SPIN
THIN
TRAP
WOOD

5
APRON
BLADE
BOGEY
CADDY
CLEEK
DORMY
DRIVE
EAGLE
GREEN
MASHY
ROUGH
SHAFT
SLICE
SOLID

5–continued
SPOOL
SPOON
TEMPO
WEDGE

6
ABSENT
BIRDIE
BISQUE
BUNKER
CADDIE
DORMIE
DRIVER
FLIGHT
FRINGE
GIMLET
HAZARD
JIGGER
MARKER
MASHIE
PUTTER
SCLAFF
SPIKES
SQUARE
STANCE
STROKE
STYMIE
TEE OFF
TEE PEG
ADDRESS

7
AIR SHOT
BRASSIE
DIMPLES
FAIRWAY
GROOVES

7–continued
HOLE OUT
MIDIRON
NIBLICK
POSTURE
SCRATCH
SCUFFED

8
APPROACH
BACKSPIN
BOUNDARY
CADDY CAR
CHIP SHOT
CLUB FACE
CLUB HEAD
HANDICAP
TAKE AWAY

9
ALBATROSS
ALIGNMENT
BACK SWING
CADDY CART
GREENSOME
HOLE IN ONE
SAND WEDGE
SWEET SPOT
SWING PATH

10
BOTTOM EDGE
GROSS SCORE
OPEN STANCE
STABLEFORD
STABLEFORD
SWING PLANE
TARGET LINE
TRAJECTORY

10–continued
VARDON GRIP

11
ANGLE OF TILT
COMPRESSION
STROKE INDEX

12
APPROACH SHOT
BASE BALL GRIP
CAVITY BACKED
CLOSED STANCE
FORWARD SWING
TEEING GROUND
THROUGH SWING

13
DISTANCE PLATE
FOLLOW THROUGH
PITCHING WEDGE
PRIMARY TARGET

14
NINETEENTH HOLE

15
ROYAL AND
  ANCIENT

17
PITCH MARK
  REPAIRER
TARGET ORIENTAT-
  ING

20
STANDARD
  SCRATCH SCORE

PATIENCE GAMES

3
FAN
FLY
USK

4
ACME
CLUB
CONE
DIAL
DUKE
ELBA
EXIT
FORT
FROG
GAPS
GATE
GIZA
GNAT
GOLF
HARP
LILY
MAZE
OPUS
PEEK
TENS
TONI
WOOD
ZEUS

5
ADELA
CLOCK
CRUEL
DEMON
DOVER
GIANT
KINGS
LANES
LINKS
LUCAS
MARIA
NINES
PENTA
SNAKE
SPIKE
STEPS
STEVE
WINGS
YUKON

6
ACES UP
ALASKA
ATHENA
BEETLE
BISLEY
BOX FAN
CADRAN

6–continued
CARPET
CASSIM
CHEOPS
CICELY
CORONA
DARWIN
DEUCES
DIEPPE
INDIAN
MADAME
MARTHA
MILLIE
MONACO
MRS MOP
MUMBAI
MUNGER
NEEDLE
NESTOR
OCTAVE
RAGLAN
REPAIR
ROBERT
SAXONY
SENATE
SKIPPY
SPIDER
SQUARE
STRATA
TETSOL
TOWERS
TUXEDO
TWENTY
ZODIAC

7
ALI BABA
AMAZONS
ANTARES
ARCHWAY
ARIZONA
BALCONY
BASTION
BIG HARP
BOUDOIR
BOX KITE
BRIGADE
BRISTOL
CARLTON
CASTILE
CITADEL
COLONEL
COLOURS
COMPASS
CORNERS
CZARINA
DIAVOLO
DOROTHY

7–continued
ECLIPSE
EIGHT ON
ELEVENS
EMPEROR
FIFTEEN
FOURS UP
FREE FAN
GRANADA
KINGDOM
LETTER H
LIMITED
MINERVA
NEW YORK
NUNAVUT
OCTAGON
OSMOSIS
OUTBACK
PAS SEUL
PENGUIN
PIGTAIL
PUSH-PIN
PYRAMID
QUEENIE
RAINBOW
SIBERIA
SIGNORA
SIMPLEX
SPIDIKE
STREETS
TERRACE
THE PLOT
THE WISH
THREE UP
TREFOIL
TWISTER
ZERLINE

8
ALHAMBRA
ARABELLA
ARACNIDA
ASSEMBLY
AUNT MARY
BACKBONE
BATSFORD
BIG APPLE
BIG DOZEN
BIG FORTY
BLOCKADE
BLOCK TEN
BRISBANE
BUSY ACES
CANFIELD
CANISTER
CHEQUERS
CHINAMAN
COLORADO

8–continued
CONGRESS
CRESCENT
CROMWELL
DEMON FAN
DIPLOMAT
DOUBLETS
DUTCHESS
EIGHT OFF
FAIR LUCY
FIFTEENS
FORECELL
FORTRESS
FORWARDS
FOURSOME
FREECELL
GEOFFREY
GOLD RUSH
HAYSTACK
IDLE ACES
JUNCTION
KINGCELL
KINGSLEY
KING'S WAY
KLONDIKE
LADY JANE
LADY PALK
LEAP YEAR
MOREHEAD
MYSTIQUE
NAPOLEON
PHARAOHS
PRIMROSE
PUTT PUTT
RAW PRAWN
REDHEADS
RESERVES
SALIC LAW
SARATOGA
SCORPION
SHIFTING
SIR TOMMY
SIXTEENS
SOLSTICE
SOMERSET
SQUADRON
ST HELENA
STRATEGY
SURPRISE
TAJ MAHAL
TAKE AWAY
TEN BY ONE
THE SPARK
TRIANGLE
TRILLIUM
TWO CELLS
VERTICAL
VINEYARD

8–continued
WATERLOO
WINDMILL

9
ACCORDION
ALL IN A ROW
APPLEGATE
BALD EAGLE
BETSY ROSS
BIG BERTHA
BIG SPIDER
BLACK HOLE
CHAMELEON
CHELICERA
CLEOPATRA
CORNELIUS
COURTYARD
DIFFUSION
DOUBLE DOT
EAGLE WING
EASTHAVEN
EIGHTEENS
FAN ALBERT
FIVE PILES
FLORADORA
FOUR BY TEN
FOURTEENS
FOUR WINDS
FORTY-NINE
GARGANTUA
INTERMENT
JOSEPHINE
LADY BETTY
LAFAYETTE
MAMY SUSAN
MARIE ROSE
MATRIMONY
MCCLELLAN
NATIONALE
NUMBER TEN
ORDER TIME
PARALLELS
PELMANISM
PITCHFORK
RIPPLE FAN
ROOSEVELT
SEA TOWERS
SHAMROCKS
SIMON SAYS
SPIDER WEB
STONEWALL
TARANTULA
THIRTEENS
THIRTY SIX
UNLIMITED
WESTCLIFF
WHITEHEAD

10

AGNES SOREL
AGNES THREE
ALEXANDRIA
ANNO DOMINI
BAKER'S GAME
BINARY STAR
BLACK WIDOW
BLIND ALLEY
BREAKWATER
CASTLES END
CHESSBOARD
CIRCLE NINE
CLOVER LEAF
CRISS CROSS
CROSSROADS
DEMONTHIEF
DOUBLE RAIL
EIGHTS DOWN
FAMILY PLOT
FOUR BY FIVE
FOURTEEN UP
GRADATIONS
GREAT WHEEL
HOW THEY RUN
HYPOTENUSE
INQUISITOR
KING ALBERT
LAST CHANCE
LITTLE GATE
LUCKY PILES
MIDSHIPMAN
MISS MUFFET
MONTE CARLO
MOVING LEFT
NUMERATION
ODD AND EVEN
OLD CARLTON
PANTAGRUEL
PARLIAMENT
PATRIARCHS
POINT SABLE
PRECEDENCE
PREFERENCE
PRINCE SERG
QUADRANGLE
RACING ACES
RAINBOW FAN
ROUGE FORTY
ROWS OF FOUR
SCORPION II
SEVEN STEPS
SEVENTEENS
SHADY LANES
SIMPLICITY
SINGLE LEFT
SINGLE RAIL
SPIDERETTE
STOREHOUSE
STRIPTEASE
STRONGHOLD
TARANTELLA

10–continued

THREE BEARS
THREE CELLS
TOURNAMENT
TRIPLE HARP
TRIPLE LEFT
TRIPLE LINE
TWIN QUEENS
TWO CASTLES
WANING MOON
WAVE MOTION
WAXING MOON
WHEATSHEAF
WHITEHORSE
YUKON KINGS

11

ACE OF HEARTS
ALTERNATION
BAKER'S DOZEN
BASTILLE DAY
BRIDESMAIDS
BUFFALO BILL
CALCULATION
CAPRICIEUSE
CASTLE MOUNT
CIRCLE EIGHT
CONTRADANCE
CORNER SUITE
DOUBLE FIVES
DOUBLET CELL
DOUBLE YUKON
EXILED KINGS
FALLING STAR
FAMOUS FIFTY
FASCINATION
FIFTEEN RUSH
FIRING SQUAD
FORTY DEVILS
FOUR COLOURS
FOUR SEASONS
FOURTEEN OUT
FRED'S SPIDER
FREE PARKING
GERMAN CROSS
GOOD MEASURE
GRANDFATHER
INTERCHANGE
INTERREGNUM
KNOTTY NINES
LADY CADOGAN
LITTLE FORTY
LITTLE GIANT
OSMOTIC CELL
PYRAMID GOLF
RANK AND FILE
RED AND BLACK
RITTENHOUSE
ROUGE ET NOIR
ROYAL FAMILY
ROYAL PARADE
RUSSIAN CELL

11–continued

SAN JUAN HILL
SEVEN BY FIVE
SEVEN BY FOUR
SEVEN DEVILS
SIMON JESTER
SIMPLE PAIRS
SIMPLE SIMON
SOLID SQUARE
SPECULATION
SPIDERCELLS
SPRINGFIELD
STALACTITES
STRATEGERIE
SUIT ELEVENS
SUSPENSEFUL
TAM O'SHANTER
THIEVES RUSH
THREE DEMONS
TREVI GARDEN
TRIPLE PEAKS
TRIPLE YUKON
YUKON PUZZLE
YUKON SPIDER

12

ACES AND KINGS
ACQUAINTANCE
ALTERNATIONS
AMERICAN TOAD
AULD LANG SYNE
BROWN RECLUSE
CANFIELD RUSH
CURDS AND WHEY
EIGHT BY EIGHT
FLOWER GARDEN
FORTY THIEVES
GRAND DUCHESS
INTELLIGENCE
KINGS AND ACES
LA BELLE LUCIE
LADIES BATTLE
LA NIVERNAISE
LITTLE BILLIE
LITTLE SPIDER
MILLIGAN CELL
MILLIGAN HARP
MISS MILLIGAN
MOUNT OLYMPUS
PATIENT PAIRS
PENELOPE'S WEB
PERSEVERANCE
PYRAMID SEVEN
RIGHT AND LEFT
SCORPION HEAD
SCORPION TAIL
SEVEN BY SEVEN
SIXTY THIEVES
STRATEGY PLUS
SUIT YOURSELF
SWEET SIXTEEN
THIRTEEN DOWN

12–continued

TOWER OF HANOI
TRIPLE DEMONS
TRUSTY TWELVE
VIRGINIA REEL
WILL O THE WISP
YUKON ONE SUIT

13

AGNES BERNAUER
BATSFORD AGAIN
BLIND PATIENCE
BRITISH SQUARE
CAPTIVE QUEENS
CARRE NAPOLEON
CHINESE SPIDER
DOUBLE OR QUITS
DOUBLE PYRAMID
DOUBLE RUSSIAN
DOUBLE SIGNORA
EIGHTY THIEVES
FIFTEEN PUZZLE
FORTUNE'S FAVOR
FORTY AND EIGHT
GREAT TRIANGLE
HEADS AND TAILS
INDEFATIGABLE
LIGHT AND SHADE
LITTLE THIEVES
LUCKY THIRTEEN
QUEEN VICTORIA
RIGHT TRIANGLE
ROMAN PATIENCE
ROYAL MARRIAGE
SIXTEEN PUZZLE
SPACES AND ACES
SPIDER ONE SUIT
STEPPING STONE
SWISS PATIENCE
THIRTEEN PACKS
THREES COMPANY
THUMB AND POUCH
TRIPLE RUSSIAN

14

CASTLES IN SPAIN
DOUBLE CANFIELD
DOUBLE FREECELL
DOUBLE KINGSLEY
DOUBLE KLONDIKE
DOUBLE SCORPION
DUTCH SOLITAIRE
EMPRESS OF ITALY
FIVE AND DIAMOND
GERMAN PATIENCE
HOUSE IN THE
    WOOD
HOUSE ON THE HILL
IMPERIAL GUARDS
INDIAN PATIENCE
KINGS AND QUEENS
KLEINE NAPOLEON

COMPUTER GAMES

14–continued
LADY OF THE MANOR
LITTLE MILLIGAN
LITTLE NAPOLEON
MIDNIGHT CLOVER
QUEENS AND JACKS
ROYAL COTILLION
SCORPION TOWERS
SCOTCH PATIENCE
SENIOR WRANGLER
SIXES AND SEVENS
SPIDER TWO SUITS
SULTAN OF TURKEY
THIEVES OF EGYPT
THREE BLIND MICE
TRAPDOOR SPIDER
TRIPLE FREECELL
TRIPLE KLONDIKE
TRIPLE SCORPION
TRIPLE TRIANGLE

15
ACEY AND KINGSLEY
BRITISH CANISTER
CHINESE KLONDIKE
DEUCES AND QUEENS
DOUBLE EASTHAVEN
DOUBLE FOURTEENS

15–continued
DOUBLE SEATOWERS
ETERNAL TRIANGLE
FORTRESS OF MERCY
FOUR LEAF CLOVERS
GLOUCESTERSHIRE
HIDDEN TREASURES
INCOMPATIBILITY
KINGSDOWN EIGHTS
NAPOLEON'S SQUARE
PATIENCE'S REWARD
PERPETUAL MOTION
PHANTOM BLOCKADE
PICTURE PATIENCE
PUSS IN THE CORNER
RESERVED PYRAMID
ROYAL RENDEZVOUS
SELECTIVE CASTLE
SPANISH PATIENCE
THIRTY-NINE STEPS
TRAVELLERS CLOCK
TRIPLE EASTHAVEN
TRIPLE FOURTEENS

16
ALGERIAN PATIENCE
AMERICAN CANISTER
BAVARIAN PATIENCE

16–continued
BIG SPIDER ONE SUIT
BOXING THE COMPASS
DEMONS AND THIEVES
GENERAL'S PATIENCE
INVERTED FREECELL
PRINCESS PATIENCE
RUSSIAN SOLITAIRE
STREETS AND ALLEYS
SUPERIOR CANFIELD

17
ALEXANDER THE GREAT
BELEAGUERED CASTLE
BIG SPIDER TWO SUITS
BRAZILIAN PATIENCE
CASTLE OF INDOLENCE
CHALLENGE FREECELL
GROUNDS FOR DIVORCE
QUADRUPLE CANFIELD
QUADRUPLE KLONDIKE
SINGLE INTERCHANGE
STRAIGHTS AND PAIRS
SUPER FLOWER GARDEN
TRIPLE INTERCHANGE

COMPUTER GAMES (mostly Trademark)

ADVENTURE
AGE OF EMPIRES
ASTEROIDS
BLOBS
BOMBARDER
BROKEN SWORD
CATCHBALL
CENTIPEDE
DONKEY KONG
DOOM
EXILE
FACTORY

FINAL FANTASY
FLIGHT SIMULATOR
FREECELL
GALAXIA
GRAND THEFT AUTO
GRAN TURISMO
HALF LIFE
HEBI
MINE SWEEPER
MISSILE COMMAND
MYST
ODYSSEY

PAC–MAN
PACPAC
POKEMON
PONG
PYRAMID
QBI
QUAKE
RESIDENT EVIL
SIMCITY
SONIC THE HEDGE-
  HOG
SPACE INVADERS

SPACEWAR
SUPER MARIO
  BROTHERS
TETRIS
THE SIMS
THIEF
TOMB RAIDER
TONY HAWK'S PRO
  SKATER
WORMS
ZELDA

EXTREME SPORTS

BASE–JUMPING
BMXING
BUNGEE JUMPING
DIRTBOARDING
DOWNHILL MOUN-
  TAIN BIKING
ENDURANCE
  RACING

EXTREME IRONING
EXTREME SKIING
FREE CLIMBING
HANG GLIDING
IN-LINE SKATING
KITEBOARDING
KITESURFING
MOTO X

PARAGLIDING
ROCK CLIMBING
SKATEBOARDING
SKYDIVING
SKYSURFING
SNOWBOARDING
SNOWMOBILES
SURFING

ULTIMATE FIGHTING
WAKEBOARDING
WATERSKIING
WHITE–WATER
  RAFTING
WINDSURFING
X–GAMES

MISCELLANEOUS

COLOURS

3
AAL
ABA
DUN
JET
RED
TAN

4
BLEU
BLUE
BOIS
BURE
CUIR
DRAB
EBON
ÉCRU
GOLD
GREY
GRIS
HOPI
IRIS
JADE
LAKE
LARK
NAVY
NOIR
ONYX
OPAL
PIED
PINK
PLUM
PUCE
ROSE
RUBY
SAND
SHOT
VERT

5
AMBER
BEIGE
BLACK
BROWN
CAMEL
CAPRI
CHAIR
COCOA
CORAL

5–continued
CREAM
CYMAR
DELFT
FLESH
GREEN
GRÈGE
HAZEL
HENNA
IVORY
JASPÉ
JAUNE
JEWEL
KHAKI
LODEN
MAIZE
MAUVE
OCHRE
OLIVE
OMBRÉ
PEACH
PEARL
PÊCHE
PRUNE
ROUGE
SEPIA
SHADE
TAUPE
TOPAZ
UMBER
WHITE

6
ACAJOU
ALESAN
ARGENT
AUBURN
BASANÉ
BISTRE
BLONDE
BRONZE
BURNET
CASTOR
CENDRÉ
CERISE
CHERRY
CHROMA
CITRON

6–continued
CLARET
COPPER
DORADO
FLAXEN
GARNET
GOLDEN
INDIGO
JASPER
MADDER
MAROON
MATARA
MOTLEY
ORANGE
ORCHID
OYSTER
PASTEL
PEARLY
PIRNED
PURPLE
RACHEL
RAISIN
RESEDA
RUSSET
SALMON
SHRIMP
SILVER
TITIAN
VIOLET
YELLOW
ZIRCON

7
ANAMITE
APRICOT
ARDOISE
AUREATE
BISCUIT
CALDRON
CARAMEL
CARMINE
CHAMOIS
CORBEAU
CRIMSON
EMERALD
FILBERT
FUCHSIA
GRIZZLE

7–continued
HEATHER
INGÉNUE
JACINTH
JONQUIL
LACQUER
LAVANDE
MAGENTA
MOTTLED
MUSTARD
NACARAT
NATURAL
NEUTRAL
OLD ROSE
PEARLED
PLATINA
SAFFRON
SCARLET
SEA BLUE
SKY BLUE
TEA ROSE
THISTLE
TILE RED
TILLEUL
TUSSORE
VIOLINE

8
ABSINTHE
ALIZARIN
AMARANTH
AURULENT
BABY BLUE
BABY PINK
BORDEAUX
BURGUNDY
CAPUCINE
CHALDERA
CHÂTAINE
CHESTNUT
CIEL BLUE
CINNAMON
CREVETTE
CYCLAMEN
EAU DE NIL
ÉCARLATE
EGGPLANT
EGGSHELL

8–continued
GRIZZLED
GUN METAL
HAZEL NUT
HYACINTH
LARKSPUR
LAVENDER
MAHOGANY
MOLE GREY
MULBERRY
NAVY BLUE
PEA GREEN
PISTACHE
POPPY RED
PRIMROSE
SAPPHIRE
SEA GREEN
SHAGREEN
SPECTRUM
VIRIDIAN

9
ALICE BLUE
AUBERGINE
AZURE BLUE
BLUE-GREEN
CADET BLUE
CADET GREY
CARNATION
CARNELIAN
CHAMPAGNE
CHOCOLATE
COCHINEAL
DELPH BLUE
DUTCH BLUE

9–continued
FLESH PINK
GREEN-BLUE
HARLEQUIN
LEAF GREEN
LIME GREEN
MOONSTONE
MOSS GREEN
NILE GREEN
OLIVE DRAB
PARCHMENT
PEARL GREY
RASPBERRY
ROYAL BLUE
TANGERINE
TOMATO RED
TURKEY RED
VERDIGRIS
VERMILION
WALLY BLUE

10
AQUAMARINE
AURICOMOUS
BOIS DE ROSE
CAFÉ AU LAIT
CASTOR GREY
COBALT BLUE
CONGO BROWN
ENSIGN BLUE
LIVER BROWN
MARINA BLUE
MARINE BLUE
OXFORD BLUE
PETROL BLUE

10–continued
POLYCHROME
POWDER BLUE
TERRACOTTA
ZENITH BLUE

11
BOTTLE GREEN
BURNT ALMOND
CARDINAL RED
CLAIR DE LUNE
FOREST GREEN
GOBELIN BLUE
HORIZON BLUE
HUNTER'S PINK
LAPIS LAZULI
LEMON YELLOW
LIPSTICK RED
PARROT GREEN
PEACOCK BLUE
POMEGRANATE
SMOKED PEARL
SOLID COLOUR
ULTRAMARINE
VERSICOLOUR
WALNUT BROWN
YELLOW OCHRE

12
BALL PARK BLUE
CANARY YELLOW
CARROT COLOUR
CASTILIAN RED
CELADON GREEN
HUNTER'S GREEN

12–continued
HYACINTH BLUE
LOGWOOD BROWN
MIDNIGHT BLUE
OVERSEAS BLUE
SAPPHIRE BLUE
SOLFERINO RED
TYRIAN PURPLE
VERDANT GREEN

13
BISHOP'S PURPLE
BISHOP'S VIOLET
CAMBRIDGE BLUE
MOTHER-OF-PEARL
MULTICOLOURED
PARTI-COLOURED
PEPPER-AND-SALT
PRIMARY COLOUR
TORTOISE SHELL
TURQUOISE BLUE

14
HEATHER MIXTURE
PERIWINKLE BLUE
PISTACHIO GREEN
TURQUOISE GREEN

15
CALEDONIAN
  BROWN
CHARTREUSE
  GREEN

16
CHARTREUSE
  YELLOW

THE SIGNS OF THE ZODIAC

SIGN (Symbol; Element; Dates)

ARIES (Ram; Fire; 21 Mar–19 Apr)
TAURUS (Bull; Earth; 20 Apr–20 May)
GEMINI (Twins; Air; 21 May–21 June)
CANCER (Crab; Water; 22 June–22 July)
LEO (Lion; Fire; 23 July–22 Aug)
VIRGO (Virgin; Earth; 23 Aug–22 Sept)

SIGN (Symbol; Dates)

LIBRA (Scales; Air; 23 Sept–23 Oct)
SCORPIO (Scorpion;Water; 24 Oct–21 Nov)
SAGITTARIUS (Archer; Fire; 22 Nov–21 Dec)
CAPRICORN (Goat; Earth; 22 Dec–19 Jan)
AQUARIUS (Water-carrier; Air; 20 Jan–18 Feb)
PISCES (Fish; Water; 19 Feb–20 Mar)

THE TWELVE SIGNS OF THE CHINESE ZODIAC

RAT
OX
TIGER
RABBIT

DRAGON
SNAKE
HORSE
SHEEP

MONKEY
ROOSTER
DOG
BOAR

CALENDARS

GREGORIAN	**HEBREW**	**CHINESE**
JANUARY	SHEVAT (Jan/Feb)	XIAO HAN (Jan)
FEBRUARY	ADAR (Feb/Mar)	DA HAN (Jan/Feb)
MARCH	NISAN (Mar/Apr)	LI CHUN (Feb)
APRIL	IYAR (Apr/May)	YU SHUI (Feb/Mar)
MAY	SIVAN (May/June)	JING ZHE (Mar)
JUNE	TAMMUZ (June/July)	CHUN FEN (Mar/Apr)
JULY	AV (July/Aug)	QING MING (Apr)
AUGUST	ELUL (Aug/Sept)	GU YU (Apr/May)
SEPTEMBER	TISHRI (Sept/Oct)	LI XIA (May)
OCTOBER	HESHVAN (Oct/Nov)	XIAO MAN (May/June)
NOVEMBER	KISLEV (Nov/Dec)	MANG ZHONG (June)
DECEMBER	TEVET (Dec/Jan)	XIA ZHI (June/July)

CHINESE (continued)
XIAO SHU (July)
DA SHU (July/Aug)

FRENCH REVOLUTIONARY	**ISLAMIC**	
VENDÉMIAIRE – Vintage (Sept)	MUHARRAM (Jan)	LI QUI (Aug)
BRUMAIRE – Fog (Oct)	SAFAR (Feb)	CHU SHU (Aug/Sept)
FRIMAIRE – Sleet (Nov)	RABIA I (Mar)	BAI LU (Sept)
NIVÔSE – Snow (Dec)	RABIA II (Apr)	QUI FEN (Sept/Oct)
PLUVIÔSE – Rain (Jan)	JUMĀDĀ I (May)	HAN LU (Oct)
VENTÔSE – Wind (Feb)	JUMĀDĀ II (June)	SHUANG JIANG (Oct/Nov)
GERMINAL – Seed (Mar)	RAJAB (July)	LI DONG (Nov)
FLOREAL – Blossom (Apr)	SHA'BAN (Aug)	XIAO XUE (Nov/Dec)
PRAIRIAL – Pasture (May)	RAMADĀN (Sept)	DA XUE (Dec)
MESSIDOR – Harvest (June)	SHAWWĀL (Oct)	DONG ZHI (Dec/Jan)
THERMIDOR – Heat (July)	DHŪAL-QA'DAH (Nov)	
FRUCTIDOR – Fruit (Aug)	DHŪAL-HIJJAH (Dec)	

BIRTHSTONES

January – GARNET	July – RUBY
February – AMETHYST	August – SARDONYX/PERIDOT
March – BLOODSTONE/AQUAMARINE	September – SAPPHIRE
April – DIAMOND	October – OPAL
May – EMERALD	November – TOPAZ
June – PEARL	December – TURQUOISE

WEDDING ANNIVERSARIES

1st – PAPER	9th – POTTERY/WILLOW	25th – SILVER
2nd – COTTON	10th – TIN/ALUMINIUM	30th – PEARL
3rd – LEATHER	11th – STEEL	35th – CORAL
4th – FRUIT/FLOWERS	12th – SILK/LINEN	40th – RUBY
5th – WOOD	13th – LACE	45th – SAPPHIRE
6th – IRON	14th – IVORY	50th – GOLD
7th – WOOL/COPPER	15th – CRYSTAL	55th – EMERALD
8th – BRONZE/POTTERY	20th – CHINA	60th – DIAMOND

PEERAGE

DUKE	DUCHESS	MARQUIS	MARCHIONESS
EARL	BARONESS	MARQUESS	VISCOUNTESS
BARON	COUNTESS	VISCOUNT	

HERALDIC TERMS

DIVISIONS OF FIELDS

PER PALE
PER FESS
PER CROSS
PER BEND
PER SALTIRE
PER CHEVRON

DESCRIPTIONS OF FIELDS

PARTY
BARRY
BURELY
BENDY
QUARTERLY
ENTY
FRETTY
GIRONNY
BEZANTY

PARTS OF THE ESCUTCHEON

DEXTER (right)
SINISTER (left)
MIDDLE
CHIEF (top)
FLANK (side)
BASE
NOMBRIL POINT
FESS POINT
HONOUR POINT
TRESSURE (border)

TINCTURES

OR (gold)
ARGENT (silver)
ERMINE
VAIR
POTENT
AZURE (blue)
GULES (red)

SABLE (black)
VERT (green)
PURPURE (purple)

CROSSES

FORMY
PATY
FLORY
MOLINE
BOTONNY
CROSLETTED
FITCHY
SALTIRE

LINES

ENGRAILED
EMBATTLED
INDENTED
INVECTED
WAVY, UNDY
NEBULY

DANCETTY
RAGULY
POTENTÉ
DOVETAILED
URDY

OTHER OBJECTS AND DECORATIONS

LOZENGE
ROUNDEL (circle)
ANNULET (ring)
FOUNTAIN (wavy line on a circle)
BILLET (upright object)
MOLET (star)
RAMPANT (rearing up)
COUCHANT (sleeping or sitting)
PASSANT (standing)
BAR

SEVEN DEADLY SINS

PRIDE	LUST	GLUTTONY	SLOTH
COVETOUSNESS	ENVY	ANGER	

SEVEN WONDERS OF THE WORLD

THE PYRAMIDS OF EGYPT
THE COLOSSUS OF RHODES
THE HANGING GARDENS OF BABYLON
THE MAUSOLEUM OF HALICARNASSUS

THE STATUE OF ZEUS AT OLYMPIA
THE TEMPLE OF ARTEMIS AT EPHESUS
THE PHAROS OF ALEXANDRIA

SEVEN VIRTUES

FAITH	HOPE	LOVE (CHARITY)	TEMPERANCE
FORTITUDE	JUSTICE	PRUDENCE	

MONEY

1&2	4–continued	5–continued	7
AS	PICE	SEMIS	ANGELOT
D	PONY	SOLDO	CAROLUS
L	QUID	STICA	CENTAVA
P	REAL	STYCA	DENARII
S	RYAL	SYCEE	DRACHMA
	TAEL	TICAL	GUILDER
3	UNIK	TICCY	JACOBUS
BIT		TOMAN	MILREIS
BOB	**5**	UNCIA	MOIDORE
COB	ANGEL	UNITE	NGUSANG
DAM	ASPER		PISTOLE
ECU	BELGA	**6**	QUARTER
FAR	BETSO	AMANIA	SEXTANS
KIP	BROAD	AUREUS	STOOTER
LAT	CONTO	BAWBEE	TESTOON
MIL	COPEC	BEZART	UNICORN
MNA	CROWN	CONDOR	
PIE	DARIC	COPANG	**8**
REE	DINAR	COPPER	AMBROSIN
REI	DUCAT	DÉCIME	DENARIUS
SHO	EAGLE	DOBLON	DIDRACHM
SOL	FRANC	DOLLAR	DOUBLOON
SOU	GROAT	ESCUDO	DUCATOON
YEN	LIARD	FLORIN	FARTHING
	LIBRA	FUORTE	FLORENCE
4	LITAS	GUINEA	JOHANNES
ANNA	LIVRE	GULDEN	KREUTZER
BEKA	LOCHO	KOPECK	LOUIS D'OR
BIGA	LOUIS	MONKEY	MARAVEDI
BUCK	MEDIO	NICKEL	NAPOLEON
CASH	MOHAR	PAGODE	PICAYUNE
CENT	MOHUR	PESETA	QUETZALE
DAUM	NOBLE	ROUBLE	SESTERCE
DIME	OBANG	SCEATT	SHILLING
DOIT	PAOLO	SEQUIN	SIXPENCE
JOEY	PENCE	STATER	
KRAN	PENGO	STIVER	**9**
LIRA	PENNY	TALARI	BOLIVIANO
MAIL	PLACK	TALENT	CUARTILLO
MARK	POUND	TANNER	DIDRACHMA
MERK	QURSH	TESTER	DUPONDIUS
MITE	RUBLE	TESTON	GOLD BROAD
OBOL	SCEAT	THALER	GOLD NOBLE
PEAG	SCUDI	TOMAUN	GOLD PENNY
PESO	SCUDO	ZECHIN	HALFPENNY

9–continued	10	10–continued	12–continued
PISTAREEN	EASTERLING	TRIPONDIUS	SILVER-STATER
RIXDOLLAR	FIRST BRASS	VENEZOLANO	TETRADRACHMA
ROSE-NOBLE	GOLD STATER		TRIBUTE PENNY
SESTERTII	QUADRUSSIS	**11**	
SOVEREIGN	SESTERTIUM	SILVER PENNY	**13**
SPUR ROYAL	SILVERLING	SPADE GUINEA	THREEPENNY BIT
YELLOW BOY	STOUR-ROYAL		
	THREEPENCE	**12**	**14**
		MILL SIXPENCE	HONG KONG DOLLAR

COLLECTIVE NAMES

ACROBATS – troupe
APES – shrewdness
ASSES – pace
BABOONS – troop
BAKERS – tabernacle
BARBERS – babble
BARMEN – promise
BAYONETS – grove
BEES – erst, swarm
BELLS – change
BISHOPS – bench, psalter
BISON – herd
BREWERS – feast
BUFFALOES – obstinacy
BULLFINCHES – bellowing
BULLOCKS – drove
BUTCHERS – goring
BUTLERS – sneer
CANONS – chapter, dignity
CATERPILLARS – army
CATTLE – herd
CHOUGHS – chattering
COBBLERS – cutting
CROCODILES – bask
CROWS – murder
DEANS – decanter, decorum
DONS – obscuration
DUCKS – paddling, safe
ELEPHANTS – herd, parade

FERRETS – busyness
FLIES – swarm
GAMBLERS – talent
GEESE – gaggle
GOLDFINCHES – charm
GOVERNESSES – galaxy
GRAMMARIANS – conjunction
HARES – down
HARPISTS – melody
HERONS – serge
HIPPOPOTAMI – bloat
HUNTERS – blast
JELLYFISH – fluther, smack
JUGGLERS – neverthriving
KITTENS – litter
LAPWING – desert
LARKS – exaltation
LEOPARDS – leap, lepe
LIONS – pride, sawt, sowse
LOCUSTS – swarm
MAGPIES – tittering
MERCHANTS – faith
MESSENGERS – diligence
MOLES – labour
MULES – span
NIGHTINGALES – watch
ORCHIDS – coterie
OWLS – parliament, stare
PAINTERS – curse, illusion

PARROTS – pandemonium
PEKINGESE – pomp
PENGUINS – parcel
PIGS – litter
PIPERS – skirl
PORPOISES – turmoil
PREACHERS – converting
RABBITS – bury
RHINOCEROS – crash
ROBBERS – band
SHEEP – flock
SHERIFFS – posse
SHIPS – fleet, armada
SHOEMAKERS – blackening
STARLINGS – murmuration
SWALLOWS – gulp
SWINE – doylt
TAILORS – disguising
TAVERNERS – closing
TROUT – hover
TURKEY – rafter
TURTLES – turn
UNDERTAKERS – unction
WIDOWS – ambush
WILDCATS – destruction, dout
WOODPECKERS – descent
WRITERS – worship
ZEBRAS – zeal

TYPEFACES

3	5	5–continued	6
DOW	ASTER	IONIC	AACHEN
	BEMBO	KABEL	ADROIT
4	BLOCK	LOTUS	AURIGA
BELL	DORIC	MITRA	BECKET
CITY	ERBAR	SABON	BODONI
GILL	FOLIO	SWIFT	BULMER
ZAPF	GOUDY	TIMES	CASLON

6–continued
COCHIN
COOPER
CORONA
FENICE
FUTURA
GLYPHA
GOTHIC
HORLEY
ITALIA
JANSON
LUCIAN
MELIOR
MODERN
OLIVER
ONDINE
OPTIMA
ROMANA

7
ANTIQUE
BASILIA
BAUHAUS
BERNARD
BOOKMAN
BRAMLEY

7–continued
CANDIDA
CENTURY
CORONET
CUSHING
ELECTRA
FLOREAL
IMPRINT
IRIDIUM
KORINNA
LUBALIN
MADISON
MEMPHIS
NEUZEIT
PLANTIN
RALEIGH
SPARTAN
STEMPEL
TIFFANY
UNIVERS
WEXFORD
WINDSOR

8
BENGUIAT
BERKELEY

8–continued
BREUGHEL
CLOISTER
CONCORDE
EGYPTIAN
EHRHARDT
FOURNIER
FRANKLIN
FRUTIGER
GALLIARD
GARAMOND
KENNERLY
NOVARESE
OLYMPIAN
PALATINO
PERPETUA
ROCKWELL
SOUVENIR

9
AMERICANA
ATHENAEUM
BARCELONA
BRITANNIC
CALEDONIA
CLARENDON

9–continued
CLEARFACE
CRITERION
DOMINANTE
EUROSTILE
EXCELSIOR
FAIRFIELD
GROTESQUE
HELVETICA
WORCESTER

10
AVANT GARDE
CHELTENHAM
CHURCHWARD
DEVANAGARI
EGYPTIENNE
LEAMINGTON

11
BASKERVILLE
COPPERPLATE

14
TRUMP MEDIAEVAL

AMERICAN INDIANS

3
FOX
OTO
UTE

4
CREE
CROW
HOPI
HUPA
IOWA
SAUK
TUPI

5
AZTEC
CADDO
CREEK
HAIDA
HURON
KASKA
KIOWA
OMAHA
OSAGE
SIOUX
SLAVE
TETON

5–continued
WAPPO
YUROK

6
ABNAKI
APACHE
ATSINA
CAYUGA
DAKOTA
DOGRIB
MANDAN
MICMAC
MIXTEC
MOHAWK
NAVAJO
NOOTKA
OJIBWA
ONEIDA
OTTAWA
PAIUTE
PAWNEE
QUAPAW
SALISH
SANTEE
SENECA

6–continued
TANANA
TOLTEC
YAKIMA

7
ARIKARA
BEOTHUK
CATAWBA
CHINOOK
CHOKTAW
HIDATSA
INGALIK
KUTCHIN
NATCHEZ
SHAWNEE
SHUSWAP
TLINGIT
WICHITA
WYANDOT

8
CHEROKEE
CHEYENNE
COMANCHE
DELAWARE
ILLINOIS

8–continued
IROQUOIS
KICKAPOO
NEZ PERCÉ
OKANOGAN
ONONDAGA
SHOSHONI
TUTCHONE

9
ALGONQUIN
BLACKFOOT
CHICKASAW
CHIPEWYAN
CHIPPEWAY
MENOMINEE
PENOBSCOT
TAHAGMIUT
TILLAMOOK
TSIMSHIAN
TUSCARORA
WINNEBAGO

10+
KAVIAGMIUT
PASAMAQUODDY
POTAWATOMI

CARTOON CHARACTERS

4
DINO
HUEY

5
BLUTO
DEWEY
GOOFY
HE-MAN
LEWEY
PLUTO
SHE-RA
SNOWY

6
BAM-BAM
BOO-BOO
DROOPY
POPEYE
SHAGGY
SNOOPY
TINTIN
TOP CAT

7
ATOM ANT
BATFINK
MR JINKS
MR MAGOO
MUTTLEY
NIBBLES
PEBBLES
RAPHAEL

8
GARFIELD
GODZILLA
LEONARDO
OLIVE OYL
PORKY PIG
SUPERTED
YOGI BEAR

9
BETTY BOOP
BUGS BUNNY
CHIP 'N' DALE
DAFFY DUCK
DAISY DUCK
DOGTANIAN
ELMER FUDD
PEPE LE PEW
SCOOBY DOO
SPIDERMAN
SYLVESTER

10
ANTHILL MOB
BARNEY BEAR
DEPUTY DAWG
DONALD DUCK
PEGLEG PETE
ROAD RUNNER
SCRAPPY DOO
TWEETIE PIE
WILY COYOTE

11
BART SIMPSON
BETTY RUBBLE
FELIX THE CAT
LISA SIMPSON
MICKEY MOUSE
MIGHTY MOUSE
MINNIE MOUSE
PETE HOTHEAD
PINK PANTHER
ROGER RABBIT
SNAGGLEPUSS
TOM AND JERRY
YOSEMITE SAM

12
BARNEY RUBBLE
HOMER SIMPSON
MARGE SIMPSON
MICHELANGELO
PETER PERFECT

13
DICK DASTARDLY
MAGGIE SIMPSON

14
CAPTAIN CAVEMAN
CAPTAIN HADDOCK
CAPTAIN PUGWASH
FOGHORN
  LEGHORN
FRED FLINTSTONE

14—continued
HONG KONG
  PHOOEY
MAGILLA GORILLA
SECRET SQUIRREL
SPEEDY GONZALES
TASMANIAN DEVIL

15
HECKLE AND
  JECKLE
PENELOPE PITSTOP
WILMA FLINTSTONE
WOODY
  WOODPECKER

16
HUCKLEBERRY
  HOUND
QUICK DRAW
  MACGRAW

17+
GERALD MCBOING
  BOING
GERTIE THE
  DINOSAUR
TEENAGE MUTANT
  NINJA TURTLES

KNOTS

3
BOW
4
BEND

5
HITCH

6
PRUSIK

7
BOWKNOT
BOWLINE
CAT'S-PAW

8
LOOP-KNOT
LOVE-KNOT
MESH KNOT
REEF KNOT

8—continued
SLIP-KNOT
WALL-KNOT
WALE-KNOT

9
HALF HITCH
SHEET BEND
THUMB KNOT
TURK'S HEAD
WATER-KNOT

10
CLOVE HITCH
GRANNY KNOT
HAWSER-BEND
SHEEPSHANK
SQUARE KNOT
SHROUD-KNOT

11
CARRICK BEND
DIAMOND KNOT
RUNNING KNOT
SAILOR'S KNOT
TIMBER HITCH
WEAVER'S KNOT
WINDSOR KNOT

12
HANGMAN'S KNOT
HARNESS HITCH
HERCULES KNOT
OVERHAND KNOT
ROLLING HITCH
SURGEON'S KNOT
TRUE-LOVE KNOT

13
ENGLISHMAN'S TIE

13—continued
MATTHEW WALKER

14
BLACKWALL HITCH
FISHERMAN'S BEND
FISHERMAN'S KNOT
RUNNING BOWLINE

17
BOWLINE ON THE
  BIGHT
FIGURE-OF-EIGHT
  KNOT

26
ROUND TURN AND
  TWO HALF
  HITCHES

LANGUAGE

LANGUAGES OF THE WORLD

2
WU

3
MIN

4
URDU

5
DUTCH
GREEK
HINDI
IRISH
MALAY
ORIYA
TAMIL
WELSH

6
ARABIC

6–continued
BIHARI
BRETON
DANISH
FRENCH
GAELIC
GERMAN
KOREAN
PAHARI
POLISH
ROMANY
SINDHI
SLOVAK
TELUGU

7
BENGALI
CATALAN
ENGLISH

7–continued
FRISIAN
ITALIAN
LATVIAN
MARATHI
PUNJABI
RUSSIAN
SLOVENE
SORBIAN
SPANISH
SWEDISH
TURKISH

8
ASSAMESE
GUJARATI
JAPANESE
JAVANESE

8–continued
KASHMIRI
MANDARIN
ROMANSCH
RUMANIAN
UKRANIAN

9
AFRIKAANS
BULGARIAN
CANTONESE
ICELANDIC
NORWEGIAN
SINHALESE

10
LITHUANIAN
PORTUGUESE
RAJASTHANI
SERBO-CROAT

THE GREEK ALPHABET

ALPHA
BETA
GAMMA
DELTA
EPSILON
ZETA

ETA
THETA
IOTA
KAPPA
LAMBDA
MU

NU
XI
OMICRON
PI
RHO
SIGMA

TAU
UPSILON
PHI
CHI
PSI
OMEGA

THE HEBREW ALPHABET

ALEPH
BETH
GIMEL
DALETH
HE
VAV

ZAYIN
CHETH
TETH
YOD
KAPH
LAMED

MEM
NUN
SAMEKH
AYIN
PE
SADI

KOPH
RESH
SHIN
SIN
TAV

FOREIGN WORDS

AND
Fr.	ET
Ger.	UND
It.	E, ED
Sp.	E
Lat.	ET

BUT
Fr.	MAIS
Ger.	ABER
It.	MA
Sp.	PERO
Lat.	SED

FOR
Fr.	POUR
Ger.	FÜR
It.	PER
Sp.	PARA, POR
Lat.	PER

TO
Fr.	À
Ger.	AUF, NACH
It.	A
Sp.	A
Lat.	AD

WITH
Fr.	AVEC
Ger.	MIT
It.	CON
Sp.	CON
Lat.	CUM

MISTER, MR
Fr.	MONSIEUR, M.
Ger.	HERR, HR., HRN.
It.	SIGNOR, SIG.
Sp.	SEÑOR, SR.
Lat.	DOMINUS

MADAME, MRS
Fr.	MADAME, MME.
Ger.	FRAU, FR.
It.	SIGNORA, SIG.A., SIG.RA.
Sp.	SEÑORA, SRA.
Lat.	DOMINA

MISS, MS
Fr.	MADEMOISELLE, MLLE
Ger.	FRÄULEIN, FRL.
It.	SIGNORINA, SIG.NA
Sp.	SEÑORITA, SRTA.

FROM
Fr.	DE
Ger.	AUS, VON
It.	DA
Sp.	DE
Lat.	AB

OF
Fr.	DE
Ger.	VON
It.	DI
Sp.	DE
Lat.	DE

GIRL
Fr.	FILLE
Ger.	MÄDCHEN
It.	RAGAZZA
Sp.	CHICA, NIÑA
Lat.	PUELLA

BOY
Fr.	GARÇON
Ger.	JUNGE
It.	RAGAZZO
Sp.	CHICO, NIÑO
Lat.	PUER

BIG
Fr.	GRAND
Ger.	GROSS
It.	GRANDE
Sp.	GRANDE
Lat.	MAGNUS

LITTLE
Fr.	PETIT
Ger.	KLEIN
It.	PICCOLO
Sp.	PEQUENO, CHICO, POCO
Lat.	PAUCUS

VERY
Fr.	TRÈS
Ger.	SEHR
It.	MOLTO
Sp.	MUCHO

FASHIONABLE
Fr.	À LA MODE
Ger.	MODISCH
It.	DI MODA
Sp.	DE MODA

GENTLEMAN
Fr.	MONSIEUR
Ger.	HERR
It.	SIGNORE
Sp.	CABALLERO
Lat.	DOMINUS

LADY
Fr.	DAME
Ger.	DAME
It.	SIGNORA
Sp.	SEÑORA
Lat.	DOMINA

MAN
Fr.	HOMME
Ger.	MANN
It.	UOMO
Sp.	HOMBRE
Lat.	HOMO

WOMAN
Fr.	FEMME
Ger.	FRAU
It.	DONNA
Sp.	DOÑA
Lat.	MULIER

WHO
Fr.	QUI
Ger.	WER
It.	CHI
Sp.	QUIÉN, QUE
Lat.	QUIS

I
Fr.	JE
Ger.	ICH
It.	IO
Sp.	YO
Lat.	EGO

YOU
Fr.	TU, VOUS
Ger.	DU, SIE, IHR
It.	TU, VOI, LEI
Sp.	TU, VOSOTROS VOSOTRAS
Lat.	TU, VOS

WHAT
Fr.	QUOI, QUEL
Ger.	WAS
It.	CHE COSA
Sp.	QUE
Lat.	QUOD

HE
Fr.	IL
Ger.	ER
It.	EGLI
Sp.	EL
Lat.	IS

SHE
Fr.	ELLE
Ger.	SIE
It.	ELLA
Sp.	ELLA
Lat.	EA

WE
Fr.	NOUS
Ger.	WIR
It.	NOI
Sp.	NOSOTROS/AS
Lat.	NOS

THEY
Fr.	ILS, ELLES
Ger.	SIE
It.	ESSI/E, LORO
Sp.	ELLOS, ELLAS
Lat.	EI, EAE

AT HOME
Fr.	CHEZ NOUS *OR* À LA MAISON
Ger.	ZU HAUSE
It.	A CASA
Sp.	EN CASA
Lat.	DOMO

HOUSE
Fr.	MAISON
Ger.	HAUS
It.	CASA
Sp.	CASA
Lat.	VILLA, DOMUS

STREET
Fr.	RUE
Ger.	STRASSE
It.	STRADA
Sp.	CALLE
Lat.	VIA

ROAD
Fr.	ROUTE
Ger.	WEG
It.	VIA
Sp.	CAMINO
Lat.	VIA

BY
Fr.	PAR
Ger.	BEI
It.	PER
Sp.	POR
Lat.	PER

BEFORE
Fr.	AVANT
Ger.	VOR
It.	PRIMA
Sp.	(DEL) ANTE
Lat.	ANTE

AFTER
Fr.	APRÈS
Ger.	NACH
It.	DOPO
Sp.	DESPUES
Lat.	POST

UNDER
Fr.	SOUS
Ger.	UNTER
It.	SOTTO
Sp.	(DE)BAJO
Lat.	SUB

OVER
Fr.	SUR
Ger.	OBER
It.	SOPRA, SU
Sp.	SOBRE
Lat.	SUPER

NEAR
Fr.	PRÈS DE
Ger.	NAHE, BEI
It.	VICINO
Sp.	CERCA
Lat.	PROPE

OUT
Fr.	DEHORS
Ger.	AUS
It.	VIA, FUORI
Sp.	FUERA
Lat.	EX

IN
Fr.	DANS
Ger.	IN
It.	IN
Sp.	EN
Lat.	IN

HOW
Fr.	COMMENT
Ger.	WIE
It.	COME
Sp.	COMO
Lat.	QUO MODO

WHY
Fr.	POURQUOI
Ger.	WARUM
It.	PERCHE
Sp.	POR QUÉ
Lat.	CUR

THE
Fr.	LE, LA, LES
Ger.	DER, DIE, DAS
It.	IL, LO, LA, I, GLI, LE
Sp.	EL, LA, LO, LOS, LAS
Lat.	ILLE

A
Fr.	UN, UNE
Ger.	EIN, EINE
It.	UN, UNO, UNA
Sp.	UN, UNA
Lat.	UNUS

RED
Fr.	ROUGE
Ger.	ROT
It.	ROSSO
Sp.	ROJO
Lat.	RUBER

BLUE
Fr.	BLEU
Ger.	BLAU
It.	AZZURRO
Sp.	AZUL
Lat.	CAERULEUS

YELLOW
Fr.	JAUNE
Ger.	GELB
It.	GIALLO
Sp.	AMARILLO
Lat.	FULVUS

GREEN
Fr.	VERT
Ger.	GRÜN
It.	VERDE
Sp.	VERDE
Lat.	VIRIDIS

BLACK
Fr.	NOIR
Ger.	SCHWARZ
It.	NERO
Sp.	NEGRO
Lat.	NIGER

WHITE
Fr.	BLANC *OR* BLANCHE
Ger.	WEISS
It.	BIANCO
Sp.	BLANCO
Lat.	ALBUS

NUMBERS

	ROMAN NUMERALS	FRENCH	GERMAN	ITALIAN	SPANISH
1	I	UN	EIN	UNO	UNO
2	II	DEUX	ZWEI	DUE	DOS
3	III	TROIS	DREI	TRE	TRES
4	IV	QUATRE	VIER	QUATTRO	CUATRO
5	V	CINQ	FÜNF	CINQUE	CINCO
6	VI	SIX	SECHS	SEI	SEIS
7	VII	SEPT	SIEBEN	SETTE	SIETE
8	VIII	HUIT	ACHT	OTTO	OCHO
9	IX	NEUF	NEUN	NOVE	NUEVE
10	X	DIX	ZEHN	DIECI	DIEZ
20	XX	VINGT	ZWANZIG	VENTI	VEINTE
30	XXX	TRENTE	DREISSIG	TRENTA	TREINTA
40	XL	QUARANTE	VIERZIG	QUARANTA	CUARENTA
50	L	CINQUANTE	FÜNFZIG	CINQUANTA	CINCUENTA
60	LX	SOIXANTE	SECHZIG	SESSANTA	SESENTA
70	LXX	SOIXANTE-DIX	SIEBZIG	SETTANTA	SETENTA
80	LXXX	QUATRE-VINGT	ACHTZIG	OTTANTA	OCHENTA
90	XC	QUATRE-VINGT-DIX	NEUNZIG	NOVANTA	NOVENTA
100	C	CENT	HUNDERT	CENTO	CIEN (CIENTO)
500	D	CINQ CENTS	FÜNFHUNDERT	CINQUECENTO	QUINIENTOS
1000	M	MILLE	TAUSEND	MILLE	MIL

FRENCH PHRASES

5
MÊLÉE – brawl
ON DIT – piece of gossip, rumour

6
DE TROP – unwelcome

7
À LA MODE – fashionable
À PROPOS – to the point
CAP-À-PIE – from head to foot
DE RÈGLE – customary
EN MASSE – all together
EN ROUTE – on the way

8
BÊTE NOIR – person or thing particularly disliked
IDÉE FIXE – obsession
MAL DE MER – seasickness
MOT JUSTE – the appropriate word

9
DE RIGUEUR – required by custom
EN PASSANT – by the way
EN RAPPORT – in harmony
ENTRE NOUS – between you and me

10
À BON MARCHÉ – cheap
BILLET DOUX – love letter
DERNIER CRI – latest fashion, the last word
NOM DE PLUME – writer's assumed name
PENSE À BIEN – think for the best

11
AMOUR PROPRE – self-esteem
GARDEZ LA FOI – keep the faith

11–continued
LÈSE MAJESTÉ – treason
NOM DE GUERRE – assumed name
RAISON D'ÊTRE – justification for existence
SAVOIR FAIRE – address, tact
TOUR DE FORCE – feat or accomplishment of great strength

12
FORCE MAJEURE – irresistible force or compulsion
HORS DE COMBAT – out of the fight, disabled
SANS DIEU RIEN – nothing without God
VENTRE À TERRE – at great speed

14
DOUBLE ENTENDRE – double meaning
ENFANT TERRIBLE – child who causes
  embarrassment
NOBLESSE OBLIGE – privilege entails
  responsibility
PREUX CHEVALIER – gallant knight
VÉRITÉ SANS PEUR – truth without fear

15
AMENDE HONORABLE – reparation

15–continued
CHERCHEZ LA FEMME – look for the woman

17
PIÈCE DE RÉSISTANCE – most outstanding
  item; main dish at a meal

20+
AUTRE TEMPS, AUTRES MOEURS – other
  times, other manners

LATIN PHRASES

4
FIAT – let it be done or made
IN RE – concerning
STET – let it stand

5
AD HOC – for this special purpose
AD LIB – to speak off the cuff, without notes
AD REM – to the point
CIRCA – about
FECIT – he did it

6
AD USUM – as customary
IN SITU – in its original situation
IN TOTO – entirely
IN VIVO – in life, describing biological
  occurrences within living bodies
PRO TEM – temporary, for the time being

7
AD FINEM – to the end
A PRIORI – by deduction
CUI BONO? – whom does it benefit?
DE FACTO – in fact
FIAT LUX – let there be light
IN VITRO – in glass, describing biological
  experiments outside a body
PECCAVI – a confession of guilt (I have sinned)
PER DIEM – by the day
SINE DIE – without a day being appointed
SUB ROSA – confidential
UNA VOCE – with one voice, unanimously

8
ALTER EGO – another self
BONA FIDE – in good faith
EMERITUS – one retired from active official
  duties
MEA CULPA – an acknowledgement of guilt
  (I am to blame)
NOTA BENE – observe or note well
PRO FORMA – for the sake of form

9
AD INTERIM – meanwhile
AD LITERAM – to the letter
AD NAUSEAM – to a disgusting, sickening
  degree
DEI GRATIA – by the grace of God
ET TU, BRUTE – and you, Brutus
EXCELSIOR – still higher
EX OFFICIO – by right of position or office
HIC ET NUNC – here and now
INTER ALIA – among other things
PRO PATRIA – for one's country
STATUS QUO – the existing situation or state of
  affairs
SUB JUDICE – under consideration
VICE VERSA – the terms being exchanged, the
  other way round
VOX POPULI – popular opinion

10
ANNO DOMINI – in the year of our Lord
DEO GRATIAS – thanks be to God
EX CATHEDRA – with authority
IN EXTREMIS – in dire straits, at the the point of
  death
IN MEMORIAM – to the memory of
LOCO CITATO – in the place quoted
POST MORTEM – after death
PRIMA FACIE – at first sight
SINE QUA NON – something indispensable
TERRA FIRMA – solid ground

11
AD INFINITUM – endlessly, to infinity
ANIMO ET FIDE – by courage and faith
DE DIE IN DIEM – from day to day
DE PROFUNDIS – from the depths of misery
EX POST FACTO – after the event
GLORIA PATRI – glory to the Father
LOCUS STANDI – the right to be heard (in a law
  case)
NON SEQUITUR – an unwarranted conclusion

11–continued
PAX VOBISCUM – peace be with you
TEMPUS FUGIT – time flies

12
ANTE MERIDIEM – before noon
CAVEAT EMPTOR – let the buyer beware
COMPOS MENTIS – of sane mind
FESTINA LENTE – hasten slowly, be quick
without impetuosity
JACTA EST ALEA – the die is cast
PERSEVERANDO – by perseverance
POST MERIDIEM – after noon
SERVABO FIDEM – I will keep faith
VENI, VIDI, VICI – I came, I saw, I conquered
VOLO NON VALEO – I am willing but unable

13
CORPUS DELICTI – body of facts that constitute
an offence
DUM SPIRO, SPERO – while I breathe, I hope
IN VINO VERITAS – there is truth in wine, that is,
the truth comes out
MODUS OPERANDI – a method of operating
NE FRONTI CREDE – trust not to appearances
VINCIT VERITAS – truth conquers
VIRTUTIS AMORE – by love of virtue

14
CETERIS PARIBUS – other things being equal
EDITIO PRINCEPS – the original edition
IN LOCO PARENTIS – in place of a parent
NIL DESPERANDUM – never despair
PRO BONO PUBLICO – for the public good

15
ANIMO NON ASTUTIA – by courage not by craft
FORTITER ET RECTE – courageously and
honourably
FORTUNA SEQUATUR – let fortune follow
INFRA DIGNITATEM – beneath one's dignity
NON COMPOS MENTIS – mentally unsound
OMNIA VINCIT AMOR – love conquers all things
PERSONA NON GRATA – an unacceptable
person

16
GLORIA IN EXCELSIS – glory to God in the
highest

17
LABOR IPSE VOLUPTAS – labour itself is
pleasure
NUNQUAM NON PARATUS – always ready
PROBUM NON PAENITET – honesty repents not
VER NON SEMPER VIRET – Spring does not
always flourish

18
NEC TEMERE NEC TIMIDE – neither rashly nor
timidly
PRO REGE, LEGE, ET GREGE – for the king,
the law, and the people
REDUCTIO AD ABSURDUM – reducing to
absurdity

19
CANDIDE ET CONSTANTER – fairly and firmly
SOLA NOBILITAS VIRTUS – virtue alone is true
nobility
VIRTUTI NON ARMIS FIDO – I trust to virtue and
not to arms

20+
DE MORTUIS NIL NISI BONUM – speak only
good of the dead
DULCE ET DECORUM EST PRO PATRIA MORI
– it is sweet and seemly to die for one's country
FORTUNA FAVET FORTIBUS – fortune favours
the brave
PATRIA CARA CARIOR LIBERTAS – my country
is dear, but liberty is dearer
QUOD ERAT DEMONSTRANDUM – which was
to be demonstrated
SIC TRANSIT GLORIA MUNDI – thus passes
the glory of the world
TIMEO DANAOS ET DONA FERENTIS – I fear
the Greeks, even when bearing gifts
VIVIT POST FUNERA VIRTUS – virtue survives
the grave

COMMON SAYINGS

PROVERBS

A bad penny always turns up.
A bad workman always blames his tools.
A bird in the hand is worth two in the bush.
Absence makes the heart grow fonder.
A cat has nine lives.
A cat may look at a king.
Accidents will happen in the best regulated families.
A chain is no stronger than its weakest link.
Actions speak louder than words.
A drowning man will clutch at a straw.
A fool and his money are soon parted.
A fool at forty is a fool indeed.
A friend in need is a friend indeed.
All cats are grey in the dark.
All good things must come to an end.
All is fair in love and war.
All roads lead to Rome.
All's grist that comes to the mill.
All's well that ends well.
All that glitters is not gold.
All the world loves a lover.
All work and no play makes Jack a dull boy.
A miss is as good as a mile.
An apple a day keeps the doctor away.
An Englishman's home is his castle.
An Englishman's word is his bond.
A nod is as good as a wink to a blind horse.
Any port in a storm.
Any publicity is good publicity.
A trouble shared is a trouble halved.

Attack is the best form of defence.
A watched pot never boils.
A woman's work is never done.
A young physician fattens the churchyard.
Bad news travels fast.
Beauty is in the eye of the beholder.
Beauty is only skin-deep.
Beggars can't be choosers.
Better be an old man's darling than a young man's slave.
Better be safe than sorry.
Better late than never.
Birds of a feather flock together.
Blood is thicker than water.
Books and friends should be few but good.
Caesar's wife must be above suspicion.
Charity begins at home.
Christmas comes but once a year.
Civility costs nothing.
Cold hands, warm heart.
Constant dripping wears away the stone.
Curiosity killed the cat.
Cut your coat according to your cloth.
Dead men tell no tales.
Death is the great leveller.
Divide and rule.
Do as I say, not as I do.
Do as you would be done by.
Dog does not eat dog.
Don't count your chickens before they are hatched.
Don't cross the bridge till you get to it.
Don't cut off your nose to spite your face.
Don't meet troubles half-way.
Don't put all your eggs in one basket.

Don't spoil the ship for a ha'porth of tar.
Don't teach your grandmother to suck eggs.
Don't throw the baby out with the bathwater.
Don't wash your dirty linen in public.
Early to bed and early to rise, makes a man healthy, wealthy and wise.
Easier said than done.
East, west, home's best.
Easy come, easy go.
Empty vessels make the greatest sound.
Even a worm will turn.
Every cloud has a silver lining.
Every dog has his day.
Every dog is allowed one bite.
Every man for himself, and the devil take the hindmost.
Everything comes to him who waits.
Experience is the best teacher.
Faith will move mountains.
Familiarity breeds contempt.
Fight fire with fire.
Fine feathers make fine birds.
Fine words butter no parsnips.
Fish and guests smell in three days.
Forewarned is forearmed.
Forgive and forget.
For want of a nail the shoe was lost; for want of a shoe the horse was lost; for want of a horse the rider was lost.
From clogs to clogs in only three generations.
Give a dog a bad name and hang him.
Give him an inch and he'll take a yard.
Great minds think alike.
Great oaks from little acorns grow.

Handsome is as handsome does.

He that fights and runs away, may live to fight another day.

He travels fastest who travels alone.

He who hesitates is lost.

He who lives by the sword dies by the sword.

He who pays the piper calls the tune.

He who sups with the devil should have a long spoon.

History repeats itself.

Honesty is the best policy.

If a job's worth doing, it's worth doing well.

If at first you don't succeed, try, try, try again.

If the mountain will not come to Mahomet, Mahomet must go to the mountain.

If you don't like the heat, get out of the kitchen.

Imitation is the sincerest form of flattery.

In for a penny, in for a pound.

In the country of the blind, the one-eyed man is king.

It is no use crying over spilt milk.

It never rains but it pours.

It's an ill wind that blows nobody any good.

It's too late to shut the stable door after the horse has bolted.

It will all come right in the wash.

It will be all the same in a hundred years.

Jack of all trades, master of none.

Keep something for a rainy day.

Kill not the goose that lays the golden egg.

Least said soonest mended.

Let bygones be bygones.

Let sleeping dogs lie.

Let the cobbler stick to his last.

Life begins at forty.

Life is just a bowl of cherries.

Life is not all beer and skittles.

Look before you leap.

Love is blind.

Love laughs at locksmiths.

Lucky at cards, unlucky in love.

Many a true word is spoken in jest.

Many hands make light work.

March comes in like a lion and goes out like a lamb.

March winds and April showers bring forth May flowers.

Marry in haste, and repent at leisure.

More haste, less speed.

Necessity is the mother of invention.

Needs must when the devil drives.

Ne'er cast a clout till May be out.

Never look a gift horse in the mouth.

No time like the present.

Old habits die hard.

Old sins cast long shadows.

One for sorrow, two for joy; three for a girl, four for a boy; five for silver, six for gold; seven for a secret, not to be told; eight for heaven, nine for hell; and ten for the devil's own sel.

One good turn deserves another.

One man's meat is another man's poison.

One swallow does not make a summer.

Out of sight, out of mind.

Patience is a virtue.

Penny wise, pound foolish.

Prevention is better than cure.

Red sky at night, shepherd's delight; red sky in the morning, shepherd's warning.

Revenge is a dish that tastes better cold.

Revenge is sweet.

See a pin and pick it up, all the day you'll have good luck; see a pin and let it lie, you'll want a pin before you die.

Seeing is believing.

See Naples and die.

Silence is golden.

Spare the rod and spoil the child.

Sticks and stones may break my bones, but words will never hurt me.

Still waters run deep.

St. Swithin's Day, if thou dost rain, for forty days it will remain; St. Swithin's Day, if thou be fair, for forty days 'twill rain no more.

Take a hair of the dog that bit you.

The darkest hour is just before the dawn.

The devil finds work for idle hands to do.

The devil looks after his own.

The early bird catches the worm.

The end justifies the means.

The exception proves the rule.

The hand that rocks the cradle rules the world.

Time is a great healer.

There is honour among thieves.

There is more than one way to skin a cat.

There is no accounting for tastes.

There is safety in numbers.

There's many a good tune played on an old fiddle.

There's many a slip' twixt the cup and the lip.

There's no place like home.

There's no smoke without fire.

The road to hell is paved with good intentions.

Time and tide wait for no man.

Time is a great healer.

Too many cooks spoil the broth.

Truth is stranger than fiction.

Two heads are better than one.

Two wrongs do not make a right.

United we stand, divided we fall.

Waste not, want not.

We must learn to walk before we can run.

What you lose on the swings you gain on the roundabouts.

When poverty comes in at the door, love flies out of the window.

When the cat's away, the mice will play.

When the wine is in, the wit is out.

Where there's a will there's a way.

Why keep a dog and bark yourself?

You can lead a horse to the water, but you can't make him drink.

You cannot run with the hare and hunt with the hounds.

You can't make an omelette without breaking eggs.

You can't teach an old dog new tricks.

You can't tell a book by its cover.

SIMILES

as bald as a coot
as black as pitch
as black as the ace of spades
as blind as a bat
as blind as a mole
as bold as brass
as bright as a button
as busy as a bee
as calm as a millpond
as cheap as dirt
as chirpy as a cricket
as clean as a whistle
as clear as a bell
as clear as crystal
as clear as mud
as cold as charity
as common as muck
as cool as a cucumber
as cross as two sticks
as daft as a brush
as dead as a dodo
as dead as a doornail
as dead as mutton
as deaf as a post
as different as chalk and
  cheese
as drunk as a lord
as dry as a bone
as dry as dust
as dull as dishwater
as easy as falling off a log
as easy as pie
as fit as a flea
as flat as a pancake
as free as a bird
as free as air

as free as the wind
as fresh as a daisy
as good as gold
as green as grass
as happy as a lark
as happy as a sandboy
as happy as Larry
as happy as the day is long
as hard as nails
as keen as mustard
as large as life
as light as a feather
as like as two peas in a pod
as lively as a cricket
as mad as a hatter
as mad as a March hare
as meek as a lamb
as merry as a cricket
as neat as a new pin
as nutty as a fruitcake
as obstinate as a mule
as old as the hills
as pale as death
as plain as a pikestaff
as plain as the nose on your
  face
as pleased as Punch
as poor as a church mouse
as poor as Lazarus
as pretty as a picture
as proud as a peacock
as pure as the driven snow
as quick as a flash
as quick as lightning
as quick as thought
as quiet as a mouse

as quiet as the grave
as red as a beetroot
as regular as clockwork
as rich as Croesus
as right as rain
as safe as houses
as sharp as a needle
as sick as a dog
as simple as falling off a log
as slippery as an eel
as snug as a bug in a rug
as sound as a bell
as steady as a rock
as stiff as a board
as stiff as a poker
as stiff as a ramrod
as straight as a die
as straight as an arrow
as stubborn as a mule
as sure as eggs is eggs
as sure as hell
as thick as thieves
as thick as two short planks
as thin as a lath
as thin as a rake
as thin as a stick
as tough as nails
as tough as old boots
as ugly as sin
as warm as toast
as weak as a kitten
as weak as dishwater
as welcome as the flowers in
  May
as white as a sheet

NURSERY RHYMES

A frog he would a-wooing go,
Heigh ho! says Rowley,
A frog he would a-wooing go,
Whether his mother would let him or no.
With a rowley, powley, gammon and spinach,
Heigh ho! says Anthony Rowley.

As I was going to St Ives,
I met a man with seven wives.
Each wife had seven sacks
Each sack had seven cats,
Each cat had seven kits,
How many were going to St Ives?

Baa, baa, black sheep,
Have you any wool?
Yes, sir, yes, sir,
Three bags full,
One for the master,
And one for the dame,
And one for the little boy
Who lives down the lane.

Bobby Shafto's gone to sea,
Silver buckles on his knee;
He'll come back and marry me,
Bonny Bobby Shafto!

Come, let's to bed
Says Sleepy-head;
Tarry a while, says Slow;
Put on the pan;
Says Greedy Nan,
Let's sup before we go.

Ding dong, bell,
Pussy's in the well.
Who put her in?
Little Johnny Green.
Who pulled her out?
Little Tommy Stout.

Doctor Foster went to Gloucester
In a shower of rain:
He stepped in a puddle,
Right up to his middle,
And never went there again.

Georgie Porgie, pudding and pie,
Kissed the girls and made them cry;
When the boys came out to play,
Georgie Porgie ran away.

Goosey, goosey gander,
Whither shall I wander?
Upstairs and downstairs
And in my lady's chamber.

Hey diddle diddle,
The cat and the fiddle,
The cow jumped over the moon;
The little dog laughed
To see such sport,
And the dish ran away with the spoon.

Hickory, dickory, dock,
The mouse ran up the clock.
The clock struck one,
The mouse ran down,
Hickory, dickory, dock.

How many miles to Babylon?
Three score miles and ten.
Can I get there by candle-light?
Yes, and back again.
If your heels are nimble and light,
You may get there by candle-light.

Humpty Dumpty sat on a wall,
Humpty Dumpty had a great fall.
All the king's horses and
All the king's men,
Couldn't put Humpty together again.

Jack and Jill went up the hill
To fetch a pail of water;
Jack fell down and broke his crown,
And Jill came tumbling after.

Jack Sprat could eat no fat,
His wife could eat no lean,
And so between them both you see,
They licked the platter clean.

Little Bo-peep has lost her sheep,
And can't tell where to find them;
Leave them alone, and they'll come home,
Bringing their tails behind them.

Little Boy Blue,
Come blow your horn,
The sheep's in the meadow,
The cow's in the corn.

Little Jack Horner
Sat in the corner,
Eating a Christmas pie;
He put in his thumb,
And pulled out a plum,
And said, What a good boy am I!

Little Miss Muffet
Sat on a tuffet,
Eating her curds and whey;
There came a big spider,
Who sat down beside her
And frightened Miss Muffet away.

Little Tommy Tucker,
Sings for his supper:
What shall we give him?
White bread and butter
How shall he cut it
Without a knife?
How will he be married
Without a wife?

Mary, Mary, quite contrary,
How does your garden grow?
With silver bells and cockle shells,
And pretty maids all in a row.

Monday's child is fair of face,
Tuesday's child is full of grace,
Wednesday's child is full of woe,
Thursday's child has far to go,
Friday's child is loving and giving,
Saturday's child works hard for his living,
And the child that is born on the Sabbath day
Is bonny and blithe, and good and gay.

Oh! the grand old Duke of York
He had ten thousand men;
He marched them up to the top of the hill,
And he marched them down again.
And when they were up they were up,
And when they were down they were down,
And when they were only half way up,
They were neither up nor down.

Old King Cole
Was a merry old soul,
And a merry old soul was he;
He called for his pipe,
And he called for his bowl,
And he called for his fiddlers three.

Old Mother Hubbard
Went to the cupboard,
To fetch her poor dog a bone;
But when she got there
The cupboard was bare
And so the poor dog had none.

One, two, Buckle my shoe;
Three, four, Knock at the door.
Five, six, Pick up sticks;
Seven, eight, Close the gate.
Nine, ten, Big fat hen;
Eleven, twelve, Dig and delve.
Thirteen, fourteen, Maids a'courting;
Fifteen, sixteen, Maids in the kitchen.
Seventeen, eighteen, Maids a'waiting;
Nineteen, twenty, My plate's empty.

Oranges and lemons,
Say the bells of St Clement's.
You owe me five farthings,
Say the bells of St Martin's.
When will you pay me?
Say the bells of Old Bailey.
When I grow rich,
Say the bells of Shoreditch.
When will that be?
Say the bells of Stepney.
I'm sure I don't know,
Says the great bell at Bow.
Here comes a candle to light you to bed,
Here comes a chopper to chop off your head.

Peter Piper picked a peck of pickled pepper;
A peck of pickled pepper Peter Piper picked;
If Peter Piper picked a peck of pickled pepper,
Where's the peck of pickled pepper Peter Piper
    picked?

Polly put the kettle on,
Polly put the kettle on,
Polly put the kettle on,
We'll all have tea.
Sukey take it off again,
Sukey take it off again,
Sukey take it off again,
They've all gone away.

Pussy cat, pussy cat, where have you been?
I've been to London to look at the queen.
Pussy cat, pussy cat, what did you there?
I frightened a little mouse under her chair.

Ride a cock-horse to Banbury Cross,
To see a fine lady upon a white horse;
Rings on her fingers and bells on her toes,
And she shall have music wherever she goes.

Ring-a-ring o'roses,
A pocket full of posies,
A-tishoo! A-tishoo!
We all fall down.

Rub-a-dub-dub,
Three men in a tub,
And who do you think they be?
The butcher, the baker,
The candlestick-maker,
And they all sailed out to sea.

See-saw, Margery Daw,
Jacky shall have a new master;
Jacky shall have but a penny a day,
Because he can't work any faster.

Simple Simon met a pieman,
Going to the fair;
Says Simple Simon to the pieman,
Let me taste your ware.
Says the pieman to Simple Simon,
Show me first your penny;
Says Simple Simon to the pieman,
Indeed I have not any.

Sing a song of sixpence,
A pocket full of rye;
Four and twenty blackbirds,
Baked in a pie.
When the pie was opened,
The birds began to sing;
Was not that a dainty dish,
To set before the king?

The king was in his counting-house,
Counting out his money;
The queen was in the parlour,
Eating bread and honey.
The maid was in the garden,
Hanging out the clothes,
When down came a blackbird,
And pecked off her nose.

Solomon Grundy,
Born on a Monday,
Christened on Tuesday,
Married on Wednesday,
Took ill on Thursday,
Worse on Friday,
Died on Saturday,
Buried on Sunday.
This is the end
Of Solomon Grundy.

The lion and the unicorn
Were fighting for the crown;
The lion beat the unicorn
All round about the town.

There was a crooked man, and he walked a
    crooked mile,
He found a crooked sixpence against a crooked
    stile:
He bought a crooked cat, which caught a crooked
    mouse,
And they all lived together in a little crooked
    house.

There was an old woman who lived in a shoe,
She had so many children she didn't know what
to do;
She gave them some broth without any bread;
She whipped them all soundly and put them to
bed.

The twelfth day of Christmas,
My true love sent to me
Twelve lords a-leaping,
Eleven ladies dancing,
Ten pipers piping,
Nine drummers drumming,
Eight maids a-milking,
Seven swans a-swimming,
Six geese a-laying,
Five gold rings,
Four colly birds,
Three French hens,
Two turtle doves, and
A partridge in a pear tree.

This little piggy went to market,
This little piggy stayed at home,
This little piggy had roast beef,
This little piggy had none,
And this little piggy cried, Wee-wee-wee-wee-
wee,
I can't find my way home.

Three blind mice, see how they run!
They all run after the farmer's wife,
Who cut off their tails with a carving knife,
Did you ever see such a thing in your life,
As three blind mice?

Tinker, Tailor,
Soldier, Sailor,
Rich man, Poor man,
Beggarman, Thief.

Tom, Tom, the piper's son,
Stole a pig and away he run;
The pig was eat
And Tom was beat,
And Tom went howling down the street.

Two little dicky birds,
Sitting on a wall;
One named Peter,
The other named Paul,
Fly away, Peter!
Fly away, Paul!
Come back, Peter!
Come back, Paul!

Wee Willie Winkie runs through the town
Upstairs and downstairs and in his nightgown,
Rapping at the window, crying through the lock,
Are the children all in bed? It's past eight o'clock.

What are little boys made of?
Frogs and snails
And puppy-dogs' tails,
That's what little boys are made of.

What are little girls made of?
Sugar and spice
And all that's nice,
That's what little girls are made of.

Who killed Cock Robin?
I, said the Sparrow,
With my bow and arrow,
I killed Cock Robin.
Who saw him die?
I, said the Fly,
With my little eye,
I saw him die.

COMMON QUOTATIONS

ARNOLD, Matthew (1822–88) British poet

The sea is calm to-night,
The tide is full, the moon lies fair
Upon the Straits.
Dover Beach

A wanderer is man from his birth.
He was born in a ship
On the breast of the river of Time.
The Future

Go, for they call you, Shepherd, from the hill.
The Scholar Gipsy

Tired of knocking at Preferment's door.
The Scholar Gipsy

Before this strange disease of modern life,
With its sick hurry, its divided aims.
The Scholar Gipsy

Truth sits upon the lips of dying men.
Sohrab and Rustum

And see all sights from pole to pole,
And glance, and nod, and bustle by;
And never once possess our soul
Before we die.
A Southern Night

AUDEN, W H (1907–73) British poet

Look, stranger, at this island now
The leaping light for your delight discovers.
Look, Stranger

To the man-in-the-street, who, I'm sorry to say
Is a keen observer of life,
The word Intellectual suggests straight away
A man who's untrue to his wife.
Note on Intellectuals

When it comes, will it come without warning
Just as I'm picking my nose?
Will it knock on my door in the morning,
Or tread in the bus on my toes?
Will it come like a change in the weather?
Will its greeting be courteous or rough?
Will it alter my life altogether?
O tell me the truth about love.
Twelve Songs, XII

AUSTEN, Jane (1775–1817) British novelist

Nobody is healthy in London, nobody can be.
Emma, Ch. 12

Business, you know, may bring money, but
friendship hardly ever does.
Emma, Ch. 34

Let other pens dwell on guilt and misery.
Mansfield Park, Ch. 48

A woman, especially if she have the misfortune of
knowing anything, should conceal it as well as
she can.
Northanger Abbey, Ch. 14

It is a truth universally acknowledged, that a
single man in possession of a good fortune must
be in want of a wife.
Pride and Prejudice, Ch. 1

Happiness in marriage is entirely a matter of
chance.
Pride and Prejudice, Ch. 6

Next to being married, a girl likes to be crossed in
love a little now and then.
Pride and Prejudice, Ch. 24

One cannot be always laughing at a man without
now and then stumbling on something witty.
Pride and Prejudice, Ch. 40

For what do we live, but to make sport for our
neighbours, and laugh at them in our turn?
Pride and Prejudice, Ch. 57

BETJEMAN, John (1906–84) British poet

You ask me what it is I do. Well actually, you know,
I'm partly a liaison man and partly P.R.O.
Essentially I integrate the current export drive
And basically I'm viable from ten o'clock till five.
Executive

I have a vision of the future, chum.
The workers' flats in fields of soya beans
Tower up like silver pencils.
The Planster's Vision

Come, friendly bombs, and fall on Slough
It isn't fit for humans now.
There isn't grass to graze a cow
Swarm over, Death!
Slough

THE BIBLE

And now abideth faith, hope, charity, these three;
but the greatest of these is charity.
I Corinthians, 13: 13

O death, where is thy sting? O grave, where is
thy victory?
I Corinthians, 15: 55

Vanity of vanities, saith the Preacher, vanity of
vanities; all is vanity.
Ecclesiastes, 1: 2

To every thing there is a season, and a time to
every purpose under the heaven:
A time to be born, and a time to die; a time to
plant, and a time to pluck up that which is
planted;
A time to kill, and a time to heal; a time to break
down, and a time to build up;
A time to weep, and a time to laugh; a time to
mourn, and a time to dance;
…
A time to love, and a time to hate; a time of war,
and a time of peace.
Ecclesiastes, 3: 1–8

I returned, and saw under the sun, that the race
is not to the swift, nor the battle to the strong,
neither yet bread to the wise, nor yet riches to
men of understanding, nor yet favour to men of
skill; but time and chance happeneth to them all.
Ecclesiastes, 9: 11

Cast thy bread upon the waters: for thou shalt
find it after many days.
Ecclesiastes, 11: 1

I am the Lord thy God, which have brought thee
out of the land of Egypt, out of the house of
bondage.
Thou shalt have no other gods before me.
Thou shalt not make unto thee any graven image,
or any likeness of any thing that is in heaven
above, or that is in the earth beneath, or that is in
the water under the earth:
Thou shalt not bow down thyself to them, nor
serve them: for I the Lord thy God am a jealous God,
visiting the iniquity of the fathers upon the
children unto the third and fourth generation of
them that hate me;
And shewing mercy unto thousands of them that
love me, and keep my commandments.
Thou shalt not take the name of the Lord thy God
in vain; for the Lord will not hold him guiltless that
taketh his name in vain.
Remember the sabbath day, to keep it holy.
Six days shalt thou labour, and do all thy work:
But the seventh day is the sabbath of the Lord thy
God: in it thou shalt not do any work, thou, nor
thy son, nor thy daughter, thy manservant, nor thy
maidservant, nor thy cattle, nor thy stranger that
is within thy gates:
For in six days the Lord made heaven and earth,
the sea, and all that in them is, and rested the

seventh day: wherefore the Lord blessed the sabbath day, and hallowed it.

Honour thy father and thy mother: that thy days may be long upon the land which the Lord thy God giveth thee.

Thou shalt not kill.

Thou shalt not commit adultery.

Thou shalt not steal.

Thou shalt not bear false witness against thy neighbour.

Thou shalt not covet thy neighbour's house, thou shalt not covet thy neighbour's wife, nor his manservant, nor his maidservant, nor his ox, nor his ass, nor any thing that is thy neighbour's.
Exodus, 20: 2–17

Eye for eye, tooth for tooth, hand for hand, foot for foot
Exodus, 21: 24

Thou shalt not suffer a witch to live.
Exodus, 22: 18

In the beginning God created the heaven and the earth.

And the earth was without form, and void; and darkness was upon the face of the deep. And the Spirit of God moved upon the face of the waters. And God said, Let there be light: and there was light.
Genesis, 1: 1–3

And God said, Let us make man in our image, after our likeness: and let them have dominion over the fish of the sea, and over the fowl of the air, and over the cattle, and over all the earth, and over every creeping thing that creepeth upon the earth.
Genesis, 1: 26

And on the seventh day God ended his work which he had made; and he rested on the seventh day from all his work which he had made.
Genesis, 2: 2

But of the tree of the knowledge of good and evil, thou shalt not eat of it: for in the day that thou eatest thereof thou shalt surely die.
Genesis, 2: 17

And the rib, which the Lord God had taken from man, made he a woman, and brought her unto the man.
Genesis, 2: 22

And the Lord said unto Cain, Where is Abel thy brother? And he said, I know not: Am I my brother's keeper?
Genesis, 4: 9

And the Lord said unto him, Therefore whosoever slayeth Cain, vengeance shall be taken on him sevenfold. And the Lord set a mark upon Cain, lest any finding him should kill him.
Genesis, 4: 15

But his wife looked back from behind him, and she became a pillar of salt.
Genesis, 19: 26

And Jacob said to Rebekah his mother, Behold, Esau my brother is a hairy man, and I am a smooth man.
Genesis, 27: 11

Therefore the Lord himself shall give you a sign; Behold, a virgin shall conceive, and bear a son, and shall call his name Immanuel.
Isaiah, 7: 14

Can the Ethiopian change his skin, or the leopard his spots? Then may ye also do good, that are accustomed to do evil.
Jeremiah, 13: 23

The next day John seeth Jesus coming unto him, and saith, Behold the Lamb of God, which taketh away the sin of the world.
John, 1: 29

So when they continued asking him, he lifted up himself, and said unto them, He that is without sin among you, let him first cast a stone at her.
John, 8: 7

And ye shall know the truth, and the truth shall make you free.
John, 8: 32

In my Father's house are many mansions: if it were not so, I would have told you. I go to prepare a place for you.
John, 14: 2

Greater love hath no man than this, that a man lay down his life for his friends.
John, 15: 13

Now the Lord had prepared a great fish to swallow up Jonah. And Jonah was in the belly of the fish three days and three nights.
Jonah, 1: 17

And it came to pass, as they still went on, and talked, that, behold, there appeared a chariot of fire, and horses of fire, and parted them both asunder; and Elijah went up by a whirlwind into heaven.
II Kings, 2: 11

And it came to pass in those days, that there went out a decree from Caesar Augustus, that all the world should be taxed.
Luke, 2: 1

And she brought forth her firstborn son, and wrapped him in swaddling clothes, and laid him in a manger; because there was no room for them in the inn.
Luke, 2: 7

Then said Jesus, Father, forgive them; for they know not what they do. And they parted his raiment, and cast lots.
Luke, 23: 34

And he asked him, What is thy name? And he answered, saying. My name is Legion: for we are many.
Mark, 5: 9

For what shall it profit a man, if he shall gain the

whole world, and lose his own soul? Or what shall a man give in exchange for his soul?
Mark, 8: 36–37

But he answered and said, It is written, Man shall not live by bread alone, but by every word that proceedeth out of the mouth of God.
Matthew, 4: 4

And he saith unto them, Follow me, and I will make you fishers of men.
Matthew, 4: 19

And if thy right eye offend thee, pluck it out, and cast it from thee: for it is profitable for thee that one of thy members should perish, and not that thy whole body should be cast into hell.
Matthew, 5: 29

Lay not up for yourselves treasures upon earth, where moth and rust doth corrupt, and where thieves break through and steal:
Matthew, 6: 19

Take therefore no thought for the morrow: for the morrow shall take thought for the things of itself. Sufficient unto the day is the evil thereof.
Matthew, 6: 33

Judge not, that ye be not judged.
Matthew, 7: 1

And why beholdest thou the mote that is in thy brother's eye, but considerest not the beam that is in thine own eye?
Matthew, 7: 3

Give not that which is holy unto the dogs, neither cast ye your pearls before swine, lest they trample them under their feet, and turn again and rend you.
Matthew, 7: 6

Because strait is the gate, and narrow is the way, which leadeth unto life, and few there be that find it.
Matthew, 7: 14

And they were offended in him. But Jesus said unto them, A prophet is not without honour, save in his own country, and in his own house.
Matthew, 13: 57

And again I say unto you, It is easier for a camel to go through the eye of a needle, than for a rich man to enter into the kingdom of God.
Matthew, 19: 24

But many that are first shall be last; and the last shall be first.
Matthew, 19: 30

Jesus said unto him, Verily I say unto thee, That this night, before the cock crow, thou shalt deny me thrice.
Matthew, 26: 34

Watch and pray, that ye enter not into temptation: the spirit indeed is willing, but the flesh is weak.
Matthew, 26: 41

Then said Jesus unto him, Put up again thy

sword into his place: for all they that take the sword shall perish with the sword.
Matthew, 26: 52

For the lips of a strange woman drop as an honeycomb, and her mouth is smoother than oil: But her end is bitter as wormwood, sharp as a two-edged sword.
Proverbs, 5: 3–4

Stolen waters are sweet, and bread eaten in secret is pleasant.
Proverbs, 9: 17

He that spareth his rod hateth his son: but he that loveth him chasteneth him betimes.
Proverbs, 13: 24

Pride goeth before destruction, and an haughty spirit before a fall.
Proverbs, 16: 18

For thou shalt heap coals of fire upon his head, and the Lord shall reward thee.
Proverbs, 25: 22

Who can find a virtuous woman? for her price is far above rubies.
Proverbs, 31: 10

And the name of the star is called Wormwood: and the third part of the waters became wormwood; and many men died of the waters, because they were made bitter.
Revelations, 8: 11

Here is wisdom. Let him that hath understanding count the number of the beast: for it is the number of a man; and his number is Six hundred threescore and six.
Revelations, 13: 18

Drink no longer water, but use a little wine for thy stomach's sake and thine often infirmities.
I Timothy, 5: 23

For the love of money is the root of all evil: which while some coveted after, they have erred from the faith, and pierced themselves through with many sorrows.
I Timothy, 6: 10

BLAKE, William (1757–1827) British poet and engraver

To see a World in a grain of sand,
And a Heaven in a wild flower,
Hold Infinity in the palm of your hand,
And Eternity in an hour.
Auguries of Innocence

And did those feet in ancient time
Walk upon England's mountains green?
And was the holy lamb of God
On England's pleasant pastures seen?
Milton, Preface (known as the hymn 'Jerusalem')

I will not cease from mental fight,
Nor shall my sword sleep in my hand,
Till we have built Jerusalem
In England's green and pleasant land.
Milton, Preface (known as the hymn 'Jerusalem')

Love seeketh not itself to please,
Nor for itself hath any care,
But for another gives its ease,
And builds a Heaven in Hell's despair.
Songs of Experience, 'The Clod and the Pebble'

Tiger! Tiger! burning bright
In the forests of the night,
What immortal hand or eye
Could frame thy fearful symmetry?
Songs of Experience, 'The Tiger'

Little Lamb, who made thee?
Dost thou know who made thee?
Songs of Innocence, 'The Lamb'

BRONTË, Charlotte (1816–55) British novelist

Reader, I married him.
Jane Eyre, Ch. 38

BROWNING, Elizabeth Barrett (1806–61)
British poet

'Yes,' I answered you last night;
'No,' this morning, sir, I say.
Colours seen by candle-light
Will not look the same by day.
The Lady's Yes

How do I love thee? Let me count the ways.
Sonnets from the Portuguese, XLIII

I love thee with the breath,
Smiles, tears, of all my life! – and, if God choose,
I shall but love thee better after death.
Sonnets from the Portuguese, XLIII

BROWNING, Robert (1812–89) British poet

Oh, to be in England
Now that April's there,
And whoever wakes in England,
Sees, some morning, unaware,
That the lowest boughs and the brushwood sheaf
Round the elm-tree bole are in tiny leaf,
While the chaffinch sings on the orchard bough
In England—now!
Home Thoughts from Abroad

Rats!
They fought the dogs and killed the cats,
And bit the babies in the cradles.
The Pied Piper of Hamelin

The year's at the spring,
And day's at the morn;
Morning's at seven;
The hill-side's dew-pearled;
The lark's on the wing;
The snail's on the thorn;
God's in His heaven –
All's right with the world.
Pippa Passes, Pt. I

BURNS, Robert (1759–96) Scottish poet

Should auld acquaintance be forgot,
And never brought to min'?
Auld Lang Syne

We'll tak a cup o' kindness yet,
For auld lang syne.
Auld Lang Syne

My love is like a red red rose
That's newly sprung in June:
My love is like the melodie
That's sweetly play'd in tune.
A Red, Red Rose

Wee, sleekit, cow'rin', tim'rous beastie,
O what a panic's in thy breastie!
To a Mouse

The best laid schemes o' mice an' men
Gang aft a-gley,
An' lea'e us nought but grief an' pain
For promis'd joy.
To a Mouse

BYRON, Lord (1788–1824) British poet

While stands the Coliseum, Rome shall stand;
When falls the Coliseum, Rome shall fall;
And when Rome falls – the World.
Childe Harold's Pilgrimage, IV

Man's love is of man's life a thing apart,
'Tis woman's whole existence.
Don Juan, I

'Tis strange – but true; for truth is always strange;
Stranger than fiction: if it could be told,
How much would novels gain by the exchange!
Don Juan, XIV

She walks in beauty, like the night
Of cloudless climes and starry skies;
And all that's best of dark and bright
Meet in her aspect and her eyes.
She Walks in Beauty

Though the night was made for loving,
And the day returns too soon,
Yet we'll go no more a roving
By the light of the moon.
So, we'll go no more a roving

CARROLL, Lewis (Charles Lutwidge Dodgson;
1832–98) British author

'What is the use of a book,' thought Alice, 'without
pictures or conversation?'
Alice's Adventures in Wonderland, Ch. 1

'Curiouser and curiouser!' cried Alice.
Alice's Adventures in Wonderland, Ch. 2

'You are old, Father William,' the young man said,
'And your hair has become very white;
And yet you incessantly stand on your head –
Do you think at your age, it is right?'
Alice's Adventures in Wonderland, Ch. 5

Twinkle, twinkle, little bat!
How I wonder what you're at!
Up above the world you fly!
Like a teatray in the sky.
Alice's Adventures in Wonderland, Ch. 7

'Off with his head!'
Alice's Adventures in Wonderland, Ch. 8

'Will you walk a little faster?' said a whiting to a snail,
'There's a porpoise close behind us, and he's treading on my tail.'
Alice's Adventures in Wonderland, Ch. 10

'Twas brillig, and the slithy toves
Did gyre and gimble in the wabe;
All mimsy were the borogoves,
And the mome raths outgrabe.
Through the Looking-Glass, Ch. 1

Tweedledum and Tweedledee
Agreed to have a battle;
For Tweedledum said Tweedledee
Had spoiled his nice new rattle.
Through the Looking-Glass, Ch. 4

'The time has come,' the Walrus said,
'To talk of many things:
Of shoes – and ships – and sealing-wax –
Of cabbages – and kings –
And why the sea is boiling hot –
And whether pigs have wings.'
Through the Looking-Glass, Ch. 4

The rule is, jam tomorrow and jam yesterday – but never jam today.
Through the Looking-Glass, Ch. 5

'You look a little shy; let me introduce you to that leg of mutton,' said the Red Queen. 'Alice – Mutton; Mutton – Alice.'
Through the Looking-Glass, Ch. 9

CERVANTES, Miguel de (1547–1616) Spanish novelist

Take care, your worship, those things over there are not giants but windmills.
Don Quixote, Pt. I, Ch. 8

Didn't I tell you, Don Quixote, sir, to turn back, for they were not armies you were going to attack, but flocks of sheep?
Don Quixote, Pt. I, Ch. 18

The best sauce in the world is hunger.
Don Quixote, Pt. II, Ch. 5

Well, now, there's a remedy for everything except death.
Don Quixote, Pt. II, Ch. 10

There are only two families in the world, my old grandmother used to say, The *Haves* and the *Have-Nots*.
Don Quixote, Pt. II, Ch. 20

A private sin is not so prejudicial in the world as a public indecency.
Don Quixote, Pt. II, Ch. 22

CHURCHILL, Sir Winston (1874–1965) British statesman and writer

We shall not flag or fail. We shall fight in France, we shall fight on the seas and oceans, we shall fight with growing confidence and growing strength in the air, we shall defend our island, whatever the cost may be, we shall fight on the beaches, we shall fight on the landing grounds,
we shall fight in the fields and in the streets, we shall fight in the hills; we shall never surrender.
Speech, House of Commons, 4 June 1940

This was their finest hour.
Speech, House of Commons, 18 June 1940
(Referring to the Dunkirk evacuation)

The battle of Britain is about to begin.
Speech, House of Commons, 1 July 1940

Never in the field of human conflict was so much owed by so many to so few.
Speech, House of Commons, 20 Aug 1940
(Referring to the Battle of Britain pilots)

COLERIDGE, Samuel Taylor (1772–1834) British poet

The frost performs its secret ministry,
Unhelped by any wind.
Frost at Midnight

In Xanadu did Kubla Khan
A stately pleasure-dome decree:
Where Alph, the sacred river, ran
Through caverns measureless to man
Down to a sunless sea.
Kubla Khan

And all should cry, Beware! Beware!
His flashing eyes, his floating hair!
Weave a circle round him thrice,
And close your eyes with holy dread,
For he on honey-dew hath fed,
And drunk the milk of Paradise.
Kubla Khan

It is an ancient Mariner,
And he stoppeth one of three.
'By thy long grey beard and glittering eye,
Now wherefore stopp'st thou me?'
The Rime of the Ancient Mariner, I

He holds him with his glittering eye—
The Wedding-Guest stood still,
And listens like a three years' child:
The Mariner hath his will.
The Rime of the Ancient Mariner, I

With my cross-bow
I shot the albatross.
The Rime of the Ancient Mariner, I

As idle as a painted ship
Upon a painted ocean.
The Rime of the Ancient Mariner, II

Water, water, every where,
Nor any drop to drink.
The Rime of the Ancient Mariner, II

Oh sleep! it is a gentle thing,
Beloved from pole to pole!
The Rime of the Ancient Mariner, V

He prayeth best, who loveth best
All things both great and small;
For the dear God who loveth us,
He made and loveth all.
The Rime of the Ancient Mariner, VII

COWARD, Sir Noël (1899–1973) British actor, dramatist, and songwriter

Don't put your daughter on the stage, Mrs Worthington.
Song title

Mad dogs and Englishmen go out in the mid-day sun.
Song title

The Stately Homes of England
How beautiful they stand,
To prove the upper classes
Have still the upper hand.
Operette, 'The Stately Homes of England'

Strange how potent cheap music is.
Private Lives

COWPER, William (1731–1800) British poet

John Gilpin was a citizen
Of credit and renown,
A train-band captain eke was he
Of famous London town.
John Gilpin

God moves in a mysterious way
His wonders to perform;
He plants his footsteps in the sea,
And rides upon the storm.
Olney Hymns, 35

I am monarch of all I survey,
My right there is none to dispute;
From the centre all round to the sea
I am lord of the foul and the brute.
Verses supposed to be written by Alexander Selkirk

DICKENS, Charles (1812–70) British novelist

This is a London particular…A fog, miss.
Bleak House, Ch. 3

'God bless us every one!' said Tiny Tim, the last of all.
A Christmas Carol

Barkis is willin'.
David Copperfield, Ch. 5

Annual income twenty pounds, annual expenditure nineteen nineteen six, result happiness. Annual income twenty pounds, annual expenditure twenty pounds ought and six, result misery.
David Copperfield, Ch. 12

I am well aware that I am the 'umblest person going.
David Copperfield, Ch. 16

Accidents will occur in the best-regulated families.
David Copperfield, Ch. 28

As she frequently remarked when she made any such mistake, it would be all the same a hundred years hence.
Martin Chuzzlewit, Ch. 9

All is gas and gaiters.
Nicholas Nickleby, Ch. 49

Oliver Twist has asked for more.
Oliver Twist, Ch. 2

Known by the *sobriquet* of 'The artful Dodger.'
Oliver Twist, Ch. 8

Take example by your father, my boy, and be very careful o' vidders all your life.
Pickwick Papers, Ch. 13

Poverty and oysters always seem to go together.
Pickwick Papers, Ch. 22

It was the best of times, it was the worst of times, it was the age of wisdom, it was the age of foolishness, it was the epoch of belief, it was the epoch of incredulity, it was the season of Light, it was the season of Darkness, it was the spring of hope, it was the winter of despair, we had everything before us, we had nothing before us, we were all going direct to Heaven, we were all going direct the other way.
A Tale of Two Cities, Bk. I, Ch. 1

It is a far, far, better thing that I do, than I have ever done; it is a far, far, better rest that I go to, than I have ever known.
A Tale of Two Cities, Bk. II, Ch. 15

DICKINSON, Emily (1830–86) US poet

Because I could not stop for Death,
He kindly stopped for me;
The carriage held but just ourselves
And Immortality.
The Chariot 'Because I could not stop for Death'

Parting is all we know of heaven,
And all we need of hell.
My Life Closed Twice Before its Close

DONNE, John (1572–1631) English poet

Come live with me, and be my love,
And we will some new pleasures prove
Of golden sands, and crystal brooks,
With silken lines, and silver hooks.
The Bait

No man is an Island, entire of itself; every man is a piece of the Continent, a part of the main.
Devotions, 17

Any man's death diminishes me, because I am involved in Mankind; And therefore never send to know for whom the bell tolls; it tolls for thee.
Devotions, 17

Go, and catch a falling star,
Get with child a mandrake root,
Tell me, where all past years are,
Or who cleft the Devil's foot.
Go and Catch a Falling Star

I am two fools, I know,
For loving, and for saying so
In whining Poetry.
The Triple Fool

DOYLE, Sir Arthur Conan (1859–1930) British writer

It is an old maxim of mine that when you have ex-

cluded the impossible, whatever remains, however improbable, must be the truth.
The Beryl Coronet

You know my method. It is founded upon the observance of trifles.
The Boscombe Valley Mystery

'Excellent!' I cried. 'Elementary,' said he.
The Crooked Man

It is quite a three-pipe problem.
The Red-Headed League

'Is there any other point to which you would wish to draw my attention?'
'To the curious incident of the dog in the night-time.'
'The dog did nothing in the night-time.'
'That was the curious incident,' remarked Sherlock Holmes.
The Silver Blaze

Mediocrity knows nothing higher than itself, but talent instantly recognizes genius.
The Valley of Fear

DRYDEN, John (1631–1700) British poet and dramatist

But far more numerous was the Herd of such,
Who think too little, and who talk too much.
Absalom and Achitophel, I

None but the Brave deserves the Fair.
Alexander's Feast

Errors, like Straws, upon the surface flow;
He who would search for Pearls must dive below.
All for Love, Prologue

By viewing Nature, Nature's handmaid, art,
Makes mighty things from small beginnings grow.
Annus Mirabilis

ELIOT, T S (1888–1965) US-born British poet and dramatist

Time present and time past
Are both perhaps present in time future,
And time future contained in time past.
Four Quartets, 'Burnt Norton'

We are the hollow men
We are the stuffed men
Leaning together
Headpiece filled with straw. Alas!
The Hollow Men

This is the way the world ends
Not with a bang but a whimper.
The Hollow Men

I have measured out my life with coffee spoons.
The Love Song of J. Alfred Prufrock

Macavity, Macavity, there's no one like Macavity,
There never was a Cat of such deceitfulness and suavity.
He always has an alibi, and one or two to spare:
At whatever time the deed took place – MACAVITY WASN'T THERE!
Old Possum's Book of Practical Cats, Macavity:
The Mystery Cat

FITZGERALD, Edward (1809–83) British poet and translator

Here with a Loaf of Bread beneath the Bough,
A Flask of Wine, a Book of Verse – and Thou
Beside me singing in the Wilderness –
And Wilderness is Paradise enow.
The Rubáiyát of Omar Khayyám (1st edn.), XI

Ah, my Belovéd, fill the Cup that clears
TO-DAY of past Regrets and Future Fears:
To-morrow! – Why, To-morrow I may be
Myself with Yesterday's Sev'n thousand Years.
The Rubáiyát of Omar Khayyám (1st edn.), XX

Ah, fill the Cup: – what boots it to repeat
How Time is slipping underneath our Feet:
Unborn TOMORROW, and dead YESTERDAY,
Why fret about them if TODAY be sweet!
The Rubáiyát of Omar Khayyám (1st edn.), XXXVII

The Moving Finger writes; and, having writ,
Moves on: nor all thy Piety nor Wit
Shall lure it back to cancel half a Line,
Nor all thy Tears wash out a Word of it.
The Rubáiyát of Omar Khayyám (1st edn.), LI

FROST, Robert Lee (1875–1963) US poet

My apple trees will never get across
And eat the cones under his pines, I tell him.
He only says, 'Good fences make good neighbours.'
North of Boston, 'Mending Wall'

Two roads diverged in a wood, and I –
I took the one less traveled by,
And that has made all the difference.
The Road Not Taken

The woods are lovely, dark, and deep,
But I have promises to keep,
And miles to go before I sleep,
And miles to go before I sleep.
Stopping by Woods on a Snowy Evening

GILBERT, Sir William Schwenk (1836–1911) British dramatist and comic writer

I'm called Little Buttercup – dear Little Buttercup,
Though I could never tell why.
HMS Pinafore, I

Stick close to your desks and never go to sea,
And you all may be Rulers of the Queen's Navee!
HMS Pinafore, I

I often think it's comical
How Nature always does contrive
That every boy and every gal
That's born into the world alive
Is either a little Liberal
Or else a little Conservative!
Iolanthe, II

As some day it may happen that a victim must be found
I've got a little list – I've got a little list
Of society offenders who might well be underground,

And who never would be missed – who never
would be missed!
The Mikado, I

Three little maids from school are we,
Pert as a school-girl well can be,
Filled to the brim with girlish glee.
The Mikado, I

My object all sublime
I shall achieve in time –
To let the punishment fit the crime –
The punishment fit the crime.
The Mikado, II

When constabulary duty's to be done –
A policeman's lot is not a happy one.
The Pirates of Penzance, II

GOLDSMITH, Oliver (1730–74) Irish-born British
writer

This is Liberty-Hall, gentlemen.
She Stoops to Conquer, II

Laws grind the poor, and rich men rule the law.
The Traveller

When lovely woman stoops to folly,
And finds too late that men betray,
What charm can soothe her melancholy,
What art can wash her guilt away?
The Vicar of Wakefield, Ch. 9

Conscience is a coward, and those faults it has
not strength enough to prevent it seldom has
justice enough to accuse.
The Vicar of Wakefield, Ch. 13

GRAY, Thomas (1716–71) British poet

The boast of heraldry, the pomp of pow'r,
And all that beauty, all that wealth e'er gave,
Awaits alike th' inevitable hour,
The paths of glory lead but to the grave.
Elegy Written in a Country Churchyard

Some village-Hampden, that with dauntless breast
The little Tyrant of his fields withstood;
Some mute inglorious Milton here may rest,
Some Cromwell guiltless of his country's blood.
Elegy Written in a Country Churchyard

Far from the madding crowd's ignoble strife,
Their sober wishes never learn'd to stray;
Along the cool sequester'd vale of life
They kept the noiseless tenor of their way.
Elegy Written in a Country Churchyard

Alas, regardless of their doom,
The little victims play!
Ode on a Distant Prospect of Eton College

Yet ah! why should they know their fate?
Since sorrow never comes too late,
And happiness too swiftly flies.
Thought would destroy their paradise.
No more; where ignorance is bliss,
'Tis folly to be wise.
Ode on a Distant Prospect of Eton College

Not all that tempts your wand'ring eyes

And heedless hearts, is lawful prize;
Nor all, that glisters, gold.
Ode on the Death of a Favourite Cat

HOUSMAN, A(lfred) E(dward) (1859–1936)
British poet

Loveliest of trees, the cherry now
Is hung with bloom along the bough,
And stands about the woodland ride
Wearing white for Eastertide.
A Shropshire Lad, '1887'

On Wenlock Edge the wood's in trouble;
His forest fleece the Wrekin heaves;
The wind, it plies the saplings double,
And thick on Severn snow the leaves.
A Shropshire Lad, 'The Welsh Marches'

East and west on fields forgotten
Bleach the bones of comrades slain,
Lovely lads and dead and rotten;
None that go return again.
A Shropshire Lad, 'The Welsh Marches'

Malt does more than Milton can
To justify God's ways to man.
A Shropshire Lad, 'The Welsh Marches'

JOHNSON, Samuel (1709–84) British
lexicographer and writer

When two Englishmen meet, their first talk is of
the weather.
The Idler

Marriage has many pains, but celibacy has no
pleasures.
Rasselas, Ch. 26

It is very strange, and very melancholy, that the
paucity of human pleasures should persuade us
ever to call hunting one of them.
Johnsonian Miscellanies (ed. G. B. Hill), Vol. I

A tavern chair is the throne of human felicity.
Johnsonian Miscellanies (ed. G. B. Hill), Vol. II

Love is the wisdom of the fool and the folly of the
wise.
Johnsonian Miscellanies (ed. G. B. Hill), Vol. II

There are few ways in which a man can be more
innocently employed than in getting money.
Life of Johnson (J. Boswell), Vol. II

A man will turn over half a library to make one
book.
Life of Johnson (J. Boswell), Vol. II

Patriotism is the last refuge of a scoundrel.
Life of Johnson (J. Boswell), Vol. II

There is nothing which has yet been contrived by
man, by which so much happiness is produced
as by a good tavern or inn.
Life of Johnson (J. Boswell), Vol. II

When a man is tired of London, he is tired of life;
for there is in London all that life can afford.
Life of Johnson (J. Boswell), Vol. III

He who praises everybody praises nobody.
Life of Johnson (J. Boswell), Vol. III

No man is a hypocrite in his pleasures.
Life of Johnson (J. Boswell), Vol. IV

KEATS, John (1795–1821) British poet

A thing of beauty is a joy for ever:
Its loveliness increases; it will never
Pass into nothingness; but still will keep
A bower quiet for us, and a sleep
Full of sweet dreams, and health, and quiet
  breathing.
Endymion, I

St Agnes' Eve – Ah, bitter chill it was!
The owl, for all his feathers, was a-cold;
The hare limp'd trembling through the frozen grass,
And silent was the flock in woolly fold.
The Eve of Saint Agnes, I

And they are gone: aye, ages long ago
These lovers fled away into the storm.
The Eve of Saint Agnes, XLII

Oh what can ail thee, knight at arms
Alone and palely loitering;
The sedge has wither'd from the lake,
And no birds sing.
La Belle Dame Sans Merci

'Beauty is truth, truth beauty,' – that is all
Ye know on earth, and all ye need to know.
Ode on a Grecian Urn

No, no, go not to Lethe, neither twist
Wolf's-bane, tight-rooted, for its poisonous wine.
Ode on Melancholy

My heart aches, and a drowsy numbness pains
My sense.
Ode to a Nightingale

O for a beaker full of the warm South,
Full of the true, the blushful Hippocrene,
With beaded bubbles winking at the brim,
And purple-stained mouth.
Ode to a Nightingale

Thou wast not born for death, immortal Bird!
No hungry generations tread thee down;
The voice I hear this passing night was heard
In ancient days by emperor and clown:
Ode to a Nightingale

Darkling I listen; and, for many a time
I have been half in love with easeful Death,
Call'd him soft names in many a musèd rhyme,
To take into the air my quiet breath;
Now more than ever seems it rich to die,
To cease upon the midnight with no pain,
While thou art pouring forth thy soul abroad
In such an ecstasy!
Ode to a Nightingale

Much have I travell'd in the realms of gold,
And many goodly states and kingdoms seen.
On first looking into Chapman's Homer

Season of mists and mellow fruitfulness,
Close bosom-friend of the maturing sun;
Conspiring with him how to load and bless

With fruit the vines that round the thatch-eaves
  run.
To Autumn

KIPLING, Rudyard (1865–1936) British writer
and poet

For the female of the species is more deadly than
  the male.
The Female of the Species

If you can talk with crowds and keep your virtue,
Or walk with Kings – nor lose the common touch,
If neither foes nor loving friends can hurt you,
If all men count with you, but none too much;
If you can fill the unforgiving minute
With sixty seconds' worth of distance run,
Yours is the Earth and everything that's in it,
And – which is more – you'll be a Man my son!
If

Ship me somewheres east of Suez, where the
  best is like the worst,
Where there aren't no Ten Commandments, an' a
  man can raise a thirst:
The Road to Mandalay

It's Tommy this, an' Tommy that, an' 'Chuck him
  out, the brute!'
But it's 'Saviour of 'is country' when the guns
  begin to shoot.
Tommy

They shut the road through the woods
Seventy years ago.
Weather and rain have undone it again,
And now you would never know
There was once a road through the woods.
The Way Through the Woods

LEAR, Edward (1812–88) British artist and writer

Far and few, far and few,
Are the lands where the Jumblies live;
Their heads are green, and their hands are blue,
And they went to sea in a sieve.
The Jumblies

The Owl and the Pussy-Cat went to sea
In a beautiful pea-green boat,
They took some honey, and plenty of money,
Wrapped up in a five-pound note.
The Owl and the Pussy-Cat

They dined on mince, and slices of quince,
Which they ate with a runcible spoon;
And hand in hand, on the edge of the sand,
They danced by the light of the moon.
The Owl and the Pussy-Cat

LONGFELLOW, Henry Wadsworth (1807–82)
US poet

The shades of night were falling fast,
As through an Alpine village passed
A youth, who bore, 'mid snow and ice,
A banner with the strange device,
Excelsior!
Excelsior

By the shore of Gitche Gumee,

By the shining Big-Sea-Water,
Stood the wigwam of Nokomis,
Daughter of the Moon, Nokomis,
The Song of Hiawatha, 'Hiawatha's Childhood'

From the waterfall he named her,
Minnehaha, Laughing Water.
The Song of Hiawatha, 'Hiawatha and Mudjekeewis'

He is dead, the sweet musician!
He is the sweetest of all singers!
He has gone from us for ever,
He has moved a little nearer
To the Master of all music,
To the Master of all singing!
O my brother, Chibiabos!
The Song of Hiawatha, 'Hiawatha's Lamentation'

Ships that pass in the night, and speak each other in passing;
Only a signal shown and a distant voice in the darkness;
So on the ocean of life we pass and speak one another,
Only a look and a voice; then darkness again and a silence.
Tales of a Wayside Inn, 'The Theologian's Tale. Elizabeth'

Under a spreading chestnut tree
The village smithy stands;
The smith, a mighty man is he,
With large and sinewy hands;
And the muscles of his brawny arms
Are strong as iron bands.
The Village Blacksmith

MARVELL, Andrew (1621–78) English poet

I have a garden of my own,
But so with roses overgrown,
And lilies, that you would it guess
To be a little wilderness.
The Nymph Complaining for the Death of her Fawn

Had we but world enough, and time,
This coyness, lady, were no crime.
To His Coy Mistress

But at my back I always hear
Time's winged chariot hurrying near;
And yonder all before us lie
Deserts of vast eternity.
To His Coy Mistress

The grave's a fine and private place,
But none, I think, do there embrace.
To His Coy Mistress

MASEFIELD, John (1878–1967) British poet

Quinquireme of Nineveh from distant Ophir
Rowing home to haven in sunny Palestine,
With a cargo of ivory,
And apes and peacocks,
Sandalwood, cedarwood, and sweet white wine.
Cargoes

Dirty British coaster with a salt-caked smoke stack,
Butting through the Channel in the mad March days,
With a cargo of Tyne coal,
Road-rail, pig-lead,
Firewood, iron-ware, and cheap tin trays.
Cargoes

I must down to the seas again, to the lonely sea and the sky,
And all I ask is a tall ship and a star to steer her by,
And the wheel's kick and the wind's song and the white sail's shaking,
And a grey mist on the sea's face and a grey dawn breaking.
Sea Fever

MILTON, John (1608–74) English poet

To sport with Amaryllis in the shade,
Or with the tangles of Neaera's hair.
Lycidas

Fame is the spur that the clear spirit doth raise
(That last infirmity of noble mind)
To scorn delights, and live laborious days.
Lycidas

Of Man's first disobedience, and the fruit
Of that forbidden tree, whose mortal taste
Brought death into the World, and all our woe…
Paradise Lost, Bk. I

What in me is dark
Illumine, what is low raise and support;
That, to the height of this great argument,
I may assert Eternal Providence,
And justify the ways of God to men.
Paradise Lost, Bk. I

To reign is worth ambition, though in Hell:
Better to reign in Hell than serve in Heaven.
Paradise Lost, Bk. I

High on a throne of royal state, which far
Outshone the wealth of Ormuz and of Ind,
Or where the gorgeous East with richest hand
Showers on her kings barbaric pearl and gold,
Satan exalted sat, by merit raised
To that bad eminence.
Paradise Lost, Bk. II

For neither man nor angel can discern
Hypocrisy, the only evil that walks
Invisible, except to God alone.
Paradise Lost, Bk. III

Ask for this great deliverer now, and find him
Eyeless in Gaza at the mill with slaves.
Samson Agonistes

When I consider how my light is spent
Ere half my days in this dark world and wide,
And that one talent which is death to hide
Lodged with me useless.
Sonnet: 'On his Blindness'

NEWBOLT, Sir Henry John (1862–1938) British poet

The sand of the desert is sodden red, –
Red with the wreck of a square that broke; –
The gatling's jammed and the colonel dead,
And the regiment blind with the dust and smoke.
The river of death has brimmed its banks
And England's far and honour a name.
But the voice of a schoolboy rallies the ranks:
'Play up! play up! and play the game!'
Vitaï Lampada

ORWELL, George (Eric Blair; 1903–50) British novelist

Man is the only creature that consumes without producing.
Animal Farm, Ch. 1

Four legs good, two legs bad.
Animal Farm, Ch. 3

All animals are equal but some animals are more equal than others.
Animal Farm, Ch. 10

Who controls the past controls the future. Who controls the present controls the past.
Nineteen Eighty-Four

If you want a picture of the future, imagine a boot stamping on a human face – for ever.
Nineteen Eighty-Four

Big Brother is watching you.
Nineteen Eighty-Four

War is Peace, Freedom is Slavery, Ignorance is Strength.
Nineteen Eighty-Four

Doublethink means the power of holding two contradictory beliefs in one's mind simultaneously, and accepting both of them.
Nineteen Eighty-Four

PARKER, Dorothy (1893–1967) US writer

He lies below, correct in cypress wood,
And entertains the most exclusive worms.
Epitaph for a Very Rich Man

Why is it no one ever sent me yet
One perfect limousine, do you suppose?
Ah no, it's always just my luck to get
One perfect rose.
One Perfect Rose

By the time you say you're his,
Shivering and sighing,
And he vows his passion is
Infinite, undying –
Lady, make a note of this:
One of you is lying.
Unfortunate Coincidence

POPE, Alexander (1688–1744) British poet

The right divine of kings to govern wrong.
The Dunciad, IV

Do good by stealth, and blush to find it fame.
Epilogue to the Satires, Dialogue I

Damn with faint praise, assent with civil leer,
And, without sneering, teach the rest to sneer.
Epistle to Dr. Arbuthnot

Of all the causes which conspire to blind
Man's erring judgment, and misguide the mind,

What the weak head with strongest bias rules,
Is Pride, the never-failing vice of fools.
An Essay on Criticism

A little learning is a dangerous thing;
Drink deep, or taste not the Pierian spring:
There shallow draughts intoxicate the brain,
And drinking largely sobers us again.
An Essay on Criticism

To err is human, to forgive, divine.
An Essay on Criticism

For fools rush in where angels fear to tread.
An Essay on Criticism

Hope springs eternal in the human breast;
Man never is, but always to be blest.
An Essay on Man, I

Know then thyself, presume not God to scan,
The proper study of Mankind is Man.
An Essay on Man, II

Where'er you walk, cool gales shall fan the glade,
Trees, where you sit, shall crowd into a shade:
Where'er you tread, the blushing flow'rs shall rise,
And all things flourish where you turn your eyes.
Pastorals, 'Summer'

SASSOON, Siegfried (1886–1967) British poet and writer

And when the war is done and youth stone dead
I'd toddle safely home and die – in bed.
Base Details

'Good morning; good morning!' the general said
When we met him last week on our way to the line.
Now the soldiers he smiled at are most of 'em dead,
And we're cursing his staff for incompetent swine.
The General

SCOTT, Sir Walter (1771–1832) Scottish writer

O Caledonia! stern and wild,
Meet nurse for a poetic child!
Land of brown heath and shaggy wood,
Land of the mountain and the flood,
Land of my sires! what mortal hand
Can e'er untie the filial band
That knits me to thy rugged strand!
The Lay of the Last Minstrel, VI

To that dark inn, the grave!
The Lord of the Isles, VI

O, young Lochinvar is come out of the west,
Through all the wide Border his steed was the best.
Marmion, V

SHAKESPEARE, William (1564–1616) English dramatist and poet

Our remedies oft in ourselves do lie,
Which we ascribe to heaven.
All's Well that Ends Well, I: 1

Where's my serpent of old Nile?
Antony and Cleopatra, I: 5

My salad days,
When I was green in judgment, cold in blood,
To say as I said then!
Antony and Cleopatra, I: 5

The barge she sat in, like a burnish'd throne,
Burn'd on the water. The poop was beaten gold;
Purple the sails, and so perfumed that
The winds were love-sick with them; the oars
    were silver,
Which to the tune of flutes kept stroke and made
The water which they beat to follow faster,
As amorous of their strokes. For her own person,
It beggar'd all description.
Antony and Cleopatra, II: 2

Age cannot wither her, nor custom stale
Her infinite variety. Other women cloy
The appetites they feed, but she makes hungry
Where most she satisfies.
Antony and Cleopatra, II: 2

She shall be buried by her Antony!
No grave upon the earth shall clip in it
A pair so famous.
Antony and Cleopatra, V: 2

Well said; that was laid on with a trowel.
As You Like It, I: 2

And this our life, exempt from public haunt,
Finds tongues in trees, books in the running
    brooks,
Sermons in stones and good in everything.
As You Like It, II: 1

All the world's a stage,
And all the men and women merely players;
They have their exits and their entrances;
And one man in his time plays many parts,
His acts being seven ages.
As You Like It, II: 7

Last scene of all,
That ends this strange eventful history,
Is second childishness and mere oblivion;
Sans teeth, sans eyes, sans taste, sans every
    thing.
As You Like It, II: 7

Men have died from time to time, and worms
have eaten them, but not for love.
As You Like It, IV: 1

Fear no more the heat o' th' sun
Nor the furious winter's rages;
Thou thy worldly task hast done,
Home art gone, and ta'en thy wages.
Golden lads and girls all must,
As chimney-sweepers, come to dust.
Cymbeline, IV: 2

But I have that within which passes show –

these but the trappings and the suits of woe.
Hamlet, I: 2

O! that this too too solid flesh would melt,
Thaw, and resolve itself into a dew.
Or that the Everlasting had not fix'd
His canon 'gainst self-slaughter! O God! O God!
How weary, stale, flat, and unprofitable,
Seem to me all the uses of this world!
Hamlet, I: 2

Frailty, thy name is woman!
Hamlet, I: 2

Foul deeds will rise,
Though all the earth o'erwhelm them, to men's
    eyes.
Hamlet, I: 2

Costly thy habit as thy purse can buy,
But not express'd in fancy; rich, not gaudy;
For the apparel oft proclaims the man.
Hamlet, I: 3

Neither a borrower nor a lender be;
For loan oft loses both itself and friend,
And borrowing dulls the edge of husbandry.
This above all: to thine own self be true,
And it must follow, as the night the day,
Thou canst not then be false to any man.
Hamlet, I: 3

Something is rotten in the state of Denmark.
Hamlet, I: 4

Murder most foul, as in the best it is;
But this most foul, strange, and unnatural.
Hamlet, I: 5

There are more things in heaven and earth,
    Horatio,
Than are dreamt of in your philosophy.
Hamlet, I: 5

Though this be madness, yet there is method in't.
Hamlet, II: 2

There is nothing either good or bad, but thinking
makes it so.
Hamlet, II: 2

What a piece of work is a man! How noble in
reason! how infinite in faculties! in form and moving, how express and admirable! in action, how
like an angel! in apprehension, how like a god!
the beauty of the world! the paragon of animals!
Hamlet, II: 2

I am but mad north-north-west; when the wind is
southerly, I know a hawk from a handsaw.
Hamlet, II: 2

The play, I remember, pleas'd not the million;
'twas caviare to the general.
Hamlet, II: 2

To be, or not to be – that is the question;
Whether 'tis nobler in the mind to suffer
The slings and arrows of outrageous fortune,
Or to take arms against a sea of troubles,
And by opposing end them? To die, to sleep –
No more; and by a sleep to say we end

The heart-ache and the thousand natural shocks
That flesh is heir to, 'tis a consummation
Devoutly to be wish'd. To die, to sleep;
To sleep, perchance to dream. Ay, there's the rub;
For in that sleep of death what dreams may come,
When we have shuffled off this mortal coil,
Must give us pause.
Hamlet, III: 1

The dread of something after death –
The undiscover'd country, from whose bourn
No traveller returns.
Hamlet, III: 1

Thus conscience does make cowards of us all;
Hamlet, III: 1

Madness in great ones must not unwatch'd go.
Hamlet, III: 1

How all occasions do inform against me,
And spur my dull revenge! What is a man,
If his chief good and market of his time
Be but to sleep and feed? a beast, no more.
Hamlet, IV: 4

When sorrows come, they come not single spies,
But in battalions!
Hamlet, IV: 5

There's rosemary, that's for remembrance; pray,
love, remember: and there is pansies, that's for
thoughts.
Hamlet, IV: 5

Alas, poor Yorick! I knew him, Horatio: a fellow of
infinite jest, of most excellent fancy.
Hamlet, V: 1

There's a divinity that shapes our ends,
Rough-hew them how we will.
Hamlet, V: 2

Out of this nettle, danger, we pluck this flower,
safety.
Henry IV, Part One, II: 3

The better part of valour is discretion; in the
which better part I have saved my life.
Henry IV, Part One, V: 4

Uneasy lies the head that wears a crown.
Henry IV, Part Two, III: 1

Once more unto the breach, dear friends, once
more;
Or close the wall up with our English dead.
Henry V, III: 1

And gentlemen in England, now a-bed
Shall think themselves accurs'd they were not
here,
And hold their manhoods cheap whiles any
speaks
That fought with us upon Saint Crispin's day.
Henry V, IV: 3

Men at some time are masters of their fates:
The fault, dear Brutus, is not in our stars,
But in ourselves, that we are underlings.
Julius Caesar, I: 2

Cry 'Havoc!' and let slip the dogs of war.
Julius Caesar, III: 1

Friends, Romans, countrymen, lend me your ears
I come to bury Caesar, not to praise him.
The evil that men do lives after them;
The good is oft interred with their bones.
Julius Caesar, III: 2

If you have tears, prepare to shed them now.
Julius Caesar, III: 2

There is a tide in the affairs of men
Which, taken at the flood, leads on to fortune;
Julius Caesar, IV: 3

How sharper than a serpent's tooth it is
To have a thankless child!
King Lear, I: 4

I am a man
More sinn'd against than sinning.
King Lear, III: 2

The worst is not
So long as we can say 'This is the worst'.
King Lear, IV: 1

As flies to wanton boys are we to th' gods –
They kill us for their sport.
King Lear, IV: 1

When shall we three meet again
In thunder, lightning, or in rain?
Macbeth, I: 1

I have no spur
To prick the sides of my intent, but only
Vaulting ambition, which o'er-leaps itself,
And falls on th' other.
Macbeth, I: 7

Is this a dagger which I see before me,
The handle toward my hand? Come, let me clutch thee:
I have thee not, and yet I see thee still.
Macbeth, II: 1

Methought I heard a voice cry, 'Sleep no more!'
Macbeth doth murder sleep,' the innocent sleep,
Sleep that knits up the ravell'd sleave of care,
The death of each day's life, sore labour's bath,
Balm of hurt minds, great nature's second course,
Chief nourisher in life's feast.
Macbeth, II: 2

Eye of newt, and toe of frog,
Wool of bat, and tongue of dog,
Adder's fork, and blind-worm's sting,
Lizard's leg, and howlet's wing,
For a charm of powerful trouble,
Like a hell-broth boil and bubble.
Macbeth, IV: 1

Be bloody bold, and resolute, laugh to scorn
The power of man, for none of woman born
Shall harm Macbeth.
Macbeth, IV: 1

Here's the smell of the blood still. All the per-
fumes of Arabia will not sweeten this little hand.
Macbeth, V: 1

Tomorrow, and tomorrow, and tomorrow,
Creeps in this petty pace from day to day
To the last syllable of recorded time,
And all our yesterdays have lighted fools
The way to dusty death. Out, out, brief candle!
Life's but a walking shadow, a poor player,
That struts and frets his hour upon the stage,
And then is heard no more; it is a tale
Told by an idiot, full of sound and fury,
Signifying nothing.
Macbeth, V: 5

The devil can cite Scripture for his purpose.
The Merchant of Venice, I: 3

You call me misbeliever, cut-throat dog,
And spit upon my Jewish gaberdine,
And all for use of that which is mine own.
The Merchant of Venice, I: 3

It is a wise father that knows his own child.
The Merchant of Venice, II: 2

Hath not a Jew eyes? Hath not a Jew hands,
organs, dimensions, senses, affections, passions,
fed with the same food, hurt with the same
weapons, subject to the same diseases, healed
by the same means, warmed and cooled by the
same winter and summer, as a Christian is? If
you prick us, do we not bleed? If you tickle us, do
we not laugh? If you poison us, do we not die?
And if you wrong us, shall we not revenge?
The Merchant of Venice, III: 1

The quality of mercy is not strain'd;
It droppeth as the gentle rain from heaven
Upon the place beneath. It is twice blest;
It blesseth him that gives and him that takes.
The Merchant of Venice, IV: 1

How far that little candle throws his beams!
So shines a good deed in a naughty world.
The Merchant of Venice, V: 1

Why, then the world's mine oyster,
Which I with sword will open.
The Merry Wives of Windsor, II: 2

For aught that I could ever read,
Could ever hear by tale or history,
The course of true love never did run smooth.
A Midsummer Night's Dream, I: 1

Ill met by moonlight, proud Titania.
A Midsummer Night's Dream, II: 1

The lunatic, the lover, and the poet,
Are of imagination all compact.
A Midsummer Night's Dream, V: 1

Doth not the appetite alter? A man loves the meat
in his youth that he cannot endure in his age.
Much Ado About Nothing, II: 3

Comparisons are odorous.
Much Ado About Nothing, III: 5

Reputation, reputation, reputation! O, I have lost
my reputation! I have lost the immortal part of
myself, and what remains is bestial.
Othello, II: 3

But he that filches from me my good name
Robs me of that which not enriches him
And makes me poor indeed.
Othello, III: 3

O, beware, my lord, of jealousy;
It is the green-ey'd monster which doth mock
The meat it feeds on.
Othello, III: 3

Then must you speak
Of one that lov'd not wisely, but too well;
Of one not easily jealous, but, being wrought,
Perplexed in the extreme; of one whose hand,
Like the base Indian, threw a pearl away
Richer than all his tribe.
Othello, V: 2

Teach thy necessity to reason thus:
There is no virtue like necessity.
Richard II, I: 3

This royal throne of kings, this sceptred isle,
This earth of majesty, this seat of Mars,
This other Eden, demi-paradise,
This fortress built by Nature for herself
Against infection and the hand of war,
This happy breed of men, this little world,
This precious stone set in the silver sea,
Which serves it in the office of a wall,
Or as a moat defensive to a house,
Against the envy of less happier lands;
This blessed plot, this earth, this realm, this
  England,
This nurse, this teeming womb of royal kings,
Fear'd by their breed, and famous by their birth.
Richard II, II: 1

Now is the winter of our discontent
Made glorious summer by this sun of York.
Richard III, I: 1

A horse! a horse! my kingdom for a horse.
Richard III, V: 4

From forth the fatal loins of these two foes
A pair of star-cross'd lovers take their life.
Romeo and Juliet, Prologue

O! she doth teach the torches to burn bright
It seems she hangs upon the cheek of night
Like a rich jewel in an Ethiop's ear;
Beauty too rich for use, for earth too dear.
Romeo and Juliet, I: 5

My only love sprung from my only hate!
Too early seen unknown, and known too late!
Romeo and Juliet, I: 5

What's in a name? That which we call a rose
By any other name would smell as sweet.
Romeo and Juliet, II: 2

Good night, good night! Parting is such sweet
  sorrow
That I shall say good night till it be morrow.
Romeo and Juliet, II: 2

A plague o' both your houses!
They have made worms' meat of me.
Romeo and Juliet, III: 1

How beauteous mankind is! O brave new world
That has such people in't!
The Tempest, V: 1

If music be the food of love, play on,
Give me excess of it, that, surfeiting,
The appetite may sicken and so die.
Twelfth Night, I: 1

Then come kiss me, sweet and twenty;
Youth's a stuff will not endure.
Twelfth Night, II: 3

Dost thou think, because thou art virtuous, there
shall be no more cakes and ale?
Twelfth Night, II: 3

Some are born great, some achieve greatness,
and some have greatness thrust upon 'em.
Twelfth Night, II: 5

Crabbed age and youth cannot live together:
Youth is full of pleasure, age is full of care;
Youth like summer morn, age like winter
   weather;
Youth like summer brave, age like winter bare.
The Passionate Pilgrim, XII

Shall I compare thee to a summer's day?
Thou art more lovely and more temperate.
Rough winds do shake the darling buds of May,
And summer's lease hath all too short a date.
Sonnet 18

Let me not to the marriage of true minds
Admit impediments. Love is not love
Which alters when it alteration finds,
Or bends with the remover to remove.
O, no! it is an ever-fixed mark,
That looks on tempests and is never shaken.
Sonnet 116

SHAW, George Bernard (1856–1950) Irish
dramatist

When a stupid man is doing something he is
ashamed of, he always declares that it is his duty.
Caesar and Cleopatra, III

He knows nothing; and he thinks he knows
everything. That points clearly to a political
career.
Major Barbara, III

He who can, does. He who cannot, teaches.
Man and Superman, 'Maxims for Revolutionists'

Gin was mother's milk to her.
Pygmalion, III

SHELLEY, Percy Bysshe (1792–1822) British
poet

Let there be light! said Liberty,
And like sunrise from the sea,
Athens arose!
Hellas, I

O Wild West Wind, thou breath of Autumn's being,
Thou, from whose unseen presence the leaves
   dead
Are driven, like ghosts from an enchanter
   fleeing,

Yellow, and black, and pale, and hectic red,
Pestilence-stricken multitudes.
Ode to the West Wind

I met a traveller from an antique land
Who said: Two vast and trunkless legs of stone
Stand in the desert.
Ozymandias

Hail to thee, blithe Spirit!
Bird thou never wert,
That from Heaven, or near it,
Pourest thy full heart
In profuse strains of unpremeditated art.
To a Skylark

STEVENSON, Robert Louis (1850–94) Scottish
writer

Fifteen men on the dead man's chest
Yo-ho-ho, and a bottle of rum!
Drink and the devil had done for the rest –
Yo-ho-ho, and a bottle of rum!
Treasure Island, Ch. 1

Under the wide and starry sky
Dig the grave and let me lie.
Glad did I live and gladly die,
 – And I laid me down with a will.
This is the verse you grave for me:
'Here he lies where he longed to be;
Home is the sailor, home from sea,
And the hunter home from the hill.'
Underwoods, Bk. I, 'Requiem'

TENNYSON, Alfred, Baron (1809–92) British
poet

'Forward the Light Brigade!'
Was there a man dismay'd?
Not tho' the soldier knew
Some one had blunder'd:
Their's not to make reply,
Their's not to reason why,
Their's but to do and die:
Into the valley of Death
Rode the six hundred.
The Charge of the Light Brigade

An arm
Rose up from out the bosom of the lake,
Clothed in white samite, mystic, wonderful.
Idylls of the King, 'The Passing of Arthur'

And slowly answer'd Arthur from the barge:
'The old order changeth, yielding place to new,
And God fulfils himself in many ways.'
Idylls of the King, 'The Passing of Arthur'

I hold it true, whate'er befall;
I feel it, when I sorrow most;
'Tis better to have loved and lost
Than never to have loved at all.
In Memoriam A.H.H., XXVII

I dreamed there would be Spring no more,
That Nature's ancient power was lost.
In Memoriam A.H.H., LXIX

Kind hearts are more than coronets,
And simple faith than Norman blood.
Lady Clara Vere de Vere, VI

On either side the river lie
Long fields of barley and of rye,
That clothe the wold and meet the sky;
And thro' the field the road runs by
To many-tower'd Camelot.
The Lady of Shalott, Pt. I

'The curse is come upon me,' cried
The Lady of Shalott.
The Lady of Shalott, Pt. III

Dear as remembered kisses after death,
And sweet as those by hopeless fancy feign'd
On lips that are for others: deep as love,
Deep as first love, and wild with all regret;
O Death in Life, the days that are no more.
The Princess, IV

THOMAS, Dylan (1914–53) Welsh poet

Though they go mad they shall be sane,
Though they sink through the sea they shall rise
    again.
Though lovers be lost love shall not;
And death shall have no dominion.
And death shall have no dominion

Do not go gentle into that good night,
Old age should burn and rave at close of day;
Rage, rage, against the dying of the light.
Do not go gentle into that good night

Now as I was young and easy under the apple
    boughs
About the lilting house and happy as the grass
    was green.
Fern Hill

Time held me green and dying
Though I sang in my chains like the sea.
Fern Hill

The hands of the clock have stayed still at half
past eleven for fifty years. It is always opening
time in the Sailors Arms.
Under Milk Wood

It is a winter's tale
That the snow blind twilight ferries over the lakes
And floating fields from the farm in the cup of the
    vales.
A Winter's Tale

TWAIN, Mark (Samuel Langhorne Clemens;
1835–1910) US writer

There are three kinds of lies: lies, damned lies,
and statistics.
Autobiography

The radical invents the views. When he has worn
them out, the conservative adopts them.
Notebooks

Adam was but human – this explains it all. He did
not want the apple for the apple's sake, he
wanted it only because it was forbidden.
Pudd'nhead Wilson's, Ch. 2

WILDE, Oscar Fingal O'Flahertie Wills
(1856–1900) Irish-born British poet and dramatist

I never saw a man who looked
With such a wistful eye
Upon that little tent of blue
Which prisoners call the sky.
The Ballad of Reading Gaol, I:3

Yet each man kills the thing he loves,
By each let this be heard,
Some do it with a bitter look,
Some with a flattering word.
The coward does it with a kiss,
The brave man with a sword!
The Ballad of Reading Gaol, I:7

To love oneself is the beginning of a lifelong
romance.
An Ideal Husband, III

Other people are quite dreadful. The only
possible society is oneself.
An Ideal Husband, III

I have invented an invaluable permanent invalid
called Bunbury, in order that I may be able to go
down into the country whenever I choose.
The Importance of Being Earnest, I

All women become like their mothers. That is
their tragedy. No man does. That's his.
The Importance of Being Earnest, I

To lose one parent, Mr Worthing, may be
regarded as a misfortune; to lose both looks like
carelessness.
The Importance of Being Earnest, I

I never travel without my diary. One should
always have something sensational to read in the
train.
The Importance of Being Earnest, II

No woman should ever be quite accurate about
her age. It looks so calculating.
The Importance of Being Earnest, III

I can resist everything except temptation.
Lady Windermere's Fan, I

It is absurd to divide people into good and bad.
People are either charming or tedious.
Lady Windermere's Fan, I

We are all in the gutter, but some of us are
looking at the stars.
Lady Windermere's Fan, III

A cigarette is the perfect type of a perfect
pleasure. It is exquisite, and it leaves one unsat-
isfied. What more can one want?
The Picture of Dorian Gray, Ch. 6

Twenty years of romance makes a woman look
like a ruin; but twenty years of marriage make her
something like a public building.
A Woman of No Importance, I

The English country gentleman galloping after a
fox – the unspeakable in full pursuit of the
uneatable.
A Woman of No Importance, I

WORDSWORTH, William (1770–1850) British poet

I travelled among unknown men
In lands beyond the sea;
Nor, England! did I know till then
What love I bore to thee.
I Travelled among Unknown Men

I wandered lonely as a cloud
That floats on high o'er vales and hills,
When all at once I saw a crowd,
A host, of golden daffodils.
I Wandered Lonely as a Cloud

For oft, when on my couch I lie
In vacant or in pensive mood,
They flash upon that inward eye
Which is the bliss of solitude.
I Wandered Lonely as a Cloud

I have learned
To look on nature, not as in the hour
Of thoughtless youth; but hearing often-times
The still, sad music of humanity.
Lines composed a few miles above Tintern Abbey

My heart leaps up when I behold
A rainbow in the sky:
So was it when my life began;
So is it now I am a man;
So be it when I shall grow old,
Or let me die!
The Child is Father of the Man;
And I could wish my days to be
Bound each to each by natural piety.
My Heart Leaps Up

Whither is fled the visionary gleam?
Where is it now, the glory and the dream?
Ode. Intimations of Immortality, IV

Fair seed-time had my soul, and I grew up
Fostered alike by beauty and by fear.
The Prelude, I

Bliss was it in that dawn to be alive,
But to be young was very heaven!
The Prelude, XI

YEATS, W(illiam) B(utler) (1865–1939) Irish poet and dramatist

O chestnut tree, great rooted blossomer,
Are you the leaf, the blossom or the bole?
O body swayed to music; O brightening glance,
How can we know the dancer from the dance?
Among School Children

Wine comes in at the mouth
And love comes in at the eye;
That's all we shall know for truth
Before we grow old and die.
A Drinking Song

For the good are always the merry,
Save by an evil chance,
And the merry love the fiddle,
And the merry love to dance
The Fiddler of Dooney

I will arise and go now, and go to Innisfree,
And a small cabin build there, of clay and wattles made;
Nine bean rows will I have there, a hive for the honey bee,
And live alone in the bee-loud glade.
The Lake Isle of Innisfree

Under bare Ben Bulben's head
In Drumcliff churchyard Yeats is laid…
On limestone quarried near the spot
By his command these words are cut:
    Cast a cold eye
    On life, on death.
    Horseman, pass by!
Under Ben Bulben, VI

When you are old and gray and full of sleep,
And nodding by the fire, take down this book,
And slowly read, and dream of the soft look
Your eyes had once, and of their shadows deep.
When you are Old

Love fled
And paced upon the mountains overhead
And hid his face amid a crowd of stars.
When you are Old

But I, being poor, have only my dreams;
I have spread my dreams under your feet;
Tread softly because you tread on my dreams.
He Wishes for the Cloths of Heaven

MOTTOES

A DEO ET REGE – By God and the King (Earl of Chesterfield)
AD MAJOREM DEI GLORIAM – to the greater glory of God (The Jesuits)
A MARI USQUE AD MARE – from sea to sea (Canada)
APRES NOUS LE DELUGE – after us the deluge (617 Squadron, 'The Dam Busters', RAF)
ARS LONGA, VITA BREVIS – art is long, life is short (Millais)
AUDI, VIDE, TACE – hear, see, keep silence (United Grand Lodge of Freemasons)
AUSPICIUM MELIORIS AEVI – the sign of a better age (Duke of St Albans, Order of St Michael and St George)

MOTTOES

BE PREPARED – Scout Association, 1908
CAVENDO TUTUS – safe by being cautious (Duke of Devonshire)
CHE SERA SERA – what will be will be (Duke of Bedford)
DARE QUAM ACCIPERE – to give rather than to receive (Guy's Hospital)
DE PRAESCIENTIA DEI – from the foreknowledge of God (Barbers' Company, 1461)
DICTUM MEUM PACTUM – my word is my bond (Stock Exchange)
DIEU ET MON DROIT – God and my right (British Sovereigns)
DILIGENT AND SECRET (College of Arms, 1484)
DOMINE DIRIGE NOS – Lord, guide us (City of London)
DOMINUS ILLUMINATIO MEA – the Lord is my light (Oxford University)
DONORUM DEI DISPENSATIO FIDELIS – faithful dispensation of the gifts of God (Harrow School)
ENTALENTÉ À PARLER D'ARMES – equipped to speak of arms (The Heraldry Society, 1957)
ESPÉRANCE EN DIEU – hope in God (Duke of Northumberland)
FIDES ATQUE INTEGRITAS – faith and integrity (Society of Incorporated Accountants and Auditors)
FLOREAT ETONA – may Eton flourish (Eton College)
FOR COUNTRY NOT FOR SELF (226 Squadron, RAF)
GARDEZ BIEN – watch well (Montgomery)
HEAVEN'S LIGHT OUR GUIDE (Order of the Star of India)
HELP (Foundling Hospital, London)
HINC LUCEM ET POCULA SACRA – hence light and sacred cups (Cambridge University)
HONI SOIT QUI MAL Y PENSE – evil be to him who evil thinks (Order of the Garter)
HONNEUR ET PATRIE – honour and country (Order of the Legion of Honour)
ICH DIEN – I serve (Prince of Wales)
IMPERATRICUS AUSPICIIS – imperial in its auspices (Order of the Indian Empire)
IN ACTION FAITHFUL AND IN HONOUR CLEAR (Order of the Companions of Honour, 1917)
IN FIDE SALUS – safety in faith (Star of Rumania)
IN SOMNO SECURITAS – security in sleep (Association of Anaesthetists of Great Britain and Ireland)
JUSTITA VIRTUTUM REGINA – justice is queen of the virtues (Goldsmiths' Company)
LABORARE EST ORARE – to labour is to pray (Benedictine Order)
LABOR VIRIS CONVENIT – labour becomes men (Richard I)
LIFE IN OUR HANDS (Institute of Hospital Engineers)
MIHI ET MEA – to me and mine (Anne Boleyn)
NATION SHALL SPEAK PEACE UNTO NATION (British Broadcasting Corporation)
NEC ASPERA TERRENT – difficulties do not daunt (3rd Foot, 'The Buffs', East Kent Regiment)
NEC CUPIAS NEC METUAS – neither desire nor fear (Earl of Hardwicke)
NEMO ME IMPUNE LACESSIT – no one injures me with impunity (Order of the Thistle)
NOLI ME TANGERE – touch me not (Graeme of Garvock, 103 Squadron, RAF)
NON EST VIVERE SED VALERE VITA – life is not living, but health is life (Royal Society of Medicine)
NON SIBI, SED PATRIAE – not for himself, but for his country (Earl of Romney)
NULLIUS IN VERBA – in no man's words (Royal Society)
PAX IN BELLO – peace in war (Godolphin, Duke of Leeds)
PEACE THROUGH UNDERSTANDING (President Eisenhower)
PER ARDUA AD ASTRA – through endeavour to the stars (RAF motto)
PER CAELUM VIA NOSTRA – our way through heaven (Guild of Air Pilots and Navigators)
PISCATORES HOMINUM – fishers of men (National Society)
POWER IN TRUST (Central Electricity Generating Board)
QUIS SEPARABIT? – who shall separate? (Order of St Patrick)
QUOD PETIS HIC EST – here is what you seek (Institute of British Engineers)
RATIONE ET CONCILIO – by reason and counsel (Magistrates Association)
RERUM COGNOSCERE CAUSAS – to know the causes of things (Institute of Brewing)
SEMPER FIDELIS – always faithful (Devonshire regiment, East Devon Militia)
SEMPER PARATUS – always prepared (207 Squadron, RAF)
SOLA VIRTUS INVICTA – virtue alone is invincible (Duke of Norfolk)
TOUCH NOT THE CAT BOT A GLOVE (Macpherson Clan)
TRIA JUNCTA IN UNO – three joined in one (Order of the Bath)
UNITATE FORTIOR – stronger by union (Building Societies Association; Army and Navy Club)
VER NON SEMPER VIRET – the spring does not always flourish
VERNON SEMPER VIRET – *Vernon* always flourishes (Lord Lyveden)
WHO DARES WINS (Special Air Service)

WORDS

PALINDROMES

3
AHA
BIB
BOB
DAD
DID
DUD
ERE
EVE
EWE
EYE
GAG
GIG
HAH
HEH
HUH
MAM
MOM
MUM

3—continued
NUN
OHO
PAP
PEP
PIP
POP
PUP
SIS
SOS
TAT
TIT
TNT
TOT
TUT
WOW

4
BOOB

4—continued
DEED
KOOK
MA'AM
NOON
PEEP
POOP
SEES
TOOT

5
CIVIC
KAYAK
LEVEL
MADAM
MINIM
RADAR
REFER
ROTOR

5—continued
SAGAS
SEXES
SHAHS
SOLOS
TENET

6
DENNED
HALLAH
HANNAH
REDDER
TERRET
TUT-TUT

9
MALAYALAM
ROTAVATOR

BACK WORDS

2
AH – HA
AM – MA
AT – TA
EH – HE
HA – AH
HE – EH
HO – OH
IT – TI
MA – AM
MP – PM
NO – ON
OH – HO
ON – NO
PM – MP
TA – AT
TI – IT

3
AND – DNA

3—continued
BAD – DAB
BAG – GAB
BAN – NAB
BAT – TAB
BIN – NIB
BOG – GOB
BOY – YOB
BUD – DUB
BUN – NUB
BUS – SUB
BUT – TUB
DAB – BAD
DAM – MAD
DEW – WED
DIM – MID
DNA – AND
DOG – GOD
DOH – HOD

3—continued
DON – NOD
DOT – TOD
DUB – BUD
EEL – LEE
GAB – BAG
GAL – LAG
GAS – SAG
GEL – LEG
GOB – BOG
GOD – DOG
GOT – TOG
GUM – MUG
GUT – TUG
HOD – DOH
JAR – RAJ
LAG – GAL
LAP – PAL
LEE – EEL

3—continued
LEG – GEL
MAD – DAM
MAR – RAM
MAY – YAM
MID – DIM
MUG – GUM
NAB – BAN
NAP – PAN
NET – TEN
NIB – BIN
NIP – PIN
NIT – TIN
NOD – DON
NOT – TON
NOW – WON
NUB – BUN
PAL – LAP
PAN – NAP

3–continued

PAR – RAP
PAT – TAP
PAY – YAP
PER – REP
PIN – NIP
PIT – TIP
POT – TOP
PUS – SUP
RAJ – JAR
RAM – MAR
RAP – PAR
RAT – TAR
RAW – WAR
REP – PER
ROT – TOR
SAG – GAS
SUB – BUS
SUP – PUS
TAB – BAT
TAP – PAT
TAR – RAT
TEN – NET
TIN – NIT
TIP – PIT
TOD – DOT
TOG – GOT
TON – NOT
TOP – POT
TOR – ROT
TUB – BUT
TUG – GUT
WAR – RAW
WAY – YAW
WED – DEW
WON – NOW
YAM – MAY
YAP – PAY
YAW – WAY
YOB – BOY

4

ABLE – ELBA
ABUT – TUBA
BARD – DRAB
BATS – STAB
BRAG – GARB
BUNS – SNUB
BUTS – STUB
DEER – REED
DIAL – LAID
DOOM – MOOD
DOOR – ROOD
DRAB – BARD
DRAW – WARD
DRAY – YARD
DUAL – LAUD
EDAM – MADE
EDIT – TIDE
ELBA – ABLE
EMIR – RIME
EMIT – TIME

4–continued

ERGO – OGRE
ET AL – LATE
EVIL – LIVE
FLOG – GOLF
FLOW – WOLF
GALS – SLAG
GARB – BRAG
GNAT – TANG
GOLF – FLOG
GULP – PLUG
GUMS – SMUG
GUNS – SNUG
HOOP – POOH
KEEL – LEEK
KEEP – PEEK
LAID – DIAL
LAIR – RIAL
LATE – ET AL
LAUD – DUAL
LEEK – KEEL
LEER – REEL
LIAR – RAIL
LIVE – EVIL
LOOP – POOL
LOOT – TOOL
MACS – SCAM
MADE – EDAM
MAPS – SPAM
MAWS – SWAM
MEET – TEEM
MOOD – DOOM
MOOR – ROOM
NAPS – SPAN
NIPS – SPIN
NUTS – STUN
OGRE – ERGO
PALS – SLAP
PANS – SNAP
PART – TRAP
PAWS – SWAP
PEEK – KEEP
PETS – STEP
PINS – SNIP
PLUG – GULP
POOH – HOOP
POOL – LOOP
POTS – STOP
RAIL – LIAR
RAPS – SPAR
RATS – STAR
REED – DEER
REEL – LEER
RIAL – LAIR
RIME – EMIR
ROOD – DOOR
ROOM – MOOR
SCAM – MACS
SLAG – GALS
SLAP – PALS
SMUG – GUMS
SNAP – PANS

4–continued

SNIP – PINS
SNOT – TONS
SNUB – BUNS
SNUG – GUNS
SPAM – MAPS
SPAN – NAPS
SPAR – RAPS
SPAT – TAPS
SPAY – YAPS
SPIN – NIPS
SPIT – TIPS
SPOT – TOPS
STAB – BATS
STAR – RATS
STEP – PETS
STEW – WETS
STOP – POTS
STUB – BUTS
STUN – NUTS
SWAM – MAWS
SWAP – PAWS
SWAY – YAWS
SWOT – TOWS
TANG – GNAT
TAPS – SPAT
TEEM – MEET
TIDE – EDIT
TIME – EMIT
TIPS – SPIT
TONS – SNOT
TOOL – LOOT
TOPS – SPOT
TORT – TROT
TOWS – SWOT
TRAP – PART
TROT – TORT
TUBA – ABUT
WARD – DRAW
WETS – STEW
WOLF – FLOW
YAPS – SPAY
YARD – DRAY
YAWS – SWAY

5

ANNAM – MANNA
ATLAS – SALTA
CARES – SERAC
DARAF – FARAD
DECAL – LACED
DENIM – MINED
DEVIL – LIVED
FARAD – DARAF
FIRES – SERIF
KEELS – SLEEK
LACED – DECAL
LAGER – REGAL
LEPER – REPEL
LEVER – REVEL
LIVED – DEVIL
LOOPS – SPOOL

5–continued

MANNA – ANNAM
MINED – DENIM
PACER – RECAP
PARTS – STRAP
POOLS – SLOOP
PORTS – STROP
REBUT – TUBER
RECAP – PACER
REGAL – LAGER
REMIT – TIMER
REPEL – LEPER
REVEL – LEVER
SALTA – ATLAS
SERAC – CARES
SERIF – FIRES
SLEEK – KEELS
SLOOP – POOLS
SMART – TRAMS
SNIPS – SPINS
SPINS – SNIPS
SPOOL – LOOPS
SPOTS – STOPS
STOPS – SPOTS
STRAP – PARTS
STRAW – WARTS
STROP – PORTS
TIMER – REMIT
TRAMS – SMART
TUBER – REBUT
WARTS – STRAW

6

ANIMAL – LAMINA
DELIAN – NAILED
DENIER – REINED
DIAPER – REPAID
DRAWER – REWARD
HARRIS – SIRRAH
LAMINA – ANIMAL
LOOTER – RETOOL
NAILED – DELIAN
PUPILS – SLIP-UP
RECAPS – SPACER
REINED – DENIER
RENNET – TENNER
REPAID – DIAPER
RETOOL – LOOTER
REWARD – DRAWER
SERVES – SEVRES
SEVRES – SERVES
SIRRAH – HARRIS
SLIP-UP – PUPILS
SNOOPS – SPOONS
SPACER – RECAPS
SPOONS – SNOOPS
TENNER – RENNET

8

DESSERTS –
  STRESSED
STRESSED –
  DESSERTS

HOMOPHONES

ACCESSARY – ACCESSORY
ACCESSORY – ACCESSARY
AERIAL – ARIEL
AERIE – AIRY
AIL – ALE
AIR – AIRE, E'ER, ERE, EYRE, HEIR
AIRE – AIR, E'ER, ERE, EYRE, HEIR
AIRSHIP – HEIRSHIP
AIRY – AERIE
AISLE – I'LL, ISLE
AIT – EIGHT, ATE
ALE – AIL
ALL – AWL, ORLE
ALMS – ARMS
ALTAR – ALTER
ALTER – ALTAR
AMAH – ARMOUR
ANTE – ANTI
ANTI – ANTE
ARC – ARK
AREN'T – AUNT
ARES – ARIES
ARIEL – AERIAL
ARIES – ARES
ARK – ARC
ARMOUR – AMAH
ARMS – ALMS
ASCENT – ASSENT
ASSENT – ASCENT
ATE – AIT, EIGHT
AUK – ORC
AUNT – AREN'T
AURAL – ORAL
AUSTERE – OSTIA
AWAY – AWEIGH
AWE – OAR, O'ER, ORE
AWEIGH – AWAY
AWL – ALL, ORLE
AXEL – AXLE
AXLE – AXEL
AY – AYE, EYE, I
AYAH – IRE
AYE – AY, EYE, I
AYES – EYES
BAA – BAH, BAR
BAAL – BASLE
BAH – BAA, BAR
BAIL – BALE
BALE – BAIL
BALL – BAWL
BALM – BARM
BALMY – BARMY
BAR – BAA, BAH
BARE – BEAR
BARM – BALM

BARMY – BALMY
BARON – BARREN
BARREN – BARON
BASE – BASS
BASLE – BAAL
BASS – BASE
BAUD – BAWD, BOARD
BAWD – BAUD, BOARD
BAWL – BALL
BAY – BEY
BEACH – BEECH
BEAN – BEEN
BEAR – BARE
BEAT – BEET
BEATER – BETA
BEAU – BOH, BOW
BEECH – BEACH
BEEN – BEAN
BEER – BIER
BEET – BEAT
BEL – BELL, BELLE
BELL – BEL, BELLE
BELLE – BEL, BELL
BERRY – BURY
BERTH – BIRTH
BETA – BEATER
BEY – BAY
BHAI – BI, BUY, BY, BYE
BI – BHAI, BUY, BY, BYE
BIER – BEER
BIGHT – BITE, BYTE
BIRTH – BERTH
BITE – BIGHT, BYTE
BLEW – BLUE
BLUE – BLEW
BOAR – BOER, BOOR, BORE
BOARD – BAUD, BAWD
BOARDER – BORDER
BOART – BOUGHT
BOER – BOAR, BOOR, BORE
BOH – BEAU, BOW
BOLE – BOWL
BOLT – BOULT
BOOR – BOAR, BOER, BORE
BOOTIE – BOOTY
BOOTY – BOOTIE
BORDER – BOARDER
BORE – BOAR, BOER, BOOR
BORN – BORNE
BORNE – BORN
BOUGH – BOW
BOUGHT – BOART
BOULT – BOLT
BOW – BEAU, BOH
BOW – BOUGH
BOWL – BOLE
BOY – BUOY

BRAKE – BREAK
BREAD – BRED
BREAK – BRAKE
BRED – BREAD
BREDE – BREED, BREID
BREED – BREDE, BREID
BREID – BREDE, BREED
BRIDAL – BRIDLE
BRIDLE – BRIDAL
BROACH – BROOCH
BROOCH – BROACH
BUNION – BUNYAN
BUNYAN – BUNION
BUOY – BOY
BURGER – BURGHER
BURGHER – BURGER
BURY – BERRY
BUS – BUSS
BUSS – BUS
BUY – BHAI, BI, BY, BYE
BUYER – BYRE
BY – BHAI, BI, BUY, BYE
BYE – BHAI, BI, BUY, BY
BYRE – BUYER
BYTE – BIGHT, BITE
CACHE – CASH
CACHOU – CASHEW
CAIN – CANE, KAIN
CALL – CAUL
CALLAS – CALLOUS, CALLUS
CALLOUS – CALLAS, CALLUS
CALLUS – CALLAS, CALLOUS
CANAPÉ – CANOPY
CANE – CAIN, KAIN
CANOPY – CANAPÉ
CARAT – CARROT, KARAT
CARROT – CARAT, KARAT
CART – CARTE, KART
CARTE – CART, KART
CASH – CACHE
CASHEW – CACHOU
CASHMERE – KASHMIR
CAST – CASTE, KARST
CASTE – CAST, KARST
CAUGHT – COURT
CAUL – CALL
CAW – COR, CORE, CORPS
CEDAR – SEEDER
CEDE – SEED
CEIL – SEEL, SEAL
CELL – SELL, SZELL
CELLAR – SELLER
CENSER – CENSOR, SENSOR
CENSOR – CENSER, SENSOR
CENT – SCENT, SENT

CERE – SEAR, SEER
CEREAL – SERIAL
CESSION – SESSION
CHAW – CHORE
CHEAP – CHEEP
CHECK – CHEQUE, CZECH
CHEEP – CHEAP
CHEQUE – CHECK, CZECH
CHOIR – QUIRE
CHOLER – COLLAR
CHORD – CORD
CHORE – CHAW
CHOTT – SHOT, SHOTT
CHOU – SHOE, SHOO
CHOUGH – CHUFF
CHUFF – CHOUGH
CHUTE – SHOOT, SHUTE
CITE – SIGHT, SITE
CLACK – CLAQUE
CLAQUE – CLACK
CLIMB – CLIME
CLIME – CLIMB
COAL – COLE, KOHL
COARSE – CORSE, COURSE
COLE – COAL, KOHL
COLLAR – CHOLER
COLONEL – KERNEL
COLOUR – CULLER
COME – CUM
COMPLEMENTARY –
    COMPLIMENTARY
COMPLIMENTARY –
    COMPLEMENTARY
COO – COUP
COOP – COUPE
COR – CAW, CORE, CORPS
CORD – CHORD
CORE – CAW, COR, CORPS
CORNFLOUR –
    CORNFLOWER
CORNFLOWER –
    CORNFLOUR
CORPS – CAW, COR, CORE
CORSE – COARSE, COURSE
COUNCIL – COUNSEL
COUNSEL – COUNCIL
COUP – COO
COUPE – COOP
COURSE – COARSE, CORSE
COURT – CAUGHT
CREAK – CREEK
CREEK – CREAK
CULLER – COLOUR
CUM – COME
CURB – KERB
CURRANT – CURRENT
CURRENT – CURRANT
CYGNET – SIGNET
CYMBAL – SYMBOL
CZECH – CHECK, CHEQUE
DAM – DAMN
DAMN – DAM

DAW – DOOR, DOR
DAYS – DAZE
DAZE – DAYS
DEAR – DEER
DEER – DEAR
DESCENT – DISSENT
DESERT – DESSERT
DESSERT – DESERT
DEW – DUE
DINAH – DINER
DINE – DYNE
DINER – DINAH
DISSENT – DESCENT
DOE – DOH, DOUGH
DOH – DOE, DOUGH
DONE – DONNE, DUN
DONNE – DONE, DUN
DOOR – DAW, DOR
DOR – DAW, DOOR
DOST – DUST
DOUGH – DOE, DOH
DRAFT – DRAUGHT
DRAUGHT – DRAFT
DROOP – DRUPE
DRUPE – DROOP
DUAL – DUEL
DUCKS – DUX
DUE – DEW
DUEL – DUAL
DUN – DONE, DONNE
DUST – DOST
DUX – DUCKS
DYEING – DYING
DYING – DYEING
DYNE – DINE
EARN – URN
EATEN – ETON
E'ER – AIR, AIRE, ERE, EYRE,
    HEIR
EERIE – EYRIE
EIDER – IDA
EIGHT – AIT, ATE
EIRE – EYRA
ELATION – ILLATION
ELICIT – ILLICIT
ELUDE – ILLUDE
ELUSORY – ILLUSORY
EMERGE – IMMERGE
EMERSED – IMMERSED
EMERSION – IMMERSION
ERE – AIR, AIRE, E'ER, EYRE,
    HEIR
ERK – IRK
ERR – UR
ESTER – ESTHER
ESTHER – ESTER
ETON – EATEN
EWE – YEW, YOU
EYE – AY, AYE, I
EYED – I'D, IDE
EYELET – ISLET
EYES – AYES

EYRA – EIRE
EYRE – AIR, AIRE, E'ER, ERE,
    HEIR
EYRIE – EERIE
FA – FAR
FAIN – FANE, FEIGN
FAINT – FEIGNT
FAIR – FARE
FANE – FAIN, FEIGN
FAR – FA
FARE – FAIR
FARO – PHARAOH
FARTHER – FATHER
FATE – FÊTE
FATHER – FARTHER
FAUGH – FOR, FOUR, FORE
FAUN – FAWN
FAWN – FAUN
FAZE – PHASE
FEAT – FEET
FEET – FEAT
FEIGN – FAIN, FANE
FEIGNT – FAINT
FELLOE – FELLOW
FELLOW – FELLOE
FELT – VELD, VELDT
FETA – FETTER
FÊTE – FATE
FETTER – FETA
FEU – FEW, PHEW
FEW – FEU, PHEW
FIR – FUR
FISHER – FISSURE
FISSURE – FISHER
FIZZ – PHIZ
FLAIR – FLARE
FLARE – FLAIR
FLAW – FLOOR
FLEA – FLEE
FLEE – FLEA
FLEW – FLU, FLUE
FLOE – FLOW
FLOOR – FLAW
FLOUR – FLOWER
FLOW – FLOE
FLOWER – FLOUR
FLU – FLEW, FLUE
FLUE – FLEW, FLU
FOR – FAUGH, FOUR, FORE
FORE – FAUGH, FOR, FOUR
FORT – FOUGHT
FORTE – FORTY
FORTH – FOURTH
FORTY – FORTE
FOUGHT – FORT
FOUL – FOWL
FOUR – FAUGH, FOR, FORE
FOURTH – FORTH
FOWL – FOUL
FRIAR – FRIER
FRIER – FRIAR
FUR – FIR

GAIL – GALE
GAIT – GATE
GALE – GAIL
GALLOP – GALLUP
GALLUP – GALLOP
GAMBLE – GAMBOL
GAMBOL – GAMBLE
GATE – GAIT
GAWKY – GORKY
GENE – JEAN
GIN – JINN
GLADDEN – GLADDON
GLADDON – GLADDEN
GNASH – NASH
GNAT – NAT
GNAW – NOR
GORKY – GAWKY
GRATER – GREATER
GREATER – GRATER
GROAN – GROWN
GROWN – GROAN
HAE – HAY, HEH, HEY
HAIL – HALE
HAIR – HARE
HALE – HAIL
HALL – HAUL
HANDEL – HANDLE
HANDLE – HANDEL
HANGAR – HANGER
HANGER – HANGAR
HARE – HAIR
HART – HEART
HAUD – HOARD, HORDE
HAUL – HALL
HAW – HOARE, WHORE
HAY – HAE, HEH, HEY
HEAR – HERE
HEART – HART
HEH – HAE, HAY, HEY
HEIR – AIR, AIRE, E'ER, ERE, EYRE
HEIRSHIP – AIRSHIP
HERE – HEAR
HEROIN – HEROINE
HEROINE – HEROIN
HEW – HUE
HEY – HAE, HAY, HEH
HIE – HIGH
HIGH – HIE
HIGHER – HIRE
HIM – HYMN
HIRE – HIGHER
HO – HOE
HOAR – HAW, WHORE
HOARD – HAUD, HORDE
HOARSE – HORSE
HOE – HO
HOLE – WHOLE
HOO – WHO
HORDE – HAUD, HOARD
HORSE – HOARSE
HOUR – OUR

HOURS – OURS
HUE – HEW
HYMN – HIM
I – AY, AYE, EYE
I'D – EYED, IDE
IDA – EIDER
IDE – EYED, I'D
IDLE – IDOL
IDOL – IDLE
I'LL – AISLE, ISLE
ILLATION – ELATION
ILLICIT – ELICIT
ILLUDE – ELUDE
ILLUSORY – ELUSORY
IMMERGE – EMERGE
IMMERSED – EMERSED
IMMERSION – EMERSION
IN – INN
INCITE – INSIGHT
INDICT – INDITE
INDITE – INDICT
INN – IN
INSIGHT – INCITE
INSOLE – INSOUL
INSOUL – INSOLE
ION – IRON
IRE – AYAH
IRK – ERK
IRON – ION
ISLE – AISLE, I'LL
ISLET – EYELET
JAM – JAMB, JAMBE
JAMB – JAM, JAMBE
JAMBE – JAM, JAMB
JEAN – GENE
JINKS – JINX
JINN – GIN
JINX – JINKS
KAIN – CAIN, CANE
KARAT – CARAT, CARROT
KARST – CAST, CASTE
KART – CART, CARTE
KASHMIR – CASHMERE
KERB – CURB
KERNEL – COLONEL
KEW – KYU, QUEUE
KEY – QUAY
KNAVE – NAVE
KNEAD – NEED
KNEW – NEW, NU
KNIGHT – NIGHT
KNIGHTLY – NIGHTLY
KNIT – NIT
KNOW – NOH, NO
KNOWS – NOES, NOSE
KOHL – COAL, COLE
KYU – KEW, QUEUE
LACKER – LACQUER
LACQUER – LACKER
LAIN – LANE
LANCE – LAUNCE
LANE – LAIN

LAUD – LORD
LAUNCE – LANCE
LAW – LORE
LAY – LEI, LEY
LAYS – LAZE
LAZE – LAYS
LEAD – LED
LEAF – LIEF
LEAH – LEAR, LEER, LEHR
LEAK – LEEK
LEANT – LENT
LEAR – LEAH, LEER, LEHR
LED – LEAD
LEEK – LEAK
LEER – LEAH, LEAR, LEHR
LEHR – LEAH, LEAR, LEER
LEI – LAY, LEY
LEMAN – LEMON
LEMON – LEMAN
LENT – LEANT
LESSEN – LESSON
LESSON – LESSEN
LEY – LAY, LEI
LIAR – LYRE
LIEF – LEAF
LINCS – LINKS, LYNX
LINKS – LINCS, LYNX
LOAD – LODE
LOAN – LONE
LODE – LOAD
LONE – LOAN
LORD – LAUD
LORE – LAW
LUMBAR – LUMBER
LUMBER – LUMBAR
LYNX – LINCS, LINKS
LYRE – LIAR
MA – MAAR, MAR
MAAR – MA, MAR
MADE – MAID
MAID – MADE
MAIL – MALE
MAIN – MAINE, MANE
MAINE – MAIN, MANE
MAIZE – MAZE
MALE – MAIL
MALL – MAUL
MANE – MAIN, MAINE
MANNA – MANNER, MANOR
MANNER – MANNA, MANOR
MANOR – MANNA, MANNER
MAQUIS – MARQUEE
MAR – MA, MAAR
MARC – MARK, MARQUE
MARE – MAYOR
MARK – MARC, MARQUE
MARQUE – MARC, MARK
MARQUEE – MAQUIS
MAUL – MALL
MAW – MOR, MORE, MOOR
MAYOR – MARE
MAZE – MAIZE

397

MEAN – MESNE, MIEN
MEAT – MEET, METE
MEDAL – MEDDLE
MEDDLE – MEDAL
MEET – MEAT, METE
MESNE – MIEN, MEAN
METAL – METTLE
METE – MEAT, MEET
METTLE – METAL
MEWS – MUSE
MIEN – MESNE, MEAN
MIGHT – MITE
MINER – MINOR
MINOR – MINER
MITE – MIGHT
MOAN – MOWN
MOAT – MOTE
MOCHA – MOCKER
MOCKER – MOCHA
MOOR – MAW, MOR, MORE
MOOSE – MOUSSE
MOR – MAW, MORE, MOOR
MORE – MAW, MOR, MOOR
MORN – MOURN
MORNING – MOURNING
MOTE – MOAT
MOURN – MORN
MOURNING – MORNING
MOUSSE – MOOSE
MOWN – MOAN
MUSCLE – MUSSEL
MUSE – MEWS
MUSSEL – MUSCLE
NAE – NAY, NEAGH, NEIGH,
  NEY
NASH – GNASH
NAT – GNAT
NAUGHT – NOUGHT
NAVAL – NAVEL
NAVE – KNAVE
NAVEL – NAVAL
NAY – NAE, NEAGH, NEIGH,
  NEY
NEAGH – NAE, NAY, NEIGH,
  NEY
NEED – KNEAD
NEIGH – NAE, NAY, NEAGH,
  NEY
NEUK – NUKE
NEW – KNEW, NU
NEY – NAE, NAY, NEAGH,
  NEIGH
NIGH – NYE
NIGHT – KNIGHT
NIGHTLY – KNIGHTLY
NIT – KNIT
NO – KNOW, NOH
NOES – KNOWS, NOSE
NOH – KNOW, NO
NONE – NUN
NOR – GNAW
NOSE – KNOWS, NOES

NOUGHT – NAUGHT
NU – KNEW, NEW
NUKE – NEUK
NUN – NONE
NYE – NIGH
OAR – AWE, O'ER, ORE
O'ER – AWE, OAR, ORE
OFFA – OFFER
OFFER – OFFA
OH – OWE
ORAL – AURAL
ORC – AUK
ORE – AWE, OAR, O'ER
ORLE – ALL, AWL
OSTIA – AUSTERE
OUR – HOUR
OURS – HOURS
OUT – OWT
OVA – OVER
OVER – OVA
OWE – OH
OWT – OUT
PA – PAH, PAR, PARR, PAS
PACKED – PACT
PACT – PACKED
PAH – PA, PAR, PARR, PAS
PAIL – PALE
PAIR – PARE, PEAR
PALATE – PALETTE, PALLET
PALE – PAIL
PALETTE – PALATE, PALLET
PALLET – PALATE, PALETTE
PANDA – PANDER
PANDER – PANDA
PAR – PA, PAH, PARR, PAS
PARE – PEAR, PAIR
PARR – PA, PAH, PAR, PAS
PAS – PA, PAH, PAR, PARR
PAW – POOR, PORE, POUR
PAWKY – PORKY
PAWN – PORN
PEA – PEE
PEACE – PIECE
PEAK – PIQUE, PEAKE,
  PEEK, PEKE
PEAL – PEEL
PEAR – PARE, PAIR
PEARL – PURL
PEARLER – PURLER
PEDAL – PEDDLE
PEDDLE – PEDAL
PEE – PEA
PEEK – PEAK, PEAKE, PEKE,
  PIQUE
PEEL – PEAL
PEKE – PEAK, PEAKE, PEEK,
  PIQUE
PER – PURR
PETREL – PETROL
PETROL – PETREL
PHARAOH – FARO
PHASE – FAZE

PHEW – FEU, FEW
PHIZ – FIZZ
PI – PIE, PYE
PIE – PI, PYE
PIECE – PEACE
PILATE – PILOT
PILOT – PILATE
PIQUE – PEAK, PEAKE,
  PEEK, PEKE
PLACE – PLAICE
PLAICE – PLACE
PLAIN – PLANE
PLANE – PLAIN
POLE – POLL
POLL – POLE
POMACE – PUMICE
POMMEL – PUMMEL
POOR – PAW, PORE, POUR
POPULACE – POPULOUS
POPULOUS – POPULACE
PORE – PAW, POOR, POUR
PORKY – PAWKY
PORN – PAWN
POUR – PAW, POOR, PORE
PRAY – PREY
PREY – PRAY
PRINCIPAL – PRINCIPLE
PRINCIPLE – PRINCIPAL
PROFIT – PROPHET
PROPHET – PROFIT
PSALTER – SALTER
PUCKA – PUCKER
PUCKER – PUCKA
PUMICE – POMACE
PUMMEL – POMMEL
PURL – PEARL
PURLER – PEARLER
PURR – PER
PYE – PI, PIE
QUAY – KEY
QUEUE – KEW, KYU
QUIRE – CHOIR
RACK – WRACK
RACKET – RACQUET
RACQUET – RACKET
RAIN – REIGN, REIN
RAINS – REINS
RAISE – RASE
RAP – WRAP
RAPT – WRAPPED
RASE – RAISE
RAW – ROAR
READ – REDE, REED
RECK – WRECK
REDE – READ, REED
REED – READ, REDE
REEK – WREAK
REIGN – RAIN, REIN
REIN – RAIN, REIGN
REINS – RAINS
RENNES – WREN
RETCH – WRETCH

REVERE – REVERS
REVERS – REVERE
RHEUM – ROOM
RHEUMY – ROOMY
RHO – ROW, ROE
RHÔNE – ROAN, RONE
RIGHT – RITE, WRIGHT,
  WRITE
RING – WRING
RINGER – WRINGER
RITE – RIGHT, WRIGHT,
  WRITE
ROAM – ROME
ROAN – RHÔNE, RONE
ROAR – RAW
ROE – RHO, ROW
ROLE – ROLL
ROLL – ROLE
ROME – ROAM
RONE – RHÔNE, ROAN
ROOD – RUDE
ROOM – RHEUM
ROOMY – RHEUMY
ROOSE – RUSE
ROOT – ROUTE
RORT – WROUGHT
ROTE – WROTE
ROUGH – RUFF
ROUTE – ROOT
ROW – RHO, ROE
RUDE – ROOD
RUFF – ROUGH
RUNG – WRUNG
RUSE – ROOSE
RYE – WRY
SAIL – SALE
SAIN – SANE, SEINE
SALE – SAIL
SALTER – PSALTER
SANE – SAIN, SEINE
SAUCE – SOURCE
SAUT – SORT, SOUGHT
SAW – SOAR, SORE
SAWN – SORN
SCENE – SEEN
SCENT – CENT, SENT
SCULL – SKULL
SEAL – CEIL, SEEL
SEAM – SEEM
SEAR – CERE, SEER
SEED – CEDE
SEEDER – CEDAR
SEEK – SEIK, SIKH
SEEL – CEIL, SEAL
SEEM – SEAM
SEEN – SCENE
SEER – CERE, SEAR
SEIK – SEEK, SIKH
SEINE – SAIN, SANE
SELL – CELL, SZELL
SELLER – CELLAR

SENSOR – CENSER,
  CENSOR
SENT – CENT, SCENT
SERF – SURF
SERGE – SURGE
SERIAL – CEREAL
SESSION – CESSION
SEW – SO, SOH, SOW
SEWN – SONE, SOWN
SHAKE – SHEIK
SHEIK – SHAKE
SHIER – SHYER, SHIRE
SHIRE – SHIER, SHYER
SHOE – CHOU, SHOO
SHOO – CHOU, SHOE
SHOOT – SHUTE, CHUTE
SHOT – SHOTT, CHOTT
SHOTT – SHOT, CHOTT
SHUTE – SHOOT, CHUTE
SHYER – SHIER, SHIRE
SIGHT – CITE, SITE
SIGN – SYN
SIGNET – CYGNET
SIKH – SEEK, SEIK
SIOUX – SOU
SITE – CITE, SIGHT
SKULL – SCULL
SKY – SKYE
SKYE – SKY
SLAY – SLEIGH
SLEAVE – SLEEVE
SLEEVE – SLEAVE
SLEIGH – SLAY
SLOE – SLOW
SLOW – SLOE
SO – SEW, SOH, SOW
SOAR – SAW, SORE
SOH – SEW, SO, SOW
SOLE – SOUL
SOME – SUM
SON – SUN, SUNN
SONE – SEWN, SOWN
SONNY – SUNNI, SUNNY
SORE – SAW, SOAR
SORN – SAWN
SORT – SAUT, SOUGHT
SOU – SIOUX
SOUGHT – SAUT, SORT
SOUL – SOLE
SOURCE – SAUCE
SOW – SEW, SO, SOH
SOWN – SEWN, SONE
STAIR – STARE
STAKE – STEAK
STALK – STORK
STARE – STAIR
STEAK – STAKE
STEAL – STEEL
STEEL – STEAL
STOREY – STORY
STORK – STALK
STORY – STOREY

SUITE – SWEET
SUM – SOME
SUN – SON, SUNN
SUNDAE – SUNDAY
SUNDAY – SUNDAE
SUNN – SON, SUN
SUNNI – SONNY, SUNNY
SUNNY – SONNY, SUNNI
SURF – SERF
SURGE – SERGE
SWAT – SWOT
SWEET – SUITE
SWOT – SWAT
SYMBOL – CYMBAL
SYN – SIGN
SZELL – CELL, SELL
TACIT – TASSET
TAI – TAILLE, THAI, TIE
TAIL – TALE
TAILLE – TAI, THAI, TIE
TALE – TAIL
TALK – TORC, TORQUE
TARE – TEAR
TASSET – TACIT
TAUGHT – TAUT, TORT,
  TORTE
TAUT – TAUGHT, TORT,
  TORTE
TEA – TEE, TI
TEAM – TEEM
TEAR – TARE
TEE – TEA, TI
TEEM – TEAM
TENNER – TENOR
TENOR – TENNER
TERNE – TURN
THAI – TAI, TAILLE, TIE
THAW – THOR
THEIR – THERE, THEY'RE
THERE – THEIR, THEY'RE
THEY'RE – THEIR, THERE
THOR – THAW
THREW – THROUGH, THRU
THROE – THROW
THRONE – THROWN
THROUGH – THREW, THRU
THROW – THROE
THROWN – THRONE
THRU – THREW, THROUGH
THYME – TIME
TI – TEA, TEE
TIC – TICK
TICK – TIC
TIDE – TIED
TIE – TAI, TAILLE, THAI
TIED – TIDE
TIER – TIRE, TYRE
TIGHTEN – TITAN
TIMBER – TIMBRE
TIMBRE – TIMBER
TIME – THYME
TIRE – TIER, TYRE

TITAN – TIGHTEN
TO – TOO, TWO
TOAD – TOED, TOWED
TOE – TOW
TOED – TOAD, TOWED
TOO – TO, TWO
TOR – TORE
TORC – TALK, TORQUE
TORE – TOR
TORQUE – TALK, TORC
TORT – TAUGHT, TAUT, TORTE
TORTE – TAUGHT, TAUT, TORT
TOW – TOE
TOWED – TOAD, TOED
TROOP – TROUPE
TROUPE – TROOP
TUNA – TUNER
TUNER – TUNA
TURN – TERNE
TWO – TO, TOO
TYRE – TIER, TIRE
UR – ERR
URN – EARN
VAIL – VALE, VEIL
VAIN – VANE, VEIN
VALE – VAIL, VEIL
VANE – VAIN, VEIN
VEIL – VAIL, VALE
VEIN – VAIN, VANE
VELD – FELT, VELDT
VELDT – FELT, VELD
WAE – WAY, WHEY
WAIL – WHALE
WAIN – WANE, WAYNE
WAIST – WASTE
WAIT – WEIGHT
WAIVE – WAVE
WANE – WAIN, WAYNE
WAR – WAUGH, WAW, WORE

WARE – WEAR, WHERE
WARN – WORN
WASTE – WAIST
WATT – WHAT, WOT
WAUGH – WAR, WAW, WORE
WAVE – WAIVE
WAW – WAR, WAUGH, WORE
WAY – WAE, WHEY
WAYNE – WAIN, WANE
WEAK – WEEK
WEAKLY – WEEKLY
WEAR – WARE, WHERE
WEAVE – WE'VE
WE'D – WEED
WEED – WE'D
WEEK – WEAK
WEEKLY – WEAKLY
WEEL – WE'LL, WHEAL, WHEEL
WEIGHT – WAIT
WE'LL – WEEL, WHEAL, WHEEL
WEN – WHEN
WERE – WHIRR
WE'VE – WEAVE
WHALE – WAIL
WHAT – WATT, WOT
WHEAL – WEEL, WE'LL, WHEEL
WHEEL – WEEL, WE'LL, WHEAL
WHEN – WEN
WHERE – WARE, WEAR
WHEY – WAE, WAY
WHICH – WITCH
WHINE – WINE
WHIRR – WERE
WHITE – WIGHT, WITE
WHITHER – WITHER
WHO – HOO
WHOA – WO, WOE

WHOLE – HOLE
WHORE – HAW, HOAR
WIGHT – WHITE, WITE
WINE – WHINE
WITCH – WHICH
WITE – WHITE, WIGHT
WITHER – WHITHER
WO – WHOA, WOE
WOE – WHOA, WO
WORE – WAR, WAUGH, WAW
WORN – WARN
WOT – WATT, WHAT
WRACK – RACK
WRAP – RAP
WRAPPED – RAPT
WREAK – REEK
WRECK – RECK
WREN – RENNES
WRETCH – RETCH
WRIGHT – RIGHT, RITE, WRITE
WRING – RING
WRINGER – RINGER
WRITE – RIGHT, RITE, WRIGHT
WROTE – ROTE
WROUGHT – RORT
WRUNG – RUNG
WRY – RYE
YAW – YORE, YOUR
YAWS – YOURS
YEW – EWE, YOU
YOKE – YOLK
YOLK – YOKE
YORE – YAW, YOUR
YOU – EWE, YEW
YOU'LL – YULE
YOUR – YAW, YORE
YOURS – YAWS
YULE – YOU'LL

TWO-WORD PHRASES

FIRST WORD

ABERDEEN – ANGUS, TERRIER
ABLE – BODIED, RATING, SEAMAN
ABSOLUTE – ALCOHOL, HUMIDITY, JUDGMENT, MAGNITUDE, MAJORITY, MONARCHY, MUSIC, PITCH, TEMPERATURE, THRESHOLD, UNIT, VALUE, ZERO
ABSTRACT – EXPRESSIONISM, NOUN
ACCESS – ROAD, TIME
ACCOMMODATION – ADDRESS, BILL, LADDER, PLATFORM
ACHILLES – HEEL, TENDON
ACID – DROP, RAIN, ROCK, SOIL, TEST, VALUE

ACT – AS, FOR, ON, OUT, UP
ACTION – COMMITTEE, GROUP, PAINTING, POTENTIAL, REPLAY, STATIONS
ACTIVE – CENTRE, LIST, SERVICE, TRANSPORT, VOCABULARY, VOLCANO
ADMIRALTY – BOARD, HOUSE, ISLANDS, MILE, RANGE
ADVANCE – BOOKING, COPY, GUARD, MAN, NOTICE, POLL, RATIO
AEOLIAN – DEPOSITS, HARP, ISLANDS, MODE
AFRICAN – LILY, MAHOGANY, TIME, VIOLET
AGONY – AUNT, COLUMN
AIR – ALERT, BAG, BED, BLADDER, BRAKE, BRIDGE, COMMODORE, CONDITIONING, CORRIDOR, COVER,

CURTAIN, CUSHION, CYLINDER, DAM, EMBOLISM, FORCE, GAS, GUN, HARDENING, HOLE, HOSTESS, JACKET, LETTER, MAIL, MARSHAL, MASS, MILE, OFFICER, PLANT, POCKET, POWER, PUMP, RAID, RIFLE, SAC, SCOOP, SCOUT, SHAFT, SHOT, SOCK, SPRAY, SPRING, STATION, TERMINAL, TRAFFIC, TURBINE, VALVE, VICE-MARSHAL

ALL – BLACK, CLEAR, FOURS, HAIL, IN, ONE, OUT, RIGHT, SQUARE, THERE, TOLD

ALPHA – CENTAURI, HELIX, IRON, PARTICLE, PRIVATIVE, RAY, RHYTHM

ALTAR – BOY, CLOTH, -PIECE

AMERICAN – ALOE, CHAMELEON, CHEESE, CLOTH, EAGLE, FOOTBALL, INDIAN, PLAN, REVOLUTION, SAMOA, WAKE

ANCHOR – MAN, PLATE, RING

ANCIENT – GREEK, HISTORY, LIGHTS, MONUMENT

ANGEL – CAKE, DUST, FALLS, FOOD, SHARK

ANGLE – BRACKET, DOZER, IRON, PLATE

ANIMAL – HUSBANDRY, KINGDOM, MAGNETISM, RIGHTS, SPIRITS, STARCH

ANT – BEAR, BIRD, COW, EATER, HEAP, HILL

APPLE – BLIGHT, BOX, BRANDY, BUTTER, GREEN, ISLE, JACK, MAGGOT, POLISHER, SAUCE

ARCTIC – CHAR, CIRCLE, FOX, HARE, OCEAN, TERN, WILLOW

ART – DECO, FORM, NOUVEAU, PAPER

ARTIFICIAL – INSEMINATION, INTELLIGENCE, RESPIRATION

ASH – BLOND, CAN, WEDNESDAY

ATOMIC – AGE, CLOCK, COCKTAIL, ENERGY, HEAT, MASS, NUMBER, PILE, POWER, STRUCTURE, THEORY, VOLUME, WEIGHT

AUTOMATIC – CAMERA, PILOT, REPEAT, TRANSMISSION, TYPESETTING

BABY – BOOM, BUGGY, CARRIAGE, GRAND, SNATCHER, TALK, TOOTH

BACK – BOILER, BURNER, COUNTRY, DOOR, DOWN, END, LIGHT, LIST, MARKER, MATTER, OUT, PASSAGE, PAY, REST, ROOM, SEAT, STRAIGHT, UP, YARD

BAD – BLOOD, FAITH, LANDS, NEWS

BALL – BEARING, BOY, COCK, GAME, VALVE

BANANA – OIL, REPUBLIC, SKIN, SPLIT

BANK – ACCEPTANCE, ACCOUNT, ANNUITIES, BILL, CARD, CLERK, DISCOUNT, HOLIDAY, MANAGER, ON, RATE, STATEMENT

BAR – BILLIARDS, CHART, CODE, DIAGRAM, FLY, GIRL, GRAPH, LINE, MITZVAH, SINISTER

BARLEY – SUGAR, WATER, WINE

BARN – DANCE, DOOR, OWL, SWALLOW

BASE – LOAD, METAL, RATE

BASKET – CASE, CHAIR, HILT, MAKER, WEAVE

BATH – BUN, CHAIR, CHAP, CUBE, OLIVER, SALTS, STONE

BATTLE – CRUISER, CRY, FATIGUE, ROYAL

BAY – LEAF, LYNX, RUM, STREET, TREE, WINDOW

BEACH – BALL, BOYS, BUGGY, FLEA, PLUM

BEAR – DOWN, GARDEN, HUG, OFF, OUT, UP, WITH

BEAUTY – QUEEN, SALON, SLEEP, SPOT

BED – JACKET, LINEN

BELL – BRONZE, BUOY, GLASS, HEATHER, JAR, MAG-PIE, METAL, MOTH, PULL, PUNCH, PUSH, SHEEP, TENT

BELLY – DANCE, FLOP, LANDING, LAUGH

BERMUDA – GRASS, RIG, SHORTS, TRIANGLE

BEST – BOY, END, GIRL, MAN, SELLER

BICYCLE – CHAIN, CLIP, PUMP

BIG – APPLE, BAND, BANG, BEN, BERTHA, BROTHER, BUSINESS, CHEESE, CHIEF, DEAL, DIPPER, END, SCREEN, SHOT, STICK, TIME, TOP, WHEEL

BINARY – CODE, DIGIT, FISSION, FORM, NOTATION, NUMBER, STAR, WEAPON

BIRD – CALL, CHERRY, DOG, PEPPER, SPIDER, STRIKE, TABLE

BIRTH – CERTIFICATE, CONTROL, RATE

BIRTHDAY – HONOURS, SUIT

BIT – PART, RATE, SLICE

BITTER – APPLE, END, LAKES, ORANGE, PRINCIPLE

BLACK – ART, BEAN, BEAR, BEETLE, BELT, BILE, BODY, BOOK, BOTTOM, BOX, COUNTRY, DEATH, DIAMOND, ECONOMY, EYE, FLY, FOREST, FRIAR, FROST, HILLS, HOLE, ICE, MAGIC, MARIA, MARK, MARKET, MASS, MONK, MOUNTAINS, PANTHER, PEPPER, PRINCE, PUDDING, ROD, ROT, SEA, SHEEP, SPOT, SWAN, TIE, TREACLE, VELVET, WATCH, WIDOW

BLANK – CARTRIDGE, CHEQUE, ENDORSEMENT, VERSE

BLANKET – BATH, FINISH, STITCH

BLIND – ALLEY, DATE, FREDDIE, GUT, SNAKE, SPOT, STAGGERS, STAMPING

BLISTER – BEETLE, COPPER, PACK, RUST

BLOCK – DIAGRAM, IN, LETTER, OUT, PRINTING, RELEASE, SAMPLING, TIN, VOTE

BLOOD – BANK, BATH, BROTHER, CELL, COUNT, DONOR, FEUD, FLUKE, GROUP, HEAT, MONEY, ORANGE, POISONING, PRESSURE, PUDDING, RED, RELATION, SPORT, TEST, TYPE, VESSEL

BLUE – BABY, BAG, BILLY, BLOOD, CHEESE, CHIP, DEVILS, ENSIGN, FUNK, GUM, JAY, MOON, MOUNTAINS, MURDER, NILE, PENCIL, PETER, RIBAND, RIBBON, VEIN

BOARDING – HOUSE, OUT, SCHOOL

BOAT – DECK, DRILL, NECK, PEOPLE, RACE, TRAIN

BOBBY – CALF, PIN, SOCKS

BODY – BLOW, BUILDING, CAVITY, CORPORATE, IMAGE, LANGUAGE, POPPING, SHOP, SNATCHER, STOCKING, WARMER

BOG – ASPHODEL, COTTON, DEAL, DOWN, IN, MOSS, MYRTLE, OAK, ORCHID, RUSH, STANDARD

BON – MOT, TON, VIVANT, VOYAGE

BONE – ASH, CHINA, IDLE, MEAL, OIL, UP

BOOBY – HATCH, PRIZE, TRAP

BOOK – CLUB, END, IN, INTO, OUT, SCORPION, TOKEN, UP

BOTTLE – GOURD, GREEN, OUT, PARTY, TREE, UP

BOTTOM – DRAWER, END, HOUSE, LINE, OUT

BOW – LEGS, OUT, TIE, WINDOW

BOWLING – ALLEY, CREASE, GREEN

BOX – CAMERA, COAT, ELDER, GIRDER, JELLYFISH, NUMBER, OFFICE, PLEAT, SEAT, SPANNER, SPRING

BRAIN – CORAL, DEATH, DRAIN, FEVER, STEM, WAVE

BRAKE – BAND, DRUM, FLUID, HORSEPOWER, LIGHT, LINING, PARACHUTE, SHOE, VAN

BRAND – IMAGE, LEADER, NAME

BRANDY – BOTTLE, BUTTER, SNAP

TWO-WORD PHRASES

BRASS – BAND, FARTHING, HAT, NECK, RUBBING, TACKS

BREAK – DANCE, DOWN, EVEN, IN, INTO, OFF, OUT, THROUGH, UP, WITH

BRING – ABOUT, DOWN, FORWARD, IN, OFF, ON, OUT, OVER, ROUND, TO, UP

BRISTOL – BOARD, CHANNEL, FASHION

BROAD – ARROW, BEAN, CHURCH, GAUGE, JUMP, SEAL

BROWN – BEAR, BOMBER, FAT, OWL, PAPER, RICE, SHIRT, SNAKE, STUDY, SUGAR

BRUSSELS – CARPET, LACE, SPROUT

BUBBLE – BATH, CAR, CHAMBER, FLOAT, GUM, MEMORY, PACK

BUCK – FEVER, RABBIT, UP

BUILDING – BLOCK, LINE, PAPER, SOCIETY

BULL – MASTIFF, NOSE, RUN, SESSION, SNAKE, TERRIER, TONGUE, TROUT

BURNT – ALMOND, OFFERING, SHALE, SIENNA, UMBER

BUS – BOY, LANE, SHELTER, STOP

BUTTER – BEAN, MUSLIN, UP

BUZZ – BOMB, OFF, SAW, WORD

CABBAGE – BUG, LETTUCE, MOTH, PALM, PALMETTO, ROSE, TREE, WHITE

CABIN – BOY, CLASS, CRUISER, FEVER

CABLE – CAR, RAILWAY, RELEASE, STITCH, TELEVISION

CALL – ALARM, BOX, DOWN, FORTH, GIRL, IN, LOAN, MONEY, NUMBER, OFF, OUT, RATE, SIGN, SLIP, UP

CAMP – DAVID, FOLLOWER, MEETING, OVEN, SITE

CANARY – CREEPER, GRASS, ISLANDS, SEED, YELLOW

CANTERBURY – BELL, LAMB, PILGRIMS

CAPE – BUFFALO, CART, COD, COLONY, COLOURED, DOCTOR, DUTCH, FLATS, GOOSEBERRY, HORN, JASMINE, PENINSULA, PIGEON, PRIMROSE, PROVINCE, SPARROW, TOWN, VERDE, YORK

CAPITAL – ACCOUNT, ALLOWANCE, ASSETS, EXPENDITURE, GAIN, GOODS, LEVY, MARKET, PUNISHMENT, SHIP, STOCK, SURPLUS

CARD – FILE, INDEX, PUNCH, READER, VOTE

CARDINAL – BEETLE, FLOWER, NUMBER, POINTS, SPIDER, VIRTUES

CARPET – BEETLE, KNIGHT, MOTH, PLOT, SHARK, SLIPPER, SNAKE, TILES

CARRIAGE – BOLT, CLOCK, DOG, LINE, TRADE

CARRIER – BAG, PIGEON, WAVE

CARRY – AWAY, BACK, FORWARD, OFF, ON, OUT, OVER, THROUGH

CARTRIDGE – BELT, CLIP, PAPER, PEN

CASH – CROP, DESK, DISCOUNT, DISPENSER, FLOW, IN, LIMIT, RATIO, REGISTER, UP

CAST – ABOUT, BACK, DOWN, IRON, ON, OUT, STEEL, UP

CAT – BURGLAR, DOOR, HOLE, LITTER, RIG, SCANNER

CATCH – BASIN, CROP, ON, OUT, PHRASE, PIT, POINTS, UP

CAULIFLOWER – CHEESE, EAR

CENTRE – BIT, FORWARD, HALF, PUNCH, SPREAD, THREE-QUARTER

CHAIN – DRIVE, GANG, GRATE, LETTER, LIGHTNING, MAIL, PRINTER, REACTION, RULE, SAW, SHOT, STITCH, STORE

CHAMBER – COUNSEL, MUSIC, ORCHESTRA, ORGAN, POT

CHARGE – ACCOUNT, DENSITY, HAND, NURSE, SHEET

CHEESE – CUTTER, MITE, SKIPPER, STRAW

CHICKEN – BREAST, FEED, LOUSE, OUT, WIRE

CHILD – ABUSE, BENEFIT, CARE, GUIDANCE, LABOUR, MINDER

CHIMNEY – BREAST, CORNER, STACK, SWALLOW, SWEEP, SWIFT

CHINA – ASTER, BARK, CLAY, INK, ROSE, SEA, TREE

CHINESE – BLOCK, CABBAGE, CHEQUERS, CHIPPENDALE, EMPIRE, GOOSEBERRY, INK, LANTERN, LEAVES, PUZZLE, WALL, WAX, WHITE, WINDLASS

CHIP – BASKET, HEATER, IN, LOG, PAN, SHOT

CHRISTMAS – BEETLE, BOX, CACTUS, CARD, DISEASE, EVE, ISLAND, PUDDING, ROSE, STOCKING, TREE

CIGARETTE – CARD, END, HOLDER, LIGHTER, PAPER

CIRCUIT – BINDING, BOARD, BREAKER, JUDGE, RIDER, TRAINING

CITY – BLUES, COMPANY, DESK, EDITOR, FATHER, HALL, MANAGER, PLANNING, SLICKER

CIVIL – DEFENCE, DISOBEDIENCE, ENGINEER, LAW, LIBERTY, LIST, MARRIAGE, RIGHTS, SERVANT, SERVICE, WAR

CLAW – BACK, HAMMER, HATCHET, OFF, SETTING

CLOCK – GOLF, OFF, ON, UP

CLOSE – CALL, COMPANY, DOWN, HARMONY, IN, OUT, PUNCTUATION, QUARTERS, SEASON, SHAVE, WITH

CLOSED – BOOK, CHAIN, CIRCUIT, CORPORATION, GAME, PRIMARY, SCHOLARSHIP, SENTENCE, SET, SHOP

CLOTHES – MOTH, PEG, POLE, PROP

CLUB – FOOT, HAND, MOSS, ROOT, SANDWICH

COAL – GAS, HEAVER, HOLE, MEASURES, OIL, POT, SACK, SCUTTLE, TAR, TIT

COCONUT – BUTTER, ICE, MATTING, OIL, PALM, SHY

COFFEE – BAG, BAR, CUP, HOUSE, MILL, MORNING, NUT, SHOP, TABLE, TREE

COLD – CALL, CHISEL, CREAM, CUTS, DUCK, FEET, FRAME, FRONT, SHOULDER, SNAP, SORE, STORAGE, SWEAT, TURKEY, WAR, WARRIOR, WAVE, WORK

COLLECTIVE – AGREEMENT, BARGAINING, FARM, FRUIT, NOUN, OWNERSHIP, SECURITY, UNCONSCIOUS

COLORADO – BEETLE, DESERT, SPRINGS

COLOUR – BAR, CODE, CONTRAST, FILTER, GUARD, INDEX, LINE, PHASE, SCHEME, SERGEANT, SUPPLEMENT, TEMPERATURE

COME – ABOUT, ACROSS, ALONG, AT, AWAY, BETWEEN, BY, FORWARD, IN, INTO, OF, OFF, OUT, OVER, ROUND, THROUGH, TO, UP, UPON

COMIC – OPERA, STRIP

COMMAND – GUIDANCE, MODULE, PAPER, PERFORMANCE, POST

COMMERCIAL – ART, BANK, COLLEGE, PAPER, TRAVELLER, VEHICLE

COMMON – COLD, DENOMINATOR, ENTRANCE, ERA, FACTOR, FEE, FRACTION, GOOD, GROUND, KNOWLEDGE, LAW, MARKET, NOUN, ROOM, SENSE, STOCK, TIME

COMMUNITY – CARE, CENTRE, CHEST, SERVICE, SINGING

COMPOUND – EYE, FLOWER, FRACTION, FRACTURE, INTEREST, LEAF, NUMBER, SENTENCE, TIME

CON – AMORE, BRIO, DOLORE, ESPRESSIONE, FUOCO, MAN, MOTO, ROD, SORDINO, SPIRITO, TRICK

CONTINENTAL – BREAKFAST, CLIMATE, DIVIDE, DRIFT, QUILT, SHELF, SYSTEM

CORAL – FERN, REEF, SEA, SNAKE, TREE

CORN – BORER, BREAD, BUNTING, DOLLY, EXCHANGE, FACTOR, LAWS, LILY, MARIGOLD, MEAL, OIL, PONE, POPPY, ROSE, ROW, SALAD, SHOCK, SHUCK, SILK, WHISKY

CORONA – AUSTRALIS, BOREALIS, DISCHARGE

COTTAGE – CHEESE, FLAT, HOSPITAL, INDUSTRY, LOAF, PIANO, PIE

COTTON – BELT, BUSH, CAKE, CANDY, FLANNEL, GRASS, ON, PICKER, SEDGE, STAINER, TO, WASTE, WOOL

COUGH – DROP, MIXTURE, UP

COUNTRY – CLUB, CODE, COUSIN, DANCE, HOUSE, MUSIC, SEAT

COURT – CARD, CIRCULAR, DRESS, MARTIAL, ROLL, SHOE

COVER – CROP, GIRL, NOTE, POINT, VERSION

CRASH – BARRIER, DIVE, HELMET, OUT, PAD

CREAM – CHEESE, CRACKER, PUFF, SAUCE, SODA, TEA

CREDIT – ACCOUNT, CARD, LINE, RATING, SQUEEZE, STANDING

CROCODILE – BIRD, CLIP, RIVER, TEARS

CRYSTAL – BALL, GAZING, MICROPHONE, PALACE, PICK-UP, SET, VIOLET

CUCKOO – BEE, CLOCK, SHRIKE, SPIT

CURTAIN – CALL, LECTURE, SPEECH, WALL

CUSTARD – APPLE, PIE, POWDER

CUT – ACROSS, ALONG, DOWN, GLASS, IN, OFF, OUT, STRING, UP

CUTTY – GRASS, SARK, STOOL

DANISH – BLUE, LOAF, PASTRY

DARK – AGES, CONTINENT, GLASSES, HORSE, LANTERN, REACTION, STAR

DAVY – JONES, LAMP

DAY – BED, LILY, NAME, NURSERY, RELEASE, RETURN, ROOM, SCHOOL, SHIFT, TRIP

DE – FACTO, FIDE, LUXE, PROFUNDIS, RIGUEUR, TROP

DEAD – BEAT, CENTRE, DUCK, END, FINISH, HAND, HEART, HEAT, LETTER, LOSS, MARCH, SEA, SET, WEIGHT

DEATH – ADDER, CAP, CELL, CERTIFICATE, DUTY, GRANT, KNELL, MASK, PENALTY, RATE, RATTLE, RAY, ROW, SEAT, VALLEY, WARRANT, WISH

DECIMAL – CLASSIFICATION, CURRENCY, FRACTION, PLACE, POINT, SYSTEM

DECK – CHAIR, HAND, OVER, TENNIS

DENTAL – CLINIC, FLOSS, HYGIENE, HYGIENIST, NURSE, PLAQUE, SURGEON

DESERT – BOOTS, COOLER, ISLAND, LYNX, OAK, PEA, RAT, SOIL

DIAMOND – ANNIVERSARY, BIRD, JUBILEE, POINT, SNAKE, WEDDING, WILLOW

DINNER – JACKET, LADY, SERVICE

DIPLOMATIC – BAG, CORPS, IMMUNITY, SERVICE

DIRECT – ACCESS, ACTION, EVIDENCE, LABOUR, METHOD, OBJECT, QUESTION, SPEECH

DISC – BRAKE, FLOWER, HARROW, JOCKEY, PLOUGH, WHEEL

DISPATCH – BOX, CASE, RIDER

DOG – BISCUIT, BOX, COLLAR, DAYS, FENNEL, HANDLER, LATIN, PADDLE, ROSE, STAR, TAG, VIOLET

DONKEY – DERBY, ENGINE, JACKET, VOTE

DOUBLE – AGENT, BACK, BAR, BASS, BASSOON, BILL, BOND, CHIN, CREAM, CROSS, DUTCH, ENTENDRE, ENTRY, EXPOSURE, FAULT, FIRST, GLAZING, GLOUCESTER, KNIT, KNITTING, NEGATION, NEGATIVE, PNEUMONIA, STANDARD, TAKE, TALK, TIME, UP

DOWN – PAYMENT, TIME, UNDER

DRAWING – BOARD, CARD, PIN, ROOM

DRESS – CIRCLE, COAT, DOWN, PARADE, REHEARSAL, SHIELD, SHIRT, SUIT, UNIFORM, UP

DRESSING – CASE, GOWN, ROOM, STATION, TABLE

DROP – AWAY, CANNON, CURTAIN, FORGE, GOAL, HAMMER, KICK, LEAF, OFF, SCONE, SHOT, TANK

DRUM – BRAKE, MAJOR, MAJORETTE, OUT, UP

DRY – BATTERY, CELL, DISTILLATION, DOCK, ICE, MARTINI, MEASURE, NURSE, OUT, ROT, RUN, UP

DUST – BOWL, COAT, COVER, DEVIL, DOWN, JACKET, SHOT, STORM

DUTCH – AUCTION, BARN, CAP, CHEESE, COURAGE, DOLL, DOOR, ELM, MEDICINE, OVEN, TREAT, UNCLE

EAR – LOBE, PIERCING, SHELL, TRUMPET

EARLY – BIRD, CLOSING, WARNING

EARTH – CLOSET, MOTHER, PILLAR, RETURN, SCIENCE, UP, WAX

EASTER – CACTUS, EGG, ISLAND, LILY

EASY – CHAIR, GAME, MEAT, MONEY, STREET

EGG – CUP, ROLL, SLICE, SPOON, TIMER, TOOTH, WHITE

ELECTRIC – BLANKET, BLUE, CHAIR, CHARGE, CONSTANT, CURRENT, EEL, EYE, FIELD, FIRE, FURNACE, GUITAR, HARE, NEEDLE, ORGAN, POTENTIAL, RAY, SHOCK, STORM

ELEPHANT – BIRD, GRASS, SEAL, SHREW

EVENING – CLASS, DRESS, PRIMROSE, STAR

EX – CATHEDRA, DIVIDEND, GRATIA, LIBRIS, OFFICIO

EYE – CONTACT, DOG, RHYME, SHADOW, SOCKET, SPLICE

FACE – CLOTH, OUT, PACK, POWDER, VALUE

FAIR – COPY, GAME, ISLE, PLAY, RENT, SEX

FAIRY – CYCLE, GODMOTHER, LIGHTS, PENGUIN, RING, SHRIMP, SWALLOW, TALE

FALL – ABOUT, AMONG, AWAY, BACK, BEHIND, DOWN, FOR, GUY, IN, OFF, ON, OVER, THROUGH, TO

FALSE – ALARM, COLOURS, DAWN, IMPRISONMENT, PRETENCES, STEP, TEETH

FAMILY – ALLOWANCE, BENEFIT, BIBLE, CIRCLE, DOCTOR, MAN, NAME, PLANNING, SKELETON, TREE

FAN – BELT, DANCE, HEATER, MAIL, VAULTING

FANCY – DRESS, GOODS, MAN, WOMAN

FAST – FOOD, LANE, MOTION, TALK

FATHER – CHRISTMAS, CONFESSOR, TIME

FIELD – ARMY, ARTILLERY, BATTERY, CENTRE, DAY, EMISSION, EVENT, GLASSES, HOSPITAL, MARSHAL, OFFICER, SPORTS, STUDY, TRIP, WORK

FIGURE – ON, OUT, SKATING

FILM – LIBRARY, PACK, SET, STAR, STRIP

FILTER – BED, OUT, PAPER, PRESS, PUMP, TIP

TWO-WORD PHRASES

FINGER – BOWL, PAINTING, POST, WAVE

FIRE – ALARM, ANT, AWAY, BRIGADE, CLAY, CONTROL, DEPARTMENT, DOOR, DRILL, ENGINE, ESCAPE, HYDRANT, INSURANCE, IRONS, RAISER, SCREEN, SHIP, STATION, WALKING, WALL, WATCHER

FIRING – LINE, ORDER, PARTY, PIN, SQUAD

FIRST – AID, BASE, CLASS, FLOOR, FRUITS, LADY, LANGUAGE, LIEUTENANT, LIGHT, MATE, NAME, NIGHT, OFFENDER, OFFICER, PERSON, POST, PRINCIPLE, READING, REFUSAL, SCHOOL, WATER

FIVE – HUNDRED, KS, NATIONS, STONES, TOWNS

FLAKE – OUT, WHITE

FLASH – BURN, CARD, ELIMINATOR, FLOOD, GUN, PHOTOGRAPHY, PHOTOLYSIS, POINT, SET, SMELTING

FLAT – CAP, KNOT, RACING, SPIN, TUNING

FLIGHT – ARROW, DECK, ENGINEER, FEATHER, FORMATION, LIEUTENANT, LINE, PATH, PLAN, RECORDER, SERGEANT, SIMULATOR, STRIP, SURGEON

FLYING – BOAT, BOMB, BRIDGE, BUTTRESS, CIRCUS, COLOURS, DOCTOR, DUTCHMAN, FISH, FOX, FROG, JIB, LEMUR, LIZARD, MARE, OFFICER, PICKET, SAUCER, SQUAD, SQUIRREL, START, WING

FOLK – DANCE, MEDICINE, MEMORY, MUSIC, SINGER, SONG, TALE, WEAVE

FOOD – ADDITIVE, CHAIN, POISONING, PROCESSOR

FOOT – BRAKE, FAULT, ROT, RULE, SOLDIER

FOREIGN – AFFAIRS, AID, BILL, CORRESPONDENT, EXCHANGE, LEGION, MINISTER, MISSION, OFFICE, SERVICE

FOUL – PLAY, SHOT, UP

FOURTH – DIMENSION, ESTATE, INTERNATIONAL, REPUBLIC, WORLD

FREE – AGENT, ASSOCIATION, CHURCH, ELECTRON, ENERGY, ENTERPRISE, FALL, FLIGHT, FORM, GIFT, HAND, HOUSE, KICK, LOVE, SPACE, SPEECH, STATE, THOUGHT, THROW, TRADE, VERSE, WILL, ZONE

FRENCH – ACADEMY, BEAN, BREAD, CHALK, CRICKET, CUFF, CURVE, DOORS, DRESSING, HORN, KISS, KNICKERS, KNOT, LEAVE, LETTER, MUSTARD, PLEAT, POLISH, SEAM, STICK, TOAST, WINDOWS

FRONT – BENCH, DOOR, LINE, MAN, MATTER

FRUIT – BAT, BODY, COCKTAIL, CUP, FLY, KNIFE, MACHINE, SALAD, SUGAR, TREE

FULL – BLOOD, BOARD, DRESS, HOUSE, MOON, NELSON, PITCH, STOP, TIME, TOSS

GALLEY – PROOF, SLAVE

GALLOWS – BIRD, HUMOUR, TREE

GAME – BIRD, CHIPS, FISH, FOWL, LAWS, PARK, POINT, THEORY, WARDEN

GARDEN – CENTRE, CITY, CRESS, FLAT, FRAME, PARTY, SNAIL, SUBURB, WARBLER

GAS – BURNER, CHAMBER, CONSTANT, ENGINE, EQUATION, FIXTURE, GANGRENE, LAWS, LIGHTER, MAIN, MANTLE, MASK, METER, OIL, OVEN, POKER, RING, STATION, TURBINE

GENERAL – ANAESTHETIC, ASSEMBLY, DELIVERY, ELECTION, HOSPITAL, PRACTITIONER, STAFF, STRIKE, SYNOD, WILL

GIN – PALACE, RUMMY, SLING

GINGER – ALE, BEER, GROUP, SNAP, UP, WINE

GIRL – FRIDAY, GUIDE, SCOUT

GIVE – AWAY, IN, OFF, ONTO, OUT, OVER, UP

GLAD – EYE, HAND, RAGS

GLOVE – BOX, COMPARTMENT, PUPPET

GOLD – BASIS, BEETLE, BRICK, CERTIFICATE, COAST, DUST, FOIL, LEAF, MEDAL, MINE, NOTE, PLATE, POINT, RECORD, RESERVE, RUSH, STANDARD, STICK

GOLDEN – AGE, ASTER, CALF, CHAIN, DELICIOUS, EAGLE, FLEECE, GATE, GOOSE, HANDSHAKE, NUMBER, OLDIE, RETRIEVER, RULE, SECTION, SYRUP

GOLF – BALL, CLUB, COURSE, LINKS

GOOD – AFTERNOON, DAY, EVENING, FRIDAY, MORNING, NIGHT, SAMARITAN, SORT, TURN

GOOSE – BARNACLE, FLESH, STEP

GRAND – CANARY, CANYON, DUCHESS, DUCHY, DUKE, FINAL, GUIGNOL, JURY, LARCENY, MAL, MARNIER, MASTER, NATIONAL, OPERA, PIANO, PRIX, SEIGNEUR, SIÈCLE, SLAM, TOUR

GRANNY – BOND, FLAT, KNOT, SMITH

GRASS – BOX, CLOTH, COURT, HOCKEY, MOTH, ROOTS, SNAKE, TREE, WIDOW

GRAVY – BOAT, TRAIN

GREASE – CUP, GUN, MONKEY

GREAT – AUK, BEAR, BRITAIN, DANE, DIVIDE, LAKES, OUSE, PLAINS, SEAL, TIT, TREK, WAR,

GREEN – BEAN, BELT, BERET, CARD, DRAGON, FINGERS, LIGHT, MONKEY, MOULD, PAPER, PEPPER, PLOVER, THUMB, TURTLE, WOODPECKER

GREGORIAN – CALENDAR, CHANT, TELESCOPE, TONE

GREY – AREA, EMINENCE, FOX, FRIAR, MARKET, MATTER, SQUIRREL, WARBLER, WHALE, WOLF

GROUND – CONTROL, COVER, ENGINEER, FLOOR, GLASS, ICE, IVY, PLAN, PLATE, PROVISIONS, RENT, RULE, SWELL

GROW – BAG, INTO, ON, UP

GUIDE – DOG, ROPE

HAIR – DRYER, FOLLICLE, GEL, LACQUER, RESTORER, SHIRT, SLIDE, SPRAY, TRIGGER

HAPPY – EVENT, HOUR, MEDIUM, RELEASE

HARD – CASH, CHEESE, COPY, CORE, COURT, DISK, FEELING, HAT, HITTER, LABOUR, LINES, ROCK, SELL, SHOULDER, STANDING

HARVEST – HOME, MITE, MOON, MOUSE

HAT – STAND, TRICK

HATCHET – JOB, MAN

HEALTH – CENTRE, FOOD, SALTS, VISITOR

HEN – HARRIER, PARTY, RUN

HIGH – ALTAR, CHURCH, COMEDY, COMMAND, COMMISSIONER, COUNTRY, COURT, DAY, EXPLOSIVE, FASHION, FIDELITY, GERMAN, HAT, HOLIDAYS, JINKS, JUMP, POINT, PRIEST, SCHOOL, SEAS, SEASON, SOCIETY, SPOT, STREET, TABLE, TEA, TECH, TECHNOLOGY, TIDE, TIME, TREASON, WATER, WIRE, WYCOMBE

HIGHLAND – CATTLE, DRESS, FLING, REGION

HIP – BATH, FLASK, JOINT, POCKET

HIT – LIST, MAN, OFF, ON, OUT, PARADE

HOLD – BACK, DOWN, FORTH, IN, OFF, ON, OUT, OVER, TOGETHER, WITH

HOLY – BIBLE, CITY, COMMUNION, DAY, FATHER, GHOST, GRAIL, ISLAND, JOE, LAND, MARY, OFFICE, ORDERS, PLACE, ROLLER, ROOD, SCRIPTURE, SEE, SEPULCHRE, SPIRIT, WAR, WATER, WEEK, WRIT

HOME – AID, COUNTIES, ECONOMICS, FARM, GROUND,

GUARD, HELP, LOAN, OFFICE, PLATE, RANGE, RULE, RUN, SECRETARY, STRAIGHT, TEACHER, TRUTH, UNIT

HORSE – AROUND, BEAN, BRASS, CHESTNUT, GUARDS, LAUGH, MACKEREL, MARINE, MUSHROOM, NETTLE, OPERA, PISTOL, SENSE, TRADING

HOT – AIR, DOG, LINE, METAL, MONEY, PEPPER, POTATO, ROD, SEAT, SPOT, SPRING, STUFF, UP, ZONE

HOUSE – ARREST, GUEST, LIGHTS, MARTIN, MOTH, ORGAN, PARTY, PHYSICIAN, PLANT, SPARROW, SPIDER

HUMAN – BEING, CAPITAL, INTEREST, NATURE, RESOURCES, RIGHTS

HURRICANE – DECK, LAMP

ICE – AGE, AXE, BAG, BLOCK, CREAM, FISH, HOCKEY, HOUSE, LOLLY, MACHINE, MAN, PACK, PICK, PLANT, POINT, SHEET, SHELF, SHOW, SKATE, STATION, WATER, YACHT

ILL – FEELING, HUMOUR, TEMPER, WILL

IN – ABSENTIA, AETERNUM, CAMERA, ESSE, EXTENSO, EXTREMIS, MEMORIAM, NOMINE, PERPETUUM, PERSONAM, RE, REM, SITU, TOTO, UTERO, VACUO, VITRO, VIVO

INDIA – PAPER, PRINT, RUBBER

INDIAN – CLUB, EMPIRE, FILE, HEMP, INK, MALLOW, MILLET, MUTINY, OCEAN, RED, RESERVE, ROPE-TRICK, SUMMER

INNER – CITY, EAR, HEBRIDES, LIGHT, MAN, MONGOLIA, TUBE

INSIDE – FORWARD, JOB, LANE, TRACK

IRISH – COFFEE, MOSS, POTATO, REPUBLIC, SEA, SETTER, STEW, TERRIER, WHISKEY, WOLFHOUND

IRON – AGE, CHANCELLOR, CROSS, CURTAIN, FILINGS, GUARD, HAND, HORSE, LUNG, MAIDEN, MAN, OUT, PYRITES, RATIONS

JACK – FROST, IN, PLANE, RABBIT, ROBINSON, RUSSELL, TAR, UP

KICK – ABOUT, IN, OFF, OUT, PLEAT, TURN, UP, UPSTAIRS

KIDNEY – BEAN, MACHINE, STONE, VETCH

KNIFE – EDGE, GRINDER, PLEAT, SWITCH

LADY – BOUNTIFUL, CHAPEL, DAY, FERN, MAYORESS, MUCK, ORCHID

LAND – AGENT, BANK, BRIDGE, CRAB, FORCES, GIRL, GRANT, LINE, MINE, OFFICE, RAIL, REFORM, TAX, UP, WITH

LAST – JUDGMENT, NAME, OUT, POST, QUARTER, RITES, STRAW, SUPPER, THING

LATIN – AMERICA, CROSS, QUARTER, SQUARE

LAY – ASIDE, AWAY, BROTHER, DAYS, DOWN, FIGURE, IN, INTO, OFF, ON, OUT, OVER, READER, TO, UP

LEADING – AIRCRAFTMAN, ARTICLE, DOG, EDGE, LIGHT, MAN, NOTE, QUESTION, REINS

LEAVE – BEHIND, OFF, OUT

LEFT – BANK, WING

LEMON – BALM, CHEESE, DROP, FISH, GERANIUM, GRASS, SOLE, SQUASH, SQUEEZER, VERBENA

LETTER – BOMB, BOX, CARD

LIBERTY – BODICE, CAP, HALL, HORSE, ISLAND, SHIP

LIE – DETECTOR, DOWN, IN, TO

LIFE – ASSURANCE, BELT, BUOY, CYCLE, EXPECTANCY, FORM, GUARDS, HISTORY, INSURANCE, INTEREST, JACKET, PEER, PRESERVER, RAFT, SCIENCE, SPAN, STYLE

LIGHT – BULB, FACE, FLYWEIGHT, HEAVYWEIGHT, HORSE, INTO, METER, MIDDLEWEIGHT, MUSIC, OPERA, OUT, SHOW, UP, WELTERWEIGHT, YEAR

LIVER – FLUKE, SALTS, SAUSAGE

LIVING – DEATH, FOSSIL, PICTURE, ROOM, WAGE

LOBSTER – MOTH, NEWBURG, POT, THERMIDOR

LOCAL – ANAESTHETIC, AUTHORITY, COLOUR, GOVERNMENT, TIME

LONE – HAND, WOLF

LONG – ARM, BEACH, FACE, HAUL, HOP, ISLAND, JENNY, JOHNS, JUMP, PARLIAMENT, SHOT, SUIT, TOM, VACATION, WEEKEND

LOOK – AFTER, BACK, DOWN, ON, OVER, THROUGH, UP

LOOSE – CHANGE, COVER, END

LORD – ADVOCATE, CHAMBERLAIN, CHANCELLOR, LIEUTENANT, MAYOR, MUCK, PROTECTOR, PROVOST

LOUNGE – LIZARD, SUIT

LOVE – AFFAIR, APPLE, CHILD, FEAST, GAME, KNOT, LETTER, LIFE, MATCH, NEST, POTION, SEAT, SET

LOW – CHURCH, COMEDY, COUNTRIES, FREQUENCY, PROFILE, TECH, TECHNOLOGY, TIDE

LUNAR – CAUSTIC, ECLIPSE, MODULE, MONTH, YEAR

LUNCHEON – CLUB, MEAT, VOUCHER

MACHINE – BOLT, GUN, HEAD, SHOP, TOOL

MACKEREL – BREEZE, SHARK, SKY

MAGIC – CARPET, EYE, LANTERN, MUSHROOM, NUMBER, SQUARE

MAGNETIC – CIRCUIT, COMPASS, CONSTANT, DISK, EQUATOR, FIELD, FLUX, INDUCTION, INK, LENS, MO-MENT, NEEDLE, NORTH, PICK-UP, POLE, STORM, TAPE

MAIDEN – NAME, OVER, VOYAGE

MAIL – DROP, ORDER

MAKE – AFTER, AWAY, BELIEVE, FOR, OF, OFF, OUT, OVER, WITH

MALT – EXTRACT, LIQUOR, WHISKY

MANDARIN – CHINESE, COLLAR, DUCK

MARCH – BROWN, HARE, PAST

MARKET – GARDEN, GARDENING, ORDER, PRICE, RENT, RESEARCH, SHARE, TOWN, VALUE

MARRIAGE – BUREAU, GUIDANCE

MARSH – ELDER, FERN, FEVER, GAS, HARRIER, HAWK, HEN, MALLOW, MARIGOLD, ORCHID, TIT

MASTER – BUILDER, CYLINDER, KEY, RACE, SERGEANT

MATINÉE – COAT, IDOL

MAUNDY – MONEY, THURSDAY

MAY – APPLE, BEETLE, BLOBS, BLOSSOM, DAY, QUEEN, TREE

MECHANICAL – ADVANTAGE, DRAWING, ENGINEERING, INSTRUMENT

MEDICAL – CERTIFICATE, EXAMINATION, EXAMINER, JURISPRUDENCE

MEDICINE – BALL, CHEST, LODGE, MAN

MELBA – SAUCE, TOAST

MEMORY – BANK, MAPPING, SPAN, TRACE

MENTAL – AGE, BLOCK, CRUELTY, DISORDER, HANDICAP

MERCHANT – BANK, NAVY, PRINCE

MERCY – FLIGHT, KILLING, SEAT

MESS – ABOUT, HALL, JACKET, KIT

MICHAELMAS – DAISY, TERM

405

TWO-WORD PHRASES

MICKEY – FINN, MOUSE
MIDDLE – AGE, AGES, C, CLASS, EAR, EAST, MANAGEMENT, NAME, SCHOOL, TEMPLE
MIDNIGHT – BLUE, SUN
MIDSUMMER – DAY, MADNESS
MILITARY – ACADEMY, HONOURS, LAW, ORCHID, PACE, POLICE
MILK – BAR, CHOCOLATE, FEVER, FLOAT, LEG, PUDDING, PUNCH, ROUND, RUN, SHAKE, STOUT, TOOTH
MINT – BUSH, JULEP, SAUCE
MINUTE – GUN, HAND, MARK, STEAK
MIRROR – CANON, CARP, FINISH, IMAGE, LENS, SYMMETRY, WRITING
MITRE – BLOCK, BOX, GEAR, JOINT, SQUARE
MIXED – BAG, BLESSING, DOUBLES, ECONOMY, FARMING, GRILL, MARRIAGE, METAPHOR
MONEY – MARKET, ORDER, SPIDER, SUPPLY
MONKEY – BREAD, BUSINESS, CLIMB, FLOWER, JACKET, NUT, ORCHID, PUZZLE, SUIT, TRICKS, WRENCH
MORNING – COAT, DRESS, SICKNESS, STAR, TEA, WATCH
MOSQUITO – BOAT, HAWK, NET
MOSS – AGATE, LAYER, PINK, ROSE, STITCH
MOTHER – COUNTRY, GOOSE, HUBBARD, LODE, SHIP, SHIPTON, SUPERIOR, TONGUE, WIT
MOTOR – CARAVAN, DRIVE, GENERATOR, SCOOTER, VEHICLE, VESSEL
MOUNTAIN – ASH, CAT, CHAIN, DEVIL, GOAT, LAUREL, LION, RANGE, SHEEP, SICKNESS
MUD – BATH, DAUBER, FLAT, HEN, MAP, PIE, PUPPY, TURTLE
MUSTARD – GAS, OIL, PLASTER
MYSTERY – PLAY, TOUR
NANSEN – BOTTLE, PASSPORT
NARROW – BOAT, GAUGE, SEAS
NATIONAL – ACCOUNTING, AGREEMENT, ANTHEM, ASSEMBLY, ASSISTANCE, DEBT, FRONT, GALLERY, GRID, SERVICE, TRUST
NERVE – CELL, CENTRE, FIBRE, GAS, IMPULSE
NEW – BROOM, FOREST, GUINEA, LOOK, MATHS, MOON, PENNY, TESTAMENT, TOWN, WAVE, WORLD, YEAR, YORK, ZEALAND
NEWS – AGENCY, CONFERENCE, VENDOR
NIGHT – BLINDNESS, DANCER, FIGHTER, NURSE, OWL, ROBE, SAFE, SCHOOL, SHIFT, WATCH, WATCHMAN
NINETEENTH – HOLE, MAN
NOBLE – ART, GAS, SAVAGE
NORFOLK – ISLAND, JACKET, TERRIER
NOSE – CONE, DIVE, OUT, RAG, RING
NUCLEAR – BOMB, ENERGY, FAMILY, FISSION, FUEL, FUSION, ISOMER, PHYSICS, POWER, REACTION, REACTOR, THRESHOLD, WINTER
NURSERY – RHYME, SCHOOL, SLOPES, STAKES
OFF – CHANCE, COLOUR, KEY, LIMITS, LINE, SEASON
OIL – BEETLE, CAKE, DRUM, HARDENING, PAINT, PAINTING, PALM, RIG, RIVERS, SHALE, SLICK, VARNISH, WELL
OLD – BAILEY, BILL, BIRD, BOY, CONTEMPTIBLES, COUNTRY, GIRL, GOLD, GUARD, HAND, HAT, LADY, MAID, MAN, MOON, NICK, PRETENDER, SCHOOL, STYLE, TESTAMENT, WORLD
OLIVE – BRANCH, BROWN, CROWN, DRAB, GREEN, OIL

ON – DIT, KEY, LINE
OPEN – AIR, BOOK, CHAIN, CIRCUIT, COURT, DAY, DOOR, HOUSE, LETTER, MARKET, PRISON, PUNCTUATION, SANDWICH, SESAME, UNIVERSITY, UP, VERDICT
OPERA – BUFFA, CLOAK, GLASSES, HAT, HOUSE, SERIA
OPIUM – DEN, POPPY, WARS
ORANGE – BLOSSOM, PEEL, PEKOE, STICK
ORDINARY – LEVEL, RATING, RAY, SEAMAN, SHARES
OXFORD – ACCENT, BAGS, BLUE, ENGLISH, FRAME, GROUP, MOVEMENT
OYSTER – BED, CRAB, PINK, PLANT, WHITE
PACK – ANIMAL, DRILL, ICE, IN, RAT, UP
PALM – BEACH, CIVET, OFF, OIL, SUGAR, SUNDAY, VAULTING, WINE
PANAMA – CANAL, CITY, HAT
PANIC – BOLT, BUTTON, BUYING, GRASS, STATIONS
PAPER – CHASE, FILIGREE, MONEY, MULBERRY, NAUTILUS, OVER, TAPE, TIGER
PAR – AVION, EXCELLENCE, VALUE
PARISH – CLERK, COUNCIL, PUMP, REGISTER
PARTY – LINE, MAN, POLITICS, WALL
PASSING – BELL, NOTE, SHOT
PASSION – FRUIT, PLAY, SUNDAY, WEEK
PATCH – BOARD, POCKET, QUILT, TEST
PAY – BACK, BED, DIRT, DOWN, FOR, IN, OFF, OUT, TELEVISION, UP
PEACE – CORPS, OFFERING, PIPE, RIVER, SIGN
PEG – CLIMBING, DOWN, LEG, OUT, TOP
PEN – FRIEND, NAME, PAL
PENNY – ARCADE, BLACK, WHISTLE
PER – ANNUM, CAPITA, CENT, CONTRA, DIEM, MENSEM, MILL, PRO, SE
PERSIAN – BLINDS, CARPET, CAT, EMPIRE, GREYHOUND, GULF, LAMB, MELON
PETIT – BOURGEOIS, FOUR, JURY, LARCENY, MAL, POINT
PETROL – BOMB, PUMP, STATION
PETTY – CASH, JURY, LARCENY, OFFICER, SESSIONS
PICTURE – CARD, HAT, HOUSE, MOULDING, PALACE, WINDOW, WRITING
PIECE – GOODS, OUT, RATE
PILLOW – BLOCK, FIGHT, LACE, LAVA, SHAM, TALK
PILOT – BALLOON, BIRD, BISCUIT, CLOTH, ENGINE, FILM, FISH, HOUSE, LAMP, LIGHT, OFFICER, PLANT, STUDY, WHALE
PIN – CURL, DOWN, JOINT, MONEY, RAIL, TUCK, WRENCH
PINE – CONE, END, MARTEN, NEEDLE, TAR
PINK – ELEPHANTS, GIN, NOISE, SALMON, SLIP
PIPE – CLEANER, DOWN, DREAM, MAJOR, ORGAN, ROLL, UP
PLACE – CARD, KICK, NAME, SETTING
PLAIN – CHOCOLATE, CLOTHES, FLOUR, SAILING, TEXT
PLAY – ALONG, DOWN, OFF, ON, OUT, UP, WITH
PLYMOUTH – BRETHREN, COLONY, ROCK
POCKET – BATTLESHIP, BILLIARDS, BOROUGH, GOPHER, MONEY, MOUSE
POETIC – JUSTICE, LICENCE
PONY – EXPRESS, TREKKING
POOR – BOX, LAW, MOUTH, RELATION, WHITE
POP – ART, OFF, SHOP

POST – CHAISE, HOC, HORN, HOUSE, MERIDIEM, OFFICE, ROAD, TOWN

POT – CHEESE, LIQUOR, MARIGOLD, ON, PLANT, ROAST, SHOT, STILL

POTATO – BEETLE, BLIGHT, CHIP, CRISP

POWDER – BLUE, BURN, COMPACT, FLASK, HORN, KEG, MONKEY, PUFF, ROOM

POWER – CUT, DIVE, DRILL, FACTOR, LINE, PACK, PLANT, POINT, POLITICS, STATION, STEERING, STRUCTURE

PRAIRIE – DOG, OYSTER, PROVINCES, SCHOONER, SOIL, TURNIP, WOLF

PRAYER – BEADS, BOOK, MEETING, RUG, SHAWL, WHEEL

PRESS – AGENCY, AGENT, BOX, CONFERENCE, GALLERY, GANG, RELEASE, STUD

PRESSURE – CABIN, COOKER, DRAG, GAUGE, GRADIENT, GROUP, HEAD, POINT, SUIT

PRICE – COMMISSION, CONTROL, DISCRIMINATION, RING, SUPPORT, TAG, WAR

PRICKLY – ASH, HEAT, PEAR, POPPY

PRIME – COST, MERIDIAN, MINISTER, MOVER, NUMBER, RATE, TIME, VERTICAL

PRIVATE – BAR, BILL, COMPANY, DETECTIVE, ENTERPRISE, EYE, HOTEL, INCOME, LANGUAGE, LIFE, MEMBER, PARTS, PATIENT, PRACTICE, PRESS, PROPERTY, SCHOOL, SECRETARY, SECTOR

PRIVY – CHAMBER, COUNCIL, PURSE, SEAL

PRIZE – COURT, MONEY, RING

PRO – FORMA, PATRIA, RATA, TEMPORE

PUBLIC – BAR, BILL, COMPANY, CONVENIENCE, COR-PORATION, DEBT, DEFENDER, ENEMY, ENTERPRISE, EXPENDITURE, FOOTPATH, GALLERY, HOLIDAY, HOUSE, LAW, NUISANCE, OPINION, OWNERSHIP, PROSECUTOR, RELATIONS, SCHOOL, SECTOR, SERVANT, SERVICE, SPEAKING, SPENDING, TRANSPORT

PUFF – ADDER, PASTRY

PULL – ABOUT, BACK, DOWN, IN, OFF, ON, OUT, THROUGH, TOGETHER, UP

PURPLE – EMPEROR, GALLINULE, HEART, MEDIC, PATCH

PUSH – ABOUT, ALONG, BUTTON, IN, OFF, ON, THROUGH

PUT – ABOUT, ACROSS, ASIDE, AWAY, BACK, BY, DOWN, FORTH, FORWARD, IN, OFF, ON, OUT, OVER, THROUGH, UP, UPON

QUANTUM – LEAP, MECHANICS, NUMBER, STATE, STATISTICS, THEORY

QUARTER – CRACK, DAY, GRAIN, HORSE, NOTE, PLATE, ROUND, SECTION, SESSIONS, TONE

QUEEN – BEE, CONSORT, DOWAGER, MAB, MOTHER, OLIVE, POST, REGENT, REGNANT, SUBSTANCE

QUEER – FISH, STREET

QUESTION – MARK, MASTER, TIME

RAIN – CHECK, GAUGE, SHADOW, TREE

REAL – ALE, ESTATE, LIFE, NUMBER, PART, PRESENCE, PROPERTY, TENNIS, WAGES

RED – ADMIRAL, ALGAE, BAG, BARK, BEDS, BIDDY, CARPET, CEDAR, CROSS, DUSTER, DWARF, ENSIGN, FLAG, HAT, HEAT, HERRING, INDIAN, MEAT, MULLET, PEPPER, RAG, RIVER, ROSE, SALMON, SEA, SETTER, SHANK, SHIFT, SNAPPER, SPIDER, SQUIRREL, TAPE

RES – ADJUDICATA, GESTAE, JUDICATA, PUBLICA

RIGHT – ABOUT, ANGLE, ASCENSION, AWAY, HONOURABLE, OFF, ON, REVEREND, WING

ROCK – BOTTOM, CAKE, CLIMBING, GARDEN, PLANT, SALT, STEADY

ROLLER – BEARING, CAPTION, COASTER, DERBY, SKATE, TOWEL

ROMAN – ARCH, CALENDAR, CANDLE, CATHOLIC, CATHOLICISM, COLLAR, EMPIRE, HOLIDAY, LAW, MILE, NOSE, NUMERALS

ROOF – GARDEN, RACK

ROOM – SERVICE, TEMPERATURE

ROOT – BEER, CANAL, CROP, NODULE, OUT, POSITION, UP

ROTARY – CLOTHESLINE, CLUB, ENGINE, PLOUGH, PRESS, PUMP

ROUGH – COLLIE, DIAMOND, OUT, PASSAGE, SPIN, STUFF, UP

ROUND – ANGLE, CLAM, DANCE, DOWN, HAND, OFF, ON, OUT, ROBIN, TABLE, TOP, TRIP, UP

ROYAL – ACADEMY, ASSENT, BLUE, BURGH, COMMISSION, DUKE, ENGINEERS, FLUSH, HIGHNESS, ICING, JELLY, MARINES, NAVY, PURPLE, ROAD, STANDARD, TENNIS, WARRANT, WORCESTER

RUBBER – BAND, BRIDGE, CEMENT, CHEQUE, GOODS, PLANT, STAMP, TREE

RUN – ACROSS, AFTER, ALONG, AROUND, AWAY, DOWN, IN, INTO, OFF, ON, OUT, OVER, THROUGH, TO, UP

RUNNING – BOARD, COMMENTARY, HEAD, LIGHT, MATE, REPAIRS, RIGGING, STITCH

RUSSIAN – DRESSING, EMPIRE, REVOLUTION, ROULETTE, SALAD, WOLFHOUND

SAFETY – BELT, CATCH, CHAIN, CURTAIN, FACTOR, FILM, FUSE, GLASS, LAMP, MATCH, NET, PIN, RAZOR, VALVE

SALAD – DAYS, DRESSING

SALLY – ARMY, LUNN

SALT – AWAY, BATH, CAKE, DOME, FLAT, LAKE, LICK, MARSH, OUT, PORK

SAND – BAR, CASTLE, EEL, FLEA, HOPPER, LANCE, LEEK, LIZARD, MARTIN, PAINTING, SHRIMP, TABLE, TRAP, VIPER, WASP, WEDGE, YACHT

SANDWICH – BOARD, CAKE, COURSE, ISLANDS, MAN

SAUSAGE – DOG, ROLL

SCARLET – FEVER, HAT, LETTER, PIMPERNEL, RUNNER, WOMAN

SCATTER – DIAGRAM, PIN, RUG

SCOTCH – BROTH, EGG, MIST, PANCAKE, SNAP, TAPE, TERRIER

SCRAPE – IN, THROUGH, TOGETHER

SCRATCH – PAD, SHEET, TEST, TOGETHER, VIDEO

SECOND – CHILDHOOD, CLASS, COMING, COUSIN, FIDDLE, FLOOR, GENERATION, GROWTH, HAND, LANGUAGE, LIEUTENANT, MATE, NAME, NATURE, READING, SIGHT, STRING, THOUGHT, WIND

SECONDARY – COLOUR, EMISSION, PICKET, PROCESSES, QUALITIES, SCHOOL, STRESS

SECRET – AGENT, POLICE, SERVICE, SOCIETY

SEE – ABOUT, INTO, OF, OFF, OUT, OVER, THROUGH

SENIOR – AIRCRAFTMAN, CITIZEN, MANAGEMENT, SERVICE

TWO-WORD PHRASES

SERVICE – AREA, CHARGE, INDUSTRY, MODULE, ROAD, STATION

SET – ABOUT, AGAINST, ASIDE, BACK, DOWN, FORTH, IN, OFF, ON, OUT, PIECE, POINT, SQUARE, THEORY, TO, UP, UPON

SETTLE – DOWN, FOR, IN, WITH

SHAKE – DOWN, OFF, UP

SHEET – ANCHOR, BEND, DOWN, LIGHTNING, METAL, MUSIC

SHOP – AROUND, ASSISTANT, FLOOR, STEWARD

SHORE – BIRD, LEAVE, PATROL

SHORT – CIRCUIT, CUT, FUSE, HEAD, LIST, ODDS, SHRIFT, STORY, STRAW, TIME, WAVE

SHOW – BILL, BUSINESS, CARD, COPY, OFF, STOPPER, TRIAL, UP

SIAMESE – CAT, TWINS

SICK – LEAVE, LIST, NOTE, PAY

SIGN – AWAY, IN, LANGUAGE, MANUAL, OFF, ON, OUT, UP

SINGLE – BOND, CREAM, DENSITY, ENTRY, FILE, TAX, THREAD, TICKET

SIT – BACK, DOWN, ON, OUT, OVER, UNDER, UP

SITTING – BULL, ROOM, TARGET, TENANT

SKI – JUMP, LIFT, PANTS, RUN, STICK, TOW

SKIN – DIVING, EFFECT, FLICK, FOOD, FRICTION, GAME, GRAFT, TEST

SLAVE – ANT, COAST, CYLINDER, DRIVER, SHIP, STATE, TRADE

SLIDE – FASTENER, GUITAR, OVER, REST, RULE, TROMBONE, VALVE

SLIP – GAUGE, RAIL, RING, ROAD, STEP, STITCH, UP

SLOW – BURN, HANDCLAP, MARCH, MOTION, TIME

SMALL – ARMS, BEER, CHANGE, FRY, HOURS, INTESTINE, SLAM, TALK

SMART – ALECK, CARD, MONEY, SET

SMOKE – BOMB, OUT, SCREEN, TREE

SNEAK – PREVIEW, THIEF

SOB – SISTER, STORY, STUFF

SOCIAL – CLIMBER, SCIENCE, SECRETARY, SECURITY, SERVICES, STUDIES, WELFARE, WORK

SODA – ASH, BISCUIT, BREAD, FOUNTAIN, JERK, LIME, NITRE, POP, SIPHON, WATER

SOFT – DRINK, FRUIT, FURNISHINGS, GOODS, LANDING, LINE, OPTION, PORN, SELL, SOAP, SPOT, TOP, TOUCH

SOLAR – ECLIPSE, FLARE, FURNACE, HEATING, MONTH, MYTH, PANEL, PLEXUS, POWER, SYSTEM, WIND, YEAR

SOUND – BARRIER, BOW, CHECK, EFFECT, HEAD, HOLE, MIXER, OFF, OUT, WAVE

SOUR – CHERRY, CREAM, GOURD, GRAPES, GUM, MASH

SPACE – AGE, BLANKET, CADET, CAPSULE, CHARACTER, HEATER, INVADERS, OPERA, PLATFORM, PROBE, SHUTTLE, STATION

SPAGHETTI – JUNCTION, WESTERN

SPARK – CHAMBER, COIL, EROSION, GAP, OFF, PLUG, TRANSMITTER

SPEAK – FOR, OUT, TO, UP

SPECIAL – ASSESSMENT, BRANCH, CASE, CONSTABLE, DELIVERY, EFFECTS, JURY, LICENCE, PLEADING, PRIVILEGE, SCHOOL, SORT

SPEED – LIMIT, TRAP, UP

SPINNING – JENNY, MULE, TOP, WHEEL

SPIRIT – GUM, LAMP, LEVEL, VARNISH

SPLIT – CANE, DECISION, INFINITIVE, PEA, PERSONALITY, SECOND, SHIFT, TIN, UP

SPONGE – BAG, BATH, CAKE, CLOTH, DOWN

SPORTS – CAR, COAT, JACKET, SHIRT

SPRING – BALANCE, CHICKEN, FEVER, LOCK, MATTRESS, ONION, ROLL, TIDE

SPUN – SILK, SUGAR, YARN

SQUARE – AWAY, BRACKET, DANCE, LEG, MEAL, NUMBER, OFF, ROOT, UP

STABLE – DOOR, FLY, LAD

STAFF – ASSOCIATION, COLLEGE, CORPORAL, NURSE, OFFICER, SERGEANT

STAG – BEETLE, PARTY

STAGE – DIRECTION, DOOR, EFFECT, FRIGHT, LEFT, MANAGER, RIGHT, WHISPER

STAMP – ACT, COLLECTING, DUTY, MILL, OUT

STAND – BY, DOWN, FOR, IN, OIL, ON, OUT, OVER, PAT, TO, UP

STAR – CHAMBER, CONNECTION, GRASS, SAPPHIRE, SHELL, STREAM, SYSTEM, THISTLE, WARS

STATUS – QUO, SYMBOL

STEEL – BAND, BLUE, GREY, GUITAR, WOOL

STICK – AROUND, AT, BY, DOWN, INSECT, OUT, TO, TOGETHER, WITH

STICKY – END, WICKET

STIRRUP – BONE, CUP, PUMP

STOCK – CAR, CERTIFICATE, COMPANY, EXCHANGE, FARM, MARKET

STOCKING – CAP, FILLER, FRAME, MASK, STITCH

STORAGE – BATTERY, CAPACITY, DEVICE, HEATER

STORM – BELT, CENTRE, CLOUD, COLLAR, CONE, DOOR, GLASS, LANTERN, PETREL, WARNING, WINDOW

STRAIGHT – BAT, FACE, FIGHT, FLUSH, MAN, OFF, UP

STRAWBERRY – BLONDE, BUSH, MARK, TOMATO, TREE

STREET – ARAB, CREDIBILITY, CRY, DOOR, PIANO, THEATRE, VALUE

STRIKE – DOWN, FAULT, NOTE, OFF, OUT, PAY, THROUGH, UP

STRING – ALONG, BAND, BASS, BEAN, COURSE, LINE, ORCHESTRA, QUARTET, TIE, VARIABLE

STRIP – CARTOON, CLUB, CROPPING, LIGHTING, MILL, MINING, OUT, POKER

SUGAR – BEET, CANDY, CANE, CORN, DADDY, DIABETES, LOAF, MAPLE

SUMMER – HOLIDAY, PUDDING, SCHOOL, SOLSTICE, TIME

SUN – BATH, BEAR, BITTERN, BLIND, BLOCK, DANCE, DECK, DISC, KING, LAMP, LOUNGE

SUPREME – BEING, COMMANDER, COURT, SACRIFICE

SURFACE – MAIL, NOISE, PLATE, STRUCTURE, TENSION

SWAN – DIVE, MAIDEN, NECK, SONG

SWEAT – GLAND, OFF, OUT, SHIRT, SUIT

SWEET – BASIL, BAY, CHERRY, CHESTNUT, CICELY, CIDER, CLOVER, CORN, FERN, FLAG, GALE, GUM, MARJORAM, MARTEN, OIL, PEA, PEPPER, POTATO, SHOP, TOOTH, WILLIAM, WOODRUFF

408

SWISS – CHARD, CHEESE, GUARD, MUSLIN, ROLL, TOURNAMENT
TABLE – BAY, D'HOTE, LICENCE, MONEY, MOUNTAIN, NAPKIN, SALT, TALK, TENNIS, WINE
TAIL – COAT, COVERT, END, FAN, GATE, OFF, OUT
TAKE – ABACK, AFTER, APART, AWAY, BACK, DOWN, FOR, IN, OFF, ON, OUT, OVER, TO, UP
TALK – ABOUT, AT, BACK, DOWN, INTO, OUT, ROUND, SHOW
TANK – ENGINE, FARMING, TOP, TRAP, UP, WAGON
TAX – AVOIDANCE, DISC, EVASION, EXILE, HAVEN, RATE, RETURN, SHELTER
TEA – BAG, BISCUIT, CLOTH, COSY, GARDEN, GOWN, LEAF, PARTY, ROSE, SERVICE, TOWEL, TROLLEY
TEAR – AWAY, DOWN, DUCT, GAS, INTO, OFF, SHEET
TELEPHONE – BOX, DIRECTORY, NUMBER
TERRA – ALBA, COTTA, FIRMA, INCOGNITA, SIGILLATA
TEST – ACT, BAN, CASE, MARKETING, MATCH, PAPER, PILOT, TUBE
THIRD – CLASS, DEGREE, DIMENSION, ESTATE, EYELID, MAN, PARTY, PERSON, READING, REICH, WORLD
THROW – ABOUT, IN, OFF, OUT, OVER, TOGETHER, UP, WEIGHT
TIME – BOMB, CAPSULE, CLOCK, IMMEMORIAL, MACHINE, SERIES, SHARING, SHEET, SIGNATURE, SWITCH, TRIAL, ZONE
TIN – CAN, GOD, HAT, LIZZIE, PLATE, SOLDIER, WHISTLE
TITLE – DEED, PAGE, ROLE
TOILET – PAPER, SET, SOAP, TRAINING, WATER
TONE – CLUSTER, COLOUR, CONTROL, DOWN, LANGUAGE, POEM, ROW, UP
TOP – BOOT, BRASS, DOG, DRAWER, END, GEAR, HAT, MANAGEMENT, OFF, OUT, UP
TORQUE – CONVERTER, METER, SPANNER, WRENCH
TOUCH – FOOTBALL, JUDGE, OFF, UP
TOWN – CLERK, CRIER, GAS, HALL, HOUSE, MEETING, PLANNING
TRACK – DOWN, EVENT, MEET, RECORD, ROD, SHOE
TRADE – ACCEPTANCE, CYCLE, DISCOUNT, GAP, JOURNAL, NAME, ON, PLATE, SCHOOL, SECRET, UNION, WIND
TRAFFIC – COP, COURT, ISLAND, JAM, LIGHT, OFFICER, PATTERN, WARDEN
TREASURY – BENCH, BILL, BOND, CERTIFICATE, NOTE, TAG
TRENCH – COAT, FEVER, FOOT, KNIFE, MORTAR, MOUTH, WARFARE
TRIPLE – ALLIANCE, BOND, ENTENTE, JUMP, POINT, TIME
TURKISH – BATH, COFFEE, DELIGHT, EMPIRE, TOBACCO, TOWEL
TURN – AGAINST, AWAY, BRIDGE, DOWN, IN, OFF, ON, OUT, OVER, TO, UP
TWELFTH – DAY, MAN, NIGHT
TWIN – BED, BILL, TOWN
UMBRELLA – BIRD, PINE, PLANT, STAND, TREE
UNION – CARD, JACK
UNIT – COST, FACTOR, PRICE, TRUST
UNITED – KINGDOM, NATIONS, PARTY, PROVINCES
VACUUM – CLEANER, FLASK
VALUE – ADDED, DATE, JUDGMENT
VENETIAN – BLIND, GLASS, RED

VENTURE – CAPITAL, SCOUT
VICAR – APOSTOLIC, FORANE, GENERAL
VICE – ADMIRAL, CHANCELLOR, PRESIDENT, SQUAD, VERSA
VIDEO – CASSETTE, GAME, NASTY, TAPE
VIRGIN – BIRTH, ISLANDS, MARY, WOOL
VIRGINIA – BEACH, CREEPER, DEER, REEL, STOCK
VOX – ANGELICA, HUMANA, POP, POPULI
VULGAR – FRACTION, LATIN
WALK – AWAY, INTO, OFF, OUT
WAR – BABY, BONNET, BRIDE, CHEST, CORRESPONDENT, CRIME, CRY, DANCE, GAME, MEMORIAL, OFFICE, PAINT, WHOOP
WASHING – MACHINE, POWDER, SODA
WATCH – CAP, CHAIN, COMMITTEE, FIRE, NIGHT, OUT
WEATHER – EYE, HOUSE, MAP, STATION, STRIP, VANE, WINDOW
WEDDING – BREAKFAST, CAKE, RING
WEIGH – DOWN, IN, UP
WELSH – CORGI, DRESSER, HARP, MOUNTAIN, POPPY, RABBIT, TERRIER
WET – BLANKET, CELL, DREAM, FISH, FLY, LOOK, NURSE, PACK, ROT, STEAM, SUIT
WHITE – ADMIRAL, AREA, BEAR, BIRCH, ELEPHANT, ENSIGN, FEATHER, FISH, FLAG, GOLD, HEAT, HORSE, HOUSE, KNIGHT, LADY, LEAD, LIE, LIGHT, MEAT, OUT, PAPER, PEPPER, SLAVE, SPIRIT, STICK, TIE, WHALE
WINDOW – BOX, ENVELOPE, SASH, SEAT, TAX
WINE – BAR, BOX, CELLAR, COOLER, TASTING
WING – CHAIR, COLLAR, COMMANDER, COVERT, LOADING, NUT, SHOT, TIP
WITCH – DOCTOR, HAZEL
WOLF – CUB, SPIDER, WHISTLE
WORD – ASSOCIATION, BLINDNESS, ORDER, PICTURE, PROCESSING, PROCESSOR, SQUARE
WORK – BACK, CAMP, ETHIC, FUNCTION, IN, OFF, ON, OUT, OVER, SHEET, STATION, THROUGH, UP
WORKING – BEE, CAPITAL, CLASS, DAY, DOG, DRAWING, PAPERS, PARTY, SUBSTANCE, WEEK
WRITE – DOWN, IN, OFF, OUT, UP
YELLOW – BELLY, CARD, FEVER, JACKET, PAGES, PERIL, RIVER, STREAK
YORKSHIRE – DALES, FOG, PUDDING, TERRIER
YOUNG – BLOOD, FOGEY, LADY, MAN, PRETENDER, TURK
YOUTH – CLUB, CUSTODY, HOSTEL

SECOND WORD

ABOUT – BRING, CAST, COME, FALL, HANG, KICK, KNOCK, MESS, MUCK, PUSH, PUT, RIGHT, SET, TALK, THROW
ABSOLUTE – ABLATIVE, DECREE
ACADEMY – FRENCH, MILITARY, ROYAL
ACCESS – DIRECT, RANDOM, SEQUENTIAL
ACCOUNT – BANK, BUDGET, CAPITAL, CHARGE, CONTROL, CREDIT, CURRENT, DEPOSIT, DRAWING, EXPENSE, JOINT, SAVINGS, SHORT, SUSPENSE, TRUST
ACCOUNTANT – CHARTERED, TURF
ACROSS – COME, CUT, GET, PUT, RUN

409

TWO-WORD PHRASES

ACT – ENABLING, HOMESTEAD, JURISTIC, LOCUTIONARY, RIOT, SPEECH, STAMP, TEST

ADMIRAL – FLEET, REAR, RED, VICE, WHITE

ADVOCATE – DEVIL'S, JUDGE, LORD

AGAINST – COUNT, GO, SET, STACK, TURN

AGENCY – ADVERTISING, EMPLOYMENT, MERCANTILE, NEWS, PRESS, TRAVEL

AGENT – CROWN, DISCLOSING, DOUBLE, ESTATE, FORWARDING, FREE, HOUSE, LAND, LAW, OXIDIZING, PRESS, REDUCING, SECRET, SHIPPING, WETTING

AGREEMENT – COLLECTIVE, GENTLEMEN'S, NATIONAL, PROCEDURAL, STANDSTILL, TECHNOLOGY

AID – ARTIFICIAL, FIRST, FOREIGN, HEARING, HOME, LEGAL, TEACHING

ALARM – CALL, FALSE, FIRE

ALCOHOL – ABSOLUTE, ALLYL, AMYL, BUTYL, ETHYL, GRAIN, LAURYL, METHYL, RUBBING, WOOD

ALE – GINGER, REAL

ALLEY – BLIND, BOWLING

ALLIANCE – DUAL, HOLY, TRIPLE

ALONG – COME, CUT, GET, GO, MUDDLE, PLAY, PUSH, RUB, RUN, SING, STRING

ANGEL – DESTROYING, HELL'S, RECORDING

ANGLE – CENTRAL, COMPLEMENTARY, CRITICAL, EXTERIOR, FACIAL, HOUR, INTERIOR, OBLIQUE, PLANE, RIGHT, STRAIGHT

ANT – AMAZON, ARMY, BULLDOG, DRIVER, FIRE, LEAFCUTTER, LEGIONARY, PHARAOH, SLAVE, VELVET, WHITE, WOOD

APPLE – ADAM'S, BALSAM, BIG, BITTER, CRAB, CUSTARD, LOVE, MAY, OAK, ROSE, SUGAR, THORN

ARCADE – AMUSEMENT, PENNY

ARCH – ACUTE, FALLEN, GOTHIC, HORSESHOE, KEEL, LANCET, NORMAN, OGEE, POINTED, ROMAN, SKEW, TRIUMPHAL, ZYGOMATIC

AREA – CATCHMENT, DEVELOPMENT, GOAL, GREY, MUSH, NO-GO, PENALTY, SERVICE

ARMS – CANTING, ORDER, SIDE, SMALL

ARMY – CHURCH, FIELD, SALLY, SALVATION, STANDING, TERRITORIAL

AROUND – BAT, GET, GO, HORSE, RUN, SHOP, SLEEP, SLOP, STICK

ART – BLACK, COMMERCIAL, FINE, NOBLE, OP, PERFORMANCE, POP

ARTS – GRAPHIC, LIBERAL, PERFORMING, VISUAL

ASH – BONE, FLY, MOUNTAIN, PEARL, PRICKLY, SODA

ASIDE – BRUSH, LAY, PUT, SET

ASSEMBLY – GENERAL, LEGISLATIVE, NATIONAL, UNLAWFUL

ATTORNEY – CROWN, DISTRICT, PROSECUTING

AWAY – BLOW, BOIL, CARRY, CLEAR, COME, EXPLAIN, FALL, FIRE, GET, GIVE, GO, KEEP, LAUGH, LAY, MAKE, PUT, RIGHT, RUN, SALT, SIGN, SOCK, SQUARE, TAKE, TEAR, TRAIL, TUCK, TURN, WALK, WHILE

BABY – BLUE, JELLY, PLUNKET, RHESUS, TEST-TUBE, WAR

BACK – ANSWER, BITE, BOUNCE, CARRY, CAST, CHOKE, CLAW, DOUBLE, FALL, FIGHT, GET, GO, HANG, HARK, HOLD, KEEP, KNOCK, LADDER, LOOK, PAY, PLOUGH, PULL, PUT, RING, SET, SIT, TAKE, TALK

BAG – AIR, BLUE, BODY, CARRIER, COFFEE, COOL, DIPLOMATIC, DOGGY, DUFFEL, GLADSTONE, GROW,

ICE, JELLY, JIFFY, LAVENDER, MIXED, SAG, SLEEPING, SPONGE, TEA, TOTE

BALLOON – BARRAGE, HOT-AIR, PILOT, TRIAL

BAND – BIG, BRAKE, BRASS, CITIZENS', CONDUCTION, ELASTIC, ENERGY, FREQUENCY, RUBBER, STEEL

BANK – BLOOD, CENTRAL, CLEARING, COMMERCIAL, COOPERATIVE, DATA, DOGGER, FOG, JODRELL, LAND, LEFT, MEMORY, MERCHANT, NATIONAL, PIGGY, RESERVE, SAVINGS, SOIL, SPERM

BAR – CAPSTAN, COFFEE, COLOUR, DOUBLE, HEEL, HORIZONTAL, INNER, MILK, OUTER, PINCH, PRIVATE, PUBLIC, SAND, SINGLES, SNACK, TORSION, WINE

BARRIER – CRASH, CRUSH, HEAT, SONIC, SOUND, THERMAL, TRANSONIC

BASE – AIR, DATA, FIRST, LEWIS, PRISONER'S, PYRIMIDINE

BASKET – CHIP, MOSES, POLLEN, WASTEPAPER

BASS – BLACK, DOUBLE, FIGURED, GROUND, LARGEMOUTH, ROCK, SEA, SMALLMOUTH, STONE, STRING, THOROUGH, WALKING

BAT – FRUIT, HORSESHOE, INSECTIVOROUS, STRAIGHT, VAMPIRE

BATH – BLANKET, BLOOD, BUBBLE, HIP, MUD, SALT, SPONGE, STEAM, SUN, SWIMMING, TURKISH

BEACON – BELISHA, LANDING, RADAR, RADIO

BEAN – ADSUKI, ADZUKI, BLACK, BROAD, BUTTER, CALABAR, CASTOR, COCOA, DWARF, FRENCH, GREEN, HORSE, JACK, JUMPING, KIDNEY, LIMA, MUNG, PINTO, RUNNER, SHELL, SNAP, SOYA, STRING, TONKA, WAX

BEAR – ANT, BLACK, BROWN, CINNAMON, GREAT, GRIZZLY, HONEY, KOALA, KODIAK, LITTLE, NATIVE, POLAR, SLOTH, SUN, TEDDY, WATER, WHITE, WOOLLY

BEAT – DEAD, MERSEY, WING

BEAUTY – BATHING, CAMBERWELL, SPRING

BED – AIR, APPLE-PIE, BUNK, FEATHER, OYSTER, PAY, SOFA, TRUCKLE, TRUNDLE, TWIN, WATER

BEE – CARPENTER, CUCKOO, HIVE, LEAFCUTTER, MASON, MINING, QUEEN, SPELLING, WORKING

BEER – BOCK, GINGER, KAFFIR, ROOT, SMALL, SPRUCE

BELL – CANTERBURY, DIVING, LUTINE, PASSING, SACRING, SANCTUS, SHARK, SILVER

BELT – BIBLE, BLACK, CARTRIDGE, CHASTITY, CONVEYOR, COPPER, COTTON, FAN, GREEN, LIFE, LONSDALE, SAFETY, SEAT, SHELTER, STOCKBROKER, STORM, SUSPENDER, SWORD

BENCH – FRONT, KING'S, OPTICAL, TREASURY

BENEFIT – CHILD, DISABLEMENT, FAMILY, FRINGE, HOUSING, INJURY, INVALIDITY, MATERNITY, SICKNESS, SUPPLEMENTARY, UNEMPLOYMENT, WIDOW'S

BILL – ACCOMMODATION, BUFFALO, DEMAND, DOUBLE, FINANCE, FOREIGN, OLD, PRIVATE, PUBLIC, REFORM, TREASURY, TRUE, TWIN

BIRD – ADJUTANT, ANT, BRAIN-FEVER, CROCODILE, DIAMOND, EARLY, ELEPHANT, GALLOWS, GAME, PARSON, WATER

BISCUIT – BOURBON, CAPTAIN'S, DIGESTIVE, DOG, PILOT, SEA, SHIP'S, SODA, TARARUA, TEA, WATER

BLACK – ALL, CARBON, GAS, IVORY, JET, LARGE, PENNY, PLATINUM

BLOCK – BREEZE, BUILDING, CAVITY, CYLINDER,

HEART, ICE, MENTAL, OFFICE, PSYCHOLOGICAL, SADDLE, STARTING, STUMBLING, SUN, WOOD

BLOOD – BAD, BLUE, BULL'S, DRAGON'S, FULL, WHOLE, YOUNG

BOARD – ABOVE, ADMIRALTY, BULLETIN, CATCHMENT, CIRCUIT, CRIBBAGE, DIVING, DRAFT, DRAINING, DRAWING, EMERY, FULL, HALF, IDIOT, IRONING, NOTICE, PATCH, RUNNING, SANDWICH, SCHOOL, SKIRTING, SOUNDING, WOBBLE

BOAT – CANAL, FLYING, GRAVY, JOLLY, MOSQUITO, NARROW, ROWING, SAILING, SAUCE, SWAMP, TORPEDO

BOMB – ATOM, BORER, BUZZ, CLUSTER, COBALT, FISSION, FLYING, FUSION, HYDROGEN, LETTER, MILLS, NEUTRON, NUCLEAR, PETROL, SMOKE, STINK, TIME, VOLCANIC

BOND – BAIL, CHEMICAL, COORDINATE, COVALENT, DATIVE, DOUBLE, ELECTROVALENT, ENGLISH, FLEMISH, GRANNY, HERRINGBONE, HYDROGEN, INCOME, IONIC, METALLIC, PAIR, PEPTIDE, SINGLE, TREASURY, TRIPLE

BONE – CANNON, CARTILAGE, COFFIN, CRAZY, FETTER, FRONTAL, FUNNY, HAUNCH, HEEL, INNOMINATE, MEMBRANE, OCCIPITAL, PARIETAL, SPHENOID, SPLINT, STIRRUP, TEMPORAL, TYMPANIC, ZYGOMATIC

BOOK – BLACK, CLOSED, COMMONPLACE, COOKERY, DOMESDAY, DOOMSDAY, HYMN, OPEN, PHRASE, PRAYER, REFERENCE, STATUTE, TALKING

BOTTLE – BRANDY, FEEDING, HOT-WATER, KLEIN, NANSEN, WATER

BOWL – BEGGING, DUST, FINGER, GOLDFISH, RICE

BOX – APPLE, BALLOT, BLACK, CHRISTMAS, COIN, DEED, DISPATCH, FUSE, FUZZ, GLOVE, JUNCTION, JURY, LETTER, MUSIC, PENALTY, PILLAR, POOR, PRESS, SENTRY, SHOOTING, SIGNAL, TELEPHONE, VOICE, WINDOW, WINE, WITNESS

BOY – ALTAR, BALL, BARROW, BEST, BEVIN, BLUE-EYED, CABIN, ERRAND, OFFICE, OLD, PRINCIPAL, RENT, TAR, TEDDY, WHIPPING

BRAKE – AIR, CENTRIFUGAL, DISC, DRUM, FOOT, HYDRAULIC, SHOOTING

BRETHREN – BOHEMIAN, ELDER, EXCLUSIVE, OPEN, PLYMOUTH, TRINITY

BRIDGE – AIR, AUCTION, BAILEY, BALANCE, BOARD, CABLE-STAYED, CANTILEVER, CLAPPER, CONTRACT, COUNTERPOISE, DUPLICATE, FLYING, FOUR-DEAL, LAND, PIVOT, RAINBOW, RUBBER, SNOW, SUSPENSION, SWING, TRANSPORTER, TRUSS, TURN, WHEATSTONE

BRIGADE – BOYS', FIRE, FUR, INTERNATIONAL

BROTHER – BIG, BLOOD, LAY

BUG – ASSASSIN, CABBAGE, CHINCH, CROTON, DAMSEL, DEBRIS, FLOWER, GROUND, HARLEQUIN, JUNE, KISSING, LACE, LIGHTNING, MAORI, MEALY, PILL, RHODODENDRON, SHIELD, SOW, SQUASH, WATER, WHEEL

BUGGY – BABY, BEACH, SWAMP

BUOY – BELL, BREECHES, CAN, LIFE, NUN, SPAR

BURNER – BACK, BUNSEN, GAS, LIME, WELSBACH

BUSH – BURNING, BUTTERFLY, CALICO, COTTON, CRANBERRY, CREOSOTE, DAISY, EMU, GOOSEBERRY, MINT, NATIVE, NEEDLE, ORCHARD, STRAWBERRY, SUGAR

BUSINESS – BIG, MONKEY, SHOW

BY – COME, DO, GET, GO, PASS, PUT, STAND, STICK

CAKE – ANGEL, BANBURY, BARM, COTTON, DUNDEE, ECCLES, FISH, GENOA, JOHNNY, LARDY, LAYER, MADEIRA, MARBLE, OIL, PONTEFRACT, POUND, ROCK, SALT, SANDWICH, SIMNEL, SPONGE, TIPSY, UPSIDE-DOWN, WEDDING

CALL – BIRD, CLOSE, COLD, CURTAIN, LINE, PHOTO, ROLL, TOLL, TRUNK

CAMERA – AUTOMATIC, BOX, CANDID, CINE, COMPACT, GAMMA, IN, MINIATURE, MOVIE, PINHOLE, REFLEX

CAMP – CONCENTRATION, HEALTH, HIGH, HOLIDAY, LABOUR, LOW, MOTOR, TRANSIT, WORK

CANAL – ALIMENTARY, ANAL, CALEDONIAN, ERIE, GRAND, HAVERSIAN, MITTELLAND, PANAMA, ROOT, SEMICIRCULAR, SPINAL, SUEZ, WELLAND

CAP – BATHING, CLOTH, CROWN, DEATH, DUNCE, DUTCH, FILLER, FLAT, FOOL'S, FUNNEL, JOCKEY, JULIET, LEGAL, LIBERTY, MILK, PERCUSSION, ROOT, SHAGGY, STOCKING, WATCH, WAX

CAPITAL – BLOCK, HUMAN, RISK, SMALL, VENTURE, WORKING

CAPSULE – SEED, SPACE, TIME

CARD – BANK, BANKER'S, CALLING, CHEQUE, CHRISTMAS, CIGARETTE, COURT, CREDIT, DONOR, DRAWING, FLASH, GREEN, ID, LASER, LETTER, PICTURE, PLACE, PLAYING, POSTAL, PUNCHED, SHOW, SMART, UNION, VISITING, YELLOW

CASE – ATTACHÉ, BASKET, COT, DISPATCH, DRESSING, LOWER, SPECIAL, SPORE, STATED, TEST, UPPER, WARDIAN, WORST, WRITING

CELL – BLOOD, CADMIUM, CLARK, COLLAR, CONDEMNED, DANIELL, DEATH, DRY, ELECTROLYTIC, FLAME, FUEL, GERM, GRAVITY, GUARD, LYMPH, MAST, NERVE, PADDED, PARIETAL, PHOTOELECTRIC, PRIMARY, SECONDARY, SELENIUM, SOLAR, SOMATIC, STANDARD, STEM, SWARM, UNIT, VOLTAIC, WET

CENTRE – ACTIVE, ATTENDANCE, CIVIC, COMMUNITY, COST, DAYCARE, DEAD, DETENTION, GARDEN, HEALTH, MUSIC, NERVE, REMAND, SHOPPING, STORM

CHAIN – BICYCLE, BRANCHED, CLOSED, DAISY, FOOD, GOLDEN, GRAND, GUNTER'S, LEARNER'S, MARKOV, MOUNTAIN, OPEN, SAFETY, SIDE, SNIGGING, STRAIGHT, SURVEYOR'S, WATCH

CHAIR – BATH, BOATSWAIN'S, DECK, EASY, ELECTRIC, ROCKING, SEDAN, STRAIGHT, SWIVEL, WINDSOR, WING

CHAMBER – BUBBLE, CLOUD, COMBUSTION, DECOMPRESSION, ECHO, FLOAT, GAS, INSPECTION, IONIZATION, LOWER, MAGMA, PRESENCE, PRIVY, SECOND, SPARK, STAR, UPPER

CHART – BAR, BREAKEVEN, CONTROL, FLOW, ORGANIZATION, PIE, PLANE

CHASE – PAPER, WILD-GOOSE

CHEST – COMMUNITY, HOPE, MEDICINE, SEA, SLOP, WAR, WIND

CHILD – FOSTER, LATCHKEY, LOVE, MOON

CHINA – BONE, COCHIN, COMMUNIST, DRESDEN, NATIONALIST, RED, WORCESTER

CHIP – BLUE, LOG, POTATO, SILICON

CIRCLE – ANTARCTIC, ARCTIC, DIP, DRESS, EQUINOCTIAL, FAMILY, GREAT, HOUR, HUT, MERIDIAN, PARQUET, PITCH, POLAR, TURNING, VERTICAL, VICIOUS

CLASS – CABIN, CRYSTAL, EVENING, FIRST, LOWER,

MIDDLE, SECOND, THIRD, UNIVERSAL, UPPER, WORKING

CLAY – BOULDER, CHINA, FIRE, PORCELAIN

CLEF – ALTO, BASS, C, F, G, SOPRANO, TENOR, TREBLE, VIOLA

CLERK – ARTICLED, BANK, DESK, FILING, PARISH, SHIPPING, TALLY, TOWN

CLIP – BICYCLE, BULLDOG, CARTRIDGE, CROCODILE, WOOL

CLOCK – ALARM, ANALOGUE, ATOMIC, BIOLOGICAL, CAESIUM, CARRIAGE, CUCKOO, DIGITAL, GRAND-FATHER, GRANDMOTHER, LONGCASE, QUARTZ, SETTLER'S, SPEAKING, TIME, TOWNHALL, WATER

CLOTH – AEROPLANE, AIRCRAFT, ALTAR, BARK, COVERT, FACE, GRASS, MONK'S, NUN'S, SPONGE, TEA, WIRE

CLUB – BOOK, CHARTERED, COUNTRY, GLEE, GOLF, INDIAN, JOCKEY, LIONS, LUNCHEON, MONDAY, PROVIDENT, PUDDING, ROTARY, STRIP, SUPPER, TRAMPING, YOUTH

COAL – BITUMINOUS, BROWN, CANNEL, GAS, HARD, SOFT, STEAM, WHITE, WOOD

COCKTAIL – ATOMIC, FRUIT, MOLOTOV

CODE – AREA, BAR, BINARY, CHARACTER, CLARENDON, COLOUR, COUNTRY, DIALLING, GENETIC, GRAY, HIGHWAY, JUSTINIAN, MORSE, NAPOLEONIC, NATIONAL, PENAL, STD, TIME, ZIP

COLLAR – CLERICAL, DOG, ETON, HEAD, MANDARIN, ROMAN, SHAWL, STORM, VANDYKE, WING

COLOUR – ACHROMATIC, CHROMATIC, COMPLEMENTARY, CROSS, LOCAL, OFF, PRIMARY, SECONDARY, TONE

COLUMN – AGONY, CORRESPONDENCE, FIFTH, PERSONAL, SPINAL, STEERING, VERTEBRAL

COMPANY – CLOSE, FINANCE, FIRE, FREE, HOLDING, JOINT-STOCK, LIMITED, PARENT, PRIVATE, PUBLIC, REPERTORY, STOCK

COMPLEX – ELECTRA, INFERIORITY, LAUNCH, OEDIPUS, PERSECUTION, SUPERIORITY

CONE – ICE-CREAM, NOSE, PINE, STORM, WIND

CORD – COMMUNICATION, SASH, SPERMATIC, SPINAL, UMBILICAL

COUNTER – CRYSTAL, GEIGER, PROPORTIONAL, REV, SCINTILLATION

COURSE – ASSAULT, BARGE, GOLF, MAGNETIC, MAIN, REFRESHER, SANDWICH

COURT – CLAY, COUNTY, CROWN, DISTRICT, DOMES-TIC, GRASS, HARD, HIGH, INFERIOR, JUSTICE, JUVE-NILE, KANGAROO, MAGISTRATES', MOOT, OPEN, PO-LICE, PRIZE, PROVOST, SHERIFF, SUPERIOR, SUPREME, TERRITORIAL, TOUT, TRAFFIC, TRIAL, WORLD

COVER – AIR, DUST, EXTRA, FIRST-DAY, GROUND, LOOSE

CREAM – BARRIER, BAVARIAN, CLOTTED, COLD, DEVONSHIRE, DOUBLE, GLACIER, ICE, PASTRY, SINGLE, SOUR, VANISHING, WHIPPING

CROP – CASH, CATCH, COVER, ETON, RIDING, ROOT

CROSS – CALVARY, CELTIC, CHARING, DOUBLE, FIERY, GEORGE, GREEK, IRON, JERUSALEM, LATIN, LORRAINE, MALTESE, NORTHERN, PAPAL, PATRIARCHAL, RED, SOUTHERN, TAU, VICTORIA

CROSSING – LEVEL, PEDESTRIAN, PELICAN, ZEBRA

CROW – CARRION, HOODED, JIM

CUP – AMERICA'S, CLARET, COFFEE, DAVIS, EGG, FA, FRUIT, GRACE, GREASE, LOVING, MOUSTACHE, STIRRUP, WORLD

CURRENCY – DECIMAL, FRACTIONAL, MANAGED, RESERVE

CURRENT – ALTERNATING, CROMWELL, DARK, DIRECT, EDDY, ELECTRIC, FOUCAULT, HUMBOLDT, JAPAN, LABRADOR, PERU, THERMIONIC, TURBIDITY

CURTAIN – AIR, BAMBOO, DROP, IRON, SAFETY

CUT – BASTARD, CREW, CULEBRA, GAILLARD, NAVY, OPEN, POWER, SHORT

DASH – EM, EN, PEBBLE, SWUNG

DAYS – DOG, EMBER, HUNDRED, JURIDICAL, LAY, ROGATION, SALAD

DEATH – BLACK, BRAIN, CIVIL, COT, CRIB, HEAT, LIVING, SUDDEN

DECK – 'TWEEN, BOAT, FLIGHT, HURRICANE, LOWER, MAIN, POOP, PROMENADE, SUN, TAPE

DELIVERY – BREECH, FORWARD, GENERAL, JAIL, RECORDED, RURAL, SPECIAL

DERBY – CROWN, DONKEY, KENTUCKY, ROLLER, SAGE

DESK – CASH, CITY, COPY, ROLL-TOP, WRITING

DEVIL – DUST, MOUNTAIN, PRINTER'S, SNOW, TASMANIAN

DIAGRAM – BAR, BLOCK, INDICATOR, RUSSELL, SCATTER, VENN

DIVE – CRASH, NOSE, POWER, SWALLOW, SWAN

DOCTOR – ANGELIC, BAREFOOT, CAPE, FAMILY, FLYING, SAW, WITCH

DOG – BACKING, BIRD, CARRIAGE, COACH, ESKIMO, EYE, GREAT, GUIDE, GUN, HEADING, HOT, KANGAROO, LEADING, LITTLE, NATIVE, PARIAH, PIG, POLICE, PRAIRIE, RACCOON, SAUSAGE, SEA, SHEPHERD, SLED, SNIFFER, SPOTTED, TOP, TRACKER, WORKING

DOOR – BACK, BARN, CAT, DUTCH, FIRE, FOLDING, FRONT, NEXT, OPEN, OVERHEAD, REVOLVING, STABLE, STAGE, STORM, STREET, SWING, TRAP

DOWN – BACK, BEAR, BEAT, BOG, BOIL, BREAK, BRING, BUCKET, BUCKLE, CALL, CAST, CHANGE, CLAMP, CLIMB, CLOSE, CRACK, CRY, CUT, DIE, DO, DRAG, DRESS, DUST, FALL, GET, GO, HAND, HOLD, HUNT, KEEP, KNOCK, LAY, LET, LIE, LIVE, LOOK, MOW, NAIL, PAY, PEG, PIN, PIPE, PLAY, PULL, PUT, RIDE, ROUND, RUB, RUN, SEND, SET, SETTLE, SHAKE, SHOOT, SHOUT, SIMMER, SIT, SLAP, SPONGE, STAND, STEP, STICK, STOP, STRIKE, TAKE, TALK, TEAR, TONE, TRACK, TURN, UPSIDE, VOTE, WASH, WEAR, WEIGH, WIND, WRITE

DRESS – ACADEMIC, COAT, COURT, EVENING, FANCY, FULL, HIGHLAND, MORNING, PINAFORE, TENT

DRESSING – FRENCH, ORE, RUSSIAN, SALAD, TOP, WELL

DRILL – BOAT, FIRE, HAMMER, KERB, PACK, POWER, TWIST

DRIVE – BEETLE, CHAIN, DISK, FLUID, FOUR-WHEEL, MOTOR, WHIST

DROP – ACID, COUGH, DELAYED, DOLLY, KNEE, LEMON, MAIL

DUCK – BLUE, BOMBAY, COLD, DEAD, HARLEQUIN, LAME, MANDARIN, MUSCOVY, MUSK, PARADISE, RUDDY, SEA, TUFTED, WOOD

DUST – ANGEL, BULL, COSMIC, GOLD

DUTY – DEATH, ESTATE, POINT, STAMP

EDGE – DECKLE, KNIFE, LEADING, TRAILING

EGG – CURATE'S, DARNING, EASTER, NEST, SCOTCH

END – BACK, BEST, BIG, BITTER, BOOK, BOTTOM, BUSINESS, CIGARETTE, COD, DEAD, EAST, FAG, GABLE, LAND'S, LOOSE, ROPE'S, STICKY, TAG, TAIL, TOP, WEST

ENGINE – AERO, BEAM, BYPASS, COMPOUND, DIESEL, DONKEY, EXTERNAL-COMBUSTION, FIRE, GAS, HEAT, INTERNAL-COMBUSTION, ION, JET, LIGHT, OVERHEAD-VALVE, PILOT, PLASMA, RADIAL, REACTION, RECIPROCATING, ROCKET, ROTARY, SIDE-VALVE, STATIONARY, STIRLING, TANK, TRACTION, TURBOJET, V-TYPE, VALVE-IN-HEAD, WANKEL

ENSIGN – BLUE, RED, WHITE

EVENT – FIELD, HAPPY, MEDIA, THREE-DAY, TRACK

EVIDENCE – CIRCUMSTANTIAL, CUMULATIVE, DIRECT, HEARSAY, KING'S, PRIMA-FACIE, QUEEN'S, STATE'S

EXCHANGE – CORN, EMPLOYMENT, FOREIGN, ION, LABOUR, PART, POST, STOCK

EYE – BEADY, BLACK, COMPOUND, ELECTRIC, EVIL, GLAD, MAGIC, MIND'S, PHEASANT'S, PINEAL, POPE'S, PRIVATE, RED, SCREW, WEATHER

FACE – BOLD, EN, LIGHT, LONG, OLD, POKER, STRAIGHT

FACTOR – COMMON, CORN, GROWTH, HOUSE, LOAD, POWER, QUALITY, RH, RHESUS, SAFETY, UNIT

FEATHER – COCK, CONTOUR, FLIGHT, SHAFT, SICKLE, WHITE

FILE – CARD, CROSSCUT, INDIAN, SINGLE

FINGER – INDEX, LADY'S, RING

FINISH – BLANKET, DEAD, MIRROR, PHOTO

FIRE – BRUSH, ELECTRIC, GREEK, LIQUID, QUICK, RAPID, RED, WATCH

FLAT – ADOBE, ALKALI, COTTAGE, DOUBLE, GARDEN, GRANNY, MUD, SALT, STUDIO

FOOD – CONVENIENCE, FAST, HEALTH, JUNK, SKIN, SOUL

FORTH – CALL, GO, HOLD, PUT, SET

FORWARD – BRING, CARRY, CENTRE, COME, INSIDE, PUT

FRACTION – COMMON, COMPLEX, COMPOUND, CONTINUED, DECIMAL, IMPROPER, PACKING, PARTIAL, PROPER, SIMPLE, VULGAR

FRACTURE – COLLES', COMMINUTED, COMPOUND, GREENSTICK, POTT'S, SIMPLE

FRAME – CLIMBING, COLD, GARDEN, HALF, OXFORD, PORTAL, SAMPLING, STILL, STOCKING

FRIDAY – GIRL, GOOD, MAN

FRONT – COLD, EYES, NATIONAL, OCCLUDED, PEOPLE'S, POLAR, POPULAR, RHODESIAN, WARM, WAVE

FROST – BLACK, JACK, SILVER, WHITE

FRUIT – ACCESSORY, COLLECTIVE, FALSE, FORBIDDEN, KEY, KIWI, MULTIPLE, PASSION, SIMPLE, SOFT, STONE, WALL

GALLERY – LADIES', NATIONAL, PRESS, PUBLIC, ROGUES', SHOOTING, STRANGER'S, TATE, WHISPERING, WINNING

GAP – CREDIBILITY, DEFLATIONARY, ENERGY, GENERA-TION, INFLATIONARY, SPARK, TRADE, WATER, WIND

GARDEN – BEAR, BOTANICAL, COVENT, KITCHEN,

KNOT, MARKET, PEBBLE, ROCK, ROOF, TEA, WINTER, ZOOLOGICAL

GAS – AIR, BOTTLED, CALOR, COAL, CS, ELECTROLYTIC, IDEAL, INERT, LAUGHING, MARSH, MUSTARD, NATURAL, NERVE, NOBLE, NORTH-SEA, PERFECT, POISON, PRODUCER, RARE, SEWAGE, TEAR, TOWN, WATER

GATE – GOLDEN, HEAD, IRON, KISSING, LICH, LYCH, MORAVIAN, STARTING, TAIL, TARANAKI, WATER

GIRL – BACHELOR, BAR, BEST, CALL, CAREER, CHORUS, CONTINUITY, COVER, DANCING, FLOWER, GIBSON, LAND, MARCHING, OLD, SWEATER

GLASS – BELL, BURNING, CHEVAL, CROWN, CUPPING, CUT, FAVRILE, FIELD, FLINT, FLOAT, GREEN, GROUND, HAND, LEAD, LIQUID, LOOKING, MAGNIFYING, MILK, MURRHINE, OBJECT, OPTICAL, PIER, PLATE, QUARTZ, REDUCING, RUBY, SAFETY, SILICA, SOLUBLE, STAINED, STORM, TIFFANY, VENETIAN, VOLCANIC, WATER, WIRE

GLASSES – DARK, FIELD, OPERA

GOAT – ANGORA, BILLY, KASHMIR, MOUNTAIN, NANNY

GOLD – FILLED, FOOL'S, FREE, MOSAIC, OLD, ROLLED, WHITE

GREEN – APPLE, BACK, BOTTLE, BOWLING, CHROME, CROWN, GRETNA, JADE, KENDAL, LIME, LINCOLN, NILE, OLIVE, PARIS, PEA, PUTTING, RIFLE, SEA

GROUND – BURIAL, CAMPING, COMMON, HOME, HUNTING, MIDDLE, PROVING, RECREATION, STAMPING, VANTAGE

GUARD – ADVANCE, COLOUR, HOME, IRON, NATIONAL, OLD, PRAETORIAN, PROVOST, RED, SECURITY, SWISS

GUIDE – BROWNIE, GIRL, HONEY, QUEEN'S

GUM – ACAROID, BLUE, BUBBLE, CHEWING, COW, FLOODED, GHOST, KAURI, RED, SNOW, SOUR, SPIRIT, SUGAR, SWEET, WATER, WHITE

HALF – BETTER, CENTRE, FLY, SCRUM

HALL – CARNEGIE, CITY, FESTIVAL, LIBERTY, MESS, MUSIC, TAMMANY, TOWN

HAND – CHARGE, CLUB, COURT, DAB, DEAD, DECK, FARM, FREE, GLAD, HELPING, HOUR, IRON, LONE, MINUTE, OLD, ROUND, SECOND, SHED, SWEEP, UPPER, WHIP

HAT – BRASS, COCKED, COSSACK, HARD, HIGH, OLD, OPERA, PANAMA, PICTURE, PORKPIE, RED, SAILOR, SCARLET, SHOVEL, SILK, SLOUCH, TEN-GALLON, TIN, TOP

HEART – BLEEDING, BULLOCK'S, DEAD, FLOATING, PURPLE, SACRED

HEAT – ATOMIC, BLACK, BLOOD, DEAD, LATENT, PRICKLY, RADIANT, RED, TOTAL, WHITE

HISTORY – ANCIENT, CASE, LIFE, NATURAL, ORAL

HITCH – BLACKWALL, CLOVE, HARNESS, MAGNUS, ROLLING, TIMBER, WEAVER'S

HOLE – AIR, BEAM, BLACK, BOLT, COAL, FUNK, GLORY, KETTLE, LUBBER'S, NINETEENTH, SOUND, SPIDER, SWALLOW, WATER, WATERING

HOLIDAY – BANK, BUSMAN'S, HALF, LEGAL, PUBLIC, ROMAN

HOME – EVENTIDE, HARVEST, MOBILE, NURSING, REMAND, STATELY, VILLA

HORSE – CHARLEY, DARK, IRON, LIBERTY, LIGHT, NIGHT, POLE, POST, QUARTER, RIVER, ROCKING,

413

SADDLE, SEA, SHIRE, TROJAN, WHEEL, WHITE, WILLING, WOODEN

HOUR – ELEVENTH, HAPPY, LUNCH, RUSH, SIDEREAL, WITCHING, ZERO

HOUSE – ACCEPTING, ADMIRALTY, BOARDING, BROILER, BUSH, CHARNEL, CHATTEL, CLEARING, COACH, COFFEE, COUNTING, COUNTRY, CUSTOM, DISCOUNT, DISORDERLY, DOWER, FASHION, FORCING, FREE, FULL, HALFWAY, ICE, ISSUING, LODGING, MANOR, MANSION, MEETING, OPEN, OPERA, PICTURE, POST, PUBLIC, ROOMING, SAFE, SOFTWARE, SPORTING, STATE, STATION, STOREY, TERRACED, THIRD, TOWN, TRINITY, UPPER, WASH, WENDY, WHITE

HUMOUR – AQUEOUS, GALLOWS, ILL, VITREOUS

HUNT – DRAG, FOX, SCAVENGER, STILL, TREASURE

ICE – BLACK, CAMPHOR, COCONUT, DRIFT, DRY, GLAZE, GROUND, PACK, PANCAKE, SHELF, SLOB, WATER

IN – ALL, BLOCK, BLOW, BOOK, BREAK, BRING, BUILD, BURN, BUY, CALL, CASH, CAVE, CHECK, CHIP, CLOSE, COME, DIG, DO, DRAG, DRAW, FALL, FILL, FIT, GET, GIVE, GO, HAND, HANG, HOLD, HORN, INK, JACK, KEEP, KEY, KICK, LAY, LET, LIE, LISTEN, LIVE, LOG, MOVE, MUCK, PACK, PAY, PHASE, PITCH, PLUG, PULL, PUSH, PUT, RAKE, REIN, RING, ROLL, ROPE, RUB, RUN, SCRAPE, SET, SETTLE, SIGN, SINK, SLEEP, STAND, START, STEP, SUCK, SWEAR, TAKE, THROW, TIE, TUCK, TUNE, TURN, WEIGH, WELL, WHIP, WORK, WRITE, ZERO, ZOOM

INTEREST – COMPOUND, CONTROLLING, HUMAN, LIFE, SIMPLE, VESTED

IRON – ALPHA, ANGLE, BETA, CAST, CHANNEL, CORRU-GATED, DELTA, GAMMA, GEM, GRAPPLING, GROZING, INGOT, LILY, MALLEABLE, PIG, PUMP, SHOOTING, SMOOTHING, SOLDERING, STEAM, TOGGLE, WROUGHT

IVY – BOSTON, GRAPE, GROUND, JAPANESE, POISON, WEEPING

JACK – JUMPING, MAN, SCREW, UNION, YELLOW

JACKET – AIR, BED, BOMBER, BUSH, DINNER, DONKEY, DUST, ETON, FLAK, HACKING, LIFE, MESS, MONKEY, NORFOLK, PEA, REEFING, SAFARI, SHELL, SMOKING, SPORTS, STEAM, WATER, YELLOW

JELLY – CALF'S-FOOT, COMB, MINERAL, PETROLEUM, ROYAL

JOE – GI, HOLY, SLOPPY

JUDGMENT – ABSOLUTE, COMPARATIVE, LAST, VALUE

JUMP – BROAD, HIGH, LONG, SKI, TRIPLE, WATER

KEY – ALLEN, CHROMA, CHURCH, CONTROL, DEAD, FUNCTION, IGNITION, MASTER, MINOR, NUT, OFF, ON, PRONG, SHIFT, SKELETON, TUNING

KICK – DROP, FLUTTER, FREE, FROG, GOAL, PENALTY, PLACE, SCISSORS, STAB

KNIFE – BOWIE, CARVING, CASE, CLASP, FLICK, FRUIT, HUNTING, PALLET, SHEATH, TRENCH

KNOT – BLACK, FISHERMAN'S, FLAT, FRENCH, GORDIAN, GRANNY, LOOP, LOVE, OVERHAND, REEF, SQUARE, STEVEDORE'S, SURGEON'S, SWORD, THUMB, TRUELOVE, WALL, WINDSOR

LACE – ALENÇON, BOBBIN, BRUSSELS, CHANTILLY, CLUNY, MECHLIN, PILLOW, POINT, SEA, TORCHON

LADY – BAG, DINNER, FIRST, NAKED, OLD, OUR, PAINTED, WHITE, YOUNG

LAMP – ALDIS, DAVY, FLUORESCENT, GLOW,

HURRICANE, INCANDESCENT, NEON, PILOT, SAFETY, SPIRIT, SUN, TUNGSTEN

LANGUAGE – BODY, COMPUTER, FIRST, FORMAL, MACHINE, NATURAL, PROGRAMMING, SECOND, SIGN

LANTERN – CHINESE, DARK, FRIAR'S, JAPANESE, MAGIC, STORM

LEAVE – FRENCH, MASS, MATERNITY, SHORE, SICK

LETTER – AIR, BEGGING, BLACK, CHAIN, COVERING, DEAD, DOMINICAL, FORM, FRENCH, LOVE, OPEN, POISON-PEN, SCARLET

LIBRARY – CIRCULATING, FILM, LENDING, MOBILE, SUBSCRIPTION

LICENCE – DRIVING, OCCASIONAL, POETIC, SPECIAL, TABLE

LIFE – FUTURE, LOVE, MEAN, PRIVATE, REAL, SHELF, STILL

LIGHT – ARC, BACK, BACK-UP, BENGAL, BRAKE, COURTESY, FIRST, GREEN, INNER, KLIEG, LEADING, PILOT, REAR, RED, REVERSING, RUSH, TRAFFIC, WHITE

LIGHTING – INDIRECT, STRIP, STROBE

LIGHTNING – CHAIN, FORKED, HEAT, SHEET

LIGHTS – ANCIENT, BRIGHT, FAIRY, HOUSE, NORTHERN, POLAR, SOUTHERN

LINE – ASSEMBLY, BAR, BOTTOM, BRANCH, CLEW, CONTOUR, DATE, FALL, FIRING, FLIGHT, FRONT, GOAL, HARD, HINDENBURG, HOT, LAND, LEAD, LEDGER, MAGINOT, MAIN, MASON-DIXON, NUMBER, ODER-NEISSE, OFF, ON, PARTY, PICKET, PLIMSOLL, PLUMB, POWER, PRODUCTION, PUNCH, SIEGFRIED, SNOW, STORY, TIMBER, WATER

LINK – CUFF, DRAG, MISSING

LION – MOUNTAIN, NEMEAN, SEA

LIST – BACK, CHECK, CIVIL, CLASS, HIT, HONOURS, MAILING, RESERVED, SHORT, SICK, TRANSFER, WAITING

LOCK – COMBINATION, FERMENTATION, MAN, MORTISE, PERCUSSION, SCALP, SPRING, STOCK, VAPOUR, WHEEL, YALE

LOVE – CALF, COURTLY, CUPBOARD, FREE, PUPPY

MACHINE – ADDING, ANSWERING, BATHING, FRUIT, KIDNEY, SEWING, SLOT, TIME, VENDING, WASHING

MAIL – AIR, CHAIN, ELECTRONIC, FAN, SURFACE

MAIN – RING, SPANISH, WATER

MAN – ADVANCE, ANCHOR, BEST, COMPANY, CON, CONFIDENCE, ENLISTED, FAMILY, FANCY, FRONT, HATCHET, HIT, ICE, INNER, IRON, LADIES', LEADING, MEDICINE, MUFFIN, NEANDERTHAL, PALAEOLITHIC, PARTY, PILTDOWN, RAG-AND-BONE, SANDWICH, STRAIGHT, TWELFTH, YES

MARCH – DEAD, FORCED, HUNGER, LONG, QUICK, SLOW

MARIA – AVE, BLACK, HENRIETTA, SANTA, TIA

MARK – BENCH, BLACK, EXCLAMATION, KITE, PUNCTUATION, QUESTION, QUOTATION

MARKET – BLACK, BUYERS', CAPITAL, CAPTIVE, COMMON, FLEA, KERB, MONEY, OPEN, SELLERS', SPOT, STOCK

MARRIAGE – CIVIL, COMMON-LAW, GROUP, MIXED

MASK – DEATH, GAS, LIFE, LOO, OXYGEN, SHADOW, STOCKING

MASTER – CAREERS, GRAND, HARBOUR, INTERNATIONAL, OLD, PAST, QUESTION

MATCH – FRICTION, LOVE, SAFETY, SHIELD, SLANGING, SLOW, TEST

MATE – FIRST, FOOL'S, RUNNING, SCHOLAR'S, SECOND, SOUL

MATTER – BACK, END, FRONT, GREY, SUBJECT, WHITE

MEDICINE – ALTERNATIVE, COMPLEMENTARY, DUTCH, FOLK, FORENSIC, PATENT

MILE – ADMIRALTY, AIR, GEOGRAPHICAL, NAUTICAL, ROMAN, SEA, STATUTE, SWEDISH

MILL – COFFEE, PEPPER, ROLLING, SMOCK, STAMP, STRIP, WATER

MITE – BULB, CHEESE, FLOUR, FOWL, GALL, HARVEST, ITCH, SPIDER, WIDOW'S

MONEY – BIG, BLOOD, CALL, CAUTION, COB, CONSCIENCE, DANGER, EASY, FOLDING, GATE, HEAD, HOT, HUSH, KEY, MAUNDY, NEAR, PAPER, PIN, PLASTIC, POCKET, PRIZE, READY, SEED, SHIP

MOON – BLUE, FULL, HARVEST, HUNTER'S, MOCK, NEW, OLD

MOTHER – EARTH, FOSTER, NURSING, QUEEN, REVEREND, SOLO

MOTION – FAST, HARMONIC, LINK, PERPETUAL, PROPER, SLOW

NAME – BRAND, CHRISTIAN, DAY, FAMILY, FIRST, GIVEN, HOUSEHOLD, LAST, MAIDEN, MIDDLE, PEN, PLACE, PROPRIETARY, SECOND, TRADE

NECK – BOAT, BRASS, CREW, SCOOP, SWAN, V

NEEDLE – CLEOPATRA'S, DARNING, DIP, ELECTRIC, ICE, MAGNETIC, PINE, SHEPHERD'S

NET – DRIFT, GILL, LANDING, MOSQUITO, POUND, SAFETY, SHARK

NIGHT – FIRST, GOOD, TWELFTH, WALPURGIS, WATCH

NOTE – ADVICE, AUXILIARY, BLUE, COVER, CURRENCY, DEMAND, EIGHTH, GOLD, GRACE, LEADING, PASSING, POSTAL, PROMISSORY, QUARTER, SICK, TREASURY, WHOLE

NUMBER – ACCESSION, ALGEBRAIC, ATOMIC, BACK, BINARY, BOX, CALL, CARDINAL, COMPLEX, COMPOSITE, COMPOUND, CONCRETE, E, GOLDEN, INDEX, MACH, MAGIC, OPPOSITE, ORDINAL, PERFECT, PRIME, REAL, REGISTRATION, SERIAL, SQUARE, TELEPHONE, WHOLE, WRONG

OFFERING – BURNT, PEACE

OFFICE – BOX, CROWN, DIVINE, ELECTRONIC, EMPLOYMENT, FOREIGN, HOLY, HOME, LAND, LEFT-LUGGAGE, PATENT, POST, REGISTER, WAR

OIL – CAMPHORATED, CASTOR, COCONUT, COD-LIVER, CORN, CRUDE, DIESEL, ESSENTIAL, FATTY, GAS, LINSEED, MACASSAR, MINERAL, MUSTARD, NUT, OLIVE, PALM, PEANUT, RAPE, SASSAFRAS, SHALE, SPERM, VEGETABLE, WHALE

OPERA – BALLAD, COMIC, GRAND, HORSE, LIGHT, SOAP, SPACE

ORANGE – AGENT, BITTER, BLOOD, MOCK, NAVEL, OSAGE, SEVILLE

ORDER – AFFILIATION, APPLE-PIE, ATTIC, BANKER'S, COMMUNITY-SERVICE, COMPENSATION, ENCLOSED, FIRING, LOOSE, MAIL, MARKET, MONEY, PECKING, POSSESSION, POSTAL, RECEIVING, SHORT, STANDING, SUPERVISION, TEUTONIC, THIRD, WORD

ORDERS – HOLY, MAJOR, MARCHING, MINOR, SEALED

ORGAN – BARREL, ELECTRIC, ELECTRONIC, END, GREAT, HAMMOND, HAND, HOUSE, MOUTH, PIPE, PORTATIVE, REED, SENSE, STEAM

OVER – BIND, BLOW, BOIL, BOWL, BRING, CARRY, CHEW, DO, FALL, GET, GIVE, GLOSS, GO, HAND, HOLD, KEEL, LAY, LOOK, MAIDEN, MAKE, PAPER, PASS, PUT, ROLL, RUN, SEE, SKATE, SLIDE, SMOOTH, SPILL, STAND, TAKE, THINK, THROW, TICK, TIDE, TURN, WARM, WORK

OYSTER – BUSH, PEARL, PRAIRIE, SEED, VEGETABLE

PACK – BLISTER, BUBBLE, COLD, FACE, FILM, ICE, POWER, WET

PAD – CRASH, HARD, LAUNCHING, LILY, SCRATCH, SHOULDER

PAINT – GLOSS, OIL, POSTER, WAR

PALACE – BUCKINGHAM, CRYSTAL, GIN, PICTURE

PAPER – ART, BALLOT, BLOTTING, BOND, BROMIDE, BROWN, BUILDING, CARBON, CARTRIDGE, CIGARETTE, COMMERCIAL, CREPE, FILTER, FLOCK, GRAPH, GREEN, INDIA, LAVATORY, LINEN, MANILA, MERCANTILE, MUSIC, ORDER, RICE, TISSUE, TOILET, TRACING, WAX, WRITING

PARK – AMUSEMENT, CAR, COUNTRY, FOREST, GAME, HYDE, NATIONAL, SAFARI, SCIENCE, THEME

PARTY – BOTTLE, COMMUNIST, CONSERVATIVE, FIRING, GARDEN, HEN, HOUSE, LABOUR, LIBERAL, NATIONAL, NATIONALIST, PEOPLE'S, REPUBLICAN, SEARCH, STAG, TEA, THIRD, WORKING

PASSAGE – BACK, BRIDGE, DRAKE, MIDDLE, MONA, NORTHEAST, NORTHWEST, ROUGH, WINDWARD

PATH – BRIDLE, FLARE, FLIGHT, GLIDE, PRIMROSE, TOWING

PAY – BACK, EQUAL, SEVERANCE, SICK, STRIKE, TAKE-HOME

PEA – BLACK-EYED, DESERT, PIGEON, SPLIT, SUGAR, SWEET

PEAR – ALLIGATOR, ANCHOVY, CONFERENCE, PRICKLY, WILLIAMS

PEN – CARTRIDGE, CATCHING, DATA, FELT-TIP, FOUNTAIN, QUILL, SEA

PENSION – EN, OCCUPATIONAL, RETIREMENT

PIANO – COTTAGE, GRAND, PLAYER, PREPARED, SQUARE, STREET, UPRIGHT

PIE – COTTAGE, CUSTARD, HUMBLE, MINCE, MUD, PORK, SHEPHERD'S

PIN – BOBBY, COTTER, DRAWING, END, FIRING, GUDGEON, PANEL, ROLLING, SAFETY, SCATTER, SHEAR, STICK, SWIVEL, TAPER, WREST, WRIST

PIPE – CORNCOB, ESCAPE, FLUE, INDIAN, JET, PEACE, PITCH, RAINWATER, REED, SOIL, WASTE

PITCH – ABSOLUTE, CONCERT, FEVER, PERFECT, WOOD

PLACE – DECIMAL, HIGH, HOLY, RESTING, WATERING

PLASTER – COURT, MUSTARD, STICKING

PLATE – ANGLE, ARMOUR, BATTEN, BUTT, ECHO, FASHION, FUTTOCK, GLACIS, GOLD, GROUND, HOME, LICENSE, NICKEL, QUARTER, REGISTRATION, SCREW, SILVER, SOUP, SURFACE, SWASH, TIN, TRADE, WALL, WOBBLE

PLAY – CHILD'S, DOUBLE, FAIR, FOUL, MATCH, MIRA-CLE, MORALITY, MYSTERY, PASSION, SHADOW, STROKE

PLEAT – BOX, FRENCH, INVERTED, KICK, KNIFE

POCKET – AIR, HIP, PATCH, SLASH, SLIT

POINT – BOILING, BREAKING, BROWNIE, CHANGE, CLOVIS, COVER, CRITICAL, CURIE, DEAD, DECIMAL, DEW, DIAMOND, DRY, END, EQUINOCTIAL, FESSE, FIXED, FLASH, FOCAL, FREEZING, GALLINAS, GAME, GOLD, HIGH, ICE, LIMIT, MATCH, MELTING, OBJECTIVE, PETIT, POWER, PRESSURE, SAMPLE, SATURATION, SET, SPECIE, STEAM, STRONG, SUSPENSION, TRANSITION, TRIG, TRIPLE, TURNING, VANISHING, VANTAGE, WEST, YIELD

POLE – BARBER'S, CELESTIAL, MAGNETIC, NORTH, SOUTH, TOTEM

POLL – ADVANCE, DEED, GALLUP, OPINION, RED, STRAW

POST – COMMAND, FINGER, FIRST, GOAL, GRADED, GRADIENT, HITCHING, LAST, LISTENING, NEWEL, OBSERVATION, REGISTERED, STAGING, TOOL, TRADING, WINNING

POT – CHAMBER, COAL, LOBSTER, MELTING, PEPPER, WATERING

POTATO – HOT, IRISH, SEED, SWEET, WHITE

POWDER – BAKING, BLACK, BLEACHING, CHILLI, CURRY, CUSTARD, FACE, GIANT, TALCUM, TOOTH, WASHING

PRESS – DRILL, FILTER, FLY, FOLDING, GUTTER, HYDRAULIC, PRINTING, PRIVATE, RACKET, STOP

PRESSURE – ATMOSPHERIC, BAROMETRIC, BLOOD, CRITICAL, FLUID, OSMOTIC, PARTIAL, VAPOUR

PRICE – ASKING, BID, BRIDE, INTERVENTION, LIST, MARKET, OFFER, RESERVE, STARTING, UNIT

PROFESSOR – ASSISTANT, ASSOCIATE, FULL, REGIUS, VISITING

PUDDING – BLACK, BLOOD, CABINET, CHRISTMAS, COLLEGE, EVE'S, HASTY, MILK, PEASE, PLUM, SUET, SUMMER, WHITE, YORKSHIRE

PUMP – AIR, BICYCLE, CENTRIFUGAL, ELECTROMAG-NETIC, FILTER, FORCE, HEAT, LIFT, PARISH, PETROL, ROTARY, STIRRUP, STOMACH, SUCTION, VACUUM

PUNCH – BELL, CARD, CENTRE, KEY, MILK, PLANTER'S, RABBIT, SUFFOLK, SUNDAY

PURSE – LONG, MERMAID'S, PRIVY, SEA

PUZZLE – CHINESE, CROSSWORD, JIGSAW, MONKEY

QUARTER – EMPTY, FIRST, LAST, LATIN

QUESTION – DIRECT, INDIRECT, LEADING, RHETORICAL

RABBIT – ANGORA, BUCK, JACK, ROCK, WELSH

RACE – ARMS, BOAT, BUMPING, CLAIMING, DRAG, EGG-AND-SPOON, MASTER, OBSTACLE, RAT, RELAY, SACK, THREE-LEGGED

RACK – CLOUD, ROOF, TOAST

RATE – BANK, BASE, BASIC, BIRTH, BIT, DEATH, EXCHANGE, LAPSE, MORTALITY, MORTGAGE, PIECE, POOR, PRIME, TAX

RECORDER – FLIGHT, INCREMENTAL, TAPE, WIRE

RED – BLOOD, BRICK, CHINESE, CHROME, CONGO, INDIAN, TURKEY, VENETIAN

RELATIONS – COMMUNITY, INDUSTRIAL, LABOUR, PUBLIC, RACE

RELIEF – HIGH, LOW, OUTDOOR, PHOTO

RENT – COST, ECONOMIC, FAIR, GROUND, MARKET, PEPPERCORN

RESERVE – CENTRAL, GOLD, INDIAN, NATURE, SCENIC

REVOLUTION – AMERICAN, BLOODLESS, CHINESE, CULTURAL, FEBRUARY, FRENCH, GLORIOUS, GREEN, INDUSTRIAL, OCTOBER, PALACE, RUSSIAN

RING – ANCHOR, ANNUAL, BENZENE, ENGAGEMENT, ETERNITY, EXTENSION, FAIRY, GAS, GROWTH, GUARD, KEEPER, NOSE, PISTON, PRICE, PRIZE, RETAINING, SEAL, SIGNET, SLIP, SNAP, TEETHING, TREE, VORTEX, WEDDING

ROAD – ACCESS, CLAY, CONCESSION, DIRT, ESCAPE, POST, RING, SERVICE, SLIP, TRUNK

ROD – AARON'S, BLACK, BLUE, CON, CONNECTING, CONTROL, DIVINING, DOWSING, DRAIN, FISHING, FLY, HOT, PISTON, STAIR, TIE, TRACK, WELDING

ROLL – BARREL, BRIDGE, COURT, DANDY, EGG, FORWARD, MUSIC, MUSTER, PIANO, PIPE, SAUSAGE, SNAP, SPRING, SWISS, VICTORY, WESTERN

ROOM – BACK, COMBINATION, COMMON, COMPOSING, CONSULTING, DAY, DINING, DRAWING, DRESSING, ENGINE, GUN, LIVING, MEN'S, OPERATIONS, ORDERLY, POWDER, PUMP, RECEPTION, RECREATION, REST, ROBING, RUMPUS, SITTING, SMOKING, STILL, TIRING, UTILITY, WAITING, WITHDRAWING

ROOT – BUTTRESS, CLUB, CUBE, CULVER'S, MALLEE, PLEURISY, PROP, SQUARE

ROT – BLACK, BROWN, DRY, FOOT, SOFT, WET

ROUND – BRING, CHANGE, COME, MILK, RALLY, SCRUB, TALK

ROW – CORN, DEATH, NOTE, SKID, TONE

ROYAL – ANNAPOLIS, BATTLE, PAIR, PORT, PRINCE, PRINCESS, RHYME

RUBBER – COLD, CREPE, HARD, INDIA, PARÁ, SMOKED, SORBO, SYNTHETIC, WILD

RULE – CHAIN, FOOT, GLOBAL, GOLDEN, GROUND, HOME, PARALLELOGRAM, PHASE, PLUMB, SETTING, SLIDE

RUN – BOMBING, BULL, DRY, DUMMY, GROUND, HEN, HOME, MILK, MOLE, SKI, TRIAL

SALAD – CORN, FRUIT, RUSSIAN, WALDORF

SALE – BOOT, BRING-AND-BUY, CAR-BOOT, JUMBLE, RUMMAGE, WHITE

SALTS – BATH, EPSOM, HEALTH, LIVER, SMELLING

SAUCE – APPLE, BÉCHAMEL, BREAD, CHILLI, CREAM, HARD, HOLLANDAISE, MELBA, MINT, MOUSSELINE, SOY, TARTAR, WHITE, WORCESTER

SAW – BACK, BAND, BUZZ, CHAIN, CIRCULAR, COMPASS, COPING, CROSSCUT, CROWN, FLOORING, FRET, GANG, PANEL, SCROLL, STONE, TENON

SCHOOL – APPROVED, BOARD, BOARDING, CHOIR, COMPREHENSIVE, CORRESPONDENCE, DAME, DAY, DIRECT-GRANT, ELEMENTARY, FINISHING, FIRST, GRAM-MAR, HIGH, INDEPENDENT, INFANT, JUNIOR, LOWER, MIDDLE, NIGHT, NURSERY, PREP, PREPARATORY, PRIMARY, PRIVATE, PUBLIC, RESIDENTIAL, SECONDARY, SPECIAL, STATE, SUMMER, SUNDAY, UPPER

SCIENCE – BEHAVIOURAL, CHRISTIAN, COGNITIVE, DOMESTIC, EARTH, HARD, INFORMATION, LIFE, NATURAL, PHYSICAL, POLICY, POLITICAL, RURAL, SOCIAL, VETERINARY

SCOUT – AIR, BOY, CUB, GIRL, KING'S, QUEEN'S, SEA, TALENT, VENTURE

SCREEN – BIG, FIRE, ORGAN, ROOD, SILVER, SMALL, SMOKE

SCREW — ARCHIMEDES', CAP, COACH, GRUB, ICE,
INTERRUPTED, LAG, LEAD, LEVELLING, LUG, MACHINE,
MICROMETER, PHILLIPS

SEASON — CLOSE, HIGH, OFF, SILLY

SEAT — BACK, BOX, BUCKET, COUNTRY, COUNTY,
DEATH, EJECTION, HOT, JUMP, LOVE, MERCY, RUMBLE,
SAFE, SLIDING, WINDOW

SECRETARY — COMPANY, HOME, PARLIAMENTARY,
PRIVATE, SOCIAL

SERVICE — ACTIVE, CIVIL, COMMUNITY, DINNER,
DIPLOMATIC, DIVINE, FOREIGN, LIP, NATIONAL, PUBLIC,
ROOM, SECRET, SENIOR, SILVER, TEA

SET — CLOSED, COMPANION, CRYSTAL, DATA, DEAD,
FILM, FLASH, JET, LOVE, NAIL, OPEN, ORDERED,
PERMANENT, POWER, SAW, SMART, SOLUTION, TOILET,
TRUTH

SHAFT — AIR, BUTT, DRIVE, ESCAPE, PROPELLER

SHEET — BALANCE, CHARGE, CRIME, DOPE, FLOW,
FLY, ICE, SCRATCH, SWINDLE, TEAR, THUNDER, TIME,
WINDING, WORK

SHIFT — BACK, BLUE, DAY, EINSTEIN, FUNCTION,
NIGHT, RED, SOUND, SPLIT, SWING

SHIRT — BOILED, BROWN, DRESS, HAIR, SPORTS,
STUFFED, SWEAT, TEE

SHOE — BLOCKED, BRAKE, COURT, GYM, HOT,
LAUNCHING, PILE, TENNIS, TRACK

SHOP — BETTING, BODY, BUCKET, CLOSED, COFFEE,
DUTY-FREE, FISH-AND-CHIP, JUNK, MACHINE, OPEN,
PRINT, SEX, SWAP, SWEET, TALKING, TUCK, UNION

SHOT — APPROACH, BIG, BOOSTER, DIRECT-MAIL,
DROP, FOUL, JUMP, LONG, PARTHIAN, PASSING, POT

SHOW — CHAT, DUMB, FLOOR, ICE, LIGHT, MINSTREL,
RAREE, ROAD, TALK

SICKNESS — ALTITUDE, BUSH, DECOMPRESSION,
FALLING, MILK, MORNING, MOTION, MOUNTAIN,
RADIATION, SERUM, SLEEPING, SWEATING

SIDE — DISTAFF, FLIP, PROMPT, SPEAR, SUNNY

SLEEVE — BALLOON, BATWING, BISHOP, DOLMAN

SOAP — CASTILE, GREEN, JOE, METALLIC, SADDLE,
SOFT, SUGAR, TOILET

SODA — CAUSTIC, CREAM, ICE-CREAM, WASHING

SOLDIER — FOOT, GALLANT, OLD, RETURNED, TIN,
UNKNOWN, WAGON, WATER

SONG — FOLK, PART, PATTER, PRICK, SWAN, THEME,
TORCH

SPEECH — CURTAIN, DIRECT, FREE, INDIRECT, KING'S,
QUEEN'S, REPORTED

SPIRIT — HOLY, PROOF, SURGICAL, TEAM, WHITE,
WOOD

SPOT — BEAUTY, BLACK, BLIND, HIGH, HOT, LEAF, SOFT,
TROUBLE

SQUAD — FIRING, FLYING, FRAUD, SNATCH, VICE

SQUARE — ALL, BEVEL, LATIN, MAGIC, MITRE, SET,
TIMES, WORD

STAMP — DATE, POSTAGE, RUBBER, TRADING

STAND — HALL, HAT, MUSIC, ONE-NIGHT, UMBRELLA

STANDARD — DOUBLE, GOLD, LAMP, ROYAL, SILVER

STAR — BINARY, BLAZING, DARK, DOG, DOUBLE,
DWARF, EVENING, EXPLODING, FALLING, FEATHER,
FILM, FIXED, FLARE, GIANT, MORNING, MULTIPLE, NEU-
TRON, NORTH, POLE, PULSATING, RADIO, SHOOTING

START — BUMP, FLYING, HEAD

STEAK — MINUTE, T-BONE, TARTAR

STICK — BIG, CANCER, COCKTAIL, CONTROL, FRENCH,
JOSS, POGO, SHOOTING, SKI, SWAGGER, SWIZZLE,
WALKING, WHITE

STITCH — BLANKET, BUTTONHOLE, CABLE, CHAIN,
GARTER, LOCK, MOSS, RUNNING, SATIN, SLIP,
STOCKING, TENT

STOCK — CAPITAL, COMMON, DEAD, JOINT, LAUGHING,
PREFERRED, ROLLING, VIRGINIA

STONE — BATH, BLARNEY, CINNAMON, COPING, FOUN-
DATION, IMPOSING, KIDNEY, MOCHA, OAMARU, PAVING,
PHILOSOPHER'S, PRECIOUS, ROSETTA, STEPPING

STOOL — CUCKING, CUTTY, DUCKING, MILKING, PIANO

STRAW — CHEESE, LAST, SHORT

STRIKE — BIRD, GENERAL, HUNGER, OFFICIAL, SIT-
DOWN, SYMPATHY, TOKEN, WILDCAT

STUDY — BROWN, CASE, FEASIBILITY, FIELD, MOTION,
NATURE, PILOT, TIME

STUFF — HOT, KIDS', ROUGH, SMALL, SOB

SUGAR — BARLEY, BEET, BROWN, CANE, CASTER,
CONFECTIONERS', FRUIT, GRANULATED, GRAPE, ICING,
INVERT, LOAF, MAPLE, MILK, PALM, SPUN, WOOD

SUIT — BATHING, BIRTHDAY, BOILER, DIVING, DRESS,
JUMP, LONG, LOUNGE, MAJOR, MAO, MINOR, MONKEY,
PATERNITY, PRESSURE, SAFARI, SAILOR, SLACK,
TROUSER, WET, ZOOT

TABLE — BIRD, COFFEE, DRESSING, GATE-LEG,
GLACIER, HIGH, LEAGUE, LIFE, MULTIPLICATION,
OCCASIONAL, OPERATING, PEMBROKE, PERIODIC,
POOL, REFECTORY, ROUND, SAND, TIDE, WATER,
WOOL, WRITING

TALK — BABY, DOUBLE, PEP, PILLOW, SALES, SMALL

TAPE — CHROME, FRICTION, GAFFER, GRIP, IDIOT,
INSULATING, MAGNETIC, MASKING, PAPER,
PERFORATED, PUNCHED, RED, SCOTCH, TICKER, VIDEO

TAR — COAL, JACK, MINERAL, PINE, WOOD

TENNIS — COURT, DECK, LAWN, REAL, ROYAL, TABLE

TERM — HALF, HILARY, INKHORN, LAW, LENT,
MICHAELMAS, TRINITY

THROUGH — BREAK, CARRY, COME, FOLLOW,
MUDDLE, PULL, PUSH, PUT, ROMP, RUN, SCRAPE, SEE,
WALK, WORK

TICKET — MEAL, ONE-WAY, PARKING, PAWN,
PLATFORM, RETURN, ROUND-TRIP, SEASON, SINGLE

TIDE — HIGH, LOW, NEAP, RED, SPRING

TIE — BLACK, BOW, CUP, ENGLISHMAN'S, STRING,
WHITE, WINDSOR

TIME — BIG, BORROWED, CLOSING, COMMON, COM-
POUND, CORE, DAYLIGHT-SAVING, DOUBLE, DOWN,
DRINKING-UP, EXTRA, FATHER, FOUR-FOUR, FULL,
HIGH, IDLE, INJURY, LIGHTING-UP, LOCAL, MEAN,
OPENING, PRIME, QUADRUPLE, QUESTION, QUICK, RE-
SPONSE, SHORT, SIX-EIGHT, SLOW, STANDARD, SUM-
MER, THREE-FOUR, TRIPLE, TWO-FOUR, UNIVERSAL

TO — BRING, COME, FALL, GO, HEAVE, KEEP, RISE, RUN,
SET, SPEAK, STAND, STICK, TAKE, TUMBLE, TURN

TOGETHER — GO, HANG, HOLD, LIVE, PULL, SCRAPE,
SCRATCH, STICK, THROW

TOM — LONG, PEEPING, UNCLE

TOOTH — BABY, EGG, MILK, SWEET, WISDOM

TOP — BIG, DOUBLE, FIGHTING, HUMMING, PEG,
ROUND, SCREW, SOFT, SPINNING, TANK

TOWN – BOOM, CAPE, COUNTY, GEORGE, GHOST, MARKET, NEW, POST, TWIN

TRADE – CARRIAGE, FREE, RAG, SLAVE

TRAIN – BOAT, DOG, GRAVY, WAGON, WAVE

TRAP – BOOBY, LIVE, POVERTY, RADAR, SAND, SPEED, STEAM, STENCH, STINK, TANK

TRIANGLE – BERMUDA, CIRCULAR, ETERNAL, PASCAL'S, RIGHT, RIGHT-ANGLED, SPHERICAL

TRICK – CON, CONFIDENCE, DIRTY, HAT, THREE-CARD

TRIP – DAY, EGO, FIELD, ROUND

TROT – JOG, RISING, SITTING, TURKEY

TUBE – CAPILLARY, CATHODE-RAY, DRIFT, ELECTRON, EUSTACHIAN, FALLOPIAN, GEISSLER, INNER, NIXIE, PICTURE, PITOT, POLLEN, SHOCK, SIEVE, SPEAKING, STATIC, TELEVISION, TEST, VACUUM

TURN – ABOUT, GOOD, KICK, LODGING, PARALLEL, STEM, THREE-POINT

UNDER – DOWN, GO, KEEP, KNUCKLE, SIT

WALL – ANTONINE, CAVITY, CELL, CHINESE, CLIMBING, CURTAIN, FIRE, HADRIAN'S, HANGING, PARTY, RETAINING, SEA, WAILING, WESTERN

WATCH – BLACK, MIDDLE, MORNING, NIGHT

WAVE – BRAIN, ELECTROMAGNETIC, FINGER, GROUND, HEAT, LONG, LONGITUDINAL, MEDIUM, NEW, PERMANENT, RADIO, SEISMIC, SHOCK, SHORT, SKY, SOUND, STANDING, STATIONARY, TIDAL

WAX – CHINESE, COBBLER'S, EARTH, JAPAN, MINERAL, MONTAN, PARAFFIN, SEALING, VEGETABLE

WAY – APPIAN, EACH, FLAMINIAN, FLY, FOSSE, MILKY, PENNINE, PERMANENT, UNDER

WHEEL – BALANCE, BIG, BUFFING, CATHERINE, CROWN, DISC, DRIVING, EMERY, ESCAPE, FERRIS, GRINDING, PADDLE, POTTER'S, PRAYER, SPINNING, STEERING, STITCH, TAIL, WATER, WIRE

WHISKEY – IRISH, CORN, MALT

WHISTLE – PENNY, STEAM, TIN, WOLF

WINDOW – BAY, BOW, COMPASS, GABLE, JESSE, LANCET, LAUNCH, PICTURE, RADIO, ROSE, SASH, STORM, WEATHER, WHEEL

WIRE – BARBED, CHICKEN, FENCING, HIGH, LIVE, RAZOR

WITH – BEAR, BREAK, CLOSE, DEAL, GO, LIVE, PLAY, SETTLE, SLEEP, STICK

WOMAN – FANCY, LITTLE, OLD, PAINTED, SCARLET, WIDOW

WORK – FIELD, NUMBER, OUTSIDE, SOCIAL

YARD – BACK, MAIN, SCOTLAND

YEAR – ASTRONOMICAL, CALENDAR, CIVIL, EQUINOCTIAL, FINANCIAL, FISCAL, GREAT, HOLY, LEAP, LIGHT, LUNAR, NEW, SABBATICAL, SCHOOL, SIDEREAL, SOLAR, TROPICAL

ZONE – ECONOMIC, ENTERPRISE, FREE, FRIGID, HOT, NUCLEAR-FREE, SKIP, SMOKELESS, TEMPERATE, TIME, TORRID, TWILIGHT

ABBREVIATIONS

AA (Alcoholics Anonymous; Automobile Association)

AAA (Amateur Athletic Association)

AB (able seaman)

ABA (Amateur Boxing Association)

ABP (archbishop)

ABTA (Association of British Travel Agents)

AC (alternating current; account)

ACA (Associate of the Institute of Chartered Accountants)

ACAS (Advisory Conciliation and Arbitration Service)

ACIS (Associate of the Chartered Institute of Secretaries)

AD (anno domini)

ADC (aide-de-camp;

amateur dramatic club)

ADJ (adjective)

ADM (Admiral)

ADV (adverb)

AD VAL (ad valorem)

AFA (Amateur Football Association)

AFC (Air Force Cross)

AFM (Air Force Medal)

AGM (annual general meeting)

AI (artificial insemination; artificial intelligence)

AIB (Associate of the Institute of Bankers)

AIDS (Acquired Immune Deficiency Syndrome)

ALA (Alabama)

AM (ante meridiem)

AMU (atomic mass unit)

ANON (anonymous)

AOB (any other business)

AOC (Air Officer Commanding)

APEX (Association of Professional, Executive, Clerical, and Computer Staff)

APOCR (Apocrypha)

APPROX (approximate)

APT (Advanced Passenger Train)

ARA (Associate of the Royal Academy)

ARAM (Associate of the Royal Academy of Music)

ARCM (Associate of the Royal College of Music)

ARCS (Associate of the Royal College of Science)

ARIBA (Associate of

the Royal Institute of British Architects)

ARIZ (Arizona)

ARK (Arkansas)

ASA (Advertising Standards Authority)

ASAP (as soon as possible)

ASH (Action on Smoking and Health)

ASLEF (Associated Society of Loco-motive Engineers and Firemen)

AT (atomic)

ATC (air traffic control; Air Training Corps)

ATS (Auxiliary Territorial Service)

ATTN (for the attention of)

ATTRIB (attributive)

AT WT (atomic weight)

AU (Ångstrom unit; astronomical unit)

AUEW (Amalgamated Union of Engineering Workers)

AUG (August)

AV (ad valorem; Authorized Version)

AVDP (avoirdupois)

AVE (avenue)

AWOL (absent without leave)

BA (Bachelor of Arts; British Academy; British Airways; British Association)

BAA (British Airports Authority)

BAFTA (British Academy of Film and Television Arts)

B ARCH (Bachelor of Architecture)

BART (baronet)

BBC (British Broadcasting Corporation)

BC (before Christ)

BCH (Bachelor of Surgery)

BCL (Bachelor of Civil Law)

BCOM (Bachelor of Commerce)

BD (Bachelor of Divinity)

BDA (British Dental Association)

BDS (Bachelor of Dental Surgery)

BE (bill of exchange)

B ED (Bachelor of Education)

B ENG (Bachelor of Engineering)

BHP (brake horsepower)

BIM (British Institute of Management)

B LITT (Bachelor of Letters)

BMA (British Medical Association)

BMC (British Medical Council)

BMJ (British Medical Journal)

BMUS (Bachelor of Music)

BN (billion)

BOC (British Oxygen Company)

BP (bishop)

BPAS (British

Pregnancy Advisory Service)

BPHARM (Bachelor of Pharmacy)

BPHIL (Bachelor of Philosophy)

BR (British Rail)

BRCS (British Red Cross Society)

BROS (brothers)

BSC (Bachelor of Science)

BSI (British Standards Institution)

BST (British Standard Time; British Summer Time)

BT (Baronet)

BTA (British Tourist Authority)

BVA (British Veterinary Association)

C (centigrade; circa)

CA (chartered accountant)

CAA (Civil Aviation Authority)

CAD (computer-aided design)

CADCAM (computer-aided design and manufacture)

CAL (California; calorie)

CAM (computer-aided manufacture)

CAMRA (Campaign for Real Ale)

C AND G (City and Guilds)

C AND W (country and western)

CANT (canticles)

CANTAB (of Cambridge – used with academic awards)

CAP (capital)

CAPT (captain)

CARD (Cardinal)

CB (Citizens' Band; Companion of the Bath)

CBE (Commander of the British Empire)

CBI (Confederation of British Industry)

CC (County Council; Cricket Club; cubic centimetre)

CDR (Commander)

CDRE (Commodore)

CE (Church of England; civil engineer)

CEGB (Central Electricity Generating Board)

C ENG (Chartered Engineer)

CENTO (Central Treaty Organization)

CERT (certificate; certified; certify)

CET (Central European Time)

CF (compare)

CFE (College of Further Education)

CFI (cost, freight, and insurance)

CGM (Conspicuous Gallantry Medal)

CH (chapter; church; Companion of Honour)

CHAS (Charles)

CI (curie; Order of the Crown of India)

CIA (Central Intelligence Agency)

CID (Criminal Investigation Department)

CIE (Companion of the Indian Empire)

CIF (cost, insurance, and freight)

CII (Chartered Insurance Institute)

C IN C (Commander in Chief)

CIS (Chartered Institute of Secretaries)

CL (centilitre)

CLLR (councillor)

CM (centimetre)

CMG (Companion of St Michael and St George)

CNAA (Council for National Academic Awards)

CND (Campaign for Nuclear Disarmament)

CO (commanding officer; company; county)

COD (cash on delivery)

C OF E (Church of England)

C OF S (Church of Scotland)

COHSE

(Confederation of Health Service Employees)

COL (colonel; Colorado; Colossians)

CONN (Connecticut)

CONT (continued)

COR (Corinthians)

COS (cosine)

CR (credit)

CRO (cathode ray oscilloscope; Criminal Records Office)

CSE (Certificate of Secondary Education)

CSI (Companion of the Star of India)

CSM (Company Sergeant Major)

CU (cubic)

CV (curriculum vitae)

CVO (Commander of the Victorian Order)

CWT (hundredweight)

D (daughter; died; penny)

DA (District Attorney)

DAK (Dakota)

DAN (Daniel)

DBE (Dame Commander of the British Empire)

DC (Detective Constable; direct current; from the beginning)

DCB (Dame Commander of the Bath)

DCL (Doctor of Civil Law)

DCM (Distinguished Conduct Medal)

DCMG (Dame Commander of St Michael and St George)

DCVO (Dame Commander of the Victorian Order)

DD (direct debit; Doctor of Divinity)

DDS (Doctor of Dental Surgery)

DEL (Delaware)

DEPT (department)

DES (Department of Education and Science)

DEUT (Deuteronomy)

DF (Defender of the Faith)

DFC (Distinguished Flying Cross)

419

DFM (Distinguished Flying Medal)
DG (by the grace of God)
DHSS (Department of Health and Social Security)
DI (Detective Inspector)
DIAL (dialect)
DIP (Diploma)
DIP ED (Diploma in Education)
DIY (do-it-yourself)
D LITT (Doctor of Literature)
DM (Doctor of Medicine)
D MUS (Doctor of Music)
DNB (Dictionary of National Biography)
DO (ditto)
DOA (dead on arrival)
DOB (date of birth)
DOE (Department of the Environment)
DOM (to God, the best and greatest)
DOZ (dozen)
DPHIL (Doctor of Philosophy)
DPP (Director of Public Prosecutions)
DR (debtor; doctor; drive)
DSC (Distinguished Service Cross; Doctor of Science)
DSM (Distinguished Service Medal)
DSO (Distinguished Service Order)
DT (delirium tremens)
DV (God willing)
DVLC (Driver and Vehicle Licensing Centre)
E (East; Easterly; Eastern)
EA (each)
EC (East Central – London postal district)
ECCLES (Ecclesiastes)
ECCLUS (Ecclesiasticus)
ECG (electrocardiogram)
ECS (European Communication Satellite)

EE (Early English)
EEC (European Economic Community)
EEG (electro-encephalogram)
EFTA (European Free Trade Association)
EG (for example)
EMA (European Monetary Agreement)
EMF (electromotive force)
ENC (enclosed; enclosure)
ENE (east-northeast)
ENSA (Entertainments National Service Association)
ENT (ear, nose and throat)
EOC (Equal Opportunities Commission)
EOF (end of file)
EP (electroplate; epistle)
EPH (Ephesians)
EPNS (electroplated nickel silver)
EPROM (erasable programmable read only memory)
ER (Edward Rex; Elizabeth Regina)
ESE (east-southeast)
ESN (educationally subnormal)
ESQ (esquire)
ESTH (Esther)
ETA (estimated time of arrival)
ETC (etcetera)
ETD (estimated time of departure)
ET SEQ (and the following one)
EX DIV (without dividend)
EX LIB (from the books)
EXOD (Exodus)
EZEK (Ezekiel)
F (Fahrenheit; franc)
FA (Football Association)
FANY (First Aid Nursing Yeomanry)
FAS (free alongside ship)
FBA (Fellow of the British Academy)
FBI (Federal Bureau of Investigation)

FC (Football Club)
FCA (Fellow of the Institute of Chartered Accountants)
FCII (Fellow of the Chartered Insurance Institute)
FCIS (Fellow of the Chartered Institute of Secretaries)
FCO (Foreign and Commonwealth Office)
FIFA (International Football Federation)
FL (flourished)
FLA (Florida)
FO (Field Officer; Flying Officer; Foreign Office)
FOB (free on board)
FOC (Father of the Chapel; free of charge)
FPA (Family Planning Association)
FRAM (Fellow of the Royal Academy of Music)
FRAS (Fellow of the Royal Astronomical Society)
FRCM (Fellow of the Royal College of Music)
FRCO (Fellow of the Royal College of Organists)
FRCOG (Fellow of the Royal College of Obstetricians and Gynaecologists)
FRCP (Fellow of the Royal College of Physicians)
FRCS (Fellow of the Royal College of Surgeons)
FRCVS (Fellow of the Royal College of Veterinary Surgeons)
FRGS (Fellow of the Royal Geographical Society)
FRIBA (Fellow of the Royal Institute of British Architects)
FRIC (Fellow of the Royal Institute of Chemistry)
FRICS (Fellow of the Royal Institution of

Chartered Surveyors)
FRPS (Fellow of the Royal Photographic Society)
FRS (Fellow of the Royal Society)
FRSA (Fellow of the Royal Society of Arts)
FSA (Fellow of the Society of Antiquaries)
FZS (Fellow of the Zoological Society)
G (gram)
GA (Georgia)
GAL (Galatians)
GATT (General Agreement on Tariffs and Trade)
GB (Great Britain)
GBE (Knight/Dame Grand Cross of the British Empire)
GBH (grievous bodily harm)
GC (George Cross)
GCB (Knight/Dame Grand Cross of the Bath)
GCE (General Certificate of Education)
GCHQ (Government Communications Headquarters)
GCIE (Grand Commander of the Indian Empire)
GCMG (Knight/Dame Grand Cross of St Michael and St George)
GCSE (General Certificate of Secondary Education)
GCVO (Knight/Dame Grand Cross of the Victorian Order)
GDP (gross domestic product)
GDR (German Democratic Republic)
GEO (George)
GER (German)
GHQ (general headquarters)
GIB (Gibraltar)
GLC (Greater London Council)
GM (George Medal; gram)

GMT (Greenwich Mean Time)
GNP (gross national product)
GOM (grand old man)
GP (general practitioner)
GPO (general post office)
H (hour)
HCF (highest common factor)
HEB (Hebrews)
HF (high frequency)
HGV (heavy goods vehicle)
HIH (His/Her Imperial Highness)
HIM (His/Her Imperial Majesty)
HM (headmaster; headmistress; His/Her Majesty)
HMI (His/Her Majesty's Inspector)
HMS (His/Her Majesty's Ship)
HMSO (His/Her Majesty's Stationery Office)
HNC (Higher National Certificate)
HND (Higher National Diploma)
HO (Home Office; house)
HON (honorary; honour; honourable)
HONS (honours)
HON SEC (Honorary Secretary)
HOS (Hosea)
HP (hire purchase; horsepower)
HQ (headquarters)
HR (holiday route; hour)
HRH (His/Her Royal Highness)
HSH (His/Her Serene Highness)
HT (height)
HV (high velocity; high-voltage)
IA (Institute of Actuaries; Iowa)
IAAF (International Amateur Athletic Federation)
IABA (International Amateur Boxing Association)

IATA (International Air Transport Association)
IB (ibidem; Institute of Bankers)
IBA (Independent Broadcasting Authority)
IBID (ibidem)
IC (in charge; integrated circuit)
ICE (Institution of Civil Engineers)
ICHEME (Institute of Chemical Engineers)
ID (idem; identification)
IE (that is)
IEE (Institution of Electrical Engineers)
IHS (Jesus)
ILL (Illinois)
I MECH E (Institution of Mechanical Engineers)
IMF (International Monetary Fund)
INC (incorporated)
INCL (included; including; inclusive)
IND (Indiana)
INST (instant)
IOM (Isle of Man)
IOW (Isle of Wight)
IPA (International Phonetic Alphabet)
IQ (intelligence quotient)
IR (Inland Revenue)
IRA (Irish Republican Army)
IS (Isaiah)
ISO (Imperial Service Order)
ITA (initial teaching alphabet)
ITAL (italic; italicized)
ITV (Independent Television)
JAM (James)
JC (Jesus Christ; Julius Caesar)
JER (Jeremiah)
JP (Justice of the Peace)
JR (junior)
KAN (Kansas)
KB (King's Bench)
KBE (Knight Commander of the British Empire)
KC (King's Counsel)

KCB (Knight Commander of the Bath)
KCIE (Knight Commander of the Indian Empire)
KCMG (Knight Commander of St Michael and St George)
KCSI (Knight Commander of the Star of India)
KCVO (Knight Commander of the Victorian Order)
KG (kilogram; Knight of the Garter)
KGB (Soviet State Security Committee)
KKK (Ku Klux Klan)
KM (kilometre)
KO (knock-out)
KP (Knight of St Patrick)
KSTJ (Knight of St John)
KT (Knight of the Thistle)
KY (Kentucky)
L (Latin; learner; pound)
LA (Louisiana)
LAT (latitude)
LB (pound)
LBW (leg before wicket)
LCD (liquid crystal display; lowest common denominator)
LCJ (Lord Chief Justice)
LEA (Local Education Authority)
LEV (Leviticus)
LF (low frequency)
LIEUT (Lieutenant)
LITT D (Doctor of Letters; Doctor of Literature)
LJ (Lord Justice)
LJJ (Lords Justices)
LLB (Bachelor of Laws)
LLD (Doctor of Laws)
LLM (Master of Laws)
LOC CIT (in the place cited)
LOQ (he/she speaks)
LPG (liquefied petroleum gas)
LPO (London Philharmonic Orchestra)

LPS (Lord Privy Seal)
LRAM (Licentiate of the Royal Academy of Music)
LS (locus sigilli)
LSD (pounds, shillings, and pence)
LSE (London School of Economics)
LSO (London Symphony Orchestra)
LTD (limited)
LW (long wave)
M (male; married; motorway; thousand)
MA (Master of Arts)
MACC (Maccabees)
MAJ (Major)
MAL (Malachi)
MASH (mobile army surgical hospital)
MASS (Massachusetts)
MATT (Matthew)
MB (Bachelor of Medicine)
MBE (Member of the British Empire)
MC (Master of Ceremonies)
MCC (Marylebone Cricket Club)
MCP (male chauvinist pig)
MD (Doctor of Medicine; Managing Director; Maryland)
ME (Maine)
MEP (Member of the European Parliament)
MET (meteorological; meteorology; metropolitan)
MF (medium frequency)
MG (milligram)
MIC (Micah)
MICH (Michigan)
MINN (Minnesota)
MISS (Mississippi)
ML (millilitre)
M LITT (Master of Letters)
MLR (minimum lending rate)
MM (millimetres)
MO (Medical Officer; Missouri)
MOD (Ministry of Defence)

MOH (Medical Officer of Health)

MONT (Montana)

MP (Member of Parliament; Metropolitan Police; Military Police)

MPG (miles per gallon)

MPH (miles per hour)

MPHIL (Master of Philosophy)

MR (Master of the Rolls)

MRCOG (Member of the Royal College of Obstetricians and Gynaecologists)

MRCP (Member of the Royal College of Physicians)

MRCS (Member of the Royal College of Surgeons)

MRCVS (Member of the Royal College of Veterinary Surgeons)

MS (manuscript; multiple sclerosis)

MSC (Master of Science)

MSM (Meritorious Service Medal)

MSS (manuscripts)

MT (Mount)

MVO (Member of the Victorian Order)

N (North)

NA (North America; not applicable)

NAAFI (Navy, Army, and Air Force Institutes)

NALGO (National and Local Government Officers Association)

NASA (National Aeronautics and Space Administration)

NAT (Nathaniel)

NATO (North Atlantic Treaty Organization)

NATSOPA (National Society of Operative Printers, Graphical and Media Personnel)

NB (note well)

NCB (National Coal Board)

NCO (non-commissioned officer)

NCP (National Car Parks)

NCT (National Childbirth Trust)

NCV (no commercial value)

NDAK (North Dakota)

NE (Northeast)

NEB (Nebraska)

NEC (National Executive Committee)

NEH (Nehemiah)

NEV (Nevada)

NFU (National Farmers' Union)

NGA (National Graphical Association)

NHS (National Health Service)

NI (National Insurance; Northern Ireland)

NNE (north-northeast)

NNW (north-northwest)

NO (not out; number)

NORM (normal)

NOS (numbers)

NP (new paragraph)

NR (near; Northern Region)

NSB (National Savings Bank)

NSPCC (National Society for the Prevention of Cruelty to Children)

NT (National Trust; New Testament)

NUBE (National Union of Bank Employees)

NUGMW (National Union of General and Municipal Workers)

NUJ (National Union of Journalists)

NUM (National Union of Mineworkers)

NUPE (National Union of Public Employees)

NUR (National Union of Railwaymen)

NUS (National Union of Seamen; National Union of Students)

NUT (National Union of Teachers)

NW (Northwest)

NY (New York)

O (Ohio)

OAP (old-age pensioner)

OB (outside broadcast)

OBAD (Obadiah)

OBE (Officer of the British Empire)

OCTU (Officer Cadets Training Unit)

OFM (Order of Friars Minor)

OHMS (On His/Her Majesty's Service)

OKLA (Oklahoma)

OM (Order of Merit)

ONC (Ordinary National Certificate)

OND (Ordinary National Diploma)

ONO (or near offer)

OP (opus)

OP CIT (in the work cited)

OPEC (Organization of Petroleum Exporting Countries)

OPS (operations)

OREG (Oregon)

OS (ordinary seaman; Ordnance Survey)

OSA (Order of St Augustine)

OSB (Order of St Benedict)

OSF (Order of St Francis)

OT (occupational therapy; Old Testament)

OTC (Officers' Training Corps)

OU (Open University)

OUDS (Oxford University Dramatic Society)

OXFAM (Oxford Committee for Famine Relief)

OZ (ounce)

P (page; penny; purl)

PA (Pennsylvania; per annum; personal assistant; public address system)

PAYE (pay as you earn)

PC (per cent; personal computer; police constable)

PD (paid)

PDSA (People's Dispensary for Sick Animals)

PE (physical education)

PEI (Prince Edward Island)

PER PRO (by the agency of)

PG (paying guest; postgraduate)

PHD (Doctor of Philosophy)

PHIL (Philippians)

PL (place; plural)

PLC (public limited company)

PLO (Palestine Liberation Organization)

PM (post meridiem; Prime Minister)

PO (Petty Officer; Pilot Officer; postal order; Post Office)

POW (prisoner of war)

PP (pages; per pro)

PPS (further postscript; Parliamentary Private Secretary)

PR (public relations)

PRAM (programmable random access memory)

PRO (Public Records Office; public relations officer)

PROM (programmable read-only memory)

PROV (Proverbs)

PS (postscript; Private Secretary)

PT (physical training)

PTA (Parent-Teacher Association)

PTO (please turn over)

PVA (polyvinyl acetate)

PVC (polyvinyl chloride)

QB (Queen's Bench)

QC (Queen's Counsel)

QED (which was to be demonstrated)

QM (quartermaster)

QR (quarter; quire)

QT (quart)

QV (which see)

R (king; queen; right; river)

RA (Royal Academy; Royal Artillery)

RAC (Royal Automobile Club)

RADA (Royal Academy of Dramatic Art)

RAF (Royal Air Force)

RAM (random access memory; Royal Academy of Music)

RAMC (Royal Army Medical Corps)

R AND D (research and development)

RBA (Royal Society of British Artists)

RBS (Royal Society of British Sculptors)

RC (Roman Catholic)

RCA (Royal College of Art)

RCM (Royal College of Music)

RCN (Royal College of Nursing)

RCP (Royal College of Physicians)

RCS (Royal College of Surgeons)

RCVS (Royal College of Veterinary Surgeons)

RD (road)

RE (religious education; Royal Engineers)

REME (Royal Electrical and Mechanical Engineers)

REV (Reverend)

RFC (Royal Flying Corps)

RH (Royal Highness; right hand)

RHA (Royal Horse Artillery)

RI (religous instruction)

RIBA (Royal Institute of British Architects)

RIC (Royal Institute of Chemistry)

RICS (Royal Institution of Chartered Surveyors)

RIP (may he rest in peace)

RK (religious knowledge)

RM (Resident Magistrate; Royal Mail; Royal Marines)

RMA (Royal Military Academy)

RN (Royal Navy)

RNIB (Royal National Institute for the Blind)

RNLI (Royal National Lifeboat Institution)

ROM (read only memory)

ROSPA (Royal Society for the Prevention of Accidents)

RPM (revolutions per minute)

RS (Royal Society)

RSA (Royal Society of Arts)

RSC (Royal Shake-speare Company)

RSM (Regimental Sergeant Major; Royal Society of Medicine)

RSPB (Royal Society for the Protection of Birds)

RSPCA (Royal Society for the Prevention of Cruelty to Animals)

RSVP (please answer)

RT HON (Right Honourable)

RT REV (Right Reverend)

RU (Rugby Union)

RUC (Royal Ulster Constabulary)

S (second; shilling; South)

SA (Salvation Army; sex appeal)

SAE (stamped addressed envelope)

SALT (Strategic Arms Limitation Talks)

SAS (Special Air Service)

SATB (soprano, alto, tenor, bass)

SAYE (save-as-you-earn)

SCD (Doctor of Science)

SE (southeast)

SEC (second; secretary)

SEN (senior; State Enrolled Nurse)

SEQ (the following)

SF (science fiction)

SGT (Sergeant)

SHAPE (Supreme Headquarters Allied Powers Europe)

SI (International System of Units)

SIN (sine)

SLADE (Society of Lithographic Artists, Designers, and Etchers)

SLR (single lens reflex)

SNCF (French National Railways)

SNP (Scottish National Party)

SNR (senior)

SOGAT (Society of Graphical and Allied Trades)

SOP (soprano)

SQ (square)

SRN (State Registered Nurse)

SSE (south-southeast)

SSW (south-southwest)

ST (saint; street)

STD (subscriber trunk dialling)

SW (southwest)

TA (Territorial Army)

TAN (tangent)

TASS (official news agency of the former Soviet Union)

TB (tubercle bacillus)

TCCB (Test and County Cricket Board)

TEFL (teaching English as a foreign language)

TENN (Tennessee)

TEX (Texas)

TGWU (Transport and General Workers' Union)

THESS (Thessalonians)

THOS (Thomas)

TM (trademark; transcendental meditation)

TOPS (Training Opportunities Scheme)

TSB (Trustee Savings Bank)

TT (teetotal; teetotaller)

TU (trade union)

TUC (Trades Union Congress)

TV (television)

UC (upper case)

UCATT (Union of Construction, Allied Trades, and Technicians)

UCCA (Universities Central Council on Admissions)

UCL (University College, London)

UDI (unilateral declaration of independence)

UEFA (Union of European Football Associations)

UHF (ultrahigh frequency)

UHT (ultrahigh temperature)

UK (United Kingdom)

ULT (ultimo)

UN (United Nations)

UNCTAD (United Nations Commission for Trade and Development)

UNESCO (United Nations Educational, Scientific, and Cultural Organization)

UNO (United Nations Organization)

UPOW (Union of Post Office Workers)

US (United States)

USA (United States of America)

USDAW (Union of Shop, Distributive, and Allied Workers)

USSR (Union of Soviet Socialist Republics)

V (verse; versus; volt)

VA (Order of Victoria and Albert; Virginia)

VAT (value-added tax)

VB (verb)

VC (Vice Chancellor; Victoria Cross)

VD (venereal disease)

VDU (visual display unit)

VE (Victory in Europe)

VG (very good)

VHF (very high frequency)

VIP (very important person)

VIZ (namely)

VLF (very low frequency)

VR (Victoria Regina; Volunteer Reserve)

VS (verse)

VSO (Voluntary Service Overseas)
VT (Vermont)
W (west)
WAAC (Women's Army Auxiliary Corps)
WAAF (Women's Auxiliary Air Force)
WC (water closet; West Central)
WI (West Indies; Women's Institute)
WIS (Wisconsin)
WK (week)
WM (William)
WNW (west-northwest)
WO (Warrant Officer)
WP (word processor)
WPC (Woman Police Constable)
WPM (words per minute)
WRAC (Women's Royal Army Corps)
WRAF (Women's Royal Air Force)
WRNS (Women's Royal Naval Service)
WRVS (Women's Royal Voluntary Service)
WSW (west-southwest)
WT (weight)
WW (Word War)
WWF (World Wildlife Fund)
WYO (Wyoming)
XL (extra large)
YHA (Youth Hostels Association)
YMCA (Young Men's Christian Association)
YR (year)
YWCA (Young Women's Christian Association)
ZECH (Zechariah)
ZEPH (Zephania)

EPONYMS

NAME – named after

ACOL – a club in Acol Road, London

ALEXANDER TECHNIQUE – Frederick Matthias (d. 1955) Australian actor who originated it

ANGSTROM – Anders J Ångström (1814–74) Swedish physicist

AXEL – Axel Paulsen (d. 1938) Norwegian skater

BADMINTON – Badminton House, where the game was first played

BAFFIN BAY – William Baffin 17th-century English navigator

BAKELITE – L H Baekeland (1863–1944) Belgian-born US inventor

BAKEWELL TART – Bakewell, Derbyshire

BALACLAVA (HELMET) – Balaklava

BANTING – William Banting (1797–1878) London undertaker

BASKERVILLE TYPE – John Baskerville (1706–75) English printer

BATH OLIVER – William Oliver (1695–1764) a physician at Bath

BEDLINGTON TERRIER – the town Bedlington in Northumberland, where they were first bred

BEEF STROGANOFF – Count Paul Stroganoff 19th-century Russian diplomat

BELISHA BEACON – Leslie Hore-Belisha (1893–1957) British politician

BERTILLON SYSTEM – Alphonse Bertillon (1853–1914) French criminal investigator

BIG BEN – Sir Benjamin Hall, Chief Commissioner of Works in 1856 when it was cast

BIRO – Laszlo Bíró (1900–85) Hungarian inventor

BLACKWOOD – Easeley F Blackwood its US inventor

BO DIDDLEY BEAT – Bo Diddley (1929–) US rhythm-and-blues performer and songwriter

BODLEIAN – Sir Thomas Bodley (1545–1613) English scholar who founded it in 1602

BORSTAL – Borstal village, Kent, where the first institution was founded

BOURBON – Bourbon County, Kentucky, where it was first made

BOWLER – John Bowler 19th-century London hatter

BRAMLEY – Matthew Bramley 19th-century English butcher, said to have first grown it

BROUGHAM – Henry Peter, Lord Brougham (1778–1868)

BROWNING GUN – John M Browning (1855–1926) US designer of firearms

CANTON CREPE – Canton, China, where it was originally made

CELSIUS – Anders Celsius (1701–44) Swedish astronomer who invented it

CHESTERFIELD – a 19th-century Earl of Chesterfield

COLT – Samuel Colt (1814–62) US inventor

COS – Kos, the Aegean island of its origin

COX'S ORANGE PIPPIN – R Cox, its English propagator

CRO-MAGNON MAN – the cave Cro-Magnon, Dordogne, France, where the remains were first found

DAIQUIRI – Daiquiri, rum-producing town in Cuba

DEMERARA – Demerara, a region of Guyana

DERBY – 12th Earl of Derby (d. 1834) who founded the horse race at Epsom Downs in 1780

DERRINGER – Henry Deringer, US gunsmith who invented it

DOILY – Doily, a London draper

DOUGLAS FIR – David Douglas (1798–1834) Scottish botanist

DOWNING STREET – Sir George Downing (1623–84) English statesman

DUMDUM – Dum-Dum, town near Calcutta where these bullets were made

EMMENTHAL CHEESE – Emmenthal, a valley in Switzerland

FERRIS WHEEL – G W G Ferris (1859–96) US engineer

FIACRE – the Hotel de St Fiacre, Paris, where these vehicles were first hired out

FOSBURY FLOP – Dick Fosbury US Olympic winner of men's high jump, 1968

GARAND RIFLE – John C Garand (1888–1974) US gun designer

GATLING GUN – R J Gatling (1818–1903) US inventor

GORGONZOLA CHEESE – Gorgonzola, Italian town where it originated

GRANNY SMITH – Maria Ann Smith, known as Granny Smith (d.1870) who first produced them at Eastwood, Sydney

GUILLOTINE – Joseph Ignace Guillotin (1738–1814) French physician

HANSARD – T C Hansard (1752–1828) who compiled the reports until 1889

HANSOM – J A Hansom (1803–82)

HEATH ROBINSON – William Heath Robinson (1872–1944) British cartoonist

HEPPLEWHITE FURNITURE – George Hepplewhite (1727–86) English cabinetmaker

HOBSON'S CHOICE – Thomas Hobson (1544–1631) English liveryman who gave his customers no choice but had them take the nearest horse

HOMBURG – Homburg, Germany, where it was originally made

HONITON LACE – Honiton, Devon, where it was first made

JACK RUSSELL – John Russell (1795–1883) English clergyman who developed the breed

KALASHNIKOV RIFLE – Mikhail Kalashnikov (1919–) its designer

KIR – Canon F Kir (1876–1968) mayor of Dijon

LEOTARD – Jules Léotard, French acrobat

LEWIS GUN – I N Lewis (1858–1931) US soldier

LLOYD'S – Edward Lloyd (d. ?1726) at whose coffee house in London the underwriters originally carried on their business

LONSDALE BELT – Hugh Cecil Lowther, 5th Earl of Lonsdale (1857–1944)

LUDDITE – Ned Ludd, an 18th-century Leicestershire workman, who destroyed industrial machinery

MACADAM – John McAdam (1756–1836) Scottish engineer

MACKINTOSH – Charles Macintosh (1760–1843) who invented it

MAGINOT LINE – André Maginot (1877–1932) French minister of war

MASOCHISM – Leopold von Sacher Masoch (1836–95) Austrian novelist

MAUSER – P P von Mauser (1838–1914) German firearms inventor

MILLS BOMB – Sir William Mills (1856–1932) English inventor

MINTON – Thomas Minton (1765–1836) English potter

MOBIUS STRIP – August Möbius (1790–1868) German mathematician

MOOG SYNTHESIZER – Robert Moogorn, US engineer

NEGUS – Col Francis Negus (d. 1732) its English inventor

NISSEN HUT – Lt Col Peter Nissen (1871–1930) British mining engineer

PETRI DISH – J R Petri (1852–1921) German bacteriologist

PILATES – Joseph Pilates (1880–1967) its German inventor

PLIMSOLL LINE – Samuel Plimsoll (1824–98) MP, who advocated its adoption

PULLMAN – George M Pullman (1831–97) the US inventor who first manufactured such coaches

QUEENSBERRY RULES – 9th Marquess of Queensberry, who originated the rules in 1869

ROLLS-ROYCE – its designers: Charles Stewart Rolls (1877–1910) and Sir Frederick Henry Royce (1863–1933)

ROQUEFORT CHEESE – Roquefort village in S France

RUBIK CUBE – Professor Erno Rubik (1944–) its Hungarian inventor

RUGBY – the public school at Rugby, where it was first played

SALLY LUNN BUN – an 18th-century English baker who invented it

SALMONELLA – Daniel E Salmon (1850–1914) US veterinary surgeon

SAM BROWNE BELT – Sir Samuel J Browne (1824–1901) British general, who devised such a belt

SANDWICH – John Montagu, 4th Earl of Sandwich (1718–92) who ate sandwiches rather than leave the gambling table for meals

SAXOPHONE – Adolphe Sax (1814–94) Belgian musical-instrument maker, who invented it (1846)

SEALYHAM TERRIER – Sealyham, village in S Wales, where it was bred in the 19th century

SHRAPNEL – H Shrapnel (1761–1842) English army officer, who invented it

SPOONERISM – W A Spooner (1844–1930) English clergyman

STANLEY KNIFE – F T Stanley, US businessman

STAYMAN – Samuel M Stayman (1909–94) US bridge expert

STETSON – John Stetson (1830–1906) US hatmaker

STILTON CHEESE – Stilton, Cambridgeshire, where it was originally sold

TATTERSALL'S – Richard Tattersall (d. 1795) English horseman, who founded the market

TONTINE – Lorenzo Tonti, Neapolitan banker who devised the scheme

TUXEDO – a country club in Tuxedo Park, New York

VENN DIAGRAM – John Venn (1834–1923) English logician

VERNIER – Paul Vernier (1580–1637) French mathematician, who described the scale

VERY LIGHT – Edward W Very (1852–1910) US naval ordnance officer

WALDORF SALAD – the Waldorf–Astoria Hotel, New York City

WELLINGTON BOOTS – the 1st Duke of Wellington

WENDY HOUSE – the house built for Wendy, the girl in J M Barrie's play *Peter Pan*

WHITWORTH SCREW THREAD – Sir Joseph Whitworth (1803–87) English engineer

WILTON CARPET – Wilton, Wiltshire

WINCHESTER RIFLE – O F Winchester (1810–80) US manufacturer

WORSTED – Worstead, a district in Norfolk

DIALECT WORDS

3	4–continued	5–continued	6–continued	7–continued
AIT	REDD	NETTY	LINHAY	PEEVERS
AN'T	REEN	NIEVE	MAUNGY	SCUNNER
DAP	ROUP	NIXER	MESTER	SHINKIN
GAN	SCAG	OXTER	MIDDEN	SHOOGLE
GEY	SILE	PEART	MISTAL	SKELLUM
HAP	SMIT	PLOAT	NOBBUT	SKIFFLE
HEN	SOOK	REEST	PASSEL	SNICKET
KEN	SPAG	REIVE	PAXWAX	SPAN–NEW
KEP	STOB	SHOON	PEERIE	STEAMIE
MIM	TAMP	SHOWD	PIZZLE	STOTTER
NEB	TASS	SKELF	PLODGE	TAMPING
TWP	TRIG	SKELP	SCALLY	WHERRET
WUS	TUMP	SKIRL	SCOUSE	
	WAFF	SNECK	SCRAMB	**8**
4	WAME	SONSY	SCROOP	BACKWORD
AGEE	WEAN	SOUGH	SCRUMP	BARM CAKE
BIDE	YAWL	SPEEL	SHEUCH	BOBOWLER
BING	YELD	SPELK	SHUGGY	CHAMPION
BIST		SPRUE	SKELLY	CHOLLERS
CHAW	**5**	STANG	SPENCE	DUNNAKIN
CLEM	ASHET	THIRL	SPUGGY	FLATLING
COOM	BEVVY	THOLE	TACKET	FORNENST
COWK	BIELD	WHEEN	THRAVE	GALLUSES
CREE	BUROO		THRAWN	PAMPHREY
DARG	CANTY	**6**	THREAP	POLLIWOG
DEEK	CHELP	ARGUFY	WAMBLE	SOUTHRON
DUNT	CLECK	BELIKE	WORRIT	
EMPT	COLLY	CAGMAG		**9**
FLEY	CUDDY	CLOUGH	**7**	BACK GREEN
GIRN	CUTTY	CODDER	BACK END	CAG–HANDED
GOWK	DIDDY	COLLOP	BOGGART	SOURDOUGH
GREE	DOUCE	COOTCH	BRODDLE	SPREATHED
GRIG	DUNNY	CROUSE	CLACHAN	WICKTHING
HAST	EMMET	DREICH	CRACKET	WUTHERING
HATH	FEEZE	EATAGE	FLEEIN'	
HEAR	FLITE	EGGLER	FOYBOAT	**10**
HOLP	GARTH	FANKLE	GRADELY	PEELY–WALLY
INBY	GUTTY	FRATCH	GROCKLE	
KEYS	HADST	GANSEY	GURRIER	**11**
LAIK	HINNY	GINNEL	HADAWAY	SWEETIEWIFE
MECK	KECKS	GIRDLE	HANDSEL	WINDLESTRAW
MOIL	LOSEL	GOUGER	HIELAND	
NARY	MARDY	HAPPEN	JIBBONS	**12**
NESH	MITCH	HOGGET	JONNOCK	CORRIE–
OOSE	MODGE	HOLDEN	MAMMOCK	FISTED
PLAT	MUTCH	LARRUP	PAN LOAF	TATTIE–PEELIN

WORD PAIRS

ALPHA AND OMEGA
APPLES AND PEARS
ASSAULT AND BATTERY
BALL AND CHAIN
BANGERS AND MASH
BAT AND BALL
BIRDS AND BEES
BLACK AND BLUE
BLOOD AND THUNDER
BREAD AND BUTTER
BRICKS AND MORTAR
BRING AND BUY
BROTHERS AND SISTERS
BUBBLE AND SQUEAK
BUCKET AND SPADE
BUTT AND BEN
BUTTONS AND BOWS
CAP AND GOWN
CASH AND CARRY
CATS AND DOGS
CHEESE AND PICKLE
COCKLES AND MUSSELS
COLLAR AND TIE
COPS AND ROBBERS
COW AND GATE
CUT AND THRUST
CUTS AND BRUISES
DUCKING AND DIVING
DUCKS AND DRAKES
DUNGEONS AND DRAGONS
DUST AND ASHES
DUSTPAN AND BRUSH
FAST AND LOOSE
FIFE AND DRUM

FINE AND DANDY
FIRE AND BRIMSTONE
FISH AND CHIPS
FLORA AND FAUNA
FOX AND HOUNDS
FRUIT AND NUT
FRUIT AND VEG
G AND T
GIN AND TONIC
GIVE AND TAKE
GRACE AND FAVOUR
HAIL AND FAREWELL
HAMMER AND TONGS
HAT AND COAT
HEART AND SOUL
HERE AND NOW
HILL AND DALE
HORSE AND CARRIAGE
HOT AND COLD
HUSBAND AND WIFE
KINGS AND QUEENS
KNIFE AND FORK
LADIES AND GENTLEMEN
LEFT AND RIGHT
LOCK AND KEY
LOVE AND KISSES
MUSTARD AND CRESS
NAME AND ADDRESS
NEEDLE AND THREAD
NIGHT AND DAY
NOUGHTS AND CROSSES
ORANGES AND LEMONS
PEN AND INK
PIG AND WHISTLE

PINS AND NEEDLES
RHUBARB AND CUSTARD
ROSE AND CROWN
SALT AND PEPPER
SHAMPOO AND SET
SHOES AND SOCKS
SLAP AND TICKLE
SLUGS AND SNAILS
SNAKES AND LADDERS
SOAP AND WATER
SONG AND DANCE
STEAK AND KIDNEY
STICKS AND STONES
STOP AND GO
STRAWBERRIES AND
  CREAM
STUFF AND NONSENSE
SUGAR AND SPICE
SWINGS AND ROUND-
  ABOUTS
TABLE AND CHAIRS
THUNDER AND LIGHTNING
TOP AND BOTTOM
TOP AND TAIL
TOWN AND COUNTRY
TRIAL AND ERROR
TRIPE AND ONIONS
TROUBLE AND STRIFE
UP AND UNDER
UPSTAIRS AND DOWN-
  STAIRS
WAR AND PEACE
WHISKY AND SODA
YOUNG AND OLD

ANAGRAM INDICATORS

ABANDONED
ABERRANT
ABNORMAL
ABOMINATION
ABORTION
ABOUND
ABROAD
ABSTRACT
ABSURD
ACCIDENTAL
ACCOMMO-
  DATED
ACCOMMODA-
  TION
ACROBATIC
ACTIVELY

ADAPT
ADAPTED
ADDLED
ADJUST
ADJUSTED
ADRIFT
ADULTERATED
AFFECT
AFFECTED
AFFLICT
AFFLICTED
AFLOAT
AFRESH
AFTER A FASH-
  ION
AFTER INJURY

AFTERMATH OF
AGITATE
AGITATED
AGITATOR
AGONY
AIEN
AILING
A LA MODE
ALCHEMY
ALIAS
ALL AT SEA
ALL CHANGE
ALL OVER
ALL OVER THE
  PLACE
ALLOY

ALL ROUND
ALLSORTS
ALL WRONG
ALTERED
ALTERNATIVE
AMALGAM
AMALGAMATE
AMAZING
AMBIGUOUS
AMEND
AMENDED
AMISS
ANALYSIS
ANARCHY
ANEW
ANGRY

ANGUISH
ANIMATED
ANNOYED
ANOMALOUS
ANOMALY
ANOTHER
ANYHOW
ANYWAY
APART
APPALLINGLY
APPEAR
APPOINTED
ARCH
ARISING FROM
AROUND
ARRANGE

427

ARRANGED
ARRANGEMENT
ARTFUL
ARTIFICIAL
AS A RESULT
ASKEW
ASSAILED
ASSAULTED
ASSEMBLE
ASSEMBLED
ASSEMBLY
ASSORTED
ASTONISHING
ASTRAY
AT FAULT
AT LIBERTY
AT ODDS
ATOMIZED
ATROCIOUS
AT SIXES AND
  SEVENS
AT VARIANCE
AUTHOR OF
AWFUL
AWFULLY
AWKWARD
AWRY
BAD
BADLY
BARMY
BARNEY
BASH
BASHED
BASTARD
BATS
BATTERED
BEAT
BEATEN–UP
BECOME
BEDEVILLED
BEDLAM
BEDRAGGLED
BEFUDDLE
BEFUDDLED
BELT
BEMUSED
BEND
BENDY
BENT
BERSERK
BEWILDERED
BIBULOUS
BIFF
BIZARRE
BLEND
BLENDED
BLIGHTED
BLITZ
BLOOMER
BLUDGEON
BLUNDER
BLUR

BOTCH
BOTCHED
BOTHER
BOTTLED
BOUNCING
BREAK
BREAKDOWN
BREAKUP
BREW
BROACH
BROADCAST
BROKE
BROKEN
BRUISE
BRUTALIZE
BUCK
BUCKLE
BUCKLED
BUCKLING
BUCKS
BUDGE
BUFFET
BUILD
BUILDING
BUMBLE
BUMP
BUNGLED
BURST
BUST
BUTCHER
BY ACCIDENT
BY ARRANGE-
  MENT
BY MISTAKE
CALAMITOUS
CALAMITOUSLY
CAMOUFLAGED
CAN BE
CANCEL
CAPER
CAPRICIOUS
CAPRICIOUSLY
CARELESSLY
CARNAGE
CASCADE
CASSEROLE
CAST
CAST OFF
CATASTROPHIC
CAUSES
CAVORT
CHANGE
CHANGEABLE
CHANGED
CHAOS
CHAOTIC
CHEW
CHEWED UP
CHICANERY
CHOPPED UP
CHOP SUEY
CHURN

CLUMSILY
CLUMSY
COBBLED
COCKSCREW
COCKTAIL
COIN
COLLAPSE
COLLAPSING
COLLECTION
COMBUSTIBLE
COME TO BE
COME TO
  GRIEF
COMMOTION
COMPACT
COMPLICATED
COMPONENTS
COMPOSE
COMPOSED
COMPOSER
COMPOSING
COMPOSITION
COMPOUND
COMPRISE
CONCEAL
CONCEALING
CONCOCTION
CONFOUND
CONFOUNDED
CONJURING
CONSTITUENTS
CONSTITUTION
CONSTRUCT
CONSTRUC-
  TION
CONTORTED
CONTRAPTION
CONTRIVANCE
CONTRIVE
CONTRIVED
CONVERSION
CONVERT
CONVERTED
CONVERTIBLE
CONVERTS
CONVULSED
COOK
COOKED
CORRECTED
CORRUPT
CORRUPTED
CORRUPTION
COULD BE
CRACK
CRACKED
CRACKERS
CRAFTY
CRASH
CRASHES
CRAZILY
CRAZY
CREATE

CREATED
CRIMINAL
CROOKED
CROSS
CRUDE
CRUMBLE
CRUMBLING
CRUMPLED
CRYPTIC
CUNNING
CURDLED
CURE
CURIOUS
CURIOUSLY
CURLY
CURRY
CUT
DAFT
DAMAGE
DAMAGED
DANCING
DEALT WITH
DEBAUCHED
DECEIT
DECEPTION
DECIPHERED
DECODED
DECOMPOSED
DEFECTIVE
DEFICIENT
DEFORMED
DEFORMITY
DELIRIOUS
DEMENTED
DEMOLISHED
DEMOLITION
DEPLORABLY
DEPLOY
DEPLOYED
DERANGED
DERIVATION
DERIVATIVE OF
DERIVED FROM
DESECRATED
DESIGN
DESPOIL
DESTROY
DESTROYED
DETERIORA-
  TION
DEVASTATE
DEVASTATED
DEVASTATION
DEVELOP
DEVELOPER
DEVELOPMENT
DEVIANT
DEVIATION
DEVILISH
DEVIOUS
DEVISE
DICKY

DIFFERENT
DIFFERENTLY
DIFFICULT
DILAPIDATED
DIRECTED TO
DISARRANGE
DISARRANGED
DISRUPTION
DISSECTED
DISSIPATED
DISSOLUTE
DISSOLVED
DISSONANT
DISTILLATION
DISTORT
DISTORTED
DISTORTION
DISTRACTED
DISTRACTEDLY
DISTRESSED
DISTRIBUTE
DISTRIBUTED
DISTRAUGHT
DISTURB
DISTURBANCE
DISTURBED
DITHERING
DIVERGENCE
DIVERGENT
DIVERSIFICA-
  TION
DIVERSIFIED
DIVERT
DIVERTING
DIZZY
DO
DOCTOR
DOCTORED
DODDERY
DOTTY
DOUBTFUL
DOUBTFULLY
DOZY
DRAWN
DREADFUL
DREADFULLY
DRESS
DRESSED
DRESSING
DRUB
DRUNK
DRUNKEN
DRUNKENLY
DUBIOUS
DUBIOUSLY
DUD
DUFF
DYNAMITE
ECCENTRIC
EDIT
EDITED
EERIE

EFFECT
EFFECTS
EFFERVES-
  CENT
ELBOW
ELFIN
EMANATED
EMBARRASSED
EMBODY
EMEND
EMENDATION
EMENDED
EMERGE FROM
EMPLOYS
ENGENDERING
ENGENDERS
ENGINEER
ENSEMBLE
ENTANGLED
ENTANGLE-
  MENT
ERRANT
ERRATIC
ERRING
ERRONEOUS
ERROR
ERUPTING
EVIL
EVOLUTION
EXCEPTIONAL
EXCEPTION-
  ALLY
EXCITE
EXCITED
EXHIBITS
EXOTIC
EXPLODE
EXPLODED
EXPLOSION
EXPLOSIVE
EXTRACT OF
EXTRAORDI-
  NARILY
EXTRAVAGANT
FABRICATED
FABRICATION
FABULOUS
FAILING
FAILURE
FAKE
FALLACIOUS
FALLING
FALSE
FALSIFIED
FALTERING
FANCIFUL
FANCY
FANTASTIC
FAR FLUNG
FASHION
FASHIONING
FAULTY

FEBRILE
FERMENT
FERMENTED
FEVERISH
FICTIONAL
FIX
FLEXIBLE
FLIGHTY
FLING
FLIP
FLOUNDER
FLUCTUATING
FLUCTUATION
FLUID
FLURRIED
FLUSTERED
FOGGY
FOMENT
FOOLISH
FOOLISHLY
FOR A CHANGE
FORCED
FOREIGN
FORGE
FORGED
FORM OF
FORMS
FORMULATING
FOUL
FOUND IN
FRACTURED
FRAGMENTS
FRANTIC
FRAUD
FREAK
FREAKISH
FREE
FREELY
FRENZIED
FRENZY
FRET
FRILLY
FRISKY
FROLIC
FUDDLE
FUDDLED
FUDGE
FULMINATE
FUNCTION
FUNNY
FUZZY
GAMBOL
GARBLE
GARBLED
GENERATES
GENERATING
GET–UP
GHASTLY
GIBBERISH
GIDDY
GIVE RISE TO
GIVES

GLEANED
  FROM
GOING TO
GONE OFF
GO OFF
GO STRAIGHT
GO TO POT
GO TO THE
  DOGS
GO WRONG
GROTESQUE
GROUND
HACK
HAMMER
HAMMERED
HANKY–PANKY
HAPHAZARD
HAPLESS
HARASSED
HARM
HASH
HASHED
HATCHES
HATCHING
HAVOC
HAYWIRE
HAZE
HELTER–SKEL-
  TER
HIDE
HIDING
HIGGLEDY PIG-
  GLEDY
HORRIBLE
HOTCH POTCH
HURT
HYBRID
IDIOTIC
ILL
ILL–COMPOSED
ILL–DISPOSED
ILL–FORMED
ILL–MADE
ILL–TREATED
ILL–USED
IMBECILE
IMPAIRED
IMPERFECT
IMPROPER
IMPROPERLY
INACCURATE
INANE
INCLUDED
INCONSTANT
INDUCE
INFAMOUS
INFIRM
INGREDIENTS
  OF
INHABITING
INJURED
IN ORDER

INORDINATELY
IN OTHER
  WORDS
IN REVOLT
IN RUINS
INSANE
IN SHREDS
INTERFERED
  WITH
INTRICATE
INVALID
INVENTION
INVOLVED
IRREGULAR
IRREGULARITY
IRRITATED
ITINERANT
JAR
JAZZ
JIG
JITTERY
JOG
JOLT
JOSTLED
JUGGLE
JUGGLED
JUMBLE
JUMBLED
KIND OF
KINK
KINKY
KNEAD
KNIT
LABYRINTHINE
LAWLESS
LEAPING
LET LOOSE
LICKED INTO
  SHAPE
LOOK SILLY
LOOSE
LOOSELY
LOUSY
LUDICROUS
LUNATIC
MAD
MADE FROM
MADE OF
MADE UP
MADLY
MAIM
MAKE
MAKE–UP
MAKING
MALADROIT
MALAISE
MALFORMA-
  TION
MALFORMED
MALFUNCTION
MALLEABLE
MALTREAT

MALTREATED
MALTREAT-
  MENT
MANAGED
MANAGER
MANGLE
MANGLED
MANIAC
MANIC
MANIFEST
MANIFESTA-
  TION
MANIPULATE
MANIPULATED
MANOEUVRE
MARRED
MARSHAL
MASH
MASHED
MASSAGE
MAUL
MAULED
MAYBE
MAY BECOME
MAYHEM
MEANDERING
MEDLEY
MELEE
MEND
MENDED
MERCURIAL
MESS
MESSILY
METAMOR-
  PHOSING
METAMORPHO-
  SIS
MIGRANT
MINCE
MINCED
MISALLIANCE
MISCONTRUED
MISDELIVERED
MISGUIDED
MISHANDLED
MISHAP
MISLED
MISREPRESEN-
  TATION
MISREPRE-
  SENTED
MISSHAPEN
MISTAKE
MISTREATED
MISUSED
MIX
MIXED
MIXTURE
MIX–UP
MOBILE
MODEL
MODELS

MODIFICATION
MODIFIED
MODIFY
MOITHER
MOLEST
MOLESTED
MONKEY WITH
MOULD
MOVED
MOVING
MUCK ABOUT
MUDDLE
MUDDLED
MUTABLE
MUTANT
MUTATION
MUTATIVE
MUTILATE
MUTILATED
MUTILATION
MUTINOUS
MYSTERIOUS
MYSTERIOUSLY
NASTY
NATURALLY
NAUGHTY
NAUSEOUS
NEATLY
NEGLECTED
NEGLIGEE
NEGOTIATED
NEGOTIATION
NERVOUSLY
NEW
NEW FORM OF
NEWLY
  FORMED
NEWLY MADE
NOBBLED
NOMADIC
NOT EXACTLY
NOT IN ORDER
NOT PROPERLY
NOT RIGHT
NOT STRAIGHT
NOVA
NOVEL
OBLIQUE
OBSCURE
OBSCURED
OBSTREPER-
  OUS
OCCASION
ODD
OF
OFF
OFF–COLOUR
OPEN
OPERATE ON
ORDER
ORDERED
ORDERLY

ORDERS
ORGANIZATION
ORGANIZED
ORIGINALLY
OTHERWISE
OUT
OUTCOME OF
OUTLANDISH
OUT OF
OUTRA-
  GEOUSLY
OVER
OVERTURN
PECULIAR
PERFIDIOUS
PERHAPS
PERPLEXED
PERVERSE
PERVERSELY
PERVERT
PERVERTED
PHONEY
PIE
PLAY
PLAYING
  TRICKS
PLYING
POLLUTED
POOR
POSING AS
POSITION
POSSIBLY
POTENTIAL
POTENTIALLY
POUND
PREPARATION
PREPARE
PREPARED
PRINT OUT
PROBLEM
PROBLEMATIC
PROBLEMATI-
  CAL
PROCESS
PROCESSING
PRODUCES
PRODUCING
PRODUCTION
PROPERLY OR-
  GANIZED
PROPERLY
  PRESENTED
PSEUDO
PULVERIZED
PUMMELLED
PUT ANOTHER
  WAY
PUT OUT
PUT RIGHT
PUT STRAIGHT
PUZZLING
QUAKING

QUEASY
QUEER
QUEER LOOK-
  ING
QUESTIONABLE
QUIRKY
QUITE DIFFER-
  ENT
QUIVERING
RABID
RAGE
RAGGED
RAKISH
RAMBLING
RANDOM
RANSACK
RAVAGED
RAVISH
RAVISHED
REACTIONARY
READJUSTED
REARRANGED
REARRANGE-
  MENT
REASSEMBLED
REASSEMBLY
REBEL
REBELLIOUS
REBUILDING
REBUILT
RECALCITRANT
RECAST
RECIPE
RECKLESS
RECON-
  STRUCTED
RECTIFICATION
RECTIFIED
REDESIGNED
REDISCOV-
  ERED
REELING
REFORMATION
REFORMED
REFRACTORY
REFURBISHED
REGULATED
REGULATION
RELAY
RELAYING
RELEASING
REMADE
REMEDY
REMODELLED
RENDERING
RENDITION
RENOVATED
RENOVATION
REORGANIZA-
  TION
REORGANIZED
REPAIR

REPAIRED
REPLACED
REPLACEMENT
REPRESENT
REPRESENTA-
  TION
REPRESENTED
REPRESENT-
  ING
REPRODUCE
REPRODUC-
  TION
RESHAPED
RESHUFFLE
RESOLUTION
RESOLVE
RESOLVED
RESORT
RESORTING
RESTLESS
RESULT
RESULTING
  FROM
REVIEW
REVISED
REVOLTING
REVOLUTION
REVOLUTION-
  ARY
REVOLUTION-
  IZED
REVOLVER
REWRITTEN
RICKETY
RIDICULOUS
RIGGED
RIOT
RIP
RIPPLING
ROCK
ROCKY
ROLLICKING
ROTARY
ROTTEN
ROUGHLY
ROUND
ROVING
ROWDY
RUBBISH
RUDE
RUFFLE
RUFFLED
RUIN
RUINED
RUINOUS
RUM
RUMPLED
RUNNING WILD
RUPTURED
SABORAGE
SACK
SADLY

SALAD
SALVAGED
  FROM
SATANIC
SAUCY
SAVAGE
SCATTER
SCATTERED
SCHEME
SCRAMBLE
SCRAMBLED
SCRATCH
SCRATCHED
SCRUFFY
SCUFFLE
SCULPTED
SEND OFF/OUT
SENSELESS
SET
SETTING
SETTLEMENT
SHAKE
SHAKEDOWN
SHAKEN
SHAKY
SHAMBLES
SHAPED
SHATTER
SHATTERED
SHELLED
SHIFT
SHIFTING
SHILLY–SHALLY
SHIMMERING
SHIP–SHAPE
SHIVER
SHIVERED
SHOCKED
SHOULD BE-
  COME
SHOWING
SHRED
SHUFFLE
SHUFFLED
SICK
SIFTED
SILLY
SKIDDING
SKIPPING
SKITTISH
SLAP–HAPPY
SLAUGHTER
SLING
SLIP
SLIPPING
SLIPSHOD
SLOPPY
SLOVENLY
SLYLY
SMASH
SMASHED
SMASHING

SOLUTION
SOMEHOW
SOMERSAULT
SORRY STATE
SORT
SORTED OUT
SORT OF
SOUP
SOZZLED
SPASMODIC
SPATTERED
SPELT OUT
SPILL
SPILT
SPIN
SPINNING
SPLASH
SPLICE
SPLICED
SPLINTER
SPLIT
SPOIL
SPOILT
SPORT
SPORTING
SPORTIVE
SPRAY
SPREAD
SPURIOUS
SQUALL
SQUASH
SQUIFFY
SQUIGGLES
STAGGER
STAGGERED
STAMPEDE
START
STATE
STEW
STEWED
STIR
STIRRED
STORM
STORMY
STRAIGHT
STRAIGHTEN

STRANGE
STRAY
STRAYING
STREWN
STRICKEN
STRUGGLE
STRUGGLING
STUPID
STUPIDLY
STYLE
SUBMERGED IN
SUPERFICIAL
SUPERFICIALLY
SURGERY
SURPRISING
SURPRISINGLY
SUSPECT
SWIRL
SWIRLING
TAILOR
TAILORED
TAMPERED
  WITH
TANGLE
TANGLED
TATTERED
TATTY
TEAR
TEASE
TEMPESTUOUS
TEMPESTU-
  OUSLY
TERRIBLE
TIDIED UP
TIDY
TILT
TIP
TIPSY
TOPSY TURVY
TO RIGHTS
TORMENT
TORN
TORTUOUS
TORTURE
TORTURED
TOSS

TOUCHED
TRAIN
TRAINED
TRANSFERRED
TRANSFORM
TRANSFORMA-
  TION
TRANSFORMED
TRANSLATE
TRANSLATED
TRANSLATION
TRANSMUTA-
  TION
TRANSMUTE
TRANSMUTED
TRANSPOSE
TRANSPOSED
TRANSPOSI-
  TION
TRAVESTY
TREATED
TREMBLING
TRICK
TRICKY
TRIP
TROUBLE
TROUBLED
TROUBLESOME
TUMBLE
TUMBLEDOWN
TUMBLING
TUMULT
TUMULTUOUS
TURBULENT
TURNED
TWIRL
TWIRLING
TWIST
TWISTED
TWISTER
UGLY
UNCERTAIN
UNCOMMON
UNCONVEN-
  TIONAL
UNDECIDED

UNDISCIPLINED
UNDOING
UNDONE
UNDULY
UNEASY
UNEVENLY
UNFAMILIAR
UNFIT
UNFORTU-
  NATELY
UNHAPPY
UNNATURAL
UNNATURALLY
UNORTHODOX
UNRAVELLED
UNRELIABLE
UNRE-
  STRAINED
UNRULY
UNSETTLED
UNSETTLING
UNSOUND
UNSTABLE
UNSTEADY
UNSTUCK
UNTIDY
UNUSUAL
UNWIND
UPSET
VACILLATING
VAGABOND
VAGUELY
VANDALIZE
VANDALIZED
VARIABLE
VARIED
VARIETY
VARIOUS
VARIOUSLY
VARY
VERSION OF
VEX
VIA
VIGOROUSLY
VILE
VIOLATE

VIOLENT
VOLATILE
WANDER
WANDERING
WARP
WARPED
WARRING
WAS
WASTED
WAVERING
WEAVE
WEIRD
WELL–FORMED
WELL–OR-
  DERED
WELL–ORGA-
  NIZED
WELL–VARIED
WHIP
WHIRL
WHIRLING
WHISK
WICKED
WILD
WILDLY
WIND
WOBBLY
WOOLLY
WORK OUT
WORRIED
WORRY
WOVEN
WRECK
WRECKED
WRENCH
WRESTED
  FROM
WRETCHED
WRITHING
WRONG
YIELDS
ZANY

SPLIT-WORD INDICATORS

ABOUT	ENCLOSURE	HOLDING PRISONER	RECEIVING
ABSORBED IN	ENCOMPASSED	HOUSED	RETAINED BY
ACCEPTED BY	ENCOMPASSING	HOUSING	RETAINING
ACCEPTING	ENGULFED	IMBIBED	RINGING
ACCOMMODATED BY	ENGULFING	IMPOUND	SEPARATED BY
ADMITTED BY	ENTERING	IMPOUNDED	SEPARATING
AMID	ENTRAPPED	IMPRISONED	SET ABOUT
AROUND	ENTRAPPING	IMPRISONING	SET IN
ASSIMILATED BY	ENTRY	INCLUDE	SHELTER
BACK	ENVELOPED	INCLUDED IN	SHELTERED BY
BACKING	ENVELOPING	INCORPORATING	SPLIT BY
BESET BY	ENVIRONMENT	INTERIOR	SPLITTING
CAPTURED BY	ENVIRONS	INTERRUPTED	STUFFING
CARRIED BY	EXTERIOR	INTERRUPTING	SURROUND
CIRCUMSCRIBED BY	FILLED BY	INTERVENING IN	SURROUNDED BY
CLUTCHED BY	FILLING	IN TWO WORDS	SWALLOWED BY
CONFINED BY	FRAMED BY	INVOLVED IN	SWALLOW UP
CONFINED IN	FRAMED IN	INVOLVING	TAKE IN
CONTAIN	FRAMING	KEEPING	TAKEN IN BY
CONTENT	GET ABOUT	LINING	TRAP
CONTENTS	GO AROUND	OCCUPIED BY	TRAPPED BY
CUT BY	GO IN	OCCUPYING	TRAPPED IN
CUTTING	GRABBED BY	OUTSIDE	TUCKED INTO
DIVIDING	GRABBING	PARTED BY	UPHEAVAL
EMBRACED	GRIPPED BY	PARTING	WITHIN
EMBRACING	GRIPPING	POCKETED BY	WITHOUT
ENCIRCLED	HARBOURED	POCKETING	WRAPPED IN
ENCIRCLING	HOLD	RECEIVED BY	WRAPPING
ENCLOSED	HOLDING CAPTIVE	RECEIVED IN	

FIRST NAMES

GIRLS' NAMES

2	3–continued	4–continued	4–continued	4–continued
DI	LYN	BEAT	GALE	LILY
EM	MAE	BELL	GAYE	LINA
JO	MAY	BESS	GERT	LISA
VI	MEG	BETA	GILL	LISE
	MEL	BETH	GINA	LITA
3	MIA	BINA	GLAD	LIZA
ADA	NAN	CARA	GWEN	LOIS
AMY	NAT	CARY	GWYN	LOLA
ANN	ONA	CASS	HEBE	LORA
AUD	PAM	CATH	HEDY	LORI
AVA	PAT	CERI	HOPE	LORN
BAB	PEG	CISS	ILMA	LUCE
BEA	PEN	CLEM	ILSE	LUCY
BEE	PIA	CLEO	IMMY	LULU
BEL	PRU	CORA	INEZ	LYNN
CIS	RAE	DAFF	IOLA	LYRA
DEB	RIA	DALE	IONA	MAIR
DEE	ROS	DANA	IRIS	MARA
DOT	SAL	DAPH	IRMA	MARY
EDA	SAM	DAWN	ISLA	MAUD
ENA	SIB	DOLL	IVAH	META
ETH	SUE	DORA	JADE	MIMA
EVA	UNA	EDEN	JAEL	MIMI
EVE	VAL	EDIE	JANE	MINA
FAN	VIV	EDNA	JEAN	MIRA
FAY	WIN	EILY	JESS	MOLL
FLO	ZOË	EIRA	JILL	MONA
GAY		ELLA	JOAN	MYRA
GUS	**4**	ELMA	JODI	NADA
IDA	ABBY	ELSA	JODY	NELL
INA	ADAH	EMMA	JOSS	NEST
ISA	ADDY	ENID	JUDI	NEVA
ITA	AINE	ERIN	JUDY	NINA
IVY	ALDA	ERYL	JUNE	NITA
JAN	ALEX	ESME	KARA	NOLA
JAY	ALIX	ETTA	KATE	NONA
JEN	ALLY	ETTY	KATH	NORA
JOY	ALMA	EVIE	KATY	NOVA
KAY	ALVA	FAYE	KERI	OLGA
KIM	ALYS	FERN	KYLE	OONA
KIT	ANIS	FIFI	LANA	OPAL
LEE	ANNA	FLOY	LELA	OZZY
LES	ANNE	FRAN	LENA	PETA
LIL	ANYA	GABI	LETA	PHIL
LIZ	AVIS	GABY	LILA	POLL
LOU	BABS	GAIL	LILI	PRUE

4–continued	5–continued	5–continued	5–continued	5–continued
RENA	AMATA	DIANE	HETTY	LUCIE
RENE	AMBER	DILYS	HILDA	LUCKY
RHEA	AMICE	DINAH	HOLLY	LYDIA
RICA	ANGEL	DIONE	HORRY	LYNDA
RIKA	ANGIE	DODIE	HULDA	LYNNE
RINA	ANITA	DOLLY	HYLDA	MABEL
RITA	ANNIE	DONNA	ILONA	MABLE
ROMA	ANNIS	DORIA	IRENE	MADDY
RONA	ANONA	DORIS	ISMAY	MADGE
ROSA	ANWEN	DREDA	JACKY	MAEVE
ROSE	APHRA	DULCE	JANET	MAGDA
ROXY	APRIL	EDITH	JANEY	MAIRE
RUBY	ASTRA	EFFIE	JANIE	MAMIE
RUTH	AUDRA	ELAIN	JANIS	MANDY
SARA	AUREA	ELENA	JAYNE	MARAH
SIAN	AVICE	ELISE	JEMMA	MARCY
SÍLE	AVRIL	ELIZA	JENNA	MARGE
SÌNE	BEATA	ELLEN	JENNY	MARGO
SUZY	BECKY	ELLIE	JEWEL	MARIA
TACY	BELLA	ELROY	JINNY	MARIE
TARA	BELLE	ELSIE	JODIE	MARLA
TESS	BERNY	ELVIE	JOSIE	MARNI
THEA	BERRY	EMILY	JOYCE	MARTA
TINA	BERTA	EMMIE	JUDOC	MARTI
TONI	BERYL	EPPIE	JULIA	MARTY
TRIS	BESSY	ERICA	JULIE	MATTY
TRIX	BETSY	ERIKA	KAREN	MAUDE
TYRA	BETTE	ESMEE	KARIN	MAURA
VERA	BETTY	ESSIE	KATHY	MAVIS
VIDA	BIDDY	ETHEL	KATIE	MEAVE
VINA	BONNY	ETHNE	KELDA	MEGAN
VITA	BRIDE	ETTIE	KELLY	MEGGY
VIVA	BRITA	EVITA	KEREN	MELBA
WYNN	BRITT	FAITH	KERRI	MELVA
ZANA	CANDY	FANNY	KERRY	MERCY
ZARA	CAREY	FARON	KEZIA	MERLE
ZENA	CARLA	FIONA	KIRBY	MERRY
ZITA	CARLY	FLEUR	KITTY	MERYL
ZOLA	CAROL	FLORA	KYLIE	MILLY
ZORA	CARYL	FLOSS	LAURA	MINNA
	CARYS	FREDA	LAURI	MINTY
5	CASEY	FREYA	LEIGH	MITZI
ABBEY	CATHY	GABBY	LEILA	MOIRA
ABBIE	CELIA	GAYLE	LENNY	MOLLY
ADDIE	CERYS	GEMMA	LEONA	MORAG
ADELA	CHLOE	GERDA	LETTY	MORNA
ADELE	CHRIS	GERRY	LIANA	MOYNA
ADLAI	CILLA	GILDA	LIBBY	MOYRA
AGGIE	CINDY	GINNY	LIDDY	MYRNA
AGNES	CISSY	GRACE	LIESL	MYSIE
AILIE	CLARA	GRETA	LILAC	NADIA
AILIS	CLARE	GUSTA	LILLA	NAHUM
AILSA	CORAL	HAGAR	LINDA	NANCE
AIMEE	DAISY	HATTY	LINDY	NANCY
ALANA	DARCY	HAZEL	LIZZY	NANNY
ALEXA	DEBRA	HEDDA	LOLLY	NAOMI
ALICE	DELIA	HEIDI	LOREN	NELLY
ALINA	DELLA	HELEN	LORNA	NERYS
ALINE	DELMA	HELGA	LORNE	NESSA
ALLIE	DERYN	HENNY	LOTTY	NESTA
ALVIE	DIANA	HEPSY	LUCIA	NETTA

5–continued	5–continued	6–continued	6–continued	6–continued
NICKY	SONYA	AILEEN	BOBBIE	EILWEN
NIKKI	SOPHY	AILITH	BONITA	EIRIAN
NOELE	STACY	AITHNE	BONNIE	EITHNE
NORAH	SUKEY	ALANNA	BRENDA	ELAINE
NORMA	SUSAN	ALBINA	BRIDIE	ELINED
NUALA	SUSIE	ALDITH	BRIGID	ELINOR
NYREE	SYBIL	ALEXIA	BRIGIT	ELISHA
ODILE	TACEY	ALEXIS	BRIONY	ELISSA
OLIFF	TAMAR	ALICIA	BRYONY	ELOISA
OLIVE	TAMMY	ALISON	CANICE	ELOISE
OLLIE	TANIA	ALTHEA	CARINA	ELSPIE
OLWEN	TANSY	ALVINA	CARITA	ELUNED
OLWYN	TANYA	AMABEL	CARMEL	ELVINA
ORIEL	TEGAN	AMALIA	CARMEN	ELVIRA
OWENA	TERRI	AMALIE	CAROLA	EMELYN
PANSY	TERRY	AMANDA	CAROLE	EMILIA
PATSY	TESSA	AMELIA	CARRIE	ESTHER
PATTI	TETTY	AMICIA	CASSIE	EUNICE
PATTY	THORA	AMINTA	CATRIN	EVADNE
PAULA	THYRA	ANDREA	CECILE	EVELYN
PEACE	TIBBY	ANDRÉE	CECILY	EVONNE
PEARL	TILDA	ANEIRA	CELINA	FARRAN
PEGGY	TILLY	ANGELA	CELINE	FARREN
PENNY	TISHA	ANNICE	CHARIS	FEDORA
PETRA	TONIA	ANNIKA	CHERIE	FELICE
PHEBE	TONYA	ANNORA	CHERRY	FINOLA
PIPPA	TOPSY	ANSTEY	CHERYL	FLAVIA
POLLY	TOTTY	ANTHEA	CICELY	FLOWER
POPPY	TRACY	ARIANE	CISSIE	FOSTER
RAINA	TRINA	ARLEEN	CLAIRE	FRANCA
RAINE	TRUDI	ARLENE	COLINA	FRANNY
REINE	TRUDY	ARLINE	CONNIE	FRIEDA
RENÉE	UNITY	ARMINA	DAGMAR	GABBIE
RENIE	VALDA	ARMINE	DANITA	GAENOR
RHIAN	VANDA	ASHLEY	DANUTA	GARNET
RHODA	VELDA	ASTRID	DAPHNE	GAYNOR
RHONA	VELMA	ATHENE	DAVIDA	GERTIE
ROBYN	VENUS	AUDREY	DAVINA	GINGER
RONNA	VERNA	AURIEL	DEANNA	GISELA
ROSIE	VICKI	AURIOL	DEANNE	GLADYS
ROWAN	VICKY	AURORA	DEBBIE	GLENDA
SADIE	VIKKI	AURORE	DECIMA	GLENIS
SALLY	VILMA	AVERIL	DELWEN	GLENNA
SAMMY	VINNY	BARBIE	DELWYN	GLENYS
SANDY	VIOLA	BARBRA	DELYTH	GLINYS
SARAH	VIVIA	BAUBIE	DENISE	GLORIA
SARAI	WANDA	BEATTY	DENNIE	GLYNIS
SARRA	WENDA	BENITA	DIANNE	GOLDIE
SELMA	WENDY	BERNIE	DIONNE	GRACIE
SENGA	WILLA	BERTHA	DORCAS	GRANIA
CHANI	WILMA	BESSIE	DOREEN	GRETEL
SHARI	WYNNE	BETHAN	DORICE	GRIZEL
SHEBA	XENIA	BETHIA	DORITA	GUSSIE
SHENA	ZELDA	BEULAH	DORRIE	GWENDA
SHIRL	ZELMA	BIANCA	DOTTIE	HAIDEE
SHONA	ZORAH	BILLIE	DULCIE	HANNAH
SIBBY		BIRDIE	DYMPNA	HATTIE
SIBYL	6	BIRGIT	EARTHA	HAYLEY
SISSY	AGACIA	BLANCH	EASTER	HEDWIG
SONIA	AGATHA	BLODYN	EDWINA	HELENA
SONJA	AGNETA	BLYTHE	EILEEN	HELENE

6–continued	6–continued	6–continued	6–continued	7–continued
HENNIE	LILIAS	NOREEN	SOPHIE	ALETHEA
HEPSEY	LILITH	ODETTE	SORCHA	ALFREDA
HEPSIE	LILLAH	ODILIA	STACEY	ALLEGRA
HERMIA	LILLIE	OLIVET	STELLA	ALLISON
HESTER	LINNET	OLIVIA	STEVIE	ALOISIA
HILARY	LIZZIE	OONAGH	SYLVIA	ALOYSIA
HONORA	LLINOS	ORIANA	SYLVIE	ANNABEL
HOWARD	LOLITA	PAMELA	TAMARA	ANNAPLE
HULDAH	LOREEN	PATTIE	TAMSIN	ANNETTE
IANTHE	LOTTIE	PEPITA	TANITH	ANOUSKA
IDONEA	LOUISA	PETULA	TEGWEN	ANSELMA
IMOGEN	LOUISE	PHEMIE	TERESA	ANSTICE
INGRID	LUCINA	PHOEBE	TESSIE	ANTOINE
ISABEL	LUELLA	PORTIA	THECLA	ANTONIA
ISEULT	MADDIE	PRISCA	THEKLA	ARIADNE
ISHBEL	MAGGIE	PRISSY	THELMA	ARIANNA
ISOBEL	MAHALA	QUEENA	THIRSA	ARLETTA
ISOLDA	MAIDIE	QUEENY	THIRZA	ARLETTE
ISOLDE	MAIRIN	RACHEL	TIRZAH	ASPASIA
JACKIE	MAISIE	RAMONA	TRACEY	AUGUSTA
JACOBA	MARCIA	REGINA	TRICIA	AURELIA
JACQUI	MARCIE	RENATA	TRISHA	AUREOLA
JANICE	MARGIE	RHONDA	TRIXIE	AUREOLE
JANINE	MARGOT	ROBINA	TRUDIE	AVELINE
JANSIS	MARIAM	ROISIN	ULRICA	BABETTE
JEANIE	MARIAN	ROSINA	URSULA	BARBARA
JEANNE	MARIEL	ROSITA	VASHTI	BARBARY
JEHANE	MARINA	ROSLYN	VERENA	BASILIA
JEMIMA	MARION	ROWENA	VERITY	BASILIE
JENNIE	MARISA	ROXANA	VERONA	BASILLA
JESSIE	MARITA	ROXANE	VICKIE	BEATRIX
JOANNA	MARLIN	RUBINA	VINNIE	BEATTIE
JOANNE	MARLYN	RUTHIE	VIOLET	BEDELIA
JOLEEN	MARNIE	SABINA	VIVIAN	BELINDA
JOLENE	MARSHA	SALENA	VIVIEN	BERNICE
JUDITH	MARTHA	SALINA	VYVYAN	BETHANY
JULIET	MARTIE	SALOME	WALLIS	BETTINA
KARINA	MATTIE	SANDIE	WINNIE	BETTRYS
KEELEY	MAUDIE	SANDRA	XANTHE	BEVERLY
KELLIE	MAXINE	SARINA	YASMIN	BLANCHE
KENDRA	MEGGIE	SARITA	YVETTE	BLODWEN
KERRIE	MEGHAN	SELENA	YVONNE	BLOSSOM
KEZIAH	MEHALA	SELINA	ZANDRA	BRANWEN
KIRSTY	MELODY	SERENA	ZILLAH	BRIDGET
LALAGE	MERCIA	SHARON	ZINNIA	BRIGHID
LAUREL	MERIEL	SHAUNA		BRONWEN
LAUREN	MIGNON	SHEENA	**7**	BRONWYN
LAURIE	MILLIE	SHEILA	ABIGAIL	CAITLIN
LAVENA	MINNIE	SHELLY	ADAMINA	CAMILLA
LAVINA	MIRIAM	SHERRI	ADELINA	CAMILLE
LEANNE	MONICA	SHERRY	ADELINE	CANDACE
LEILAH	MURIEL	SHERYL	ADRIANA	CANDICE
LENNIE	MYRTLE	SIBBIE	AINSLEY	CANDIDA
LENORE	NADINE	SIDONY	AINSLIE	CARLEEN
LEONIE	NELLIE	SILVIA	AISLING	CARLENE
LESLEY	NERINA	SIMONA	AISLINN	CARMELA
LESLIE	NESSIE	SIMONE	ALBERTA	CAROLYN
LETTIE	NETTIE	SINEAD	ALBINIA	CECILIA
LIANNE	NICOLA	SISLEY	ALBREDA	CECILIE
LIESEL	NICOLE	SISSIE	ALDREDA	CEINWEN
LILIAN	NOELLE	SOPHIA	ALEDWEN	CELESTE

7–continued	7–continued	7–continued	7–continued	7–continued
CHARITY	FRANNIE	LILLIAS	NICHOLA	SILVANA
CHARLEY	GENEVRA	LINDSAY	NINETTE	SIOBHAN
CHARLIE	GEORGIA	LINDSEY	NOELEEN	SUSANNA
CHATTIE	GEORGIE	LINETTE	NOELINE	SUSANNE
CHRISSY	GILLIAN	LISBETH	OCTAVIA	SUZANNA
CHRISTY	GINETTE	LISETTE	OLYMPIA	SUZANNE
CLARICE	GINEVRA	LIZANNE	OPHELIA	SUZETTE
CLARRIE	GISELLE	LIZBETH	OTTILIA	SYBELLA
CLAUDIA	GRAINNE	LORAINE	OTTILIE	SYBILLA
CLODAGH	GRIZZEL	LORETTA	PAMELIA	TABITHA
COLETTE	GWLADYS	LORETTE	PANDORA	TALITHA
COLLEEN	GWYNEDD	LORINDA	PASCALE	TATIANA
CORALIE	GWYNETH	LOUELLA	PAULINE	THERESA
CORINNA	HALCYON	LOVEDAY	PEARLIE	THÉRÈSE
CORINNE	HARRIET	LUCASTA	PERDITA	TIFFANY
CRYSTAL	HEATHER	LUCETTA	PERONEL	TRISSIE
CYNTHIA	HÉLOÏSE	LUCETTE	PETRINA	VALERIA
DAMARIS	HEULWEN	LUCIANA	PHILLIS	VALERIE
DANETTE	HILLARY	LUCILLA	PHYLLIS	VANESSA
DARLENE	HONORIA	LUCILLE	QUEENIE	VENETIA
DAVINIA	HORATIA	LUCINDA	RACHAEL	VIVIANA
DEBORAH	HYPATIA	LUCRECE	RAELENE	YOLANDA
DEIRDRE	ISADORA	LYNETTE	RAFAELA	YOLANDE
DELILAH	ISIDORA	MABELLA	REBECCA	ZENOBIA
DEMELZA	JACINTA	MABELLE	REBEKAH	ZULEIKA
DESIREE	JACINTH	MAHALAH	RHONWEN	
DIAMOND	JANETTA	MAHALIA	RICARDA	**8**
DOLORES	JANETTE	MALVINA	RICHMAL	ADELAIDE
DONALDA	JASMINE	MANUELA	ROBERTA	ADELHEID
DORETTE	JEANNIE	MARILYN	ROMAINE	ADRIANNE
DORINDA	JENIFER	MARISSA	RONALDA	ADRIENNE
DOROTHY	JESSICA	MARLENE	ROSABEL	ANGELICA
DYMPHNA	JILLIAN	MARTINA	ROSALIA	ANGELINA
EILUNED	JOCASTA	MARTINE	ROSALIE	ANGELINE
ELDREDA	JOCELYN	MATILDA	ROSALYN	ANGHARAD
ELEANOR	JOHANNA	MAUREEN	ROSANNA	ANNALISA
ELFREDA	JONQUIL	MEHALAH	ROSANNE	ANTONINA
ELFRIDA	JOSEPHA	MEHALIA	ROSEANN	ANTONNIA
ELSPETH	JOSETTE	MEIRION	ROSELYN	APPOLINA
EMELINE	JUANITA	MELANIA	ROSETTA	APPOLINE
EMERALD	JULIANA	MELANIE	ROSSLYN	ARABELLA
ESTELLA	JULITTA	MELINDA	ROXANNA	ARAMINTA
ESTELLE	JUSTINA	MELIORA	ROXANNE	BEATRICE
EUGENIA	JUSTINE	MELISSA	RUPERTA	BERENICE
EUGENIE	KATHRYN	MELODIE	SABRINA	BEVERLEY
EULALIA	KATRINA	MELVINA	SAFFRON	BIRGITTA
EULALIE	KATRINE	MERILYN	SANCHIA	BRIGITTA
EVELEEN	KETURAH	MERRION	SARANNA	BRIGITTE
EVELINA	KIRSTEN	MICHELE	SCARLET	BRITTANY
EVELINE	KRISTEN	MILDRED	SEPTIMA	BRUNETTA
FABIANA	KRISTIN	MINERVA	SHANNON	CARLOTTA
FELICIA	LARAINE	MIRABEL	SHARRON	CAROLINA
FENELLA	LARISSA	MIRANDA	SHEILAH	CAROLINE
FEODORA	LAUREEN	MODESTY	SHELAGH	CATHLEEN
FIDELIA	LAURINA	MONIQUE	SHELLEY	CATRIONA
FLORRIE	LAVERNE	MYFANWY	SHIRLEY	CERIDWEN
FLOSSIE	LAVINIA	NANETTE	SIBELLA	CHARISSA
FORTUNE	LEONORA	NATALIA	SIBILLA	CHARLENE
FRANCES	LETITIA	NATALIE	SIBYLLA	CHARMIAN
FRANCIE	LETTICE	NATASHA	SIDONIA	CHRISSIE
FRANKIE	LILLIAN	NERISSA	SIDONIE	CHRISTIE

8–continued	8–continued	8–continued	9–continued
CLARIBEL	JOSCELIN	ROSALIND	CELESTINA
CLARINDA	JULIANNE	ROSALINE	CELESTINE
CLARISSA	JULIENNE	ROSAMOND	CHARLOTTE
CLAUDINE	JULIETTE	ROSAMUND	CHARMAINE
CLEMENCE	KATHLEEN	ROSEANNA	CHRISTIAN
CLEMENCY	KIMBERLY	ROSEANNE	CHRISTINA
CLOTILDA	KRISTINA	ROSELINE	CHRISTINE
CONCEPTA	KRISTINE	ROSEMARY	CHRISTMAS
CONCETTA	LAETITIA	SAMANTHA	CLAUDETTE
CORDELIA	LARRAINE	SAPPHIRA	CLEMENTIA
CORNELIA	LAURAINE	SAPPHIRE	CLEOPATRA
COURTNEY	LAURETTA	SCARLETT	COLUMBINA
CRESSIDA	LAURETTE	SHEELAGH	COLUMBINE
CYTHEREA	LAURINDA	SHUSHANA	CONSTANCE
DANIELLA	LORRAINE	STEFANIE	CONSTANCY
DANIELLE	LUCIENNE	SUSANNAH	COURTENAY
DELPHINE	LUCRETIA	TALLULAH	DESDEMONA
DIONYSIA	LUCREZIA	TAMASINE	DOMINIQUE
DOMINICA	LYNNETTE	THEODORA	DONALDINA
DOROTHEA	MADELINA	THERESIA	ELISABETH
DOWSABEL	MADELINE	THOMASIN	ELIZABETH
DRUSILLA	MAGDALEN	TIMOTHEA	EMMANUELA
ELEANORA	MAGNOLIA	TRYPHENA	ERNESTINE
ELEONORA	MARCELLA	VERONICA	ESMERALDA
EMANUELA	MARCELLE	VICTORIA	ETHELINDA
EMMELINE	MARGARET	VIOLETTA	FIONNUALA
EUPHEMIA	MARIAMNE	VIOLETTE	FRANCESCA
EUSTACIA	MARIANNE	VIRGINIA	FRANCISCA
FAUSTINA	MARIETTA	VIVIENNE	FREDERICA
FELICITY	MARIETTE	WALBURGA	FREDERIKA
FLORENCE	MARIGOLD	WILFREDA	GABRIELLA
FLORETTA	MARJORIE	WILFRIDA	GABRIELLE
FLORETTE	MELICENT	WINEFRED	GENEVIEVE
FLORINDA	MELISENT	WINIFRED	GEORGETTE
FRANCINE	MELLONEY		GEORGIANA
FREDRICA	MERCEDES	**9**	GERALDINE
FREDRIKA	MEREDITH	ALBERTINA	GHISLAINE
GEORGINA	MERRILYN	ALBERTINE	GUENDOLEN
GERMAINE	MICHAELA	ALEXANDRA	GUINEVERE
GERTRUDE	MICHELLE	AMARYLLIS	GWENDOLEN
GILBERTA	MORWENNA	AMBROSINA	GWENDOLYN
GRETCHEN	MYRTILLA	AMBROSINE	GWENLLIAN
GRISELDA	PATIENCE	ANASTASIA	HARRIETTE
GULIELMA	PATRICIA	ANGELIQUE	HENRIETTA
GWYNNETH	PAULETTE	ANNABELLA	HENRIETTE
HADASSAH	PENELOPE	ANNABELLE	HEPHZIBAH
HELEWISE	PERPETUA	ANNELIESE	HILDEGARD
HEPZIBAH	PHILIPPA	APOLLONIA	HIPPOLYTA
HERMIONE	PHILLIDA	ARTEMISIA	HORTENSIA
HORTENSE	PHILLIPA	ARTHURINA	HYACINTHA
HYACINTH	PHYLLIDA	ARTHURINE	JACQUELYN
INGEBORG	PRIMROSE	AUGUSTINA	JACQUETTA
IOLANTHE	PRUDENCE	BATHSHEBA	JEANNETTE
ISABELLA	PRUNELLA	BENEDICTA	JESSAMINE
ISABELLE	RAPHAELA	BERNADINA	JOSEPHINE
JACOBINA	RAYMONDE	BERNADINE	KATHARINE
JAMESINA	RHIANNON	BRITANNIA	KATHERINE
JEANETTE	RICHENDA	CARMELITA	KIMBERLEY
JEANNINE	ROCHELLE	CASSANDRA	LAURENCIA
JENNIFER	RONNETTE	CATHARINE	LAURENTIA
JESSAMYN	ROSALEEN	CATHERINE	MADELEINE

9–continued
MAGDALENA
MAGDALENE
MARGARETA
MARGARITA
MEHETABEL
MEHITABEL
MÉLISANDE
MILLICENT
MIRABELLA
MIRABELLE
NICOLETTE
PARTHENIA
PHILLIPPA
PHILOMENA
PLEASANCE
POLLYANNA
PRISCILLA
ROSABELLA
ROSABELLE
ROSALINDA
ROSEMARIE

9–continued
SERAPHINA
SHUSHANNA
SOPHRONIA
STEPHANIE
THEODOSIA
THEOPHILA
THOMASINA
THOMASINE
VALENTINA
VALENTINE
VÉRONIQUE
VICTORINE
VINCENTIA
WINNIFRED

10
ALEXANDRIA
ALPHONSINE
ANTOINETTE
ARTHURETTA
BERENGARIA

10–continued
BERNADETTE
BERNARDINA
BERNARDINE
CHRISTABEL
CHRISTIANA
CINDERELLA
CLEMENTINA
CLEMENTINE
CONSTANTIA
DULCIBELLA
ERMINTRUDE
ERMYNTRUDE
ETHELDREDA
EVANGELINA
EVANGELINE
GILBERTINE
GWENDOLINE
HILDEGARDE
JACQUELINE
KINBOROUGH
MARGARETTA

10–continued
MARGUERITA
MARGUERITE
MARIABELLA
MILBOROUGH
PETRONELLA
PETRONILLA
TEMPERANCE
THEOPHANIA
WILHELMINA
WILLIAMINA

11
ALEXANDRINA
CHRISTIANIA
FIONNGHUALA

12
KERENHAPPUCH
PHILADELPHIA

BOYS' NAMES

2
AL
CY
ED
TY

3
ABE
ALF
ART
ASA
BAS
BAT
BAZ
BEN
BOB
BUD
CAI
DAI
DAN
DEE
DEL
DES
DON
DUD
ELI
ERN
GIB
GIL
GUS
GUY

3–continued
HAL
HAM
HEW
HOB
HUW
IAN
IKE
IRA
IVO
JAN
JAY
JED
JEM
JIM
JOB
JOE
JON
KAY
KEN
KIM
KIT
LEE
LEN
LEO
LES
LEW
LEX
LOU
LYN
MAT

3–continued
MAX
MEL
NAT
NED
NYE
ODO
PAT
PIP
RAB
RAY
REG
REX
ROB
ROD
RON
ROY
SAM
SEB
SID
SIM
STU
SYD
TAM
TED
TEL
TEX
TIM
TOM
VIC
VIN

3–continued
WAL
WAT
WIN
ZAK

4
ABEL
ADAM
ALAN
ALDO
ALEC
ALED
ALEX
ALGY
ALUN
ALVA
AMOS
ANDY
ARTY
AXEL
BART
BEAU
BERT
BILL
BING
BOAZ
BOYD
BRAD
BRAM
BRET

4–continued
BRYN
BURT
CARL
CARY
CERI
CHAD
CHAS
CHAY
CLEM
COLM
CONN
CURT
DALE
DANA
DAVE
DAVY
DEAN
DEWI
DICK
DION
DIRK
DOUG
DREW
DUKE
EARL
EBEN
EDDY
EDEN
EDOM
EMIL

4–continued	4–continued	4–continued	5–continued	5–continued
ENOS	LUKE	WILF	BLAIR	DONNY
ERIC	LYLE	WILL	BLAKE	DORAN
ERIK	MARC	WYNN	BLANE	DROGO
ERLE	MARK	YVES	BLASE	DUANE
ESAU	MATT	ZACK	BOBBY	DYLAN
ESME	MERV	ZANE	BONAR	EAMON
EVAN	MICK	ZEKE	BORIS	EDDIE
EWAN	MIKE		BOYCE	EDGAR
EWEN	MILO	**5**	BRENT	EDWIN
EZRA	MORT	AARON	BRETT	EDWYN
FRED	MOSS	ABNER	BRIAN	ELDON
GARY	MUIR	ABRAM	BRICE	ELIAS
GENE	NEAL	ADAIR	BROCK	ELIHU
GLEN	NEIL	ADOLF	BRUCE	ELIOT
GLYN	NICK	AIDAN	BRUNO	ELLIS
GREG	NOAH	ALAIN	BRYAN	ELMER
GWYN	NOEL	ALBAN	BRYCE	ELTON
HAMO	NORM	ALBIN	BYRON	ELVIN
HANK	OLAF	ALDEN	CADEL	ELVIS
HANS	OLAV	ALDIS	CAIUS	ELWYN
HERB	OMAR	ALDUS	CALEB	EMERY
HUEY	OSSY	ALFIE	CALUM	EMILE
HUGH	OTHO	ALGAR	CAREY	EMLYN
HUGO	OTIS	ALGER	CARLO	EMRYS
IAGO	OTTO	ALGIE	CAROL	ENOCH
IAIN	OWEN	ALICK	CASEY	EPPIE
IFOR	PAUL	ALLAN	CECIL	ERNIE
IGOR	PETE	ALLEN	CHRIS	ERROL
IOLO	PHIL	ALVAH	CHUCK	ETHAN
IVAN	RAFE	ALVAR	CLARK	FARON
IVES	RENÉ	ALVIE	CLAUD	FELIX
IVOR	RHYS	ALVIN	CLIFF	FIDEL
JACK	RICH	ALVIS	CLINT	FLOYD
JAGO	RICK	ALWYN	CLIVE	FRANK
JAKE	ROLF	AMIAS	CLYDE	GAIUS
JEFF	ROLY	AMYAS	COLIN	GARRY
JOCK	RORY	ANCEL	COLUM	GARTH
JOEL	ROSS	ANDRÉ	CONAN	GAVIN
JOEY	RUDI	ANGEL	CONOR	GEOFF
JOHN	RUDY	ANGUS	COSMO	GERRY
JOSÉ	RUSS	ANSEL	CRAIG	GILES
JOSH	RYAN	ANTON	CUDDY	GLENN
JUAN	SAUL	ARCHY	CYRIL	GRANT
JUDD	SEAN	ARMIN	CYRUS	GREGG
JUDE	SETH	ARTIE	DAMON	GUIDO
KANE	SHAW	ASHER	DANNY	GYLES
KARL	SHEM	ATHOL	DANTE	HAMON
KEIR	STAN	AULAY	DARBY	HARDY
KENT	STEW	AVERY	DARCY	HARRY
KING	THEO	BARON	DARYL	HAYDN
KIRK	THOM	BARRY	DAVID	HEATH
KRIS	TOBY	BASIE	DENIS	HEBER
KURT	TODD	BASIL	DENNY	HENRI
KYLE	TONY	BENET	DENYS	HENRY
LARS	TREV	BENJY	DERBY	HERVÉ
LEON	TROY	BENNY	DEREK	HIRAM
LEVI	VERE	BERNY	DERRY	HOMER
LIAM	VICK	BERRY	DERYK	HONOR
LORI	WADE	BEVIS	DICKY	HORRY
LORN	WALT	BILLY	DIGBY	HOWEL
LUDO	WARD	BJORN	DONAL	HUMPH

5–continued	5–continued	5–continued	6–continued	6–continued
HYMAN	MORTY	SHANE	AUSTEN	DOUGIE
HYMIE	MOSES	SHAUN	AUSTIN	DUDLEY
HYWEL	MOSHE	SHAWN	AYLMER	DUGALD
IDRIS	MUNGO	SILAS	AYLWIN	DUGGIE
INIGO	MYLES	SIMON	BALDIE	DUNCAN
IRVIN	MYRON	SOLLY	BARNET	DURAND
IRWIN	NEDDY	STEVE	BARNEY	DUSTIN
ISAAC	NEILL	TAFFY	BARRIE	DWAYNE
ITHEL	NEVIL	TEDDY	BARRON	DWIGHT
IZAAK	NIALL	TERRI	BARTLE	EAMONN
JABEZ	NICKY	TERRY	BENITO	EASTER
JACKY	NICOL	TIMMY	BENNET	EDMOND
JACOB	NIGEL	TITUS	BERNIE	EDMUND
JAMES	NIKKI	TOLLY	BERTIE	EDWARD
JAMIE	NOLAN	TOMMY	BETHEL	EGBERT
JARED	OGDEN	TUDOR	BILLIE	ELDRED
JASON	OLAVE	ULRIC	BLAINE	ELIJAH
JEMMY	OLLIE	UPTON	BLAISE	ELLERY
JERRY	ORSON	URBAN	BOBBIE	ELLIOT
JESSE	ORVAL	URIAH	BONAMY	EOGHAN
JESUS	OSCAR	URIAH	BOTOLF	ERNEST
JIMMY	OSSIE	VINCE	BOTULF	ESMOND
JONAH	OSWIN	VITUS	BUSTER	EUGENE
JONAS	OWAIN	WALDO	CADELL	EVELYN
JUDAH	OZZIE	WALLY	CAESAR	FABIAN
JUDAS	PABLO	WAYNE	CALLUM	FARRAN
JULES	PADDY	WILLY	CALVIN	FARREN
KAROL	PAOLO	WYATT	CARLOS	FERGIE
KEITH	PARRY	WYNNE	CAROLE	FERGUS
KENNY	PEDRO	**6**	CARTER	FINLAY
KEVIN	PERCE	ADOLPH	CASPAR	FLURRY
KIRBY	PERCY	ADRIAN	CEDRIC	FRANCO
LABAN	PERRY	AENEAS	CERDIC	FRASER
LANCE	PETER	ALARIC	CLAUDE	FRAZER
LANTY	PIERS	ALBANY	COLLEY	FREDDY
LARRY	PIRAN	ALBERT	CONNOR	GARETH
LAURI	QUINN	ALDOUS	CONRAD	GARNET
LEIGH	RALPH	ALDRED	CORMAC	GARRET
LEROY	RAMON	ALDWIN	CORNEY	GASPAR
LEWIS	RANDY	ALDWYN	COSIMO	GAWAIN
LLOYD	RAOUL	ALEXIS	CUDDIE	GEORGE
LOREN	RICKI	ALFRED	CURTIS	GERALD
LORIN	RICKY	ALONSO	DAFYDD	GERARD
LORNE	RIKKI	ALONZO	DAMIAN	GERWYN
LOUIE	ROALD	ALURED	DAMIEN	GETHIN
LOUIS	ROBIN	ANDREW	DANIEL	GIDEON
LUCAS	RODDY	ANGELO	DARREL	GILROY
LYULF	RODGE	ANSELL	DARREN	GODWIN
MADOC	ROGER	ANSELM	DARRYL	GORDON
MANNY	ROLLO	ANTONY	DECLAN	GRAEME
MANUS	ROLLY	AQUILA	DENNIS	GRAHAM
MARCO	ROLPH	ARCHER	DENZIL	GREGOR
MARIO	ROWAN	ARCHIE	DERMOT	GROVER
MARTY	ROYAL	ARMAND	DERYCK	GUNTER
MICAH	RUFUS	ARNAUD	DEXTER	GUSSIE
MICKY	SACHA	ARNOLD	DICKIE	GUSTAF
MILES	SAMMY	ARTHUR	DICKON	GUSTAV
MITCH	SAXON	ASHLEY	DILLON	GWILYM
MONTE	SCOTT	AUBERT	DONALD	GWYLIM
MONTY	SELBY	AUBREY	DORIAN	HAMISH
MORAY	SERGE	AUGUST	DOUGAL	HAMLET

6–continued	6–continued	6–continued	6–continued	7–continued
HAMLYN	LESTER	PRINCE	WARREN	CHAUNCY
HAMNET	LIONEL	QUINCY	WESLEY	CHESTER
HARLEY	LONNIE	RABBIE	WILBUR	CHRISTY
HAROLD	LOVELL	RAFAEL	WILLIE	CLAYTON
HARVEY	LOWELL	RAINER	WILLIS	CLEDWYN
HAYDEN	LUCIAN	RAMSAY	WILMER	CLEMENT
HAYDON	LUCIEN	RAMSEY	WILMOT	CLIFTON
HECTOR	LUCIUS	RANALD	WINNIE	CLINTON
HEDLEY	LUTHER	RANDAL	WYBERT	COLUMBA
HERBIE	LYNDON	RAYNER	WYSTAN	CRISPIN
HERMAN	LYULPH	RAYNOR	XAVIER	CRYSTAL
HERVEY	MAGNUS	REGGIE	YEHUDI	CYPRIAN
HILARY	MALISE	REUBEN		DARRELL
HOBART	MALORY	RICHIE	**7**	DECIMUS
HOLDEN	MALVIN	ROBBIE	ABRAHAM	DENHOLM
HONOUR	MANLEY	ROBERT	ABSALOM	DERRICK
HORACE	MANSEL	RODGER	ABSOLON	DESMOND
HOWARD	MANUEL	RODNEY	ADAMNAN	DIGGORY
HOWELL	MARCEL	ROLAND	ADOLPHE	DOMINIC
HUBERT	MARCUS	RONALD	AINSLEY	DONOVAN
HUGHIE	MARIUS	RONNIE	AINSLIE	DOUGLAS
INGRAM	MARTIN	RUDOLF	ALBERIC	DUNSTAN
IRVINE	MARTYN	RUPERT	ALDHELM	EARNEST
IRVING	MARVIN	RUSSEL	ALFONSO	ELEAZAR
ISAIAH	MARVYN	SAMSON	AMBROSE	ELKANAH
ISRAEL	MELVIN	SAMUEL	ANDREAS	ELLIOTT
JACKIE	MELVYN	SEAMUS	ANEIRIN	EMANUEL
JACQUI	MERLIN	SEFTON	ANEURIN	EPHRAIM
JARRED	MERTON	SELWYN	ANTHONY	ERASMUS
JARROD	MERVIN	SERGEI	ANTONIO	EUSTACE
JARVIS	MERVYN	SERGIO	ARTEMAS	EVERARD
JASPER	MICKEY	SEUMAS	ARTEMUS	EZEKIEL
JEREMY	MILTON	SEWARD	AUBERON	FEARGUS
JEROME	MORGAN	SEXTUS	AZARIAH	FITZROY
JETHRO	MORRIS	SHAMUS	BALDWIN	FLORIAN
JOHNNY	MURRAY	SHELLY	BARCLAY	FRANCIS
JOLYON	NATHAN	SHOLTO	BARNABY	FRANKIE
JORDAN	NEDDIE	SIDNEY	BARNARD	FREDDIE
JOSEPH	NELSON	SIMEON	BARRETT	FREDRIC
JOSHUA	NEWTON	STEVEN	BARTLET	FULBERT
JOSIAH	NINIAN	STEVIE	BASTIAN	GABRIEL
JOSIAS	NORMAN	ST JOHN	BEDFORD	GARRETT
JOTHAM	NORRIS	STUART	BENNETT	GARRICK
JULIAN	NORTON	SYDNEY	BENTLEY	GAYLORD
JULIUS	NOWELL	TALBOT	BERNARD	GEORDIE
JUNIOR	OBERON	TAYLOR	BERTRAM	GEORGIE
JUSTIN	OLIVER	TEDDIE	BETHELL	GERAINT
KELVIN	ORRELL	THOMAS	BOTOLPH	GERRARD
KENDAL	OSBERT	TOBIAS	BRADLEY	GERSHOM
KENELM	OSBORN	TRAVIS	BRANDAN	GERVAIS
KENTON	OSMOND	TREFOR	BRANDON	GERVASE
KESTER	OSMUND	TREVOR	BRENDAN	GILBERT
KIERAN	OSWALD	TYBALT	CAMERON	GILLEAN
LAUNCE	PALMER	TYRONE	CARADOC	GILLIAN
LAUREN	PARKER	VAUGHN	CARADOG	GODFREY
LAURIE	PASCAL	VERNON	CARLTON	GOLDWIN
LAWRIE	PASCOE	VICTOR	CAROLUS	GOLDWYN
LAYTON	PELHAM	VIRGIL	CEDRYCH	GRAHAME
LEMUEL	PHILIP	WALLIS	CHARLES	GREGORY
LENNOX	PIERRE	WALTER	CHARLEY	GUNTHER
LESLIE	POLDIE	WARNER	CHARLIE	GUSTAVE

7–continued	7–continued	8	8–continued
GWYNFOR	PATRICK	ADOLPHUS	HARRISON
HADRIAN	PHILLIP	ALASDAIR	HERCULES
HAMMOND	PHINEAS	ALASTAIR	HEREWARD
HARTLEY	PRESTON	ALGERNON	HEZEKIAH
HERBERT	QUENTIN	ALISTAIR	HUMPHREY
HERMANN	QUINTIN	ALOYSIUS	IGNATIUS
HILLARY	RANDALL	ALPHONSE	IORWERTH
HORATIO	RAPHAEL	ALPHONSO	JEDIDIAH
HUMBERT	RAYMOND	AUGUSTIN	JEPHTHAH
ICHABOD	REDVERS	AUGUSTUS	JEREMIAH
ISIDORE	REYNARD	AURELIAN	JEREMIAS
JACQUES	REYNOLD	BARDOLPH	JERMAINE
JAPHETH	RICARDO	BARNABAS	JOHANNES
JEFFERY	RICHARD	BARTLETT	JONATHAN
JEFFREY	RODOLPH	BENEDICK	JOSCELIN
JILLIAN	RODRIGO	BENEDICT	KIMBERLY
JOACHIM	ROWLAND	BENJAMIN	KINGSLEY
JOCELYN	ROYSTON	BERENGER	LANCELOT
JOHNNIE	RUDOLPH	BERKELEY	LAURENCE
KENDALL	RUSSELL	BERNHARD	LAWRENCE
KENNETH	SALAMON	BERTHOLD	LEIGHTON
KENRICK	SAMPSON	BERTRAND	LLEWELYN
KIMBALL	SERGIUS	BEVERLEY	MANASSEH
LACHLAN	SEYMOUR	BONIFACE	MANASSES
LAMBERT	SHANNON	CAMILLUS	MARSHALL
LAZARUS	SHELDON	CAMPBELL	MATTHIAS
LEANDER	SHELLEY	CARLETON	MELVILLE
LEOFRIC	SIGMUND	CARTHACH	MEREDITH
LEOLINE	SOLOMON	CHARLTON	MITCHELL
LEONARD	SPENCER	CHAUNCEY	MONTAGUE
LEOPOLD	STANLEY	CHRISTIE	MORDECAI
LINCOLN	STEPHEN	CHRYSTAL	MORTIMER
LINDSAY	STEWART	CLARENCE	NAPOLEON
LORENZO	SWITHIN	CLAUDIUS	NEHEMIAH
LUDOVIC	TANCRED	CLIFFORD	NICHOLAS
MALACHI	TERENCE	CONSTANT	OCTAVIAN
MALACHY	TERTIUS	COURTNEY	OCTAVIUS
MALCOLM	THORLEY	CRISPIAN	PERCEVAL
MALLORY	TIMOTHY	CUTHBERT	PERCIVAL
MANFRED	TORQUIL	DIARMAIT	PHILEMON
MANSELL	TRAVERS	DIARMUID	PHINEHAS
MATTHEW	TRISTAN	DOMINICK	RADCLIFF
MAURICE	ULYSSES	EBENEZER	RANDOLPH
MAXWELL	VAUGHAN	EMMANUEL	REGINALD
MAYNARD	VINCENT	ETHELRED	RODERICK
MEIRION	WALLACE	FARQUHAR	SALVADOR
MERRION	WARWICK	FERNANDO	SEPTIMUS
MICHAEL	WENDELL	FLETCHER	SHERIDAN
MILBURN	WILBERT	FLORENCE	SILVANUS
MONTAGU	WILFRED	FLUELLEN	SINCLAIR
MURDOCH	WILFRID	FRANKLIN	STAFFORD
MURTAGH	WILLARD	FREDERIC	STANFORD
NEVILLE	WILLIAM	FREDRICK	STIRLING
NICOLAS	WINDSOR	GAMALIEL	SYLVANUS
NORBERT	WINFRED	GARFIELD	TALIESIN
OBADIAH	WINFRID	GEOFFREY	TERRENCE
OLIVIER	WINSTON	GRAYBURN	THADDEUS
ORLANDO	WOODROW	GRIFFITH	THEOBALD
ORVILLE	WYNDHAM	GUSTAVUS	THEODORE
OSBORNE	WYNFORD	HAMILTON	THORNTON
PADRAIG	ZACHARY	HANNIBAL	THURSTAN

8–continued
THURSTON
TRISTRAM
TURLOUGH
WINTHROP
ZEDEKIAH

9
ALEXANDER
ALPHONSUS
AMBROSIUS
ARCHELAUS
ARCHIBALD
ATHELSTAN
AUGUSTINE
BALTHASAR
BALTHAZAR
BRODERICK
CADWALADR
CHRISTIAN
CHRISTMAS
CORNELIUS

9–continued
COURTENAY
DIONYSIUS
ENDEAVOUR
ETHELBERT
FERDINAND
FRANCESCO
FRANCISCO
FREDERICK
GERONTIUS
GRANVILLE
GRENVILLE
JEFFERSON
KENTIGERN
KIMBERLEY
LAUNCELOT
LLEWELLYN
MARCELLUS
MARMADUKE
NATHANAEL
NATHANIEL

9–continued
NICODEMUS
ONUPHRIUS
PEREGRINE
PHILIBERT
RADCLIFFE
SALVATORE
SEBASTIAN
SIEGFRIED
SIGISMUND
SILVESTER
STANISLAS
SYLVESTER
THEODORIC
VALENTINE
ZACCHAEUS
ZACHARIAH
ZACHARIAS
ZECHARIAH
ZEPHANIAH

10
BARRINGTON
CARACTACUS
FORTUNATUS
HIERONYMUS
HILDEBRAND
HIPPOLYTUS
MAXIMILIAN
MONTGOMERY
STANISLAUS
THEOPHILUS
WASHINGTON
WILLOUGHBY

11
BARTHOLOMEW
CADWALLADER
CHRISTOPHER
CONSTANTINE
SACHEVERELL

INDEX

Entries in bold face type (e.g. **COUNTRIES OF THE WORLD** 1) refer to sections, tables, or lists in the text, with their page numbers. Other index entries suggest tables that might be useful (e.g. SHELLS *see* SEASHELLS, or INSTRUMENT *try* MUSICAL INSTRUMENTS; TOOLS. We have also included a selection of cue words for cryptic clues (e.g. the word ZERO often indicates the letter O).

I

INDIAN DISHES 330

INDIANS *see* AMERICAN INDIANS

INDIAN STATES AND UNION TERRITORIES 18

INDICATORS *see* ANAGRAM INDICATORS; SPLIT-WORD INDICATORS

INFECTIONS *try* ANIMAL DISEASES AND INFECTIONS; MEDICAL FIELDS AND SPECIALITIES

IN FRANCE, PARIS, SPAIN *etc. may indicate a foreign word e.g.* man in Paris = M (monsieur); *try* FOREIGN WORDS; NUMBERS

INITIALLY *may indicate the first letter of a word to be used in forming a new word*

INSECTS 69

IN SHORT *may indicate an abbreviation*

INSTRUMENT *try* MUSICAL INSTRUMENTS; TOOLS

INTERNATIONAL AIRPORTS 305

INTERNATIONAL CAR REGISTRATIONS 308

INVENTORS *see* ENGINEERS AND INVENTORS; *try* COMPUTER SCIENTISTS; ENTREPRENEURS AND INDUSTRIALISTS; SCIENTISTS

ISLAND GROUPS 38

ISLANDS 37

ITALIAN REGIONS 17

J

JEWELLERY 320; *see also* BIRTHSTONES; GEMSTONES

JOINTS OF MEAT 326

K

KINGS *see* RULERS OF ENGLAND; SCOTTISH RULERS; king *may also indicate* K, R, REX

KITCHEN UTENSILS AND TABLEWARE 322

KNITTING TERMS 351

KNOTS 362

L

LAKES, LOCHS, AND LOUGHS 43

LÄNDER *see* GERMAN STATES

LANGUAGE 363–368

LANGUAGE *try* COMPUTER LANGUAGES; FIGURES OF SPEECH; LANGUAGES OF THE WORLD; LITERARY TERMS

LANGUAGES OF THE WORLD 363

LARGE NUMBER *may indicate the letters* M *or* D (*Roman numerals*)

LATIN PHRASES 367

LAW *see section* HISTORY, POLITICS, GOVERNMENT, AND LAW; *try* LEGAL TERMS

LEARNER *may indicate the letter* L

LEFT *may indicate* L, SINISTER, PORT

LEGAL TERMS 219

LEGEND *see* ARTHURIAN LEGEND; CHARACTERS FROM THE TALES OF ROBIN HOOD; MYTHOLOGICAL AND IMAGINARY BEINGS; *see also* AFRICAN MYTHOLOGY; AUSTRALIAN MYTHOLOGY; CELTIC MYTHOLOGY; CENTRAL AND SOUTH AMERICAN MYTHOLOGY; EGYPTIAN MYTHOLOGY; GREEK AND ROMAN MYTHOLOGY; NORSE MYTHOLOGY; NORTH AMERICAN MYTHOLOGY

LIQUEUR *see* DRINKS

LITERARY TERMS 164

LOCAL AUTHORITIES *see* ENGLISH COUNTIES AND SELECTED LOCAL AUTHORITIES; SCOTTISH REGIONS, COUNTIES, AND SELECTED LOCAL AUTHORITIES; WELSH COUNTIES AND SELECTED LOCAL AUTHORITIES

LOCHS *see* LAKES, LOCHS, and LOUGHS

LOCOMOTIVES 312

LOVE *may indicate the letter* O

LOVERS OF FACT AND FICTION 206

M

MAJOR ARTERIES 247

MAJOR RUGBY UNION CLUBS 341

MAJOR VEINS 247

MANNED SPACE PROGRAMS 240

MANY *may indicate the letters* D *or* M (*Roman numerals*)

MARSUPIALS 68

MATERIALS 317

MATHEMATICAL TERMS 231; *see also* GEOMETRIC FIGURES AND CURVES

MEASURES *see* PAPER MEASURES; WEIGHTS AND MEASURES

MEAT *try* JOINTS OF MEAT

MEDALS *see* BRITISH DECORATIONS AND MEDALS; US DECORATIONS AND MEDALS

MEDIC *may indicate the letters* DR, MD, MO, MB

MEDICAL FIELDS AND SPECIALITIES 247

MEDICATION 252

MEDICINE AND HEALTH 247–260

MEMBERS OF NATO 217

MEMBERS OF THE COMMONWEALTH 217

METEOR SHOWERS 239

MILITARY LEADERS 84

MILITARY TERMS 288–302

MINERALS *see* ROCKS AND MINERALS

MINISTER *try* CLERGY

MISCELLANEOUS 355–362

MIXED *may indicate an anagram*

MONEY 359; *see also* CURRENCIES; FORMER EUROPEAN CURRENCIES

MOTHS 71

MOTORING TERMS 307

MOTORWAY *may indicate the letters* M, MI (M1)

MOTORWAY SERVICE STATIONS 311

MOTTOES 391

MOUNTAINS AND HILLS 46

MOVED *may indicate an anagram*

MURDERERS 154

MUSCLES 249

MUSEUMS AND GALLERIES 169

MUSICAL INSTRUMENTS 174